FIRE FORCE

04 OMNIBUS
ATSUSHI OHKUBO

CONTENTS

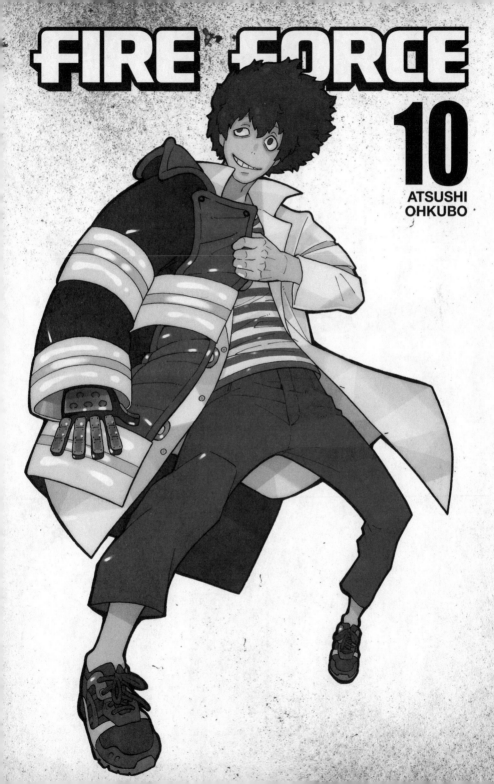

FIRE FORCE

10

ATSUSHI OHKUBO

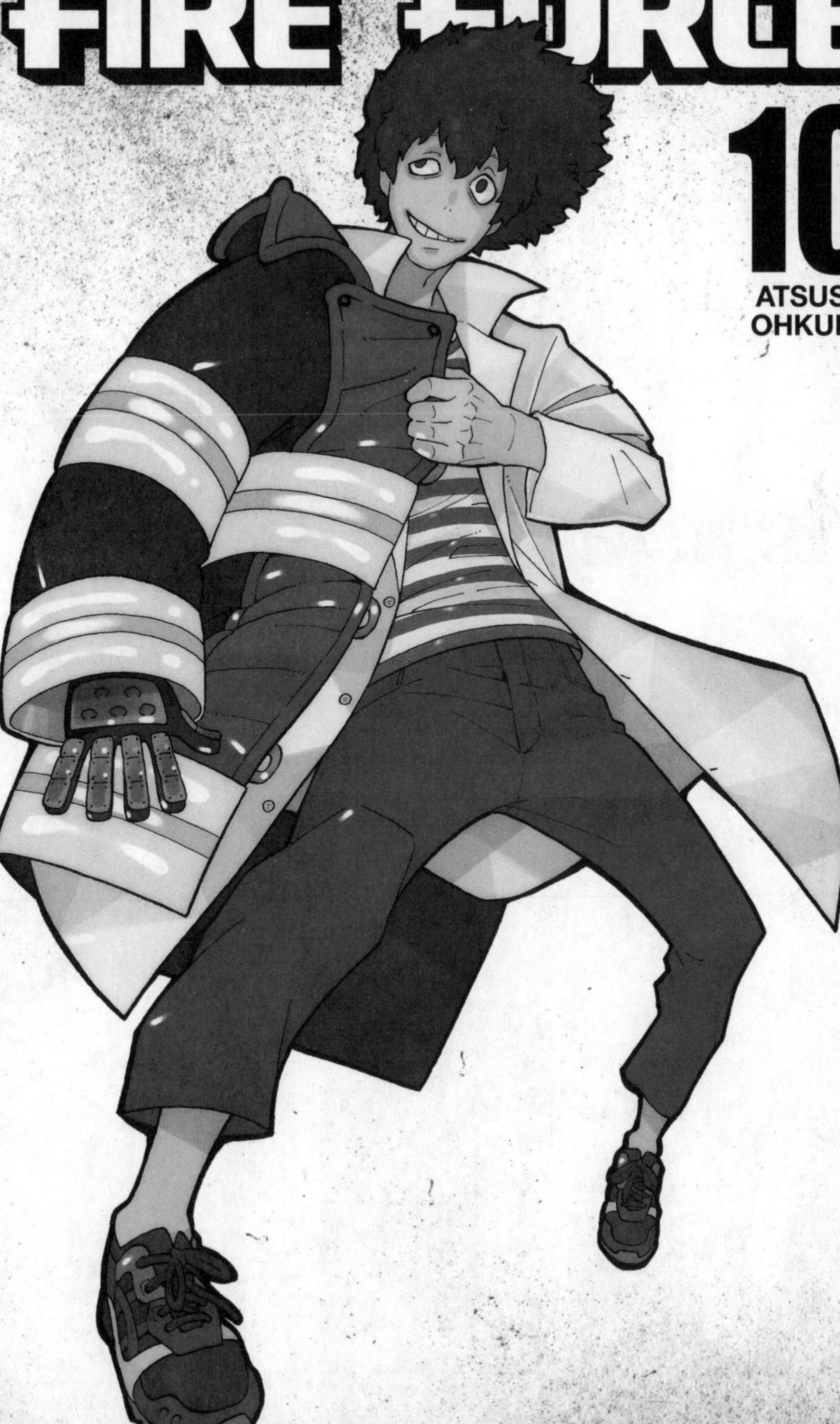

two, or . . . ?

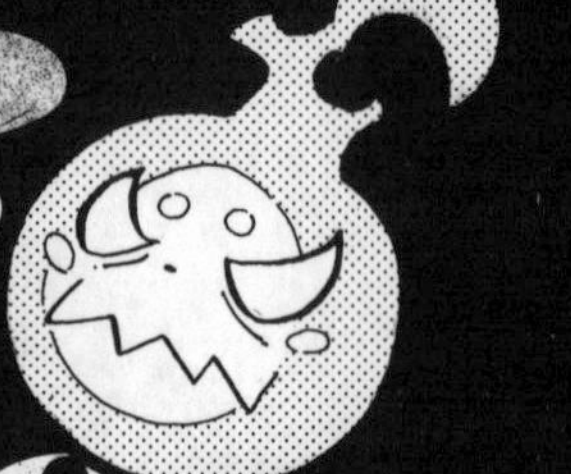

divine can shed the truth.

VOL. 10

ATSUSHI OHKUBO

Is it time that separates the

Only the flame light on

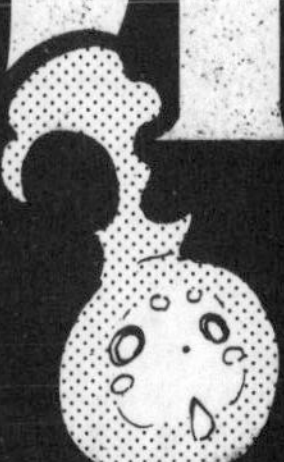

FIRE FORCE

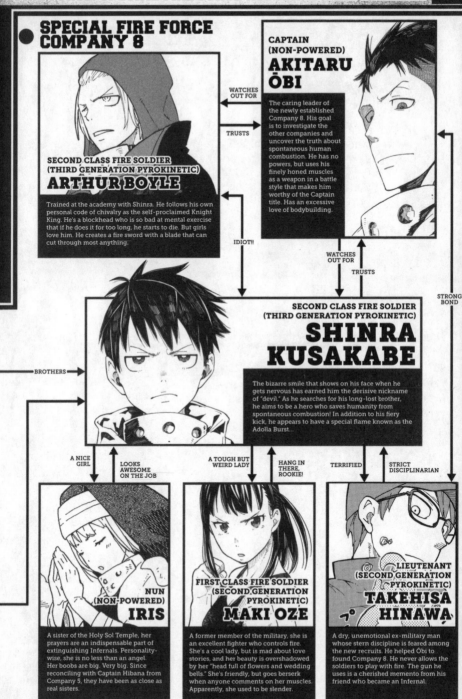

SPECIAL FIRE FORCE COMPANY 8

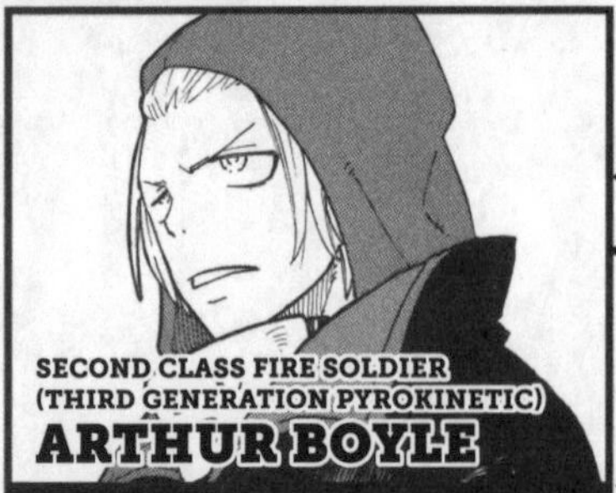

SECOND CLASS FIRE SOLDIER (THIRD GENERATION PYROKINETIC)

ARTHUR BOYLE

Trained at the academy with Shinra. He follows his own personal code of chivalry as the self-proclaimed Knight King. He's a blockhead who is so bad at mental exercise that if he does it for too long, he starts to die. But girls love him. He creates a fire sword with a blade that can cut through most anything.

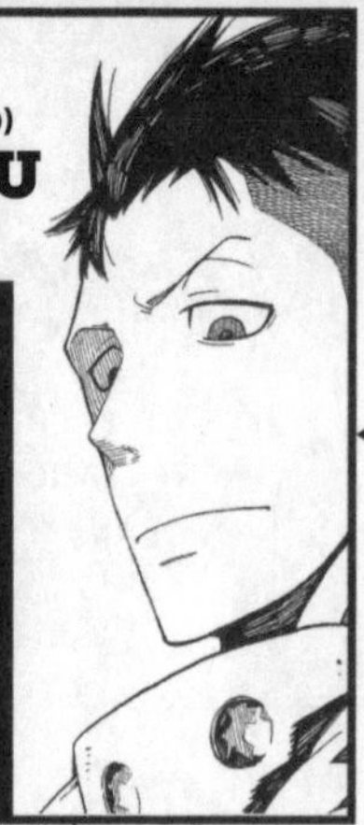

CAPTAIN (NON-POWERED)

AKITARU ŌBI

The caring leader of the newly established Company 8. His goal is to investigate the other companies and uncover the truth about spontaneous human combustion. He has no powers, but uses his finely honed muscles as a weapon in a battle style that makes him worthy of the Captain title. Has an excessive love of bodybuilding.

WATCHES OUT FOR

TRUSTS

IDIOT!!

WATCHES OUT FOR

TRUSTS

STRONG BOND

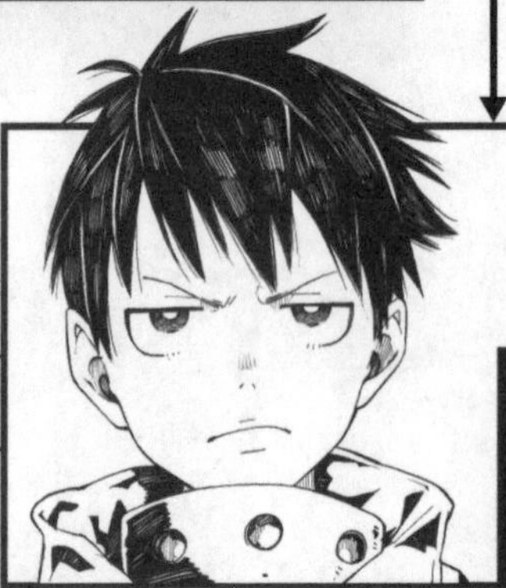

SECOND CLASS FIRE SOLDIER (THIRD GENERATION PYROKINETIC)

SHINRA KUSAKABE

The bizarre smile that shows on his face when he gets nervous has earned him the derisive nickname of "devil." As he searches for his long-lost brother, he aims to be a hero who saves humanity from spontaneous combustion! In addition to his fiery kick, he appears to have a special flame known as the Adolla Burst...

BROTHERS

A NICE GIRL

LOOKS AWESOME ON THE JOB

A TOUGH BUT WEIRD LADY

HANG IN THERE, ROOKIE!

TERRIFIED

STRICT DISCIPLINARIAN

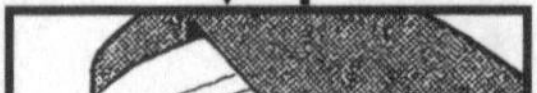

NUN (NON-POWERED)

IRIS

A sister of the Holy Sol Temple, her prayers are an indispensable part of extinguishing Infernals. Personality-wise, she is no less than an angel. Her boobs are big. Very big. Since reconciling with Captain Hibana from Company 5, they have been as close as real sisters.

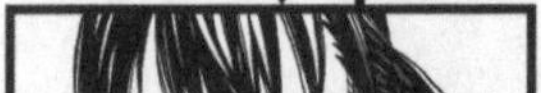

FIRST CLASS FIRE SOLDIER (SECOND GENERATION PYROKINETIC)

MAKI OZE

A former member of the military, she is an excellent fighter who controls fire. She's a cool lady, but is mad about love stories, and her beauty is overshadowed by her "head full of flowers and wedding bells." She's friendly, but goes berserk when anyone comments on her muscles. Apparently, she used to be slender.

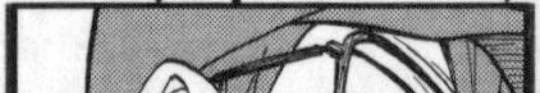

LIEUTENANT (SECOND GENERATION PYROKINETIC)

TAKEHISA HINAWA

A dry, unemotional ex-military man whose stern discipline is feared among the new recruits. He helped Ōbi to found Company 8. He never allows the soldiers to play with fire. The gun he uses is a cherished memento from his friend who became an Infernal.

THE GIRLS' CLUB

RESPECTS

● FOLLOWERS OF THE EVANGELIST

CAPTAIN OF SPECIAL FIRE FORCE COMPANY 3 (SECOND GENERATION PYROKINETIC?)
DR. GIOVANNI

A traitor who started working for the Evangelist despite being a captain in the Special Fire Force. He fights by using fire to control mechanical limbs. It is his policy to knock on a stone bridge multiple times before crossing it.

SUB-ORD-INATE →

(THIRD GENERATION PYROKINETIC)
LISA

Had been living in Vulcan's home after he took her in, but was actually a spy sent by Dr. Giovanni. Controls tentacles of flame.

COMMANDER OF THE KNIGHTS OF THE ASHEN FLAME
SHŌ KUSAKABE

Shinra's long-lost brother, the commander of an order of knights that works for the Evangelist. His powers are still shrouded in mystery, but anyway, he's ridiculously strong!!

WHITE-CLAD
YONA

A white-clad soldier of the Evangelist with inhuman features. Has the power to mold and reshape others' faces.

WE'RE FAMILY! ↕   YOU GULLIBLE BLEEDING HEART! ↕

ENGINEER
VULCAN

The greatest engineer of the day, renowned as the God of Fire and the Forge. He originally hated the Fire Force, but he sympathized with Obi's and Shinra's ideals and agreed to join Company 8 as their engineer. His dream is to revive the world's extinct animals!

SCIENCE TEAM
VIKTOR LICHT

A morally ambiguous man deployed from Haijima Industries to fill the vacancy in Company 8's science department. Apparently a genius.

SECOND CLASS FIRE SOLDIER (THIRD GENERATION PYROKINETIC)
TAMAKI KOTATSU

Originally a rookie member of Company 1, she was caught up in the treasonous plot of her superior officer Hoshimiya, and is currently being disciplined under Company 8's watch. A tough girl with an unfortunate "lucky lecher lure" condition, she nevertheless has a pure heart.

HAS HIM ON HER MIND →

SUMMARY...

After venturing into the Nether, Company 8 is split apart by the Evangelist's soldiers' divide-and-conquer tactics. Led by an Adolla Link, Shinra finally finds his brother, but Shō's blind faith in the Evangelist deafens him to Shinra's words. Now Shinra's only option is to beat the snot out of Shō and drag him back home!! After 12 years apart, a battle breaks out between the long-lost brothers!!

SPUTT
SPUTT

FIRE FORCE

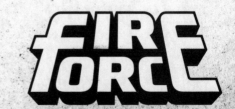

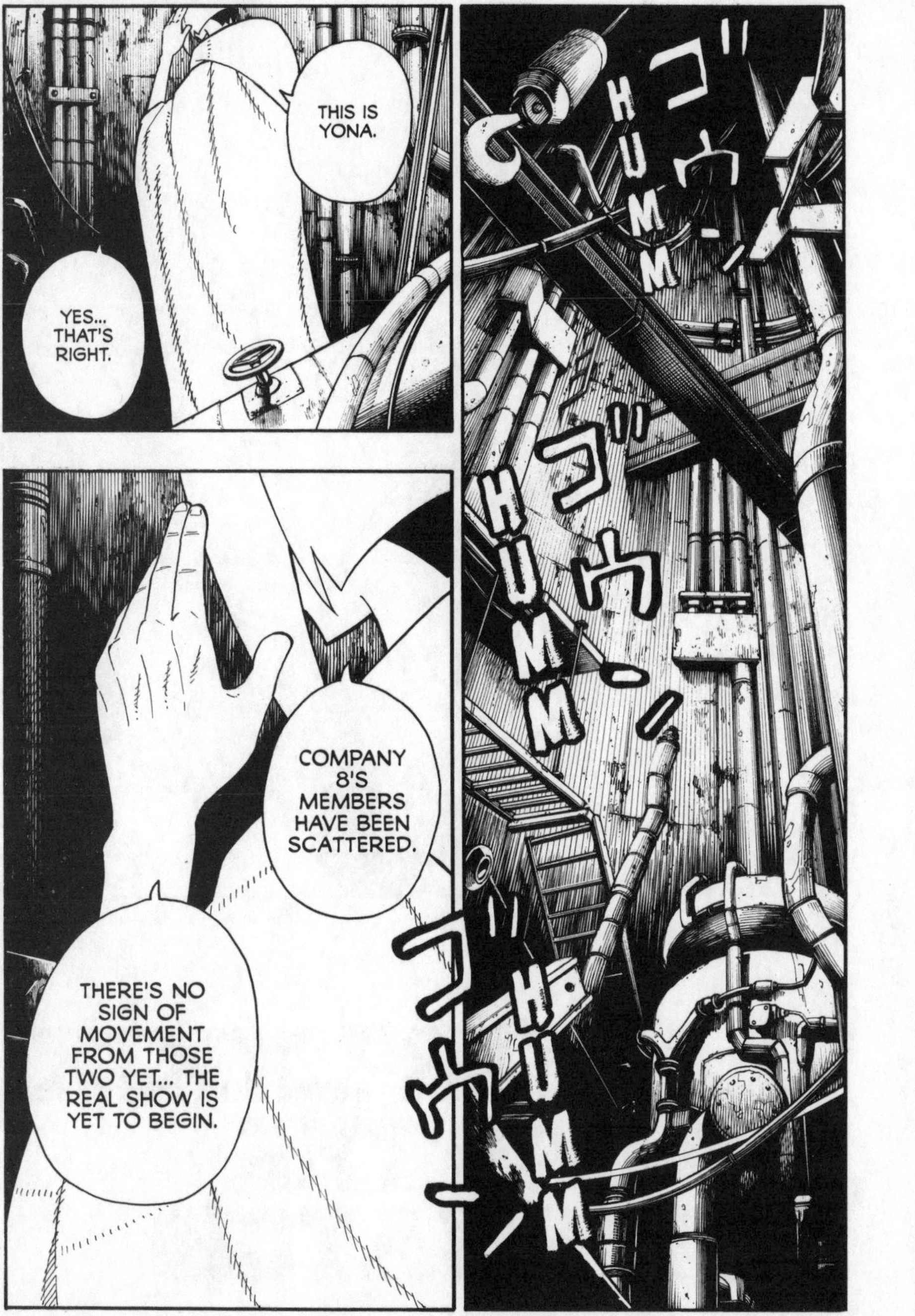
ゴウー
HUMM
ゴウー
HUMM
ゴウー
HUMM
THIS IS YONA.
YES... THAT'S RIGHT.
COMPANY 8'S MEMBERS HAVE BEEN SCATTERED.
THERE'S NO SIGN OF MOVEMENT FROM THOSE TWO YET... THE REAL SHOW IS YET TO BEGIN.

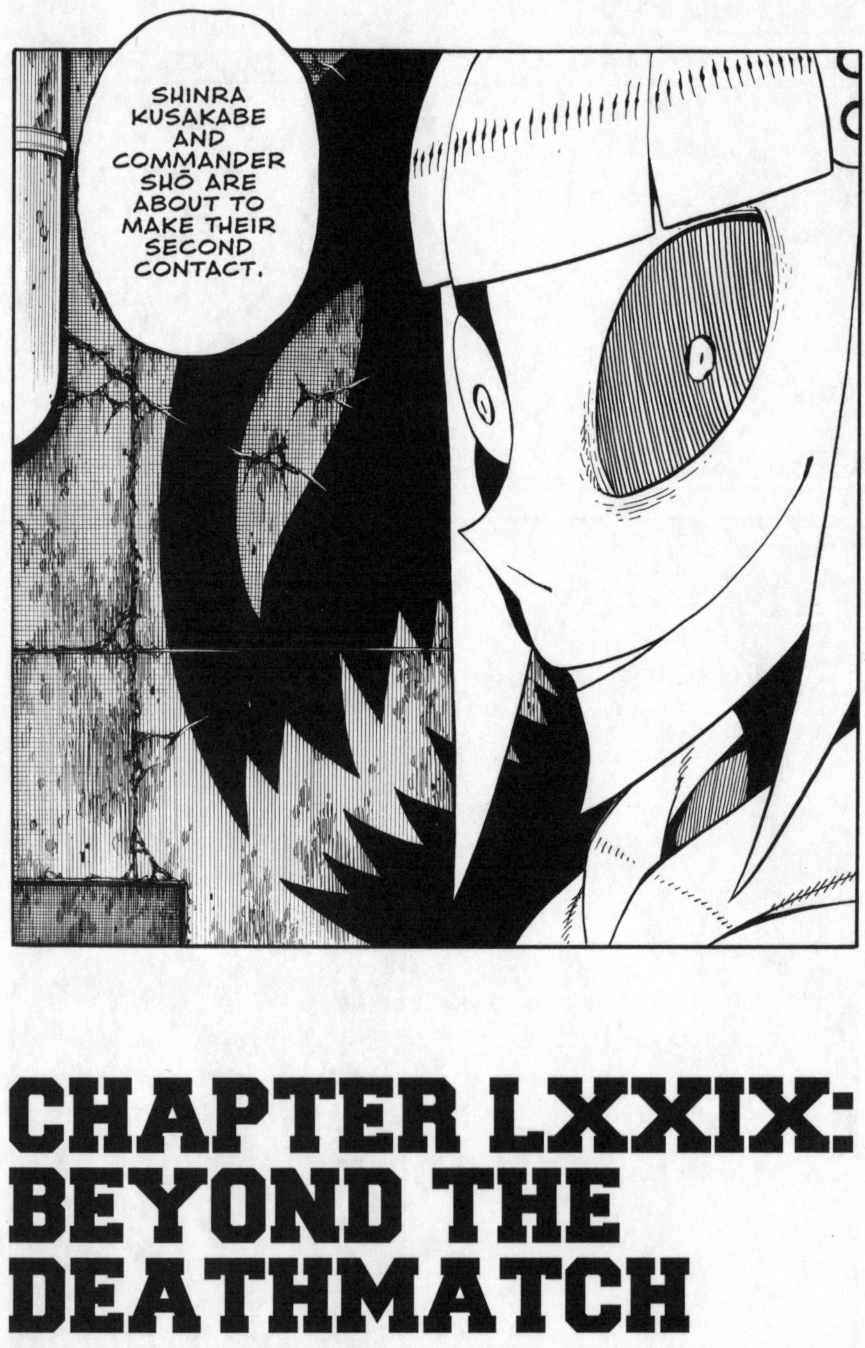
SHINRA KUSAKABE AND COMMANDER SHŌ ARE ABOUT TO MAKE THEIR SECOND CONTACT.

CHAPTER LXXIX: BEYOND THE DEATHMATCH

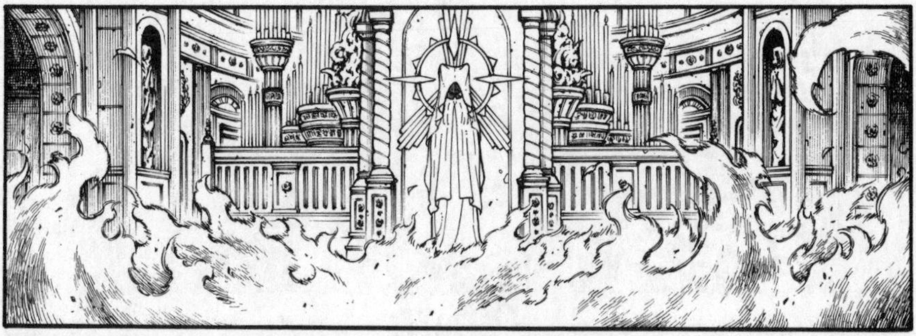

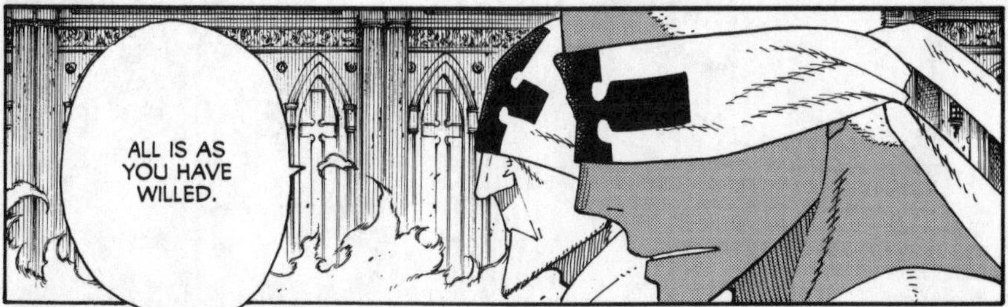
ALL IS AS YOU HAVE WILLED.

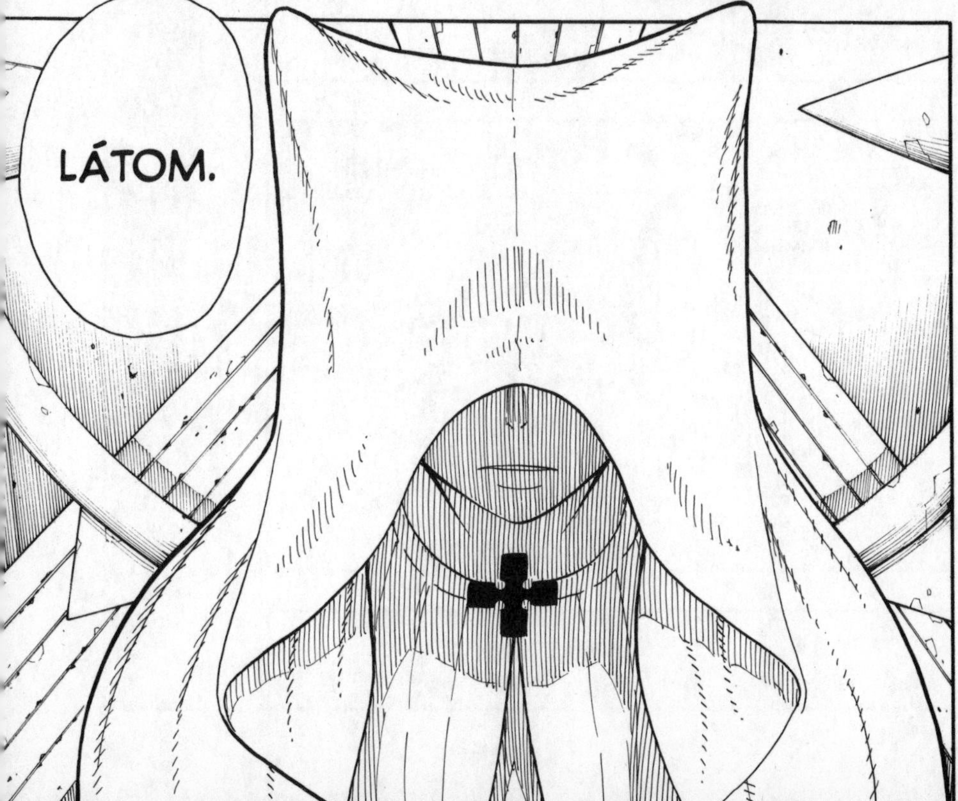
LÁTOM.

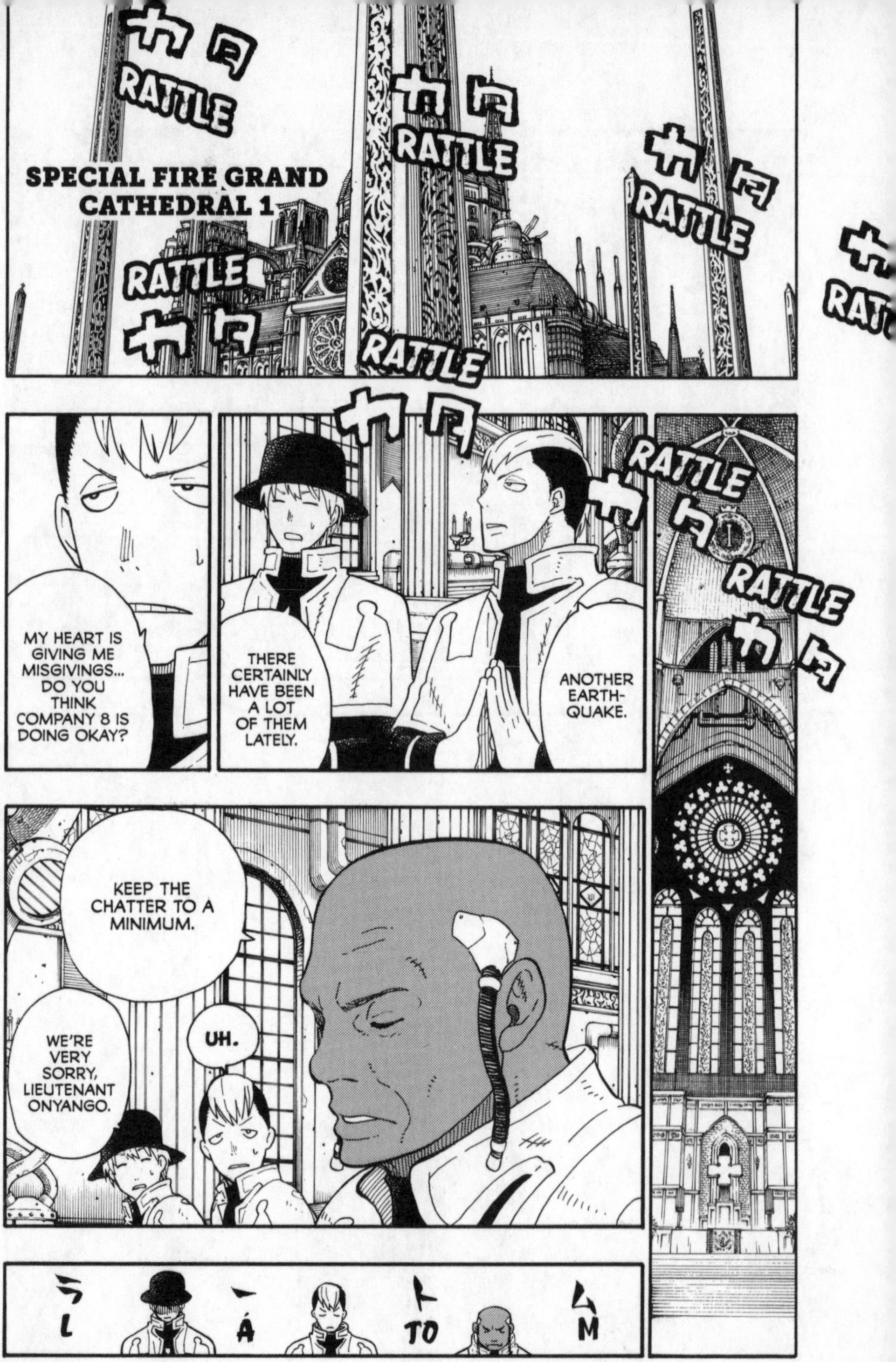

カタ
RATTLE
カタ
RATTLE
カタ
RATTLE
SPECIAL FIRE GRAND CATHEDRAL 1
RATTLE
カタ
RATTLE
カタ
RATTLE
カタ
RATTLE
カタ
ANOTHER EARTHQUAKE.
THERE CERTAINLY HAVE BEEN A LOT OF THEM LATELY.
MY HEART IS GIVING ME MISGIVINGS... DO YOU THINK COMPANY 8 IS DOING OKAY?
KEEP THE CHATTER TO A MINIMUM.
UH.
WE'RE VERY SORRY, LIEUTENANT ONYANGO.
ラ ー ト ム
L Á TO M

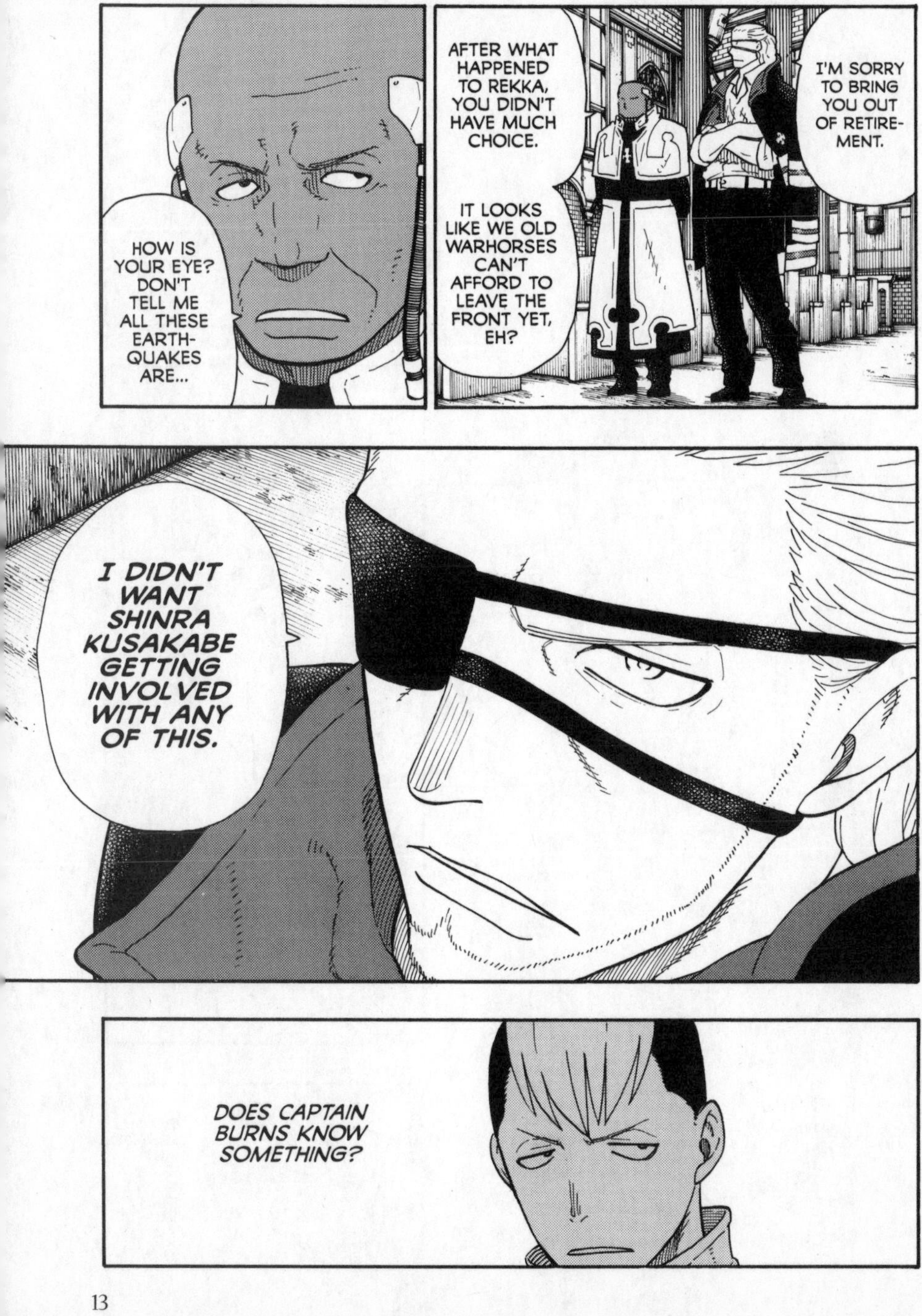
I'M SORRY TO BRING YOU OUT OF RETIRE-MENT.
AFTER WHAT HAPPENED TO REKKA, YOU DIDN'T HAVE MUCH CHOICE.
IT LOOKS LIKE WE OLD WARHORSES CAN'T AFFORD TO LEAVE THE FRONT YET, EH?
HOW IS YOUR EYE? DON'T TELL ME ALL THESE EARTH-QUAKES ARE...
I DIDN'T WANT SHINRA KUSAKABE GETTING INVOLVED WITH ANY OF THIS.
DOES CAPTAIN BURNS KNOW SOMETHING?

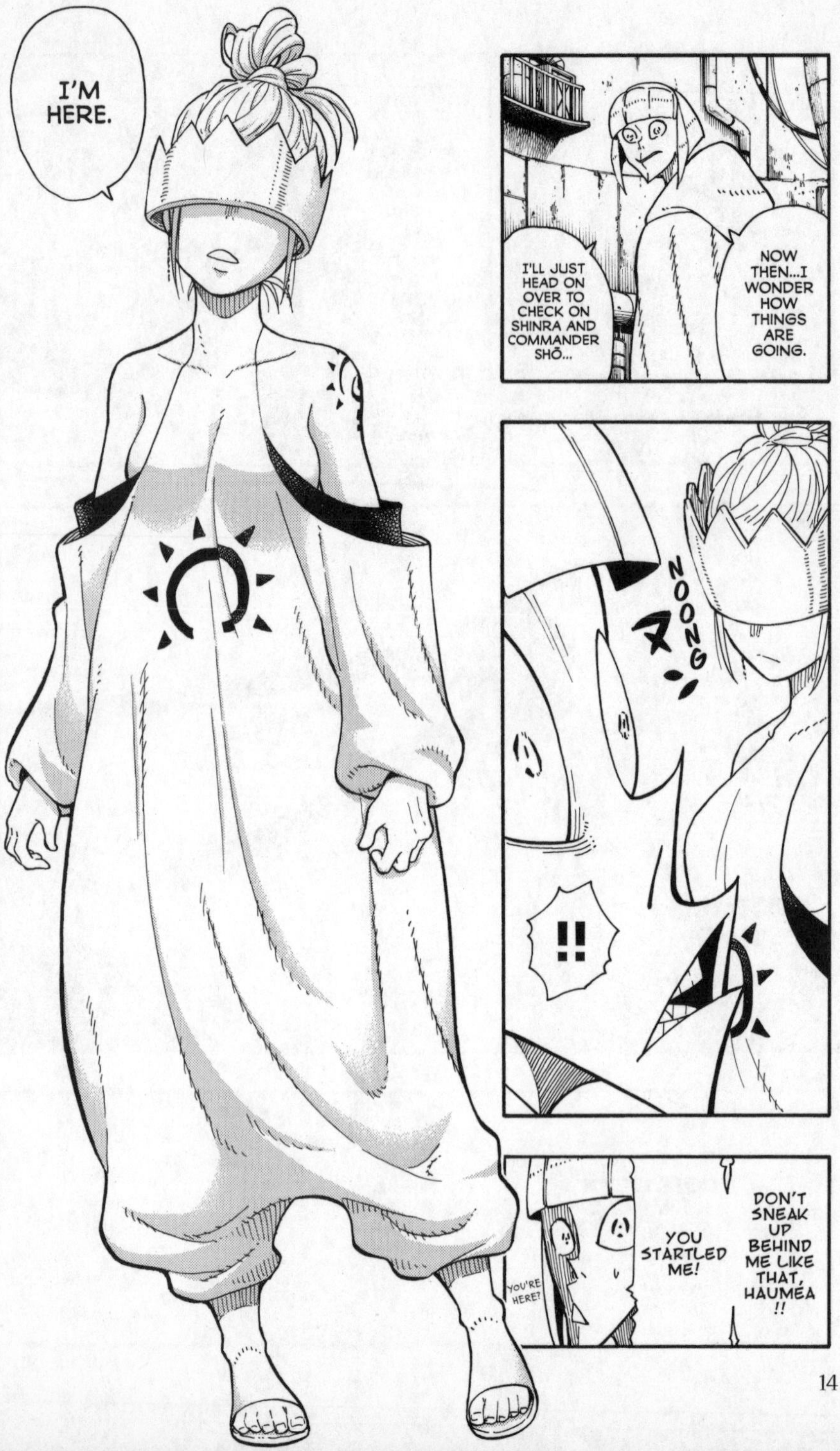
NOW THEN...I WONDER HOW THINGS ARE GOING.
I'LL JUST HEAD ON OVER TO CHECK ON SHINRA AND COMMANDER SHŌ...
NOONG
!!
DON'T SNEAK UP BEHIND ME LIKE THAT, HAUMEA!!
YOU STARTLED ME!
YOU'RE HERE?
I'M HERE.

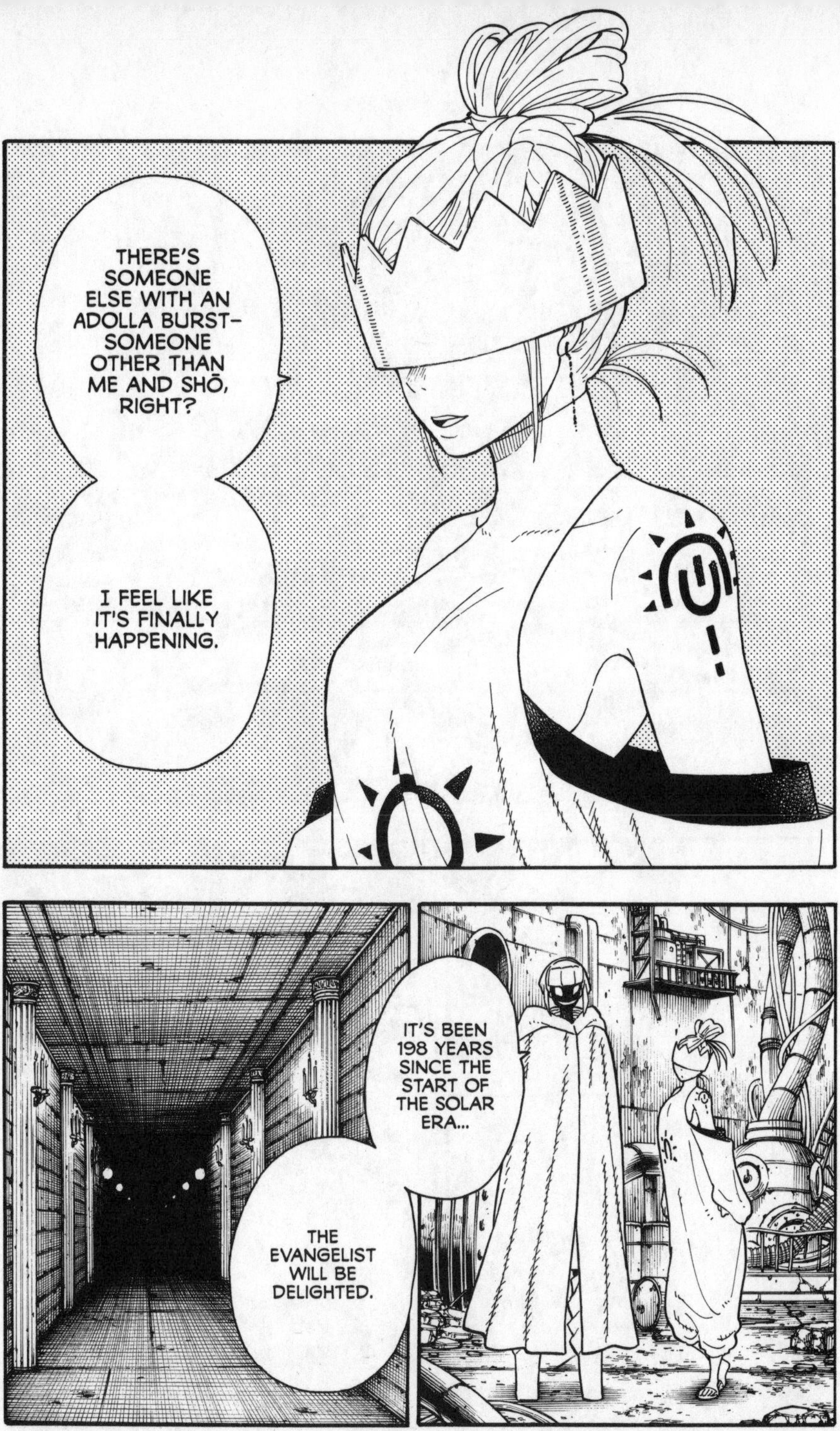
THERE'S SOMEONE ELSE WITH AN ADOLLA BURST–SOMEONE OTHER THAN ME AND SHŌ, RIGHT?
I FEEL LIKE IT'S FINALLY HAPPENING.
IT'S BEEN 198 YEARS SINCE THE START OF THE SOLAR ERA...
THE EVANGELIST WILL BE DELIGHTED.

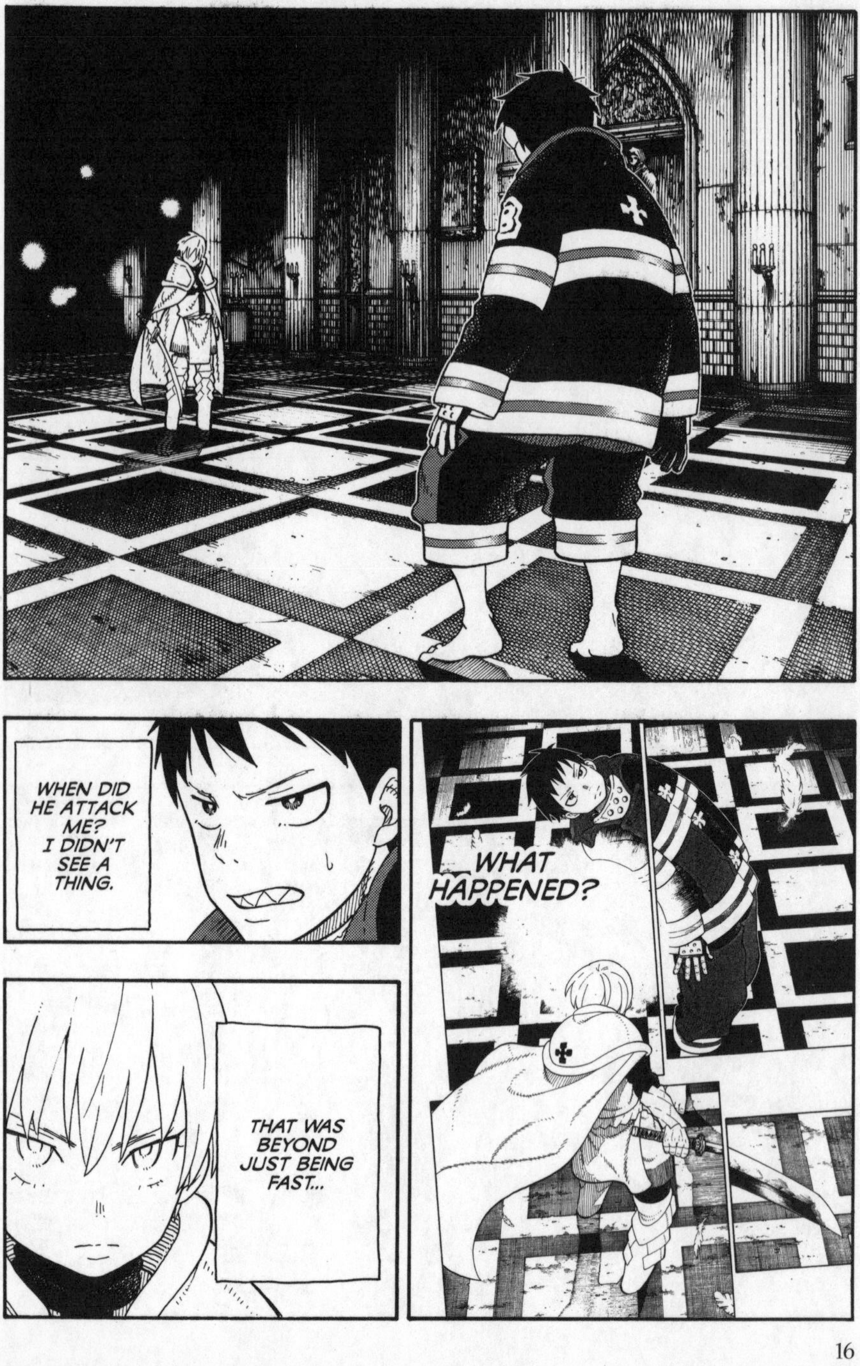
WHAT HAPPENED?
WHEN DID HE ATTACK ME? I DIDN'T SEE A THING.
THAT WAS BEYOND JUST BEING FAST...

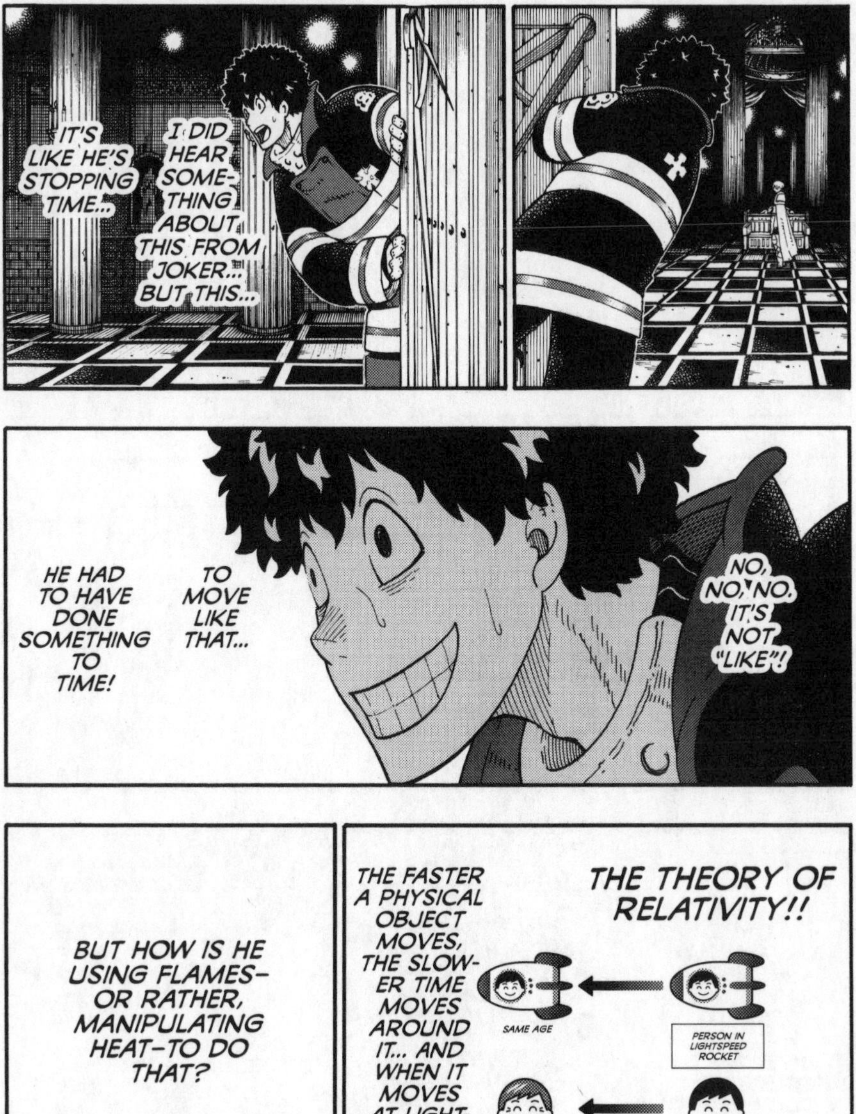
I DID HEAR SOME-THING ABOUT THIS FROM JOKER... BUT THIS...
IT'S LIKE HE'S STOPPING TIME...
NO, NO, NO. IT'S NOT "LIKE"!
TO MOVE LIKE THAT...
HE HAD TO HAVE DONE SOMETHING TO TIME!
THE THEORY OF RELATIVITY!!
THE FASTER A PHYSICAL OBJECT MOVES, THE SLOW-ER TIME MOVES AROUND IT... AND WHEN IT MOVES AT LIGHT-SPEED, TIME STOPS!!
PERSON IN LIGHTSPEED ROCKET
SAME AGE
NORMAL PERSON
10 EARTH YEARS
10 YEARS OLDER
BUT HOW IS HE USING FLAMES–OR RATHER, MANIPULATING HEAT–TO DO THAT?

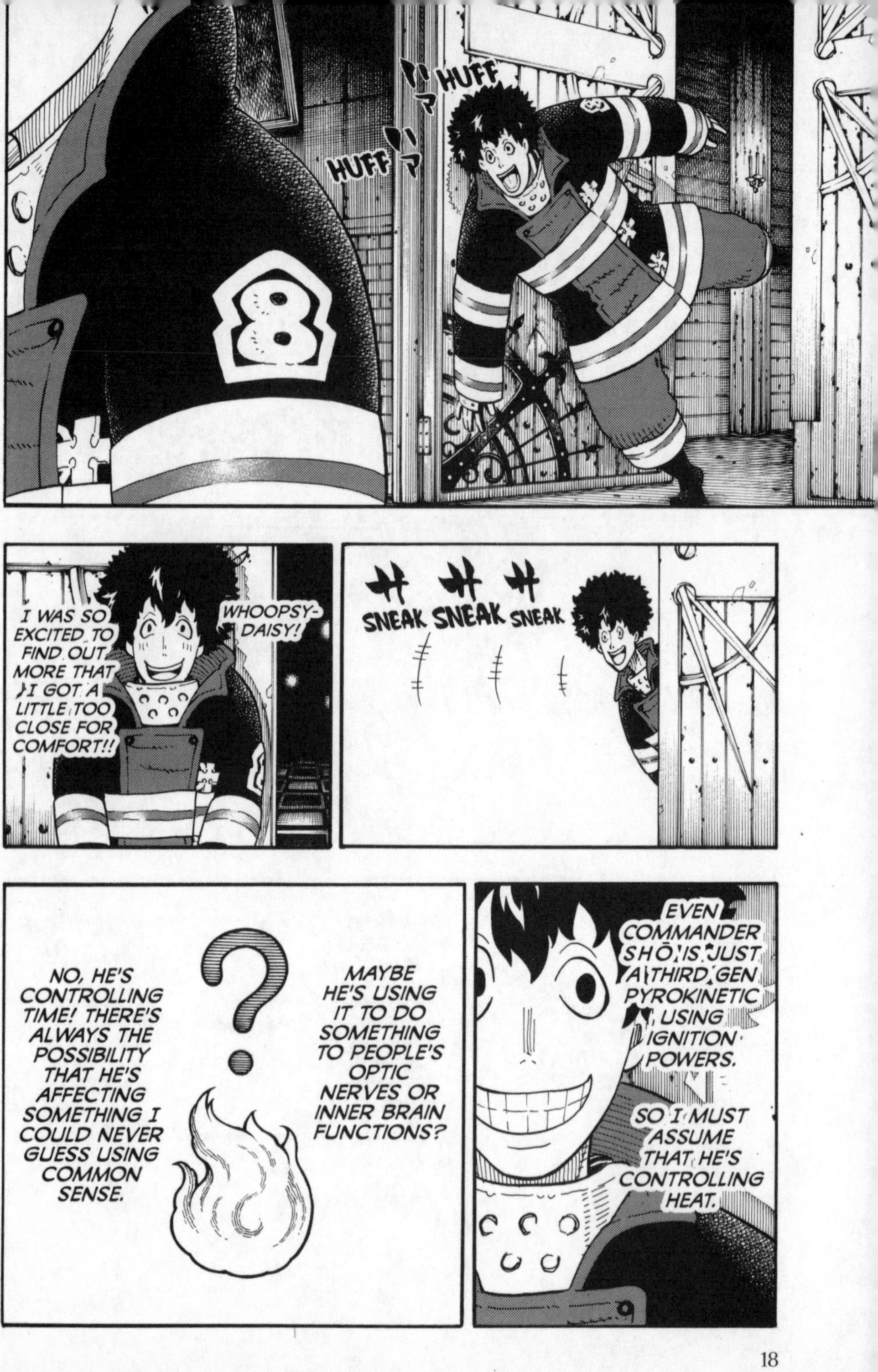
HUFF
HUFF
SNEAK SNEAK SNEAK
WHOOPSY-DAISY!
I WAS SO EXCITED TO FIND OUT MORE THAT I GOT A LITTLE TOO CLOSE FOR COMFORT!!
EVEN COMMANDER SHŌ IS JUST A THIRD GEN PYROKINETIC USING IGNITION POWERS.
SO I MUST ASSUME THAT HE'S CONTROLLING HEAT.
MAYBE HE'S USING IT TO DO SOMETHING TO PEOPLE'S OPTIC NERVES OR INNER BRAIN FUNCTIONS?
NO, HE'S CONTROLLING TIME! THERE'S ALWAYS THE POSSIBILITY THAT HE'S AFFECTING SOMETHING I COULD NEVER GUESS USING COMMON SENSE.

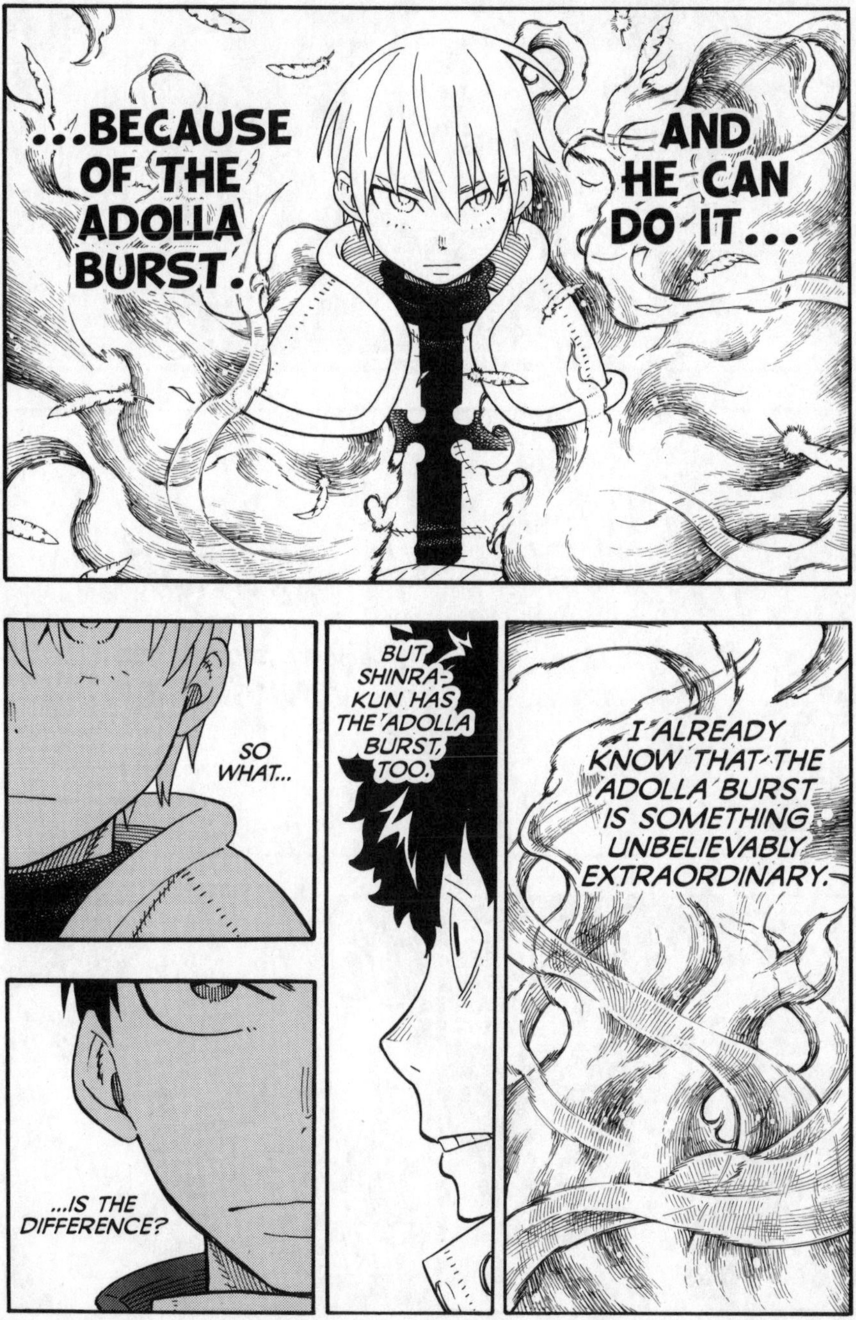
AND HE CAN DO IT...
...BECAUSE OF THE ADOLLA BURST.
I ALREADY KNOW THAT THE ADOLLA BURST IS SOMETHING UNBELIEVABLY EXTRAORDINARY.
BUT SHINRA-KUN HAS THE ADOLLA BURST, TOO.
SO WHAT...
...IS THE DIFFERENCE?

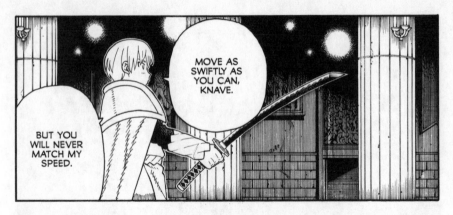

MOVE AS SWIFTLY AS YOU CAN, KNAVE.
BUT YOU WILL NEVER MATCH MY SPEED.
YOU AND I EXIST IN TWO SEPARATE UNIVERSES.
HAAH?! WHAT ARE YOU TALKING ABOUT?
?!
UNI-VERSE...?
IDIOMATICALLY, IT WOULD BE MORE NATURAL TO SAY "WE'RE ON DIFFERENT LEVELS."
THE POWER TO CONTROL FLAME... TIME... THE UNIVERSE...?!

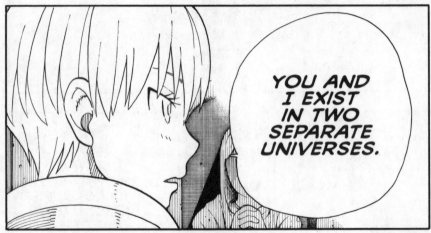

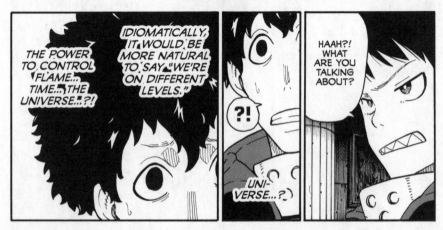

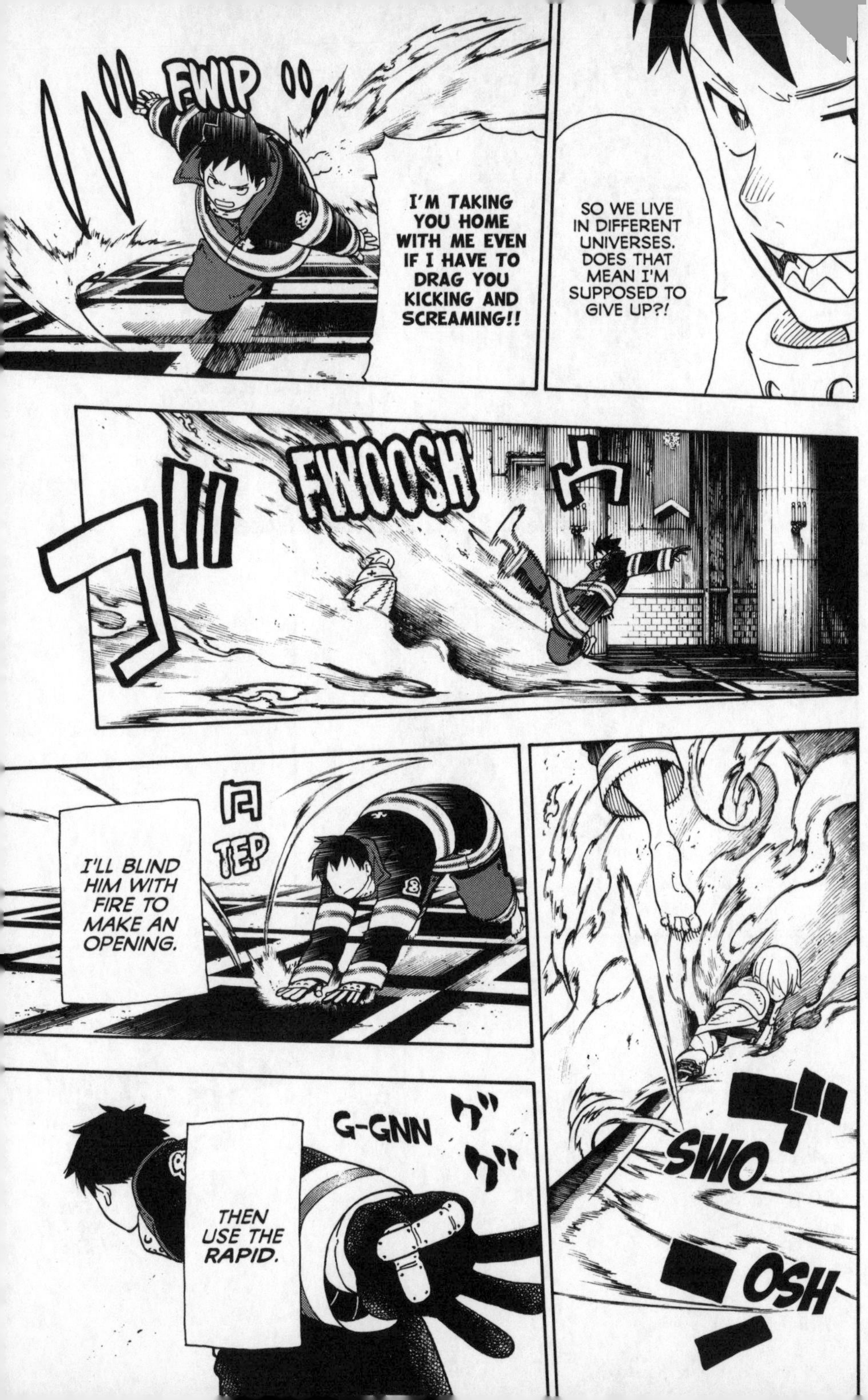
SO WE LIVE IN DIFFERENT UNIVERSES. DOES THAT MEAN I'M SUPPOSED TO GIVE UP?!
FWIP
I'M TAKING YOU HOME WITH ME EVEN IF I HAVE TO DRAG YOU KICKING AND SCREAMING!!
FWOOSH
SWO
OSH
TEP
I'LL BLIND HIM WITH FIRE TO MAKE AN OPENING.
G-GNN
THEN USE THE RAPID.

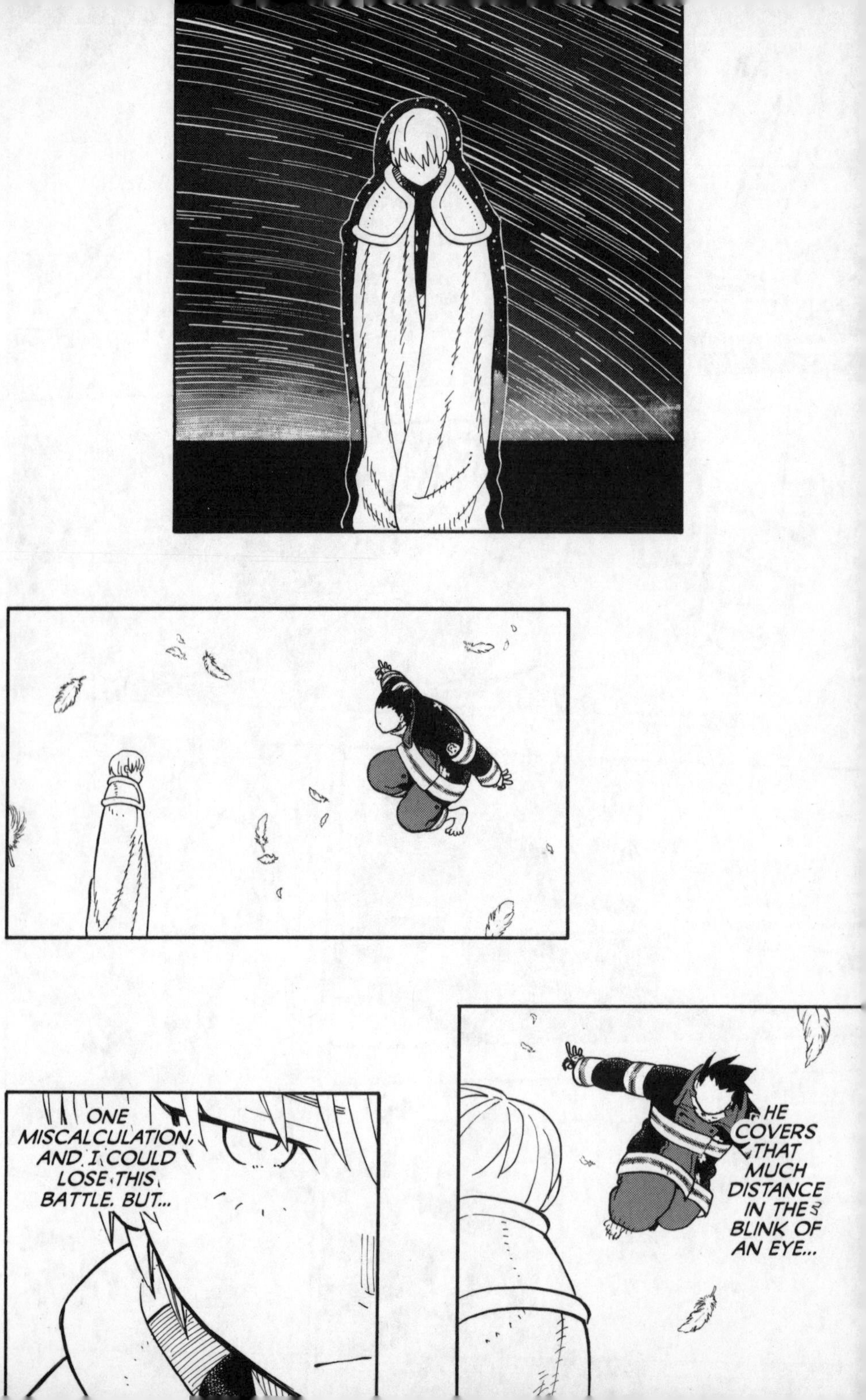
HE COVERS THAT MUCH DISTANCE IN THE BLINK OF AN EYE...
ONE MISCALCULATION, AND I COULD LOSE THIS BATTLE. BUT...

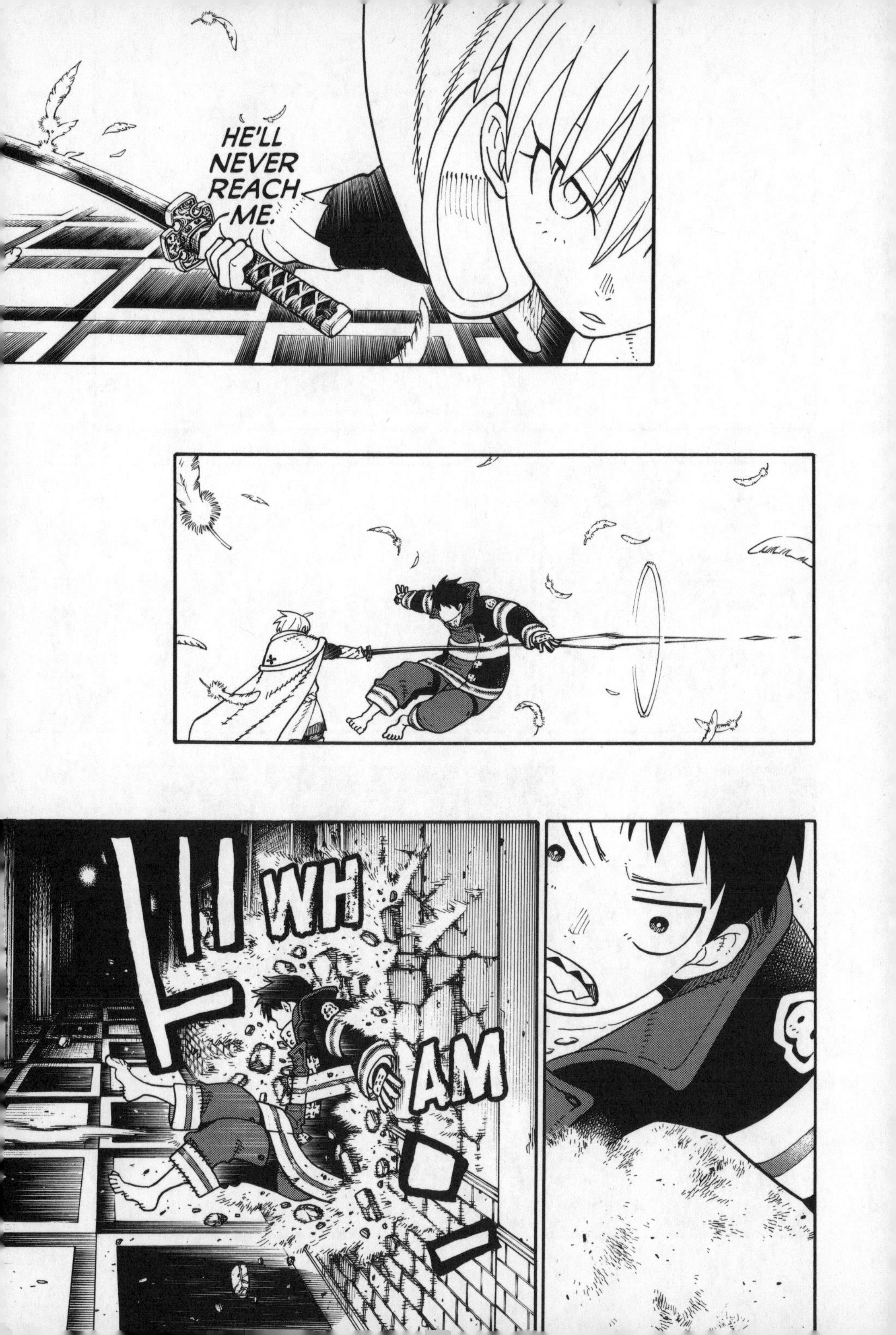
HE'LL NEVER REACH ME.
WHAM

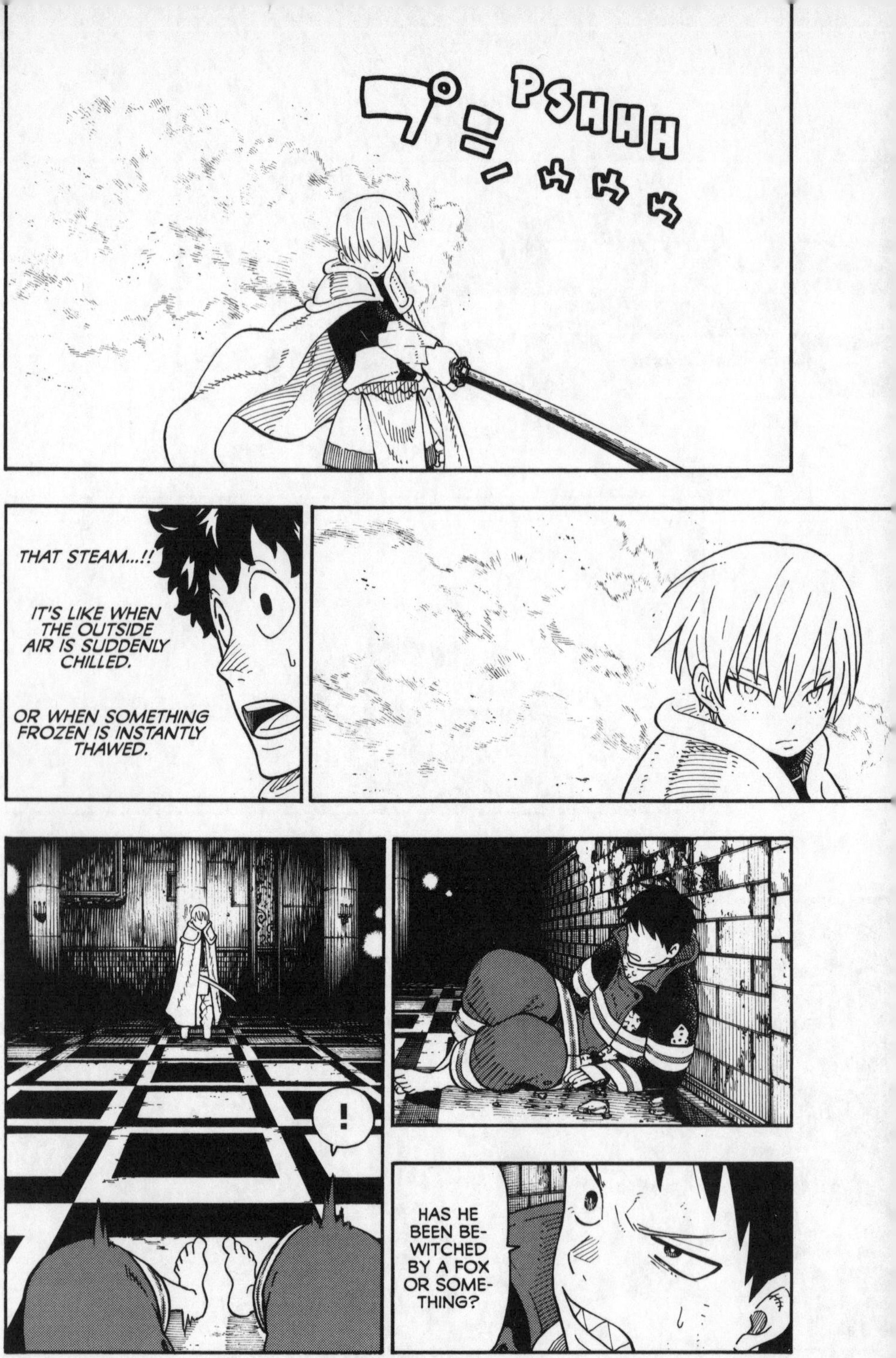
PSHHH
THAT STEAM...!!
IT'S LIKE WHEN THE OUTSIDE AIR IS SUDDENLY CHILLED.
OR WHEN SOMETHING FROZEN IS INSTANTLY THAWED.
HAS HE BEEN BE-WITCHED BY A FOX OR SOME-THING?
!

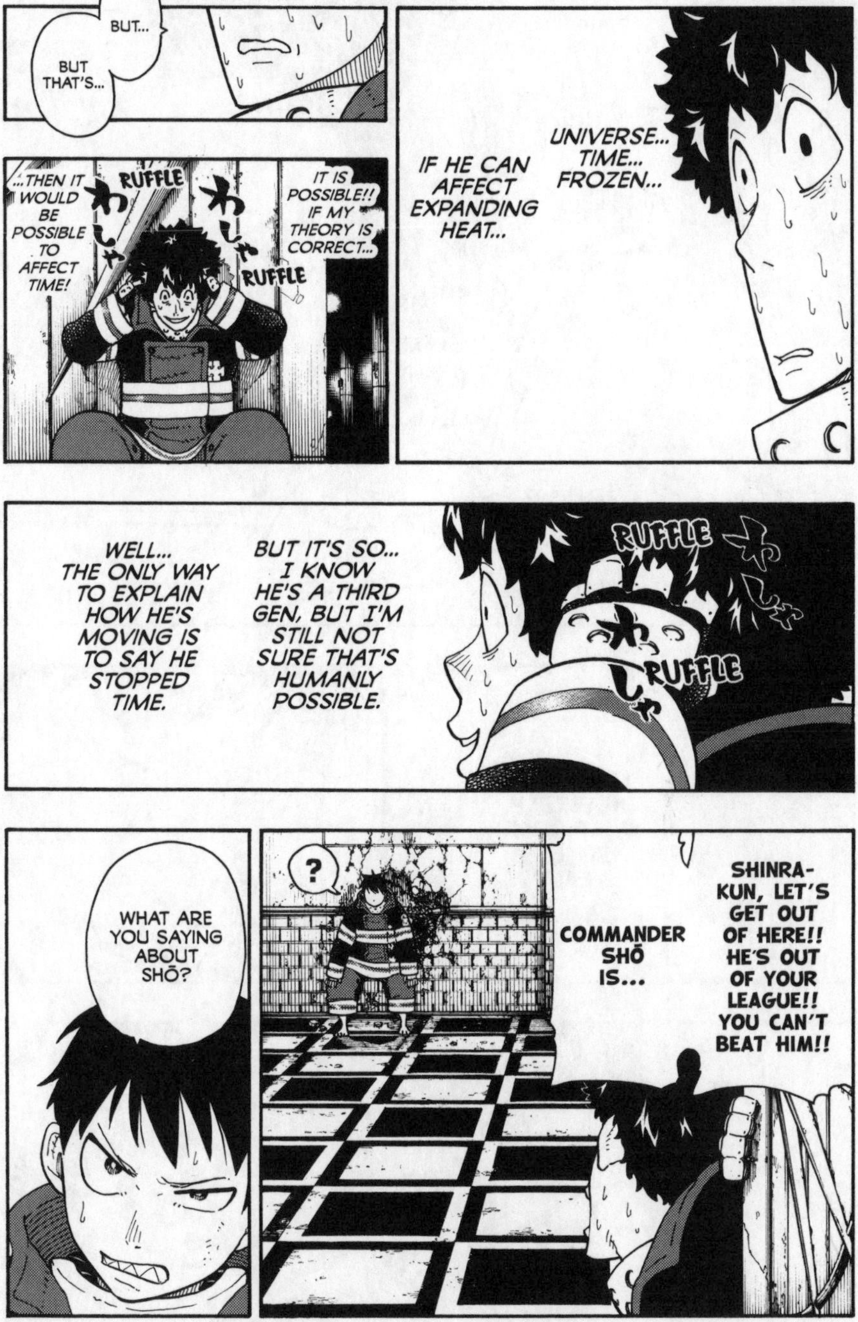
UNIVERSE... TIME... FROZEN...
IF HE CAN AFFECT EXPANDING HEAT...
BUT...
BUT THAT'S...
IT IS POSSIBLE!! IF MY THEORY IS CORRECT...
わしゃ
RUFFLE
...THEN IT WOULD BE POSSIBLE TO AFFECT TIME!
わしゃ
RUFFLE
RUFFLE
わしゃ
わしゃ
RUFFLE
BUT IT'S SO... I KNOW HE'S A THIRD GEN, BUT I'M STILL NOT SURE THAT'S HUMANLY POSSIBLE.
WELL... THE ONLY WAY TO EXPLAIN HOW HE'S MOVING IS TO SAY HE STOPPED TIME.
SHINRA-KUN, LET'S GET OUT OF HERE!! HE'S OUT OF YOUR LEAGUE!! YOU CAN'T BEAT HIM!!
COMMANDER SHŌ IS...
?
WHAT ARE YOU SAYING ABOUT SHŌ?

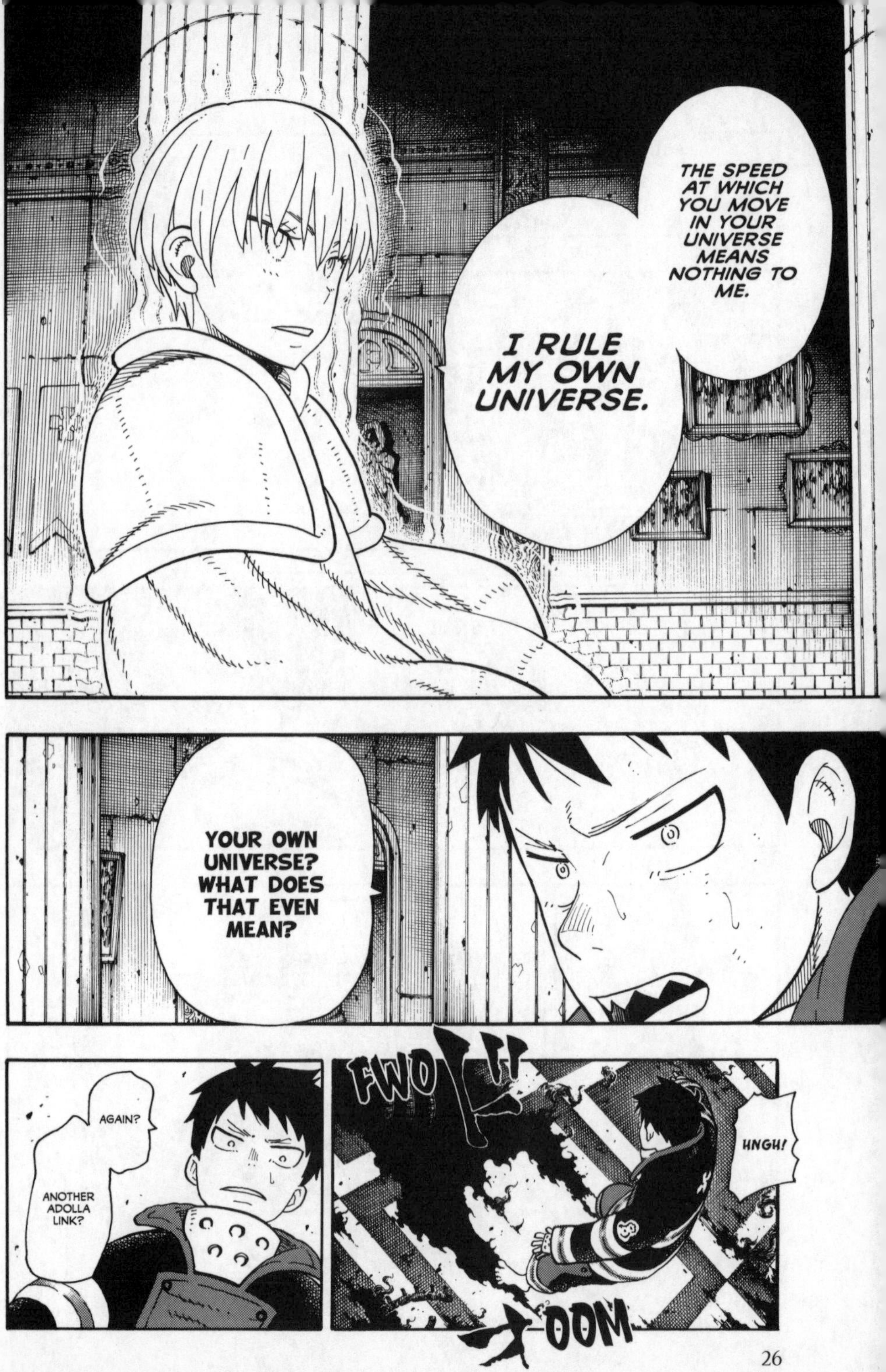
THE SPEED AT WHICH YOU MOVE IN YOUR UNIVERSE MEANS NOTHING TO ME.
I RULE MY OWN UNIVERSE.
YOUR OWN UNIVERSE? WHAT DOES THAT EVEN MEAN?
FWO
OOM
UNGH!
AGAIN?
ANOTHER ADOLLA LINK?

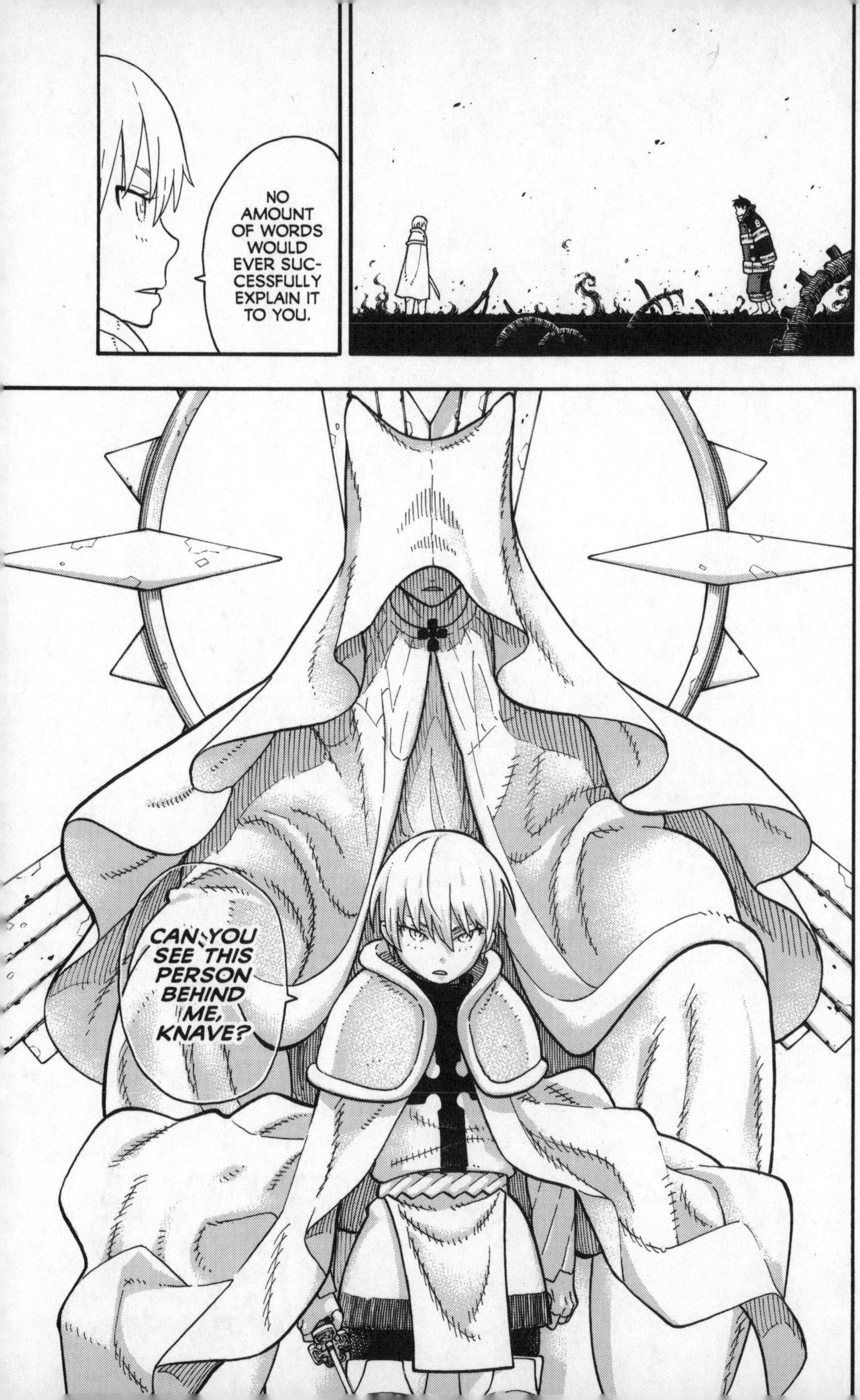
NO AMOUNT OF WORDS WOULD EVER SUC-CESSFULLY EXPLAIN IT TO YOU.
CAN YOU SEE THIS PERSON BEHIND ME, KNAVE?

FIRE FORCE

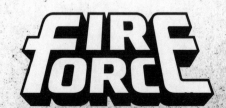

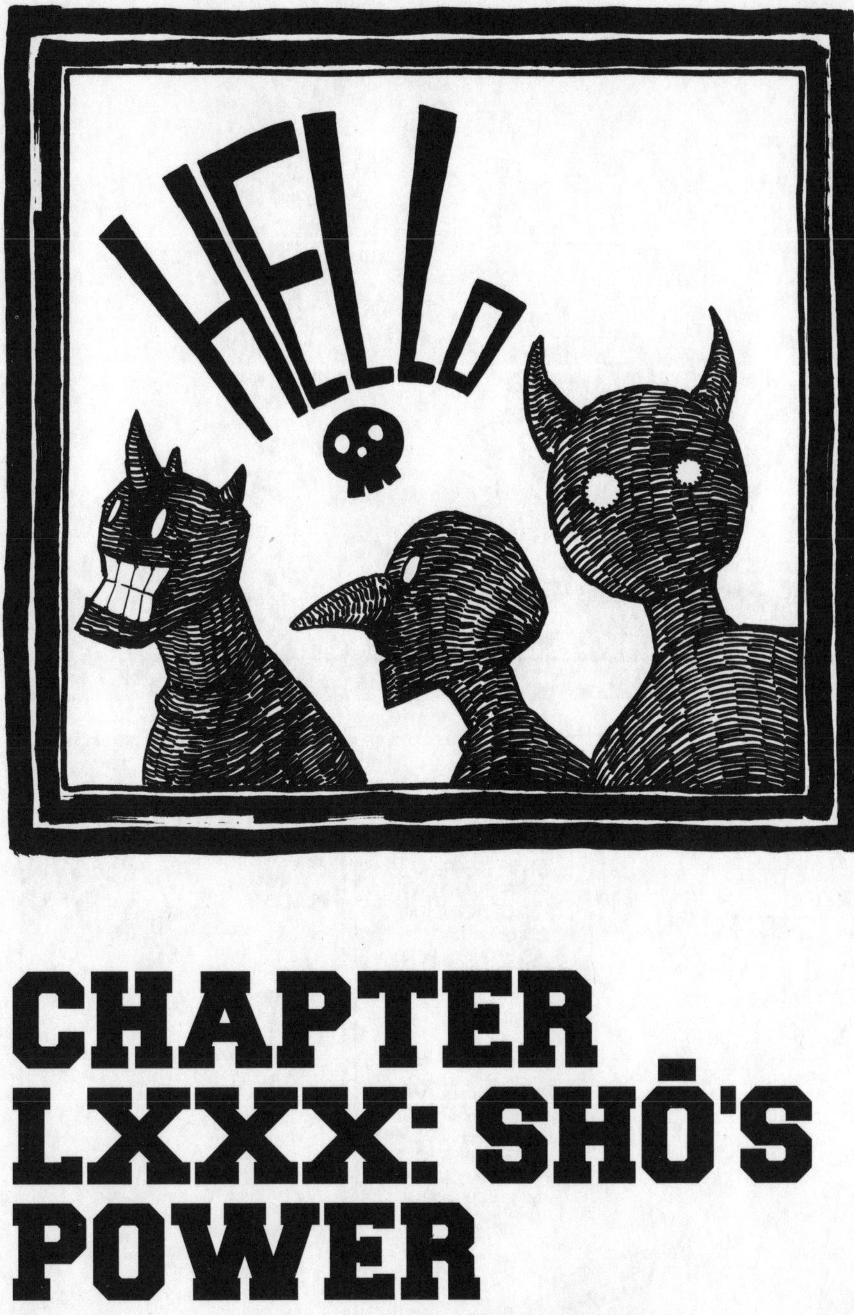
HELLO

CHAPTER LXXX: SHŌ'S POWER

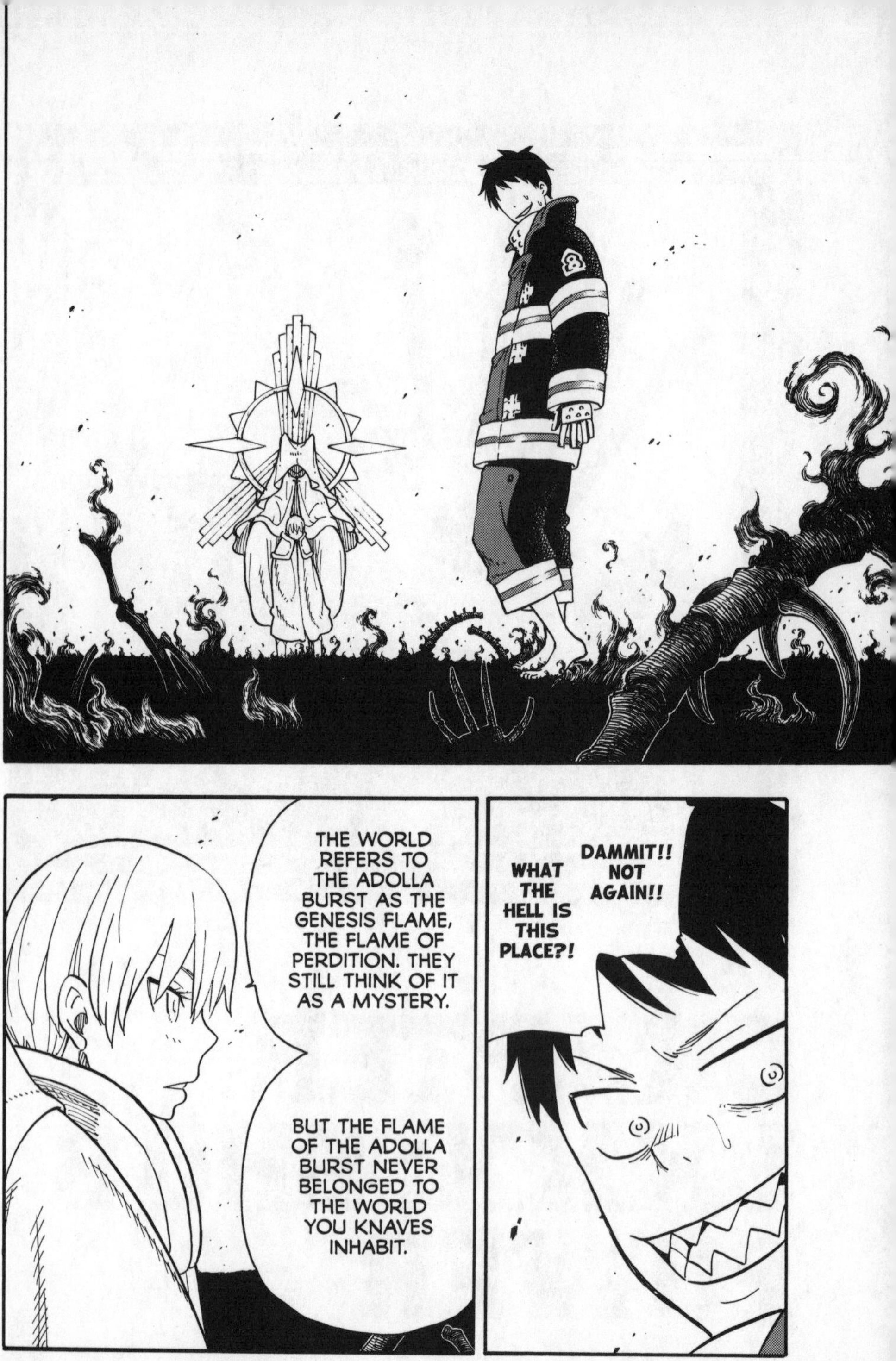
DAMMIT!! NOT AGAIN!!
WHAT THE HELL IS THIS PLACE?!
THE WORLD REFERS TO THE ADOLLA BURST AS THE GENESIS FLAME, THE FLAME OF PERDITION. THEY STILL THINK OF IT AS A MYSTERY.
BUT THE FLAME OF THE ADOLLA BURST NEVER BELONGED TO THE WORLD YOU KNAVES INHABIT.

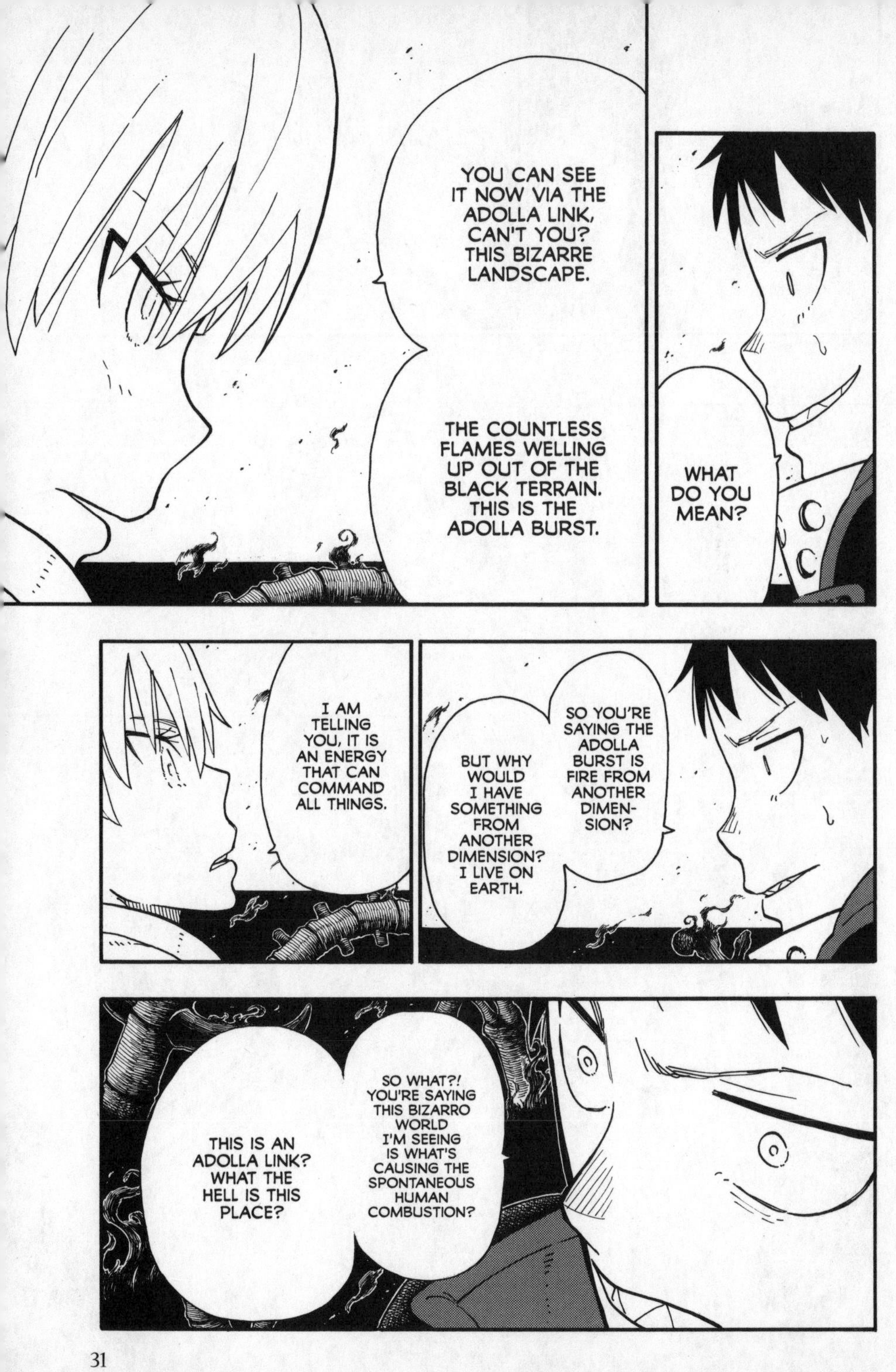
WHAT DO YOU MEAN?
YOU CAN SEE IT NOW VIA THE ADOLLA LINK, CAN'T YOU? THIS BIZARRE LANDSCAPE.
THE COUNTLESS FLAMES WELLING UP OUT OF THE BLACK TERRAIN. THIS IS THE ADOLLA BURST.
SO YOU'RE SAYING THE ADOLLA BURST IS FIRE FROM ANOTHER DIMEN-SION?
BUT WHY WOULD I HAVE SOMETHING FROM ANOTHER DIMENSION? I LIVE ON EARTH.
I AM TELLING YOU, IT IS AN ENERGY THAT CAN COMMAND ALL THINGS.
SO WHAT?! YOU'RE SAYING THIS BIZARRO WORLD I'M SEEING IS WHAT'S CAUSING THE SPONTANEOUS HUMAN COMBUSTION?
THIS IS AN ADOLLA LINK? WHAT THE HELL IS THIS PLACE?

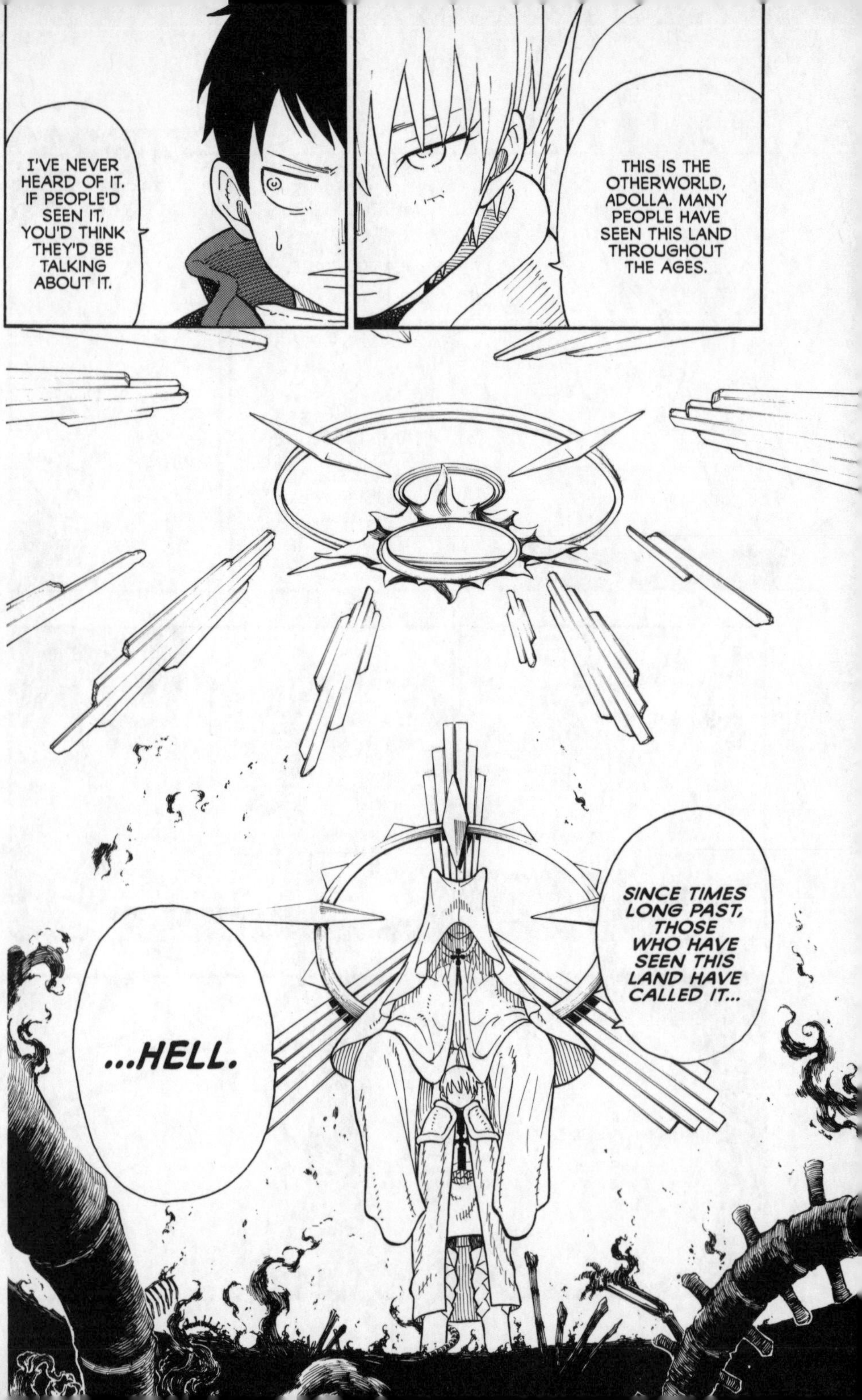
THIS IS THE OTHERWORLD, ADOLLA. MANY PEOPLE HAVE SEEN THIS LAND THROUGHOUT THE AGES.
I'VE NEVER HEARD OF IT. IF PEOPLE'D SEEN IT, YOU'D THINK THEY'D BE TALKING ABOUT IT.
SINCE TIMES LONG PAST, THOSE WHO HAVE SEEN THIS LAND HAVE CALLED IT...
...HELL.

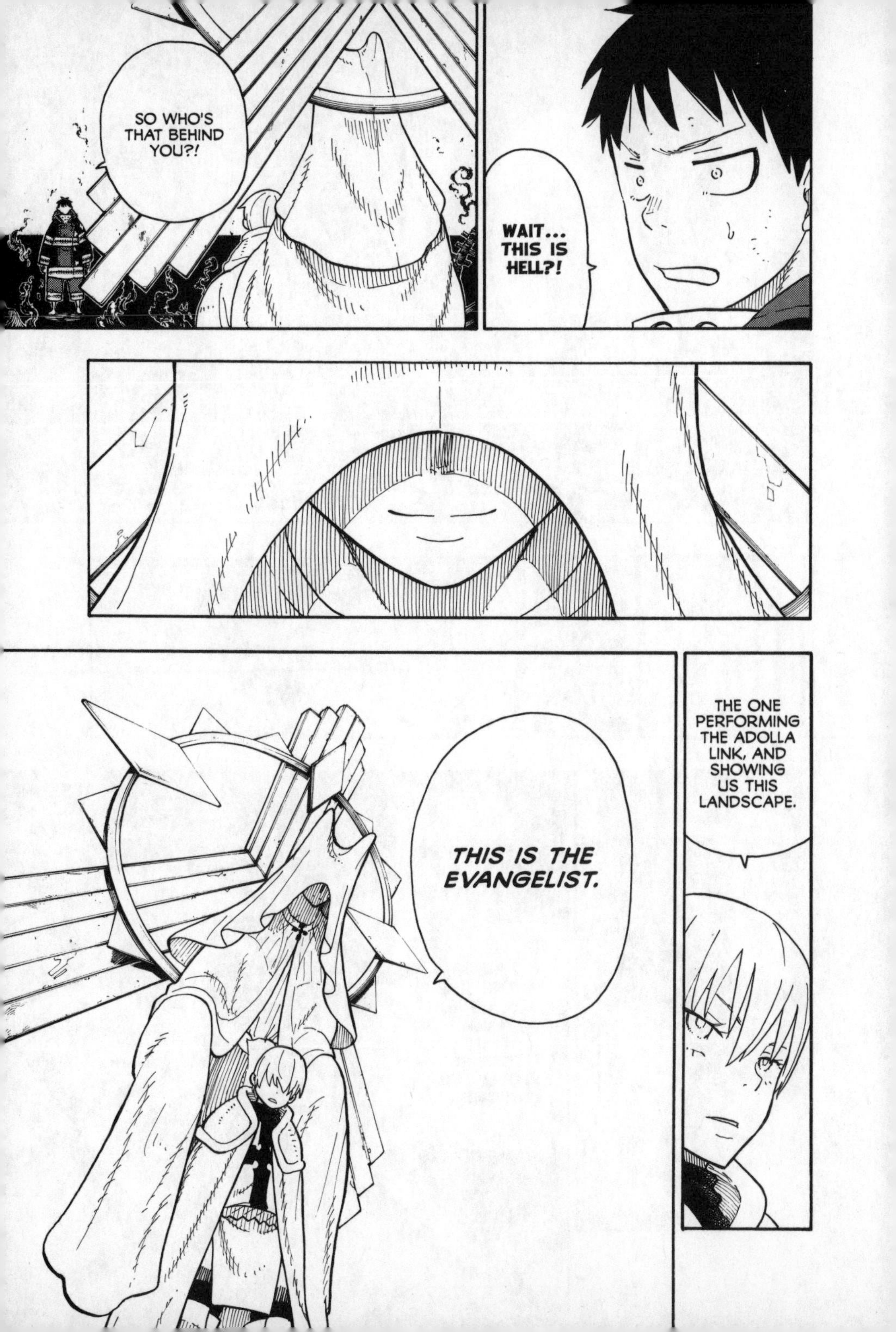
WAIT... THIS IS HELL?!
SO WHO'S THAT BEHIND YOU?!
THE ONE PERFORMING THE ADOLLA LINK, AND SHOWING US THIS LANDSCAPE.
THIS IS THE EVANGELIST.

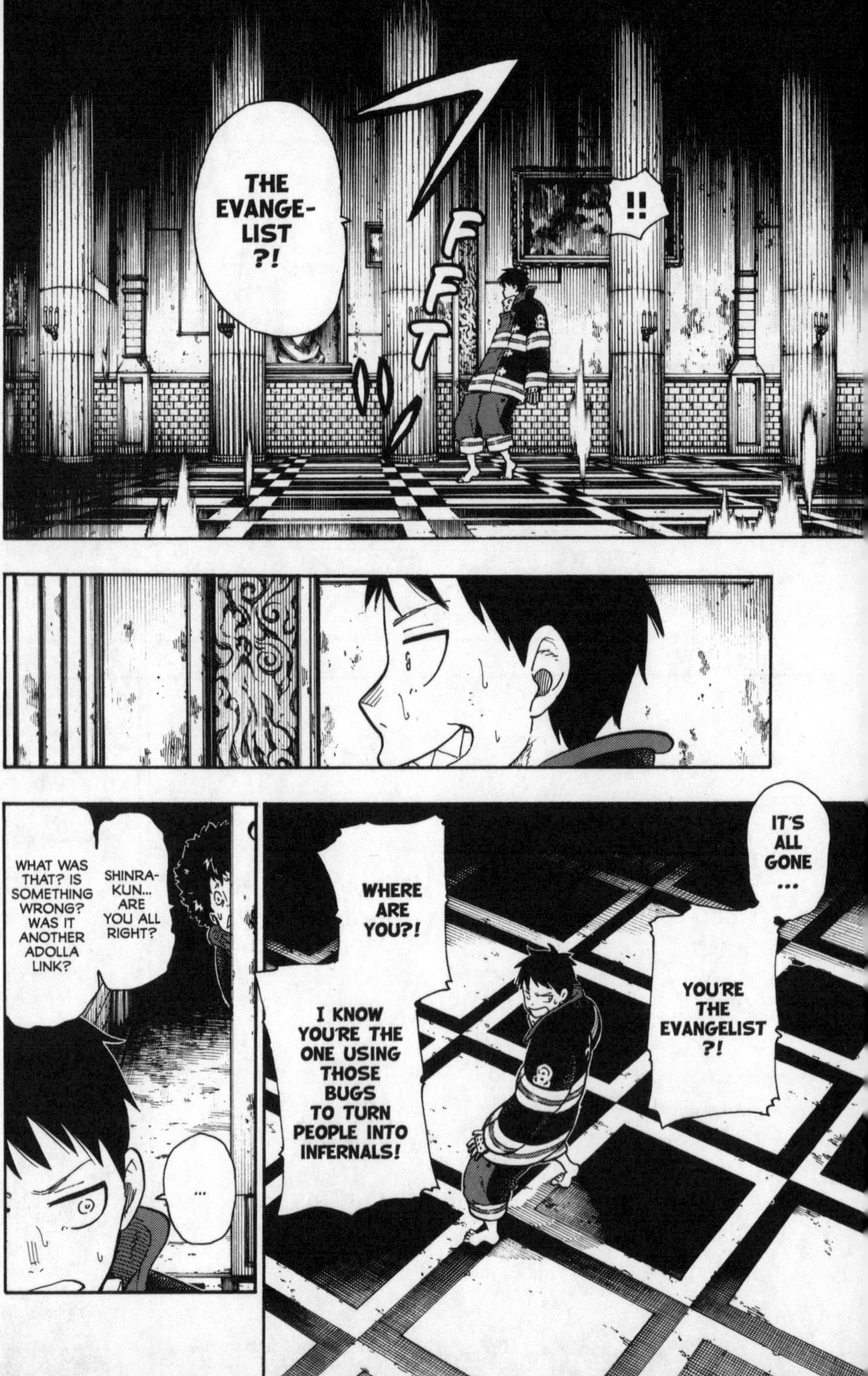
THE EVANGE-LIST?!
!!
FFFT
IT'S ALL GONE...
WHERE ARE YOU?!
YOU'RE THE EVANGELIST?!
I KNOW YOU'RE THE ONE USING THOSE BUGS TO TURN PEOPLE INTO INFERNALS!
SHINRA-KUN... ARE YOU ALL RIGHT?
WHAT WAS THAT? IS SOMETHING WRONG? WAS IT ANOTHER ADOLLA LINK?
...

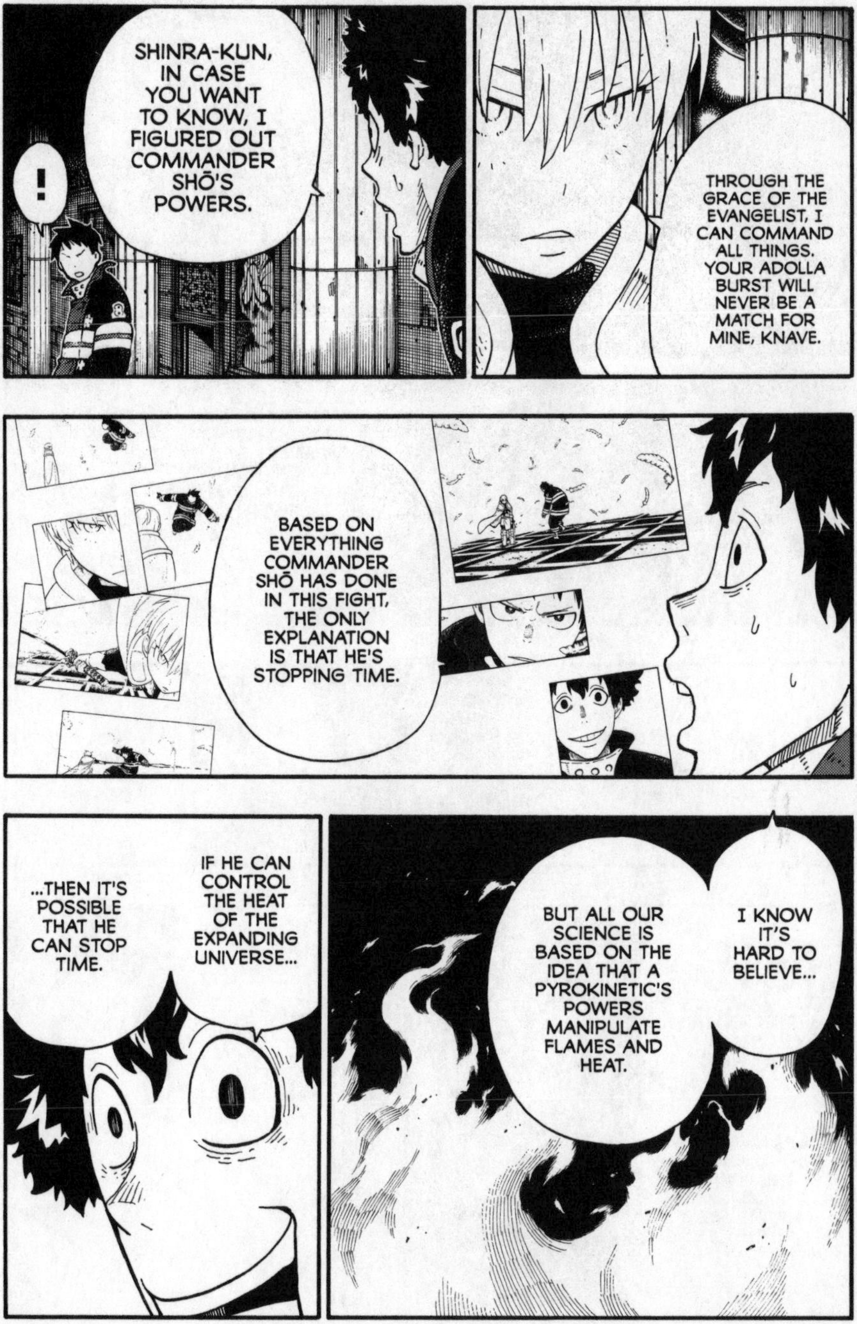
THROUGH THE GRACE OF THE EVANGELIST, I CAN COMMAND ALL THINGS. YOUR ADOLLA BURST WILL NEVER BE A MATCH FOR MINE, KNAVE.
SHINRA-KUN, IN CASE YOU WANT TO KNOW, I FIGURED OUT COMMANDER SHŌ'S POWERS.
!
BASED ON EVERYTHING COMMANDER SHŌ HAS DONE IN THIS FIGHT, THE ONLY EXPLANATION IS THAT HE'S STOPPING TIME.
I KNOW IT'S HARD TO BELIEVE...
BUT ALL OUR SCIENCE IS BASED ON THE IDEA THAT A PYROKINETIC'S POWERS MANIPULATE FLAMES AND HEAT.
IF HE CAN CONTROL THE HEAT OF THE EXPANDING UNIVERSE...
...THEN IT'S POSSIBLE THAT HE CAN STOP TIME.

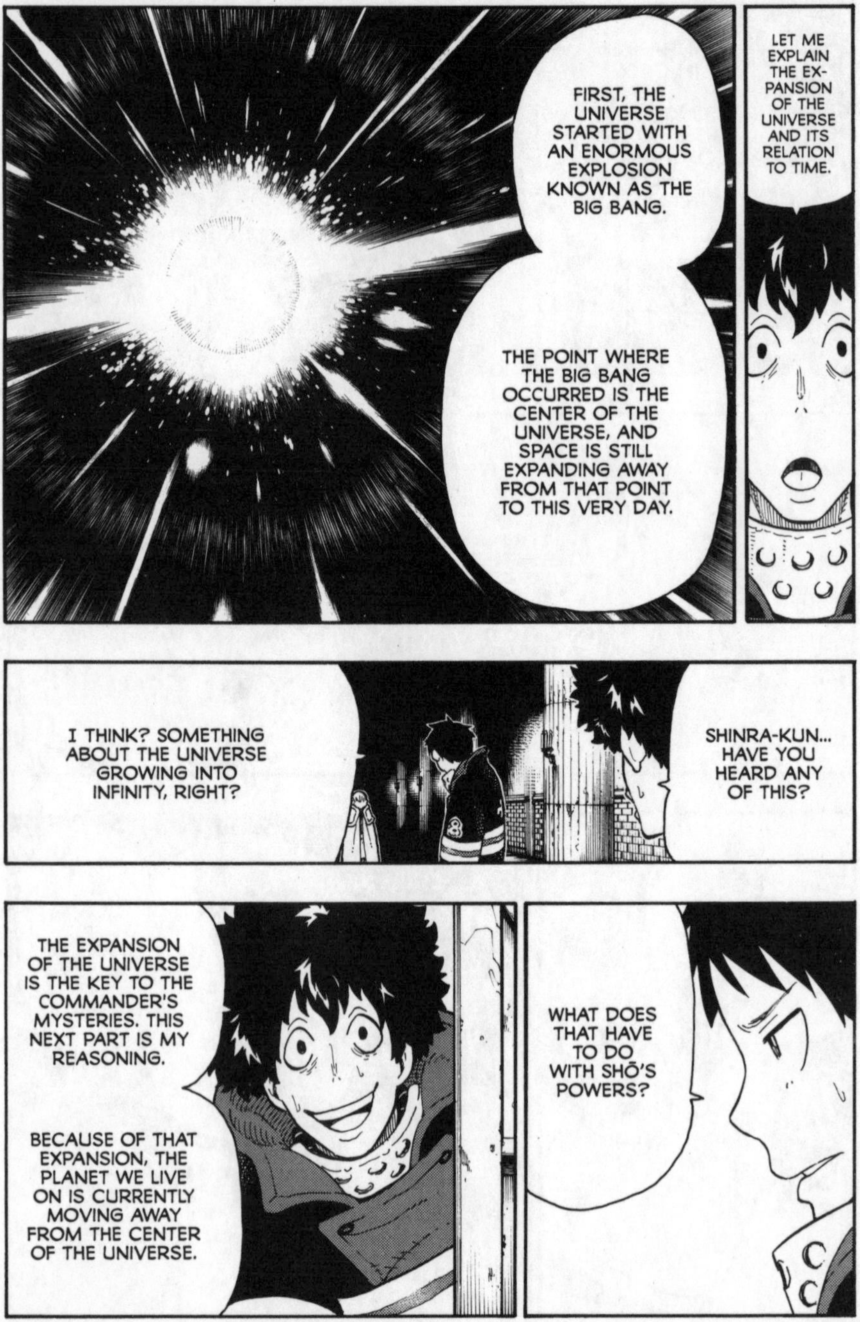
LET ME EXPLAIN THE EX-PANSION OF THE UNIVERSE AND ITS RELATION TO TIME.
FIRST, THE UNIVERSE STARTED WITH AN ENORMOUS EXPLOSION KNOWN AS THE BIG BANG.
THE POINT WHERE THE BIG BANG OCCURRED IS THE CENTER OF THE UNIVERSE, AND SPACE IS STILL EXPANDING AWAY FROM THAT POINT TO THIS VERY DAY.
SHINRA-KUN... HAVE YOU HEARD ANY OF THIS?
I THINK? SOMETHING ABOUT THE UNIVERSE GROWING INTO INFINITY, RIGHT?
WHAT DOES THAT HAVE TO DO WITH SHŌ'S POWERS?
THE EXPANSION OF THE UNIVERSE IS THE KEY TO THE COMMANDER'S MYSTERIES. THIS NEXT PART IS MY REASONING.
BECAUSE OF THAT EXPANSION, THE PLANET WE LIVE ON IS CURRENTLY MOVING AWAY FROM THE CENTER OF THE UNIVERSE.

*REGARDING THE SPEED OF EXPANSION
*THE EXPANSION SPEED OF POINT B ON THE OUTSIDE IS FASTER THAN THAT OF POINT A.
ACCORDING TO HUBBLE'S LAW, THE FARTHER YOU GET AWAY FROM THE CENTER OF THE UNIVERSE, THE FASTER THINGS ARE EXPANDING.
Big Bang
POINT A
POINT B
EARTH
*REGARDING TIME
*POINT B IS MOVING FASTER THAN POINT A, SO ITS TIME IS MOVING SLOWER.
AND ACCORDING TO THE THEORY OF RELATIVITY, THE FASTER AN OBJECT MOVES, THE SLOWER TIME MOVES FOR THAT OBJECT.
POINT A
POINT B
EARTH
IN OTHER WORDS, WE CAN ASSUME THAT THINGS ON THE OUTSIDE ARE MOVING FASTER, AND THEREFORE THEIR TIME IS SLOWER, WHILE THINGS ON THE INSIDE ARE MOVING SLOWER, ERGO THEIR TIME IS FASTER.

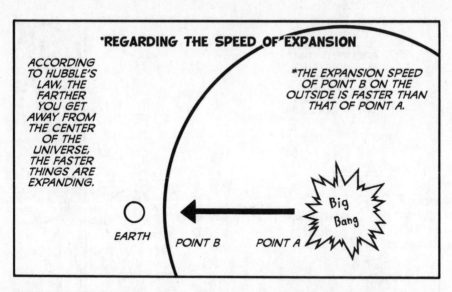

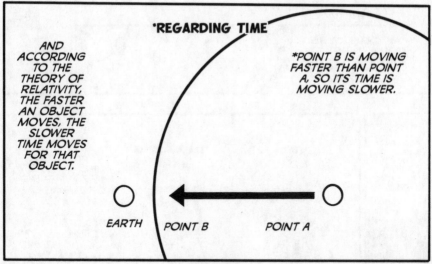

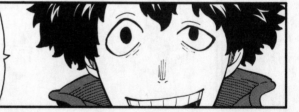

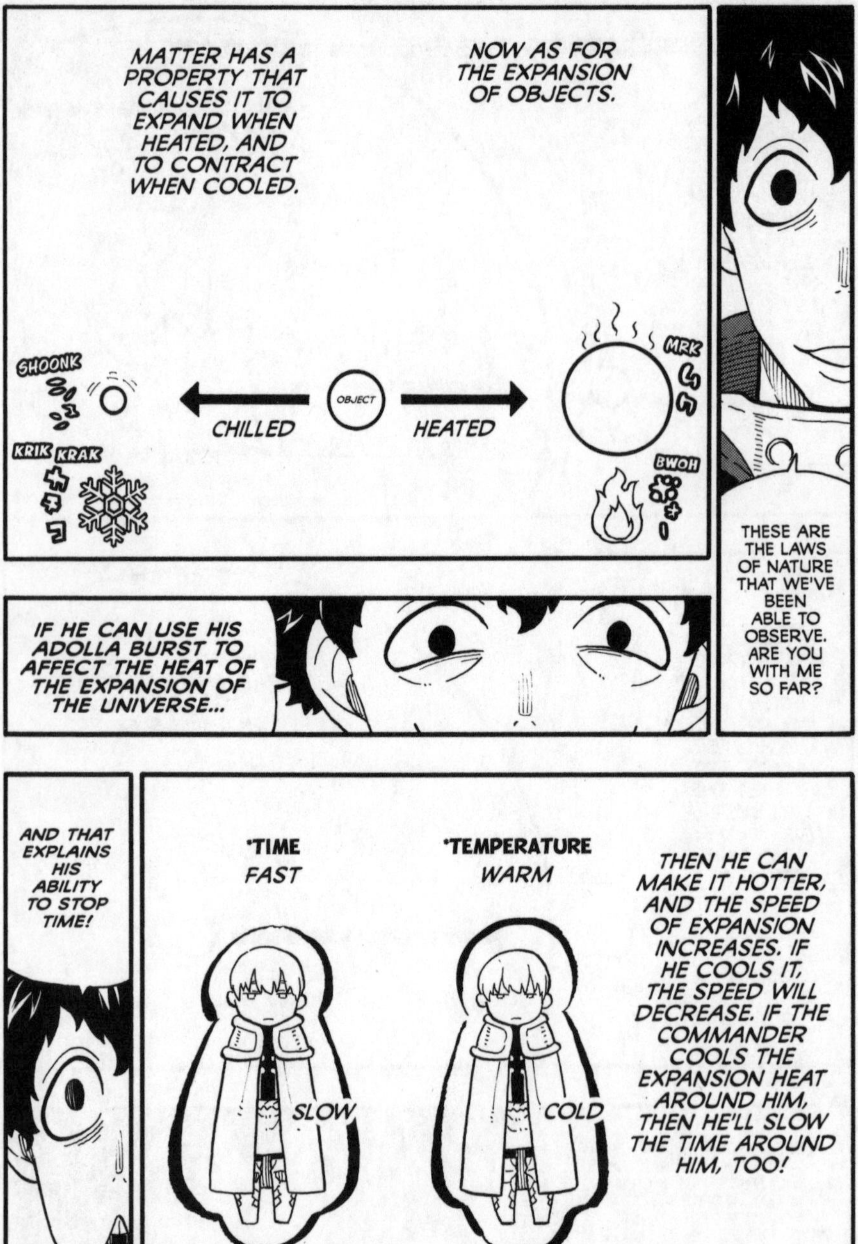
THESE ARE THE LAWS OF NATURE THAT WE'VE BEEN ABLE TO OBSERVE. ARE YOU WITH ME SO FAR?
NOW AS FOR THE EXPANSION OF OBJECTS.
MATTER HAS A PROPERTY THAT CAUSES IT TO EXPAND WHEN HEATED, AND TO CONTRACT WHEN COOLED.
MRK
BWOH
HEATED
OBJECT
CHILLED
SHOONK
KRIK
KRAK
IF HE CAN USE HIS ADOLLA BURST TO AFFECT THE HEAT OF THE EXPANSION OF THE UNIVERSE...
THEN HE CAN MAKE IT HOTTER, AND THE SPEED OF EXPANSION INCREASES. IF HE COOLS IT, THE SPEED WILL DECREASE. IF THE COMMANDER COOLS THE EXPANSION HEAT AROUND HIM, THEN HE'LL SLOW THE TIME AROUND HIM, TOO!
*TEMPERATURE
WARM
COLD
*TIME
FAST
SLOW
AND THAT EXPLAINS HIS ABILITY TO STOP TIME!

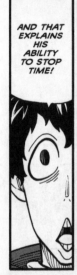

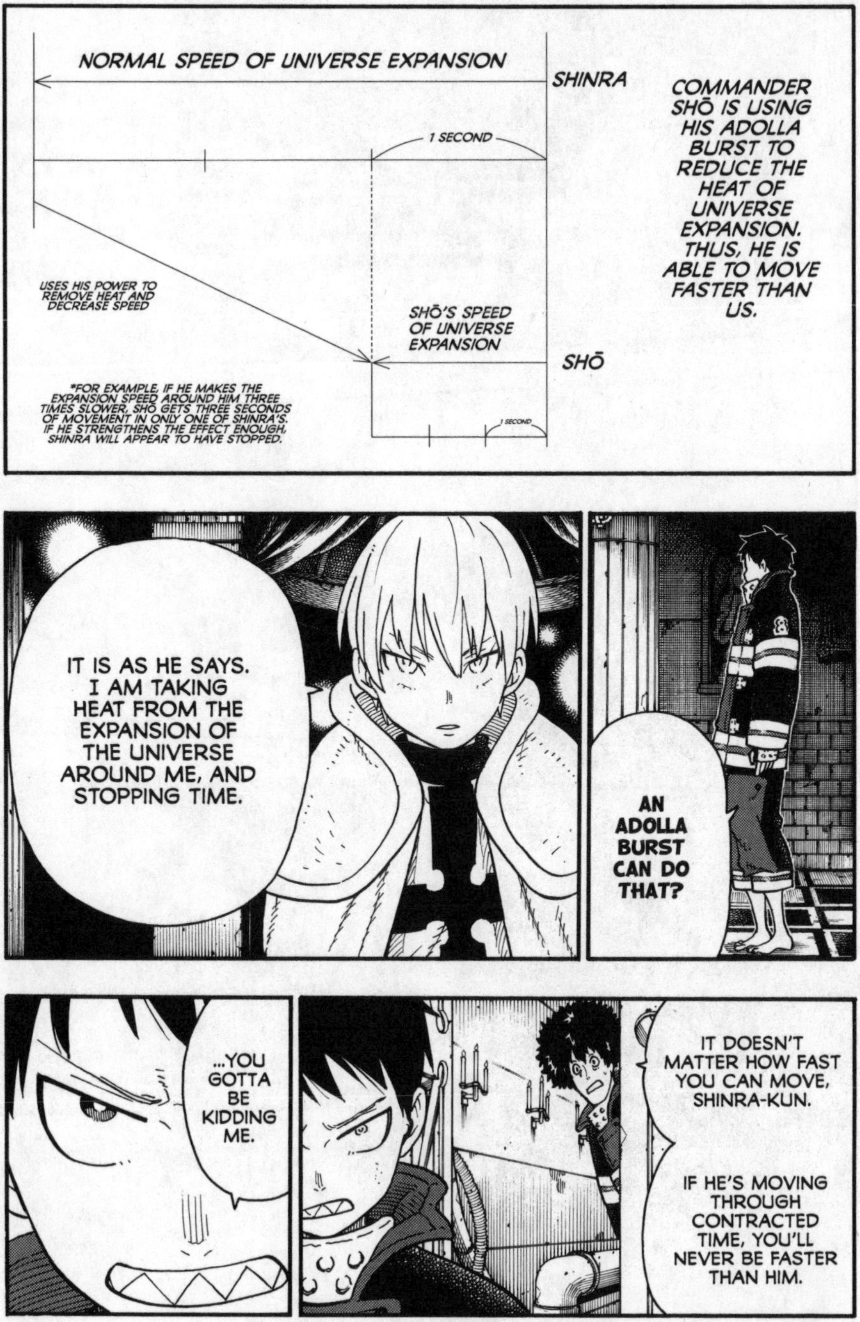
COMMANDER SHŌ IS USING HIS ADOLLA BURST TO REDUCE THE HEAT OF UNIVERSE EXPANSION. THUS, HE IS ABLE TO MOVE FASTER THAN US.
NORMAL SPEED OF UNIVERSE EXPANSION
SHINRA
1 SECOND
USES HIS POWER TO REMOVE HEAT AND DECREASE SPEED
SHŌ'S SPEED OF UNIVERSE EXPANSION
SHŌ
1 SECOND
*FOR EXAMPLE, IF HE MAKES THE EXPANSION SPEED AROUND HIM THREE TIMES SLOWER, SHŌ GETS THREE SECONDS OF MOVEMENT IN ONLY ONE OF SHINRA'S. IF HE STRENGTHENS THE EFFECT ENOUGH, SHINRA WILL APPEAR TO HAVE STOPPED.
AN ADOLLA BURST CAN DO THAT?
IT IS AS HE SAYS. I AM TAKING HEAT FROM THE EXPANSION OF THE UNIVERSE AROUND ME, AND STOPPING TIME.
IT DOESN'T MATTER HOW FAST YOU CAN MOVE, SHINRA-KUN.
IF HE'S MOVING THROUGH CONTRACTED TIME, YOU'LL NEVER BE FASTER THAN HIM.
...YOU GOTTA BE KIDDING ME.

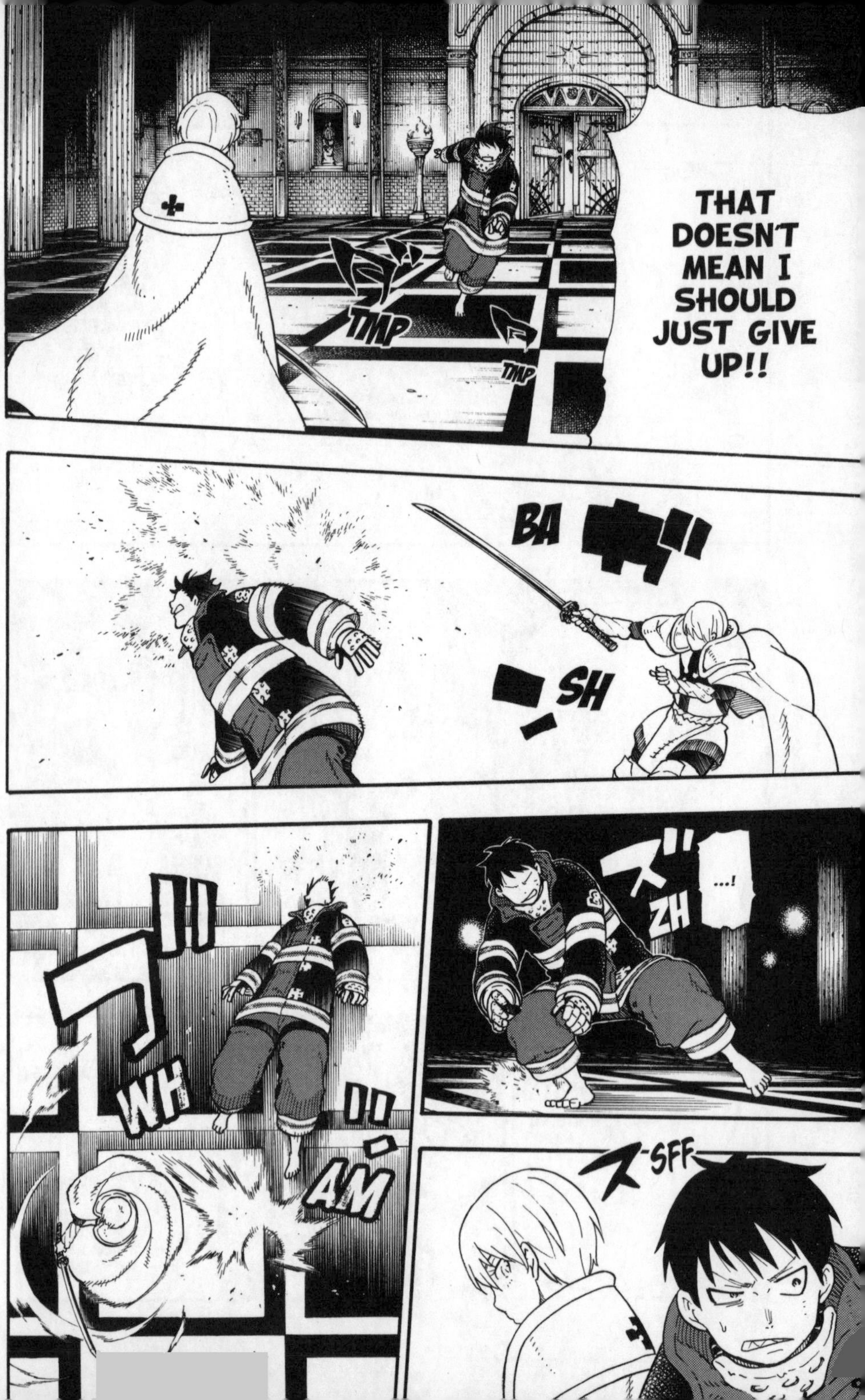
THAT DOESN'T MEAN I SHOULD JUST GIVE UP!!
TMP
TMP
BA
SH
...!
ZH
SFF
WH
AM

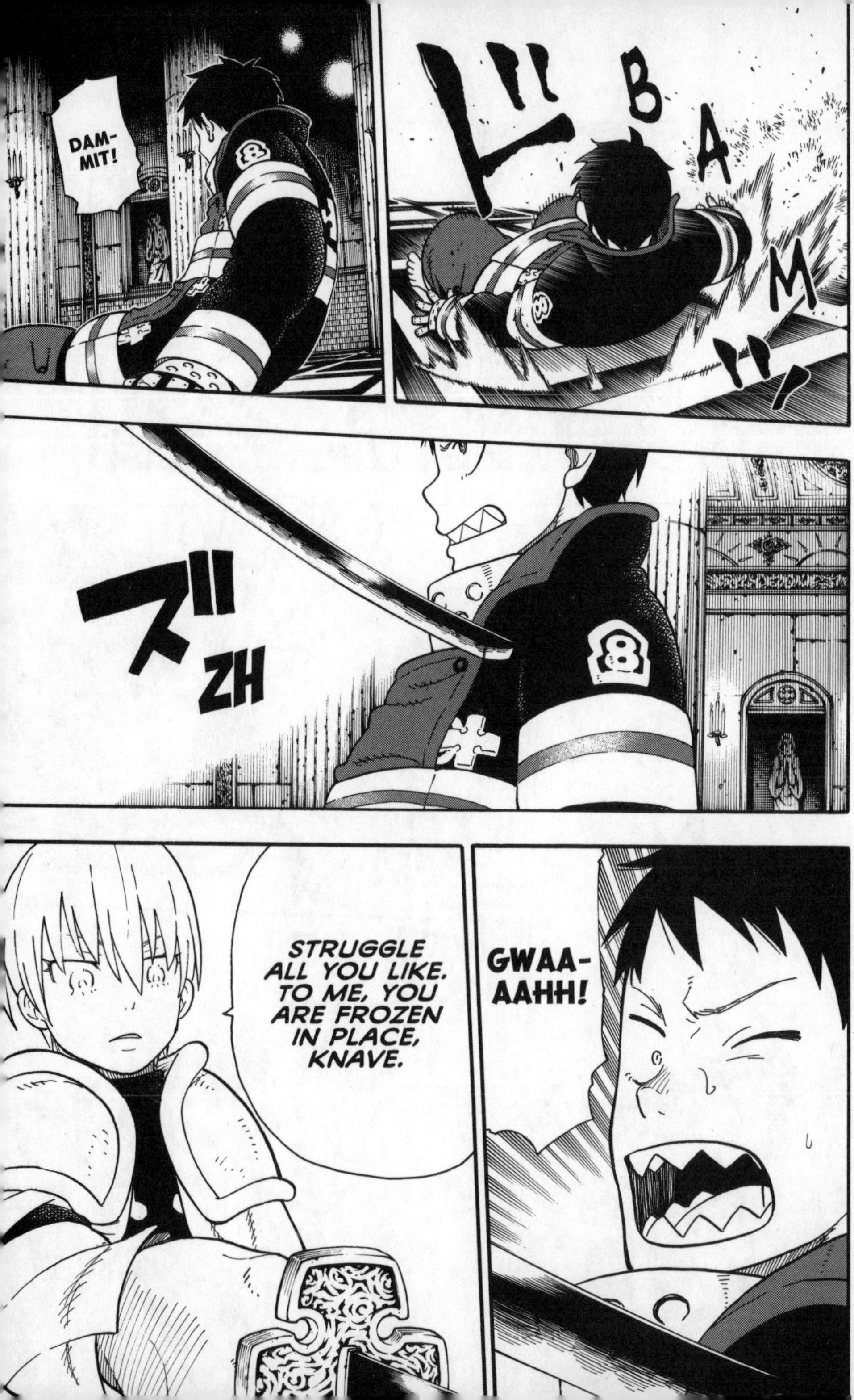
BAM
DAM-MIT!
ズ
ZH
GWAA-AAHH!
STRUGGLE ALL YOU LIKE. TO ME, YOU ARE FROZEN IN PLACE, KNAVE.

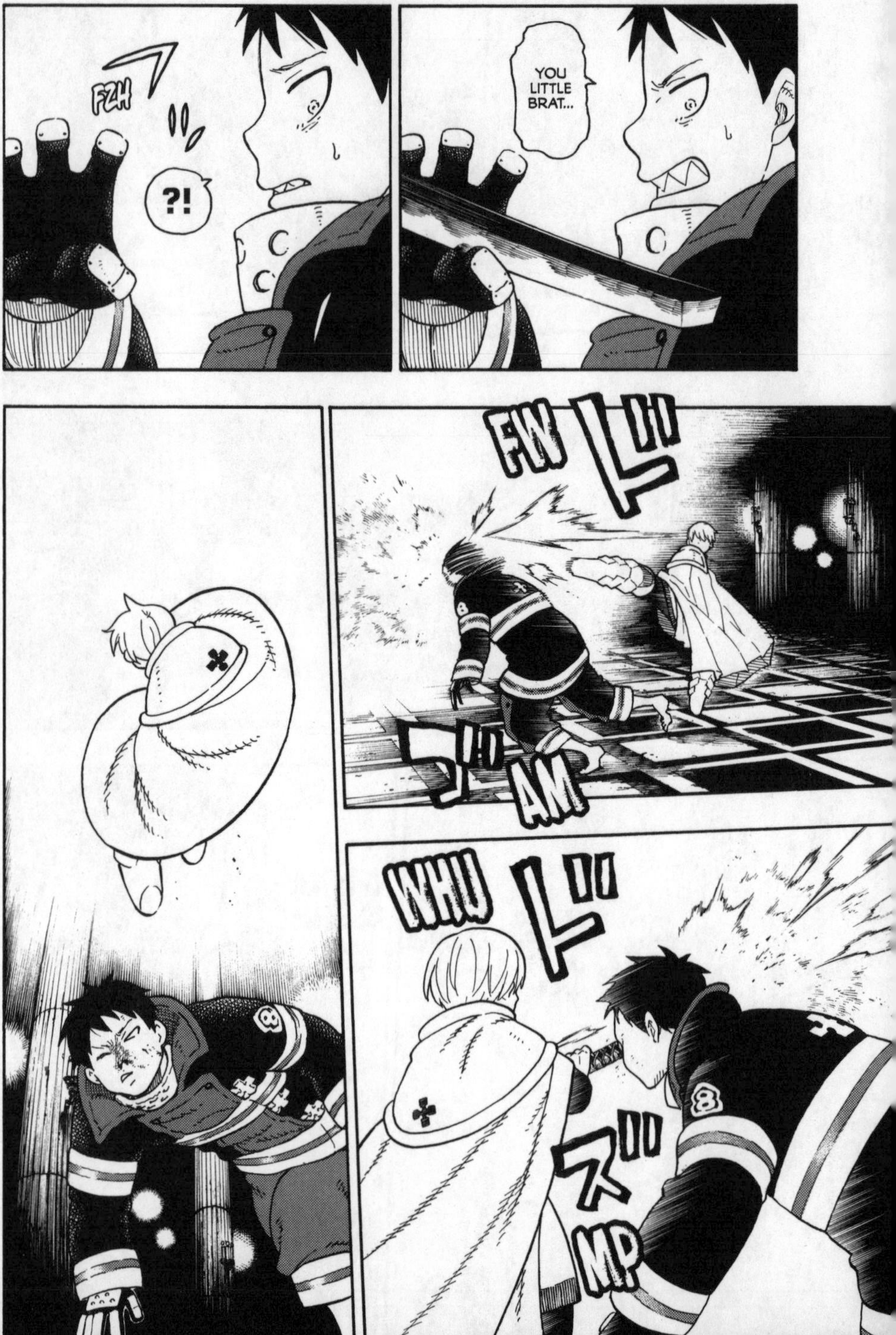
YOU LITTLE BRAT...
FZH
?!
FW ドッ
AM
WHU ドッ
スッ
MP

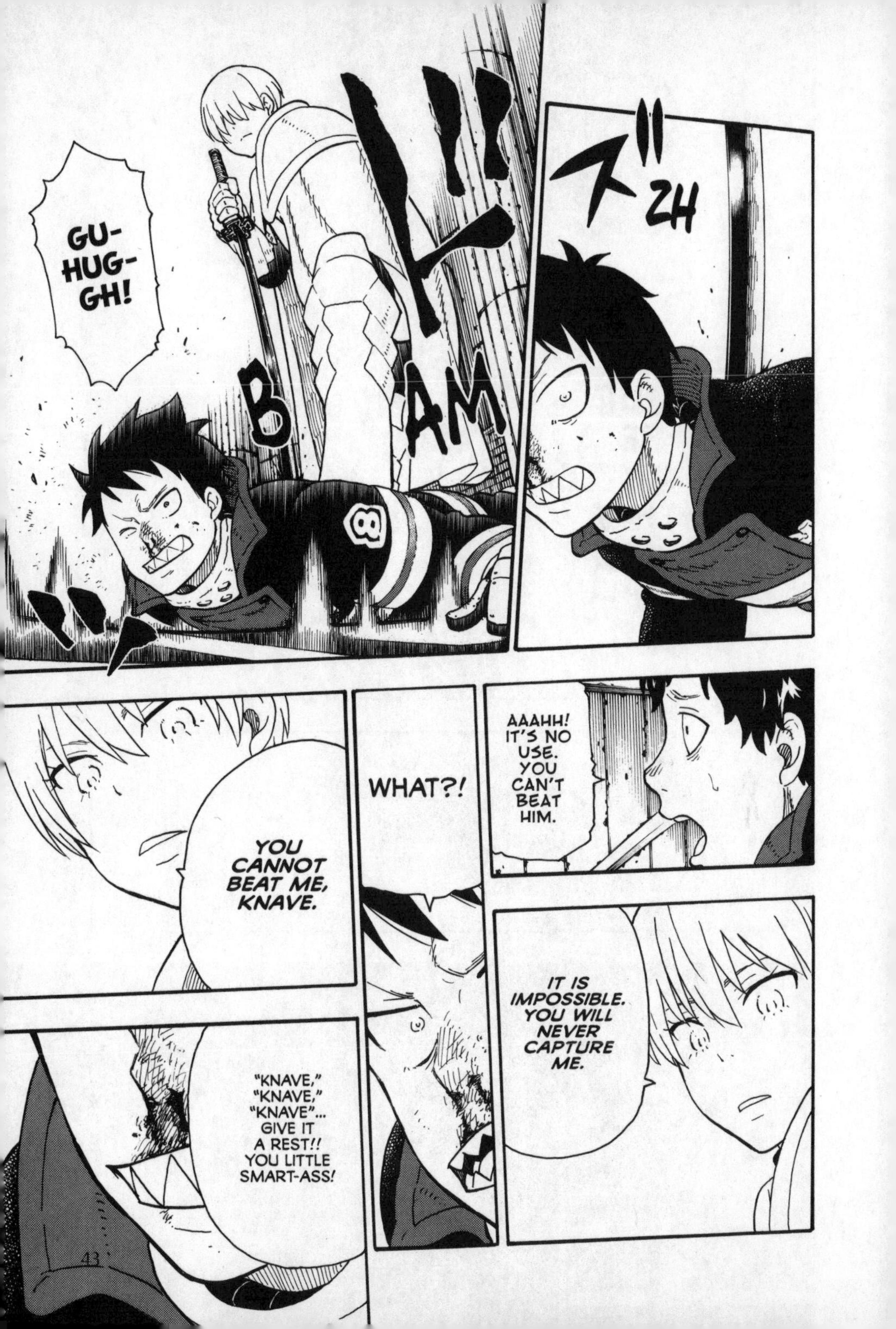
ズ
ZH
BAM
GU-
HUG-
GH!
AAAHH! IT'S NO USE. YOU CAN'T BEAT HIM.
WHAT?!
YOU CANNOT BEAT ME, KNAVE.
IT IS IMPOSSIBLE. YOU WILL NEVER CAPTURE ME.
"KNAVE," "KNAVE," "KNAVE"... GIVE IT A REST!! YOU LITTLE SMART-ASS!

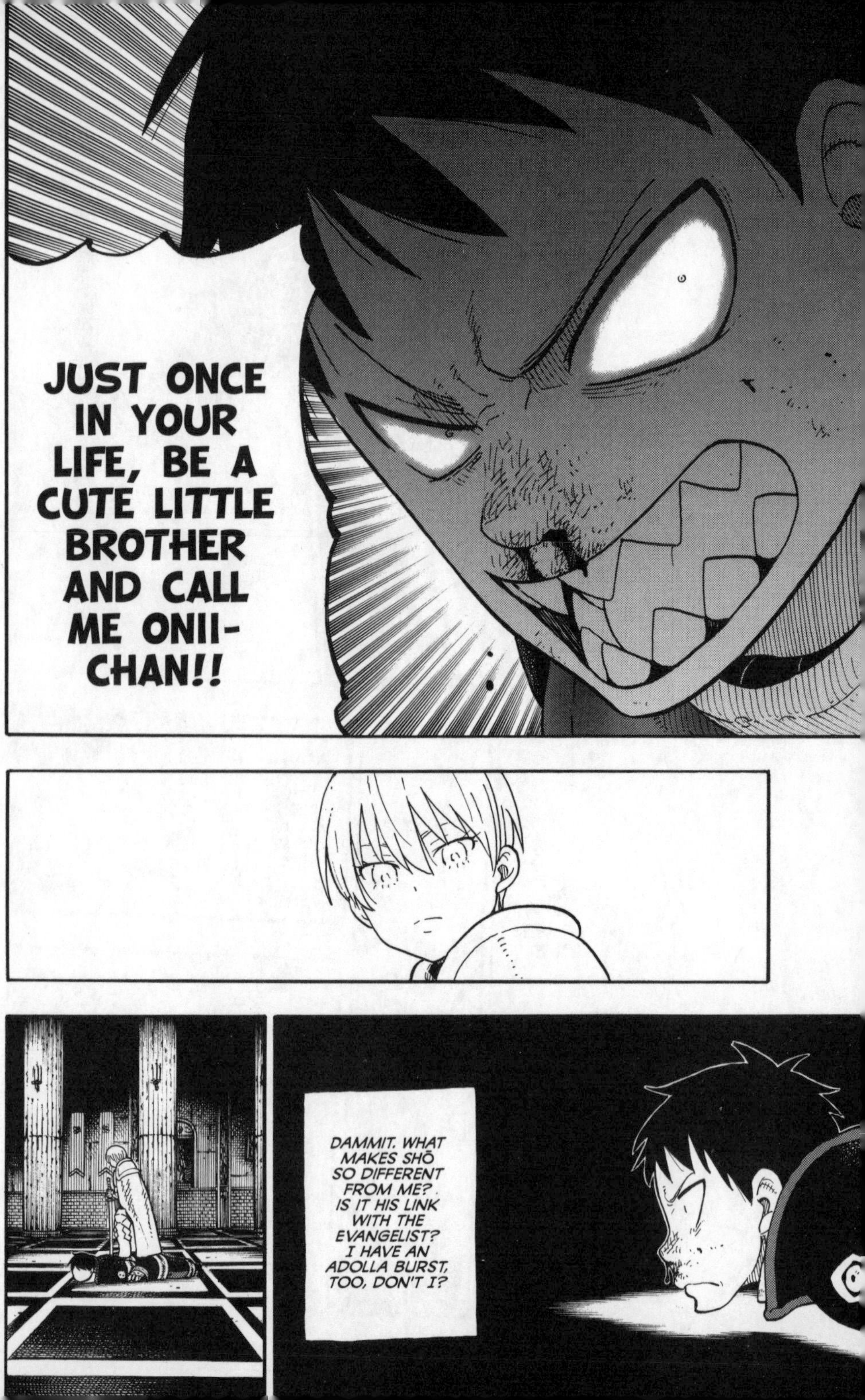
JUST ONCE IN YOUR LIFE, BE A CUTE LITTLE BROTHER AND CALL ME ONII-CHAN!!
DAMMIT. WHAT MAKES SHŌ SO DIFFERENT FROM ME? IS IT HIS LINK WITH THE EVANGELIST? I HAVE AN ADOLLA BURST, TOO, DON'T I?

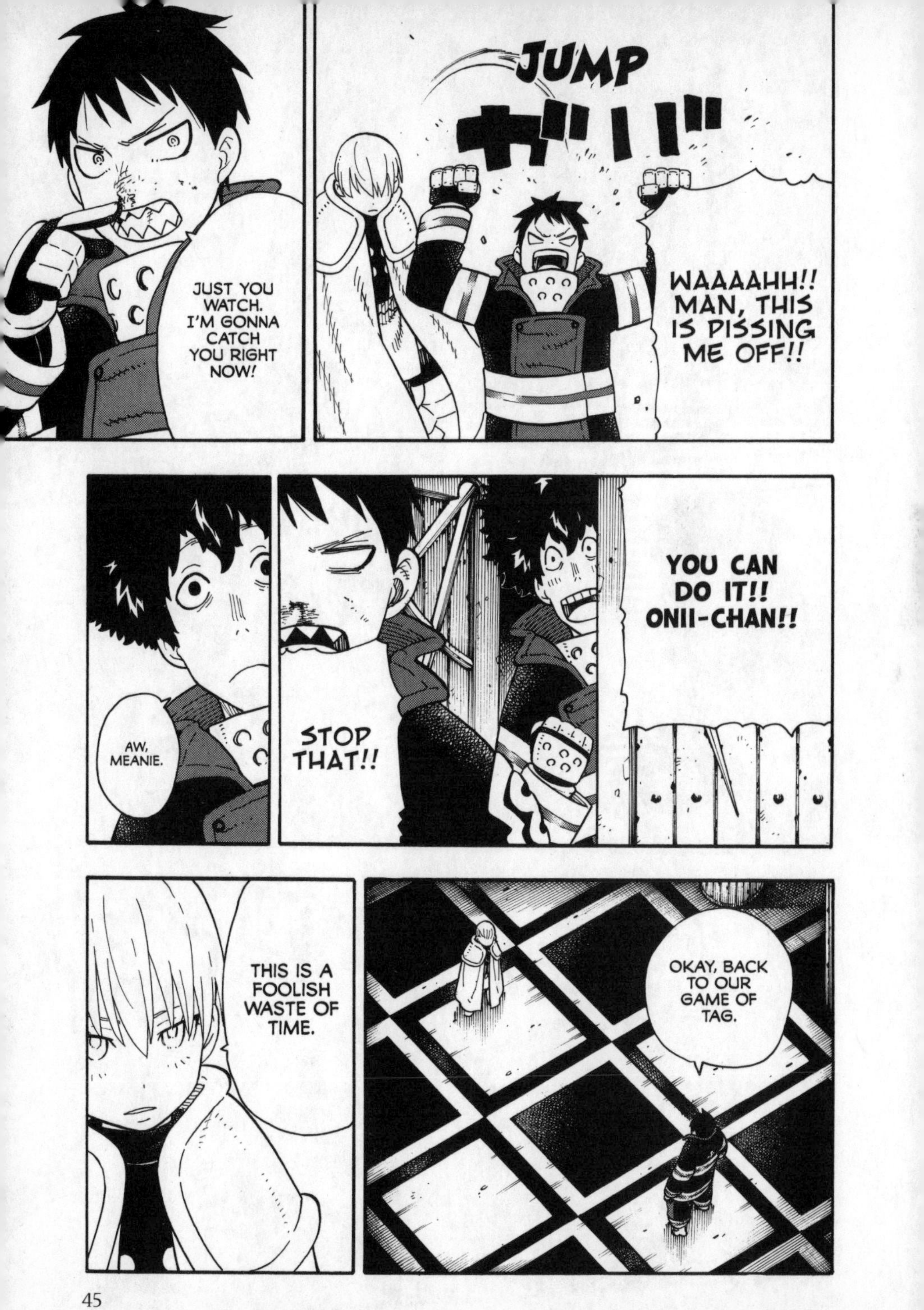
JUMP
WAAAAHH!! MAN, THIS IS PISSING ME OFF!!
JUST YOU WATCH. I'M GONNA CATCH YOU RIGHT NOW!
YOU CAN DO IT!! ONII-CHAN!!
STOP THAT!!
AW, MEANIE.
OKAY, BACK TO OUR GAME OF TAG.
THIS IS A FOOLISH WASTE OF TIME.

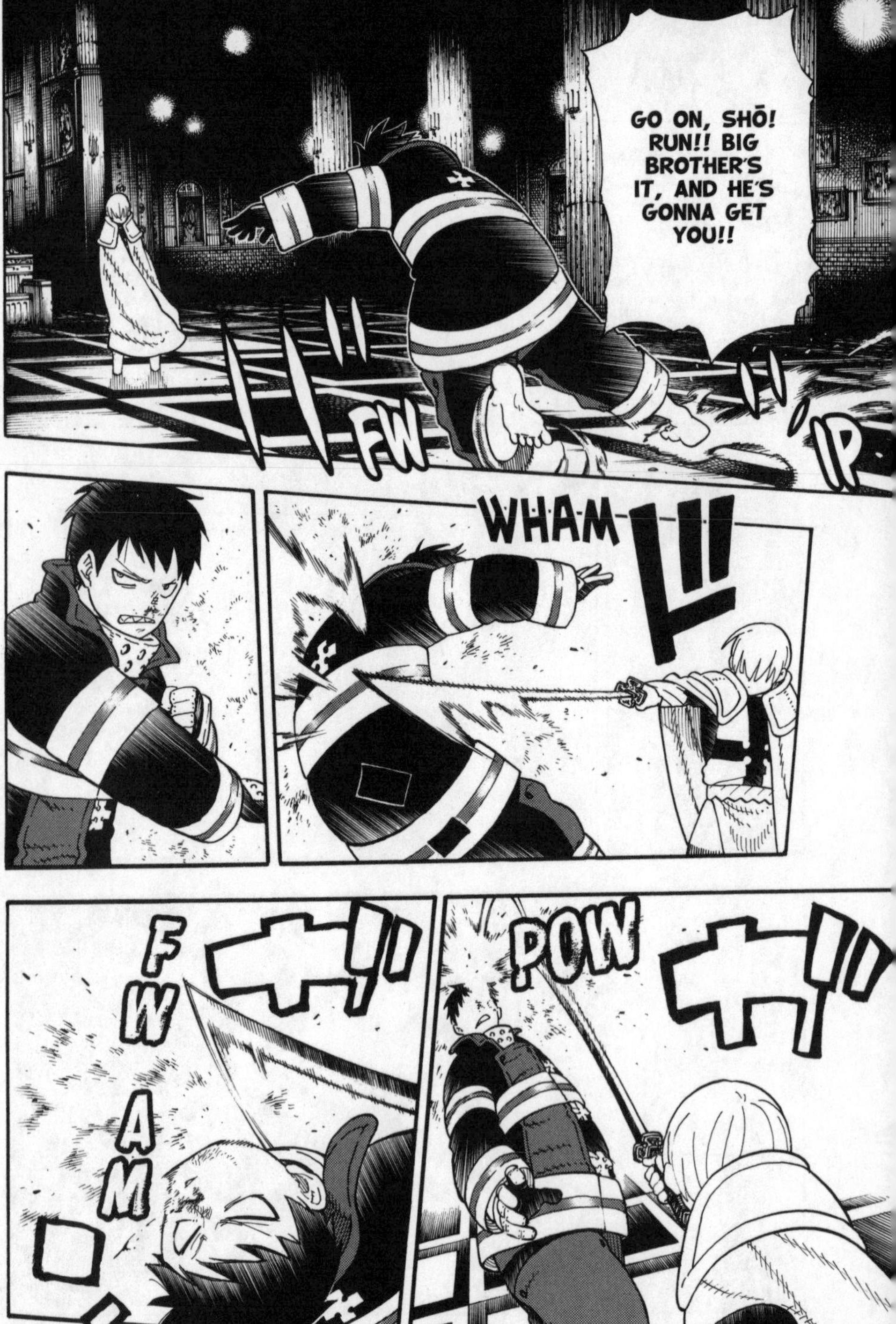
GO ON, SHŌ! RUN!! BIG BROTHER'S IT, AND HE'S GONNA GET YOU!!
FW
IP
WHAM
POW
FWAM

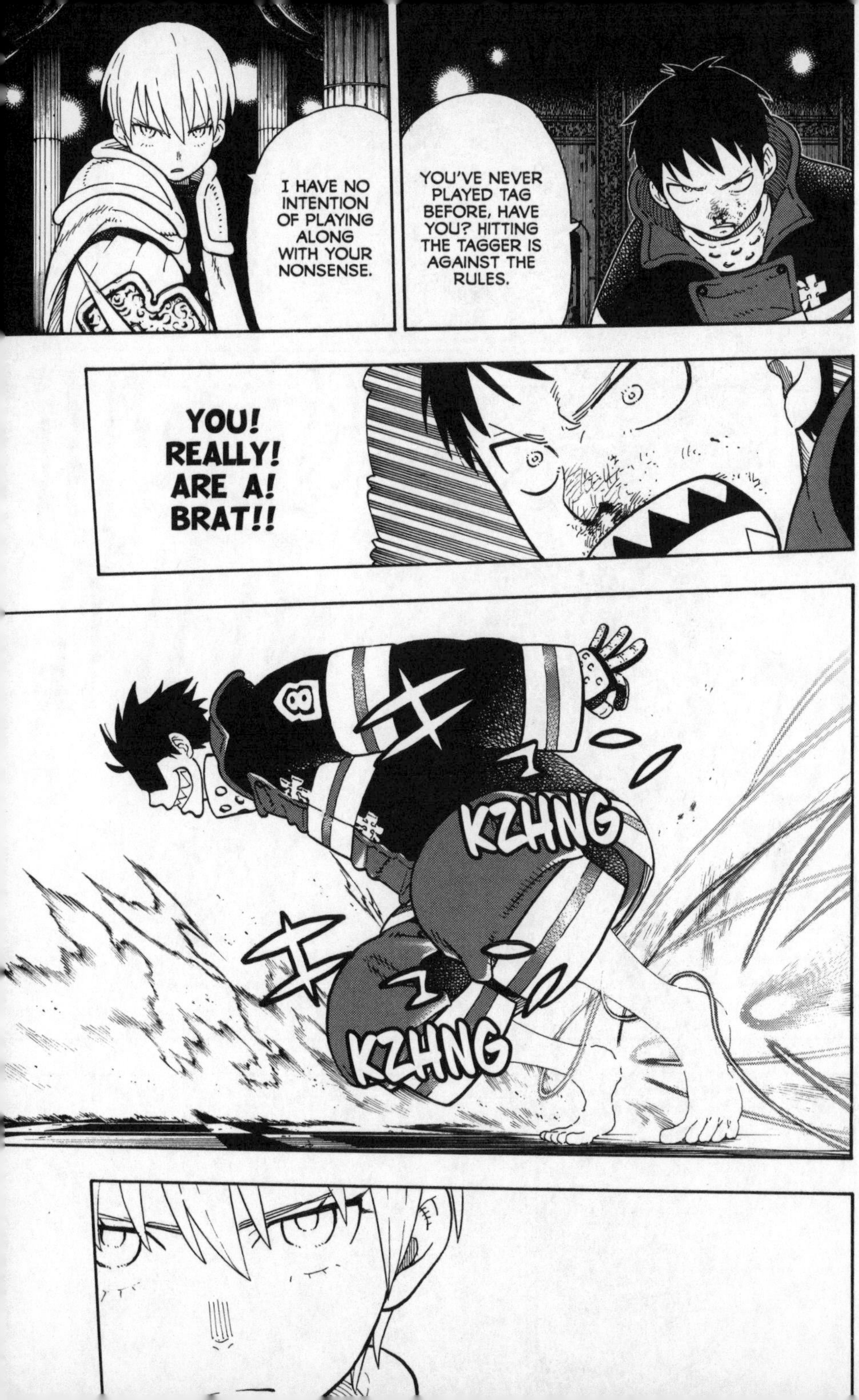
YOU'VE NEVER PLAYED TAG BEFORE, HAVE YOU? HITTING THE TAGGER IS AGAINST THE RULES.
I HAVE NO INTENTION OF PLAYING ALONG WITH YOUR NONSENSE.
YOU! REALLY! ARE A! BRAT!!
KZHNG
KZHNG

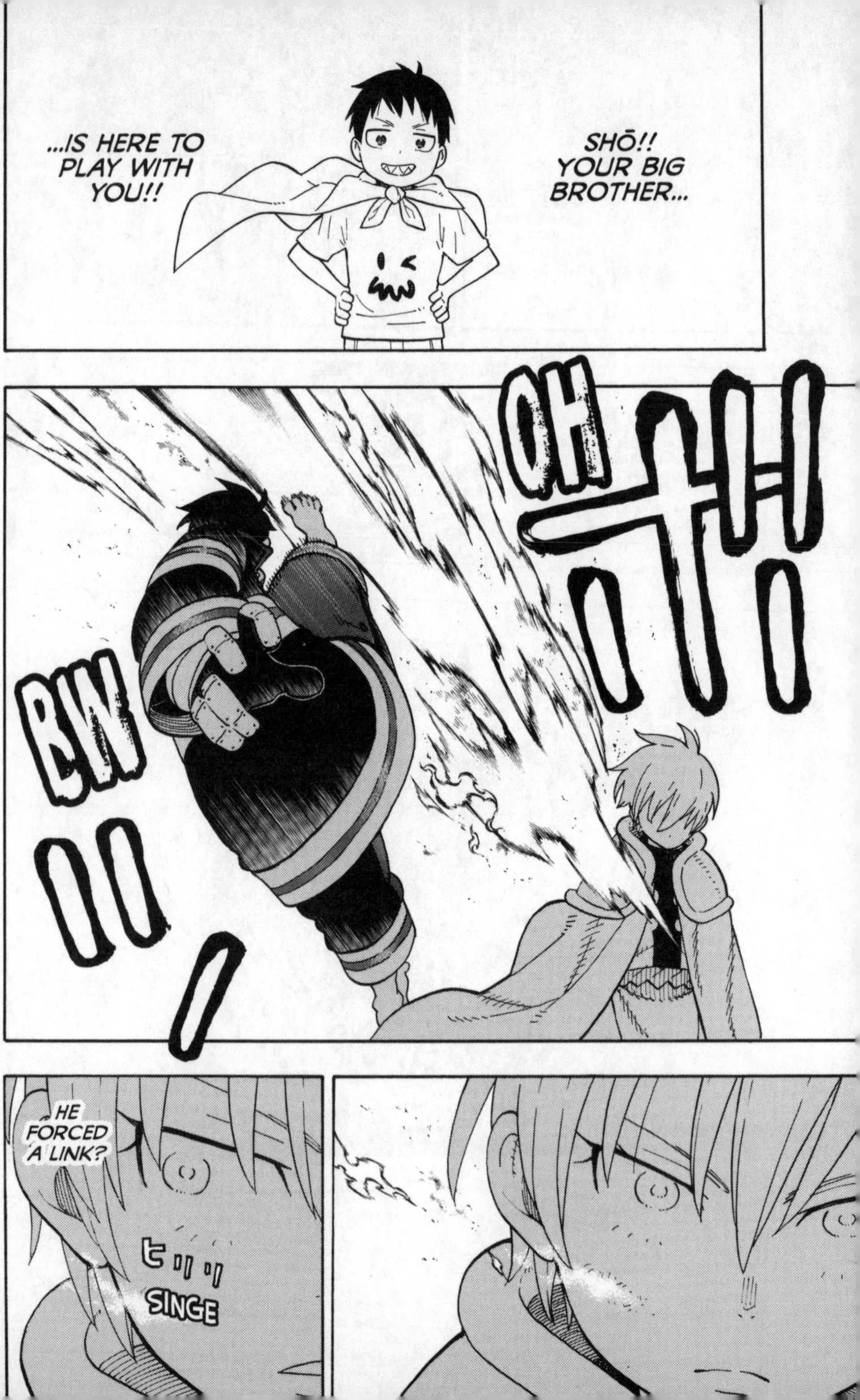
SHŌ!! YOUR BIG BROTHER...
...IS HERE TO PLAY WITH YOU!!
HE FORCED A LINK?
SINGE

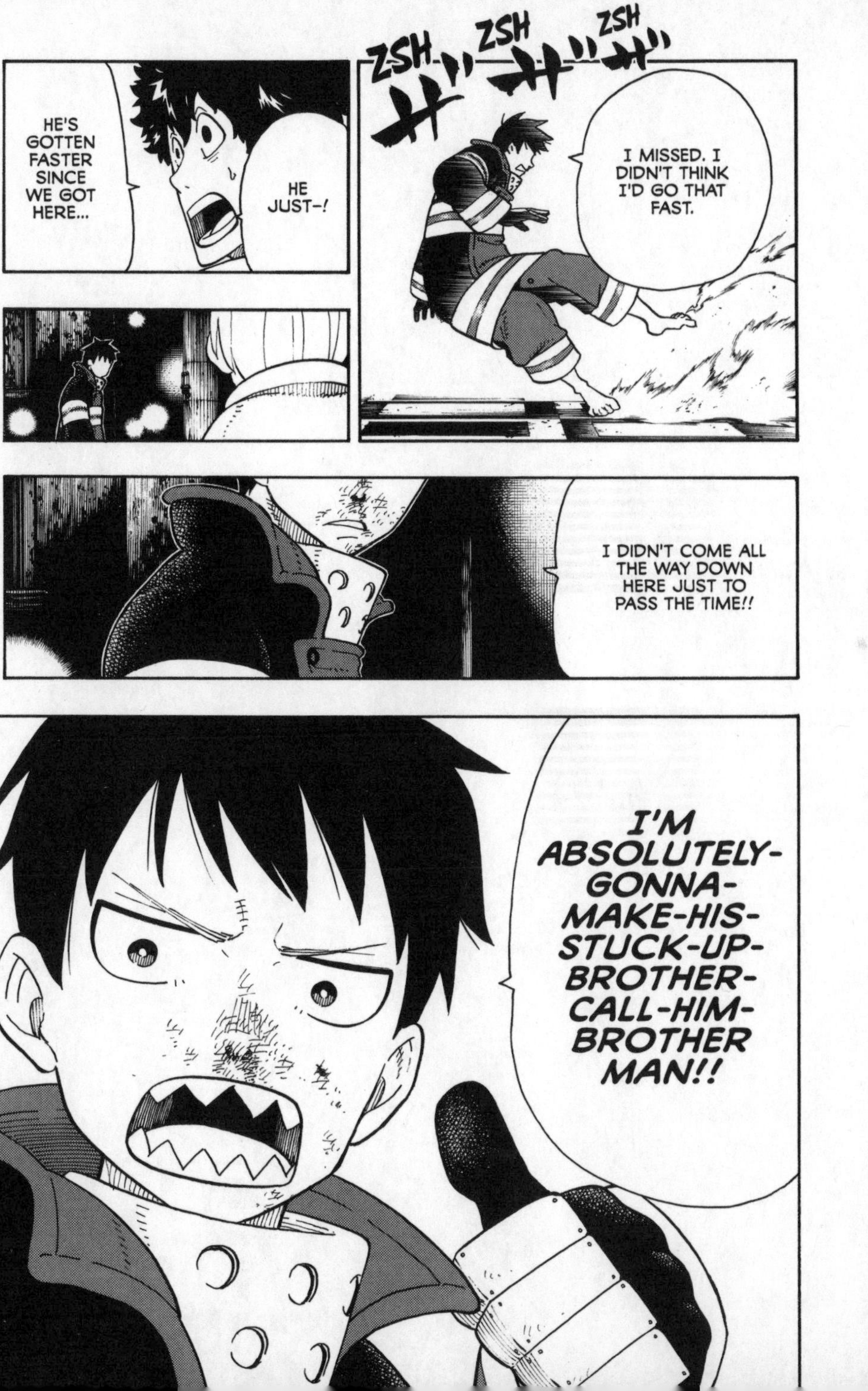
ZSH
ZSH
ZSH
I MISSED. I DIDN'T THINK I'D GO THAT FAST.
HE JUST-!
HE'S GOTTEN FASTER SINCE WE GOT HERE...
I DIDN'T COME ALL THE WAY DOWN HERE JUST TO PASS THE TIME!!
I'M ABSOLUTELY-GONNA-MAKE-HIS-STUCK-UP-BROTHER-CALL-HIM-BROTHER MAN!!

FIRE FORCE

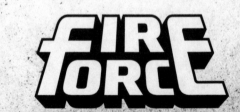

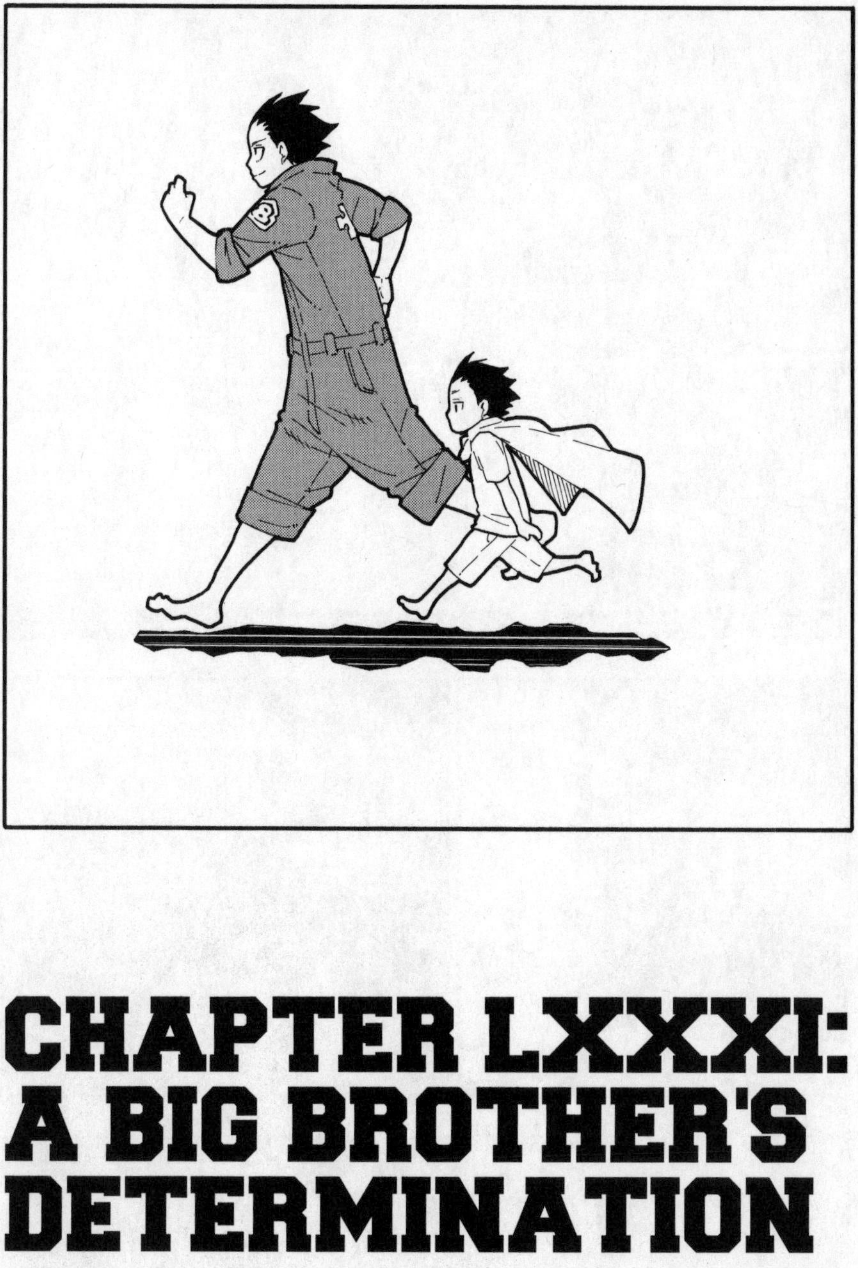

CHAPTER LXXXI: A BIG BROTHER'S DETERMINATION

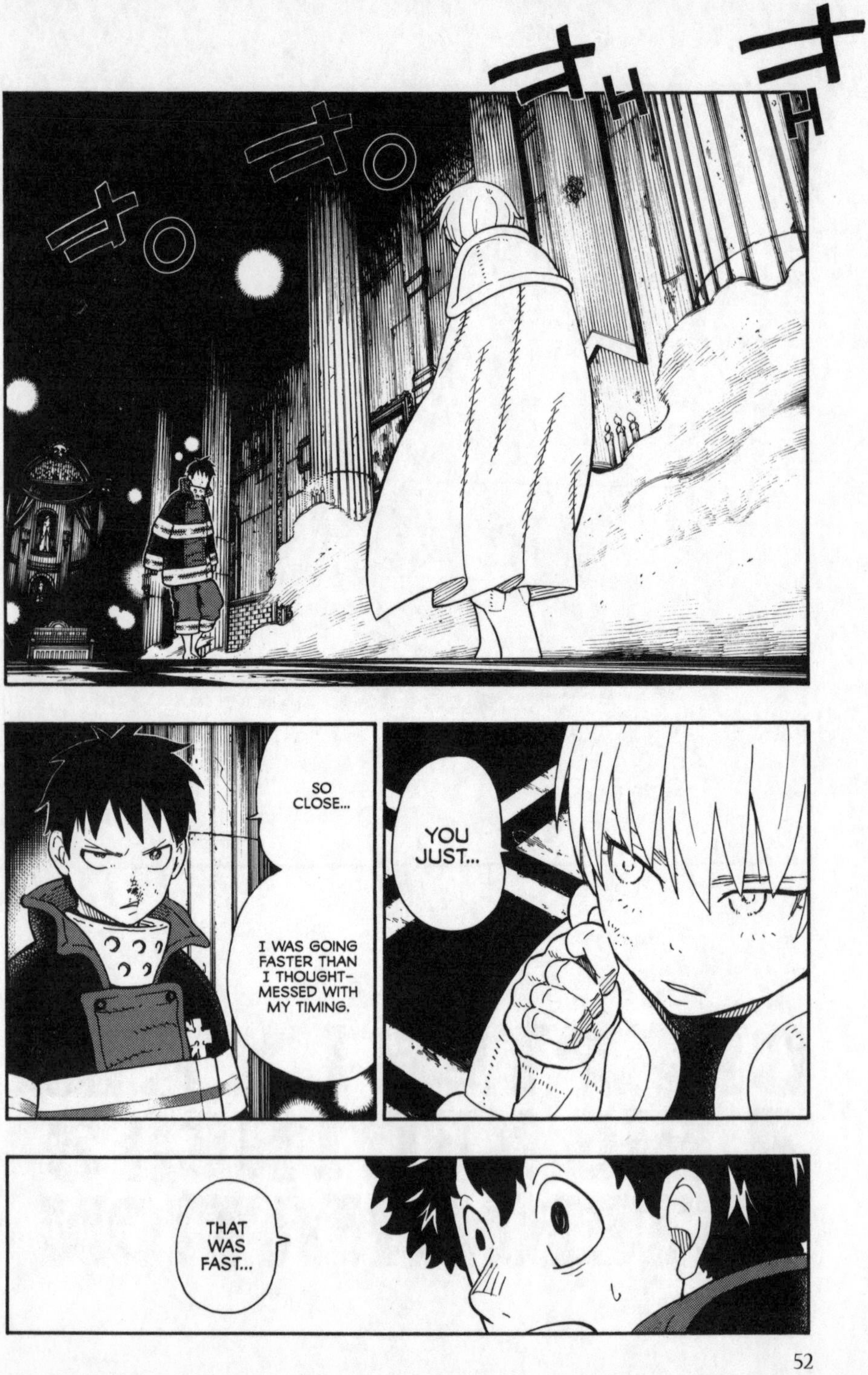
YOU JUST...
SO CLOSE...
I WAS GOING FASTER THAN I THOUGHT—MESSED WITH MY TIMING.
THAT WAS FAST...

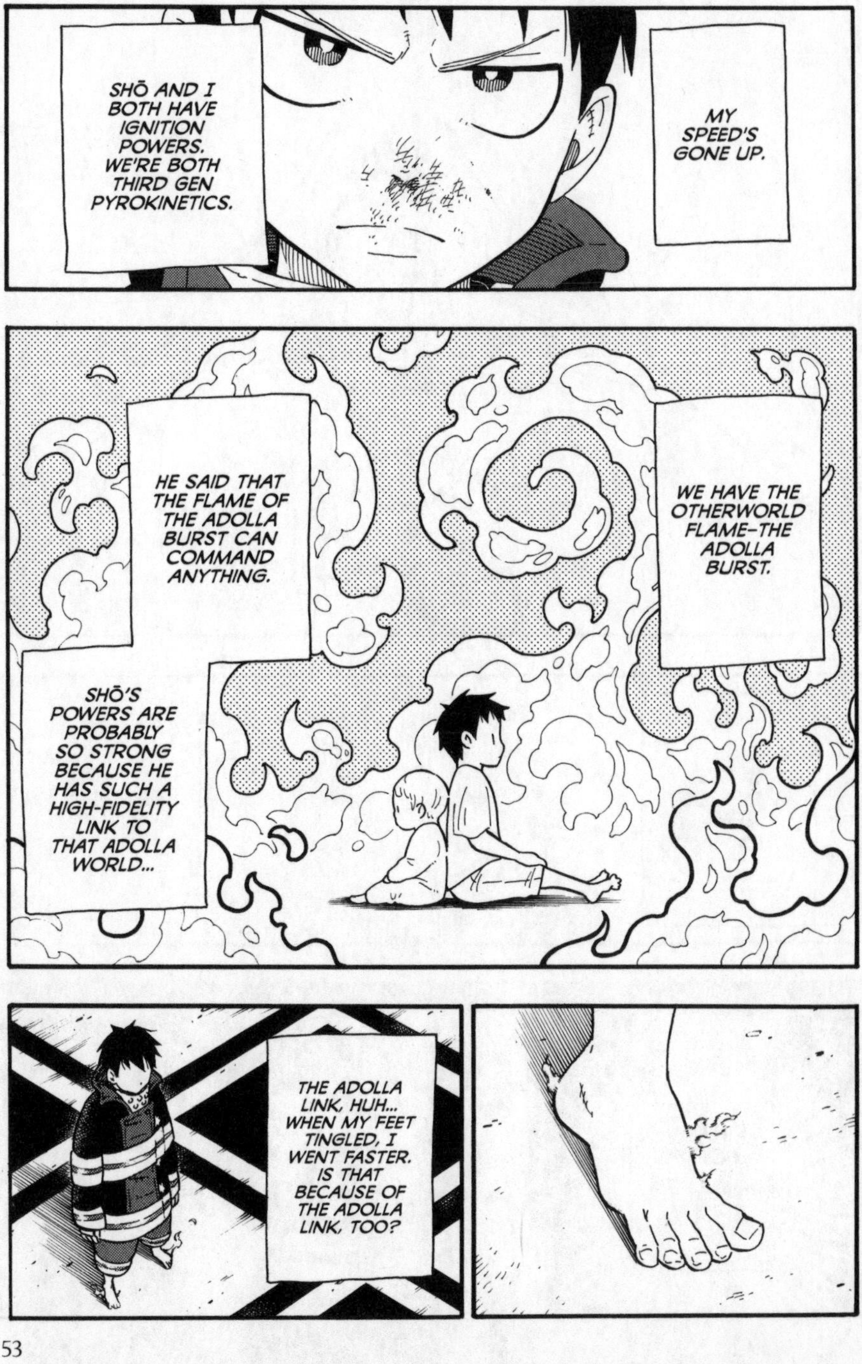
MY SPEED'S GONE UP.
SHŌ AND I BOTH HAVE IGNITION POWERS. WE'RE BOTH THIRD GEN PYROKINETICS.
WE HAVE THE OTHERWORLD FLAME—THE ADOLLA BURST.
HE SAID THAT THE FLAME OF THE ADOLLA BURST CAN COMMAND ANYTHING.
SHŌ'S POWERS ARE PROBABLY SO STRONG BECAUSE HE HAS SUCH A HIGH-FIDELITY LINK TO THAT ADOLLA WORLD...
THE ADOLLA LINK, HUH... WHEN MY FEET TINGLED, I WENT FASTER. IS THAT BECAUSE OF THE ADOLLA LINK, TOO?

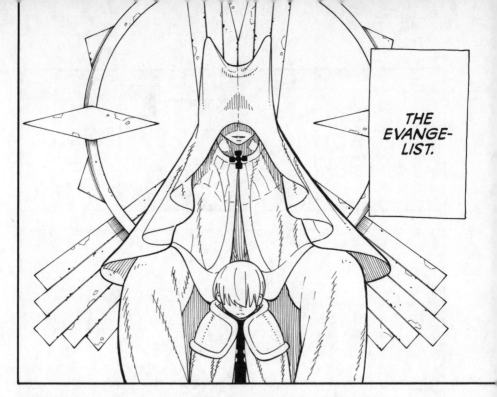

THE EVANGE-LIST.

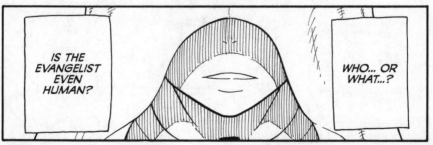

IS THE EVANGELIST EVEN HUMAN?

WHO... OR WHAT...?

BUT... HOW?

IF MY ADOLLA BURST CAN GET ME THE "GRACE OF THE EVANGELIST" OR WHATEVER IT IS, THEN I'LL BE STRONGER.

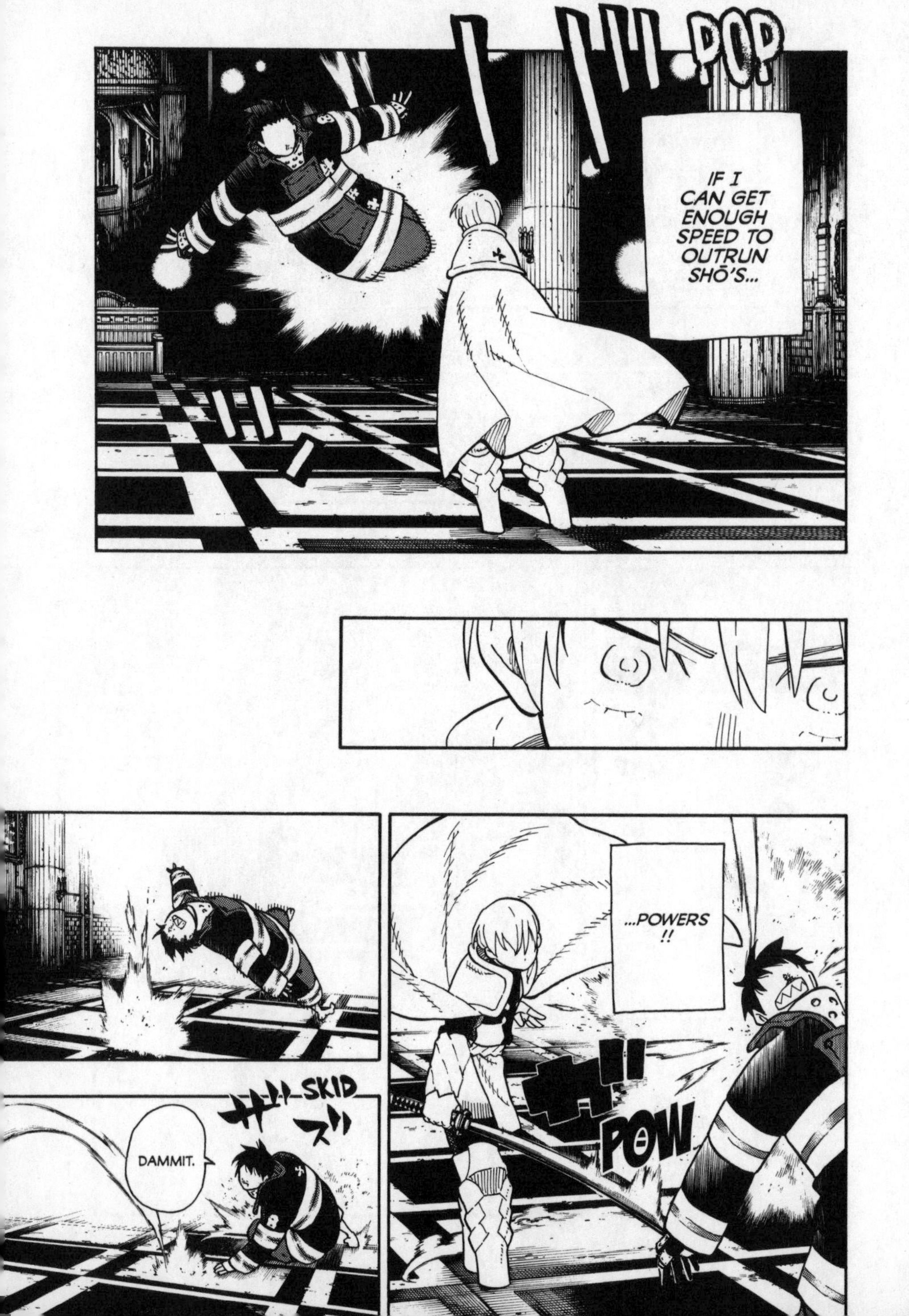
POP
IF I CAN GET ENOUGH SPEED TO OUTRUN SHŌ'S...
...POWERS !!
POW
SKID
DAMMIT.

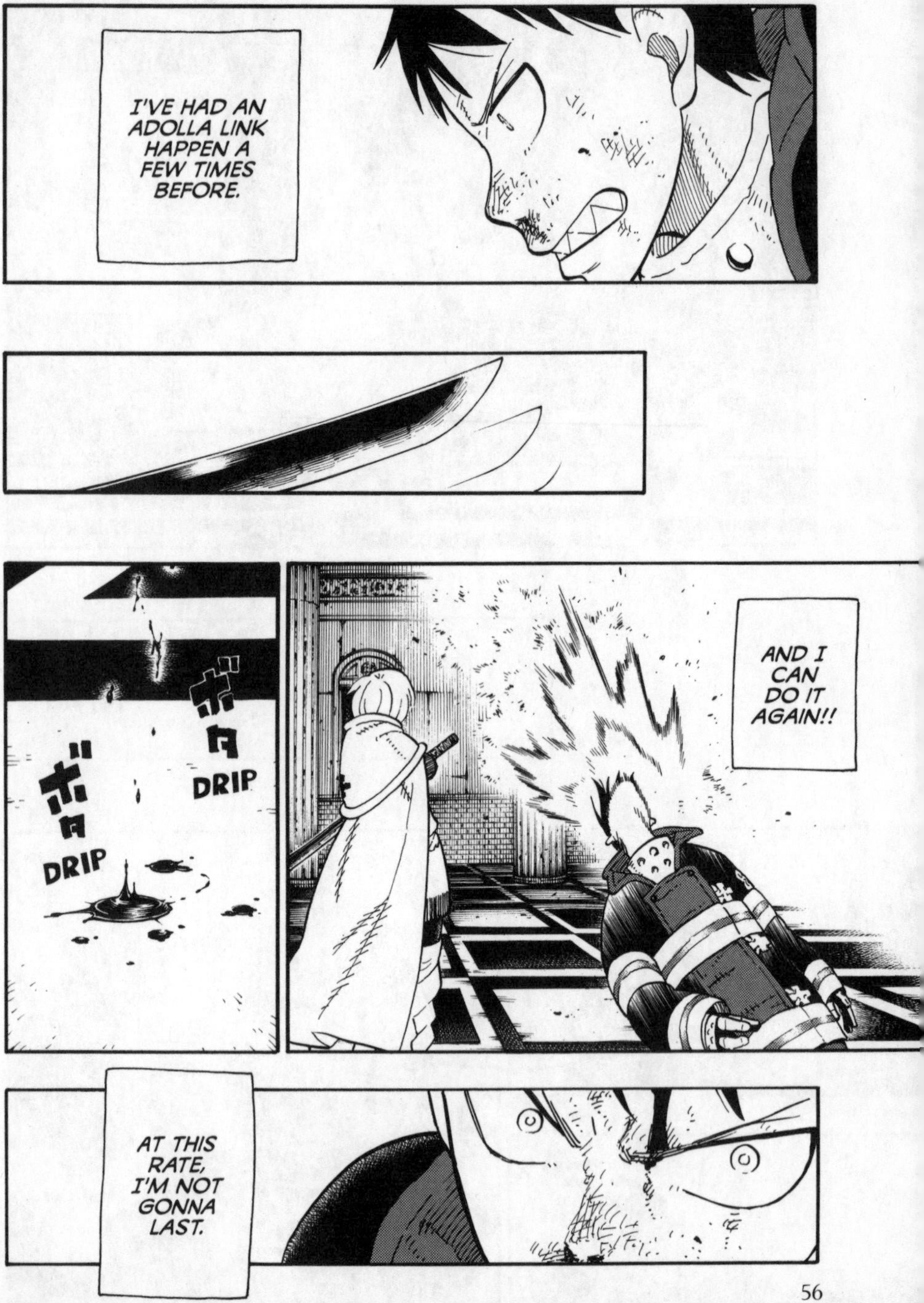

I'VE HAD AN ADOLLA LINK HAPPEN A FEW TIMES BEFORE.
AND I CAN DO IT AGAIN!!
ボタ
DRIP
ボタ
DRIP
AT THIS RATE, I'M NOT GONNA LAST.

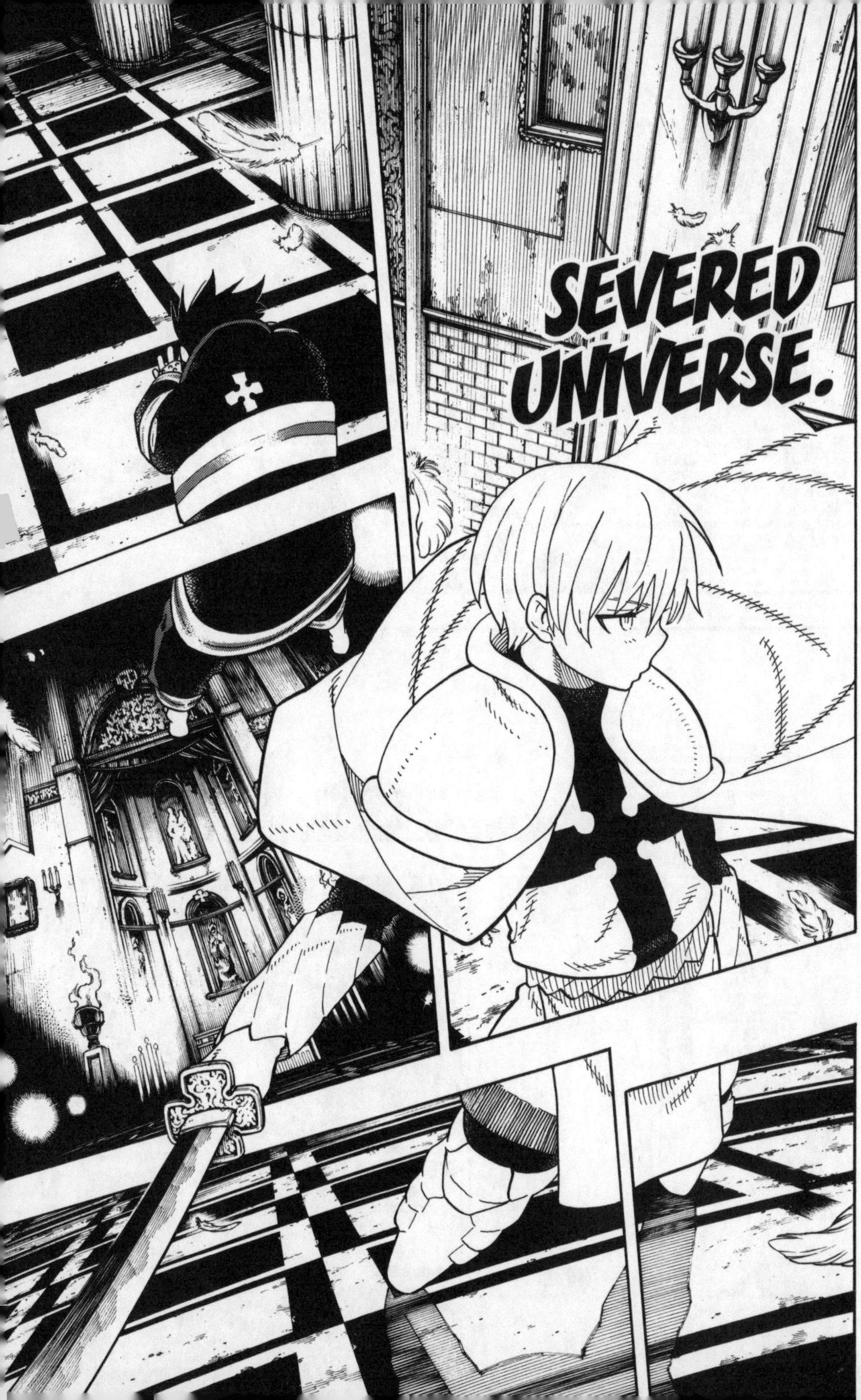
SEVERED UNIVERSE.

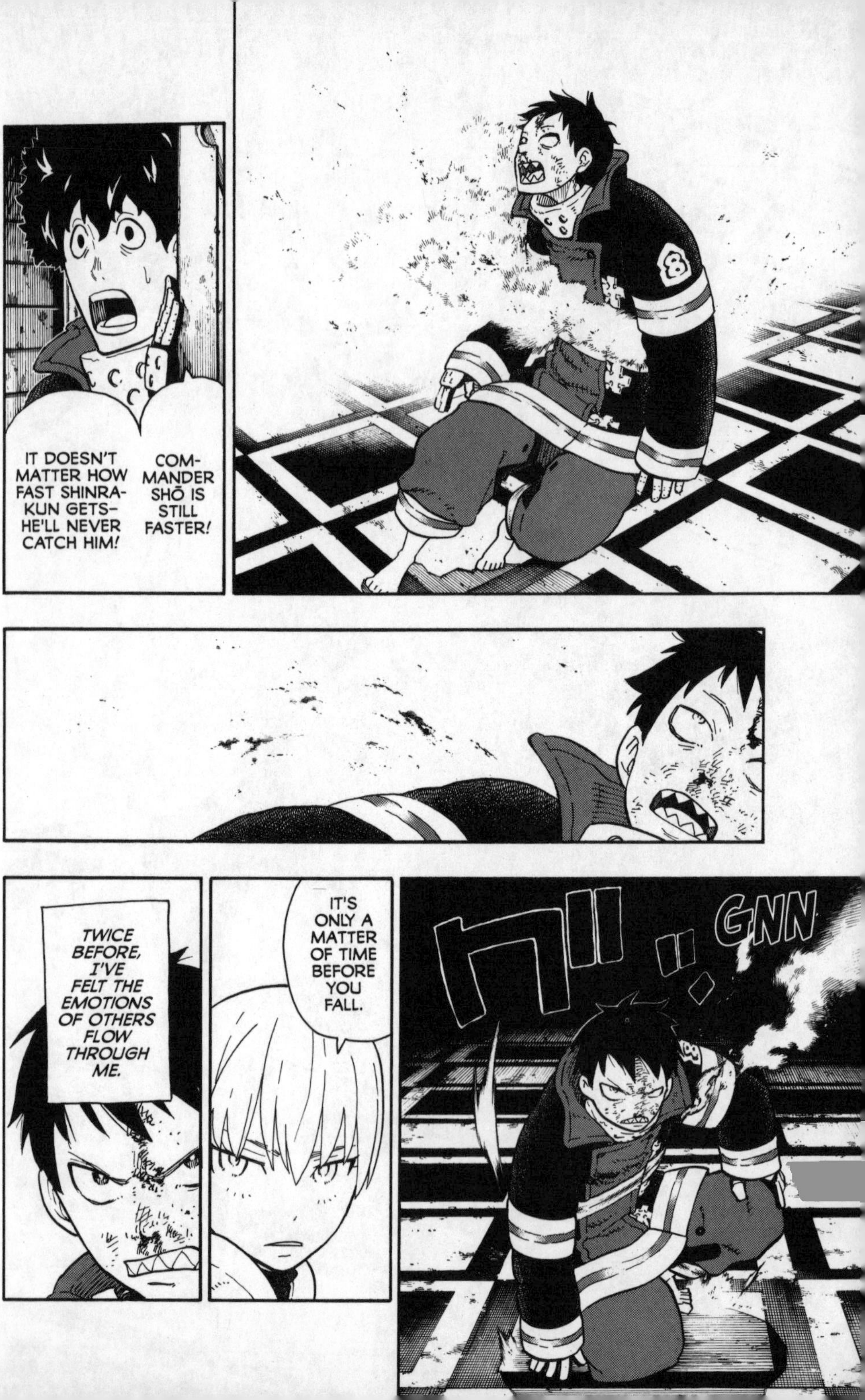
COM-MANDER SHŌ IS STILL FASTER!
IT DOESN'T MATTER HOW FAST SHINRA-KUN GETS– HE'LL NEVER CATCH HIM!
GNN
IT'S ONLY A MATTER OF TIME BEFORE YOU FALL.
TWICE BEFORE, I'VE FELT THE EMOTIONS OF OTHERS FLOW THROUGH ME.

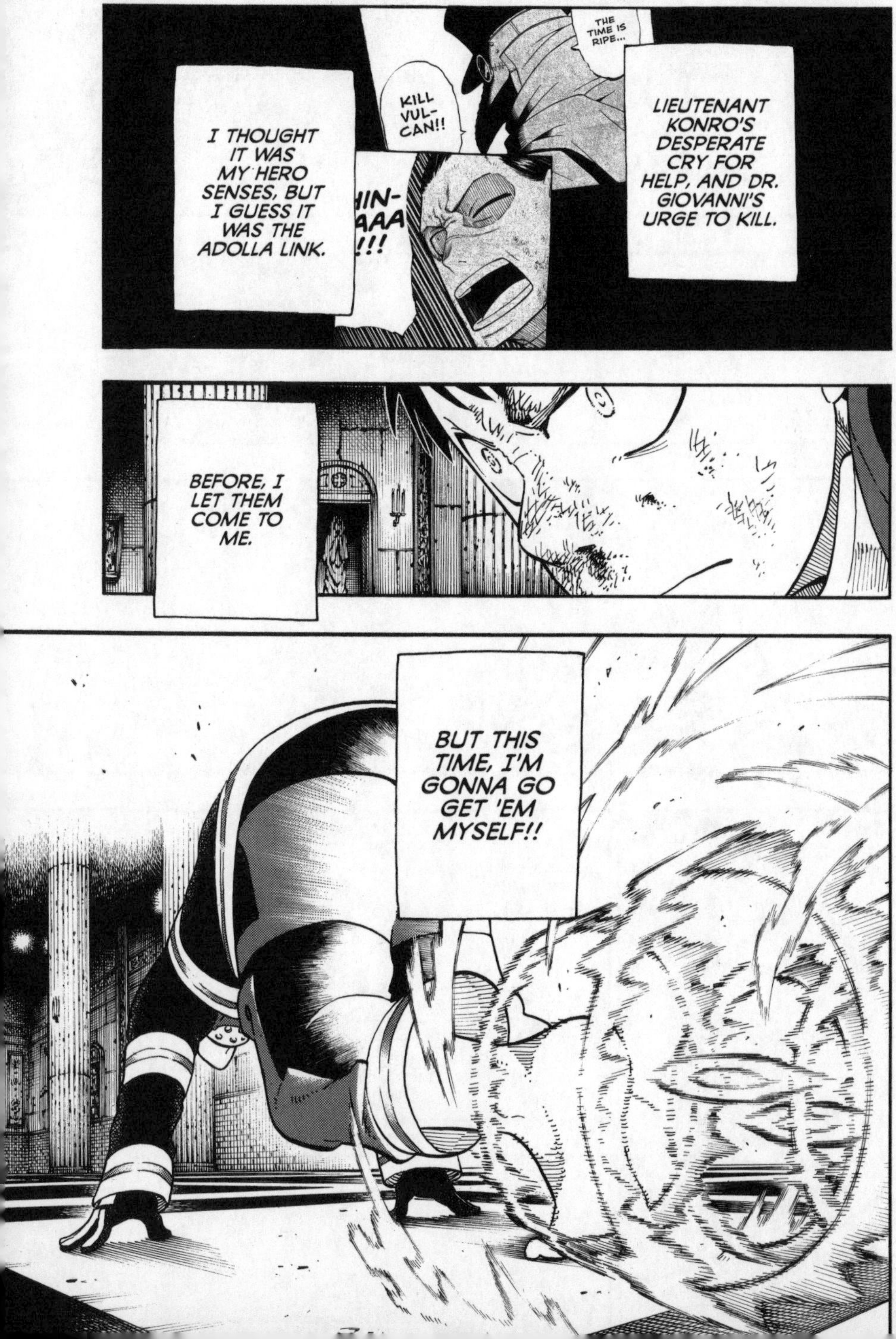
THE TIME IS RIPE...
LIEUTENANT KONRO'S DESPERATE CRY FOR HELP, AND DR. GIOVANNI'S URGE TO KILL.
KILL VUL-CAN!!
I THOUGHT IT WAS MY HERO SENSES, BUT I GUESS IT WAS THE ADOLLA LINK.
BEFORE, I LET THEM COME TO ME.
BUT THIS TIME, I'M GONNA GO GET 'EM MYSELF!!

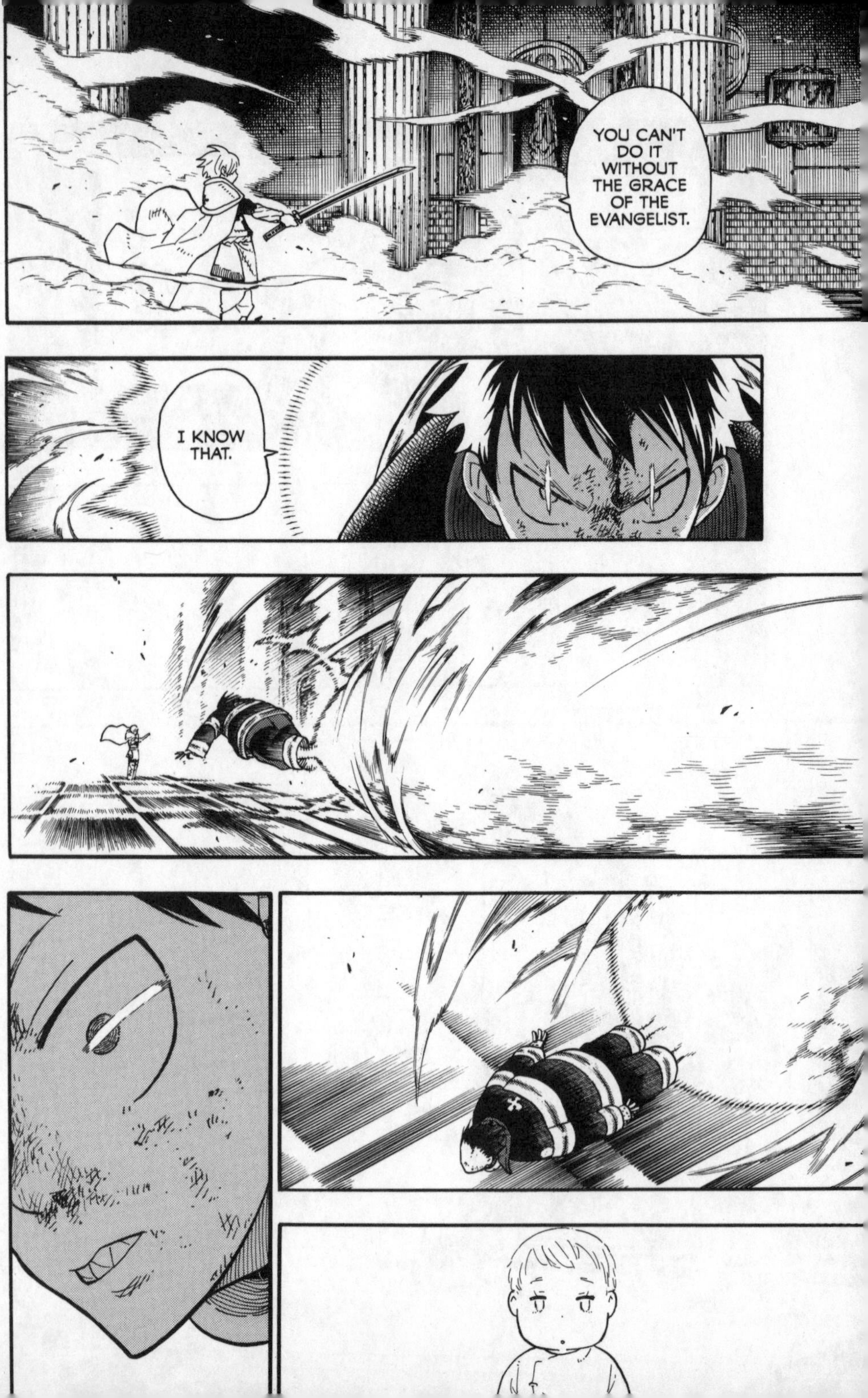
YOU CAN'T DO IT WITHOUT THE GRACE OF THE EVANGELIST.
I KNOW THAT.

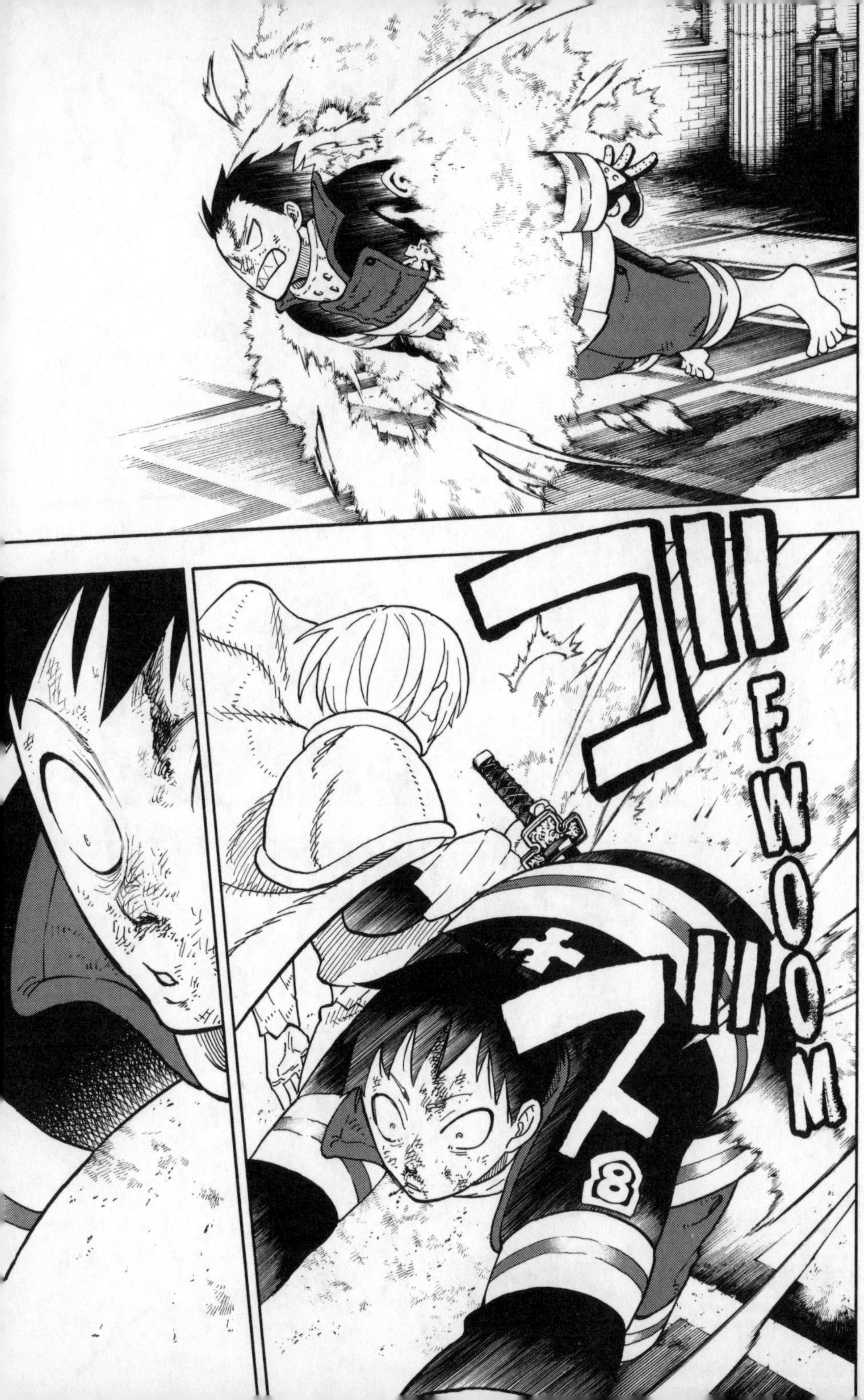
FWOOM

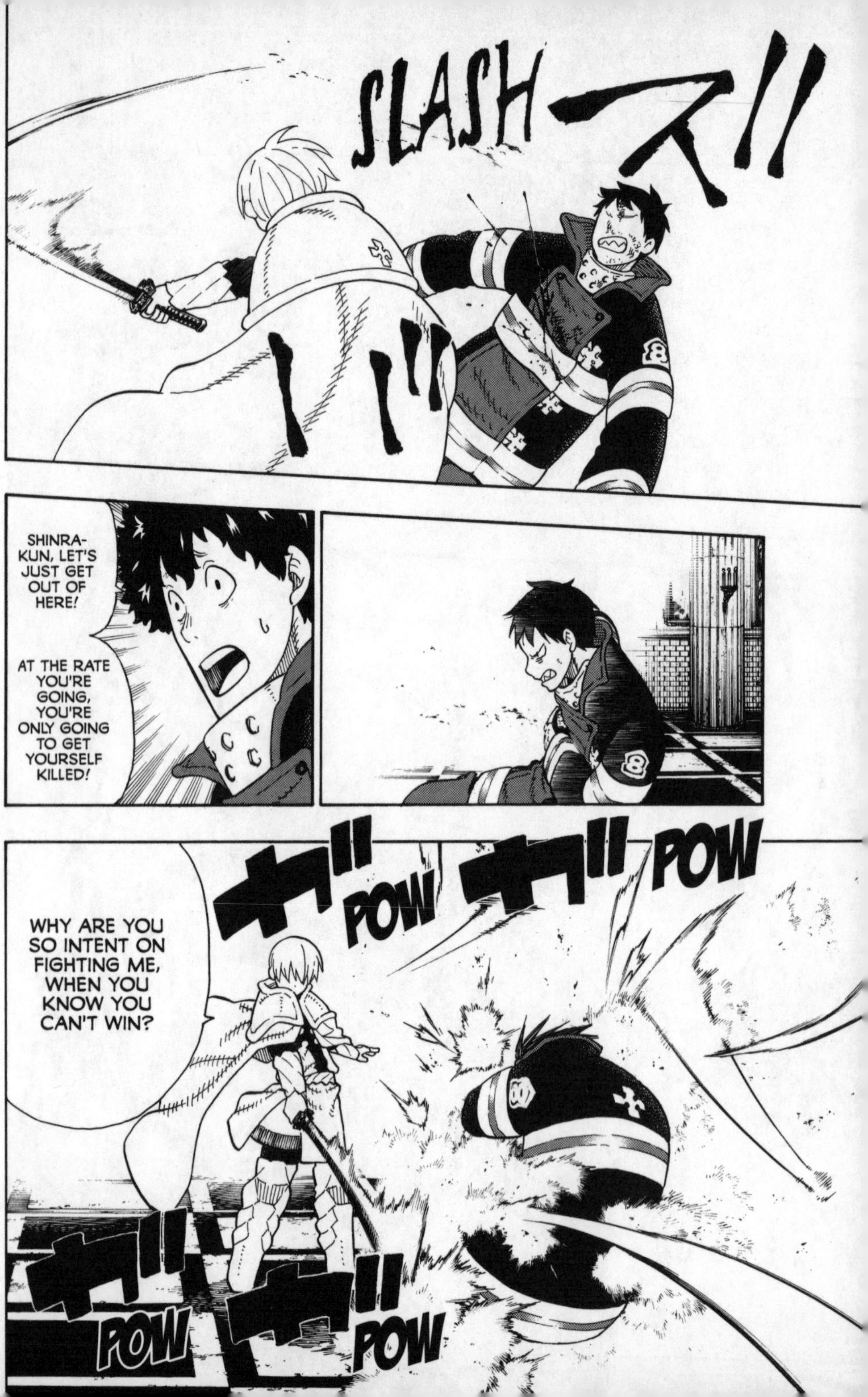
SLASH
SHINRA-KUN, LET'S JUST GET OUT OF HERE!
AT THE RATE YOU'RE GOING, YOU'RE ONLY GOING TO GET YOURSELF KILLED!
POW
POW
WHY ARE YOU SO INTENT ON FIGHTING ME, WHEN YOU KNOW YOU CAN'T WIN?
POW
POW

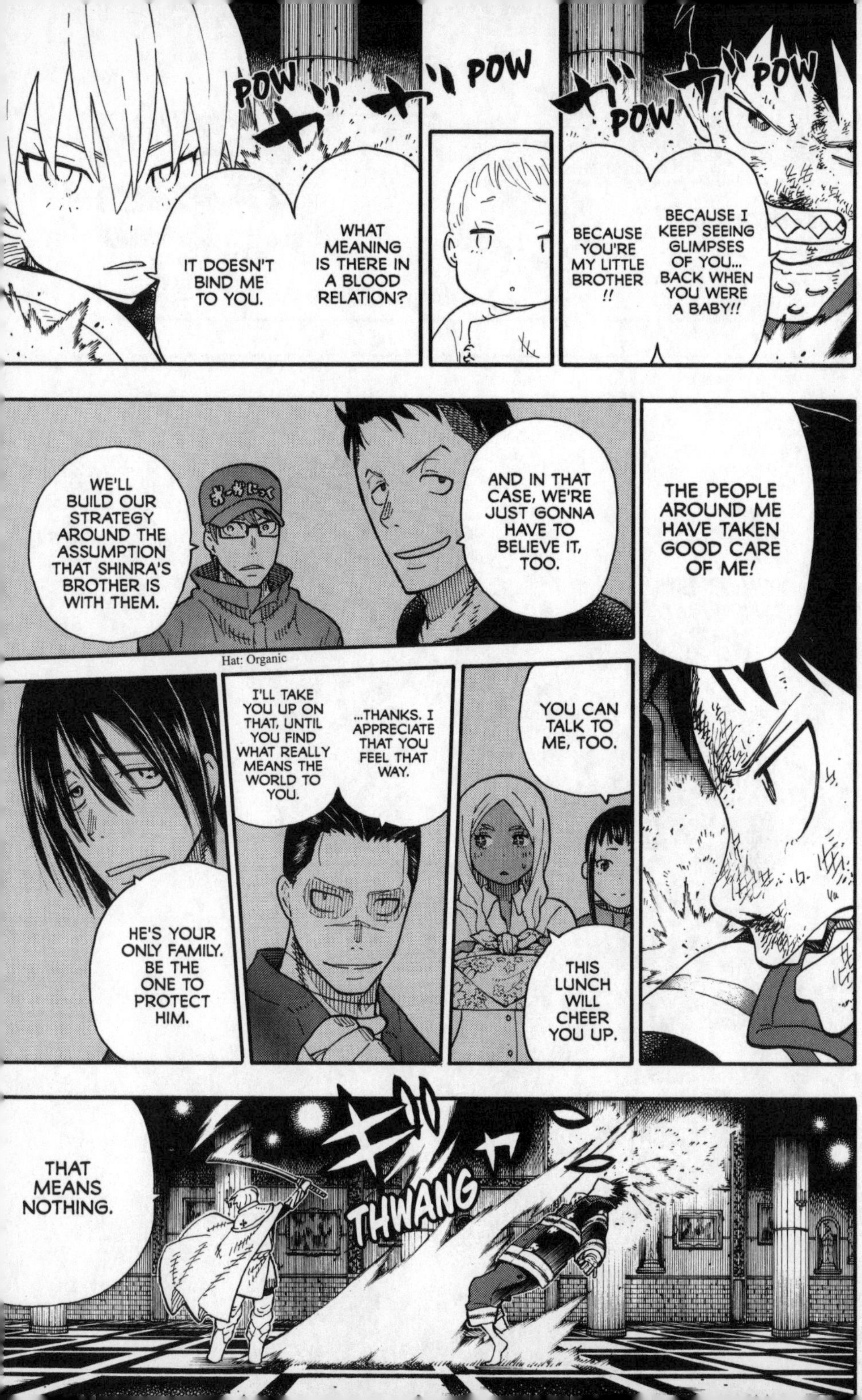
POW
POW
POW
POW
BECAUSE I KEEP SEEING GLIMPSES OF YOU... BACK WHEN YOU WERE A BABY!!
BECAUSE YOU'RE MY LITTLE BROTHER!!
WHAT MEANING IS THERE IN A BLOOD RELATION?
IT DOESN'T BIND ME TO YOU.
THE PEOPLE AROUND ME HAVE TAKEN GOOD CARE OF ME!
AND IN THAT CASE, WE'RE JUST GONNA HAVE TO BELIEVE IT, TOO.
WE'LL BUILD OUR STRATEGY AROUND THE ASSUMPTION THAT SHINRA'S BROTHER IS WITH THEM.
Hat: Organic
YOU CAN TALK TO ME, TOO.
THIS LUNCH WILL CHEER YOU UP.
...THANKS. I APPRECIATE THAT YOU FEEL THAT WAY.
I'LL TAKE YOU UP ON THAT, UNTIL YOU FIND WHAT REALLY MEANS THE WORLD TO YOU.
HE'S YOUR ONLY FAMILY. BE THE ONE TO PROTECT HIM.
THWANG
THAT MEANS NOTHING.

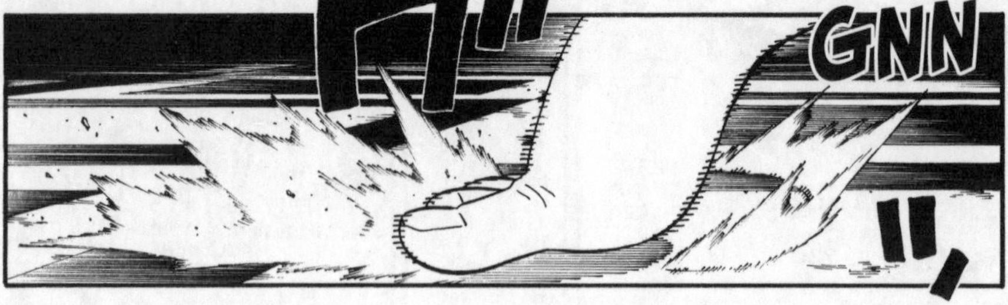
GNN
ガ
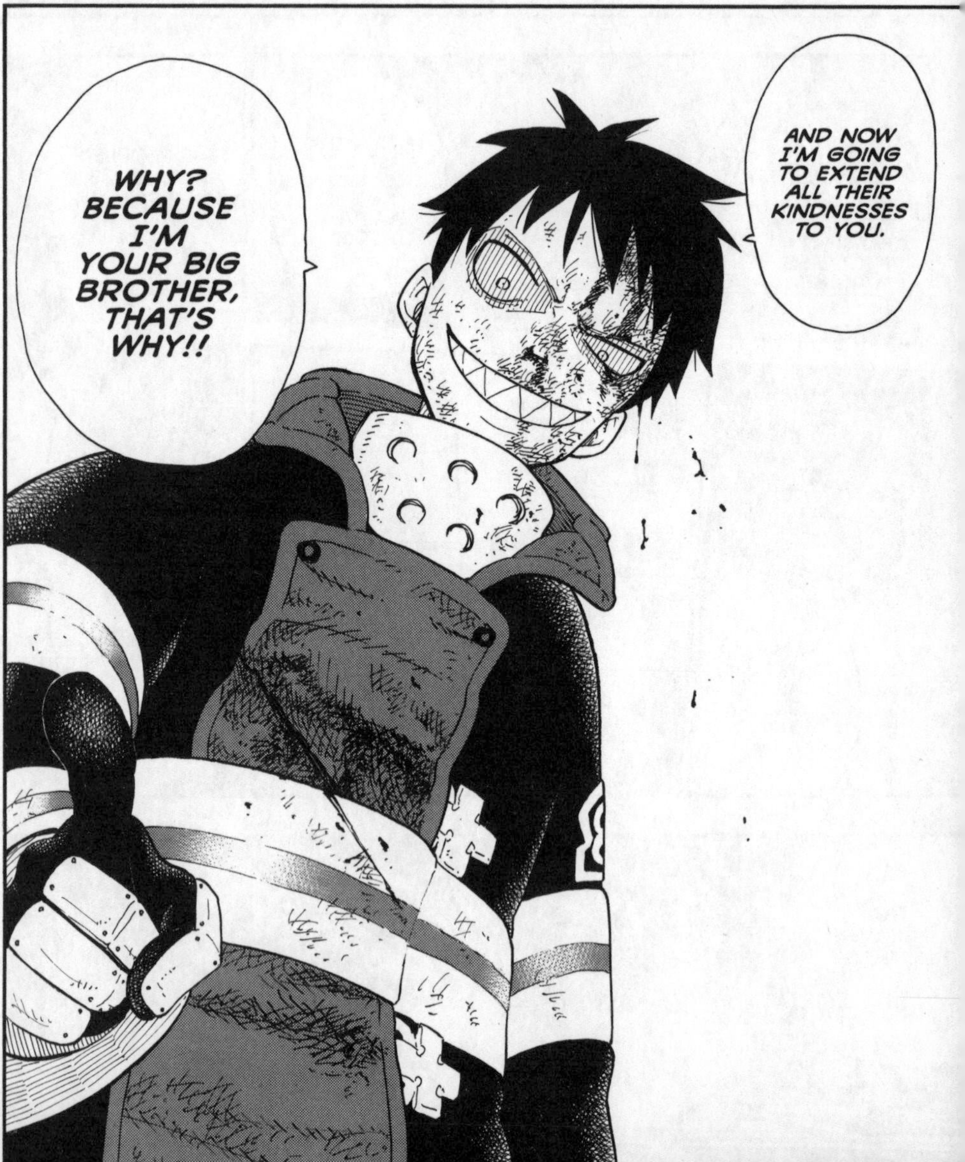
AND NOW I'M GOING TO EXTEND ALL THEIR KINDNESSES TO YOU.
WHY? BECAUSE I'M YOUR BIG BROTHER, THAT'S WHY!!

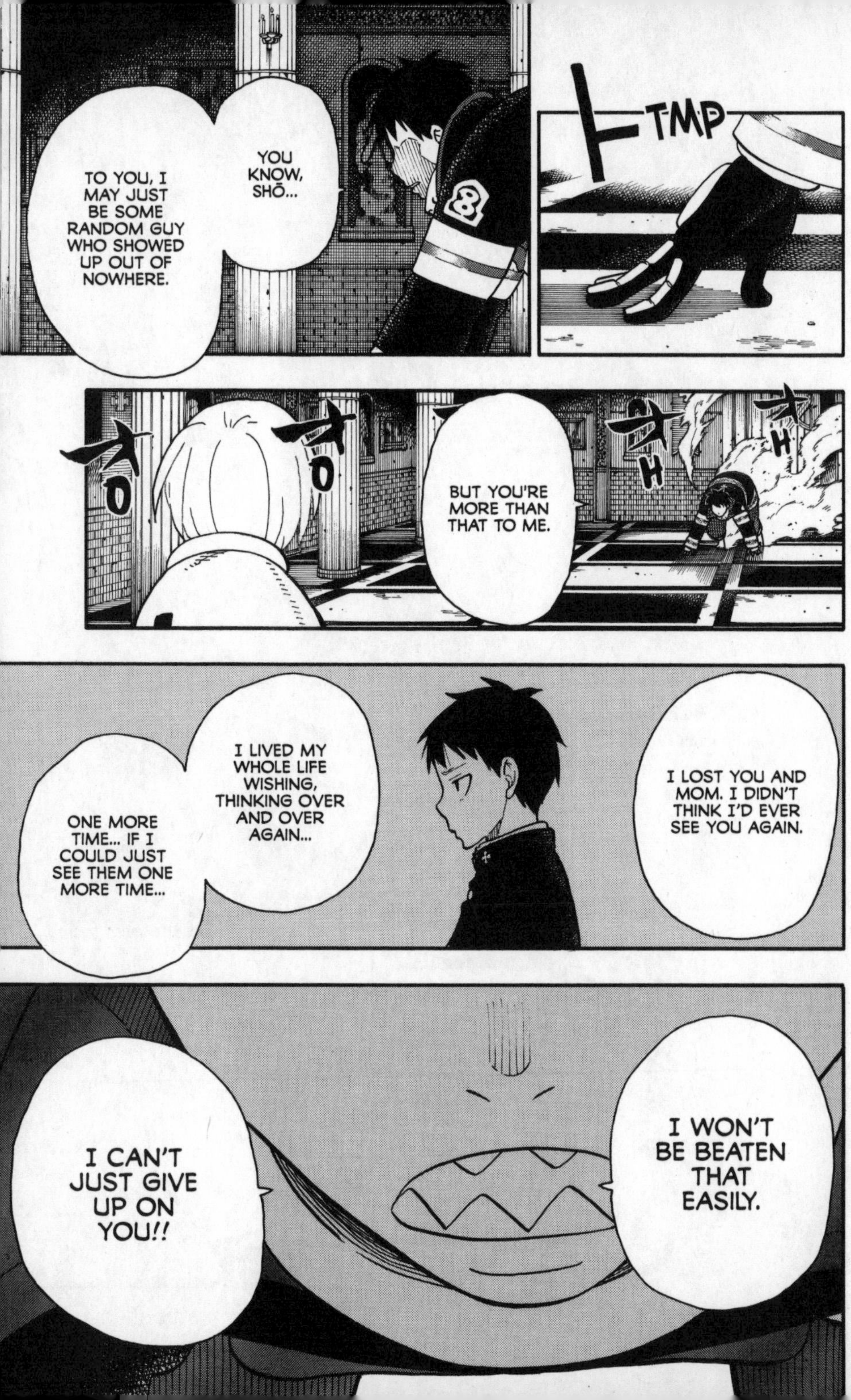
TMP
YOU KNOW, SHŌ...
TO YOU, I MAY JUST BE SOME RANDOM GUY WHO SHOWED UP OUT OF NOWHERE.
H
H
BUT YOU'RE MORE THAN THAT TO ME.
O
O
I LOST YOU AND MOM. I DIDN'T THINK I'D EVER SEE YOU AGAIN.
I LIVED MY WHOLE LIFE WISHING, THINKING OVER AND OVER AGAIN...
ONE MORE TIME... IF I COULD JUST SEE THEM ONE MORE TIME...
I WON'T BE BEATEN THAT EASILY.
I CAN'T JUST GIVE UP ON YOU!!

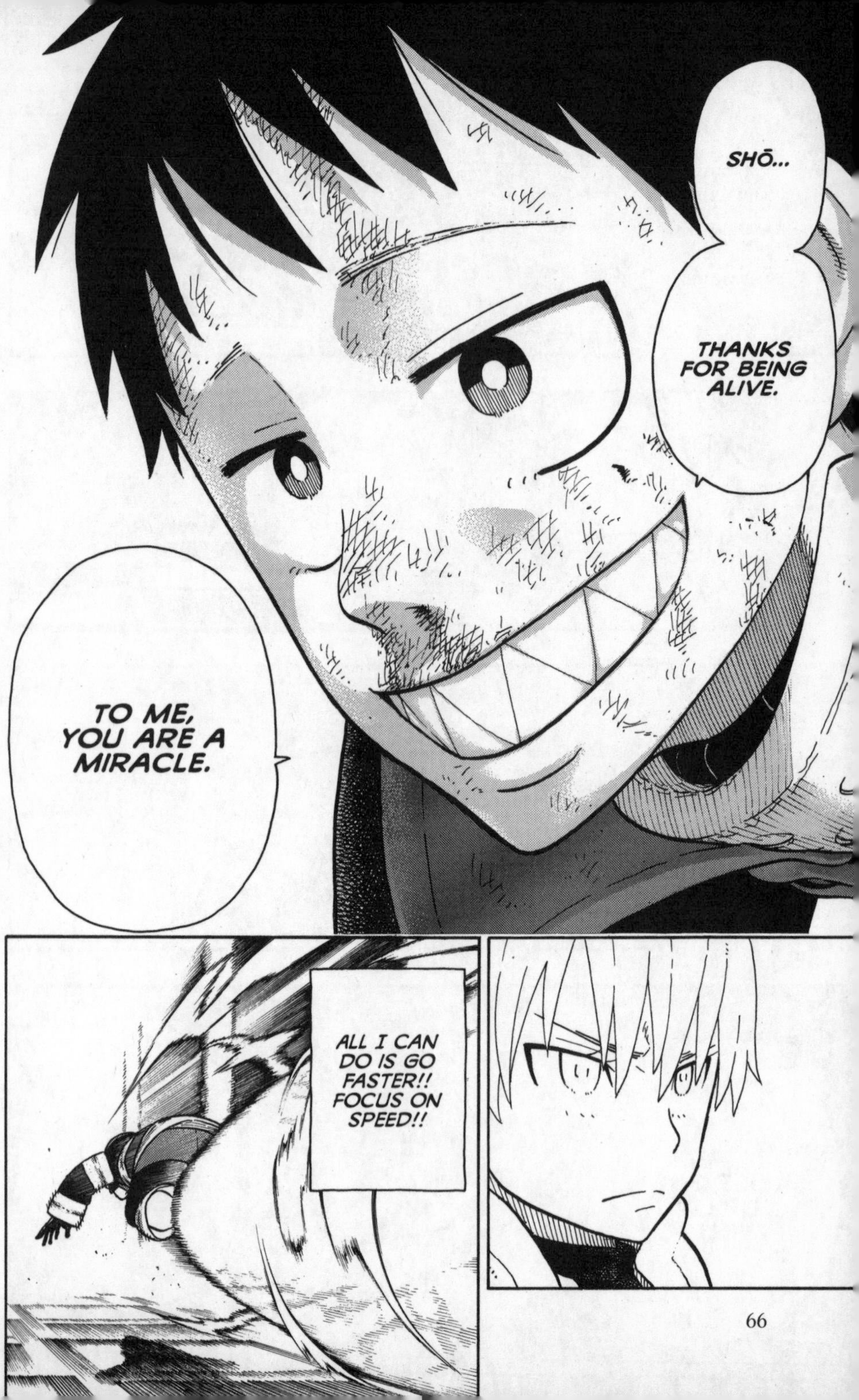
SHŌ...
THANKS FOR BEING ALIVE.
TO ME, YOU ARE A MIRACLE.
ALL I CAN DO IS GO FASTER!! FOCUS ON SPEED!!

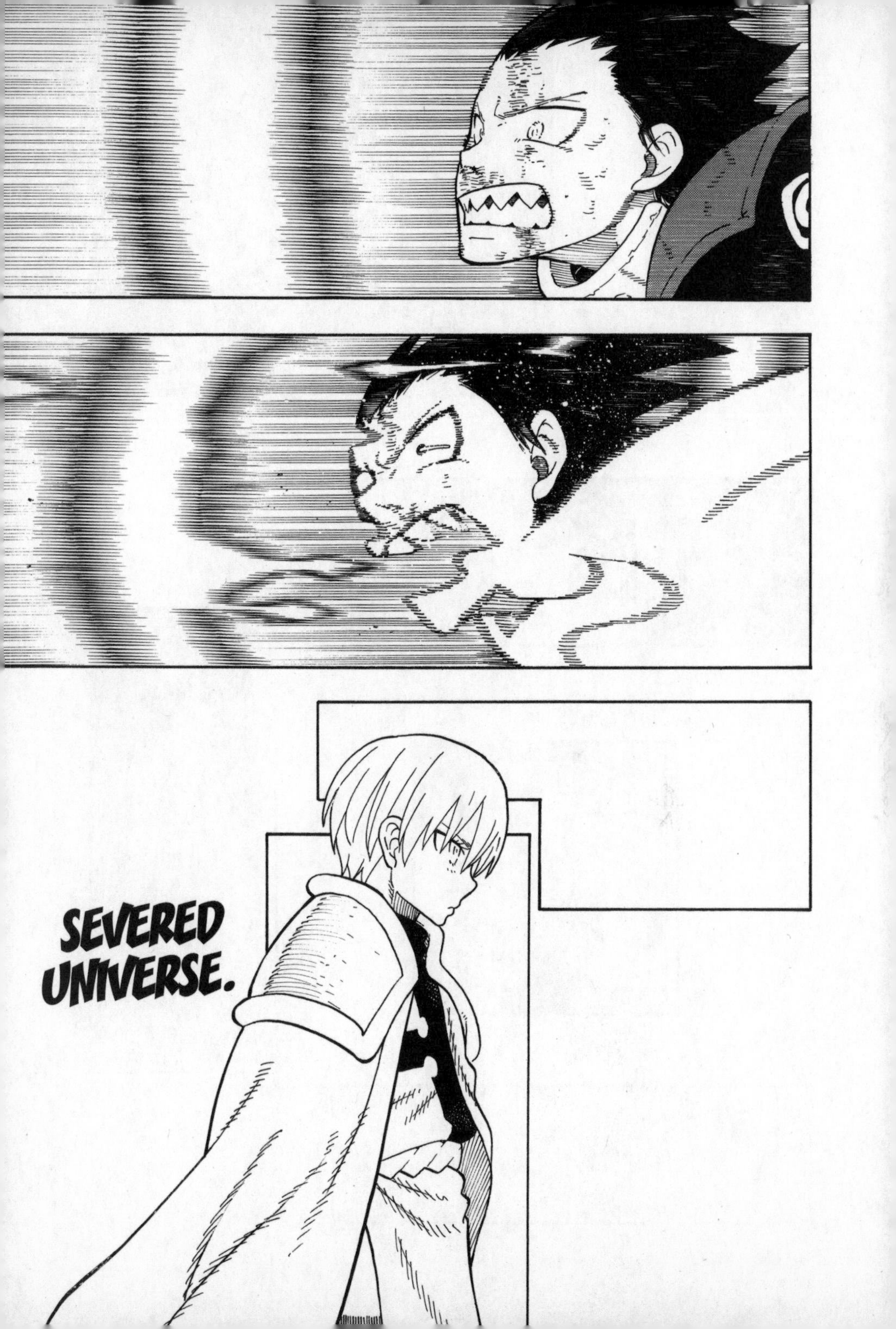
SEVERED UNIVERSE.

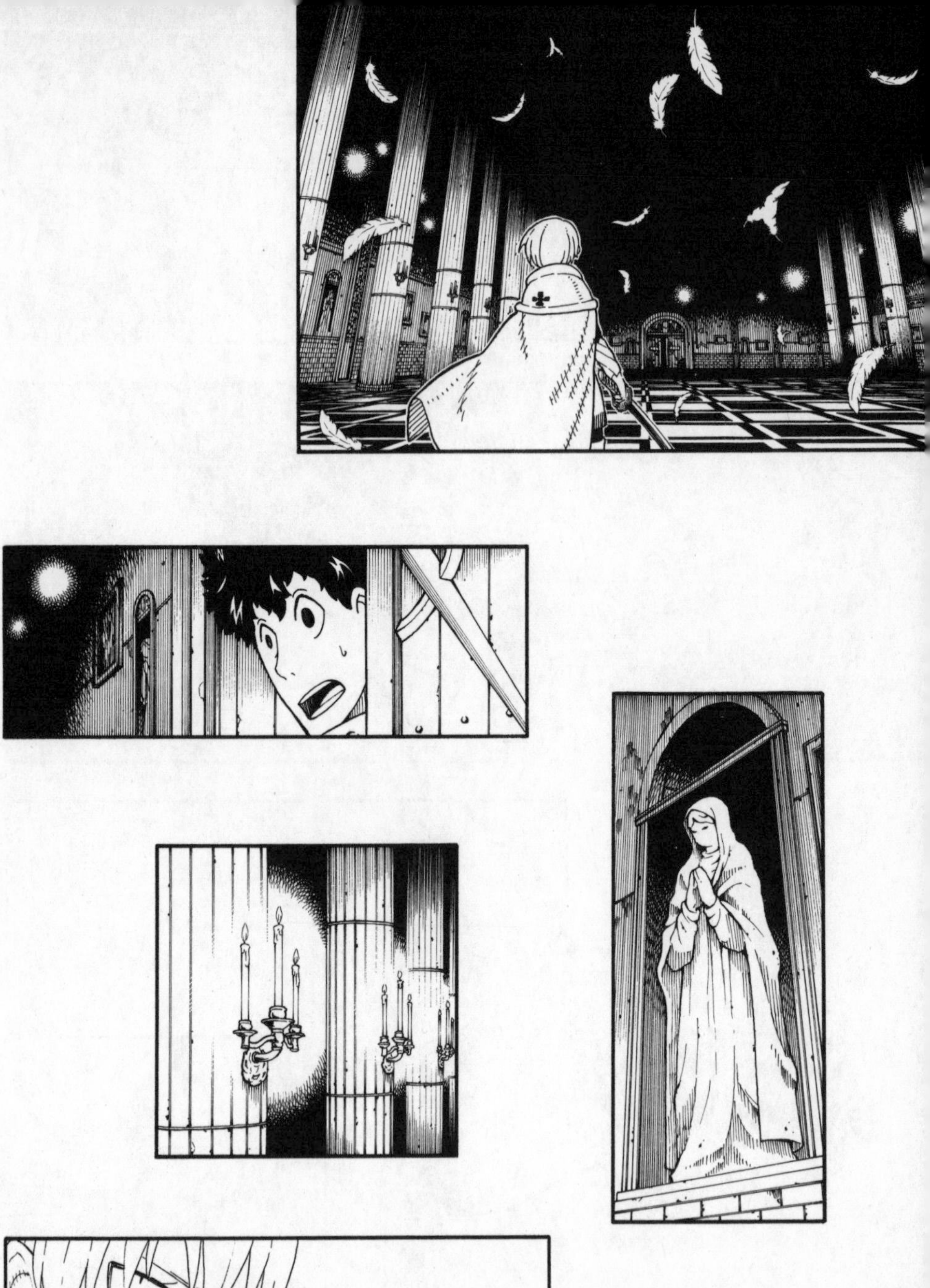

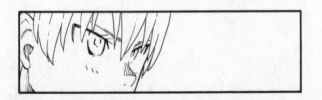

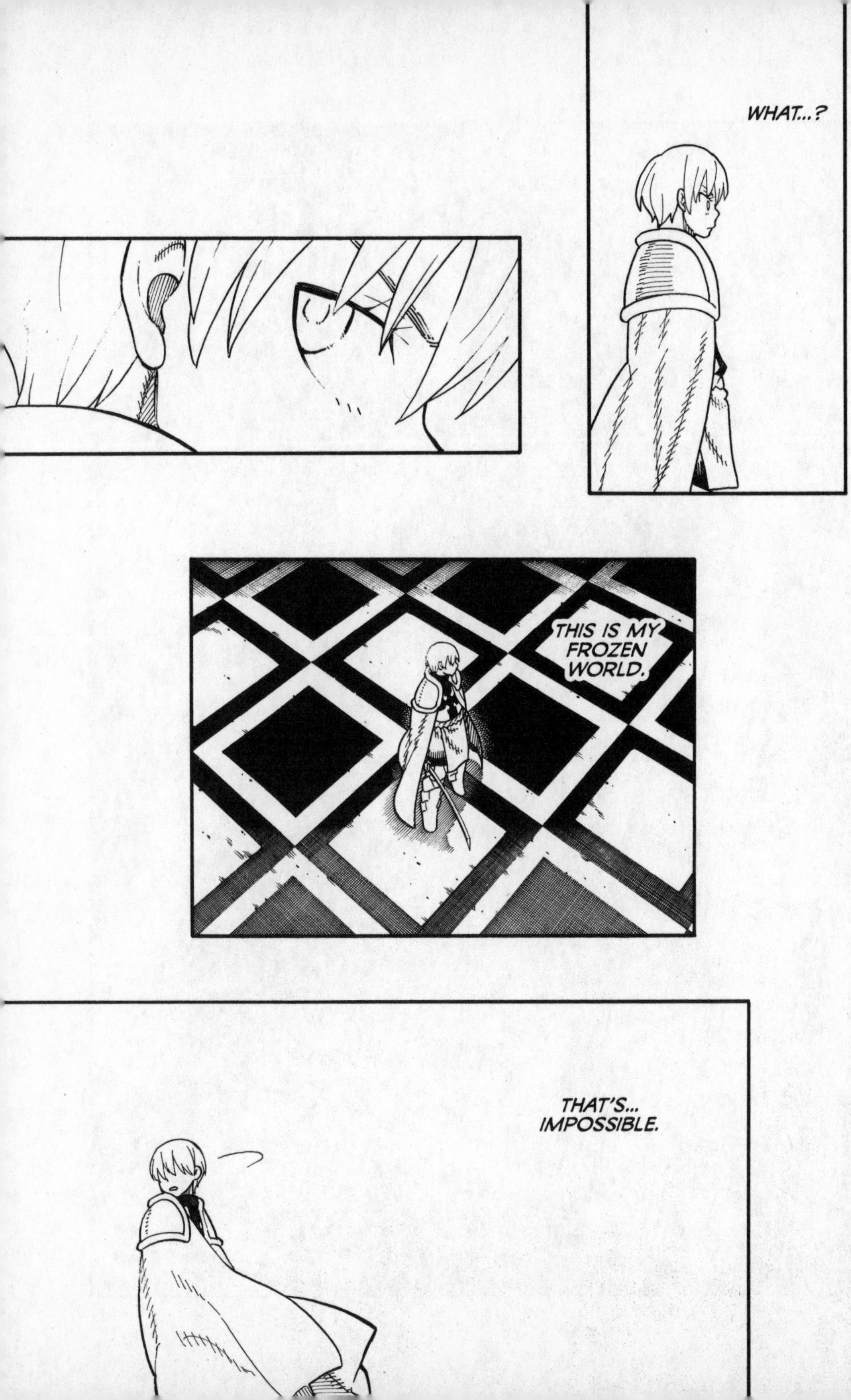
WHAT...?
THIS IS MY FROZEN WORLD.
THAT'S... IMPOSSIBLE.

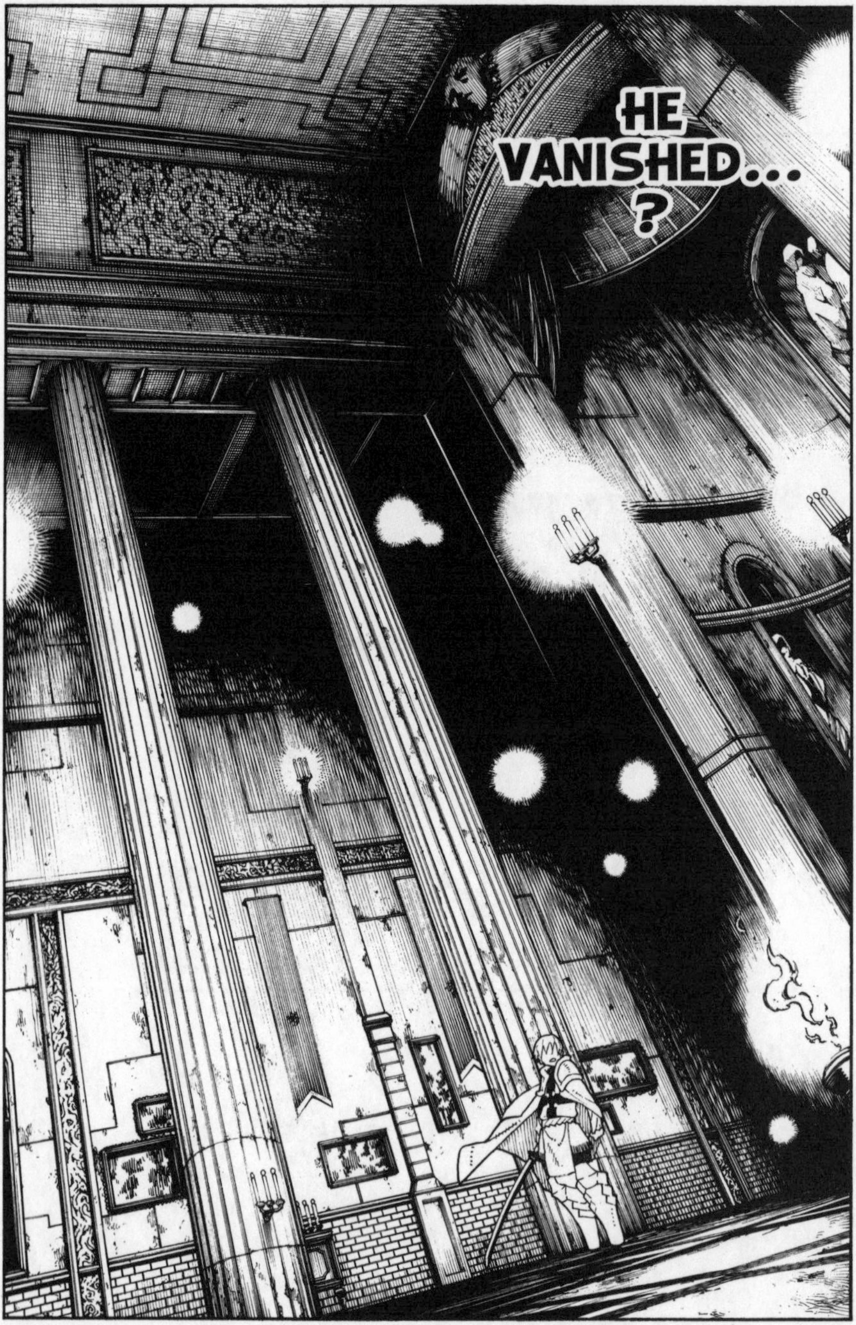
HE VANISHED...?

FIRE FORCE

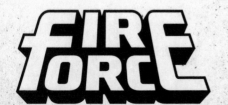

FIRE FORCE

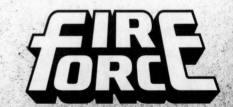

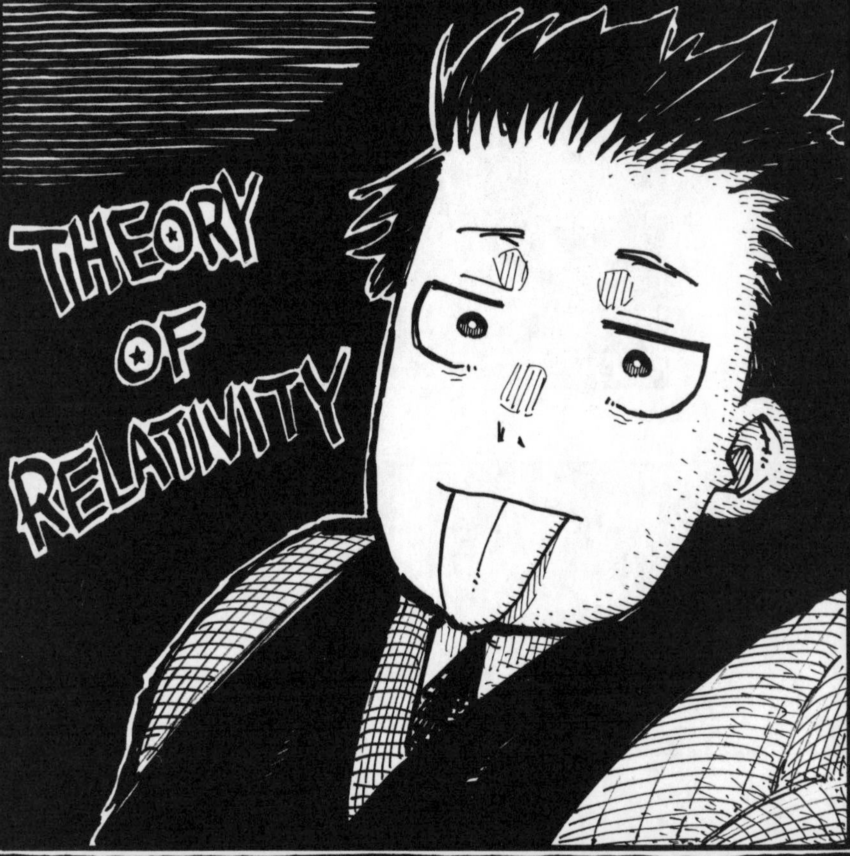
THEORY OF RELATIVITY

CHAPTER LXXXII: THE GRACE OF THE EVANGELIST

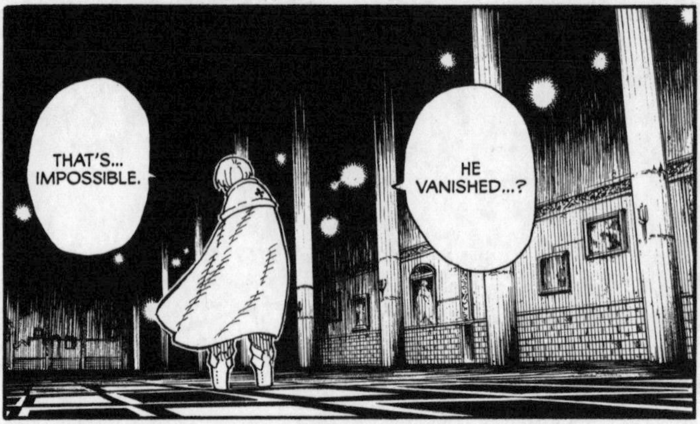
HE VANISHED...?
THAT'S... IMPOSSIBLE.

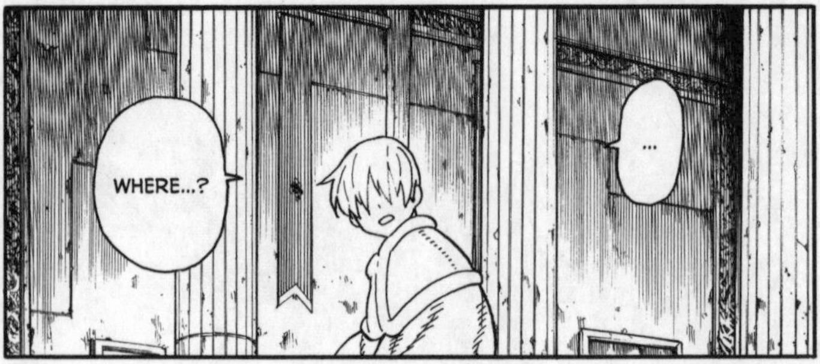
...
WHERE...?

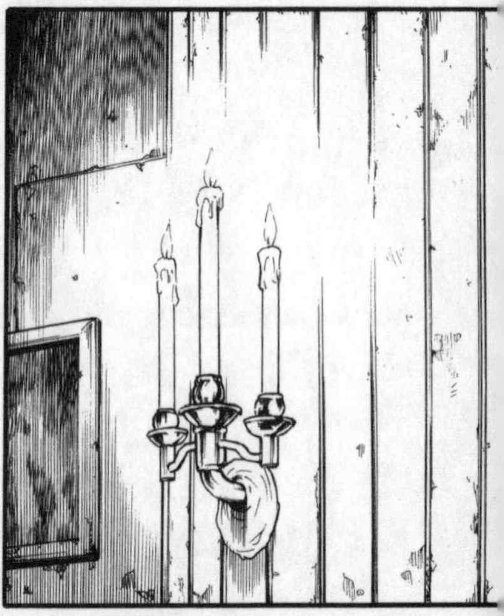

WHERE IS SHINRA KUSAKABE?

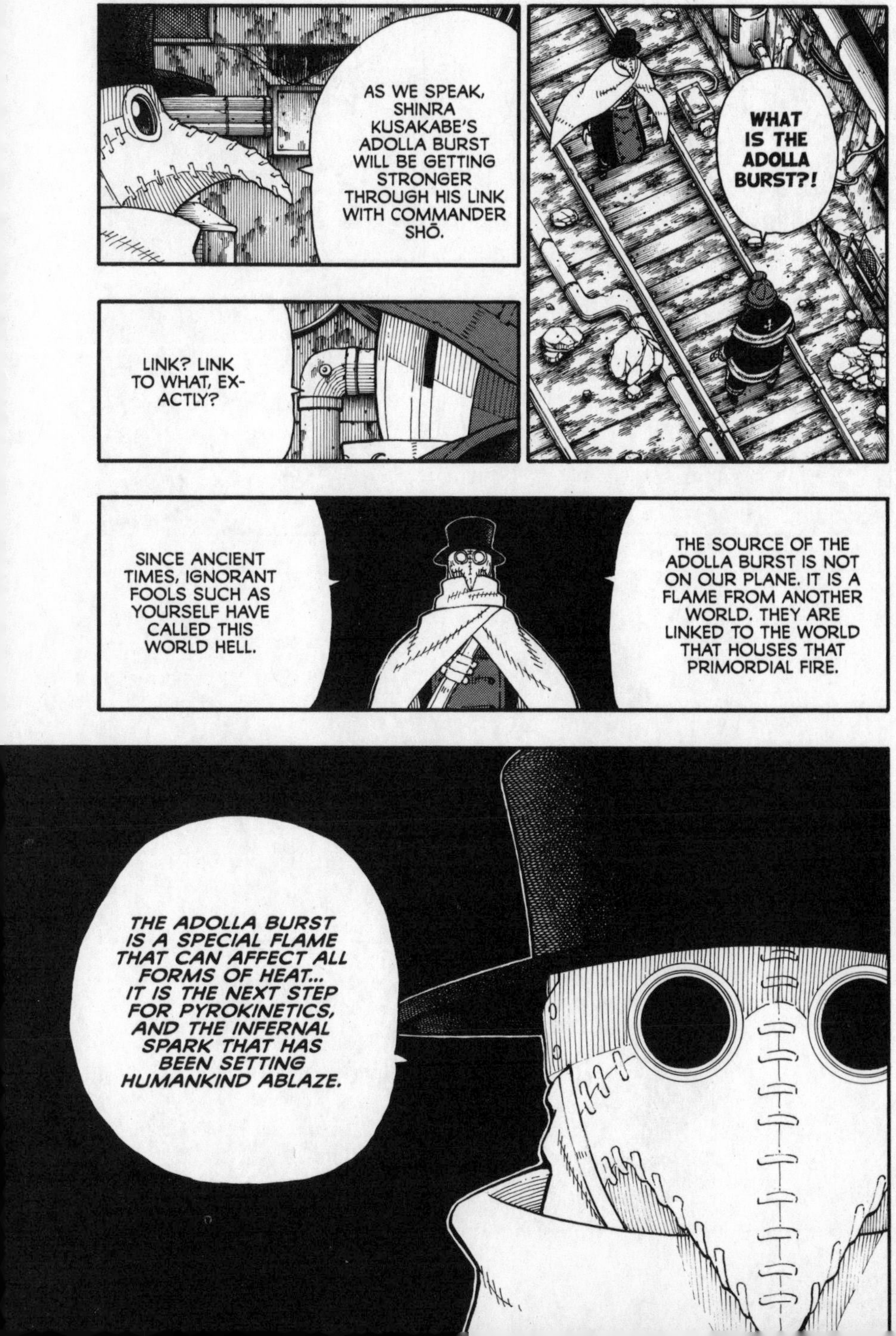
WHAT IS THE ADOLLA BURST?!
AS WE SPEAK, SHINRA KUSAKABE'S ADOLLA BURST WILL BE GETTING STRONGER THROUGH HIS LINK WITH COMMANDER SHŌ.
LINK? LINK TO WHAT, EX-ACTLY?
THE SOURCE OF THE ADOLLA BURST IS NOT ON OUR PLANE. IT IS A FLAME FROM ANOTHER WORLD. THEY ARE LINKED TO THE WORLD THAT HOUSES THAT PRIMORDIAL FIRE.
SINCE ANCIENT TIMES, IGNORANT FOOLS SUCH AS YOURSELF HAVE CALLED THIS WORLD HELL.
THE ADOLLA BURST IS A SPECIAL FLAME THAT CAN AFFECT ALL FORMS OF HEAT... IT IS THE NEXT STEP FOR PYROKINETICS, AND THE INFERNAL SPARK THAT HAS BEEN SETTING HUMANKIND ABLAZE.

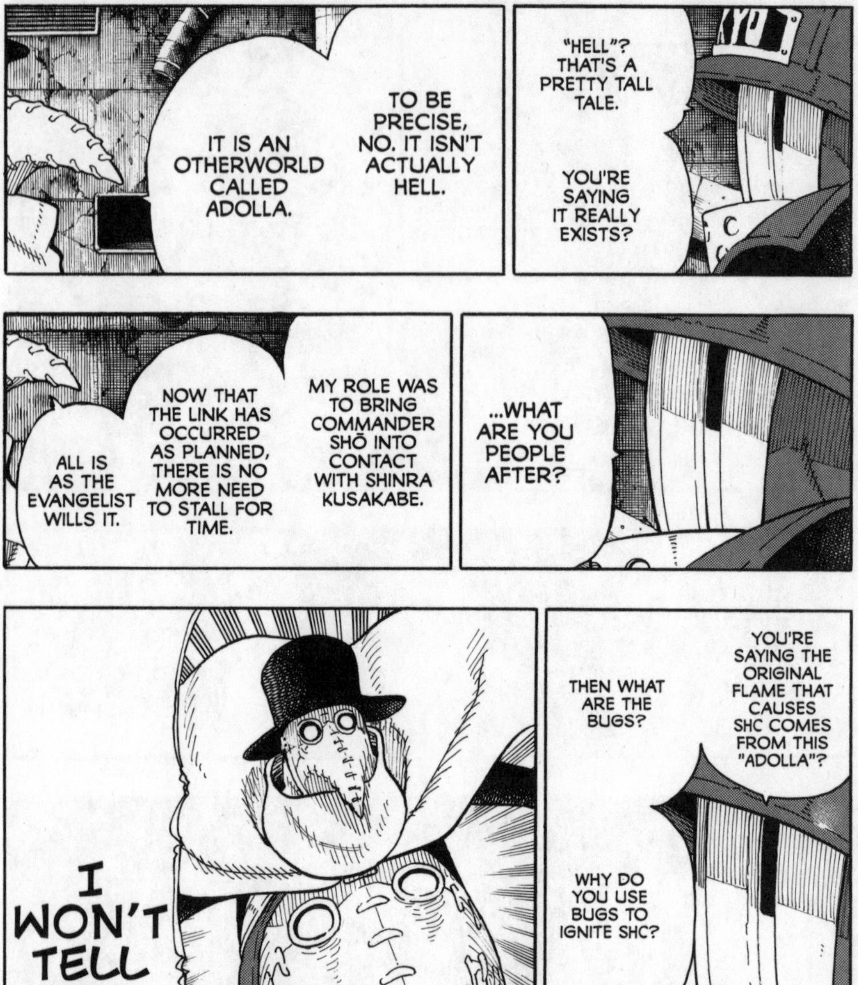
"HELL"? THAT'S A PRETTY TALL TALE.
YOU'RE SAYING IT REALLY EXISTS?
TO BE PRECISE, NO. IT ISN'T ACTUALLY HELL.
IT IS AN OTHERWORLD CALLED ADOLLA.
...WHAT ARE YOU PEOPLE AFTER?
MY ROLE WAS TO BRING COMMANDER SHŌ INTO CONTACT WITH SHINRA KUSAKABE.
NOW THAT THE LINK HAS OCCURRED AS PLANNED, THERE IS NO MORE NEED TO STALL FOR TIME.
ALL IS AS THE EVANGELIST WILLS IT.
YOU'RE SAYING THE ORIGINAL FLAME THAT CAUSES SHC COMES FROM THIS "ADOLLA"?
THEN WHAT ARE THE BUGS?
WHY DO YOU USE BUGS TO IGNITE SHC?
YOU WISH TO KNOW HOW THE BUGS AND THE FLAME ARE RE-LATED?
HEH HEH HEH... WELL, YOU SEE...
I WON'T TELL YOU!!!!

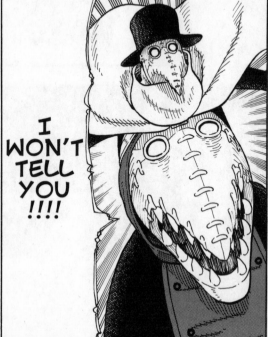

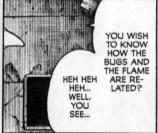

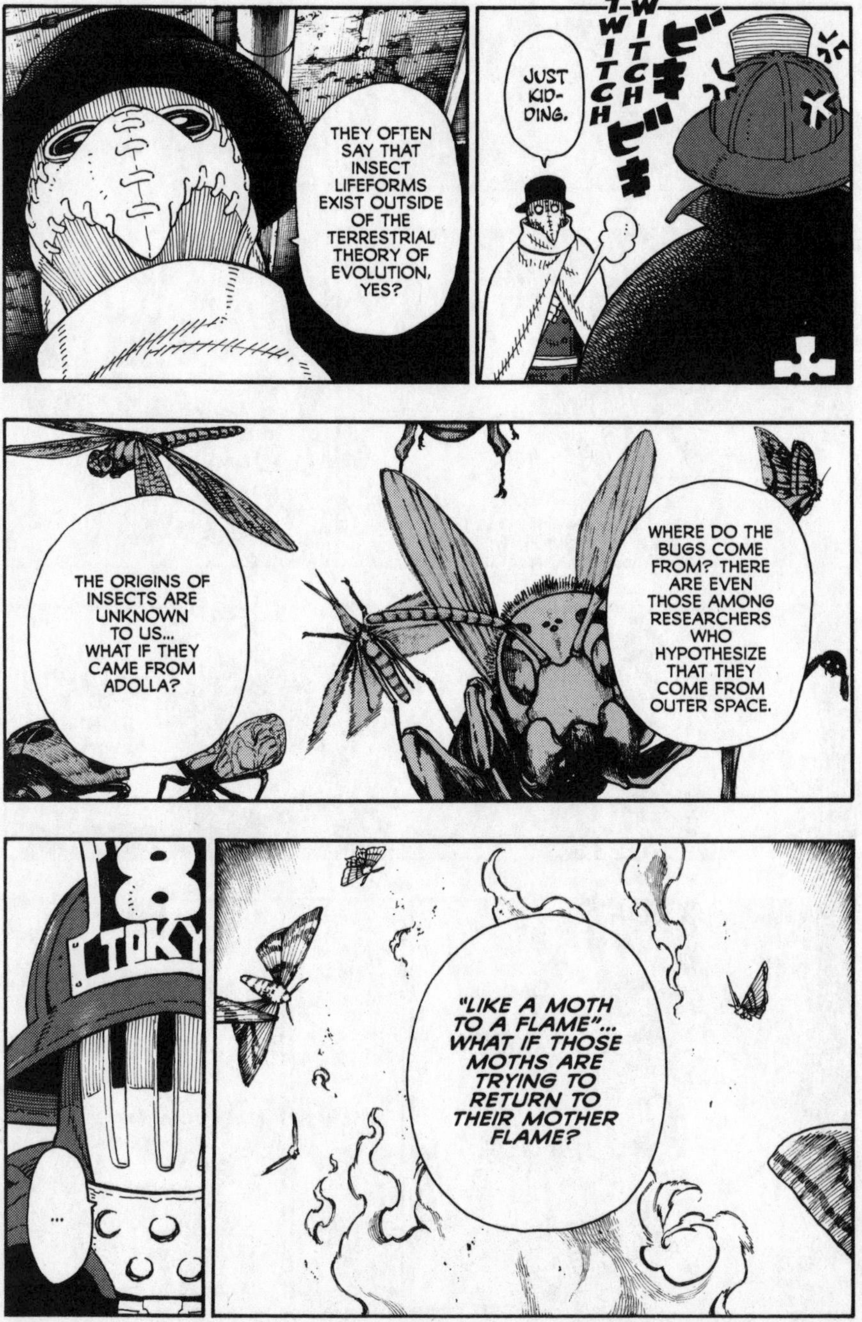
ビキビキ
TWITCH TWITCH
JUST KID-DING.
THEY OFTEN SAY THAT INSECT LIFEFORMS EXIST OUTSIDE OF THE TERRESTRIAL THEORY OF EVOLUTION, YES?
WHERE DO THE BUGS COME FROM? THERE ARE EVEN THOSE AMONG RESEARCHERS WHO HYPOTHESIZE THAT THEY COME FROM OUTER SPACE.
THE ORIGINS OF INSECTS ARE UNKNOWN TO US... WHAT IF THEY CAME FROM ADOLLA?
"LIKE A MOTH TO A FLAME"... WHAT IF THOSE MOTHS ARE TRYING TO RETURN TO THEIR MOTHER FLAME?
8
TOKY
...

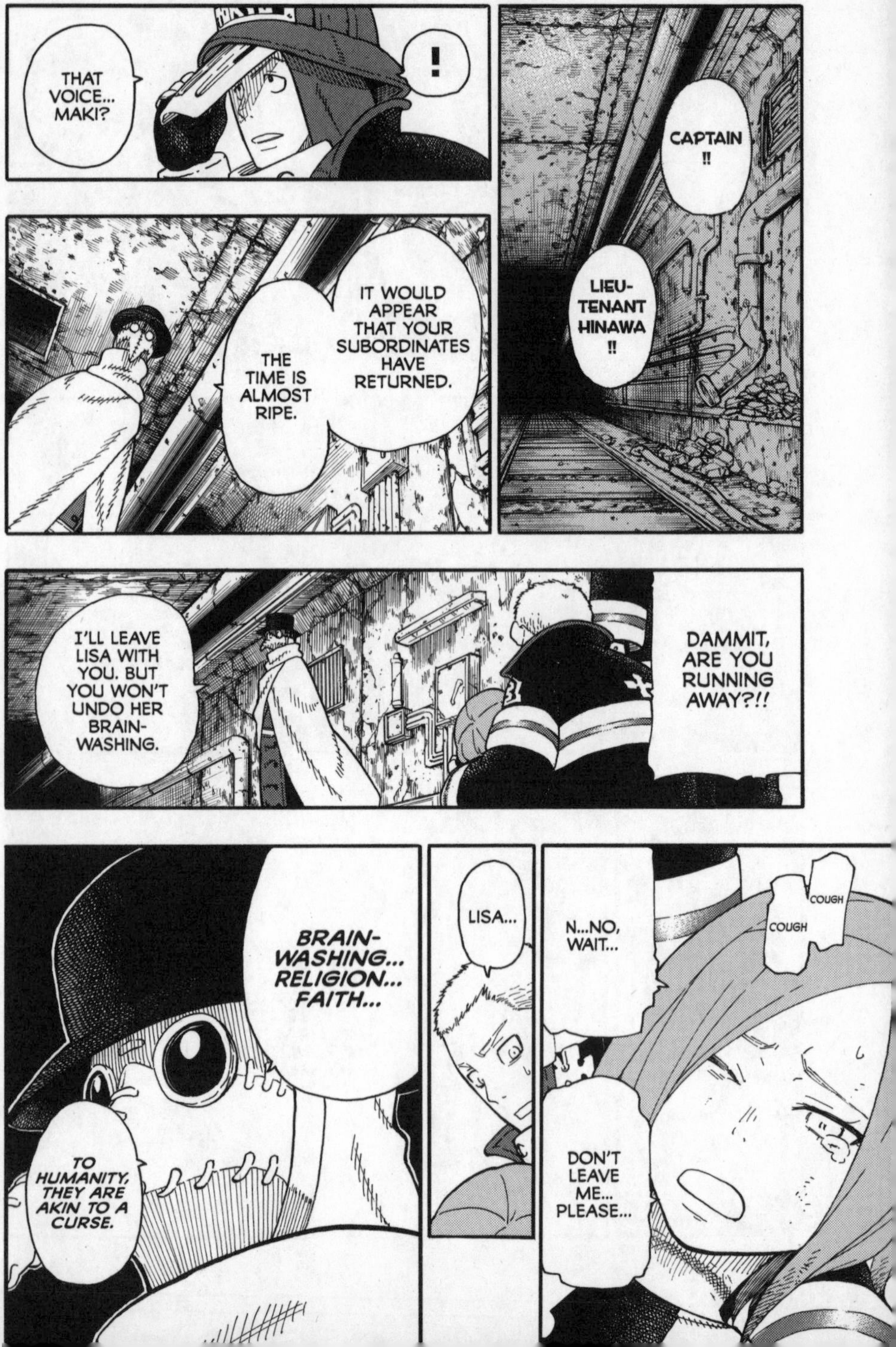
CAPTAIN !!
LIEU-TENANT HINAWA !!
!
THAT VOICE... MAKI?
IT WOULD APPEAR THAT YOUR SUBORDINATES HAVE RETURNED.
THE TIME IS ALMOST RIPE.
DAMMIT, ARE YOU RUNNING AWAY?!!
I'LL LEAVE LISA WITH YOU. BUT YOU WON'T UNDO HER BRAIN-WASHING.
COUGH
COUGH
N...NO, WAIT...
DON'T LEAVE ME... PLEASE...
LISA...
BRAIN-WASHING... RELIGION... FAITH...
TO HUMANITY, THEY ARE AKIN TO A CURSE.

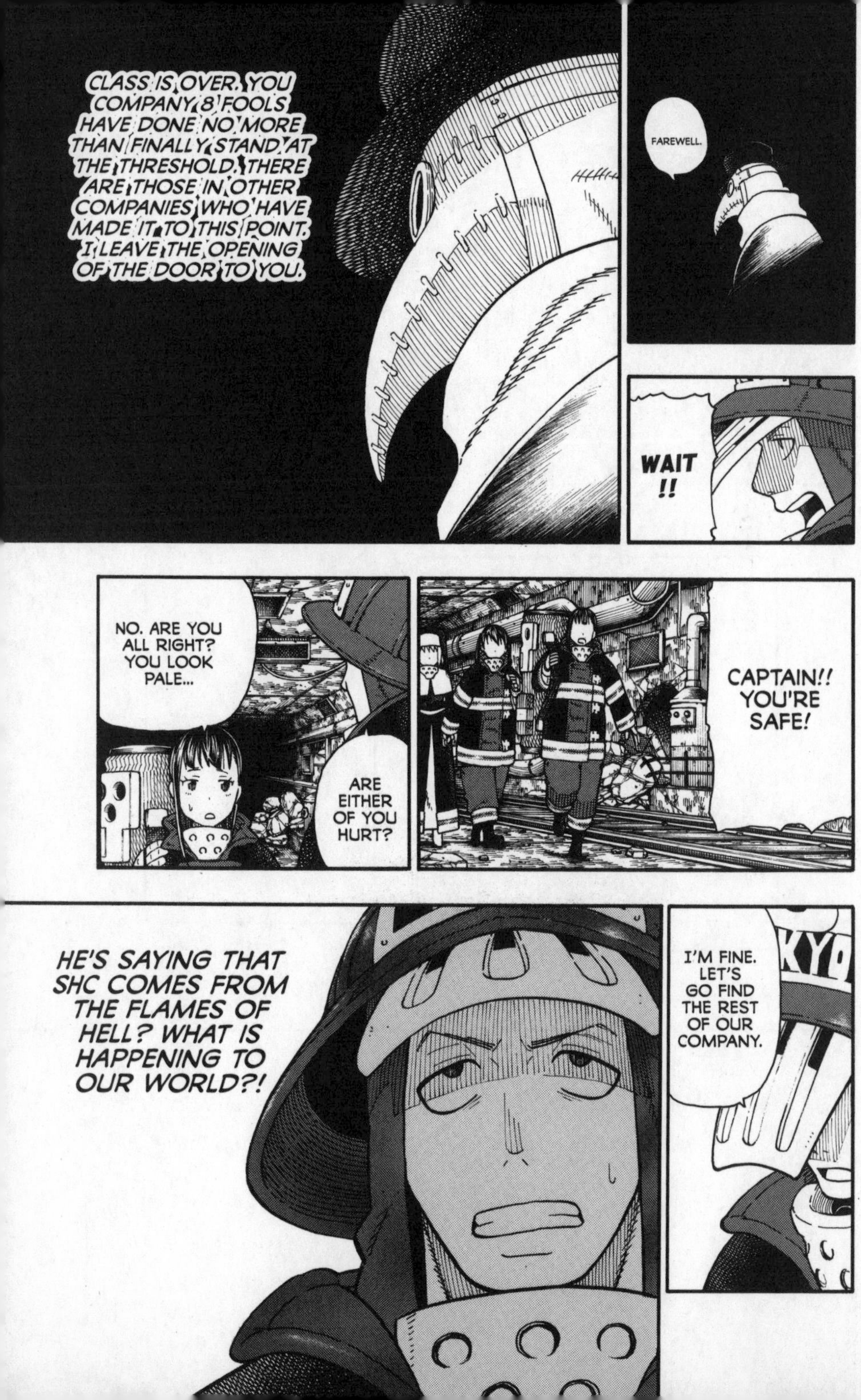
FAREWELL.
WAIT !!
CLASS IS OVER. YOU COMPANY 8 FOOLS HAVE DONE NO MORE THAN FINALLY STAND AT THE THRESHOLD. THERE ARE THOSE IN OTHER COMPANIES WHO HAVE MADE IT TO THIS POINT. I LEAVE THE OPENING OF THE DOOR TO YOU.
CAPTAIN!! YOU'RE SAFE!
ARE EITHER OF YOU HURT?
NO. ARE YOU ALL RIGHT? YOU LOOK PALE...
I'M FINE. LET'S GO FIND THE REST OF OUR COMPANY.
HE'S SAYING THAT SHC COMES FROM THE FLAMES OF HELL? WHAT IS HAPPENING TO OUR WORLD?!

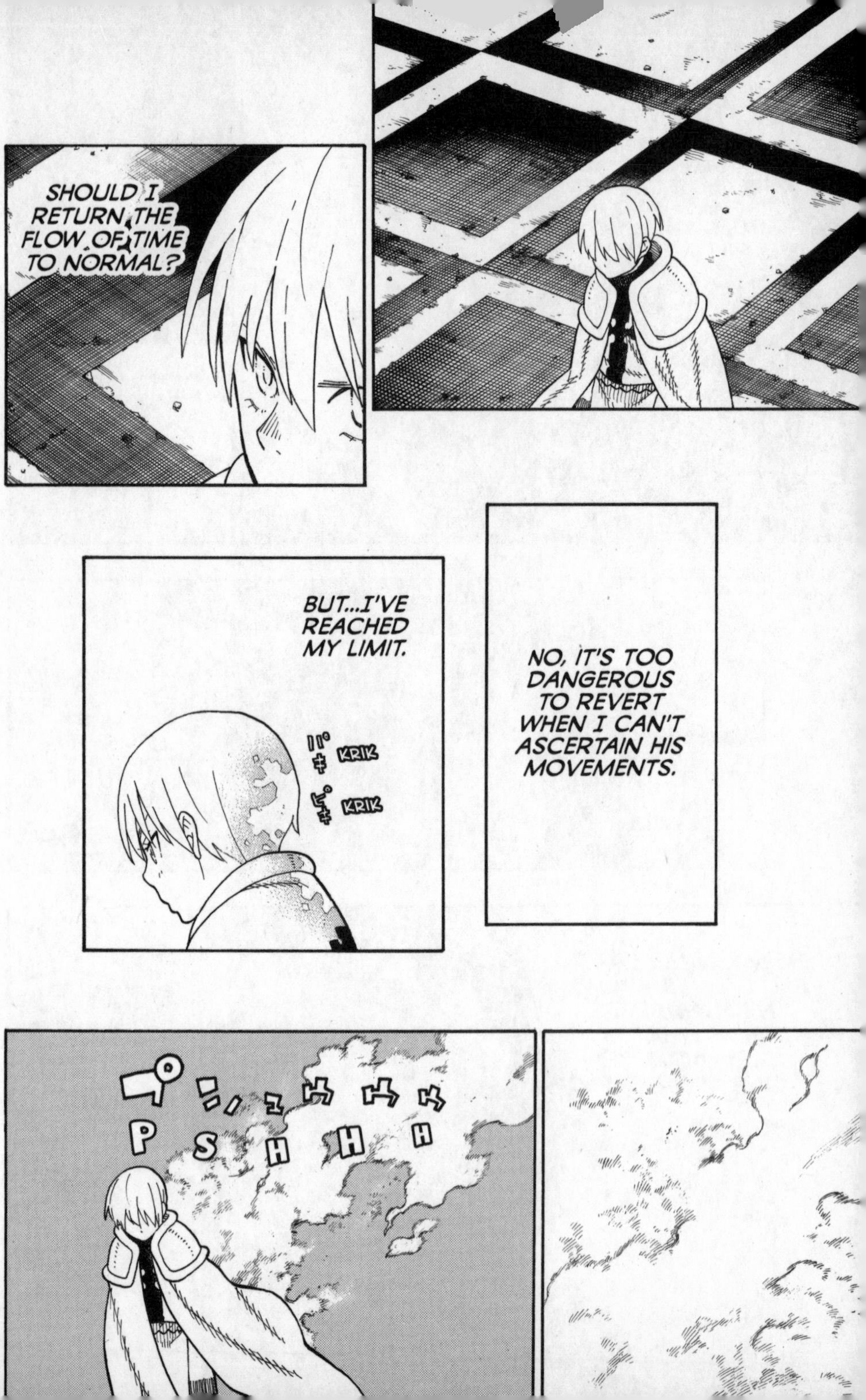

SHOULD I RETURN THE FLOW OF TIME TO NORMAL?
NO, IT'S TOO DANGEROUS TO REVERT WHEN I CAN'T ASCERTAIN HIS MOVEMENTS.
BUT...I'VE REACHED MY LIMIT.
KRIK
KRIK
PSHHH

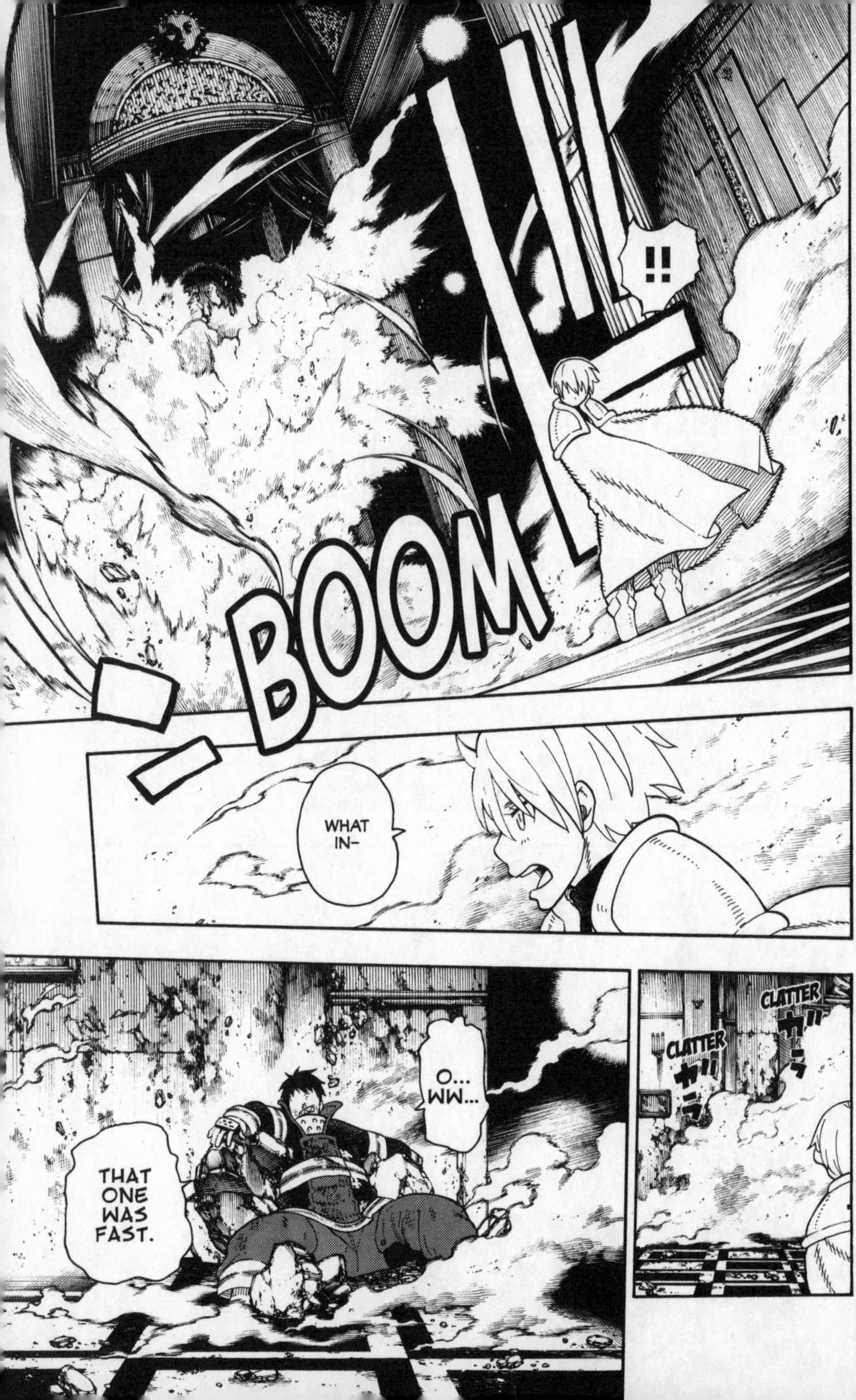
!!
BOOM
WHAT IN-
CLATTER
CLATTER
O... WW...
THAT ONE WAS FAST.

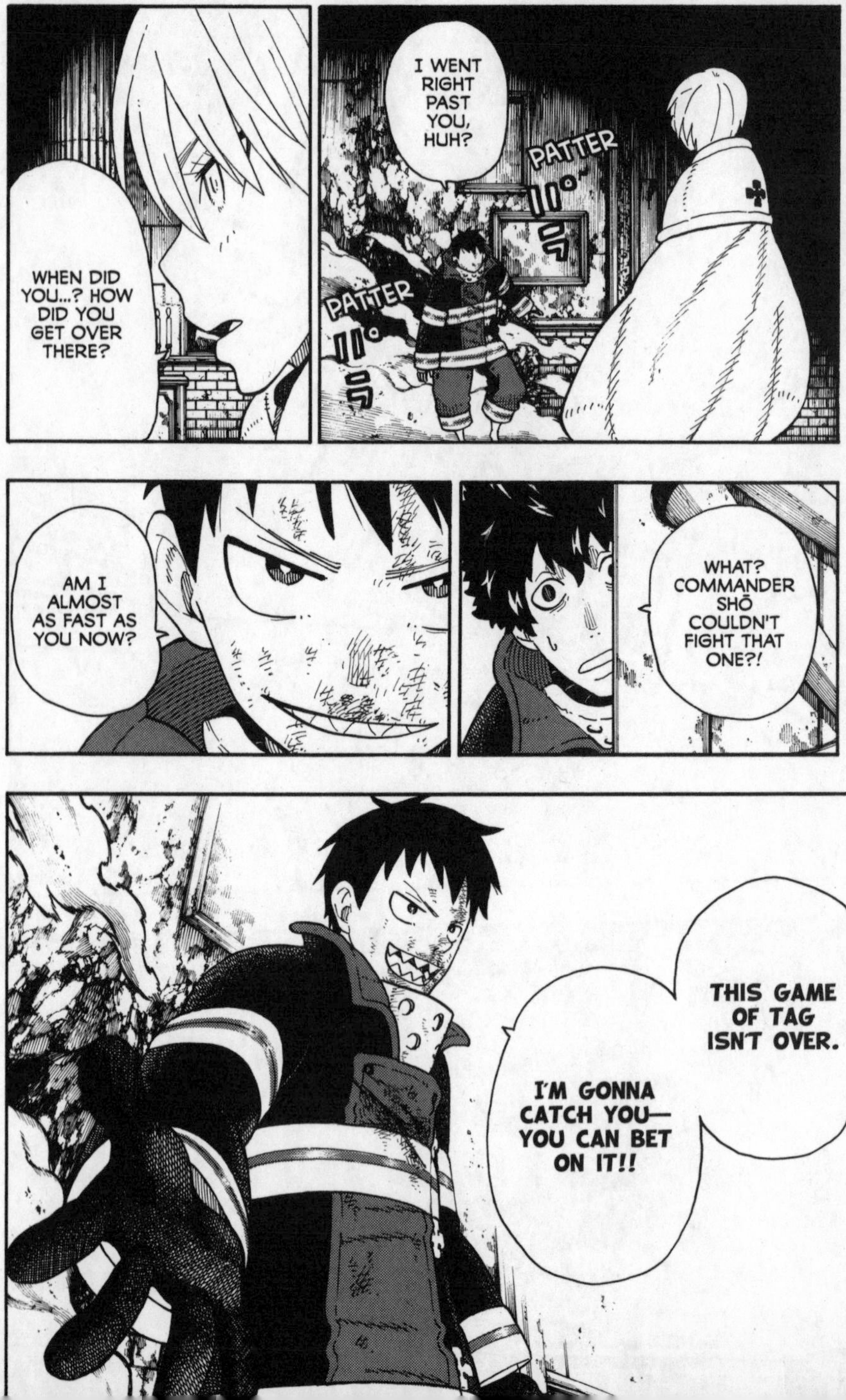
I WENT RIGHT PAST YOU, HUH?
PATTER
PATTER
WHEN DID YOU...? HOW DID YOU GET OVER THERE?
WHAT? COMMANDER SHŌ COULDN'T FIGHT THAT ONE?!
AM I ALMOST AS FAST AS YOU NOW?
THIS GAME OF TAG ISN'T OVER.
I'M GONNA CATCH YOU— YOU CAN BET ON IT!!

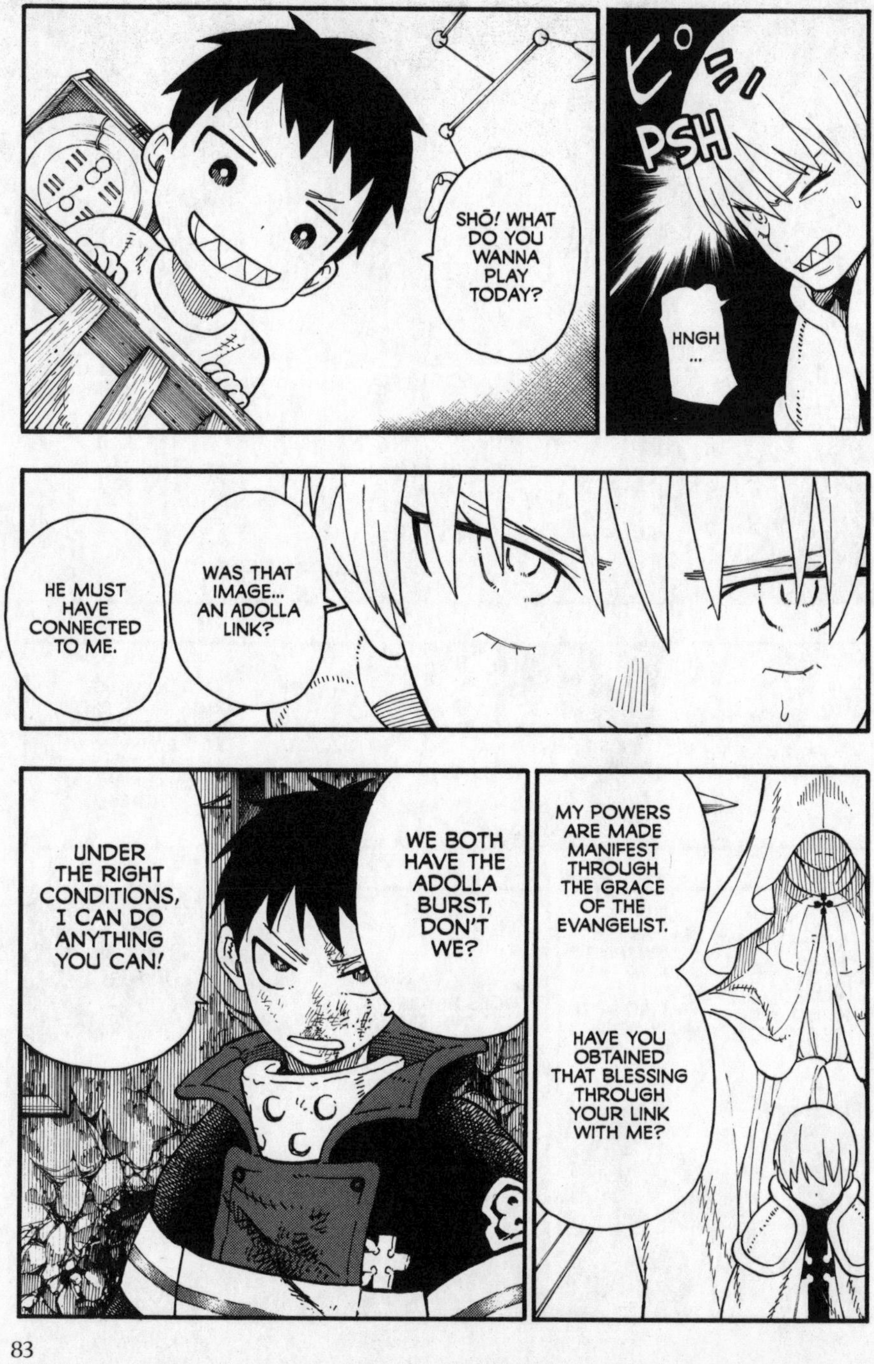
ピ
PSH
HNGH ...
SHŌ! WHAT DO YOU WANNA PLAY TODAY?
WAS THAT IMAGE... AN ADOLLA LINK?
HE MUST HAVE CONNECTED TO ME.
MY POWERS ARE MADE MANIFEST THROUGH THE GRACE OF THE EVANGELIST.
HAVE YOU OBTAINED THAT BLESSING THROUGH YOUR LINK WITH ME?
WE BOTH HAVE THE ADOLLA BURST, DON'T WE?
UNDER THE RIGHT CONDITIONS, I CAN DO ANYTHING YOU CAN!

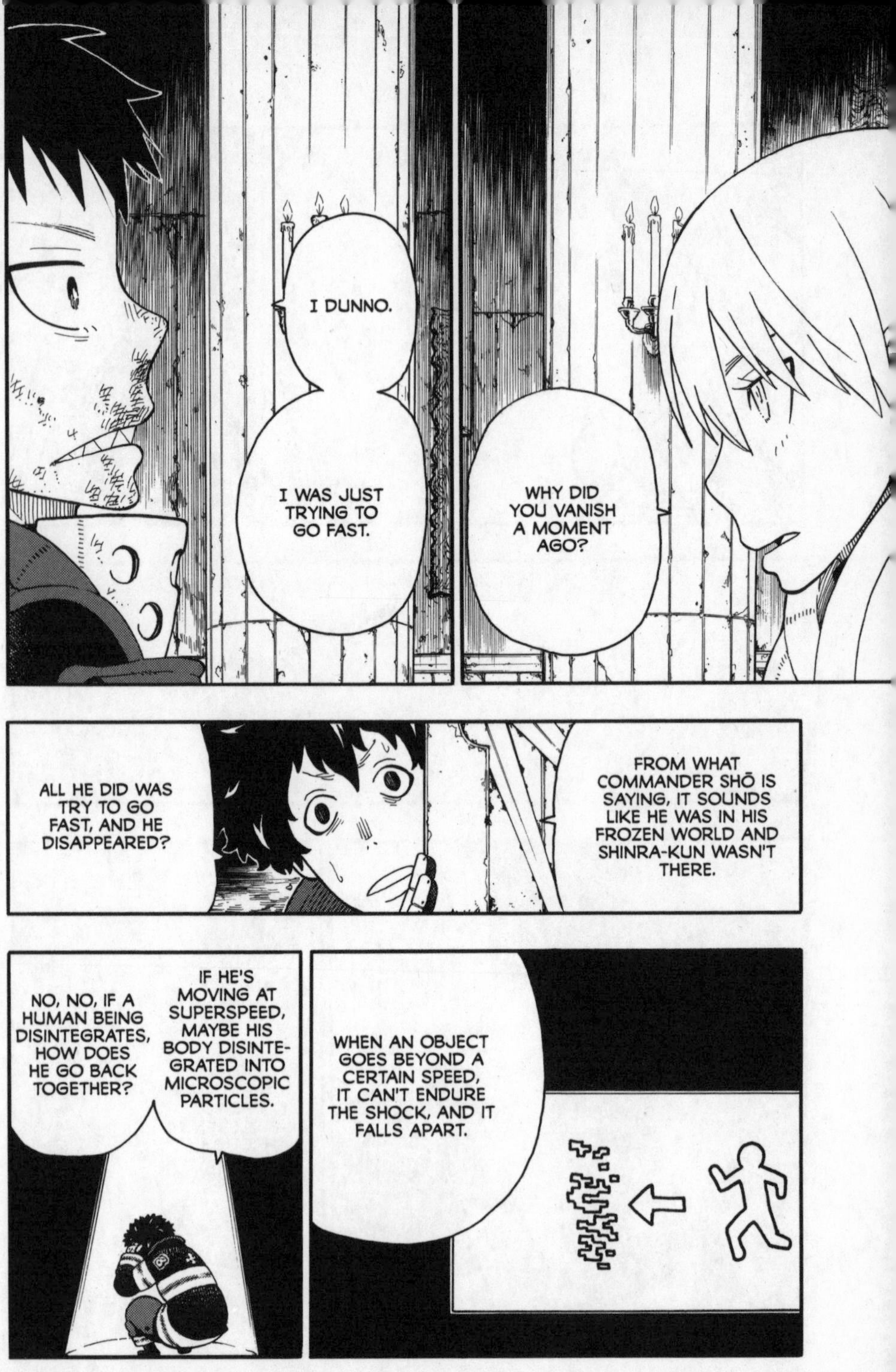
WHY DID YOU VANISH A MOMENT AGO?
I DUNNO.
I WAS JUST TRYING TO GO FAST.
FROM WHAT COMMANDER SHŌ IS SAYING, IT SOUNDS LIKE HE WAS IN HIS FROZEN WORLD AND SHINRA-KUN WASN'T THERE.
ALL HE DID WAS TRY TO GO FAST, AND HE DISAPPEARED?
WHEN AN OBJECT GOES BEYOND A CERTAIN SPEED, IT CAN'T ENDURE THE SHOCK, AND IT FALLS APART.
IF HE'S MOVING AT SUPERSPEED, MAYBE HIS BODY DISINTE-GRATED INTO MICROSCOPIC PARTICLES.
NO, NO, IF A HUMAN BEING DISINTEGRATES, HOW DOES HE GO BACK TOGETHER?

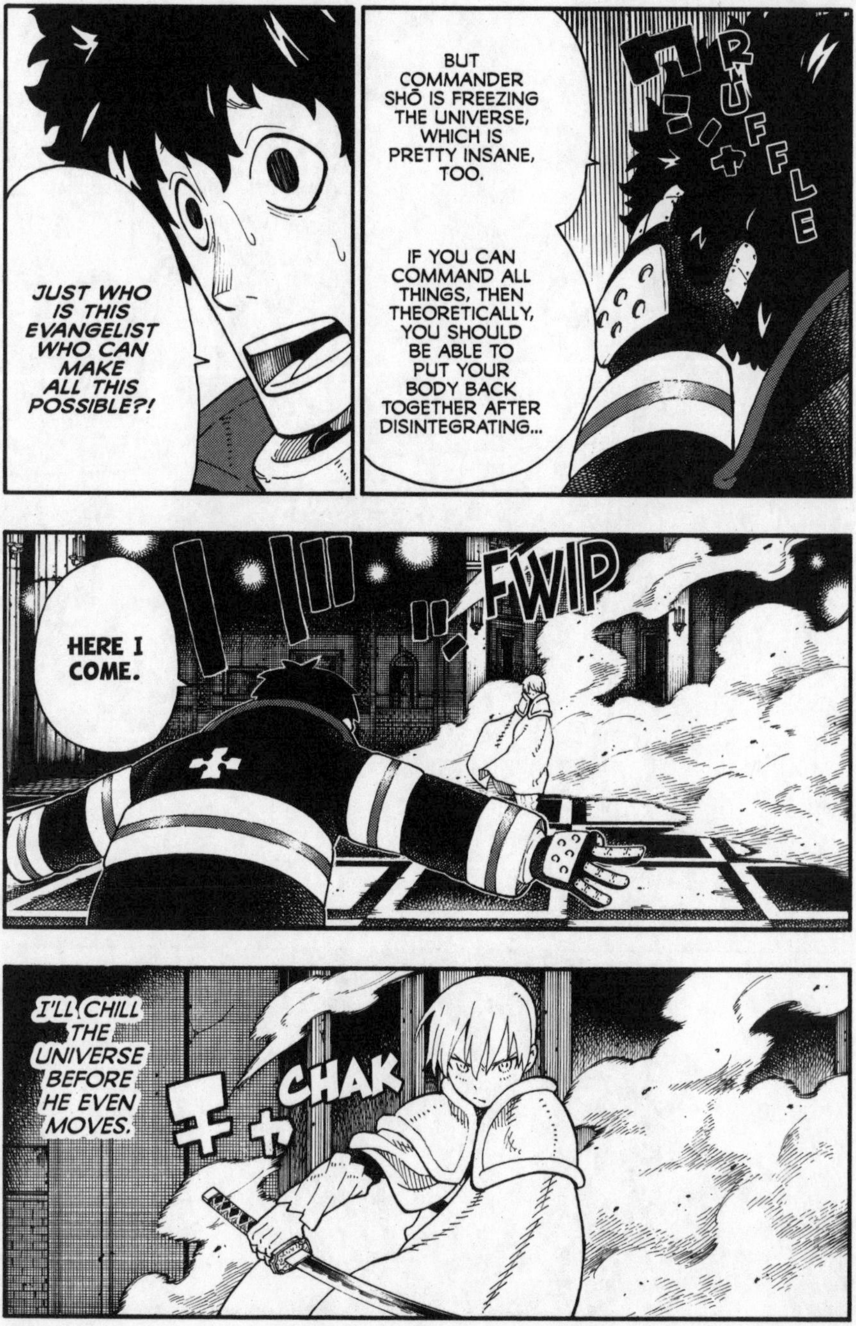
RUFFLE
BUT COMMANDER SHŌ IS FREEZING THE UNIVERSE, WHICH IS PRETTY INSANE, TOO.
IF YOU CAN COMMAND ALL THINGS, THEN THEORETICALLY, YOU SHOULD BE ABLE TO PUT YOUR BODY BACK TOGETHER AFTER DISINTEGRATING...
JUST WHO IS THIS EVANGELIST WHO CAN MAKE ALL THIS POSSIBLE?!
FWIP
HERE I COME.
I'LL CHILL THE UNIVERSE BEFORE HE EVEN MOVES.
CHAK

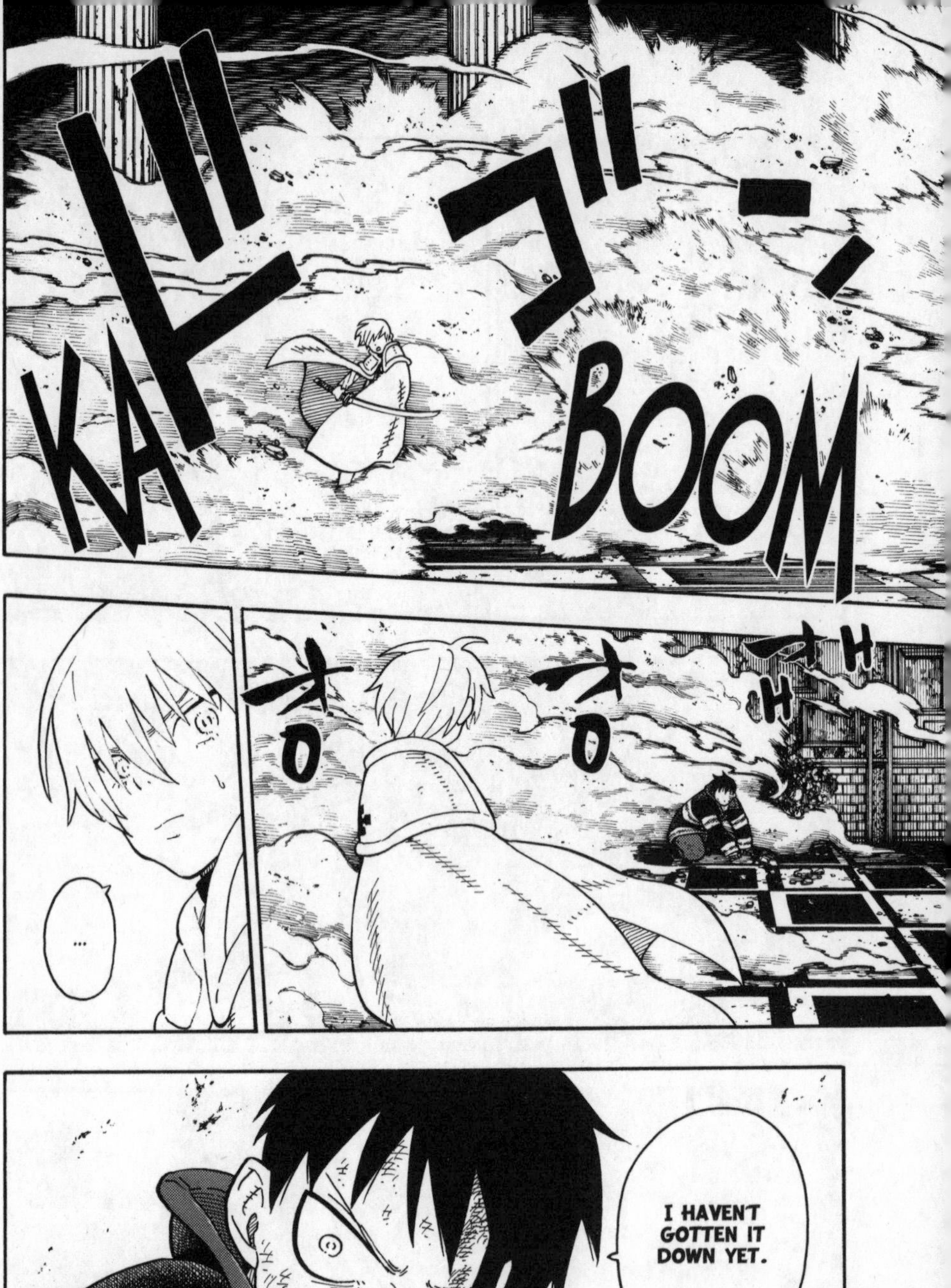
KABOOM
...
I HAVEN'T GOTTEN IT DOWN YET.

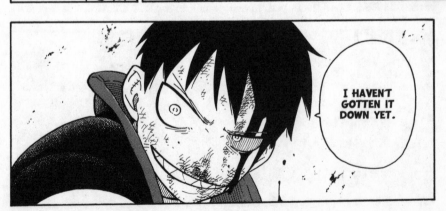

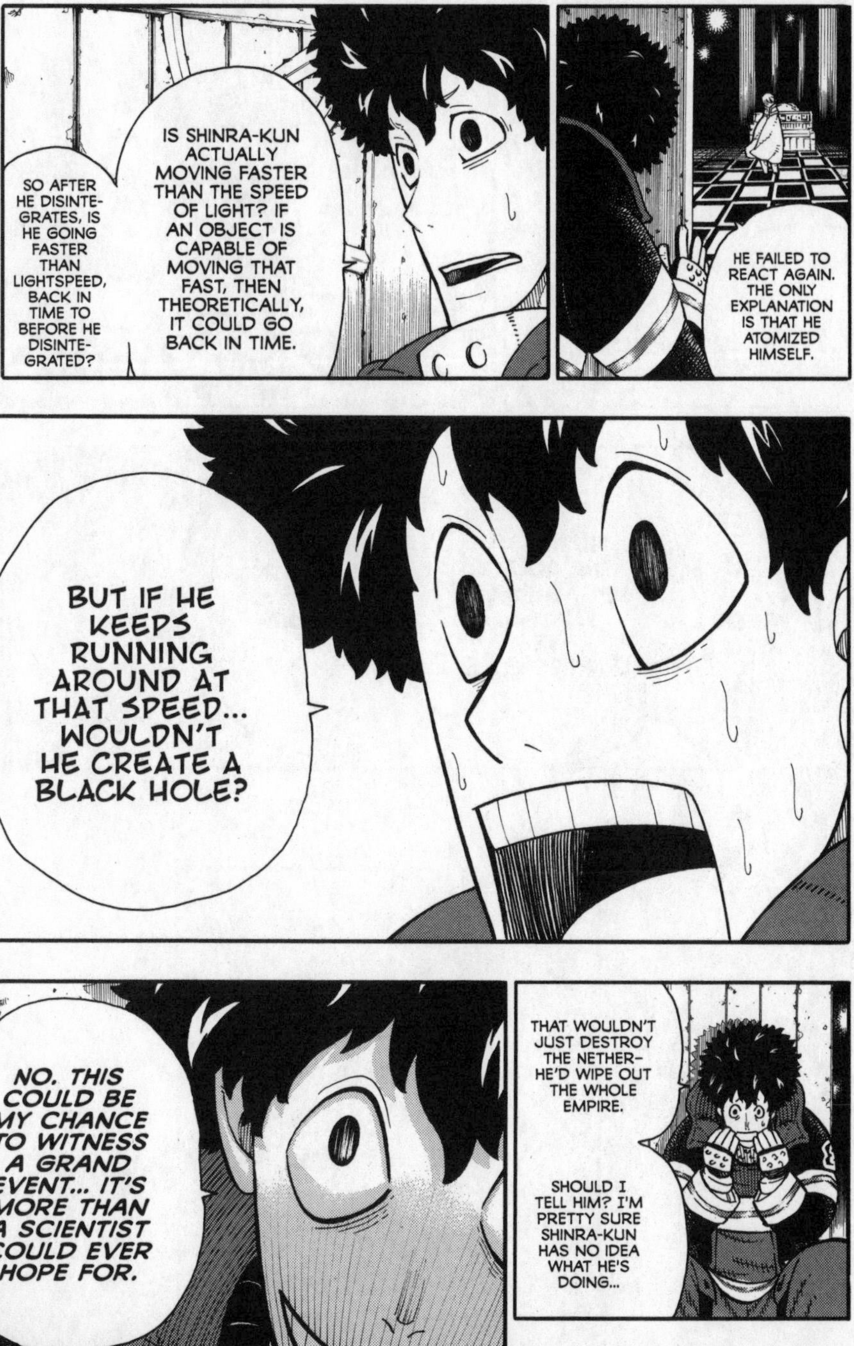
HE FAILED TO REACT AGAIN. THE ONLY EXPLANATION IS THAT HE ATOMIZED HIMSELF.
IS SHINRA-KUN ACTUALLY MOVING FASTER THAN THE SPEED OF LIGHT? IF AN OBJECT IS CAPABLE OF MOVING THAT FAST, THEN THEORETICALLY, IT COULD GO BACK IN TIME.
SO AFTER HE DISINTEGRATES, IS HE GOING FASTER THAN LIGHTSPEED, BACK IN TIME TO BEFORE HE DISINTEGRATED?
BUT IF HE KEEPS RUNNING AROUND AT THAT SPEED... WOULDN'T HE CREATE A BLACK HOLE?
THAT WOULDN'T JUST DESTROY THE NETHER- HE'D WIPE OUT THE WHOLE EMPIRE.
SHOULD I TELL HIM? I'M PRETTY SURE SHINRA-KUN HAS NO IDEA WHAT HE'S DOING...
NO. THIS COULD BE MY CHANCE TO WITNESS A GRAND EVENT... IT'S MORE THAN A SCIENTIST COULD EVER HOPE FOR.

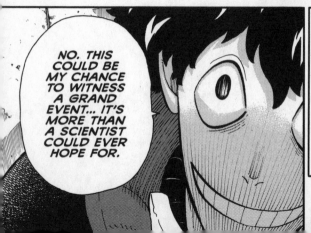

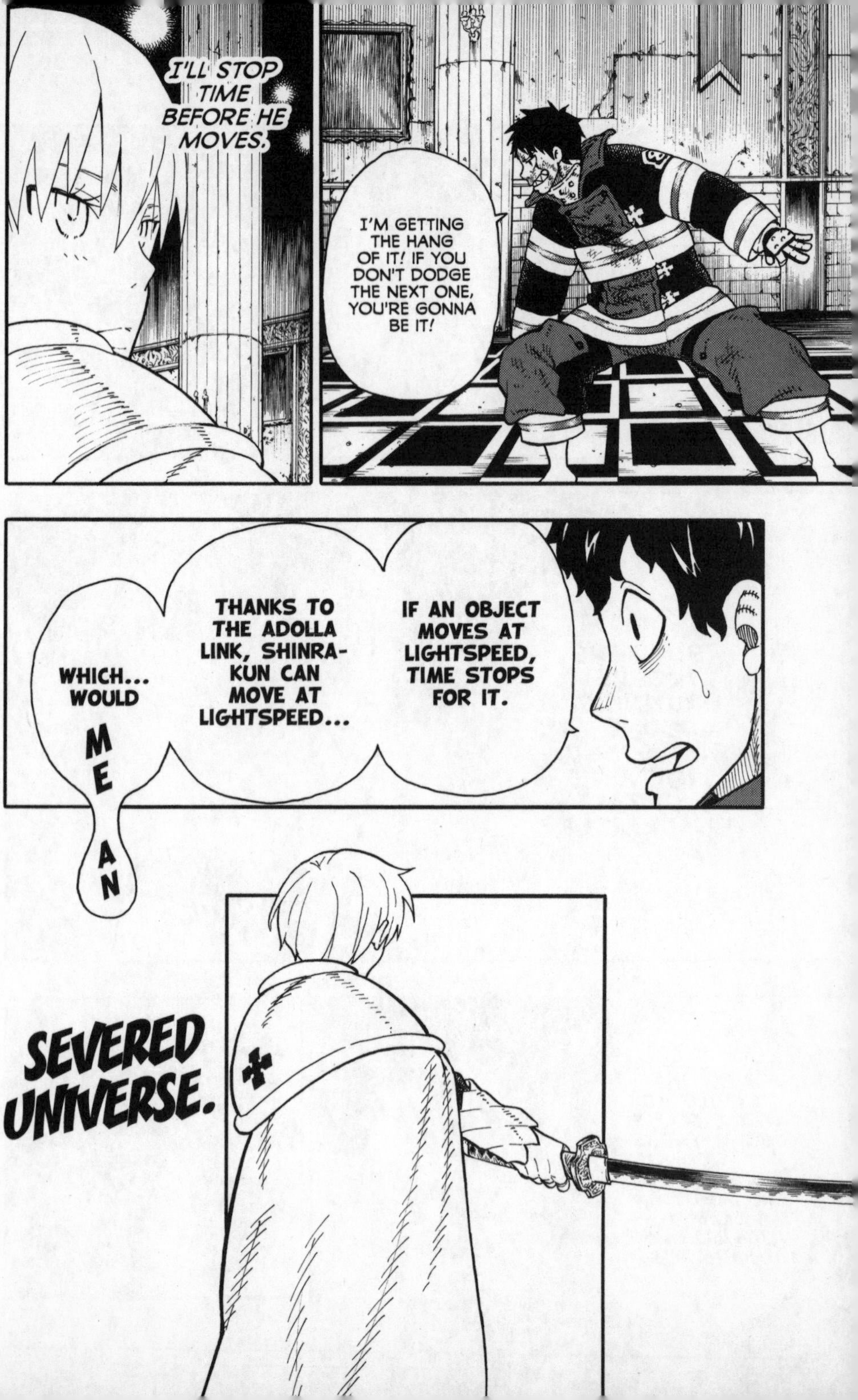
I'M GETTING THE HANG OF IT! IF YOU DON'T DODGE THE NEXT ONE, YOU'RE GONNA BE IT!
I'LL STOP TIME BEFORE HE MOVES.
IF AN OBJECT MOVES AT LIGHTSPEED, TIME STOPS FOR IT.
THANKS TO THE ADOLLA LINK, SHINRA-KUN CAN MOVE AT LIGHTSPEED...
WHICH... WOULD MEAN AN
SEVERED UNIVERSE.

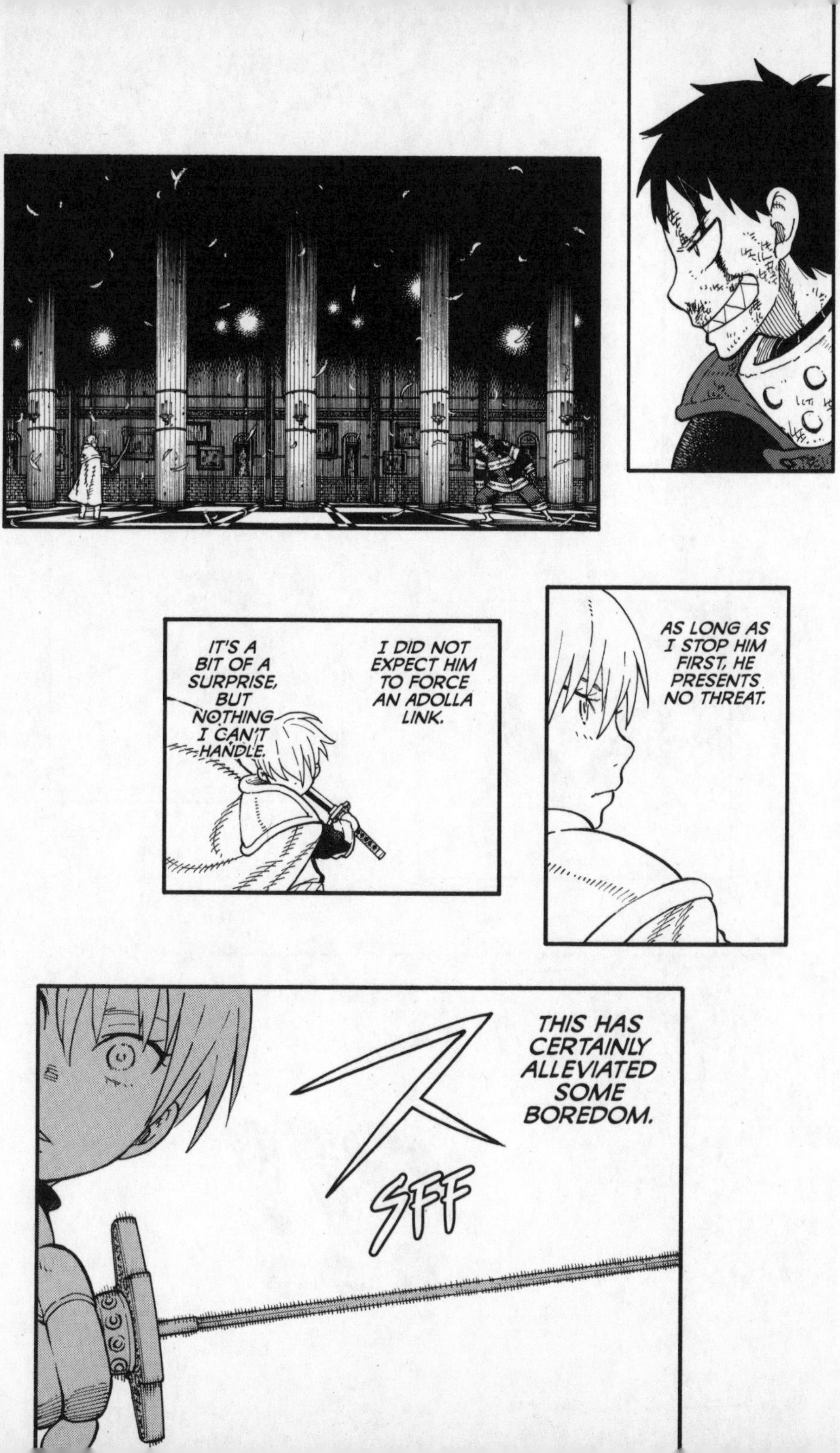
AS LONG AS I STOP HIM FIRST, HE PRESENTS NO THREAT.
I DID NOT EXPECT HIM TO FORCE AN ADOLLA LINK.
IT'S A BIT OF A SURPRISE, BUT NOTHING I CAN'T HANDLE.
THIS HAS CERTAINLY ALLEVIATED SOME BOREDOM.
SFF

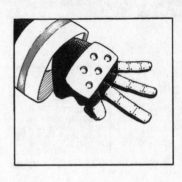

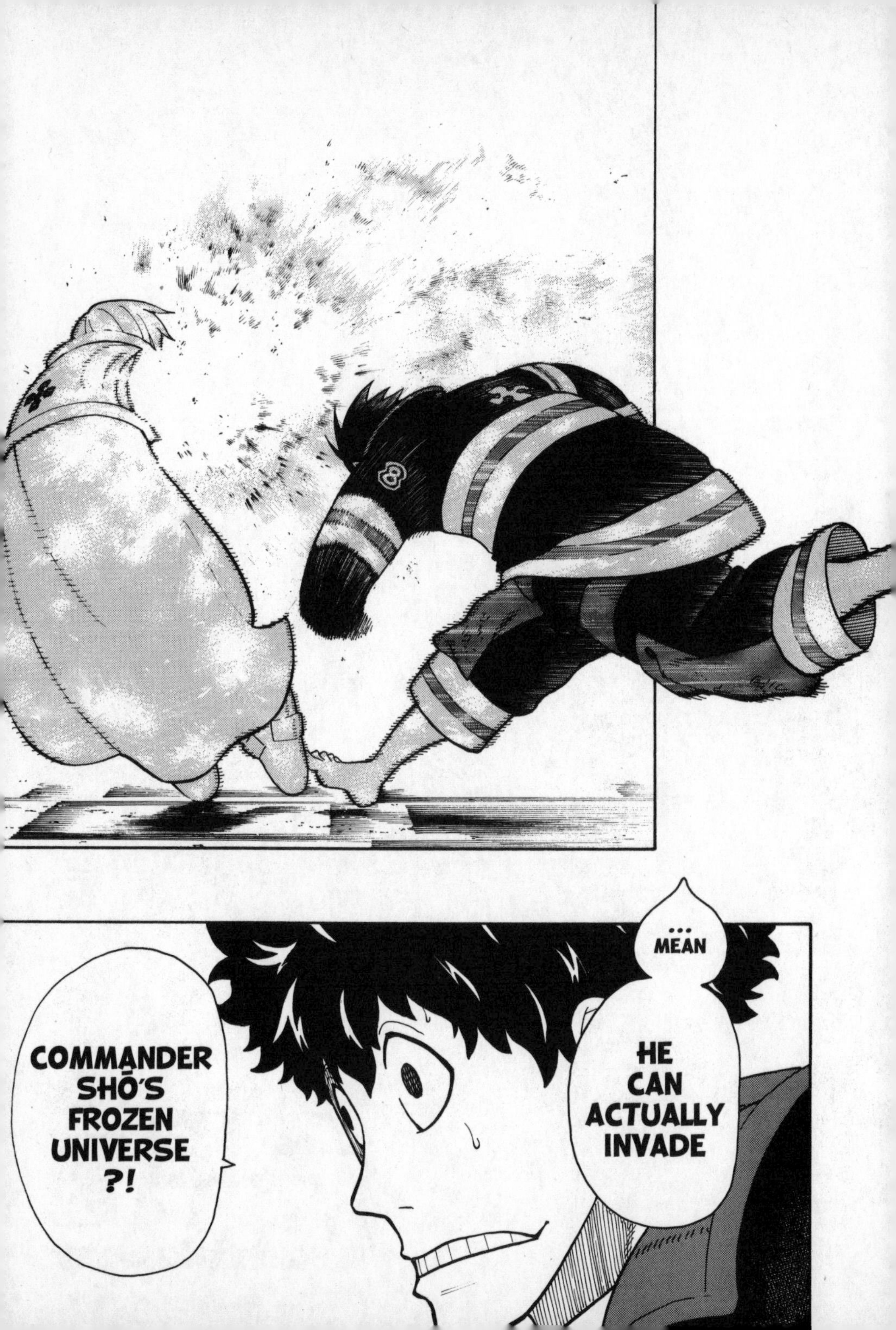
...MEAN
HE CAN ACTUALLY INVADE
COMMANDER SHŌ'S FROZEN UNIVERSE ?!

FIRE FORCE

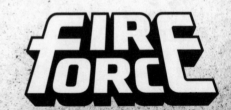

CHAPTER LXXXIII: FOURTH GENERATION

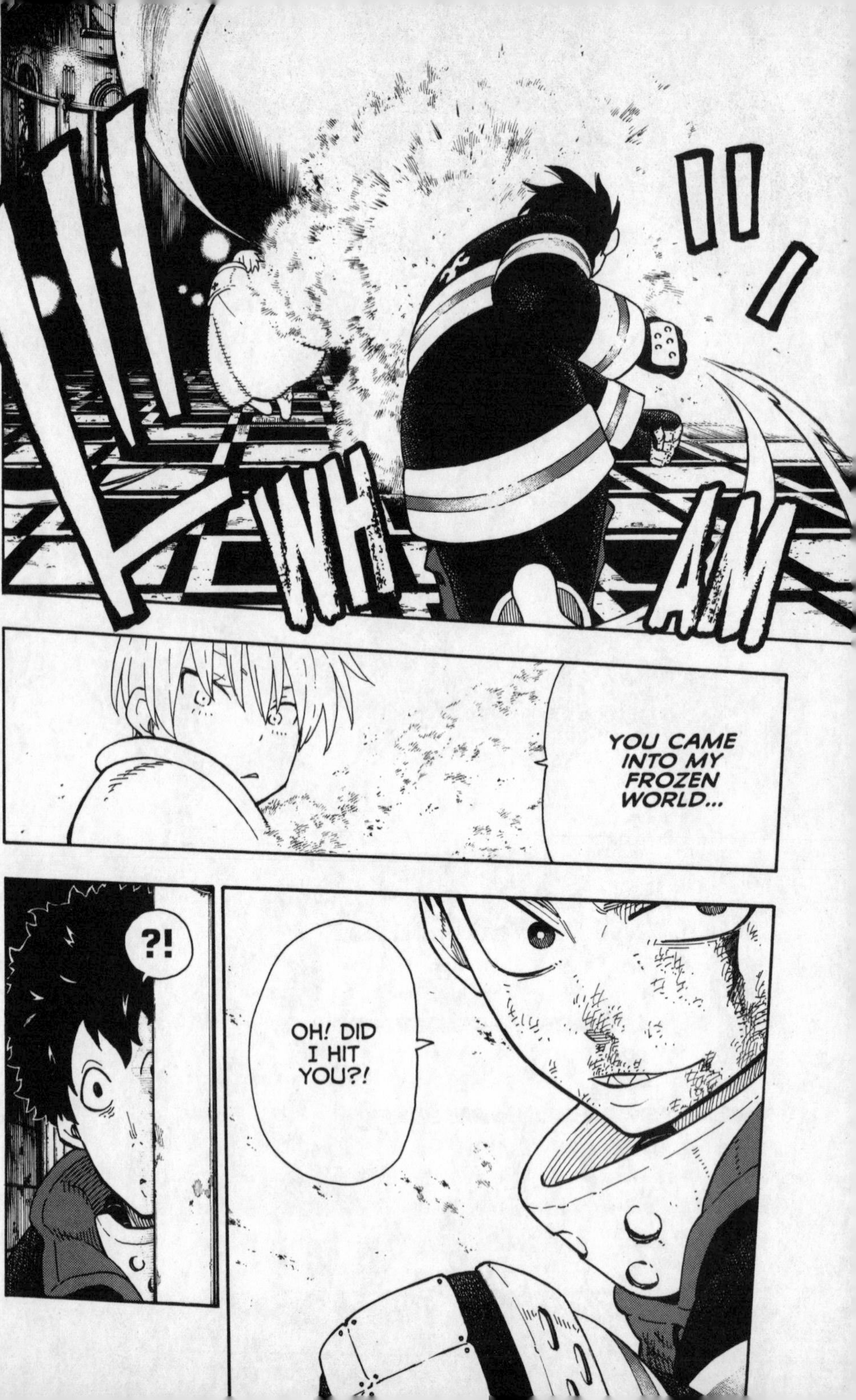
WHAM
YOU CAME INTO MY FROZEN WORLD...
OH! DID I HIT YOU?!
?!

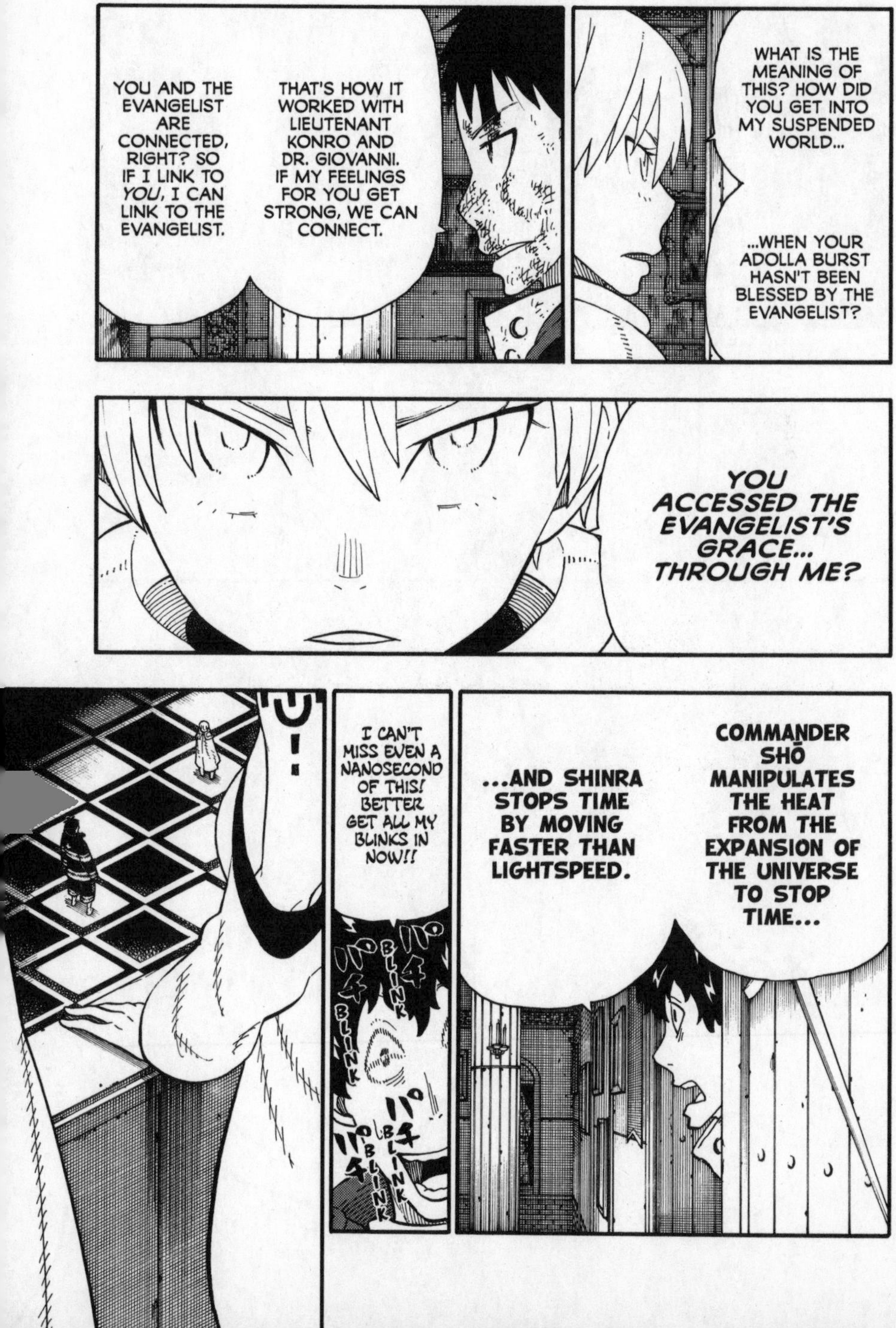
WHAT IS THE MEANING OF THIS? HOW DID YOU GET INTO MY SUSPENDED WORLD...
...WHEN YOUR ADOLLA BURST HASN'T BEEN BLESSED BY THE EVANGELIST?
THAT'S HOW IT WORKED WITH LIEUTENANT KONRO AND DR. GIOVANNI. IF MY FEELINGS FOR YOU GET STRONG, WE CAN CONNECT.
YOU AND THE EVANGELIST ARE CONNECTED, RIGHT? SO IF I LINK TO *YOU*, I CAN LINK TO THE EVANGELIST.
YOU ACCESSED THE EVANGELIST'S GRACE... THROUGH ME?
COMMANDER SHŌ MANIPULATES THE HEAT FROM THE EXPANSION OF THE UNIVERSE TO STOP TIME...
...AND SHINRA STOPS TIME BY MOVING FASTER THAN LIGHTSPEED.
I CAN'T MISS EVEN A NANOSECOND OF THIS! BETTER GET ALL MY BLINKS IN NOW!!
パチ BLINK
パチ BLINK
パチ BLINK
パチ BLINK

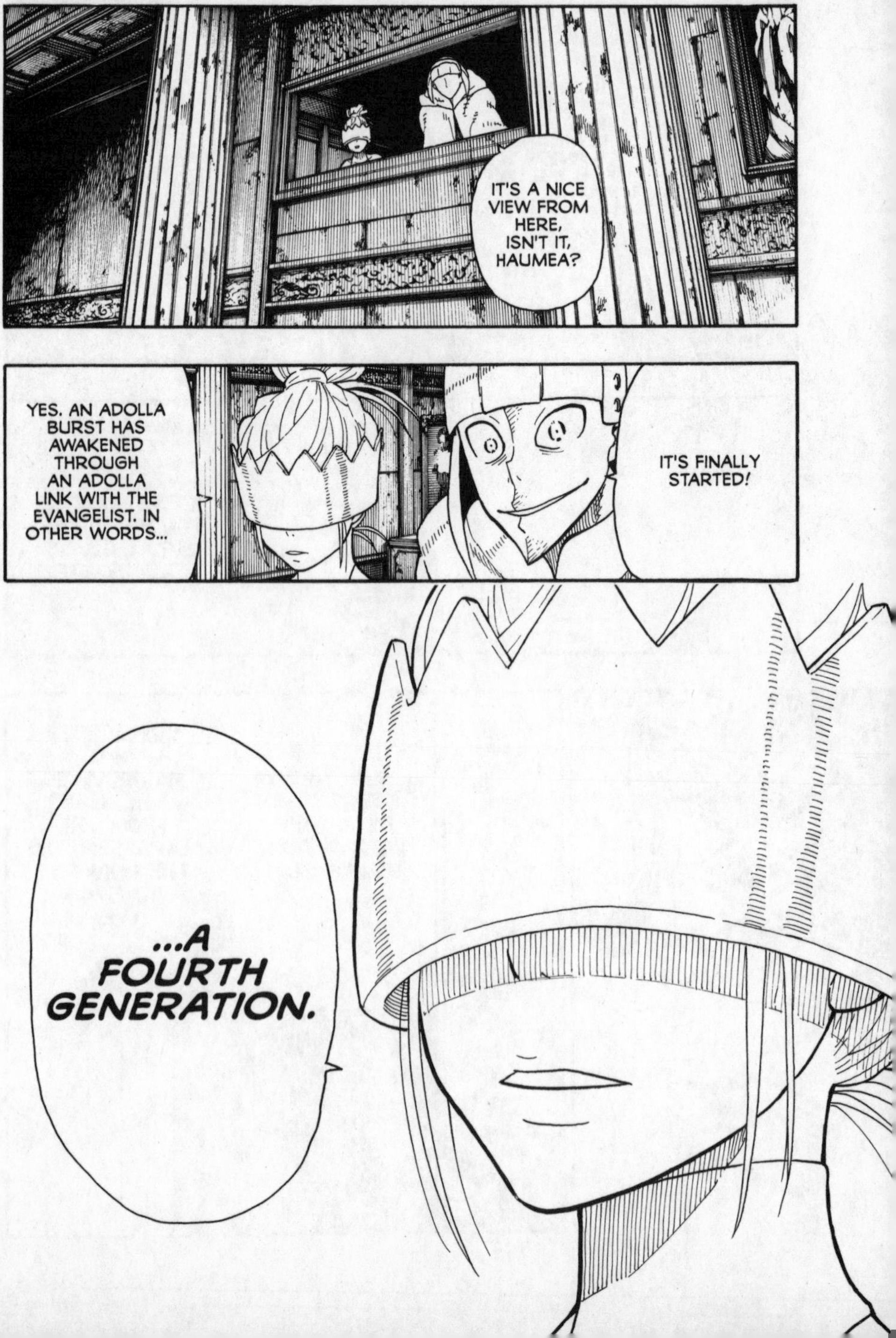

IT'S A NICE VIEW FROM HERE, ISN'T IT, HAUMEA?
IT'S FINALLY STARTED!
YES. AN ADOLLA BURST HAS AWAKENED THROUGH AN ADOLLA LINK WITH THE EVANGELIST. IN OTHER WORDS...
...A FOURTH GENERATION.

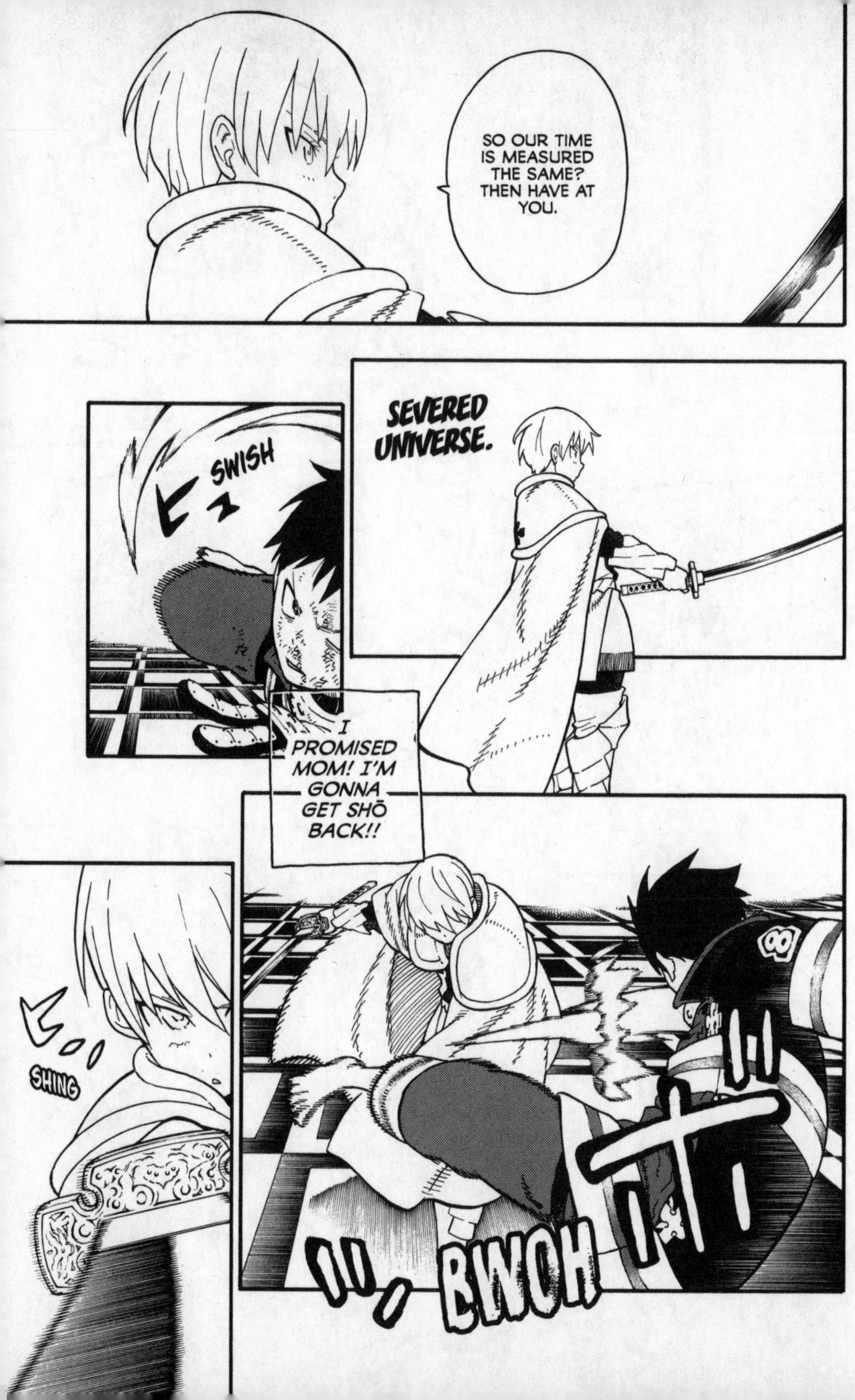
SO OUR TIME IS MEASURED THE SAME? THEN HAVE AT YOU.
SEVERED UNIVERSE.
SWISH
I PROMISED MOM! I'M GONNA GET SHŌ BACK!!
BWOH
SHING

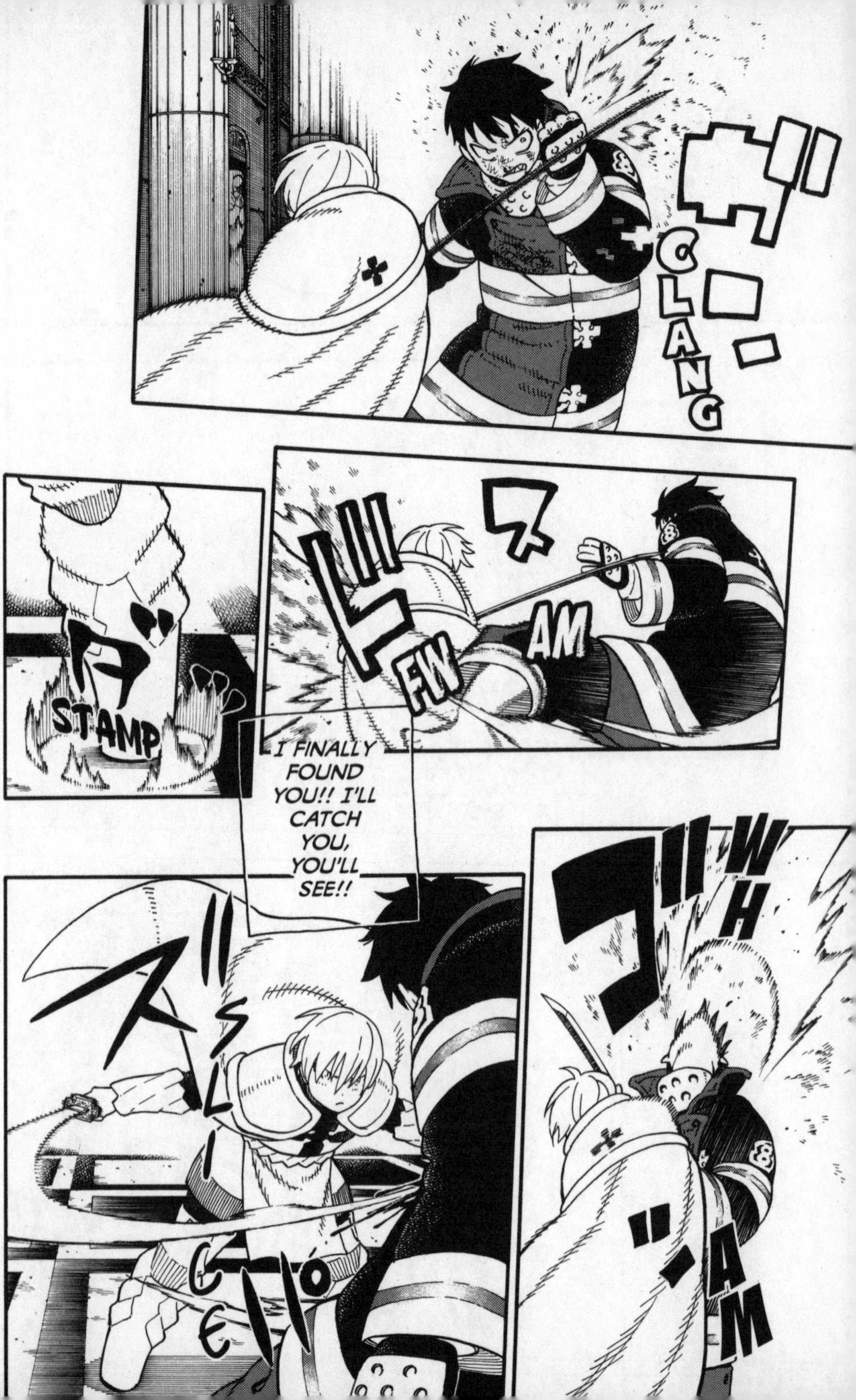
CLANG
FWAM
I FINALLY FOUND YOU!! I'LL CATCH YOU, YOU'LL SEE!!
STAMP
WHAM
SLICE

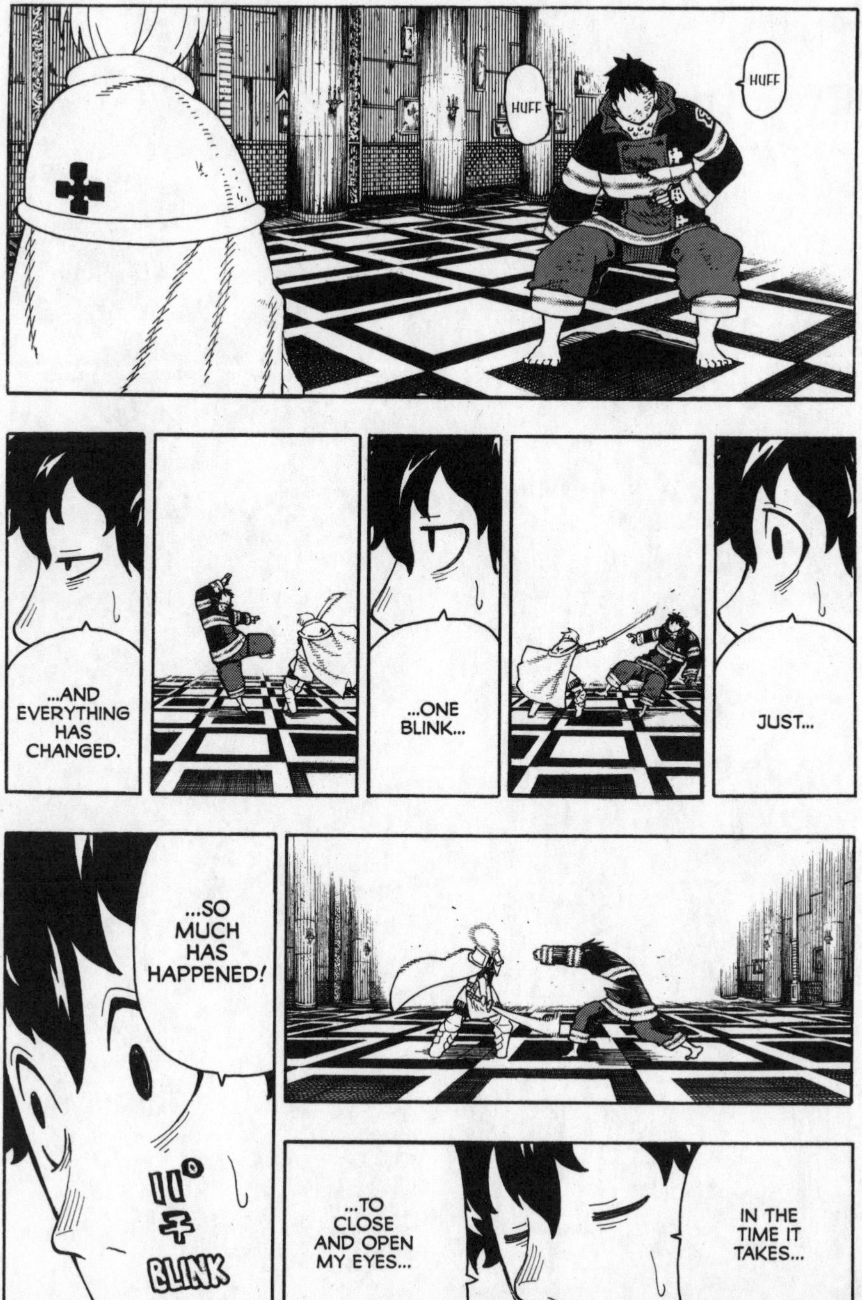
HUFF
HUFF
JUST...
...ONE BLINK...
...AND EVERYTHING HAS CHANGED.
IN THE TIME IT TAKES...
...TO CLOSE AND OPEN MY EYES...
...SO MUCH HAS HAPPENED!
BLINK

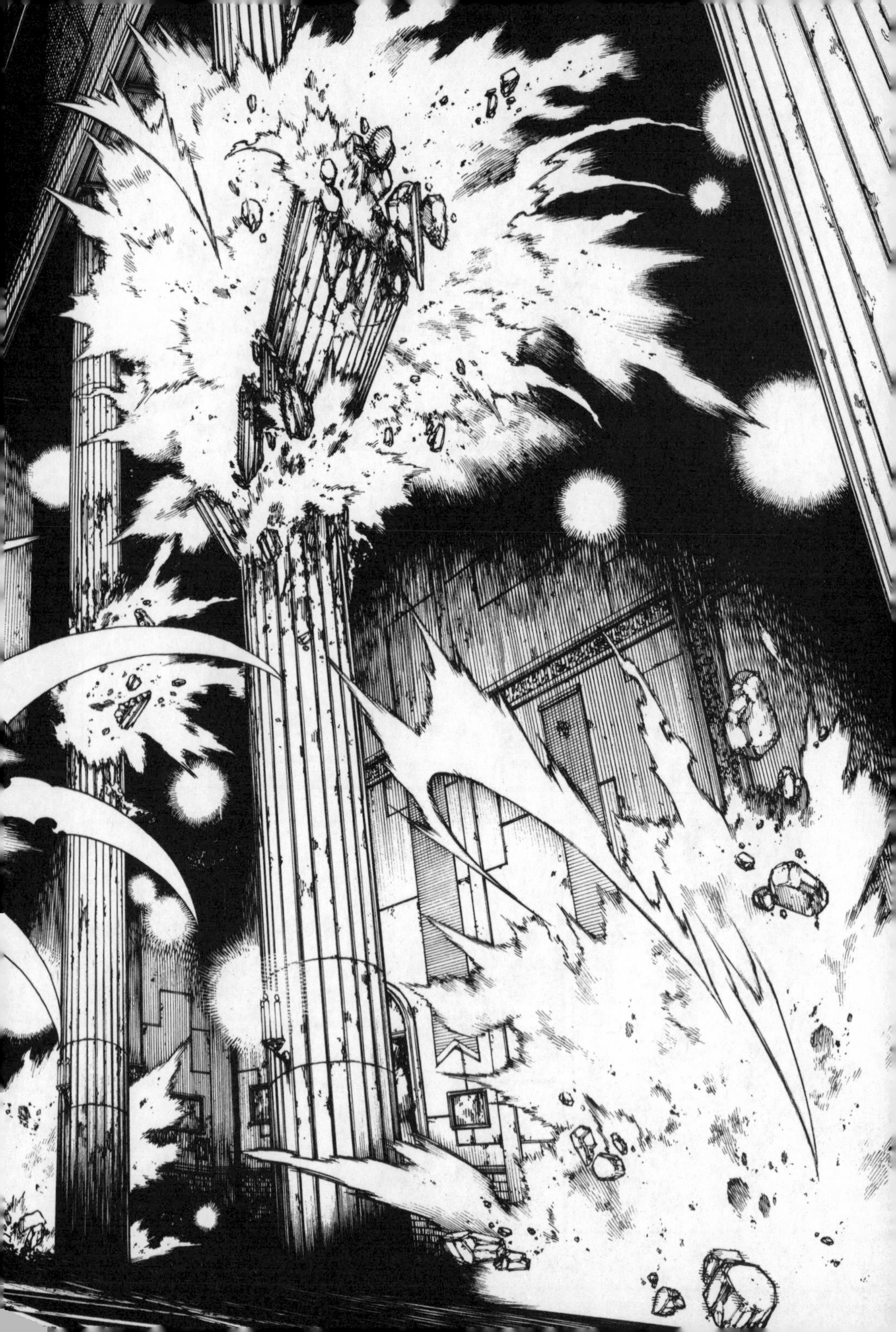

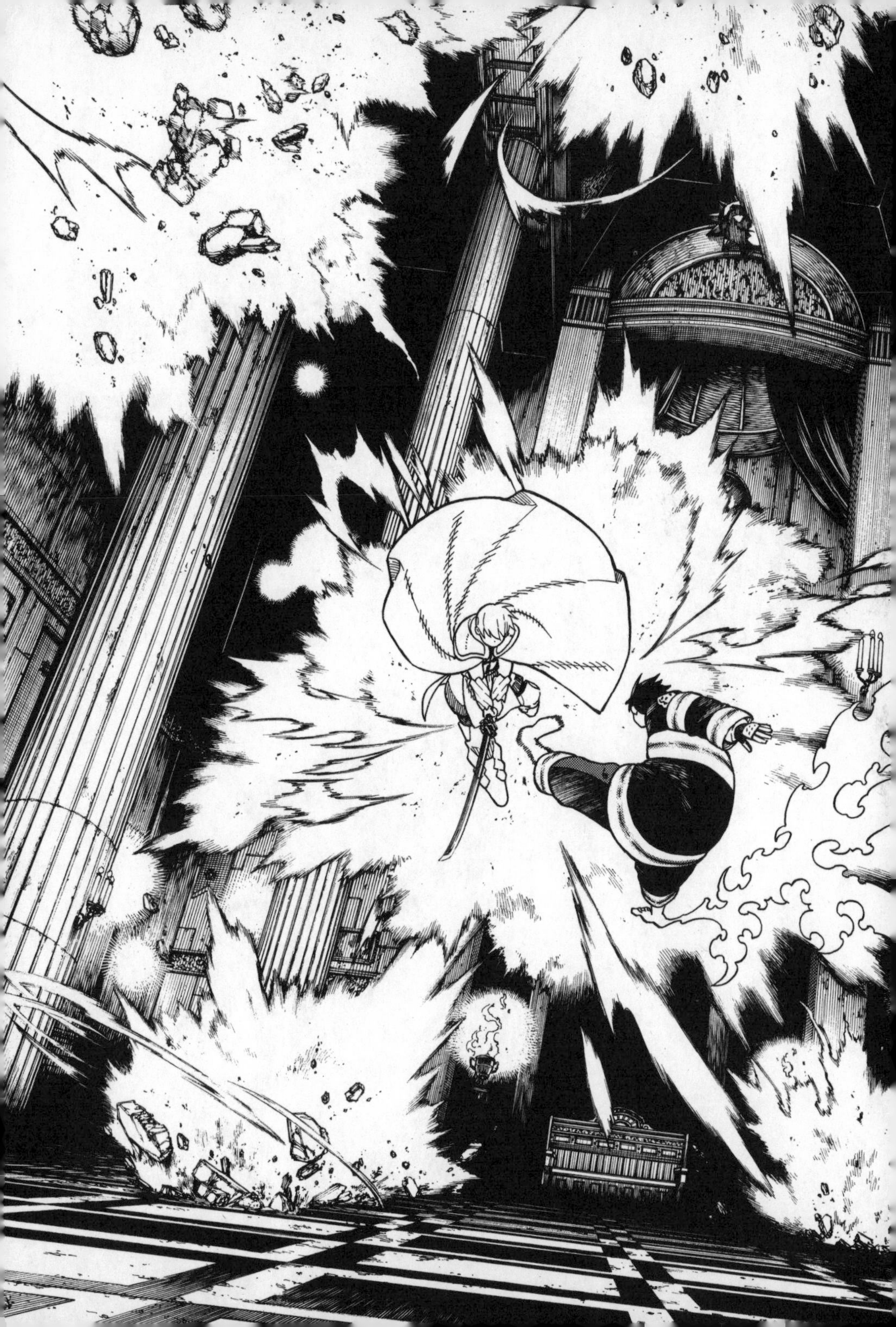

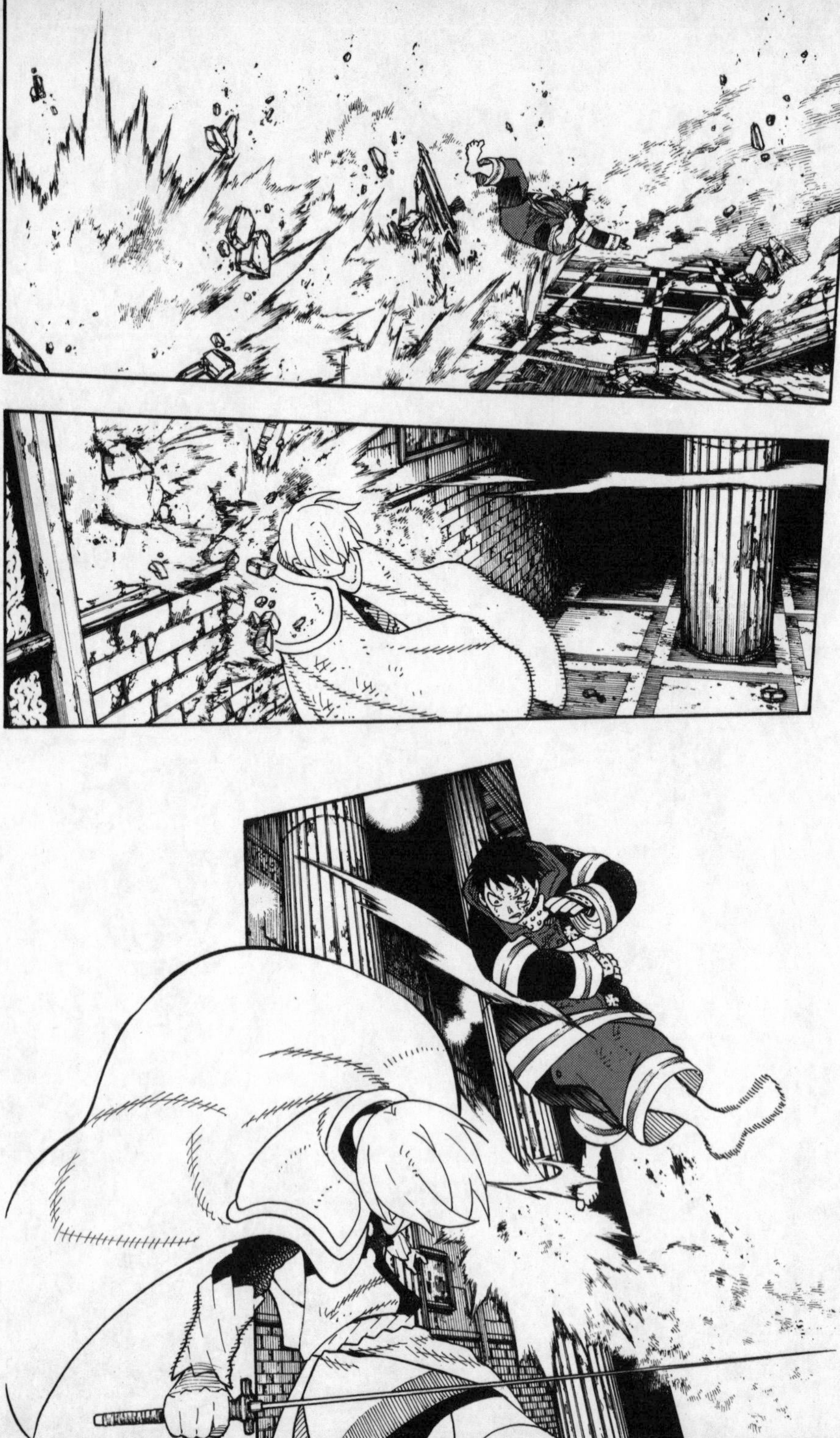

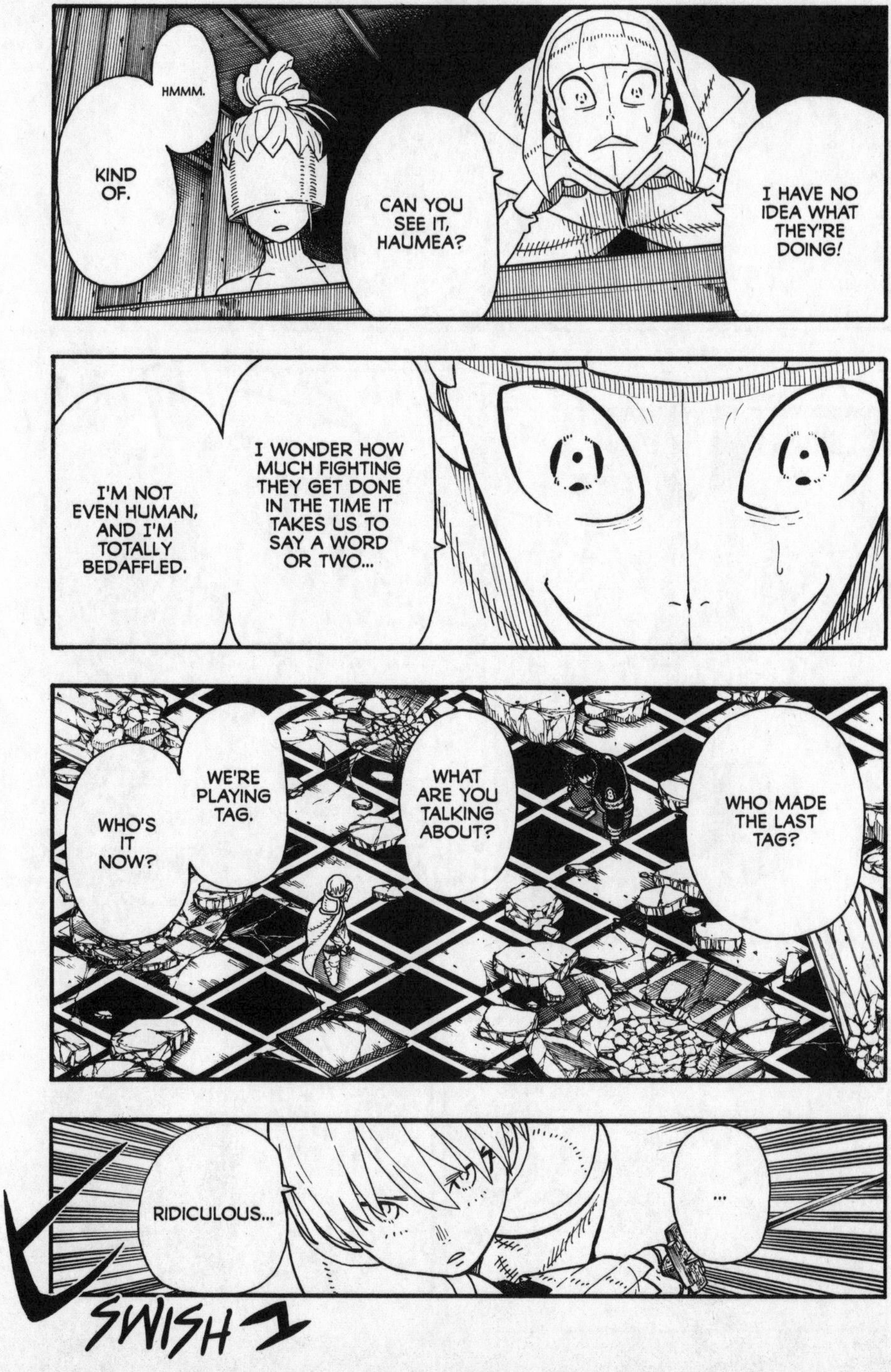
I HAVE NO IDEA WHAT THEY'RE DOING!
CAN YOU SEE IT, HAUMEA?
HMMM.
KIND OF.
I WONDER HOW MUCH FIGHTING THEY GET DONE IN THE TIME IT TAKES US TO SAY A WORD OR TWO...
I'M NOT EVEN HUMAN, AND I'M TOTALLY BEDAFFLED.
WHO MADE THE LAST TAG?
WHAT ARE YOU TALKING ABOUT?
WE'RE PLAYING TAG.
WHO'S IT NOW?
...
RIDICULOUS...
SWISH

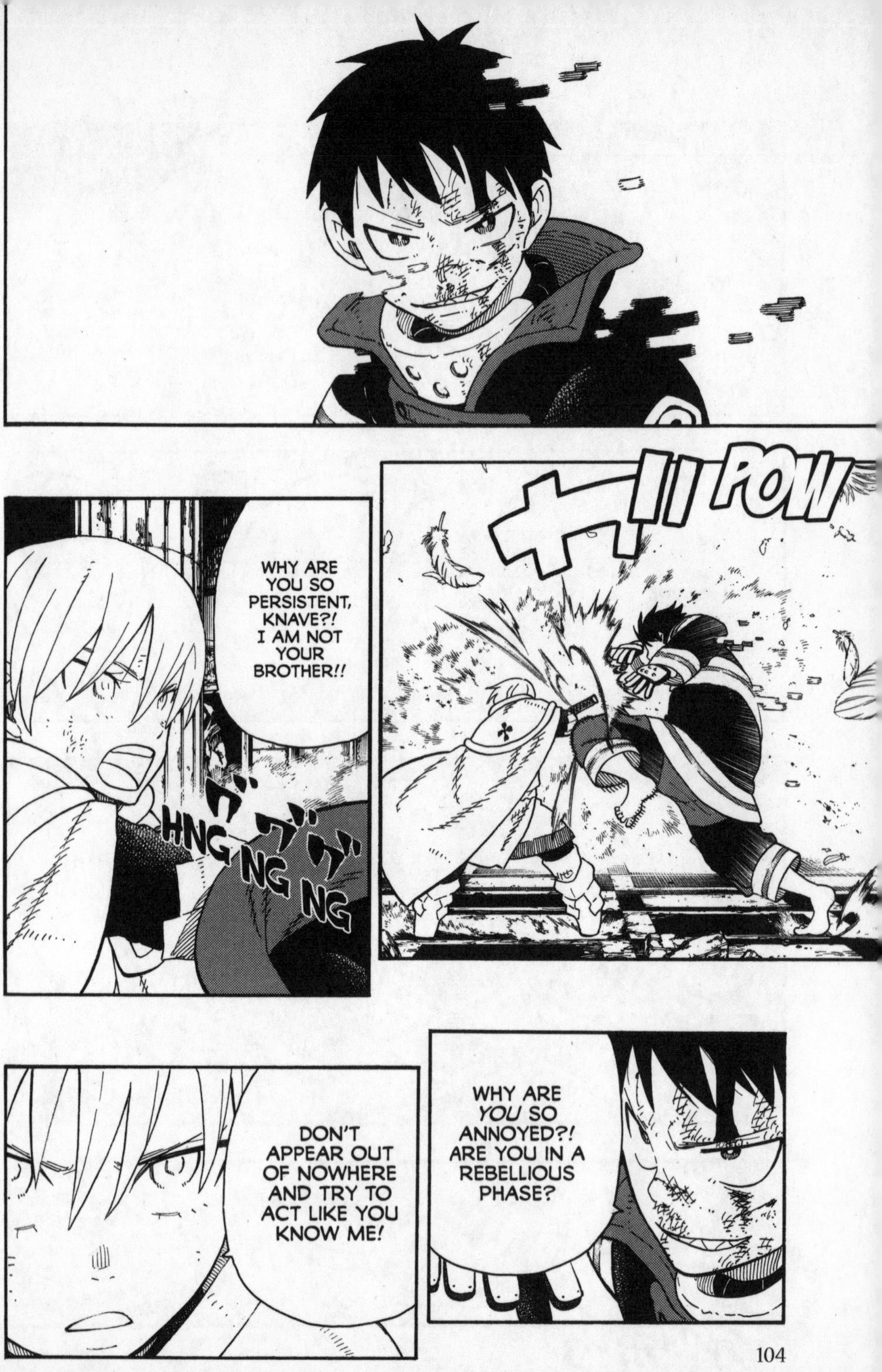
POW
WHY ARE YOU SO PERSISTENT, KNAVE?! I AM NOT YOUR BROTHER!!
HNG NG NG
WHY ARE *YOU* SO ANNOYED?! ARE YOU IN A REBELLIOUS PHASE?
DON'T APPEAR OUT OF NOWHERE AND TRY TO ACT LIKE YOU KNOW ME!

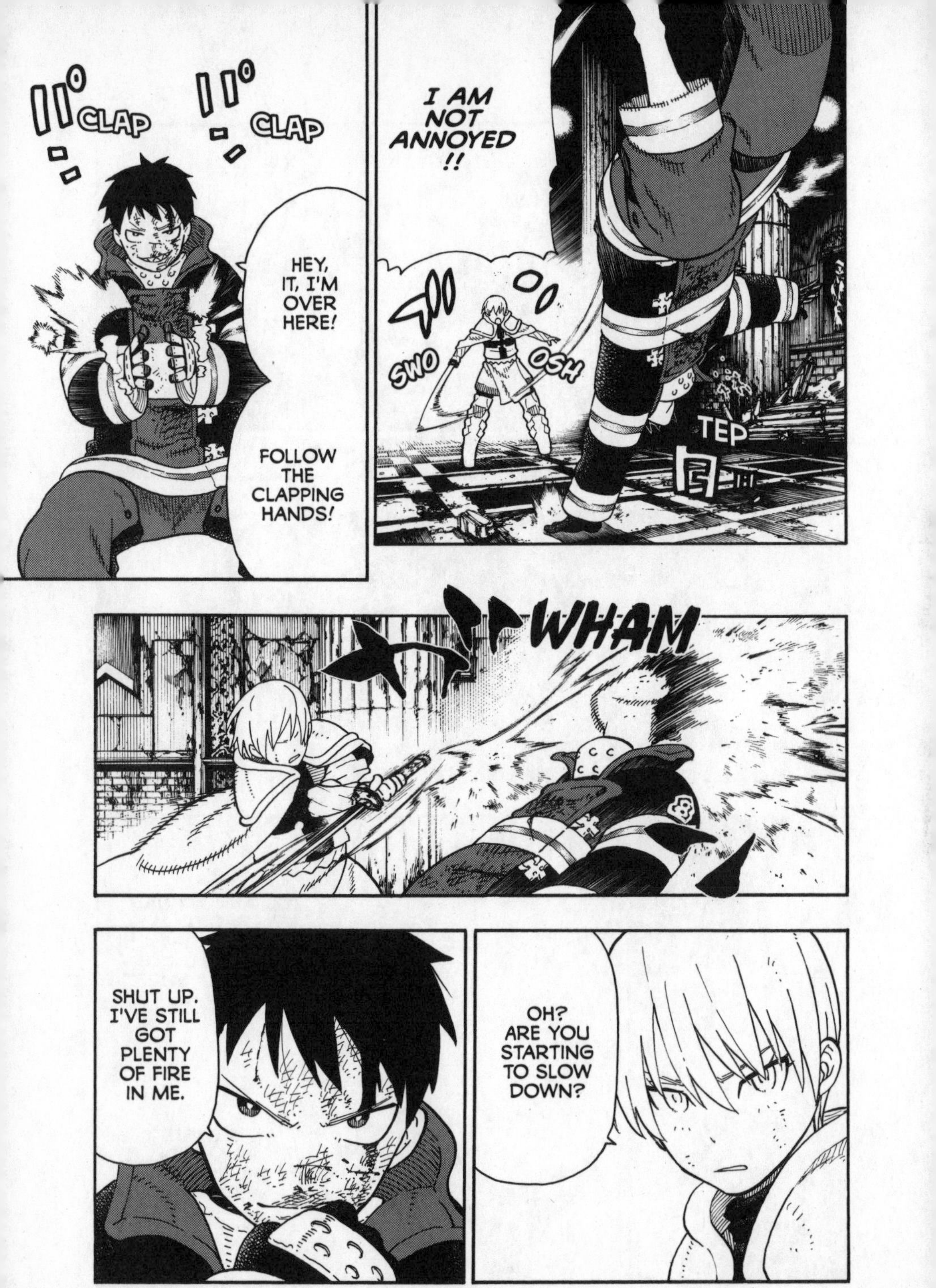
I AM NOT ANNOYED !!
SWO
OSH
TEP
CLAP
CLAP
HEY, IT, I'M OVER HERE!
FOLLOW THE CLAPPING HANDS!
WHAM
OH? ARE YOU STARTING TO SLOW DOWN?
SHUT UP. I'VE STILL GOT PLENTY OF FIRE IN ME.

—GH!!

NGH
...

...RGH.

DRIP DRIP

YOU'RE BADLY
INJURED,
AND YOU'RE
CLOSE TO
OVERHEATING.

HUFF

HUFF

...

YOU ALMOST HAD
ME... BUT YOU'VE
NOT HAD AS MUCH
PRACTICE USING
THE ADOLLA BURST
AS I HAVE.

IT'S OVER. I'M
TAKING YOU TO
THE EVANGELIST.
WE NEED YOUR
FLAMES.

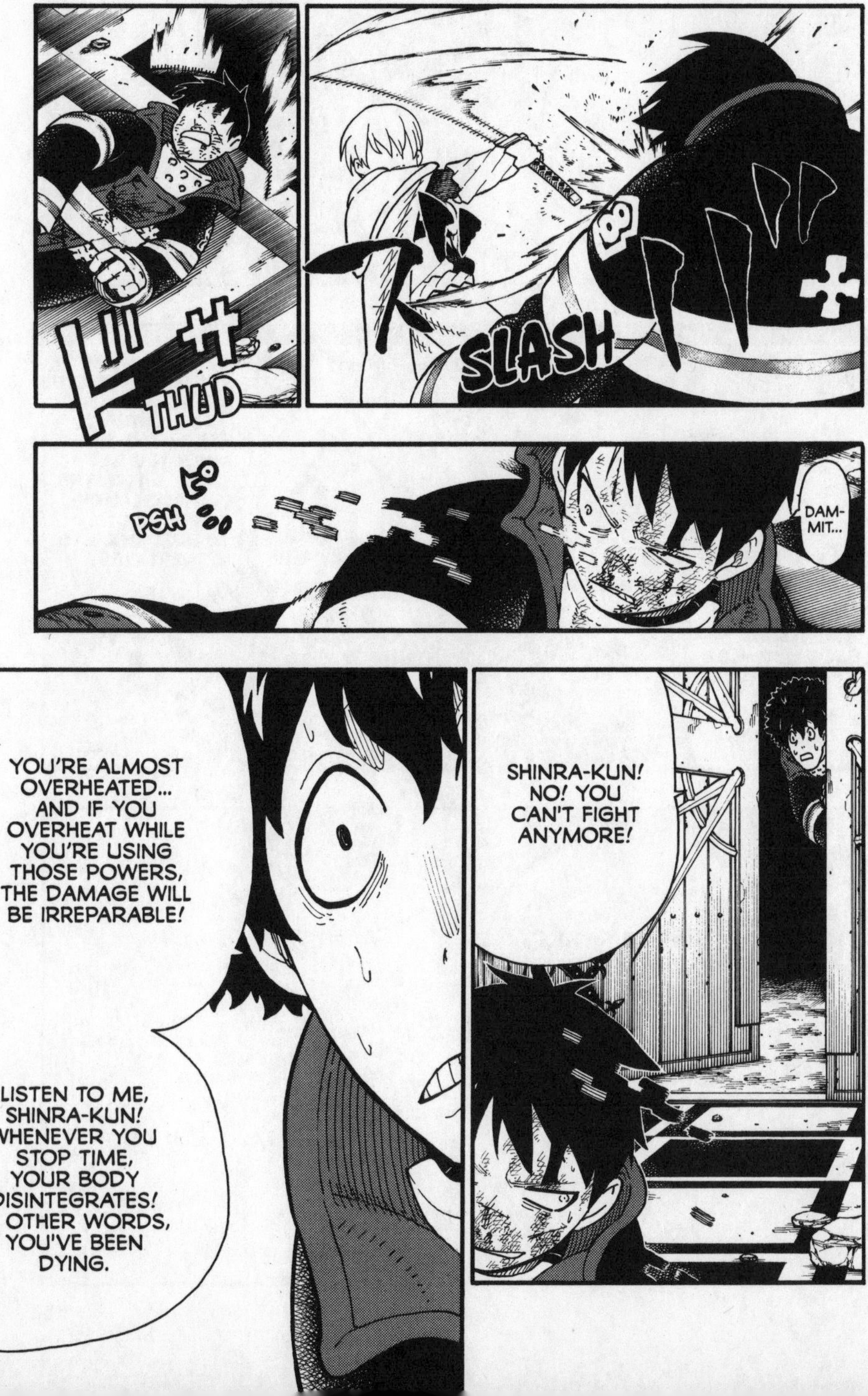
SLASH
THUD
DAM-MIT...
PSH
SHINRA-KUN! NO! YOU CAN'T FIGHT ANYMORE!
YOU'RE ALMOST OVERHEATED... AND IF YOU OVERHEAT WHILE YOU'RE USING THOSE POWERS, THE DAMAGE WILL BE IRREPARABLE!
LISTEN TO ME, SHINRA-KUN! WHENEVER YOU STOP TIME, YOUR BODY DISINTEGRATES! IN OTHER WORDS, YOU'VE BEEN DYING.

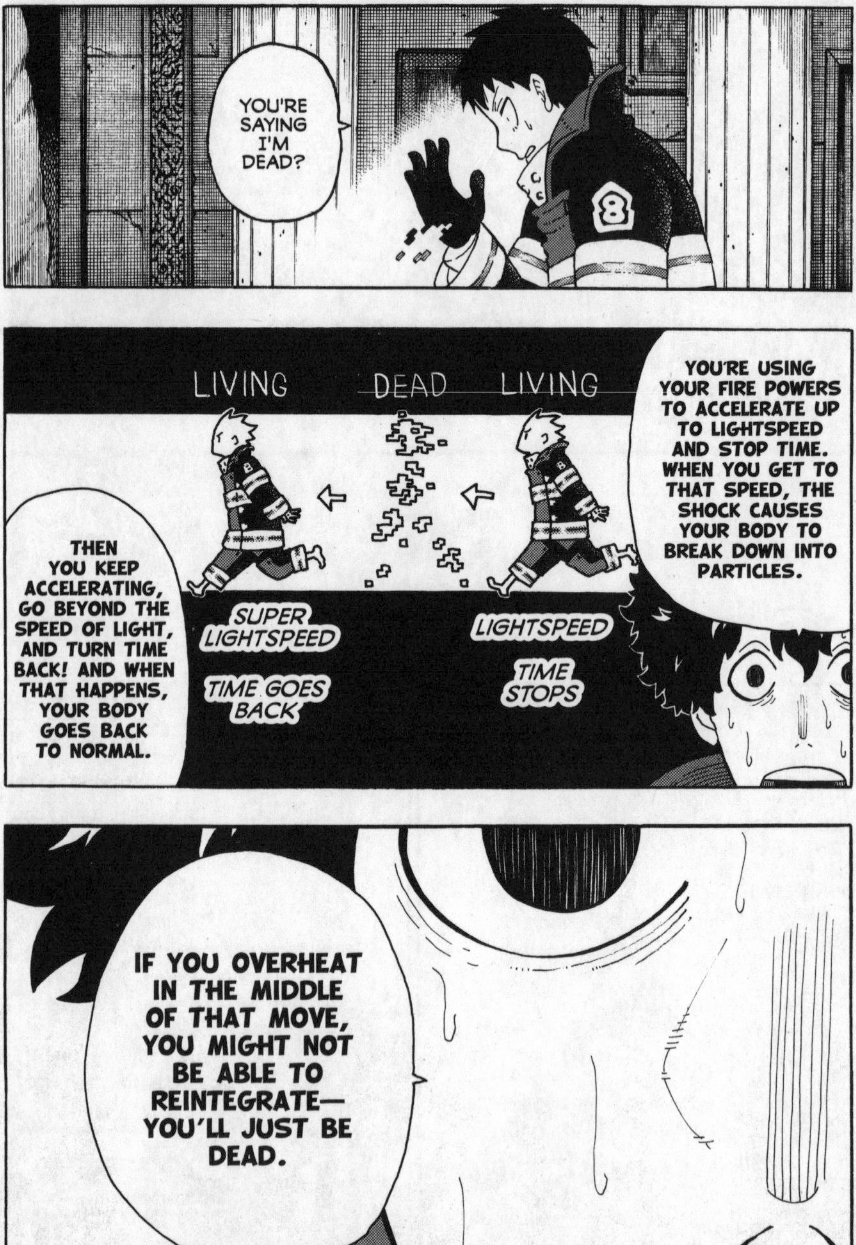
YOU'RE SAYING I'M DEAD?
YOU'RE USING YOUR FIRE POWERS TO ACCELERATE UP TO LIGHTSPEED AND STOP TIME. WHEN YOU GET TO THAT SPEED, THE SHOCK CAUSES YOUR BODY TO BREAK DOWN INTO PARTICLES.
LIVING DEAD LIVING
LIGHTSPEED
TIME STOPS
THEN YOU KEEP ACCELERATING, GO BEYOND THE SPEED OF LIGHT, AND TURN TIME BACK! AND WHEN THAT HAPPENS, YOUR BODY GOES BACK TO NORMAL.
SUPER LIGHTSPEED
TIME GOES BACK
IF YOU OVERHEAT IN THE MIDDLE OF THAT MOVE, YOU MIGHT NOT BE ABLE TO REINTEGRATE— YOU'LL JUST BE DEAD.

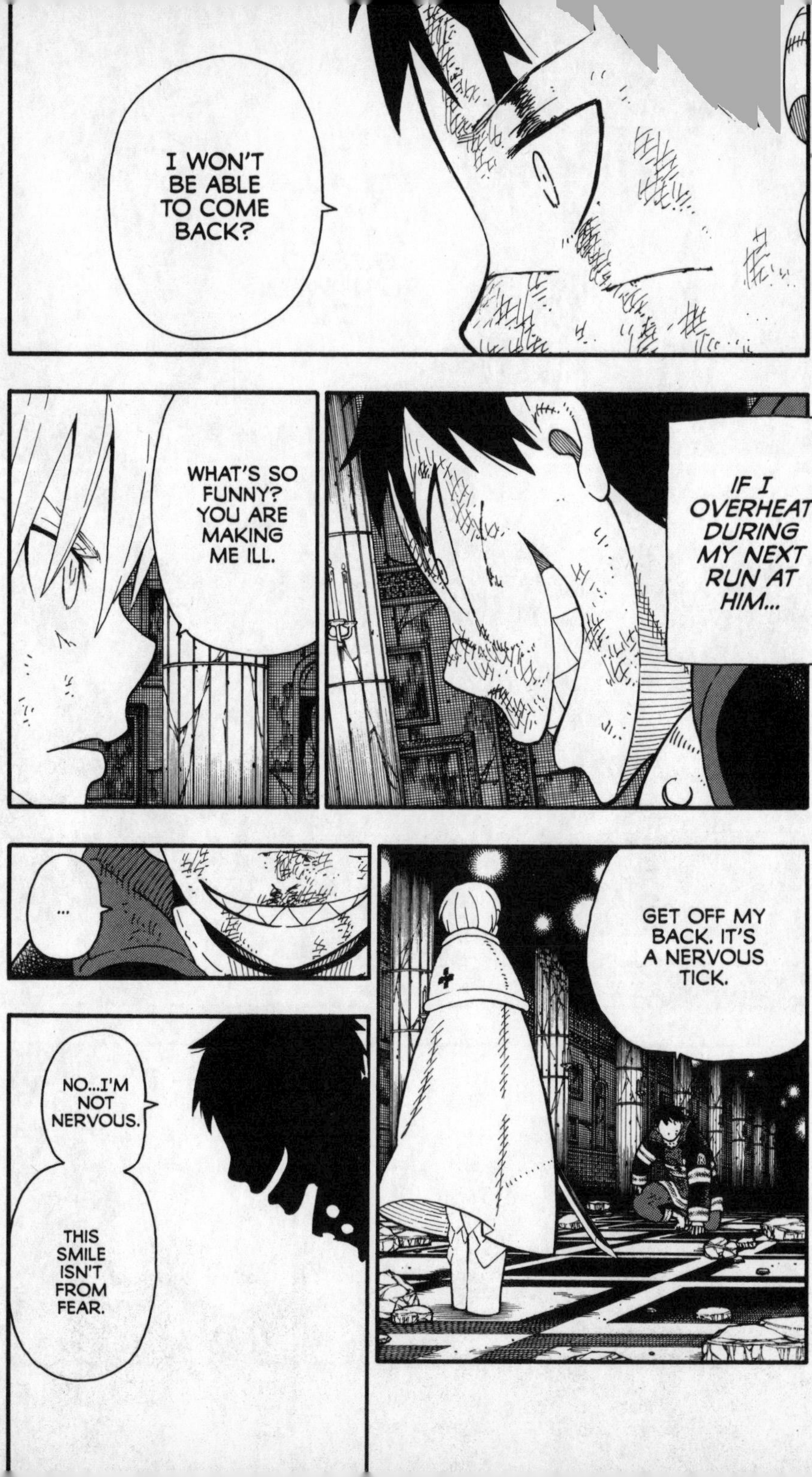
I WON'T BE ABLE TO COME BACK?
IF I OVERHEAT DURING MY NEXT RUN AT HIM...
WHAT'S SO FUNNY? YOU ARE MAKING ME ILL.
GET OFF MY BACK. IT'S A NERVOUS TICK.
...
NO...I'M NOT NERVOUS.
THIS SMILE ISN'T FROM FEAR.

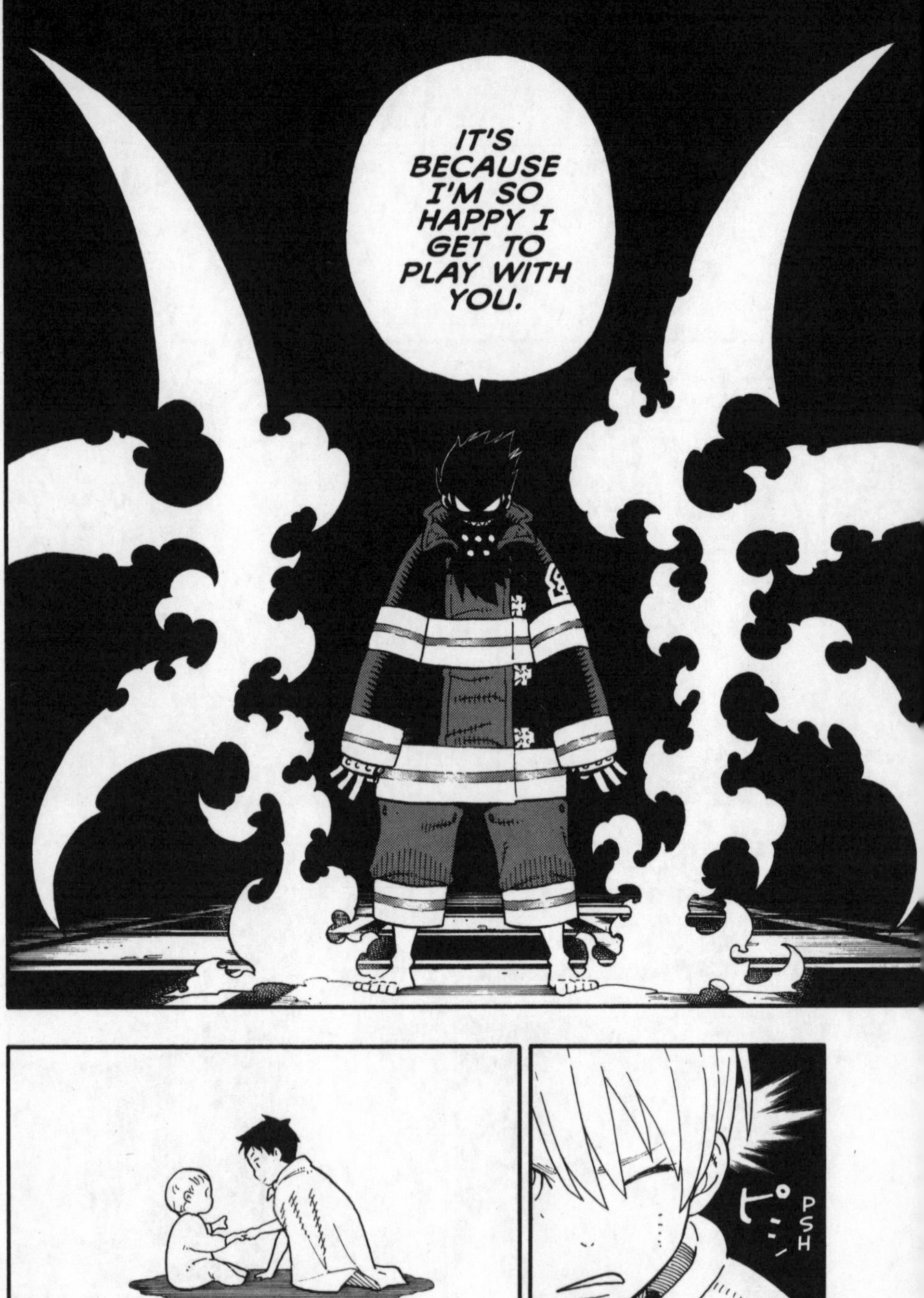
IT'S BECAUSE I'M SO HAPPY I GET TO PLAY WITH YOU.
ピ
PSH

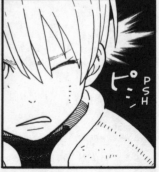

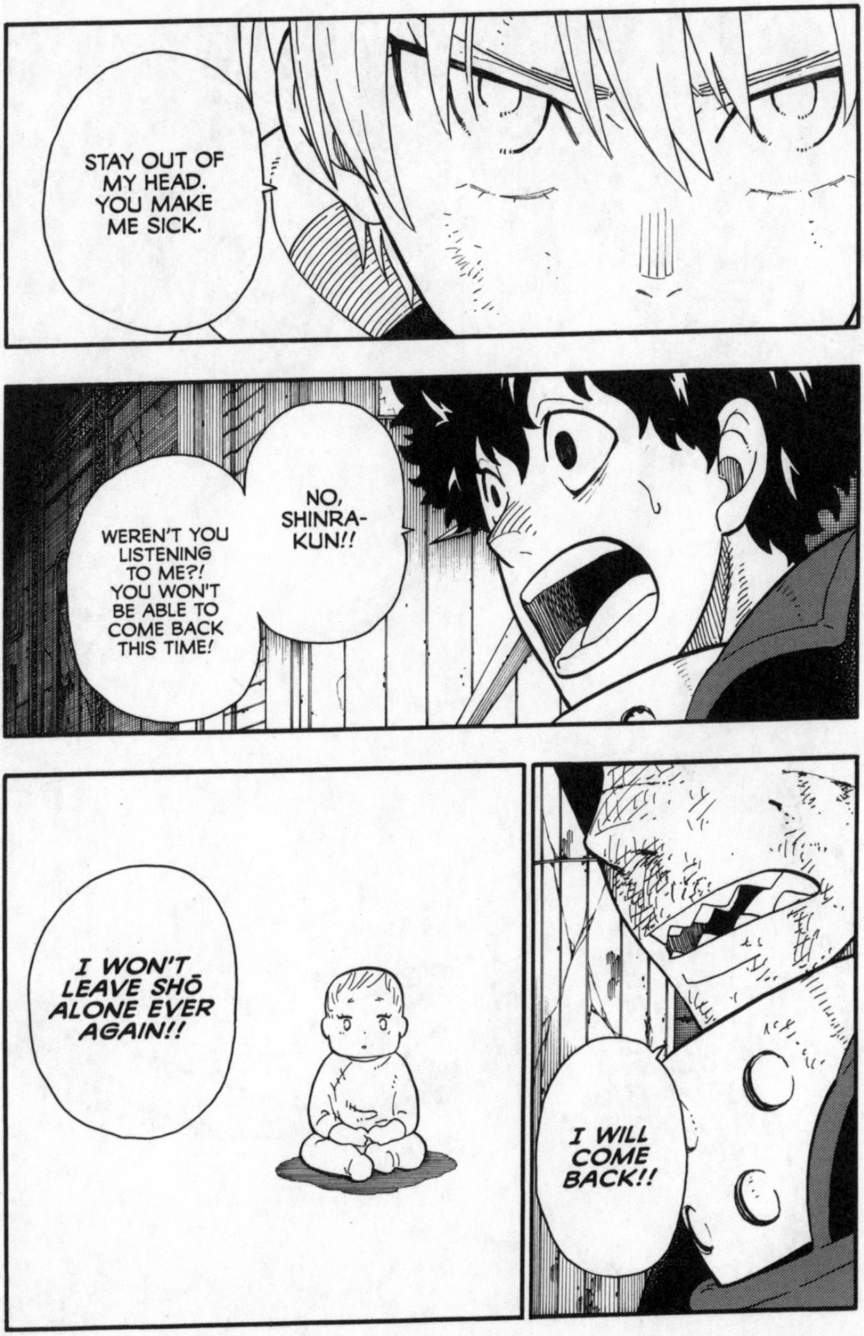
STAY OUT OF MY HEAD. YOU MAKE ME SICK.
NO, SHINRA-KUN!!
WEREN'T YOU LISTENING TO ME?! YOU WON'T BE ABLE TO COME BACK THIS TIME!
I WILL COME BACK!!
I WON'T LEAVE SHŌ ALONE EVER AGAIN!!

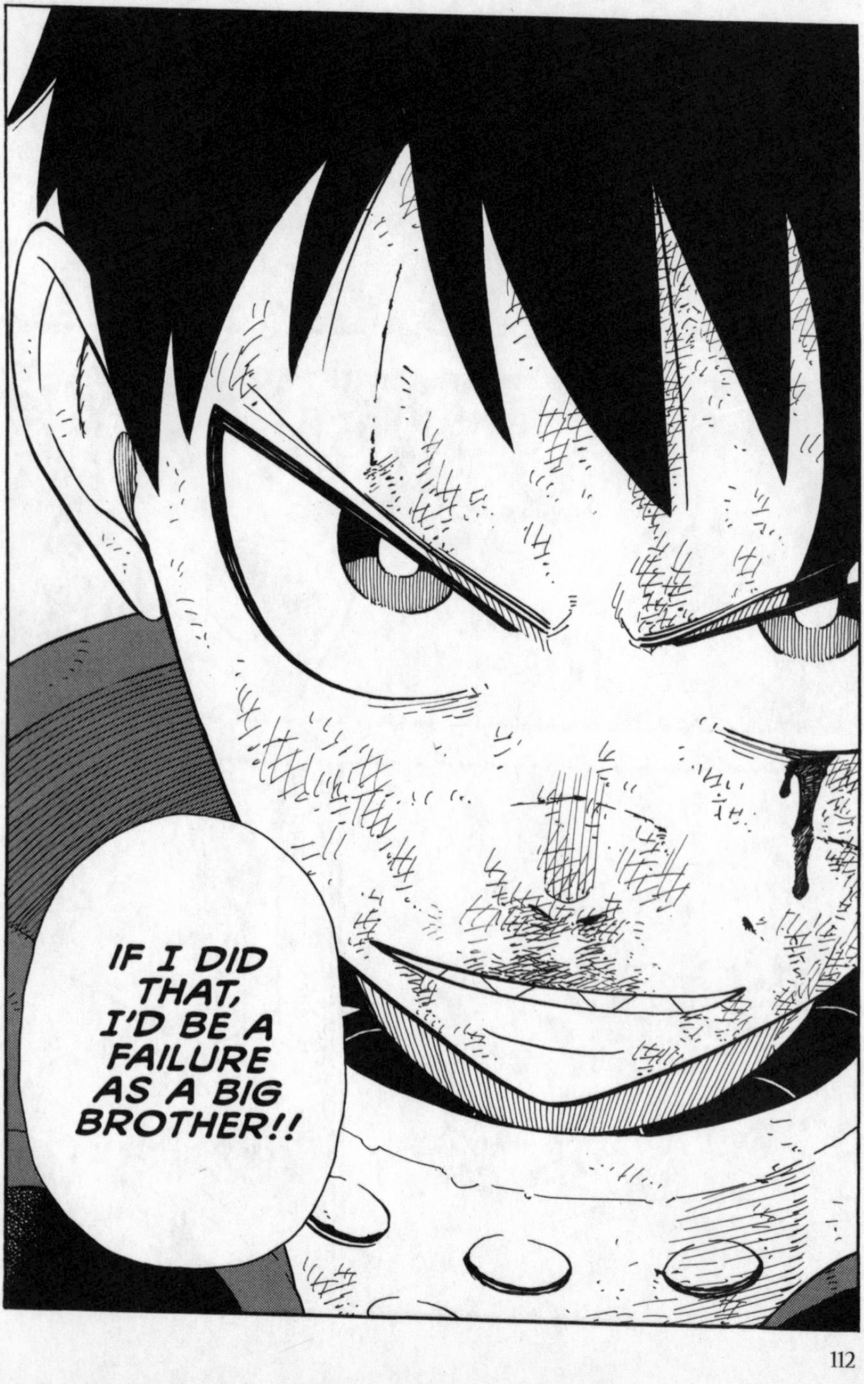
IF I DID THAT, I'D BE A FAILURE AS A BIG BROTHER!!

FIRE FORCE

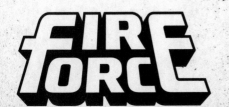

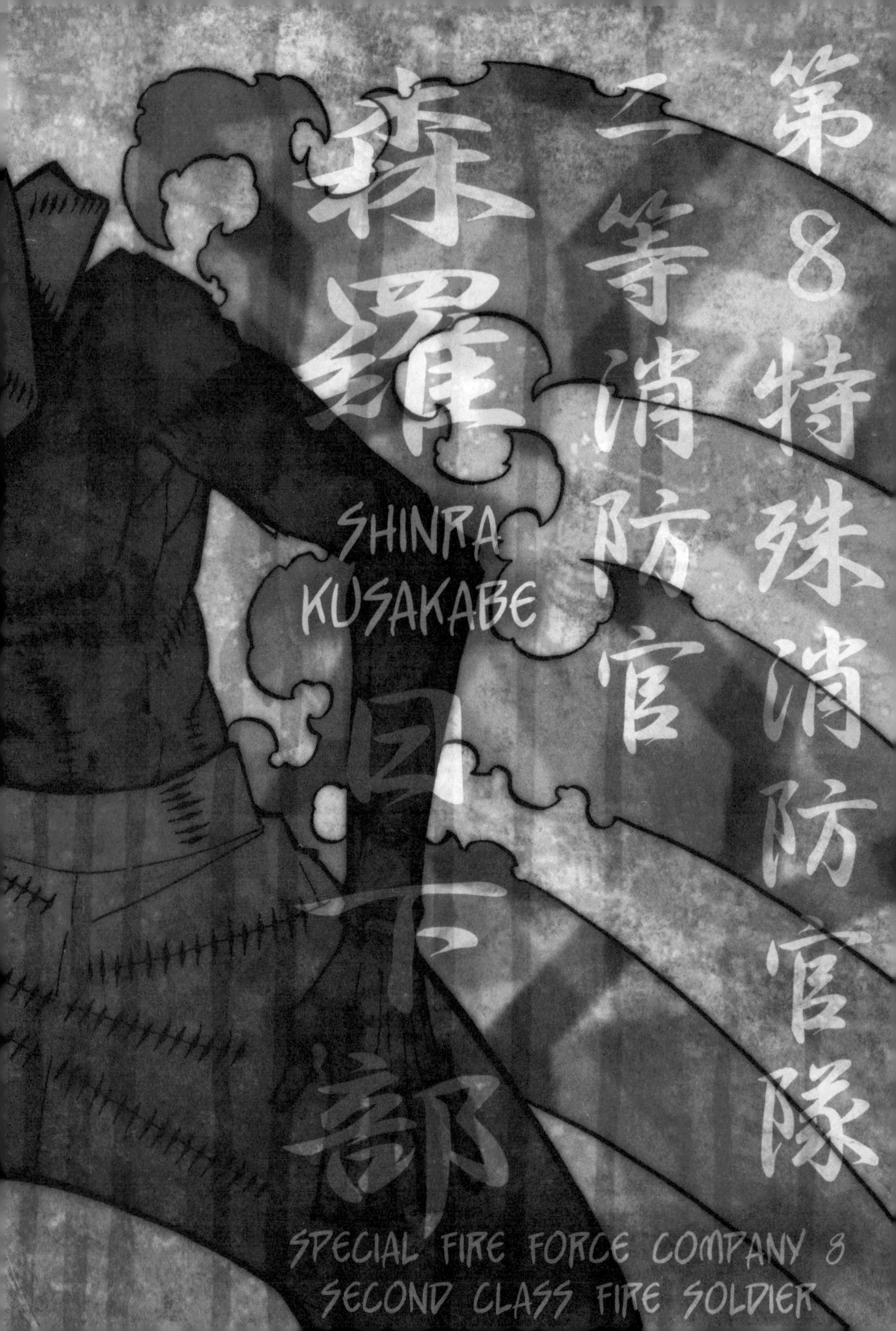
第8特殊消防官隊
二等消防官
森羅
日下部
SHINRA KUSAKABE
SPECIAL FIRE FORCE COMPANY 8
SECOND CLASS FIRE SOLDIER

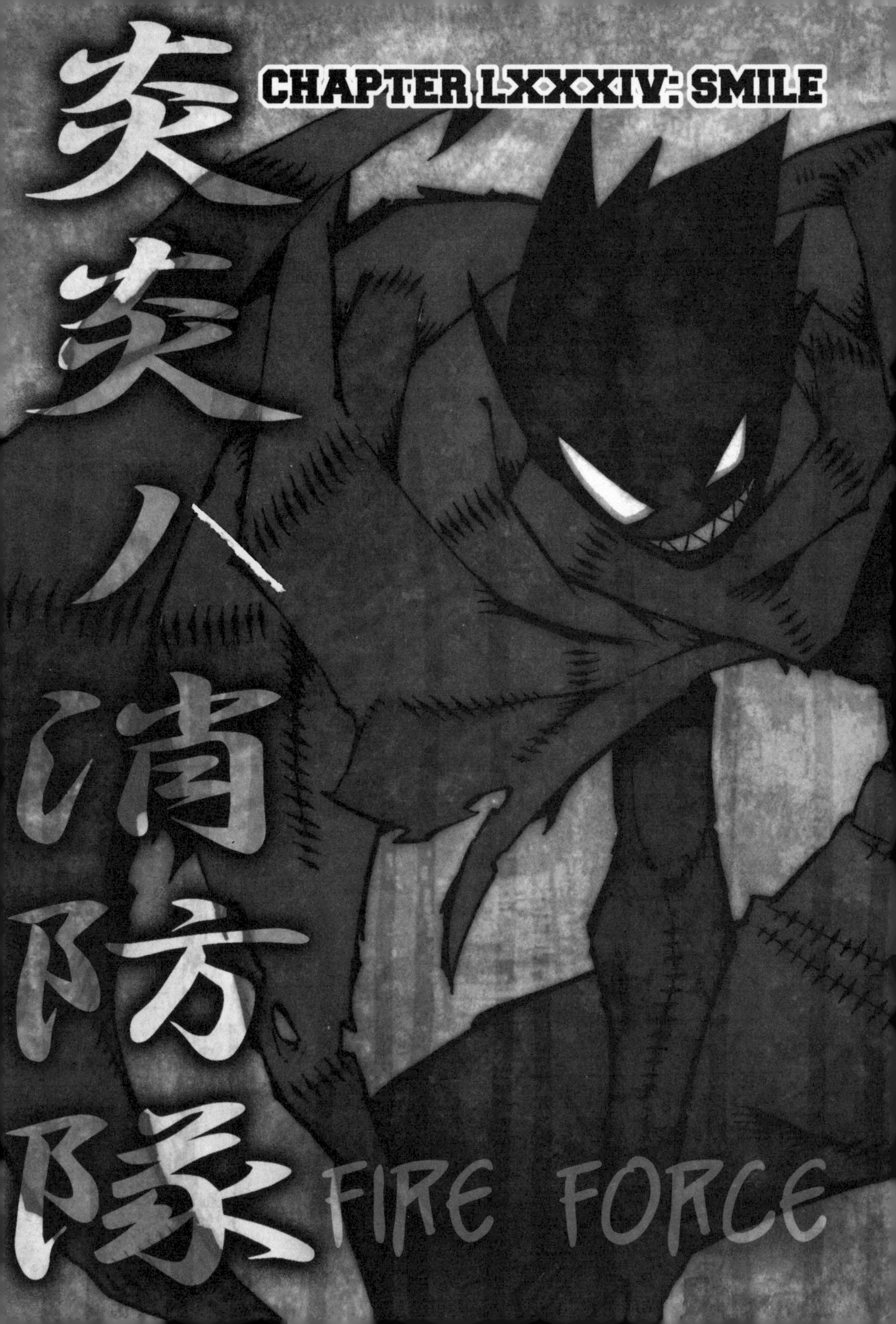
CHAPTER LXXXIV: SMILE
炎炎ノ消防隊
FIRE FORCE

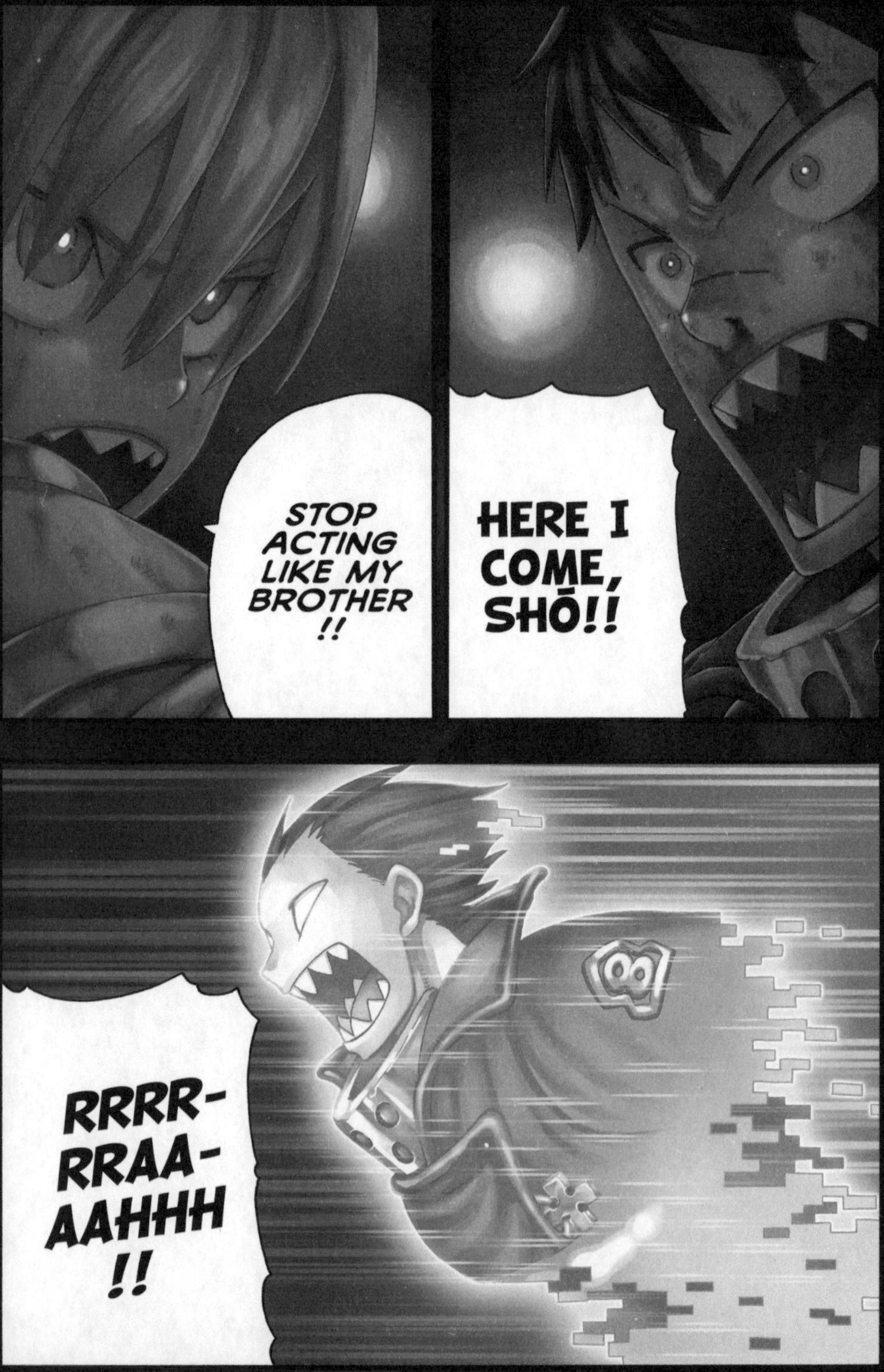
HERE I COME, SHŌ!!
STOP ACTING LIKE MY BROTHER!!
RRRR-RRAA-AHHHH!!

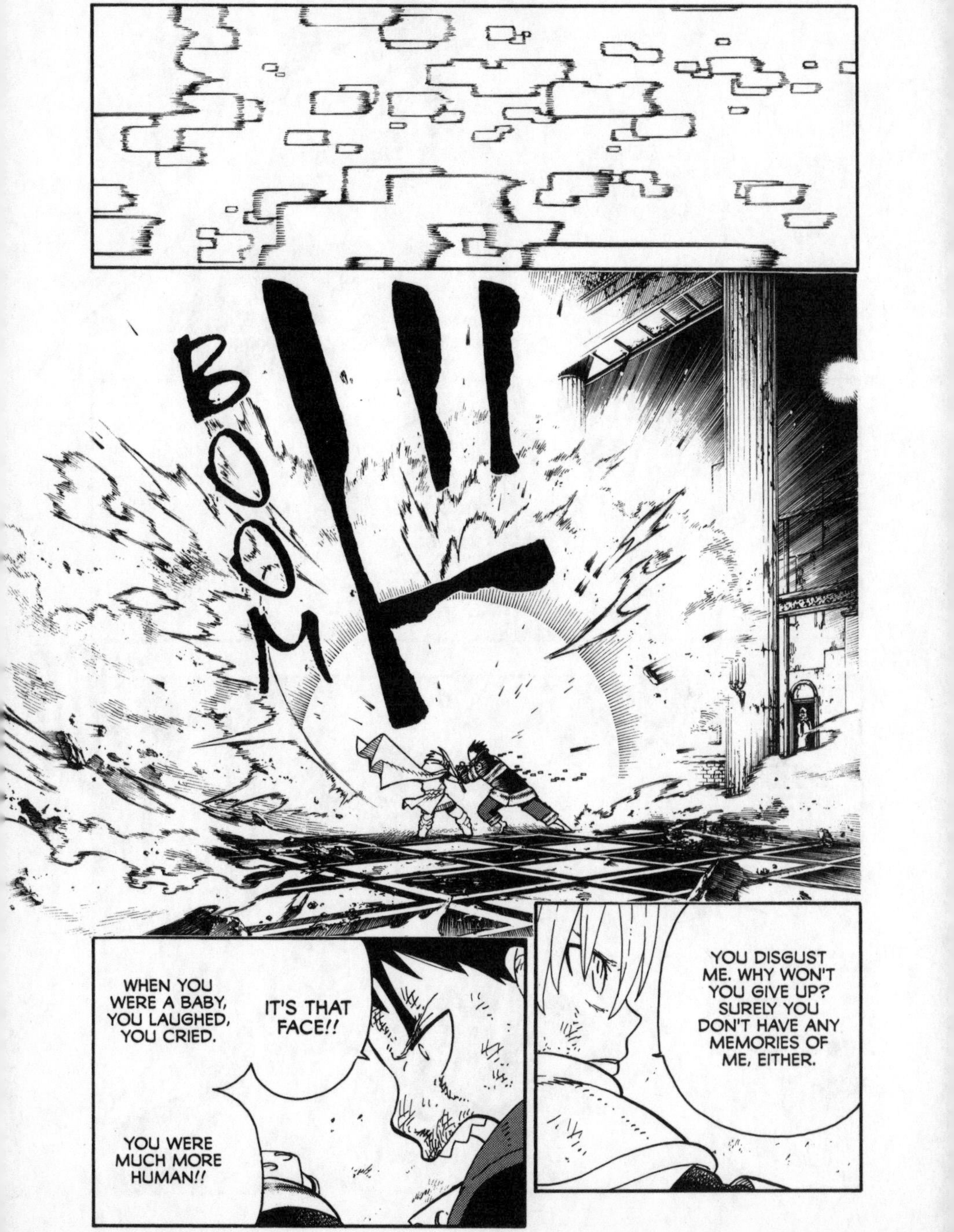
BOOOM
YOU DISGUST ME. WHY WON'T YOU GIVE UP? SURELY YOU DON'T HAVE ANY MEMORIES OF ME, EITHER.
IT'S THAT FACE!!
WHEN YOU WERE A BABY, YOU LAUGHED, YOU CRIED.
YOU WERE MUCH MORE HUMAN!!

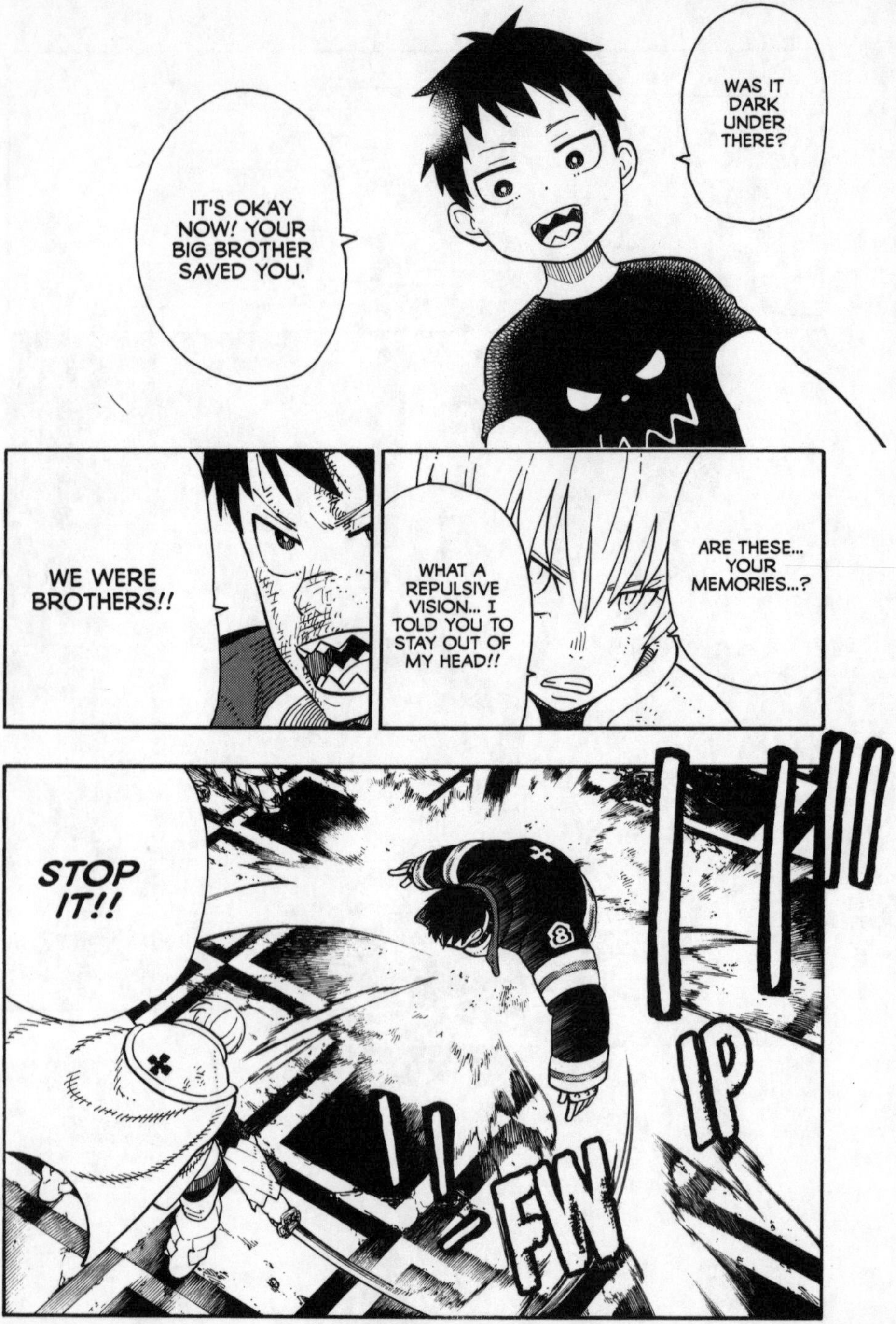

WAS IT DARK UNDER THERE?
IT'S OKAY NOW! YOUR BIG BROTHER SAVED YOU.
ARE THESE... YOUR MEMORIES...?
WHAT A REPULSIVE VISION... I TOLD YOU TO STAY OUT OF MY HEAD!!
WE WERE BROTHERS!!
STOP IT!!
FWIP

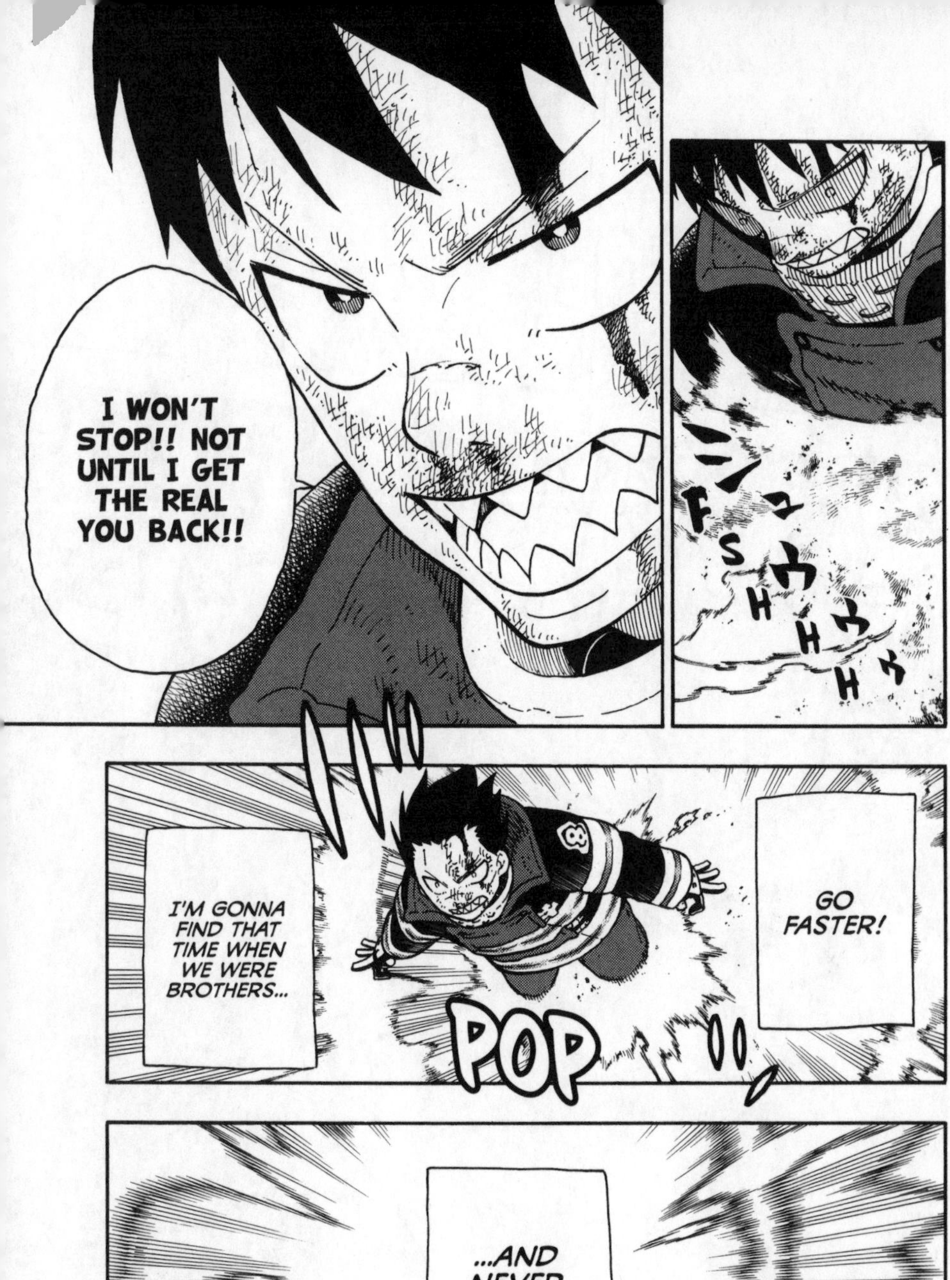
FSHHHH
I WON'T STOP!! NOT UNTIL I GET THE REAL YOU BACK!!
GO FASTER!
I'M GONNA FIND THAT TIME WHEN WE WERE BROTHERS...
POP
...AND NEVER LET IT GO!

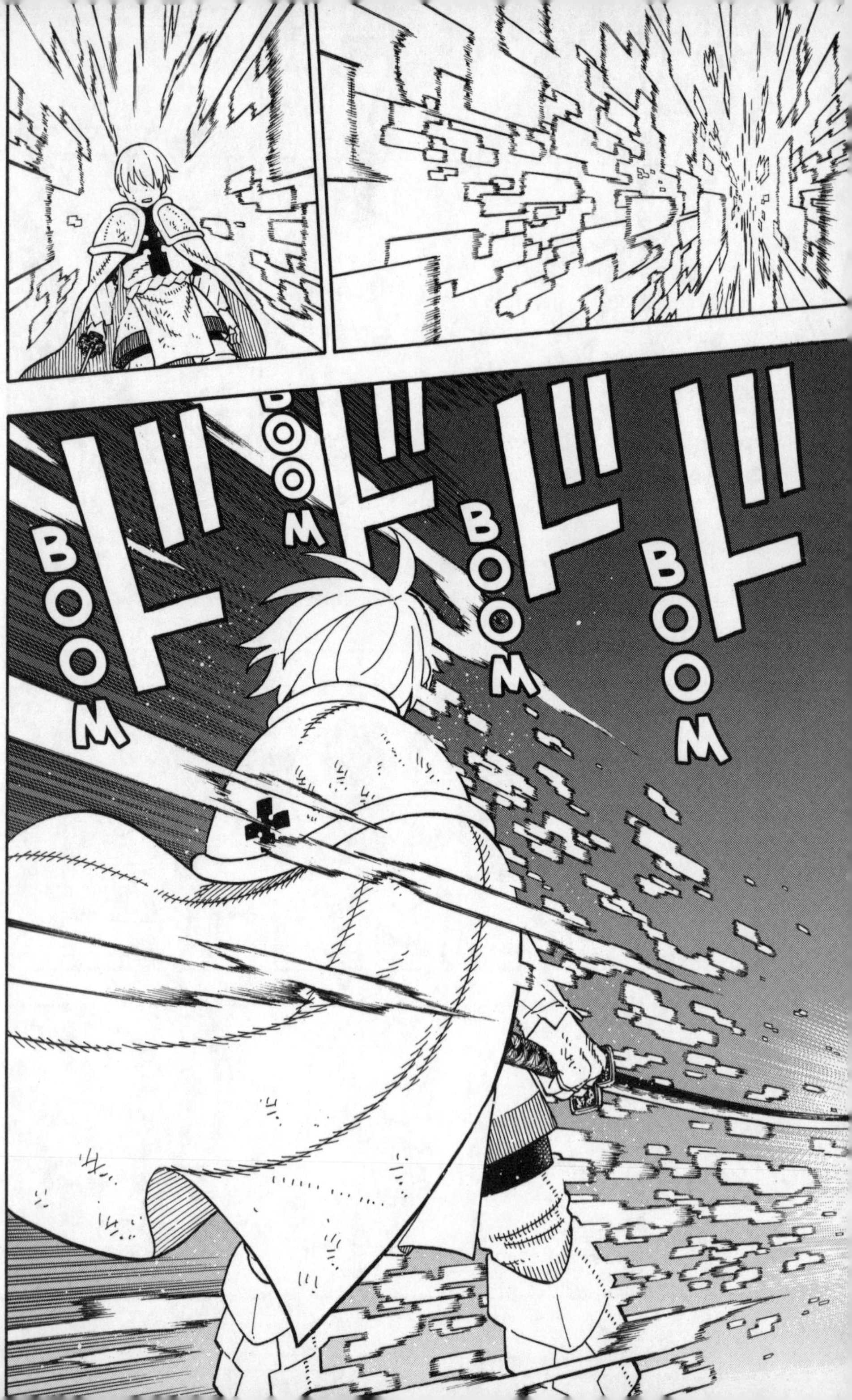
ド BOOM
ド BOOM
ド BOOM
ド BOOM

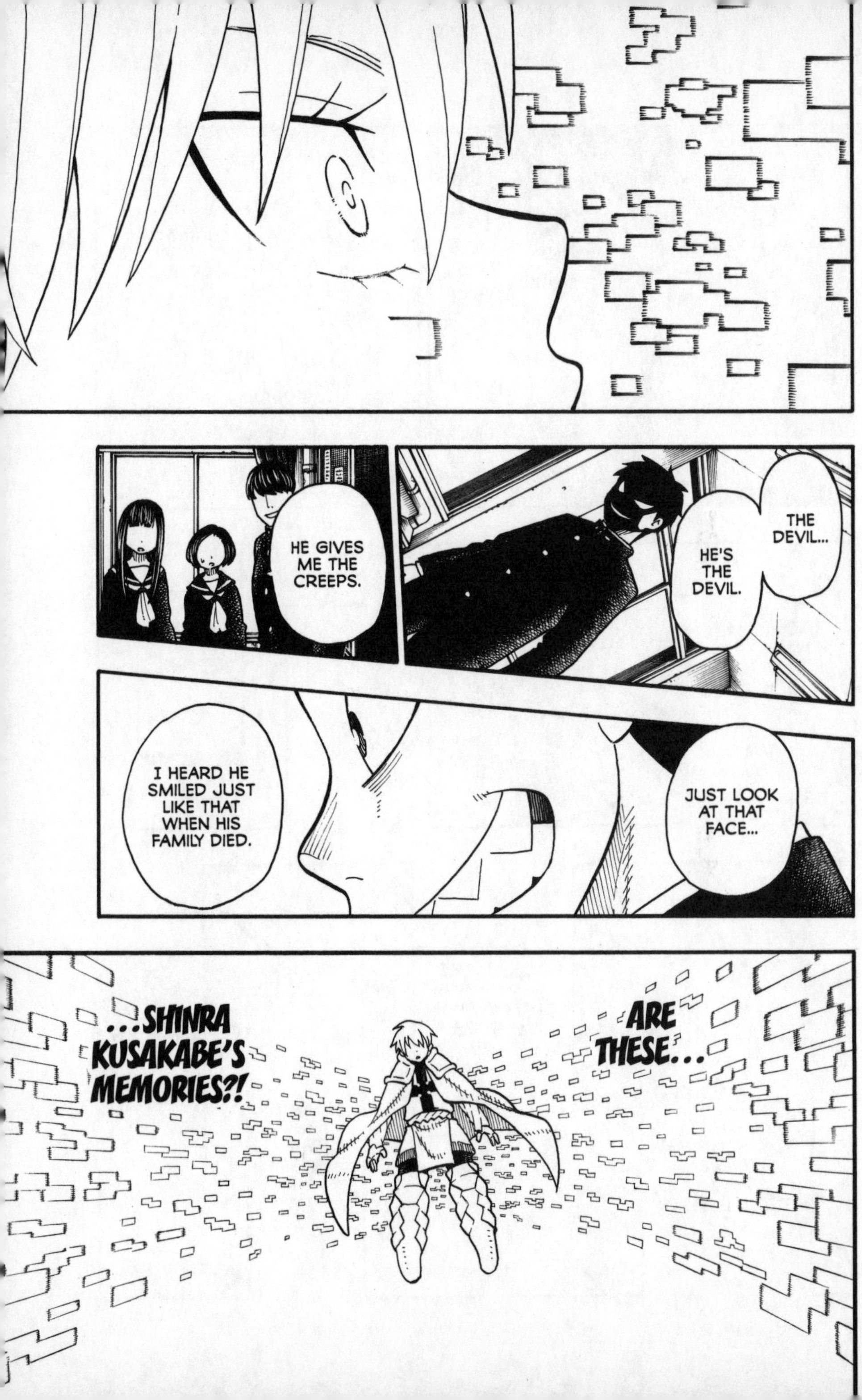
THE DEVIL...
HE'S THE DEVIL.
HE GIVES ME THE CREEPS.
JUST LOOK AT THAT FACE...
I HEARD HE SMILED JUST LIKE THAT WHEN HIS FAMILY DIED.
ARE THESE...
...SHINRA KUSAKABE'S MEMORIES?!

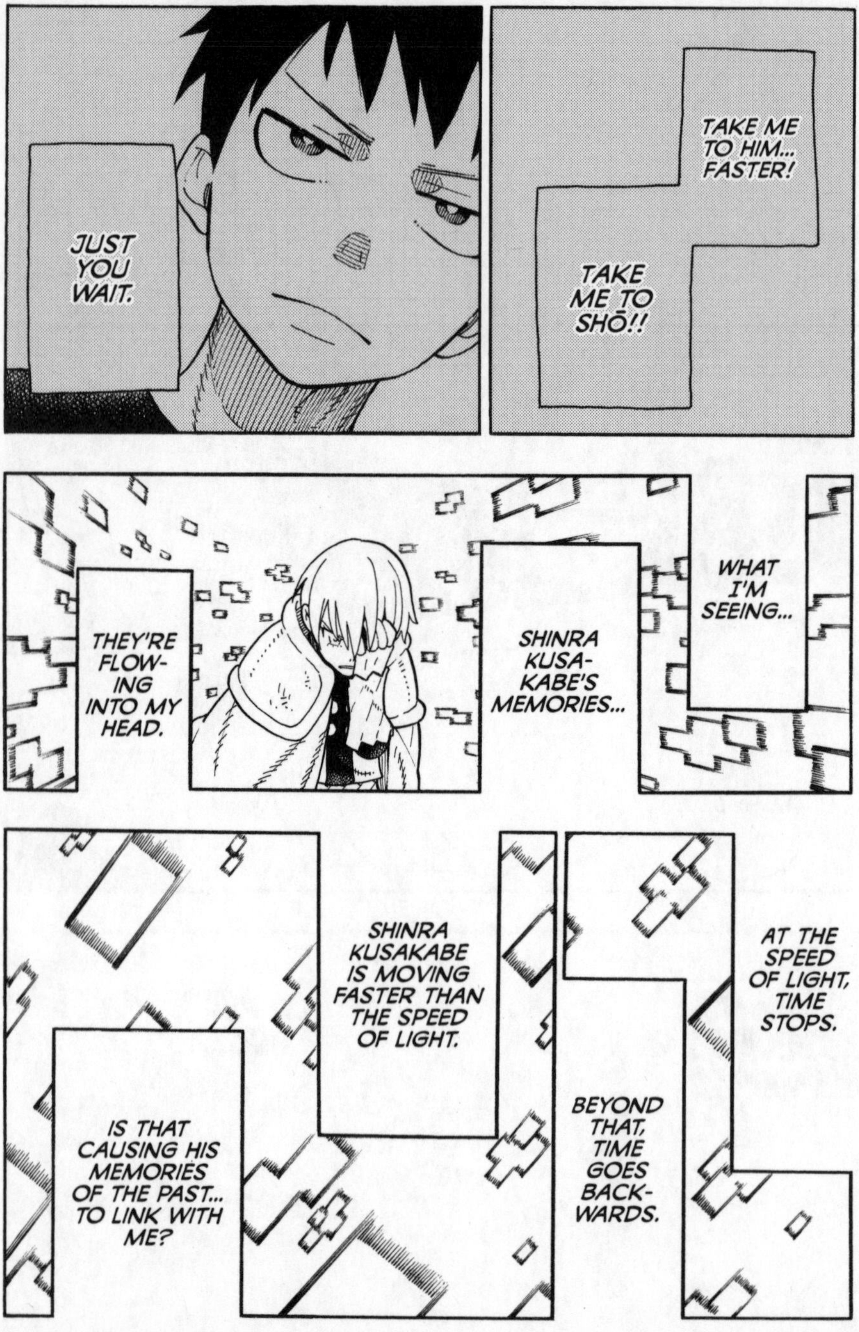
TAKE ME TO HIM... FASTER!
TAKE ME TO SHŌ!!
JUST YOU WAIT.
WHAT I'M SEEING...
SHINRA KUSAKABE'S MEMORIES...
THEY'RE FLOWING INTO MY HEAD.
AT THE SPEED OF LIGHT, TIME STOPS.
BEYOND THAT, TIME GOES BACKWARDS.
SHINRA KUSAKABE IS MOVING FASTER THAN THE SPEED OF LIGHT.
IS THAT CAUSING HIS MEMORIES OF THE PAST... TO LINK WITH ME?

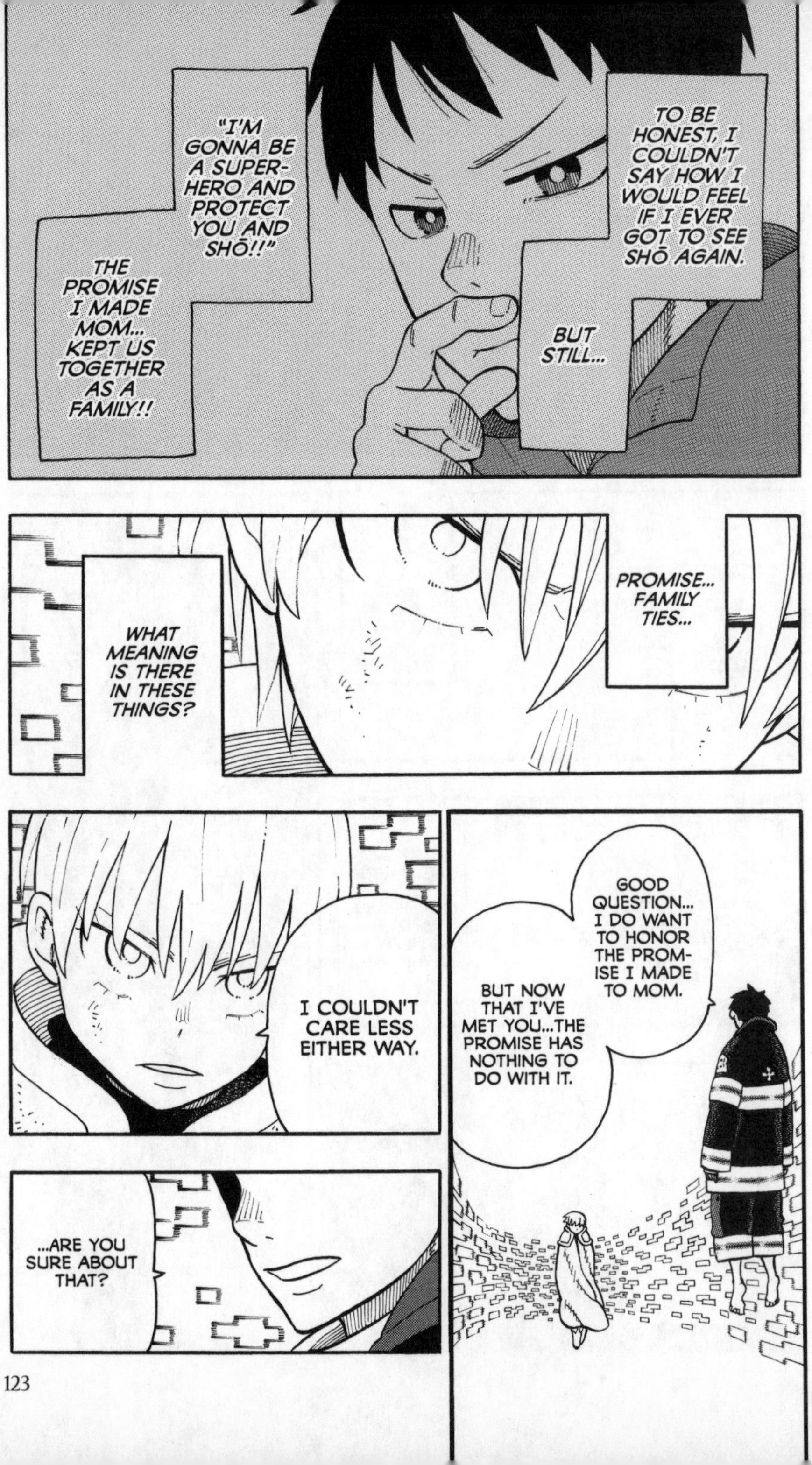
TO BE HONEST, I COULDN'T SAY HOW I WOULD FEEL IF I EVER GOT TO SEE SHŌ AGAIN.
BUT STILL...
"I'M GONNA BE A SUPER-HERO AND PROTECT YOU AND SHŌ!!"
THE PROMISE I MADE MOM... KEPT US TOGETHER AS A FAMILY!!
PROMISE... FAMILY TIES...
WHAT MEANING IS THERE IN THESE THINGS?
GOOD QUESTION... I DO WANT TO HONOR THE PROM-ISE I MADE TO MOM.
BUT NOW THAT I'VE MET YOU...THE PROMISE HAS NOTHING TO DO WITH IT.
I COULDN'T CARE LESS EITHER WAY.
...ARE YOU SURE ABOUT THAT?

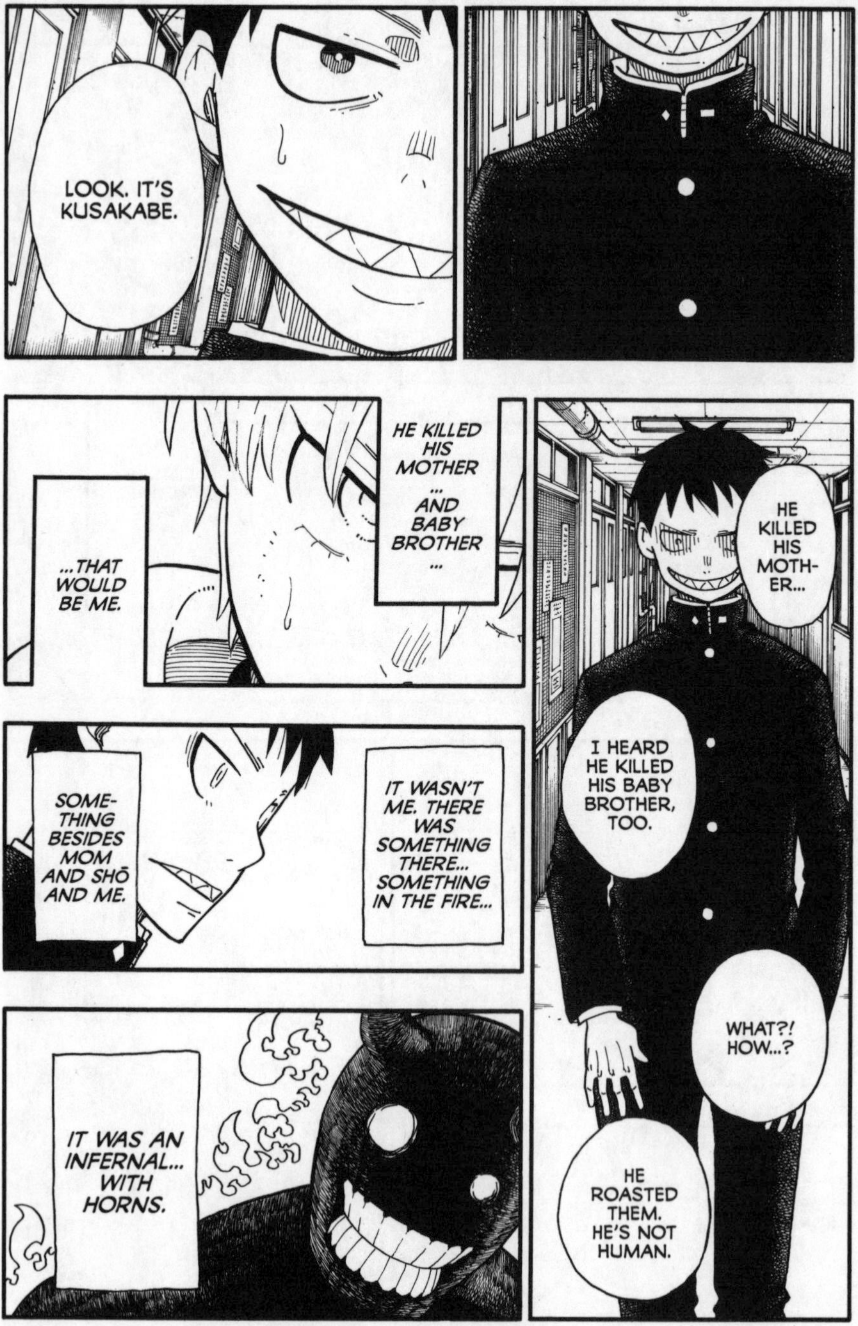
LOOK. IT'S KUSAKABE.
HE KILLED HIS MOTHER...
I HEARD HE KILLED HIS BABY BROTHER, TOO.
WHAT?! HOW...?
HE ROASTED THEM. HE'S NOT HUMAN.
HE KILLED HIS MOTHER ... AND BABY BROTHER ...
...THAT WOULD BE ME.
IT WASN'T ME. THERE WAS SOMETHING THERE... SOMETHING IN THE FIRE...
SOMETHING BESIDES MOM AND SHŌ AND ME.
IT WAS AN INFERNAL... WITH HORNS.

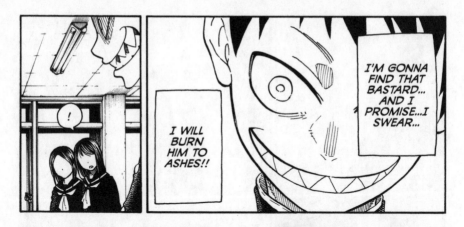

I'M GONNA FIND THAT BASTARD... AND I PROMISE...I SWEAR...
I WILL BURN HIM TO ASHES!!
!
DID YOU JUST SEE HIS FACE?
HE'S A DEVIL...
GET OFF MY BACK. MY FACE TENSES UP INTO THAT SMILE, EVER SINCE THE FIRE.
I KILLED SHŌ?
SINCE THEN, WHENEVER I FEEL NERVOUS, I TENSE UP INTO THAT WEIRD SMILE.
I AM NOT A DEVIL!

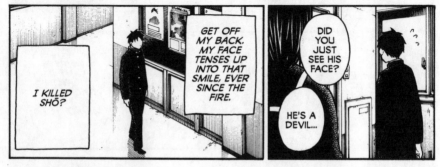

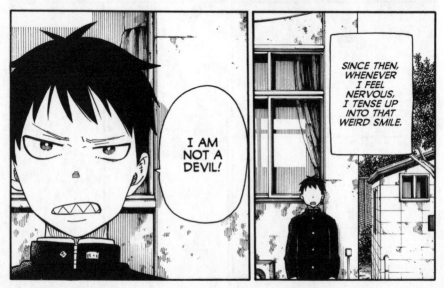

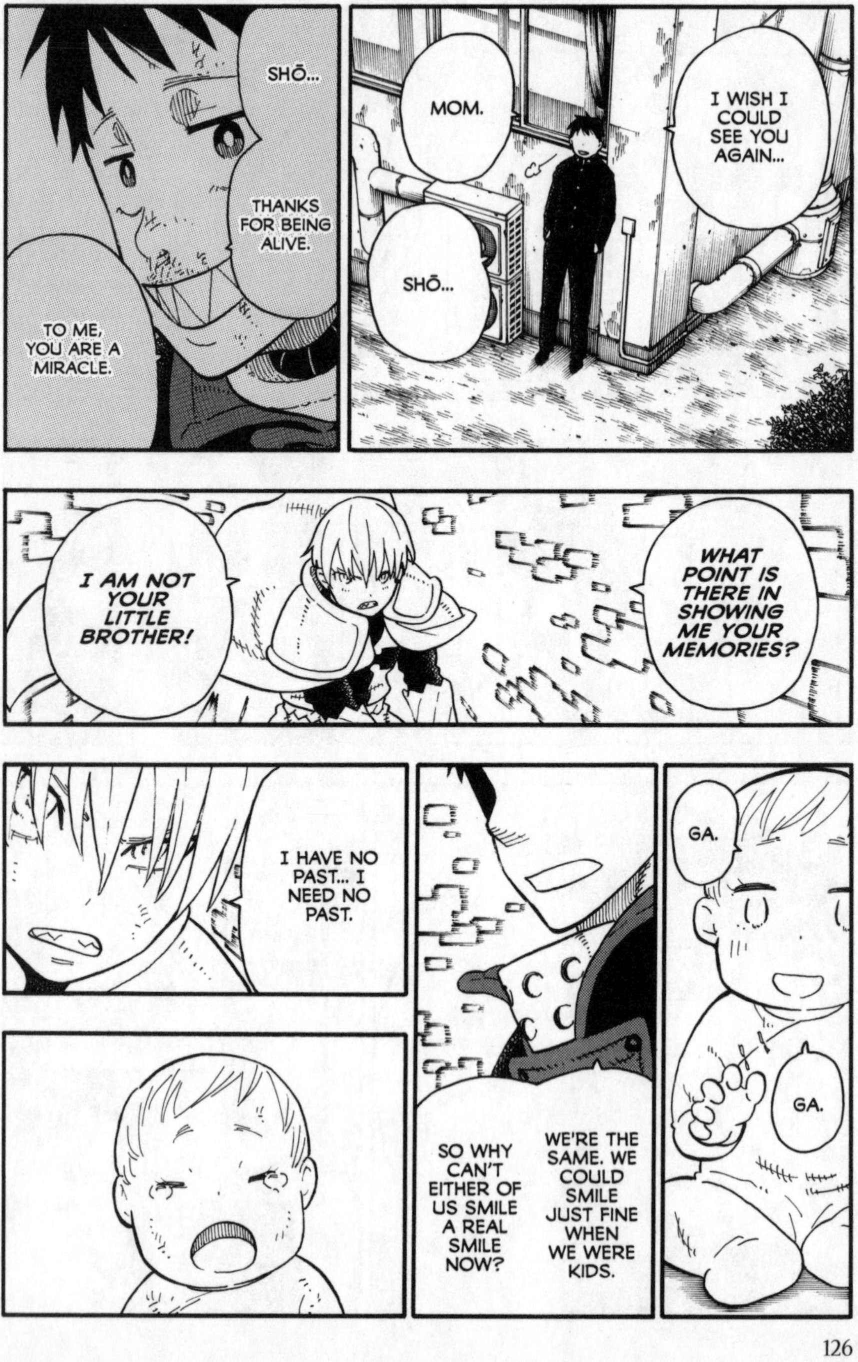
I WISH I COULD SEE YOU AGAIN...
MOM.
SHŌ...
SHŌ...
THANKS FOR BEING ALIVE.
TO ME, YOU ARE A MIRACLE.
WHAT POINT IS THERE IN SHOWING ME YOUR MEMORIES?
I AM NOT YOUR LITTLE BROTHER!
GA.
GA.
WE'RE THE SAME. WE COULD SMILE JUST FINE WHEN WE WERE KIDS.
SO WHY CAN'T EITHER OF US SMILE A REAL SMILE NOW?
I HAVE NO PAST... I NEED NO PAST.

CHILD, YOU HOLD THE ADOLLA BURST... COME WITH ME, AND WE WILL OPEN THE DOOR.

IS IT MINE? IS IT A MEMORY I LOST?

THIS MEMORY...

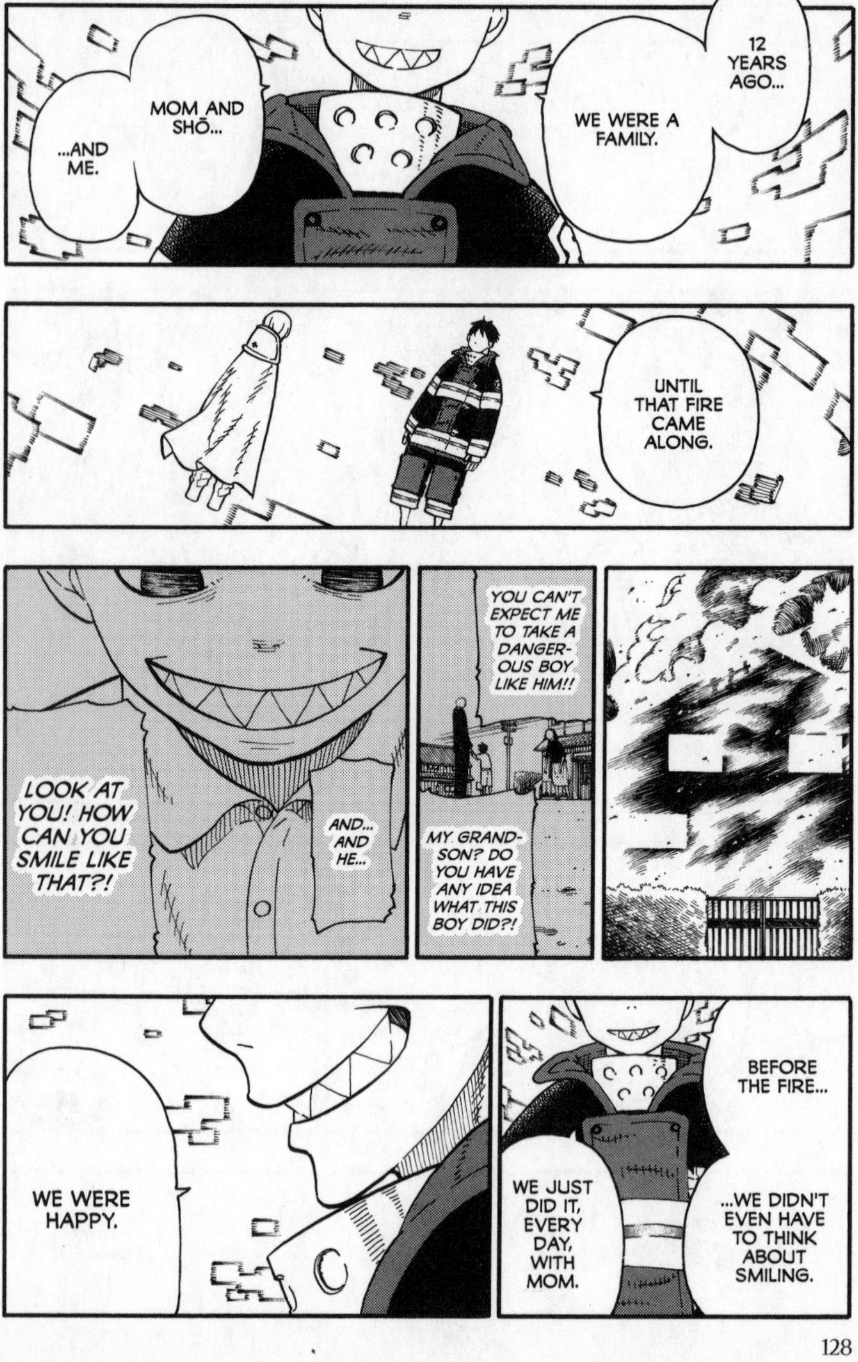
12 YEARS AGO...
WE WERE A FAMILY.
MOM AND SHŌ...
...AND ME.
UNTIL THAT FIRE CAME ALONG.
YOU CAN'T EXPECT ME TO TAKE A DANGEROUS BOY LIKE HIM!!
MY GRANDSON? DO YOU HAVE ANY IDEA WHAT THIS BOY DID?!
AND... AND HE...
LOOK AT YOU! HOW CAN YOU SMILE LIKE THAT?!
BEFORE THE FIRE...
...WE DIDN'T EVEN HAVE TO THINK ABOUT SMILING.
WE JUST DID IT, EVERY DAY, WITH MOM.
WE WERE HAPPY.

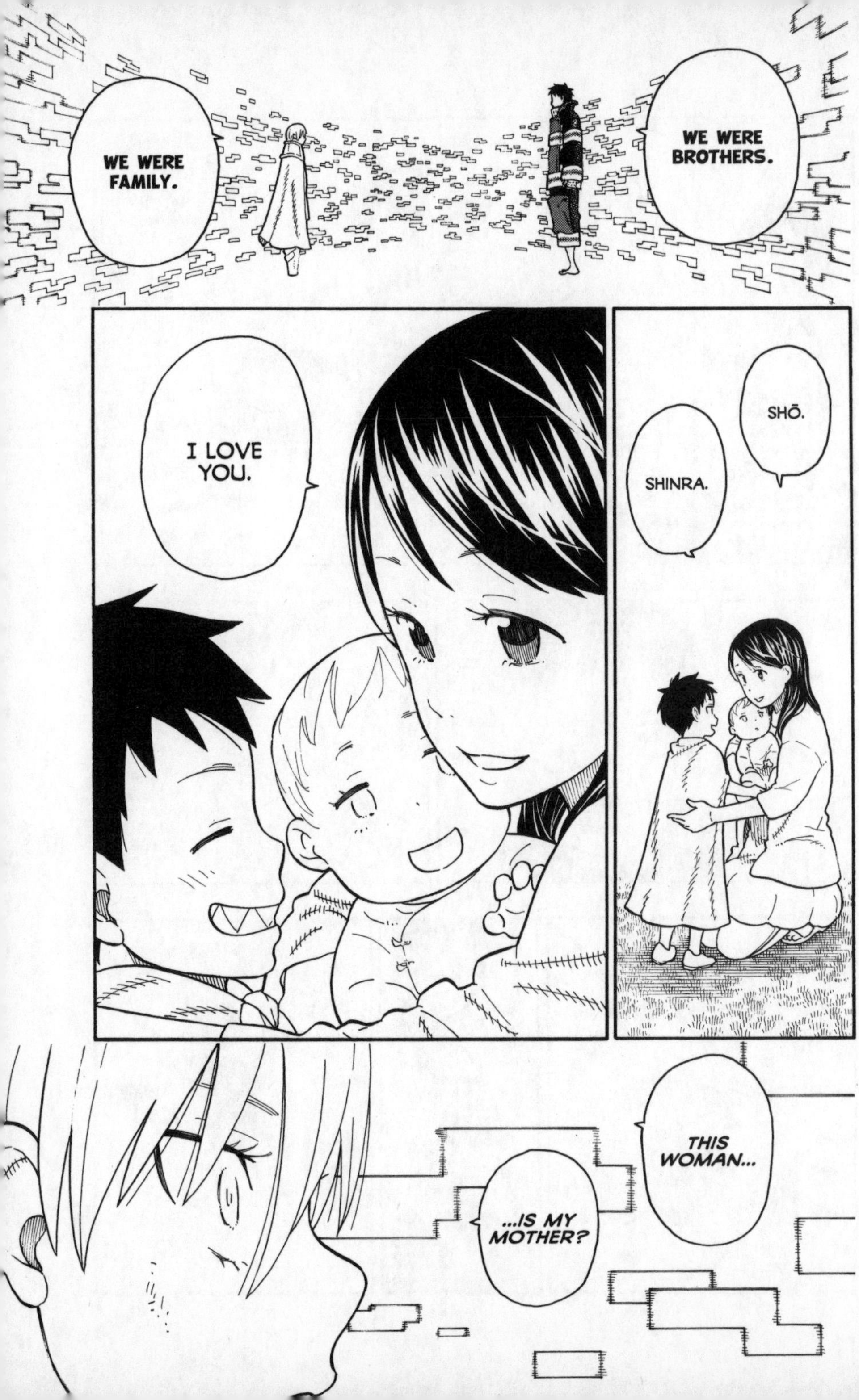
WE WERE BROTHERS.
WE WERE FAMILY.
SHŌ.
SHINRA.
I LOVE YOU.
THIS WOMAN...
...IS MY MOTHER?

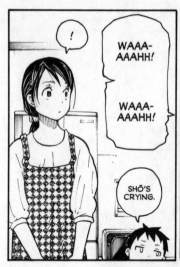

WHATCHA MAKING, MOM?
HAMBURG STEAK!!
If you open it, close it!
YESSS!
!
WAAA-AAAHH!
WAAA-AAAHH!
SHŌ'S CRYING.
OH, MY, MY, WHAT DO I DO?
I JUST FED HIM AND PUT HIM TO SLEEP.
JUST HOLD ON A MINUTE! I'LL GO WASH MY HANDS!
I'LL DO IT, MOM!
I'LL GO SAVE THE DAY!
STOMP だ
I'M ON MY WAY, SHŌ!!
STOMP だ
STOMP だ
クス
HEE HEE
WAAAA-AAHH!
ARE YOU OKAY?! YOU CAN RELAX NOW–YOUR BROTHER'S HERE!
ざざん
ZA-ZAM

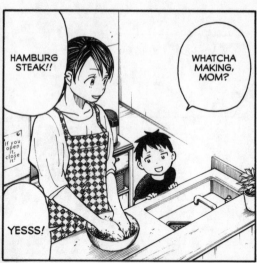

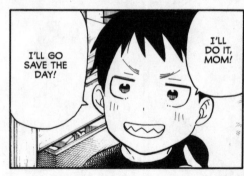

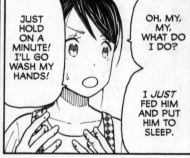

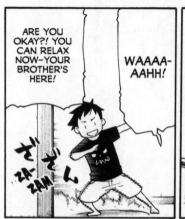

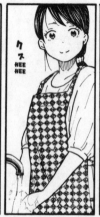

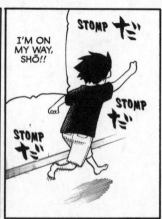

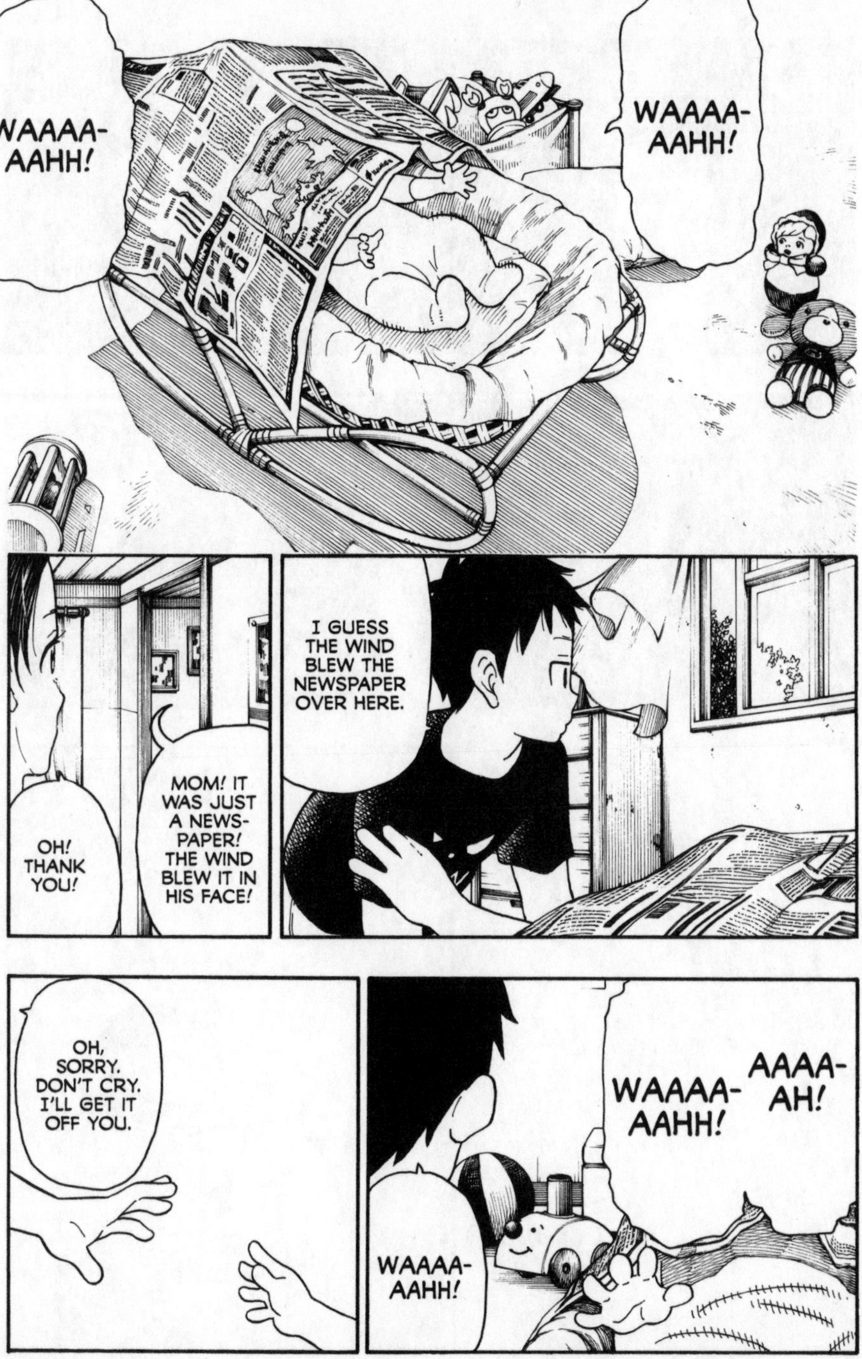
WAAAA-AAHH!
WAAAA-AAHH!
I GUESS THE WIND BLEW THE NEWSPAPER OVER HERE.
MOM! IT WAS JUST A NEWS-PAPER! THE WIND BLEW IT IN HIS FACE!
OH! THANK YOU!
AAAA-AH!
WAAAA-AAHH!
WAAAA-AAHH!
OH, SORRY. DON'T CRY. I'LL GET IT OFF YOU.

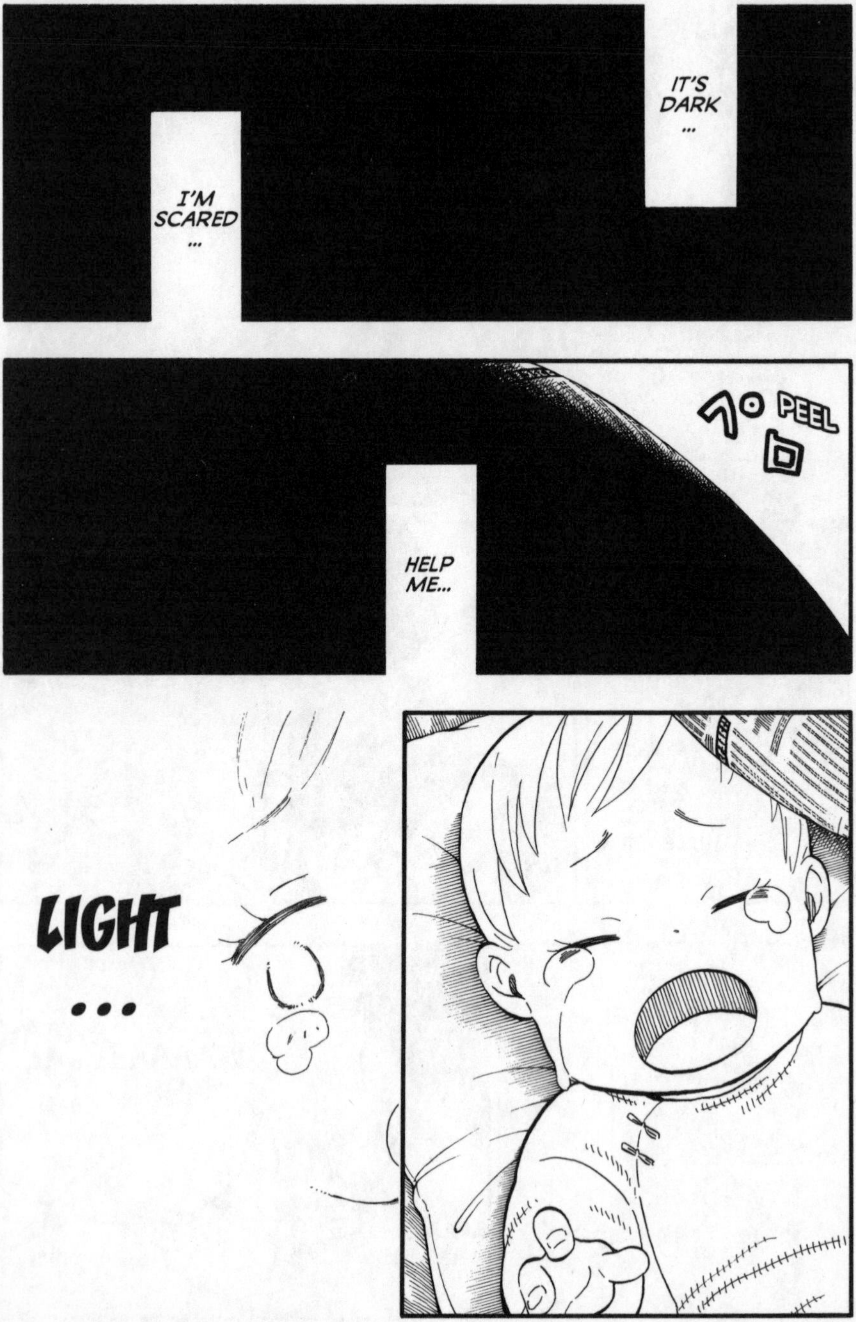
IT'S DARK ...
I'M SCARED ...
PEEL
HELP ME...
LIGHT ...

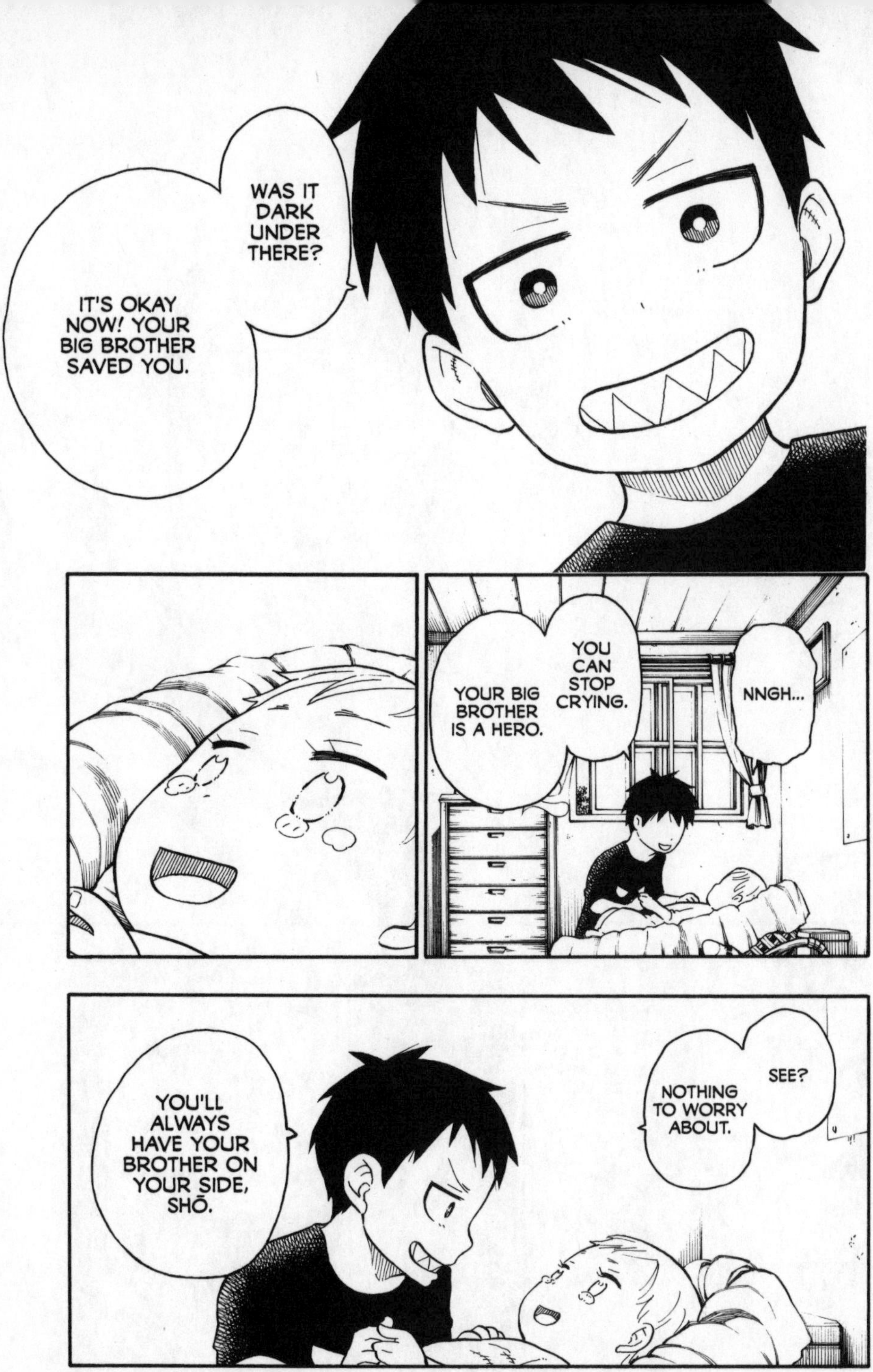
WAS IT DARK UNDER THERE?
IT'S OKAY NOW! YOUR BIG BROTHER SAVED YOU.
NNGH...
YOU CAN STOP CRYING.
YOUR BIG BROTHER IS A HERO.
SEE?
NOTHING TO WORRY ABOUT.
YOU'LL ALWAYS HAVE YOUR BROTHER ON YOUR SIDE, SHŌ.

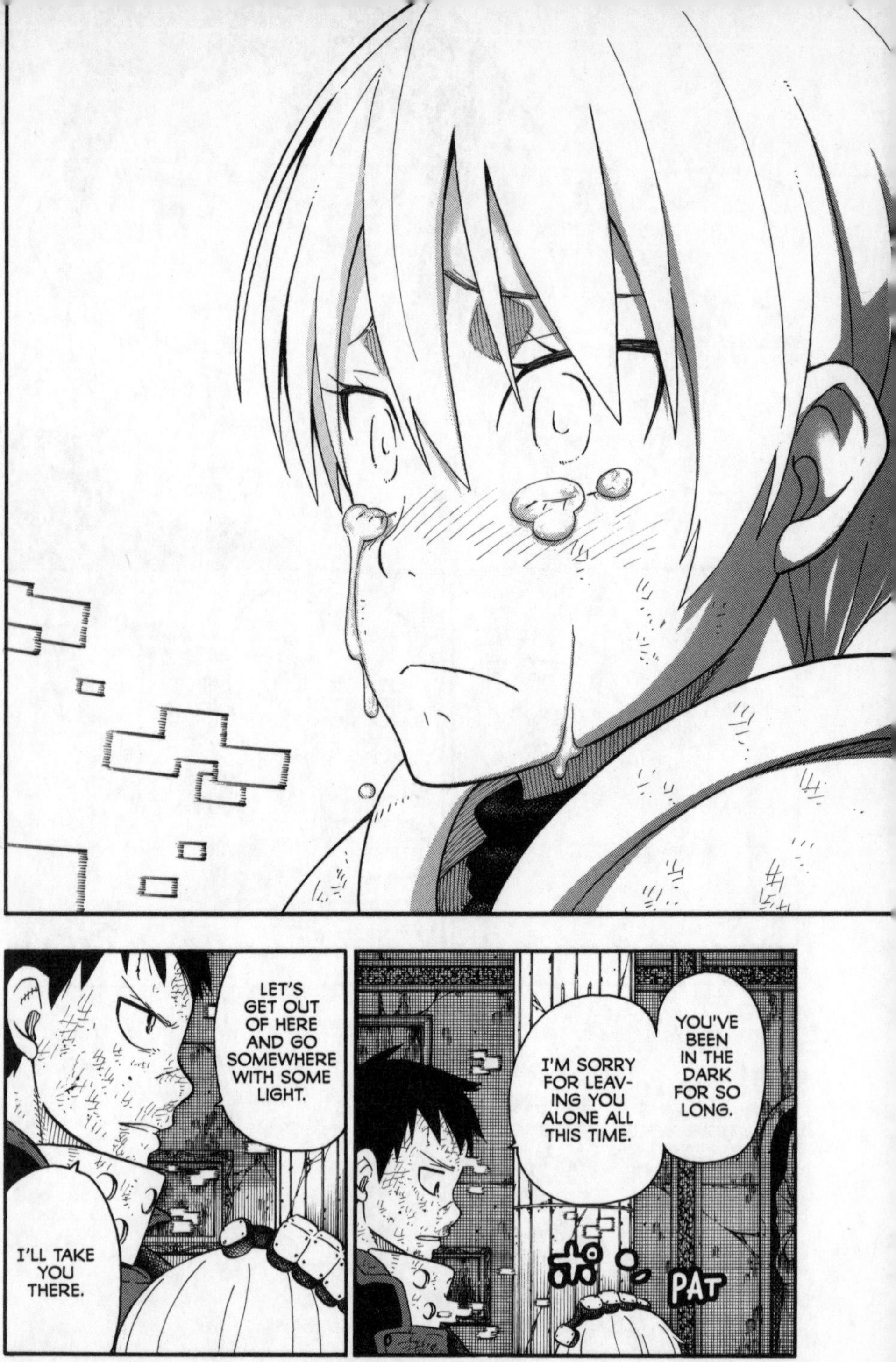
YOU'VE BEEN IN THE DARK FOR SO LONG.
I'M SORRY FOR LEAVING YOU ALONE ALL THIS TIME.
PAT
LET'S GET OUT OF HERE AND GO SOMEWHERE WITH SOME LIGHT.
I'LL TAKE YOU THERE.

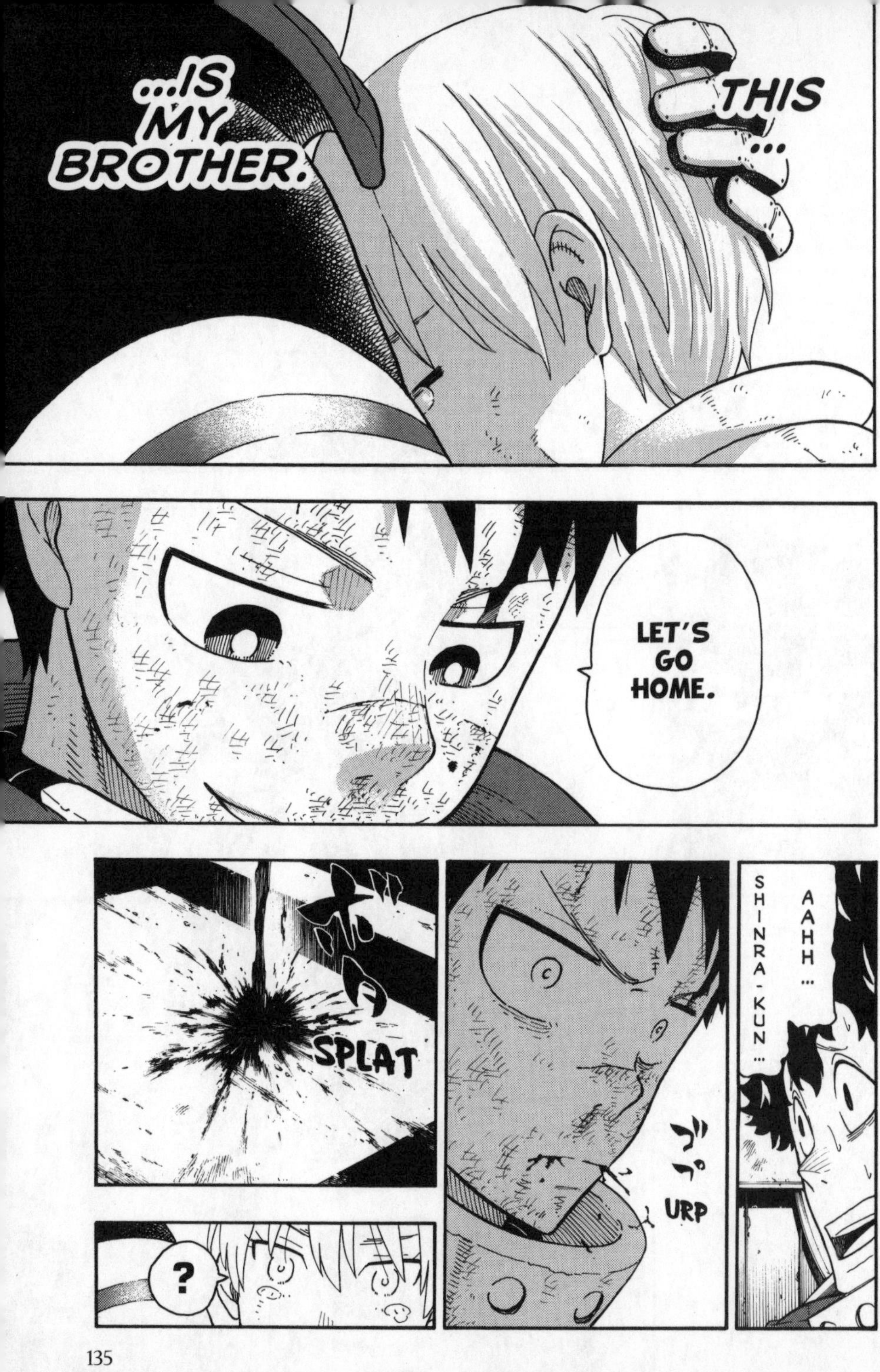
THIS...
...IS MY BROTHER.
LET'S GO HOME.
AAHH...
SHINRA-KUN...
URP
SPLAT
?

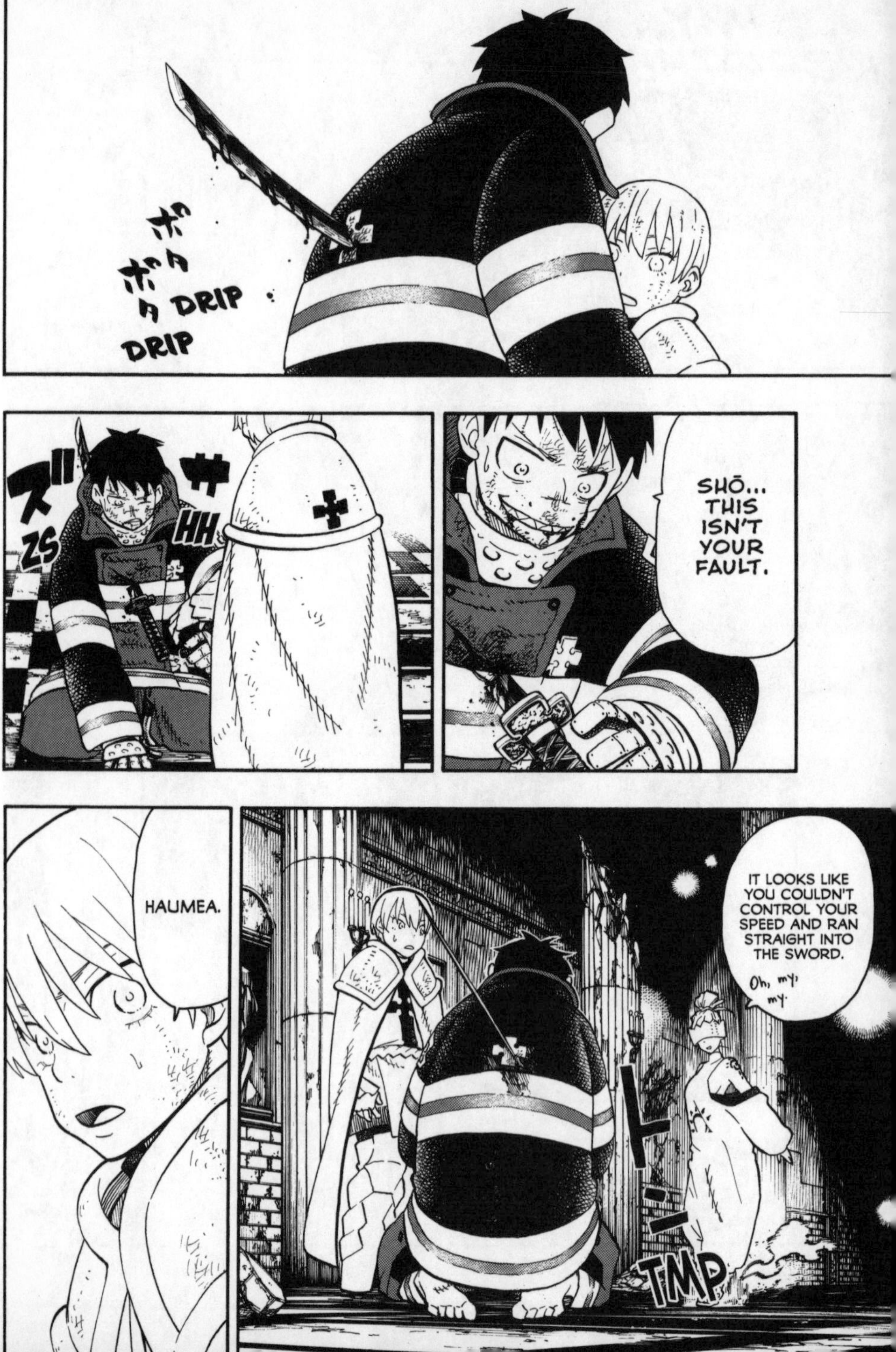
ボタ
ボタ
DRIP
DRIP
SHŌ... THIS ISN'T YOUR FAULT.
ズ
ザ
ZS
HH
IT LOOKS LIKE YOU COULDN'T CONTROL YOUR SPEED AND RAN STRAIGHT INTO THE SWORD.
Oh, my, my.
ドー
TMP
HAUMEA.

FIRE FORCE

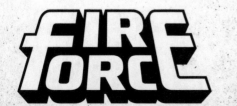

FIRE FORCE

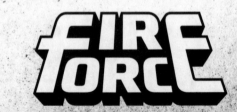

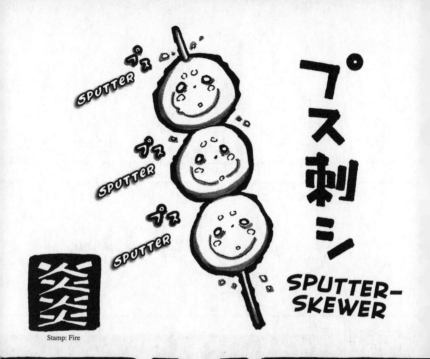

SPUTTER
プス

SPUTTER
プス

SPUTTER
プス

プス刺シ

SPUTTER-
SKEWER

Stamp: Fire

CHAPTER LXXXV: A PLOT REVEALED

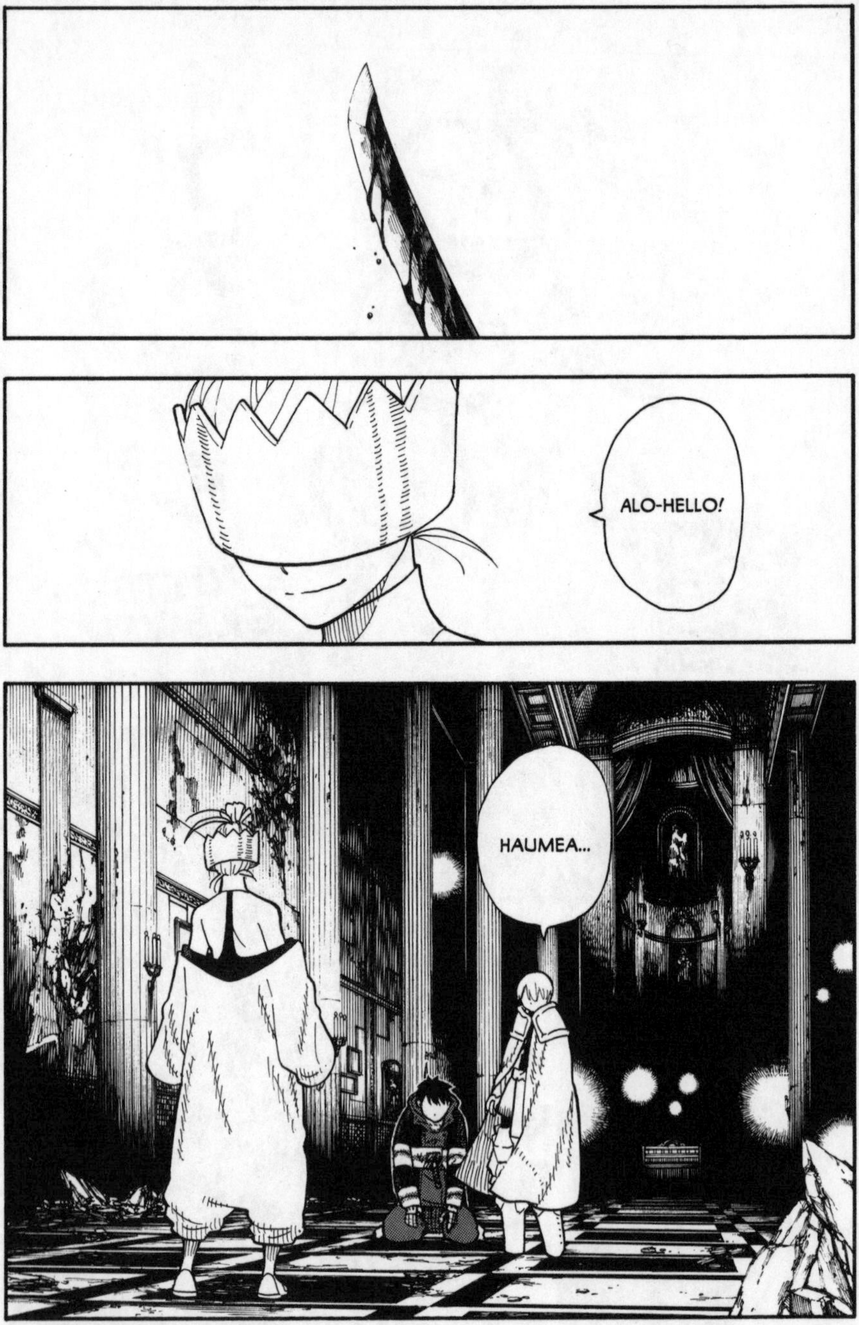
ALO-HELLO!
HAUMEA...

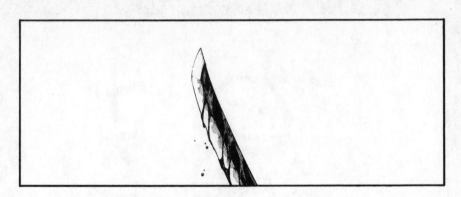

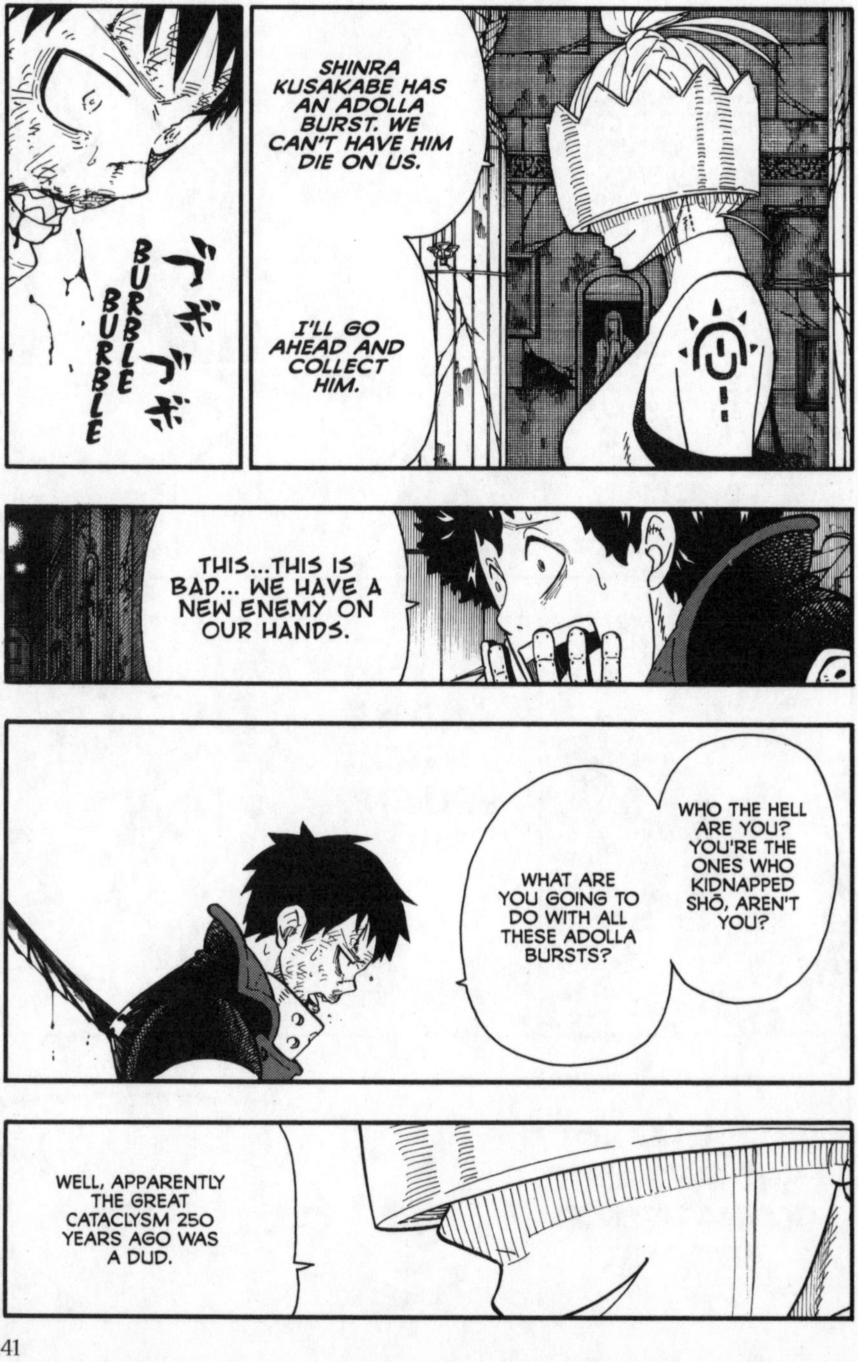
SHINRA KUSAKABE HAS AN ADOLLA BURST. WE CAN'T HAVE HIM DIE ON US.
I'LL GO AHEAD AND COLLECT HIM.
ゴボゴボ
BURBLE BURBLE
THIS...THIS IS BAD... WE HAVE A NEW ENEMY ON OUR HANDS.
WHO THE HELL ARE YOU? YOU'RE THE ONES WHO KIDNAPPED SHŌ, AREN'T YOU?
WHAT ARE YOU GOING TO DO WITH ALL THESE ADOLLA BURSTS?
WELL, APPARENTLY THE GREAT CATACLYSM 250 YEARS AGO WAS A DUD.

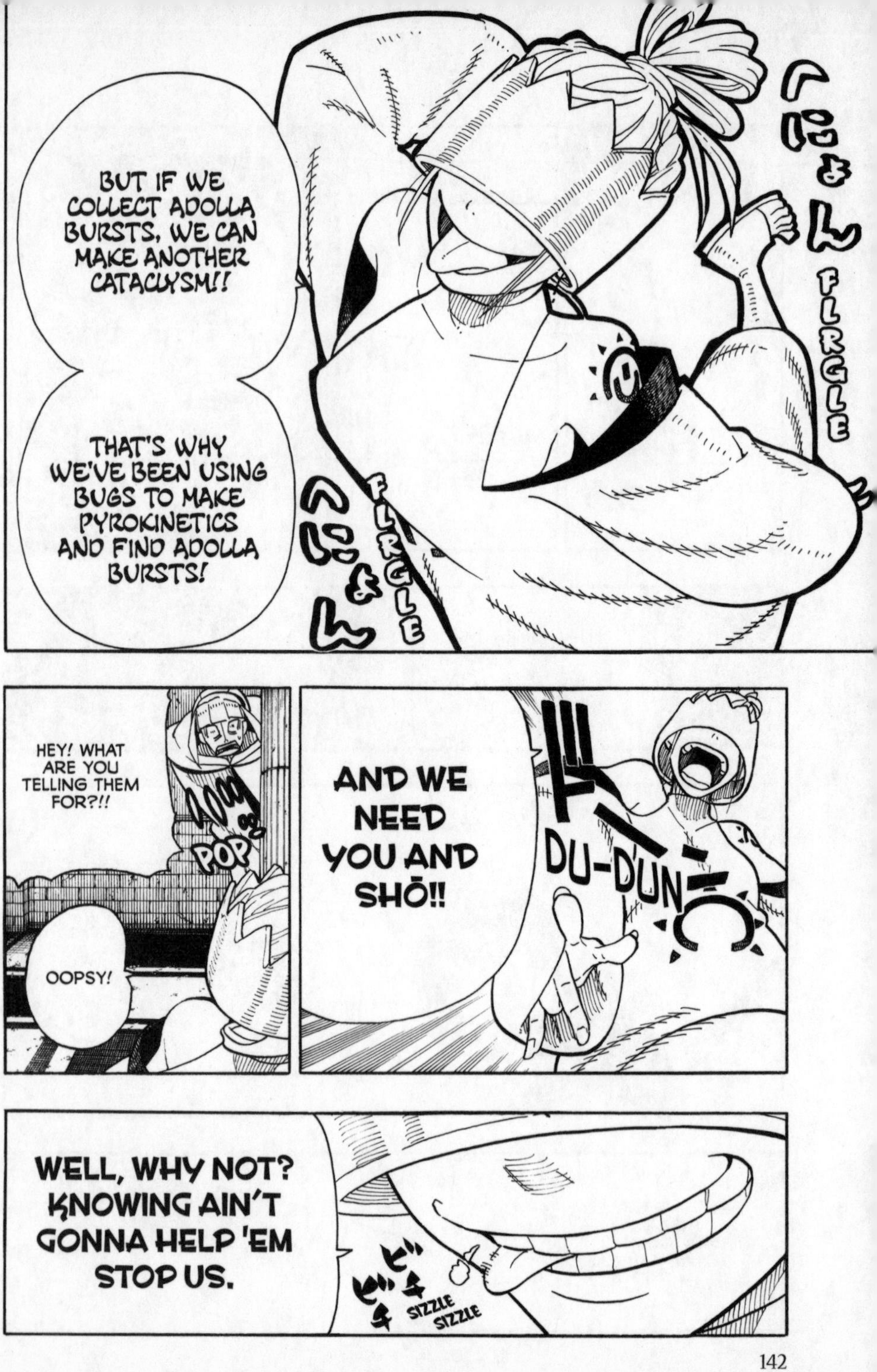
へにょん
FLRGLE
BUT IF WE COLLECT ADOLLA BURSTS, WE CAN MAKE ANOTHER CATACLYSM!!
THAT'S WHY WE'VE BEEN USING BUGS TO MAKE PYROKINETICS AND FIND ADOLLA BURSTS!
へにょん
FLRGLE
AND WE NEED YOU AND SHŌ!!
ドン
DU-DUN
HEY! WHAT ARE YOU TELLING THEM FOR?!!
POP
OOPSY!
WELL, WHY NOT? KNOWING AIN'T GONNA HELP 'EM STOP US.
SIZZLE SIZZLE

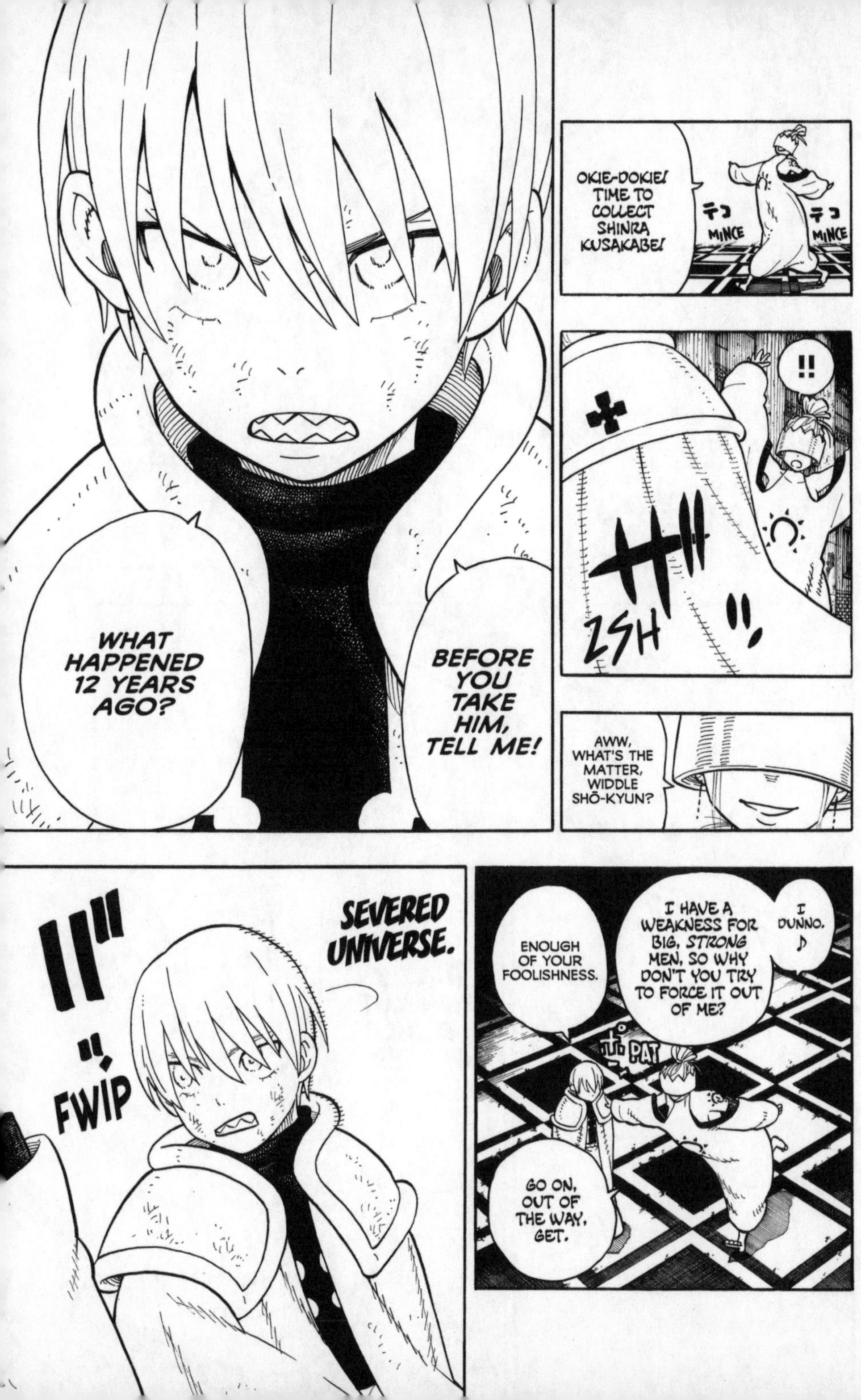
OKIE-DOKIE! TIME TO COLLECT SHINRA KUSAKABE!
テコ MINCE
テコ MINCE
!!
ZSH
AWW, WHAT'S THE MATTER, WIDDLE SHŌ-KYUN?
BEFORE YOU TAKE HIM, TELL ME!
WHAT HAPPENED 12 YEARS AGO?
I DUNNO. ♪
I HAVE A WEAKNESS FOR BIG, STRONG MEN, SO WHY DON'T YOU TRY TO FORCE IT OUT OF ME?
ENOUGH OF YOUR FOOLISHNESS.
PAT
GO ON, OUT OF THE WAY, GET.
SEVERED UNIVERSE.
FWIP

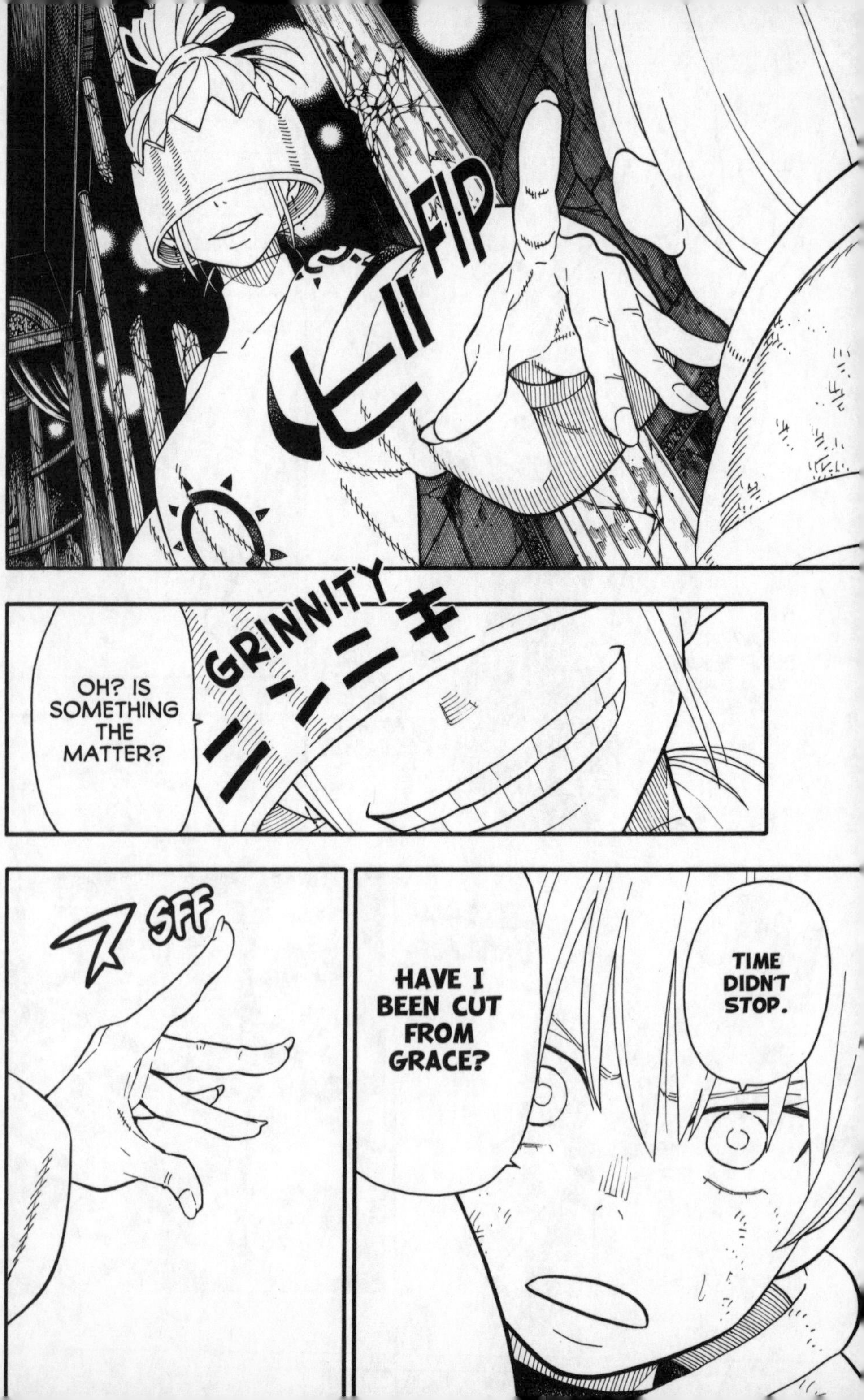
FIP
GRINNITY
OH? IS SOMETHING THE MATTER?
TIME DIDN'T STOP.
HAVE I BEEN CUT FROM GRACE?
SFF

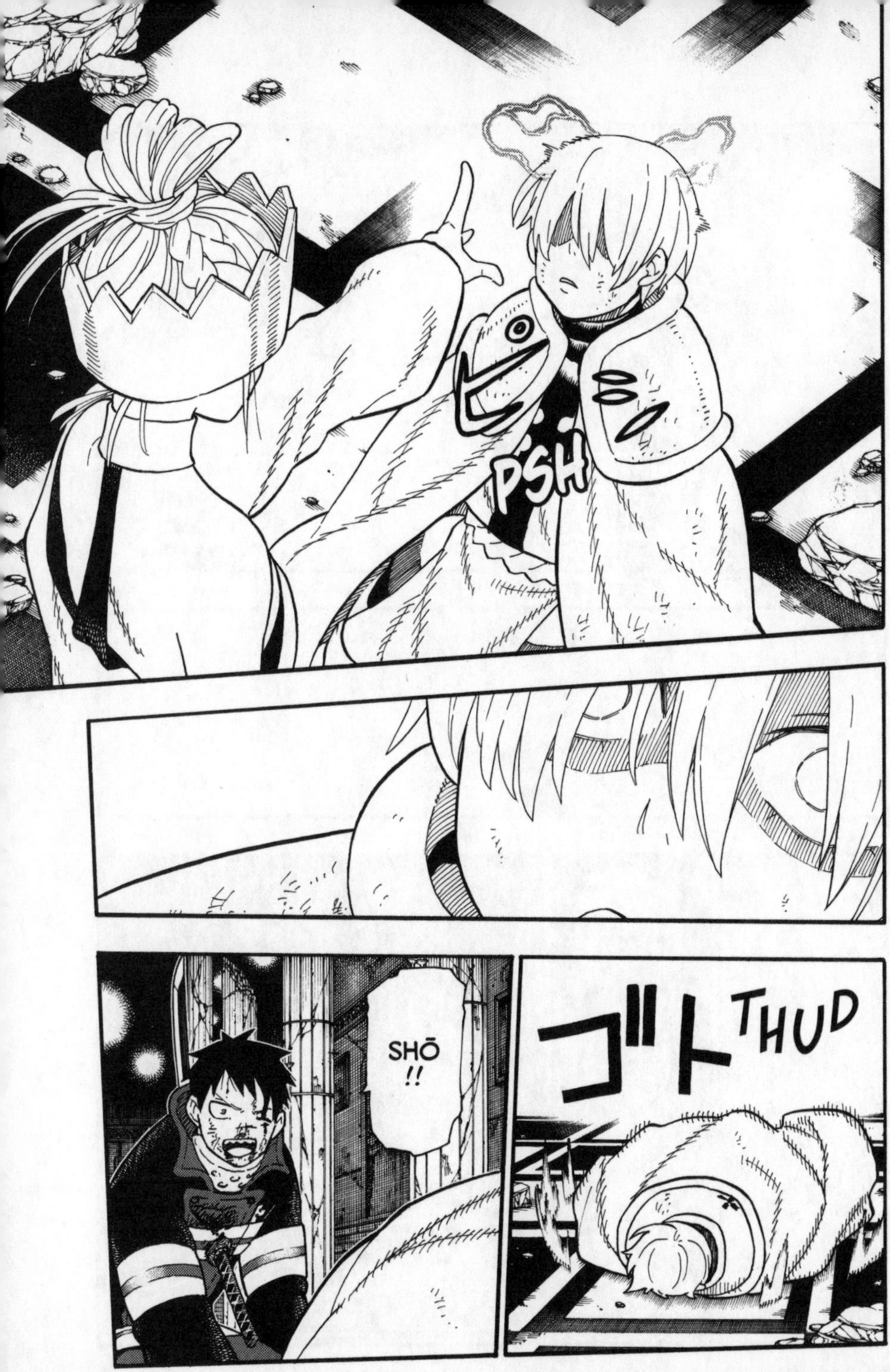
PSH
ゴト THUD
SHŌ!!

MRK
SHŌ!
SFF
...?!

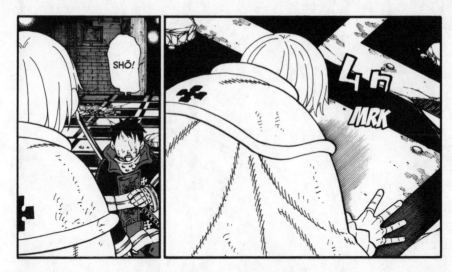

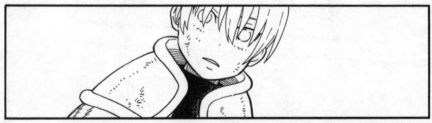

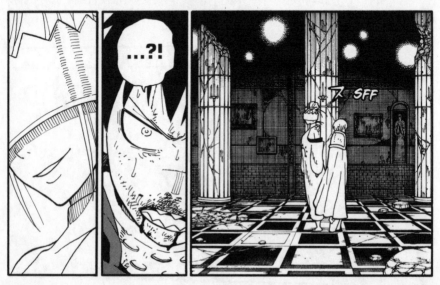

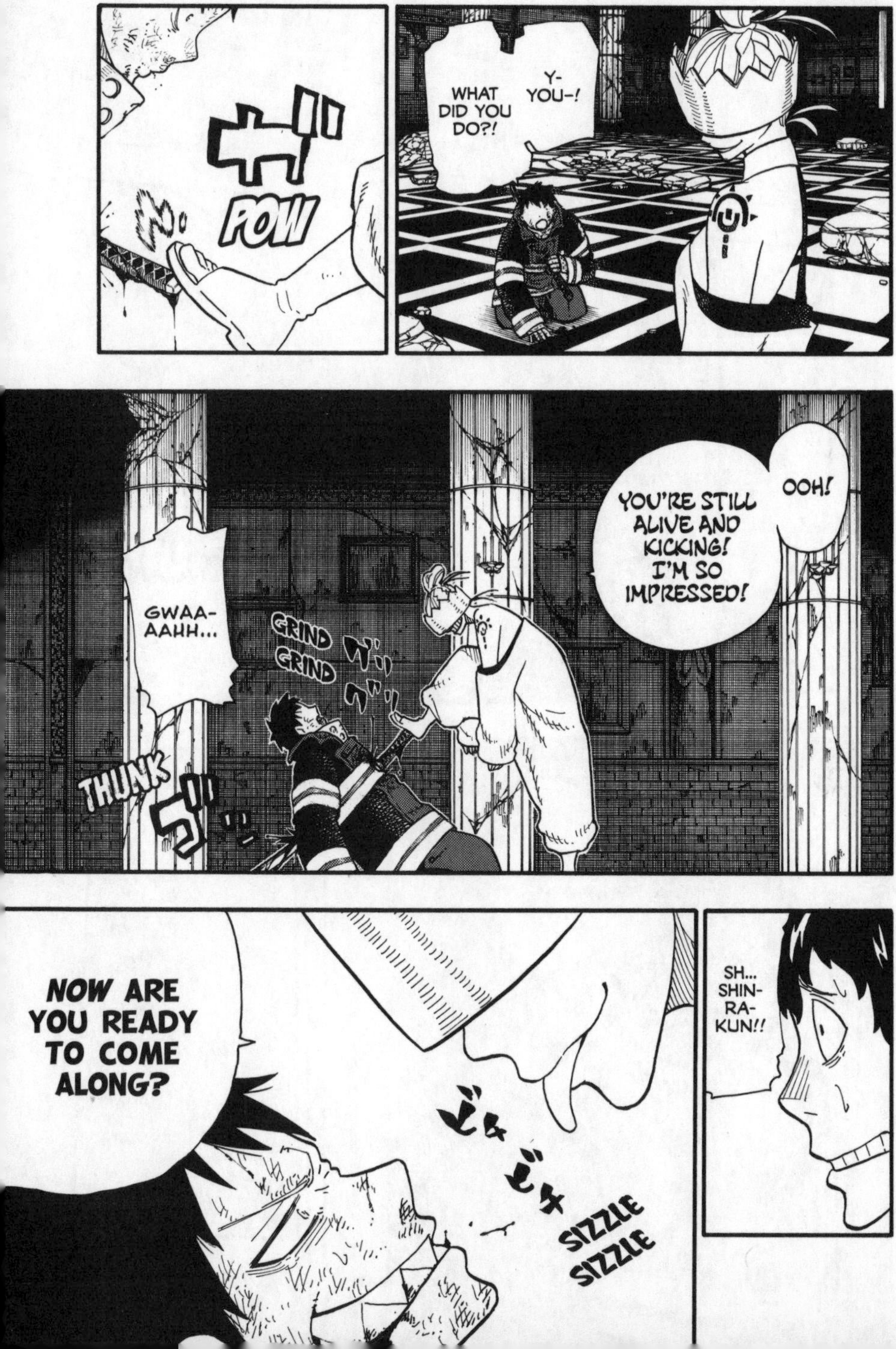
Y- YOU-!
WHAT DID YOU DO?!
POW
OOH!
YOU'RE STILL ALIVE AND KICKING! I'M SO IMPRESSED!
GRIND GRIND
GWAA-AAHH...
THUNK
SH... SHIN-RA-KUN!!
NOW ARE YOU READY TO COME ALONG?
SIZZLE SIZZLE

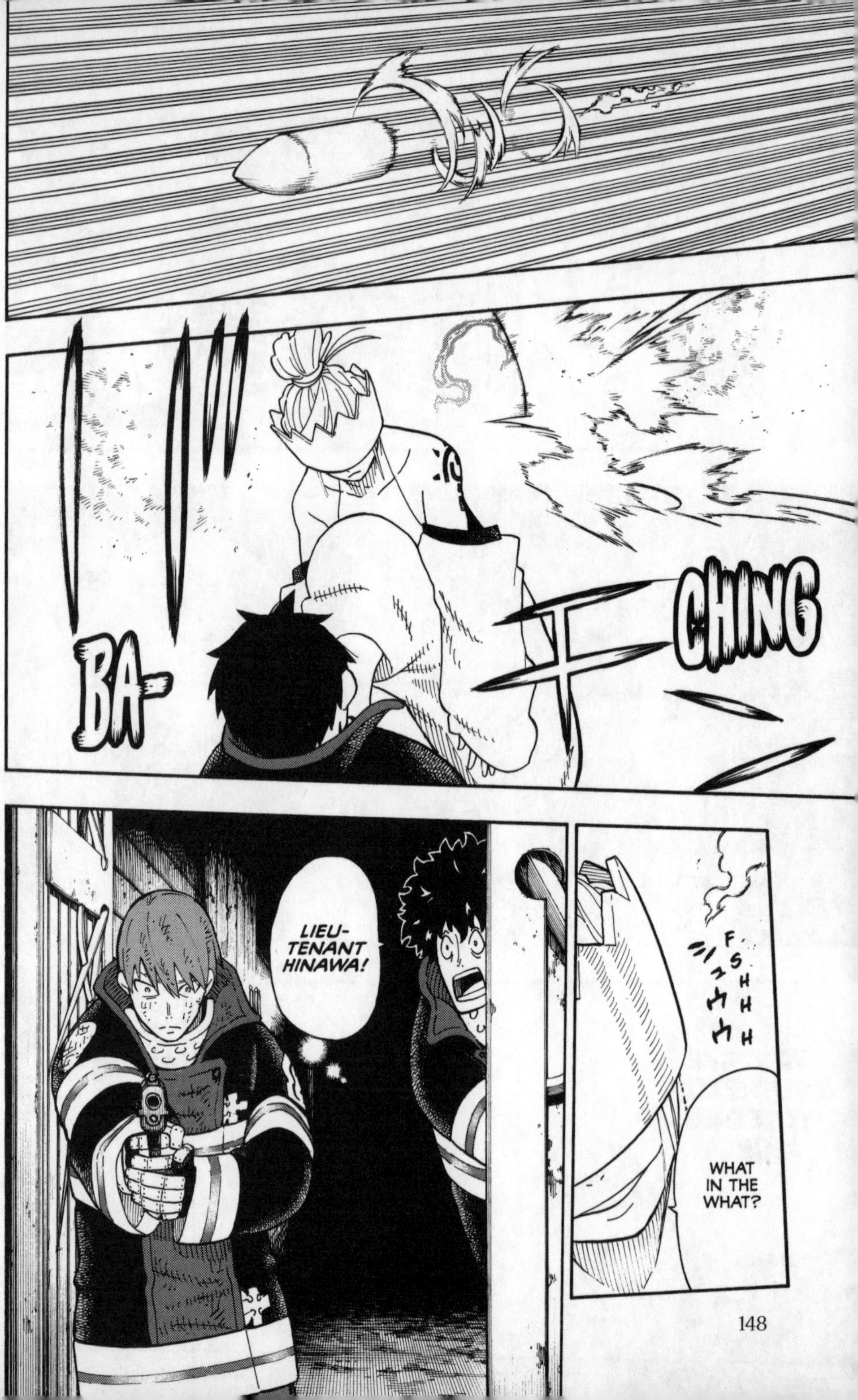
BA-
CHING
FSHHHH
WHAT IN THE WHAT?
LIEU-TENANT HINAWA!

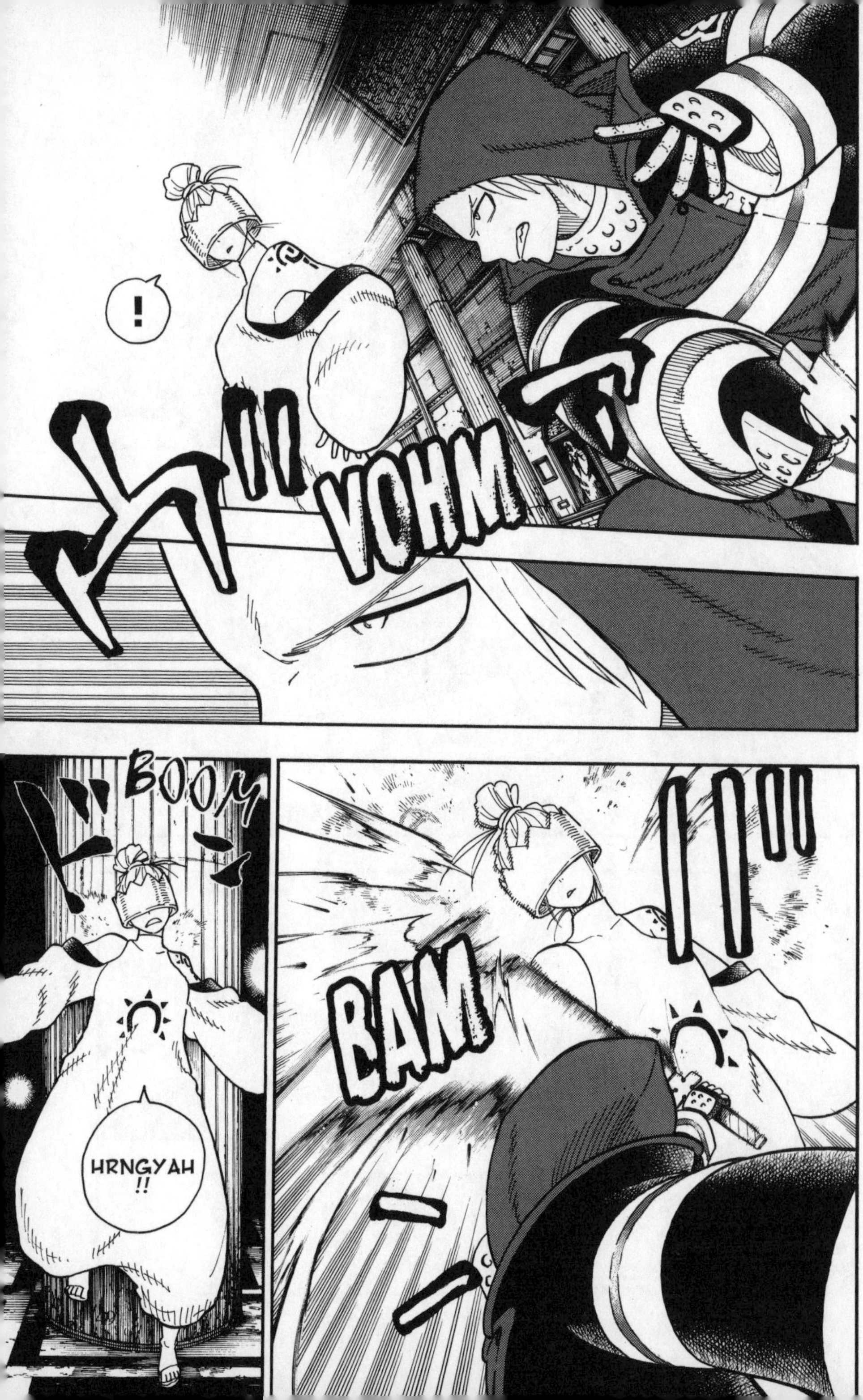
!
VOHM
BAM
BOOM
HRNGYAH !!

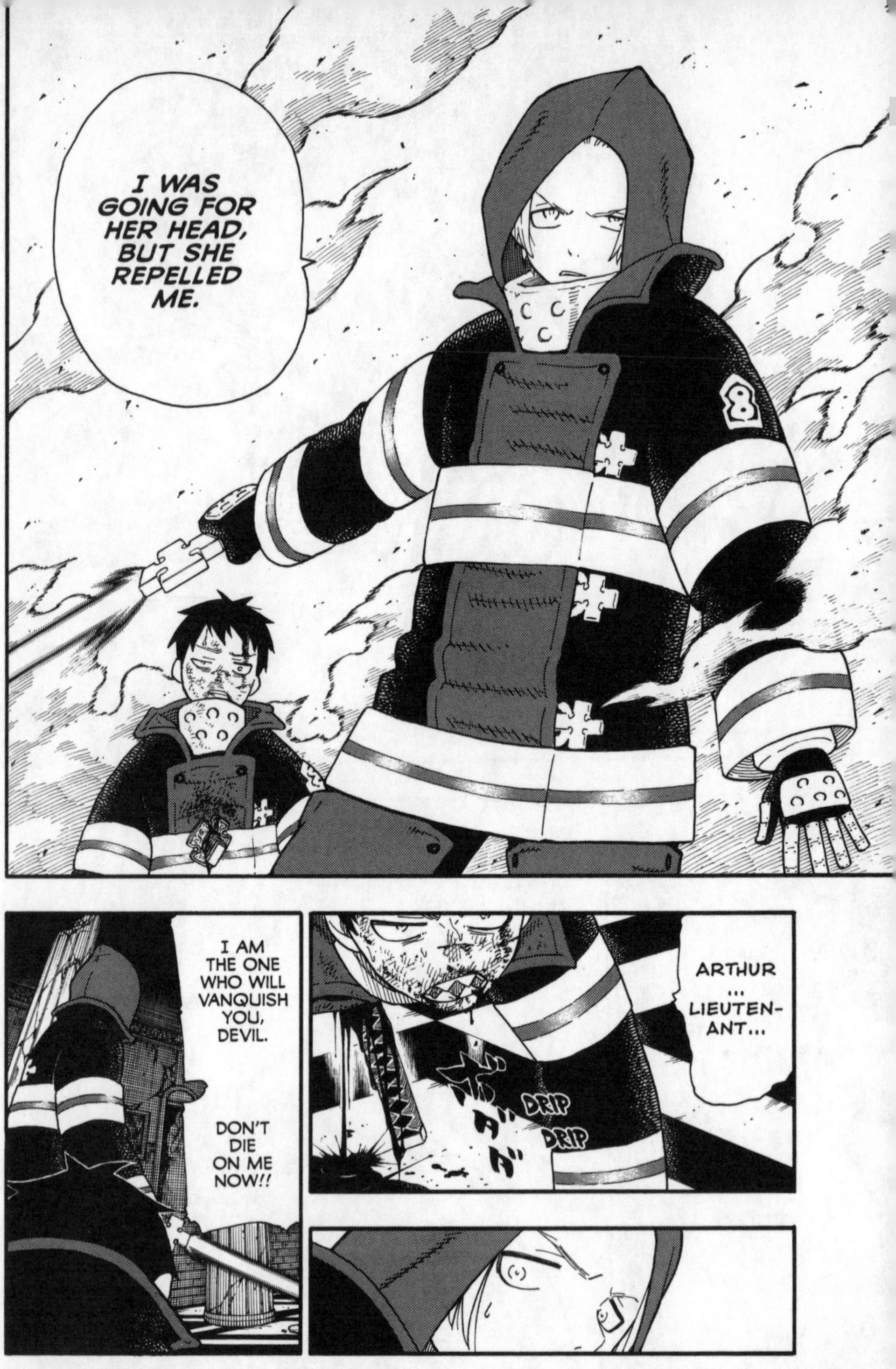
I WAS GOING FOR HER HEAD, BUT SHE REPELLED ME.
ARTHUR ... LIEUTEN-ANT...
DRIP
DRIP
I AM THE ONE WHO WILL VANQUISH YOU, DEVIL.
DON'T DIE ON ME NOW!!

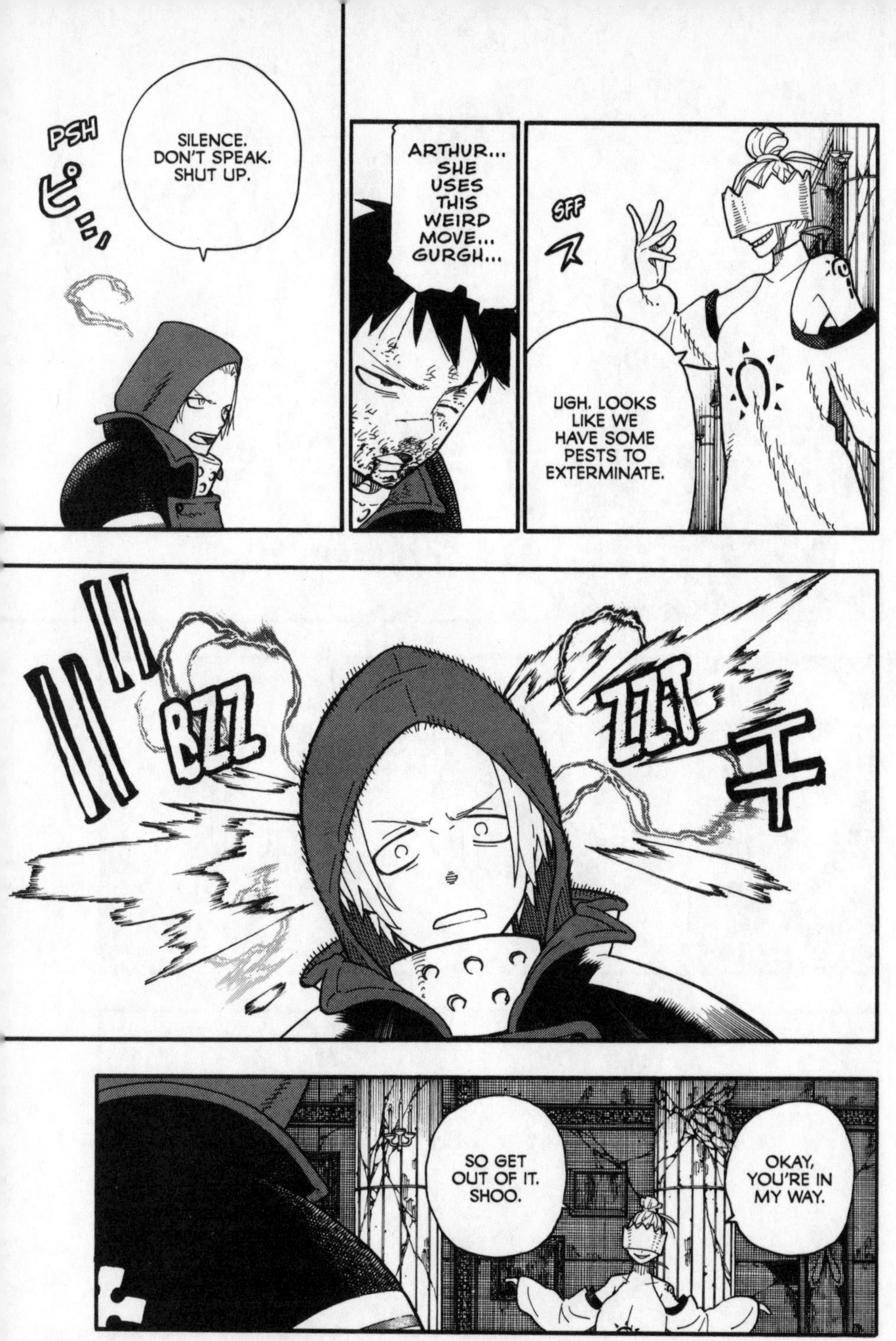
SFF
UGH. LOOKS LIKE WE HAVE SOME PESTS TO EXTERMINATE.
ARTHUR... SHE USES THIS WEIRD MOVE... GURGH...
PSH
SILENCE. DON'T SPEAK. SHUT UP.
ZZZT
BZZ
OKAY, YOU'RE IN MY WAY.
SO GET OUT OF IT. SHOO.

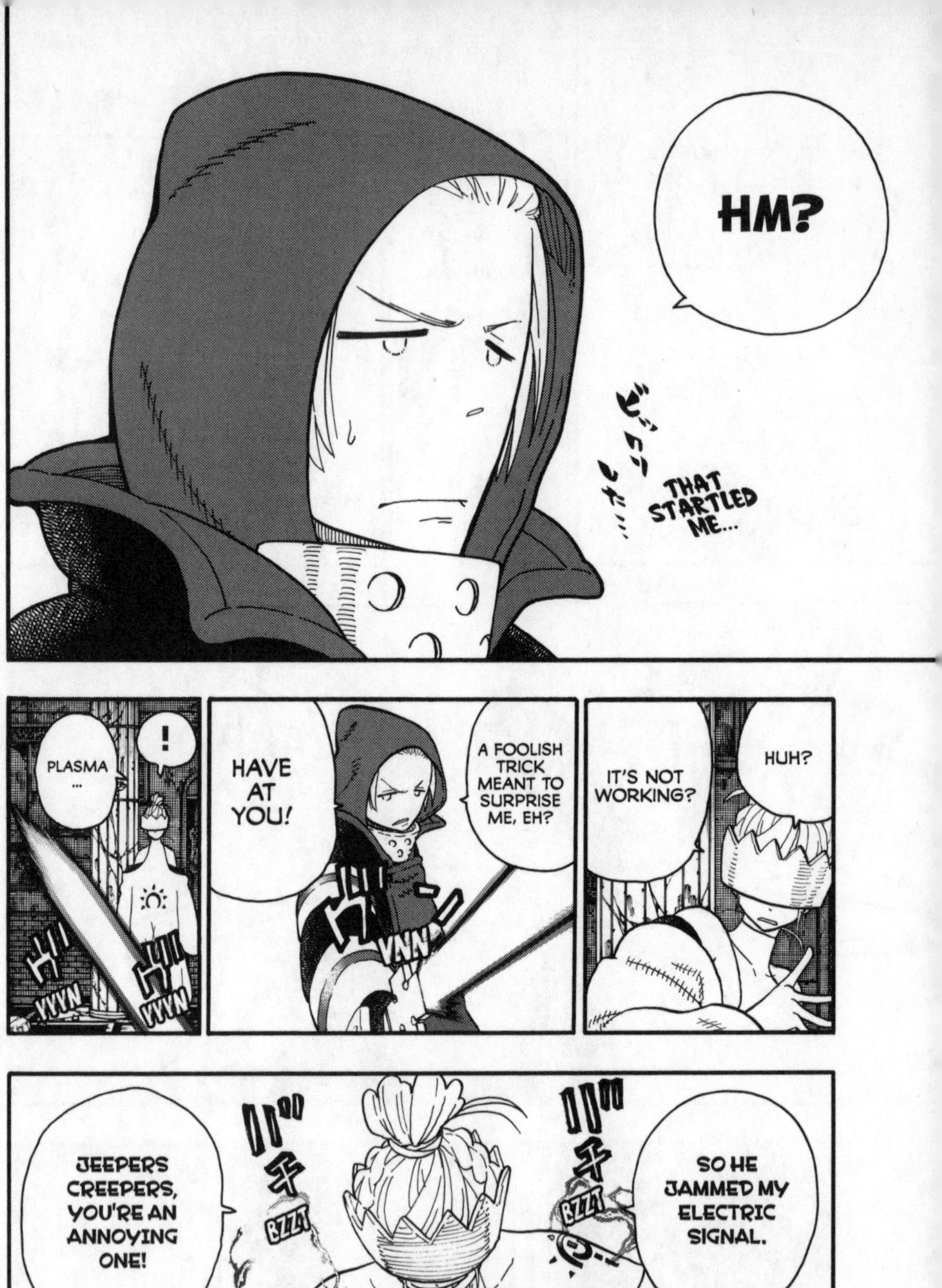
HM?
ビクッ した…
THAT STARTLED ME...
HUH?
IT'S NOT WORKING?
A FOOLISH TRICK MEANT TO SURPRISE ME, EH?
HAVE AT YOU!
VNN
!
PLASMA ...
VVVN
VVVN
SO HE JAMMED MY ELECTRIC SIGNAL.
BZZZT
JEEPERS CREEPERS, YOU'RE AN ANNOYING ONE!
BZZZT

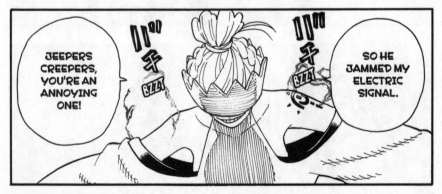

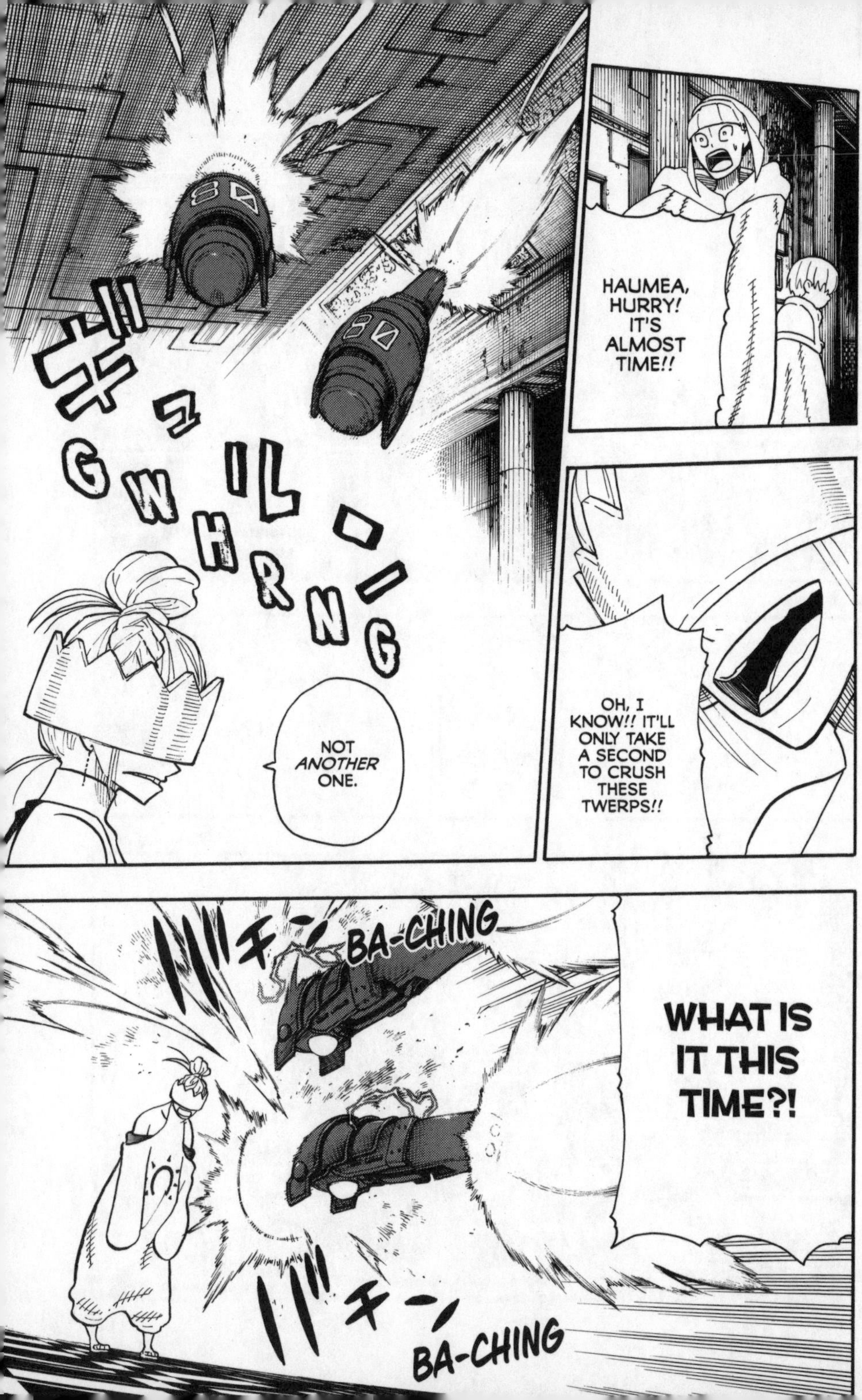
HAUMEA, HURRY! IT'S ALMOST TIME!!
OH, I KNOW!! IT'LL ONLY TAKE A SECOND TO CRUSH THESE TWERPS!!
GWHRNG
NOT *ANOTHER* ONE.
BA-CHING
WHAT IS IT THIS TIME?!
BA-CHING

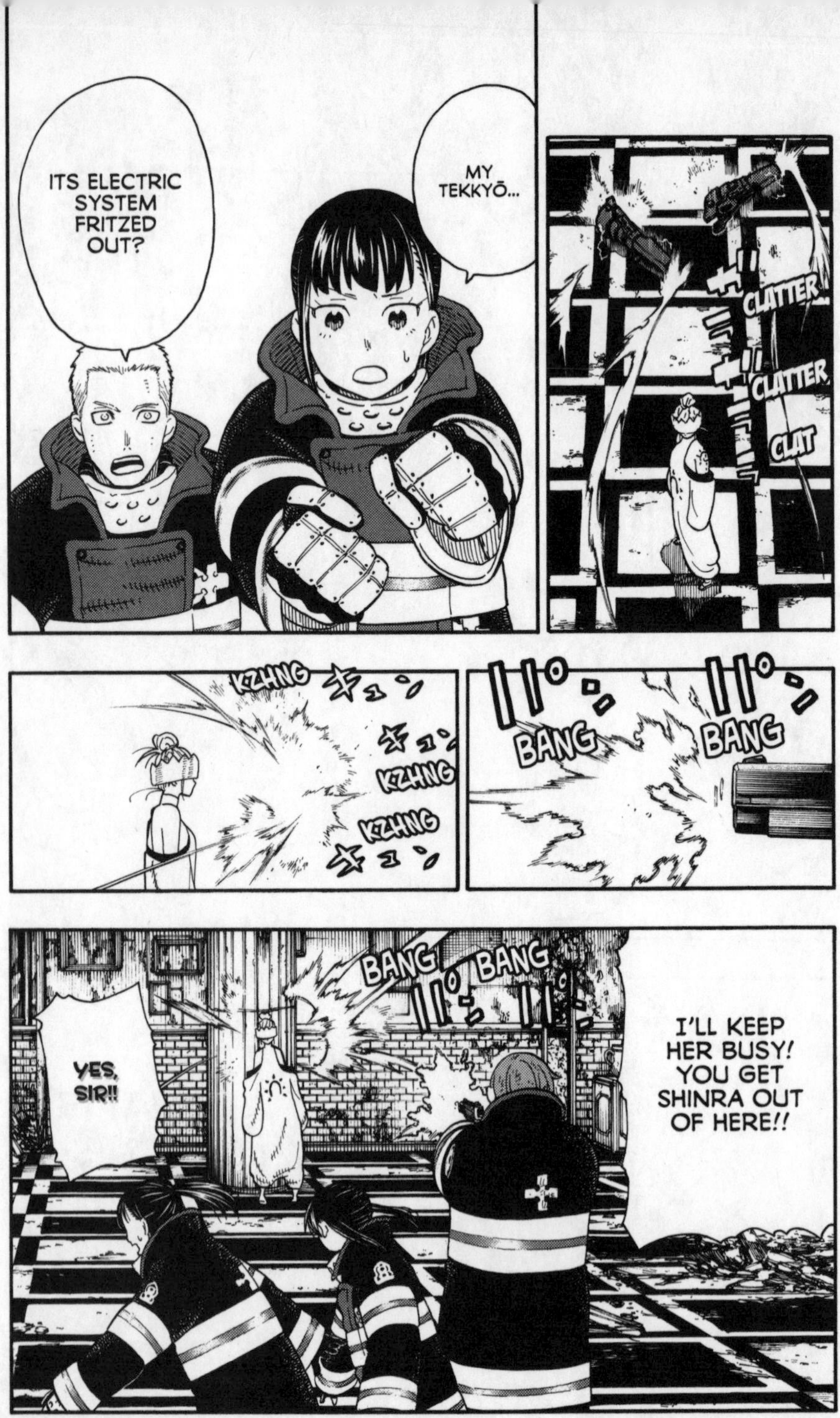
CLATTER
CLATTER
CLAT
MY TEKKYŌ...
ITS ELECTRIC SYSTEM FRITZED OUT?
BANG
BANG
KZHNG
KZHNG
KZHNG
BANG
BANG
I'LL KEEP HER BUSY! YOU GET SHINRA OUT OF HERE!!
YES, SIR!!

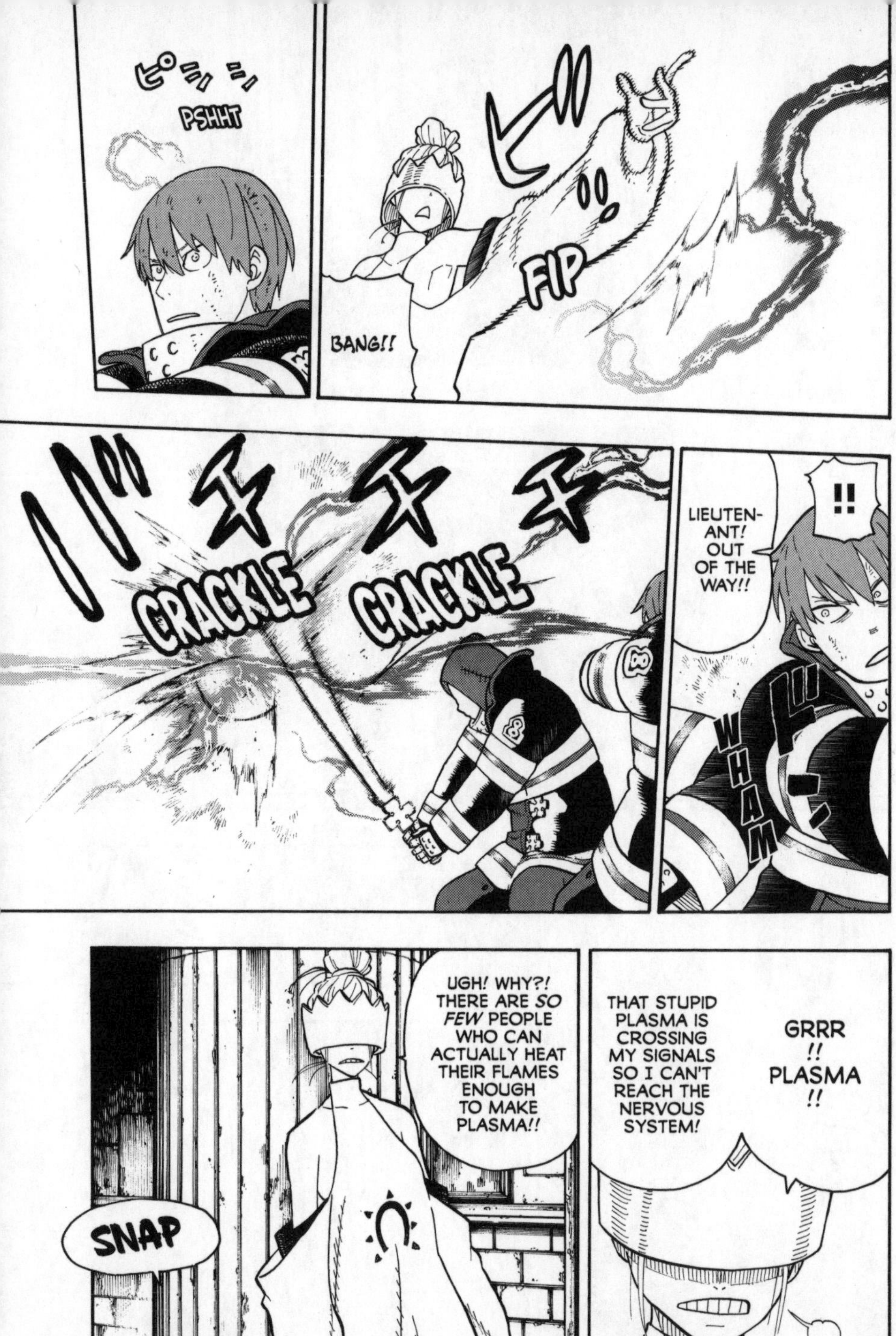
FIP
BANG!!
PSHHT
!!
LIEUTEN-ANT! OUT OF THE WAY!!
WHAM
CRACKLE
CRACKLE
GRRR!! PLASMA!!
THAT STUPID PLASMA IS CROSSING MY SIGNALS SO I CAN'T REACH THE NERVOUS SYSTEM!
UGH! WHY?! THERE ARE *SO FEW* PEOPLE WHO CAN ACTUALLY HEAT THEIR FLAMES ENOUGH TO MAKE PLASMA!!
SNAP

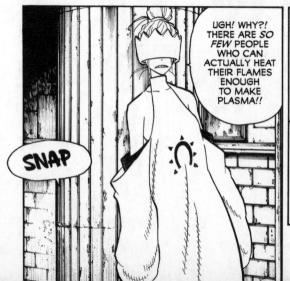

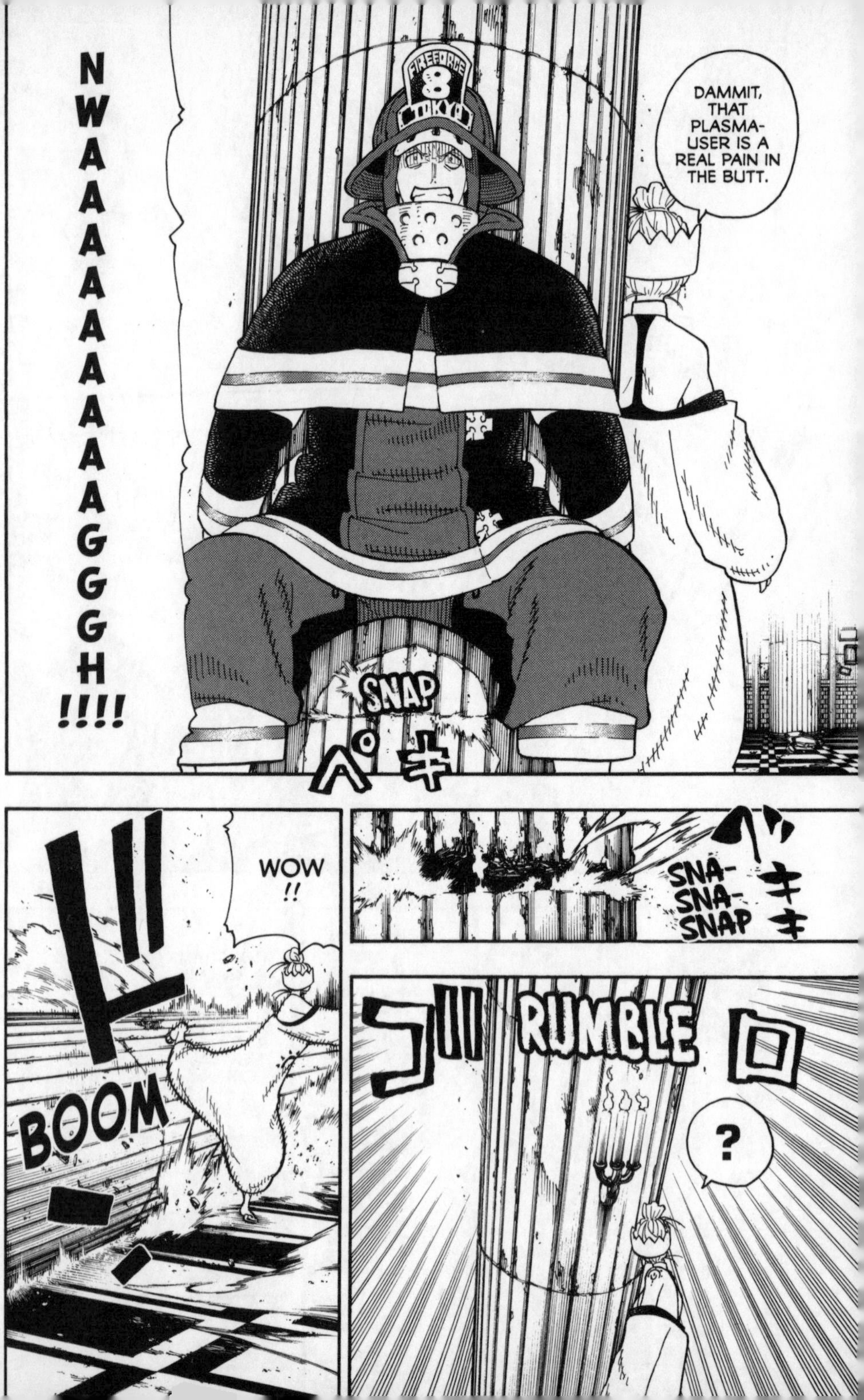
DAMMIT, THAT PLASMA-USER IS A REAL PAIN IN THE BUTT.
NWAAAAAAAAAAAAAGGGGH!!!!
SNAP
ペキ
SNA-SNA-SNAP
ベキキ
ゴロ
RUMBLE
?
WOW!!
ド
BOOM

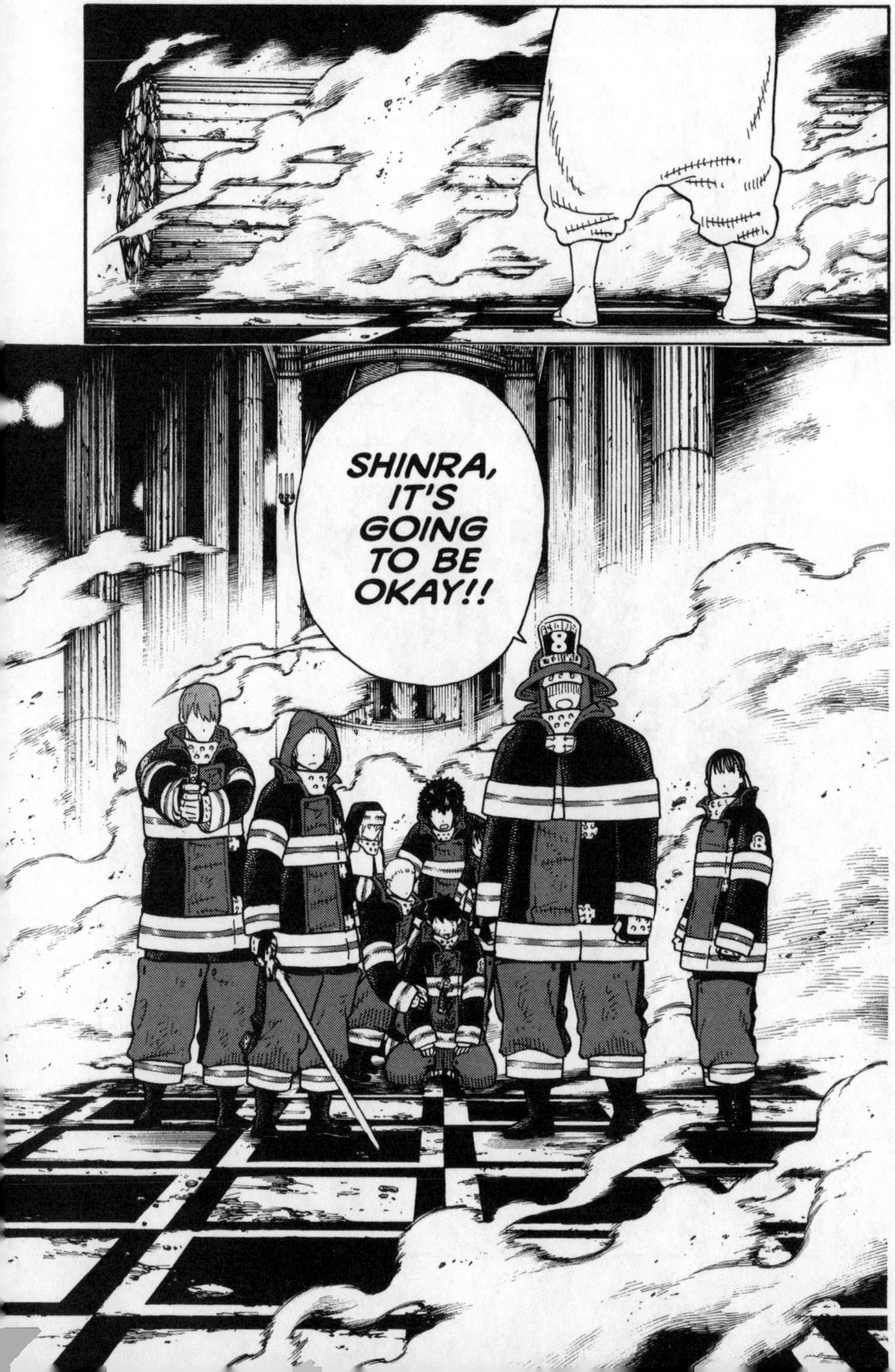
SHINRA, IT'S GOING TO BE OKAY!!

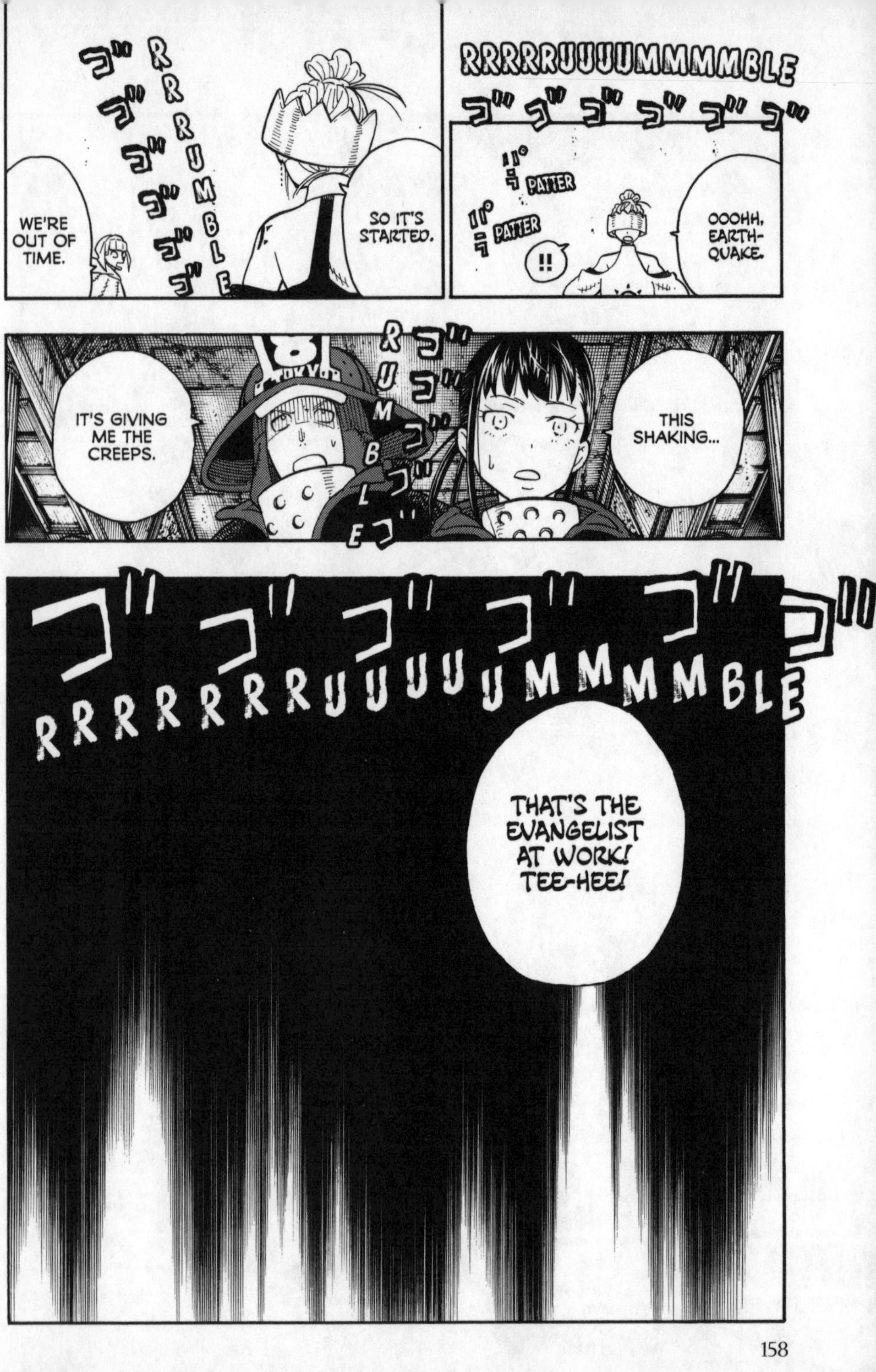
RRRRRUUUUMMMMMBLE
ゴゴゴゴゴゴ
OOOHH, EARTH-QUAKE.
パラ PATTER
パラ PATTER
!!
SO IT'S STARTED.
ゴゴゴゴゴゴ RRRUMBLE
WE'RE OUT OF TIME.
THIS SHAKING...
ゴゴゴゴゴゴ RUMBLE
IT'S GIVING ME THE CREEPS.
ゴゴゴゴゴゴ
RRRRRRRUUUUUMMMMMBLE
THAT'S THE EVANGELIST AT WORK! TEE-HEE!

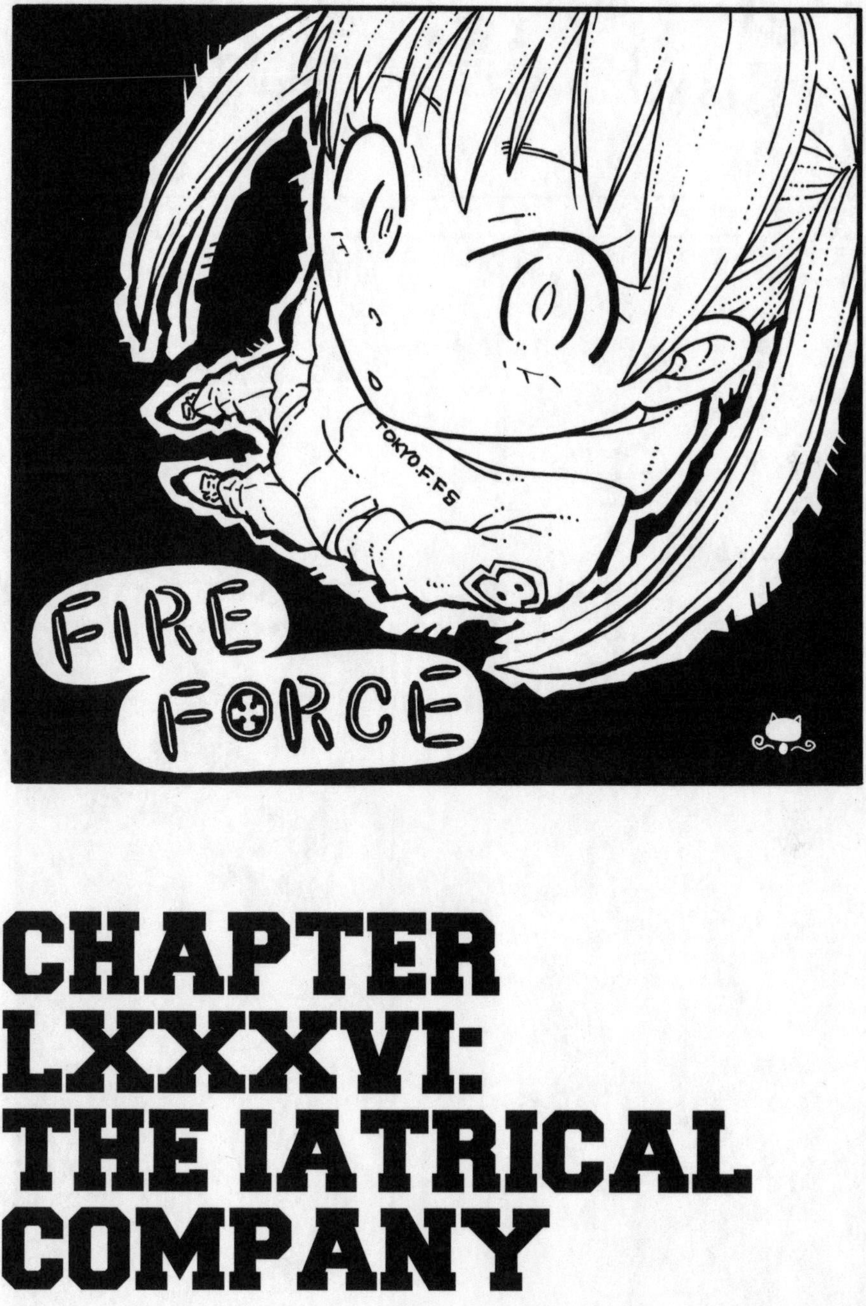
TOKYO.F.F.S
FIRE
FORCE

CHAPTER LXXXVI: THE IATRICAL COMPANY

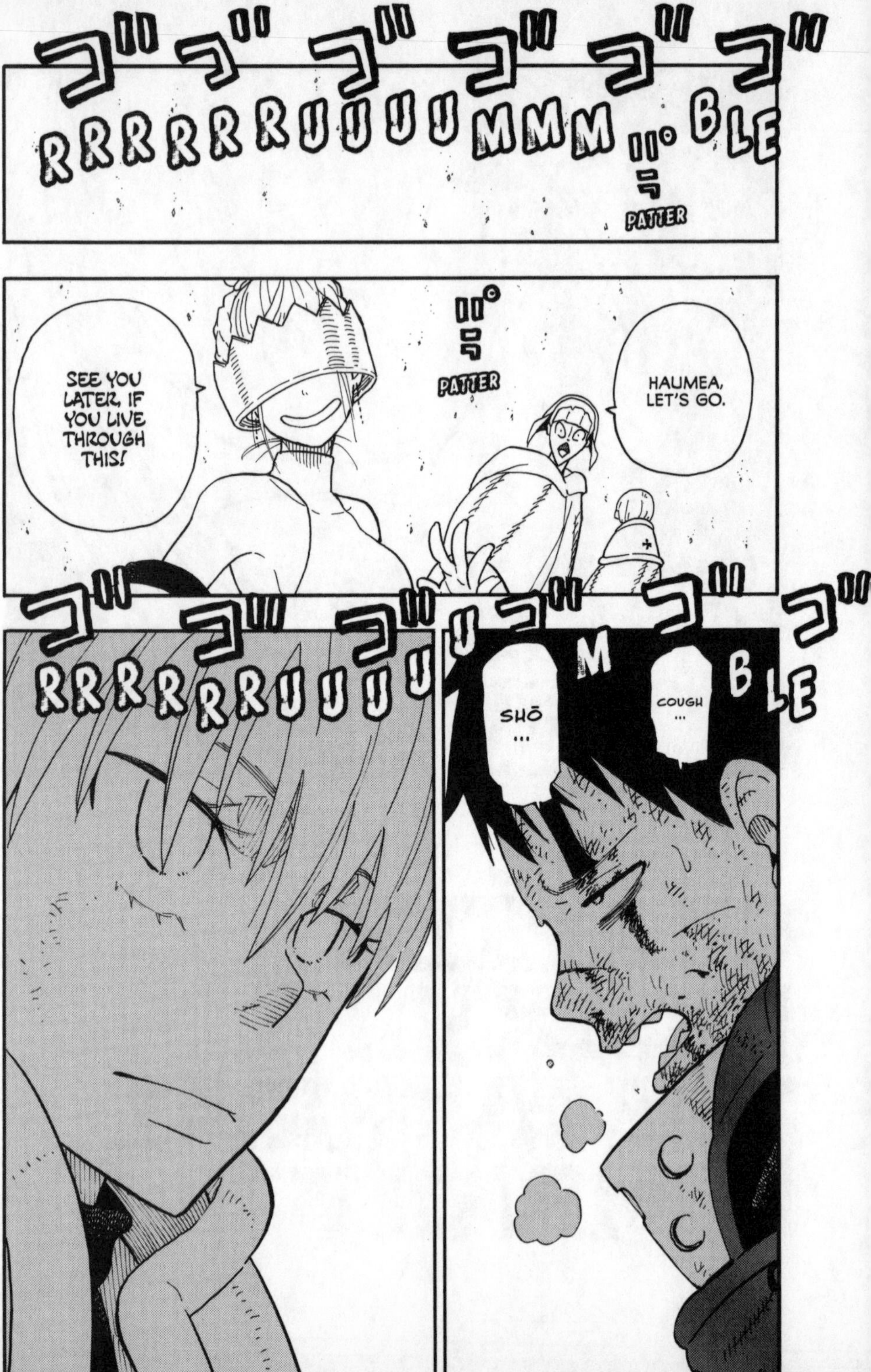
ゴゴゴゴゴゴ
RRRRRUUUUUMMMMBLE
パラ
PATTER
HAUMEA, LET'S GO.
パラ
PATTER
SEE YOU LATER, IF YOU LIVE THROUGH THIS!
ゴゴゴゴゴゴ
RRRRRRUUUUUMBLE
COUGH ...
SHŌ ...

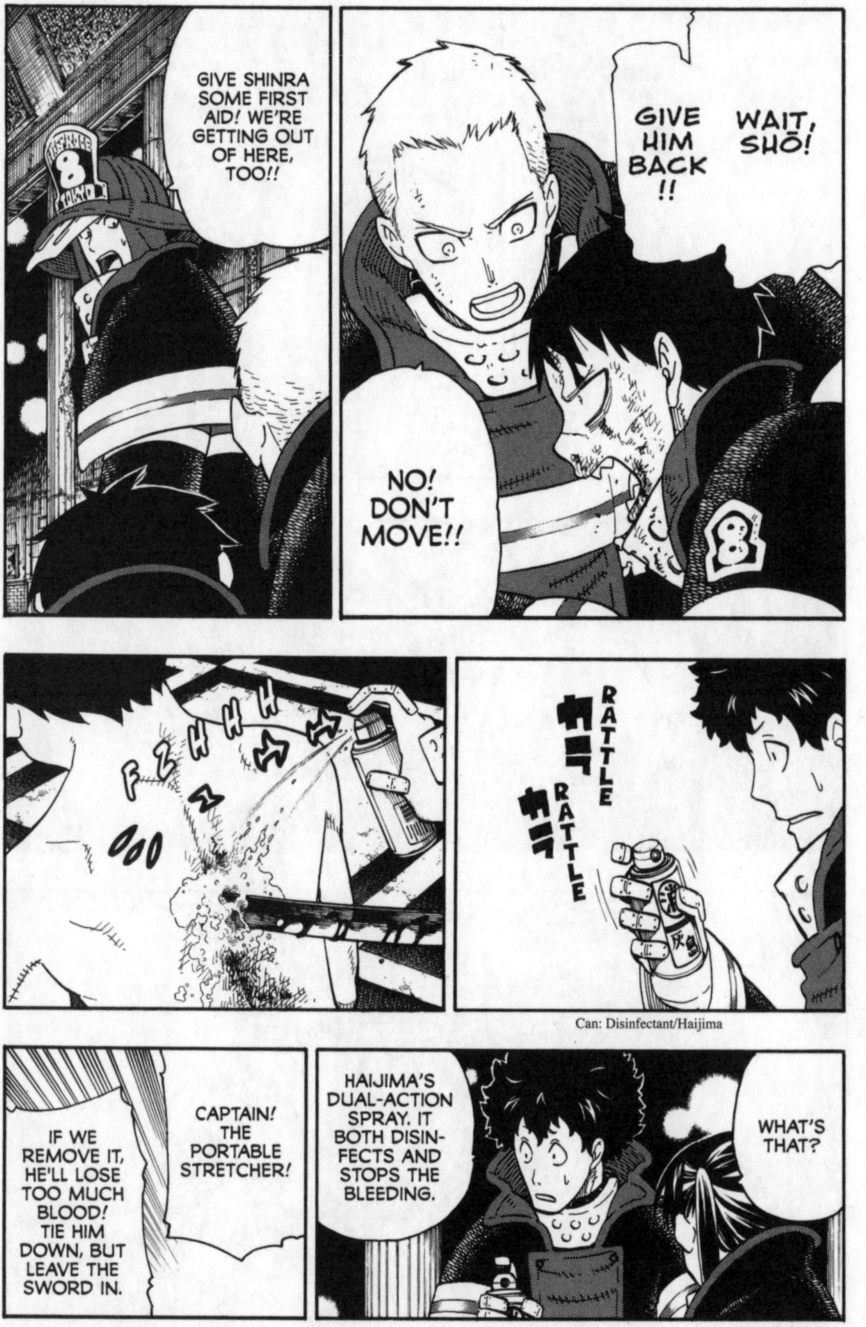
WAIT, SHŌ!
GIVE HIM BACK!!
NO! DON'T MOVE!!
GIVE SHINRA SOME FIRST AID! WE'RE GETTING OUT OF HERE, TOO!!
RATTLE
RATTLE
FZHHHH
WHAT'S THAT?
HAIJIMA'S DUAL-ACTION SPRAY. IT BOTH DISIN-FECTS AND STOPS THE BLEEDING.
CAPTAIN! THE PORTABLE STRETCHER!
IF WE REMOVE IT, HE'LL LOSE TOO MUCH BLOOD! TIE HIM DOWN, BUT LEAVE THE SWORD IN.
Can: Disinfectant/Haijima

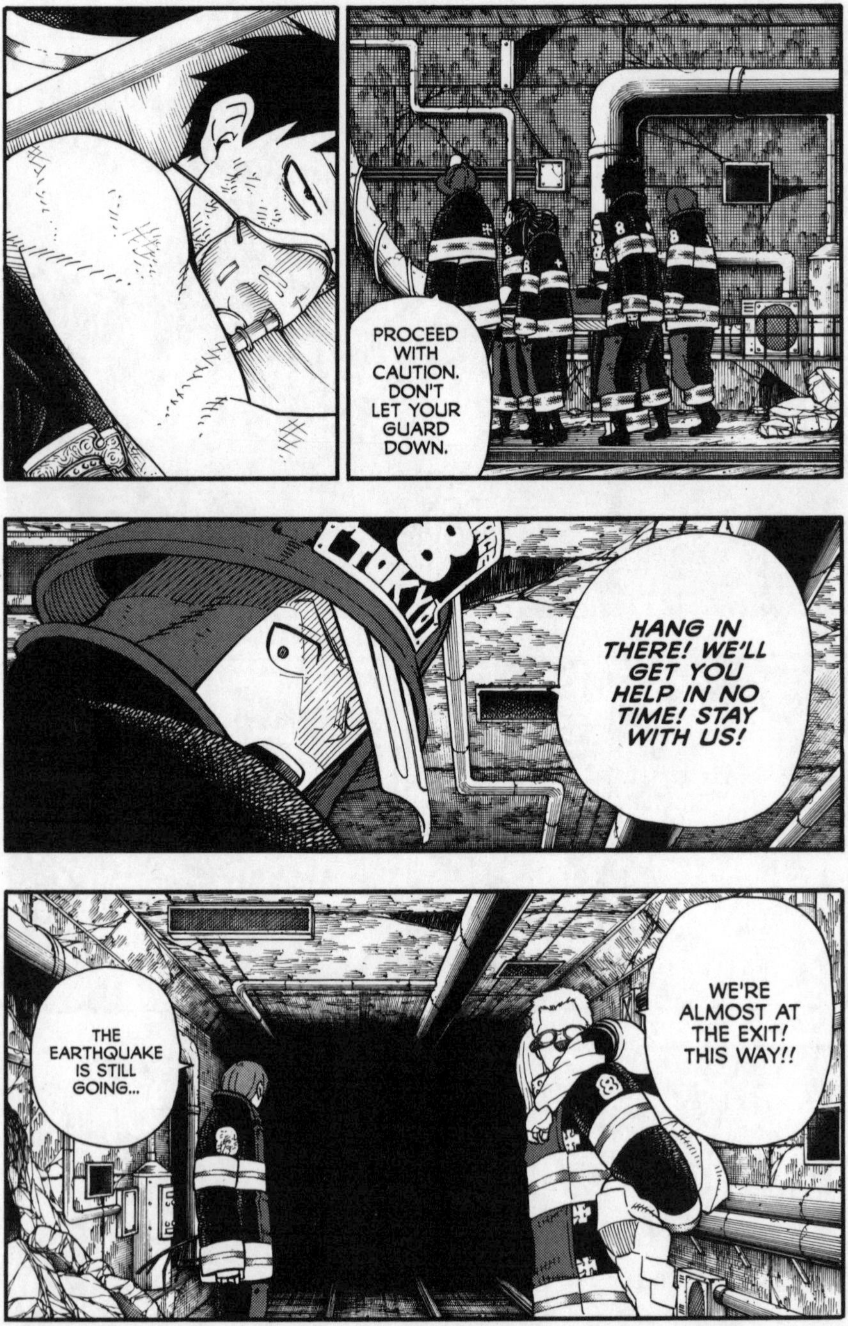
PROCEED WITH CAUTION. DON'T LET YOUR GUARD DOWN.
HANG IN THERE! WE'LL GET YOU HELP IN NO TIME! STAY WITH US!
WE'RE ALMOST AT THE EXIT! THIS WAY!!
THE EARTHQUAKE IS STILL GOING...

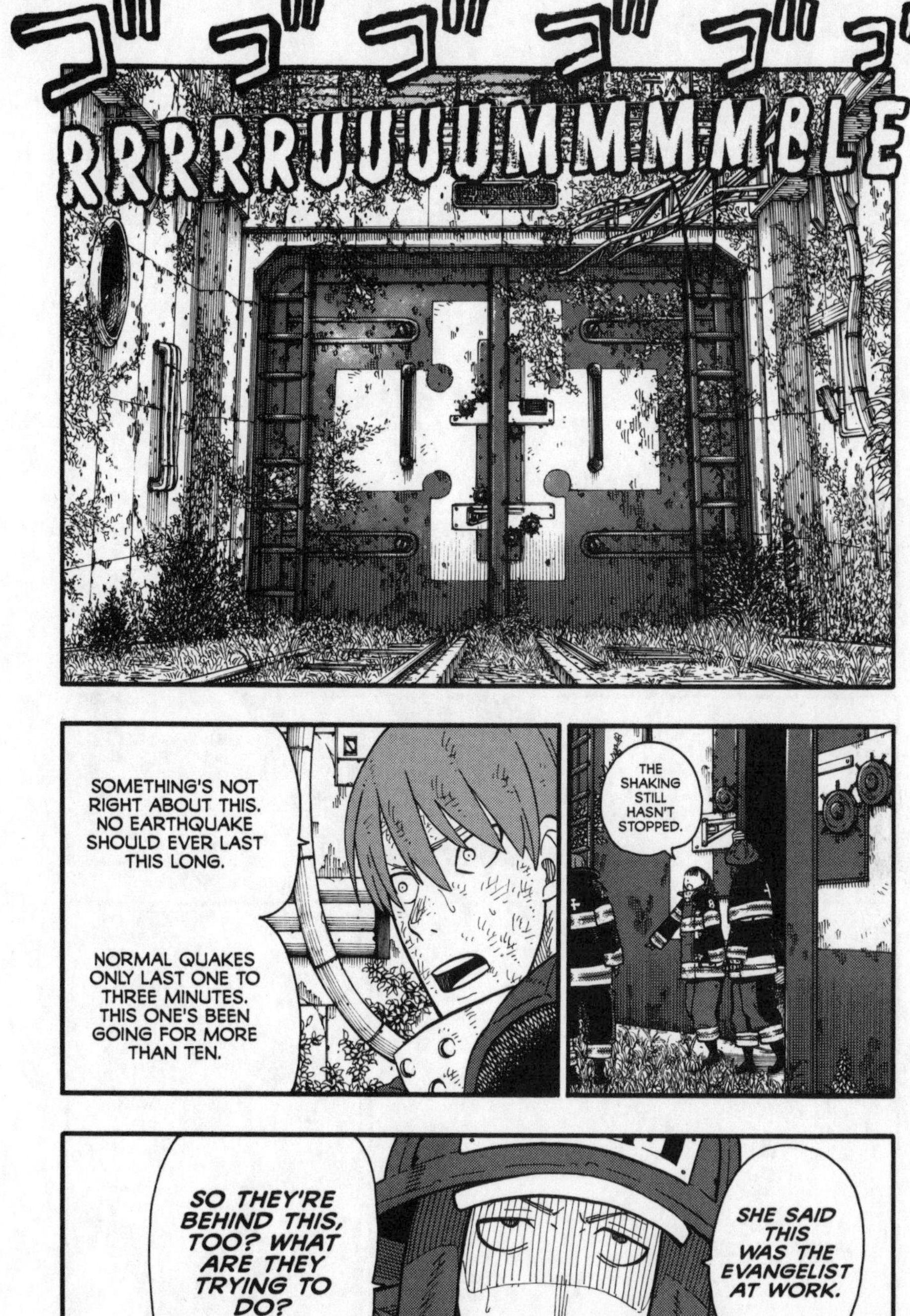
ゴゴゴゴゴゴ
RRRRRUUUUUMMMMMBLE
THE SHAKING STILL HASN'T STOPPED.
SOMETHING'S NOT RIGHT ABOUT THIS. NO EARTHQUAKE SHOULD EVER LAST THIS LONG.
NORMAL QUAKES ONLY LAST ONE TO THREE MINUTES. THIS ONE'S BEEN GOING FOR MORE THAN TEN.
SHE SAID THIS WAS THE EVANGELIST AT WORK.
SO THEY'RE BEHIND THIS, TOO? WHAT ARE THEY TRYING TO DO?

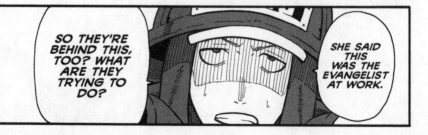

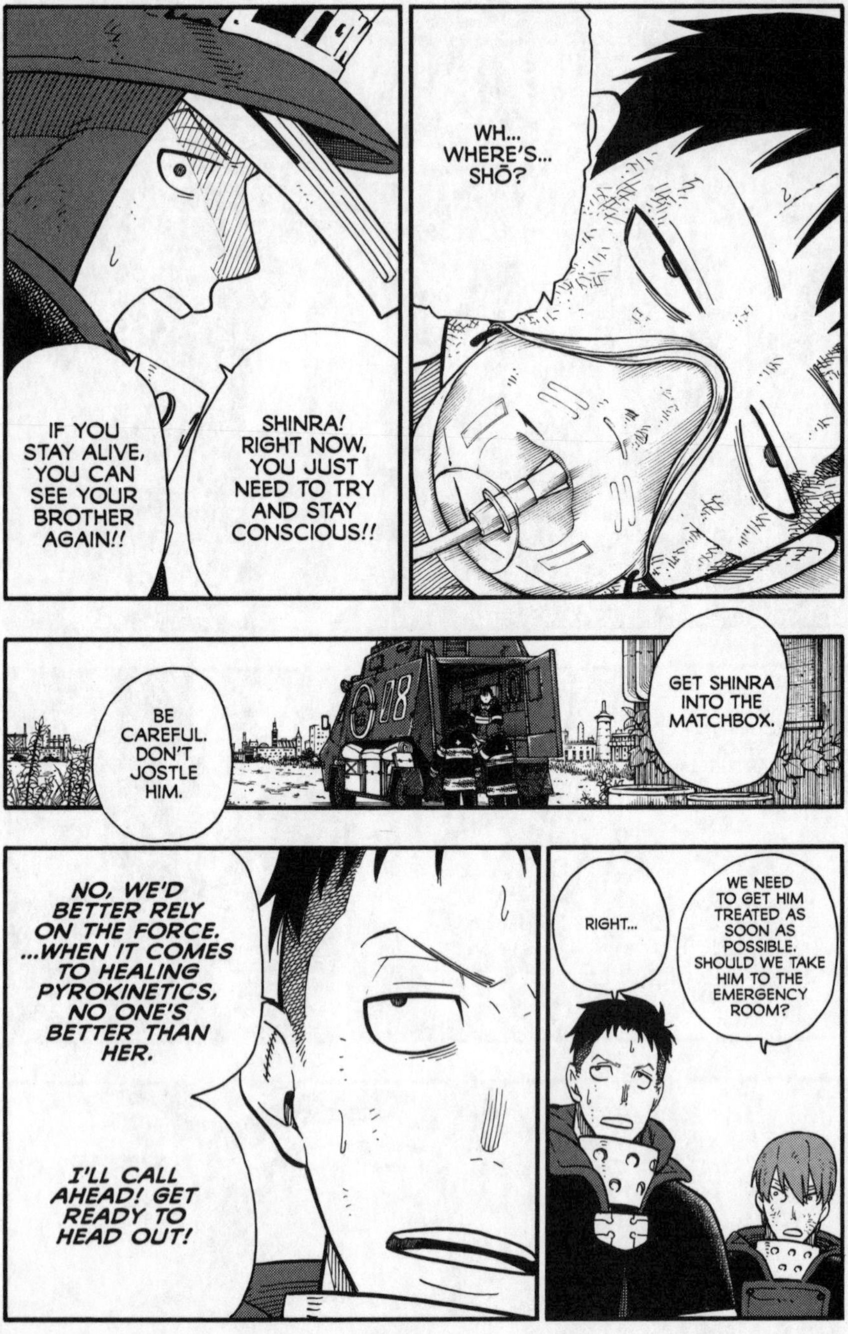
WH... WHERE'S... SHŌ?
SHINRA! RIGHT NOW, YOU JUST NEED TO TRY AND STAY CONSCIOUS!!
IF YOU STAY ALIVE, YOU CAN SEE YOUR BROTHER AGAIN!!
GET SHINRA INTO THE MATCHBOX.
BE CAREFUL. DON'T JOSTLE HIM.
WE NEED TO GET HIM TREATED AS SOON AS POSSIBLE. SHOULD WE TAKE HIM TO THE EMERGENCY ROOM?
RIGHT...
NO, WE'D BETTER RELY ON THE FORCE. ...WHEN IT COMES TO HEALING PYROKINETICS, NO ONE'S BETTER THAN HER.
I'LL CALL AHEAD! GET READY TO HEAD OUT!

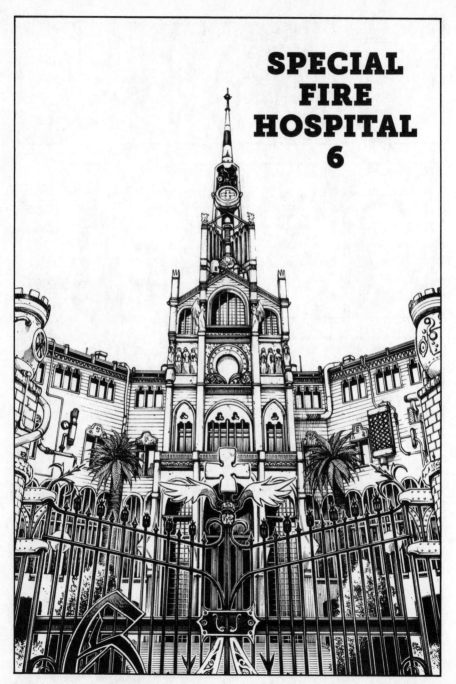

SPECIAL
FIRE
HOSPITAL
6

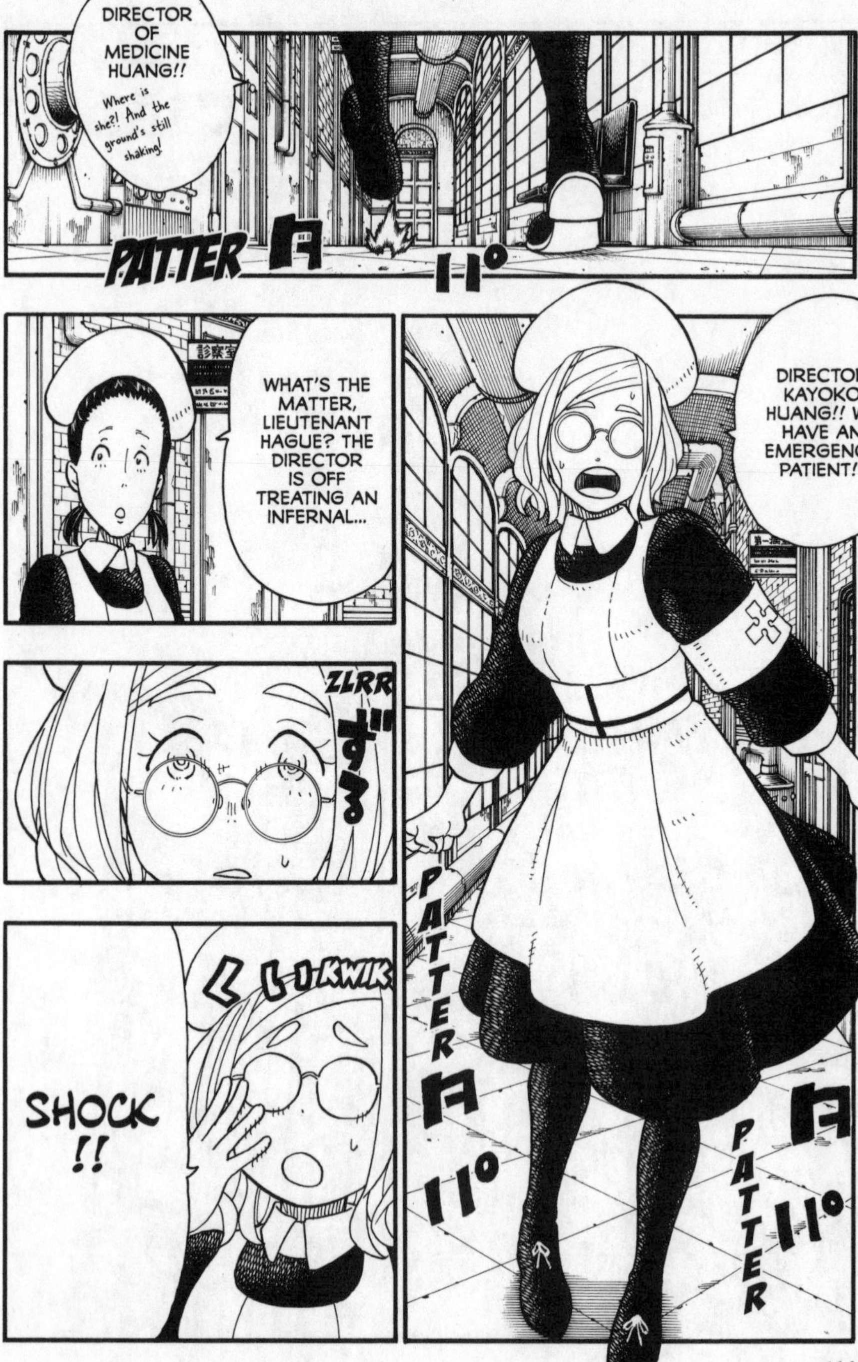
DIRECTOR OF MEDICINE HUANG!!
Where is she?! And the ground's still shaking!
PATTER
DIRECTOR KAYOKO HUANG!! WE HAVE AN EMERGENCY PATIENT!!
PATTER
PATTER
WHAT'S THE MATTER, LIEUTENANT HAGUE? THE DIRECTOR IS OFF TREATING AN INFERNAL...
ZLRR
ずる
KWIK
SHOCK !!

RRRUUUMMBLE

WEE-OO

DIRECTOR HUANG WILL BE PERFORMING THE OPERATION PERSONALLY!

WE'RE READY TO BEGIN! THIS WAY, DIRECTOR!

FIRE FORCE 6 TOKYO

ZSH

ZSH

ZSH

I WILL NOW PERFORM THE EXTINGUISHING PROCEDURE FOR THIS IN-FERNAL.

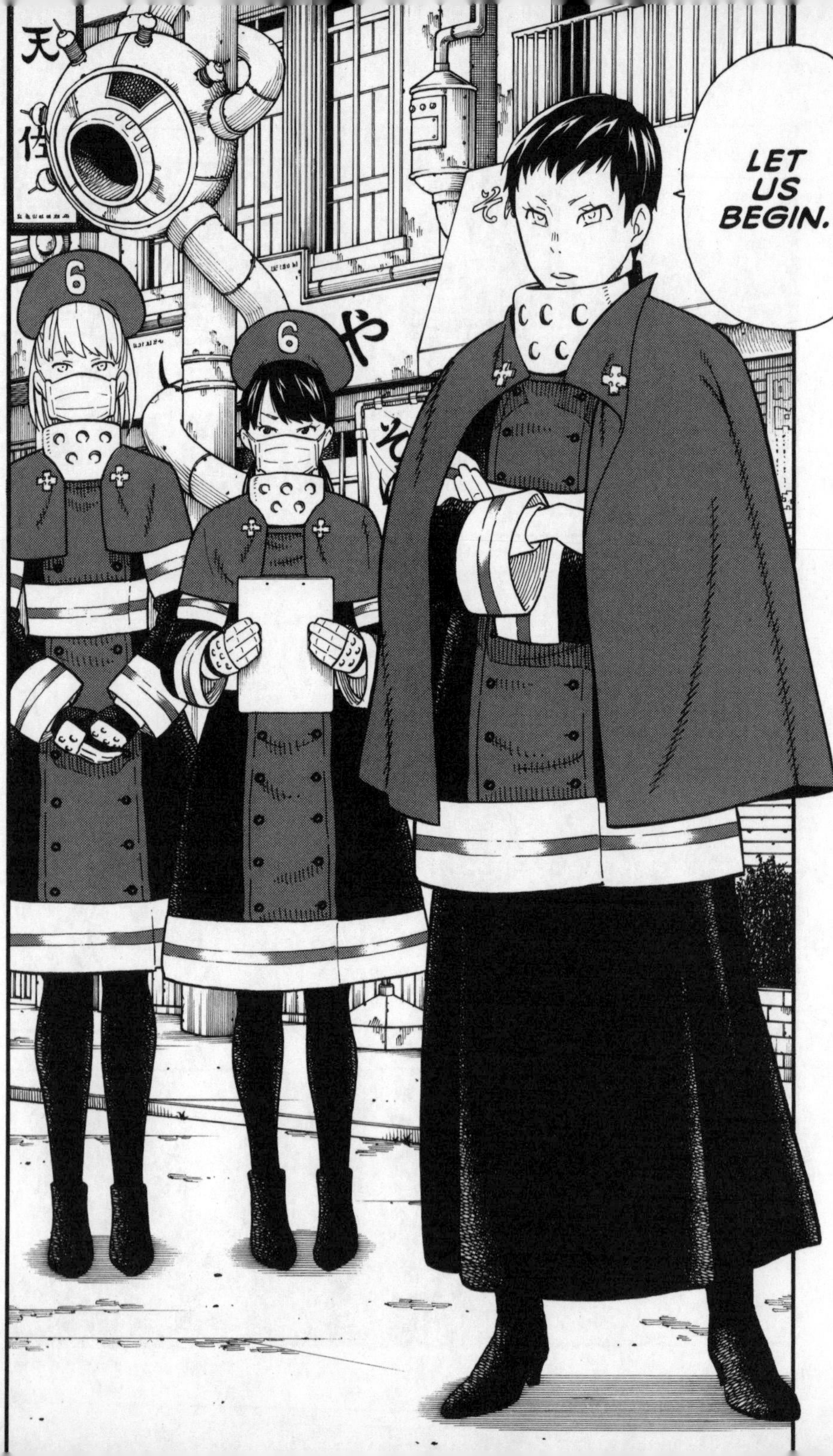
LET US BEGIN.

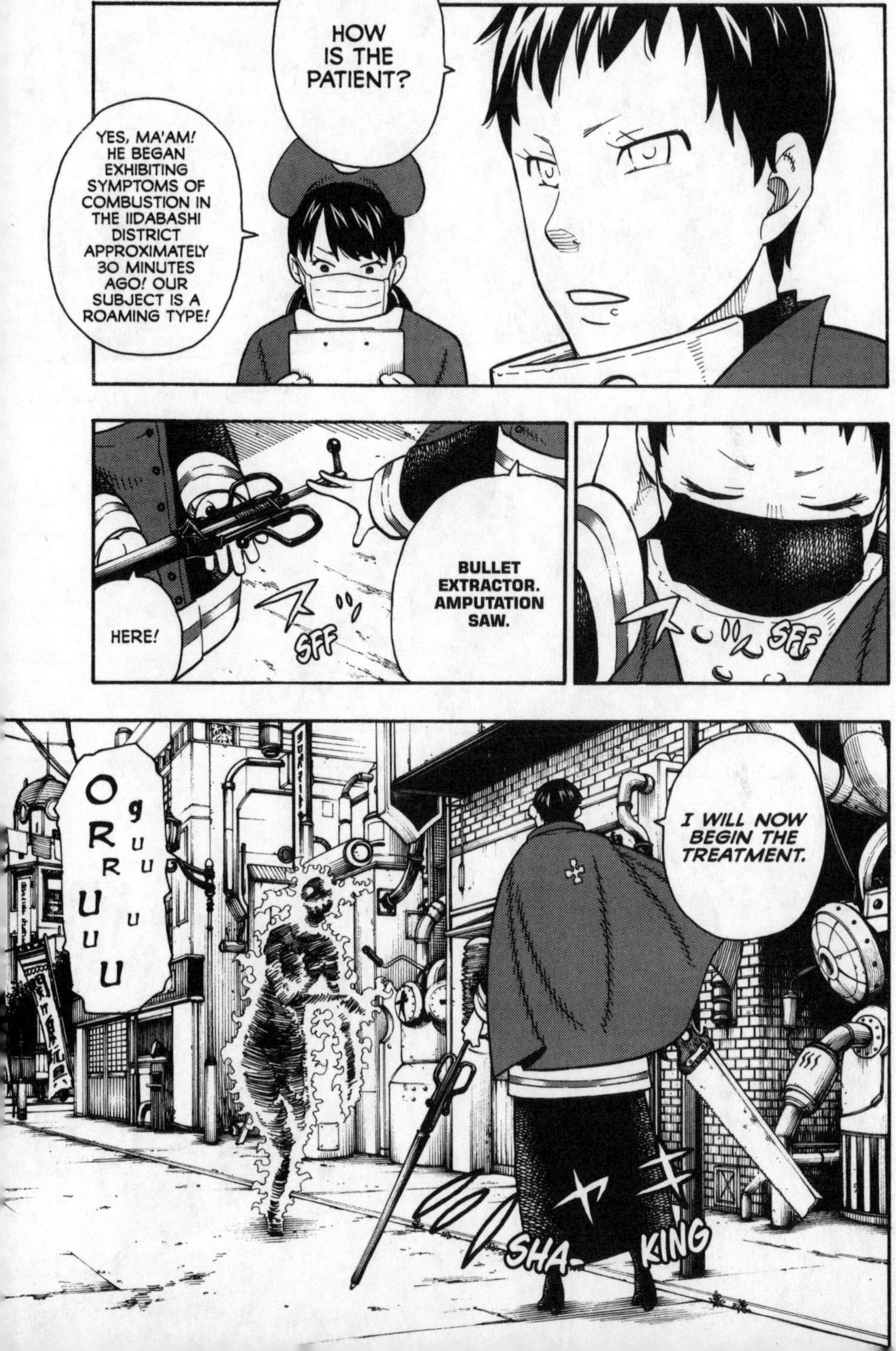
HOW IS THE PATIENT?
YES, MA'AM! HE BEGAN EXHIBITING SYMPTOMS OF COMBUSTION IN THE IIDABASHI DISTRICT APPROXIMATELY 30 MINUTES AGO! OUR SUBJECT IS A ROAMING TYPE!
SFF
BULLET EXTRACTOR. AMPUTATION SAW.
HERE!
SFF
I WILL NOW BEGIN THE TREATMENT.
ORRUUU
SHA-KING

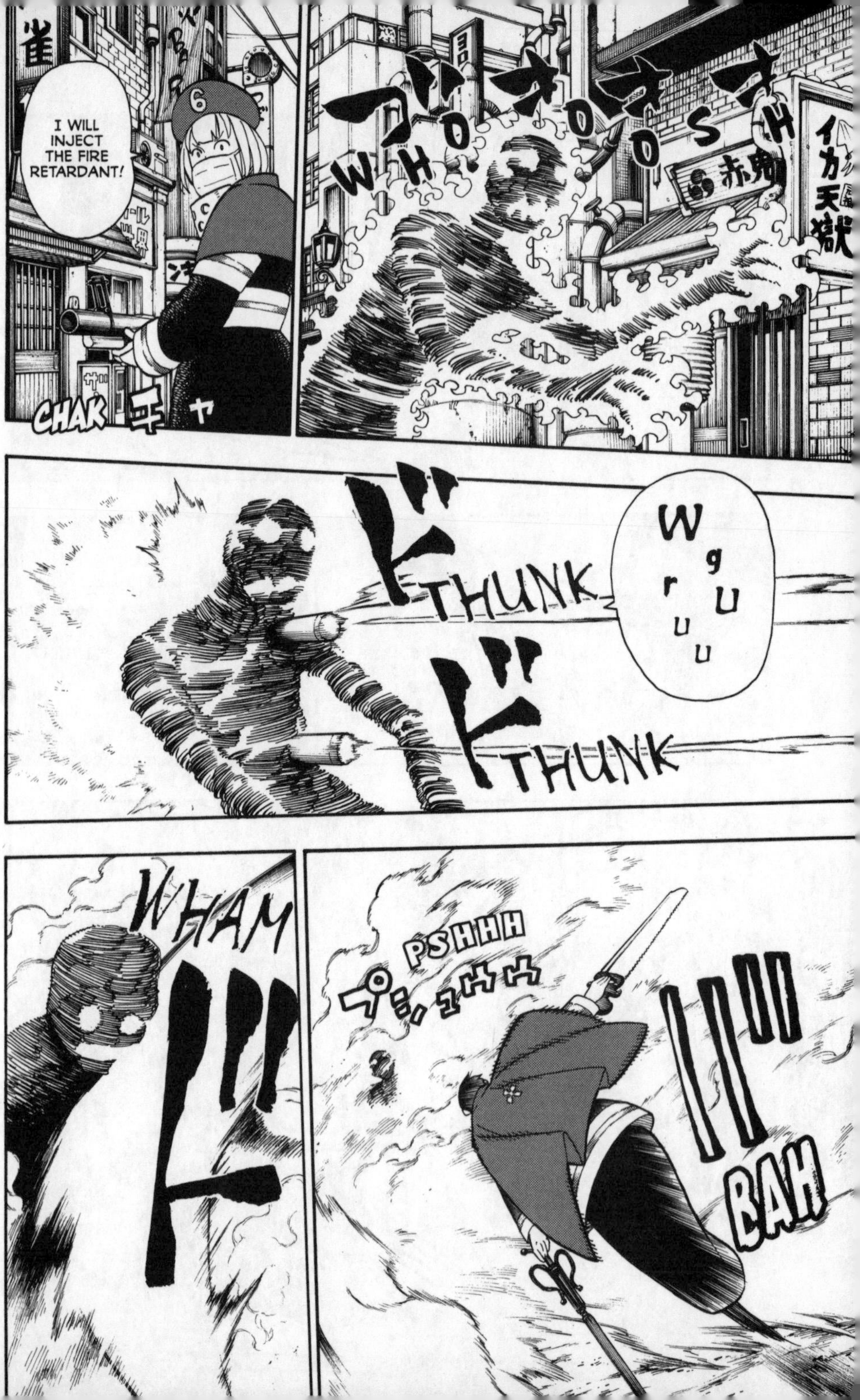
WHOOSH
I WILL INJECT THE FIRE RETARDANT!
CHAK
THUNK
Wgruuu
THUNK
PSHHH
BAH
WHAM

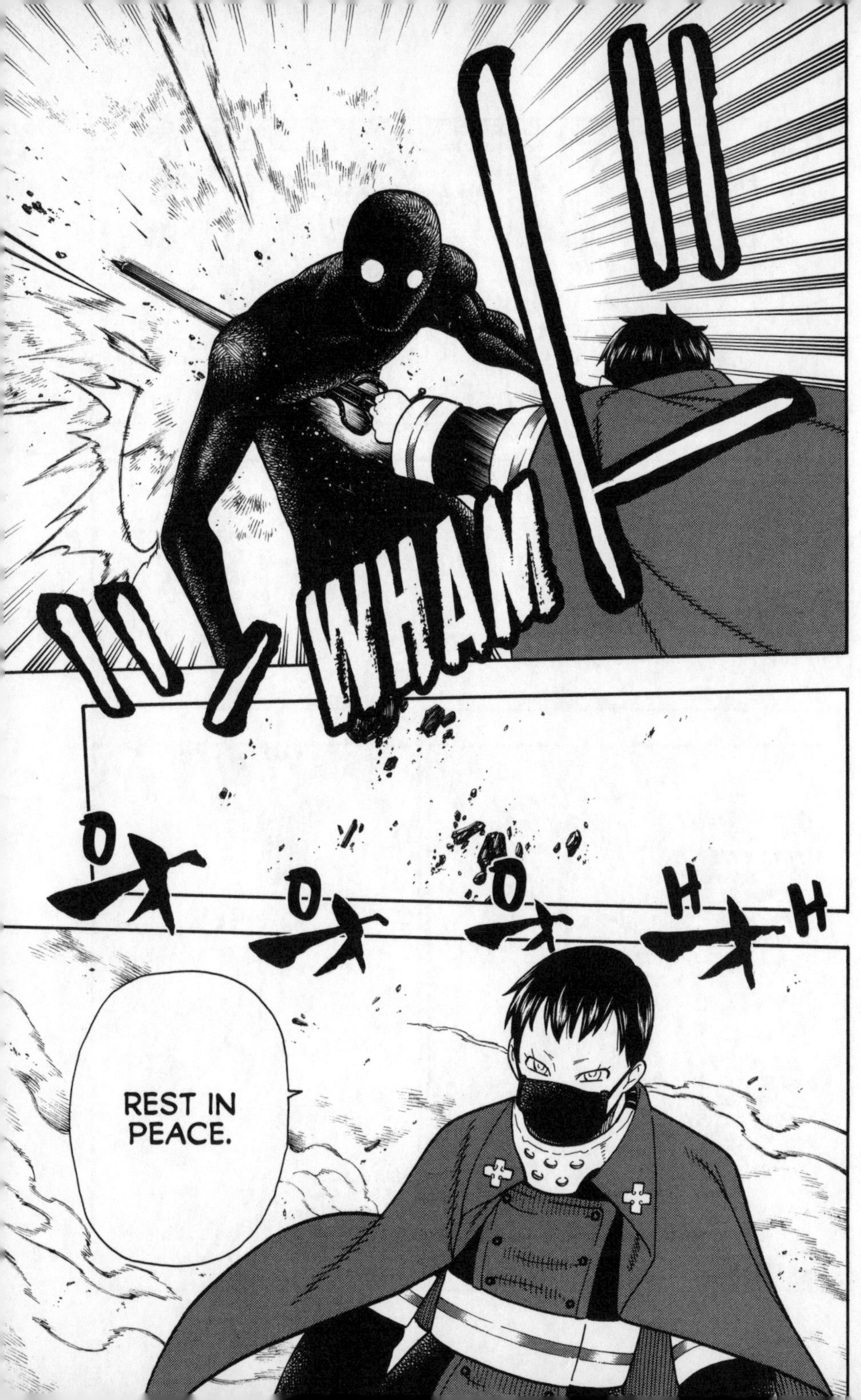
WHAM!!
OOOHH
REST IN PEACE.

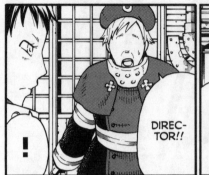

THE REST IS UP TO YOU, FATHER.
WELL DONE, MA'AM.
DIREC-TOR!!
!
WE HAVE AN EMERGENCY PATIENT AT HOSPITAL 6! WILL YOU PLEASE COME BACK WITH ME?!
WE RECEIVED A CALL FROM COMPANY 8. ONE OF THEIR SOLDIERS HAS BEEN BADLY INJURED!
BUT WHY WOULD THEY COME TO US?
IF A SOLDIER GETS INJURED ON A CALL, ANY HOSPITAL CAN TREAT THEM.
THE PATIENT IS A PYROKINETIC. WHAT'S MORE, HE HAS THE ADOLLA BURST!
HE IS IN EXTREMELY CRITICAL CONDITION! THEY NEED YOUR HELP!

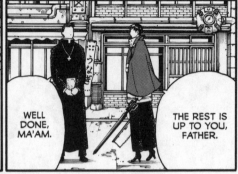

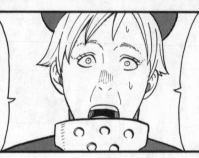

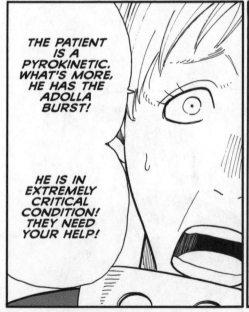

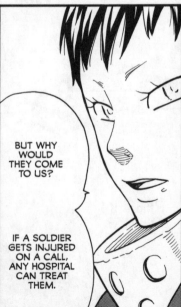

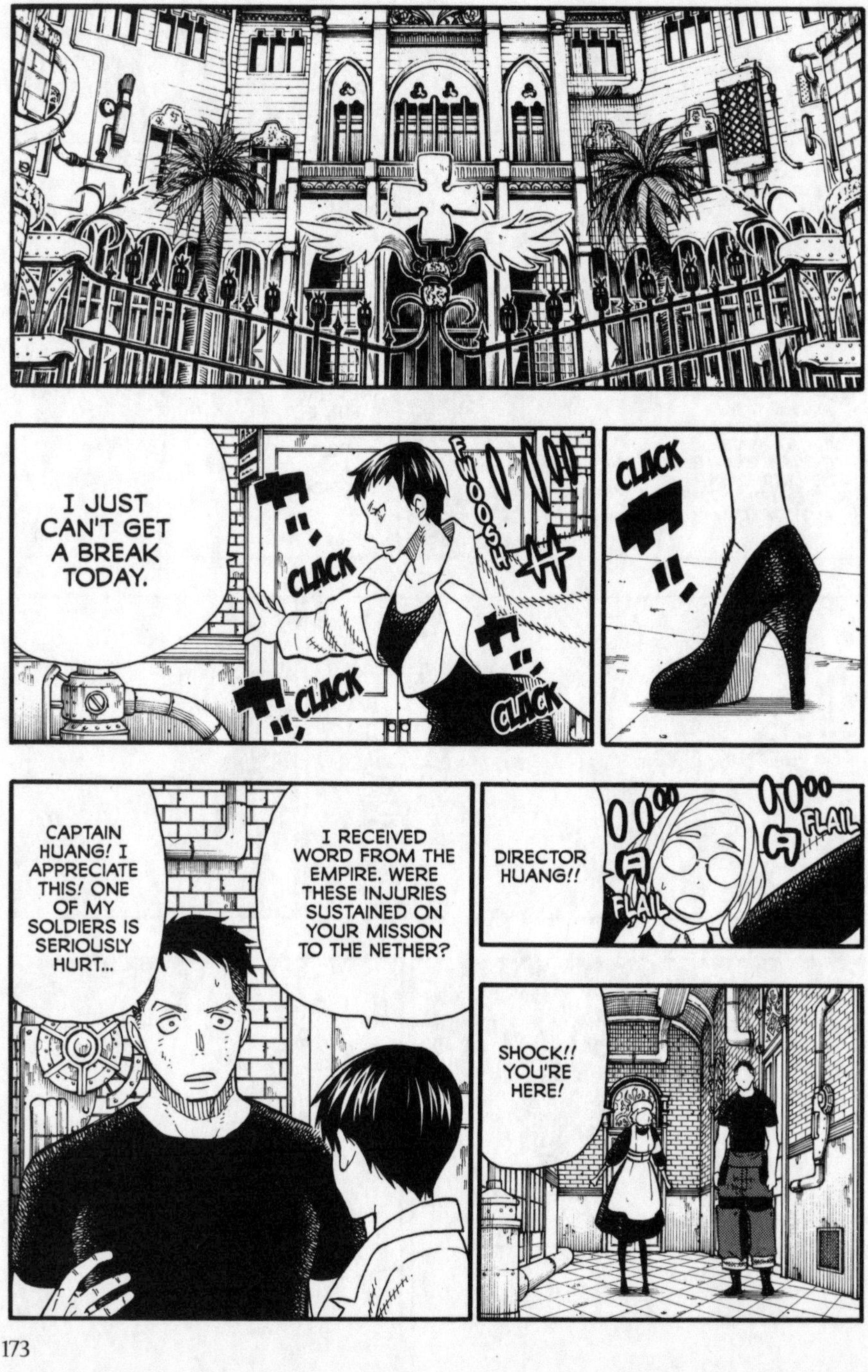
CLACK
I JUST CAN'T GET A BREAK TODAY.
FWOOSH
CLACK
CLACK
CLACK
DIRECTOR HUANG!!
FLAIL
FLAIL
SHOCK!! YOU'RE HERE!
I RECEIVED WORD FROM THE EMPIRE. WERE THESE INJURIES SUSTAINED ON YOUR MISSION TO THE NETHER?
CAPTAIN HUANG! I APPRECIATE THIS! ONE OF MY SOLDIERS IS SERIOUSLY HURT...

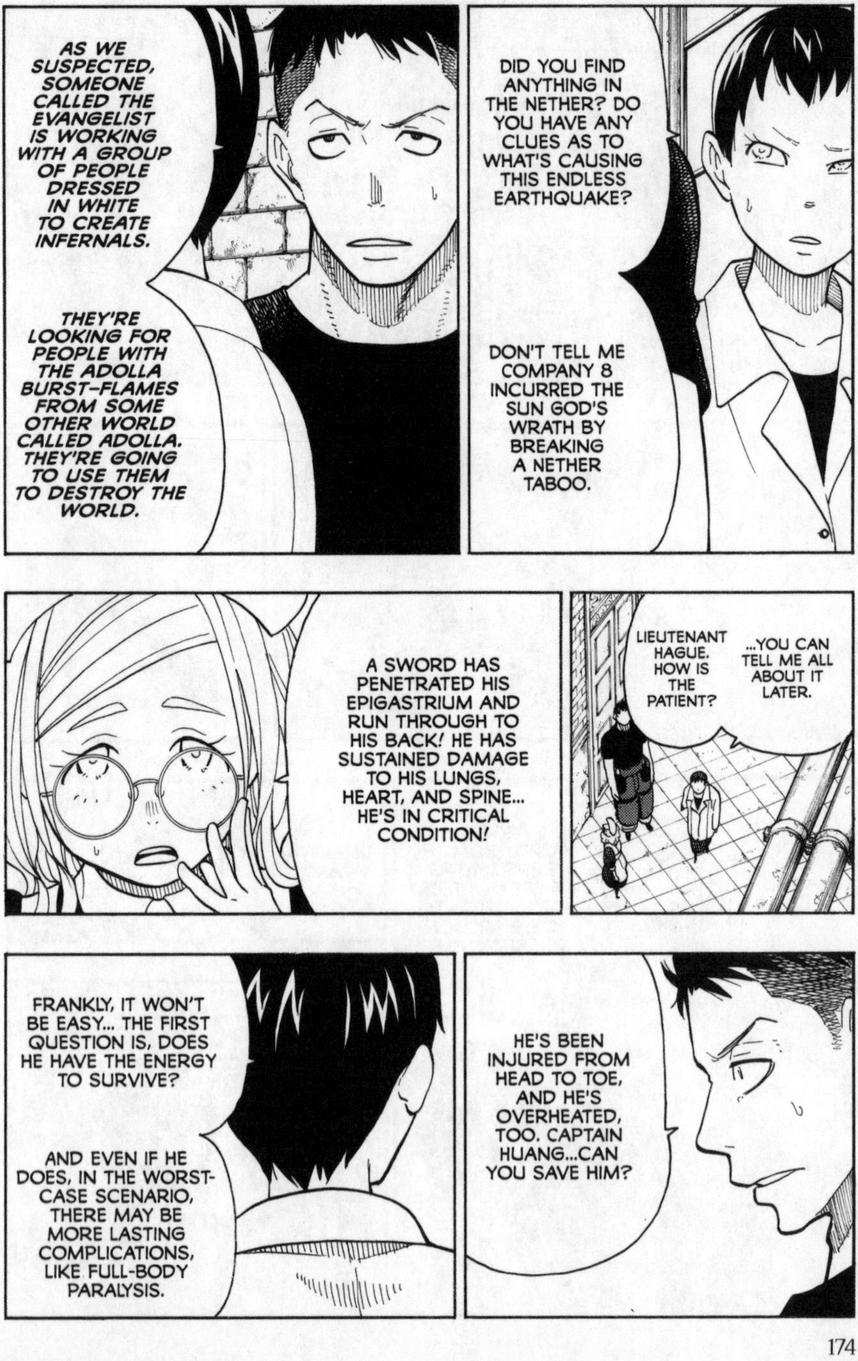
DID YOU FIND ANYTHING IN THE NETHER? DO YOU HAVE ANY CLUES AS TO WHAT'S CAUSING THIS ENDLESS EARTHQUAKE?
DON'T TELL ME COMPANY 8 INCURRED THE SUN GOD'S WRATH BY BREAKING A NETHER TABOO.
AS WE SUSPECTED, SOMEONE CALLED THE EVANGELIST IS WORKING WITH A GROUP OF PEOPLE DRESSED IN WHITE TO CREATE INFERNALS.
THEY'RE LOOKING FOR PEOPLE WITH THE ADOLLA BURST-FLAMES FROM SOME OTHER WORLD CALLED ADOLLA. THEY'RE GOING TO USE THEM TO DESTROY THE WORLD.
...YOU CAN TELL ME ALL ABOUT IT LATER.
LIEUTENANT HAGUE. HOW IS THE PATIENT?
A SWORD HAS PENETRATED HIS EPIGASTRIUM AND RUN THROUGH TO HIS BACK! HE HAS SUSTAINED DAMAGE TO HIS LUNGS, HEART, AND SPINE... HE'S IN CRITICAL CONDITION!
HE'S BEEN INJURED FROM HEAD TO TOE, AND HE'S OVERHEATED, TOO. CAPTAIN HUANG...CAN YOU SAVE HIM?
FRANKLY, IT WON'T BE EASY... THE FIRST QUESTION IS, DOES HE HAVE THE ENERGY TO SURVIVE?
AND EVEN IF HE DOES, IN THE WORST-CASE SCENARIO, THERE MAY BE MORE LASTING COMPLICATIONS, LIKE FULL-BODY PARALYSIS.

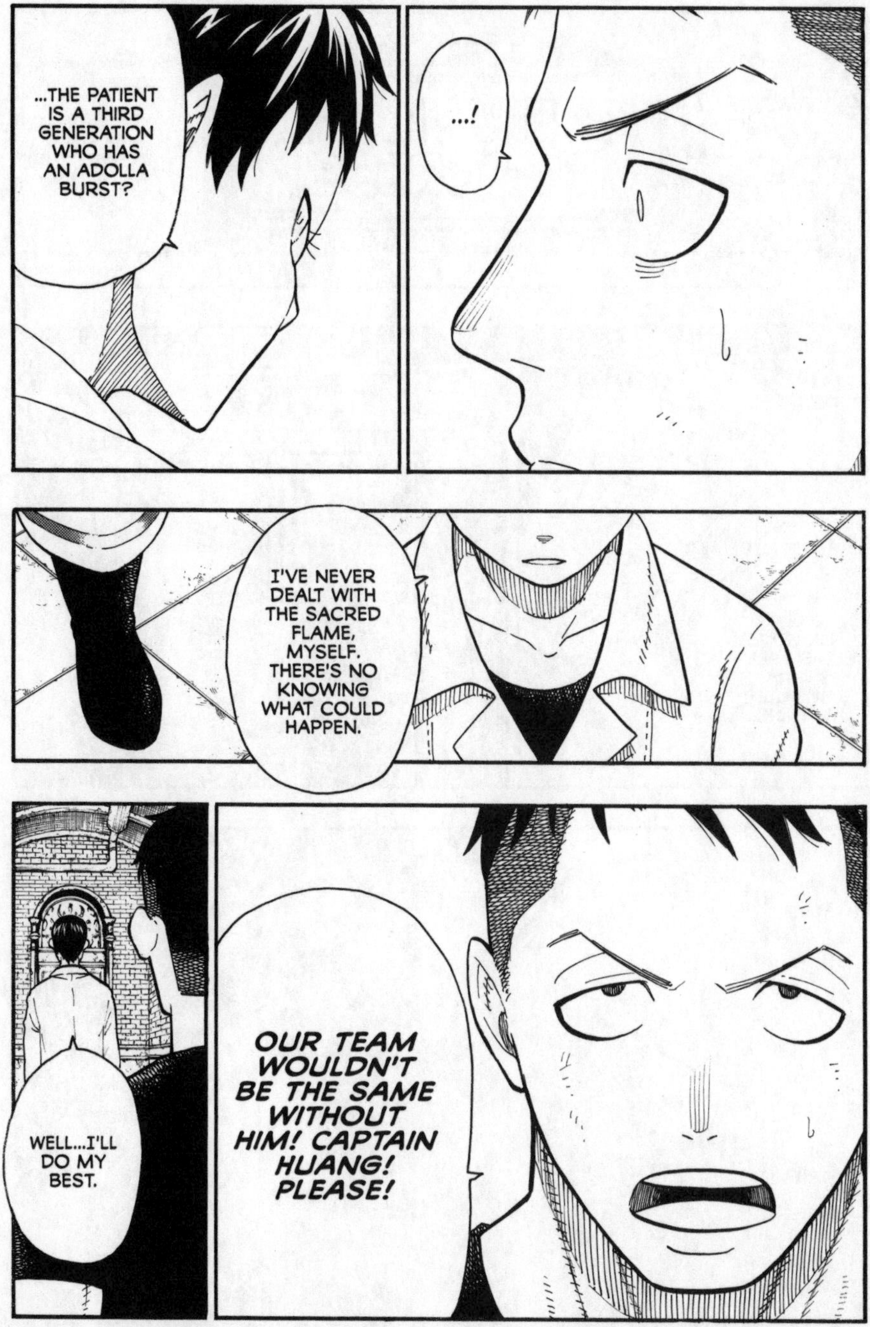
...!
...THE PATIENT IS A THIRD GENERATION WHO HAS AN ADOLLA BURST?
I'VE NEVER DEALT WITH THE SACRED FLAME, MYSELF. THERE'S NO KNOWING WHAT COULD HAPPEN.
OUR TEAM WOULDN'T BE THE SAME WITHOUT HIM! CAPTAIN HUANG! PLEASE!
WELL...I'LL DO MY BEST.

OPERATION IN PROGRESS

GREAT SUN GOD... PLEASE, KEEP SHINRA-SAN'S LIGHT BURNING.

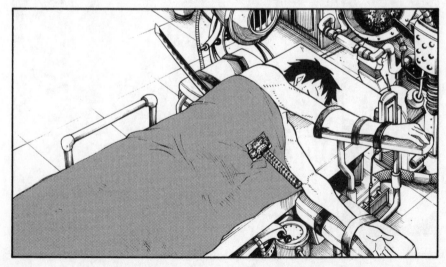

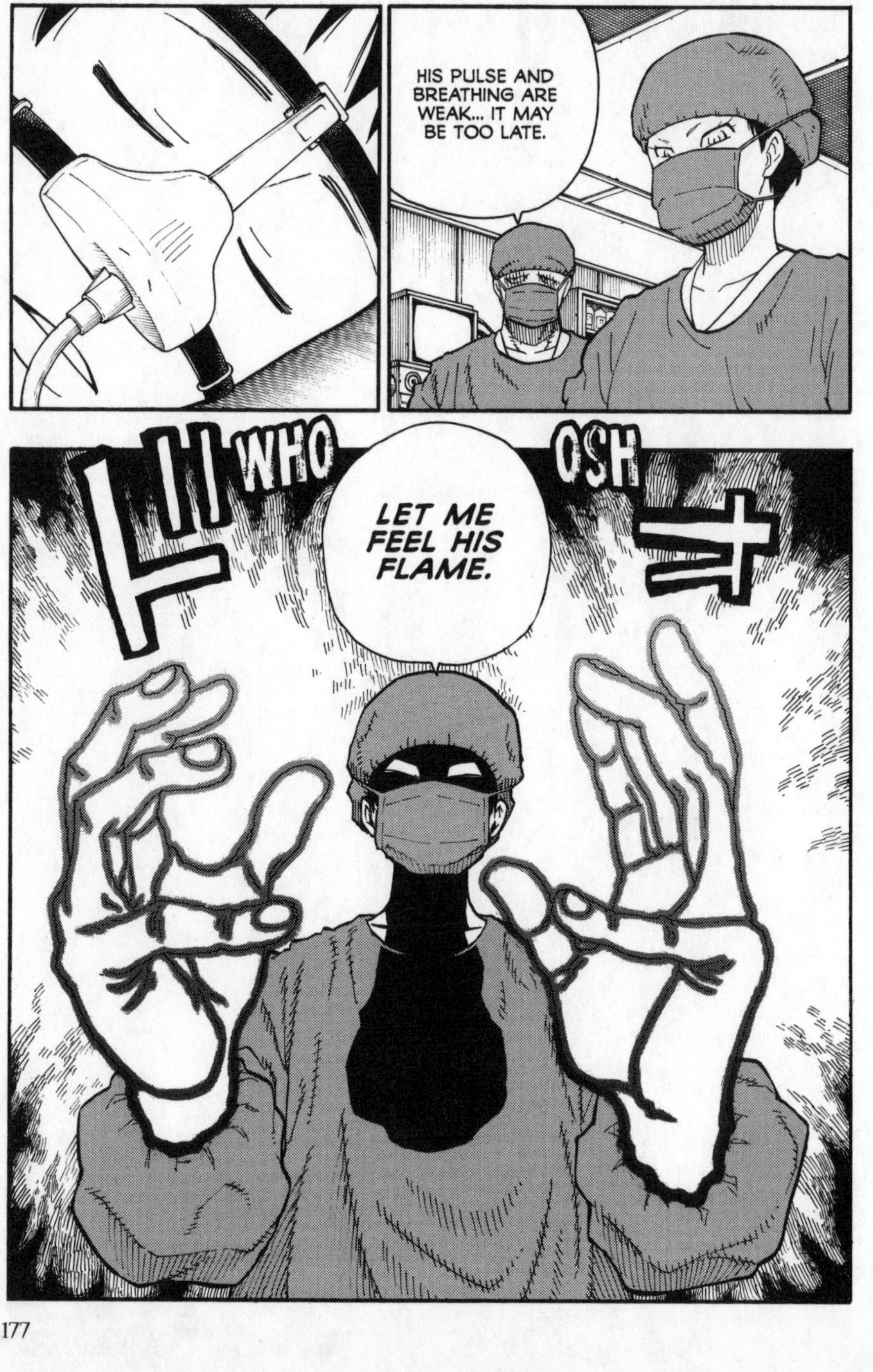
HIS PULSE AND BREATHING ARE WEAK... IT MAY BE TOO LATE.
WHO OSH
ドオ
LET ME FEEL HIS FLAME.

FIRE FORCE

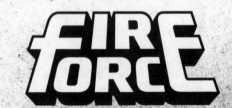

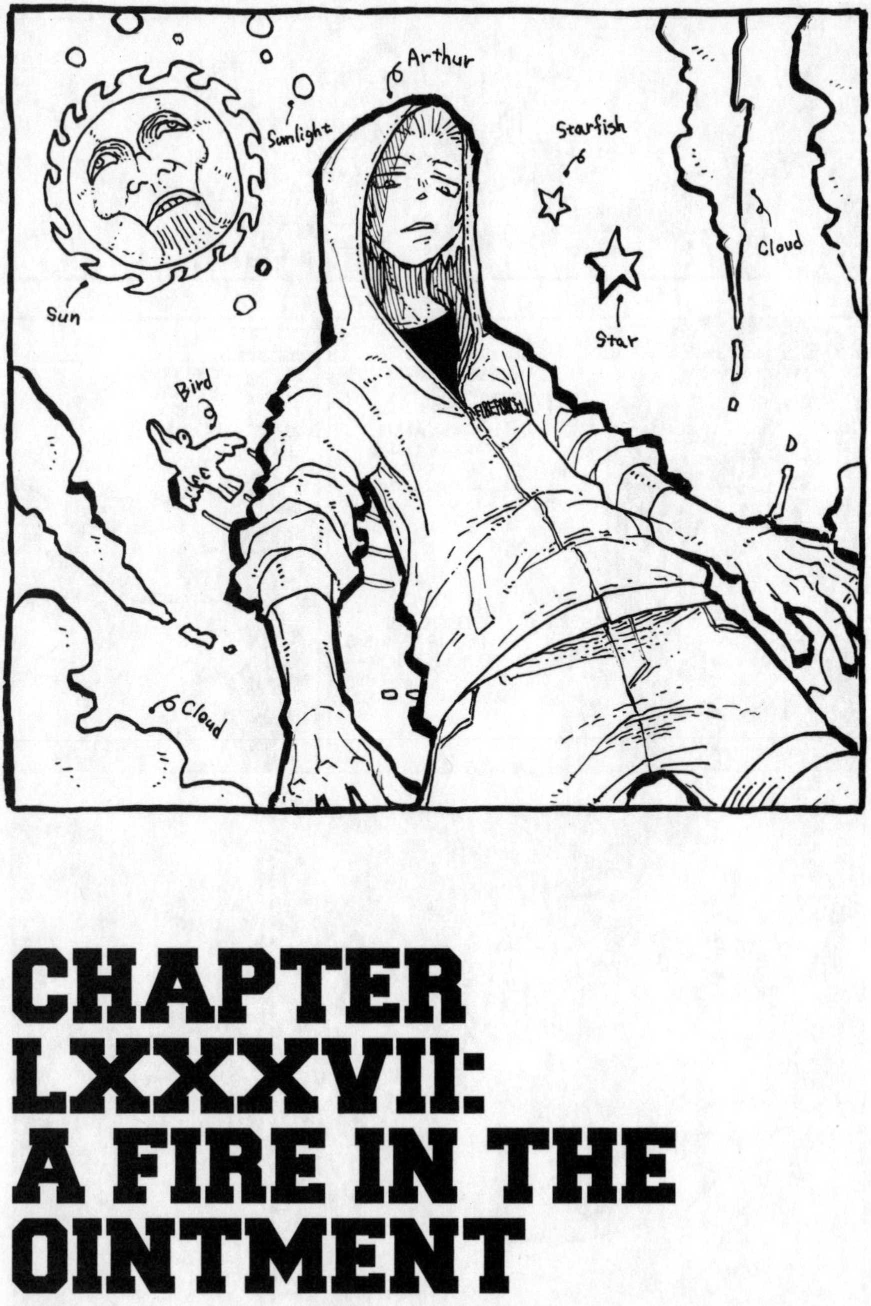
Arthur
Sunlight
Starfish
Cloud
Sun
Star
Bird
FIRE FORCE
Cloud

CHAPTER LXXXVII: A FIRE IN THE OINTMENT

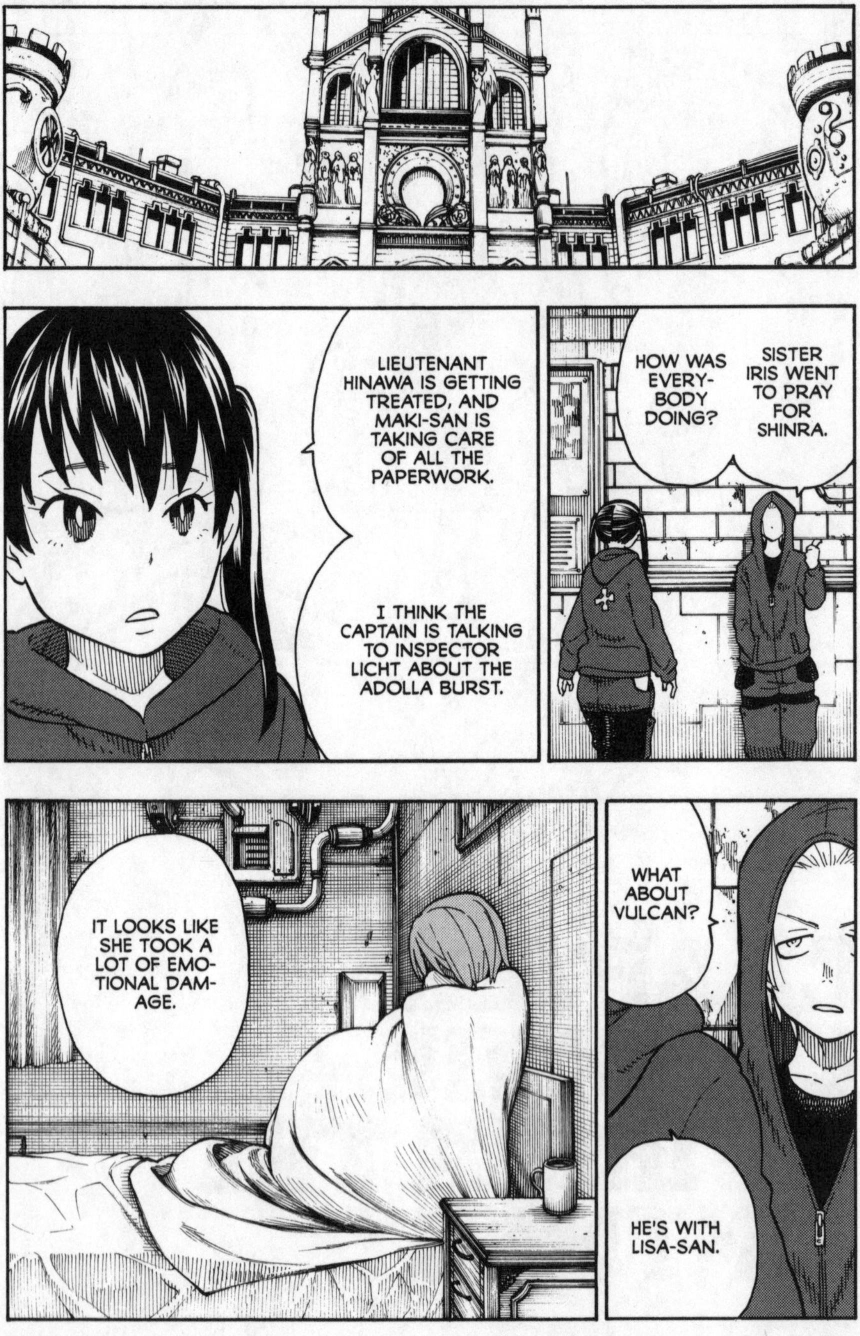
SISTER IRIS WENT TO PRAY FOR SHINRA.
HOW WAS EVERY-BODY DOING?
LIEUTENANT HINAWA IS GETTING TREATED, AND MAKI-SAN IS TAKING CARE OF ALL THE PAPERWORK.
I THINK THE CAPTAIN IS TALKING TO INSPECTOR LICHT ABOUT THE ADOLLA BURST.
WHAT ABOUT VULCAN?
HE'S WITH LISA-SAN.
IT LOOKS LIKE SHE TOOK A LOT OF EMO-TIONAL DAM-AGE.

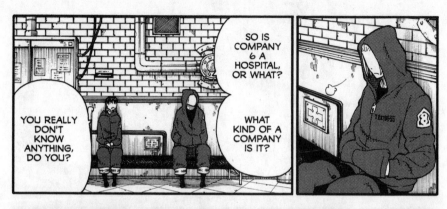

SO IS COMPANY 6 A HOSPITAL, OR WHAT?
WHAT KIND OF A COMPANY IS IT?
YOU REALLY DON'T KNOW ANYTHING, DO YOU?
FIRE FORCE
6
TOKYO
YOU KNOW THAT MEDICAL CARE IN THE EMPIRE CONSISTS OF RELIGIOUS RITES THAT CAN ONLY LEGALLY BE PERFORMED BY MEMBERS OF THE HOLY SOL TEMPLE, RIGHT?
SO LIKE COMPANY 1, MOST OF COMPANY 6'S SOLDIERS ARE MEMBERS OF THE CHURCH, BUT IT SPECIALIZES IN MEDICINE.
WHICH MEANS WE'RE EITHER IN A CHURCH OR A HOSPITAL.
IT'S A SPECIAL FIRE FORCE COMPANY!
ははぁ~ん
UH-HUH.
APPARENTLY NO ONE CAN COMPARE TO COMPANY 6'S CAPTAIN HUANG WHEN IT COMES TO HEALING PYROKINETICS.
I HEARD SHE USES HER SPECIAL ABILITY TO TREAT HER PATIENTS...

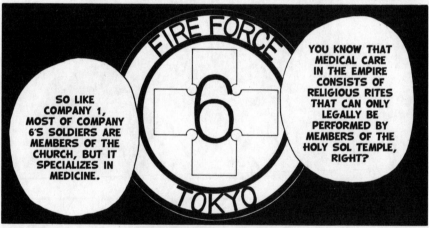

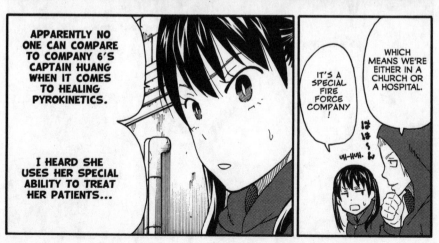

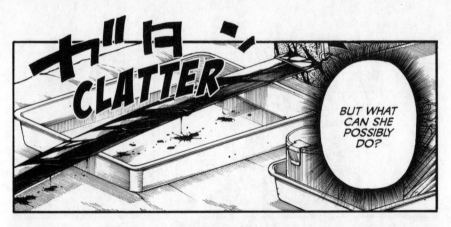

ガタン
CLATTER
BUT WHAT CAN SHE POSSIBLY DO?
WE HAVE SUCCESSFULLY EXTRACTED THE SWORD... HIS VITALS ARE STABLE.
NOW I JUST NEED TO TREAT HIM WITH MY POWERS.
STILL, WITH THESE INJURIES...I DON'T KNOW IF MY POWER WILL BE ENOUGH.
THIS IS GOING TO DEPEND ON THE STRENGTH OF HIS FLAME.

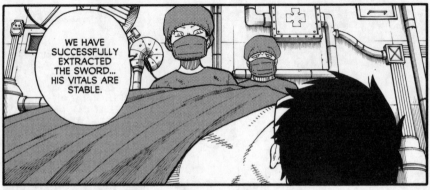

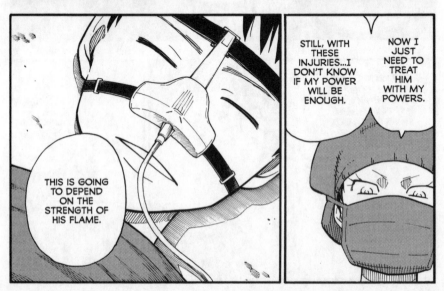

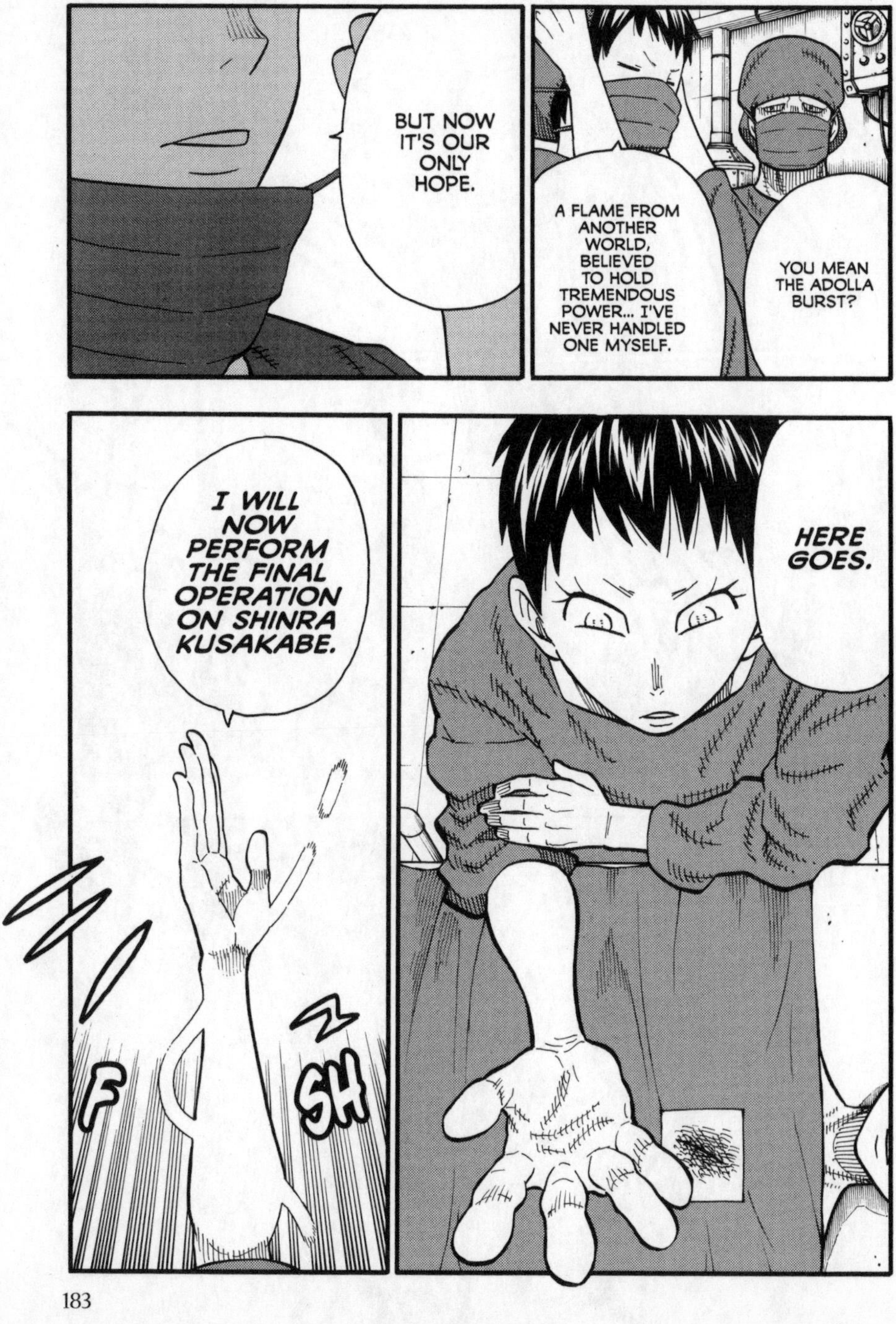
YOU MEAN THE ADOLLA BURST?
A FLAME FROM ANOTHER WORLD, BELIEVED TO HOLD TREMENDOUS POWER... I'VE NEVER HANDLED ONE MYSELF.
BUT NOW IT'S OUR ONLY HOPE.
HERE GOES.
I WILL NOW PERFORM THE FINAL OPERATION ON SHINRA KUSAKABE.
FSH

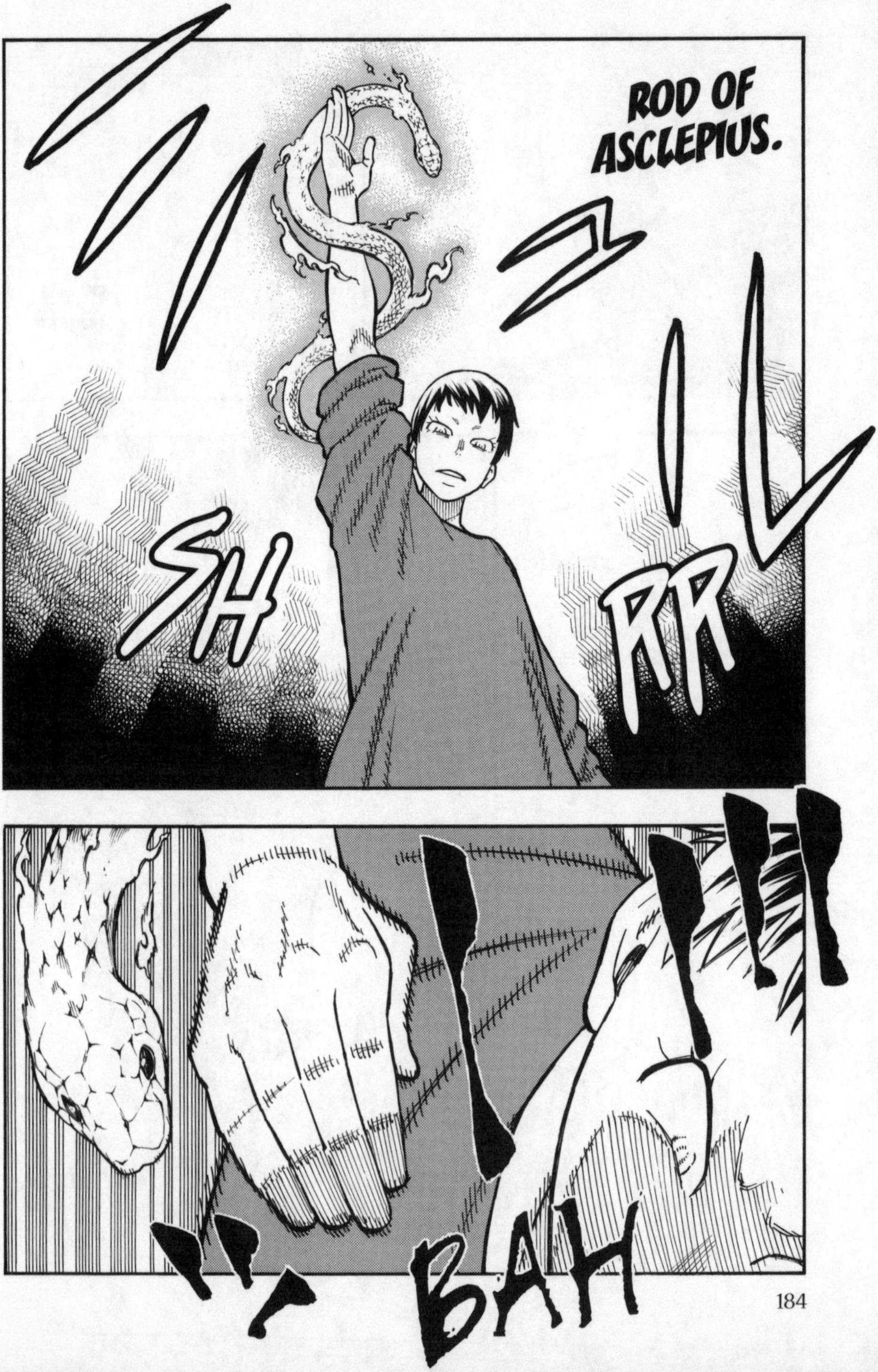
ROD OF ASCLEPIUS.
SH
RR
BAH

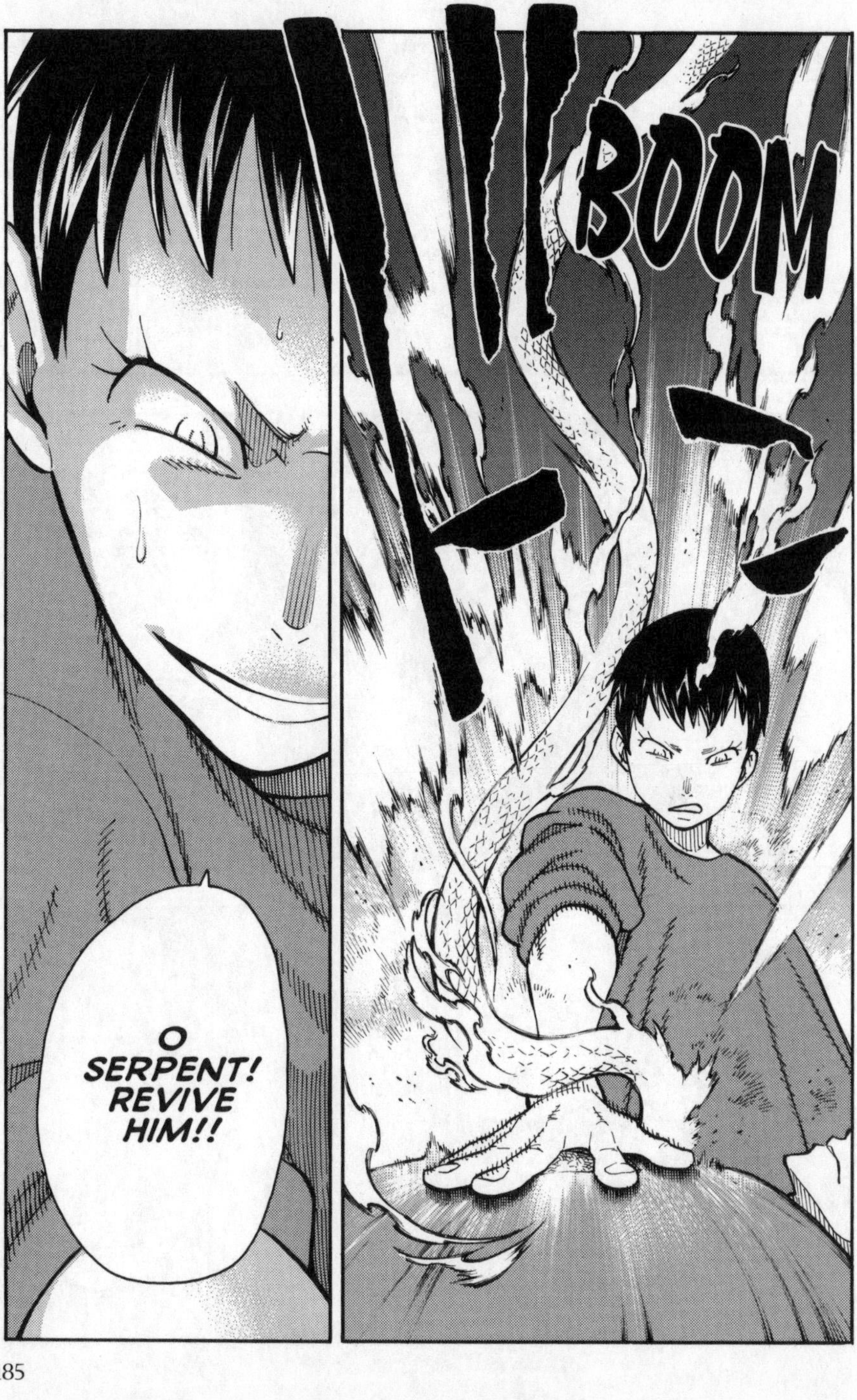
BOOM
O SERPENT! REVIVE HIM!!

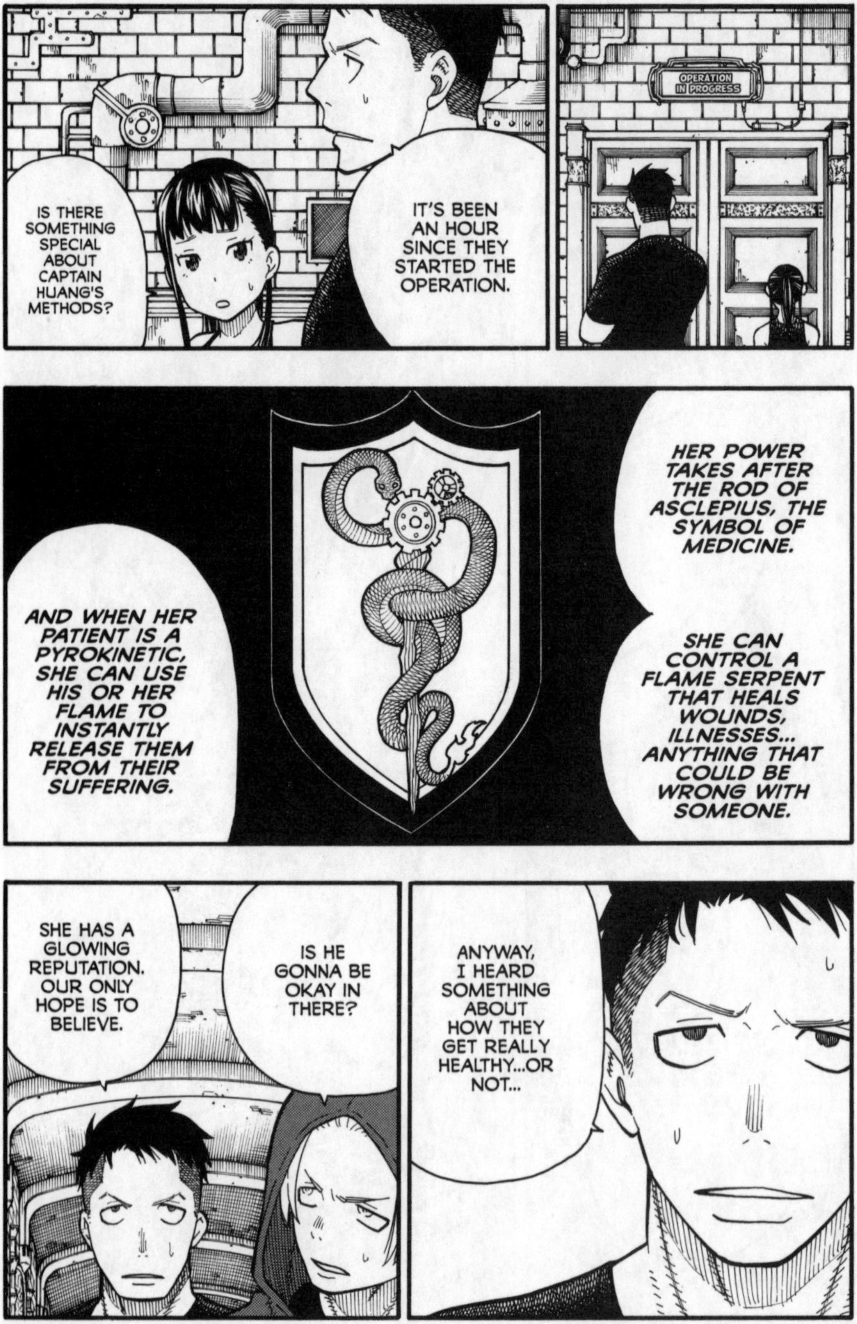
OPERATION IN PROGRESS
IT'S BEEN AN HOUR SINCE THEY STARTED THE OPERATION.
IS THERE SOMETHING SPECIAL ABOUT CAPTAIN HUANG'S METHODS?
HER POWER TAKES AFTER THE ROD OF ASCLEPIUS, THE SYMBOL OF MEDICINE.
SHE CAN CONTROL A FLAME SERPENT THAT HEALS WOUNDS, ILLNESSES... ANYTHING THAT COULD BE WRONG WITH SOMEONE.
AND WHEN HER PATIENT IS A PYROKINETIC, SHE CAN USE HIS OR HER FLAME TO INSTANTLY RELEASE THEM FROM THEIR SUFFERING.
ANYWAY, I HEARD SOMETHING ABOUT HOW THEY GET REALLY HEALTHY...OR NOT...
IS HE GONNA BE OKAY IN THERE?
SHE HAS A GLOWING REPUTATION. OUR ONLY HOPE IS TO BELIEVE.

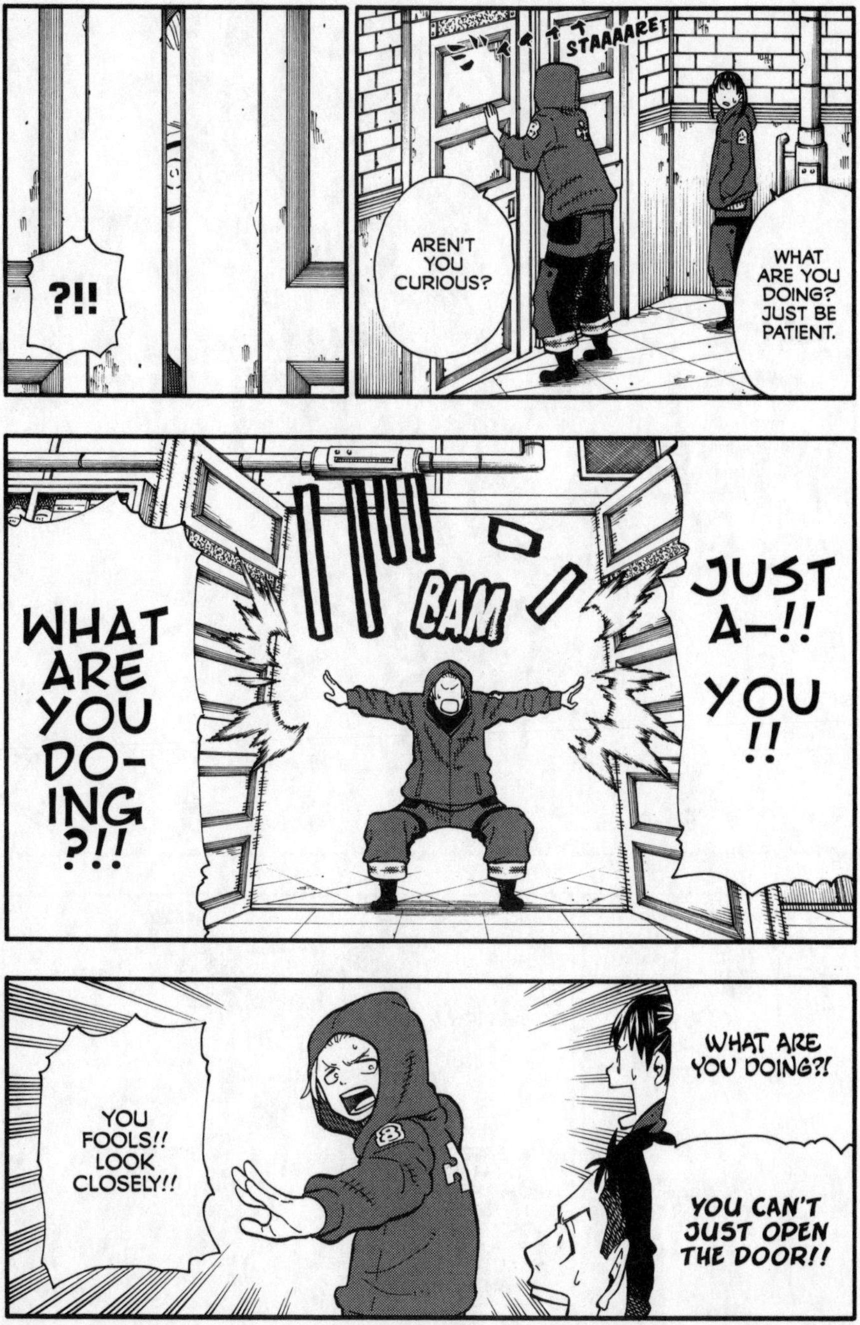
STAAAARE
WHAT ARE YOU DOING? JUST BE PATIENT.
AREN'T YOU CURIOUS?
?!!
JUST A-!!
YOU!!
BAM
WHAT ARE YOU DO-ING?!!
WHAT ARE YOU DOING?!
YOU CAN'T JUST OPEN THE DOOR!!
YOU FOOLS!! LOOK CLOSELY!!

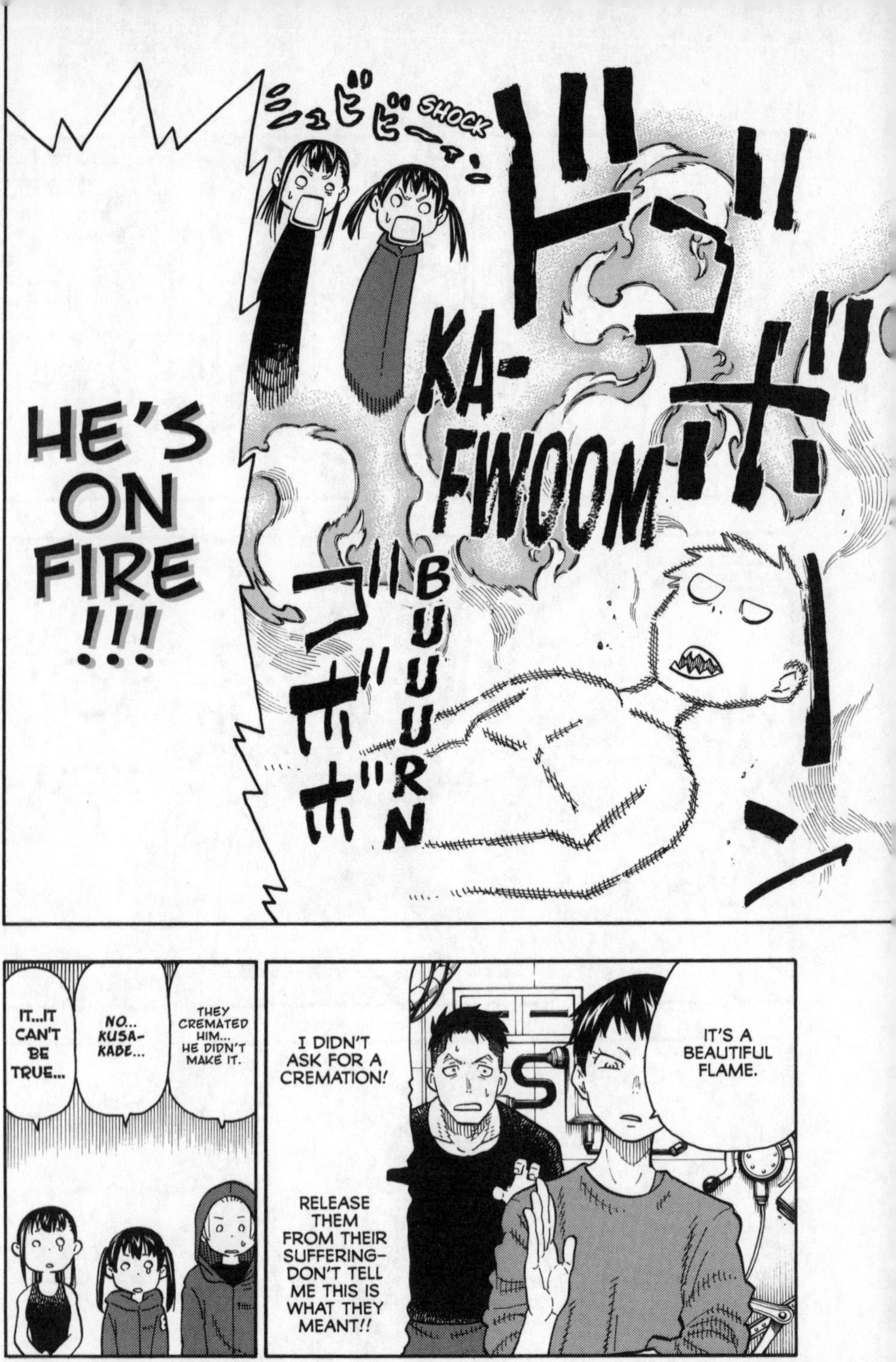
SHOCK
KA-FWOOM
BUUUURN
HE'S ON FIRE!!!
IT'S A BEAUTIFUL FLAME.
I DIDN'T ASK FOR A CREMATION!
RELEASE THEM FROM THEIR SUFFERING- DON'T TELL ME THIS IS WHAT THEY MEANT!!
THEY CREMATED HIM... HE DIDN'T MAKE IT.
NO... KUSA-KABE...
IT...IT CAN'T BE TRUE...

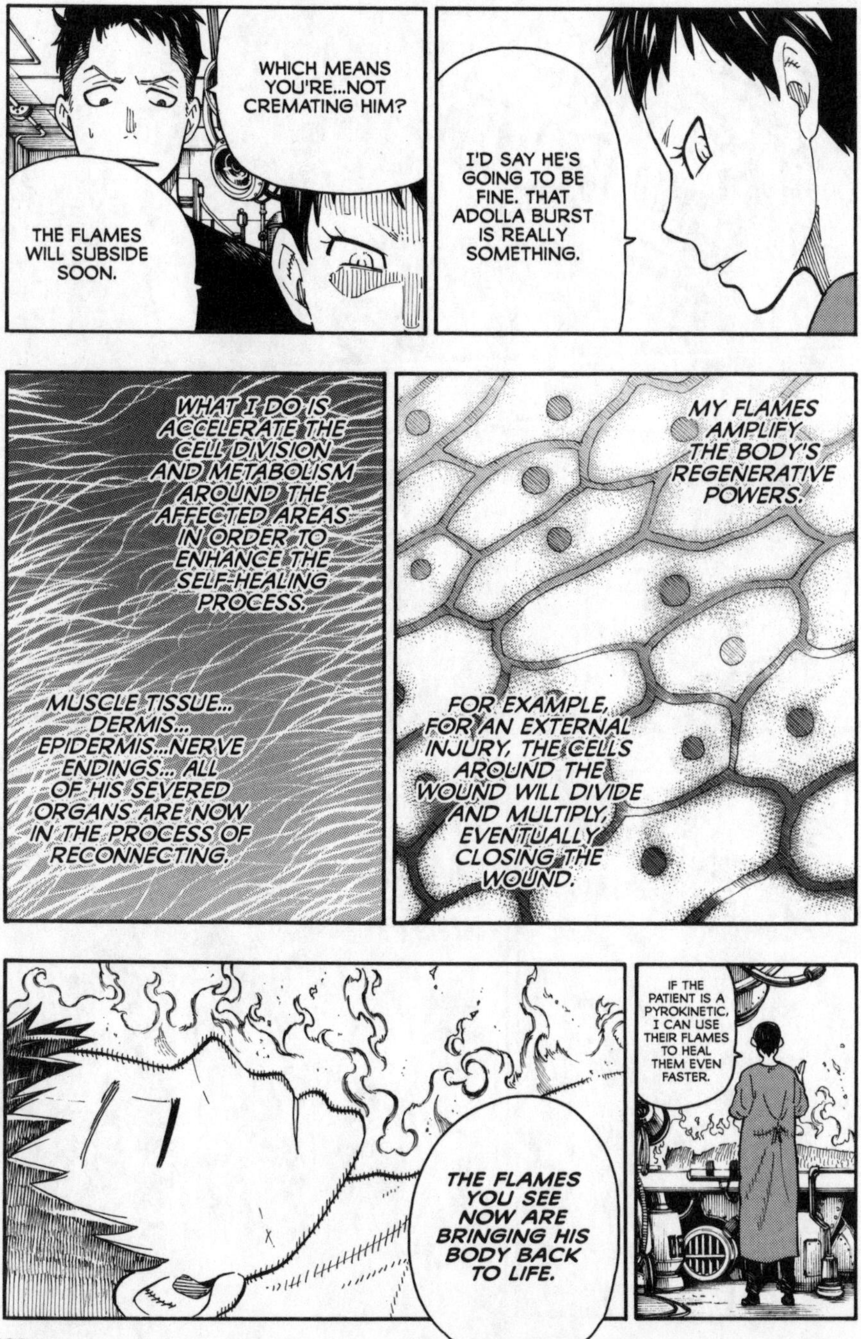
I'D SAY HE'S GOING TO BE FINE. THAT ADOLLA BURST IS REALLY SOMETHING.
WHICH MEANS YOU'RE...NOT CREMATING HIM?
THE FLAMES WILL SUBSIDE SOON.
MY FLAMES AMPLIFY THE BODY'S REGENERATIVE POWERS.
FOR EXAMPLE, FOR AN EXTERNAL INJURY, THE CELLS AROUND THE WOUND WILL DIVIDE AND MULTIPLY, EVENTUALLY CLOSING THE WOUND.
WHAT I DO IS ACCELERATE THE CELL DIVISION AND METABOLISM AROUND THE AFFECTED AREAS IN ORDER TO ENHANCE THE SELF-HEALING PROCESS.
MUSCLE TISSUE... DERMIS... EPIDERMIS...NERVE ENDINGS... ALL OF HIS SEVERED ORGANS ARE NOW IN THE PROCESS OF RECONNECTING.
IF THE PATIENT IS A PYROKINETIC, I CAN USE THEIR FLAMES TO HEAL THEM EVEN FASTER.
THE FLAMES YOU SEE NOW ARE BRINGING HIS BODY BACK TO LIFE.

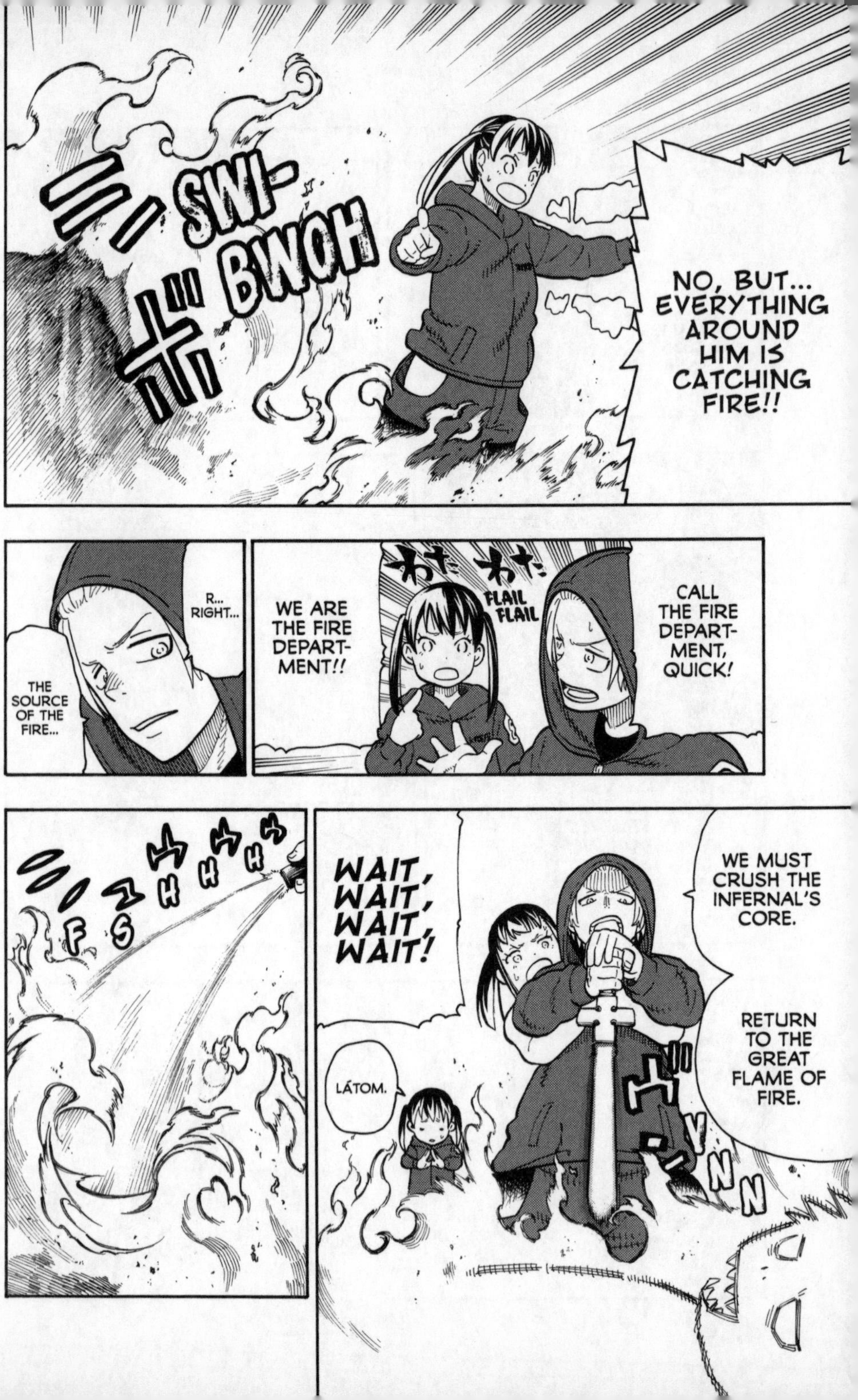
SWI-BWOH
NO, BUT... EVERYTHING AROUND HIM IS CATCHING FIRE!!
わたわた
FLAIL FLAIL
CALL THE FIRE DEPARTMENT, QUICK!
WE ARE THE FIRE DEPARTMENT!!
R... RIGHT...
THE SOURCE OF THE FIRE...
WE MUST CRUSH THE INFERNAL'S CORE.
WAIT, WAIT, WAIT, WAIT!
RETURN TO THE GREAT FLAME OF FIRE.
VNN
LÁTOM.
FSHHHH

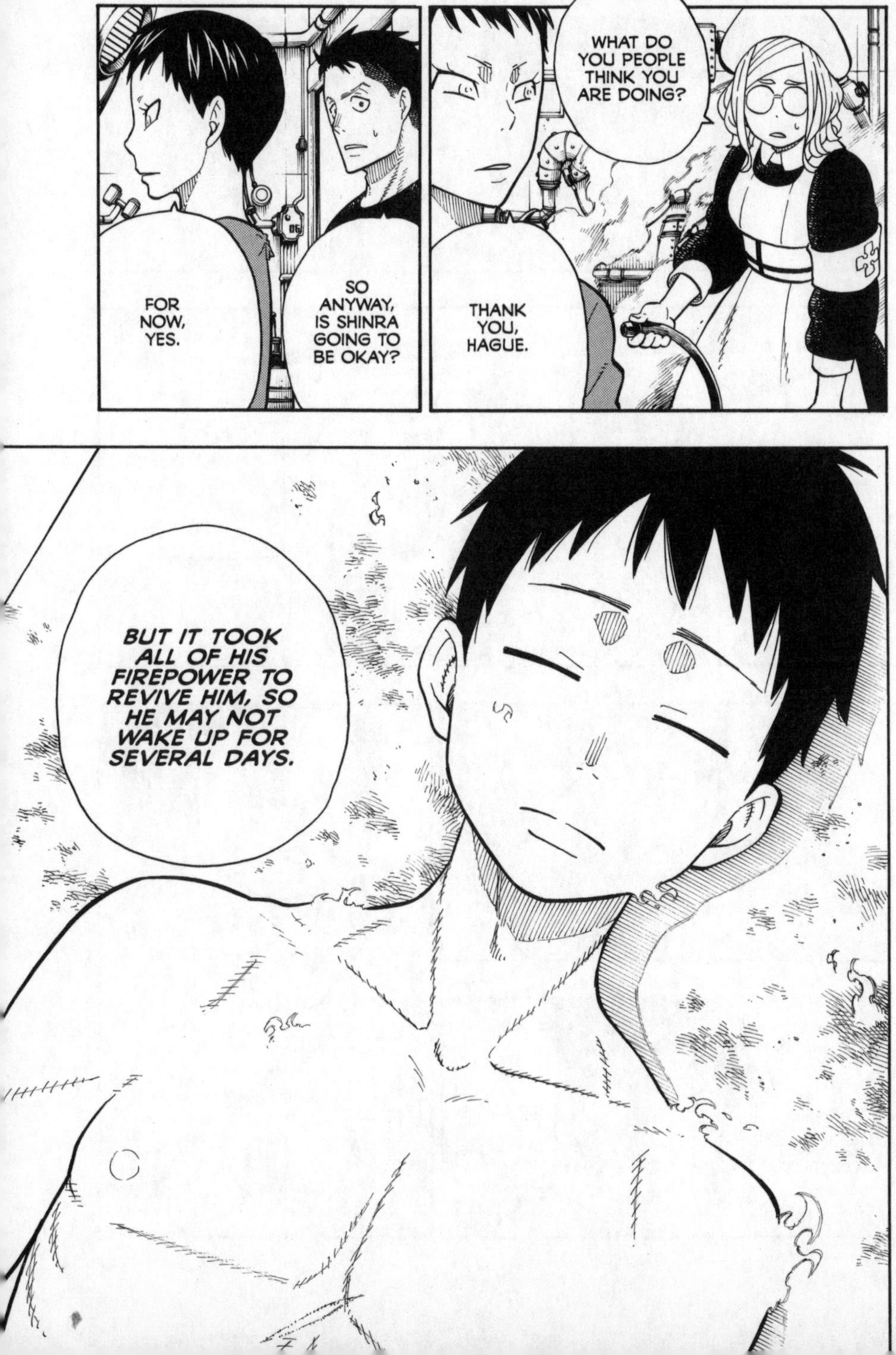
WHAT DO YOU PEOPLE THINK YOU ARE DOING?
THANK YOU, HAGUE.
SO ANYWAY, IS SHINRA GOING TO BE OKAY?
FOR NOW, YES.
BUT IT TOOK ALL OF HIS FIREPOWER TO REVIVE HIM, SO HE MAY NOT WAKE UP FOR SEVERAL DAYS.

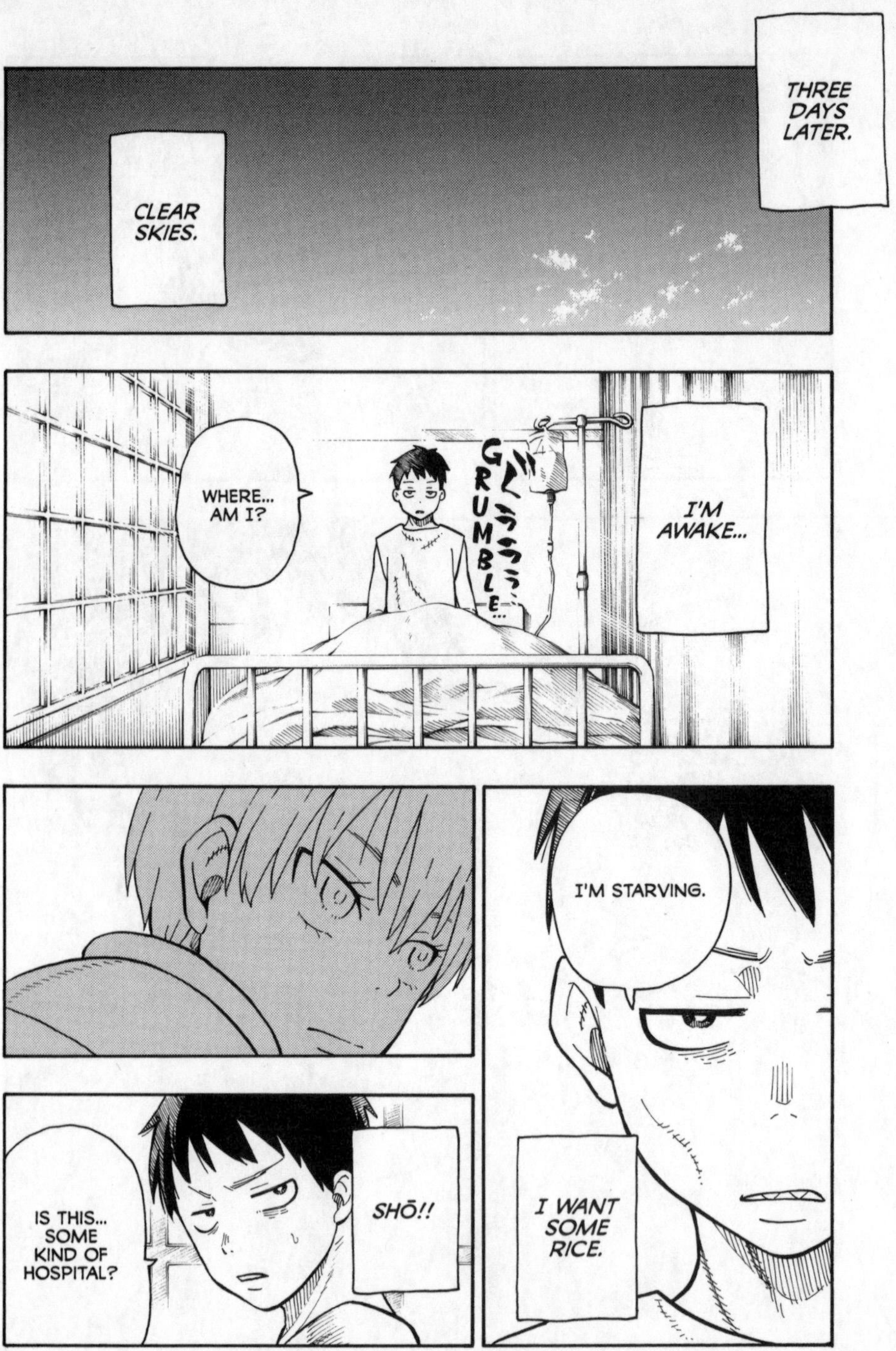
THREE DAYS LATER.
CLEAR SKIES.
I'M AWAKE...
GRUMBLE...
WHERE... AM I?
I'M STARVING.
I WANT SOME RICE.
SHŌ!!
IS THIS... SOME KIND OF HOSPITAL?

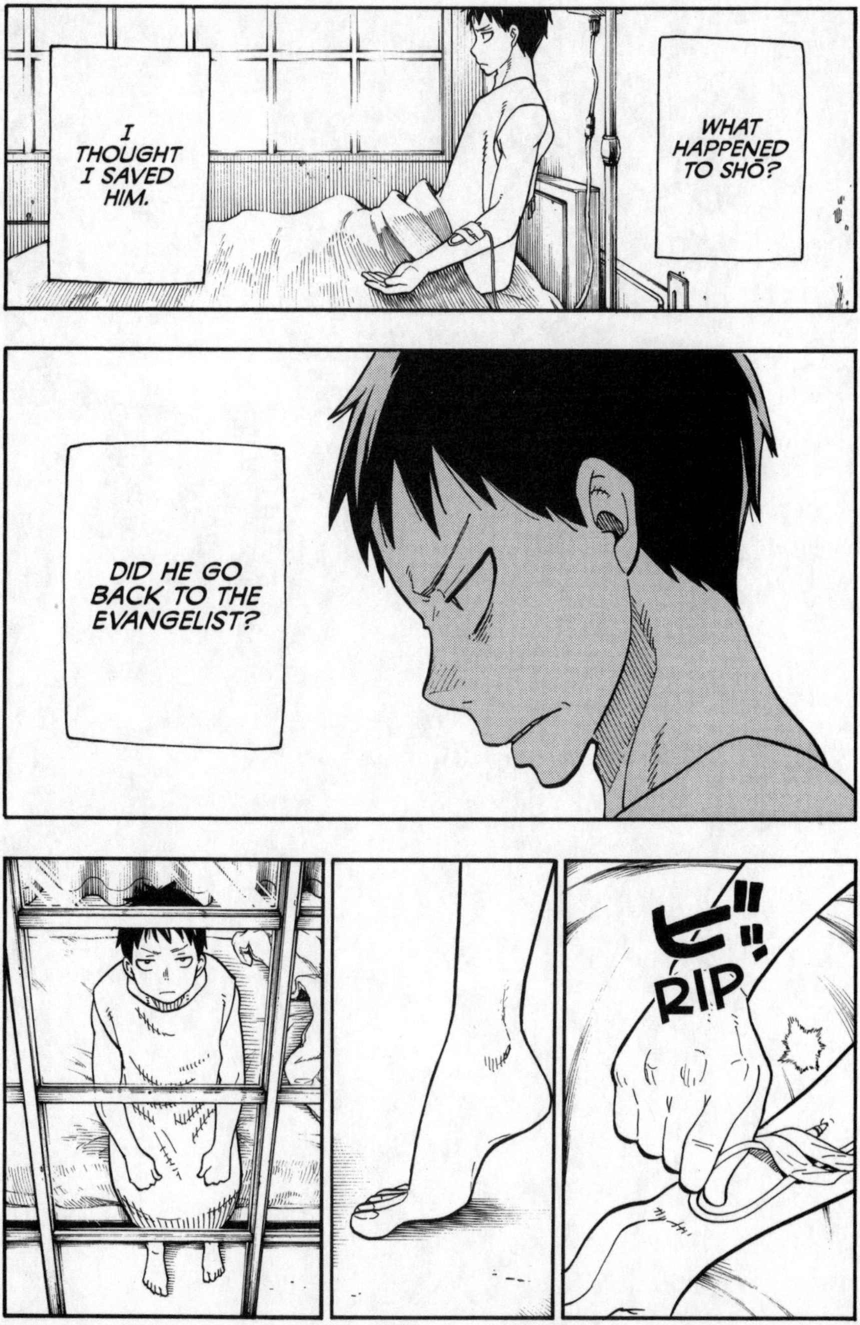
WHAT HAPPENED TO SHŌ?
I THOUGHT I SAVED HIM.
DID HE GO BACK TO THE EVANGELIST?
ビッ
RIP

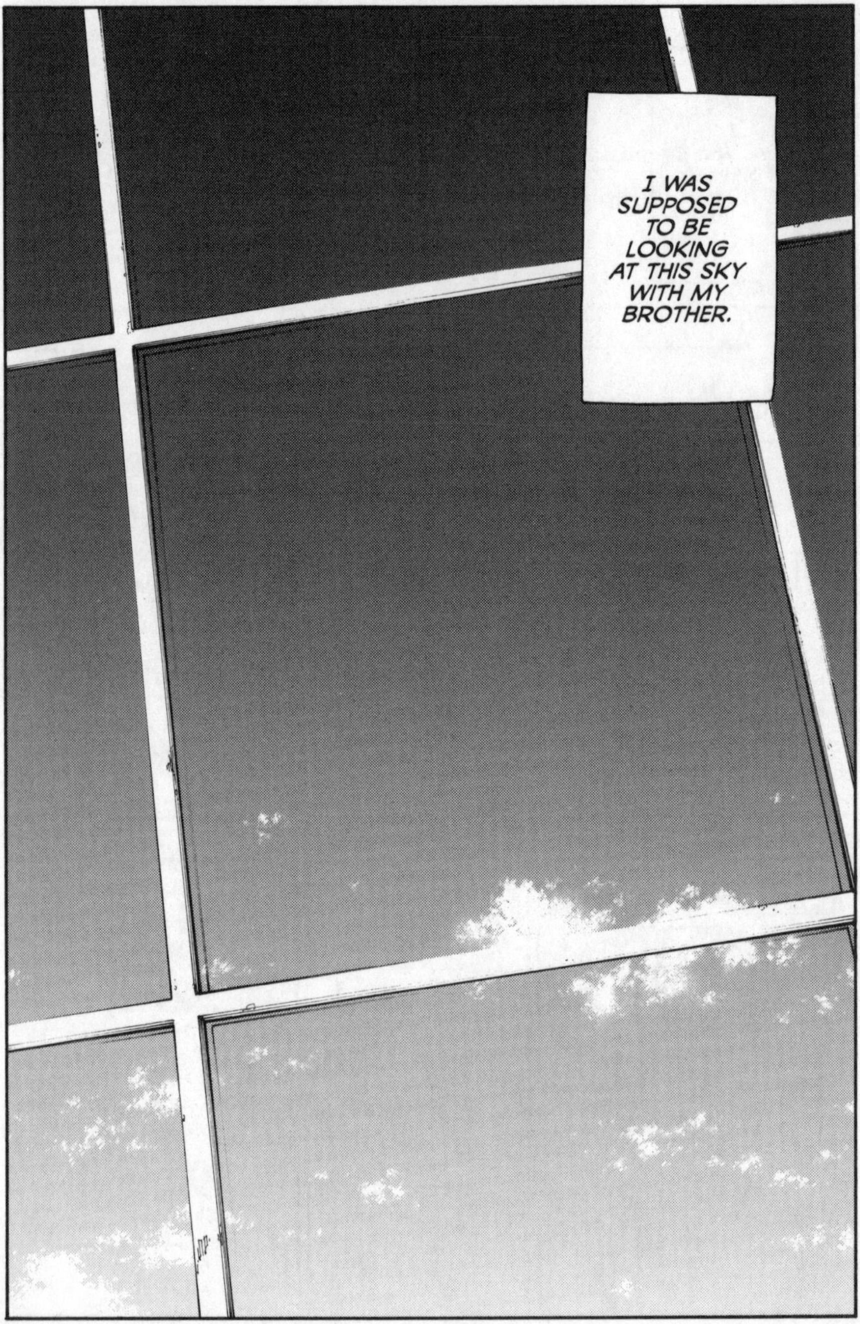
I WAS SUPPOSED TO BE LOOKING AT THIS SKY WITH MY BROTHER.

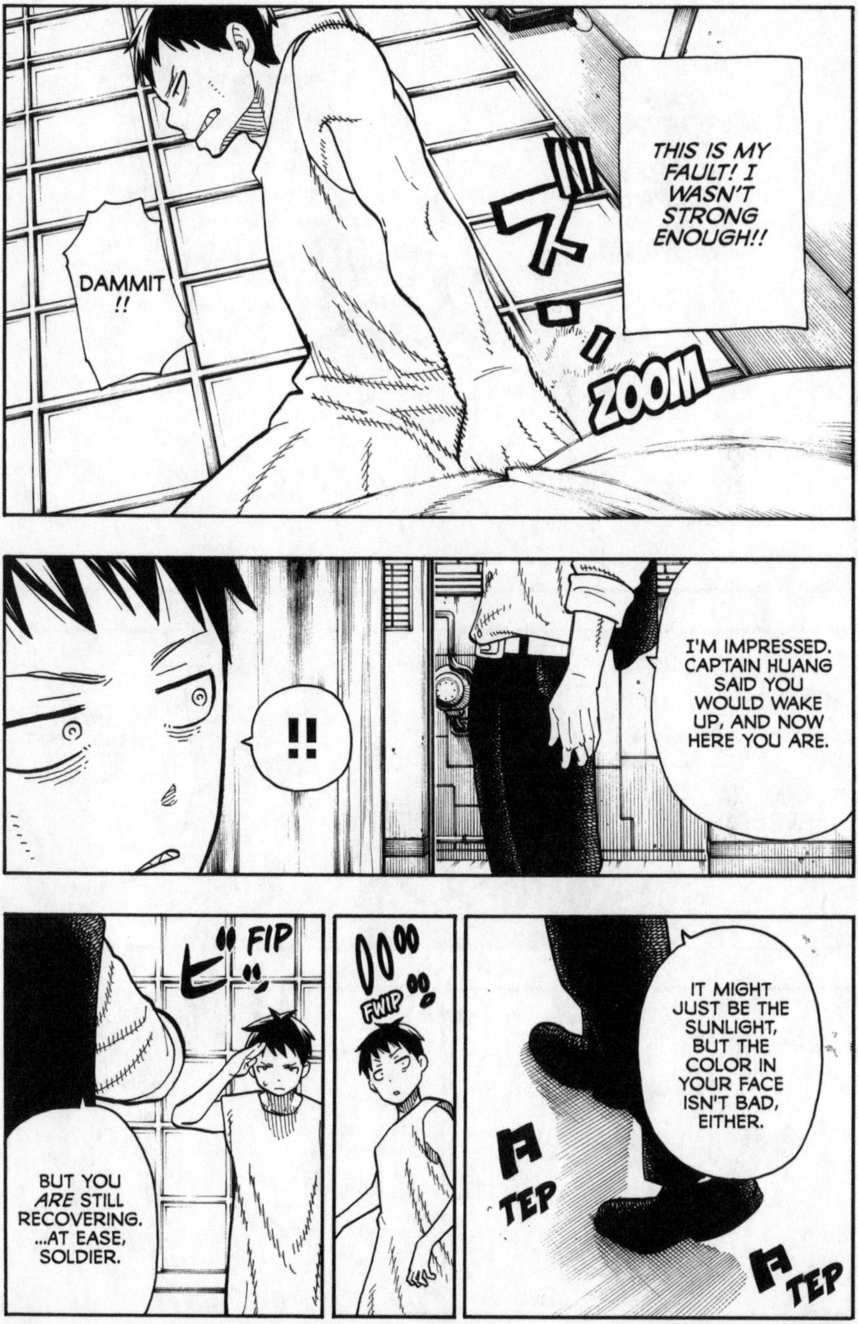
THIS IS MY FAULT! I WASN'T STRONG ENOUGH!!
ZOOM
DAMMIT!!
I'M IMPRESSED. CAPTAIN HUANG SAID YOU WOULD WAKE UP, AND NOW HERE YOU ARE.
!!
IT MIGHT JUST BE THE SUNLIGHT, BUT THE COLOR IN YOUR FACE ISN'T BAD, EITHER.
TEP
TEP
FWIP
FIP
BUT YOU ARE STILL RECOVERING. ...AT EASE, SOLDIER.

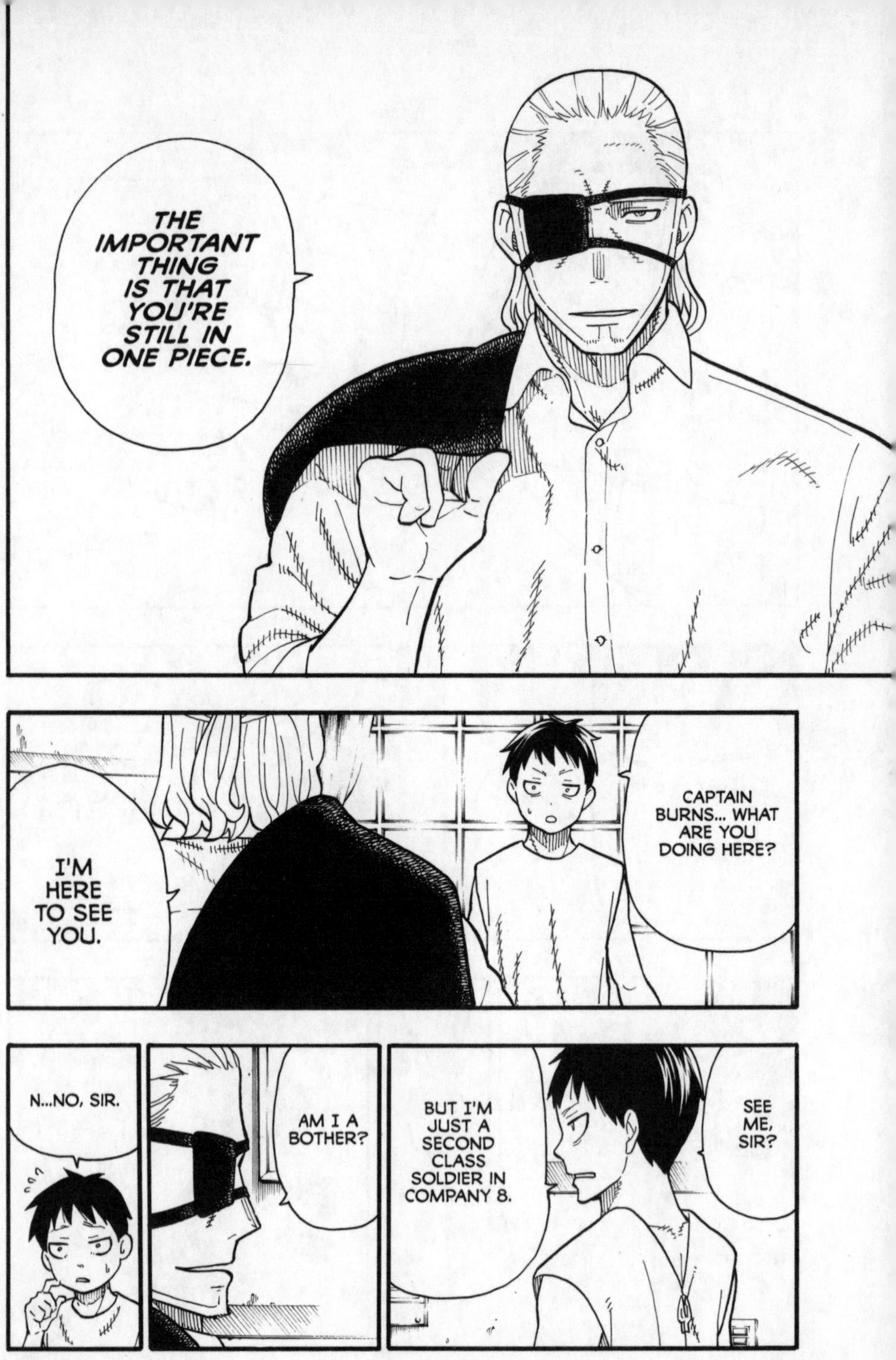
THE IMPORTANT THING IS THAT YOU'RE STILL IN ONE PIECE.
CAPTAIN BURNS... WHAT ARE YOU DOING HERE?
I'M HERE TO SEE YOU.
SEE ME, SIR?
BUT I'M JUST A SECOND CLASS SOLDIER IN COMPANY 8.
AM I A BOTHER?
N...NO, SIR.

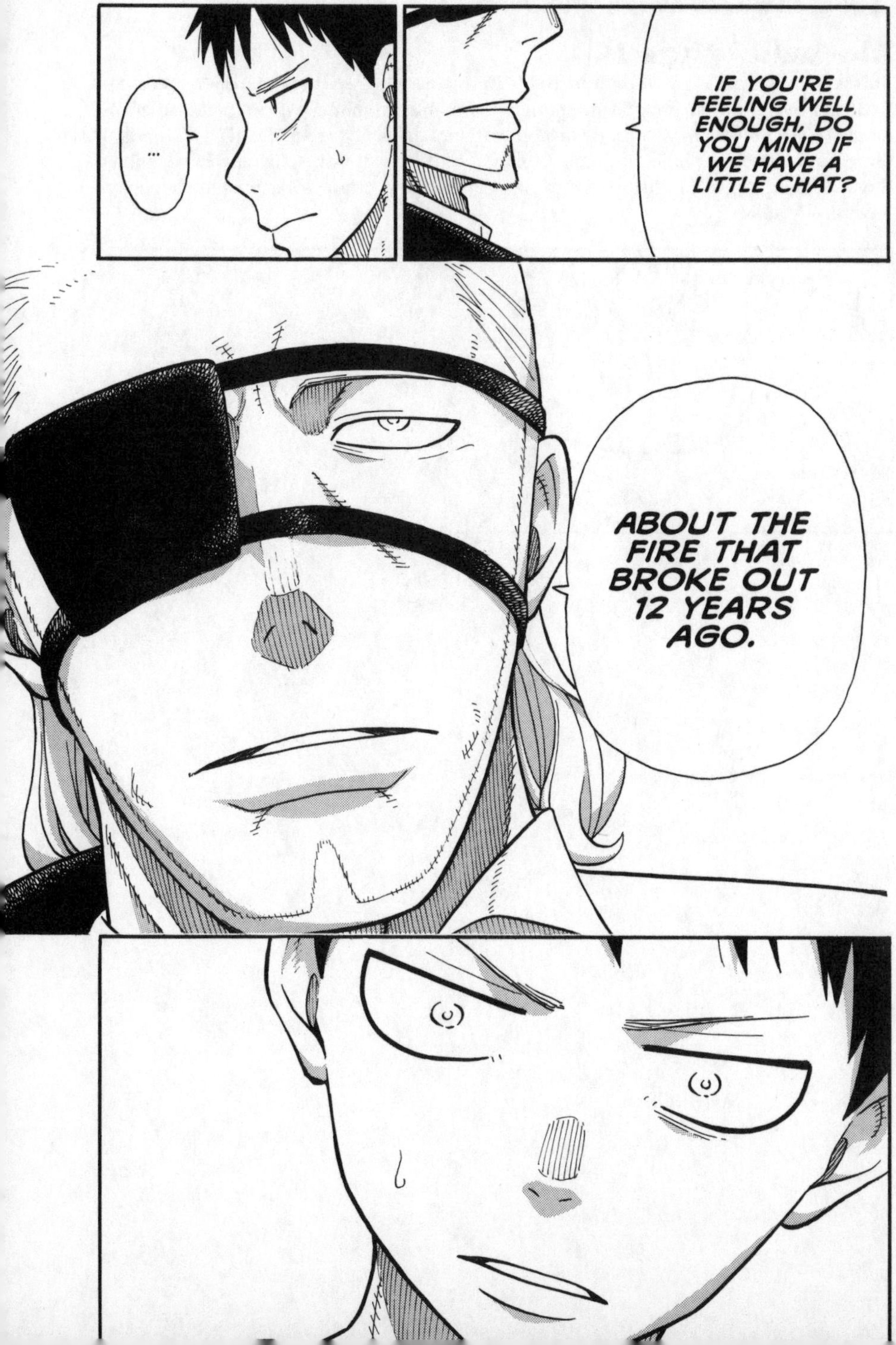
IF YOU'RE FEELING WELL ENOUGH, DO YOU MIND IF WE HAVE A LITTLE CHAT?
...
ABOUT THE FIRE THAT BROKE OUT 12 YEARS AGO.

Translation Note:

Alo-hello, page 140

This is a combination of "aloha" and "hello." In the original Japanese, Haumea greets Shō with *oharō*, a combination of the Japanese *ohayō* and a Japanese pronunciation of the English *hello*. This term was made famous in Japan by Rinoa Heartilly of *Final Fantasy VIII* fame. To replicate the cute language mixing, for this version the translators combined Hawaiian and English, because of Haumea's Hawaiian name, and because they feel it sounds adorable.

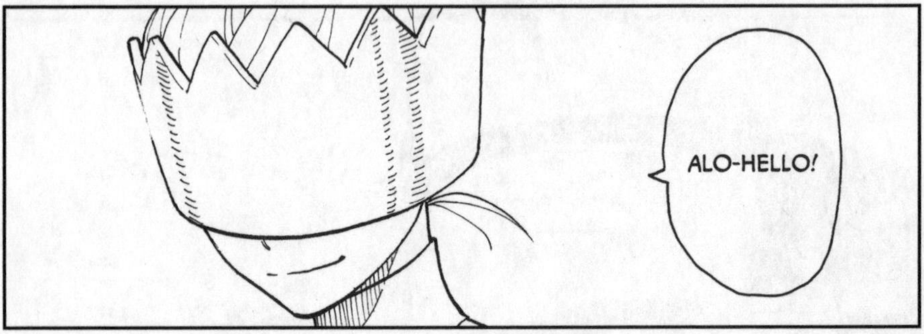
ALO-HELLO!

FIRE FORCE

AFTERWORD MANGA: ATSUSHIYA

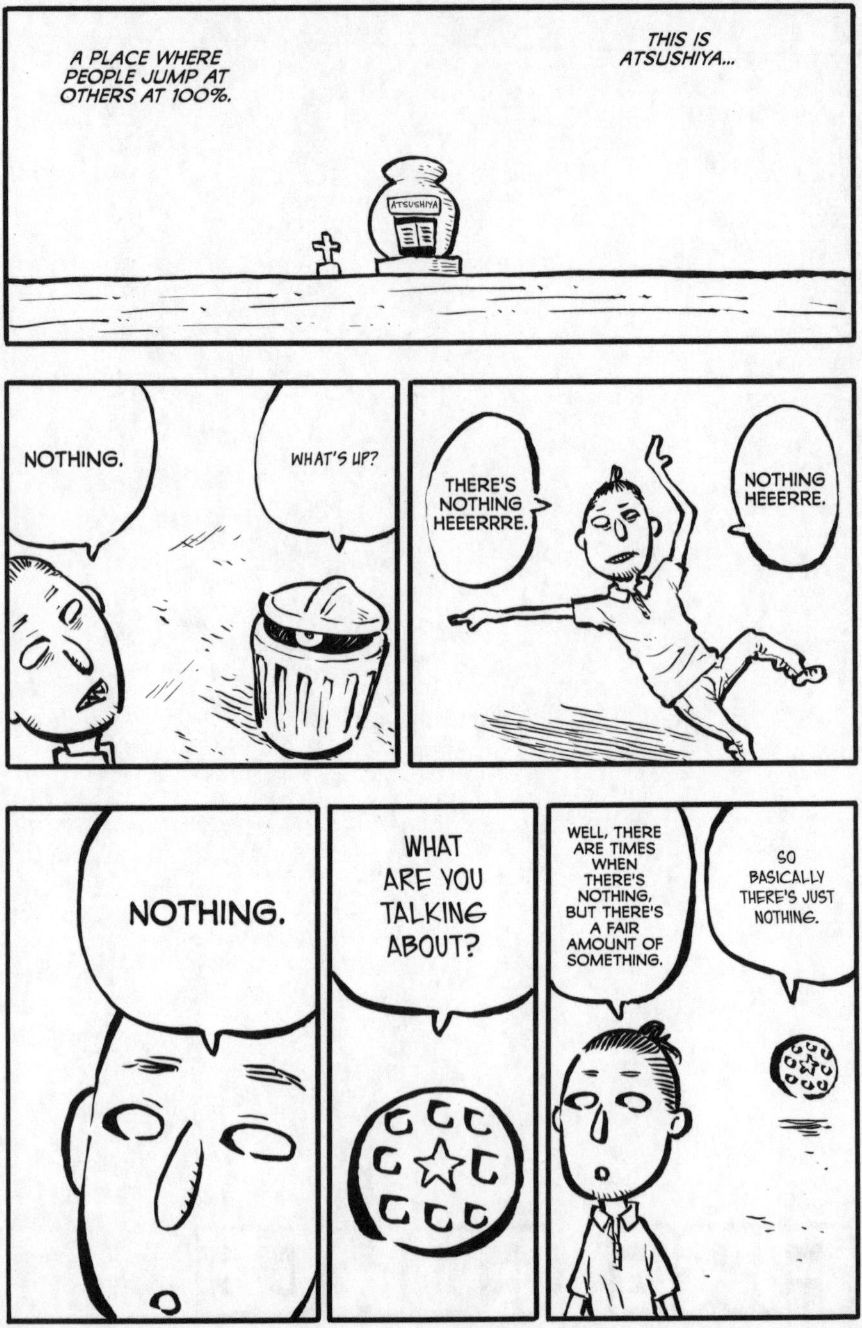
THIS IS ATSUSHIYA...
A PLACE WHERE PEOPLE JUMP AT OTHERS AT 100%.
ATSUSHIYA
NOTHING HEEERRE.
THERE'S NOTHING HEEERRRE.
WHAT'S UP?
NOTHING.
SO BASICALLY THERE'S JUST NOTHING.
WELL, THERE ARE TIMES WHEN THERE'S NOTHING, BUT THERE'S A FAIR AMOUNT OF SOMETHING.
WHAT ARE YOU TALKING ABOUT?
NOTHING.

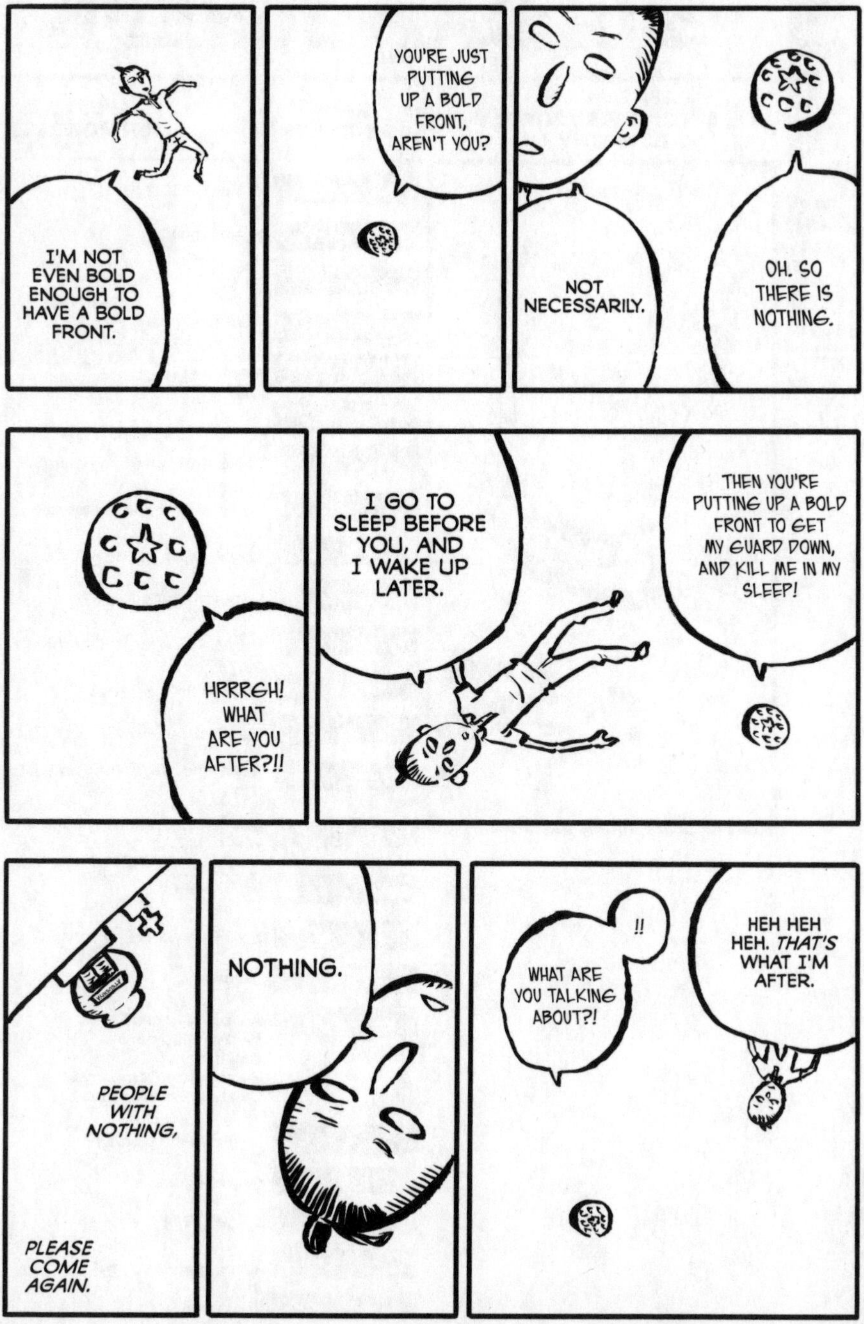
OH. SO THERE IS NOTHING.
NOT NECESSARILY.
YOU'RE JUST PUTTING UP A BOLD FRONT, AREN'T YOU?
I'M NOT EVEN BOLD ENOUGH TO HAVE A BOLD FRONT.
THEN YOU'RE PUTTING UP A BOLD FRONT TO GET MY GUARD DOWN, AND KILL ME IN MY SLEEP!
I GO TO SLEEP BEFORE YOU, AND I WAKE UP LATER.
HRRRGH! WHAT ARE YOU AFTER?!!
HEH HEH HEH. *THAT'S* WHAT I'M AFTER.
!!
WHAT ARE YOU TALKING ABOUT?!
NOTHING.
PEOPLE WITH NOTHING,
PLEASE COME AGAIN.

VULCAN JOSEPH

FIRE FORCE

AFFILIATION:	RANK:	ABILITY:
SPECIAL FIRE FORCE COMPANY 8	**ENGINEER**	**NON-POWERED**

Height	178 cm [5'10'']
Weight	72 kg [159 lbs.]
Age	18
Birthday	April 18
Sign	Aries
Bloodtype	B
Nickname	Fire Soldier Loather, Haijima Hater
Self-Proclaimed	I dunno! Just call me turdface.
Favorite Foods	Lisa's cooking! Fries! Soda!!
Least Favorite Food	I wouldn't hate food!
Favorite Music	Punk! With a lot of distortion!!
Favorite Animal	All of them!
Favorite Color	Metallic!
His Type	A girl who plays along and eats a lot!
Who He Respects	Dad and Grandpa, my ancestors who made Amaterasu
Who He Has Trouble Around	Dr. Giovanni
Who He's Afraid Of	No one in particular
Hobbies	Drums!
Daily Routine	Animal watching! Mech maintenance Catch with Yū Remodeling Company 8 Cleaning up after Iris...
Dream	To revive the world!!!!
Shoe Size	28.5 cm [10.5]
Eyesight	1.5 [20/12.5]
Favorite Subject	Technology! Biology!
Least Favorite Subject	The annoying ones

CHARACTER PROFILE

FIRE FORCE

VIKTOR LICHT

AFFILIATION: SPECIAL FIRE FORCE COMPANY 8

RANK: SCIENCE TEAM (FIRST CLASS FIRE SOLDIER) HEAD OF RESEARCH (HAIJIMA)

ABILITY: NON-POWERED

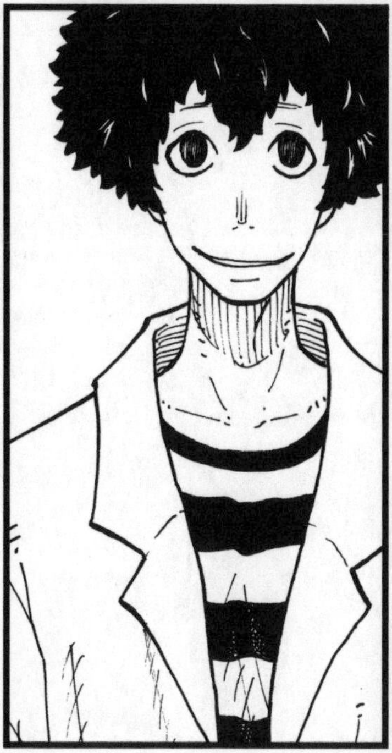

Height	187.236 cm [6'1.71496"] (measured exactly one hour after getting out of bed)
Weight	(Averaging numbers taken throughout the week) 72.358 kg [159.54939 lbs.]
Age	23 and 115 days (at time of recording)
Birthday	March 14 02:35 (@ Delivery Room 3, in Imperial Central Hospital West Wing)
Sign	Pisces
Bloodtype	AO Rh+
Nickname	Weirdo (I do understand common sense, whether or not I choose to use it.)
Self-Proclaimed	"Self-proclaimed" essentially refers to unverified information that a person uses to describe him or herself regardless of the truth behind it. Is this understanding correct?
Favorite Foods	I eat what will give me a balanced diet based on its nutritional elements.
Least Favorite Food	I avoid what will not give me a balanced diet based on its nutritional elements.
Favorite Music	EDM like dubstep and house. I listen to reggae and rap, too.
Favorite Animal	Humans
Favorite Color	DIC99(65%) + Y(11%)
His Type	Large-breasted
Who He Respects	I respect aaall of you.
Who He Has Trouble Around	People who set research budgets
Who He's Afraid Of	People who cut research funding
Hobbies	DJing
Daily Routine	I eat and sleep.
Dream	Last night, it involved a countless number of fairies hanging onto the hair at the nape of my neck.
Shoe Size	29.224 cm [11.7224]
Eyesight	1.35 [20/14.815]
Favorite Subject	Independent study
Least Favorite Subject	I don't divide my study into categories.

FIRE FORCE

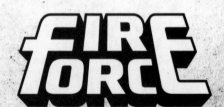

FIRE FORCE

11

ATSUSHI
OHKUBO

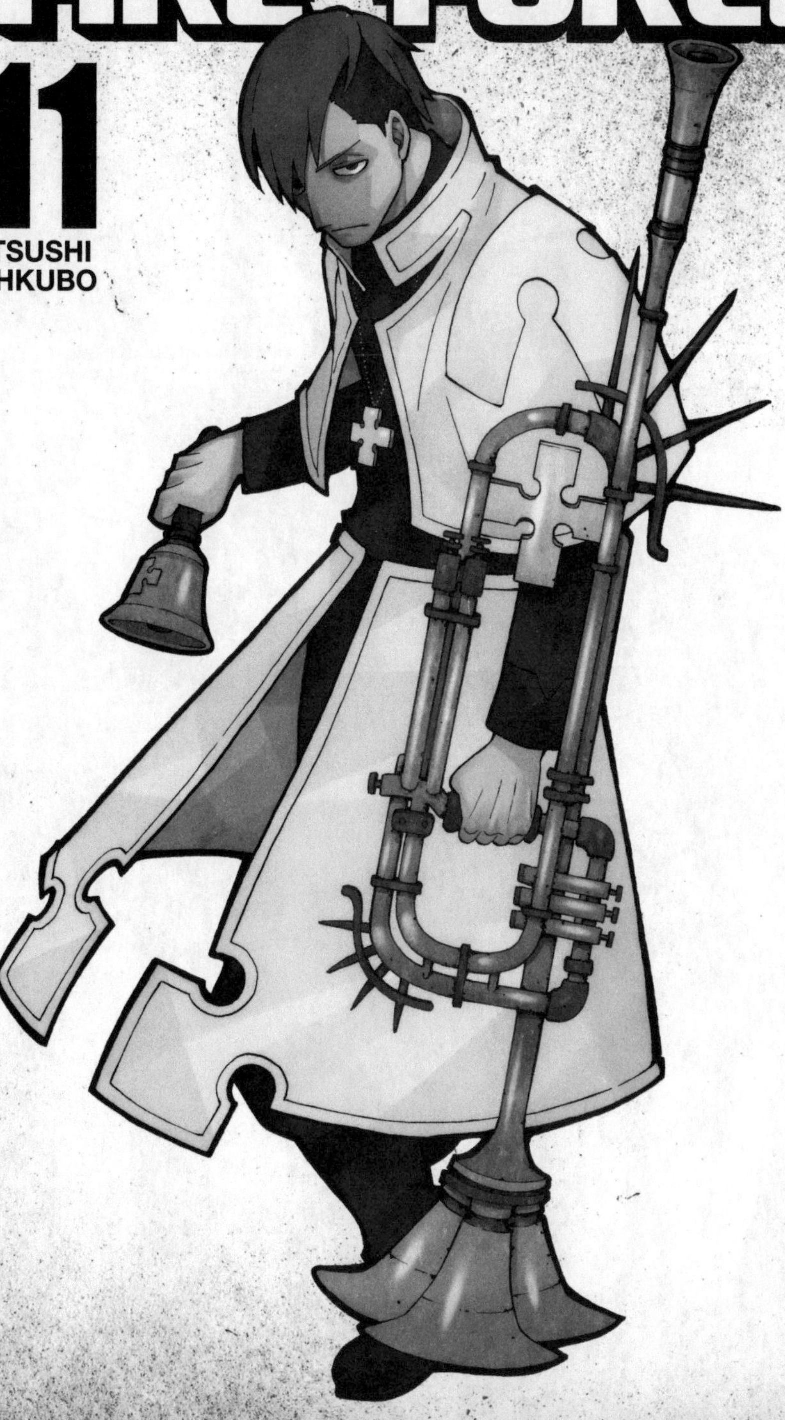

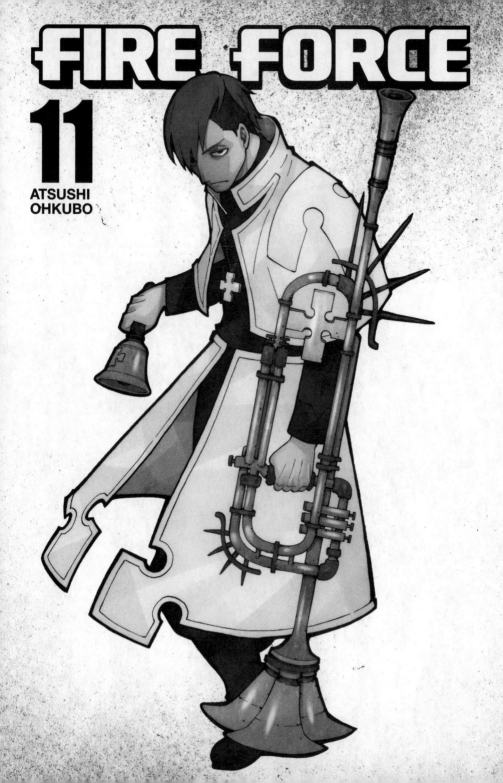

Ready Truth?

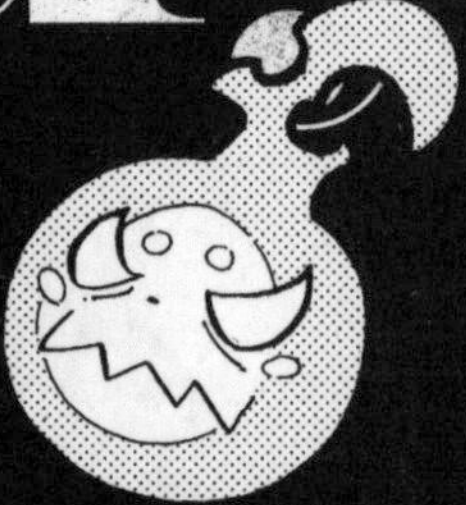

VOL. 11

ATSUSHI OHKUBO

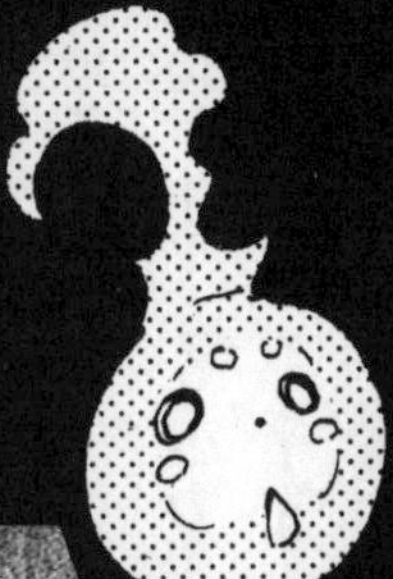

Are You For The

FIRE FORCE

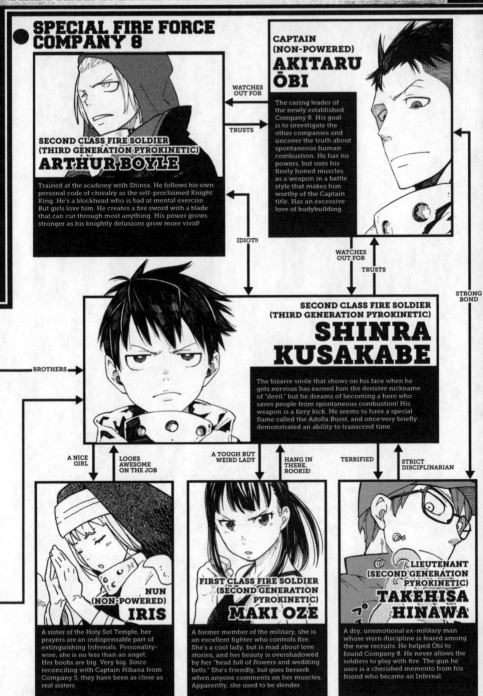

SPECIAL FIRE FORCE COMPANY 8

CAPTAIN (NON-POWERED) AKITARU ŌBI

The caring leader of the newly established Company 8. His goal is to investigate the other companies and uncover the truth about spontaneous human combustion. He has no powers, but uses his finely honed muscles as a weapon in a battle style that makes him worthy of the Captain title. Has an excessive love of bodybuilding.

WATCHES OUT FOR

TRUSTS

SECOND CLASS FIRE SOLDIER (THIRD GENERATION PYROKINETIC) ARTHUR BOYLE

Trained at the academy with Shinra. He follows his own personal code of chivalry as the self-proclaimed Knight King. He's a blockhead who is bad at mental exercise. But girls love him. He creates a fire sword with a blade that can cut through most anything. His power grows stronger as his knightly delusions grow more vivid!

IDIOT!!

WATCHES OUT FOR

TRUSTS

STRONG BOND

SECOND CLASS FIRE SOLDIER (THIRD GENERATION PYROKINETIC) SHINRA KUSAKABE

The bizarre smile that shows on his face when he gets nervous has earned him the derisive nickname of "devil," but he dreams of becoming a hero who saves people from spontaneous combustion! His weapon is a fiery kick. He seems to have a special flame called the Adolla Burst, and once very briefly demonstrated an ability to transcend time.

BROTHERS

A NICE GIRL

LOOKS AWESOME ON THE JOB

A TOUGH BUT WEIRD LADY

HANG IN THERE, ROOKIE!

TERRIFIED

STRICT DISCIPLINARIAN

LIEUTENANT (SECOND GENERATION PYROKINETIC) TAKEHISA HINAWA

A dry, unemotional ex-military man whose stern discipline is feared among the new recruits. He helped Ōbi to found Company 8. He never allows the soldiers to play with fire. The gun he uses is a cherished memento from his friend who became an Infernal.

FIRST CLASS FIRE SOLDIER (SECOND GENERATION PYROKINETIC) MAKI OZE

A former member of the military, she is an excellent fighter who controls fire. She's a cool lady, but is mad about love stories, and her beauty is overshadowed by her "head full of flowers and wedding bells." She's friendly, but goes berserk when anyone comments on her muscles. Apparently, she used to be slender.

NUN (NON-POWERED) IRIS

A sister of the Holy Sol Temple, her prayers are an indispensable part of extinguishing Infernals. Personality-wise, she is no less than an angel. Her boobs are big. Very big. Since reconciling with Captain Hibana from Company 5, they have been as close as real sisters.

THE GIRLS' CLUB

RESPECTS

SPECIAL FIRE FORCE COMPANY 1

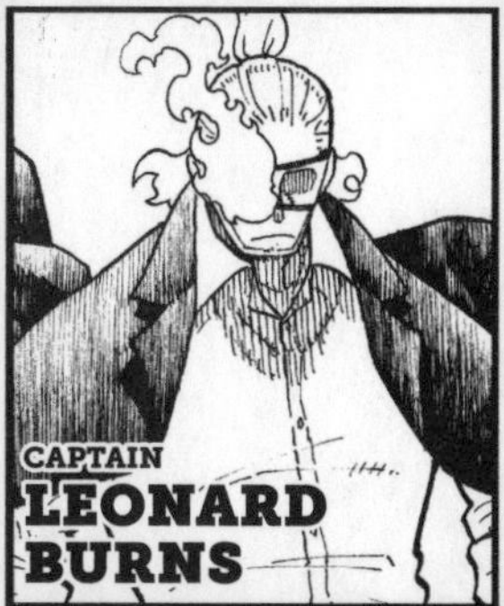

CAPTAIN
LEONARD BURNS

A fire soldier who ran to the scene of the fire that took Shinra's family when he was young. He commands the elite Company 1 and has overwhelming skill. He holds some kind of secret...?

FOLLOWERS OF THE EVANGELIST

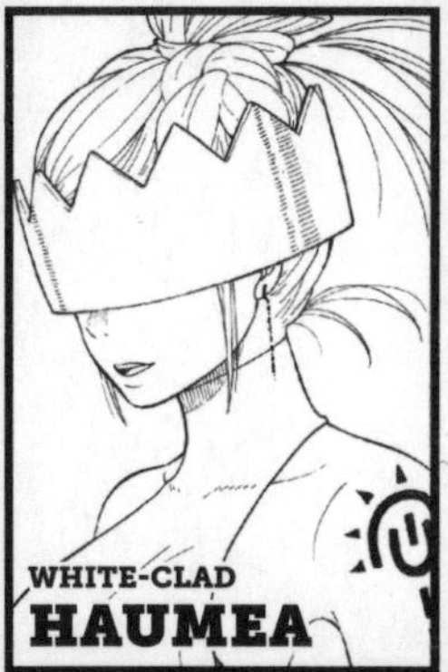

WHITE-CLAD
HAUMEA

One of the Evangelist's white-clad combatants. After Shō begins to open his heart to Shinra, she neutralizes the knight commander with a power still shrouded in mystery and takes him back to the Evangelist.

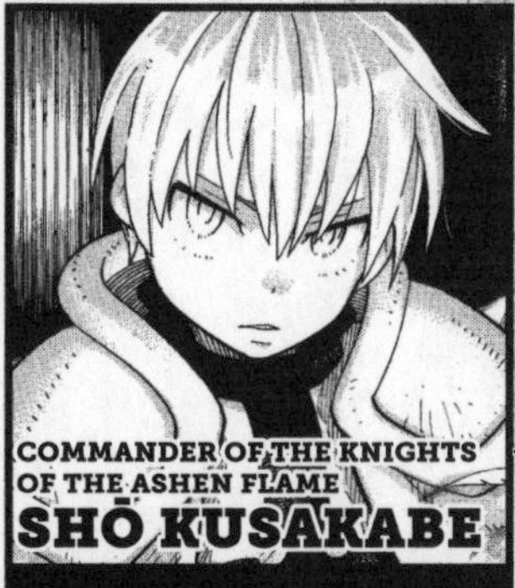

COMMANDER OF THE KNIGHTS OF THE ASHEN FLAME
SHŌ KUSAKABE

Shinra's long-lost brother, the commander of an order of knights that works for the Evangelist. He has the astounding ability to stop time for all but himself! Through a direct confrontation with Shinra, the two begin to regain their brotherly bond, but Haumea intervenes.

SPECIAL FIRE FORCE COMPANY 6

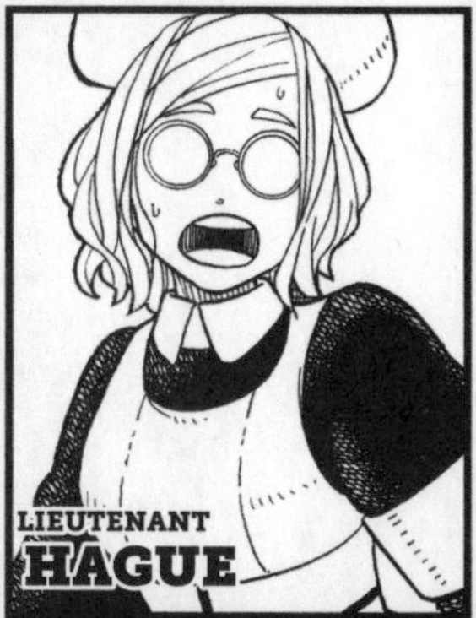

LIEUTENANT
HAGUE

A soldier at Special Fire Hospital 6, where Shinra was taken for emergency treatment after his fight with Shō. She has a mild-mannered personality, and her catchphrase is "Shock!!"

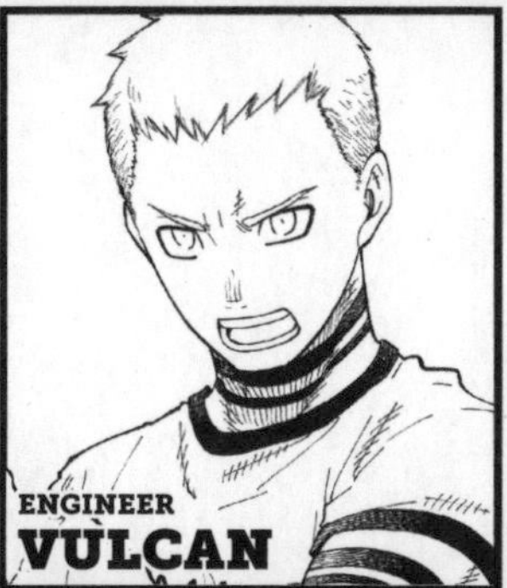

ENGINEER
VULCAN

The greatest engineer of the day, renowned as the God of Fire and the Forge. He originally hated the Fire Force, but he sympathized with Ōbi's and Shinra's ideals and agreed to join Company 8 as their engineer. His dream is to revive the world's extinct animals!

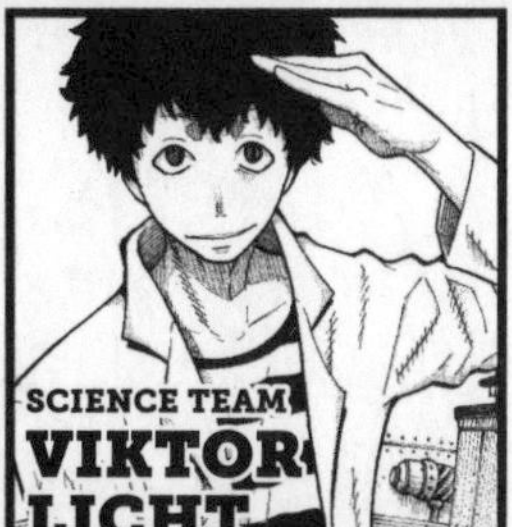

SCIENCE TEAM
VIKTOR LICHT

A morally ambiguous man deployed from Haijima Industries to fill the vacancy in Company 8's science department. Apparently a genius.

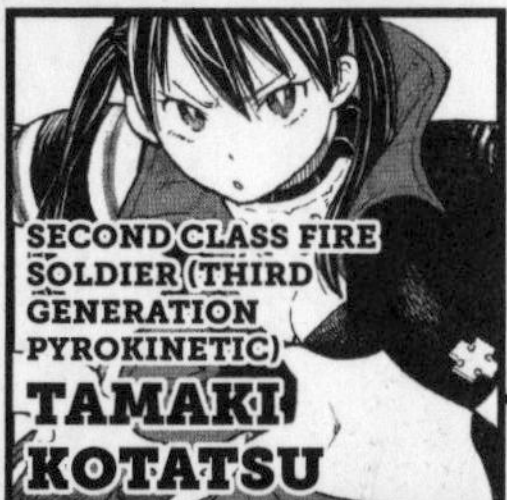

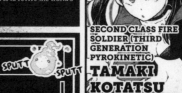

SECOND CLASS FIRE SOLDIER (THIRD GENERATION PYROKINETIC)
TAMAKI KOTATSU

HAS HIM ON HER MIND

Originally a rookie member of Company 1, she was caught up in the treasonous plot of her superior officer Hoshimiya, and is currently being disciplined under Company 8's watch. A tough girl with an unfortunate "lucky lecher lure" condition, she nevertheless has a pure heart.

SUMMARY...

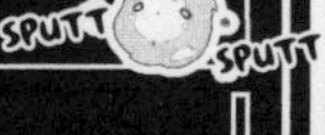
SPUTT
SPUTT

Shinra fights for his life after his touching reunion with Shō results in a possibly fatal injury. He is taken to Special Fire Hospital 6, a facility that specializes in treating pyrokinetics, and his life is saved. When he wakes from his coma, who should appear before Shinra but Captain Burns of Special Fire Force Company 1. He says he has come to discuss the fire that took Shinra's family 12 years ago, but what is he really after...?!

FIRE FORCE

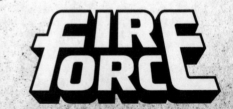

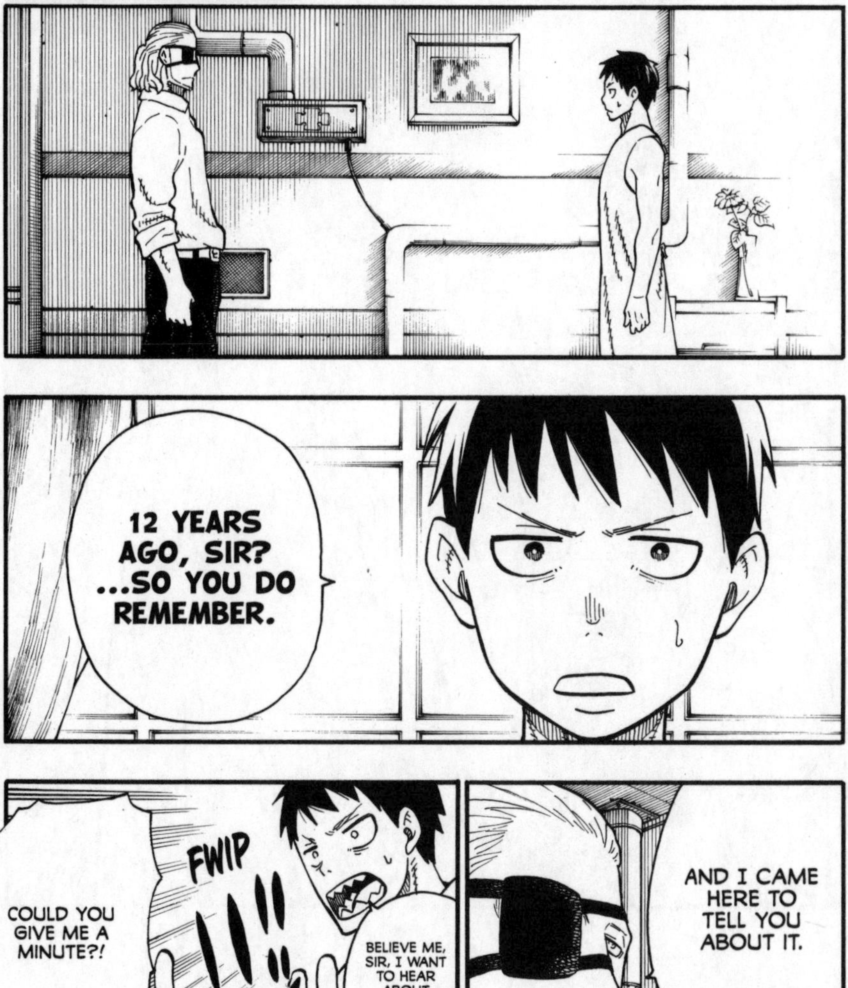
12 YEARS AGO, SIR? ...SO YOU DO REMEMBER.
AND I CAME HERE TO TELL YOU ABOUT IT.
IT'S A LONG STORY. GET COMFORTABLE.
BELIEVE ME, SIR, I WANT TO HEAR ABOUT THIS MORE THAN ANYTHING, BUT...
FWIP
COULD YOU GIVE ME A MINUTE?!
IS SOMETHING THE MATTER?

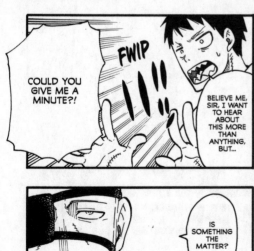

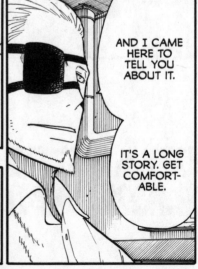

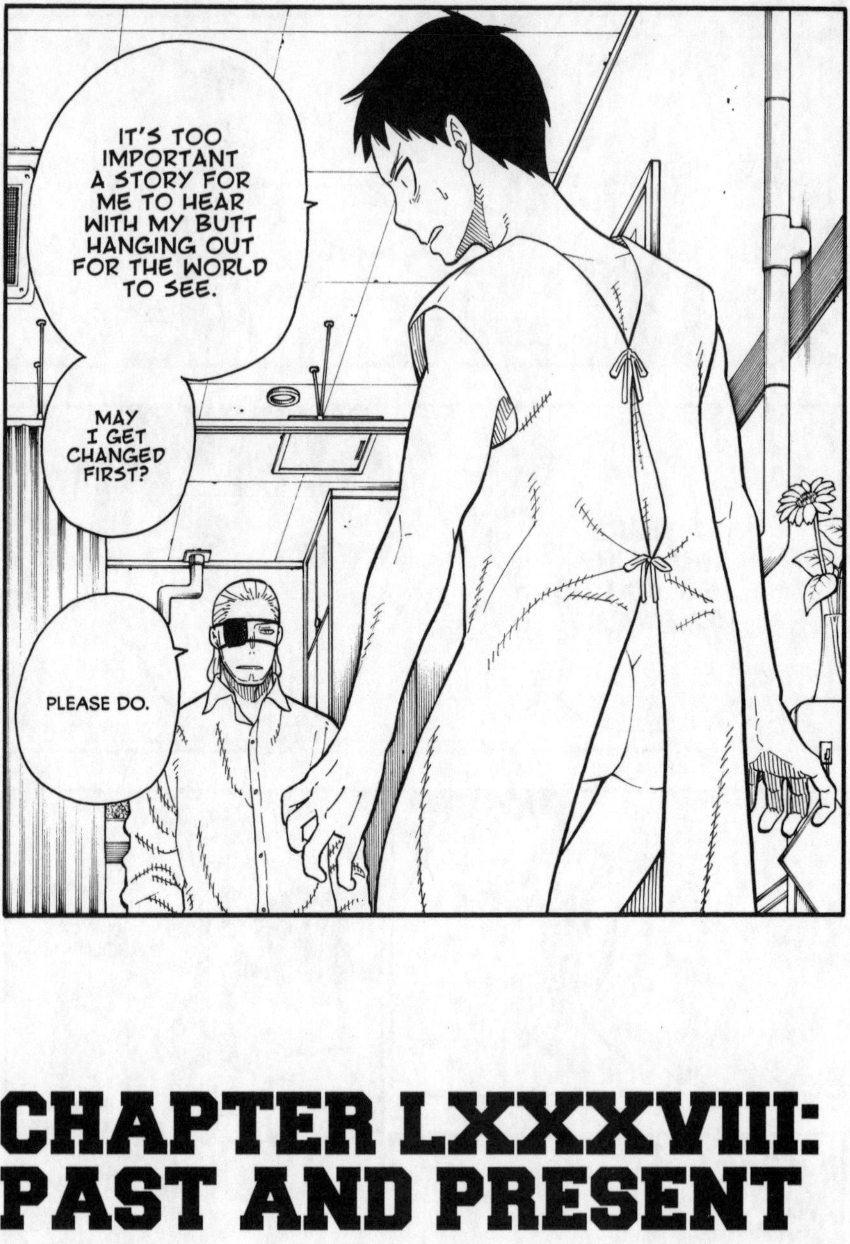
IT'S TOO IMPORTANT A STORY FOR ME TO HEAR WITH MY BUTT HANGING OUT FOR THE WORLD TO SEE.
MAY I GET CHANGED FIRST?
PLEASE DO.

CHAPTER LXXXVIII: PAST AND PRESENT

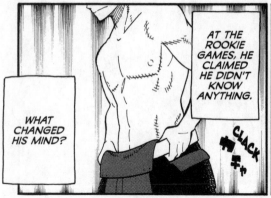

FWO OSH
AT THE ROOKIE GAMES, HE CLAIMED HE DIDN'T KNOW ANYTHING.
WHAT CHANGED HIS MIND?
CLACK
!
NO STITCHES OR ANYTHING. IT ALREADY LOOKS LIKE AN OLD SCAR.
I SAW THE COMPANY 6 CREST OUTSIDE THE WINDOW... SO I GUESS THEY'RE THE ONES THAT FIXED ME UP.
FIRE FO
6
TOKYO

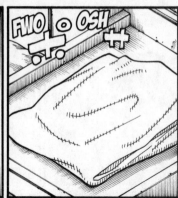

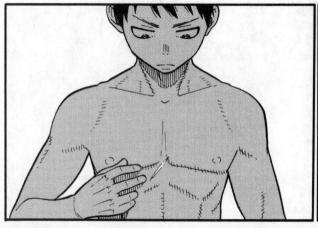

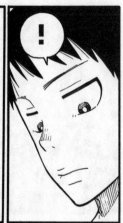

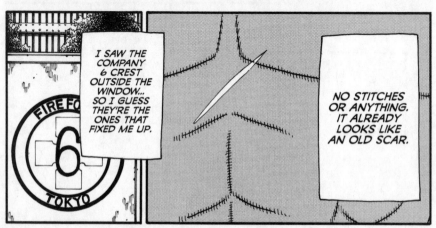

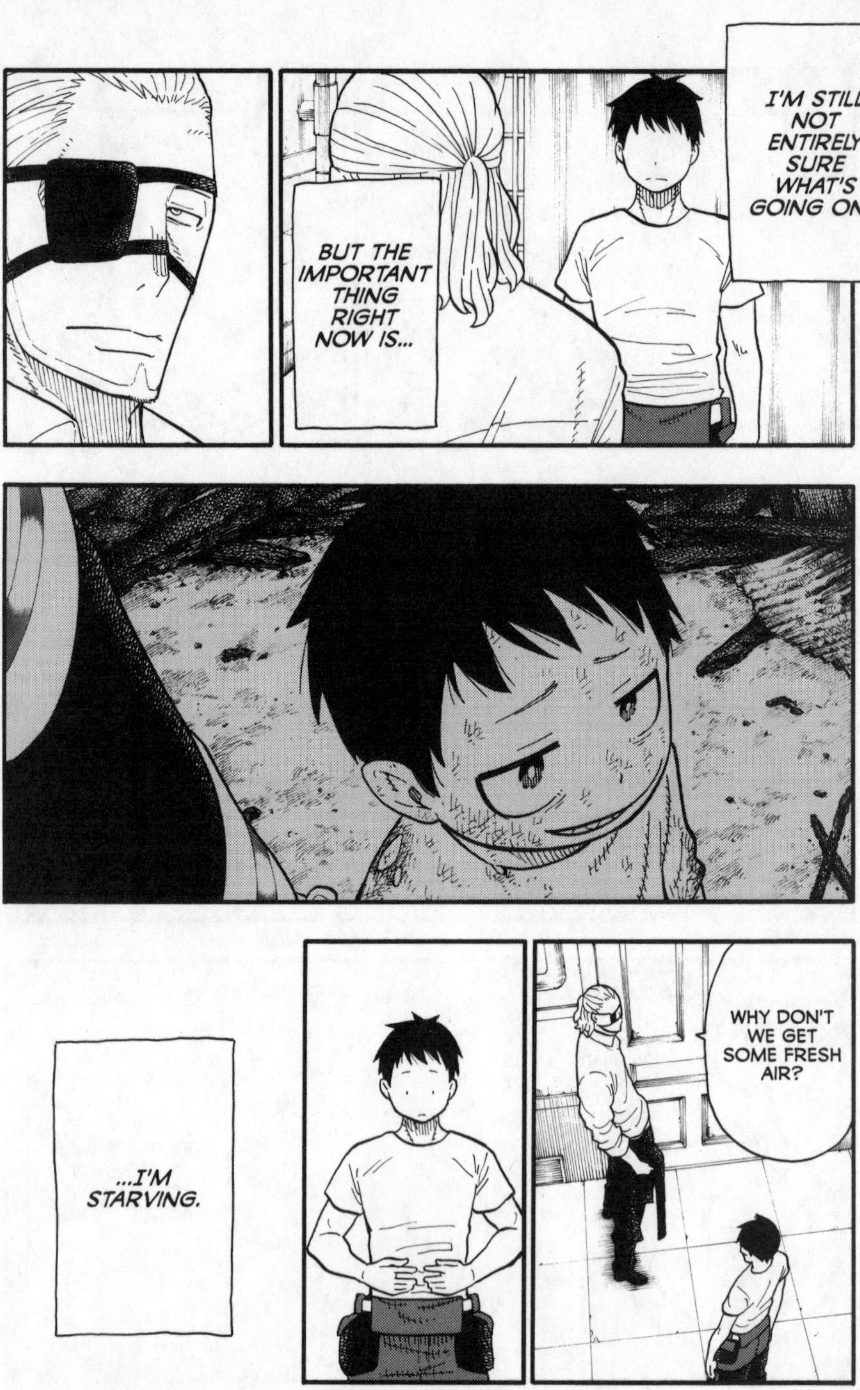
I'M STILL NOT ENTIRELY SURE WHAT'S GOING ON...
BUT THE IMPORTANT THING RIGHT NOW IS...
WHY DON'T WE GET SOME FRESH AIR?
...I'M STARVING.

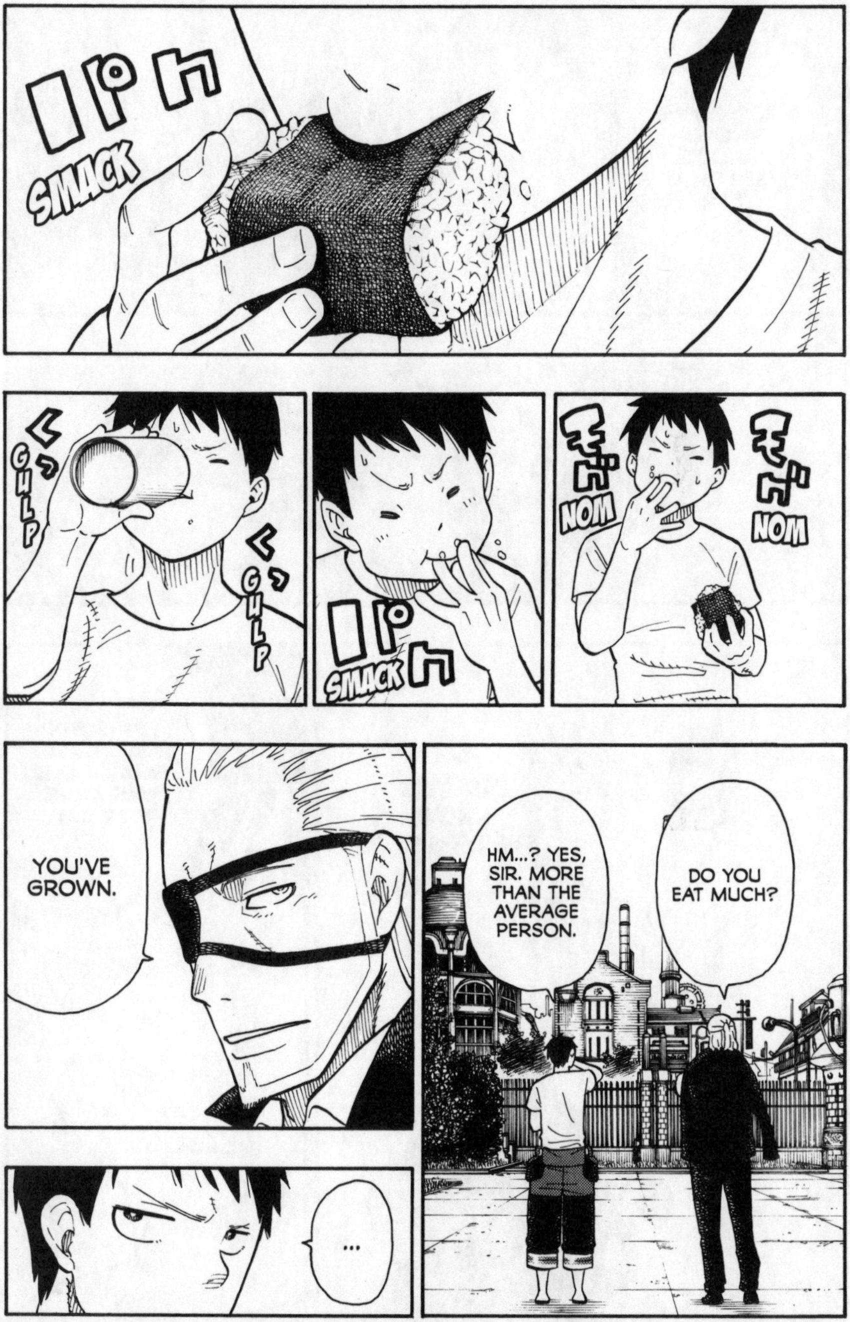
SMACK
NOM
NOM
SMACK
GULP
GULP
DO YOU EAT MUCH?
HM...? YES, SIR. MORE THAN THE AVERAGE PERSON.
YOU'VE GROWN.
...

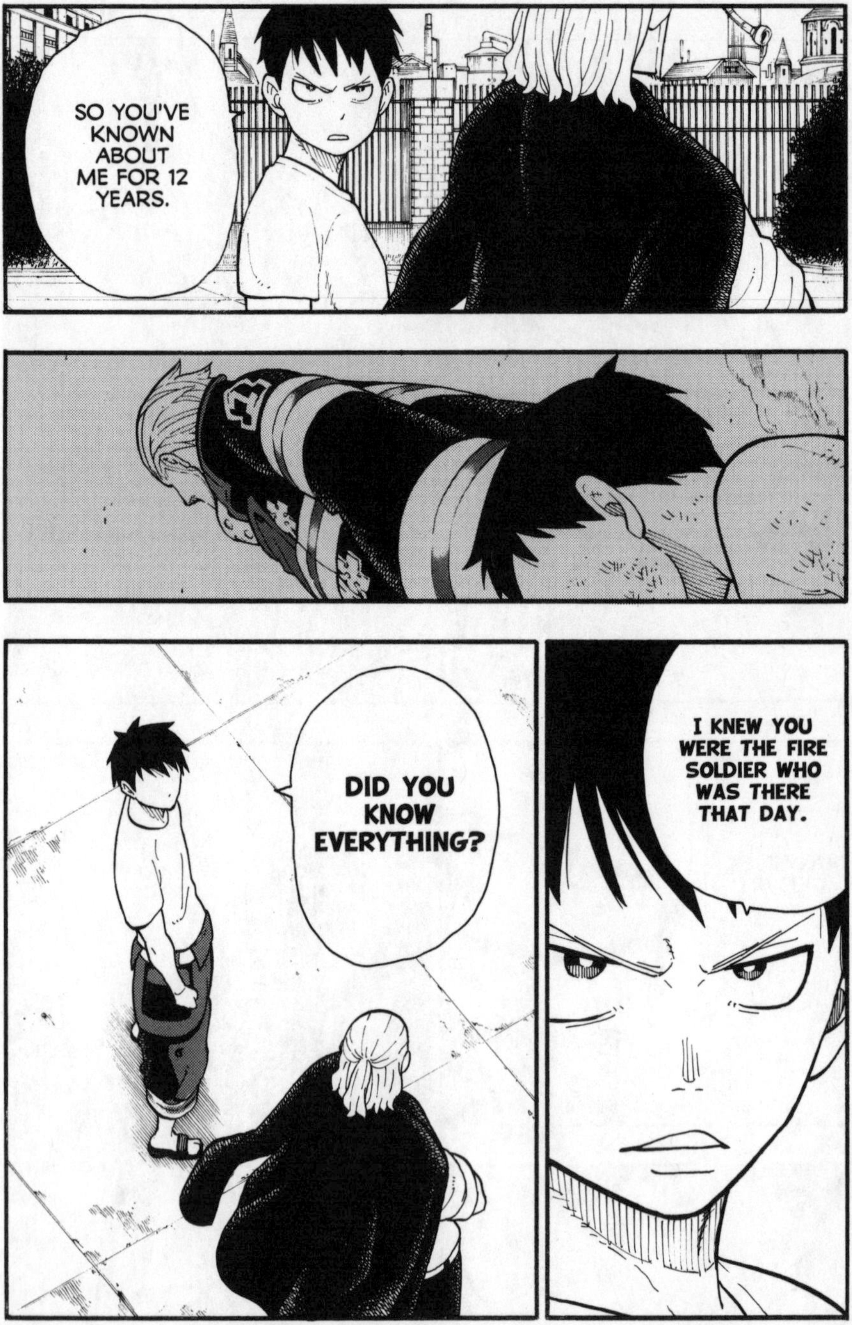
SO YOU'VE KNOWN ABOUT ME FOR 12 YEARS.
I KNEW YOU WERE THE FIRE SOLDIER WHO WAS THERE THAT DAY.
DID YOU KNOW EVERYTHING?

I DON'T CARE ABOUT ME!!

DID YOU KNOW THAT SHŌ WAS ALIVE, CAPTAIN BURNS?

YES.

IF I HAD REPORTED THE TRUTH ABOUT THAT FIRE, YOU WOULD HAVE BEEN SPARED YOUR BADGE OF INFAMY–NO ONE WOULD HAVE SUSPECTED YOU OF KILLING YOUR OWN FAMILY.

DOES THAT MEAN YOU KNEW HE'D BEEN TAKEN BY THE EVANGELIST'S CRONIES, SIR?!

YES.

YES.

I KNEW.

I KNEW.

!!

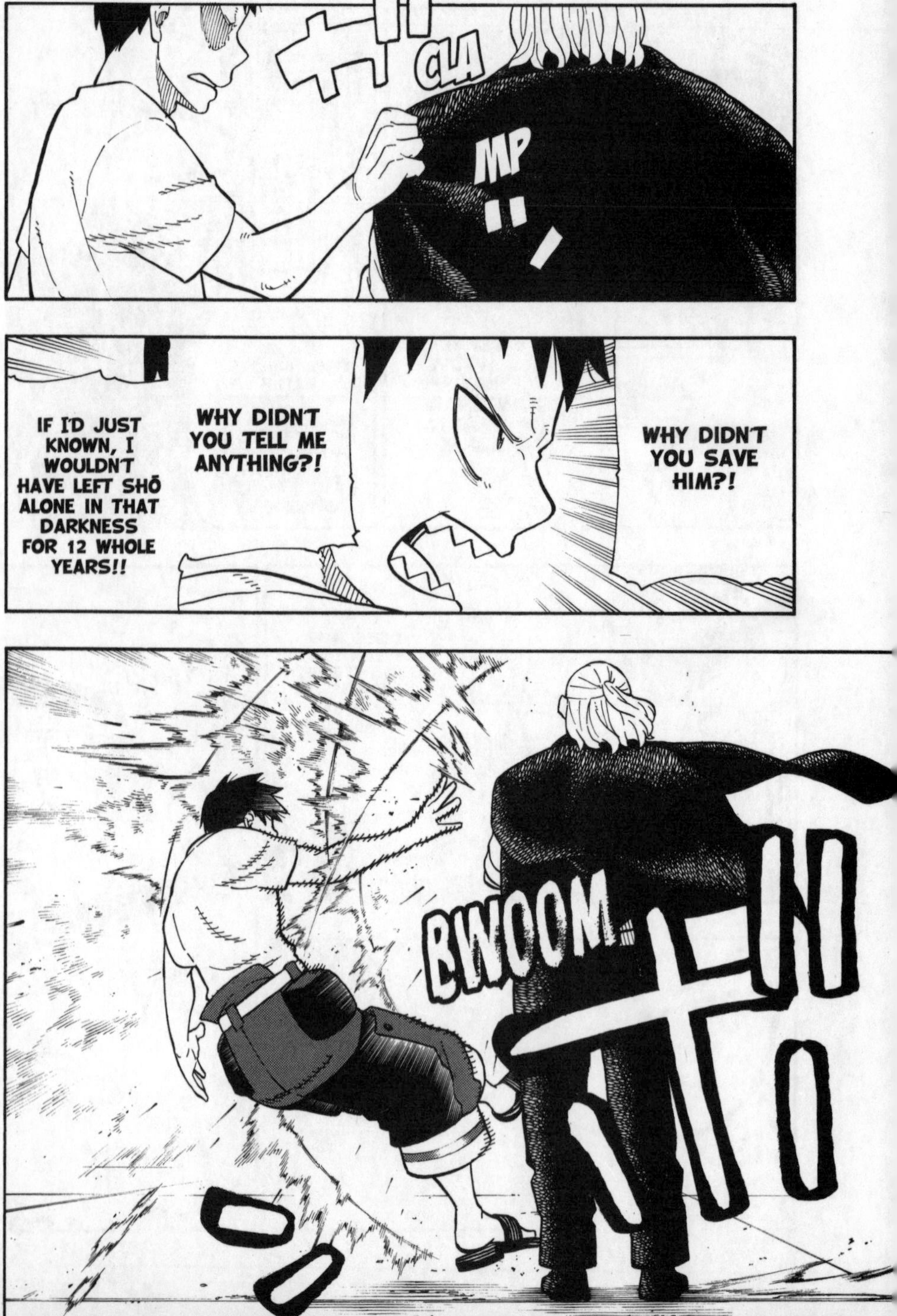
CLAMP
WHY DIDN'T YOU SAVE HIM?!
WHY DIDN'T YOU TELL ME ANYTHING?!
IF I'D JUST KNOWN, I WOULDN'T HAVE LEFT SHŌ ALONE IN THAT DARKNESS FOR 12 WHOLE YEARS!!
BWOOM

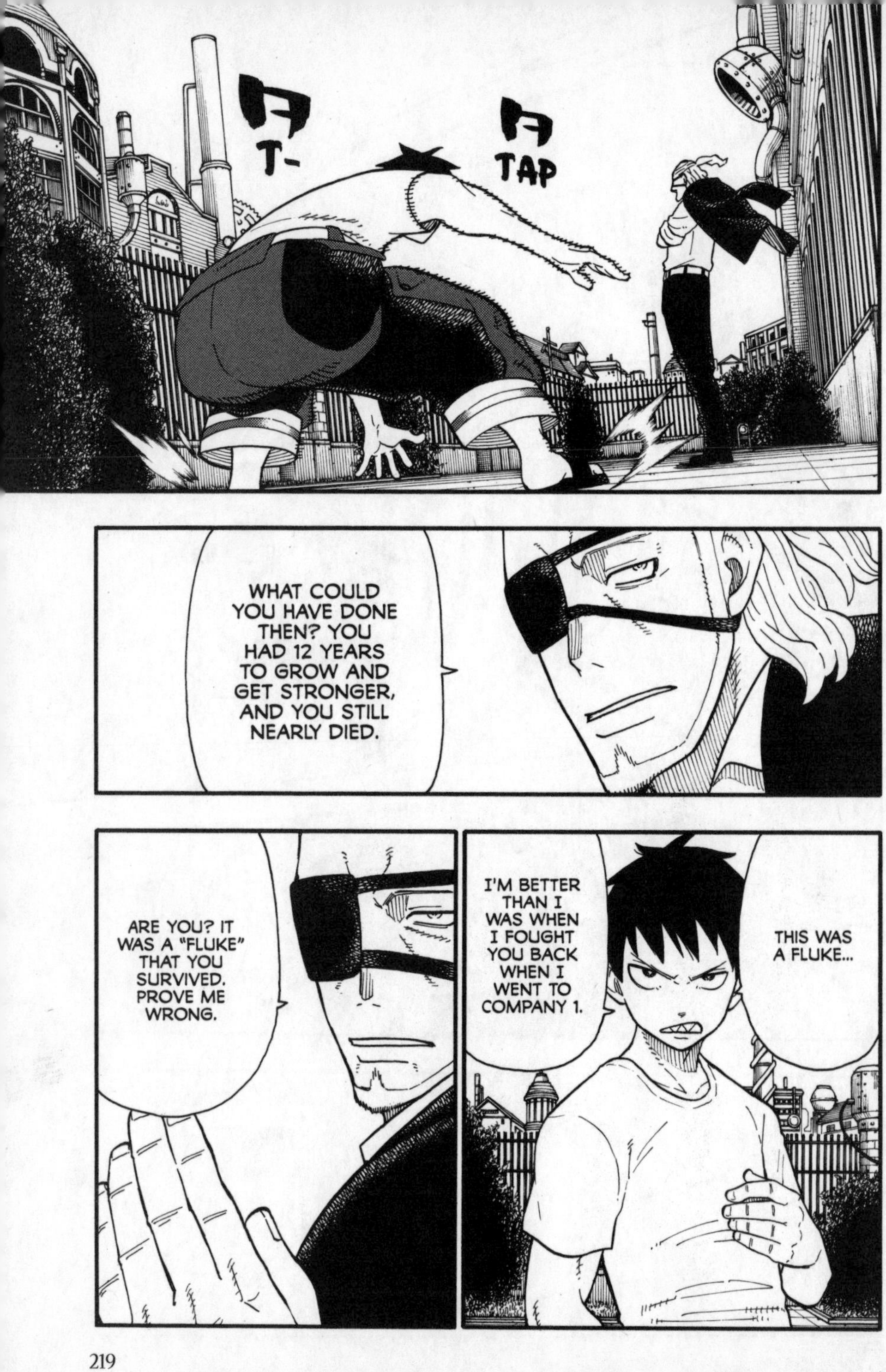
T-
TAP
WHAT COULD YOU HAVE DONE THEN? YOU HAD 12 YEARS TO GROW AND GET STRONGER, AND YOU STILL NEARLY DIED.
THIS WAS A FLUKE...
I'M BETTER THAN I WAS WHEN I FOUGHT YOU BACK WHEN I WENT TO COMPANY 1.
ARE YOU? IT WAS A "FLUKE" THAT YOU SURVIVED. PROVE ME WRONG.

IF I'D KNOWN, I WOULDN'T HAVE LEFT SHŌ ALONE FOR SO LONG!

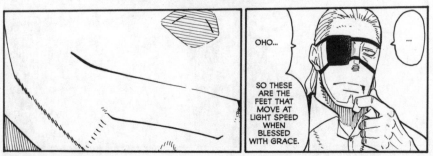

OHO...

SO THESE ARE THE FEET THAT MOVE AT LIGHT SPEED WHEN BLESSED WITH GRACE.

...

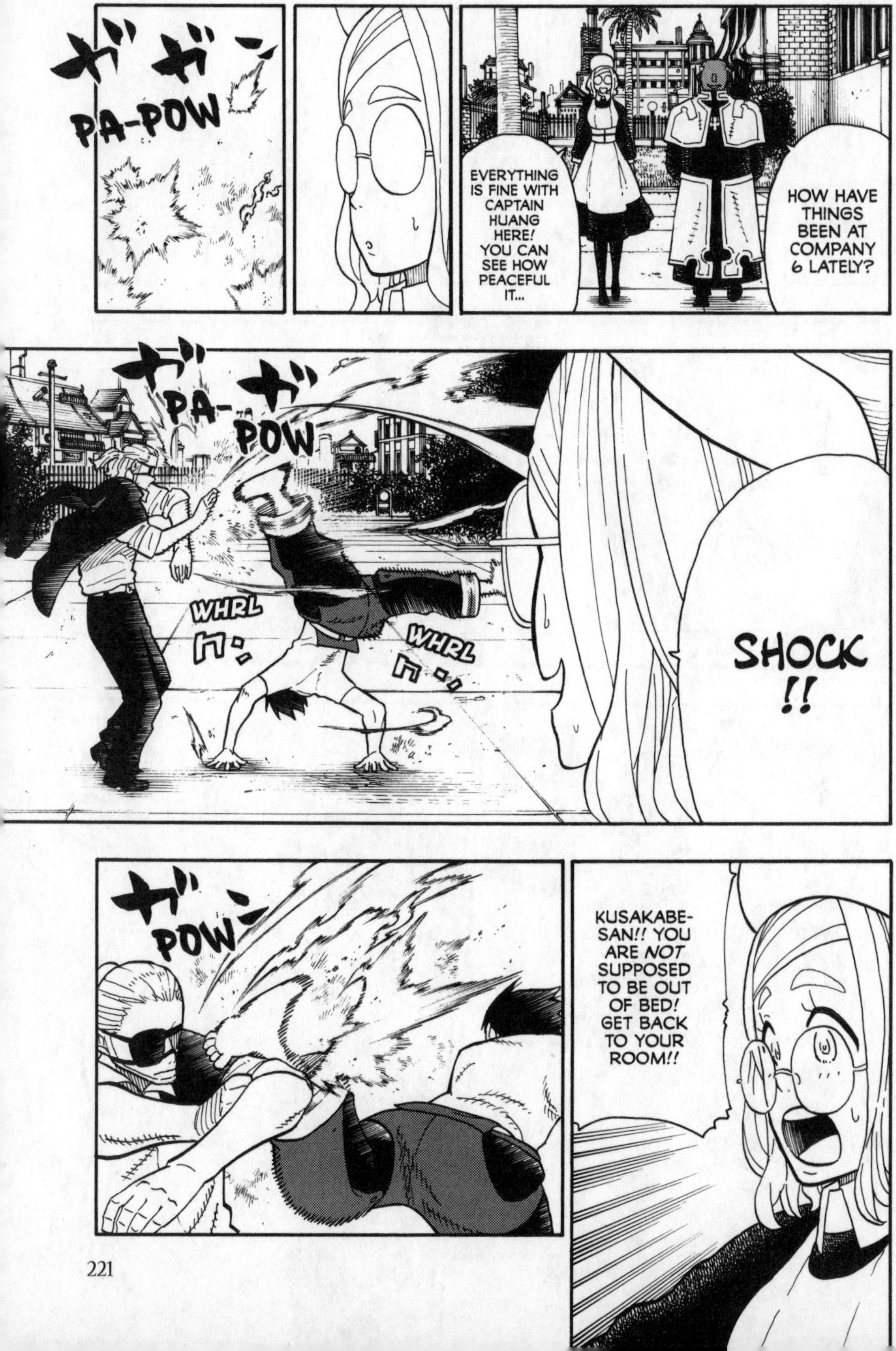
HOW HAVE THINGS BEEN AT COMPANY 6 LATELY?
EVERYTHING IS FINE WITH CAPTAIN HUANG HERE! YOU CAN SEE HOW PEACEFUL IT...
PA-POW
SHOCK!!
PA-POW
WHRL
WHRL
KUSAKABE-SAN!! YOU ARE *NOT* SUPPOSED TO BE OUT OF BED! GET BACK TO YOUR ROOM!!
POW

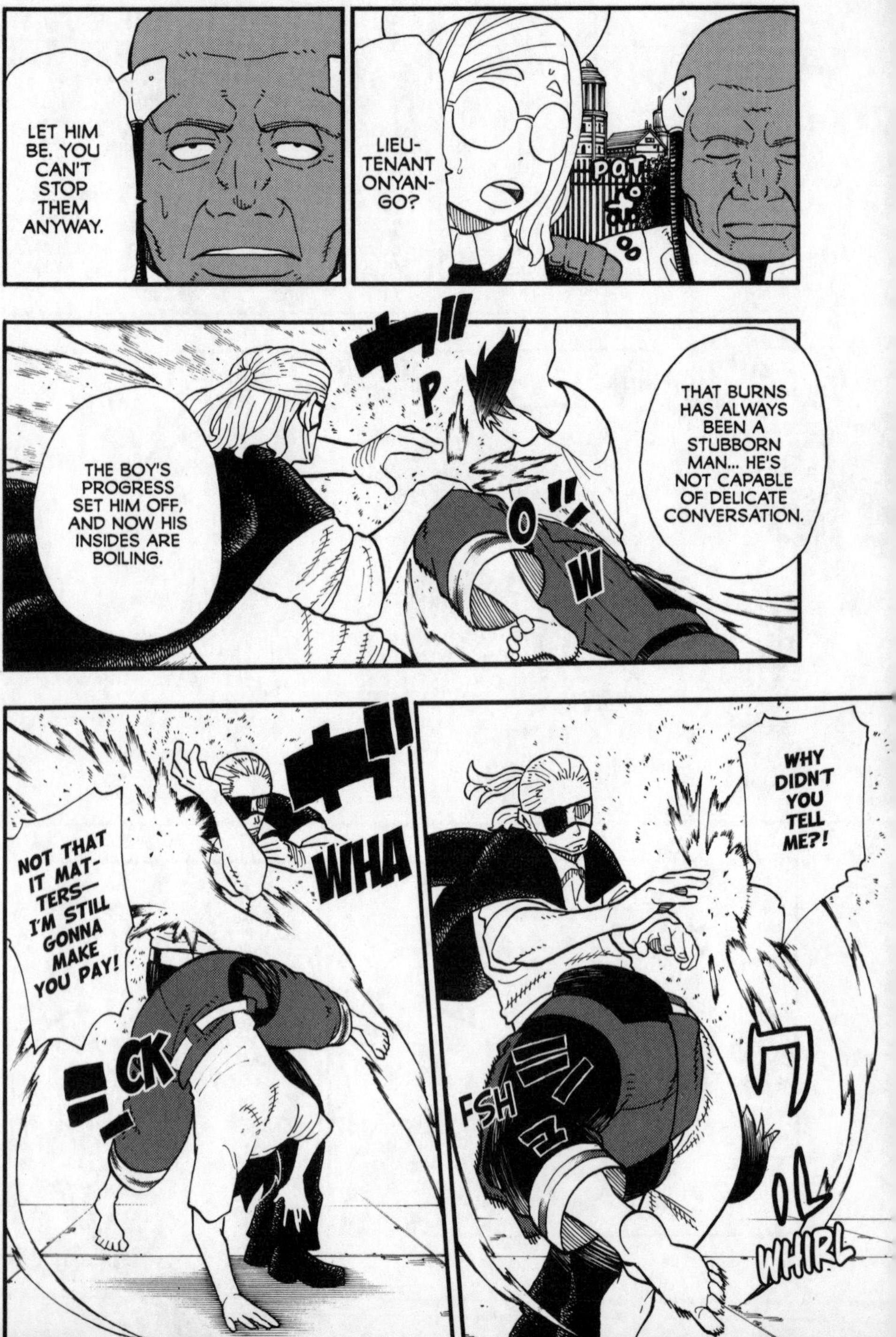
LIEU-TENANT ONYAN-GO?
PAT PAT
LET HIM BE. YOU CAN'T STOP THEM ANYWAY.
THAT BURNS HAS ALWAYS BEEN A STUBBORN MAN... HE'S NOT CAPABLE OF DELICATE CONVERSATION.
P
O
W
THE BOY'S PROGRESS SET HIM OFF, AND NOW HIS INSIDES ARE BOILING.
WHY DIDN'T YOU TELL ME?!
FSH
WHIRL
WHA
NOT THAT IT MAT-TERS— I'M STILL GONNA MAKE YOU PAY!
CK

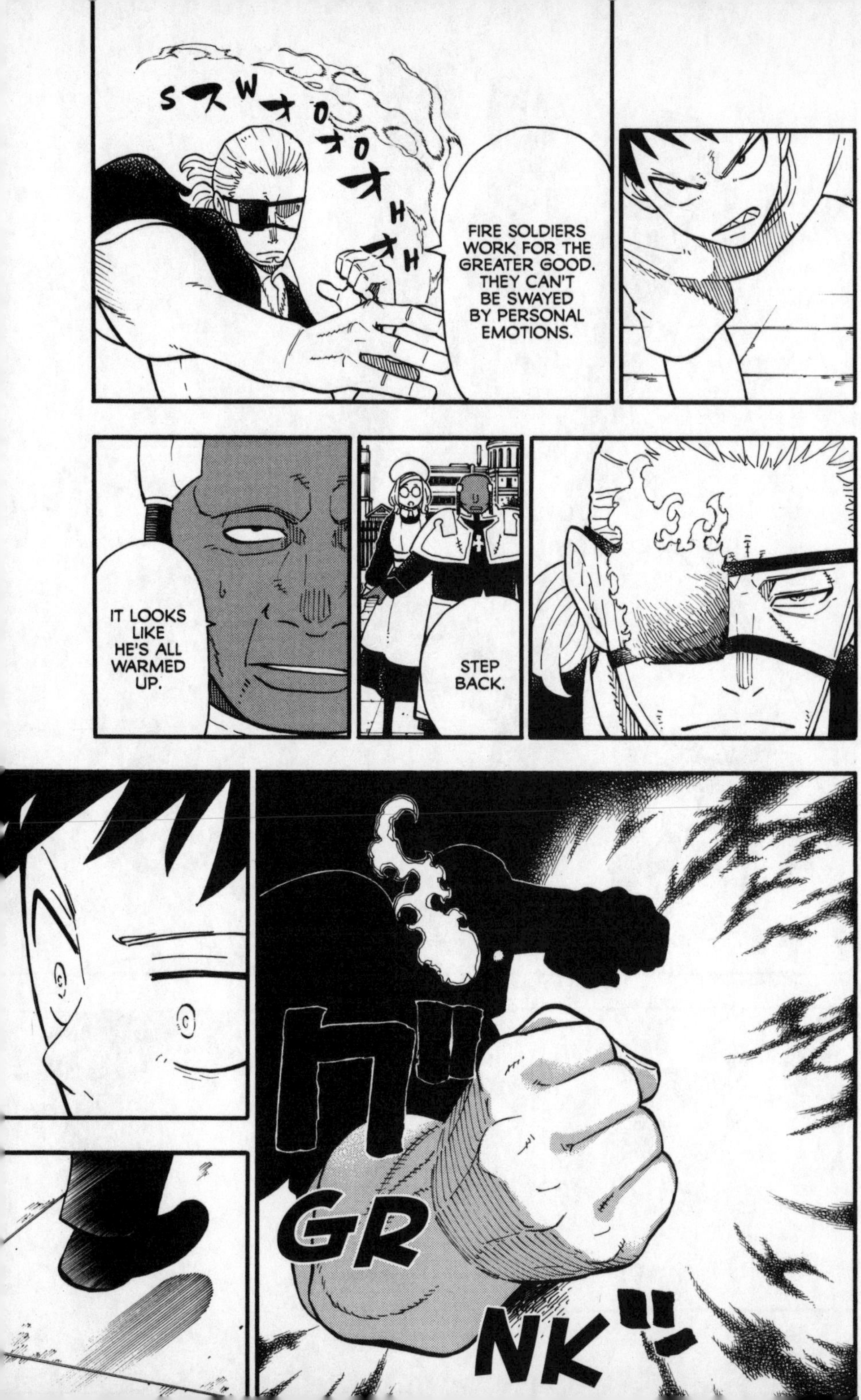
SWOOHH
FIRE SOLDIERS WORK FOR THE GREATER GOOD. THEY CAN'T BE SWAYED BY PERSONAL EMOTIONS.
STEP BACK.
IT LOOKS LIKE HE'S ALL WARMED UP.
GRNK

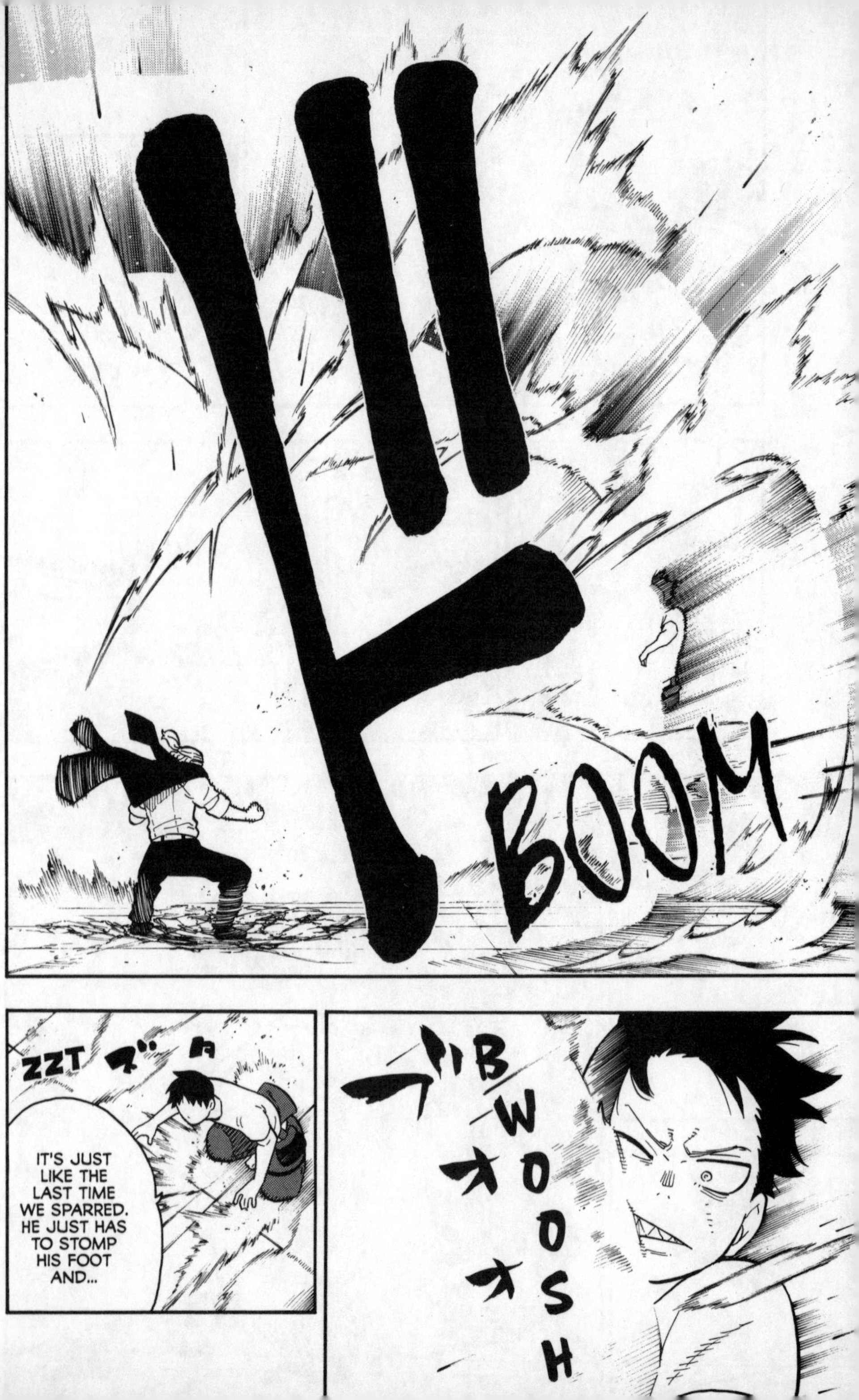
ド
BOOM
BWOOSH
ZZT
IT'S JUST LIKE THE LAST TIME WE SPARRED. HE JUST HAS TO STOMP HIS FOOT AND...

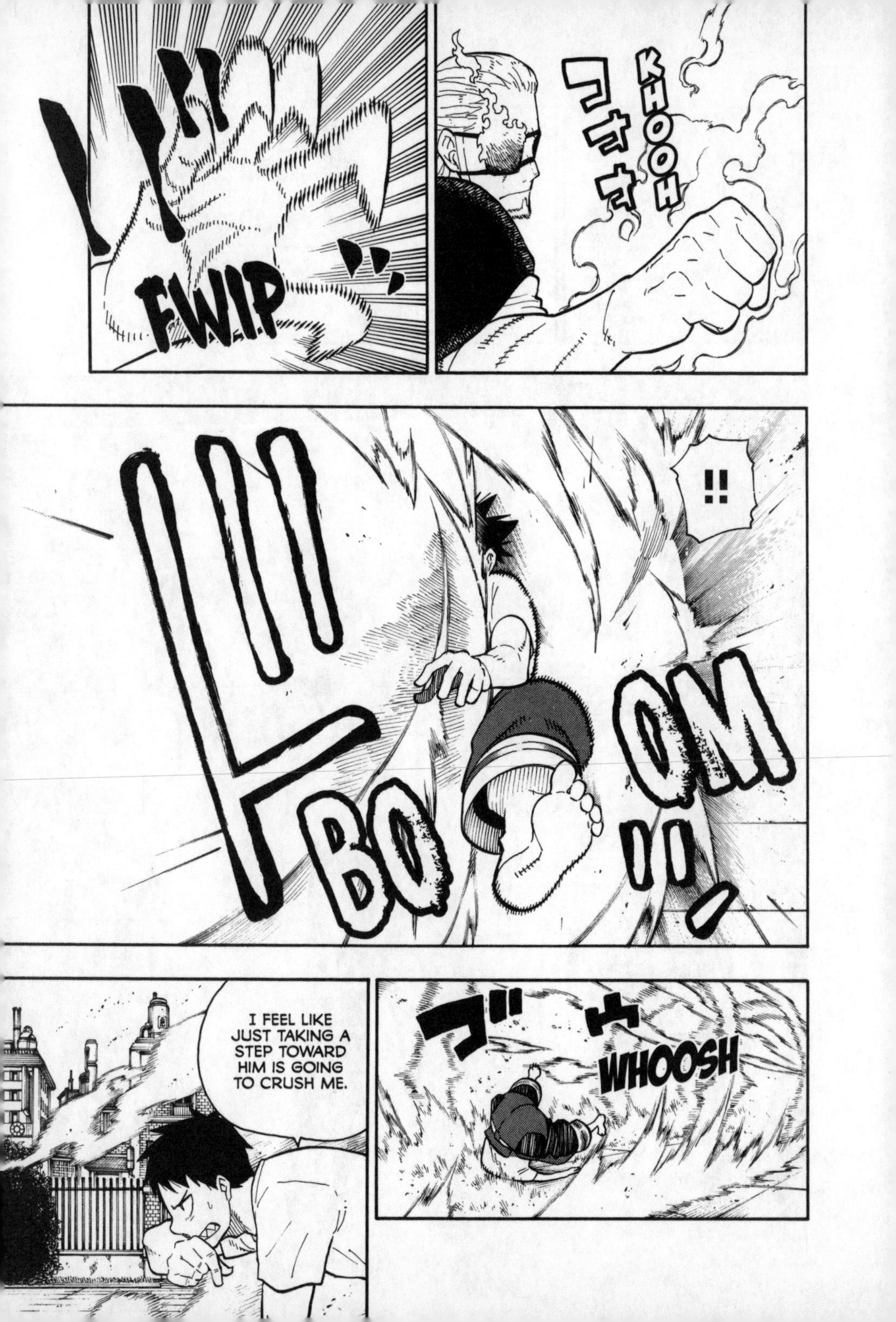

KHOOH
フォオ
FWIP
!!
BOOM
WHOOSH
I FEEL LIKE JUST TAKING A STEP TOWARD HIM IS GOING TO CRUSH ME.

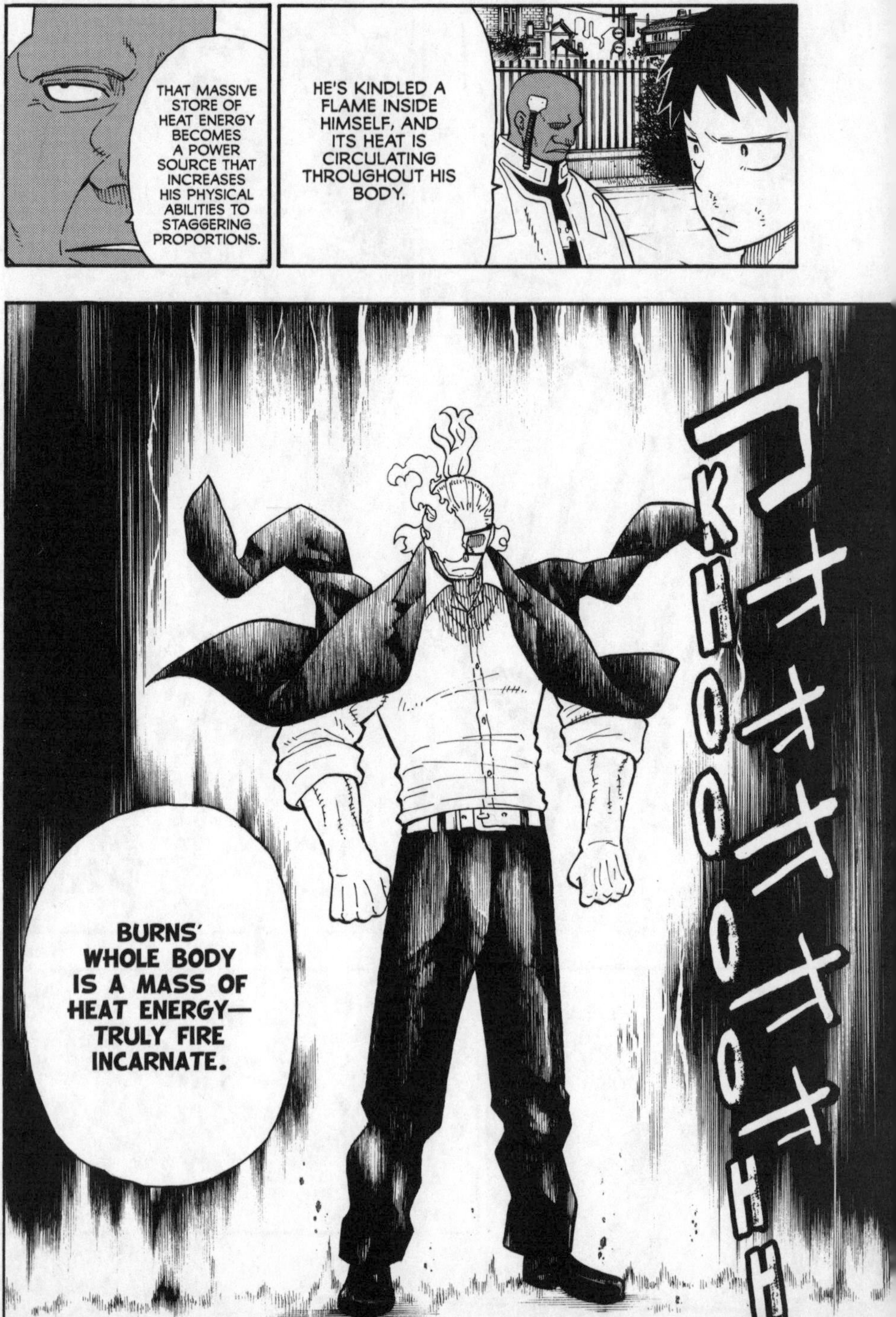
HE'S KINDLED A FLAME INSIDE HIMSELF, AND ITS HEAT IS CIRCULATING THROUGHOUT HIS BODY.
THAT MASSIVE STORE OF HEAT ENERGY BECOMES A POWER SOURCE THAT INCREASES HIS PHYSICAL ABILITIES TO STAGGERING PROPORTIONS.
KHOOOOHH
BURNS' WHOLE BODY IS A MASS OF HEAT ENERGY—TRULY FIRE INCARNATE.

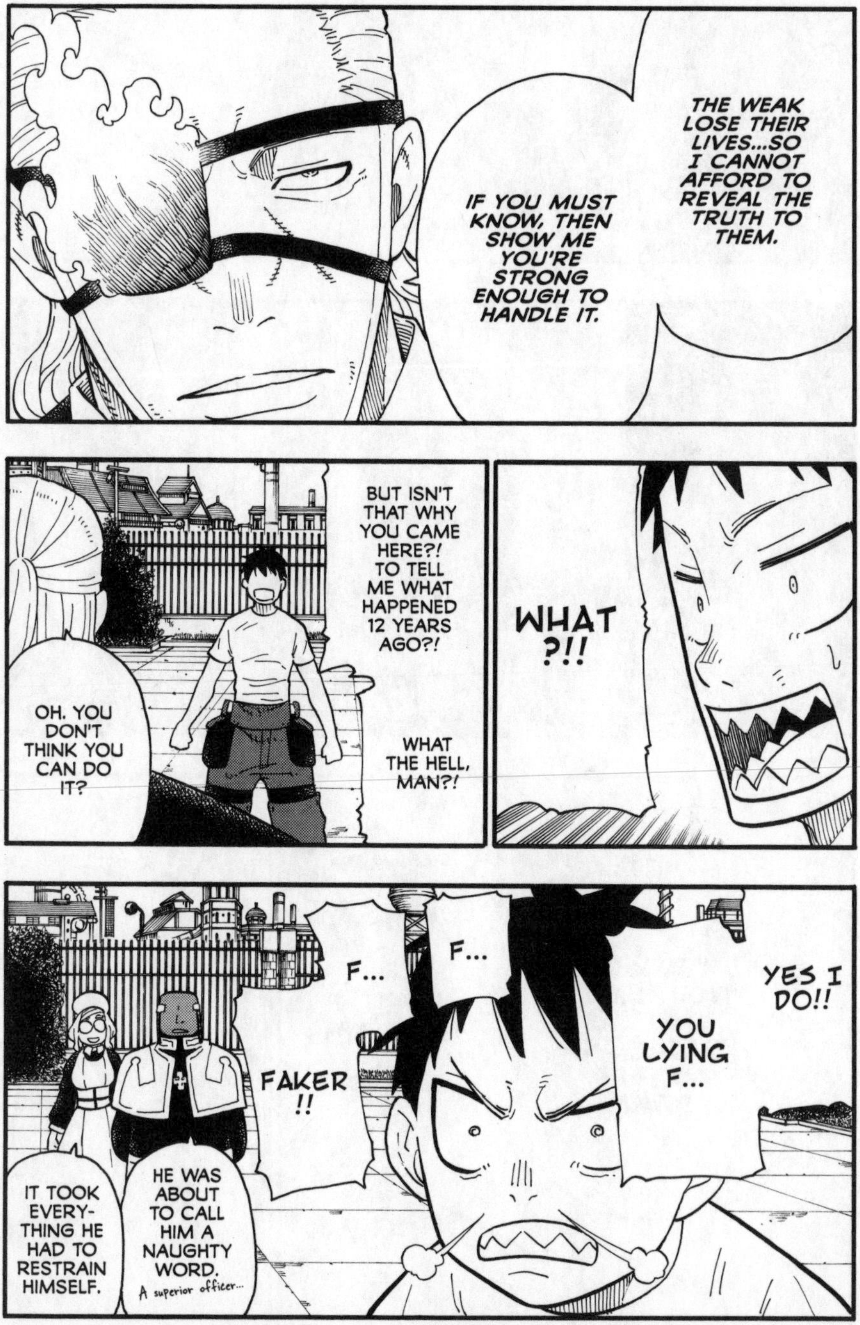
THE WEAK LOSE THEIR LIVES...SO I CANNOT AFFORD TO REVEAL THE TRUTH TO THEM.
IF YOU MUST KNOW, THEN SHOW ME YOU'RE STRONG ENOUGH TO HANDLE IT.
WHAT ?!!
BUT ISN'T THAT WHY YOU CAME HERE?! TO TELL ME WHAT HAPPENED 12 YEARS AGO?!
WHAT THE HELL, MAN?!
OH. YOU DON'T THINK YOU CAN DO IT?
YES I DO!!
YOU LYING F...
F...
F...
FAKER !!
HE WAS ABOUT TO CALL HIM A NAUGHTY WORD.
A superior officer...
IT TOOK EVERY-THING HE HAD TO RESTRAIN HIMSELF.

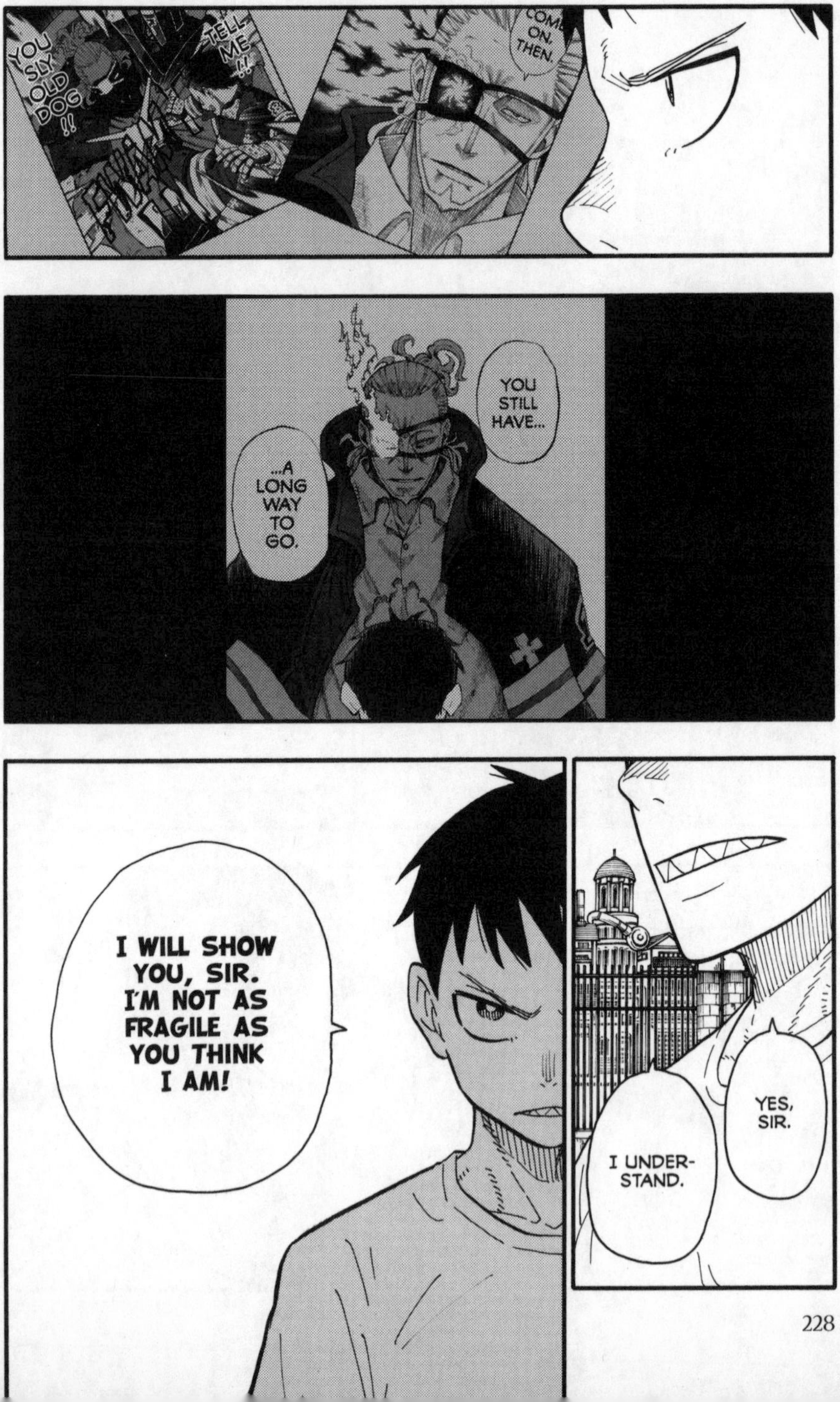
COME ON. THEN.
TELL ME!!
YOU SLY OLD DOG!!
YOU STILL HAVE...
...A LONG WAY TO GO.
YES, SIR.
I UNDER-STAND.
I WILL SHOW YOU, SIR. I'M NOT AS FRAGILE AS YOU THINK I AM!

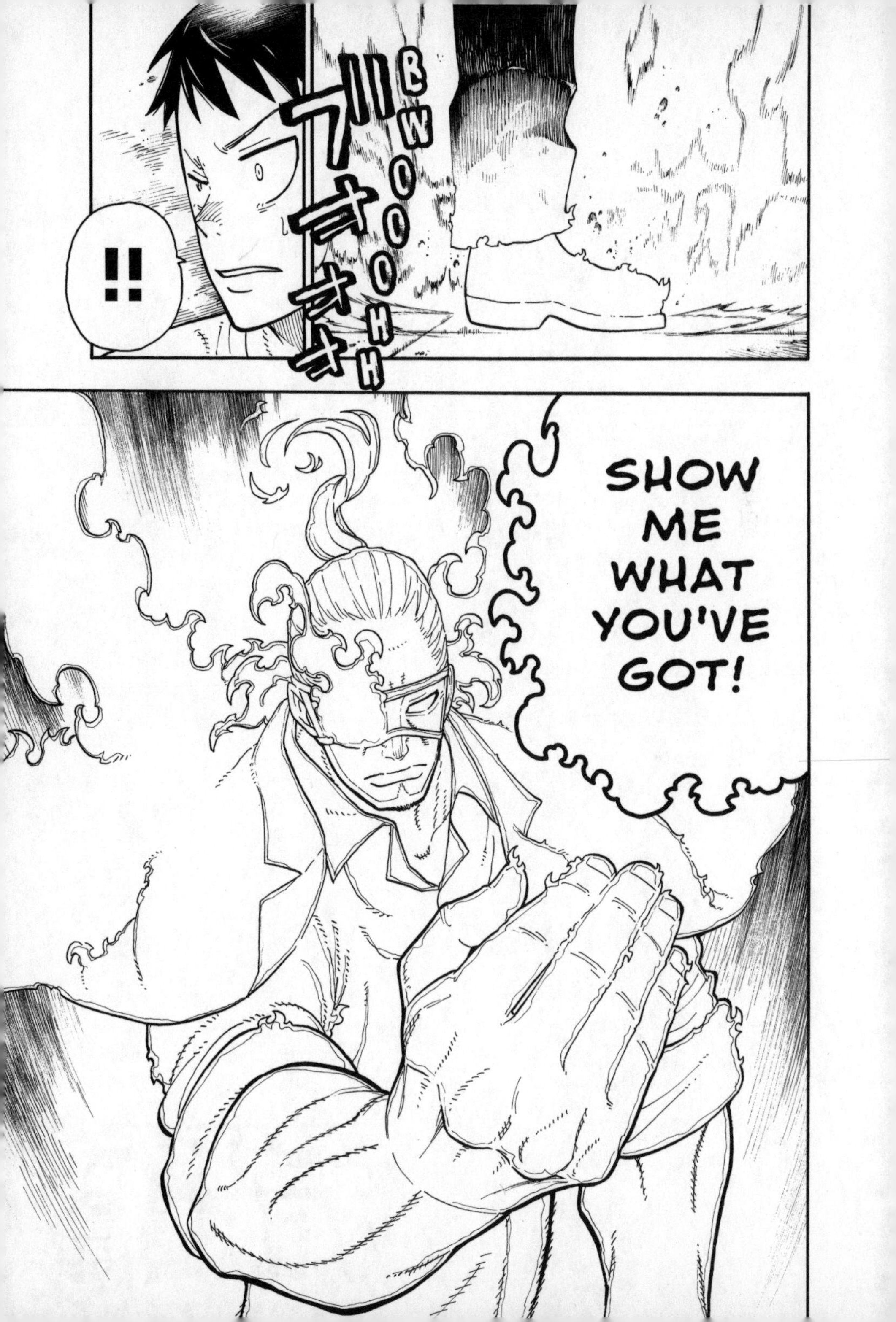
!!
BWOOOHHH
SHOW ME WHAT YOU'VE GOT!

FIRE FORCE

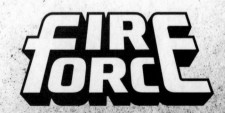

CHAPTER LXXXIX: FIERY PAST

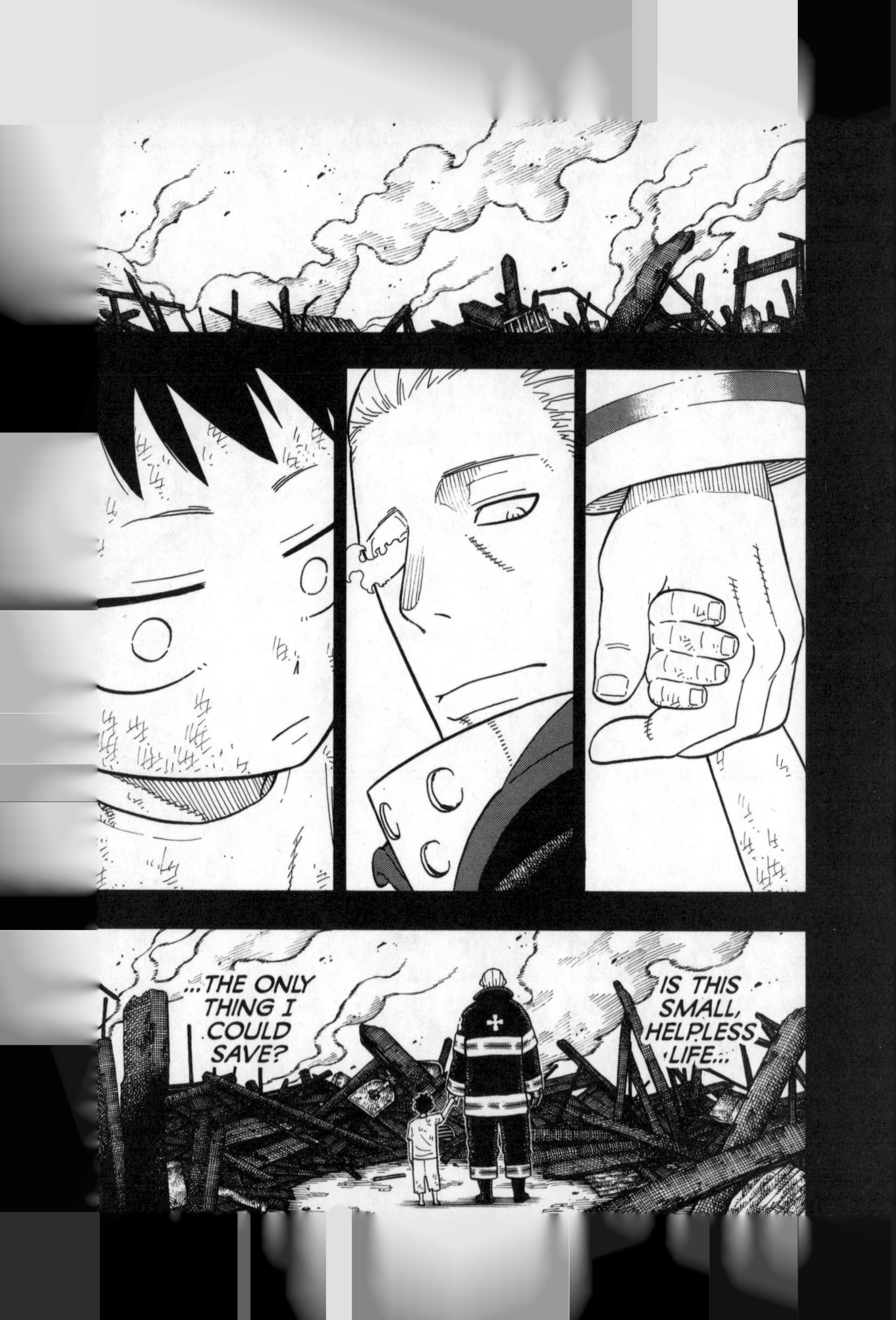
IS THIS SMALL, HELPLESS LIFE...
...THE ONLY THING I COULD SAVE?

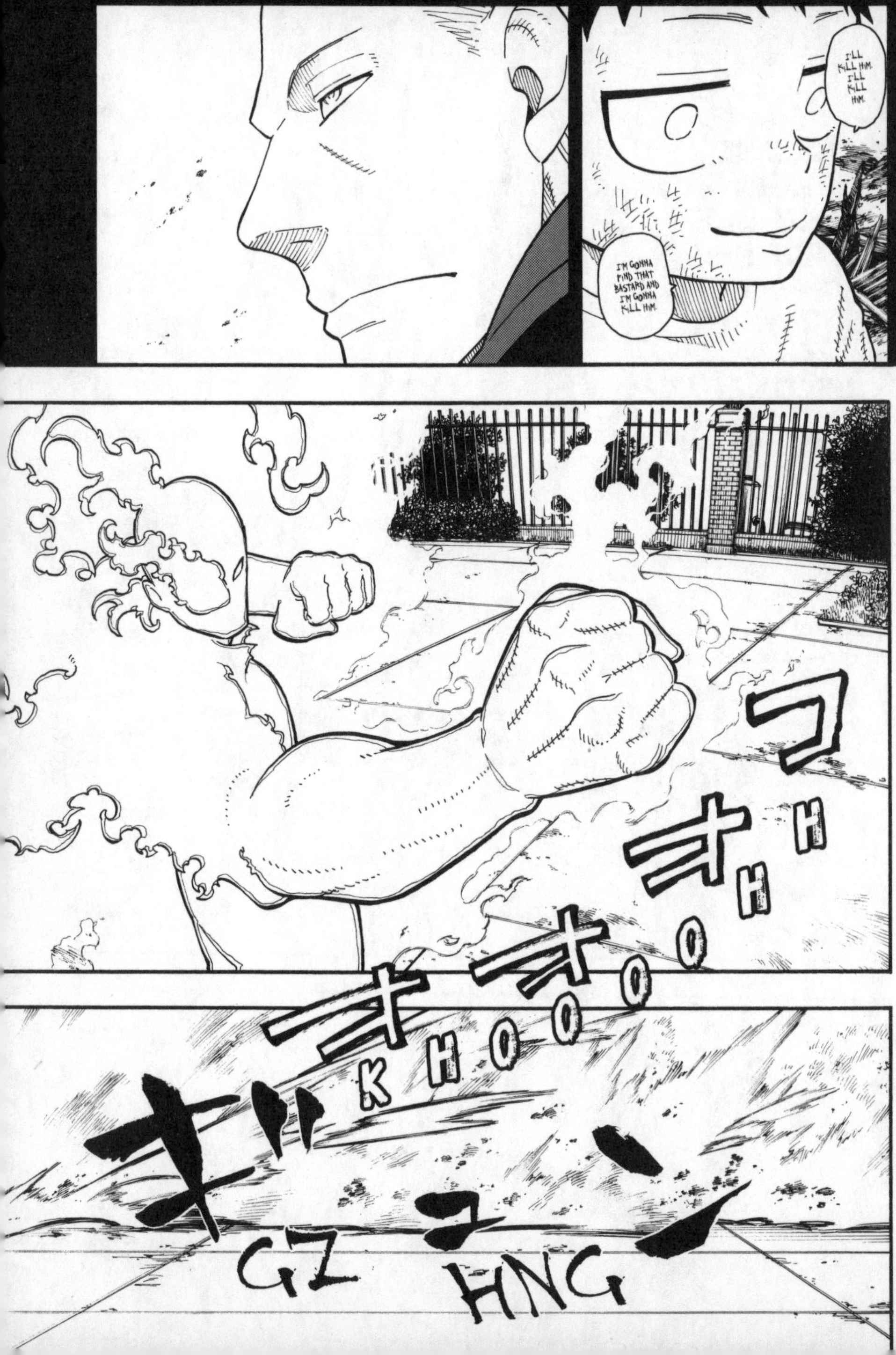
I'LL KILL HIM. I'LL KILL HIM.
I'M GONNA FIND THAT BASTARD AND I'M GONNA KILL HIM.
KHOOOOHH
GZ
HNG

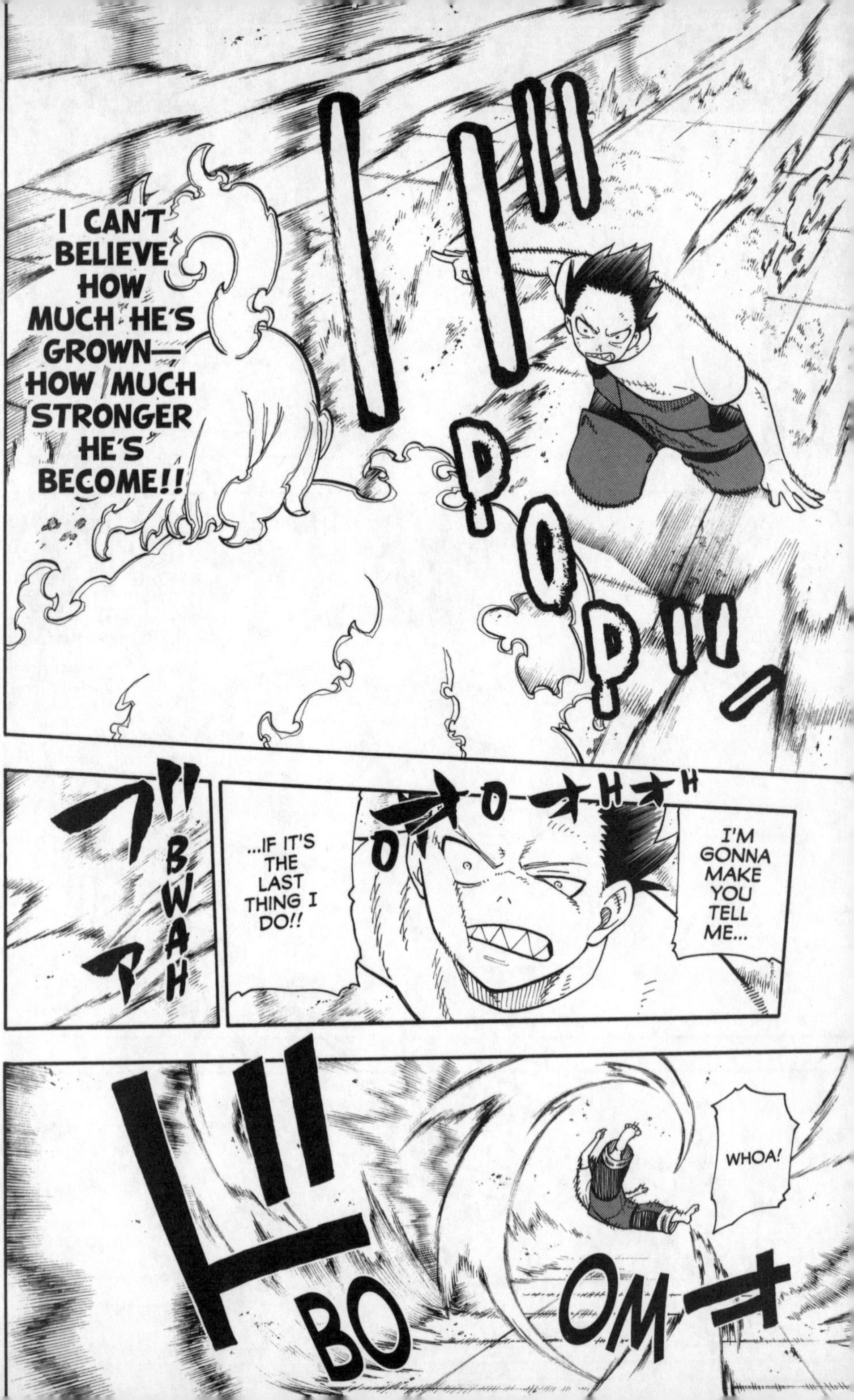
POP!!
I CAN'T BELIEVE HOW MUCH HE'S GROWN—HOW MUCH STRONGER HE'S BECOME!!
I'M GONNA MAKE YOU TELL ME...
...IF IT'S THE LAST THING I DO!!
BWAH
WHOA!
BOOM

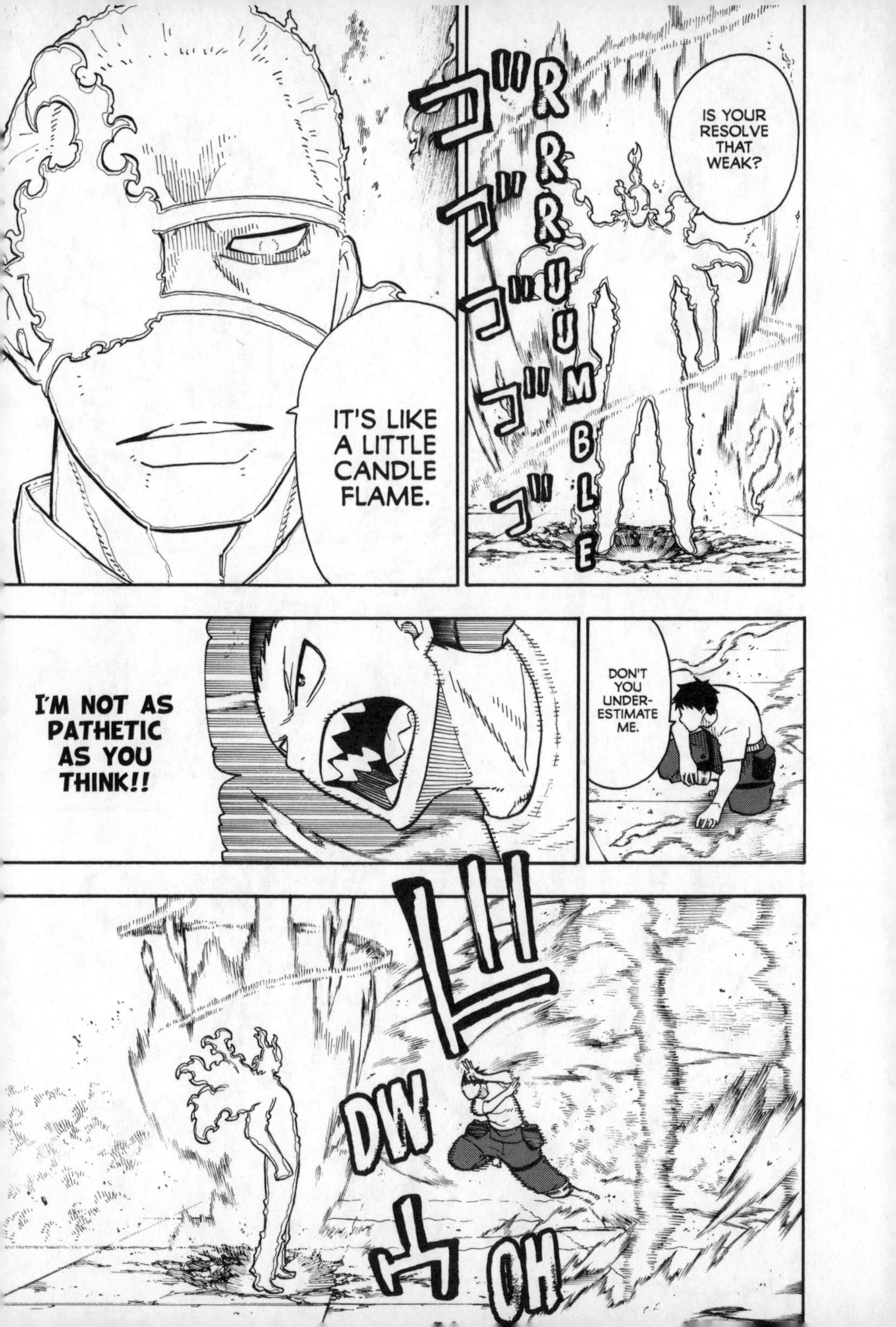
IS YOUR RESOLVE THAT WEAK?
RRRUMBLE
IT'S LIKE A LITTLE CANDLE FLAME.
DON'T YOU UNDER-ESTIMATE ME.
I'M NOT AS PATHETIC AS YOU THINK!!
DW
OH

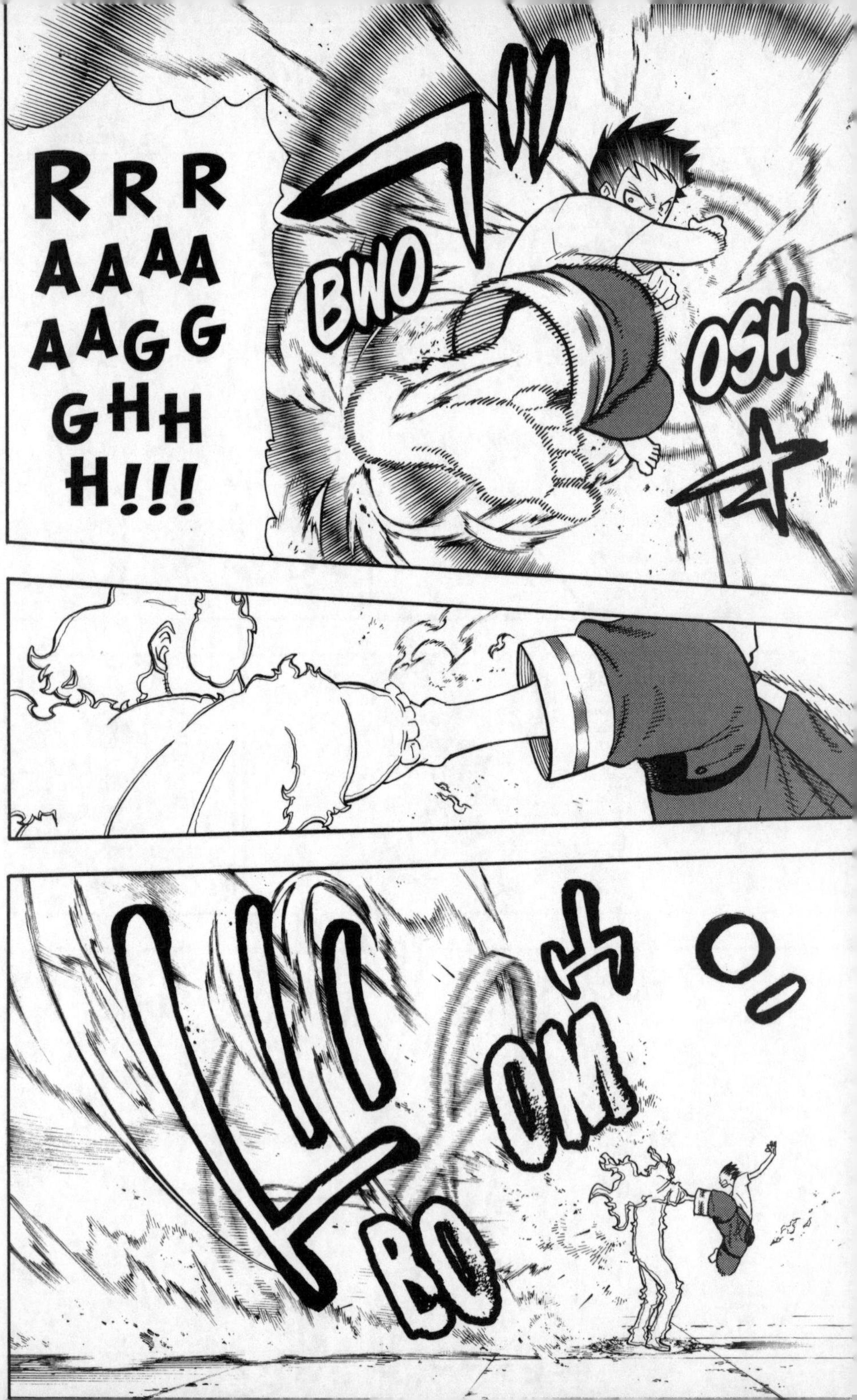
BWO
OSH
RRRAAAAAAGGGHHH!!!
BO
OM

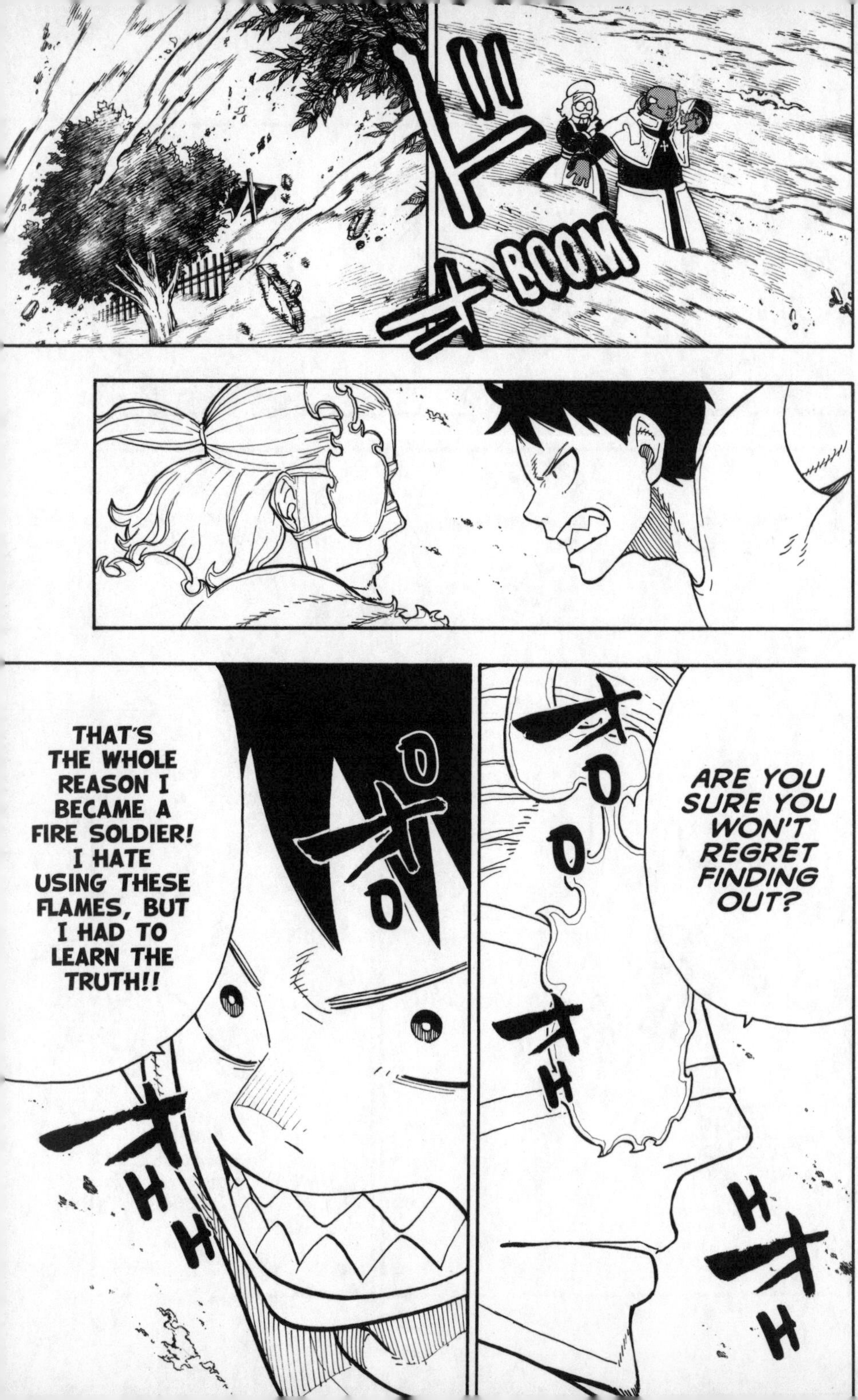
BOOM
ARE YOU SURE YOU WON'T REGRET FINDING OUT?
THAT'S THE WHOLE REASON I BECAME A FIRE SOLDIER! I HATE USING THESE FLAMES, BUT I HAD TO LEARN THE TRUTH!!

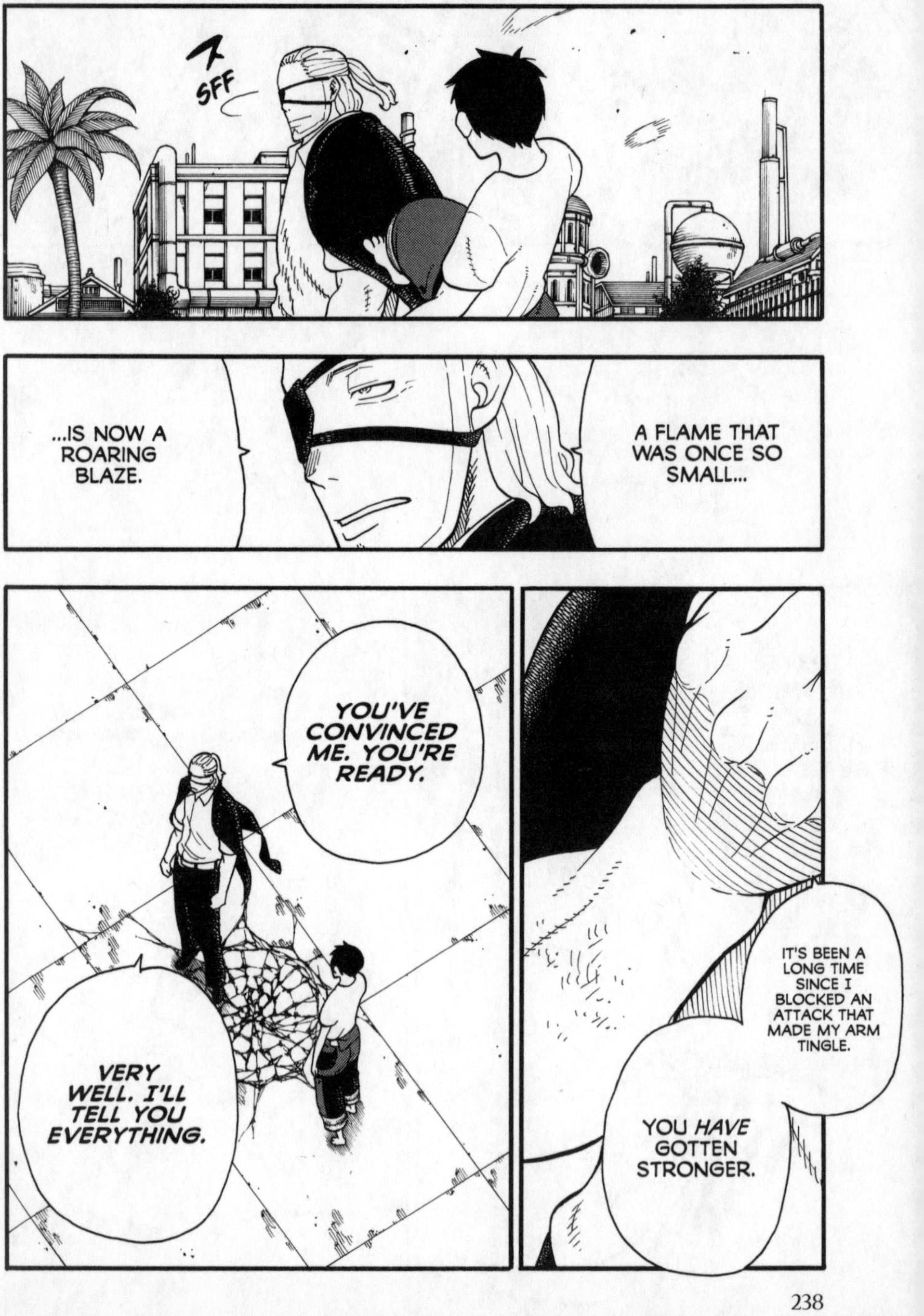
SFF
A FLAME THAT WAS ONCE SO SMALL...
...IS NOW A ROARING BLAZE.
IT'S BEEN A LONG TIME SINCE I BLOCKED AN ATTACK THAT MADE MY ARM TINGLE.
YOU *HAVE* GOTTEN STRONGER.
YOU'VE CONVINCED ME. YOU'RE READY.
VERY WELL. I'LL TELL YOU EVERYTHING.

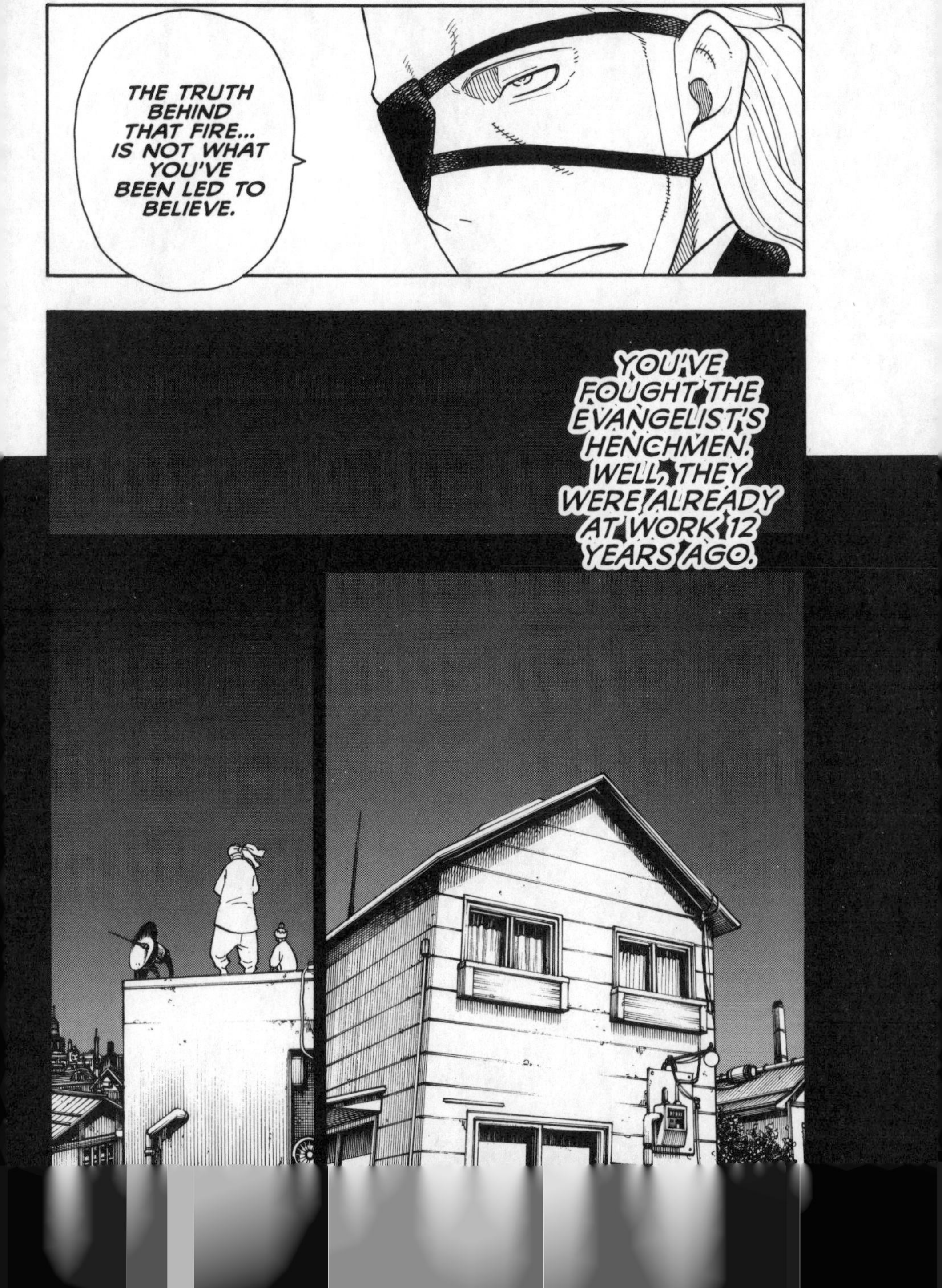
THE TRUTH BEHIND THAT FIRE... IS NOT WHAT YOU'VE BEEN LED TO BELIEVE.
YOU'VE FOUGHT THE EVANGELIST'S HENCHMEN. WELL, THEY WERE ALREADY AT WORK 12 YEARS AGO.

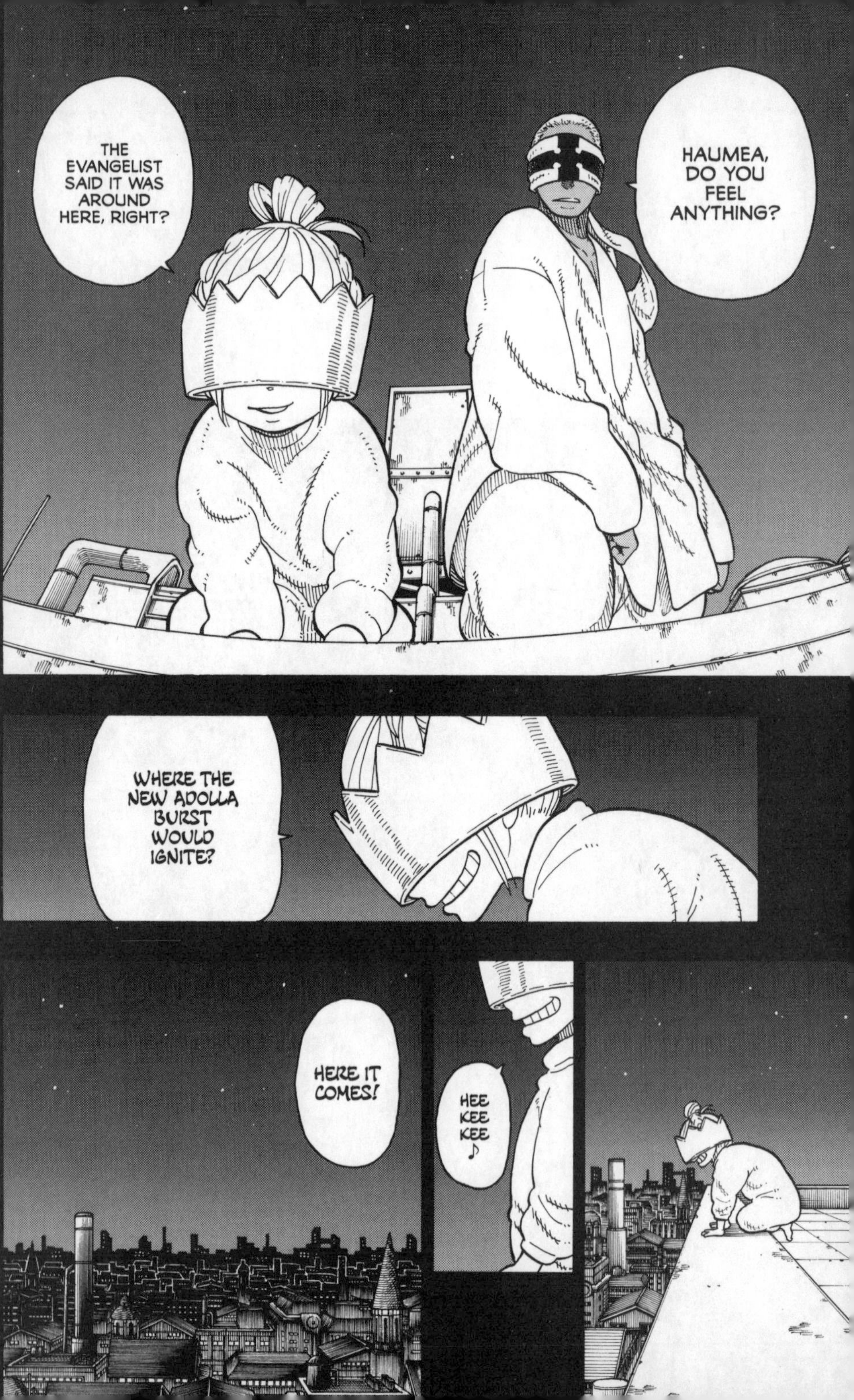
HAUMEA, DO YOU FEEL ANYTHING?
THE EVANGELIST SAID IT WAS AROUND HERE, RIGHT?
WHERE THE NEW ADOLLA BURST WOULD IGNITE?
HEE KEE KEE ♪
HERE IT COMES!

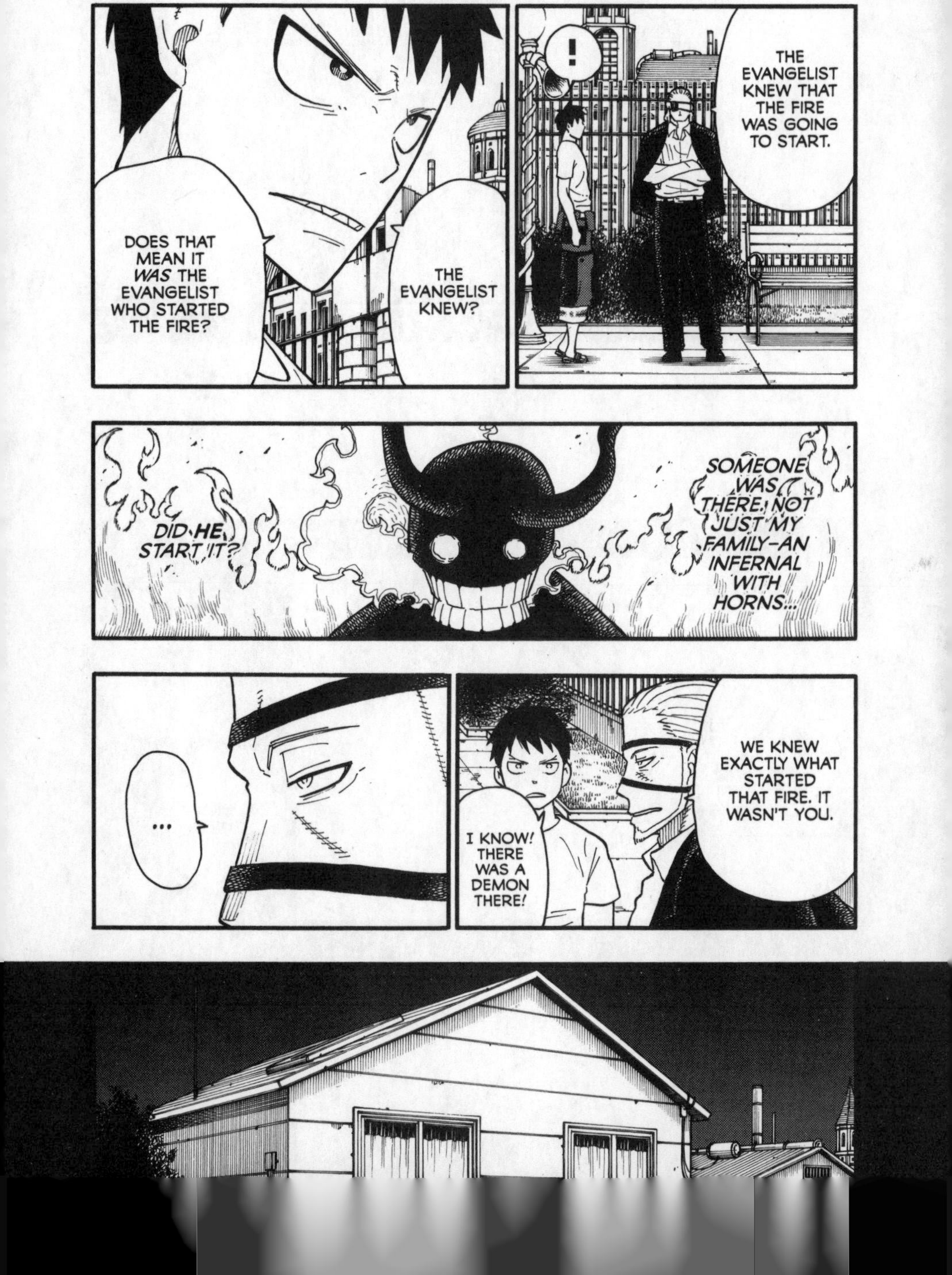
!
THE EVANGELIST KNEW THAT THE FIRE WAS GOING TO START.
THE EVANGELIST KNEW?
DOES THAT MEAN IT *WAS* THE EVANGELIST WHO STARTED THE FIRE?
SOMEONE WAS THERE. NOT JUST MY FAMILY—AN INFERNAL WITH HORNS...
DID HE START IT?
WE KNEW EXACTLY WHAT STARTED THAT FIRE. IT WASN'T YOU.
I KNOW! THERE WAS A DEMON THERE!
...

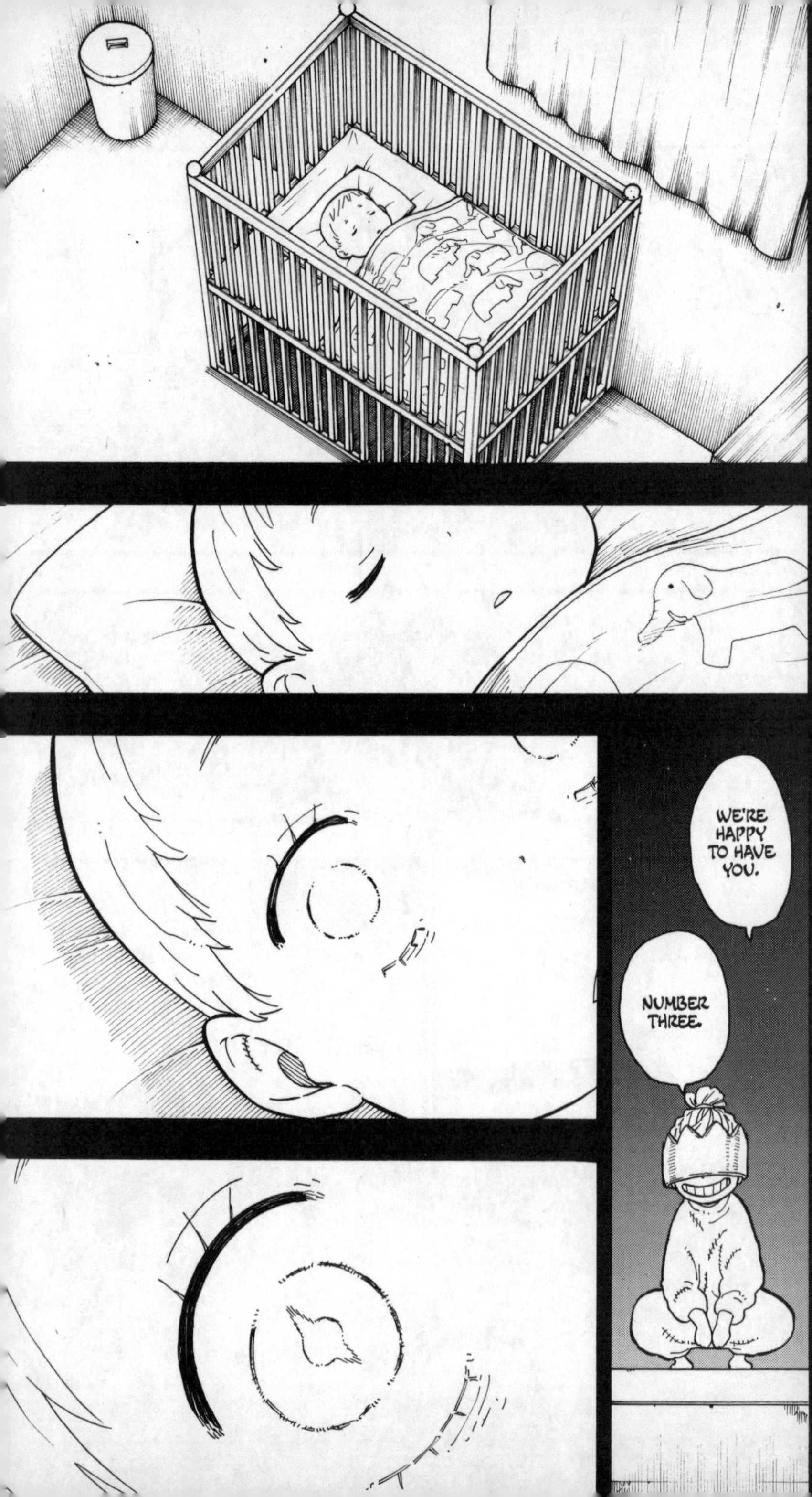
WE'RE HAPPY TO HAVE YOU.
NUMBER THREE.

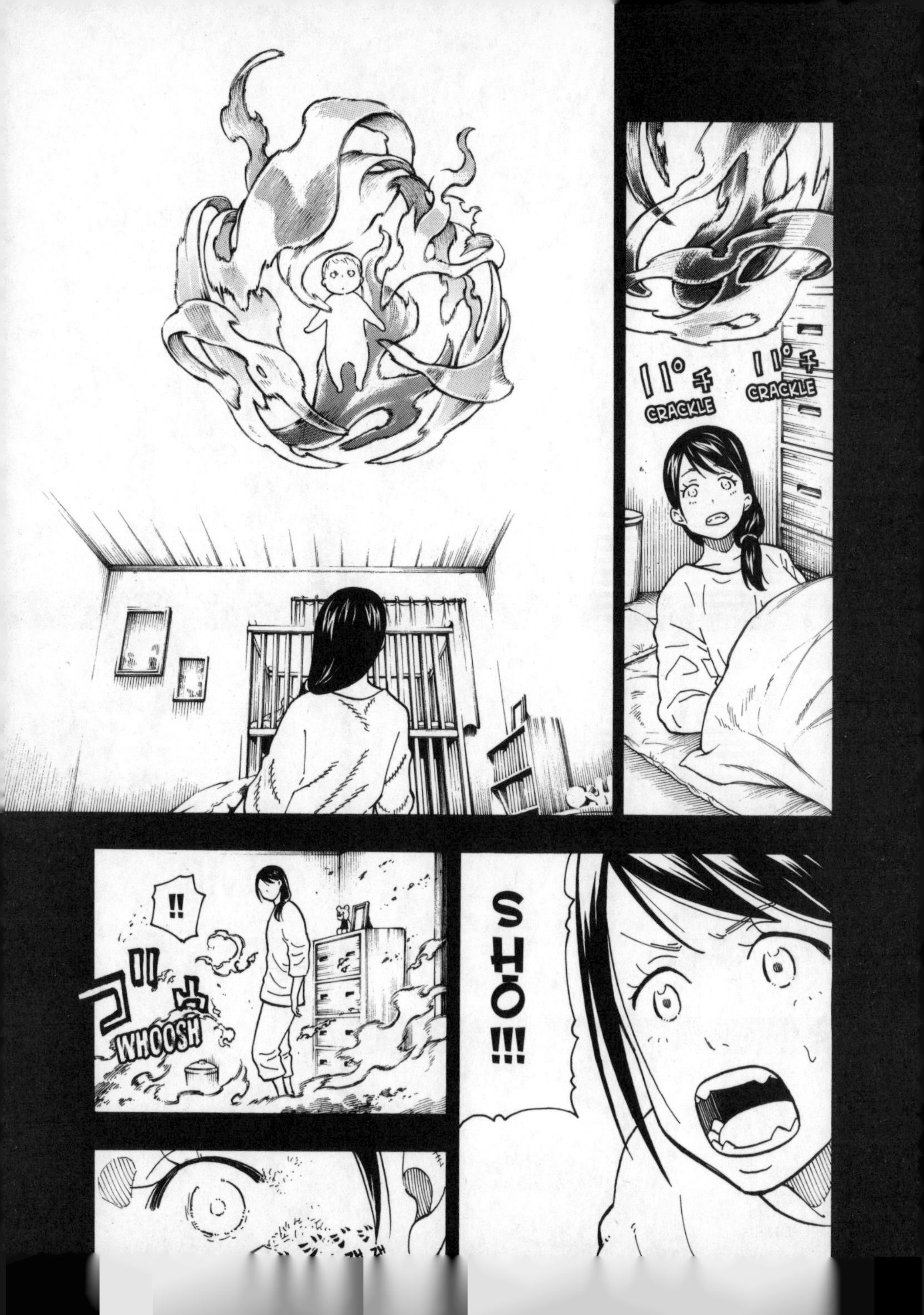
CRACKLE
CRACKLE
SHŌ!!!
!!
WHOOSH
ZH ZH

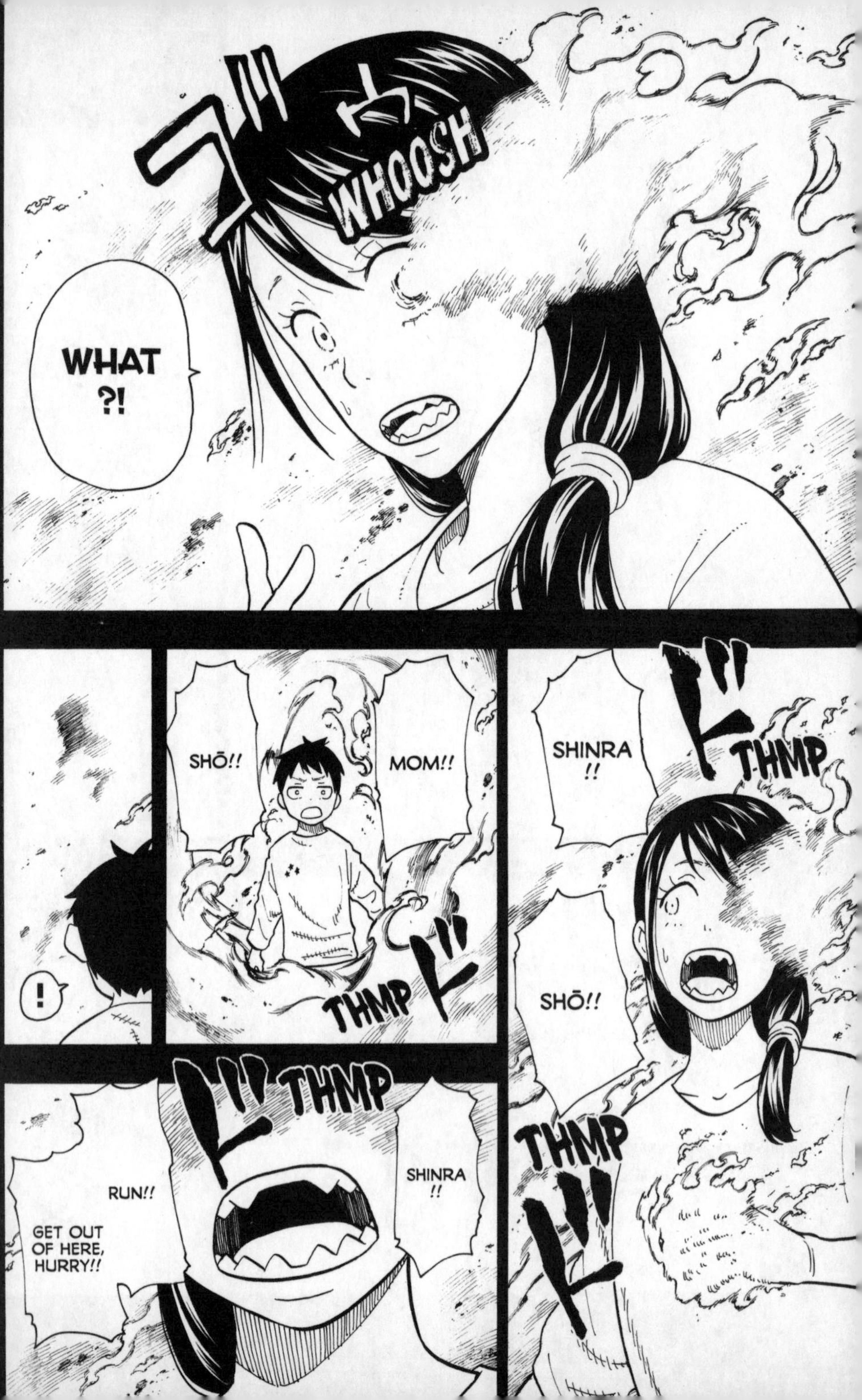
WHOOSH
WHAT ?!
SHINRA !!
THMP
SHŌ!!
THMP
MOM!!
SHŌ!!
THMP
!
THMP
SHINRA !!
RUN!!
GET OUT OF HERE, HURRY!!

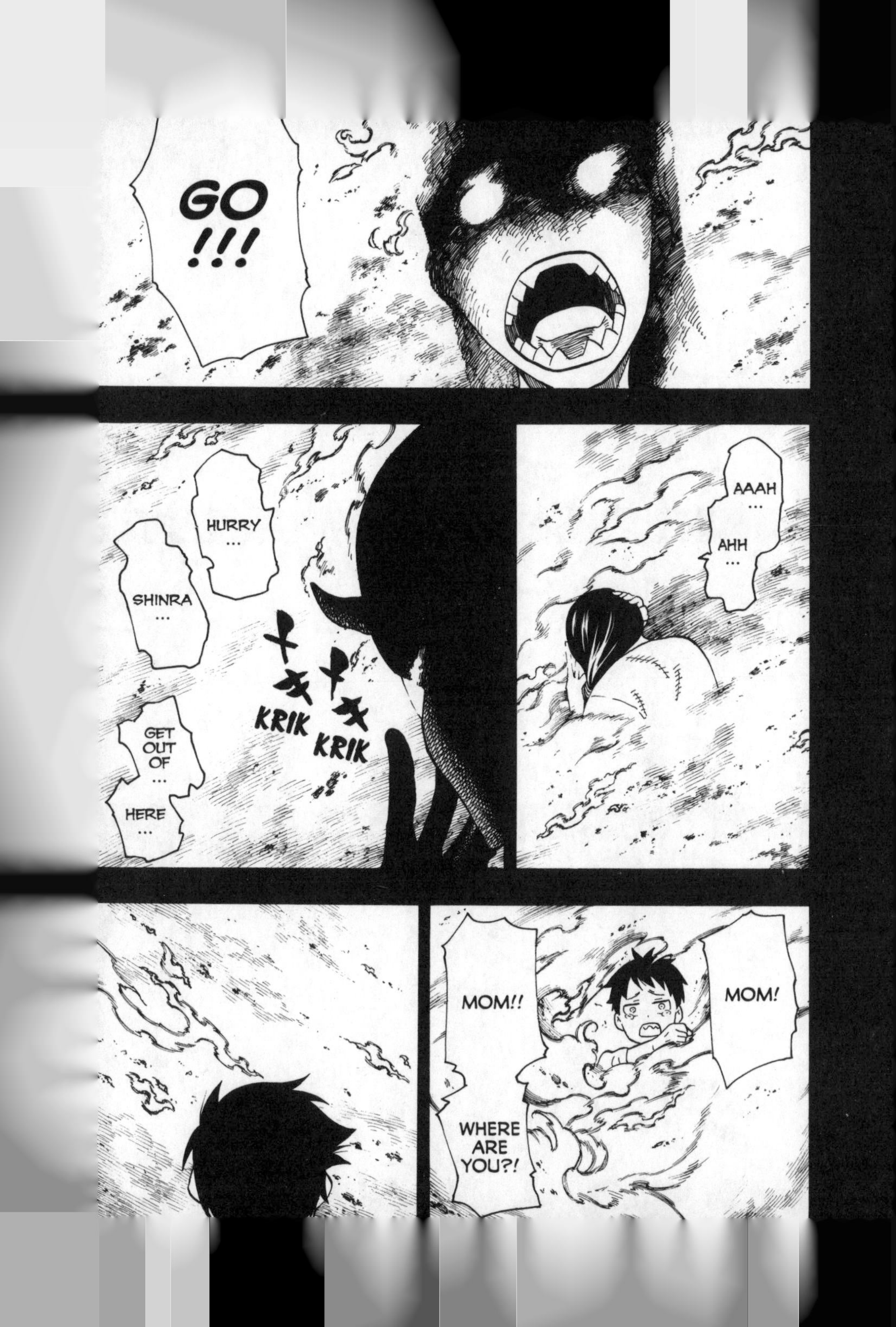
GO !!!
AAAH … AHH …
HURRY …
SHINRA …
KRIK KRIK
GET OUT OF … HERE …
MOM!
MOM!!
WHERE ARE YOU?!

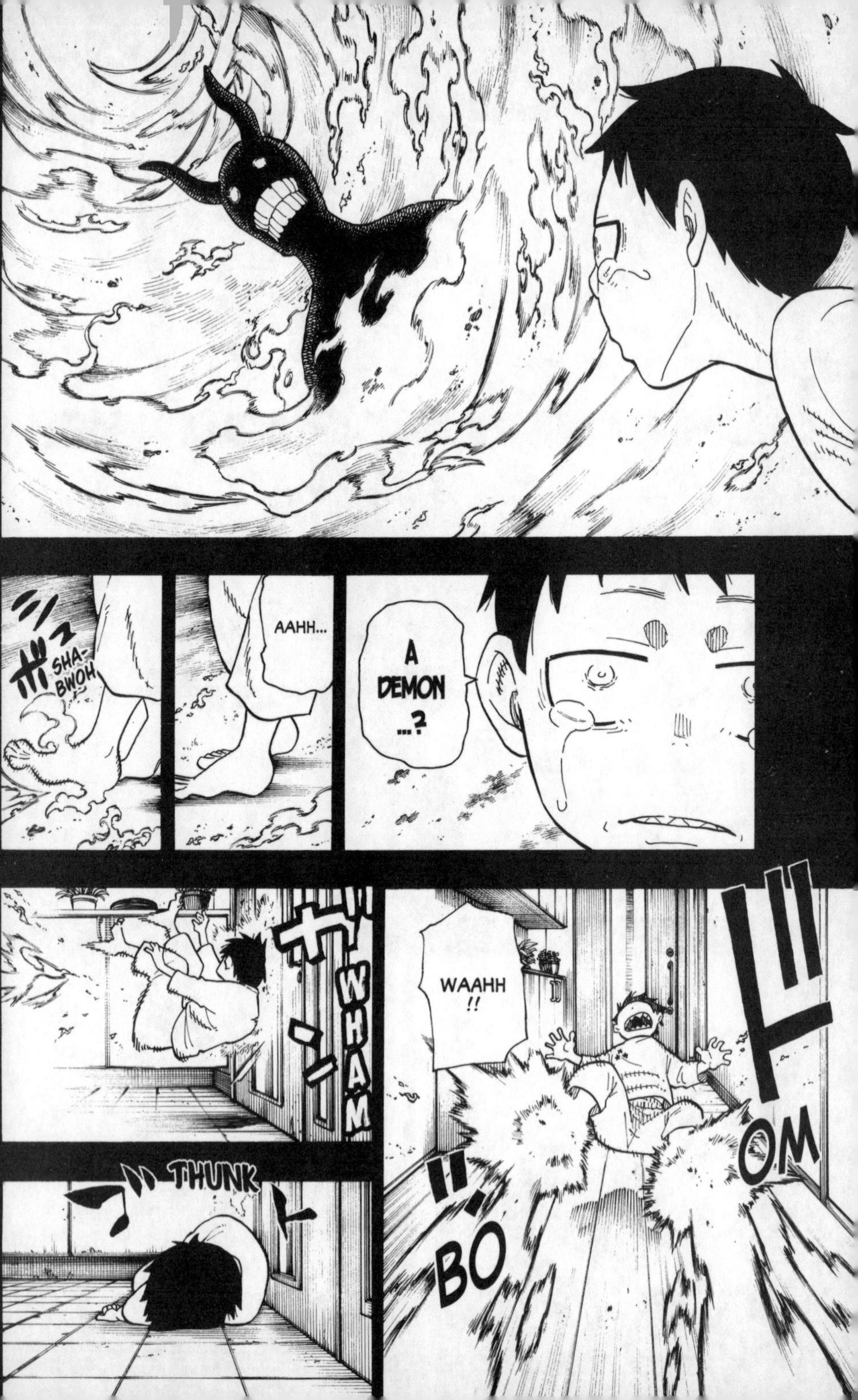
A DEMON ...?
AAHH...
SHA-BWOH
WAAHH !!
BO-OM
WHAM
THUNK

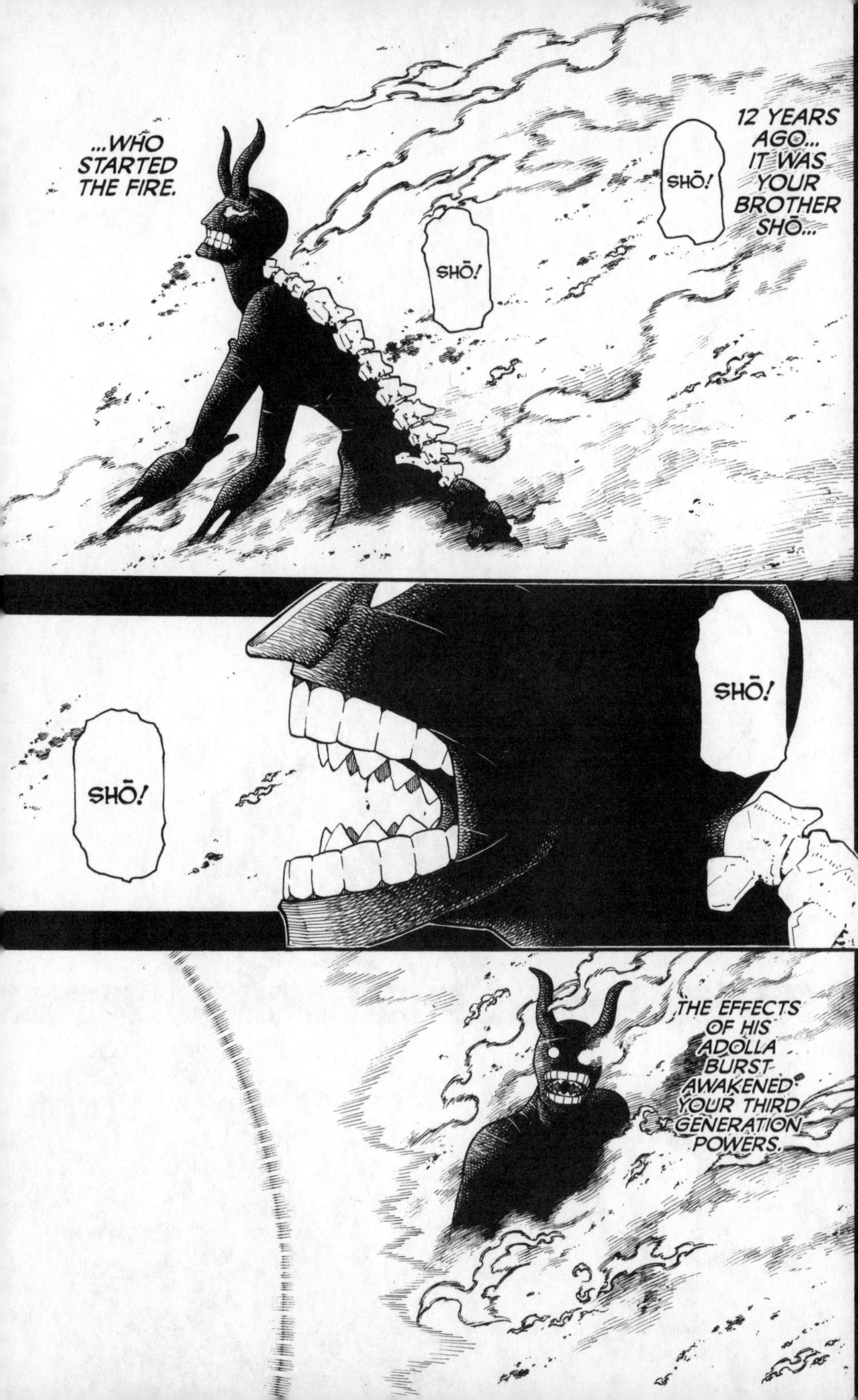
12 YEARS AGO... IT WAS YOUR BROTHER SHŌ...
SHŌ!
SHŌ!
...WHO STARTED THE FIRE.
SHŌ!
SHŌ!
THE EFFECTS OF HIS ADOLLA BURST AWAKENED YOUR THIRD GENERATION POWERS.

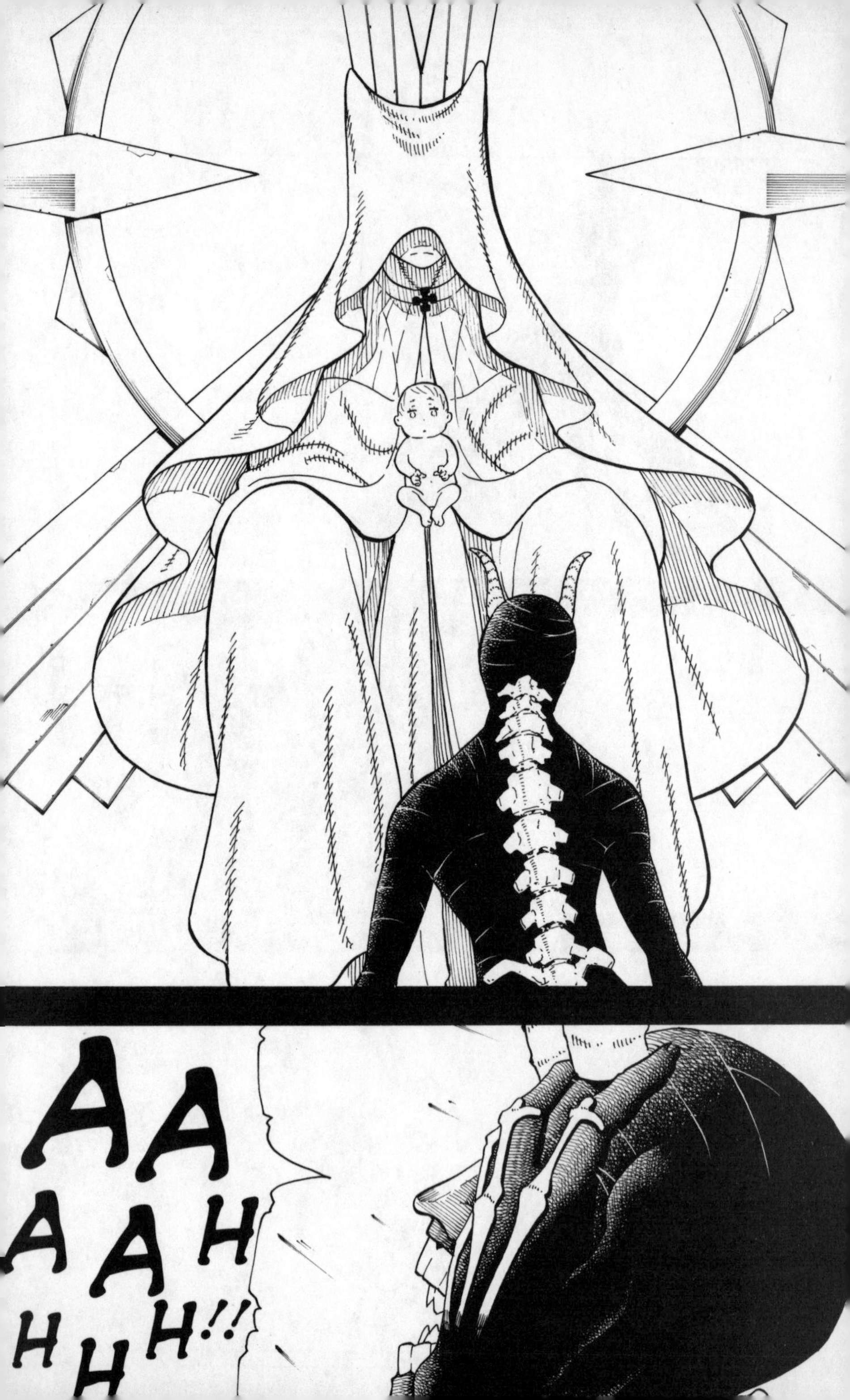
AAAAHHHH!!

YOU KNOW WHY WE HIDE OUR EYES, DON'T YOU?

YEAH. DUH.

BECAUSE WHEN YOU LOOK DIRECTLY INTO THE SUN, IT BURNS YOUR EYES.

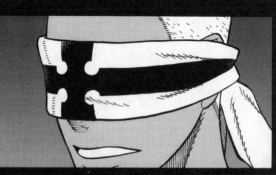

ALTHOUGH THE SUN DOTH SPARKLE, IT IS UNSEEABLE TO THE CHILDREN OF MEN. ALL WHO WISH TO APPROACH THE WORLD OF THE GODS MUST FEEL IT IN THEIR HEARTS.

THE HORNED INFERNAL YOU CLAIM YOU SAW...

グチ GRK

グ GRK

グチチチ GR-GRK

グチ GRK

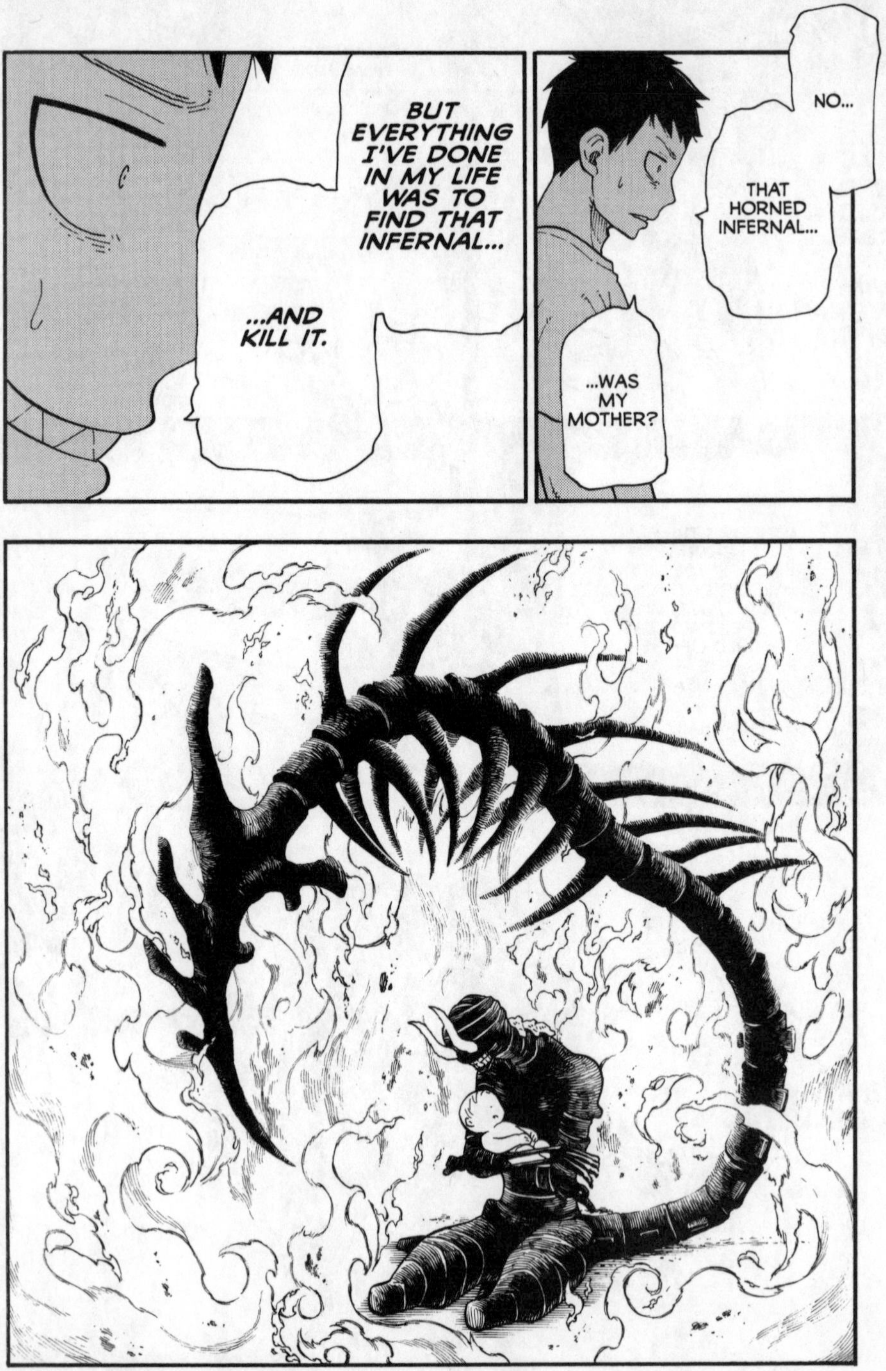
NO...
THAT HORNED INFERNAL...
...WAS MY MOTHER?
BUT EVERYTHING I'VE DONE IN MY LIFE WAS TO FIND THAT INFERNAL...
...AND KILL IT.

CHAPTER XC:
AT TRAGEDY'S END

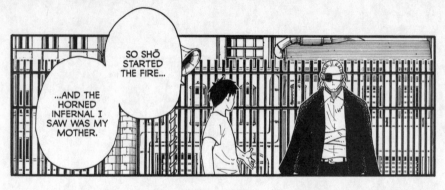

SO SHŌ STARTED THE FIRE...
...AND THE HORNED INFERNAL I SAW WAS MY MOTHER.
BUT THEN... WHAT HAPPENED TO HER?
I ARRIVED AT THE SCENE 15 MINUTES AFTER THE FIRE BROKE OUT.
FWOOOOOOO
ANY SURVIVORS INSIDE?!
WHY AREN'T YOU DOING ANYTHING TO PUT OUT THE FIRE?!!
THEY'RE NOT NORMAL FLAMES!! OUR HOSES DON'T EVEN SLOW THEM DOWN.

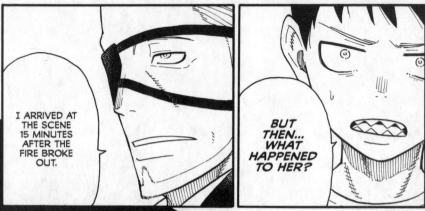

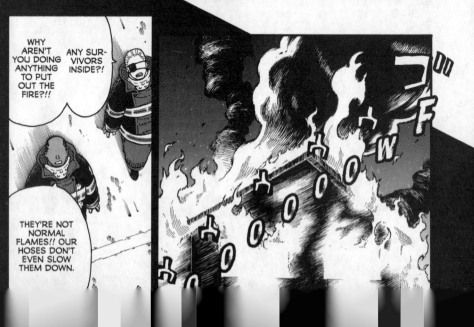

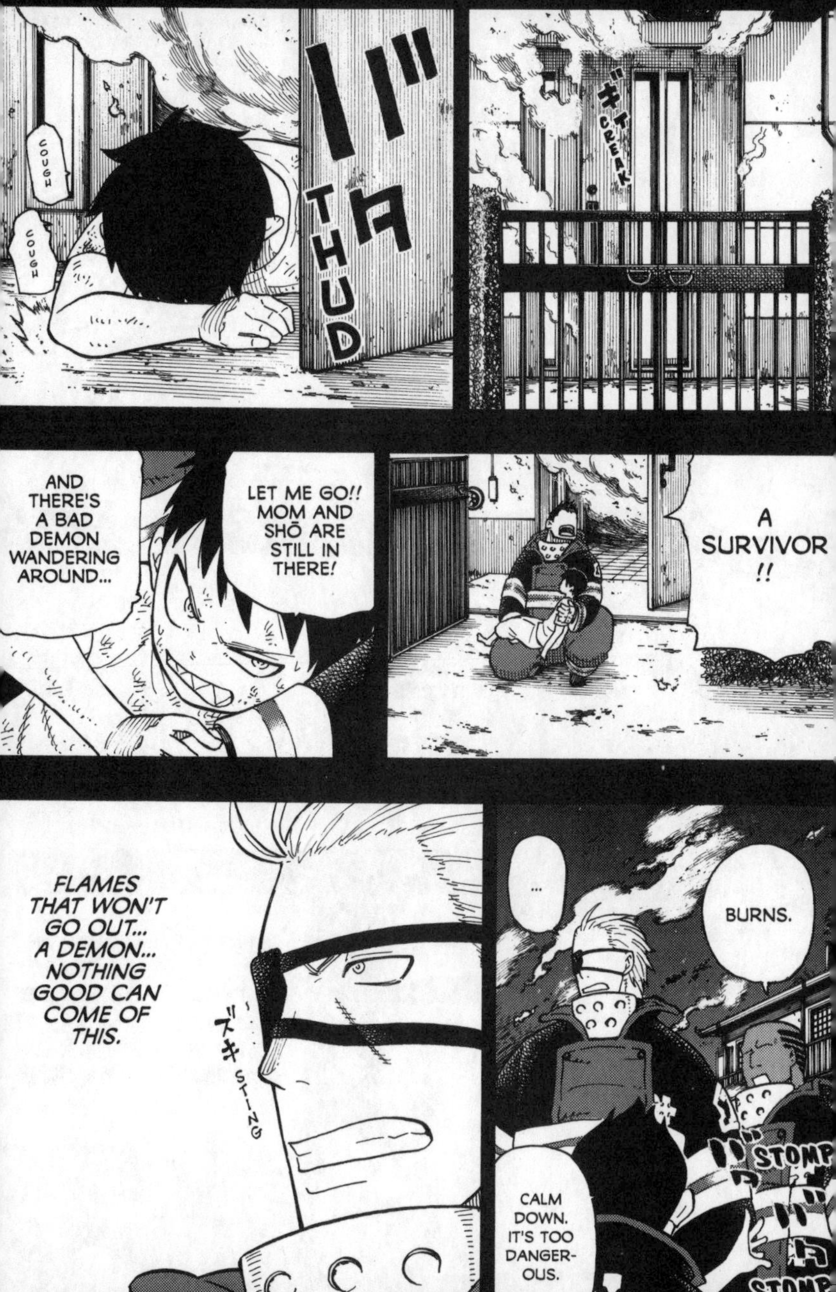
ギ
CREAK
バタ
THUD
COUGH
COUGH
A SURVIVOR!!
LET ME GO!! MOM AND SHŌ ARE STILL IN THERE!
AND THERE'S A BAD DEMON WANDERING AROUND...
BURNS.
...
STOMP
CALM DOWN. IT'S TOO DANGER-OUS.
STOMP
FLAMES THAT WON'T GO OUT... A DEMON... NOTHING GOOD CAN COME OF THIS.
ズキ
STING

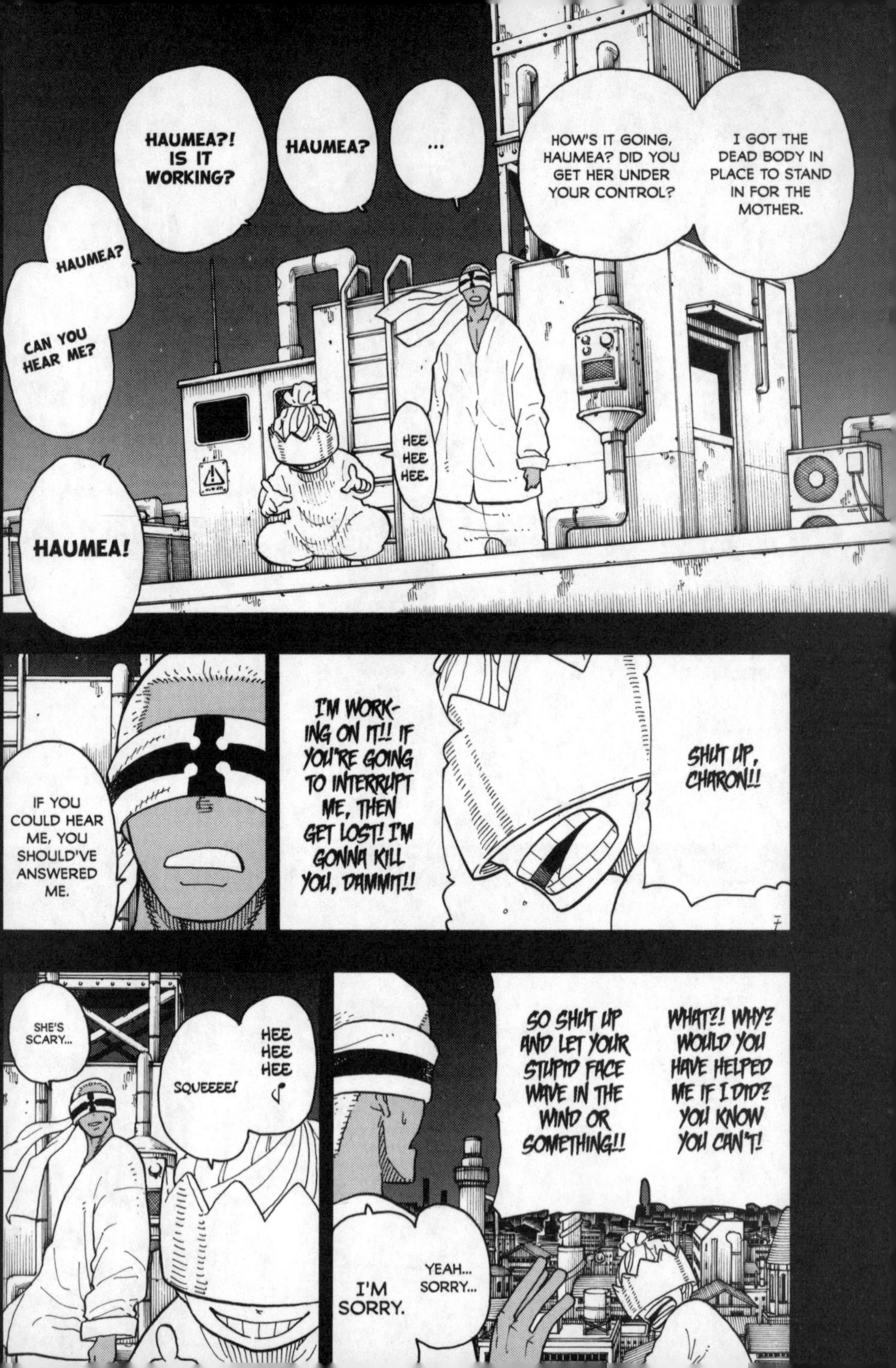

I GOT THE DEAD BODY IN PLACE TO STAND IN FOR THE MOTHER.
HOW'S IT GOING, HAUMEA? DID YOU GET HER UNDER YOUR CONTROL?
...
HAUMEA?
HAUMEA?! IS IT WORKING?
HAUMEA?
CAN YOU HEAR ME?
HEE HEE HEE.
HAUMEA!
SHUT UP, CHARON!!
I'M WORKING ON IT!! IF YOU'RE GOING TO INTERRUPT ME, THEN GET LOST! I'M GONNA KILL YOU, DAMMIT!!
IF YOU COULD HEAR ME, YOU SHOULD'VE ANSWERED ME.
WHAT?! WHY? WOULD YOU HAVE HELPED ME IF I DID? YOU KNOW YOU CAN'T!
SO SHUT UP AND LET YOUR STUPID FACE WAVE IN THE WIND OR SOMETHING!!
YEAH... SORRY...
I'M SORRY.
HEE HEE HEE
SQUEEEE!
SHE'S SCARY...

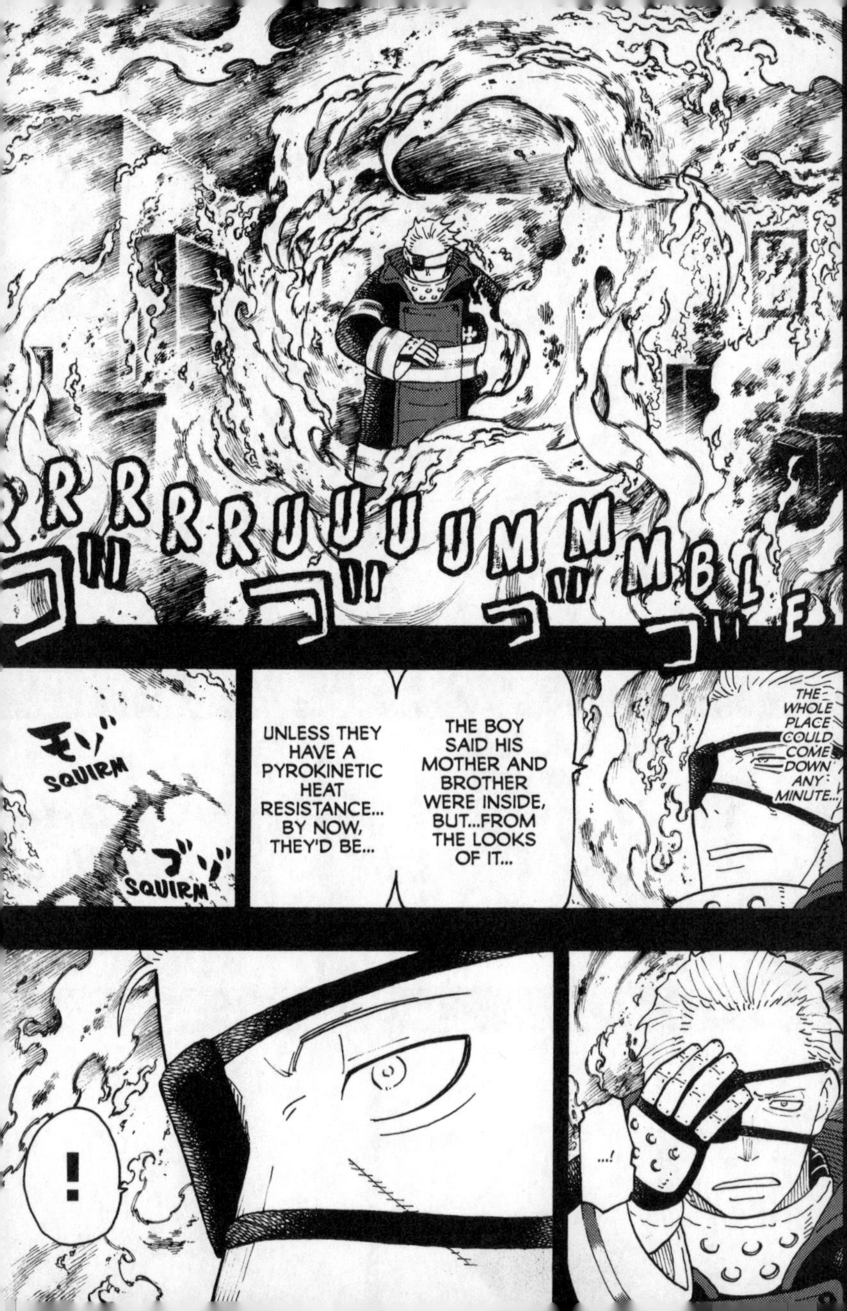
RRRRRUUUUMMMBLE
THE WHOLE PLACE COULD COME DOWN ANY MINUTE...
THE BOY SAID HIS MOTHER AND BROTHER WERE INSIDE, BUT...FROM THE LOOKS OF IT...
UNLESS THEY HAVE A PYROKINETIC HEAT RESISTANCE... BY NOW, THEY'D BE...
SQUIRM
SQUIRM
...!
!

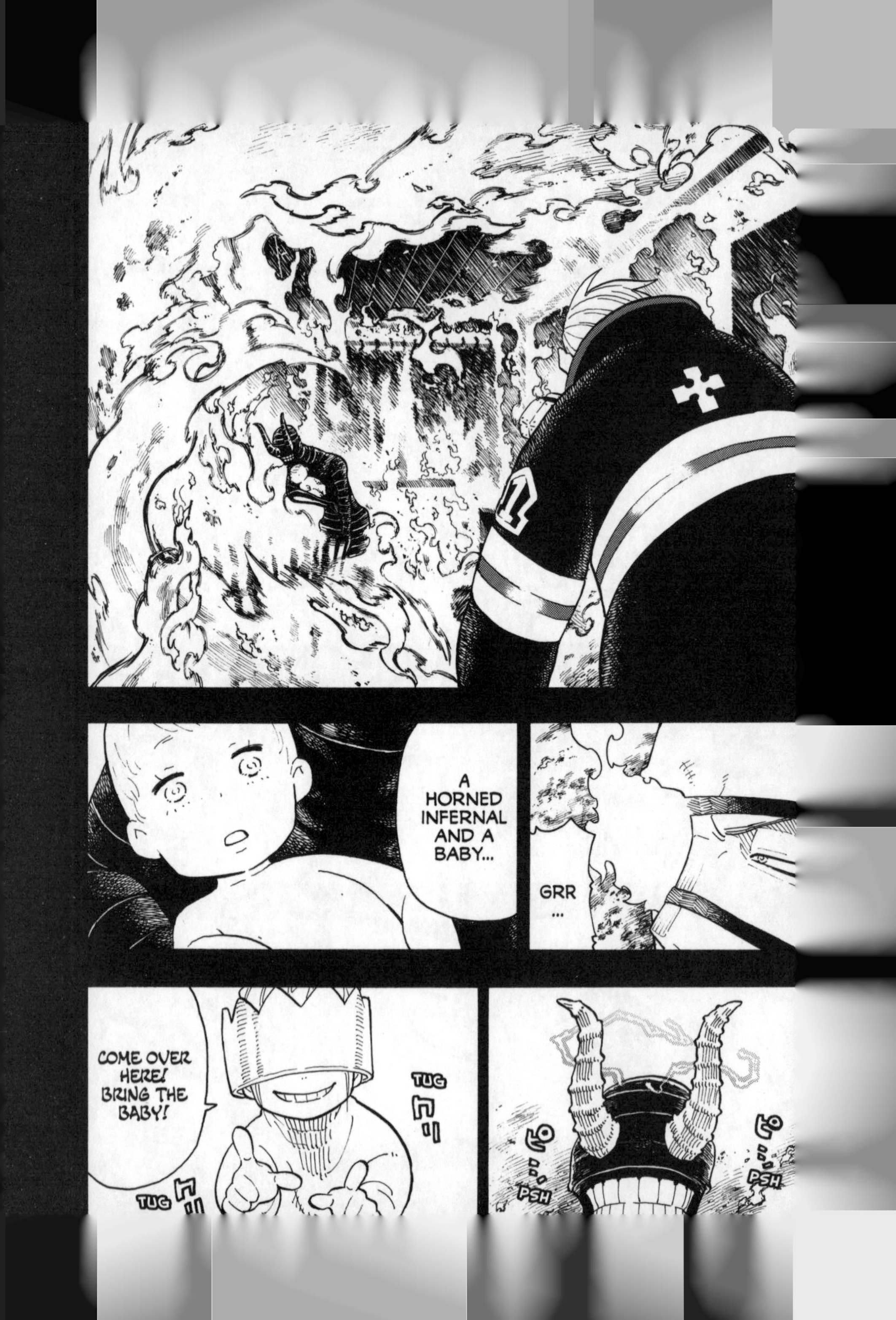
GRR ...
A HORNED INFERNAL AND A BABY...
PSH
PSH
COME OVER HERE! BRING THE BABY!
TUG
TUG

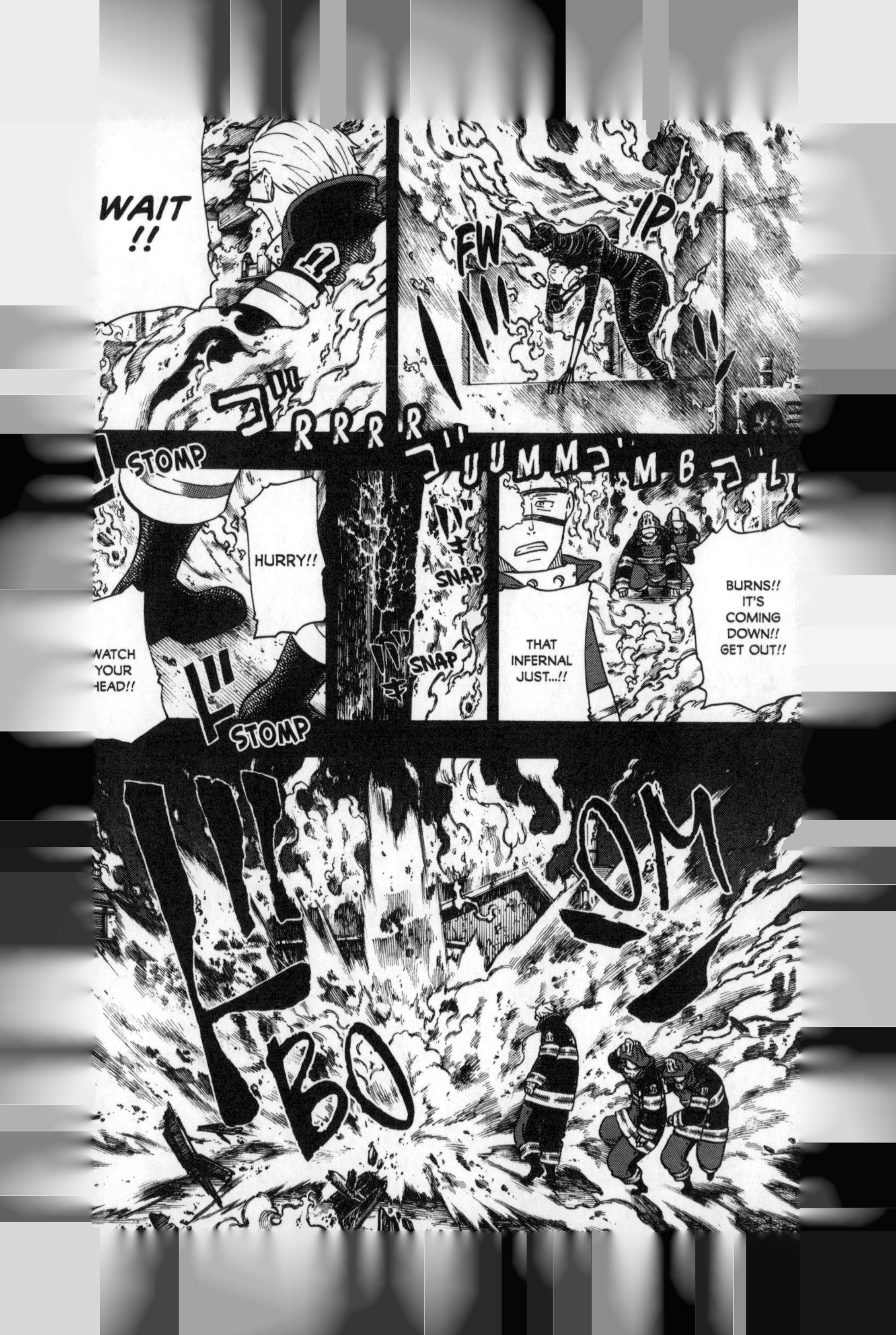
FWIP
WAIT!!
RRRRUUMMMB
BURNS!! IT'S COMING DOWN!! GET OUT!!
THAT INFERNAL JUST...!!
SNAP
SNAP
HURRY!!
STOMP
WATCH YOUR HEAD!!
STOMP
BOOM

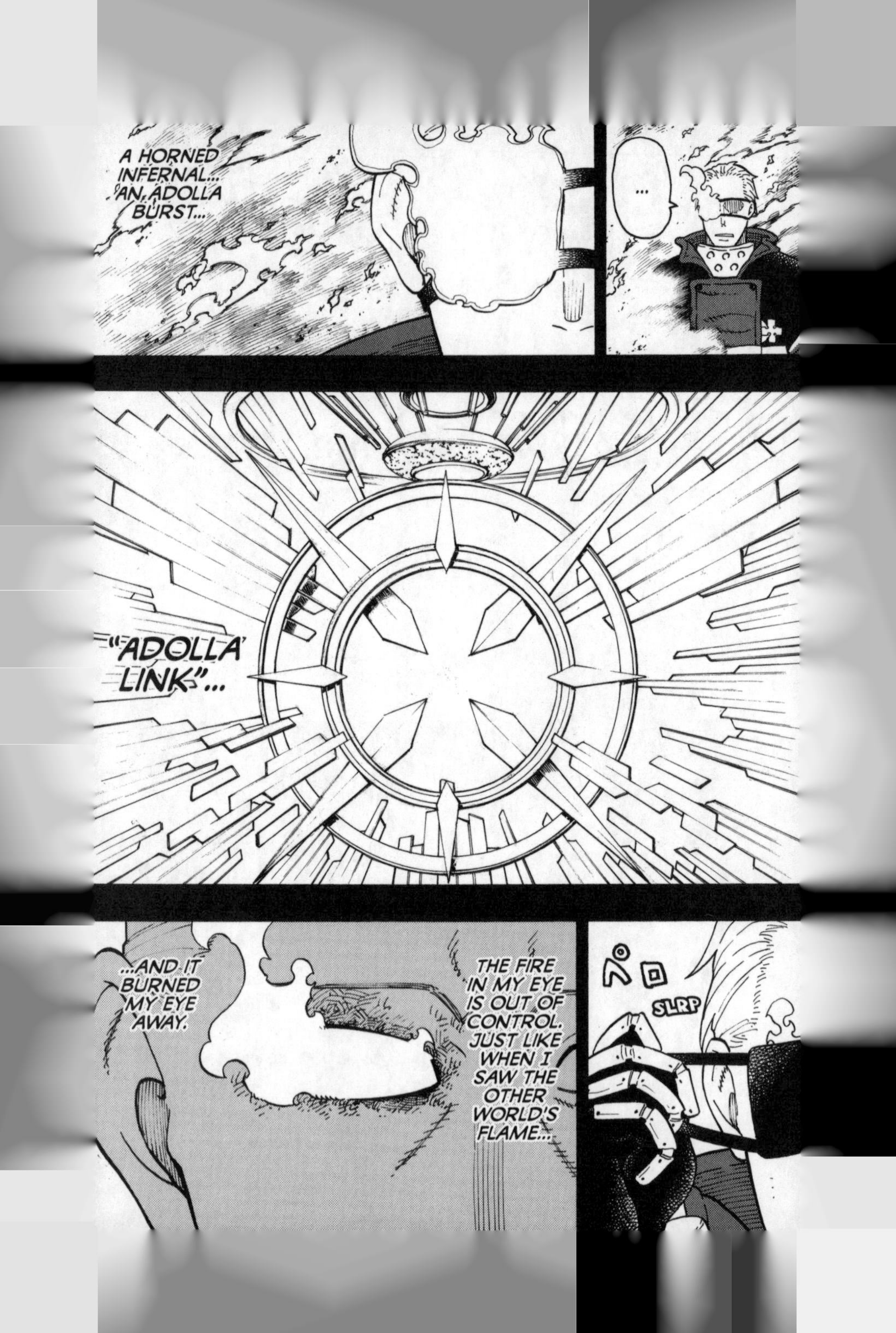
...
A HORNED INFERNAL... AN ADOLLA BURST...
"ADOLLA LINK"...
ペロ
SLRP
THE FIRE IN MY EYE IS OUT OF CONTROL. JUST LIKE WHEN I SAW THE OTHER WORLD'S FLAME...
...AND IT BURNED MY EYE AWAY.

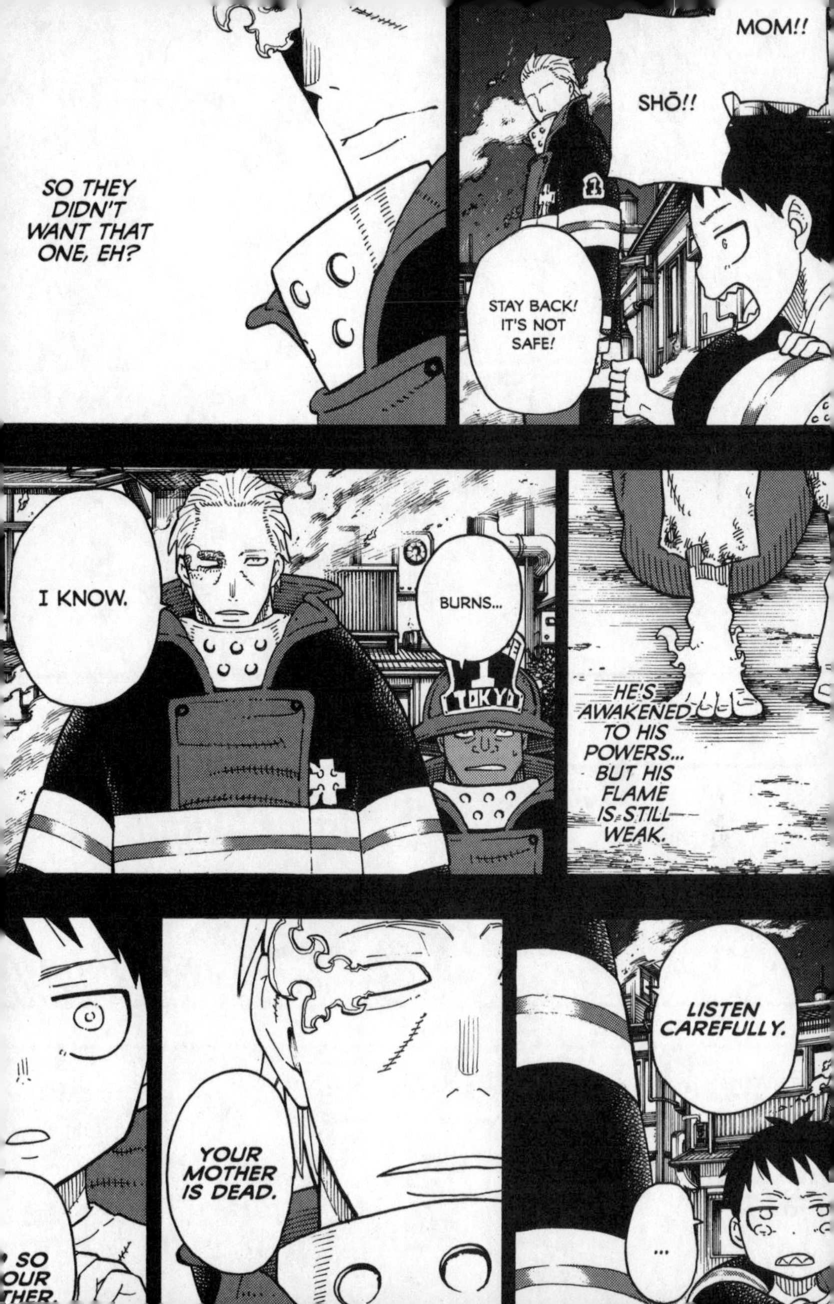
MOM!!
SHŌ!!
STAY BACK! IT'S NOT SAFE!
SO THEY DIDN'T WANT THAT ONE, EH?
HE'S AWAKENED TO HIS POWERS... BUT HIS FLAME IS STILL WEAK.
BURNS...
I KNOW.
LISTEN CAREFULLY.
...
YOUR MOTHER IS DEAD.

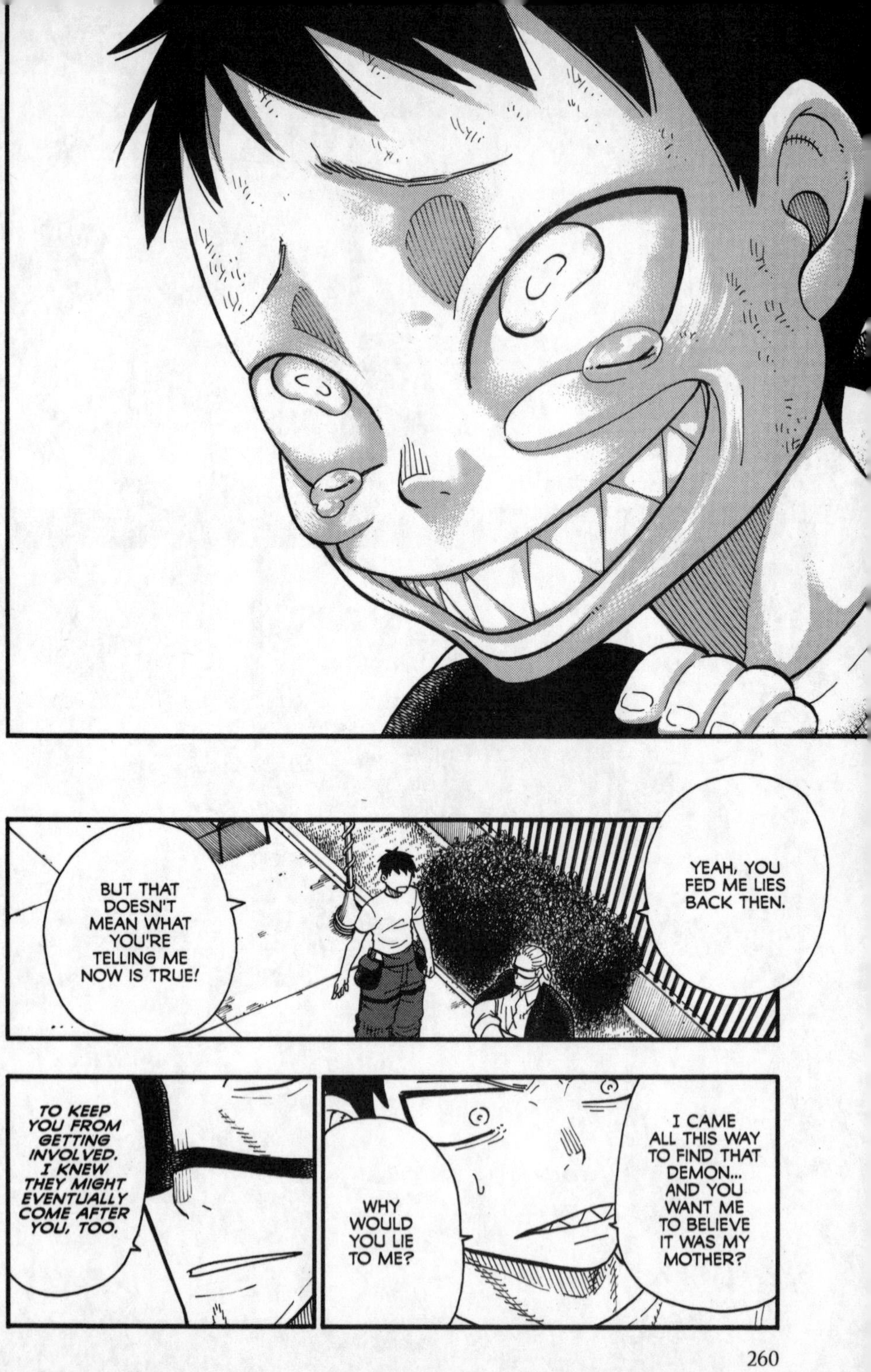
YEAH, YOU FED ME LIES BACK THEN.
BUT THAT DOESN'T MEAN WHAT YOU'RE TELLING ME NOW IS TRUE!
I CAME ALL THIS WAY TO FIND THAT DEMON... AND YOU WANT ME TO BELIEVE IT WAS MY MOTHER?
WHY WOULD YOU LIE TO ME?
TO KEEP YOU FROM GETTING INVOLVED. I KNEW THEY MIGHT EVENTUALLY COME AFTER YOU, TOO.

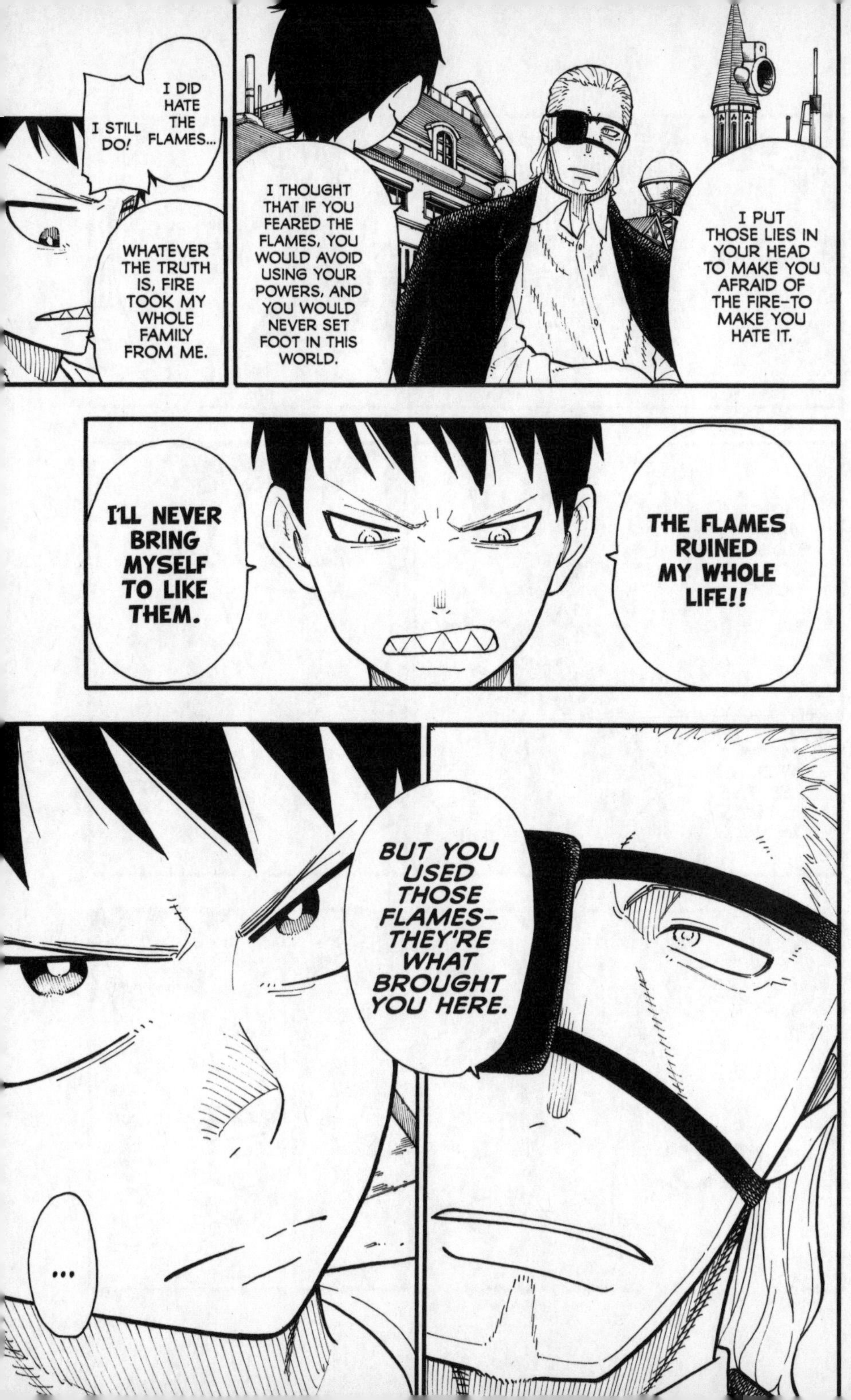
I PUT THOSE LIES IN YOUR HEAD TO MAKE YOU AFRAID OF THE FIRE—TO MAKE YOU HATE IT.
I THOUGHT THAT IF YOU FEARED THE FLAMES, YOU WOULD AVOID USING YOUR POWERS, AND YOU WOULD NEVER SET FOOT IN THIS WORLD.
I DID HATE THE FLAMES...
I STILL DO!
WHATEVER THE TRUTH IS, FIRE TOOK MY WHOLE FAMILY FROM ME.
THE FLAMES RUINED MY WHOLE LIFE!!
I'LL NEVER BRING MYSELF TO LIKE THEM.
BUT YOU USED THOSE FLAMES—THEY'RE WHAT BROUGHT YOU HERE.
...

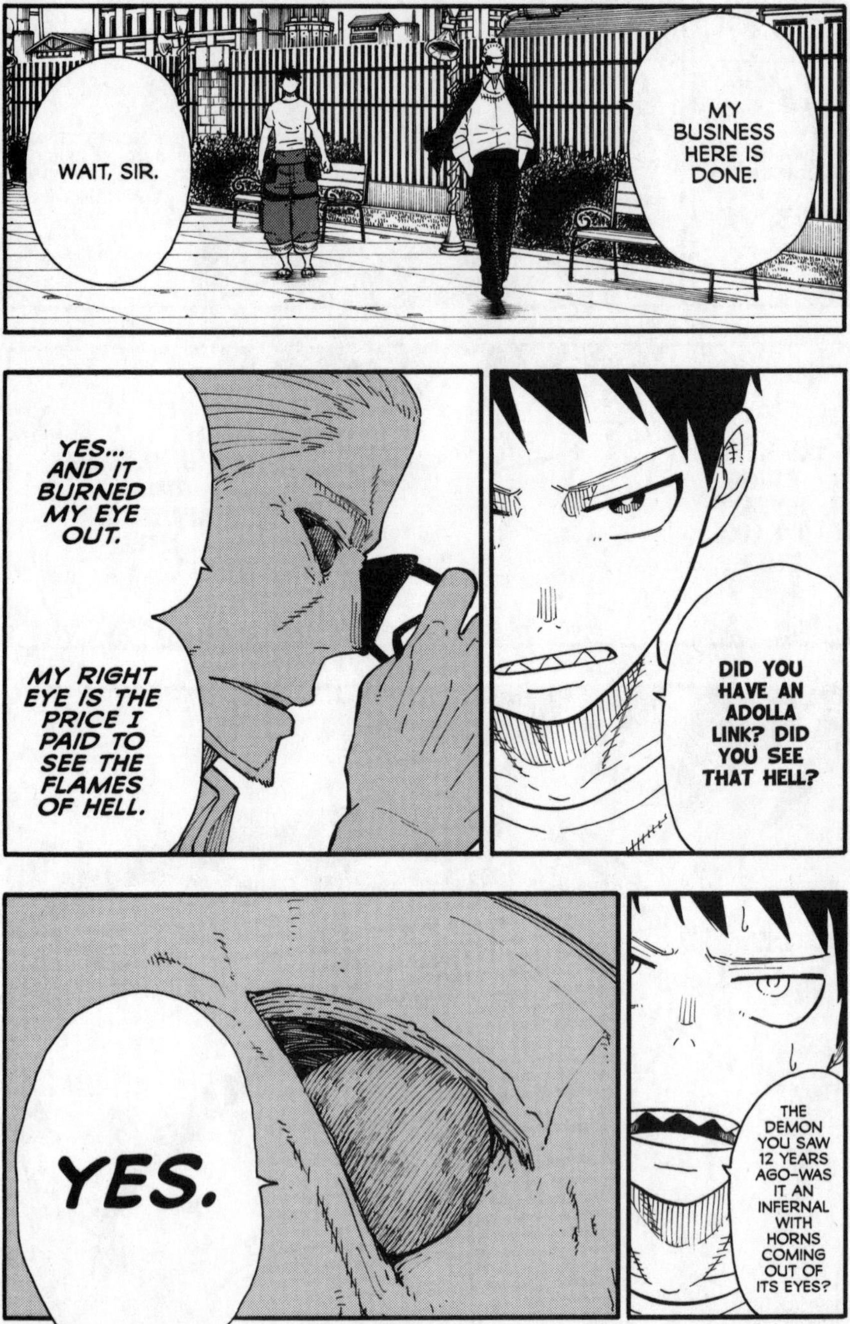
MY BUSINESS HERE IS DONE.
WAIT, SIR.
DID YOU HAVE AN ADOLLA LINK? DID YOU SEE THAT HELL?
YES... AND IT BURNED MY EYE OUT.
MY RIGHT EYE IS THE PRICE I PAID TO SEE THE FLAMES OF HELL.
THE DEMON YOU SAW 12 YEARS AGO—WAS IT AN INFERNAL WITH HORNS COMING OUT OF ITS EYES?
YES.

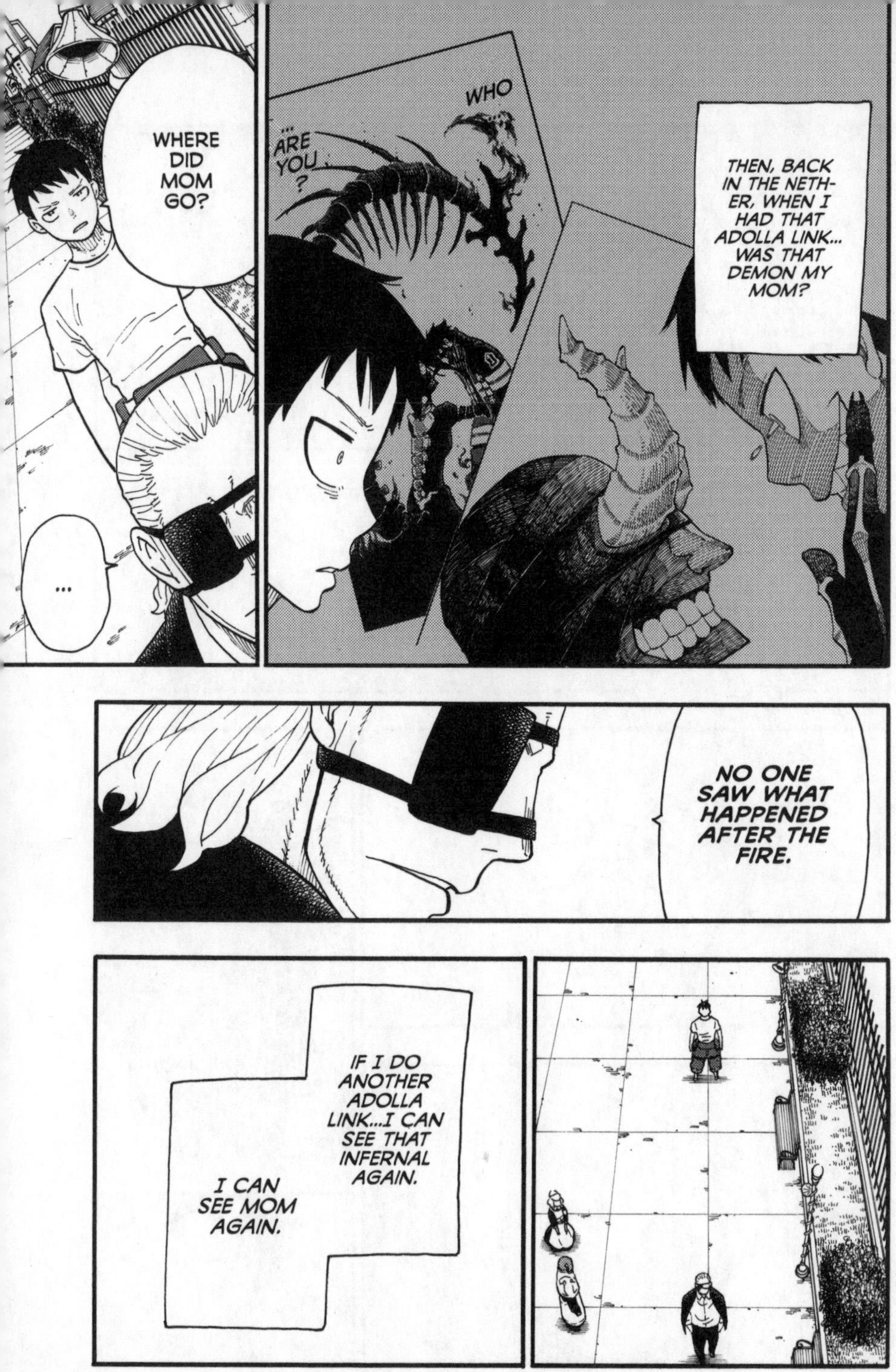
THEN, BACK IN THE NETHER, WHEN I HAD THAT ADOLLA LINK... WAS THAT DEMON MY MOM?
WHO ... ARE YOU?
WHERE DID MOM GO?
...
NO ONE SAW WHAT HAPPENED AFTER THE FIRE.
IF I DO ANOTHER ADOLLA LINK...I CAN SEE THAT INFERNAL AGAIN.
I CAN SEE MOM AGAIN.

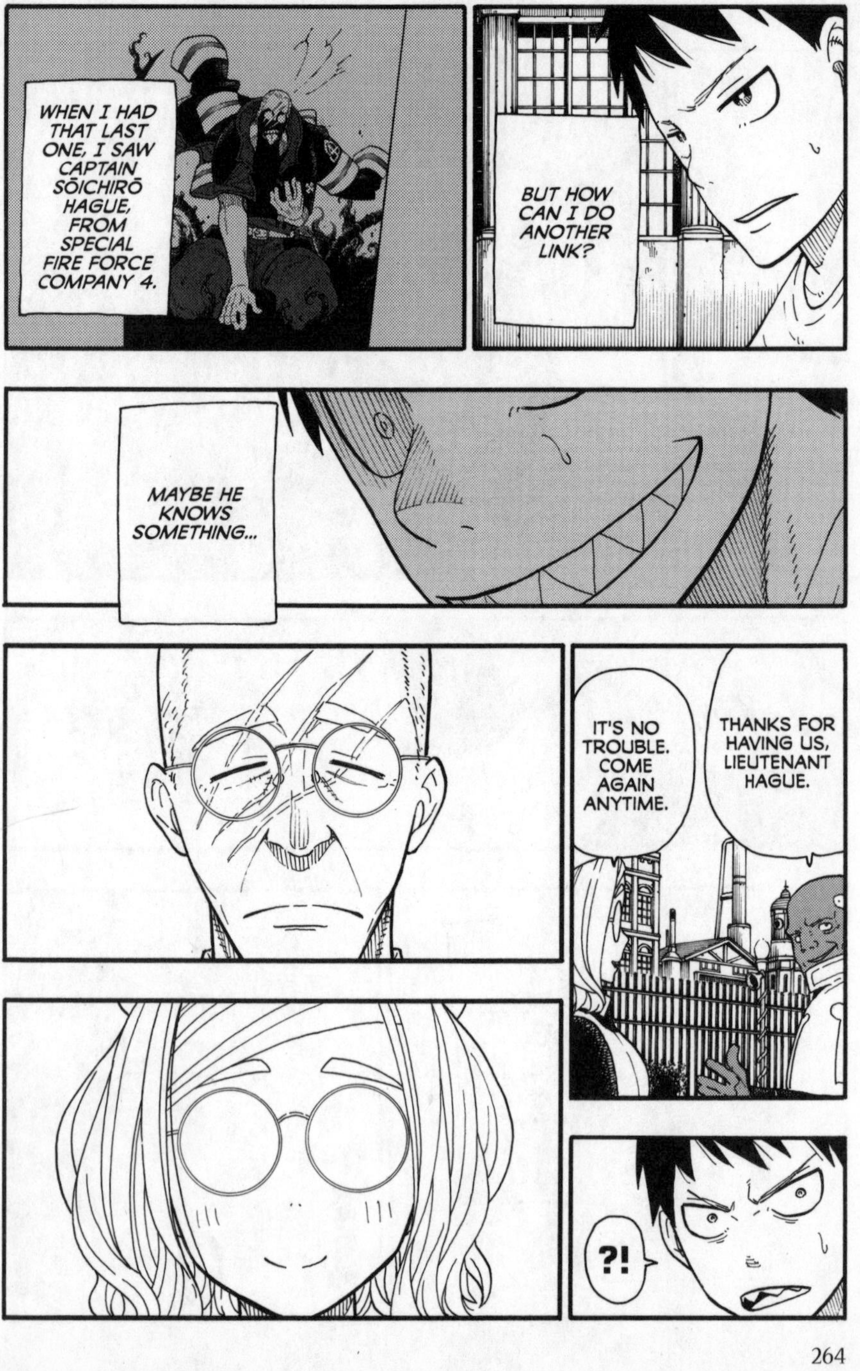
BUT HOW CAN I DO ANOTHER LINK?
WHEN I HAD THAT LAST ONE, I SAW CAPTAIN SŌICHIRŌ HAGUE, FROM SPECIAL FIRE FORCE COMPANY 4.
MAYBE HE KNOWS SOMETHING...
THANKS FOR HAVING US, LIEUTENANT HAGUE.
IT'S NO TROUBLE. COME AGAIN ANYTIME.
?!

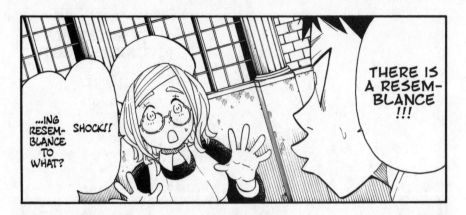

THERE IS A RESEMBLANCE!!!
...ING RESEMBLANCE TO WHAT?
SHOCK!!
UMMM, LIEUTENANT HAGUE?
YES? ?
ARE YOU, BY ANY CHANCE, RELATED TO COMPANY 4'S...
OH! YES! COMPANY 4 CAPTAIN SŌICHIRŌ HAGUE IS MY GRANDFATHER!
WAIT. WHY DO YOU ASK? DO I LOOK THAT MUCH LIKE HIM?
NO!! JUST CERTAIN KEY FEATURES. DON'T WORRY ABOUT IT.
DON'T WORRY?
DO YOU THINK I COULD MEET WITH CAPTAIN HAGUE?
MEET WITH THE CAPTAIN...?

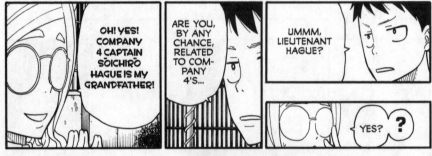

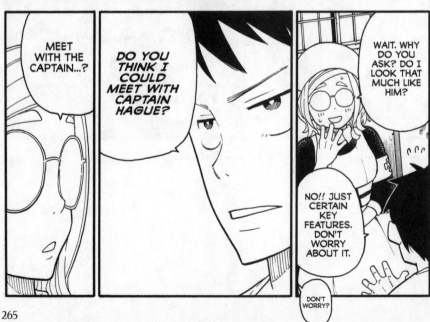

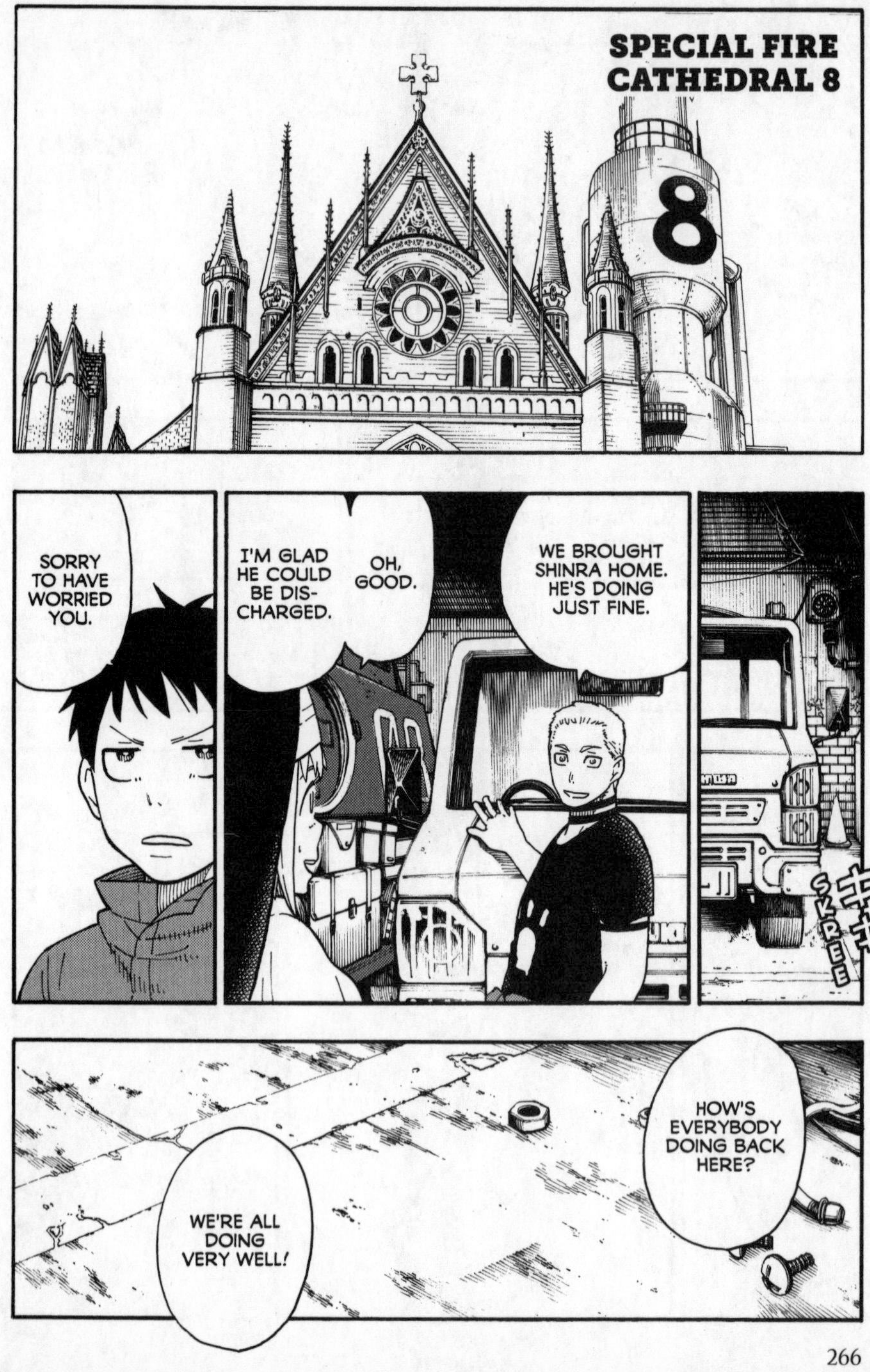
SPECIAL FIRE CATHEDRAL 8
8
キキキ
SKREE
WE BROUGHT SHINRA HOME. HE'S DOING JUST FINE.
OH, GOOD.
I'M GLAD HE COULD BE DIS-CHARGED.
SORRY TO HAVE WORRIED YOU.
HOW'S EVERYBODY DOING BACK HERE?
WE'RE ALL DOING VERY WELL!

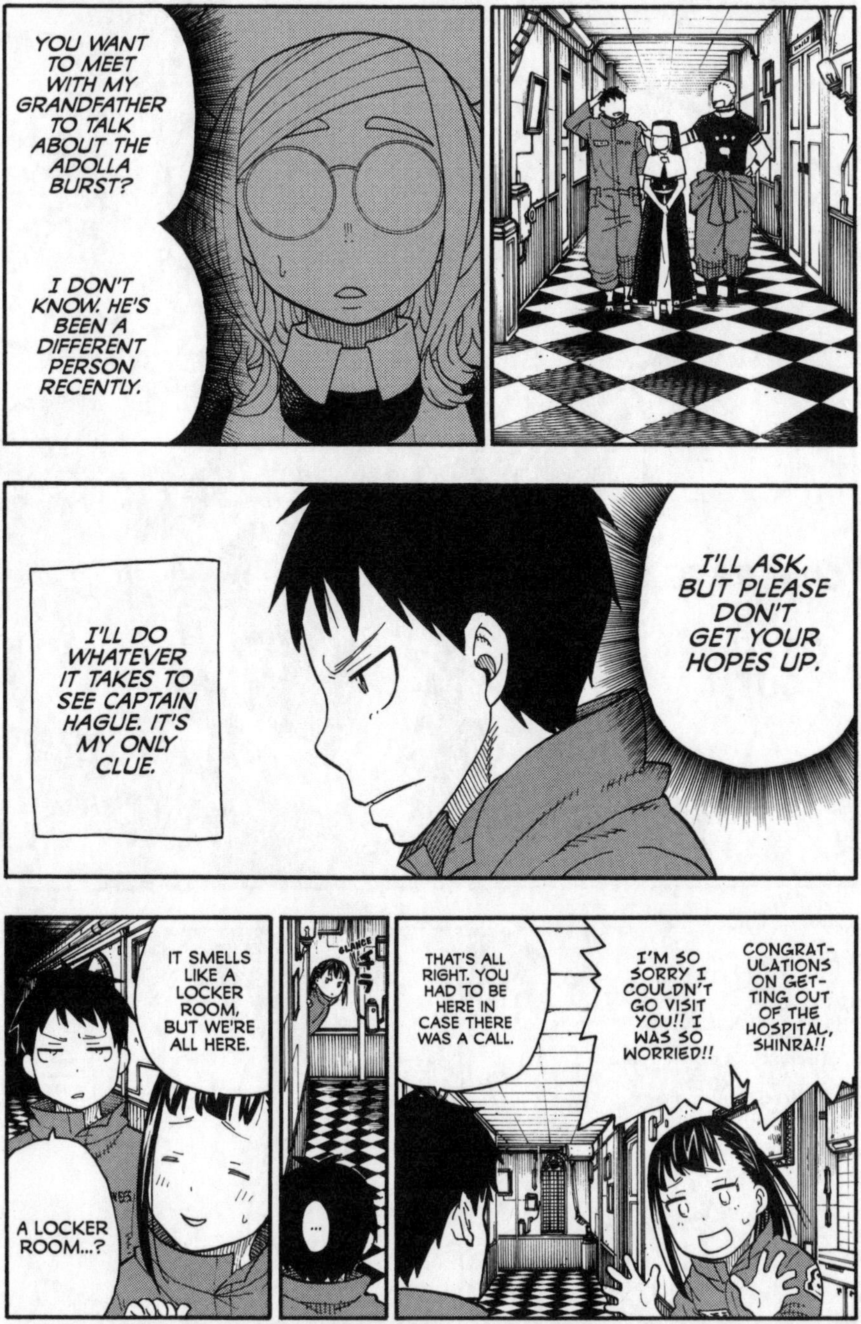
YOU WANT TO MEET WITH MY GRANDFATHER TO TALK ABOUT THE ADOLLA BURST?
I DON'T KNOW. HE'S BEEN A DIFFERENT PERSON RECENTLY.
I'LL ASK, BUT PLEASE DON'T GET YOUR HOPES UP.
I'LL DO WHATEVER IT TAKES TO SEE CAPTAIN HAGUE. IT'S MY ONLY CLUE.
CONGRAT-ULATIONS ON GET-TING OUT OF THE HOSPITAL, SHINRA!!
I'M SO SORRY I COULDN'T GO VISIT YOU!! I WAS SO WORRIED!!
THAT'S ALL RIGHT. YOU HAD TO BE HERE IN CASE THERE WAS A CALL.
...
GLANCE
IT SMELLS LIKE A LOCKER ROOM, BUT WE'RE ALL HERE.
A LOCKER ROOM...?

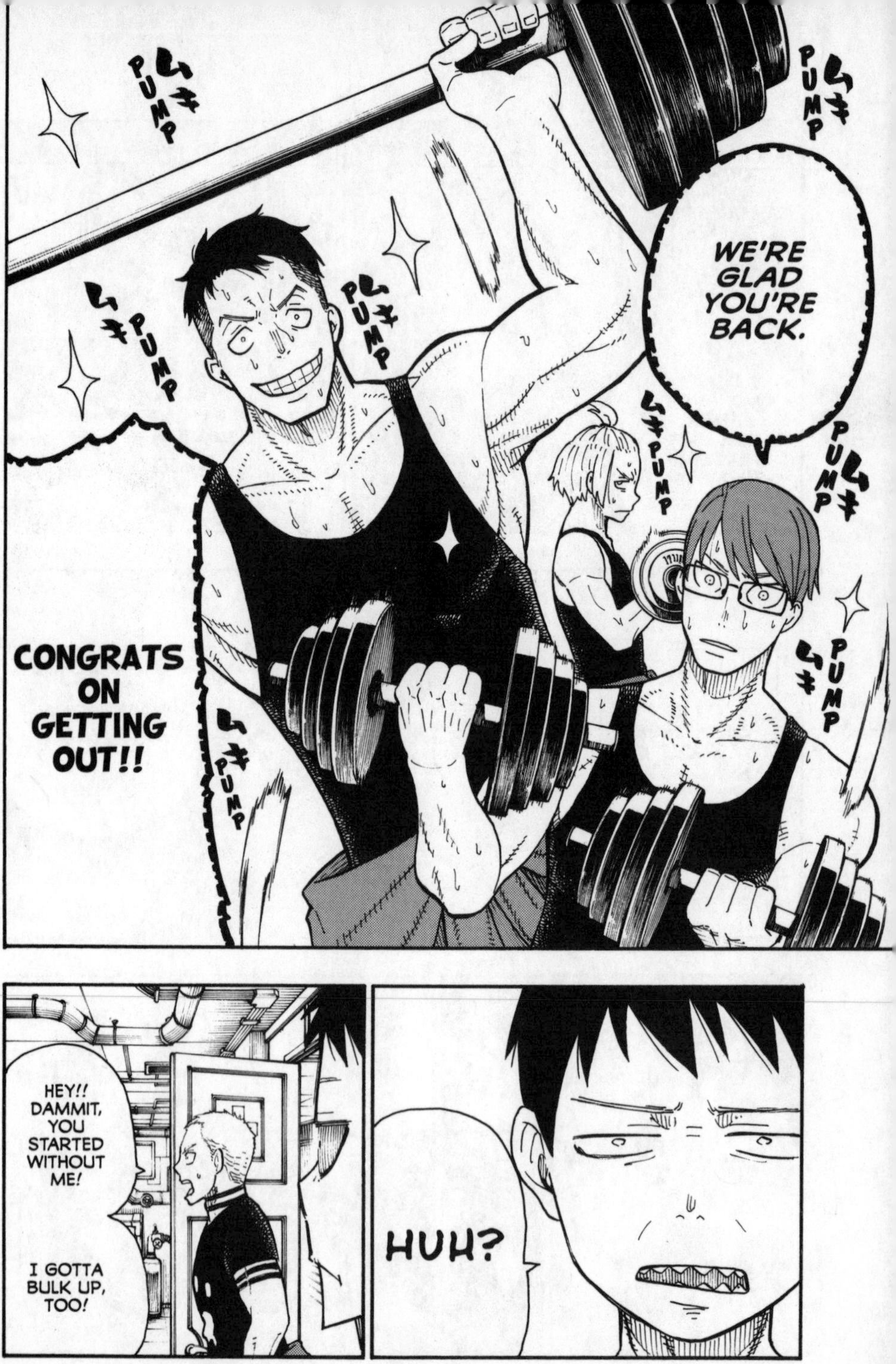
ムキ PUMP
WE'RE GLAD YOU'RE BACK.
ムキ PUMP
ムキ PUMP
ムキ PUMP
ムキ PUMP
ムキ PUMP
ムキ PUMP
ムキ PUMP
CONGRATS ON GETTING OUT!!
ムキ PUMP
HUH?
HEY!! DAMMIT, YOU STARTED WITHOUT ME!
I GOTTA BULK UP, TOO!

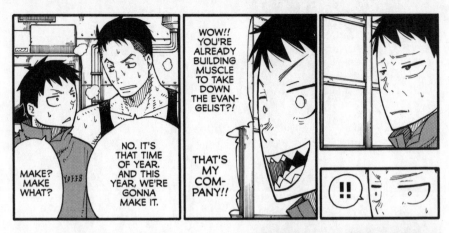

!!
WOW!! YOU'RE ALREADY BUILDING MUSCLE TO TAKE DOWN THE EVAN-GELIST?!
THAT'S MY COM-PANY!!
NO. IT'S THAT TIME OF YEAR. AND THIS YEAR, WE'RE GONNA MAKE IT.
MAKE? MAKE WHAT?
THE SPECIAL FIRE FORCE NUDE CALENDAR!!
WHA-AAA?!
WHAT HAPPENED WHILE I WAS UNCON-SCIOUS?!
SHOULD I FEAR FOR THE FUTURE OF SPECIAL FIRE FORCE COMPANY 8?!

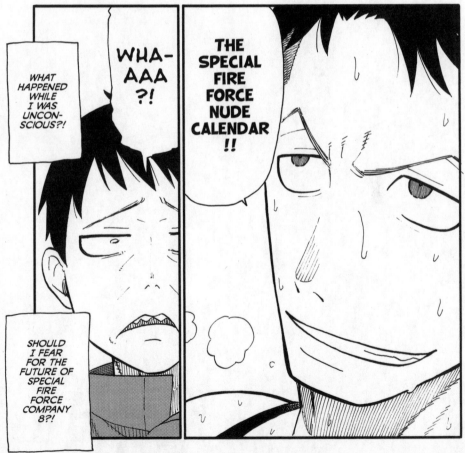

FIRE FORCE

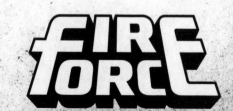

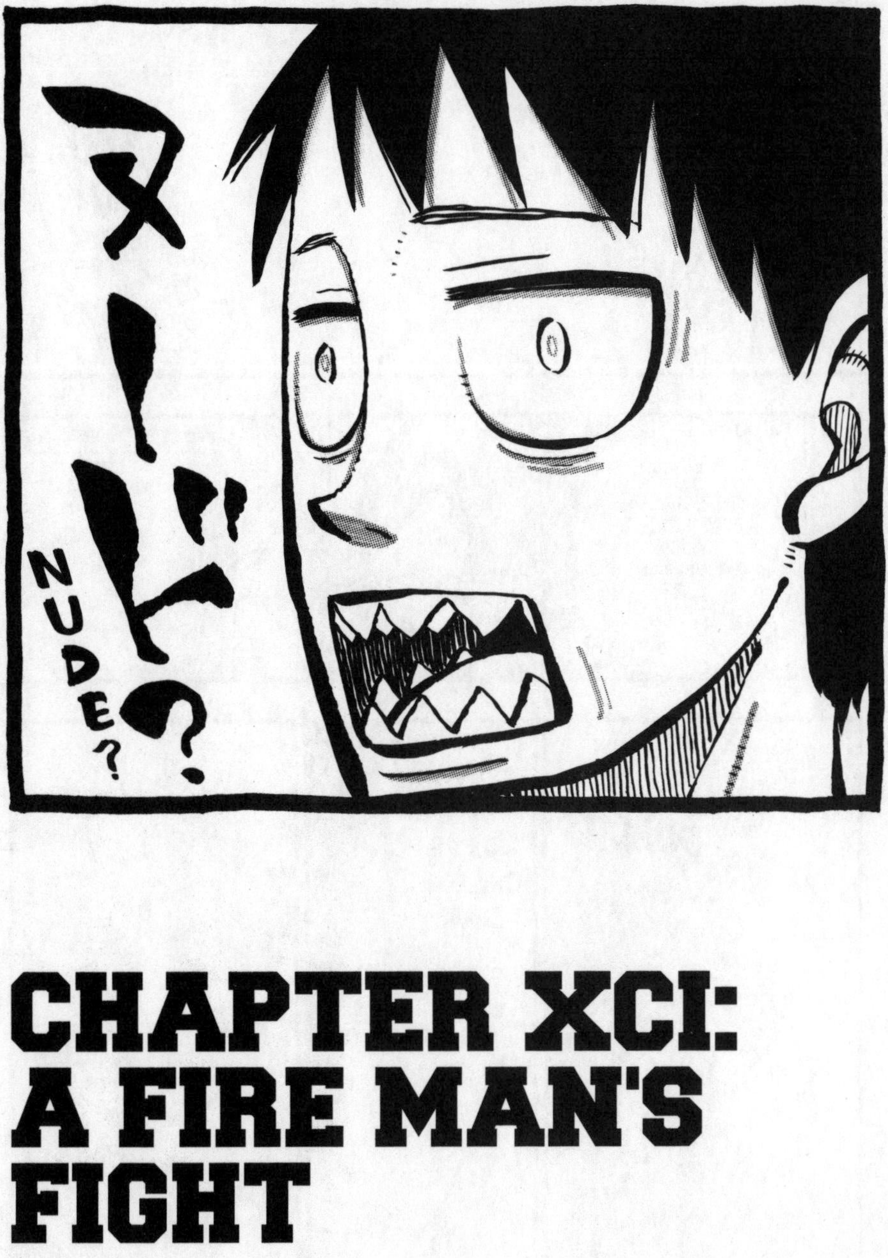
ヌード?
NUDE?

CHAPTER XCI:
A FIRE MAN'S FIGHT

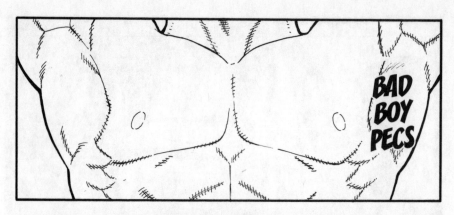

BAD BOY PECS
UH...
THE SPECIAL FIRE FORCE NUDE CALENDAR... SIR?
ASSERTIVE ABS
YES, THE NUDE CALEN-DAR.
SHY DORSALS

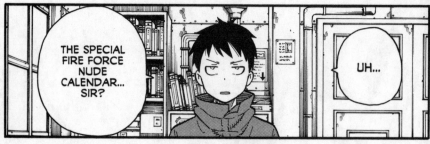

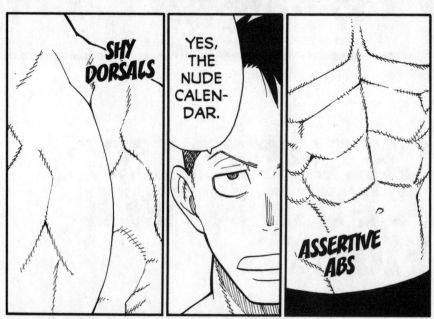

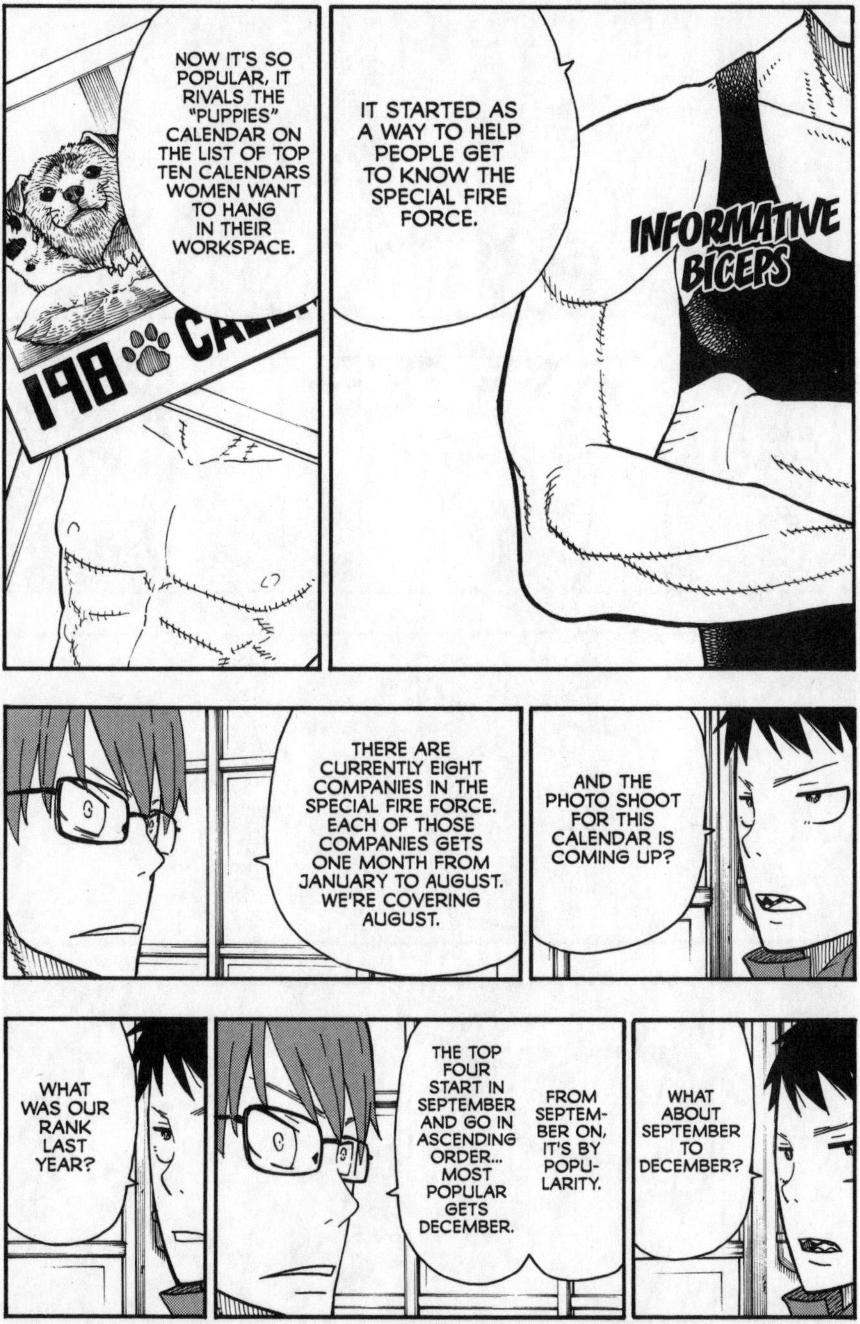
IT STARTED AS A WAY TO HELP PEOPLE GET TO KNOW THE SPECIAL FIRE FORCE.
INFORMATIVE BICEPS
NOW IT'S SO POPULAR, IT RIVALS THE "PUPPIES" CALENDAR ON THE LIST OF TOP TEN CALENDARS WOMEN WANT TO HANG IN THEIR WORKSPACE.
AND THE PHOTO SHOOT FOR THIS CALENDAR IS COMING UP?
THERE ARE CURRENTLY EIGHT COMPANIES IN THE SPECIAL FIRE FORCE. EACH OF THOSE COMPANIES GETS ONE MONTH FROM JANUARY TO AUGUST. WE'RE COVERING AUGUST.
WHAT ABOUT SEPTEMBER TO DECEMBER?
FROM SEPTEMBER ON, IT'S BY POPULARITY.
THE TOP FOUR START IN SEPTEMBER AND GO IN ASCENDING ORDER... MOST POPULAR GETS DECEMBER.
WHAT WAS OUR RANK LAST YEAR?

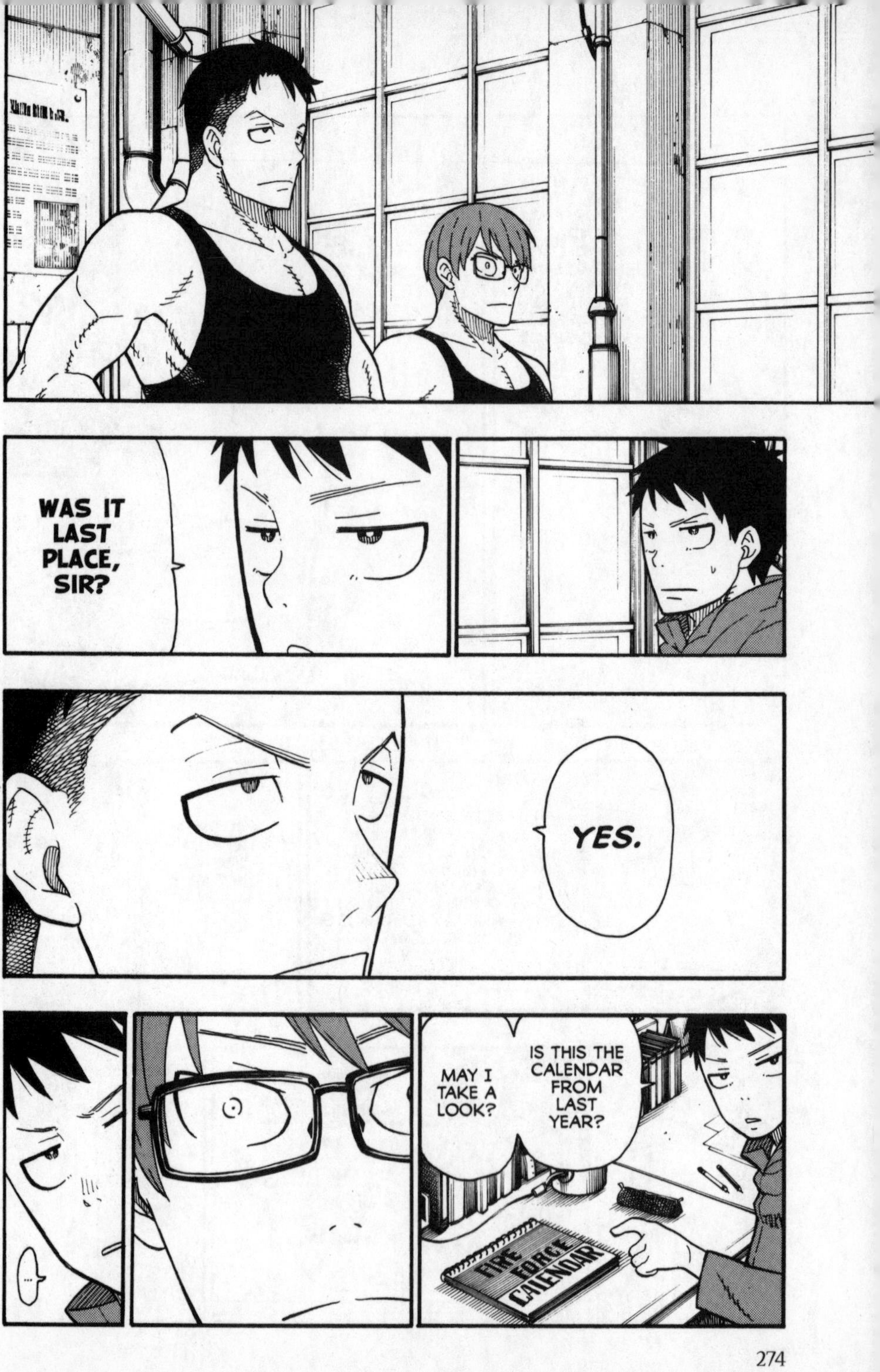
WAS IT LAST PLACE, SIR?
YES.
IS THIS THE CALENDAR FROM LAST YEAR?
MAY I TAKE A LOOK?
FIRE FORCE CALENDAR
...

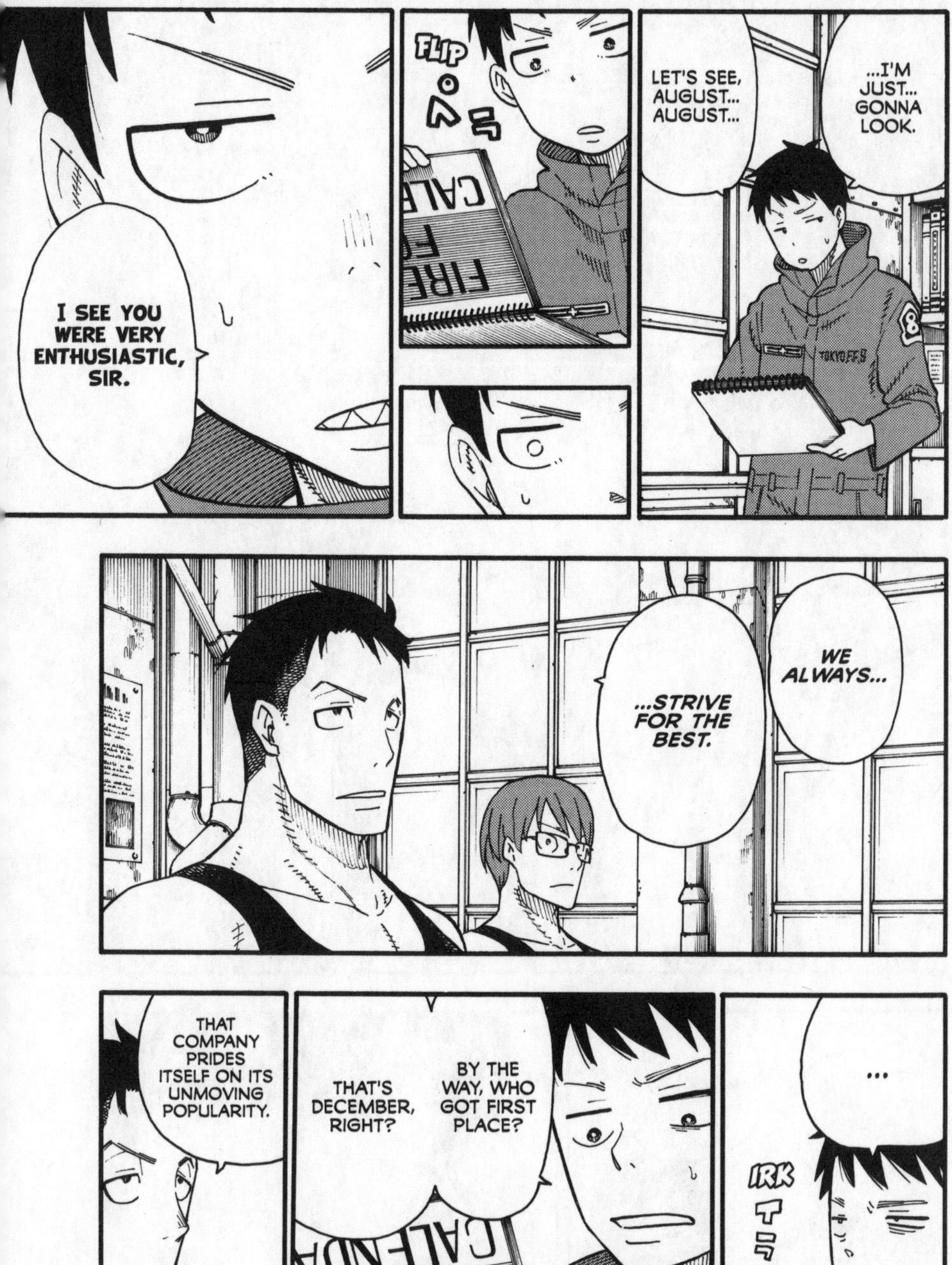
...I'M JUST... GONNA LOOK.
LET'S SEE, AUGUST... AUGUST...
FLIP
I SEE YOU WERE VERY ENTHUSIASTIC, SIR.
WE ALWAYS...
...STRIVE FOR THE BEST.
...
IRK
BY THE WAY, WHO GOT FIRST PLACE?
THAT'S DECEMBER, RIGHT?
THAT COMPANY PRIDES ITSELF ON ITS UNMOVING POPULARITY.

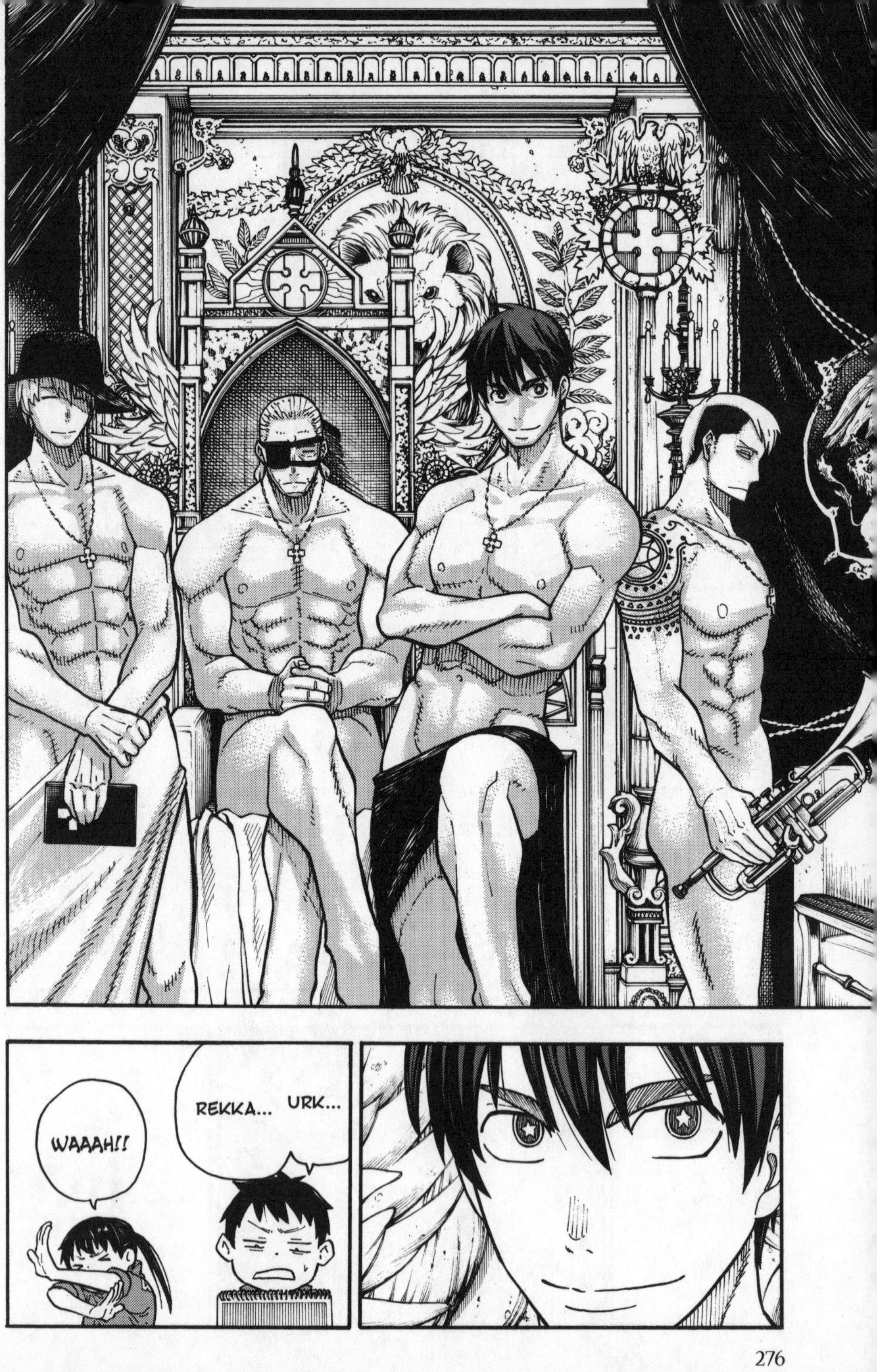
REKKA... URK...
WAAAH!!

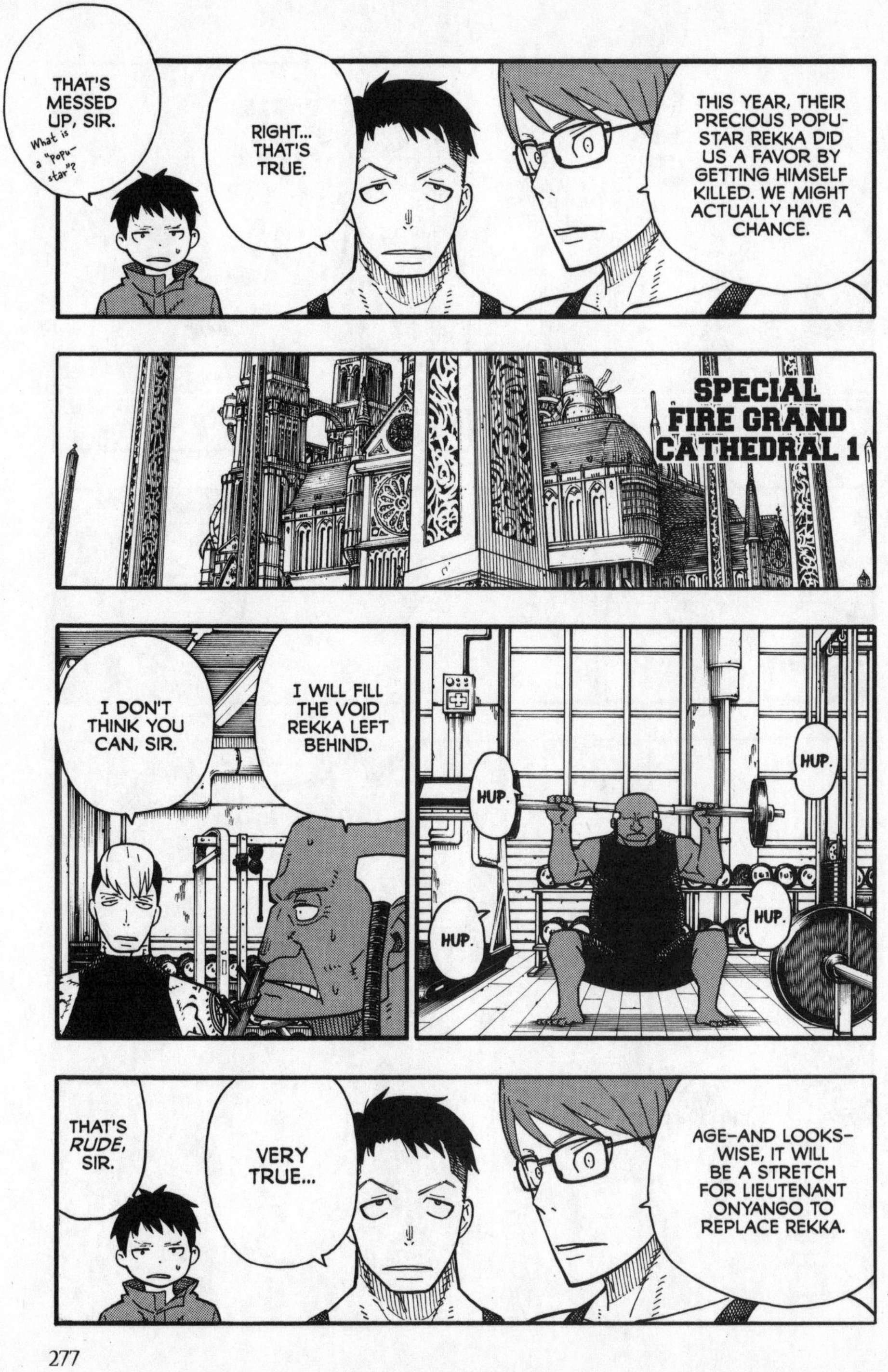

THIS YEAR, THEIR PRECIOUS POPU-STAR REKKA DID US A FAVOR BY GETTING HIMSELF KILLED. WE MIGHT ACTUALLY HAVE A CHANCE.
RIGHT... THAT'S TRUE.
THAT'S MESSED UP, SIR.
What is a "Popu-star"?
SPECIAL FIRE GRAND CATHEDRAL 1
HUP.
HUP.
HUP.
HUP.
I WILL FILL THE VOID REKKA LEFT BEHIND.
I DON'T THINK YOU CAN, SIR.
AGE-AND LOOKS-WISE, IT WILL BE A STRETCH FOR LIEUTENANT ONYANGO TO REPLACE REKKA.
VERY TRUE...
THAT'S *RUDE*, SIR.

SPECIAL FIRE BASE 2
COME *ON*!! JUGGERNAUT!!
TAKE 'EM OFF ALREADY!! THAT'S AN ORDER FROM A SUPERIOR OFFICER!!
N...NOOOO! PLEASE, SIR! I'M TOO EMBARRASSED!!
I CAN'T DO A NUDE SHOOT!!
COME TO THINK OF IT, DR. GIOVANNI'S IN COMPANY 3...
MAYBE I CAN ACTUALLY SEE INSIDE THAT THING!
ペラ
FLIP
THAT HAS GOT TO BE FAKE.
DAMMIT!
GO TO HELL!!

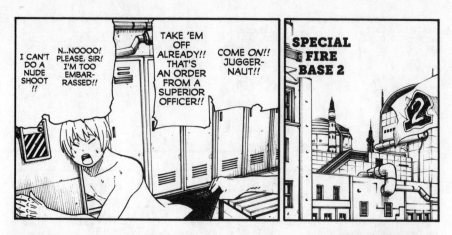

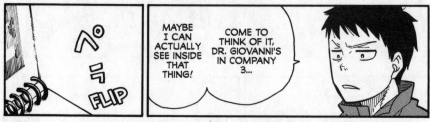

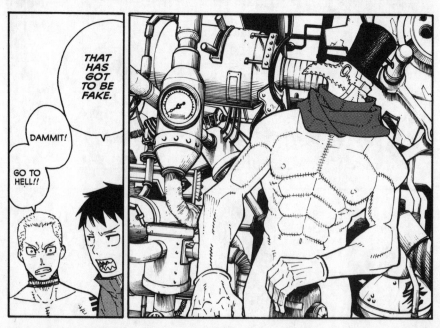

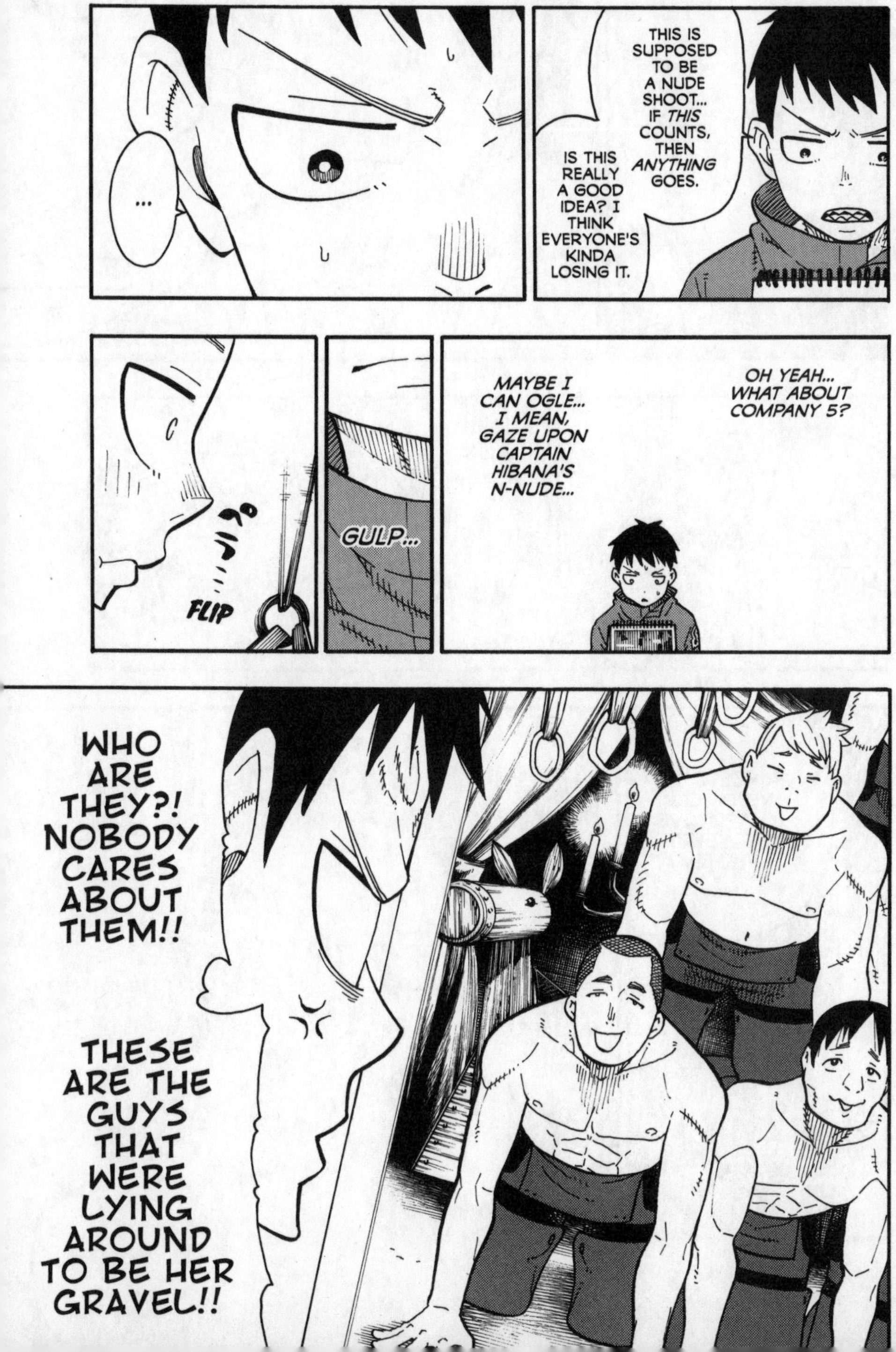
THIS IS SUPPOSED TO BE A NUDE SHOOT... IF THIS COUNTS, THEN ANYTHING GOES.
IS THIS REALLY A GOOD IDEA? I THINK EVERYONE'S KINDA LOSING IT.
...
OH YEAH... WHAT ABOUT COMPANY 5?
MAYBE I CAN OGLE... I MEAN, GAZE UPON CAPTAIN HIBANA'S N-NUDE...
GULP...
FLIP
WHO ARE THEY?! NOBODY CARES ABOUT THEM!!
THESE ARE THE GUYS THAT WERE LYING AROUND TO BE HER GRAVEL!!

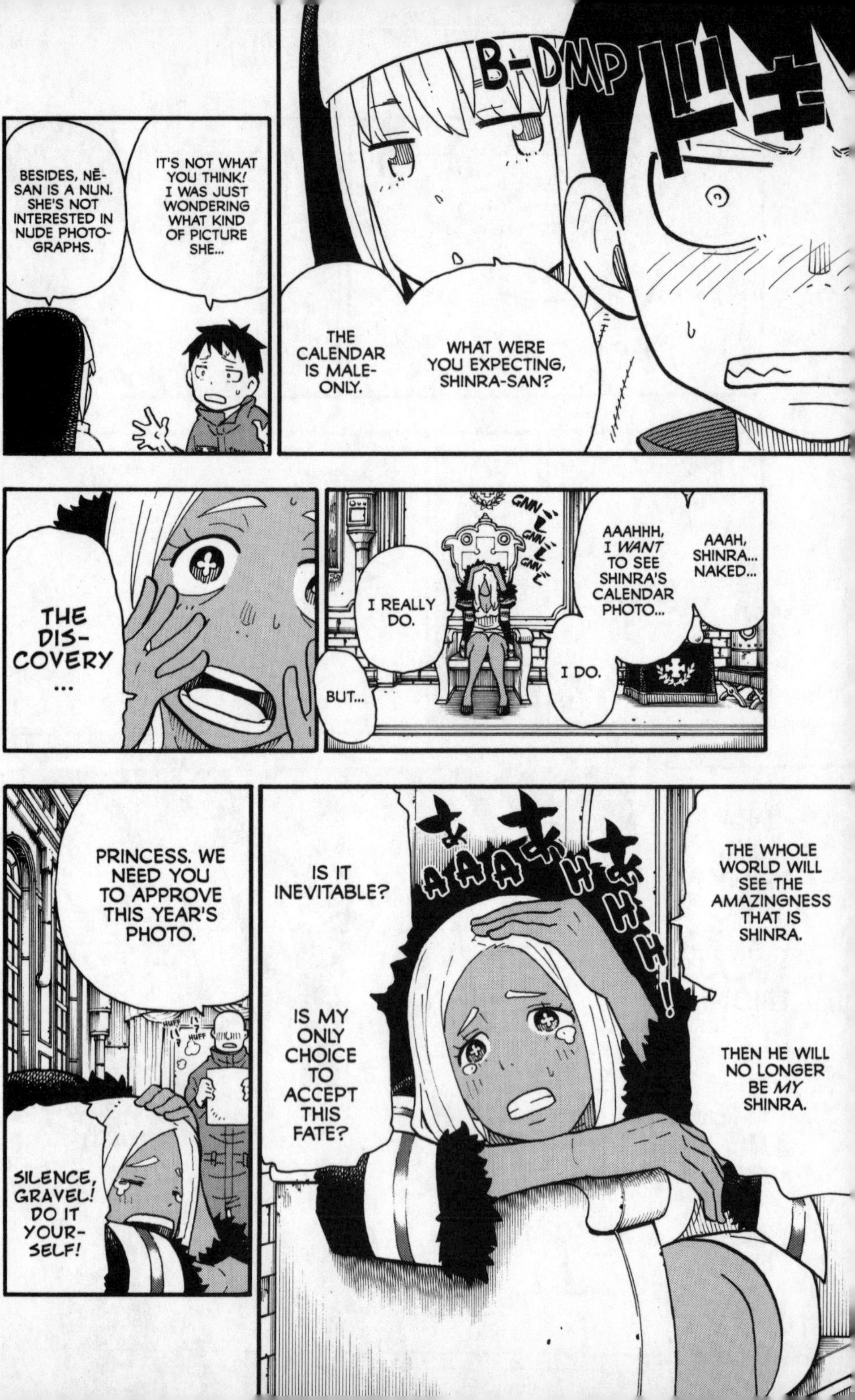
B-DMP
WHAT WERE YOU EXPECTING, SHINRA-SAN?
THE CALENDAR IS MALE-ONLY.
IT'S NOT WHAT YOU THINK! I WAS JUST WONDERING WHAT KIND OF PICTURE SHE...
BESIDES, NĒ-SAN IS A NUN. SHE'S NOT INTERESTED IN NUDE PHOTOGRAPHS.
AAAH, SHINRA... NAKED...
AAAHHH, I *WANT* TO SEE SHINRA'S CALENDAR PHOTO...
GNN GNN GNN
I DO.
I REALLY DO.
BUT...
THE DISCOVERY...
THE WHOLE WORLD WILL SEE THE AMAZINGNESS THAT IS SHINRA.
AAAAHHHHH!
IS IT INEVITABLE?
THEN HE WILL NO LONGER BE *MY* SHINRA.
IS MY ONLY CHOICE TO ACCEPT THIS FATE?
PRINCESS. WE NEED YOU TO APPROVE THIS YEAR'S PHOTO.
HUFF HUFF
SILENCE, GRAVEL! DO IT YOURSELF!

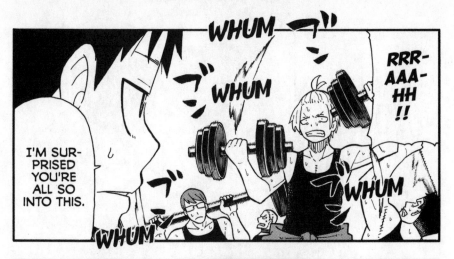

WHUM
RRR-AAA-HH!!
WHUM
WHUM
I'M SUR-PRISED YOU'RE ALL SO INTO THIS.
WHUM
THERE'S NOT A CHANCE COMPANY 7 CARES ABOUT THIS IN ANY WAY, RIGHT?
CAPTAIN SHINMON IS A PRETTY BIG POPU-STAR.
COULD YOU PLEASE STOP SAYING "POPU-STAR"?
TOKYO F.F.S
WAIT.
YOU MEAN *THE* CAPTAIN SHINMON?
I MEAN, I GET THAT PEOPLE LIKE HIM.
BUT HE WOULDN'T ACTUALLY PARTICIPATE IN THIS, WOULD HE?!
JULY...
JULY...
Sun
FLIP

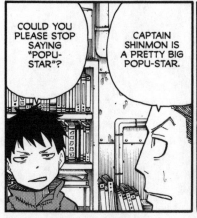

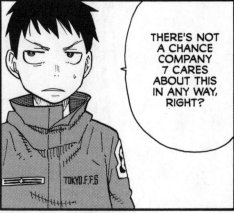

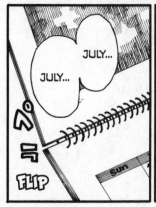

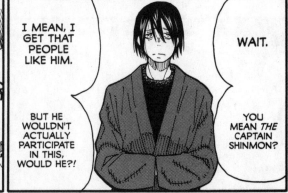

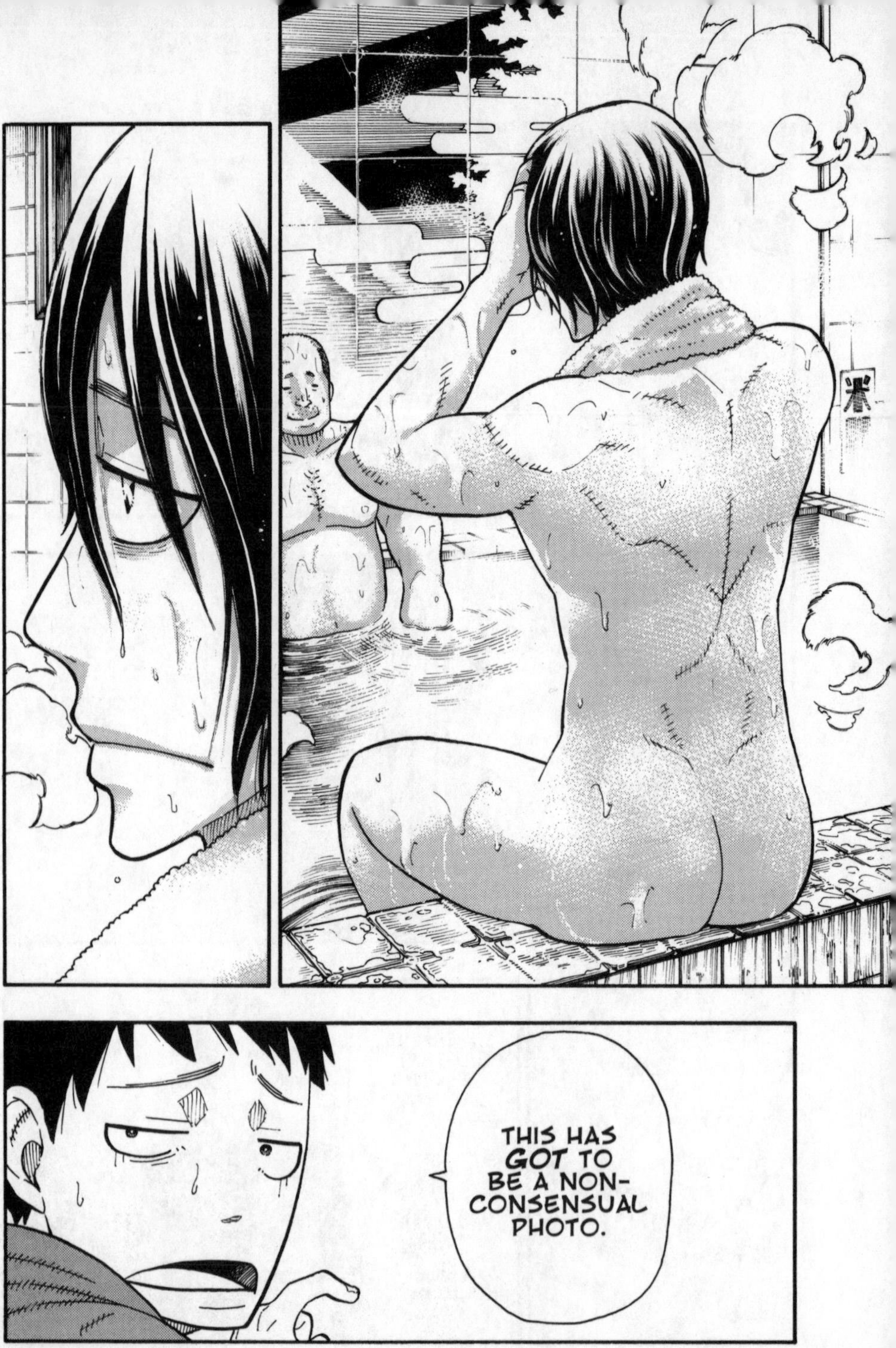
THIS HAS GOT TO BE A NON-CONSENSUAL PHOTO.

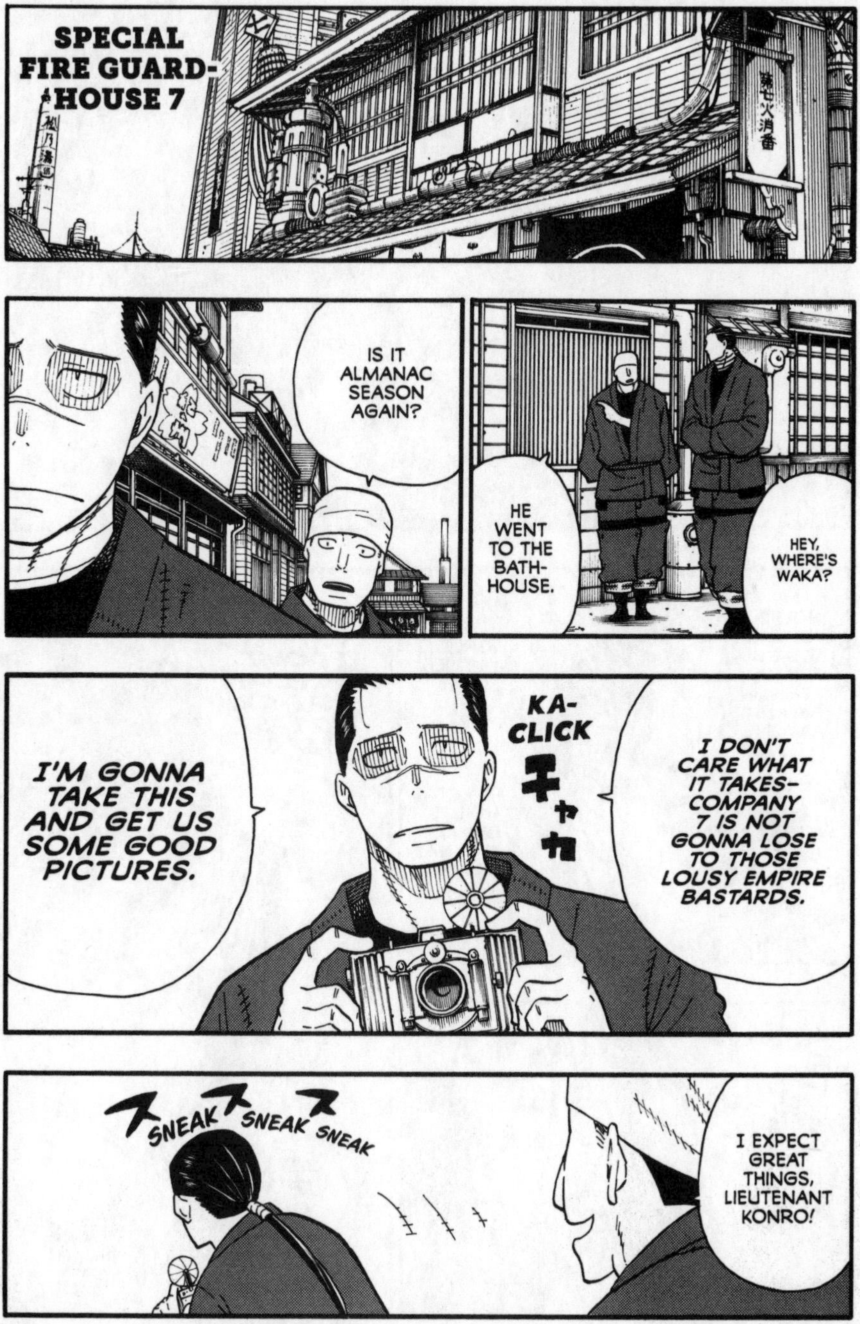
SPECIAL FIRE GUARD-HOUSE 7
HEY, WHERE'S WAKA?
HE WENT TO THE BATH-HOUSE.
IS IT ALMANAC SEASON AGAIN?
I DON'T CARE WHAT IT TAKES— COMPANY 7 IS NOT GONNA LOSE TO THOSE LOUSY EMPIRE BASTARDS.
KA-CLICK
チャカ
I'M GONNA TAKE THIS AND GET US SOME GOOD PICTURES.
I EXPECT GREAT THINGS, LIEUTENANT KONRO!
ス SNEAK ス SNEAK ス SNEAK

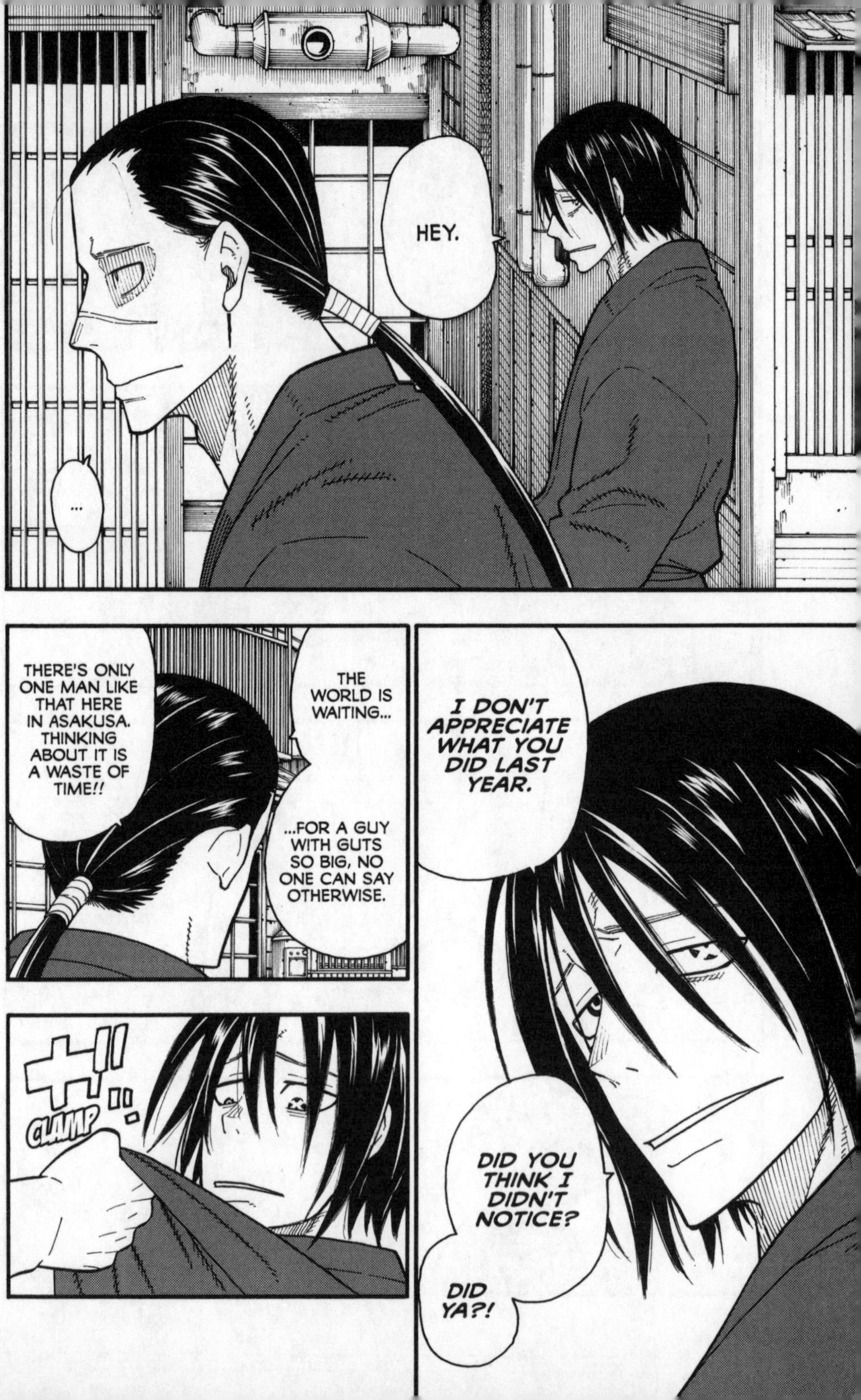
HEY.
...
I DON'T APPRECIATE WHAT YOU DID LAST YEAR.
DID YOU THINK I DIDN'T NOTICE?
DID YA?!
THE WORLD IS WAITING...
...FOR A GUY WITH GUTS SO BIG, NO ONE CAN SAY OTHERWISE.
THERE'S ONLY ONE MAN LIKE THAT HERE IN ASAKUSA. THINKING ABOUT IT IS A WASTE OF TIME!!
CLAMP

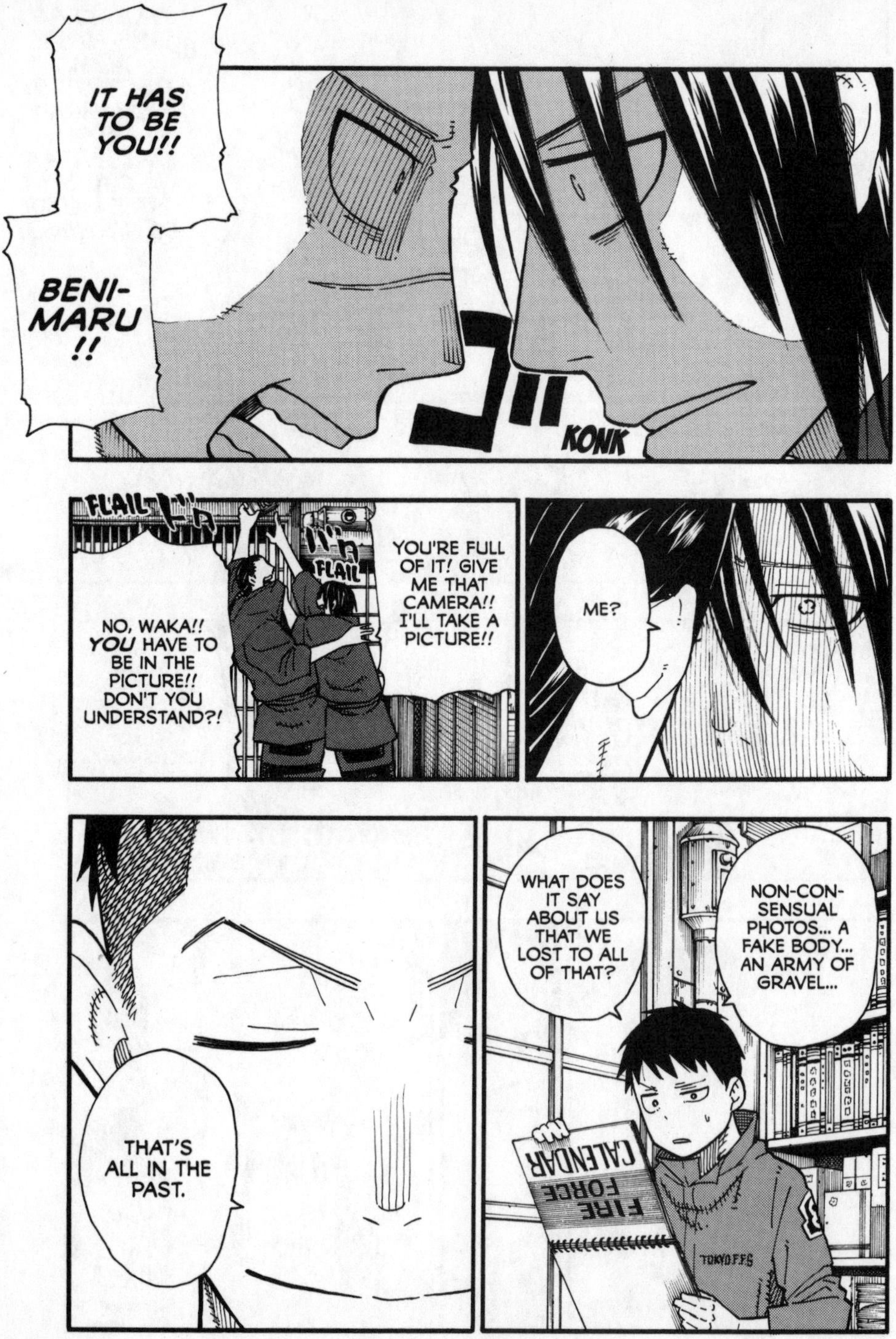
IT HAS TO BE YOU!!
BENI-MARU!!
KONK
ME?
FLAIL
YOU'RE FULL OF IT! GIVE ME THAT CAMERA!! I'LL TAKE A PICTURE!!
NO, WAKA!! *YOU* HAVE TO BE IN THE PICTURE!! DON'T YOU UNDERSTAND?!
FLAIL
NON-CON-SENSUAL PHOTOS... A FAKE BODY... AN ARMY OF GRAVEL...
WHAT DOES IT SAY ABOUT US THAT WE LOST TO ALL OF THAT?
FIRE FORCE CALENDAR
TOKYO F.F.S
THAT'S ALL IN THE PAST.

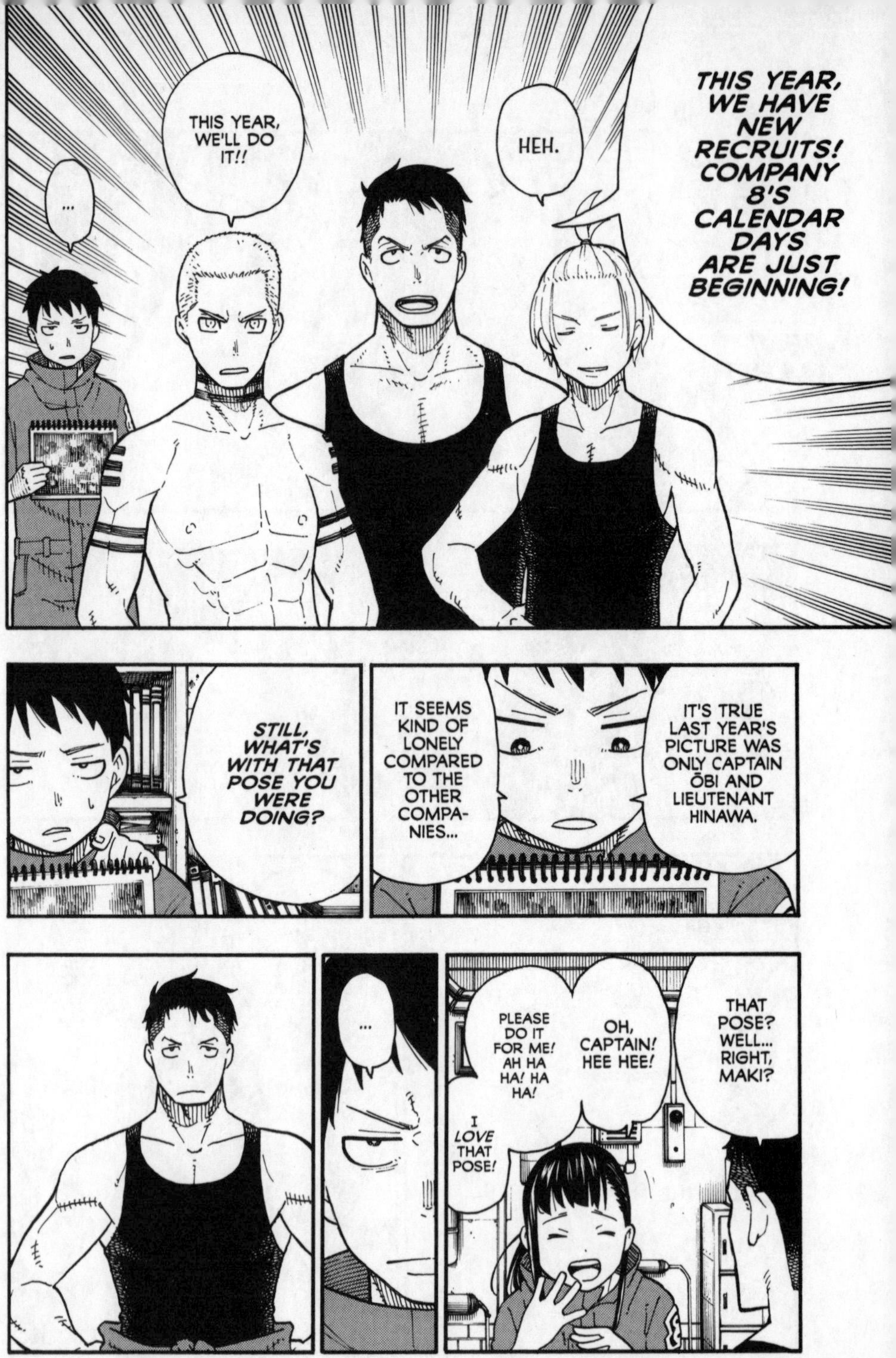
THIS YEAR, WE HAVE NEW RECRUITS! COMPANY 8'S CALENDAR DAYS ARE JUST BEGINNING!
HEH.
THIS YEAR, WE'LL DO IT!!
...
IT'S TRUE LAST YEAR'S PICTURE WAS ONLY CAPTAIN ŌBI AND LIEUTENANT HINAWA.
IT SEEMS KIND OF LONELY COMPARED TO THE OTHER COMPANIES...
STILL, WHAT'S WITH THAT POSE YOU WERE DOING?
THAT POSE? WELL... RIGHT, MAKI?
OH, CAPTAIN! HEE HEE!
PLEASE DO IT FOR ME! AH HA HA! HA HA!
I LOVE THAT POSE!
...

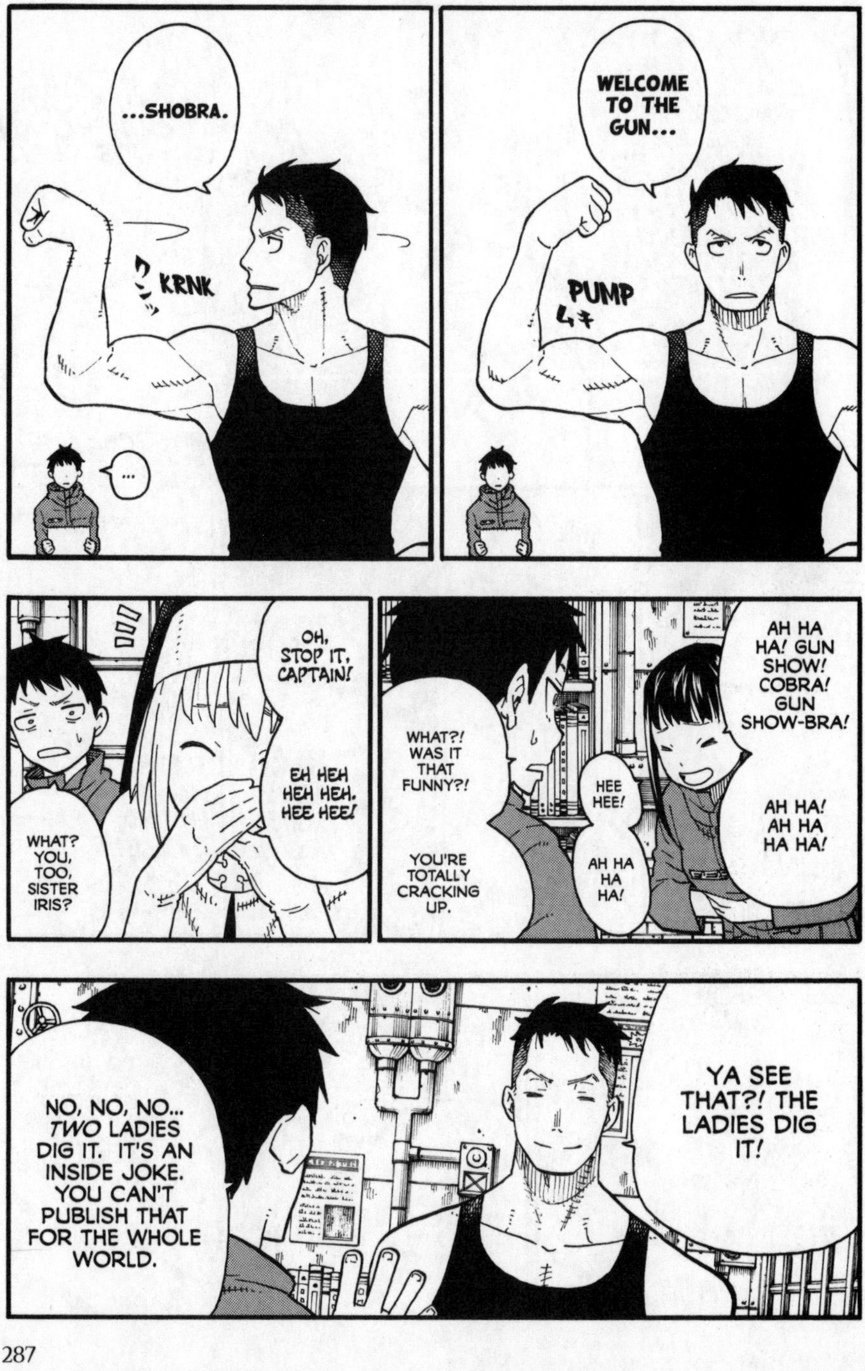
WELCOME TO THE GUN...
PUMP
ムキ
...SHOBRA.
KRNK
...
AH HA HA! GUN SHOW! COBRA! GUN SHOW-BRA!
AH HA! AH HA HA HA!
WHAT?! WAS IT THAT FUNNY?!
HEE HEE!
AH HA HA HA!
YOU'RE TOTALLY CRACKING UP.
OH, STOP IT, CAPTAIN!
EH HEH HEH HEH. HEE HEE!
WHAT? YOU, TOO, SISTER IRIS?
YA SEE THAT?! THE LADIES DIG IT!
NO, NO, NO... *TWO* LADIES DIG IT. IT'S AN INSIDE JOKE. YOU CAN'T PUBLISH THAT FOR THE WHOLE WORLD.

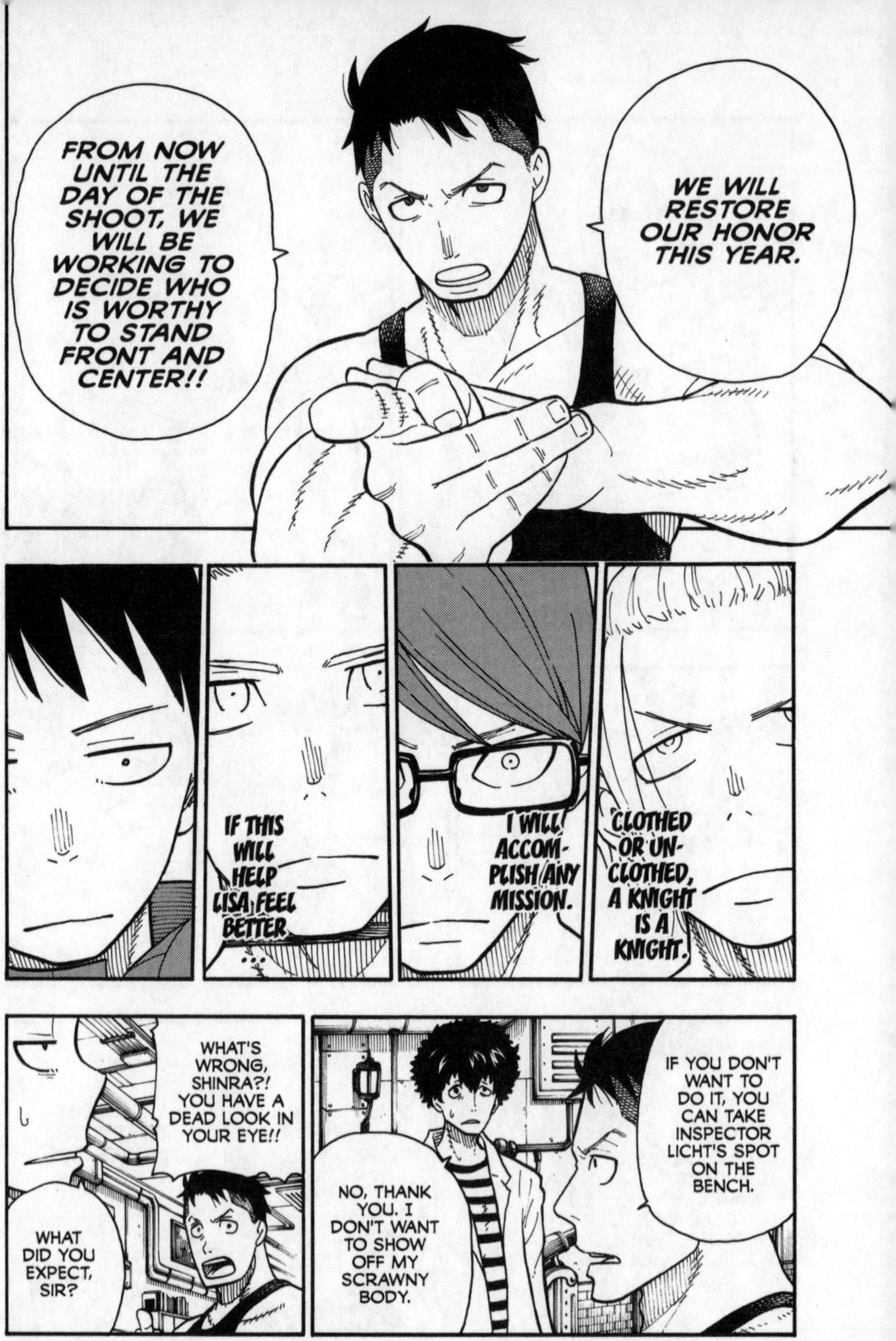
WE WILL RESTORE OUR HONOR THIS YEAR.
FROM NOW UNTIL THE DAY OF THE SHOOT, WE WILL BE WORKING TO DECIDE WHO IS WORTHY TO STAND FRONT AND CENTER!!
CLOTHED OR UN-CLOTHED, A KNIGHT IS A KNIGHT.
I WILL ACCOM-PLISH ANY MISSION.
IF THIS WILL HELP LISA FEEL BETTER
IF YOU DON'T WANT TO DO IT, YOU CAN TAKE INSPECTOR LICHT'S SPOT ON THE BENCH.
NO, THANK YOU. I DON'T WANT TO SHOW OFF MY SCRAWNY BODY.
WHAT'S WRONG, SHINRA?! YOU HAVE A DEAD LOOK IN YOUR EYE!!
WHAT DID YOU EXPECT, SIR?

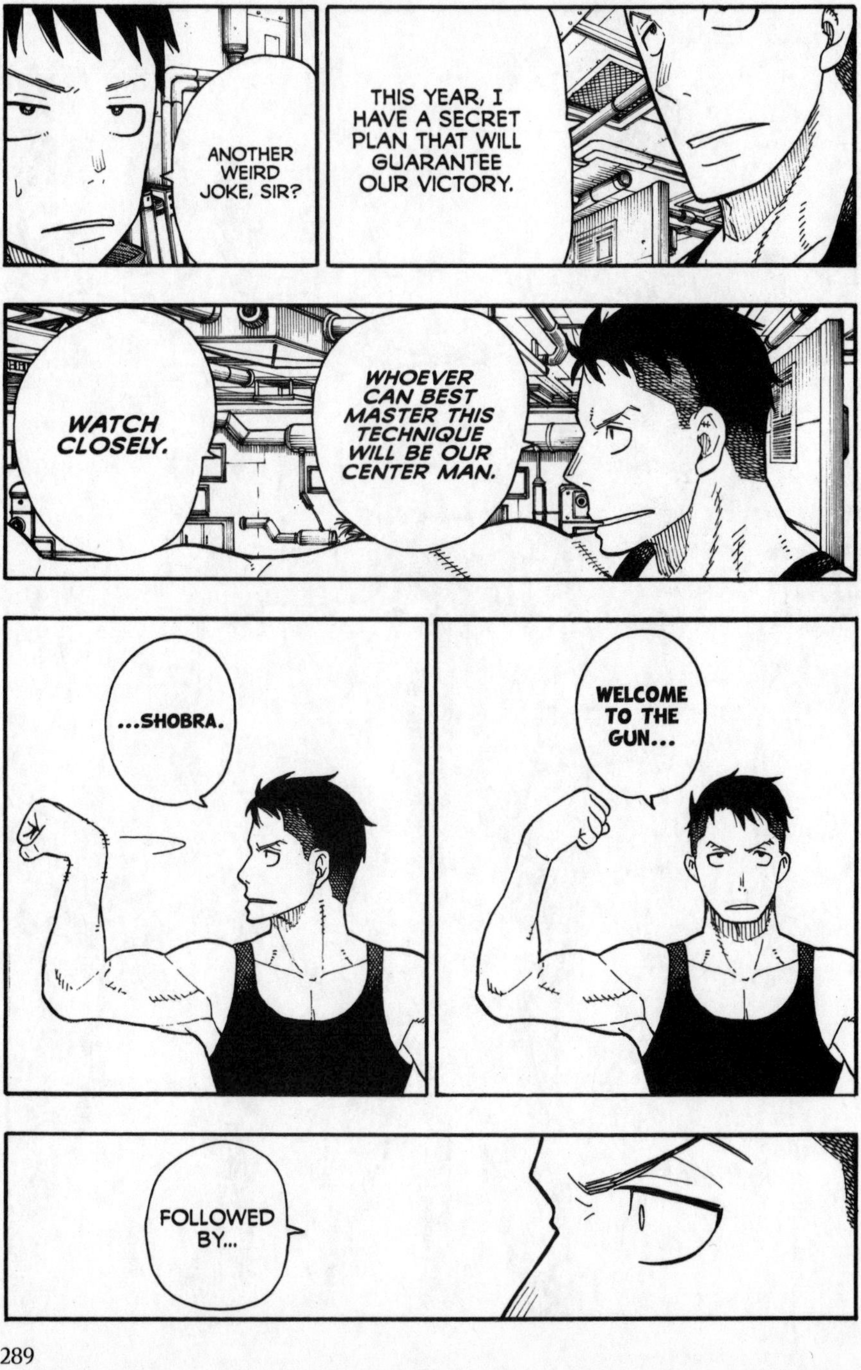
THIS YEAR, I HAVE A SECRET PLAN THAT WILL GUARANTEE OUR VICTORY.
ANOTHER WEIRD JOKE, SIR?
WHOEVER CAN BEST MASTER THIS TECHNIQUE WILL BE OUR CENTER MAN.
WATCH CLOSELY.
WELCOME TO THE GUN...
...SHOBRA.
FOLLOWED BY...

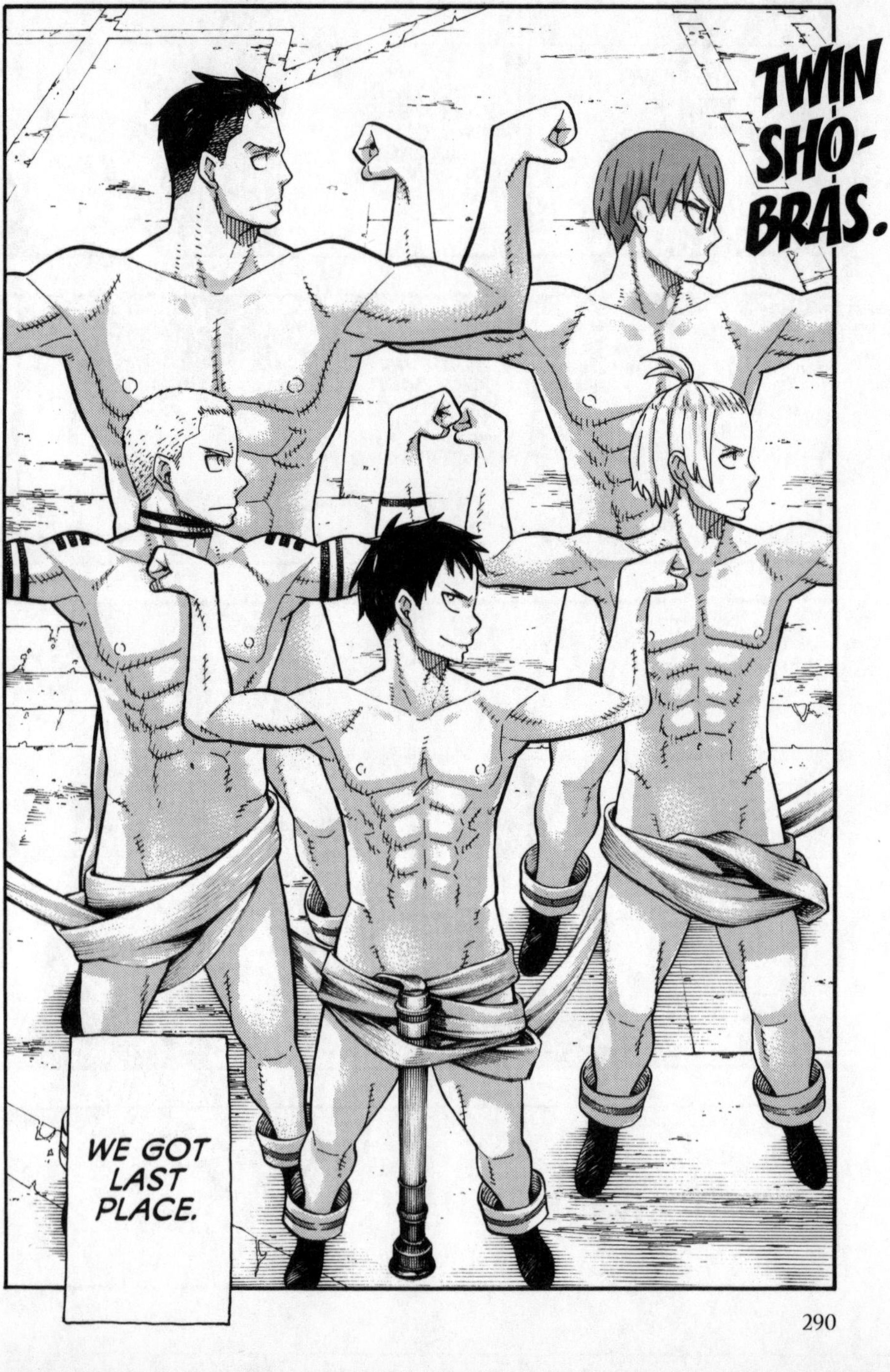
TWIN SHŌ-BRAS.
WE GOT LAST PLACE.

CHAPTER XCII: THE LIEUTENANT REMODELING PROJECT

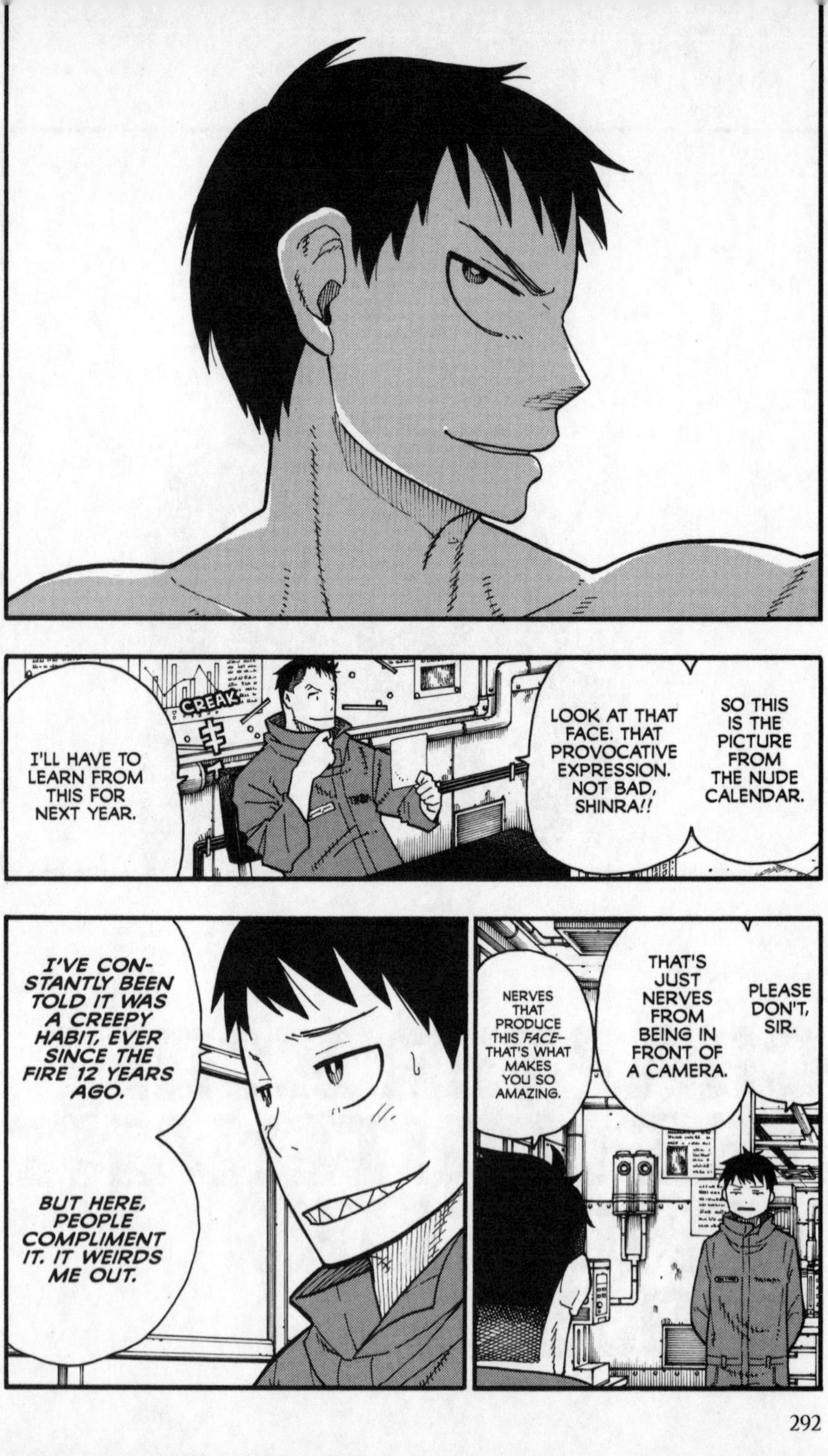
SO THIS IS THE PICTURE FROM THE NUDE CALENDAR.
LOOK AT THAT FACE. THAT PROVOCATIVE EXPRESSION. NOT BAD, SHINRA!!
CREAK
キ
I'LL HAVE TO LEARN FROM THIS FOR NEXT YEAR.
PLEASE DON'T, SIR.
THAT'S JUST NERVES FROM BEING IN FRONT OF A CAMERA.
NERVES THAT PRODUCE THIS FACE—THAT'S WHAT MAKES YOU SO AMAZING.
I'VE CONSTANTLY BEEN TOLD IT WAS A CREEPY HABIT, EVER SINCE THE FIRE 12 YEARS AGO.
BUT HERE, PEOPLE COMPLIMENT IT. IT WEIRDS ME OUT.

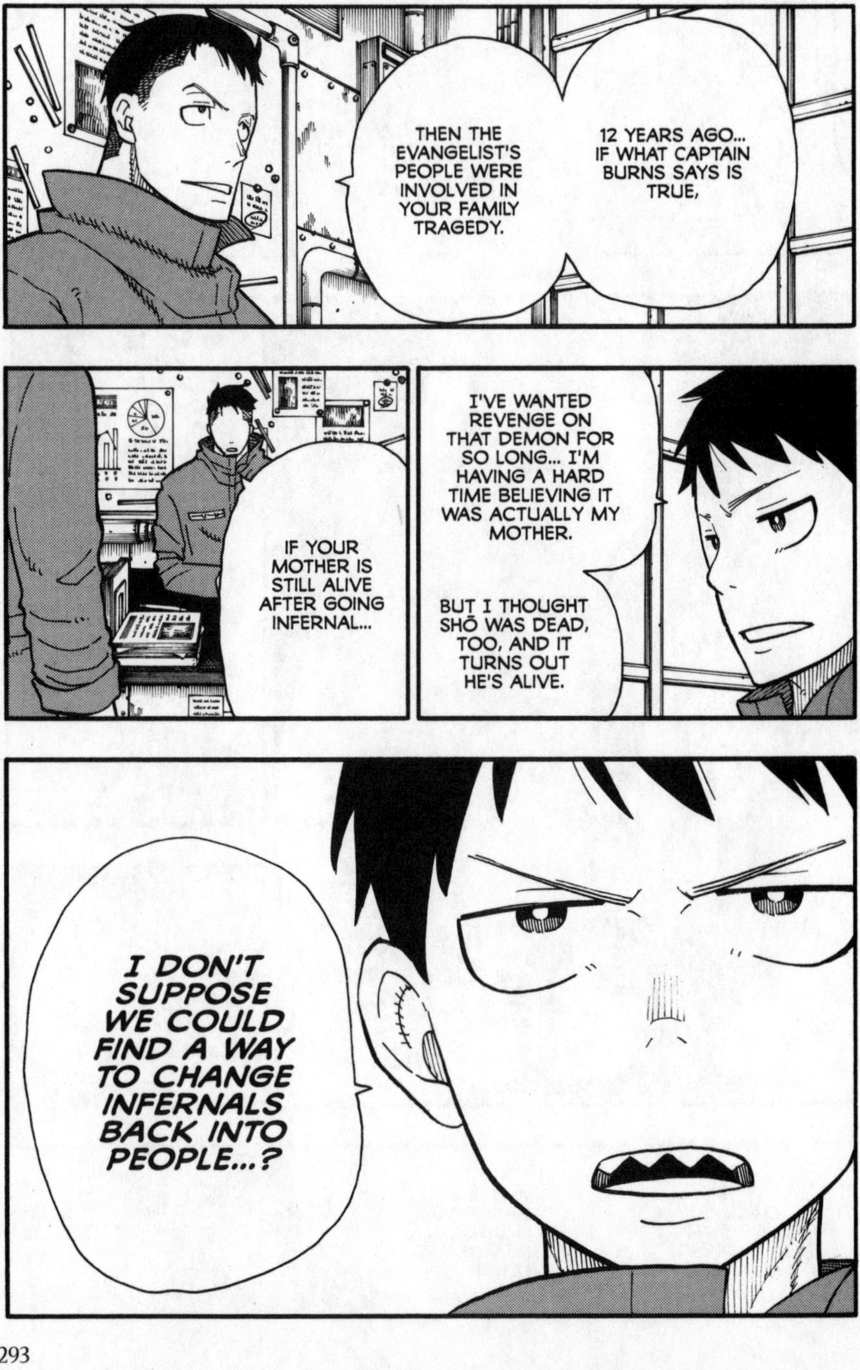
12 YEARS AGO... IF WHAT CAPTAIN BURNS SAYS IS TRUE,
THEN THE EVANGELIST'S PEOPLE WERE INVOLVED IN YOUR FAMILY TRAGEDY.
I'VE WANTED REVENGE ON THAT DEMON FOR SO LONG... I'M HAVING A HARD TIME BELIEVING IT WAS ACTUALLY MY MOTHER.
BUT I THOUGHT SHŌ WAS DEAD, TOO, AND IT TURNS OUT HE'S ALIVE.
IF YOUR MOTHER IS STILL ALIVE AFTER GOING INFERNAL...
I DON'T SUPPOSE WE COULD FIND A WAY TO CHANGE INFERNALS BACK INTO PEOPLE...?

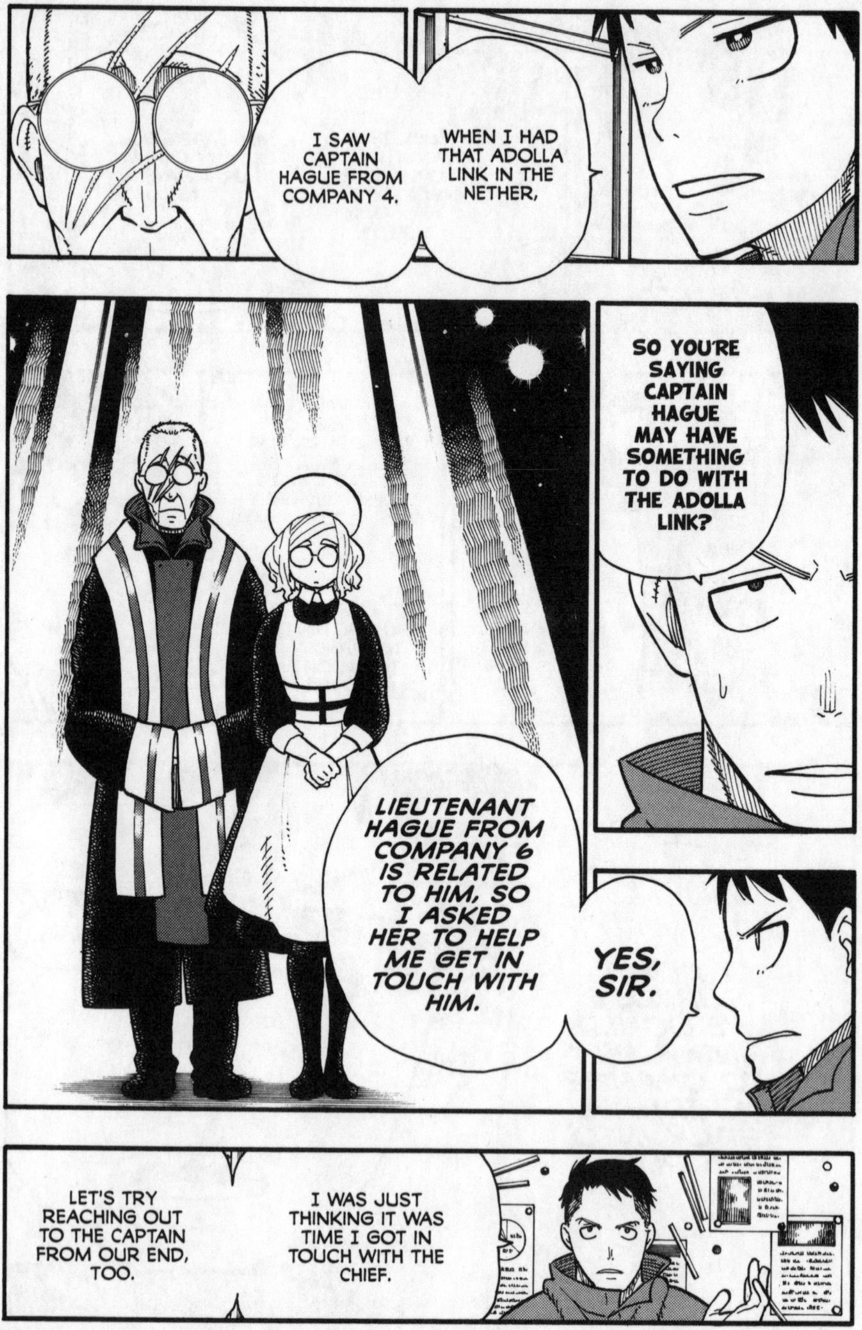
WHEN I HAD THAT ADOLLA LINK IN THE NETHER,
I SAW CAPTAIN HAGUE FROM COMPANY 4.
SO YOU'RE SAYING CAPTAIN HAGUE MAY HAVE SOMETHING TO DO WITH THE ADOLLA LINK?
YES, SIR.
LIEUTENANT HAGUE FROM COMPANY 6 IS RELATED TO HIM, SO I ASKED HER TO HELP ME GET IN TOUCH WITH HIM.
I WAS JUST THINKING IT WAS TIME I GOT IN TOUCH WITH THE CHIEF.
LET'S TRY REACHING OUT TO THE CAPTAIN FROM OUR END, TOO.

ANYWAY, YOU FINALLY GET A DAY OFF TOMORROW, SO GET PLENTY OF REST.

THANK YOU VERY MUCH, SIR!

WE DON'T GET MANY VACATION DAYS. DO YOU HAVE ANY PLANS?

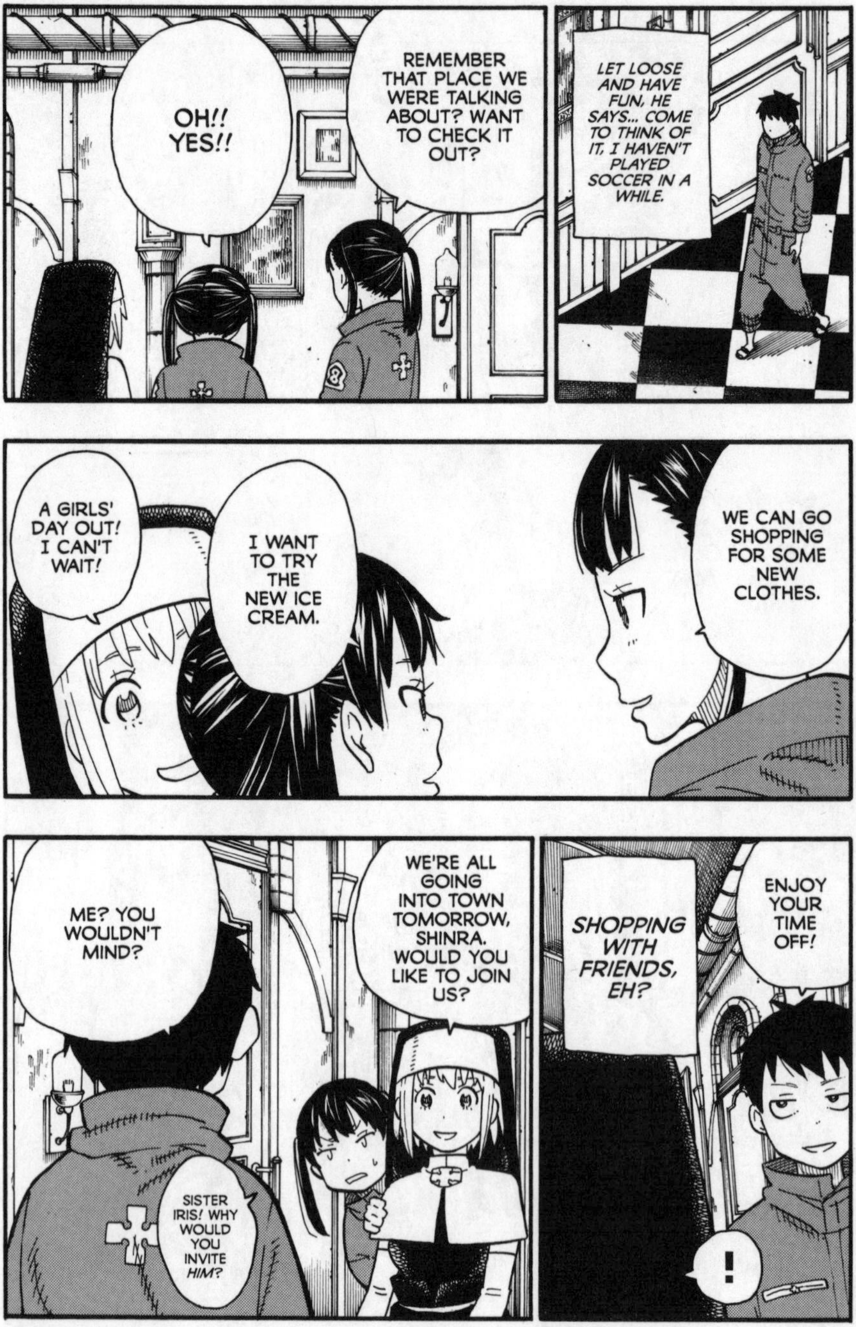
LET LOOSE AND HAVE FUN, HE SAYS... COME TO THINK OF IT, I HAVEN'T PLAYED SOCCER IN A WHILE.
REMEMBER THAT PLACE WE WERE TALKING ABOUT? WANT TO CHECK IT OUT?
OH!! YES!!
WE CAN GO SHOPPING FOR SOME NEW CLOTHES.
I WANT TO TRY THE NEW ICE CREAM.
A GIRLS' DAY OUT! I CAN'T WAIT!
ENJOY YOUR TIME OFF!
SHOPPING WITH FRIENDS, EH?
!
WE'RE ALL GOING INTO TOWN TOMORROW, SHINRA. WOULD YOU LIKE TO JOIN US?
ME? YOU WOULDN'T MIND?
SISTER IRIS! WHY WOULD YOU INVITE HIM?

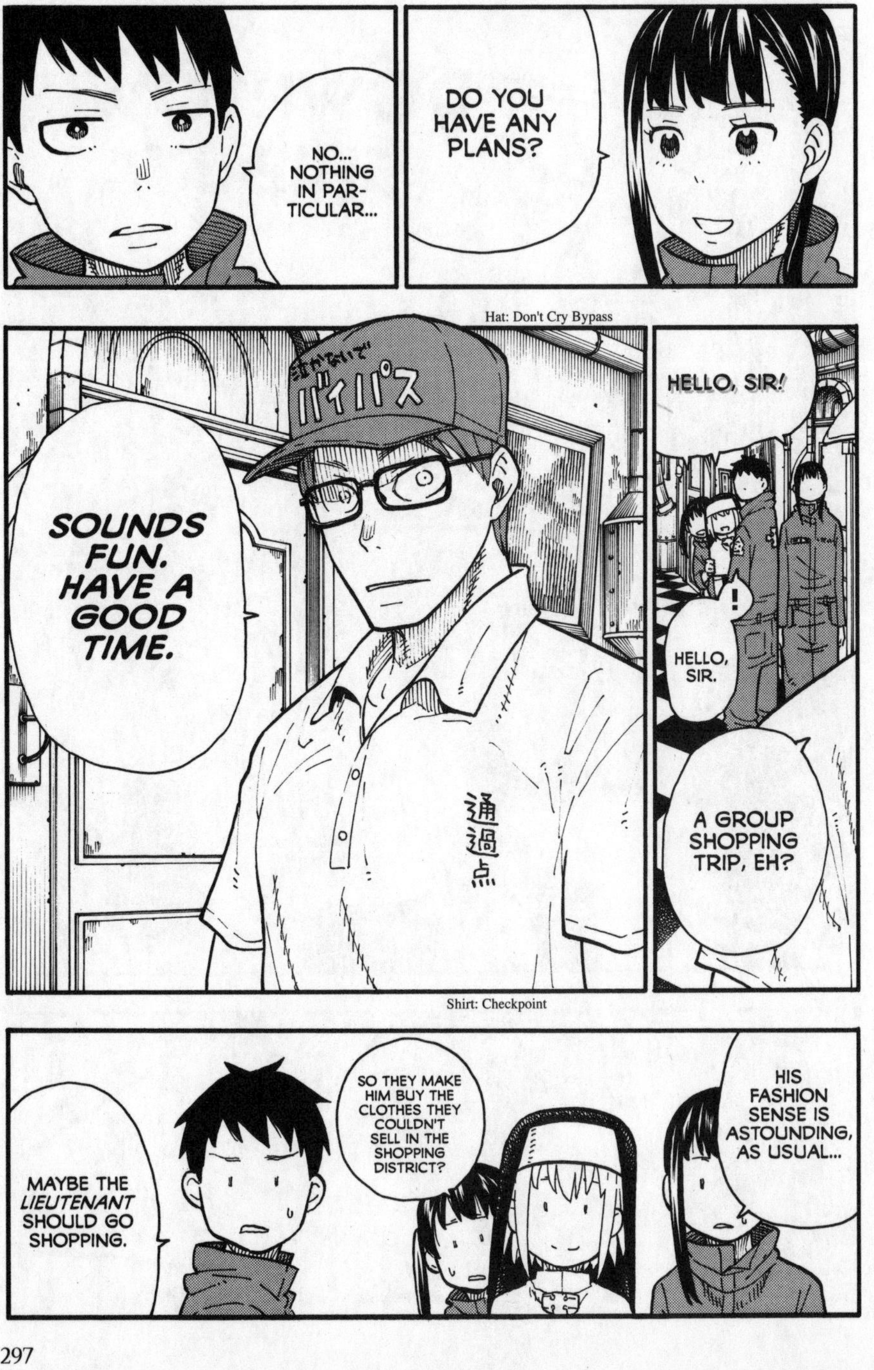
DO YOU HAVE ANY PLANS?
NO... NOTHING IN PARTICULAR...
HELLO, SIR!
!
HELLO, SIR.
A GROUP SHOPPING TRIP, EH?
泣かないで バイパス
SOUNDS FUN. HAVE A GOOD TIME.
通過点
HIS FASHION SENSE IS ASTOUNDING, AS USUAL...
SO THEY MAKE HIM BUY THE CLOTHES THEY COULDN'T SELL IN THE SHOPPING DISTRICT?
MAYBE THE *LIEUTENANT* SHOULD GO SHOPPING.

Hat: Don't Cry Bypass

Shirt: Checkpoint

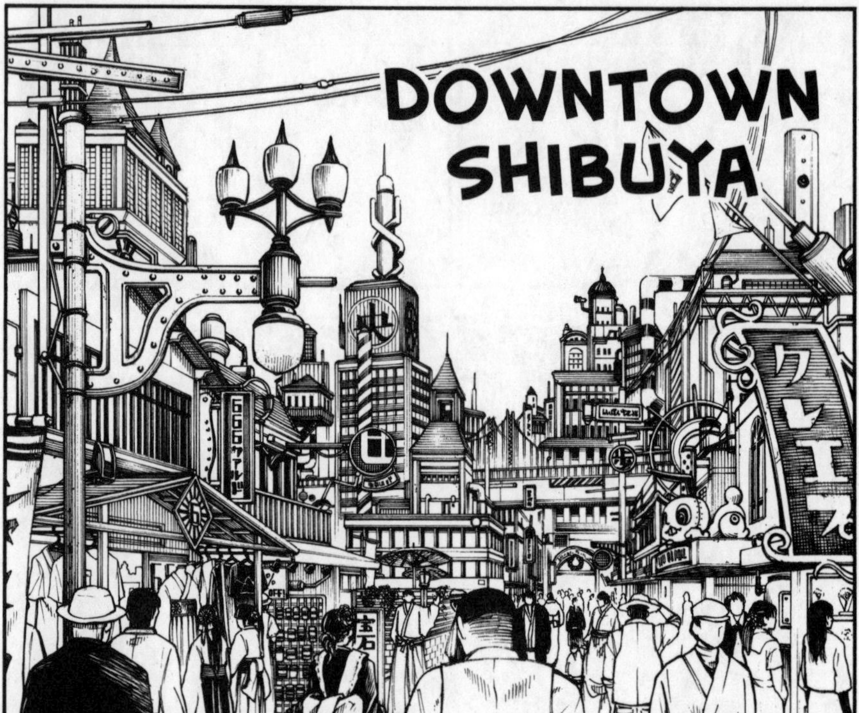
DOWNTOWN SHIBUYA
宝石

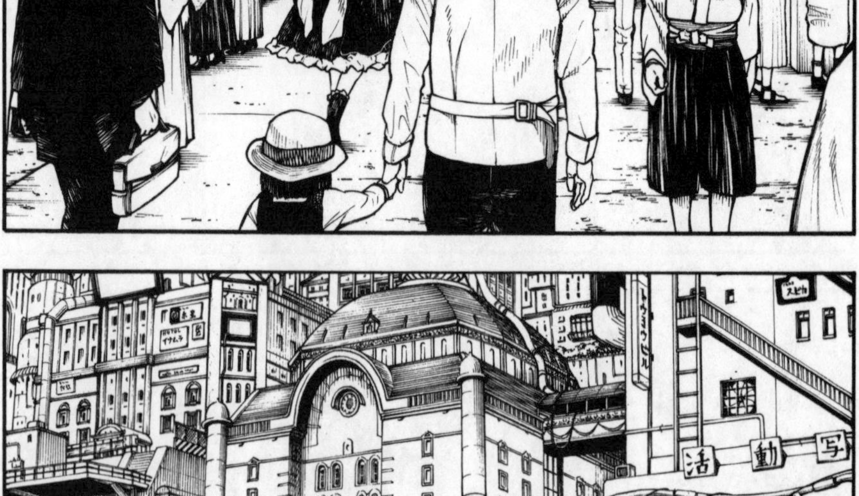
活動写

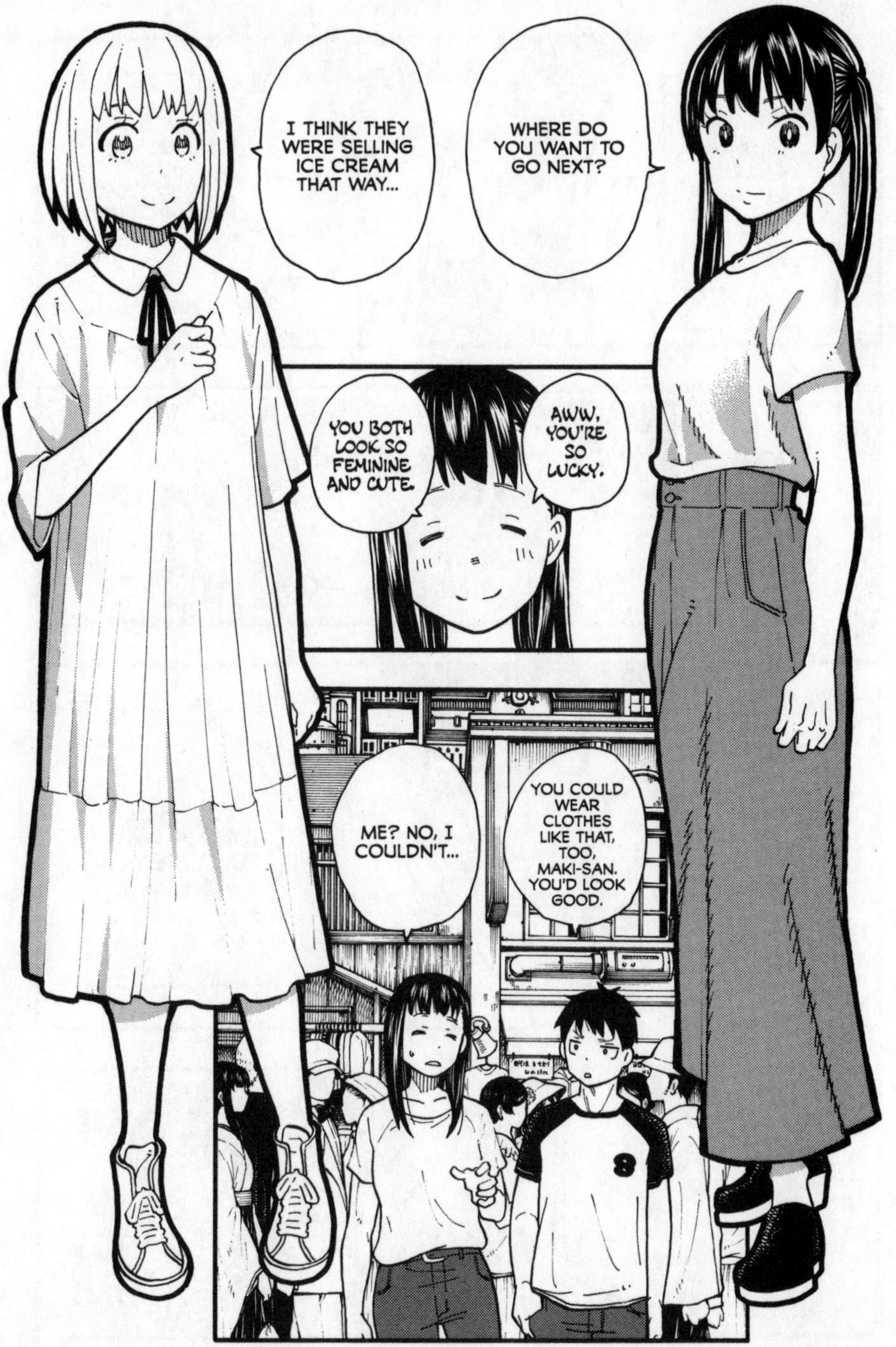
WHERE DO YOU WANT TO GO NEXT?
I THINK THEY WERE SELLING ICE CREAM THAT WAY...
AWW, YOU'RE SO LUCKY.
YOU BOTH LOOK SO FEMININE AND CUTE.
YOU COULD WEAR CLOTHES LIKE THAT, TOO, MAKI-SAN. YOU'D LOOK GOOD.
ME? NO, I COULDN'T...

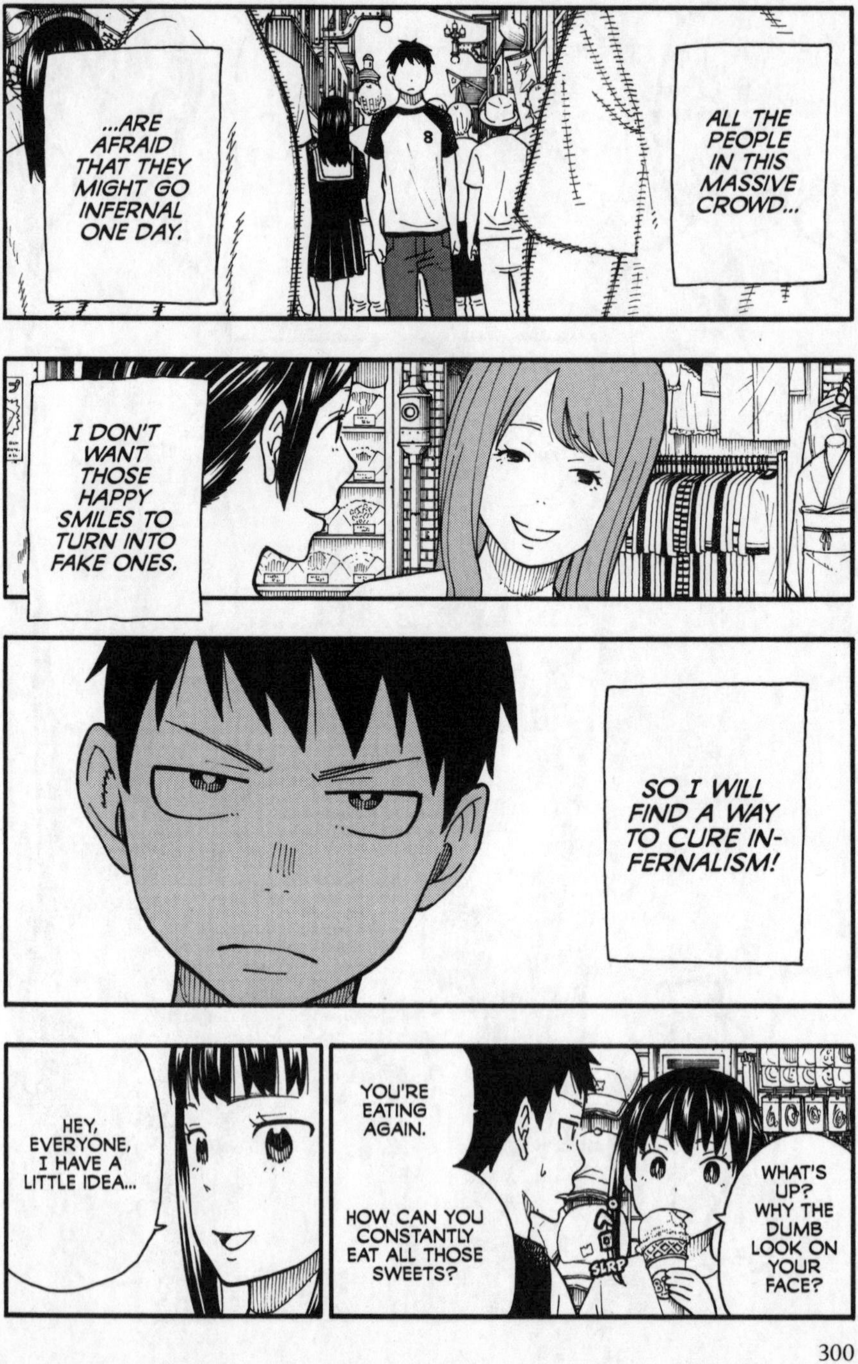
ALL THE PEOPLE IN THIS MASSIVE CROWD...
...ARE AFRAID THAT THEY MIGHT GO INFERNAL ONE DAY.
I DON'T WANT THOSE HAPPY SMILES TO TURN INTO FAKE ONES.
SO I WILL FIND A WAY TO CURE IN-FERNALISM!
WHAT'S UP? WHY THE DUMB LOOK ON YOUR FACE?
SLRP
YOU'RE EATING AGAIN.
HOW CAN YOU CONSTANTLY EAT ALL THOSE SWEETS?
HEY, EVERYONE, I HAVE A LITTLE IDEA...

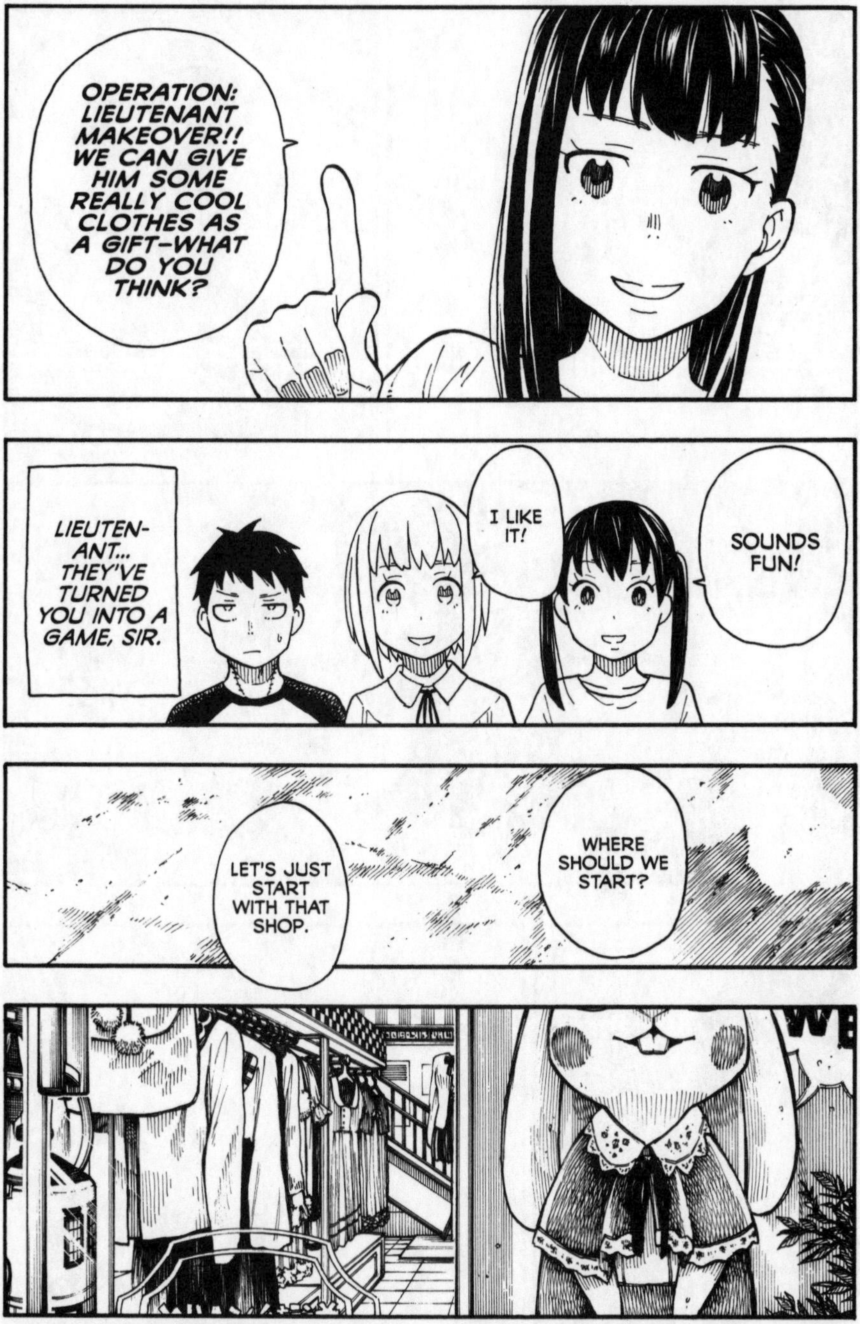
OPERATION: LIEUTENANT MAKEOVER!! WE CAN GIVE HIM SOME REALLY COOL CLOTHES AS A GIFT—WHAT DO YOU THINK?
SOUNDS FUN!
I LIKE IT!
LIEUTEN-ANT... THEY'VE TURNED YOU INTO A GAME, SIR.
WHERE SHOULD WE START?
LET'S JUST START WITH THAT SHOP.

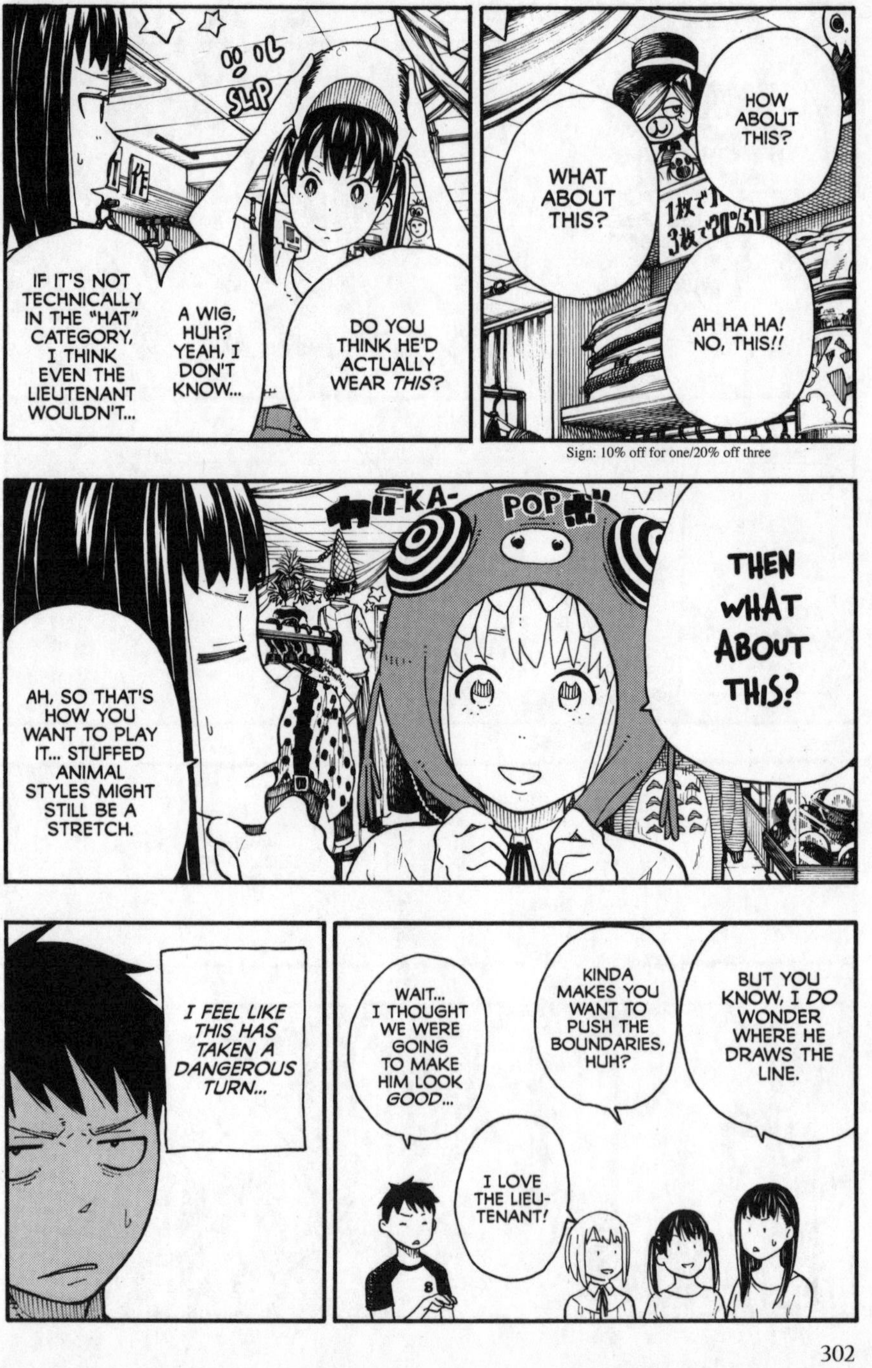
HOW ABOUT THIS?
WHAT ABOUT THIS?
AH HA HA! NO, THIS!!
SLIP
DO YOU THINK HE'D ACTUALLY WEAR *THIS*?
A WIG, HUH? YEAH, I DON'T KNOW...
IF IT'S NOT TECHNICALLY IN THE "HAT" CATEGORY, I THINK EVEN THE LIEUTENANT WOULDN'T...
KA-POP
THEN WHAT ABOUT THIS?
AH, SO THAT'S HOW YOU WANT TO PLAY IT... STUFFED ANIMAL STYLES MIGHT STILL BE A STRETCH.
BUT YOU KNOW, I *DO* WONDER WHERE HE DRAWS THE LINE.
KINDA MAKES YOU WANT TO PUSH THE BOUNDARIES, HUH?
WAIT... I THOUGHT WE WERE GOING TO MAKE HIM LOOK *GOOD*...
I LOVE THE LIEU-TENANT!
I FEEL LIKE THIS HAS TAKEN A DANGEROUS TURN...

Sign: 10% off for one/20% off three

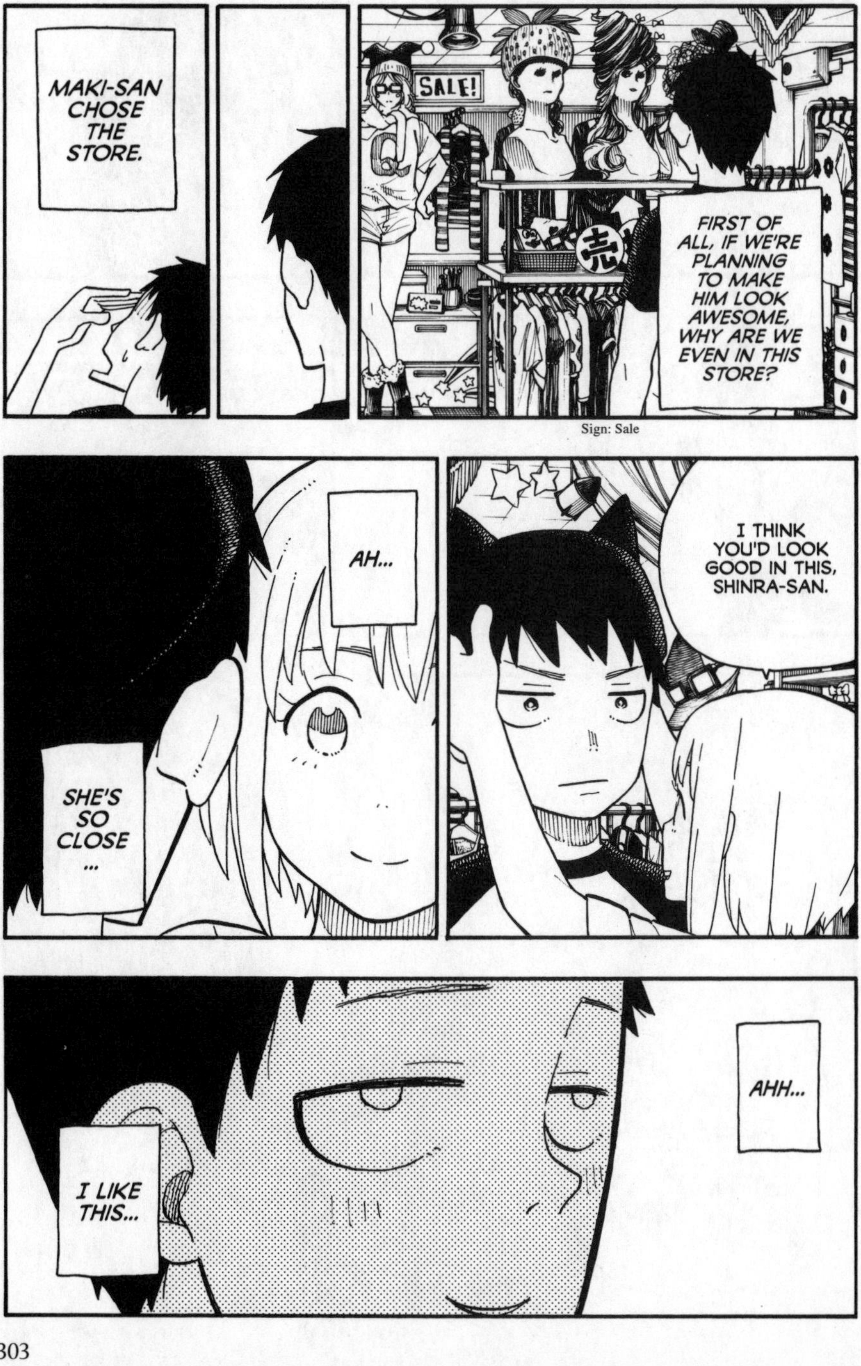
FIRST OF ALL, IF WE'RE PLANNING TO MAKE HIM LOOK AWESOME, WHY ARE WE EVEN IN THIS STORE?
SALE!
MAKI-SAN CHOSE THE STORE.
I THINK YOU'D LOOK GOOD IN THIS, SHINRA-SAN.
AH...
SHE'S SO CLOSE ...
AHH...
I LIKE THIS...

Sign: Sale

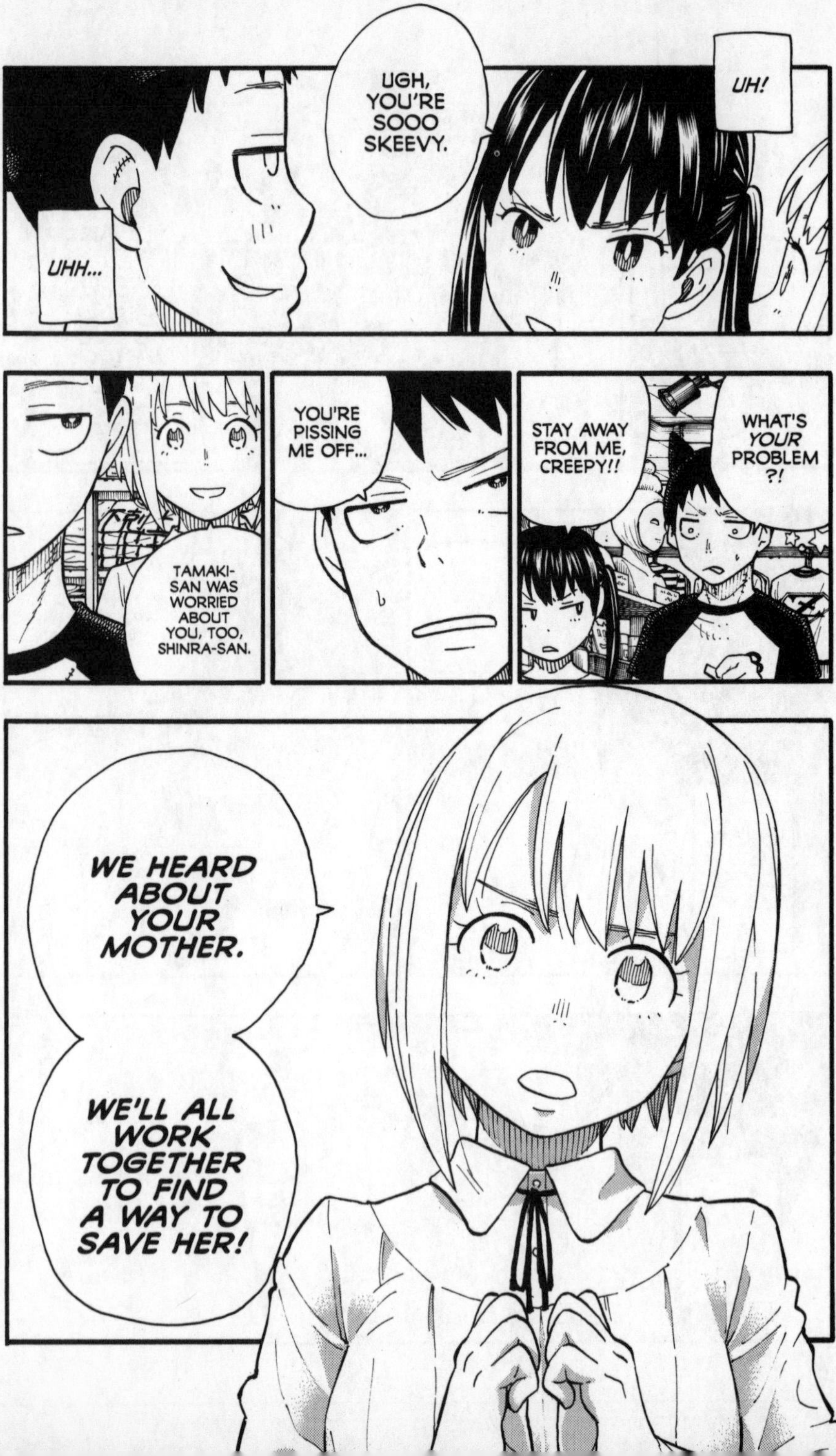
UH!
UGH, YOU'RE SOOO SKEEVY.
UHH...
WHAT'S *YOUR* PROBLEM ?!
STAY AWAY FROM ME, CREEPY!!
YOU'RE PISSING ME OFF...
TAMAKI-SAN WAS WORRIED ABOUT YOU, TOO, SHINRA-SAN.
WE HEARD ABOUT YOUR MOTHER.
WE'LL ALL WORK TOGETHER TO FIND A WAY TO SAVE HER!

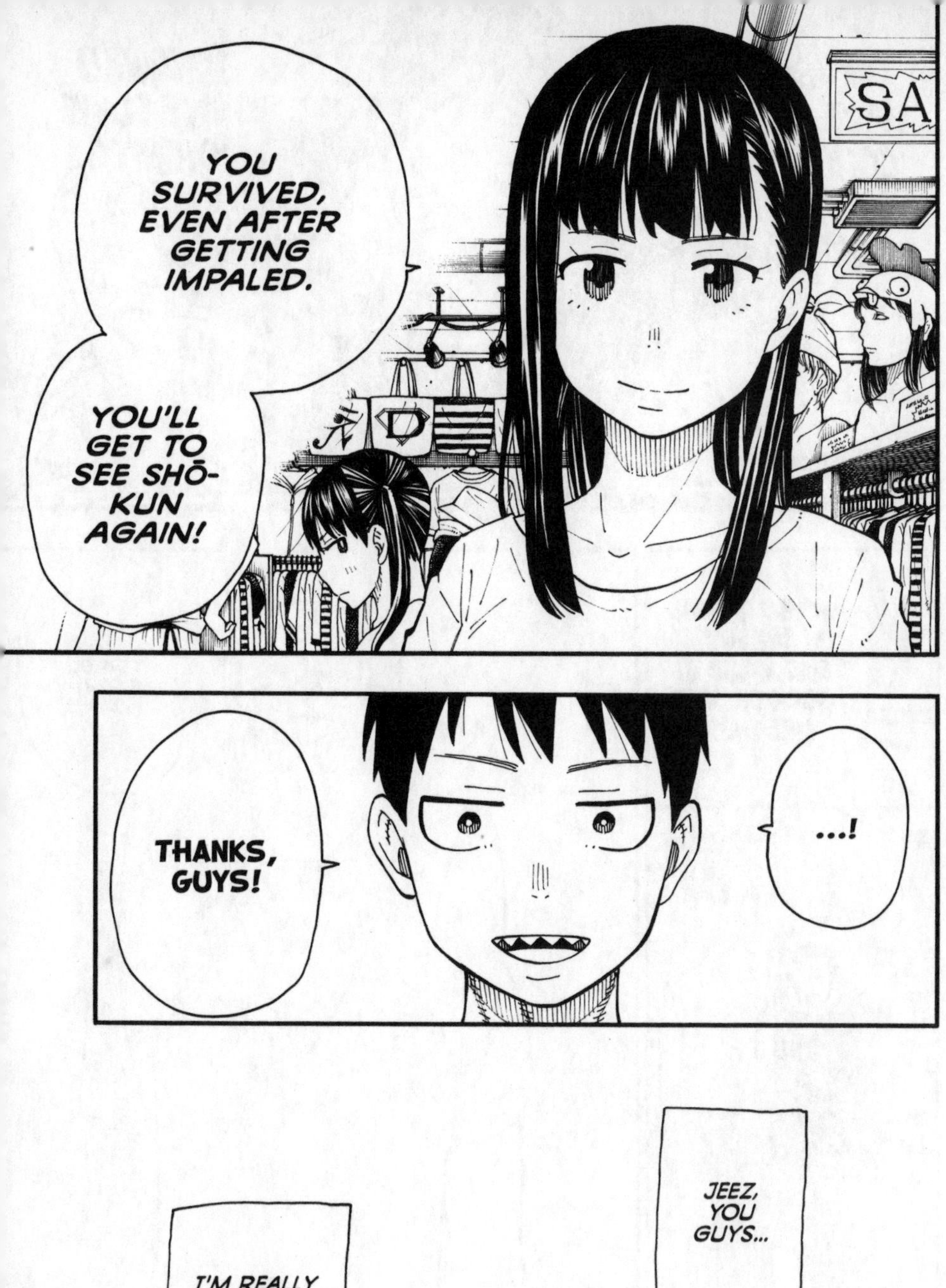
YOU SURVIVED, EVEN AFTER GETTING IMPALED.
YOU'LL GET TO SEE SHŌ-KUN AGAIN!
...!
THANKS, GUYS!
JEEZ, YOU GUYS...
I'M REALLY GLAD I'M IN COMPANY 8!

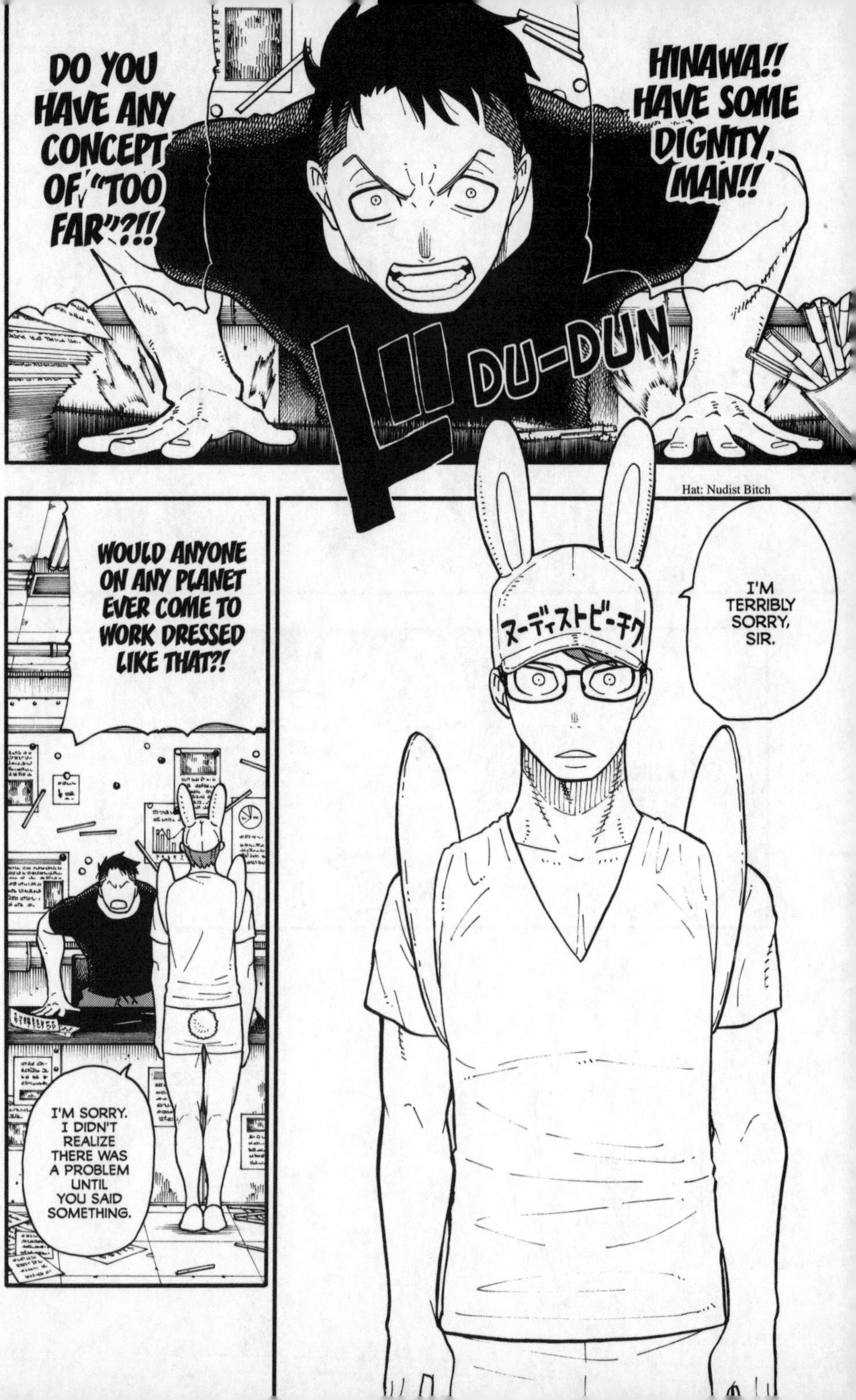
HINAWA!! HAVE SOME DIGNITY, MAN!!
DO YOU HAVE ANY CONCEPT OF "TOO FAR"?!!
DU-DUN
Hat: Nudist Bitch
ヌーディストビーチク
I'M TERRIBLY SORRY, SIR.
WOULD ANYONE ON ANY PLANET EVER COME TO WORK DRESSED LIKE THAT?!
I'M SORRY. I DIDN'T REALIZE THERE WAS A PROBLEM UNTIL YOU SAID SOMETHING.

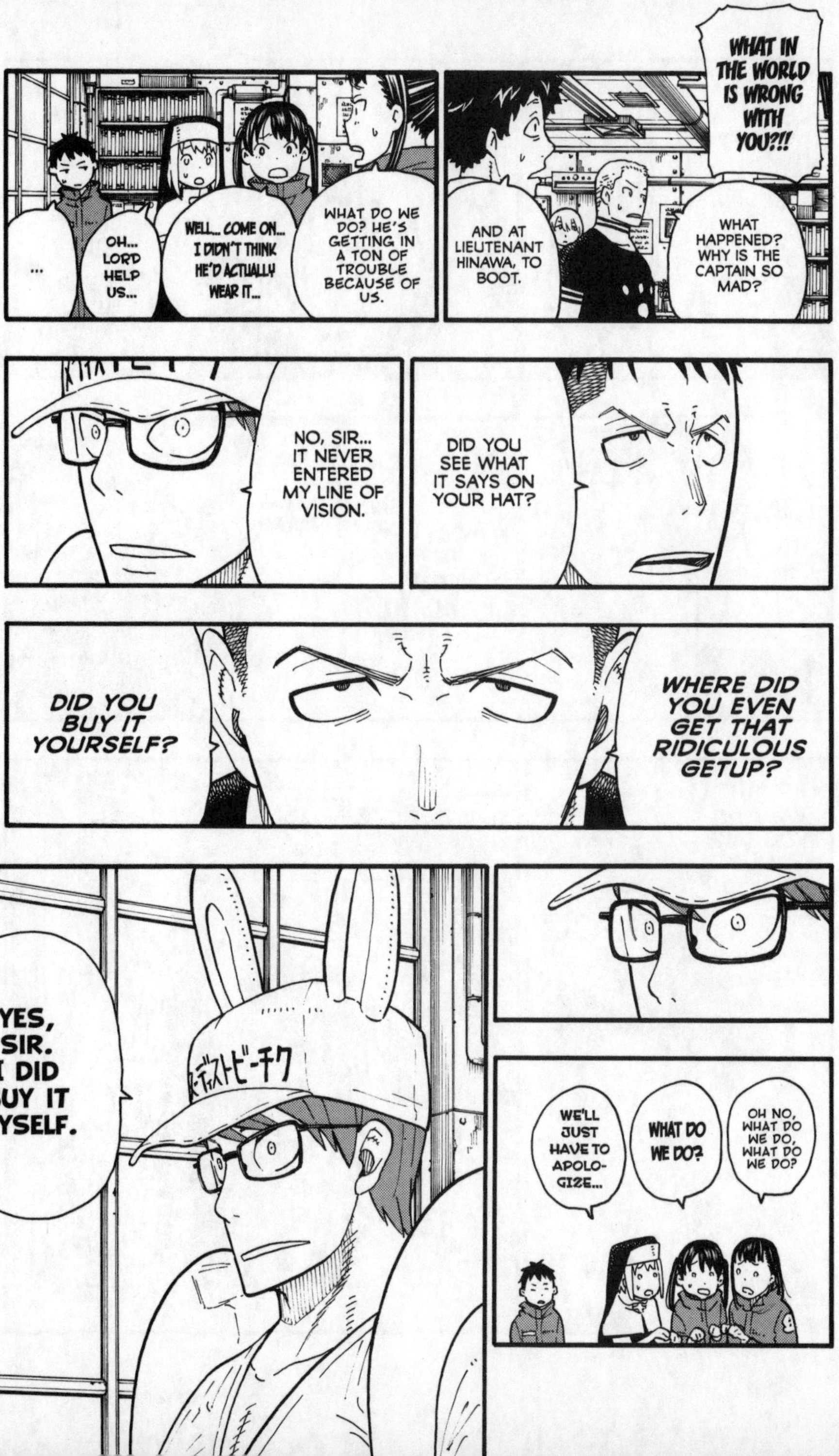
WHAT IN THE WORLD IS WRONG WITH YOU?!!
WHAT HAPPENED? WHY IS THE CAPTAIN SO MAD?
AND AT LIEUTENANT HINAWA, TO BOOT.
WHAT DO WE DO? HE'S GETTING IN A TON OF TROUBLE BECAUSE OF US.
WELL... COME ON... I DIDN'T THINK HE'D ACTUALLY WEAR IT...
OH... LORD HELP US...
...
DID YOU SEE WHAT IT SAYS ON YOUR HAT?
NO, SIR... IT NEVER ENTERED MY LINE OF VISION.
WHERE DID YOU EVEN GET THAT RIDICULOUS GETUP?
DID YOU BUY IT YOURSELF?
OH NO, WHAT DO WE DO, WHAT DO WE DO?
WHAT DO WE DO?
WE'LL JUST HAVE TO APOLOGIZE...
YES, SIR. I DID BUY IT MYSELF.

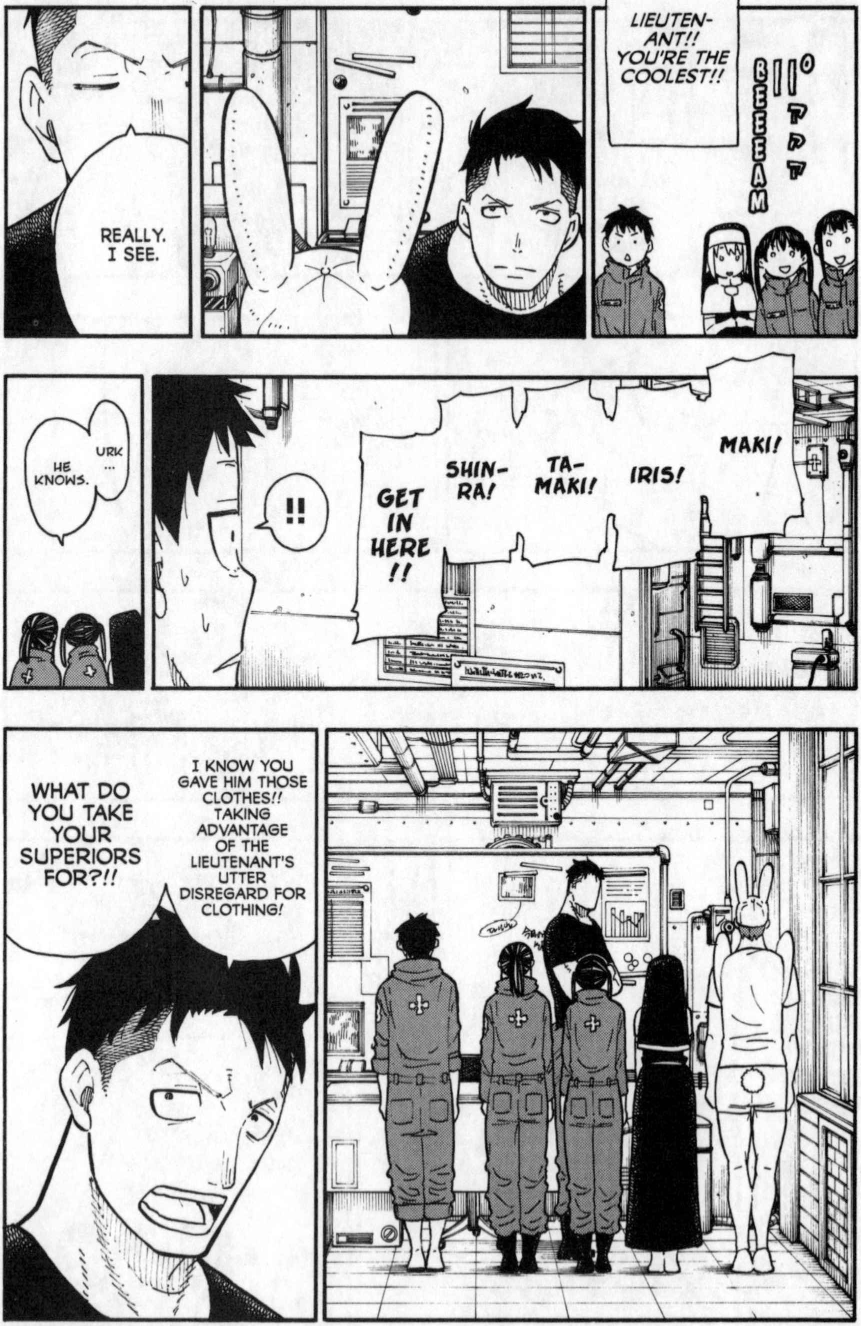
LIEUTEN-ANT!! YOU'RE THE COOLEST!!
BEEEEAM
REALLY. I SEE.
GET IN HERE!! SHIN-RA! TA-MAKI! IRIS! MAKI!
!!
URK... HE KNOWS.
I KNOW YOU GAVE HIM THOSE CLOTHES!! TAKING ADVANTAGE OF THE LIEUTENANT'S UTTER DISREGARD FOR CLOTHING!
WHAT DO YOU TAKE YOUR SUPERIORS FOR?!!

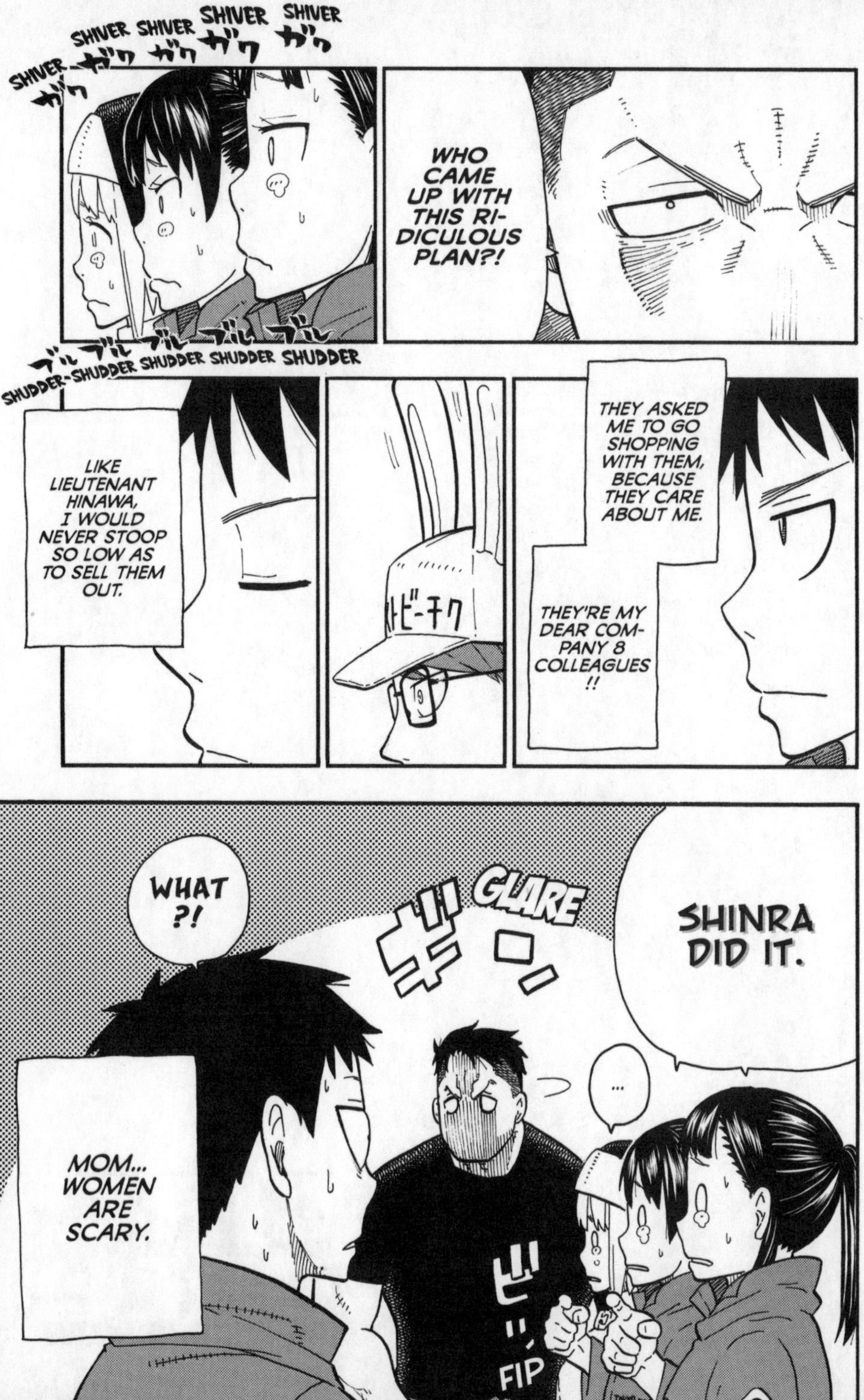

WHO CAME UP WITH THIS RI-DICULOUS PLAN?!
SHIVER SHIVER SHIVER SHIVER SHIVER
SHUDDER-SHUDDER SHUDDER SHUDDER SHUDDER
THEY ASKED ME TO GO SHOPPING WITH THEM, BECAUSE THEY CARE ABOUT ME.
THEY'RE MY DEAR COMPANY 8 COLLEAGUES !!
LIKE LIEUTENANT HINAWA, I WOULD NEVER STOOP SO LOW AS TO SELL THEM OUT.
SHINRA DID IT.
...
GLARE
WHAT ?!
MOM... WOMEN ARE SCARY.
FIP

FIRE FORCE

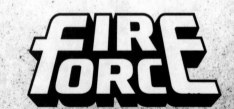

CHAPTER XCIII: SPECIAL FIRE FORCE COMPANY 4

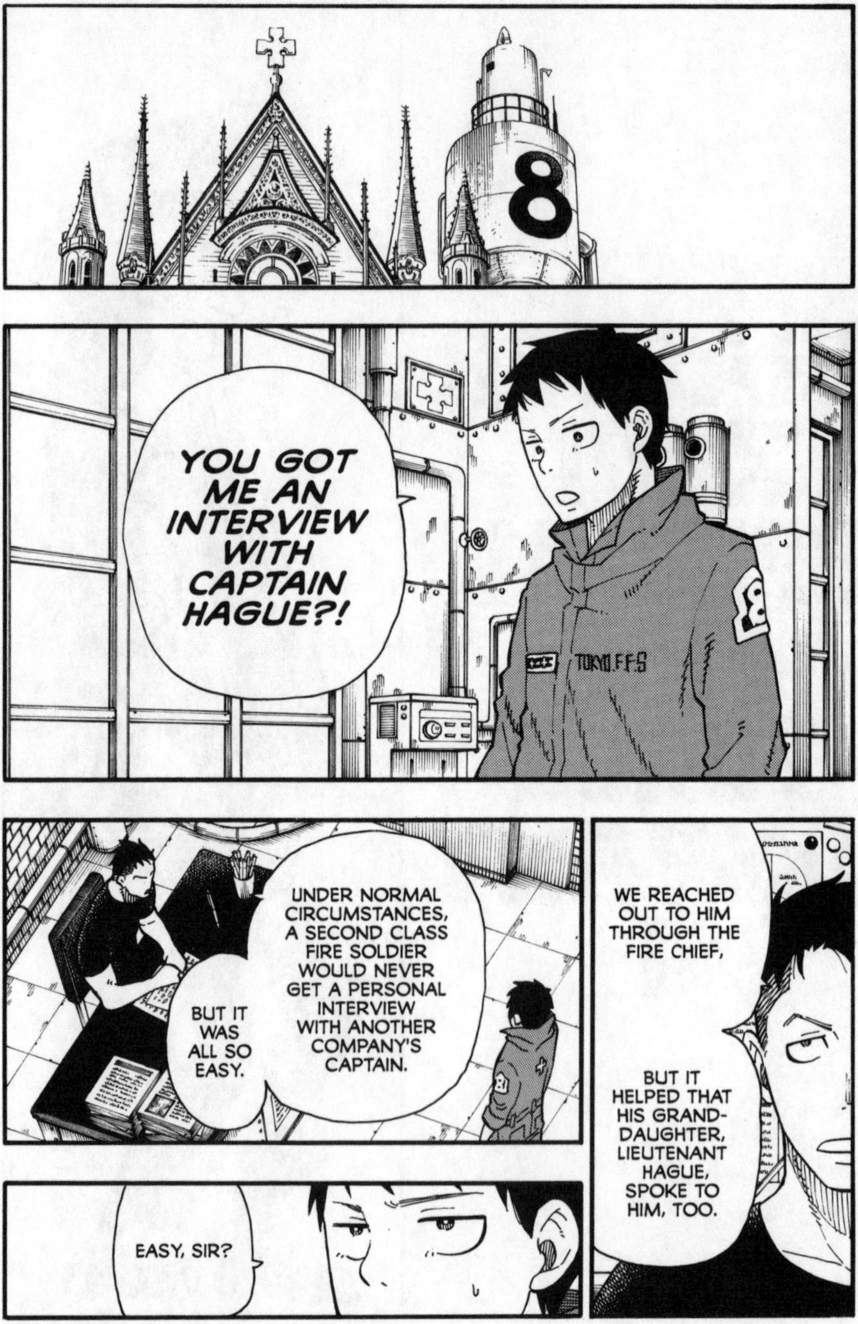
YOU GOT ME AN INTERVIEW WITH CAPTAIN HAGUE?!
TOKYO.F.F.S
WE REACHED OUT TO HIM THROUGH THE FIRE CHIEF,
BUT IT HELPED THAT HIS GRAND-DAUGHTER, LIEUTENANT HAGUE, SPOKE TO HIM, TOO.
UNDER NORMAL CIRCUMSTANCES, A SECOND CLASS FIRE SOLDIER WOULD NEVER GET A PERSONAL INTERVIEW WITH ANOTHER COMPANY'S CAPTAIN.
BUT IT WAS ALL SO EASY.
EASY, SIR?

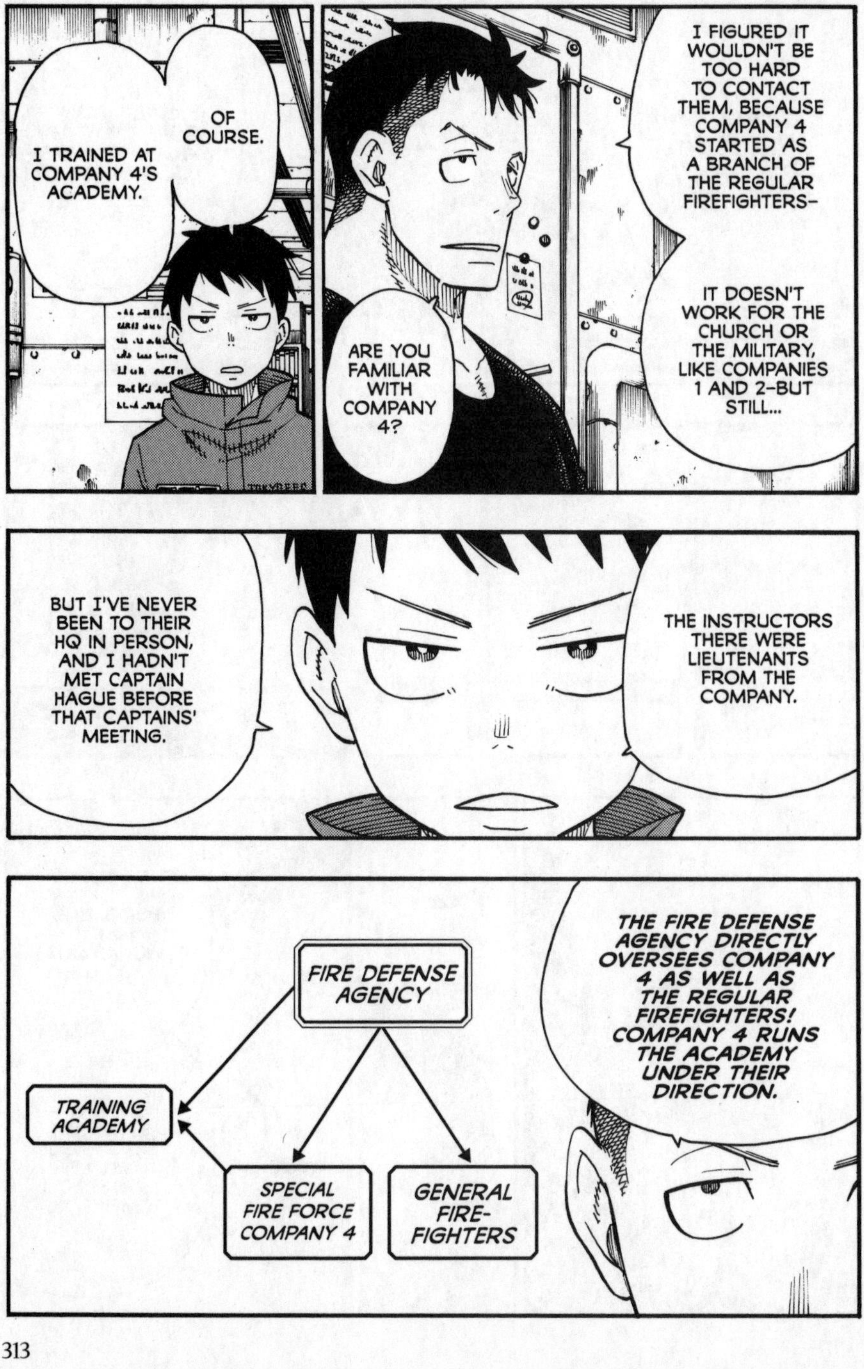
I FIGURED IT WOULDN'T BE TOO HARD TO CONTACT THEM, BECAUSE COMPANY 4 STARTED AS A BRANCH OF THE REGULAR FIREFIGHTERS–
IT DOESN'T WORK FOR THE CHURCH OR THE MILITARY, LIKE COMPANIES 1 AND 2–BUT STILL...
ARE YOU FAMILIAR WITH COMPANY 4?
OF COURSE.
I TRAINED AT COMPANY 4'S ACADEMY.
THE INSTRUCTORS THERE WERE LIEUTENANTS FROM THE COMPANY.
BUT I'VE NEVER BEEN TO THEIR HQ IN PERSON, AND I HADN'T MET CAPTAIN HAGUE BEFORE THAT CAPTAINS' MEETING.
THE FIRE DEFENSE AGENCY DIRECTLY OVERSEES COMPANY 4 AS WELL AS THE REGULAR FIREFIGHTERS! COMPANY 4 RUNS THE ACADEMY UNDER THEIR DIRECTION.
FIRE DEFENSE AGENCY
TRAINING ACADEMY
SPECIAL FIRE FORCE COMPANY 4
GENERAL FIRE-FIGHTERS

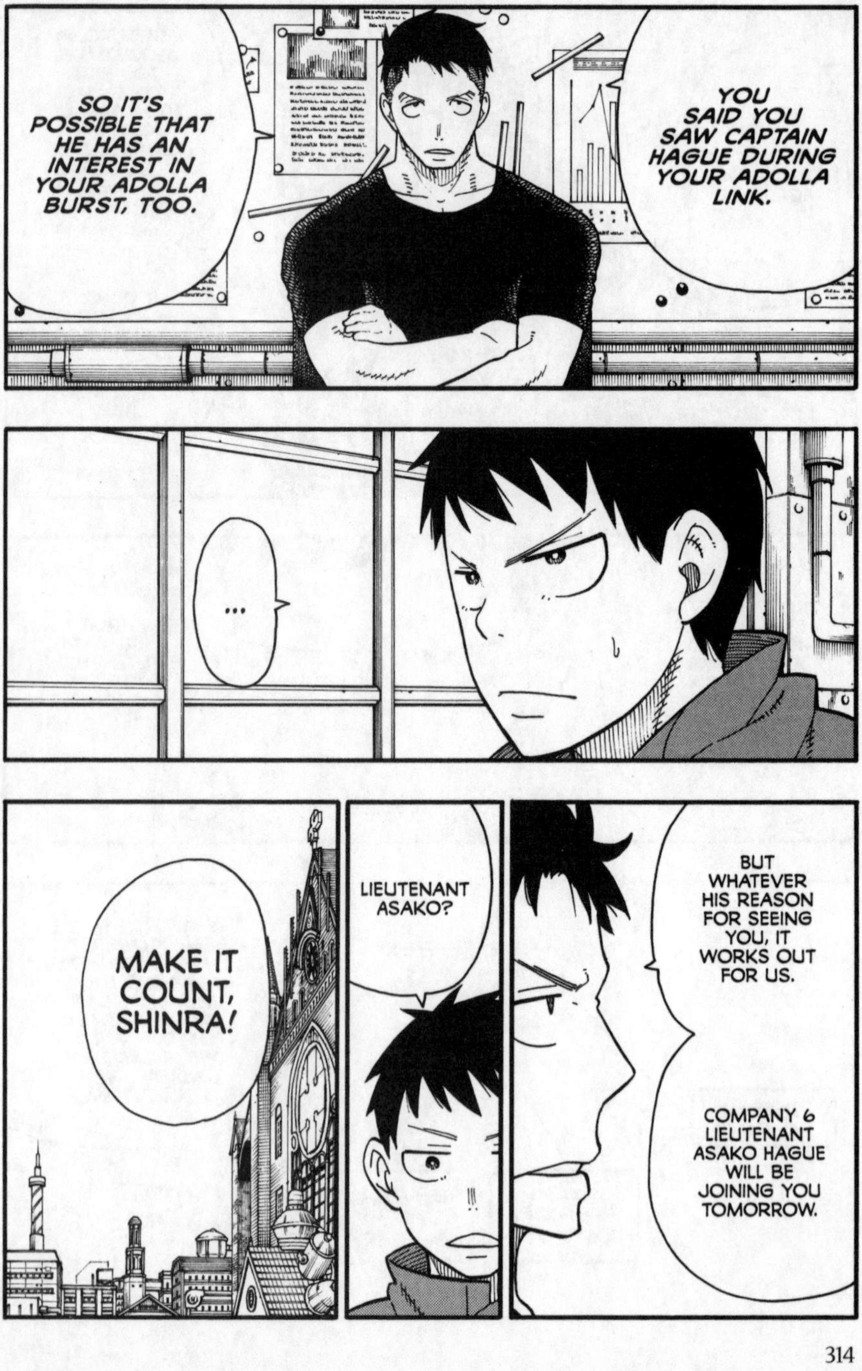
YOU SAID YOU SAW CAPTAIN HAGUE DURING YOUR ADOLLA LINK.
SO IT'S POSSIBLE THAT HE HAS AN INTEREST IN YOUR ADOLLA BURST, TOO.
...
BUT WHATEVER HIS REASON FOR SEEING YOU, IT WORKS OUT FOR US.
COMPANY 6 LIEUTENANT ASAKO HAGUE WILL BE JOINING YOU TOMORROW.
LIEUTENANT ASAKO?
MAKE IT COUNT, SHINRA!

SPECIAL FIRE STATION 4

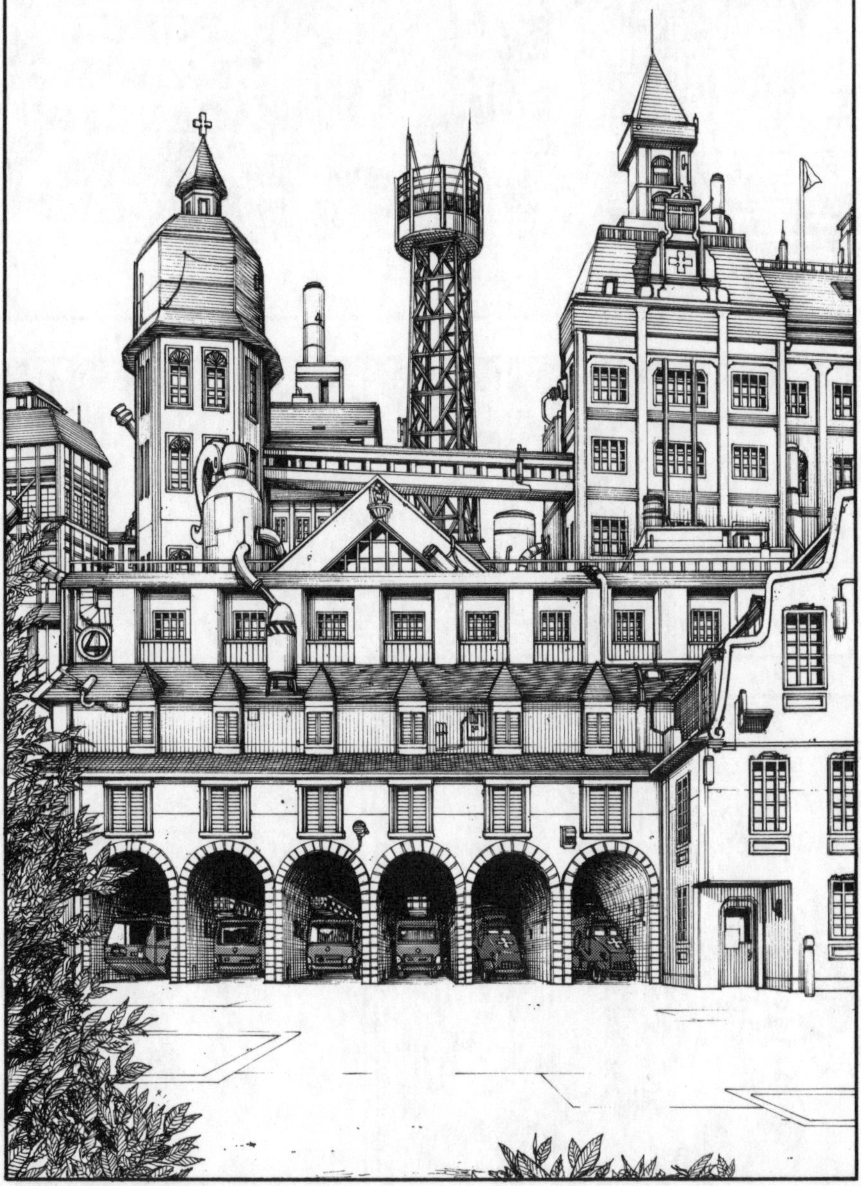

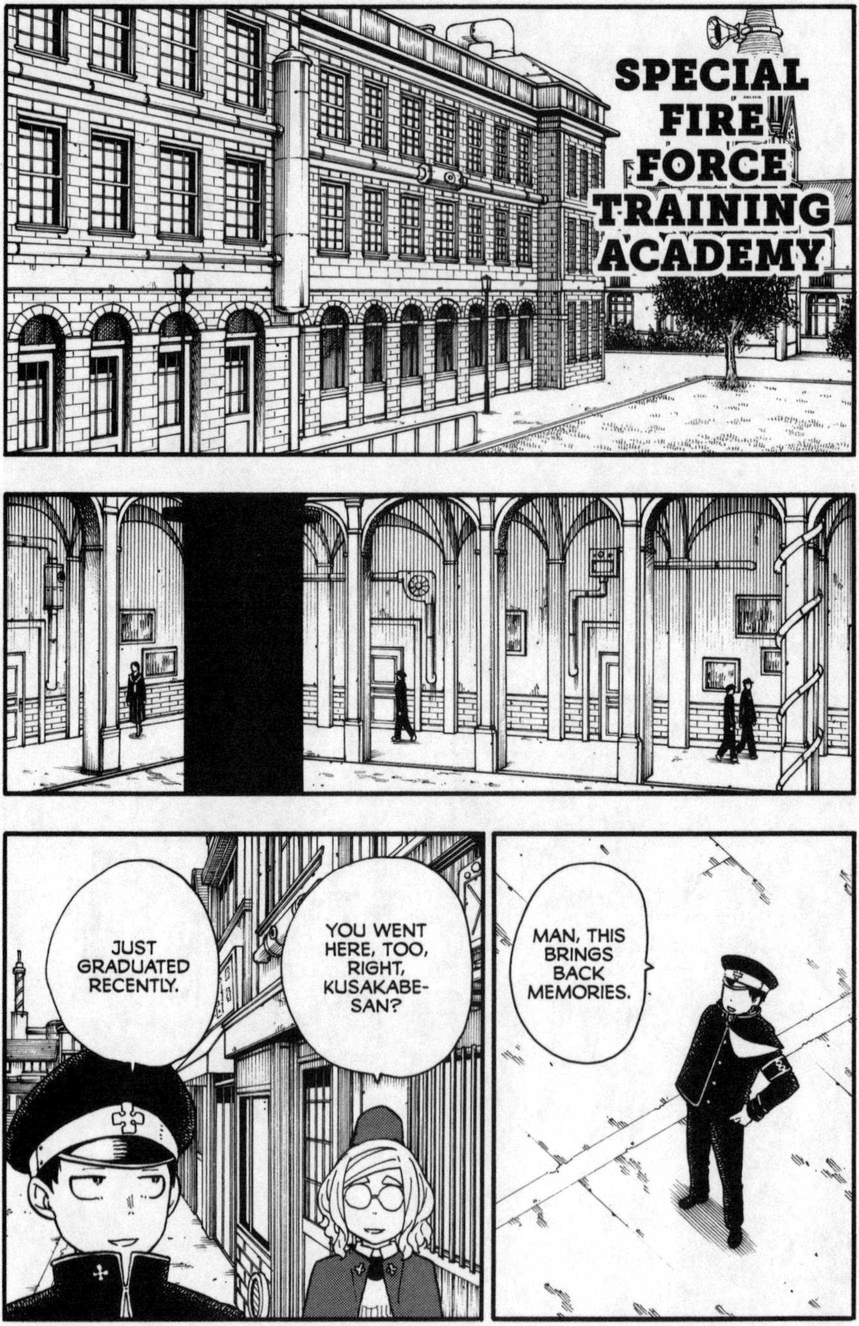
SPECIAL FIRE FORCE TRAINING ACADEMY
MAN, THIS BRINGS BACK MEMORIES.
YOU WENT HERE, TOO, RIGHT, KUSAKABE-SAN?
JUST GRADUATED RECENTLY.

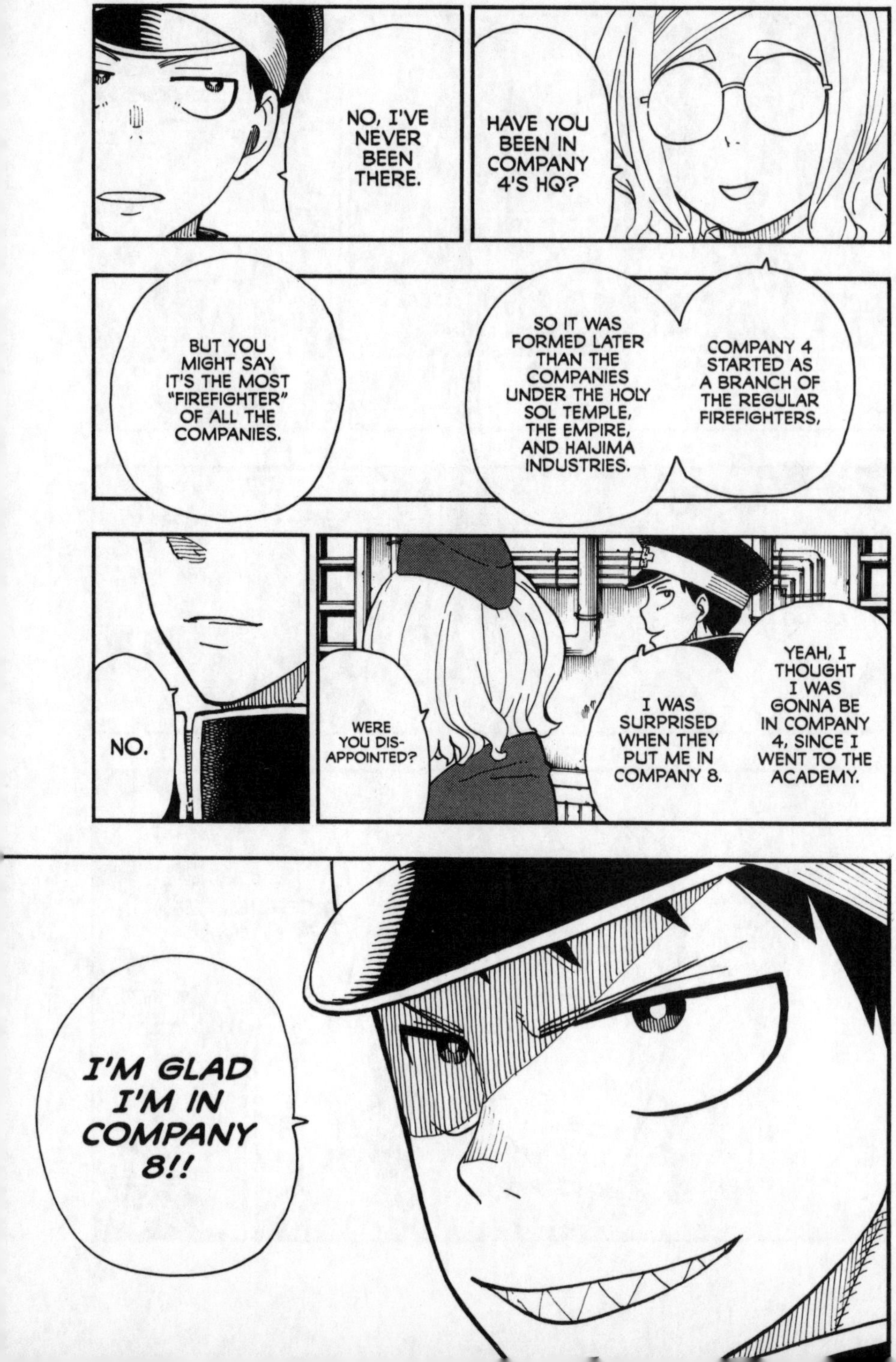
HAVE YOU BEEN IN COMPANY 4'S HQ?
NO, I'VE NEVER BEEN THERE.
COMPANY 4 STARTED AS A BRANCH OF THE REGULAR FIREFIGHTERS,
SO IT WAS FORMED LATER THAN THE COMPANIES UNDER THE HOLY SOL TEMPLE, THE EMPIRE, AND HAIJIMA INDUSTRIES.
BUT YOU MIGHT SAY IT'S THE MOST "FIREFIGHTER" OF ALL THE COMPANIES.
YEAH, I THOUGHT I WAS GONNA BE IN COMPANY 4, SINCE I WENT TO THE ACADEMY.
I WAS SURPRISED WHEN THEY PUT ME IN COMPANY 8.
WERE YOU DIS-APPOINTED?
NO.
I'M GLAD I'M IN COMPANY 8!!

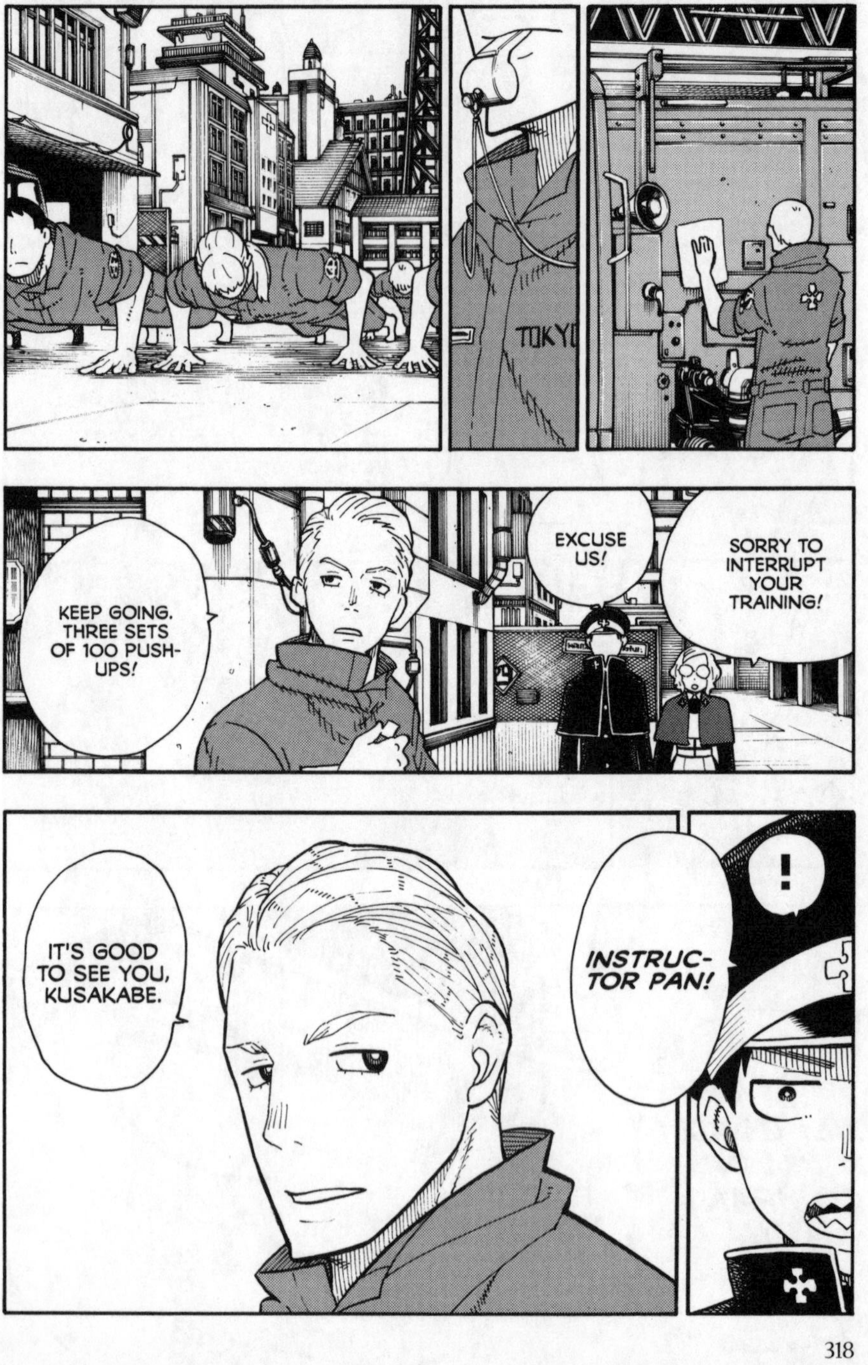
SORRY TO INTERRUPT YOUR TRAINING!
EXCUSE US!
KEEP GOING. THREE SETS OF 100 PUSH-UPS!
!
INSTRUCTOR PAN!
IT'S GOOD TO SEE YOU, KUSAKABE.

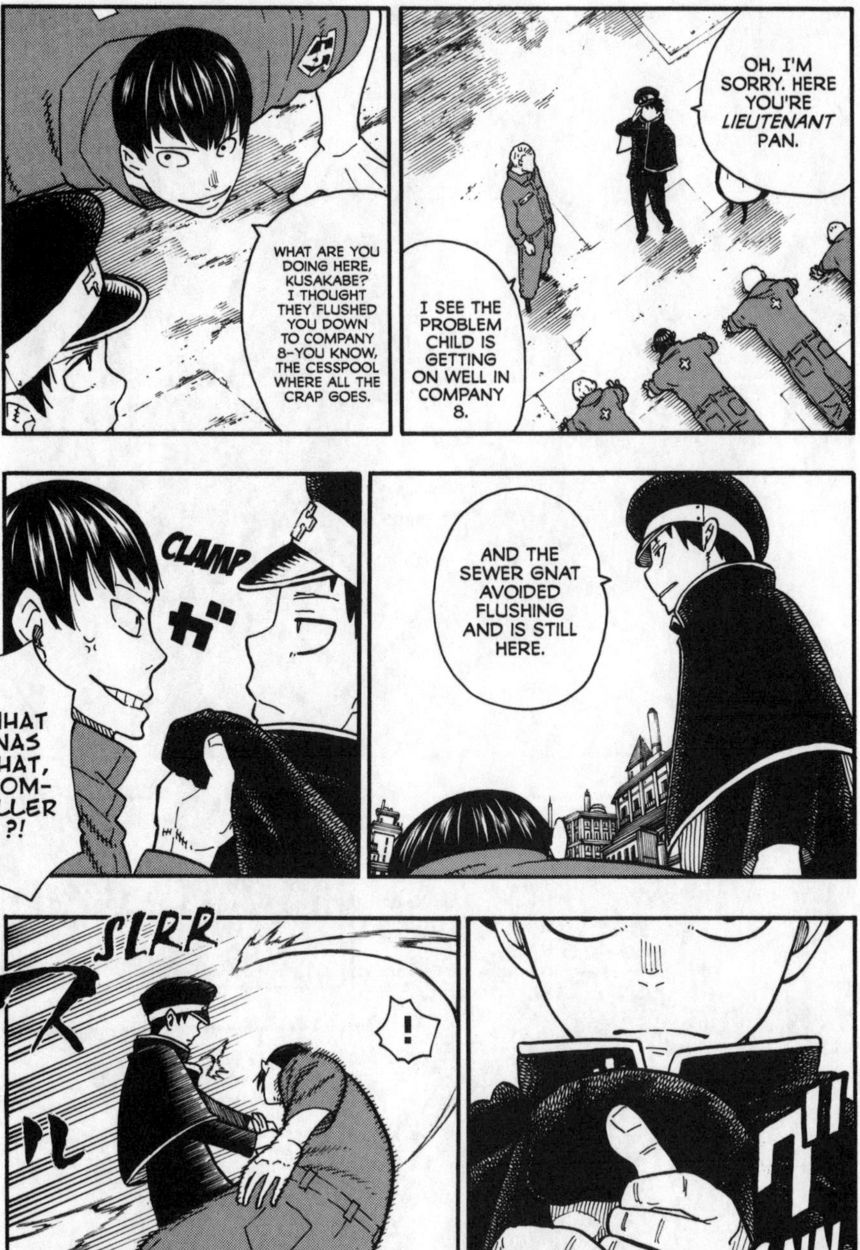

OH, I'M SORRY. HERE YOU'RE *LIEUTENANT* PAN.
I SEE THE PROBLEM CHILD IS GETTING ON WELL IN COMPANY 8.
WHAT ARE YOU DOING HERE, KUSAKABE? I THOUGHT THEY FLUSHED YOU DOWN TO COMPANY 8–YOU KNOW, THE CESSPOOL WHERE ALL THE CRAP GOES.
AND THE SEWER GNAT AVOIDED FLUSHING AND IS STILL HERE.
CLAMP
ガ
WHAT WAS THAT, MOM-KILLER?!
GNN
SLRR
!

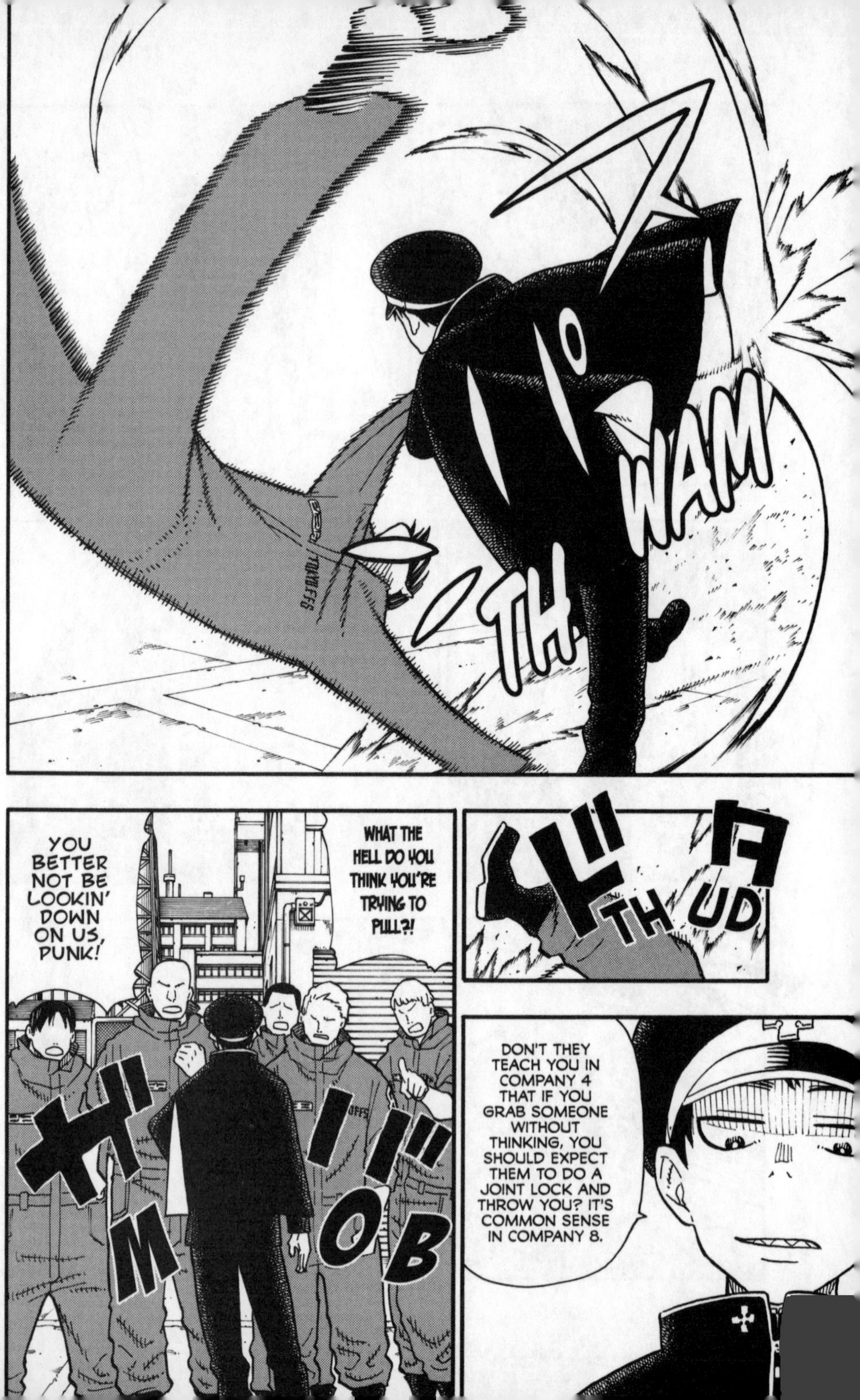
THWAM
THUD
WHAT THE HELL DO YOU THINK YOU'RE TRYING TO PULL?!
YOU BETTER NOT BE LOOKIN' DOWN ON US, PUNK!
DON'T THEY TEACH YOU IN COMPANY 4 THAT IF YOU GRAB SOMEONE WITHOUT THINKING, YOU SHOULD EXPECT THEM TO DO A JOINT LOCK AND THROW YOU? IT'S COMMON SENSE IN COMPANY 8.
MOB

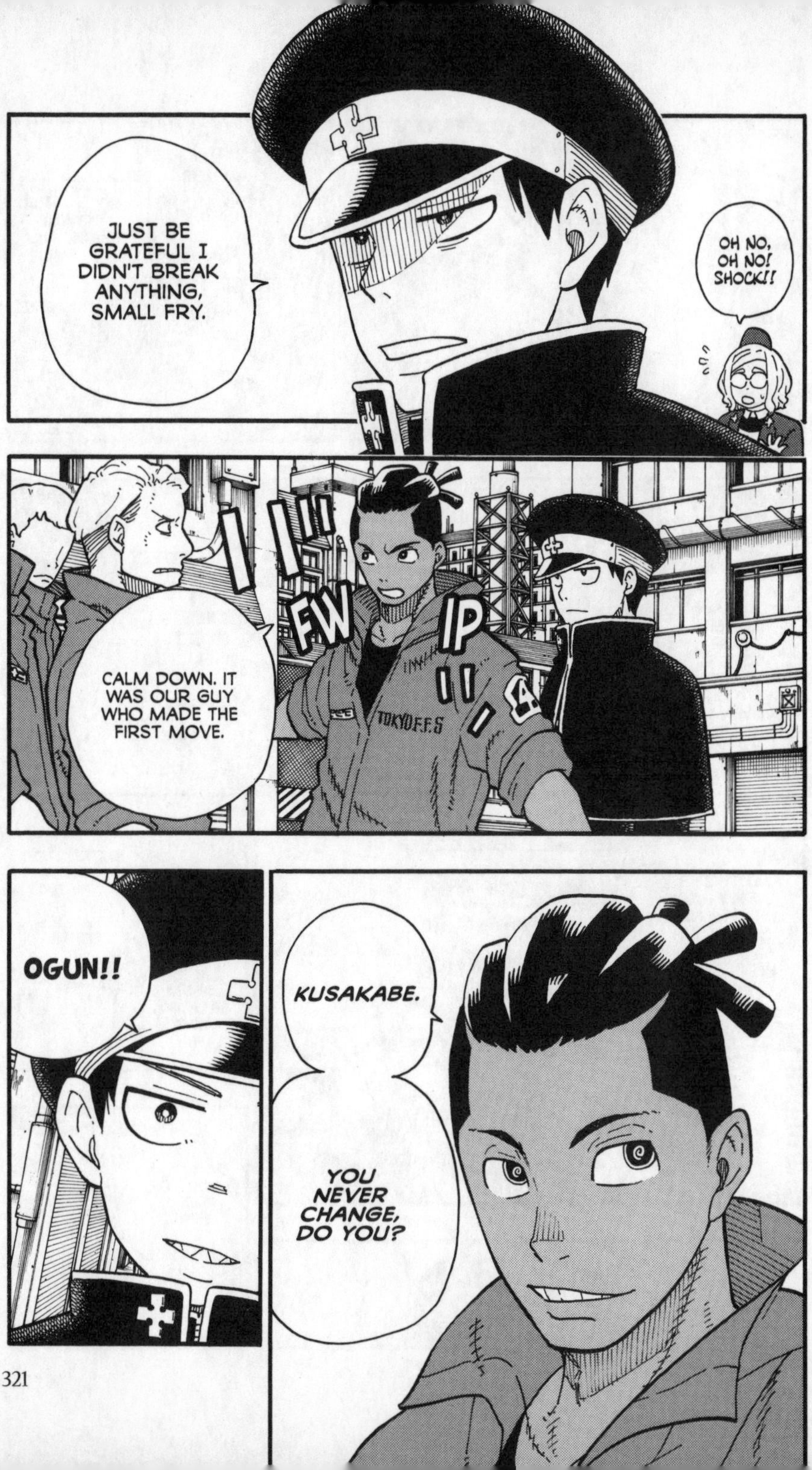
OH NO, OH NO! SHOCK!!
JUST BE GRATEFUL I DIDN'T BREAK ANYTHING, SMALL FRY.
FWIP
CALM DOWN. IT WAS OUR GUY WHO MADE THE FIRST MOVE.
KUSAKABE.
YOU NEVER CHANGE, DO YOU?
OGUN!!

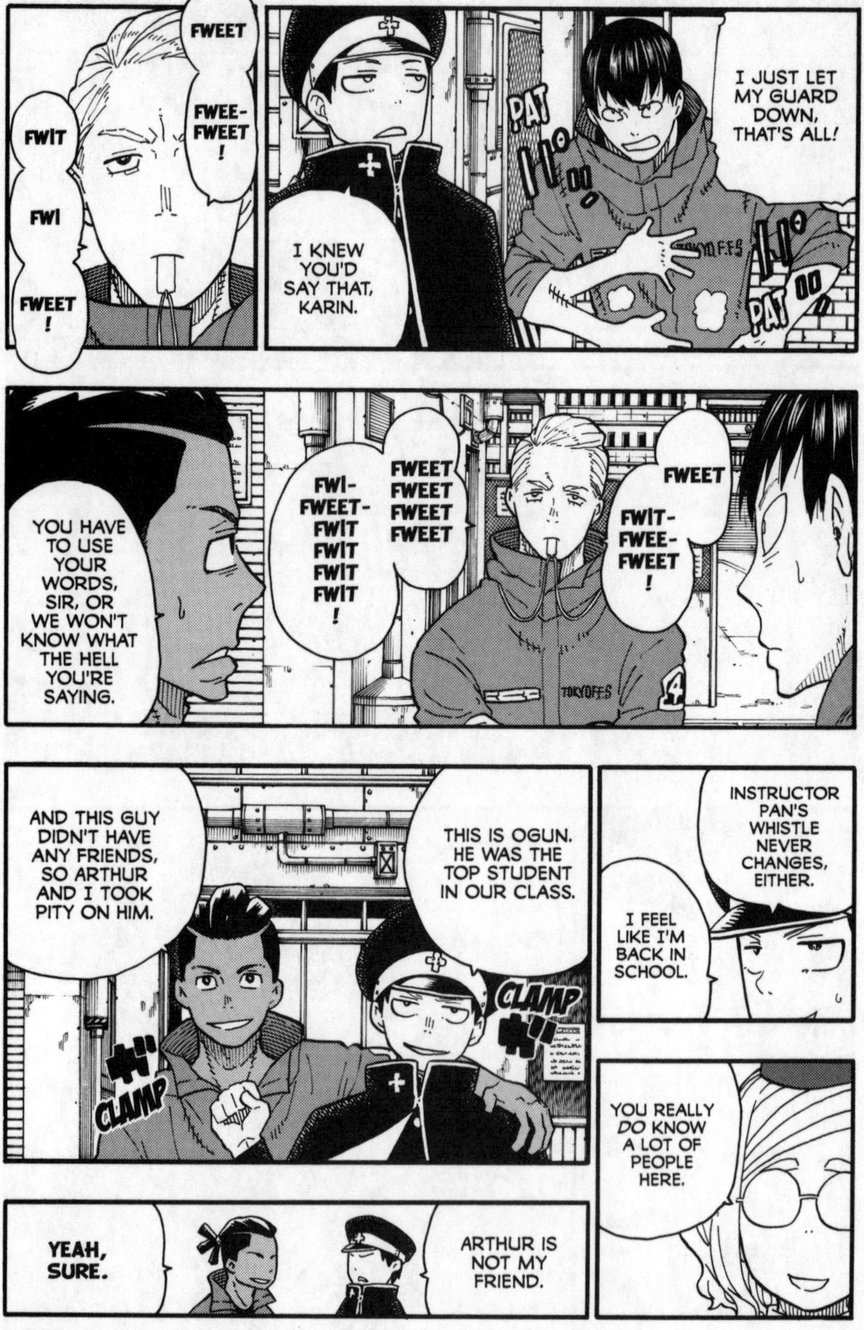
I JUST LET MY GUARD DOWN, THAT'S ALL!
PAT
PAT
I KNEW YOU'D SAY THAT, KARIN.
FWEET
FWEE-FWEET!
FWIT
FWI
FWEET!
FWEET
FWIT-FWEE-FWEET!
FWEET FWEET FWEET FWEET
FWI-FWEET-FWIT FWIT FWIT FWIT!
YOU HAVE TO USE YOUR WORDS, SIR, OR WE WON'T KNOW WHAT THE HELL YOU'RE SAYING.
INSTRUCTOR PAN'S WHISTLE NEVER CHANGES, EITHER.
I FEEL LIKE I'M BACK IN SCHOOL.
YOU REALLY *DO* KNOW A LOT OF PEOPLE HERE.
THIS IS OGUN. HE WAS THE TOP STUDENT IN OUR CLASS.
AND THIS GUY DIDN'T HAVE ANY FRIENDS, SO ARTHUR AND I TOOK PITY ON HIM.
CLAMP
CLAMP
ARTHUR IS NOT MY FRIEND.
YEAH, SURE.

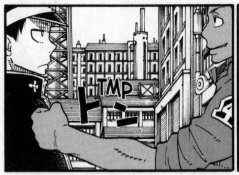

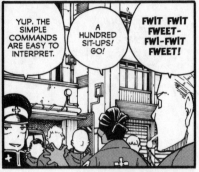

FWIT FWIT FWEET-FWI-FWIT FWEET!
A HUNDRED SIT-UPS! GO!
YUP. THE SIMPLE COMMANDS ARE EASY TO INTERPRET.
TMP
SOUNDS LIKE YOU'RE DOING ALL RIGHT IN COMPANY 8.
YOU, TOO!
FWIT!
FWEET FWIT FWEET, FWEET FWEET FWEET, FWI-FWIT, FWEET FWEET FWEET!
LIEUTENANT PAN SAYS HE'LL TAKE US TO THE CAPTAIN! THANKS FOR YOUR HELP, SIR!
I'M SURPRISED YOU UNDER-STOOD THAT.

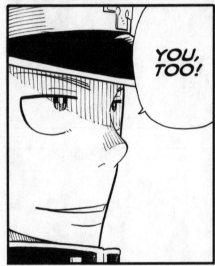

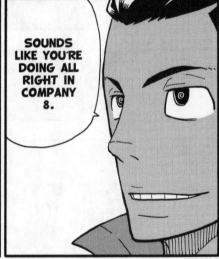

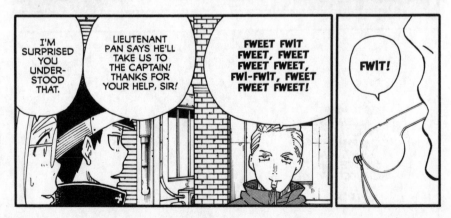

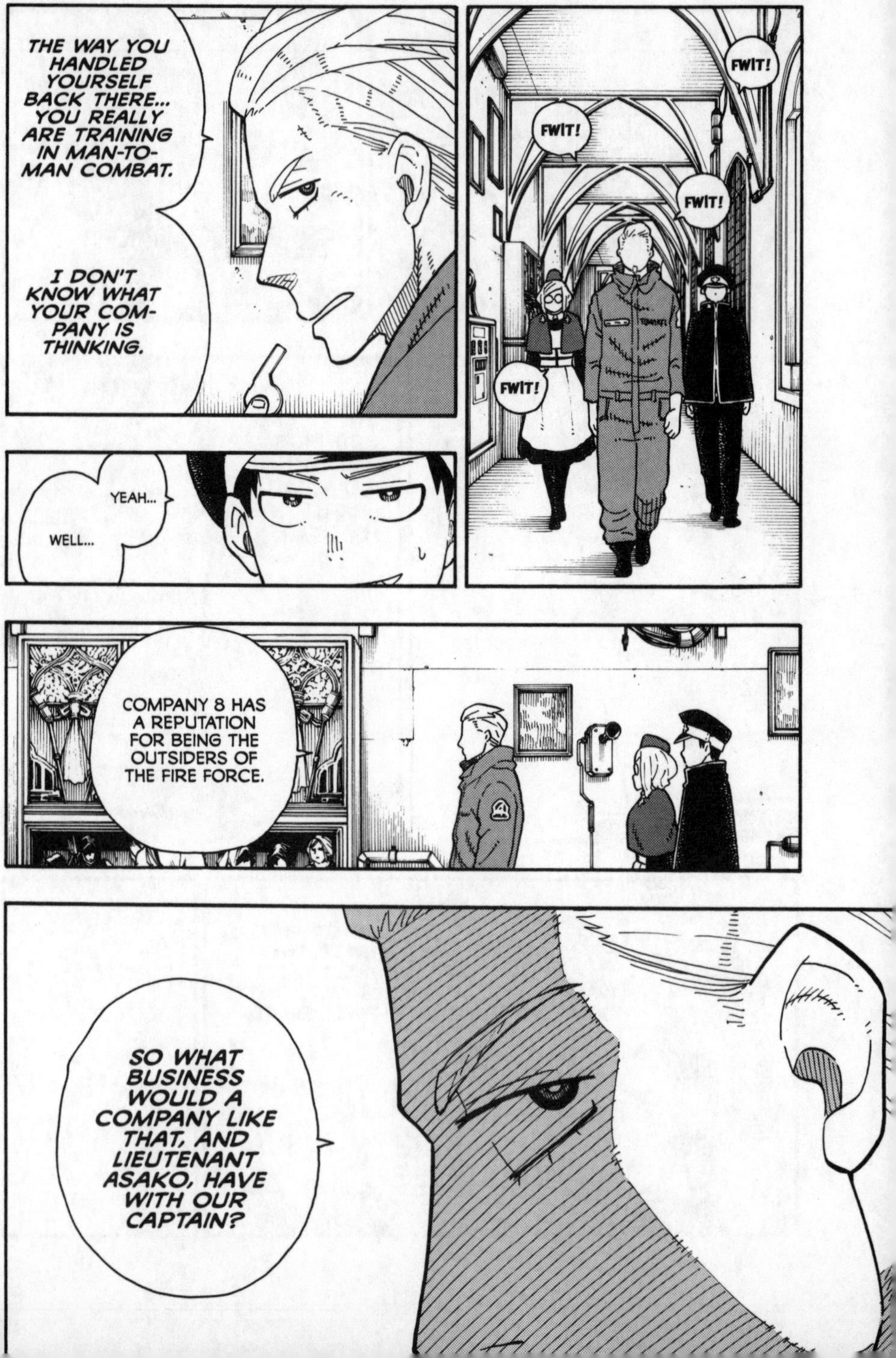
FWIT!
FWIT!
FWIT!
FWIT!
THE WAY YOU HANDLED YOURSELF BACK THERE... YOU REALLY ARE TRAINING IN MAN-TO-MAN COMBAT.
I DON'T KNOW WHAT YOUR COMPANY IS THINKING.
YEAH...
WELL...
COMPANY 8 HAS A REPUTATION FOR BEING THE OUTSIDERS OF THE FIRE FORCE.
SO WHAT BUSINESS WOULD A COMPANY LIKE THAT, AND LIEUTENANT ASAKO, HAVE WITH OUR CAPTAIN?

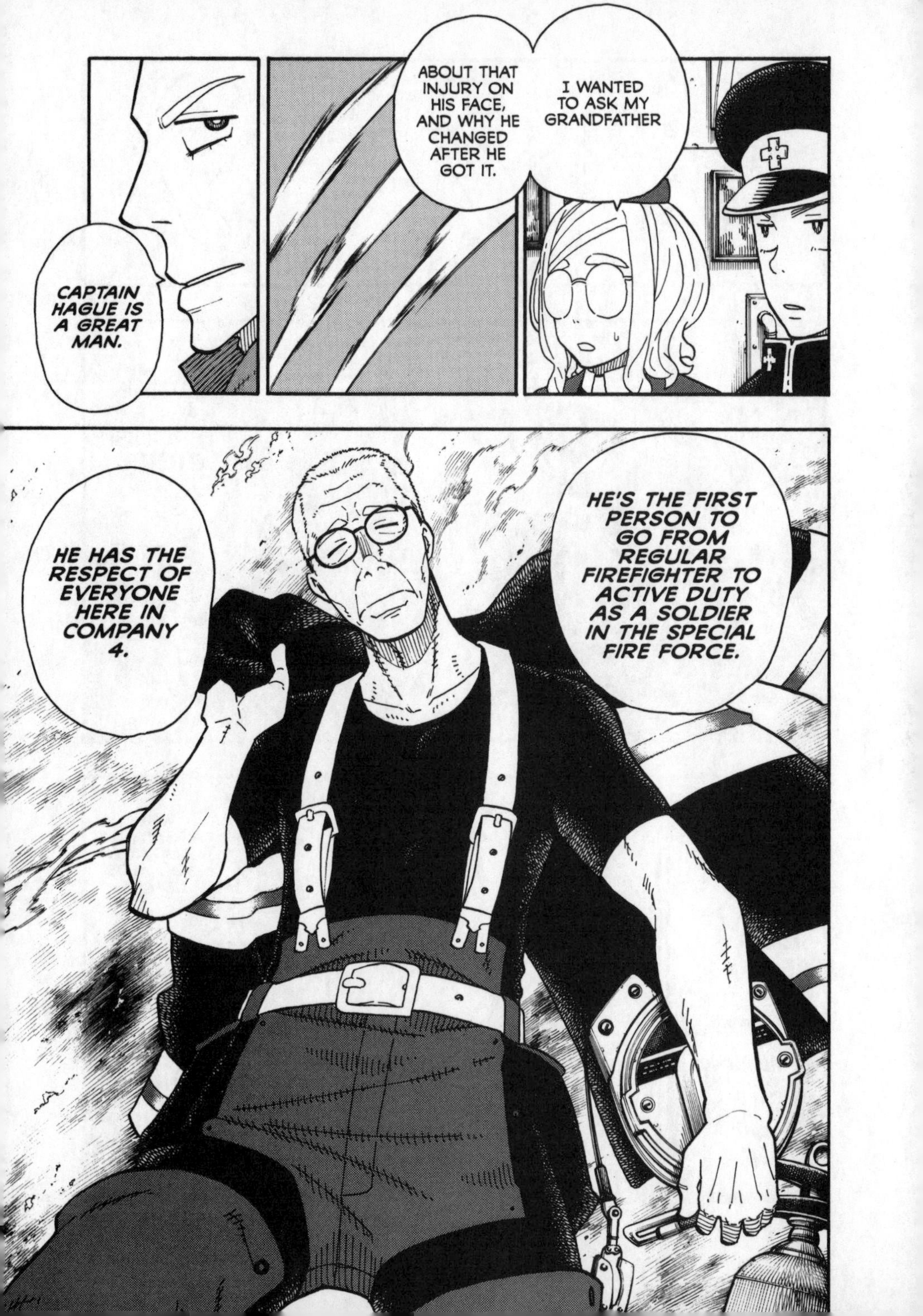
I WANTED TO ASK MY GRANDFATHER
ABOUT THAT INJURY ON HIS FACE, AND WHY HE CHANGED AFTER HE GOT IT.
CAPTAIN HAGUE IS A GREAT MAN.
HE'S THE FIRST PERSON TO GO FROM REGULAR FIREFIGHTER TO ACTIVE DUTY AS A SOLDIER IN THE SPECIAL FIRE FORCE.
HE HAS THE RESPECT OF EVERYONE HERE IN COMPANY 4.

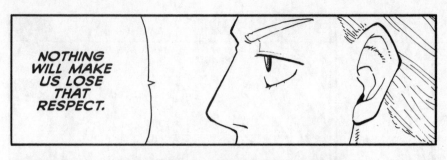

NOTHING WILL MAKE US LOSE THAT RESPECT.
CAPTAIN HAGUE IS THROUGH THERE.
WE'VE ALREADY LET HIM KNOW YOU WERE COMING.
KUSAKABE IS TO SEE HIM ALONE.
TOKYO F.F.S
ALONE, SIR?
I TOLD HIM THAT YOU WANTED TO ASK HIM ABOUT THE ADOLLA BURST.
IT'S PROBABLY BETTER FOR ME NOT TO GO IN WITH YOU. I WOULDN'T WANT TO INTERFERE.
I UNDER-STAND.
HERE GOES...
ME, ALONE WITH THE CAPTAIN... THAT MAKES ME NERVOUS.

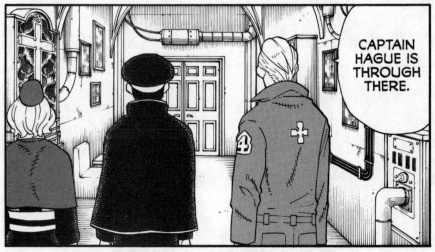

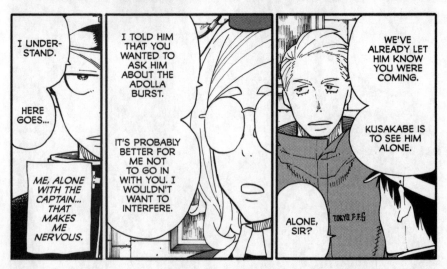

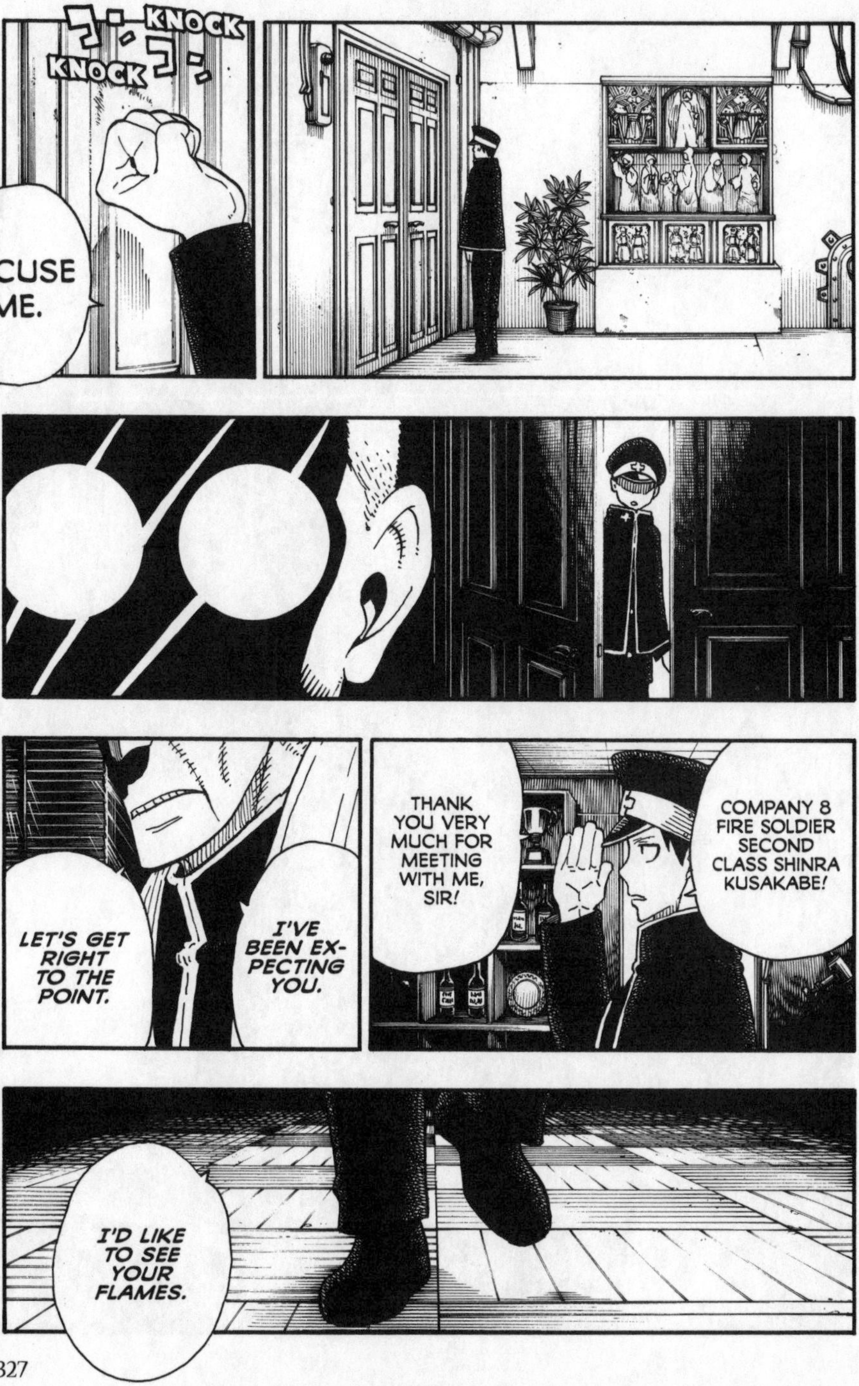
KNOCK
KNOCK
EXCUSE ME.
COMPANY 8 FIRE SOLDIER SECOND CLASS SHINRA KUSAKABE!
THANK YOU VERY MUCH FOR MEETING WITH ME, SIR!
I'VE BEEN EX-PECTING YOU.
LET'S GET RIGHT TO THE POINT.
I'D LIKE TO SEE YOUR FLAMES.

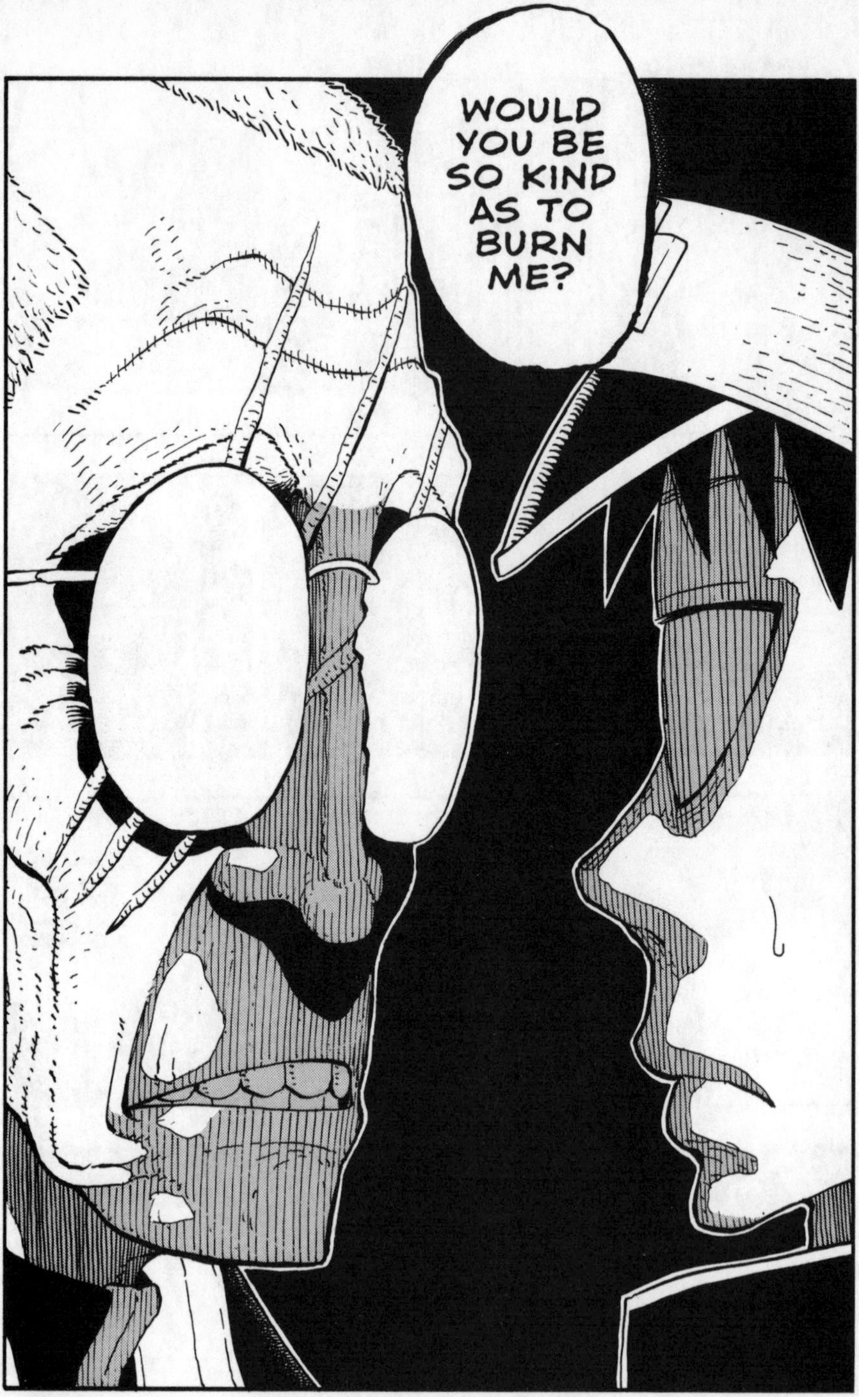
WOULD YOU BE SO KIND AS TO BURN ME?

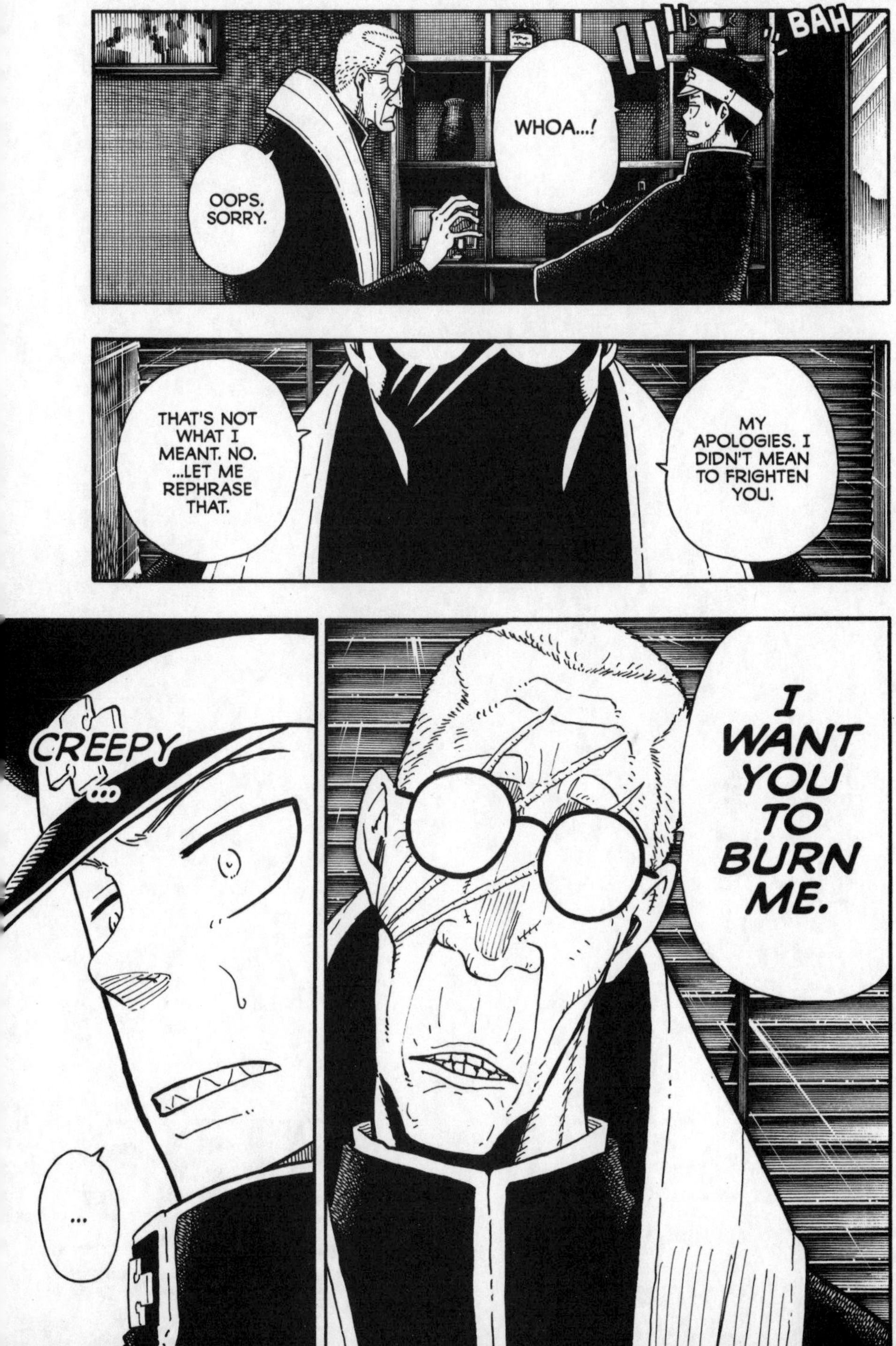
BAH
WHOA...!
OOPS. SORRY.
MY APOLOGIES. I DIDN'T MEAN TO FRIGHTEN YOU.
THAT'S NOT WHAT I MEANT. NO. ...LET ME REPHRASE THAT.
I WANT YOU TO BURN ME.
CREEPY...
...

FIRE FORCE

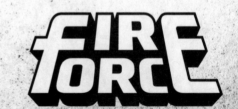

CHAPTER XCIV: SŌICHIRŌ HAGUE

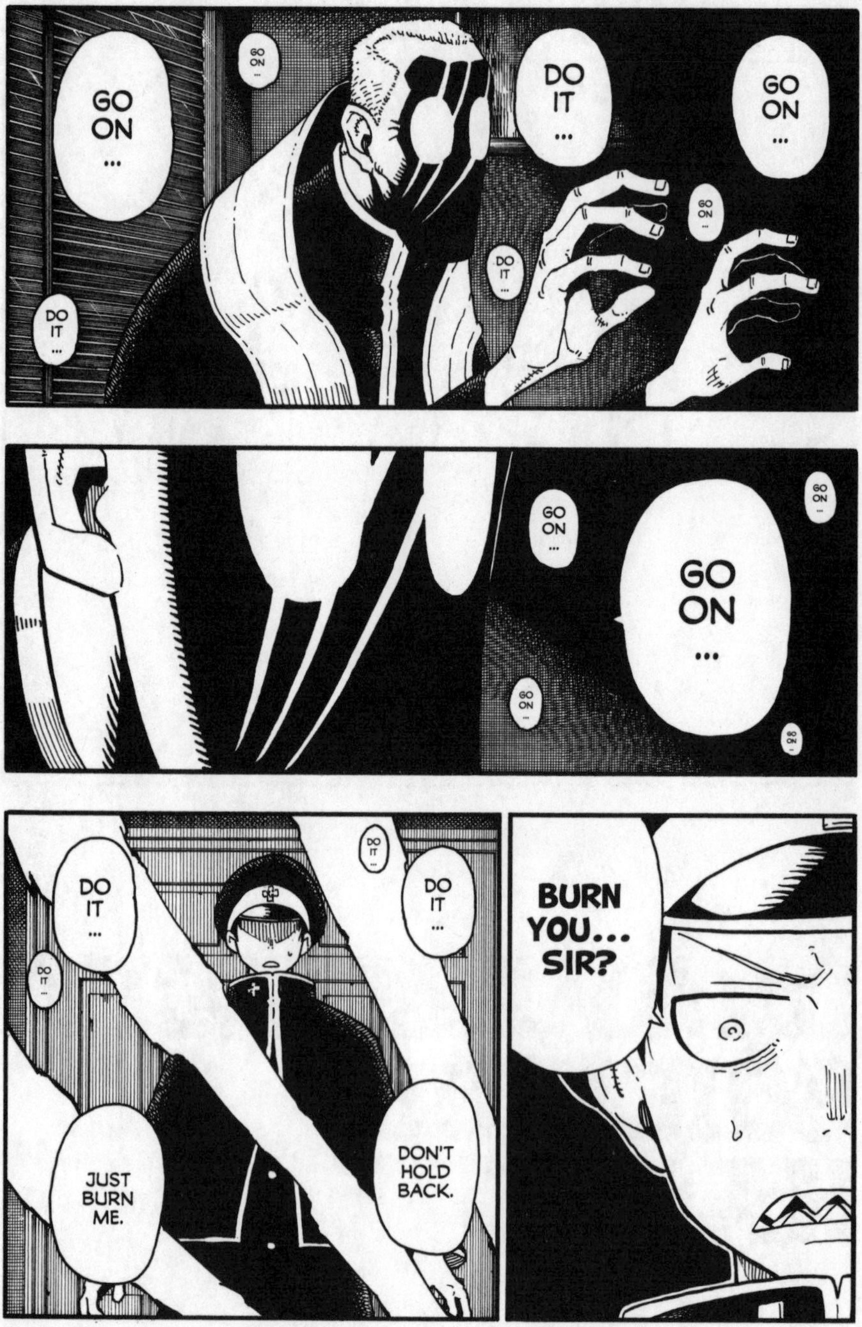
GO ON ...
GO ON ...
DO IT ...
GO ON ...
DO IT ...
GO ON ...
DO IT ...
GO ON ...
GO ON ...
GO ON ...
GO ON ...
GO ON ...
BURN YOU... SIR?
DO IT ...
DO IT ...
DO IT ...
DO IT ...
DON'T HOLD BACK.
JUST BURN ME.

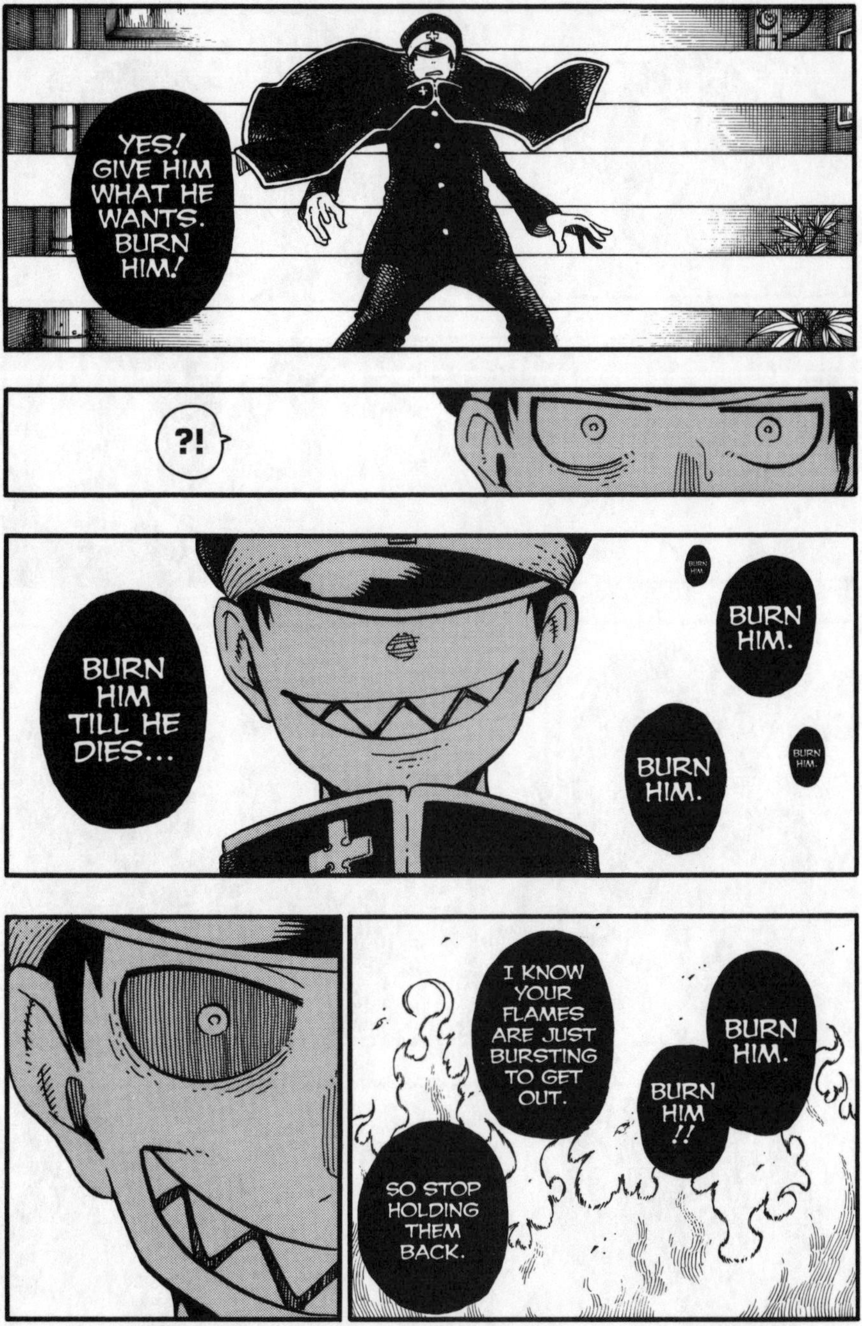
YES! GIVE HIM WHAT HE WANTS. BURN HIM!
?!
BURN HIM
BURN HIM.
BURN HIM.
BURN HIM.
BURN HIM TILL HE DIES...
BURN HIM.
BURN HIM!!
I KNOW YOUR FLAMES ARE JUST BURSTING TO GET OUT.
SO STOP HOLDING THEM BACK.

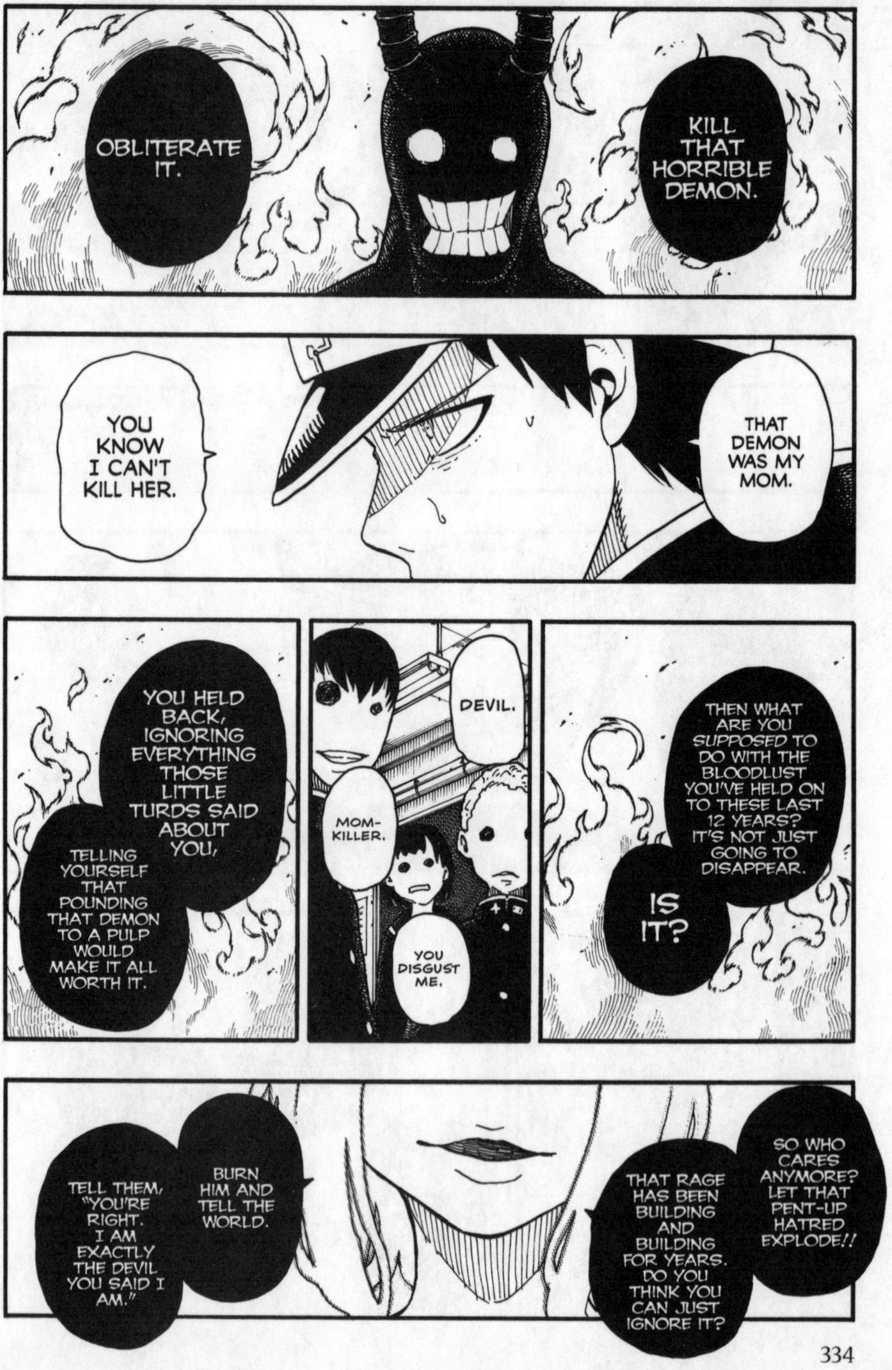
KILL THAT HORRIBLE DEMON.
OBLITERATE IT.
THAT DEMON WAS MY MOM.
YOU KNOW I CAN'T KILL HER.
THEN WHAT ARE YOU *SUPPOSED* TO DO WITH THE BLOODLUST YOU'VE HELD ON TO THESE LAST 12 YEARS? IT'S NOT JUST GOING TO DISAPPEAR.
IS IT?
DEVIL.
MOM-KILLER.
YOU DISGUST ME.
YOU HELD BACK, IGNORING EVERYTHING THOSE LITTLE TURDS SAID ABOUT YOU,
TELLING YOURSELF THAT POUNDING THAT DEMON TO A PULP WOULD MAKE IT ALL WORTH IT.
THAT RAGE HAS BEEN BUILDING AND BUILDING FOR YEARS. DO YOU THINK YOU CAN JUST IGNORE IT?
SO WHO CARES ANYMORE? LET THAT PENT-UP HATRED *EXPLODE!!*
BURN HIM AND TELL THE WORLD.
TELL THEM, "YOU'RE RIGHT. I AM EXACTLY THE DEVIL YOU SAID I AM."

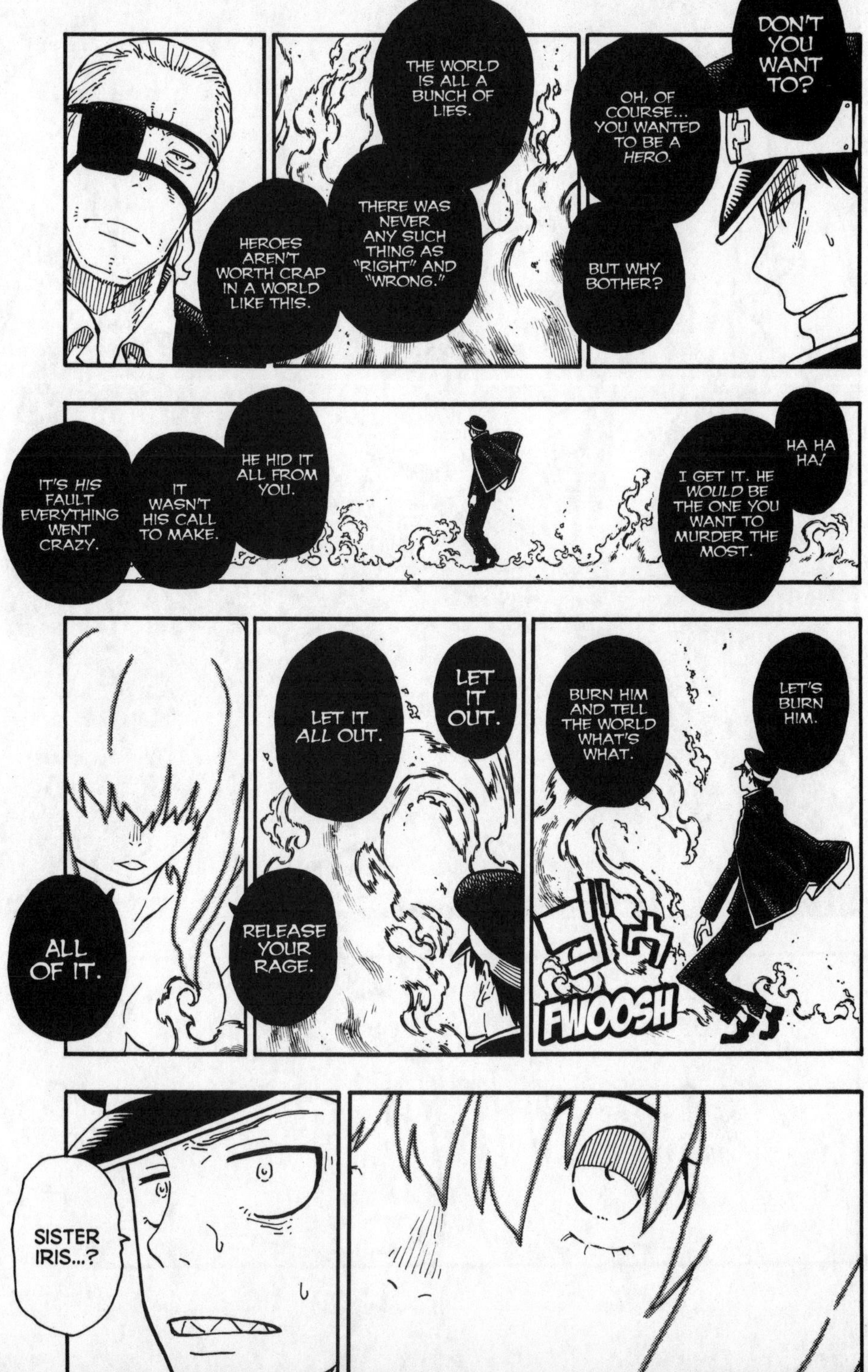
DON'T YOU WANT TO?
OH, OF COURSE... YOU WANTED TO BE A *HERO*.
BUT WHY BOTHER?
THE WORLD IS ALL A BUNCH OF LIES.
THERE WAS NEVER ANY SUCH THING AS "RIGHT" AND "WRONG."
HEROES AREN'T WORTH CRAP IN A WORLD LIKE THIS.
HA HA HA!
I GET IT. HE *WOULD* BE THE ONE YOU WANT TO MURDER THE MOST.
HE HID IT ALL FROM YOU.
IT WASN'T HIS CALL TO MAKE.
IT'S *HIS* FAULT EVERYTHING WENT CRAZY.
LET'S BURN HIM.
BURN HIM AND TELL THE WORLD WHAT'S WHAT.
FWOOSH
LET IT OUT.
LET IT *ALL* OUT.
RELEASE YOUR RAGE.
ALL OF IT.
SISTER IRIS...?

BURY EVERYTHING IN A SEA OF YOUR OWN FLAMES!

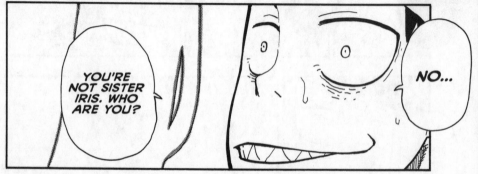

YOU'RE NOT SISTER IRIS. WHO ARE YOU?

NO...

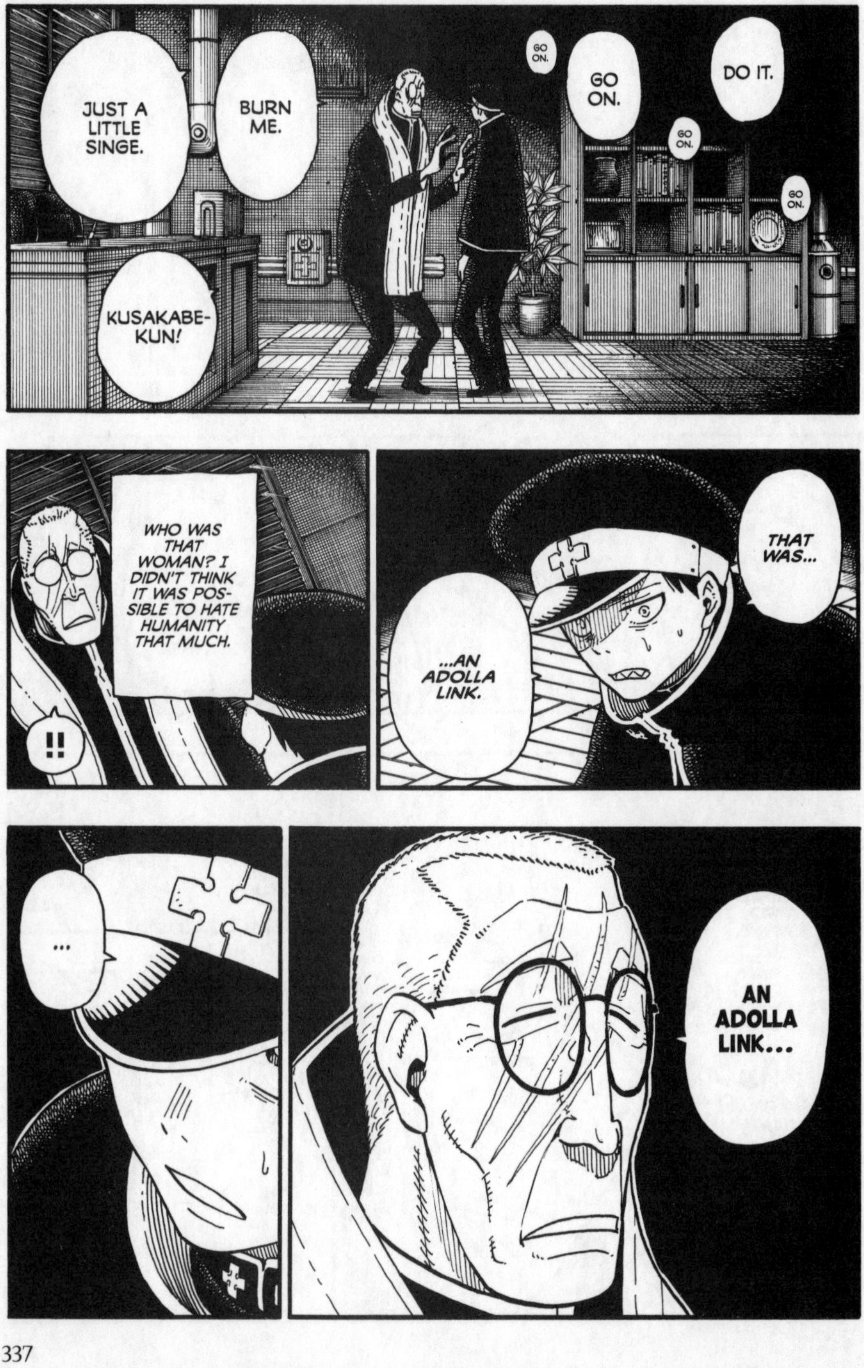
DO IT.
GO ON.
GO ON.
GO ON.
GO ON.
BURN ME.
JUST A LITTLE SINGE.
KUSAKABE-KUN!
THAT WAS...
...AN ADOLLA LINK.
WHO WAS THAT WOMAN? I DIDN'T THINK IT WAS POSSIBLE TO HATE HUMANITY THAT MUCH.
!!
AN ADOLLA LINK...
...

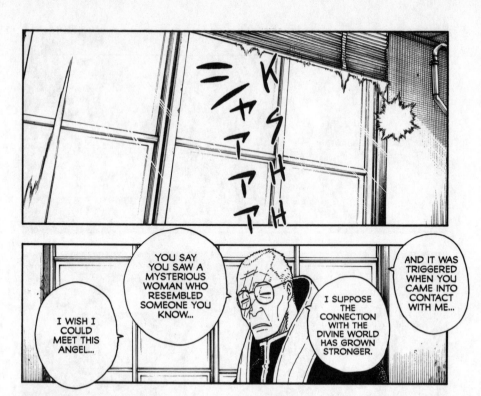

KSHHH
AND IT WAS TRIGGERED WHEN YOU CAME INTO CONTACT WITH ME...
I SUPPOSE THE CONNECTION WITH THE DIVINE WORLD HAS GROWN STRONGER.
YOU SAY YOU SAW A MYSTERIOUS WOMAN WHO RESEMBLED SOMEONE YOU KNOW...
I WISH I COULD MEET THIS ANGEL...
I WANT YOU TO BURN ME MORE AND MORE.
EEK!
...
THAT'S WHY I'M HERE TODAY—TO ASK ABOUT THE ADOLLA LINK.
HAVE *YOU* EVER HAD AN ADOLLA LINK, CAPTAIN HAGUE?
IF THAT'S WHAT IT'S CALLED, THEN I SUPPOSE I HAVE.
IT WAS A MAGNIFICENT EXPERIENCE.

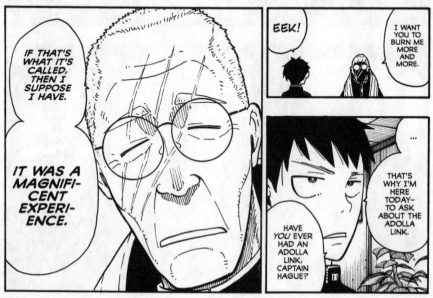

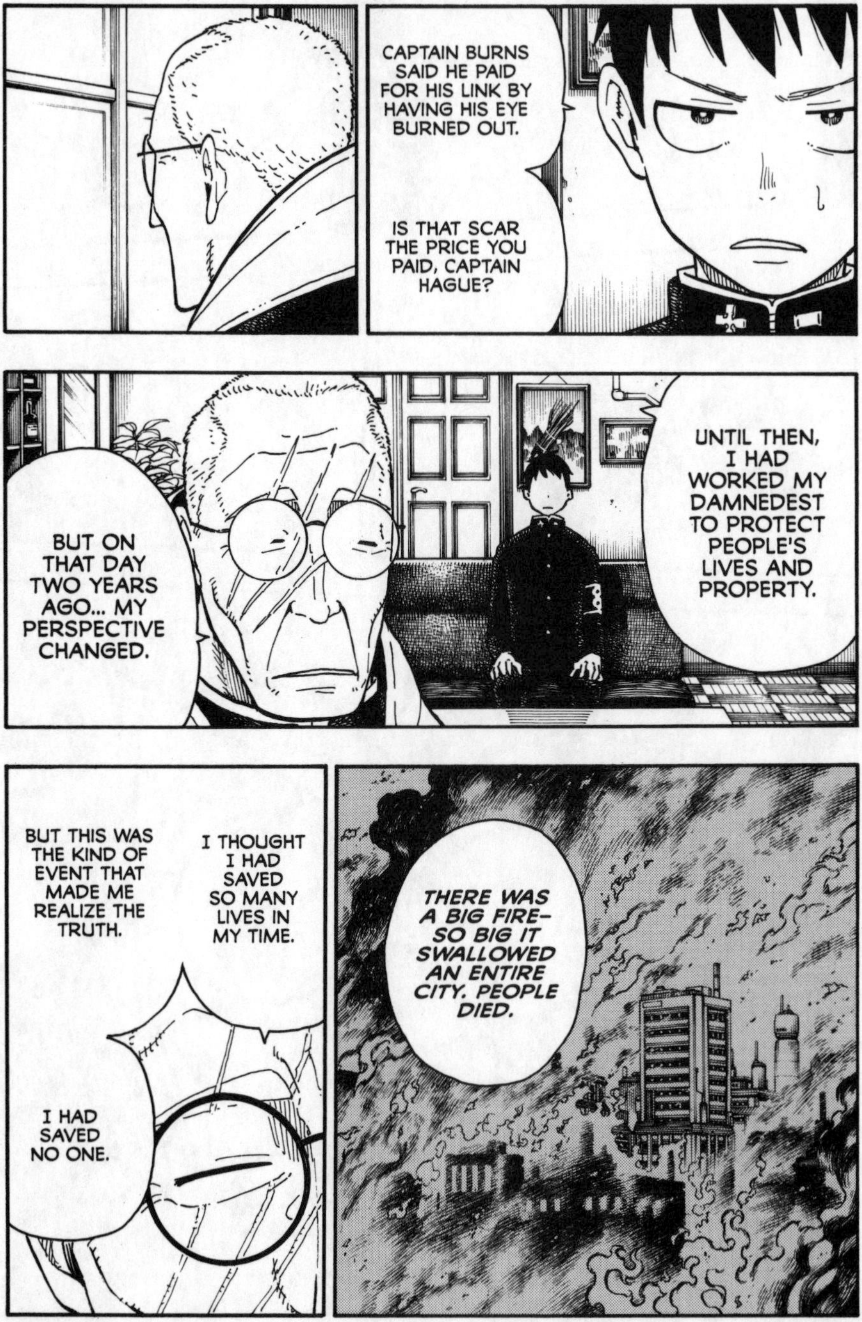
CAPTAIN BURNS SAID HE PAID FOR HIS LINK BY HAVING HIS EYE BURNED OUT.
IS THAT SCAR THE PRICE YOU PAID, CAPTAIN HAGUE?
UNTIL THEN, I HAD WORKED MY DAMNEDEST TO PROTECT PEOPLE'S LIVES AND PROPERTY.
BUT ON THAT DAY TWO YEARS AGO... MY PERSPECTIVE CHANGED.
THERE WAS A BIG FIRE— SO BIG IT SWALLOWED AN ENTIRE CITY. PEOPLE DIED.
I THOUGHT I HAD SAVED SO MANY LIVES IN MY TIME.
BUT THIS WAS THE KIND OF EVENT THAT MADE ME REALIZE THE TRUTH.
I HAD SAVED NO ONE.

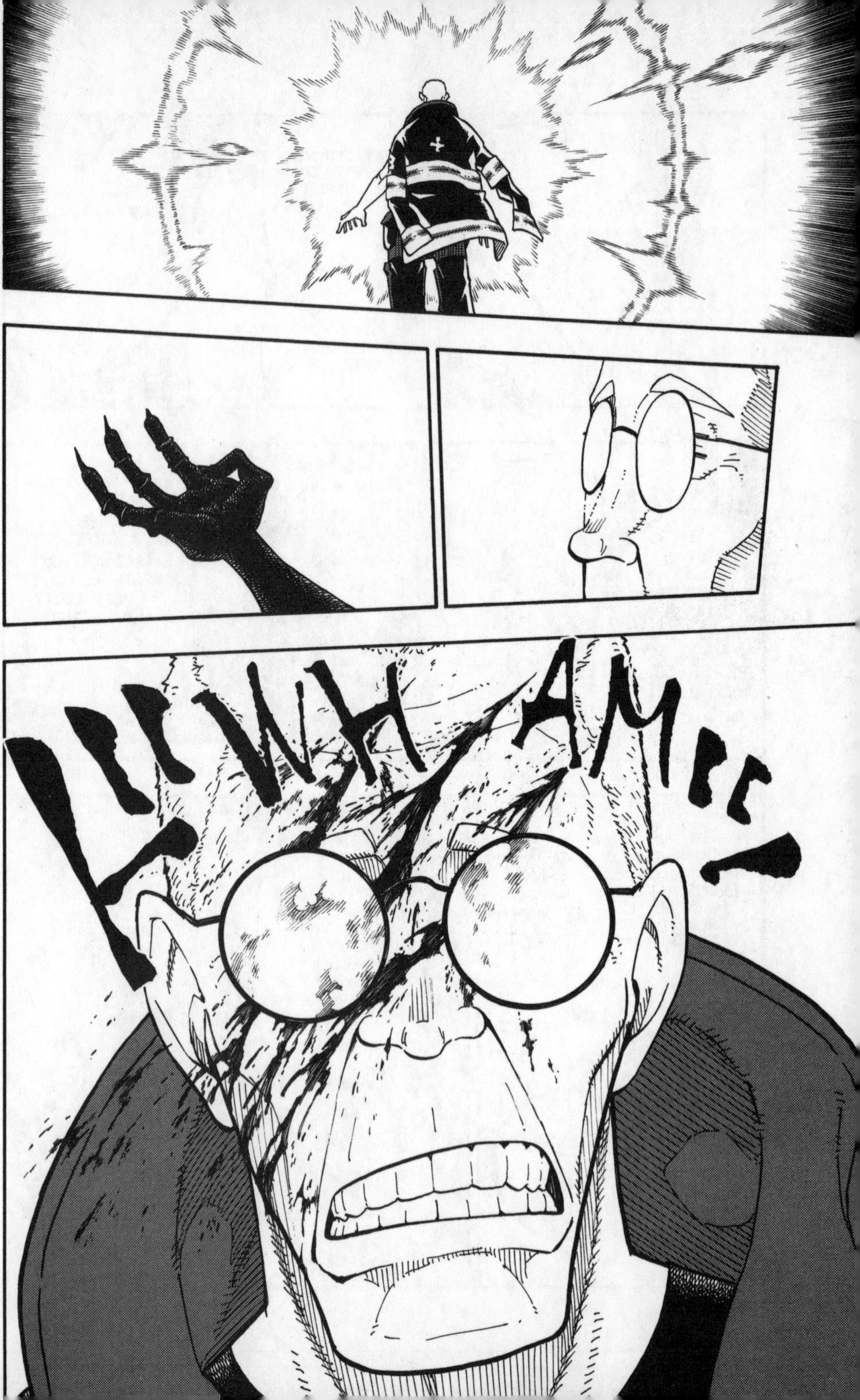
KWHAM!

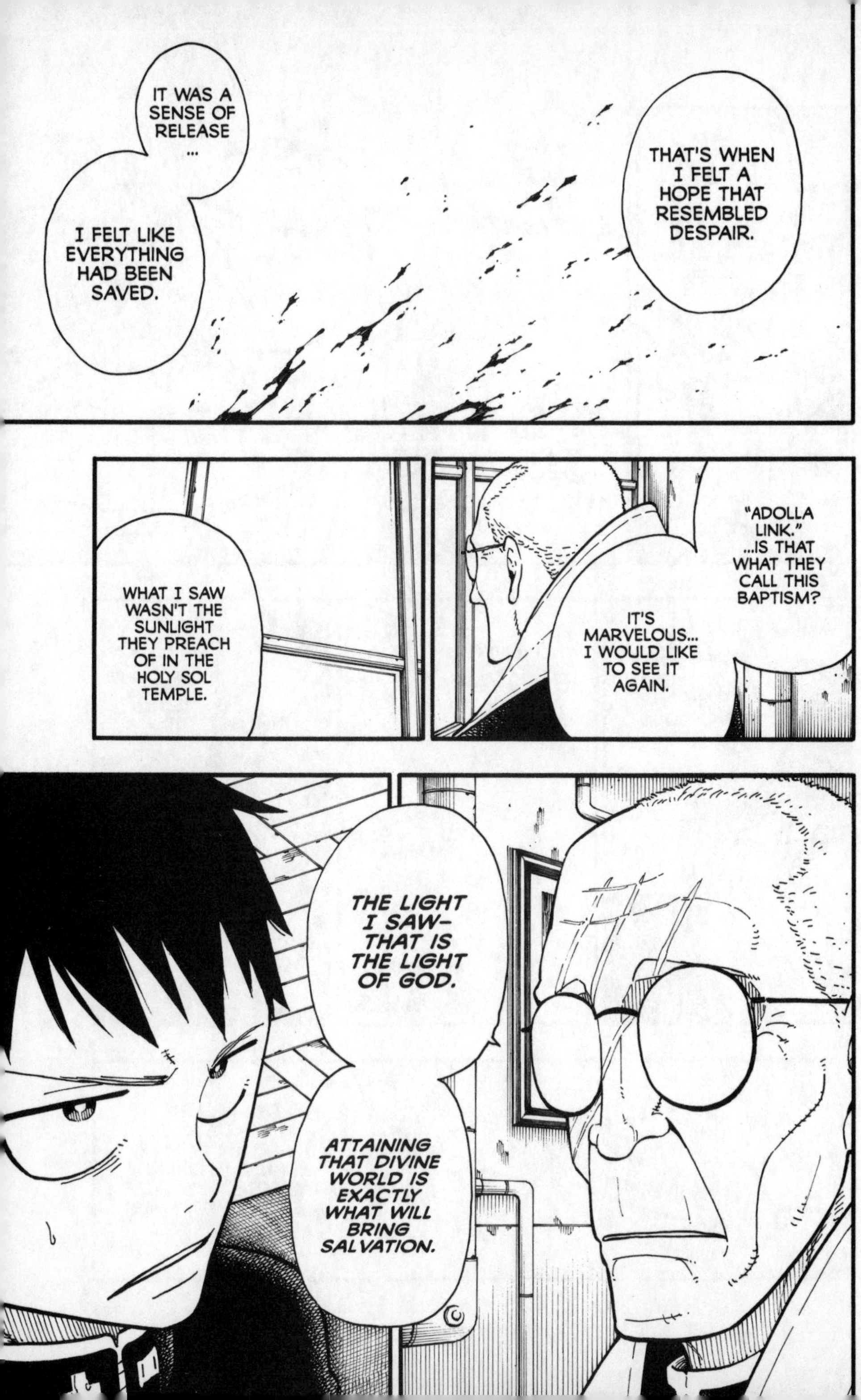
THAT'S WHEN I FELT A HOPE THAT RESEMBLED DESPAIR.
IT WAS A SENSE OF RELEASE ...
I FELT LIKE EVERYTHING HAD BEEN SAVED.
"ADOLLA LINK." ...IS THAT WHAT THEY CALL THIS BAPTISM?
IT'S MARVELOUS... I WOULD LIKE TO SEE IT AGAIN.
WHAT I SAW WASN'T THE SUNLIGHT THEY PREACH OF IN THE HOLY SOL TEMPLE.
THE LIGHT I SAW—THAT IS THE LIGHT OF GOD.
ATTAINING THAT DIVINE WORLD IS EXACTLY WHAT WILL BRING SALVATION.

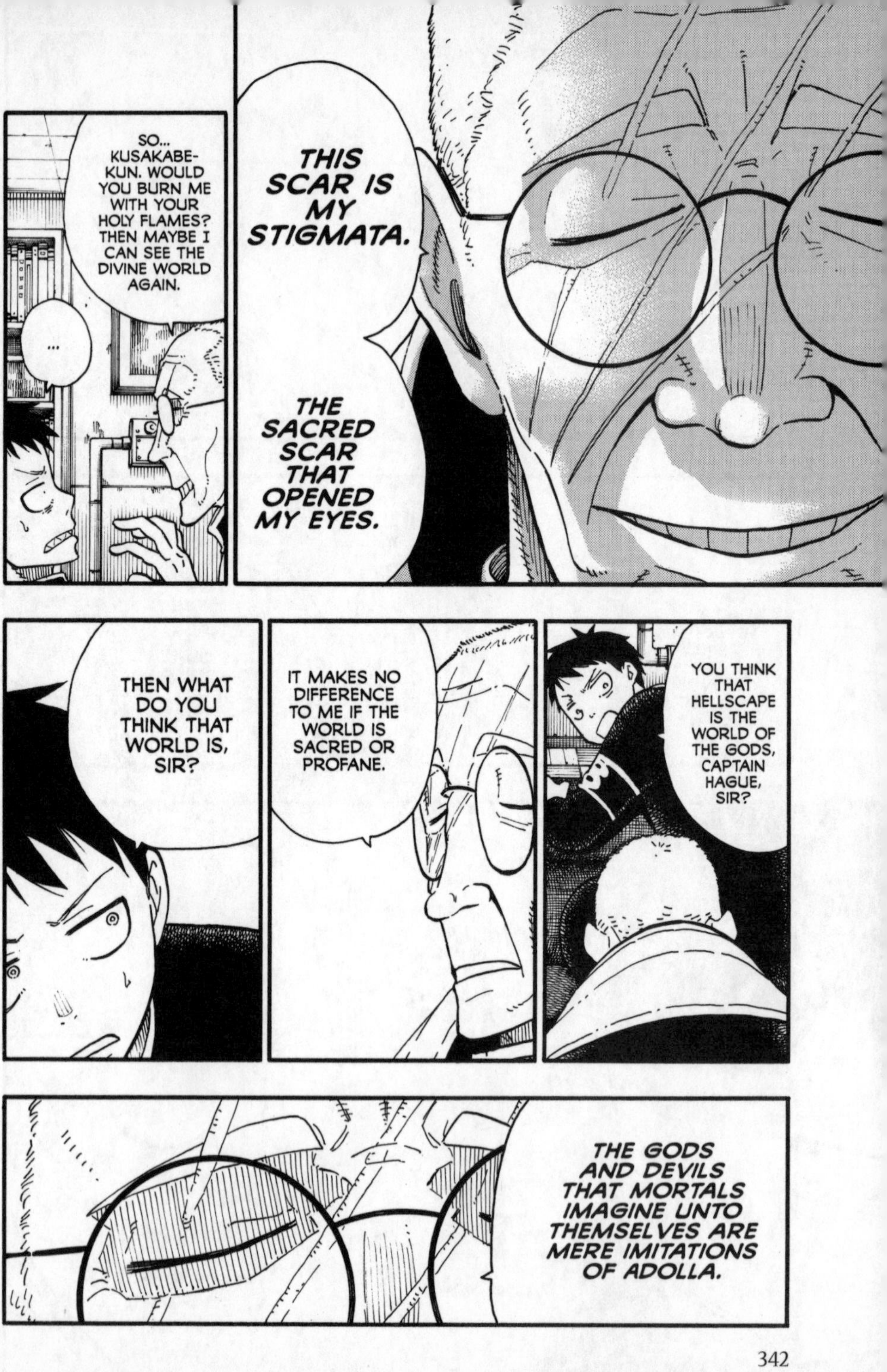
THIS SCAR IS MY STIGMATA.
THE SACRED SCAR THAT OPENED MY EYES.
SO... KUSAKABE-KUN. WOULD YOU BURN ME WITH YOUR HOLY FLAMES? THEN MAYBE I CAN SEE THE DIVINE WORLD AGAIN.
...
YOU THINK THAT HELLSCAPE IS THE WORLD OF THE GODS, CAPTAIN HAGUE, SIR?
IT MAKES NO DIFFERENCE TO ME IF THE WORLD IS SACRED OR PROFANE.
THEN WHAT DO YOU THINK THAT WORLD IS, SIR?
THE GODS AND DEVILS THAT MORTALS IMAGINE UNTO THEMSELVES ARE MERE IMITATIONS OF ADOLLA.

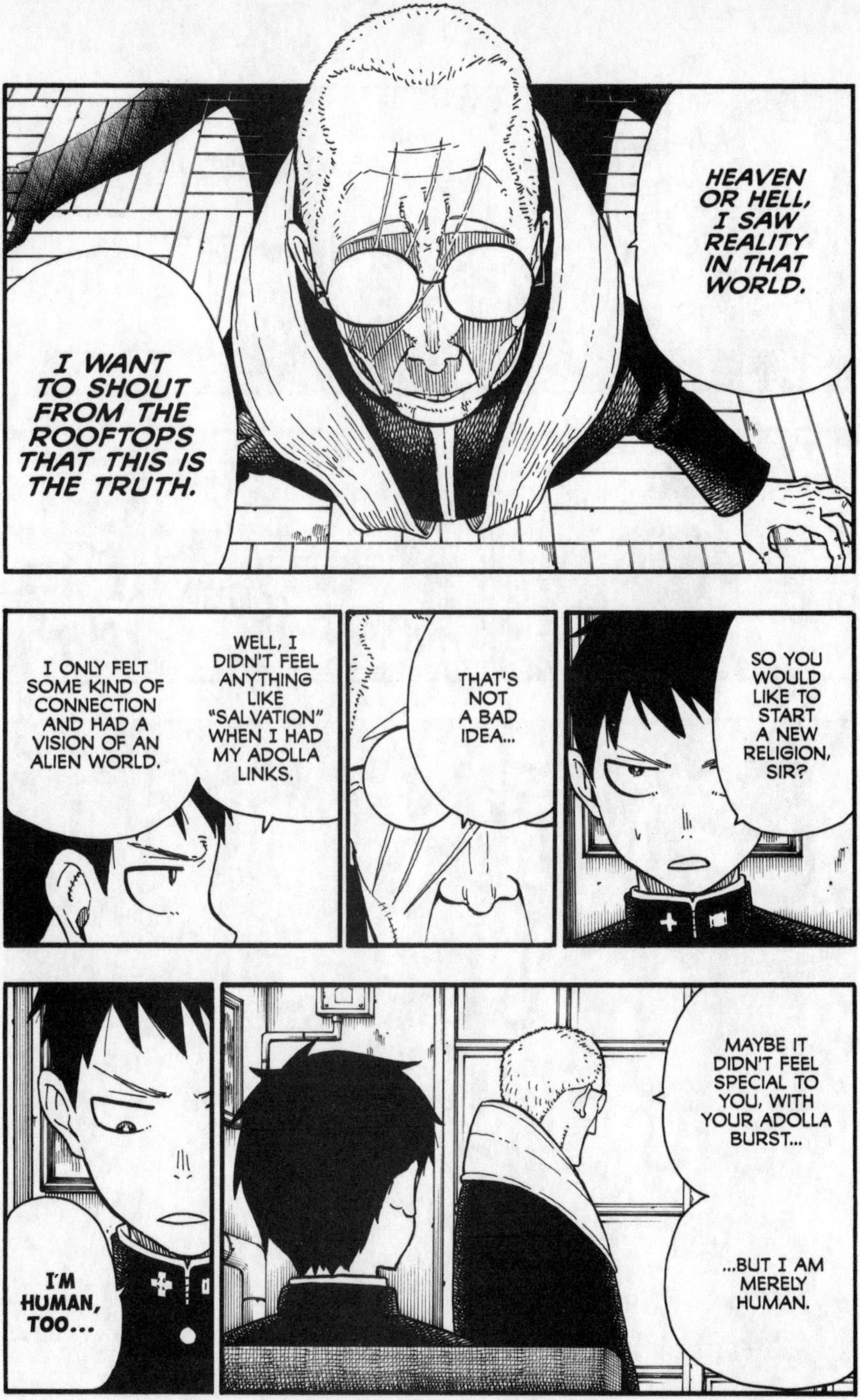
HEAVEN OR HELL, I SAW REALITY IN THAT WORLD.
I WANT TO SHOUT FROM THE ROOFTOPS THAT THIS IS THE TRUTH.
SO YOU WOULD LIKE TO START A NEW RELIGION, SIR?
THAT'S NOT A BAD IDEA...
WELL, I DIDN'T FEEL ANYTHING LIKE "SALVATION" WHEN I HAD MY ADOLLA LINKS.
I ONLY FELT SOME KIND OF CONNECTION AND HAD A VISION OF AN ALIEN WORLD.
MAYBE IT DIDN'T FEEL SPECIAL TO YOU, WITH YOUR ADOLLA BURST...
...BUT I AM MERELY HUMAN.
I'M HUMAN, TOO...

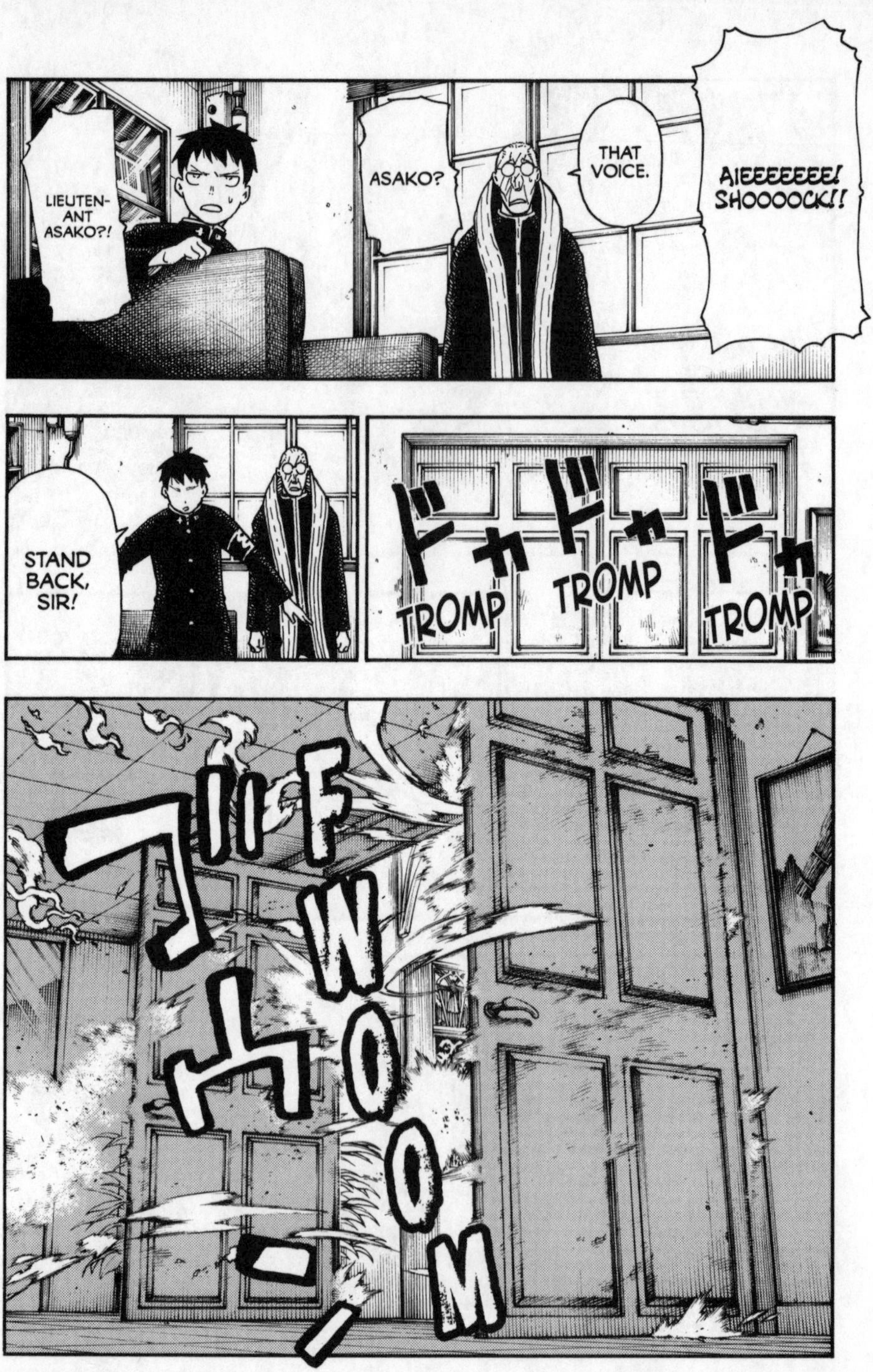
AIEEEEEEE! SHOOOOCK!!
THAT VOICE.
ASAKO?
LIEUTEN-ANT ASAKO?!
TROMP
TROMP
TROMP
STAND BACK, SIR!
FWOOOM

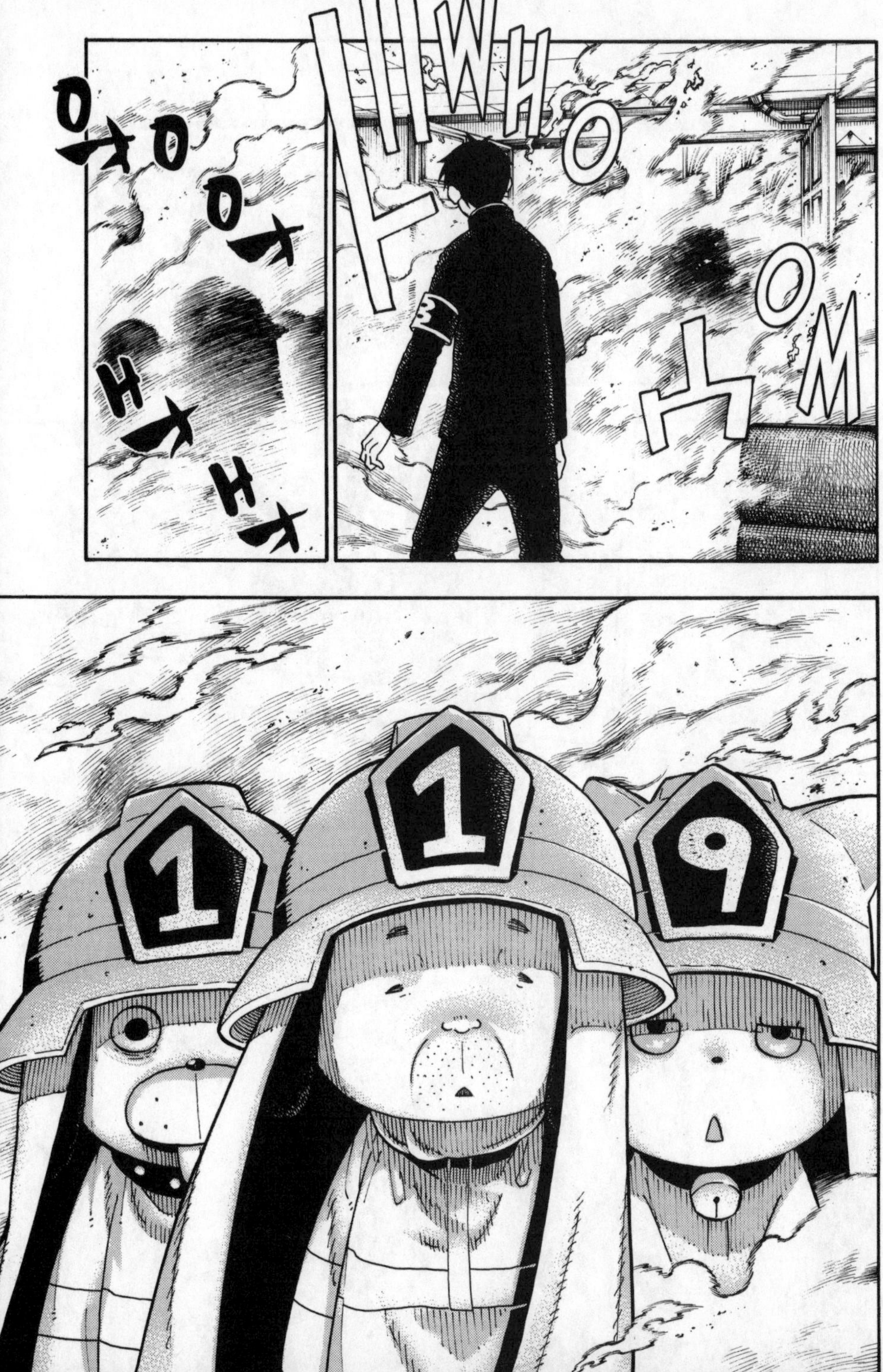
WHOOOM

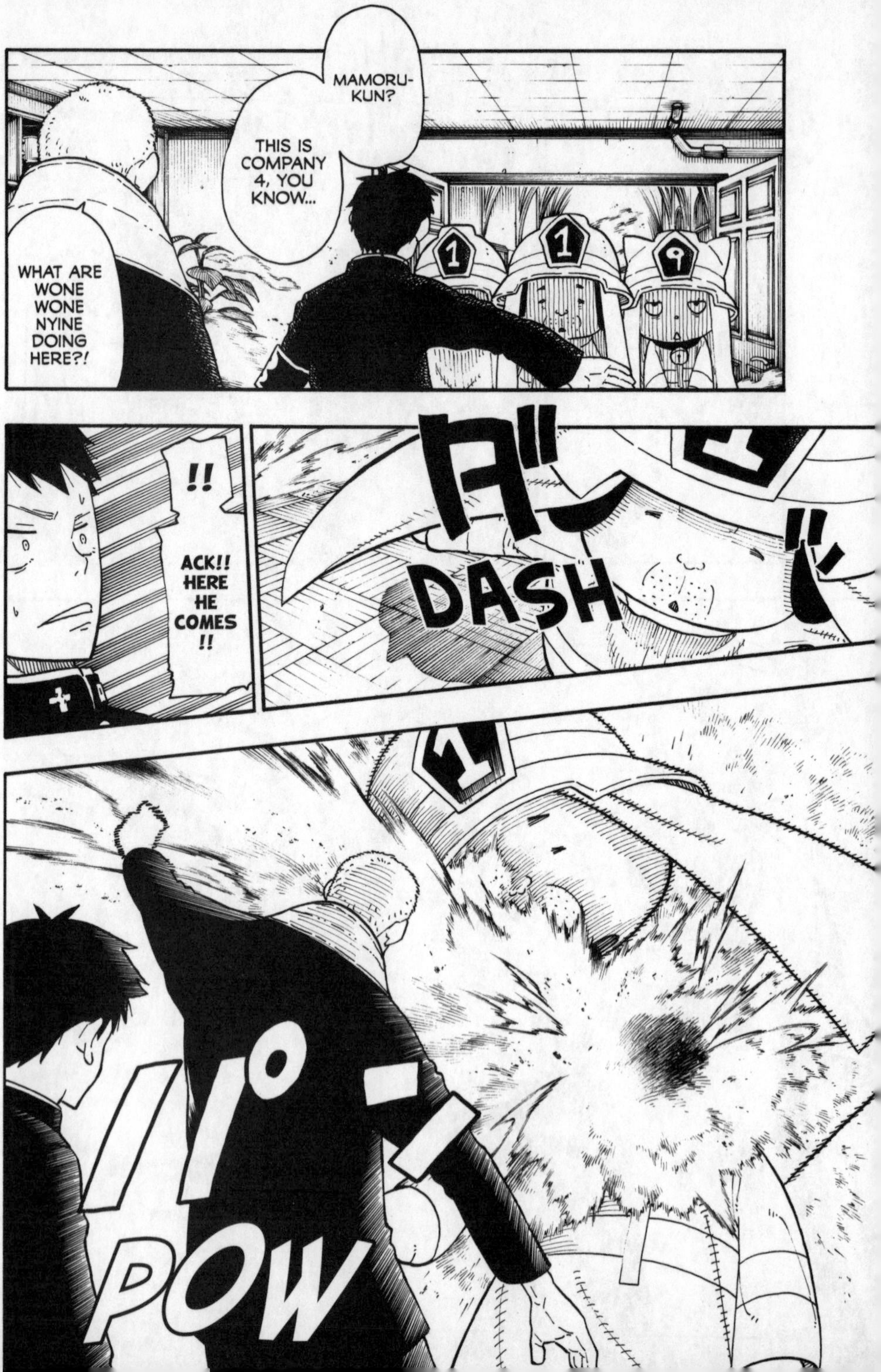

MAMORU-KUN?
THIS IS COMPANY 4, YOU KNOW...
WHAT ARE WONE WONE NYINE DOING HERE?!
DASH
!!
ACK!! HERE HE COMES!!
POW

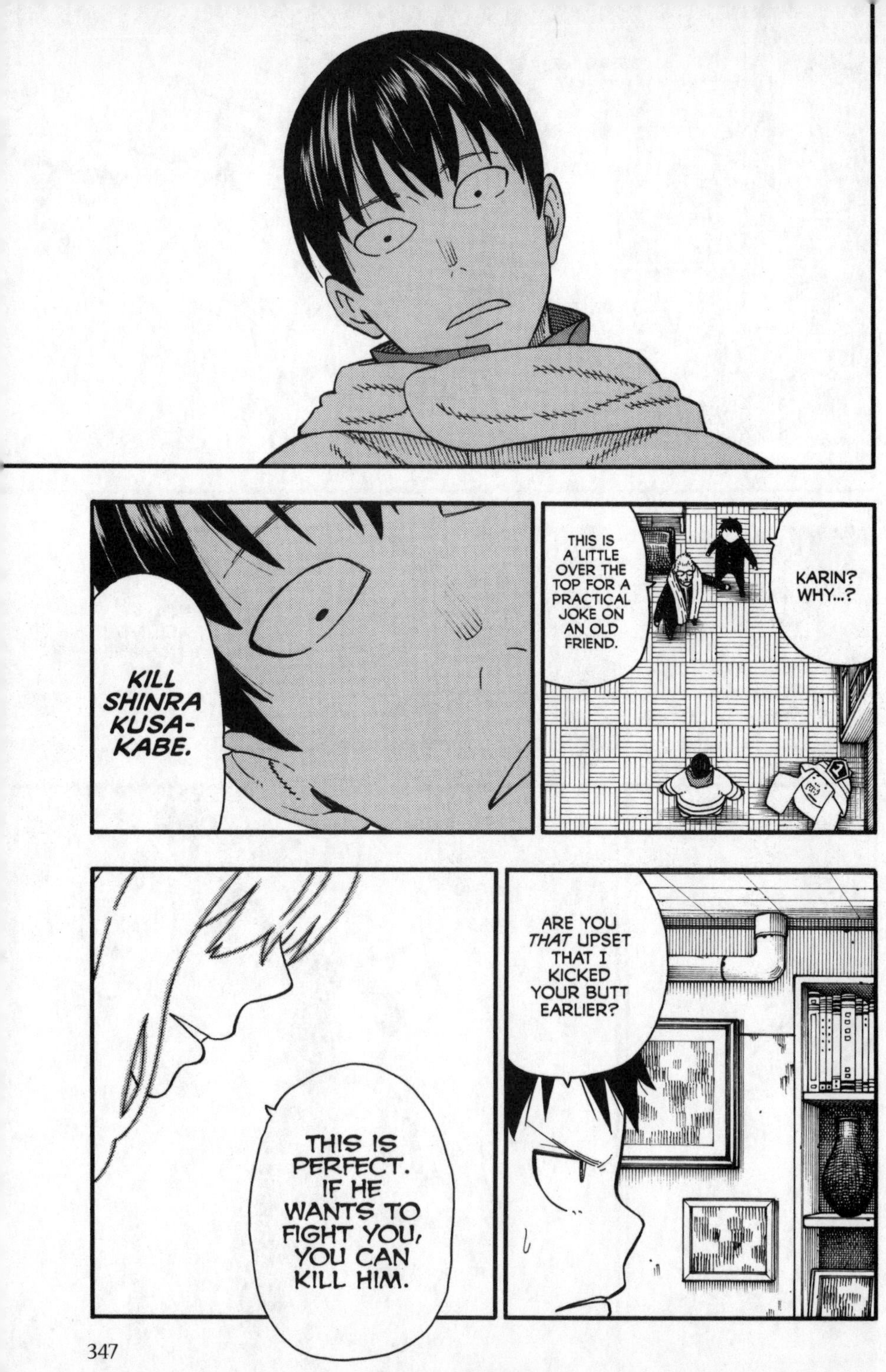
KARIN? WHY...?
THIS IS A LITTLE OVER THE TOP FOR A PRACTICAL JOKE ON AN OLD FRIEND.
KILL SHINRA KUSA-KABE.
ARE YOU *THAT* UPSET THAT I KICKED YOUR BUTT EARLIER?
THIS IS PERFECT. IF HE WANTS TO FIGHT YOU, YOU CAN KILL HIM.

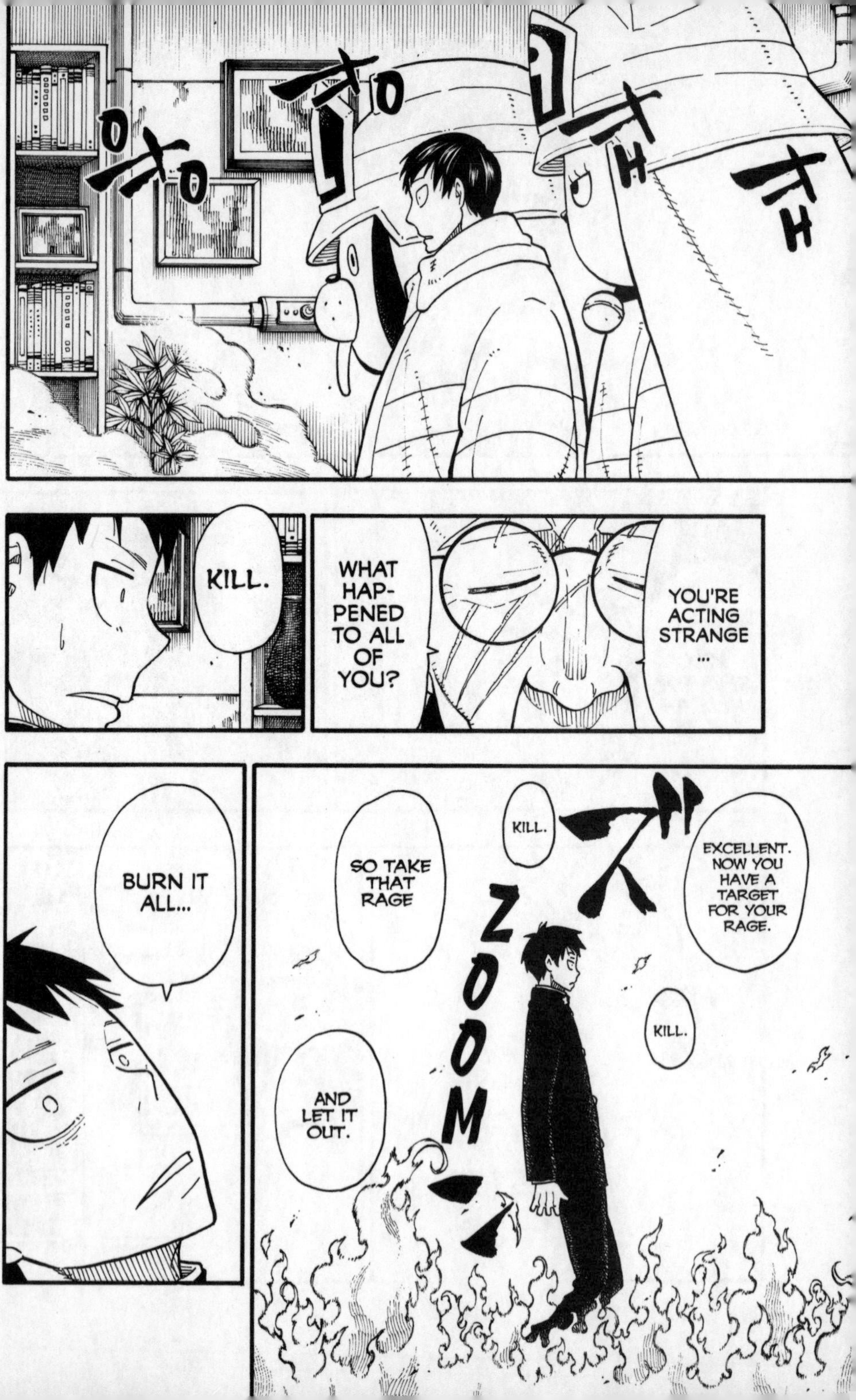
YOU'RE ACTING STRANGE ...
WHAT HAP-PENED TO ALL OF YOU?
KILL.
EXCELLENT. NOW YOU HAVE A TARGET FOR YOUR RAGE.
KILL.
SO TAKE THAT RAGE
KILL.
ZOOM
AND LET IT OUT.
BURN IT ALL...

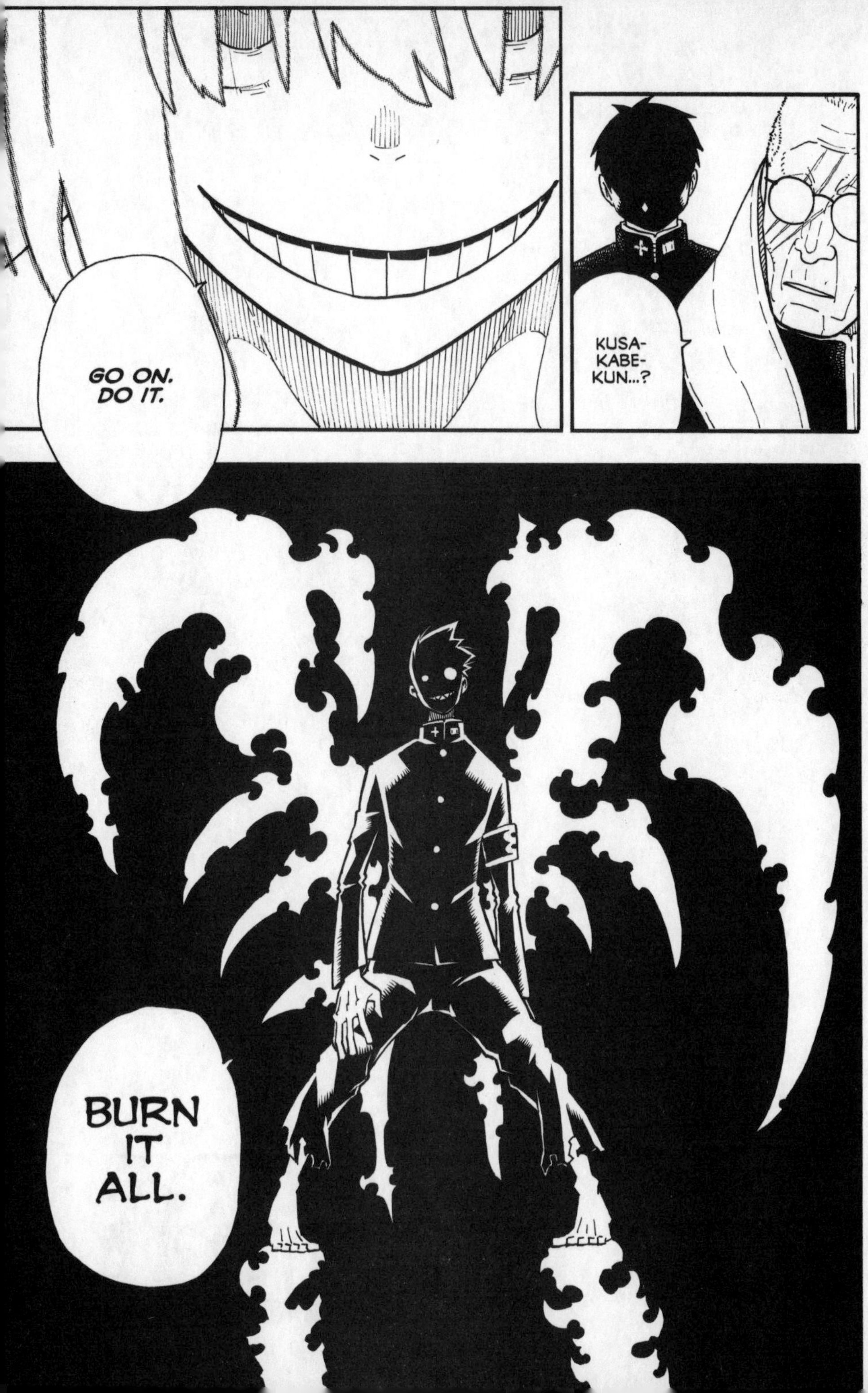
KUSA-KABE-KUN...?
GO ON. DO IT.
BURN IT ALL.

FIRE FORCE

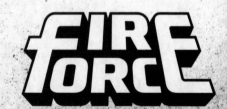

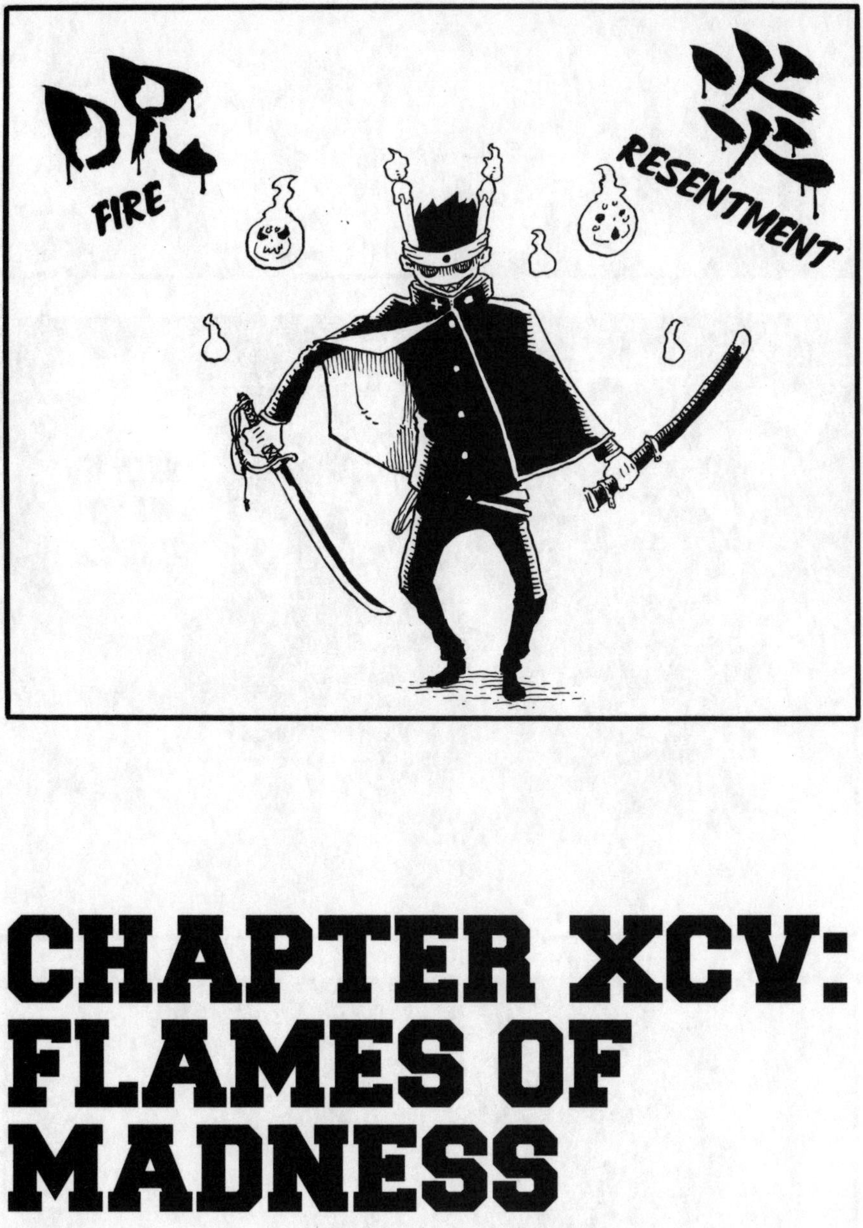
呪
FIRE
炎
RESENTMENT

CHAPTER XCV: FLAMES OF MADNESS

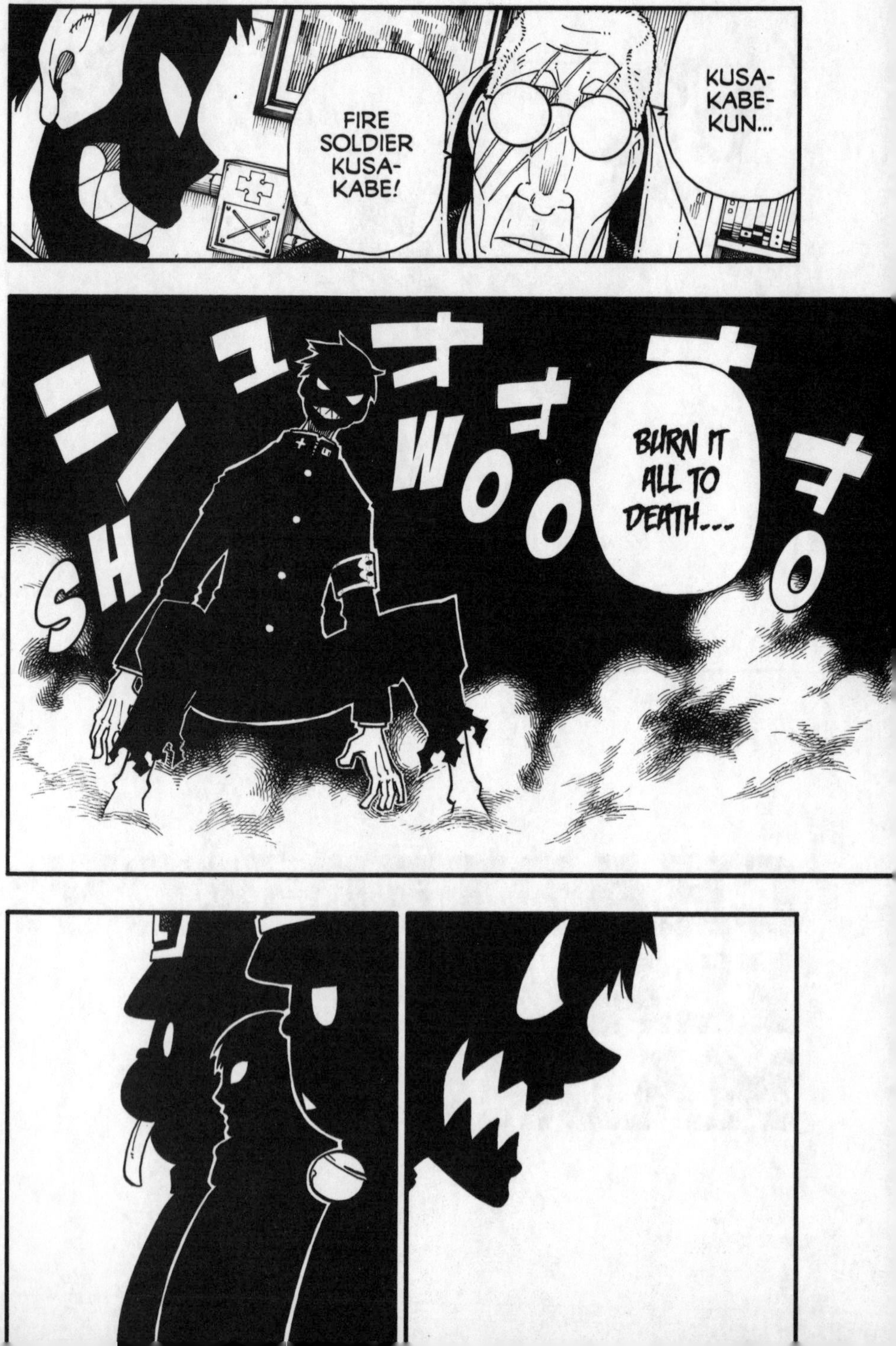
KUSA-
KABE-
KUN...
FIRE
SOLDIER
KUSA-
KABE!
SHWOOO
BURN IT
ALL TO
DEATH...

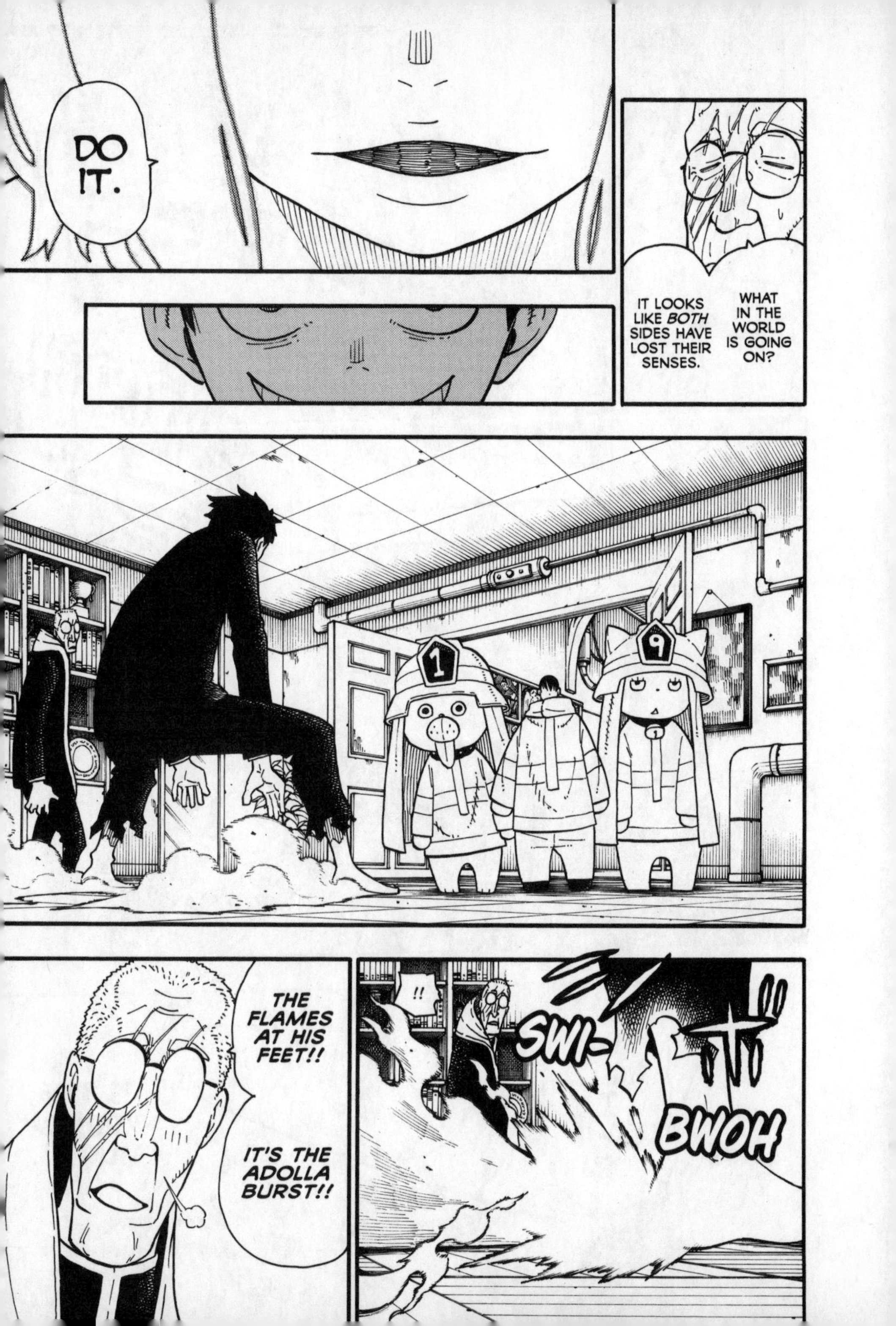
WHAT IN THE WORLD IS GOING ON?
IT LOOKS LIKE *BOTH* SIDES HAVE LOST THEIR SENSES.
DO IT.
!!
SWI-
BWOH
THE FLAMES AT HIS FEET!!
IT'S THE ADOLLA BURST!!

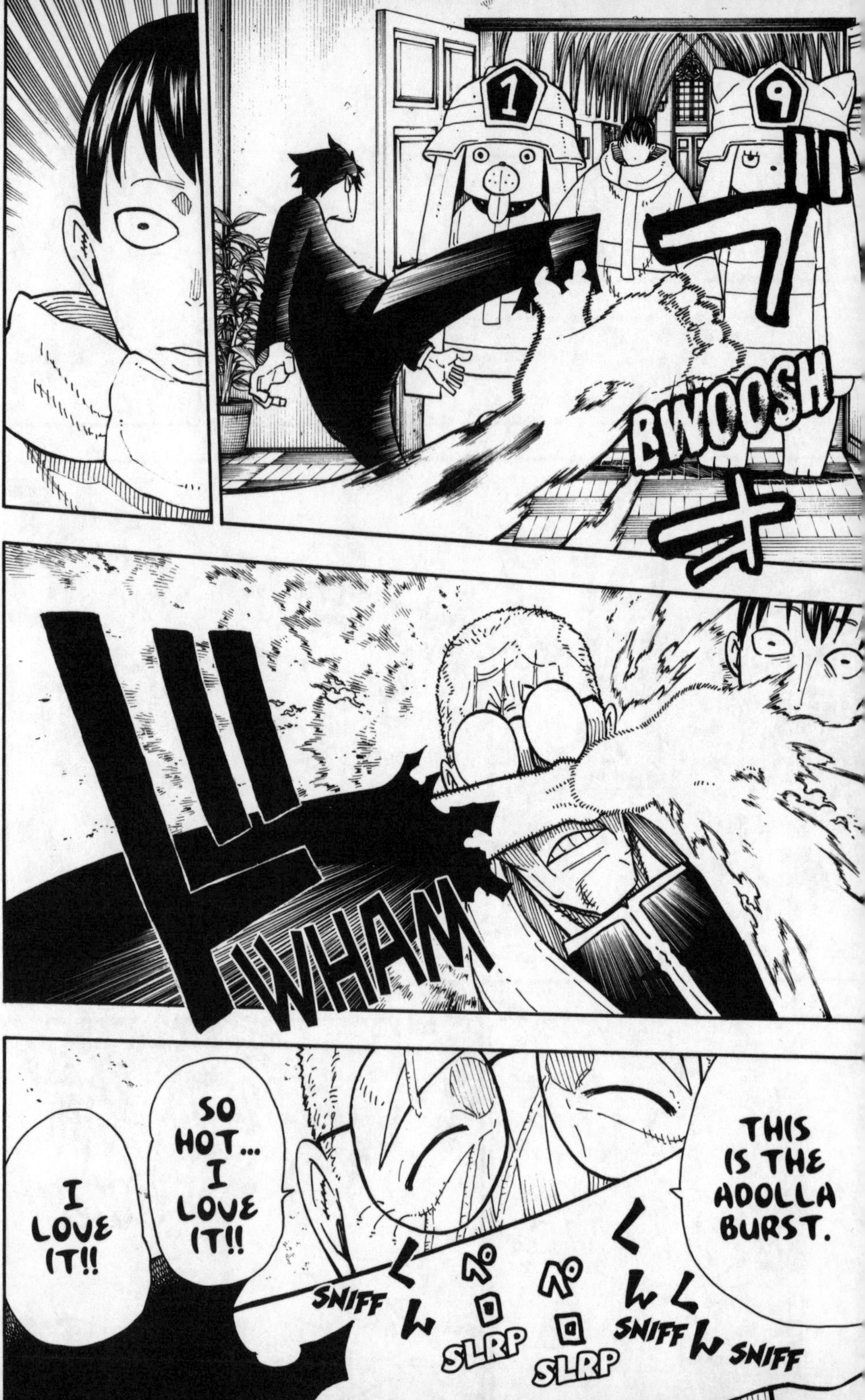
BWOOSH
WHAM
THIS IS THE ADOLLA BURST.
SNIFF
SNIFF
SLRP
SLRP
SNIFF
SO HOT... I LOVE IT!!
I LOVE IT!!

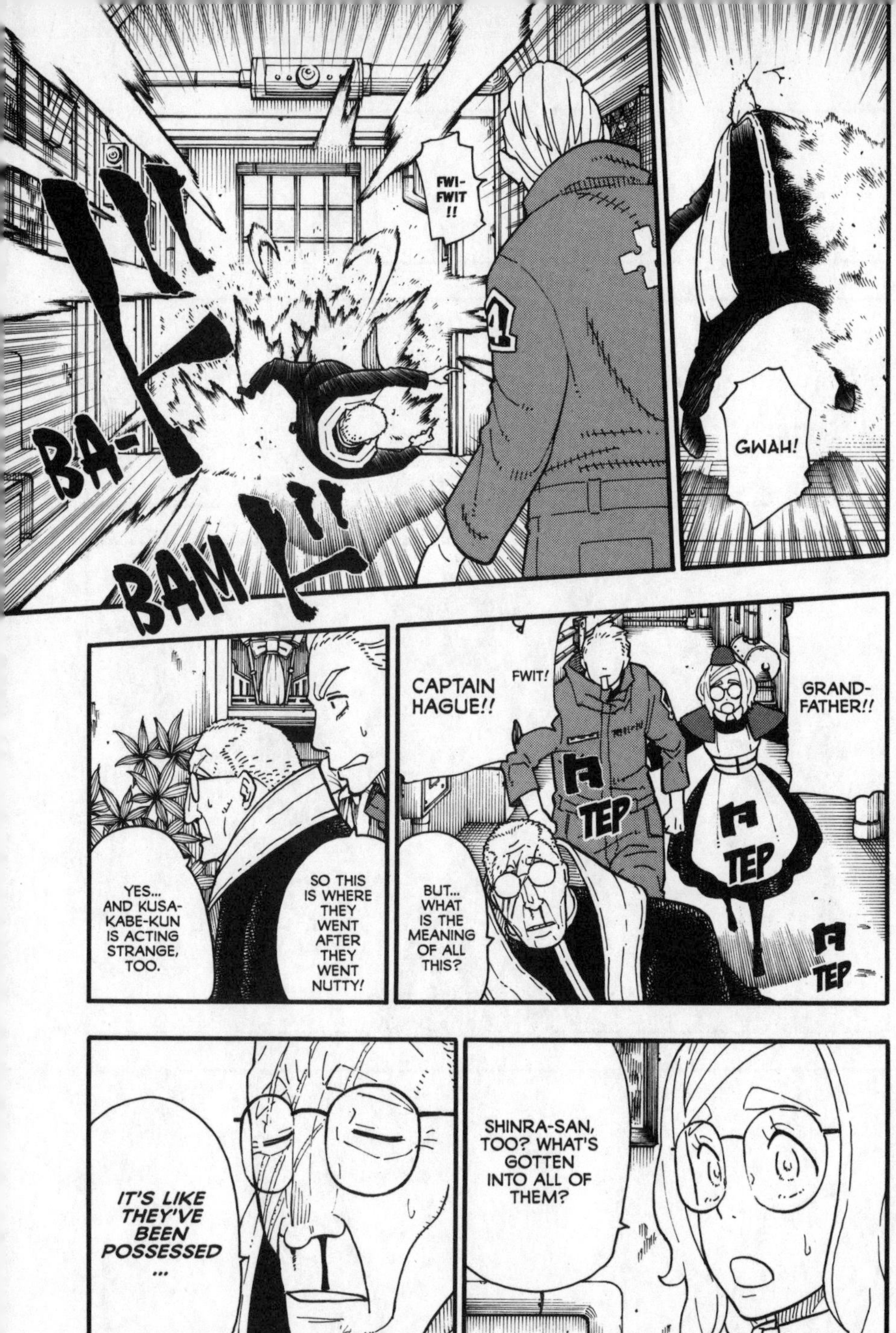

GWAH!
FWI-FWIT!!
BA-
BAM
GRAND-FATHER!!
FWIT!
CAPTAIN HAGUE!!
TEP
TEP
TEP
BUT... WHAT IS THE MEANING OF ALL THIS?
SO THIS IS WHERE THEY WENT AFTER THEY WENT NUTTY!
YES... AND KUSA-KABE-KUN IS ACTING STRANGE, TOO.
SHINRA-SAN, TOO? WHAT'S GOTTEN INTO ALL OF THEM?
IT'S LIKE THEY'VE BEEN POSSESSED...

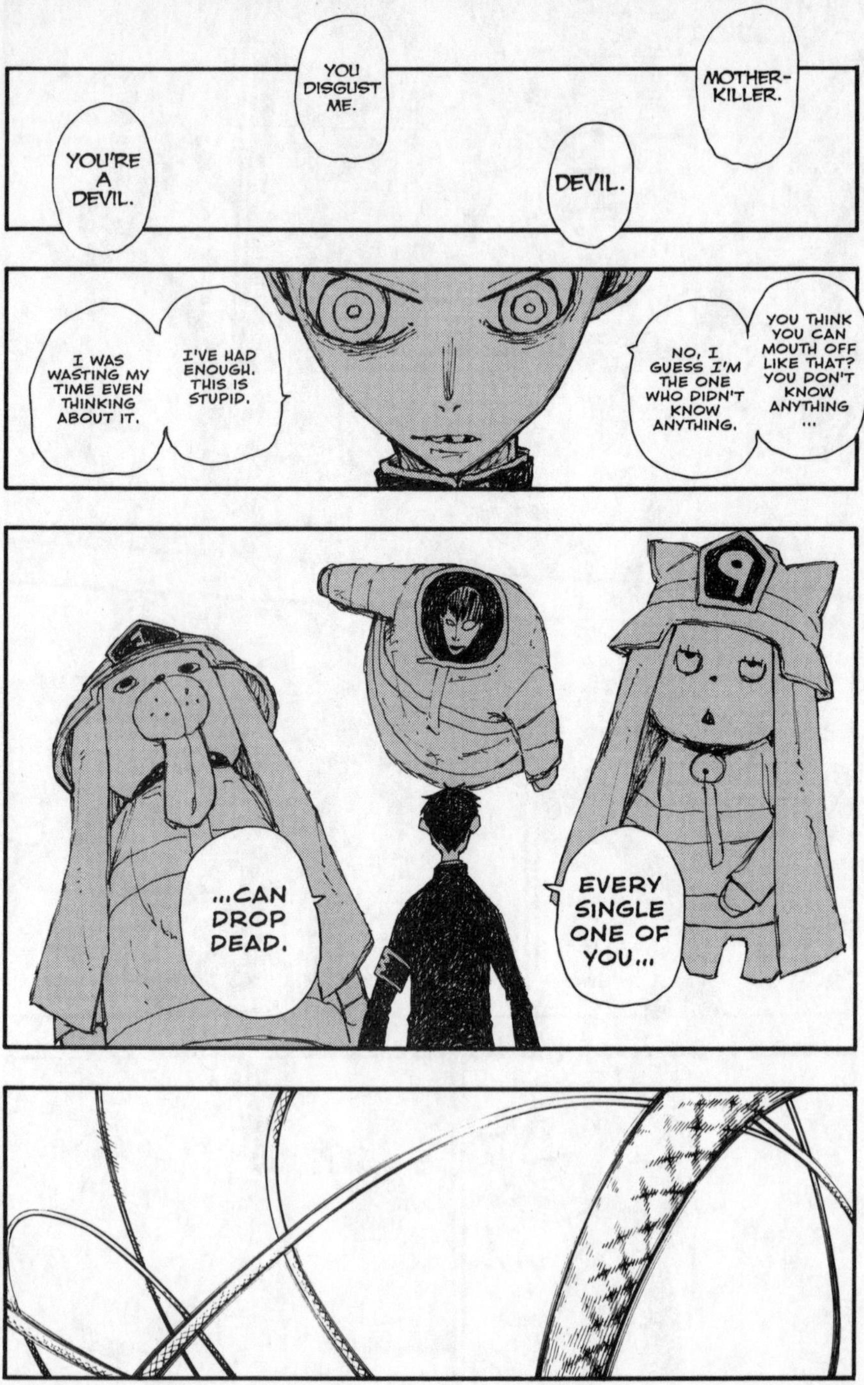
MOTHER-KILLER.
DEVIL.
YOU DISGUST ME.
YOU'RE A DEVIL.
YOU THINK YOU CAN MOUTH OFF LIKE THAT? YOU DON'T KNOW ANYTHING ...
NO, I GUESS I'M THE ONE WHO DIDN'T KNOW ANYTHING.
I'VE HAD ENOUGH. THIS IS STUPID.
I WAS WASTING MY TIME EVEN THINKING ABOUT IT.
EVERY SINGLE ONE OF YOU...
...CAN DROP DEAD.

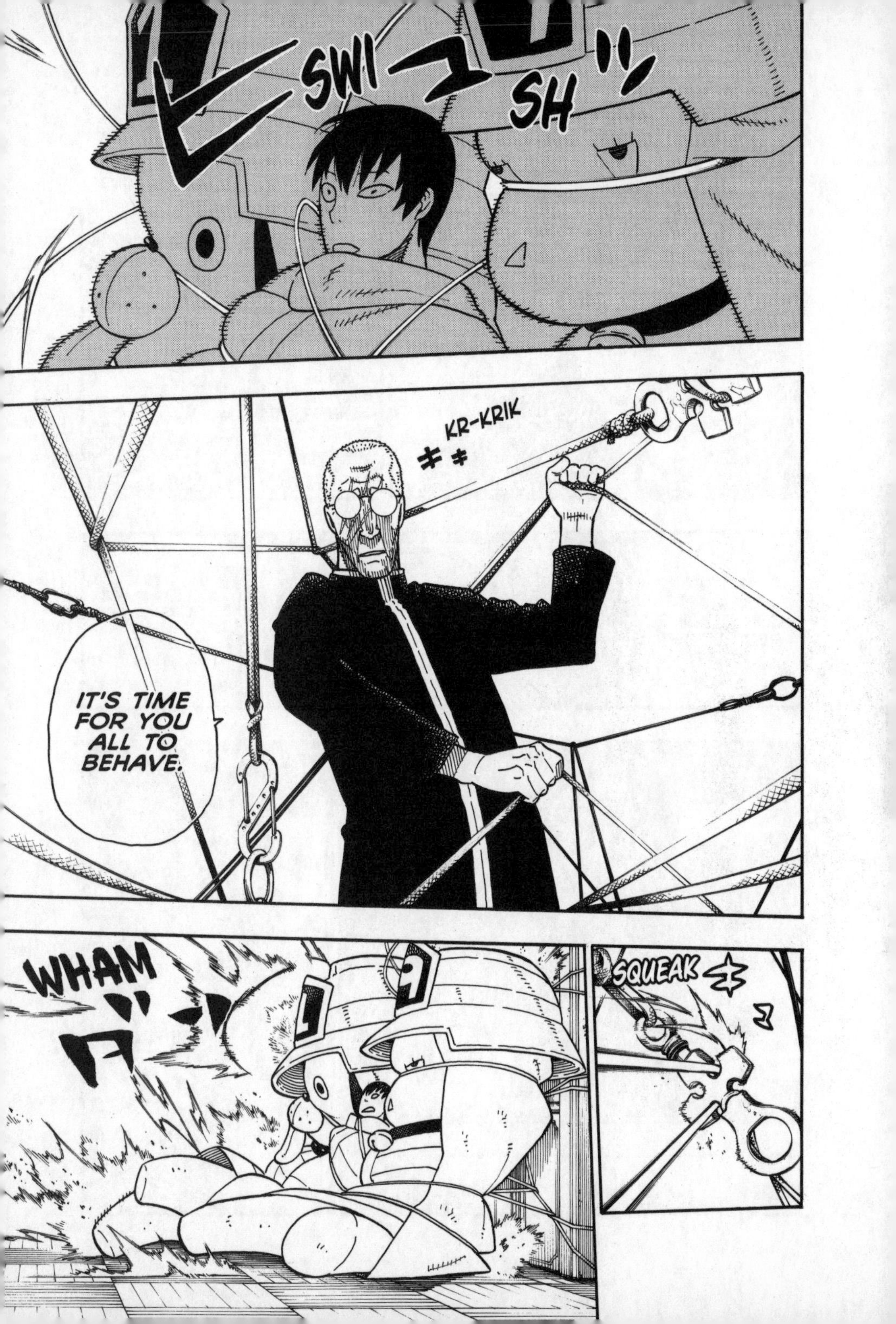
SWI
SH
KR-KRIK
IT'S TIME FOR YOU ALL TO BEHAVE.
SQUEAK
WHAM

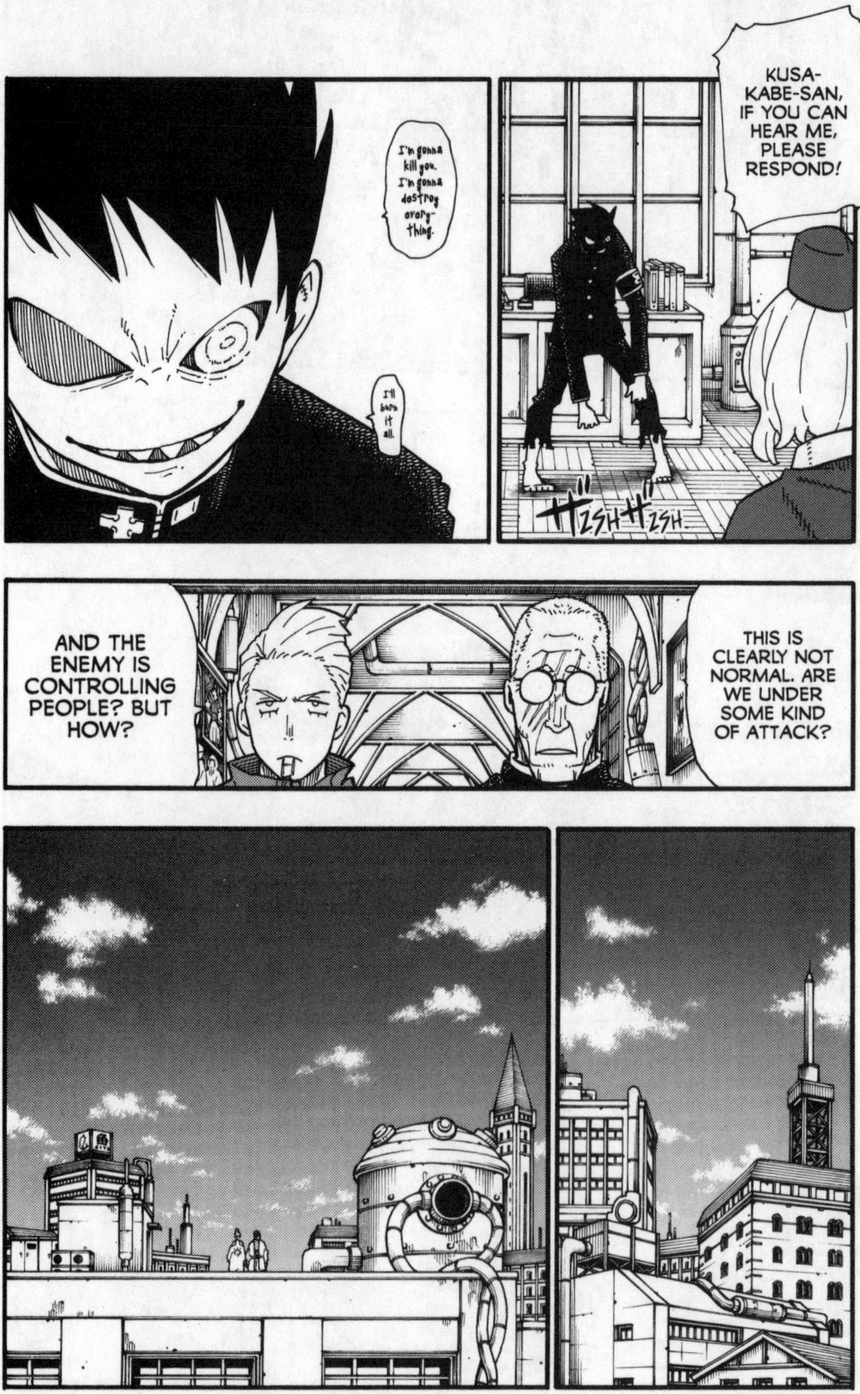
KUSA-KABE-SAN, IF YOU CAN HEAR ME, PLEASE RESPOND!
ZSH ZSH
I'm gonna kill you. I'm gonna destroy every-thing.
I'll burn it all.
THIS IS CLEARLY NOT NORMAL. ARE WE UNDER SOME KIND OF ATTACK?
AND THE ENEMY IS CONTROLLING PEOPLE? BUT HOW?

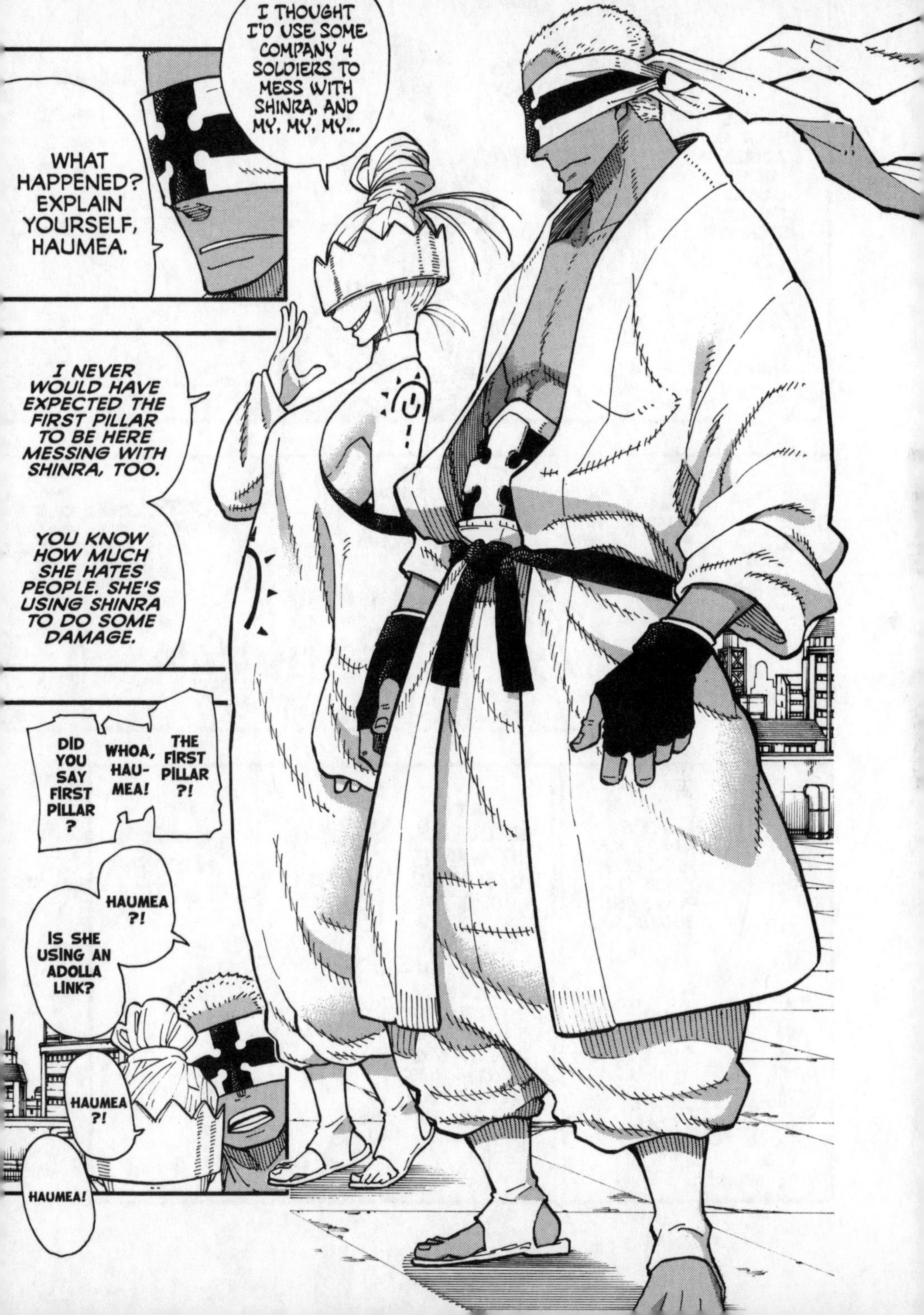
WHAT HAPPENED? EXPLAIN YOURSELF, HAUMEA.
I THOUGHT I'D USE SOME COMPANY 4 SOLDIERS TO MESS WITH SHINRA, AND MY, MY, MY...
I NEVER WOULD HAVE EXPECTED THE FIRST PILLAR TO BE HERE MESSING WITH SHINRA, TOO.
YOU KNOW HOW MUCH SHE HATES PEOPLE. SHE'S USING SHINRA TO DO SOME DAMAGE.
THE FIRST PILLAR ?!
WHOA, HAU-MEA!
DID YOU SAY FIRST PILLAR ?
HAUMEA ?!
IS SHE USING AN ADOLLA LINK?
HAUMEA ?!
HAUMEA!

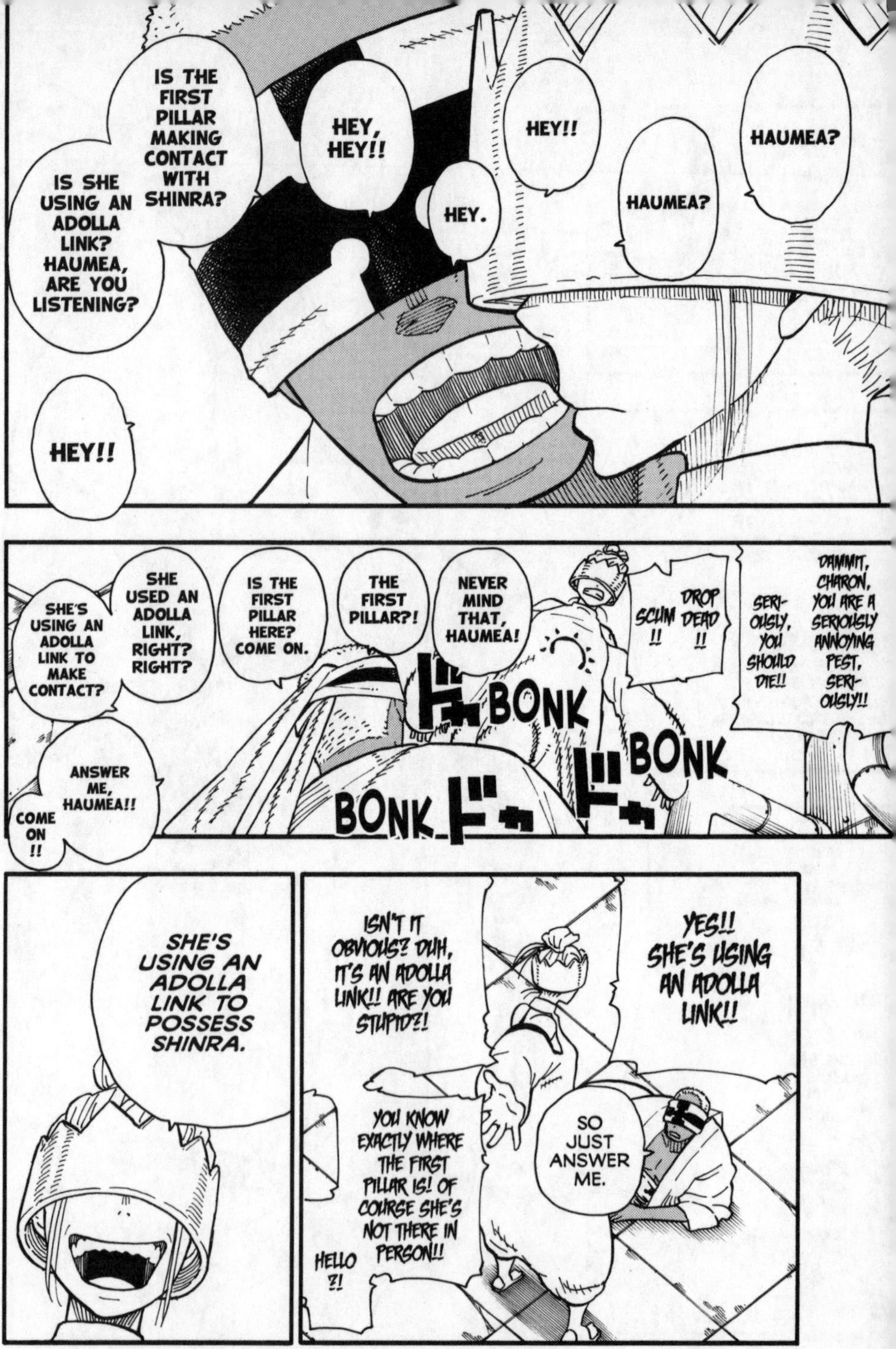
HAUMEA?
HAUMEA?
HEY!!
HEY.
HEY, HEY!!
IS THE FIRST PILLAR MAKING CONTACT WITH SHINRA?
IS SHE USING AN ADOLLA LINK? HAUMEA, ARE YOU LISTENING?
HEY!!
DAMMIT, CHARON, YOU ARE A SERIOUSLY ANNOYING PEST, SERIOUSLY!!
SERIOUSLY, YOU SHOULD DIE!!
DROP DEAD!!
SCUM!!
NEVER MIND THAT, HAUMEA!
THE FIRST PILLAR?!
IS THE FIRST PILLAR HERE? COME ON.
SHE USED AN ADOLLA LINK, RIGHT? RIGHT?
SHE'S USING AN ADOLLA LINK TO MAKE CONTACT?
BONK
BONK
BONK
ANSWER ME, HAUMEA!!
COME ON!!
YES!! SHE'S USING AN ADOLLA LINK!!
ISN'T IT OBVIOUS? DUH, IT'S AN ADOLLA LINK!! ARE YOU STUPID?!
SO JUST ANSWER ME.
YOU KNOW EXACTLY WHERE THE FIRST PILLAR IS! OF COURSE SHE'S NOT THERE IN PERSON!!
HELLO?!
SHE'S USING AN ADOLLA LINK TO POSSESS SHINRA.

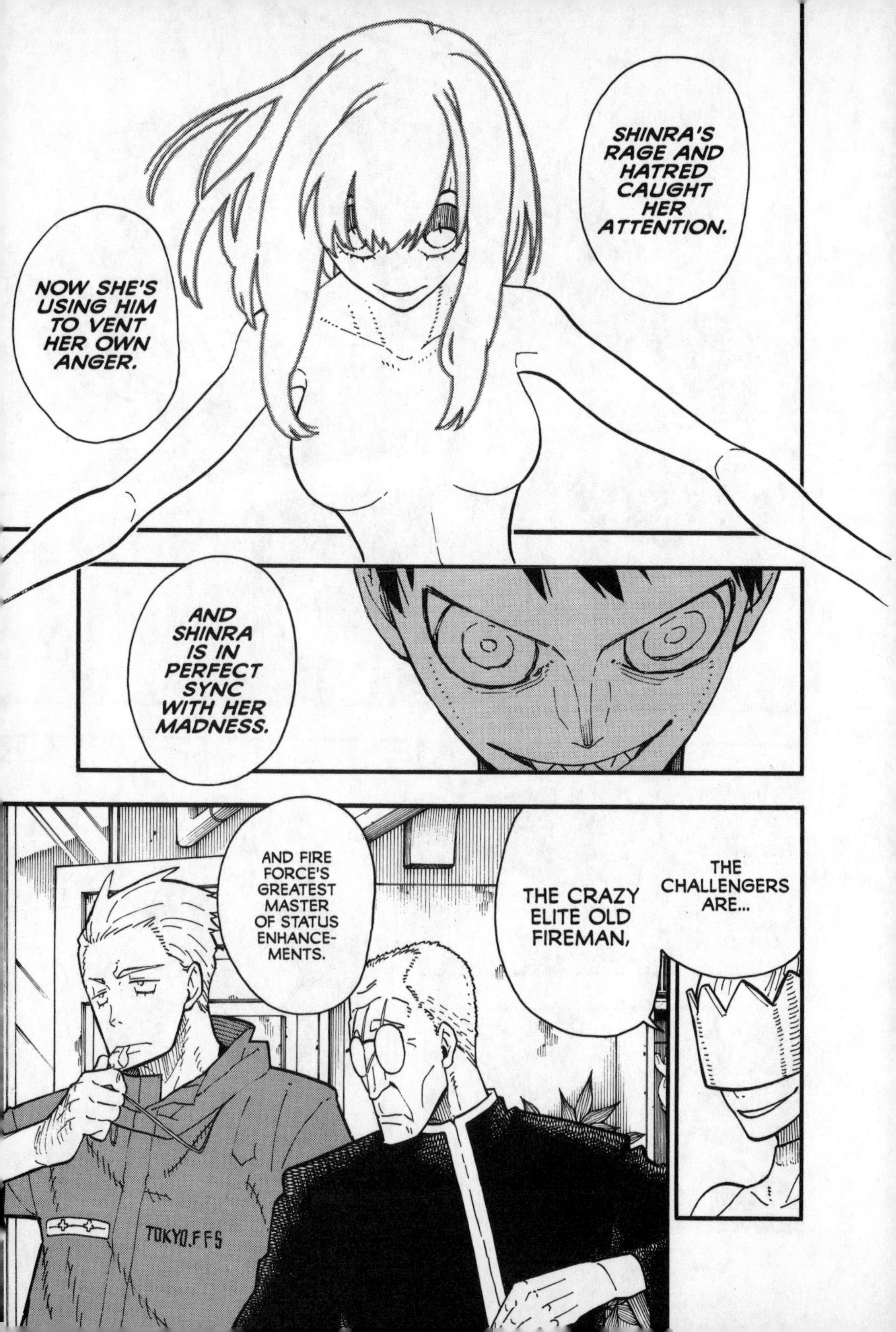
SHINRA'S RAGE AND HATRED CAUGHT HER ATTENTION.
NOW SHE'S USING HIM TO VENT HER OWN ANGER.
AND SHINRA IS IN PERFECT SYNC WITH HER MADNESS.
THE CHALLENGERS ARE...
THE CRAZY ELITE OLD FIREMAN,
AND FIRE FORCE'S GREATEST MASTER OF STATUS ENHANCE-MENTS.
TOKYO.FFS

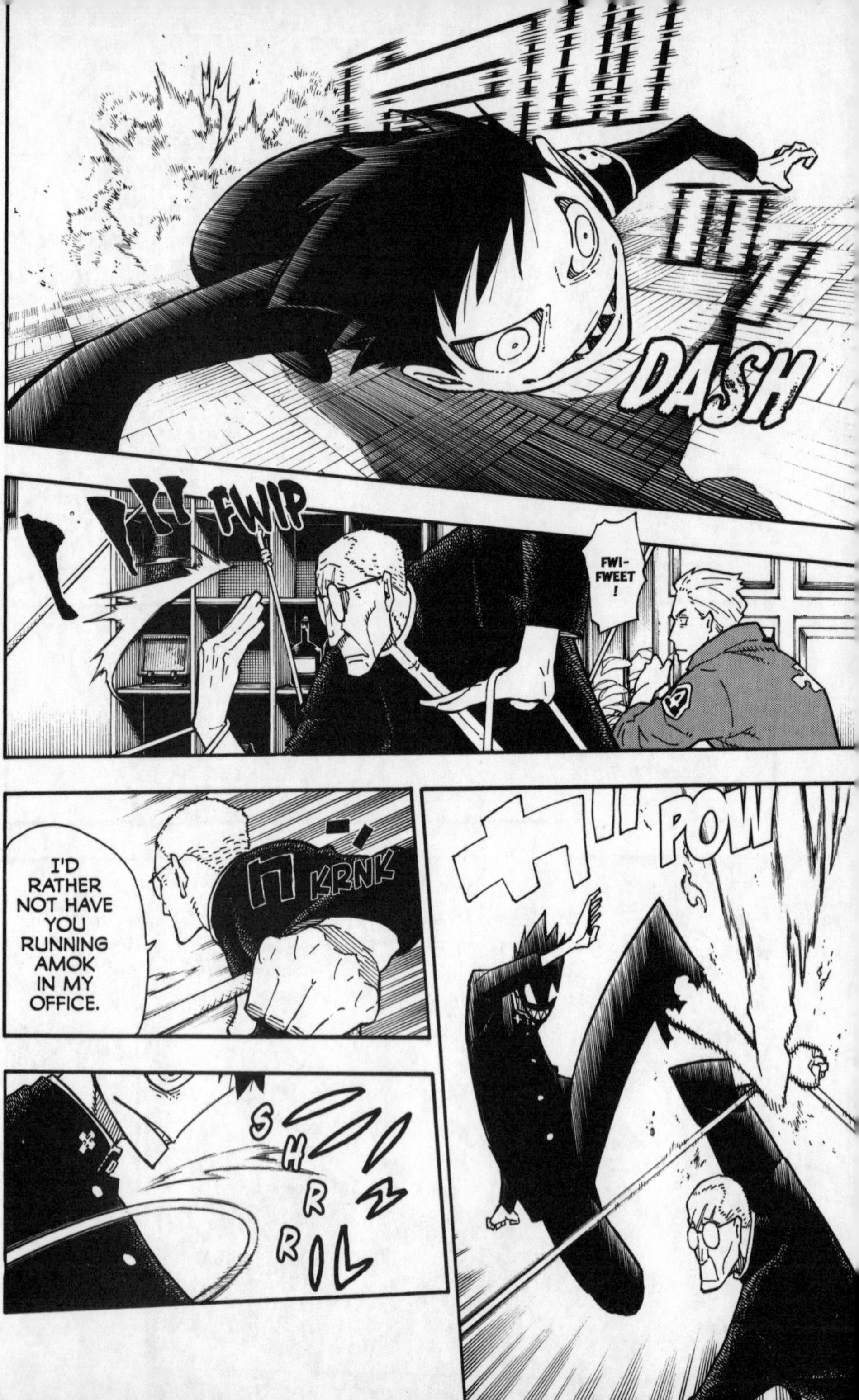
DASH
FWI-FWEET!
FWIP
POW
I'D RATHER NOT HAVE YOU RUNNING AMOK IN MY OFFICE.
KRNK
SHRRIL

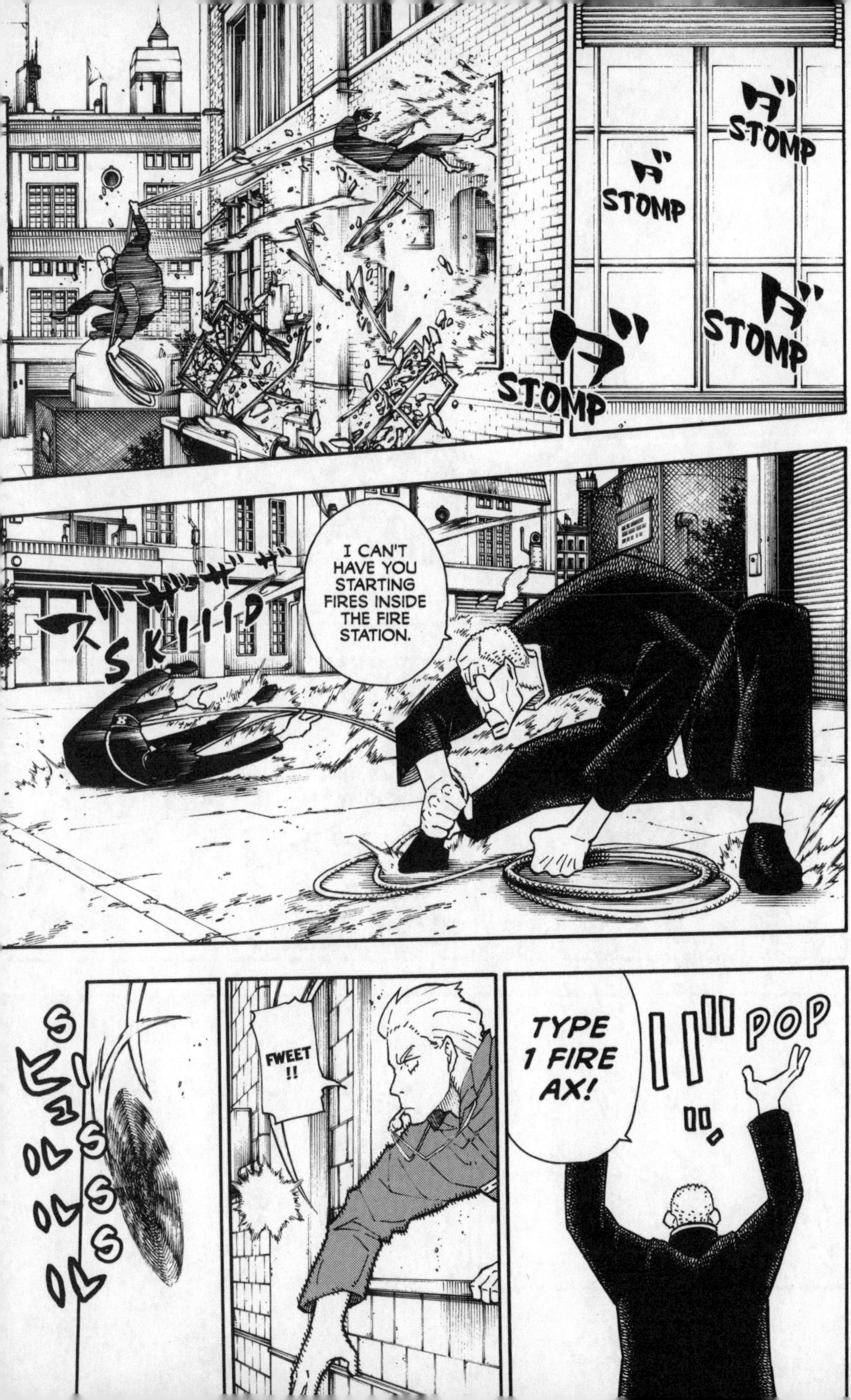
STOMP
STOMP
STOMP
STOMP
I CAN'T HAVE YOU STARTING FIRES INSIDE THE FIRE STATION.
SKIIID
TYPE 1 FIRE AX!
POP
FWEET !!
SSSS

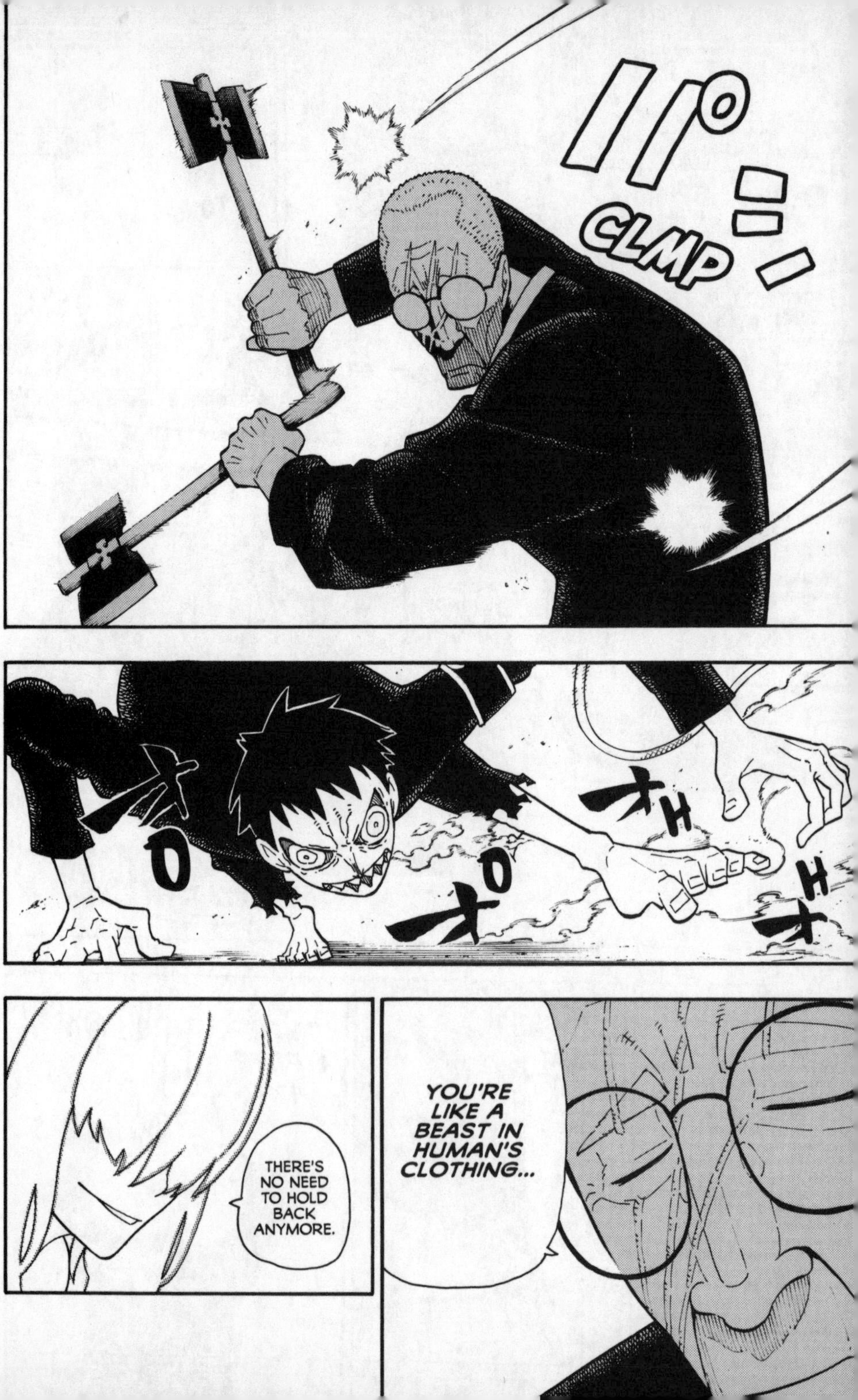
CLMP
YOU'RE LIKE A BEAST IN HUMAN'S CLOTHING...
THERE'S NO NEED TO HOLD BACK ANYMORE.

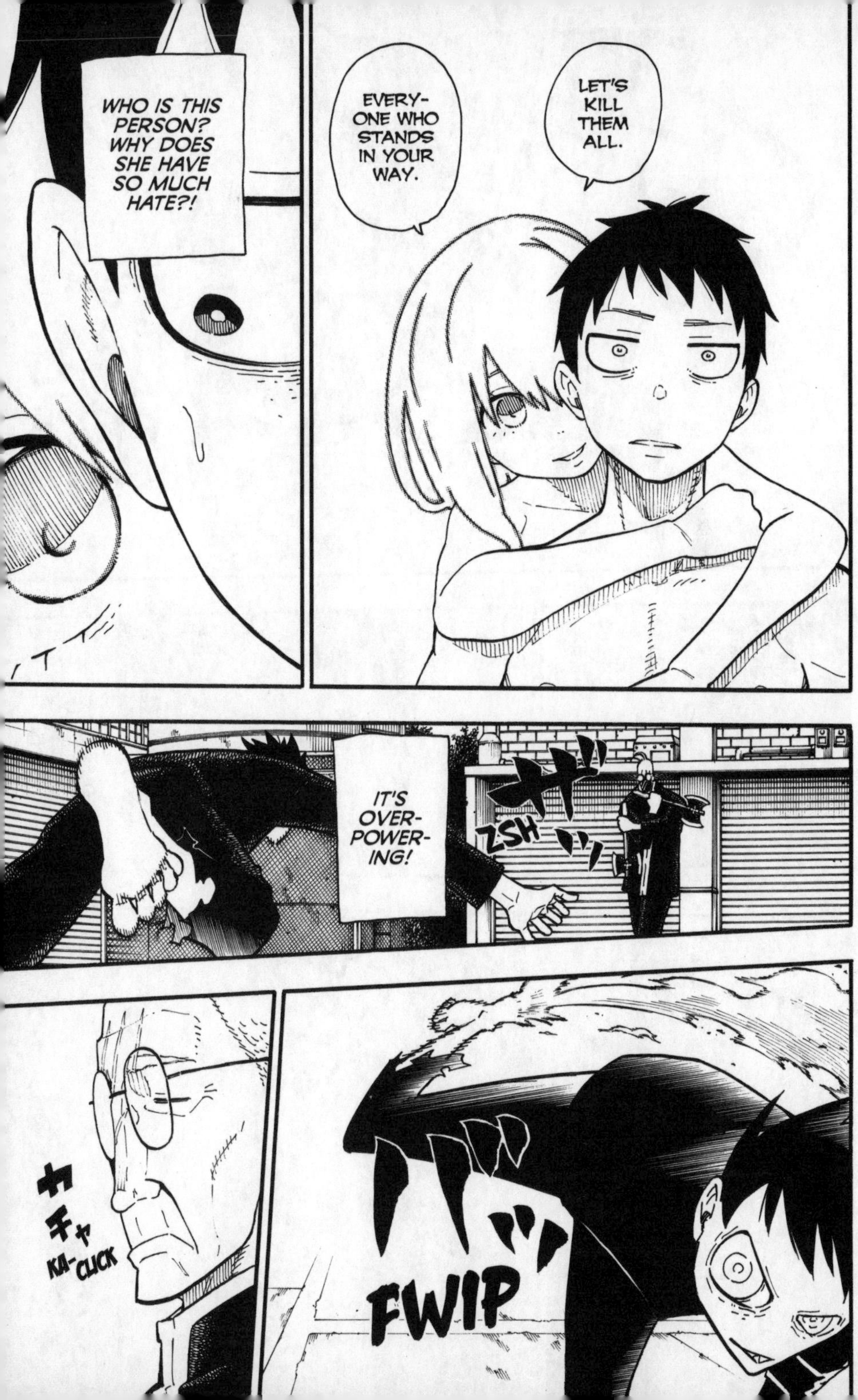
LET'S KILL THEM ALL.
EVERY-ONE WHO STANDS IN YOUR WAY.
WHO IS THIS PERSON? WHY DOES SHE HAVE SO MUCH HATE?!
ZSH
IT'S OVER-POWERING!
FWIP
カチャ
KA-CLICK

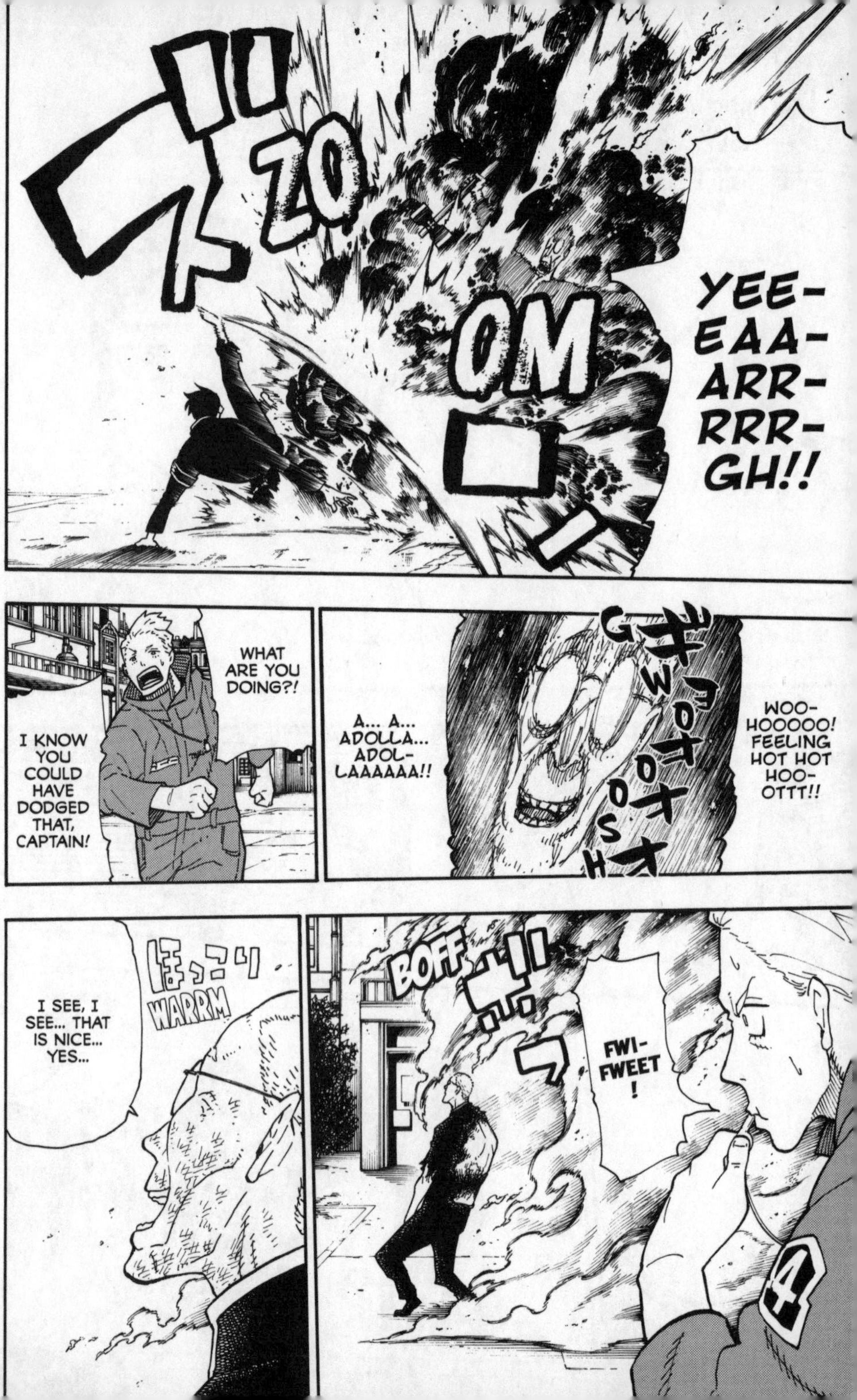

YEE-EAA-ARR-RRR-GH!!
ZO
OM
WOO-HOOOOO! FEELING HOT HOT HOO-OTTT!!
GWOOOSH
A... A... ADOLLA... ADOL-LAAAAAA!!
WHAT ARE YOU DOING?!
I KNOW YOU COULD HAVE DODGED THAT, CAPTAIN!
FWI-FWEET!
BOFF
WARRM
I SEE, I SEE... THAT IS NICE... YES...

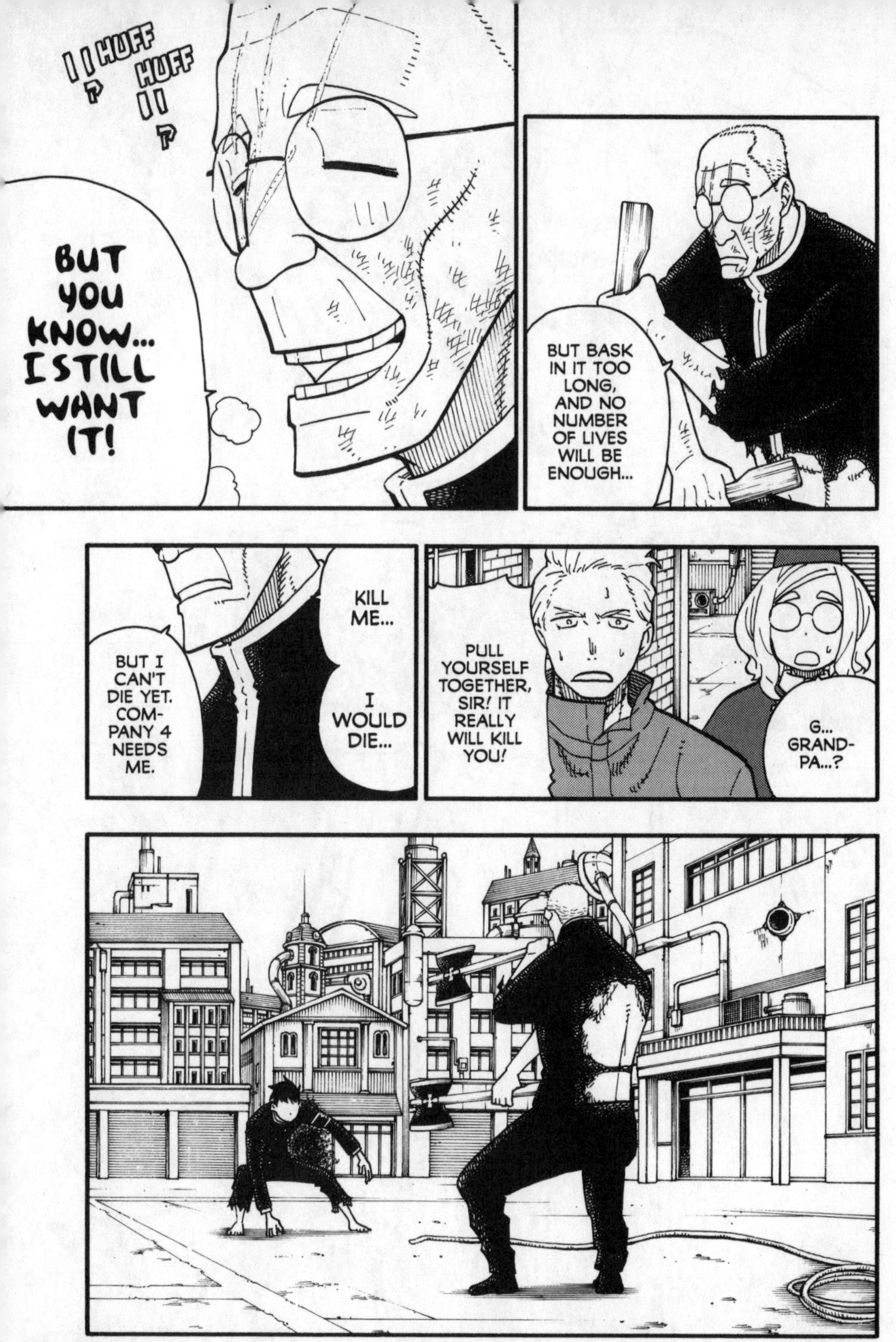
BUT BASK IN IT TOO LONG, AND NO NUMBER OF LIVES WILL BE ENOUGH...
HUFF
HUFF
BUT YOU KNOW... I STILL WANT IT!
G... GRANDPA...?
PULL YOURSELF TOGETHER, SIR! IT REALLY WILL KILL YOU!
KILL ME...
I WOULD DIE...
BUT I CAN'T DIE YET. COMPANY 4 NEEDS ME.

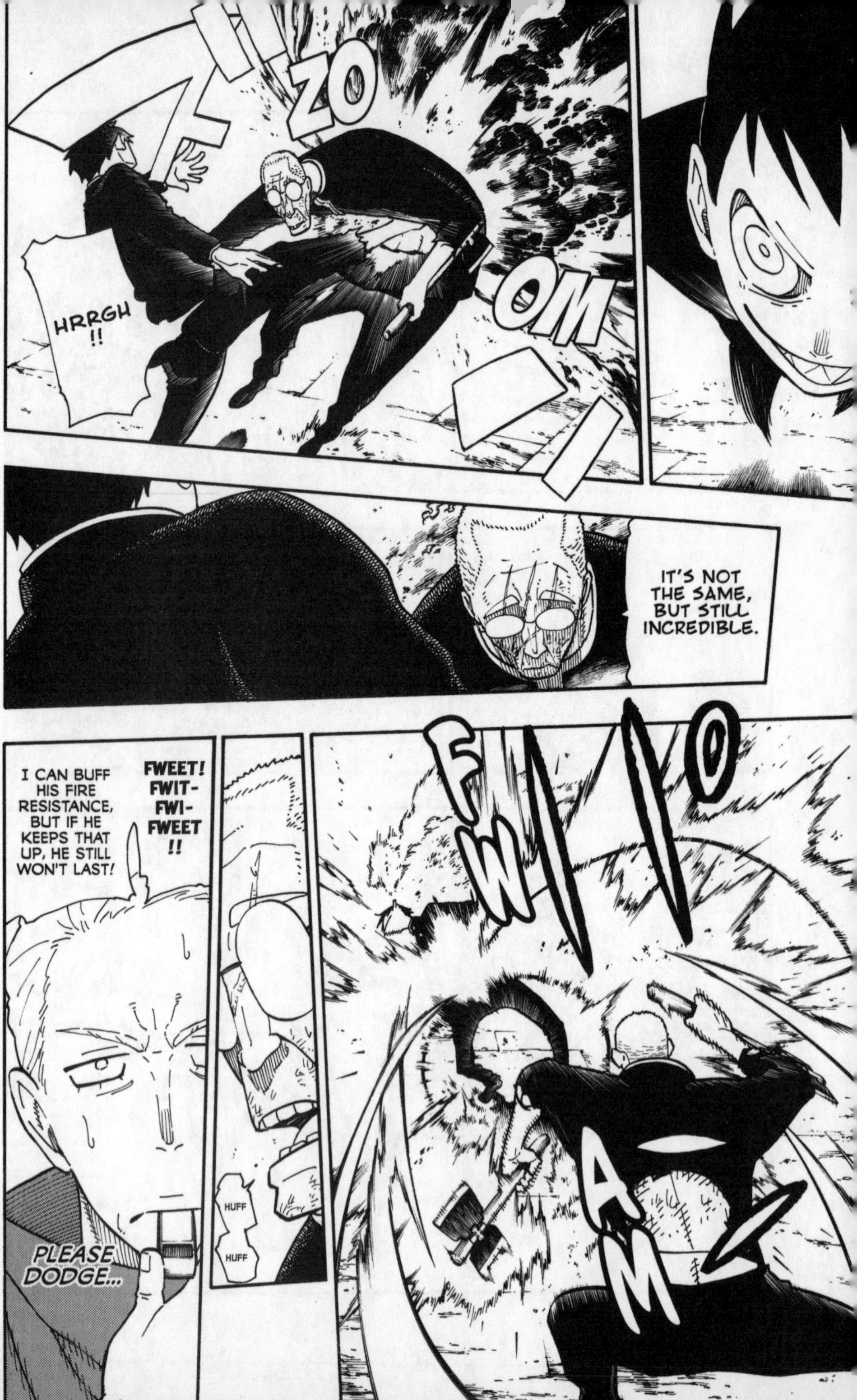
HRRGH !!
IT'S NOT THE SAME, BUT STILL INCREDIBLE.
FWEET! FWIT-FWI-FWEET !!
HUFF
HUFF
I CAN BUFF HIS FIRE RESISTANCE, BUT IF HE KEEPS THAT UP, HE STILL WON'T LAST!
PLEASE DODGE...

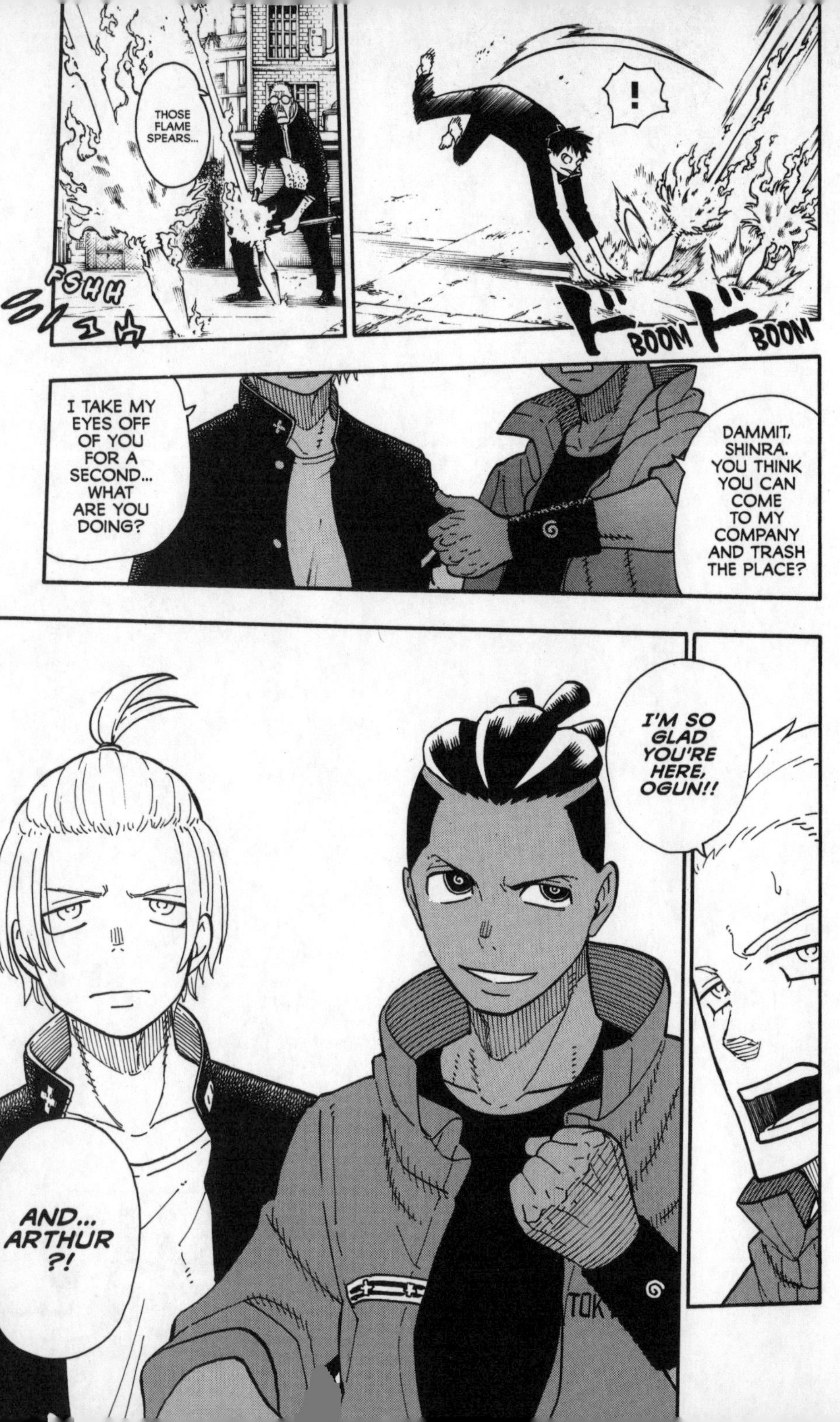
!
BOOM
BOOM
THOSE FLAME SPEARS...
FSHH
DAMMIT, SHINRA. YOU THINK YOU CAN COME TO MY COMPANY AND TRASH THE PLACE?
I TAKE MY EYES OFF OF YOU FOR A SECOND... WHAT ARE YOU DOING?
I'M SO GLAD YOU'RE HERE, OGUN!!
AND... ARTHUR?!

FIRE FORCE

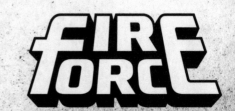

CHAPTER XCVI: OLD FRIENDS UNITED

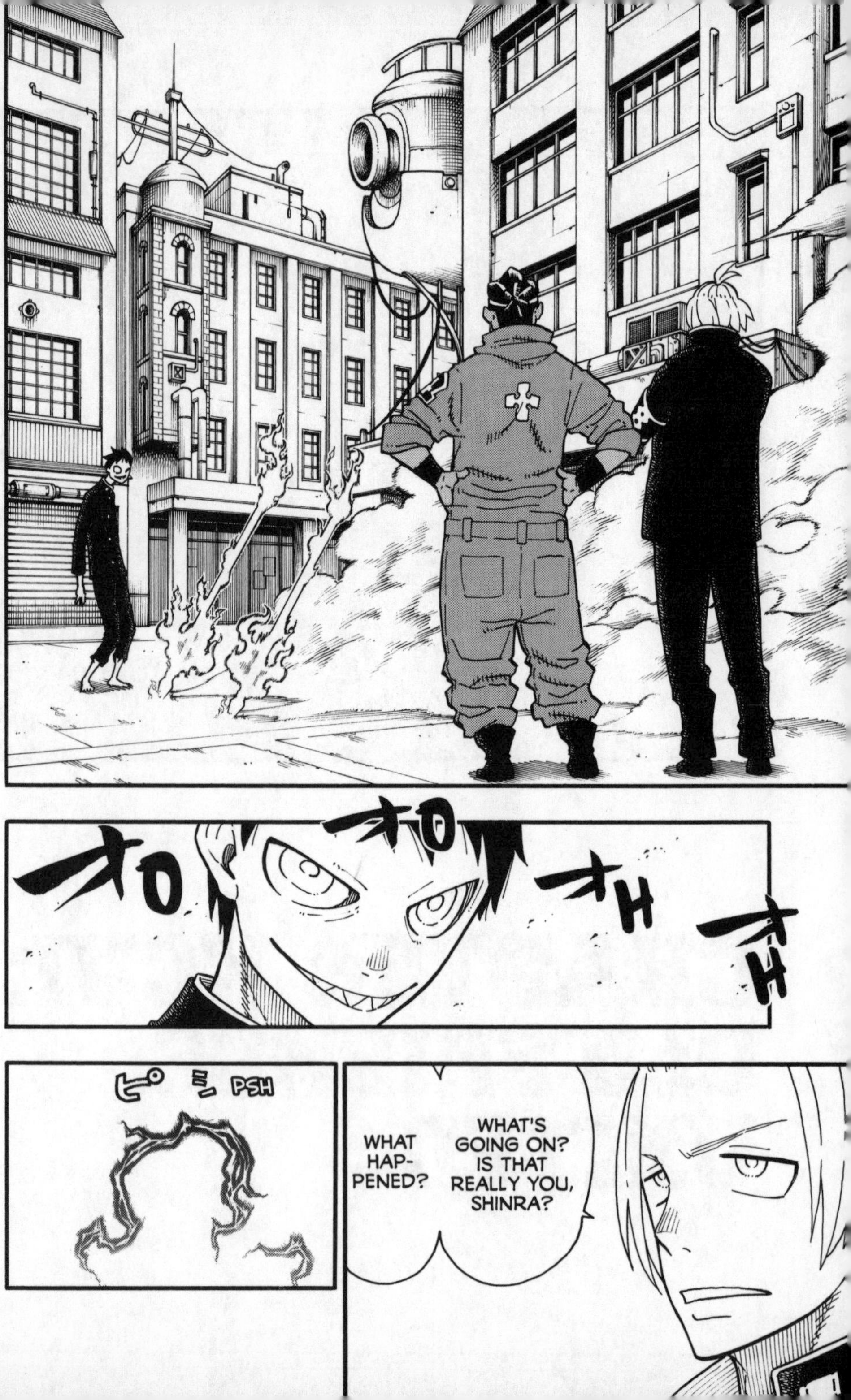
WHAT'S GOING ON? IS THAT REALLY YOU, SHINRA?
WHAT HAP-PENED?
PSH

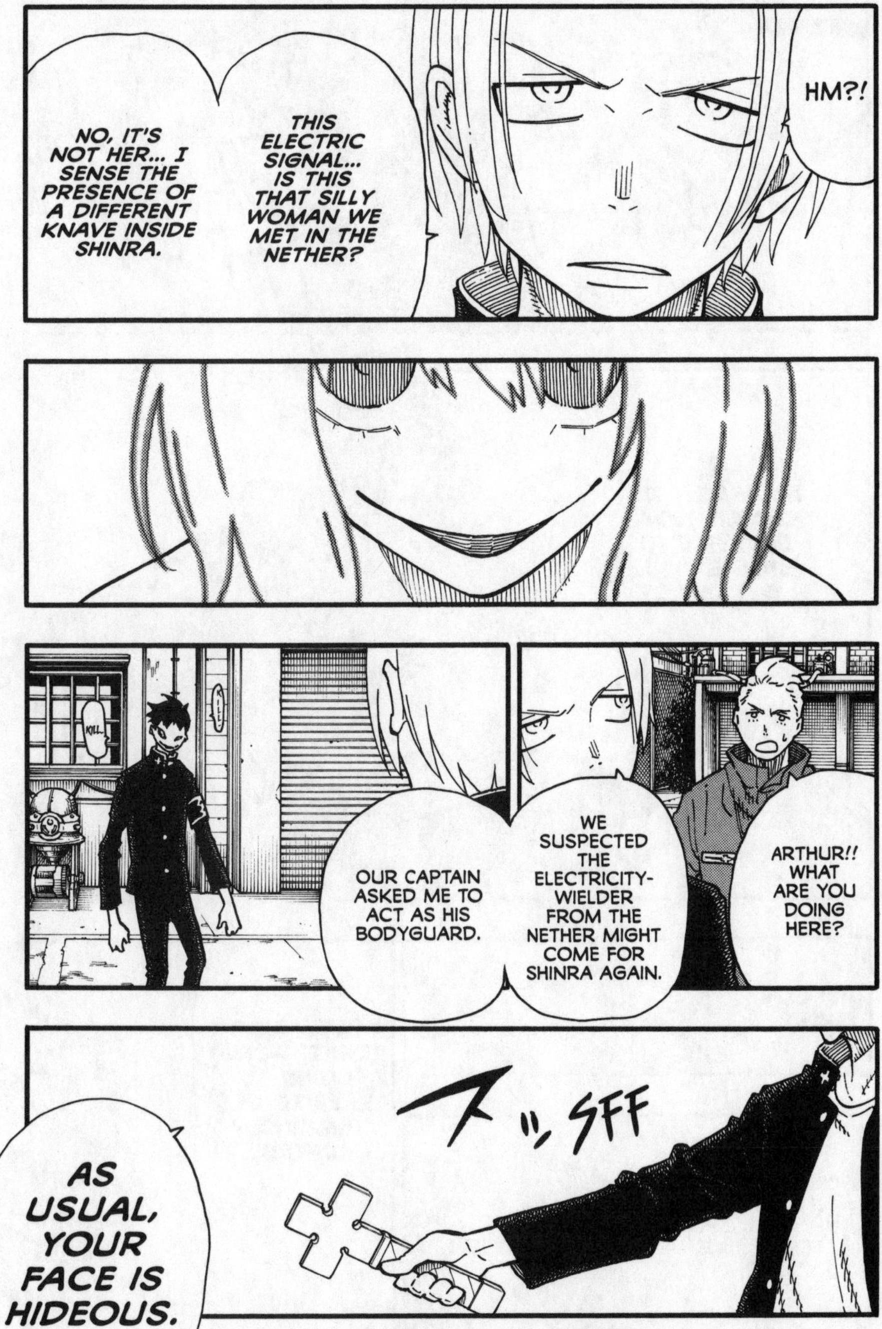
HM?!
THIS ELECTRIC SIGNAL... IS THIS THAT SILLY WOMAN WE MET IN THE NETHER?
NO, IT'S NOT HER... I SENSE THE PRESENCE OF A DIFFERENT KNAVE INSIDE SHINRA.
ARTHUR!! WHAT ARE YOU DOING HERE?
WE SUSPECTED THE ELECTRICITY-WIELDER FROM THE NETHER MIGHT COME FOR SHINRA AGAIN.
OUR CAPTAIN ASKED ME TO ACT AS HIS BODYGUARD.
KILL...
SFF
AS USUAL, YOUR FACE IS HIDEOUS.

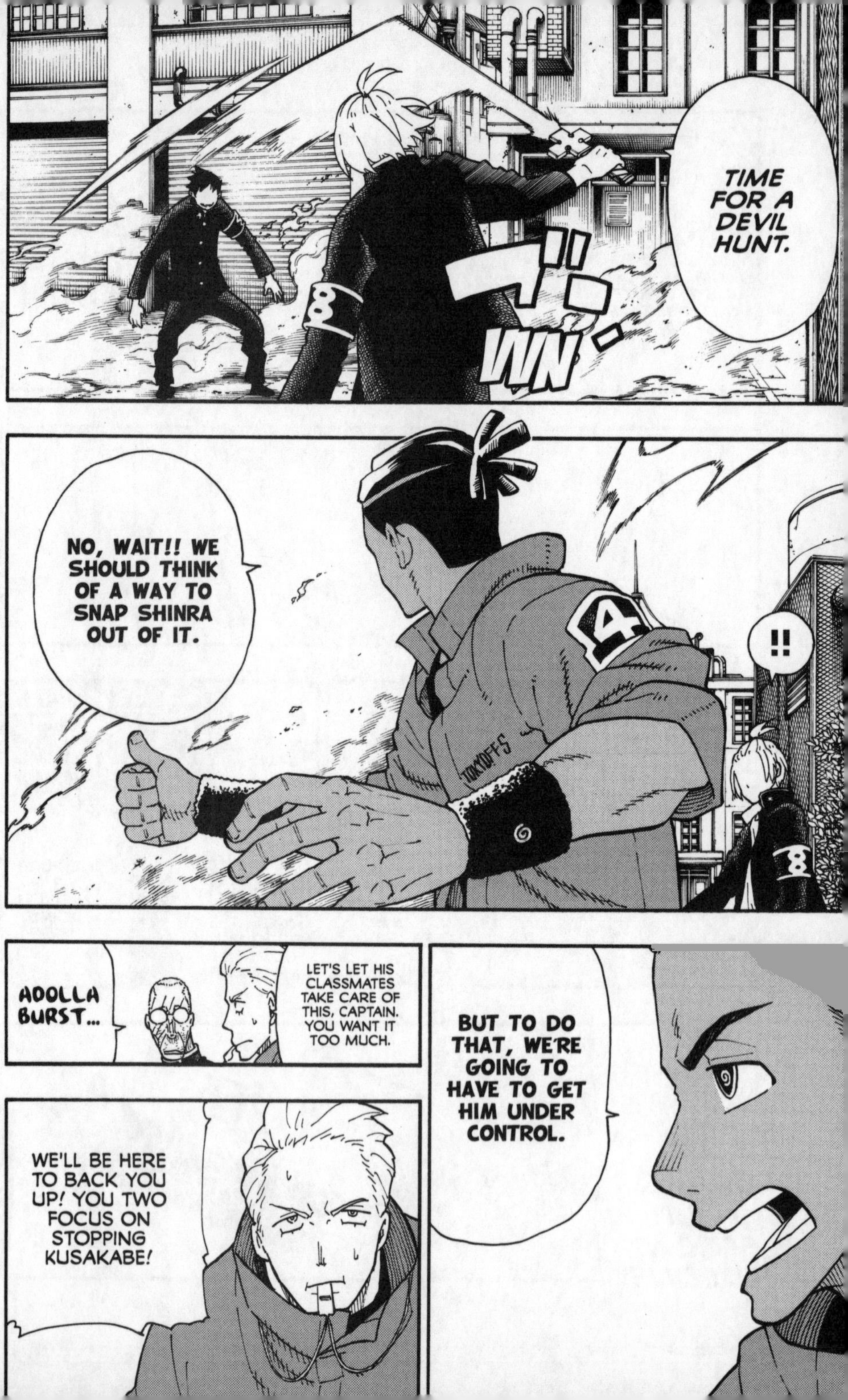
TIME FOR A DEVIL HUNT.
VVN
NO, WAIT!! WE SHOULD THINK OF A WAY TO SNAP SHINRA OUT OF IT.
!!
BUT TO DO THAT, WE'RE GOING TO HAVE TO GET HIM UNDER CONTROL.
LET'S LET HIS CLASSMATES TAKE CARE OF THIS, CAPTAIN. YOU WANT IT TOO MUCH.
ADOLLA BURST...
WE'LL BE HERE TO BACK YOU UP! YOU TWO FOCUS ON STOPPING KUSAKABE!

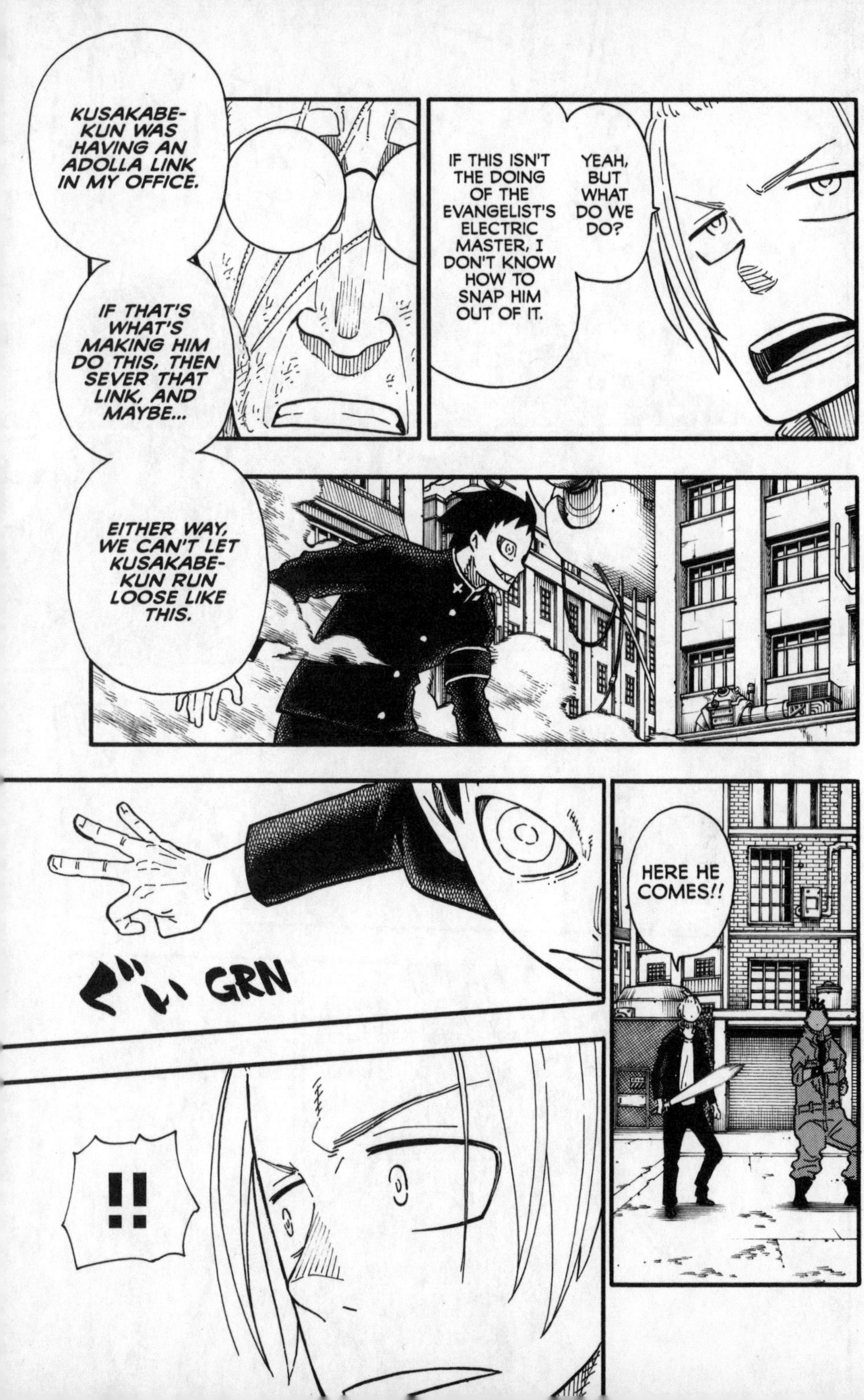
YEAH, BUT WHAT DO WE DO?
IF THIS ISN'T THE DOING OF THE EVANGELIST'S ELECTRIC MASTER, I DON'T KNOW HOW TO SNAP HIM OUT OF IT.
KUSAKABE-KUN WAS HAVING AN ADOLLA LINK IN MY OFFICE.
IF THAT'S WHAT'S MAKING HIM DO THIS, THEN SEVER THAT LINK, AND MAYBE...
EITHER WAY, WE CAN'T LET KUSAKABE-KUN RUN LOOSE LIKE THIS.
HERE HE COMES!!
ぐい GRN
!!

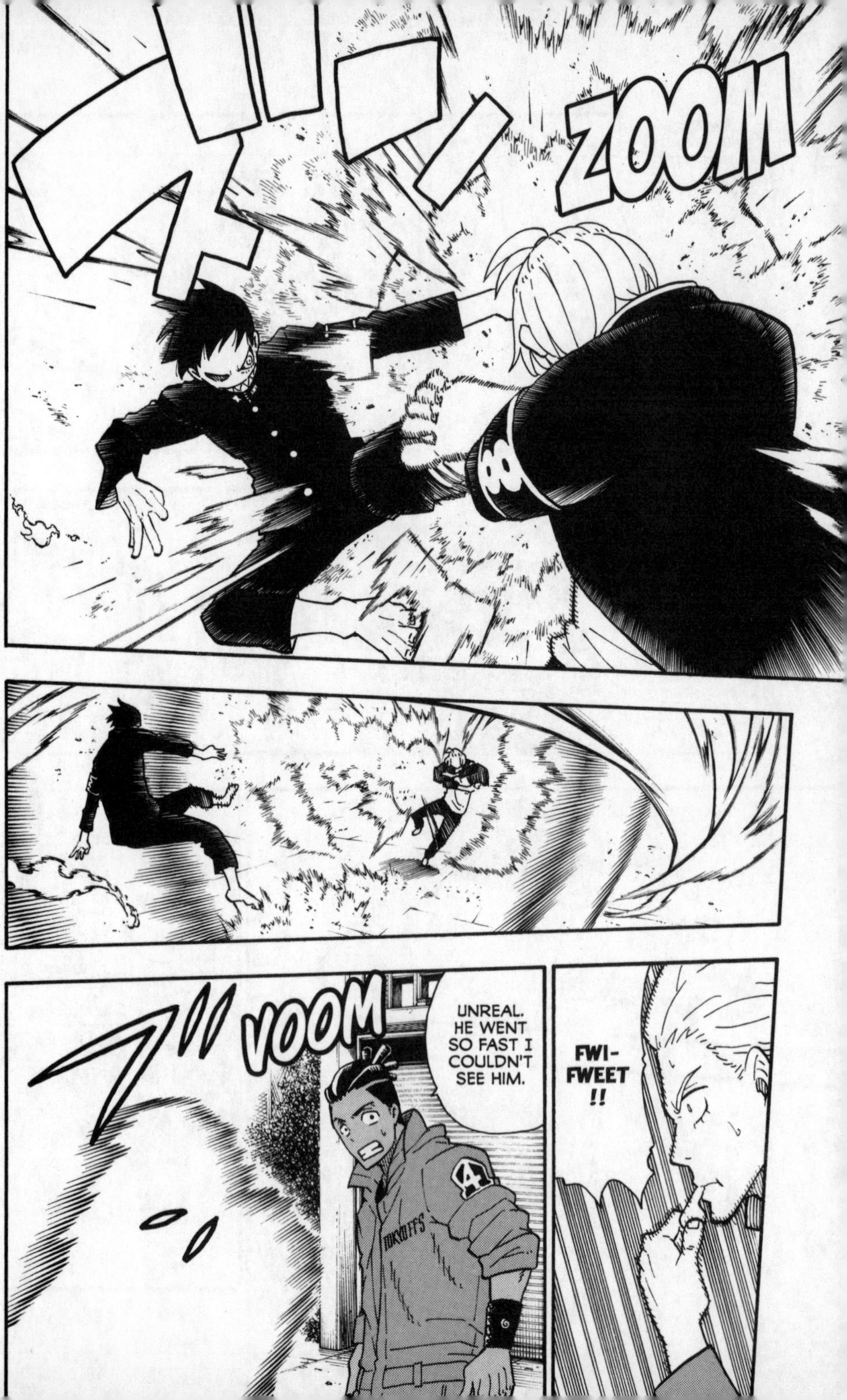
ZOOM
FWI-
FWEET
!!
VOOM
UNREAL. HE WENT SO FAST I COULDN'T SEE HIM.

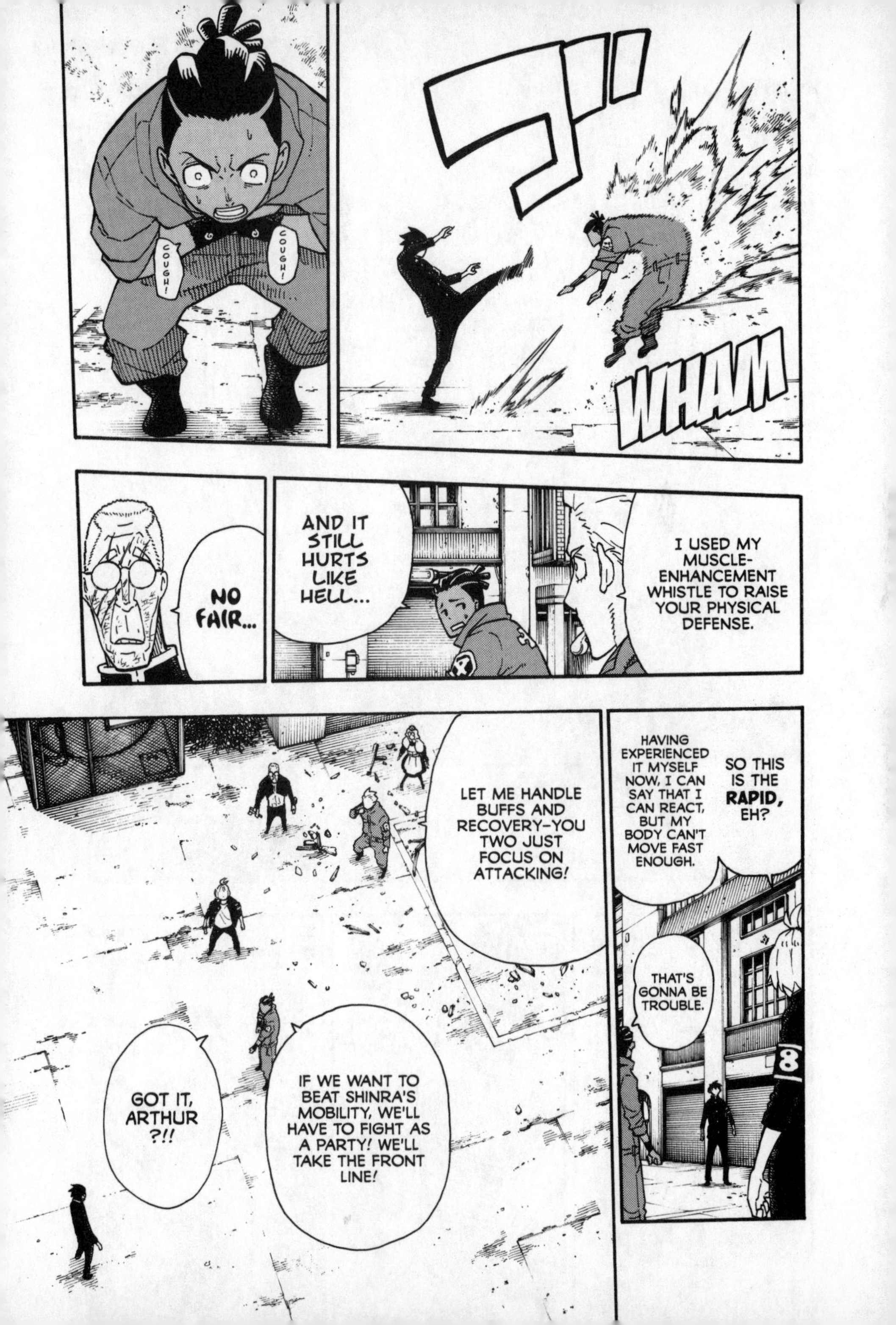

ゴ
WHAM
COUGH!
COUGH!
I USED MY MUSCLE-ENHANCEMENT WHISTLE TO RAISE YOUR PHYSICAL DEFENSE.
AND IT STILL HURTS LIKE HELL...
NO FAIR...
SO THIS IS THE **RAPID,** EH?
HAVING EXPERIENCED IT MYSELF NOW, I CAN SAY THAT I CAN REACT, BUT MY BODY CAN'T MOVE FAST ENOUGH.
THAT'S GONNA BE TROUBLE.
LET ME HANDLE BUFFS AND RECOVERY–YOU TWO JUST FOCUS ON ATTACKING!
IF WE WANT TO BEAT SHINRA'S MOBILITY, WE'LL HAVE TO FIGHT AS A PARTY! WE'LL TAKE THE FRONT LINE!
GOT IT, ARTHUR?!!

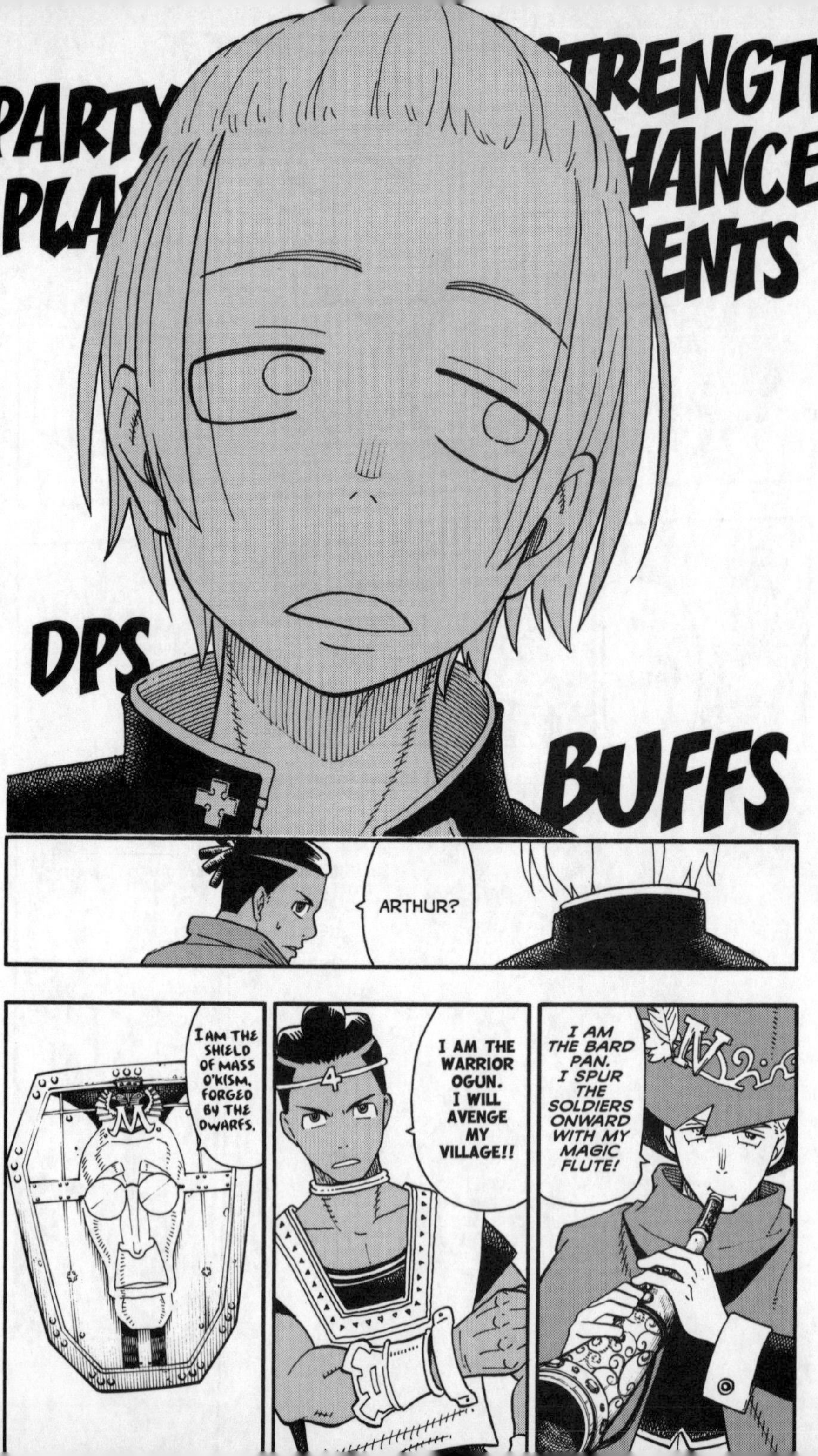

STRENGTH
HANCE-
ENTS
PARTY
PLA
DPS
BUFFS
ARTHUR?
I AM THE BARD PAN. I SPUR THE SOLDIERS ONWARD WITH MY MAGIC FLUTE!
I AM THE WARRIOR OGUN. I WILL AVENGE MY VILLAGE!!
I AM THE SHIELD OF MASS O'KISM, FORGED BY THE DWARFS.

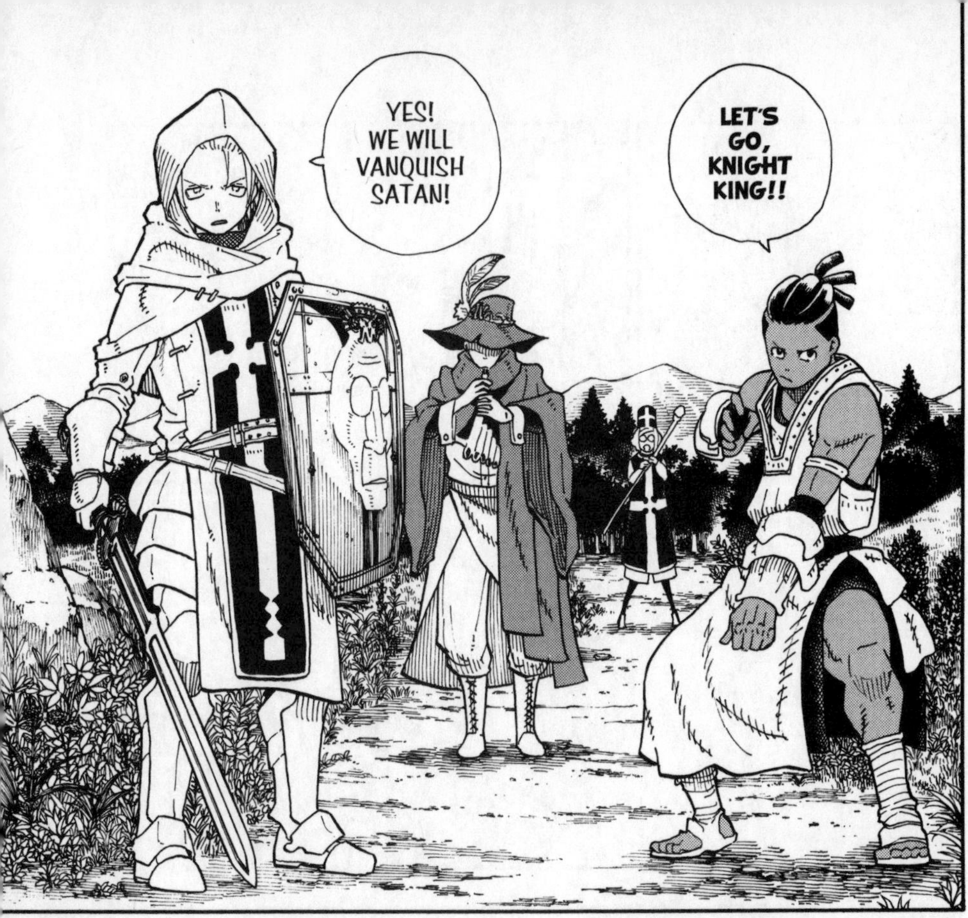
LET'S GO, KNIGHT KING!!
YES! WE WILL VANQUISH SATAN!
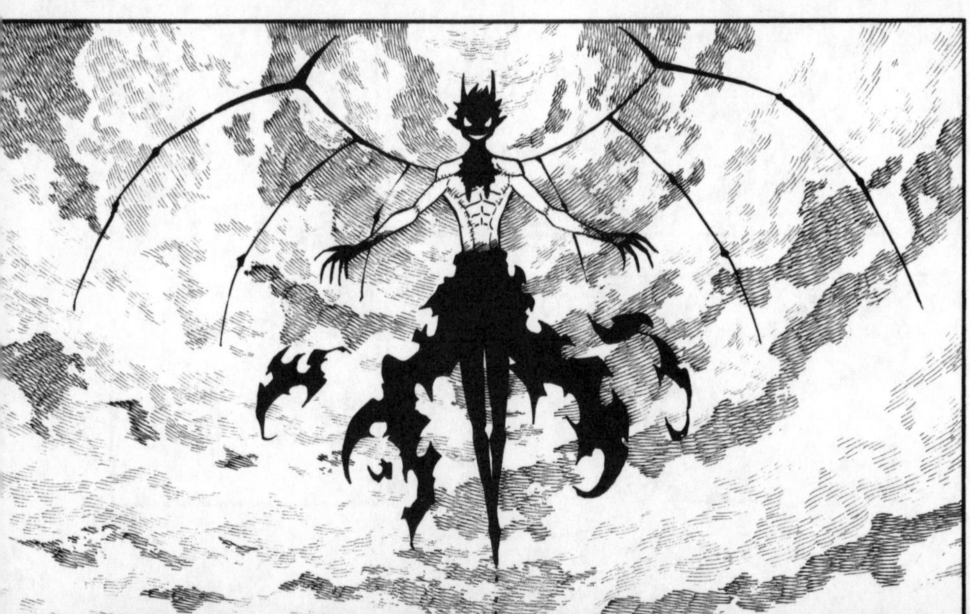

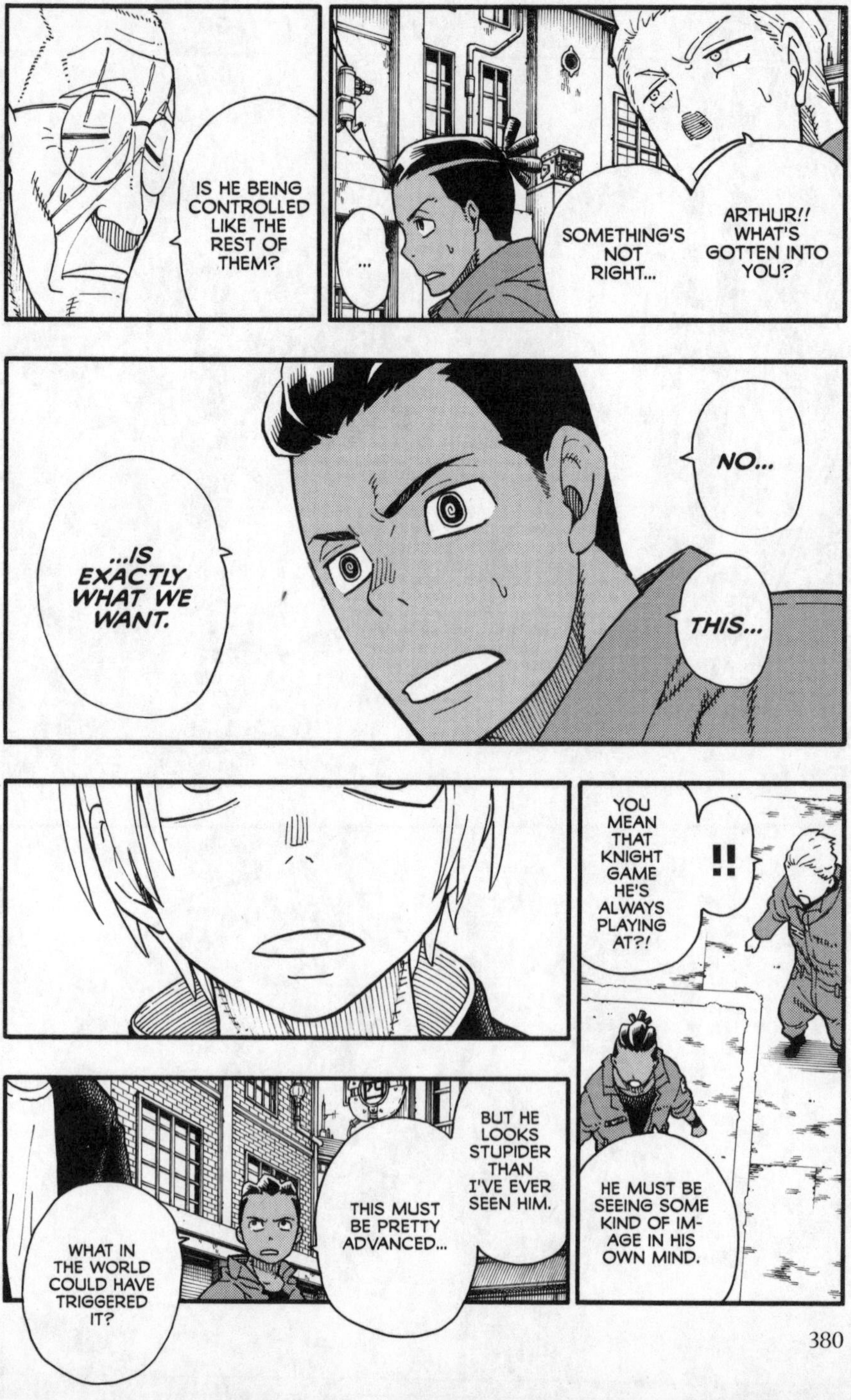
ARTHUR!! WHAT'S GOTTEN INTO YOU?
SOMETHING'S NOT RIGHT...
...
IS HE BEING CONTROLLED LIKE THE REST OF THEM?
NO...
THIS...
...IS EXACTLY WHAT WE WANT.
YOU MEAN THAT KNIGHT GAME HE'S ALWAYS PLAYING AT?!
!!
HE MUST BE SEEING SOME KIND OF IM-AGE IN HIS OWN MIND.
BUT HE LOOKS STUPIDER THAN I'VE EVER SEEN HIM.
THIS MUST BE PRETTY ADVANCED...
WHAT IN THE WORLD COULD HAVE TRIGGERED IT?

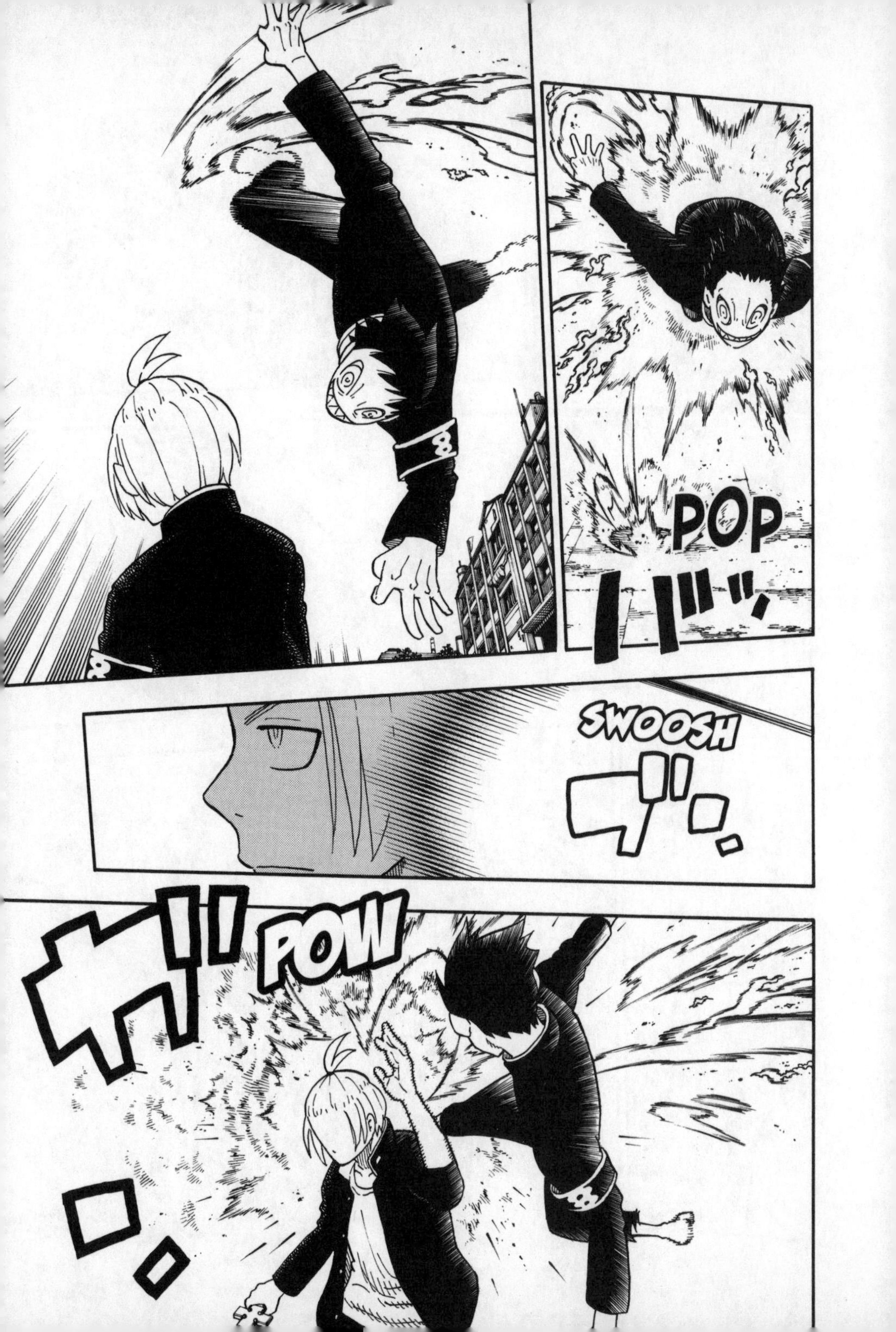
POP
SWOOSH
POW

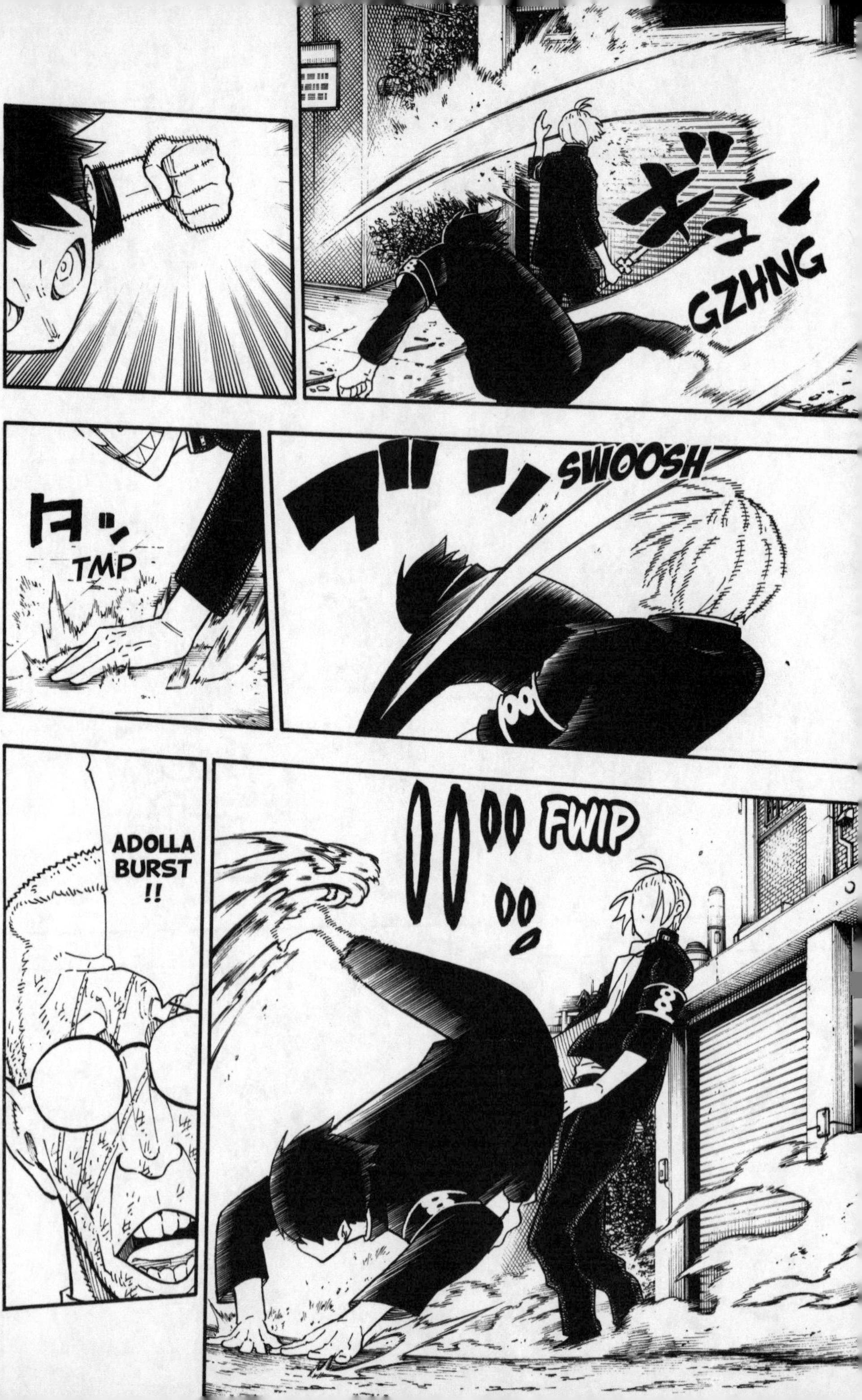
GZHNG
SWOOSH
TMP
FWIP
ADOLLA BURST !!

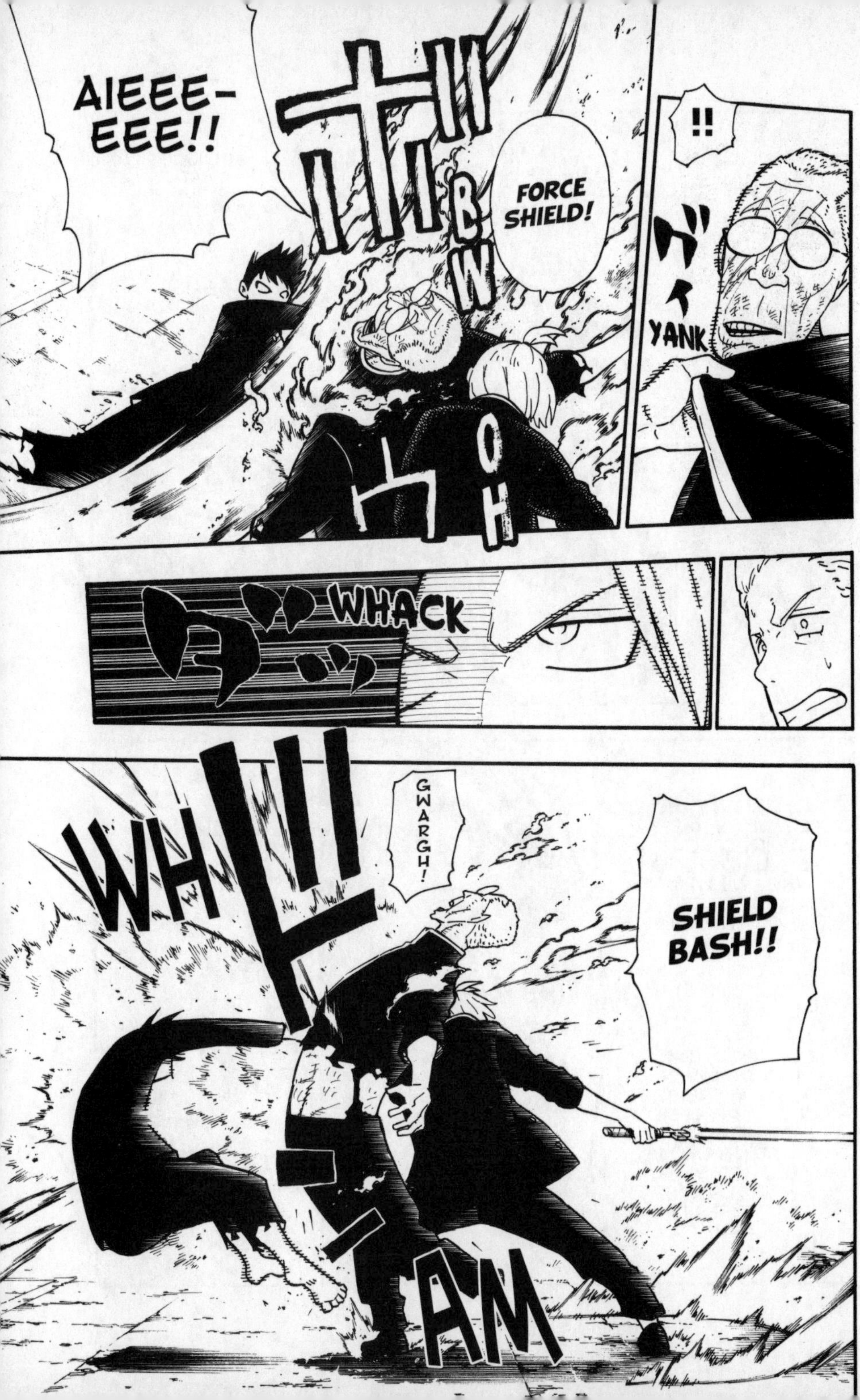
!!
YANK
FORCE SHIELD!
BWOH
AIEEE-EEE!!
WHACK
SHIELD BASH!!
GWARGH!
WHAM

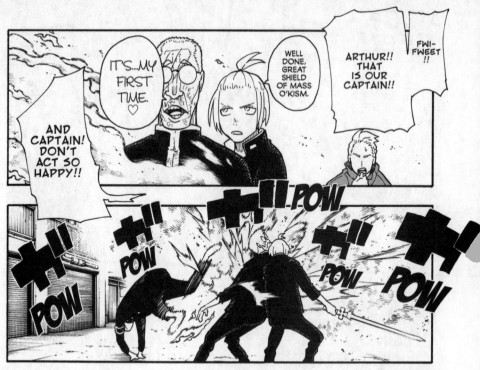

FWI-FWEET!!
ARTHUR!! THAT IS OUR CAPTAIN!!
WELL DONE, GREAT SHIELD OF MASS O'KISM.
IT'S...MY FIRST TIME. ♡
AND CAPTAIN! DON'T ACT SO HAPPY!!
POW
POW
POW
POW
POW
POW
I HARDLY RECOGNIZE THEM FROM THEIR DAYS IN THE ACADEMY.
DO THE PROPERTIES OF PLASMA HAVE ANYTHING TO DO WITH ARTHUR'S STRENGTH?
TOKYOFFS
YES, SIR! ARTHUR'S POWER IS PRETTY UNIQUE, BUT HE'S AN IDIOT, SO WHEN WE WERE STUDENTS, I DID A LOT OF RESEARCH FOR HIM.
I LEARNED THAT THIS THING HE DOES, WHERE HE GETS STRONGER OR WEAKER DEPENDING ON HIS CIRCUMSTANCES, IS A LOT LIKE THE PROPERTIES OF PLASMA.

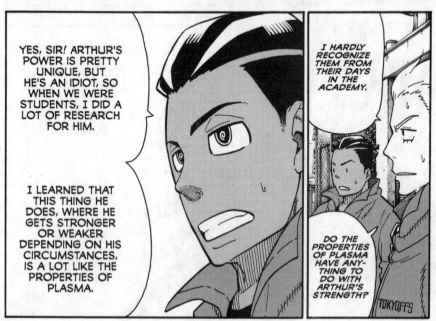

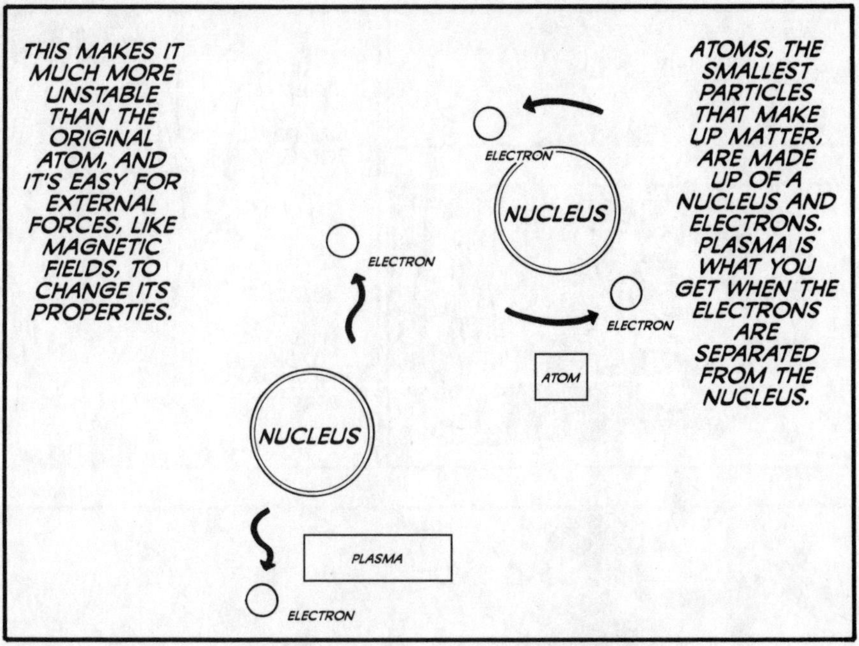
ATOMS, THE SMALLEST PARTICLES THAT MAKE UP MATTER, ARE MADE UP OF A NUCLEUS AND ELECTRONS. PLASMA IS WHAT YOU GET WHEN THE ELECTRONS ARE SEPARATED FROM THE NUCLEUS.
ELECTRON
NUCLEUS
ELECTRON
ATOM
ELECTRON
NUCLEUS
PLASMA
ELECTRON
THIS MAKES IT MUCH MORE UNSTABLE THAN THE ORIGINAL ATOM, AND IT'S EASY FOR EXTERNAL FORCES, LIKE MAGNETIC FIELDS, TO CHANGE ITS PROPERTIES.

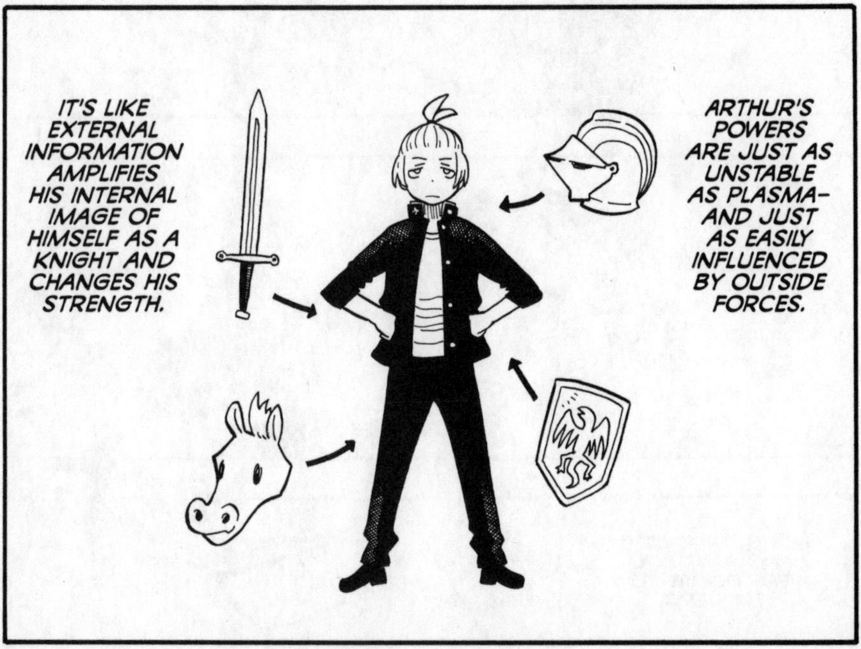
ARTHUR'S POWERS ARE JUST AS UNSTABLE AS PLASMA— AND JUST AS EASILY INFLUENCED BY OUTSIDE FORCES.
IT'S LIKE EXTERNAL INFORMATION AMPLIFIES HIS INTERNAL IMAGE OF HIMSELF AS A KNIGHT AND CHANGES HIS STRENGTH.

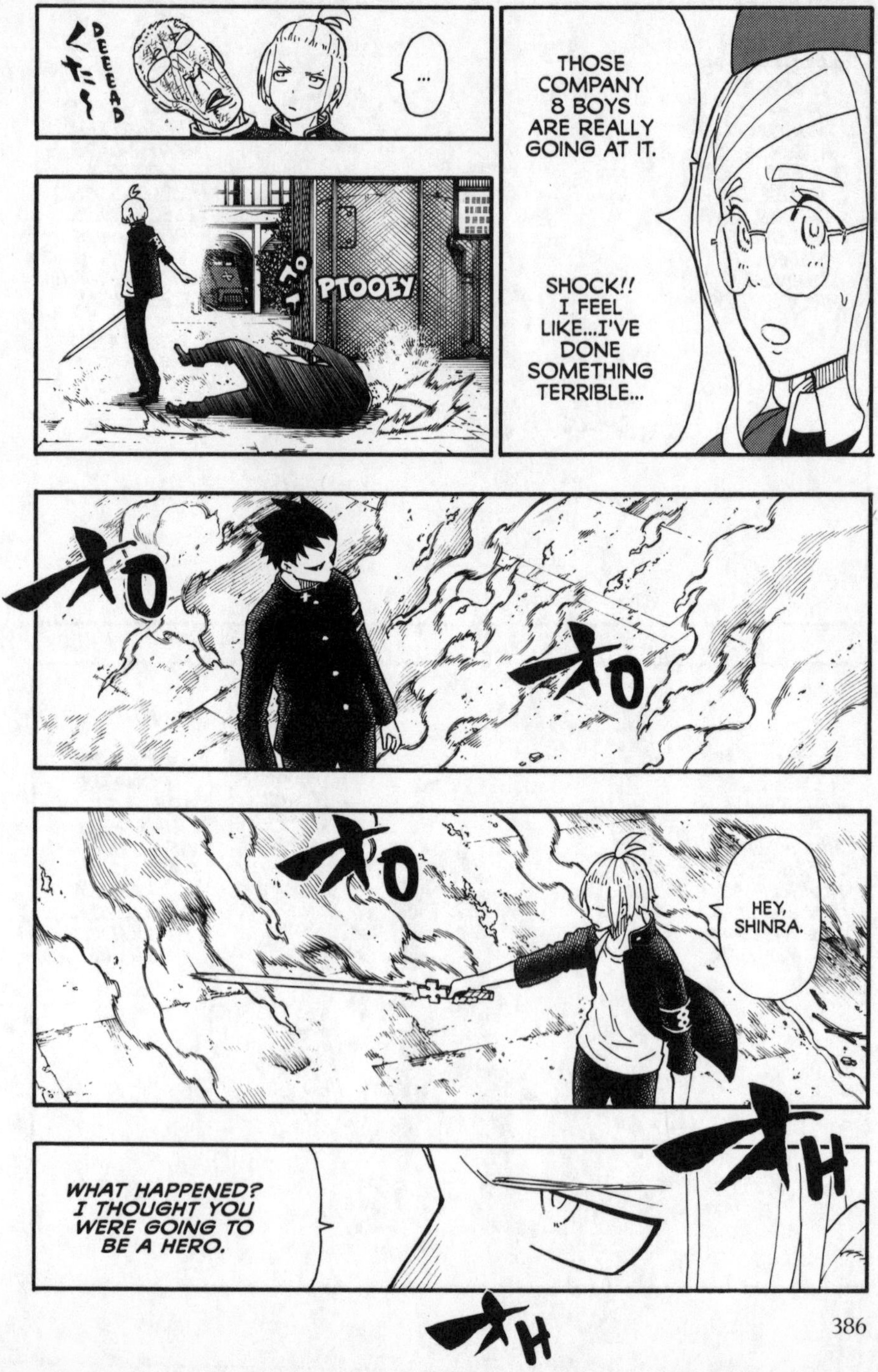
THOSE COMPANY 8 BOYS ARE REALLY GOING AT IT.
SHOCK!! I FEEL LIKE...I'VE DONE SOMETHING TERRIBLE...
DEEEAD
...
PTOOEY
HEY, SHINRA.
WHAT HAPPENED? I THOUGHT YOU WERE GOING TO BE A HERO.

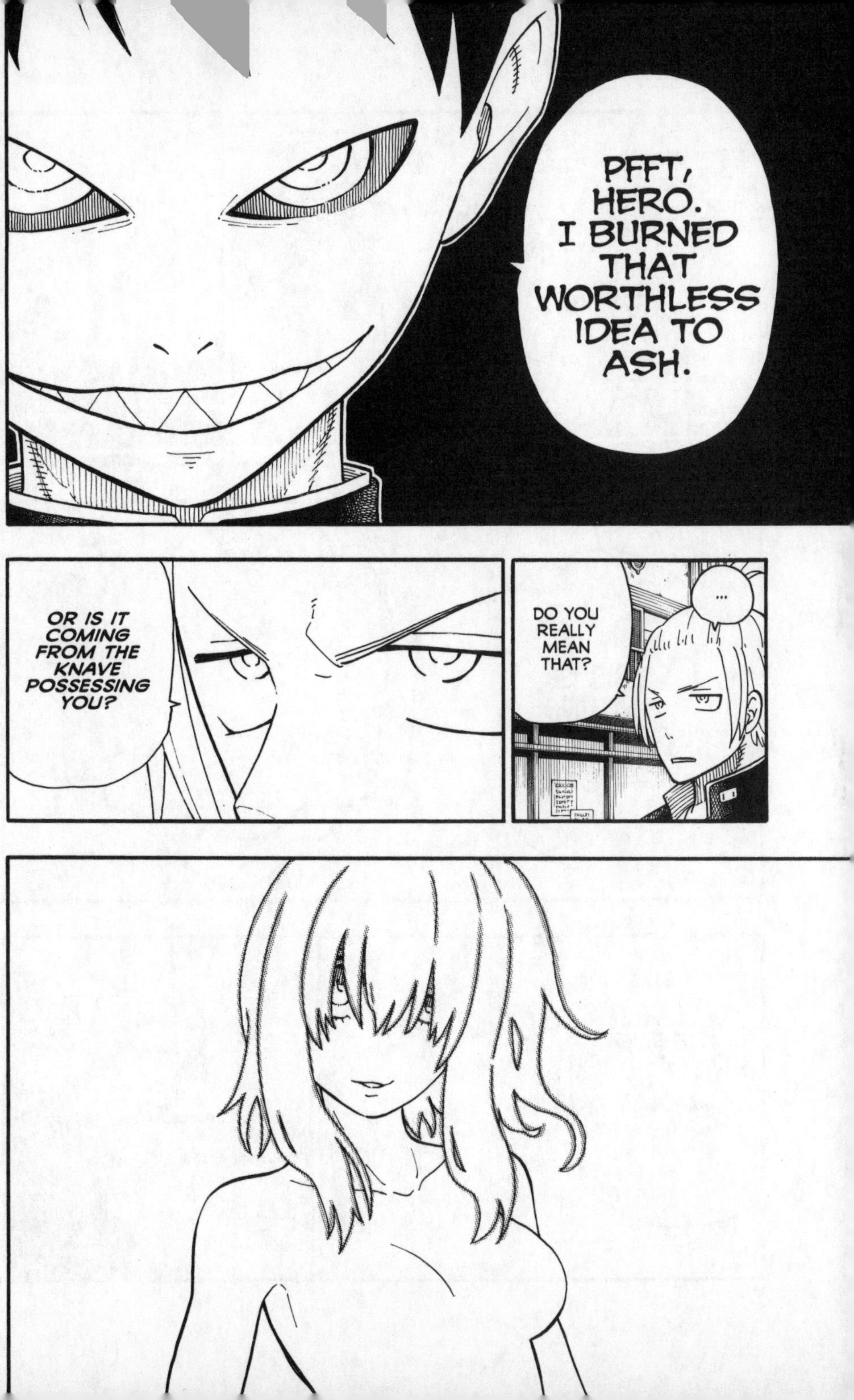
PFFT, HERO. I BURNED THAT WORTHLESS IDEA TO ASH.
...
DO YOU REALLY MEAN THAT?
OR IS IT COMING FROM THE KNAVE POSSESSING YOU?

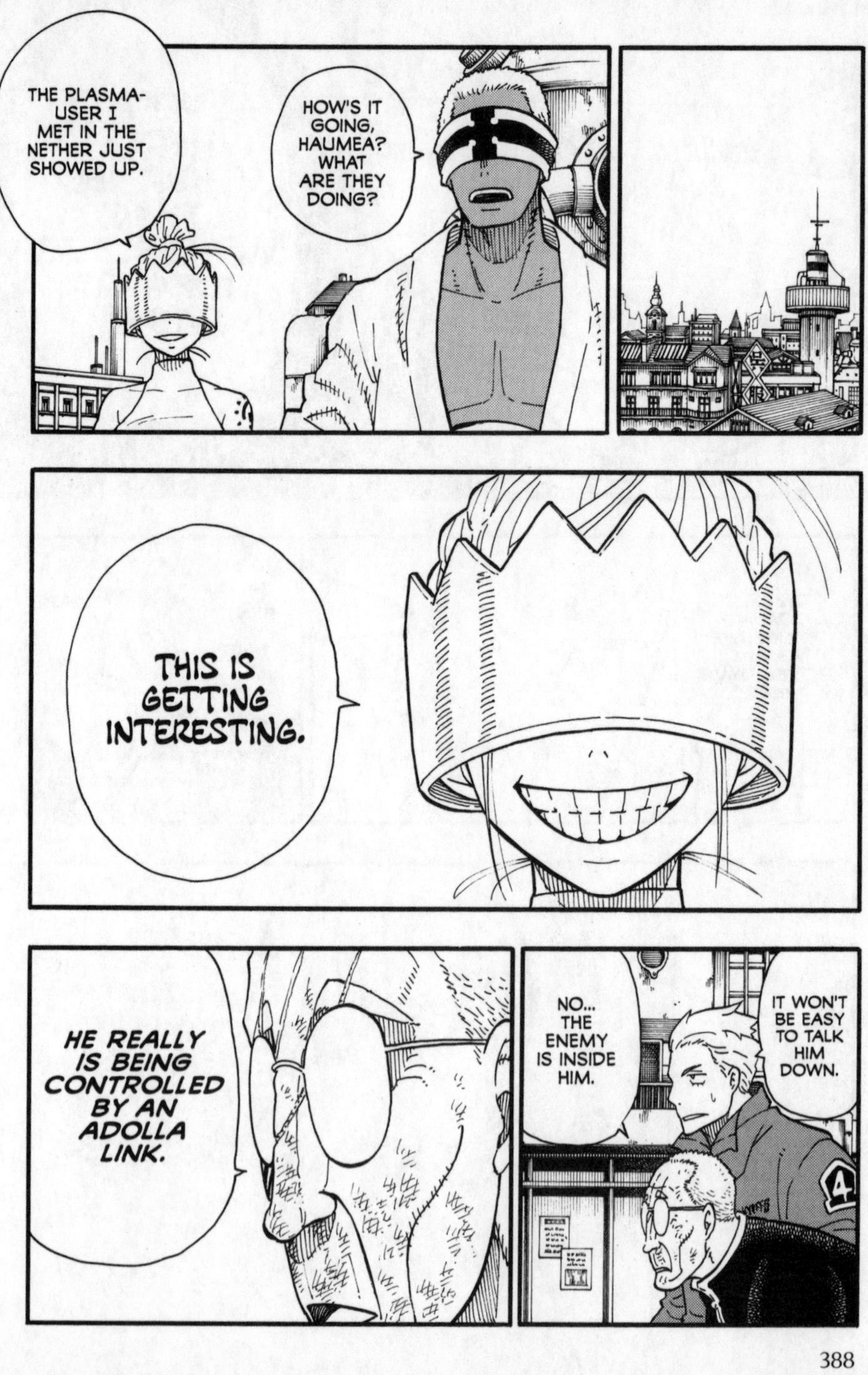
HOW'S IT GOING, HAUMEA? WHAT ARE THEY DOING?
THE PLASMA-USER I MET IN THE NETHER JUST SHOWED UP.
THIS IS GETTING INTERESTING.
IT WON'T BE EASY TO TALK HIM DOWN.
NO... THE ENEMY IS INSIDE HIM.
HE REALLY IS BEING CONTROLLED BY AN ADOLLA LINK.

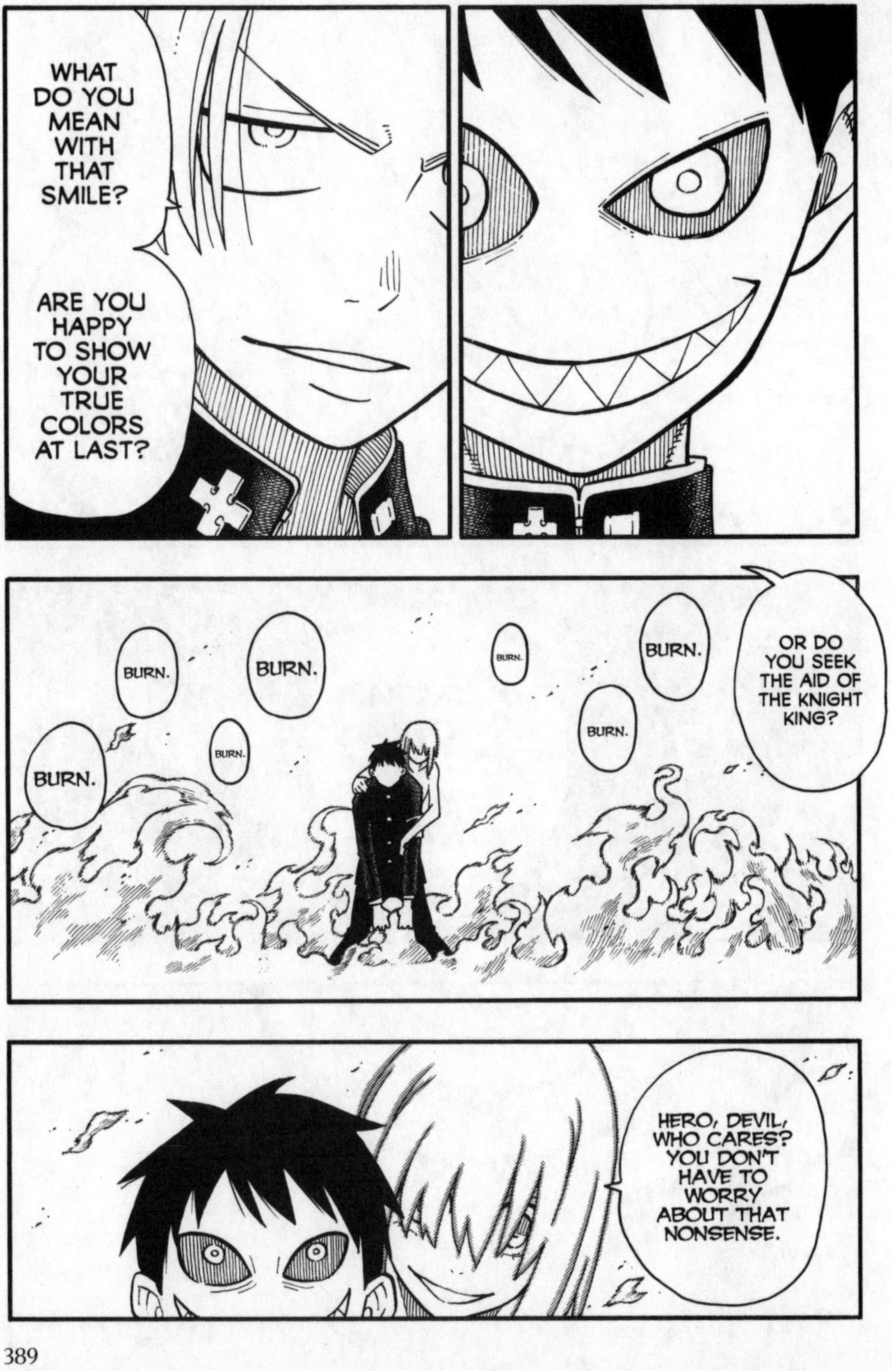
WHAT DO YOU MEAN WITH THAT SMILE?
ARE YOU HAPPY TO SHOW YOUR TRUE COLORS AT LAST?
OR DO YOU SEEK THE AID OF THE KNIGHT KING?
BURN.
BURN.
BURN.
BURN.
BURN.
BURN.
BURN.
HERO, DEVIL, WHO CARES? YOU DON'T HAVE TO WORRY ABOUT THAT NONSENSE.

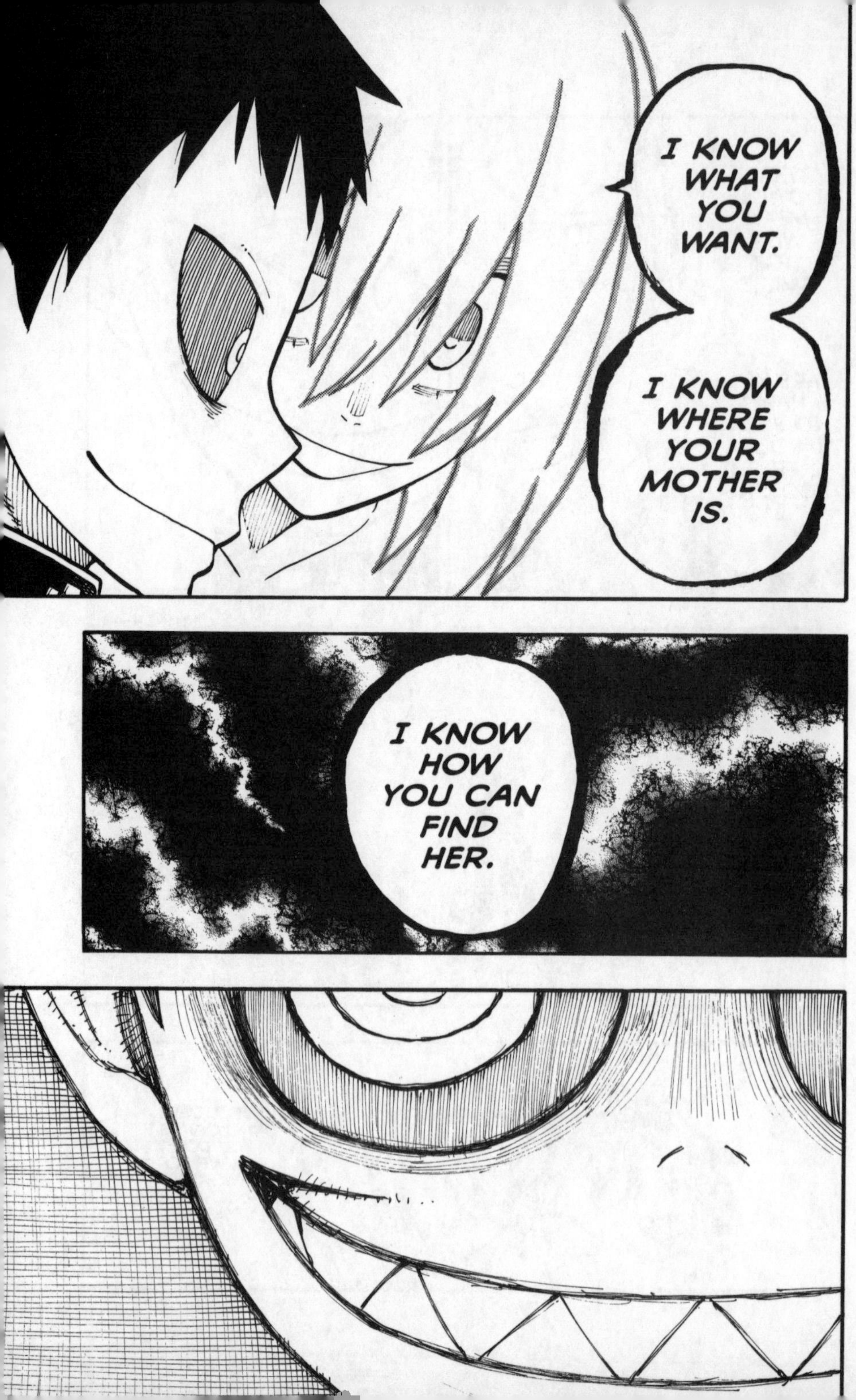
I KNOW WHAT YOU WANT.
I KNOW WHERE YOUR MOTHER IS.
I KNOW HOW YOU CAN FIND HER.

Translation Notes:

January and August, page 273

Before the Solar Era, many of the English names for months came from Roman gods and rulers, or just from Latin numbers. They may or may not have been changed when the Solar Era began, but in Japanese, the months are all named for the order they appear in the calendar: Ichigatsu (Month One), Nigatsu (Month Two), etc. This did not change with the new era, so there's no telling what the real English names of these months would be, but the translators have opted to use what the readers will readily recognize. Of course, naming the months after numbers makes it very easy to determine which company will adorn the calendar page of which month.

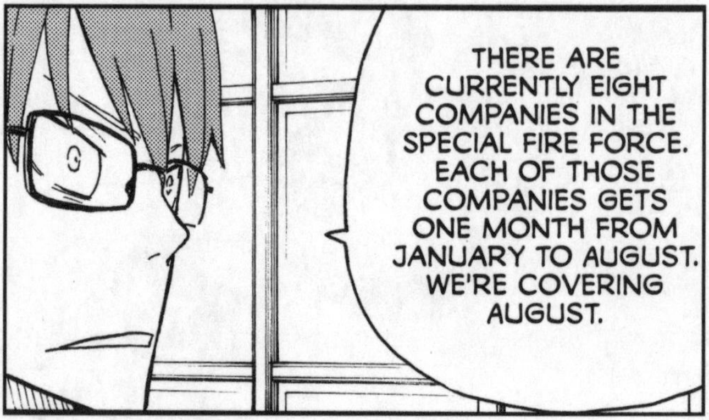
THERE ARE CURRENTLY EIGHT COMPANIES IN THE SPECIAL FIRE FORCE. EACH OF THOSE COMPANIES GETS ONE MONTH FROM JANUARY TO AUGUST. WE'RE COVERING AUGUST.

Welcome to the gun shobra, page 287

The translators would like to apologize for their very sorry attempt at recreating this pun. The Japanese word for "flexed biceps" is *chikara-kobu*, which literally means "strength lump." Captain Ōbi added a "-ra" to the end to make it *chikara-kobura*, which is now a portmanteau of "flexed bicep" and "cobra."

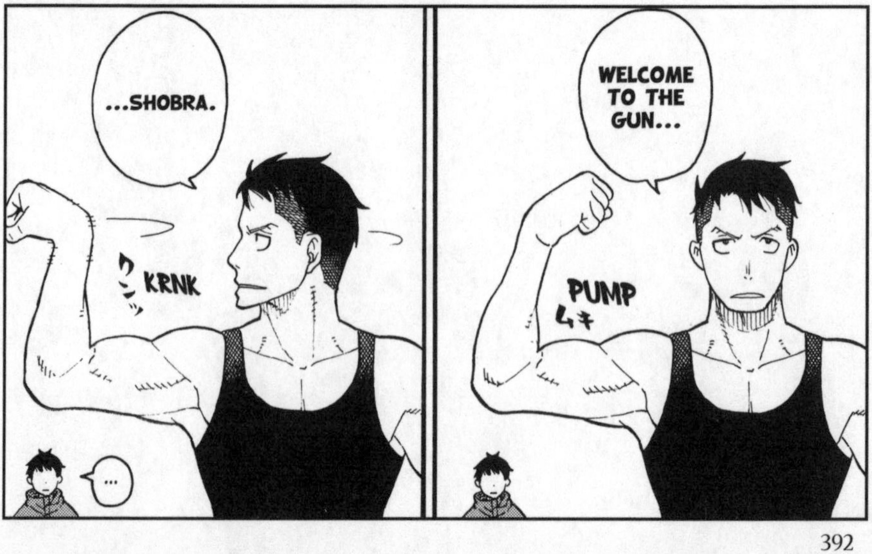
WELCOME TO THE GUN...
PUMP
...SHOBRA.
KRNK
...

Hat: Nudist Bitch

I'M TERRIBLY SORRY, SIR.

Nudist Bitch, page 306

The Japanese on Hinawa's hat here is actually "*nudisto bichiku*," with "*bichiku*" being a portmanteau of the word "beach" and the swapped syllables of the word "*chikubi*" (meaning "teats"). Whether it's Nudist Bitch or Nudist Beach-Teats, Hinawa's new hat is definitely unacceptable office wear.

Where would he go for research, page 394

In Japan, chapters of manga are published in a magazine on a weekly or monthly basis, and when enough chapters have been released, they are compiled into a graphic novel. Every so often, a magazine will come out and be missing a chapter of, perhaps, a favorite manga. The editors will inform the readers that the author of said manga has taken a break for research purposes. This is a code meaning, "The artist missed the deadline."

THERE HAVEN'T BEEN ANY SUDDEN ILLNESSES OR SUDDEN DISAPPEARANCES MAKING THE READERS THINK, "WHERE IN THE HECK WOULD HE BE GOING FOR RESEARCH?"

THE SERIES HAS GONE ON WITH PERFECT ATTENDANCE.

TWO YEA[R]S WITH N[O] ACCIDENT[S] AND N[O] VIOLATION[S]

AFTERWORD MANGA: ATSUSHIYA

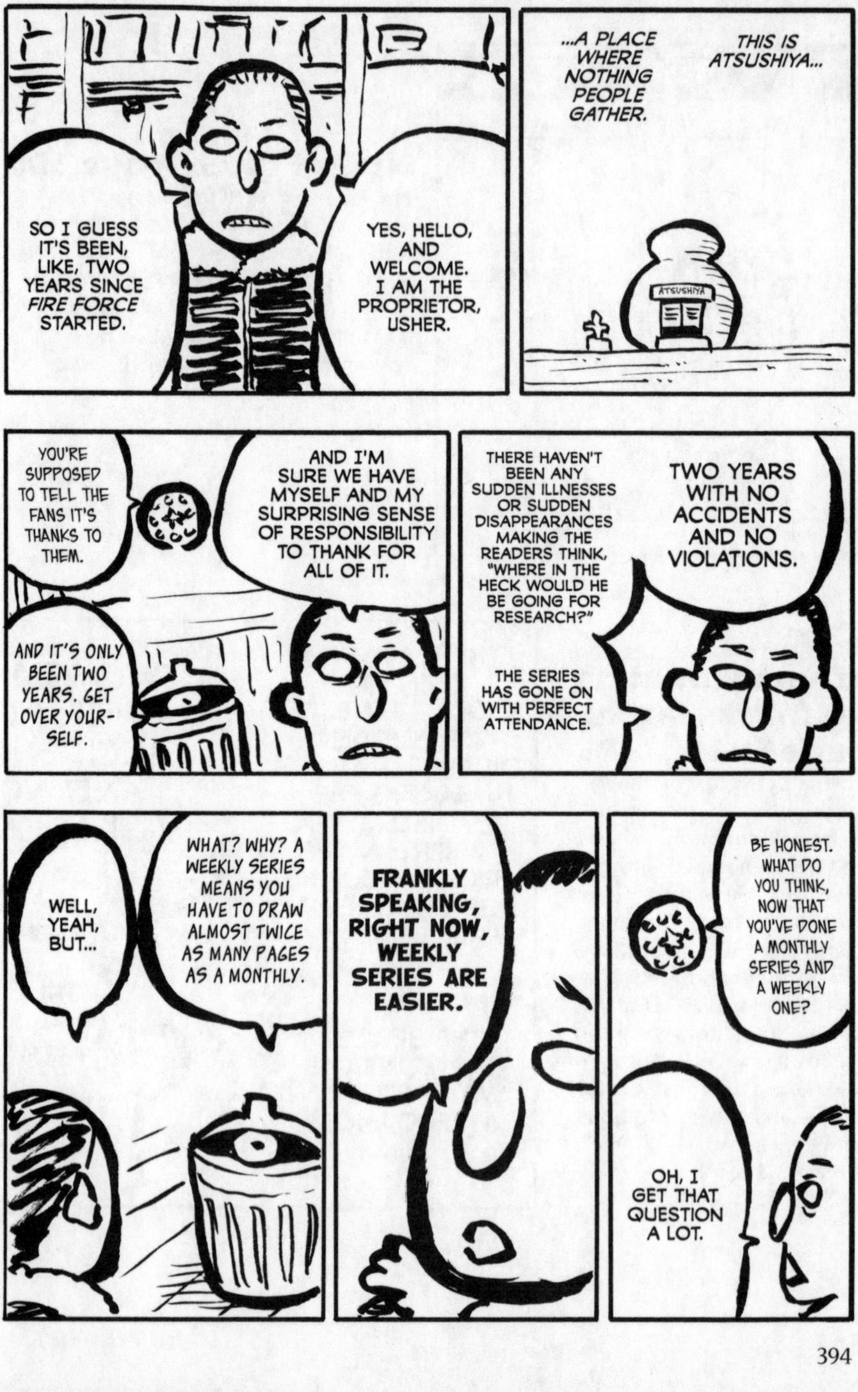
THIS IS ATSUSHIYA...
...A PLACE WHERE NOTHING PEOPLE GATHER.
ATSUSHIYA
YES, HELLO, AND WELCOME. I AM THE PROPRIETOR, USHER.
SO I GUESS IT'S BEEN, LIKE, TWO YEARS SINCE *FIRE FORCE* STARTED.
TWO YEARS WITH NO ACCIDENTS AND NO VIOLATIONS.
THERE HAVEN'T BEEN ANY SUDDEN ILLNESSES OR SUDDEN DISAPPEARANCES MAKING THE READERS THINK, "WHERE IN THE HECK WOULD HE BE GOING FOR RESEARCH?"
THE SERIES HAS GONE ON WITH PERFECT ATTENDANCE.
AND I'M SURE WE HAVE MYSELF AND MY SURPRISING SENSE OF RESPONSIBILITY TO THANK FOR ALL OF IT.
YOU'RE SUPPOSED TO TELL THE FANS IT'S THANKS TO THEM.
AND IT'S ONLY BEEN TWO YEARS. GET OVER YOUR-SELF.
BE HONEST. WHAT DO YOU THINK, NOW THAT YOU'VE DONE A MONTHLY SERIES AND A WEEKLY ONE?
OH, I GET THAT QUESTION A LOT.
FRANKLY SPEAKING, RIGHT NOW, WEEKLY SERIES ARE EASIER.
WHAT? WHY? A WEEKLY SERIES MEANS YOU HAVE TO DRAW ALMOST TWICE AS MANY PAGES AS A MONTHLY.
WELL, YEAH, BUT...

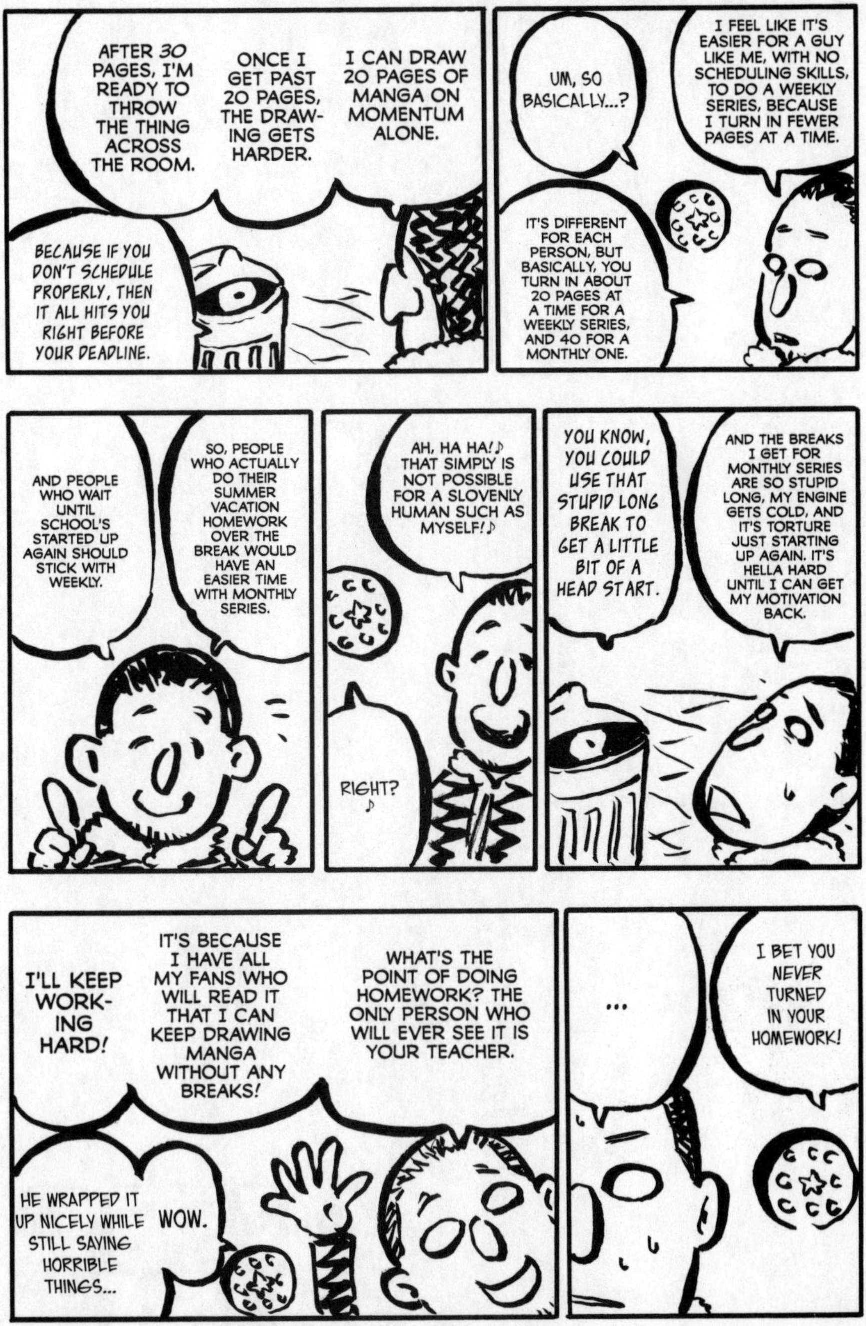
I FEEL LIKE IT'S EASIER FOR A GUY LIKE ME, WITH NO SCHEDULING SKILLS, TO DO A WEEKLY SERIES, BECAUSE I TURN IN FEWER PAGES AT A TIME.
UM, SO BASICALLY...?
IT'S DIFFERENT FOR EACH PERSON, BUT BASICALLY, YOU TURN IN ABOUT 20 PAGES AT A TIME FOR A WEEKLY SERIES, AND 40 FOR A MONTHLY ONE.
I CAN DRAW 20 PAGES OF MANGA ON MOMENTUM ALONE.
ONCE I GET PAST 20 PAGES, THE DRAWING GETS HARDER.
AFTER 30 PAGES, I'M READY TO THROW THE THING ACROSS THE ROOM.
BECAUSE IF YOU DON'T SCHEDULE PROPERLY, THEN IT ALL HITS YOU RIGHT BEFORE YOUR DEADLINE.
AND THE BREAKS I GET FOR MONTHLY SERIES ARE SO STUPID LONG, MY ENGINE GETS COLD, AND IT'S TORTURE JUST STARTING UP AGAIN. IT'S HELLA HARD UNTIL I CAN GET MY MOTIVATION BACK.
YOU KNOW, YOU COULD USE THAT STUPID LONG BREAK TO GET A LITTLE BIT OF A HEAD START.
AH, HA HA!♪ THAT SIMPLY IS NOT POSSIBLE FOR A SLOVENLY HUMAN SUCH AS MYSELF!♪
RIGHT? ♪
SO, PEOPLE WHO ACTUALLY DO THEIR SUMMER VACATION HOMEWORK OVER THE BREAK WOULD HAVE AN EASIER TIME WITH MONTHLY SERIES.
AND PEOPLE WHO WAIT UNTIL SCHOOL'S STARTED UP AGAIN SHOULD STICK WITH WEEKLY.
I BET YOU NEVER TURNED IN YOUR HOMEWORK!
...
WHAT'S THE POINT OF DOING HOMEWORK? THE ONLY PERSON WHO WILL EVER SEE IT IS YOUR TEACHER.
IT'S BECAUSE I HAVE ALL MY FANS WHO WILL READ IT THAT I CAN KEEP DRAWING MANGA WITHOUT ANY BREAKS!
I'LL KEEP WORKING HARD!
WOW.
HE WRAPPED IT UP NICELY WHILE STILL SAYING HORRIBLE THINGS...

FIRE FORCE

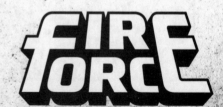

FIRE FORCE

12

ATSUSHI OHKUBO

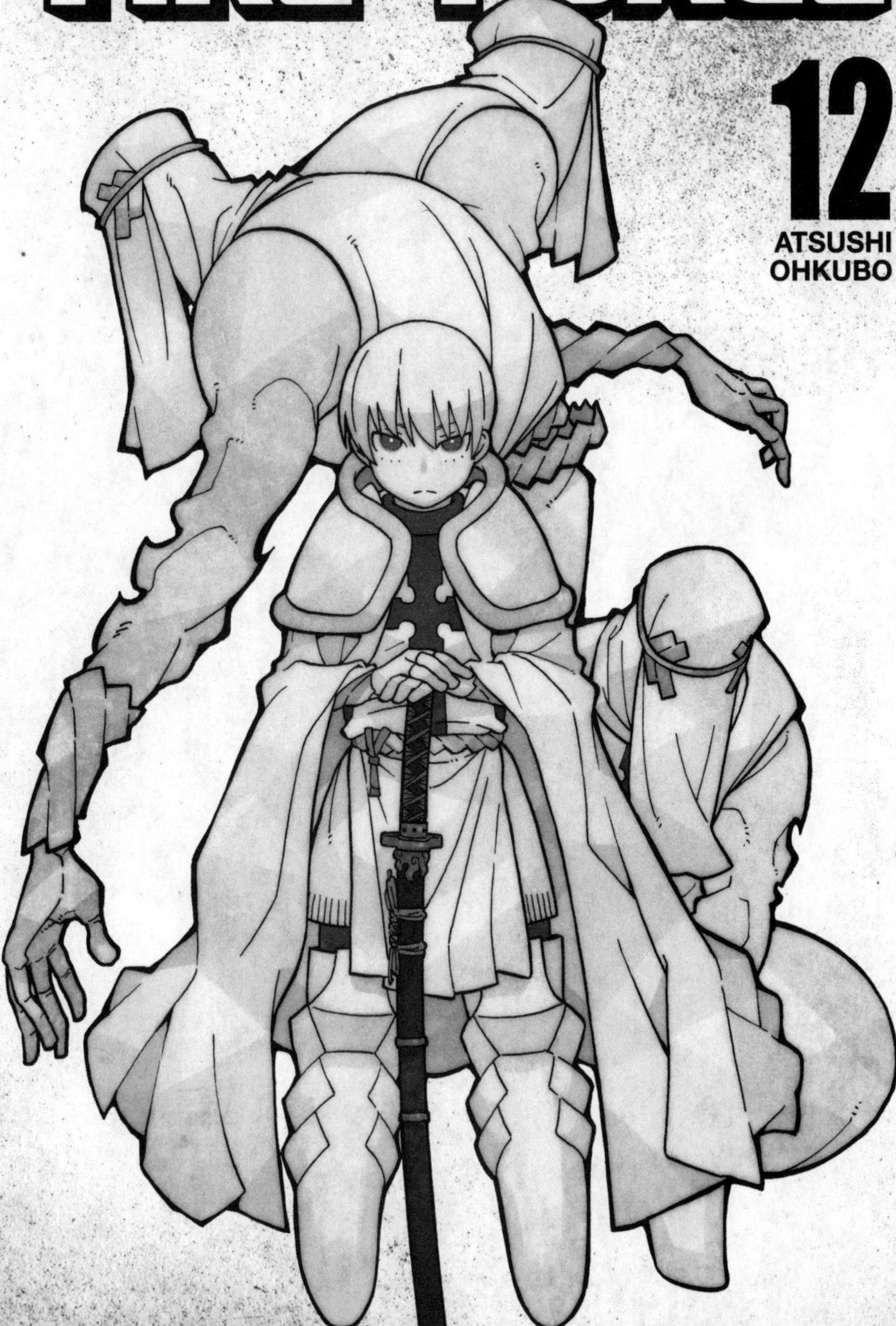

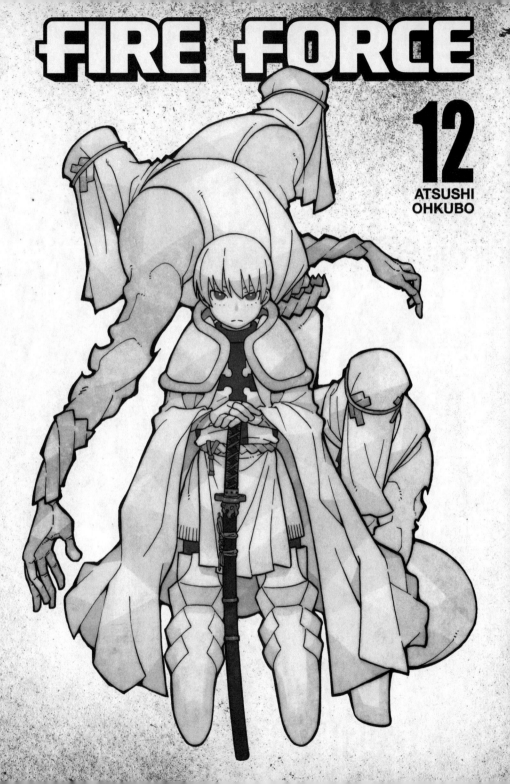

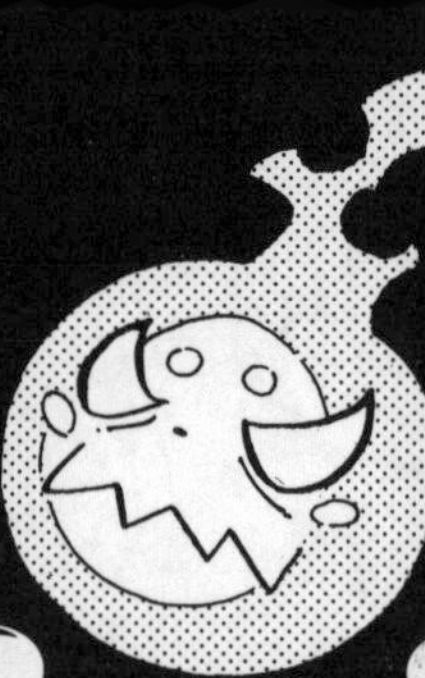

offering to world?

VOL. 12

ATSUSHI OHKUBO

What if you were the burnt needed save the

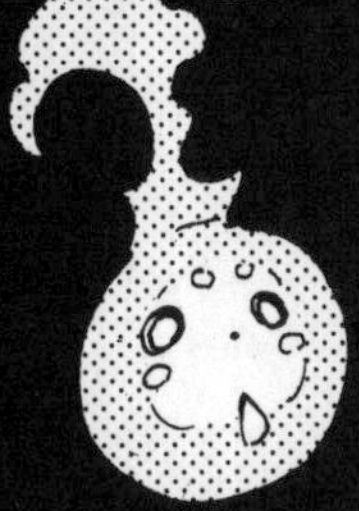

FIRE FORCE

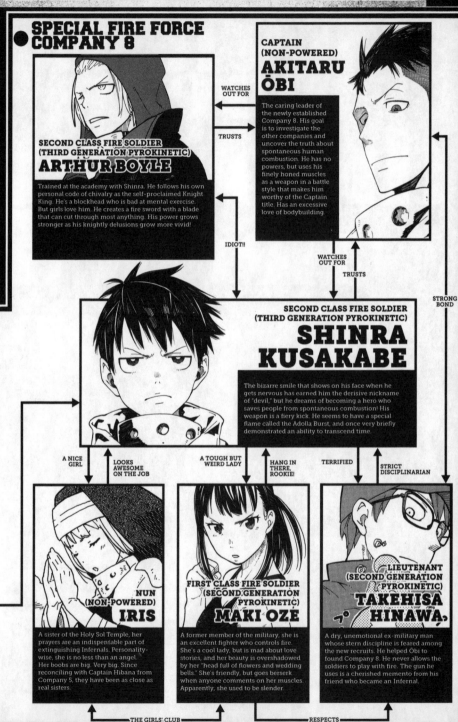

SPECIAL FIRE FORCE COMPANY 8

CAPTAIN (NON-POWERED) AKITARU ŌBI

The caring leader of the newly established Company 8. His goal is to investigate the other companies and uncover the truth about spontaneous human combustion. He has no powers, but uses his finely honed muscles as a weapon in a battle style that makes him worthy of the Captain title. Has an excessive love of bodybuilding.

SECOND CLASS FIRE SOLDIER (THIRD GENERATION PYROKINETIC) ARTHUR BOYLE

Trained at the academy with Shinra. He follows his own personal code of chivalry as the self-proclaimed Knight King. He's a blockhead who is bad at mental exercise. But girls love him. He creates a fire sword with a blade that can cut through most anything. His power grows stronger as his knightly delusions grow more vivid!

WATCHES OUT FOR

TRUSTS

IDIOT!!

WATCHES OUT FOR

TRUSTS

STRONG BOND

SECOND CLASS FIRE SOLDIER (THIRD GENERATION PYROKINETIC) SHINRA KUSAKABE

The bizarre smile that shows on his face when he gets nervous has earned him the derisive nickname of "devil," but he dreams of becoming a hero who saves people from spontaneous combustion! His weapon is a fiery kick. He seems to have a special flame called the Adolla Burst, and once very briefly demonstrated an ability to transcend time.

A NICE GIRL

LOOKS AWESOME ON THE JOB

A TOUGH BUT WEIRD LADY

HANG IN THERE, ROOKIE!

TERRIFIED

STRICT DISCIPLINARIAN

LIEUTENANT (SECOND GENERATION PYROKINETIC) TAKEHISA HINAWA

A dry, unemotional ex-military man whose stern discipline is feared among the new recruits. He helped Ōbi to found Company 8. He never allows the soldiers to play with fire. The gun he uses is a cherished memento from his friend who became an Infernal.

FIRST CLASS FIRE SOLDIER (SECOND GENERATION PYROKINETIC) MAKI OZE

A former member of the military, she is an excellent fighter who controls fire. She's a cool lady, but is mad about love stories, and her beauty is overshadowed by her "head full of flowers and wedding bells." She's friendly, but goes berserk when anyone comments on her muscles. Apparently, she used to be slender.

NUN (NON-POWERED) IRIS

A sister of the Holy Sol Temple, her prayers are an indispensable part of extinguishing Infernals. Personality-wise, she is no less than an angel. Her boobs are big. Very big. Since reconciling with Captain Hibana from Company 5, they have been as close as real sisters.

THE GIRLS' CLUB

RESPECTS

SPECIAL FIRE FORCE COMPANY 4

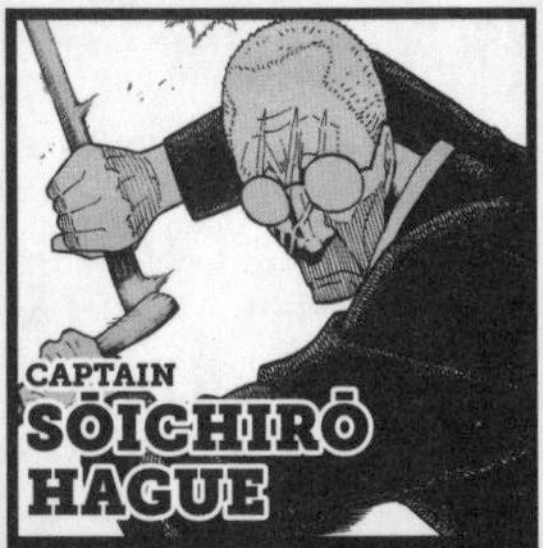

CAPTAIN
SŌICHIRŌ HAGUE

There are rumors that he has changed since his close encounter with an Adolla Burst, but he is normally a lovable old man. He just likes a little bit of pain, that's all.♥ He is loved and respected by his company.

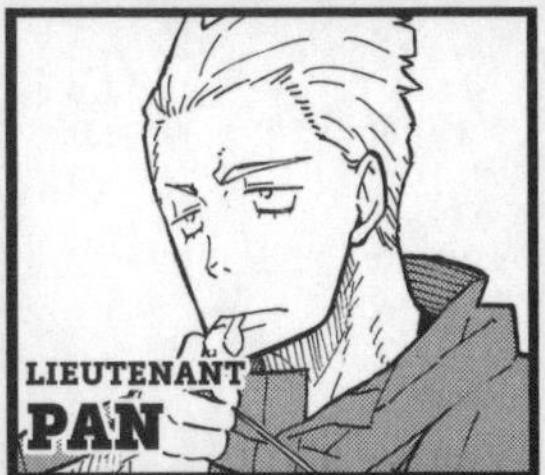

LIEUTENANT
PAN

Served as Shinra and Arthur's instructor at the academy. The Fire Force's greatest master of status enhancements.

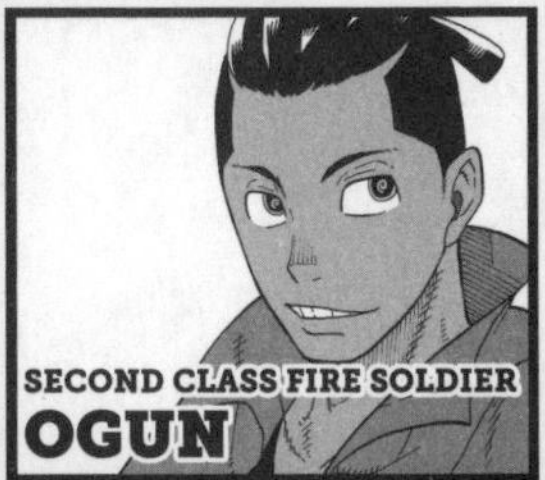

SECOND CLASS FIRE SOLDIER
OGUN

A friend of Shinra and Arthur's from the academy, and top of his class. A good-natured and friendly soldier who controls fire spears.

FOLLOWERS OF THE EVANGELIST

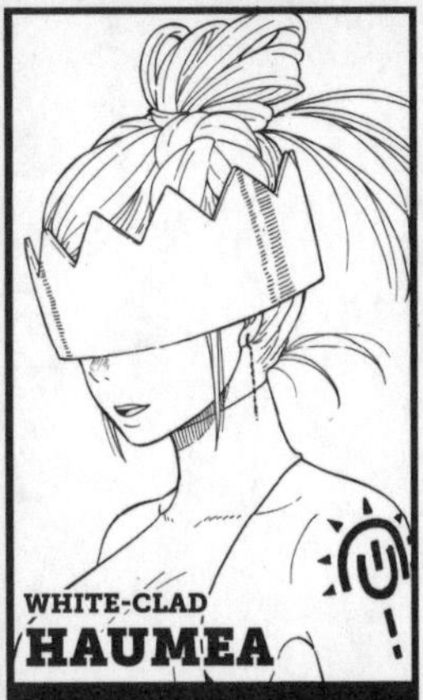

WHITE-CLAD
HAUMEA

One of the Evangelist's white-clad combatants. She is a troublesome opponent who can control others with her mind-jacking powers, and she has a foul mouth.

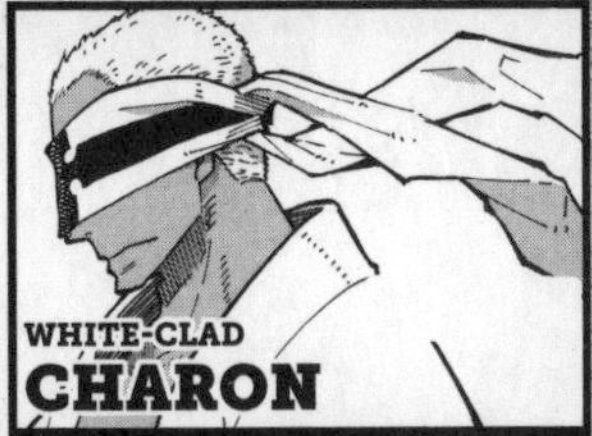

WHITE-CLAD
CHARON

A talkative man who won't stop asking questions until he gets an answer. His powers are unknown, but he must be powerful if he's hanging out with Haumea, right?

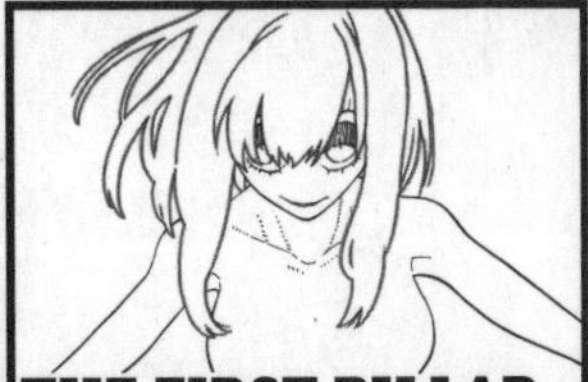

THE FIRST PILLAR

A mysterious woman who has used an Adolla Link to take over Shinra's mind.

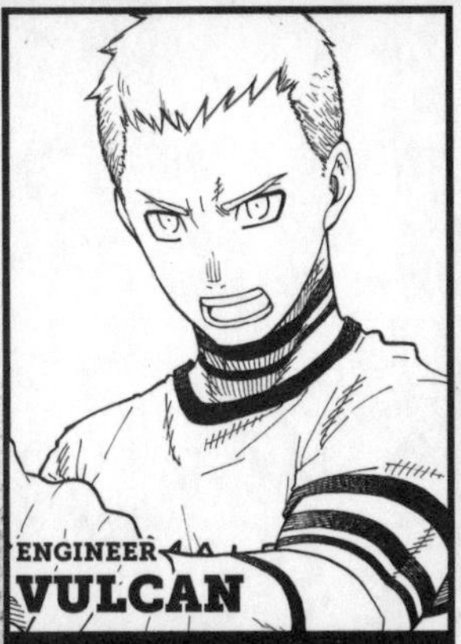

ENGINEER
VULCAN

The greatest engineer of the day, renowned as the God of Fire and the Forge. He sympathized with Ōbi's and Shinra's ideals and agreed to join Company 8 as their engineer.

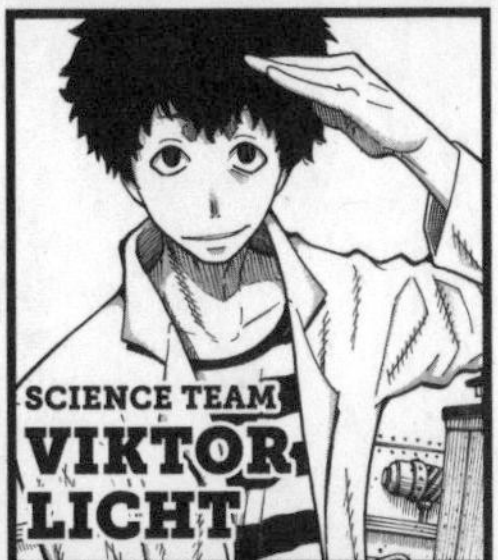

SCIENCE TEAM
VIKTOR LICHT

A morally ambiguous man deployed from Haijima Industries to fill the vacancy in Company 8's science department. Apparently a genius.

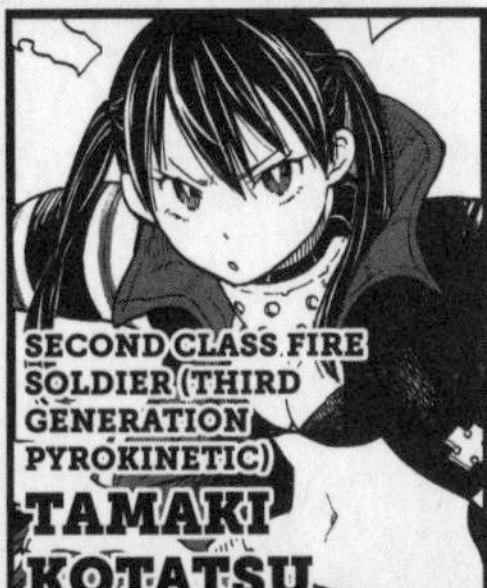

SECOND CLASS FIRE SOLDIER (THIRD GENERATION PYROKINETIC)
TAMAKI KOTATSU

HAS HIM ON HER MIND

Originally a headstrong rookie member of Company 1, she is currently being disciplined under Company 8's watch. Although she has a "lucky lecher lure" condition, she nevertheless has a pure heart.

SUMMARY...

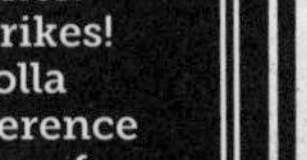
SPUTT
SPUTT

After learning that his mother has become a demon, Shinra gains an interview with Captain Sōichirō Hague of Special Fire Force Company 4 in his quest to learn more about the Adolla Link and find her. But in the middle of their meeting, trouble strikes! Someone known as the First Pillar has an Adolla Burst like Shinra's and is using mental interference to drive Shinra to insanity!! The elite members of Company 4 and Arthur attempt to stop him, but...?!

FIRE FORCE

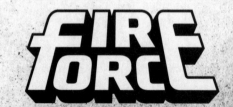

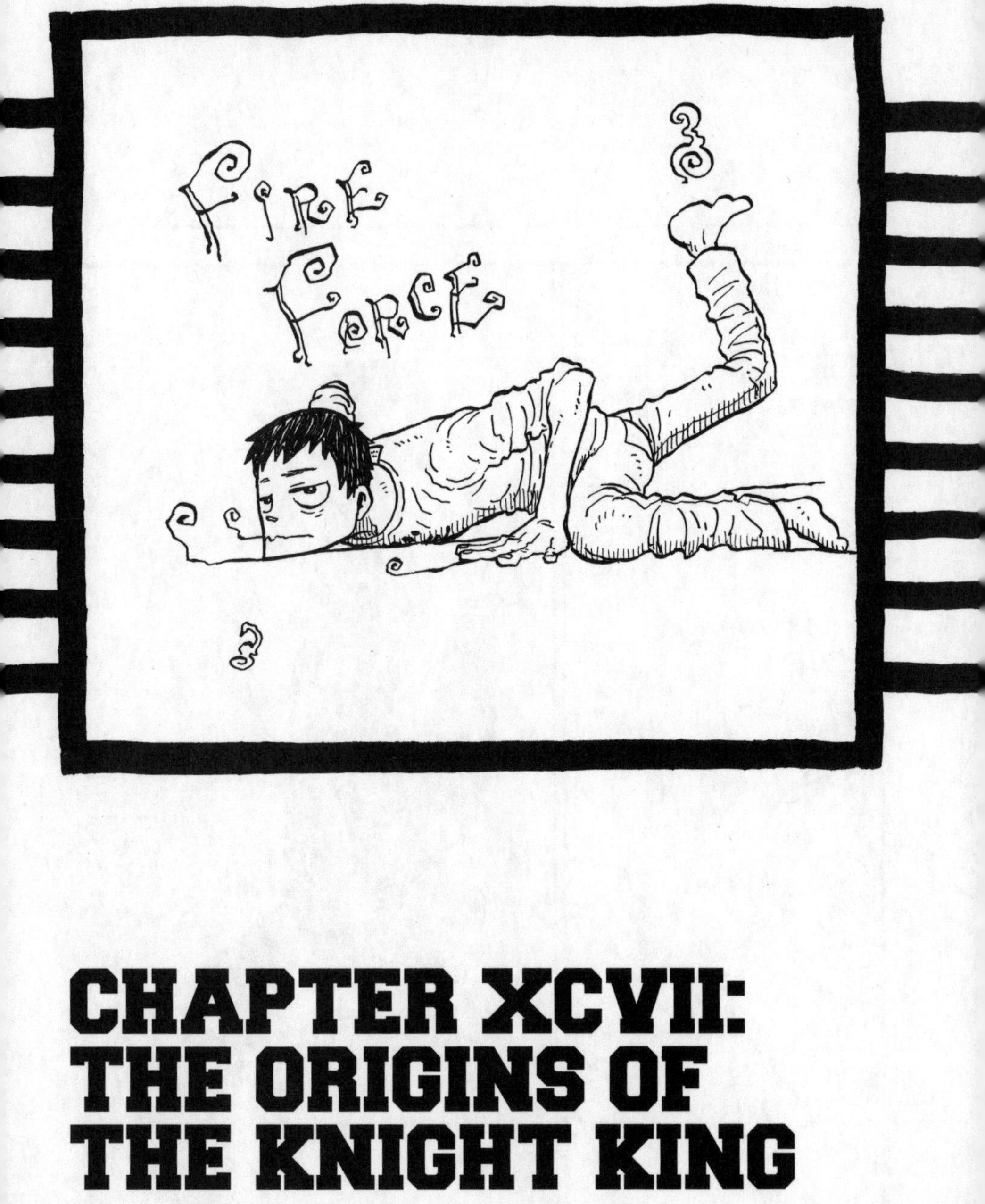
FIRE FORCE

CHAPTER XCVII: THE ORIGINS OF THE KNIGHT KING

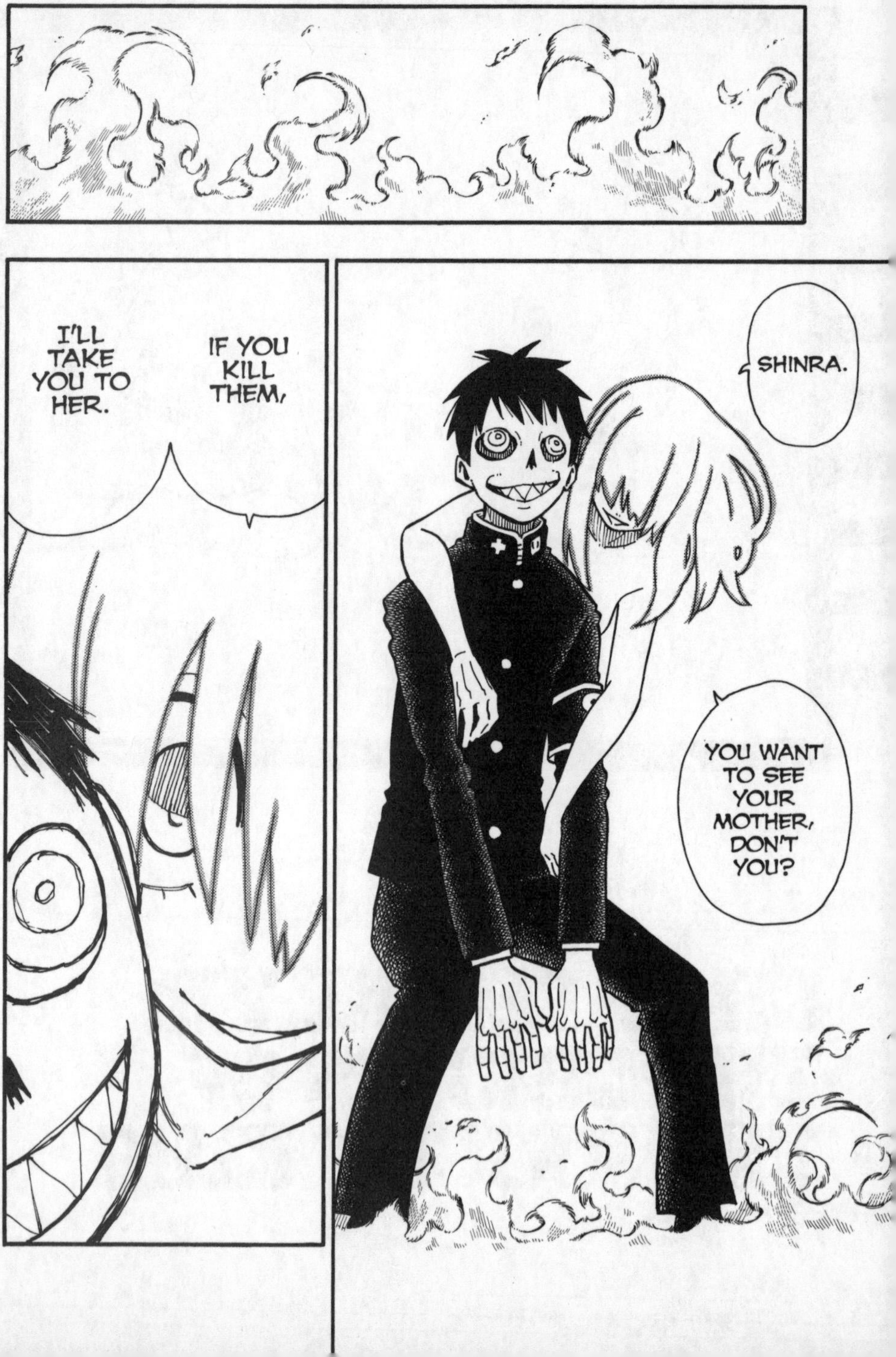
SHINRA.
YOU WANT TO SEE YOUR MOTHER, DON'T YOU?
IF YOU KILL THEM,
I'LL TAKE YOU TO HER.

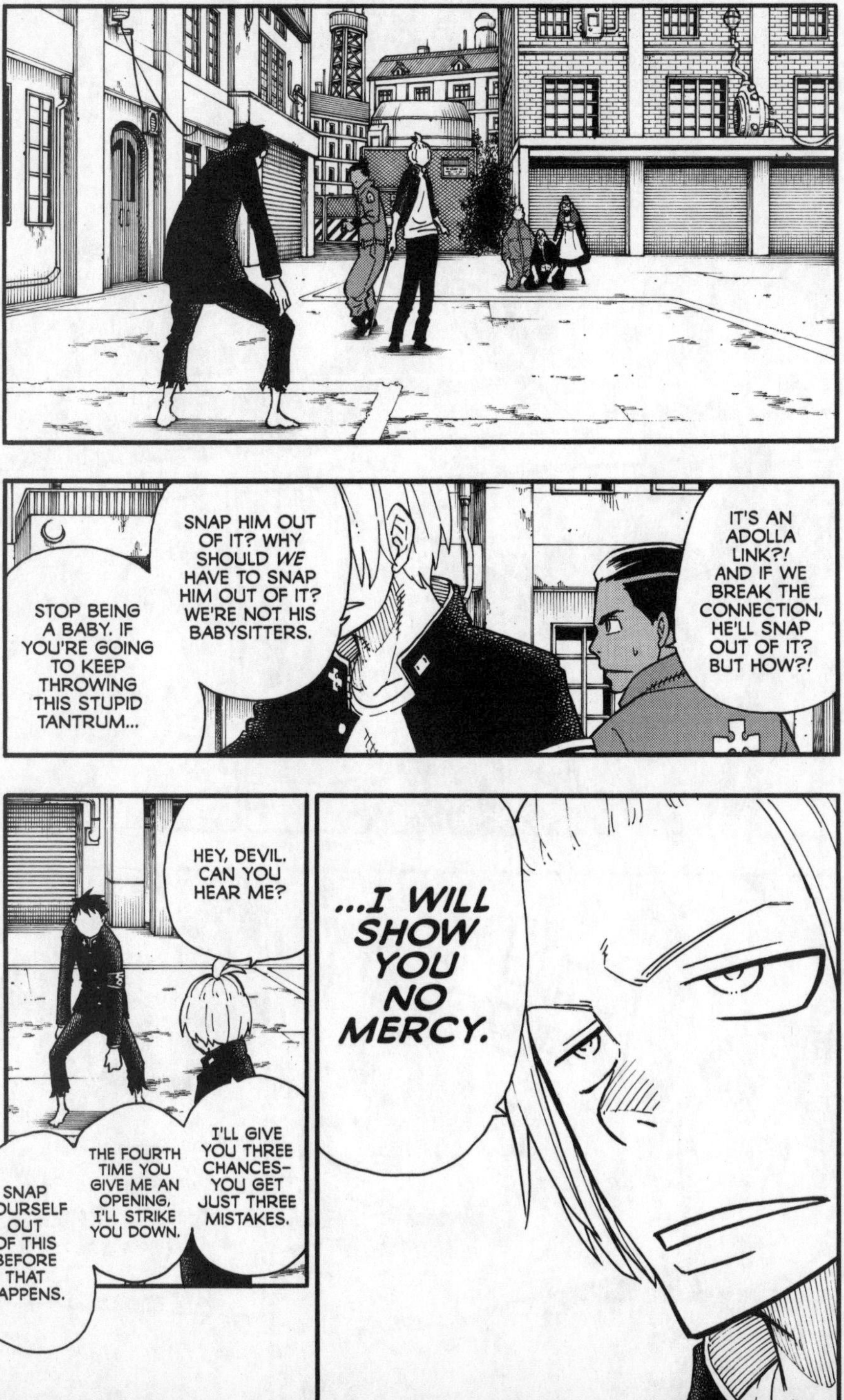
IT'S AN ADOLLA LINK?! AND IF WE BREAK THE CONNECTION, HE'LL SNAP OUT OF IT? BUT HOW?!
SNAP HIM OUT OF IT? WHY SHOULD *WE* HAVE TO SNAP HIM OUT OF IT? WE'RE NOT HIS BABYSITTERS.
STOP BEING A BABY. IF YOU'RE GOING TO KEEP THROWING THIS STUPID TANTRUM...
...I WILL SHOW YOU NO MERCY.
HEY, DEVIL. CAN YOU HEAR ME?
I'LL GIVE YOU THREE CHANCES– YOU GET JUST THREE MISTAKES.
THE FOURTH TIME YOU GIVE ME AN OPENING, I'LL STRIKE YOU DOWN.
SNAP YOURSELF OUT OF THIS BEFORE THAT HAPPENS.

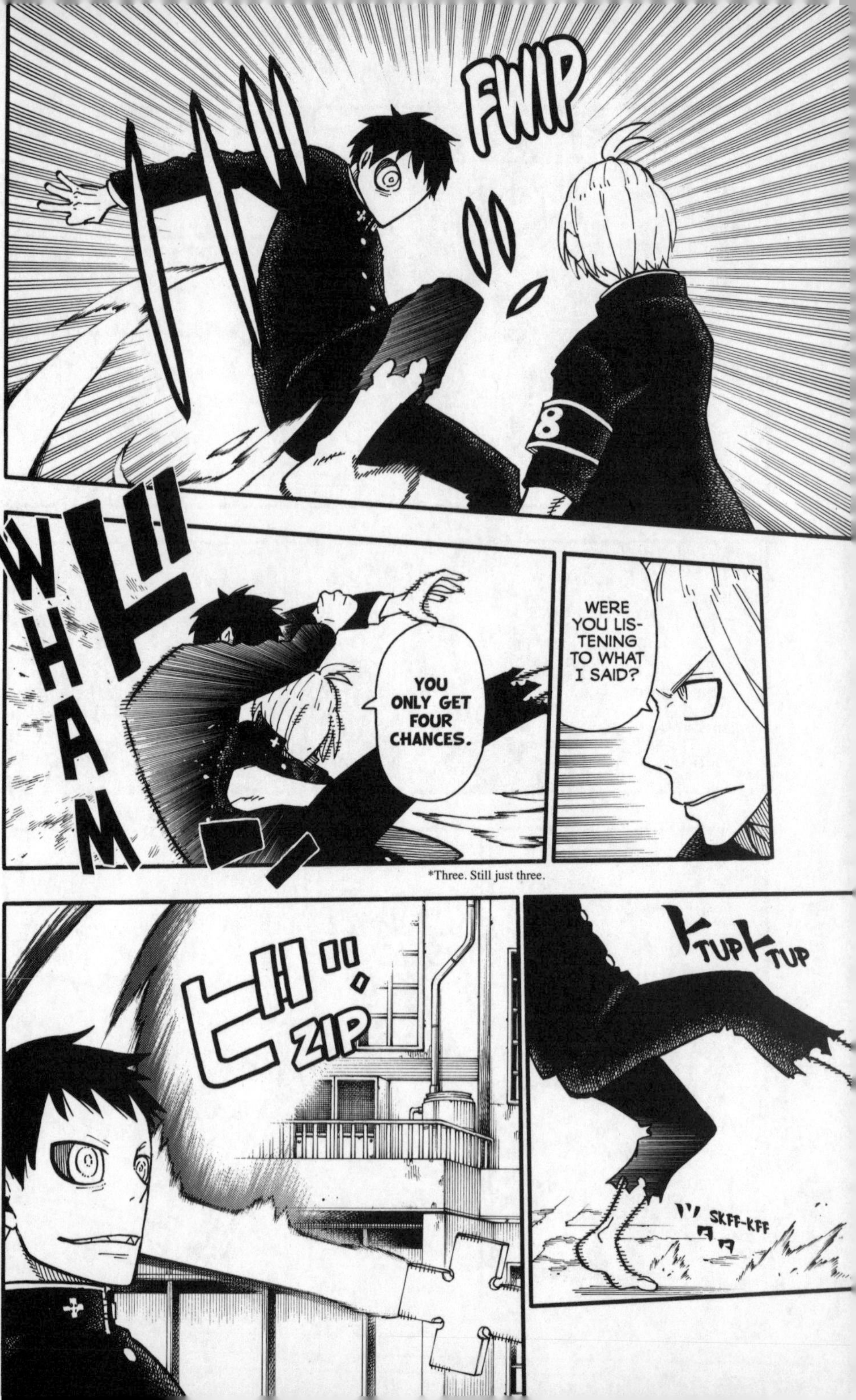
FWIP
WERE YOU LISTENING TO WHAT I SAID?
YOU ONLY GET FOUR CHANCES.
WHAM
TUP TUP
SKFF-KFF
ZIP
*Three. Still just three.

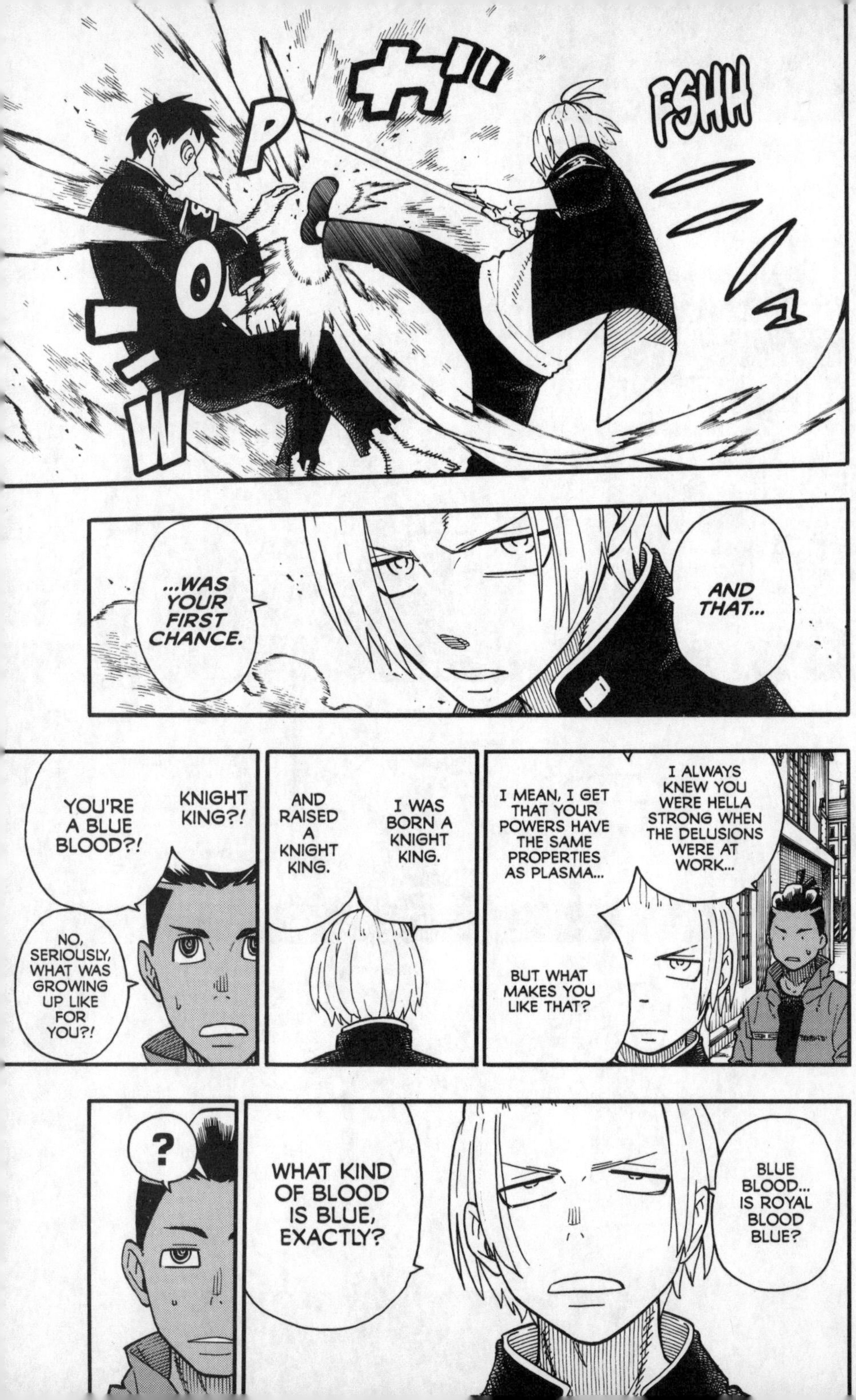
FSHH
POW
AND THAT...
...WAS YOUR FIRST CHANCE.
I ALWAYS KNEW YOU WERE HELLA STRONG WHEN THE DELUSIONS WERE AT WORK...
I MEAN, I GET THAT YOUR POWERS HAVE THE SAME PROPERTIES AS PLASMA...
BUT WHAT MAKES YOU LIKE THAT?
I WAS BORN A KNIGHT KING.
AND RAISED A KNIGHT KING.
KNIGHT KING?!
YOU'RE A BLUE BLOOD?!
NO, SERIOUSLY, WHAT WAS GROWING UP LIKE FOR YOU?!
BLUE BLOOD... IS ROYAL BLOOD BLUE?
WHAT KIND OF BLOOD IS BLUE, EXACTLY?
?

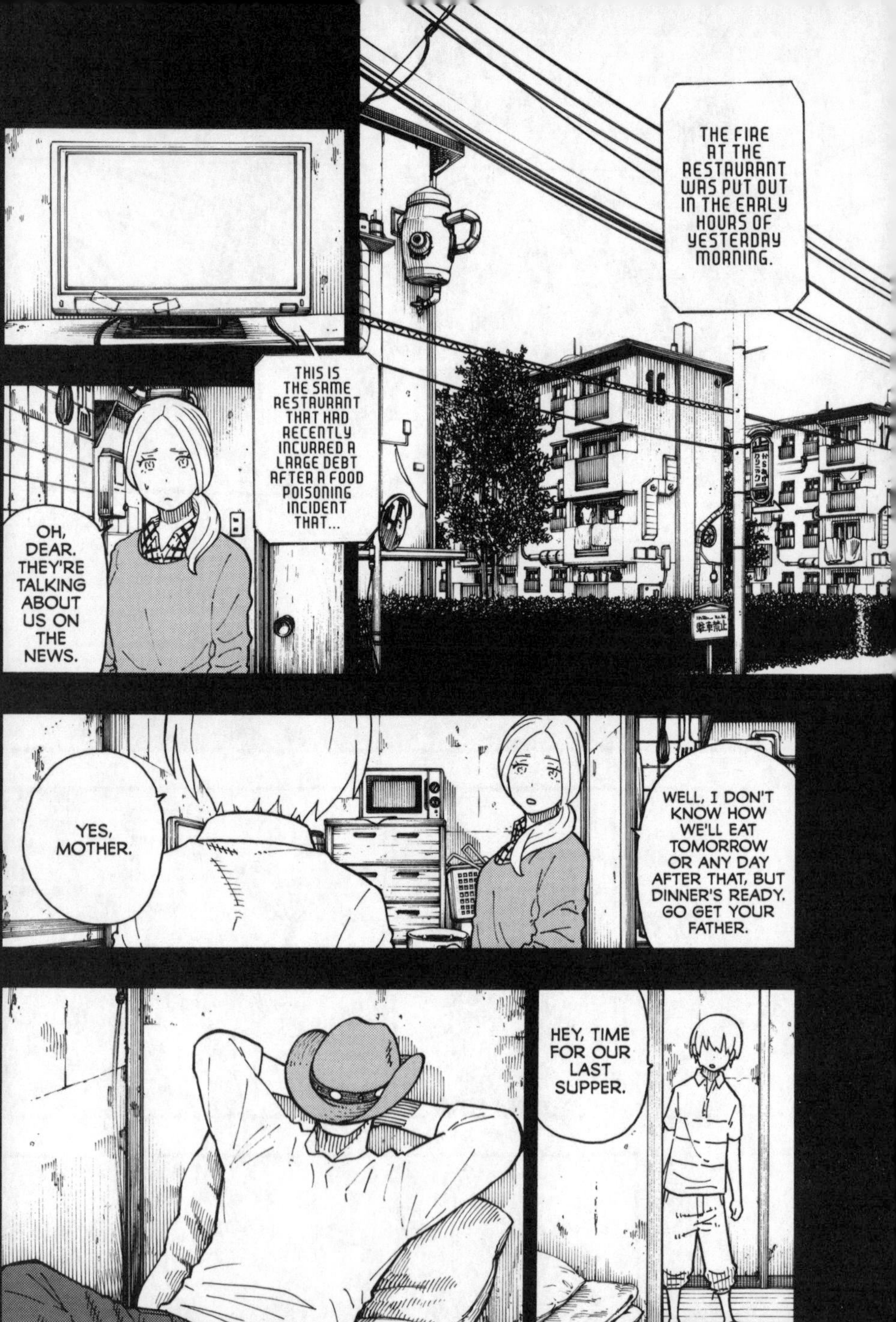
THE FIRE AT THE RESTAURANT WAS PUT OUT IN THE EARLY HOURS OF YESTERDAY MORNING.
THIS IS THE SAME RESTAURANT THAT HAD RECENTLY INCURRED A LARGE DEBT AFTER A FOOD POISONING INCIDENT THAT...
OH, DEAR. THEY'RE TALKING ABOUT US ON THE NEWS.
WELL, I DON'T KNOW HOW WE'LL EAT TOMORROW OR ANY DAY AFTER THAT, BUT DINNER'S READY. GO GET YOUR FATHER.
YES, MOTHER.
HEY, TIME FOR OUR LAST SUPPER.

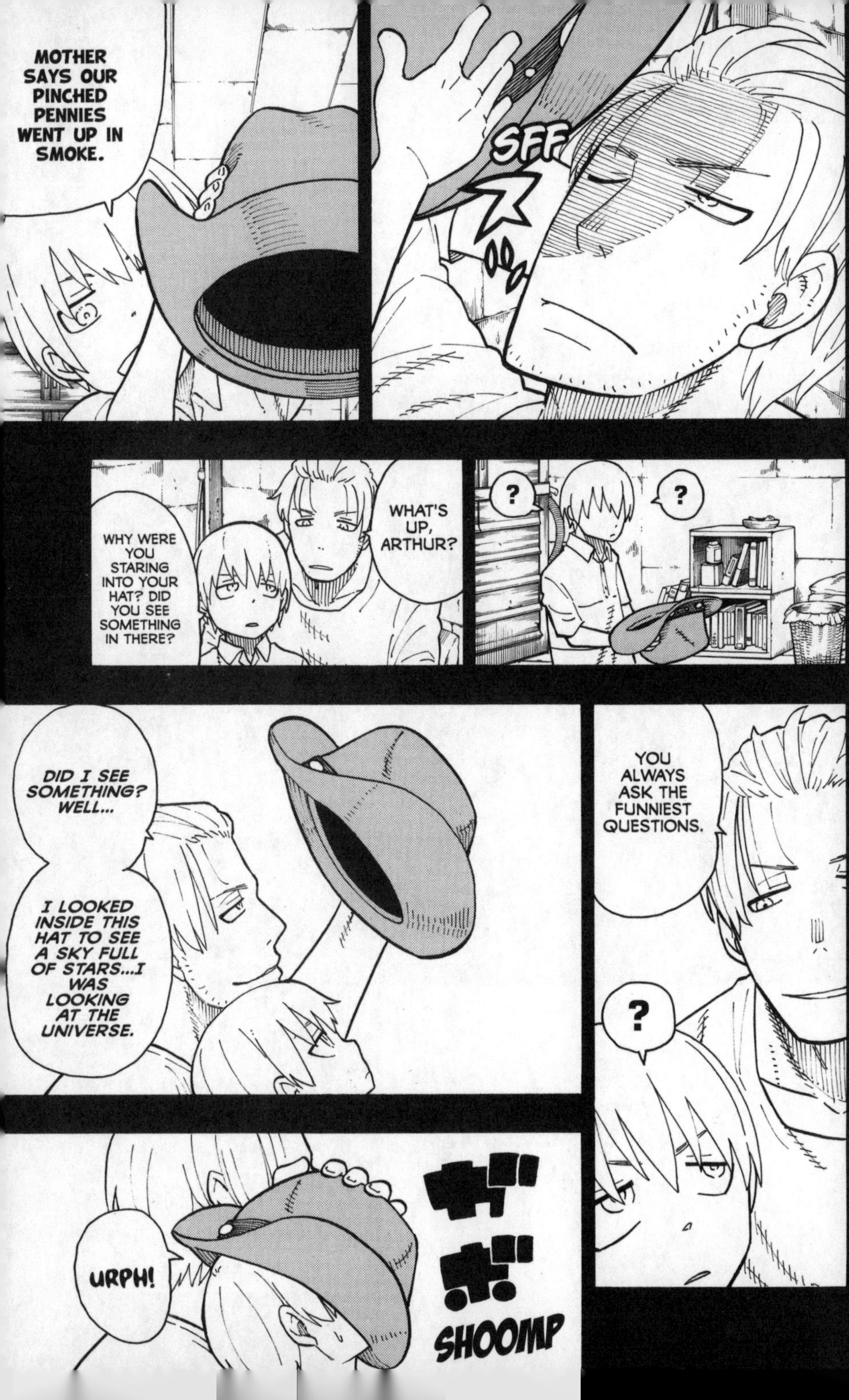
SFF
MOTHER SAYS OUR PINCHED PENNIES WENT UP IN SMOKE.
?
?
WHAT'S UP, ARTHUR?
WHY WERE YOU STARING INTO YOUR HAT? DID YOU SEE SOMETHING IN THERE?
YOU ALWAYS ASK THE FUNNIEST QUESTIONS.
?
DID I SEE SOMETHING? WELL...
I LOOKED INSIDE THIS HAT TO SEE A SKY FULL OF STARS...I WAS LOOKING AT THE UNIVERSE.
SHOOMP
URPH!

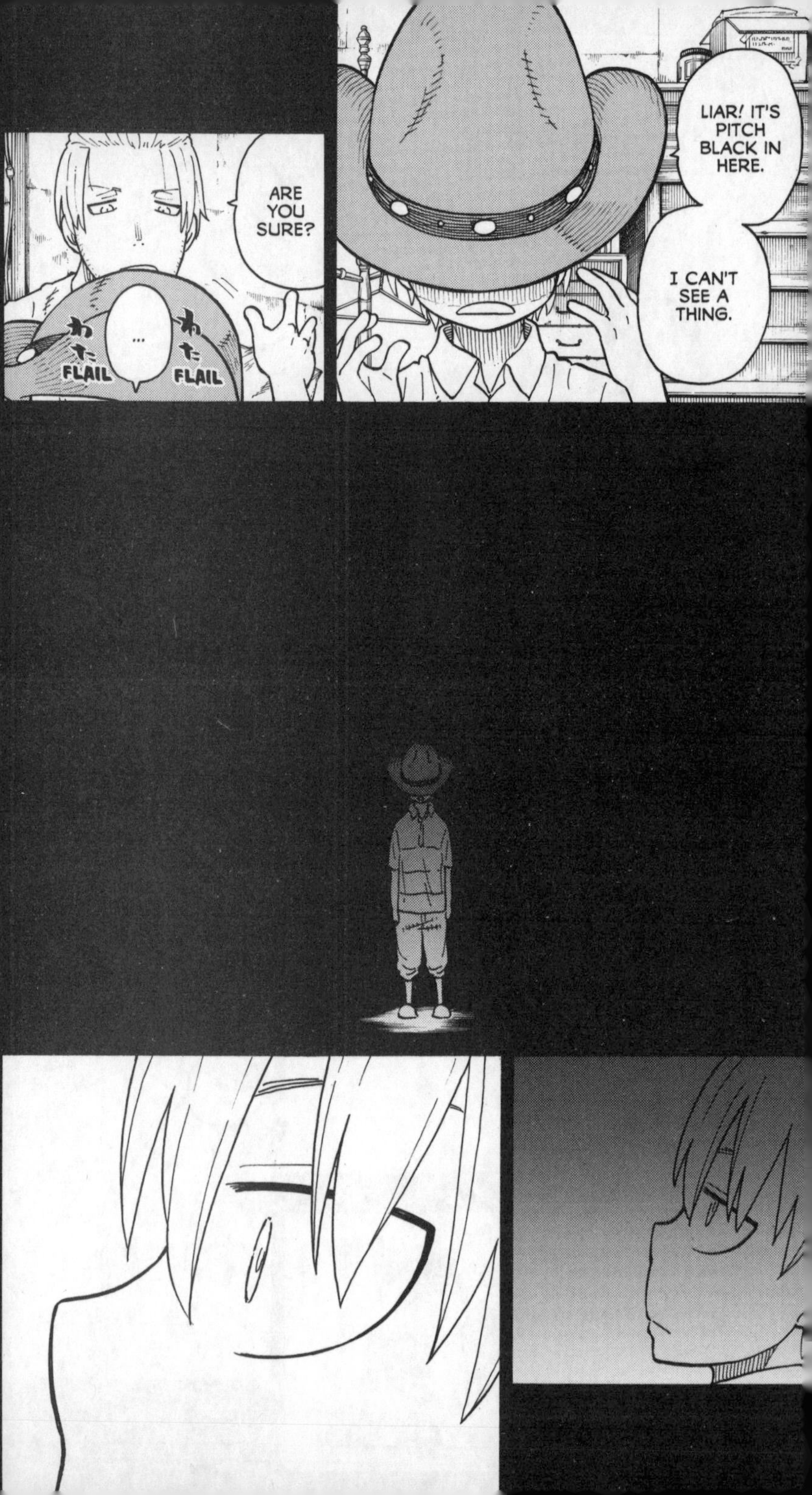
LIAR! IT'S PITCH BLACK IN HERE.
I CAN'T SEE A THING.
ARE YOU SURE?
...
わた FLAIL
わた FLAIL

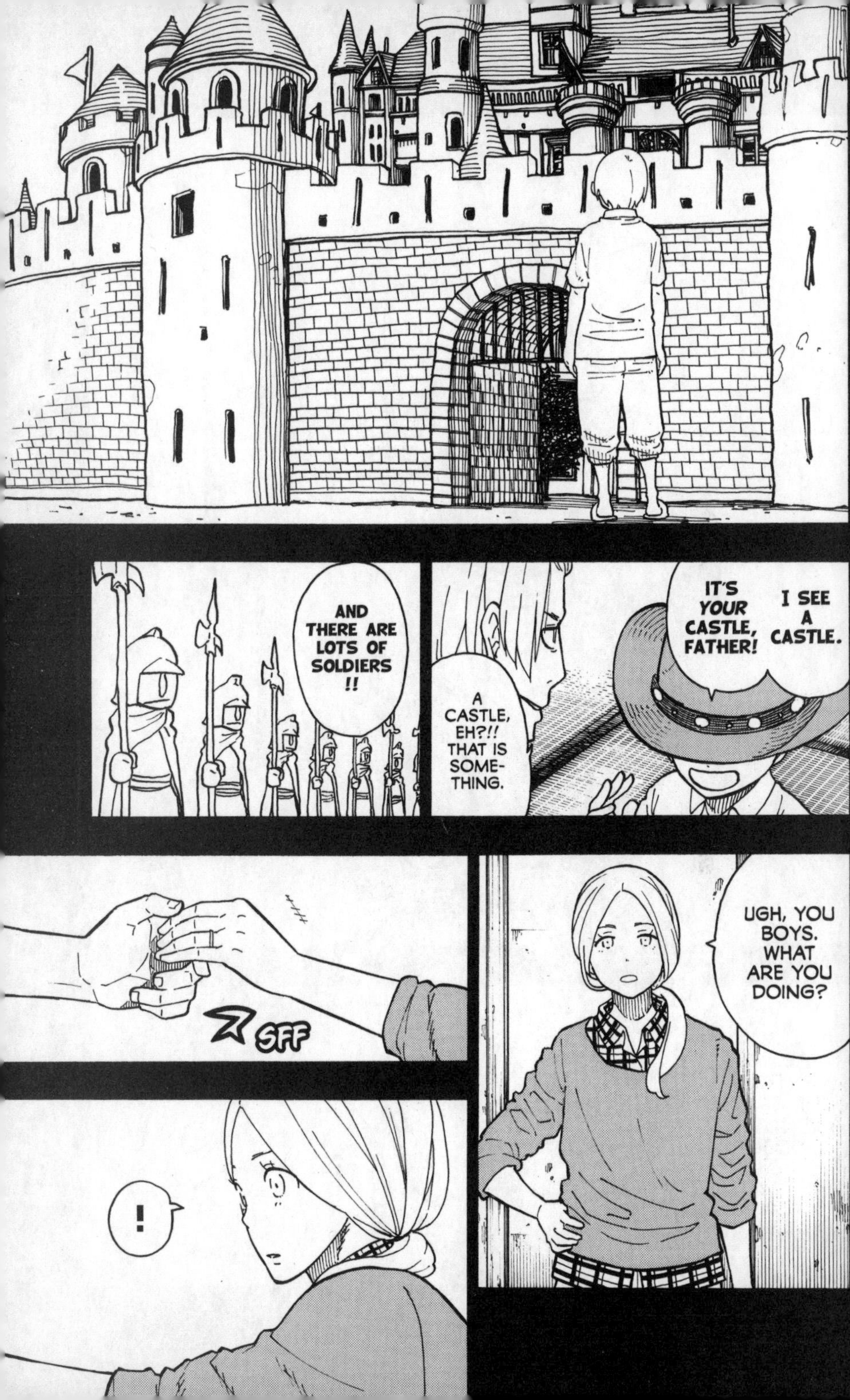
I SEE A CASTLE.
IT'S *YOUR* CASTLE, FATHER!
A CASTLE, EH?!! THAT IS SOME-THING.
AND THERE ARE LOTS OF SOLDIERS!!
UGH, YOU BOYS. WHAT ARE YOU DOING?
SFF
!

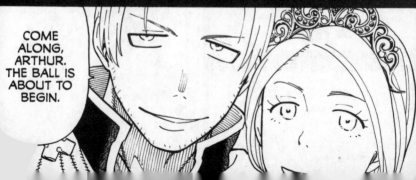

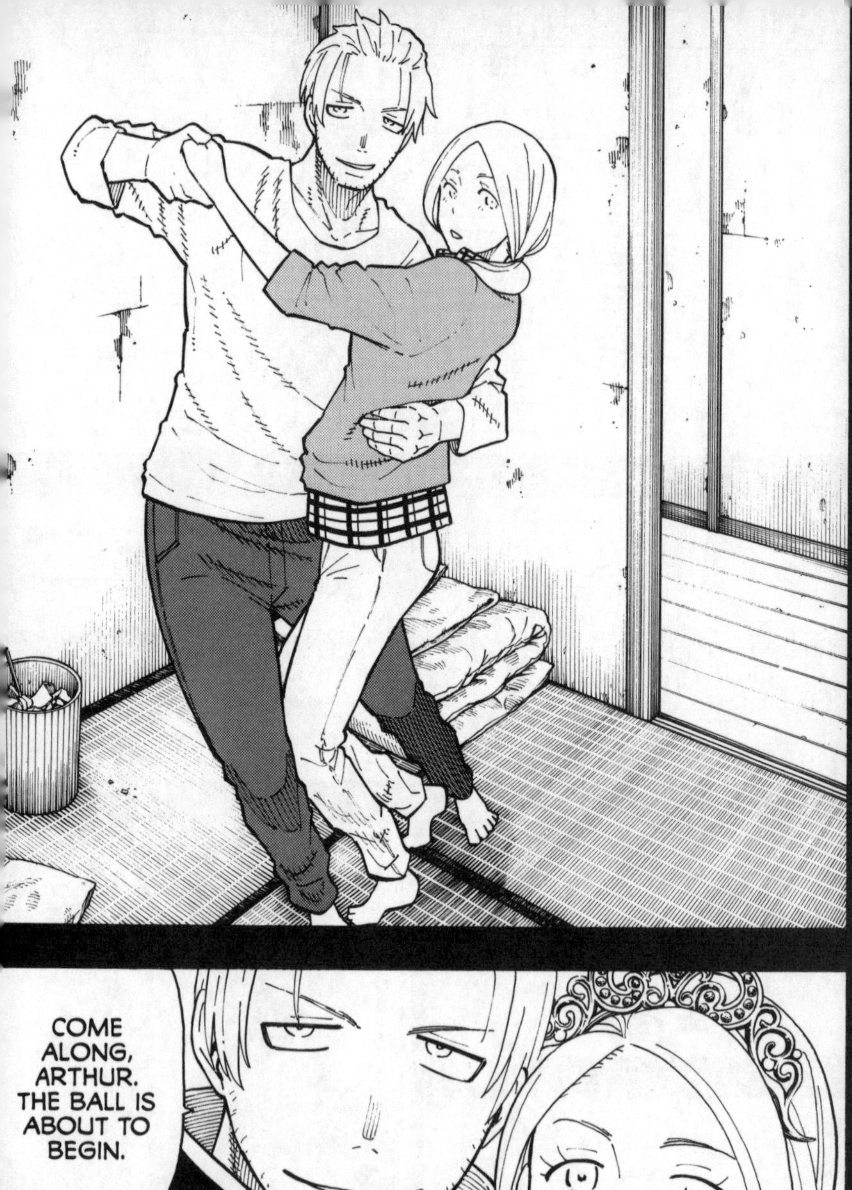
COME ALONG, ARTHUR. THE BALL IS ABOUT TO BEGIN.

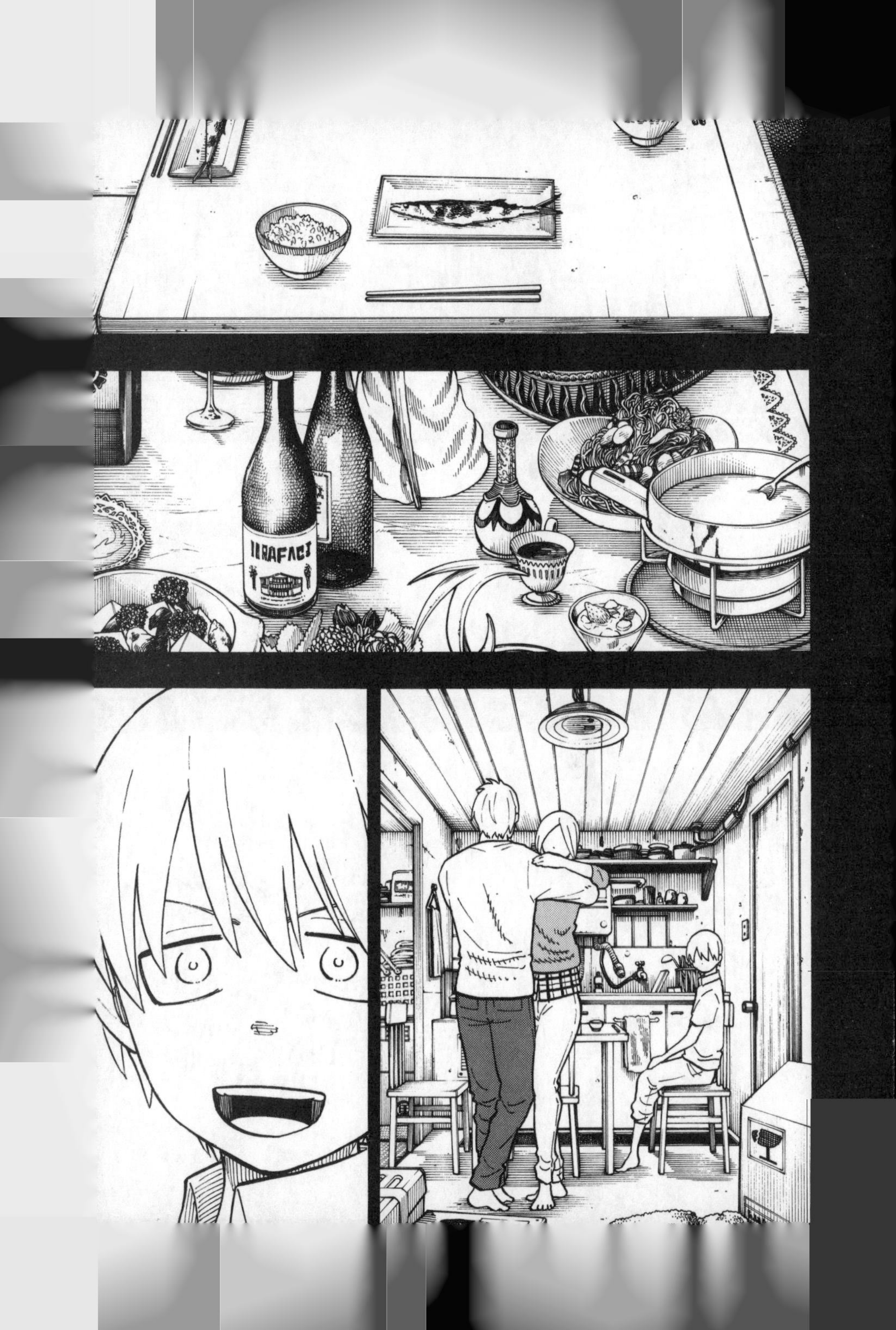

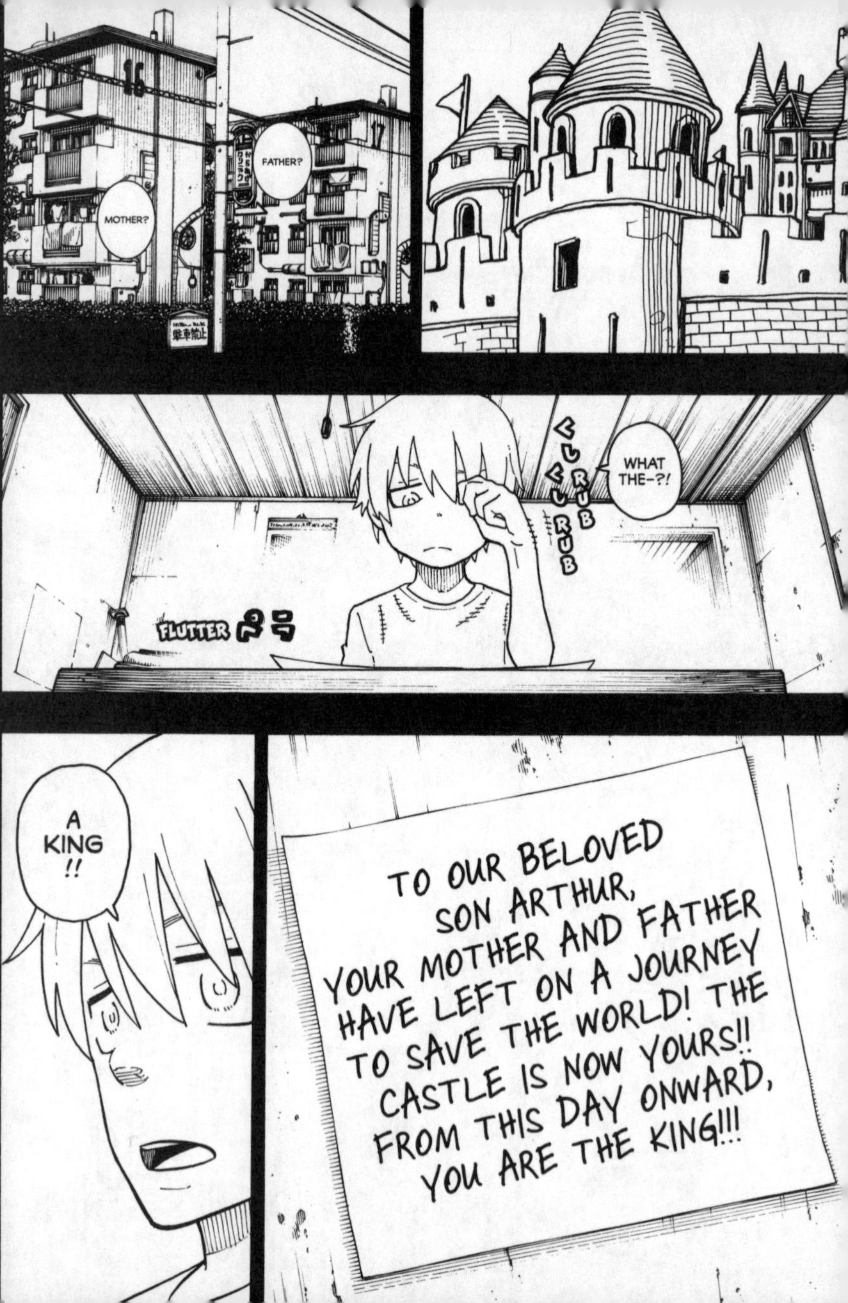
FATHER?
MOTHER?
WHAT THE-?!
RUB RUB
FLUTTER
TO OUR BELOVED SON ARTHUR, YOUR MOTHER AND FATHER HAVE LEFT ON A JOURNEY TO SAVE THE WORLD! THE CASTLE IS NOW YOURS!! FROM THIS DAY ONWARD, YOU ARE THE KING!!!
A KING !!

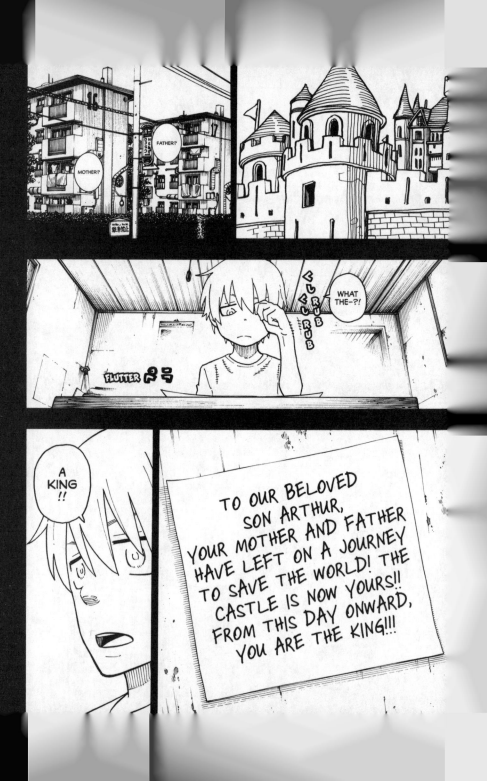

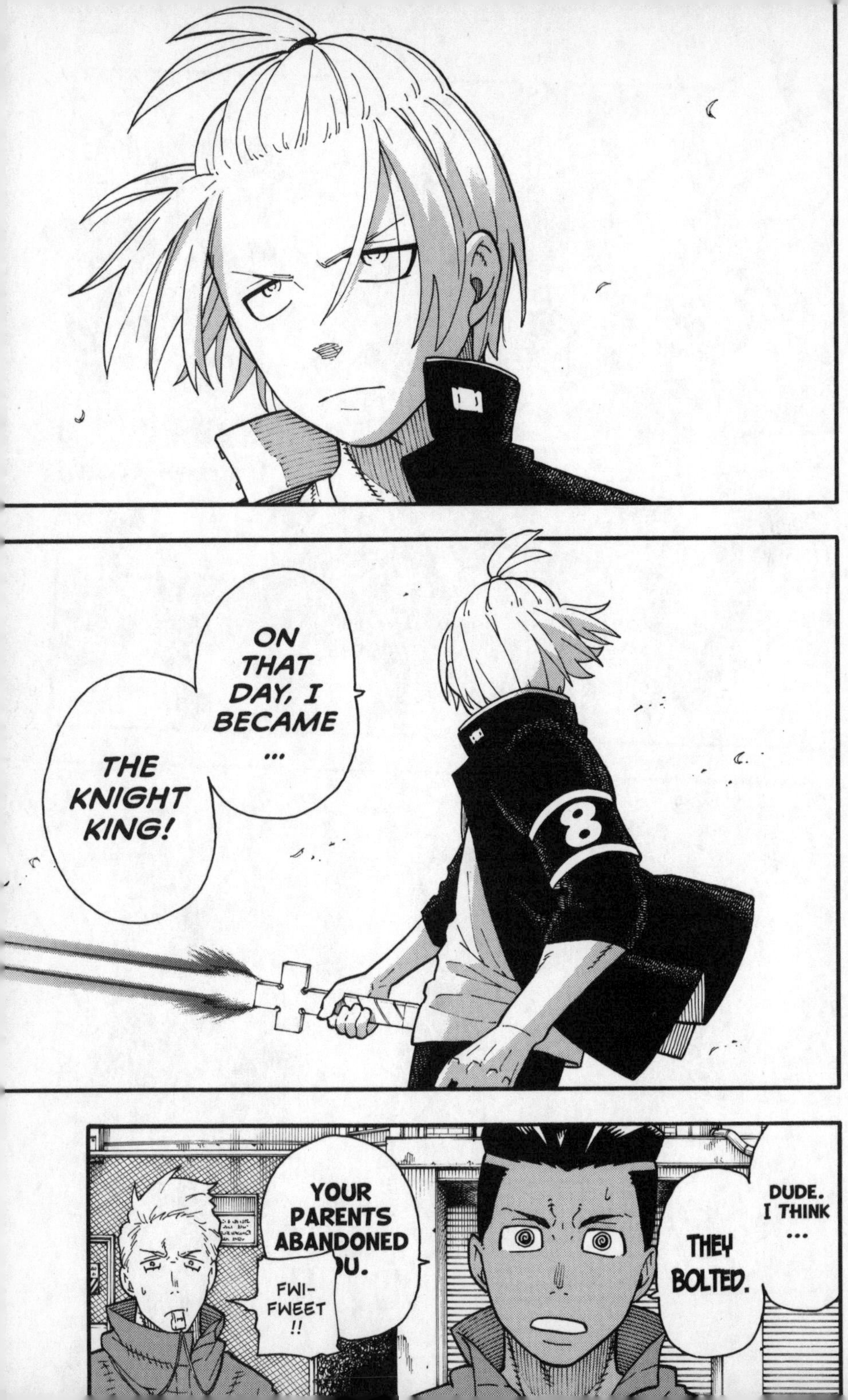
ON THAT DAY, I BECAME ...
THE KNIGHT KING!
DUDE. I THINK ...
THEY BOLTED.
YOUR PARENTS ABANDONED U.
FWI-FWEET !!

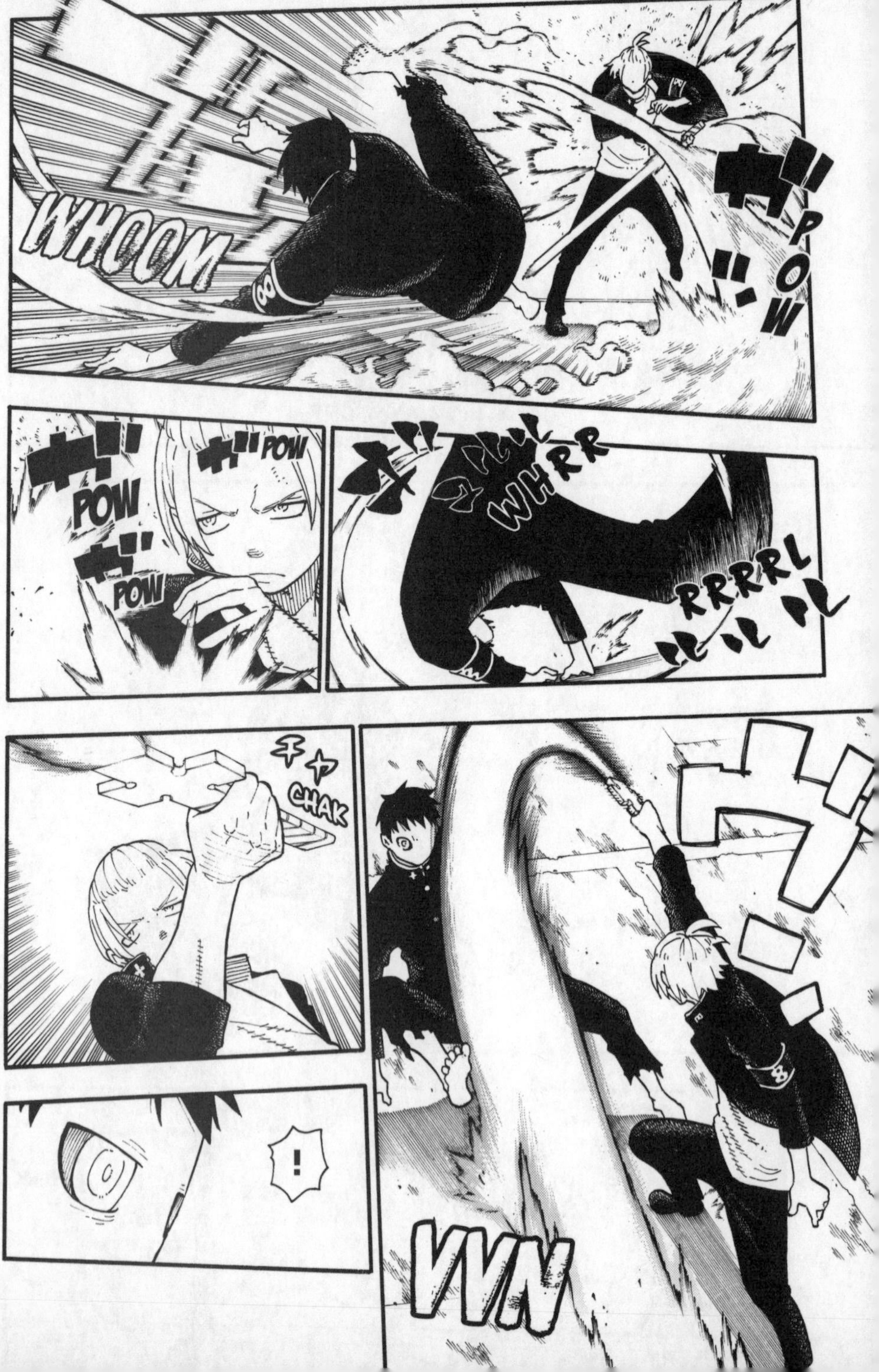
POW
WHOOM
WHRR
RRRRL
POW
POW
POW
VVN
CHAK
!

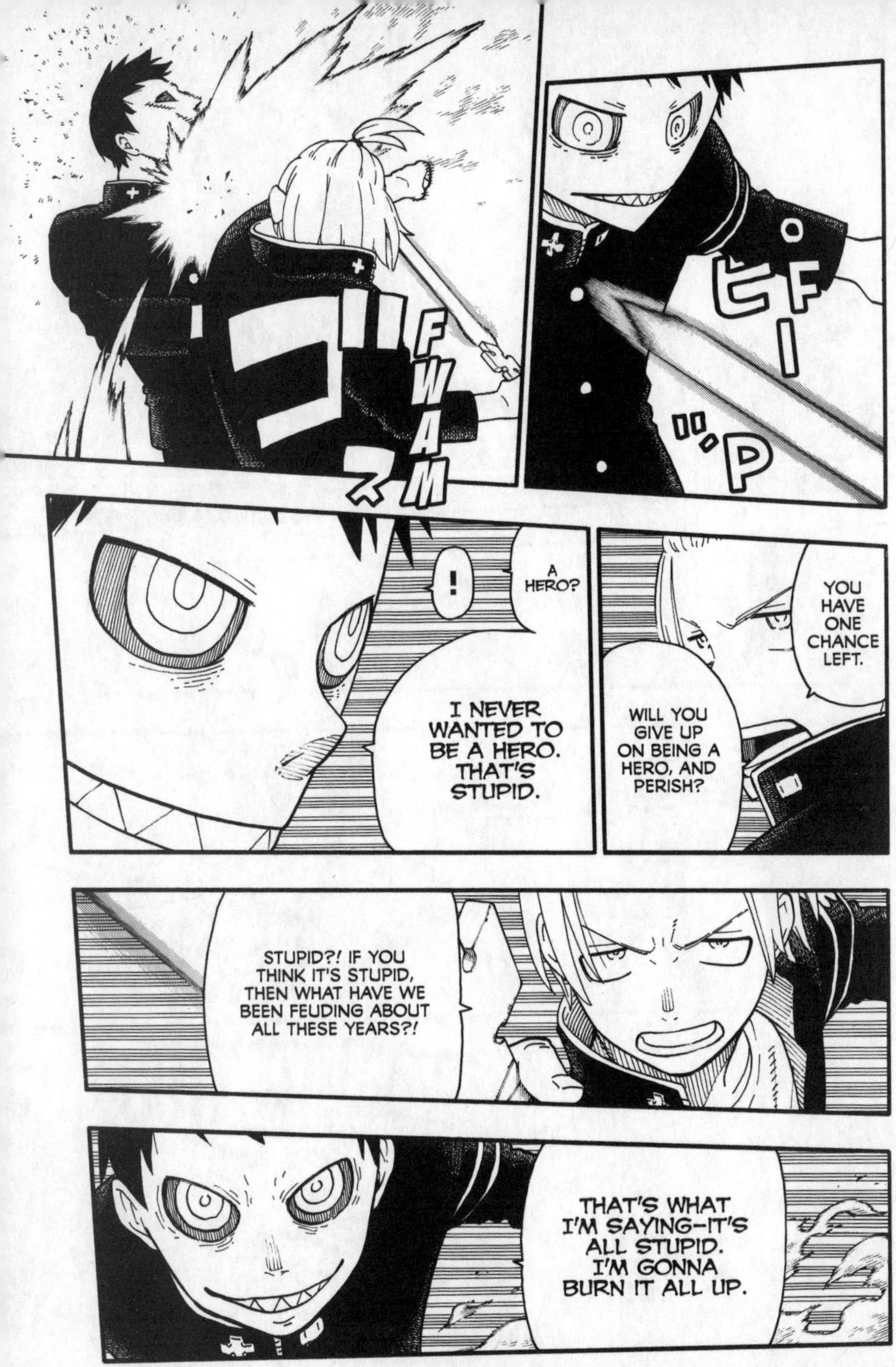
FIP
FWAM
YOU HAVE ONE CHANCE LEFT.
WILL YOU GIVE UP ON BEING A HERO, AND PERISH?
A HERO?
!
I NEVER WANTED TO BE A HERO. THAT'S STUPID.
STUPID?! IF YOU THINK IT'S STUPID, THEN WHAT HAVE WE BEEN FEUDING ABOUT ALL THESE YEARS?!
THAT'S WHAT I'M SAYING–IT'S ALL STUPID. I'M GONNA BURN IT ALL UP.

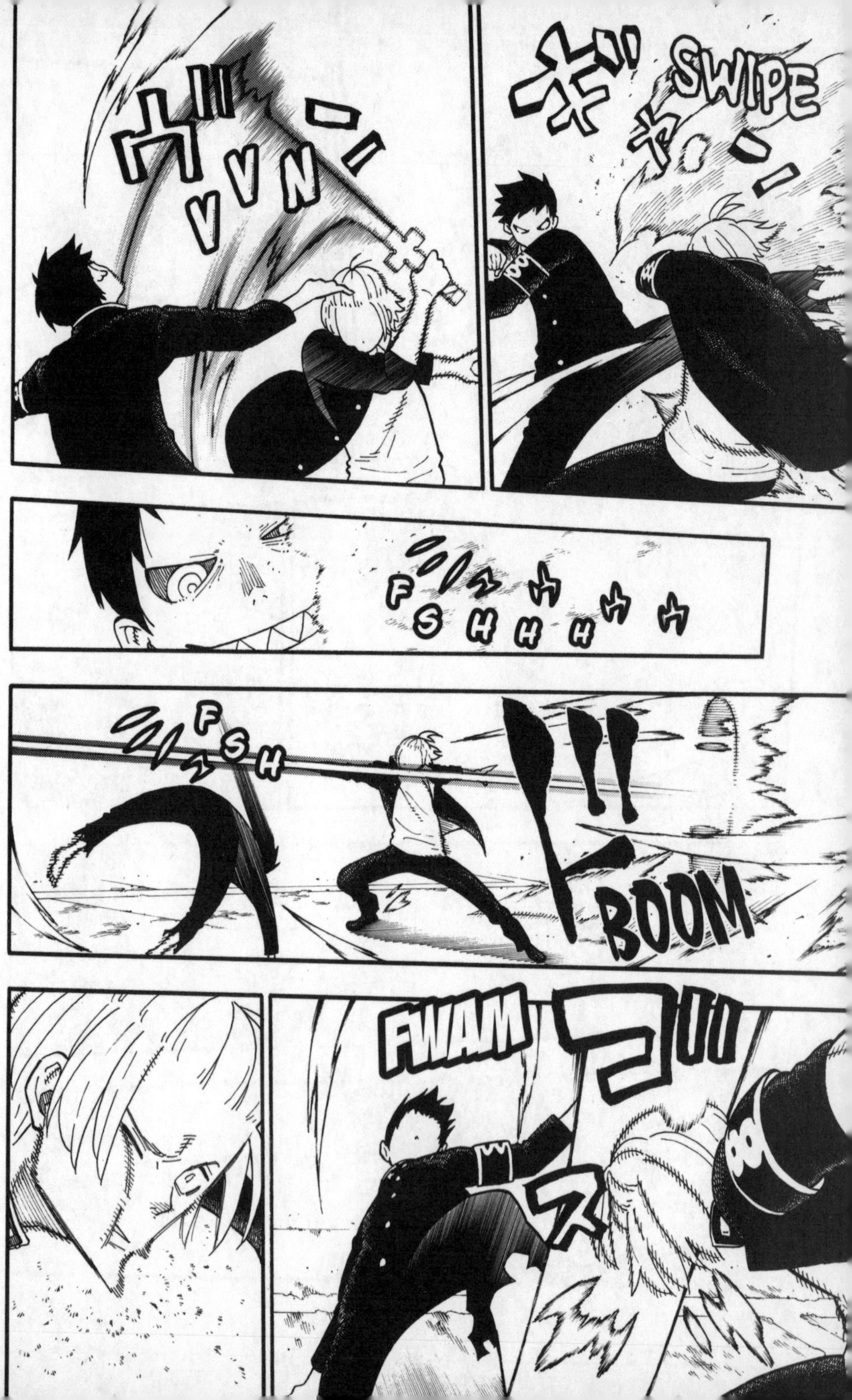
SWIPE
VVN
FSHHHH
FSH
BOOM
FWAM

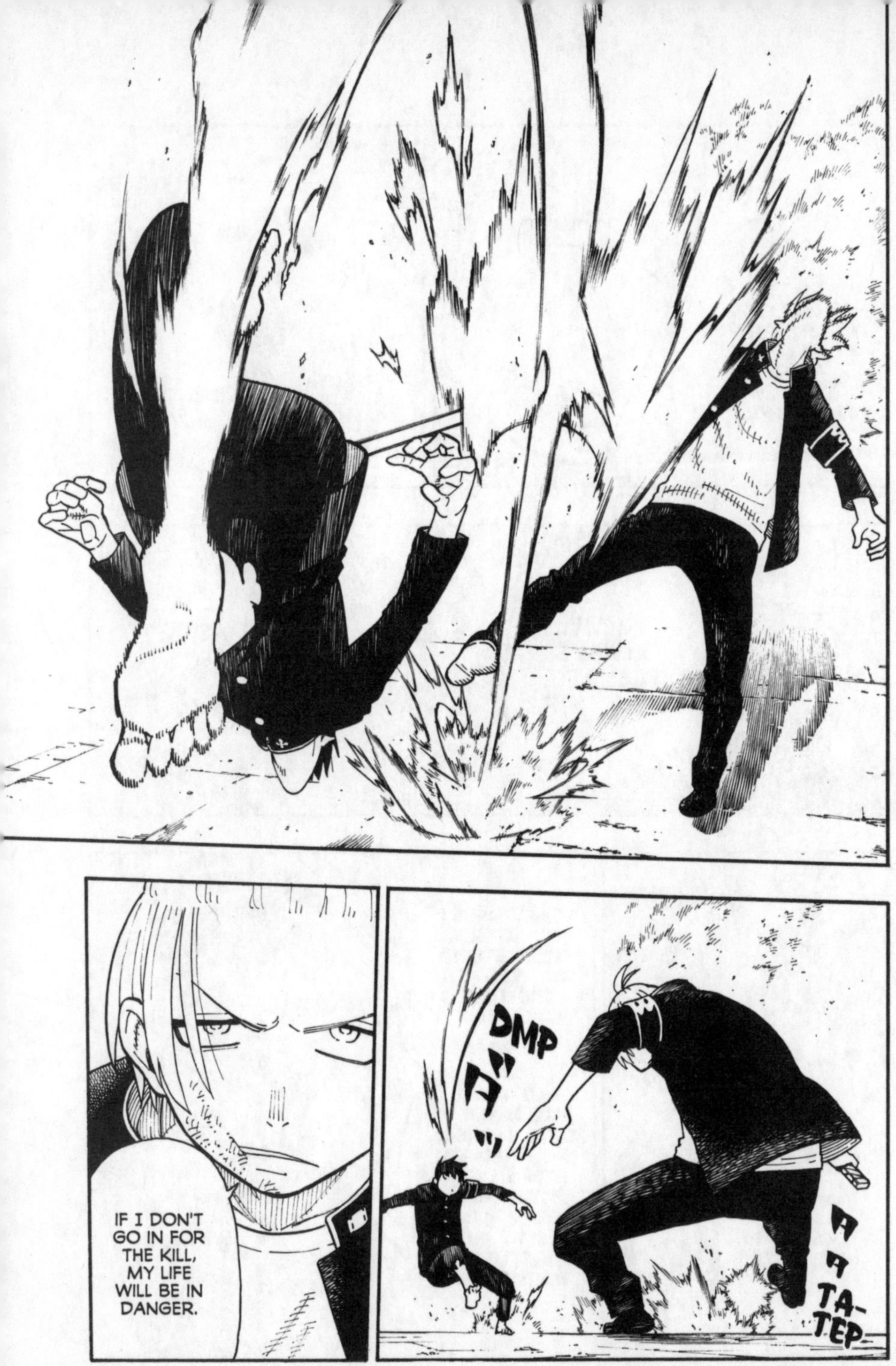
DMP
ダッ
TA-TEP
タタ
IF I DON'T GO IN FOR THE KILL, MY LIFE WILL BE IN DANGER.

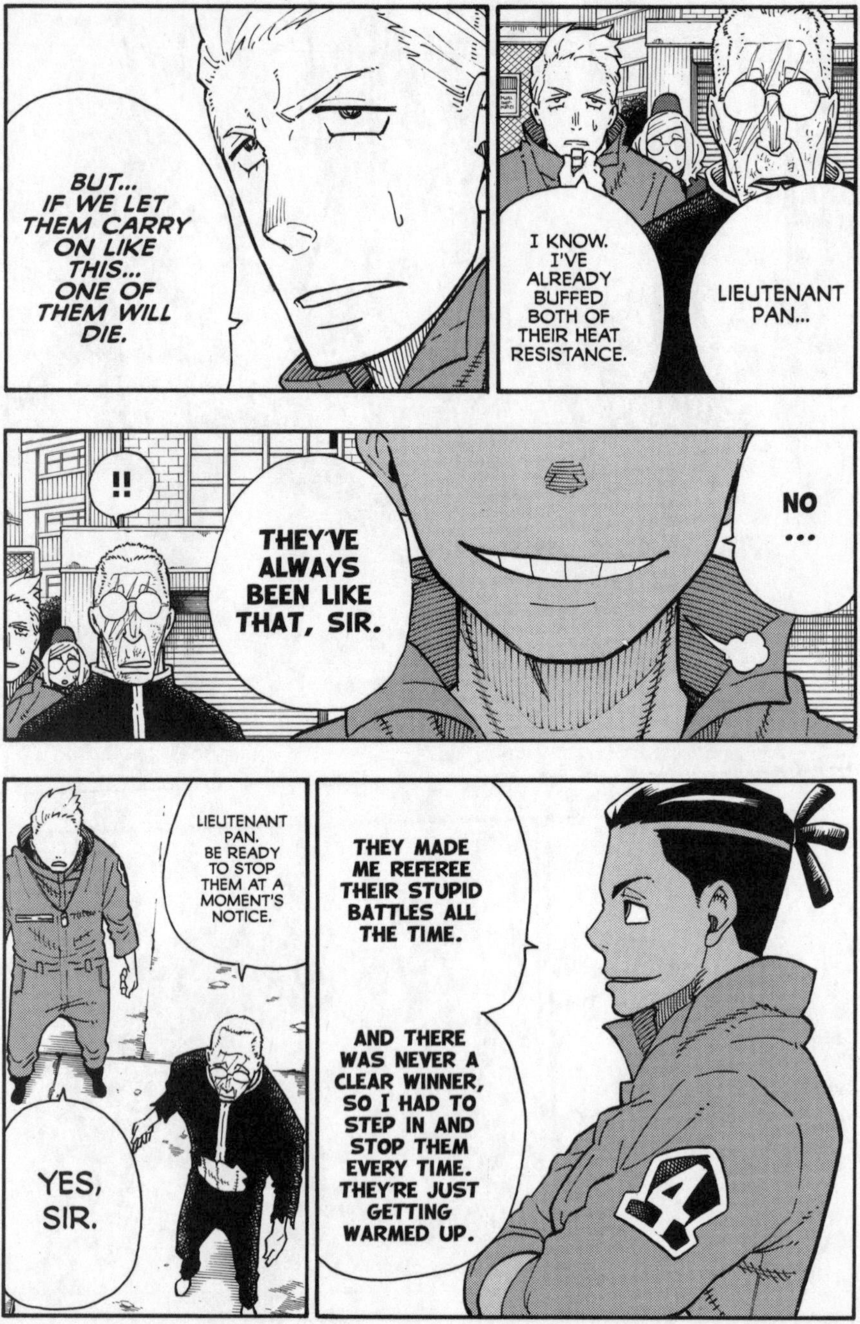
LIEUTENANT PAN...
I KNOW. I'VE ALREADY BUFFED BOTH OF THEIR HEAT RESISTANCE.
BUT... IF WE LET THEM CARRY ON LIKE THIS... ONE OF THEM WILL DIE.
NO ...
THEY'VE ALWAYS BEEN LIKE THAT, SIR.
!!
THEY MADE ME REFEREE THEIR STUPID BATTLES ALL THE TIME.
AND THERE WAS NEVER A CLEAR WINNER, SO I HAD TO STEP IN AND STOP THEM EVERY TIME. THEY'RE JUST GETTING WARMED UP.
LIEUTENANT PAN. BE READY TO STOP THEM AT A MOMENT'S NOTICE.
YES, SIR.

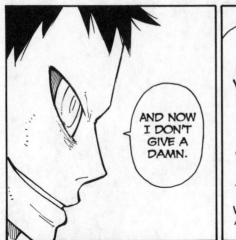

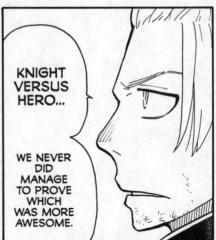

KNIGHT VERSUS HERO...
WE NEVER DID MANAGE TO PROVE WHICH WAS MORE AWESOME.
AND NOW I DON'T GIVE A DAMN.
...
I SEE. YOU'VE ABANDONED YOUR CONVICTIONS.
THEN I HAVE NO MORE NEED TO HOLD BACK.

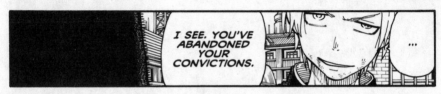

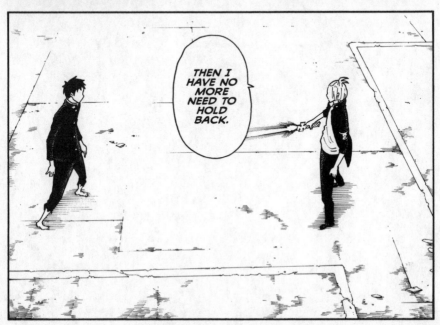

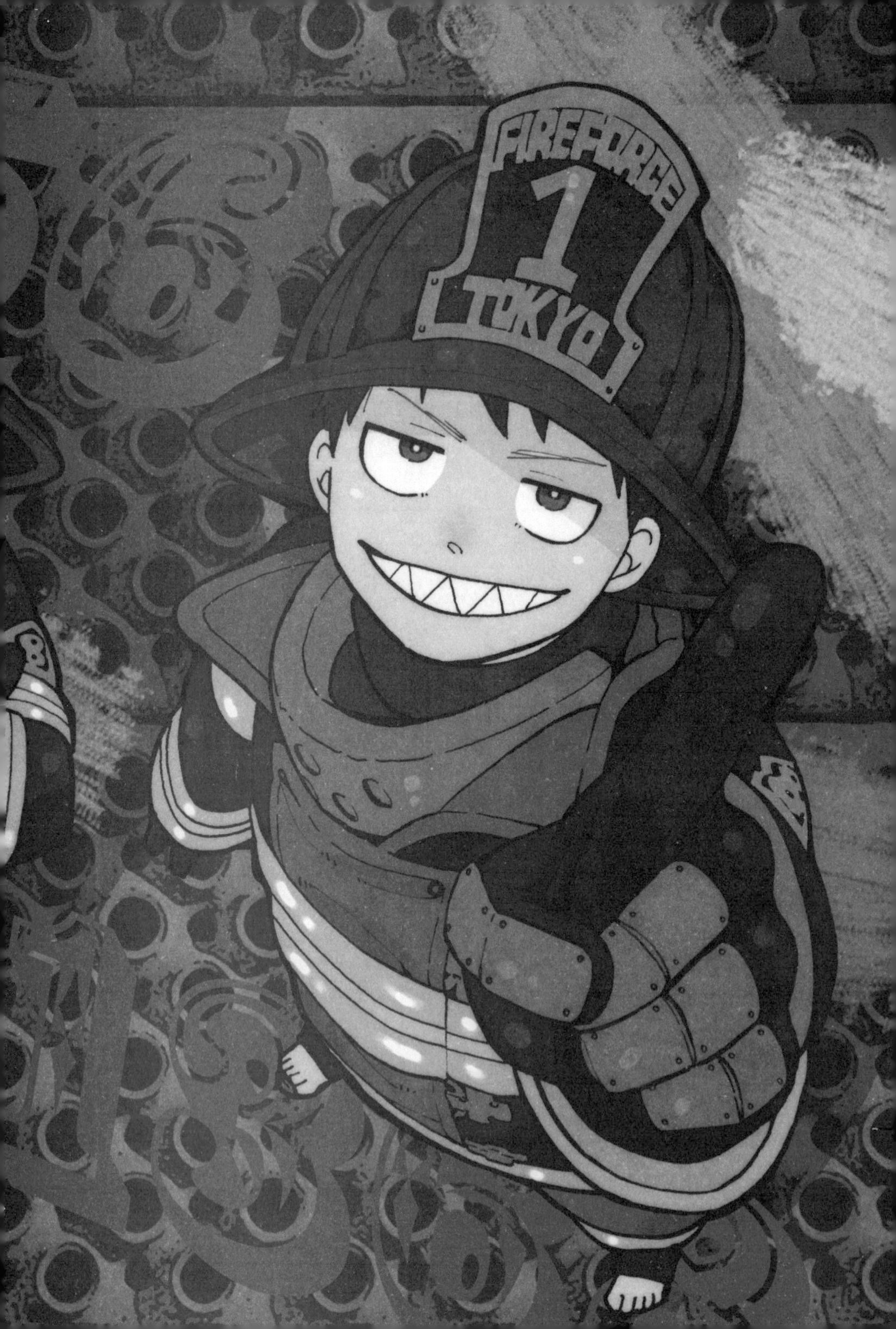
FIREFORCE
1
TOKYO

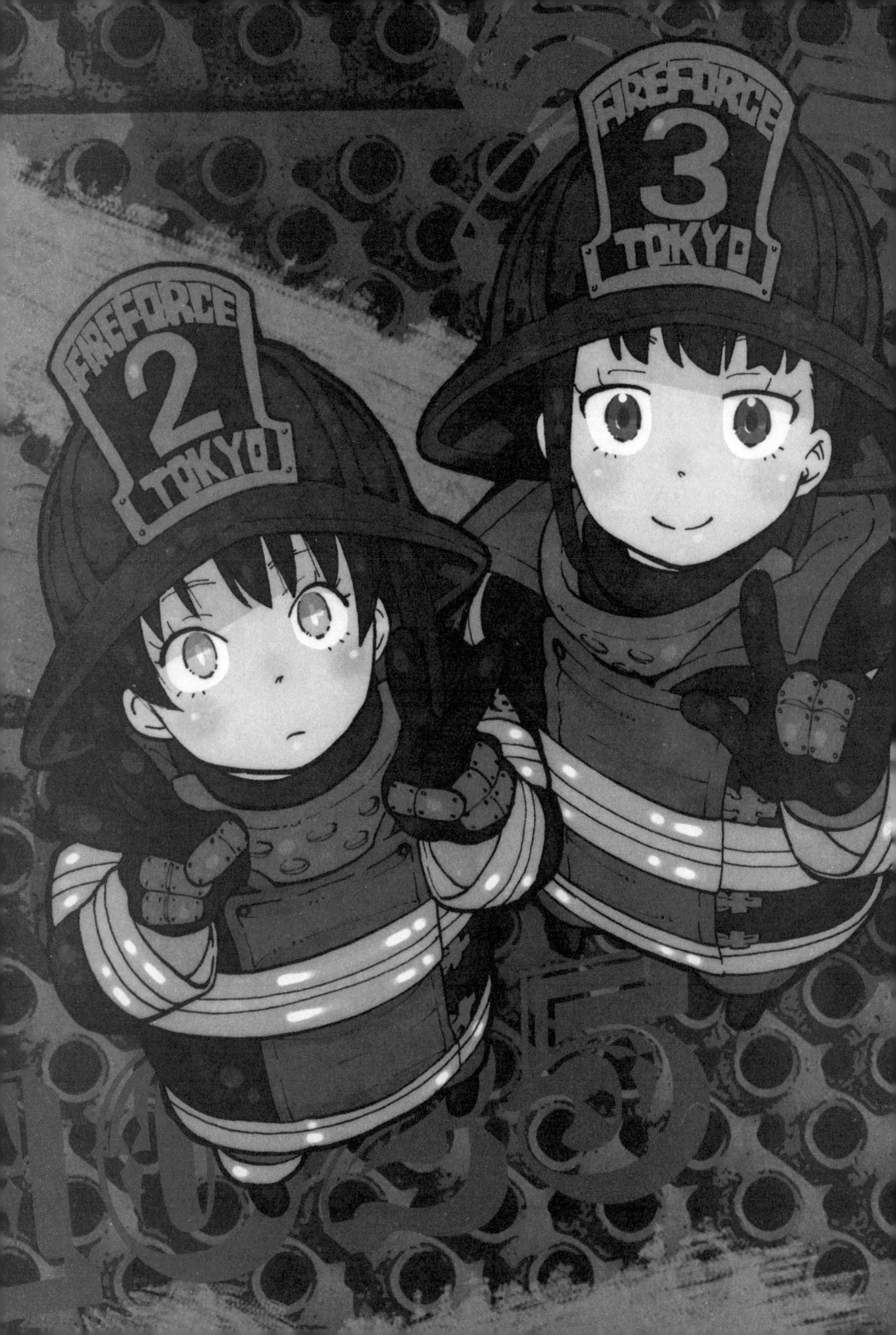
FIREFORCE
2
TOKYO
FIREFORCE
3
TOKYO

FIRE FORCE

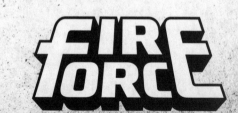

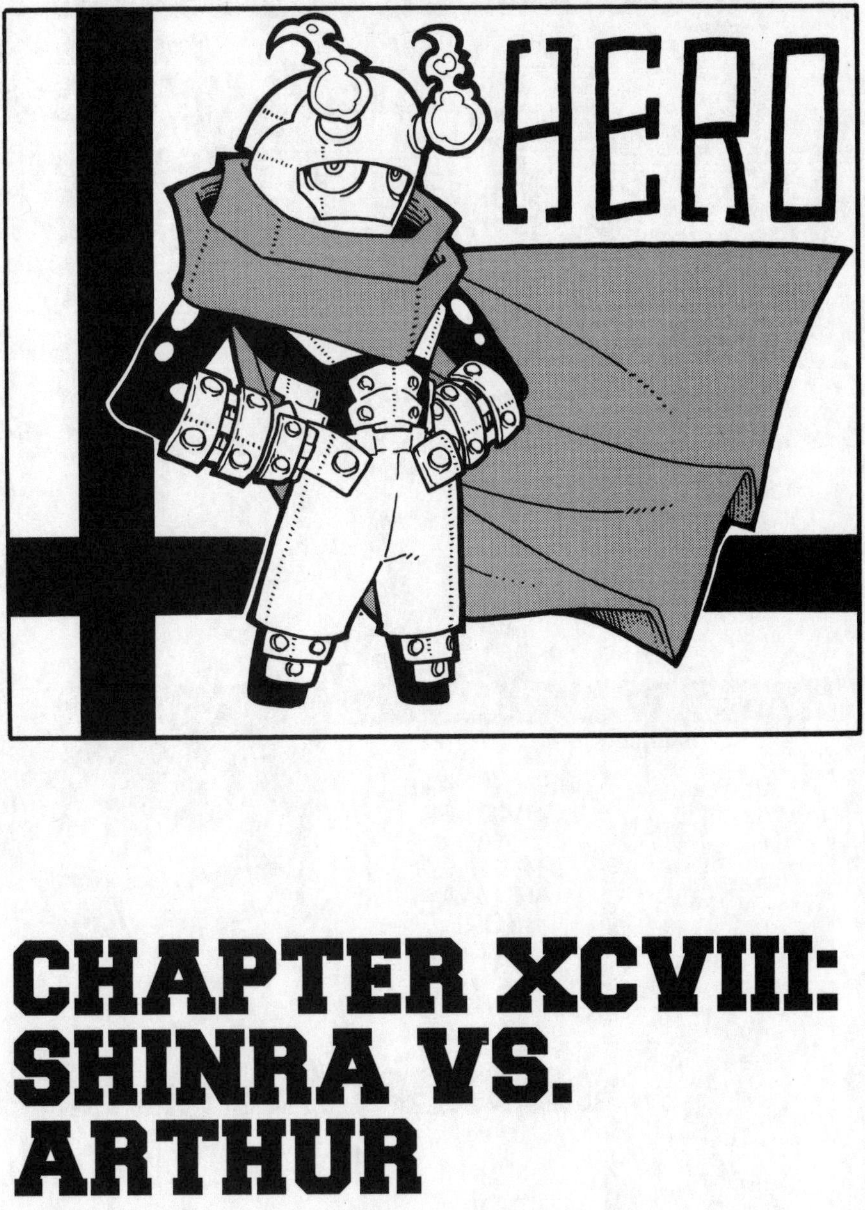
HERO

CHAPTER XCVIII: SHINRA VS. ARTHUR

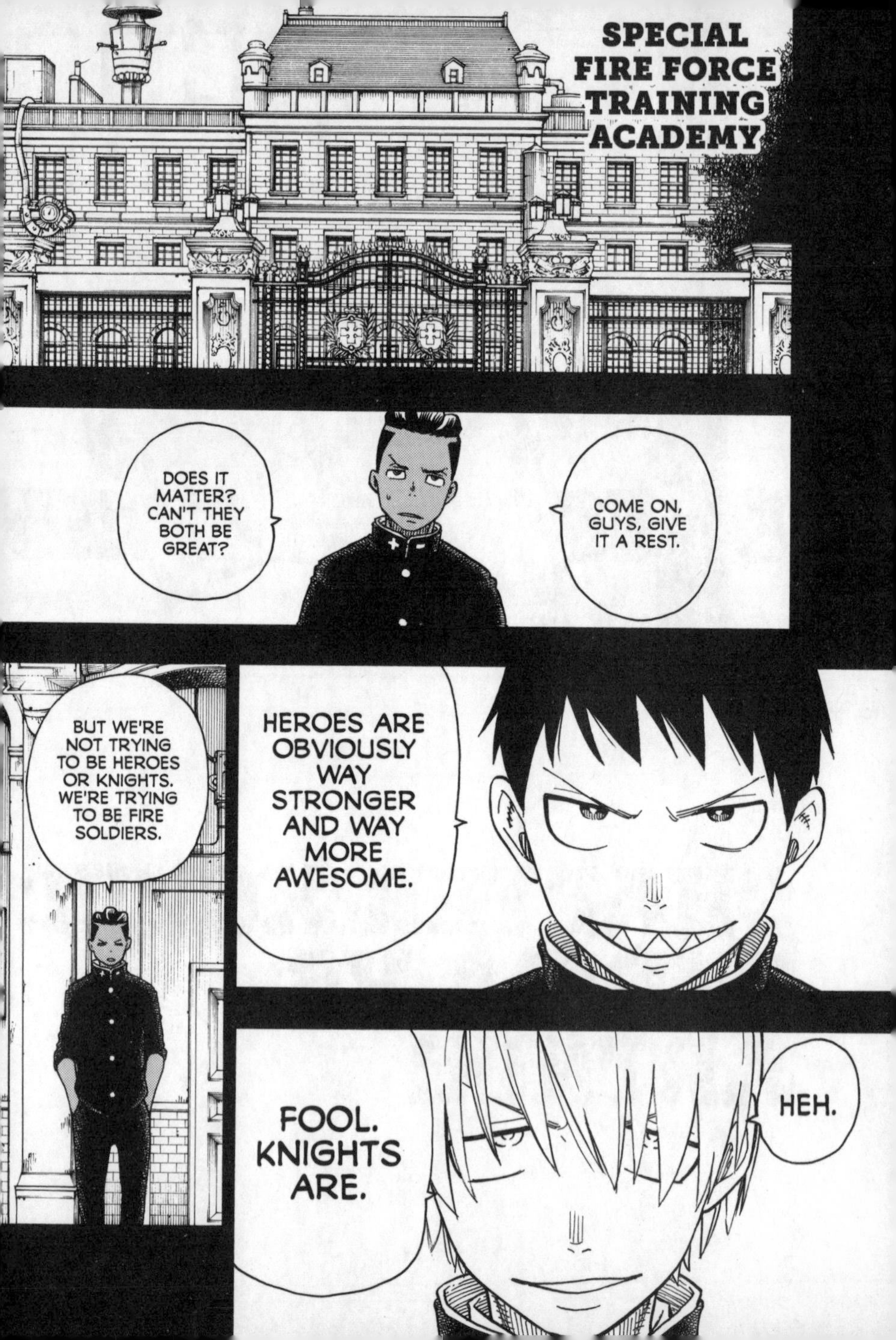
SPECIAL FIRE FORCE TRAINING ACADEMY
COME ON, GUYS, GIVE IT A REST.
DOES IT MATTER? CAN'T THEY BOTH BE GREAT?
HEROES ARE OBVIOUSLY WAY STRONGER AND WAY MORE AWESOME.
HEH.
FOOL. KNIGHTS ARE.
BUT WE'RE NOT TRYING TO BE HEROES OR KNIGHTS. WE'RE TRYING TO BE FIRE SOLDIERS.

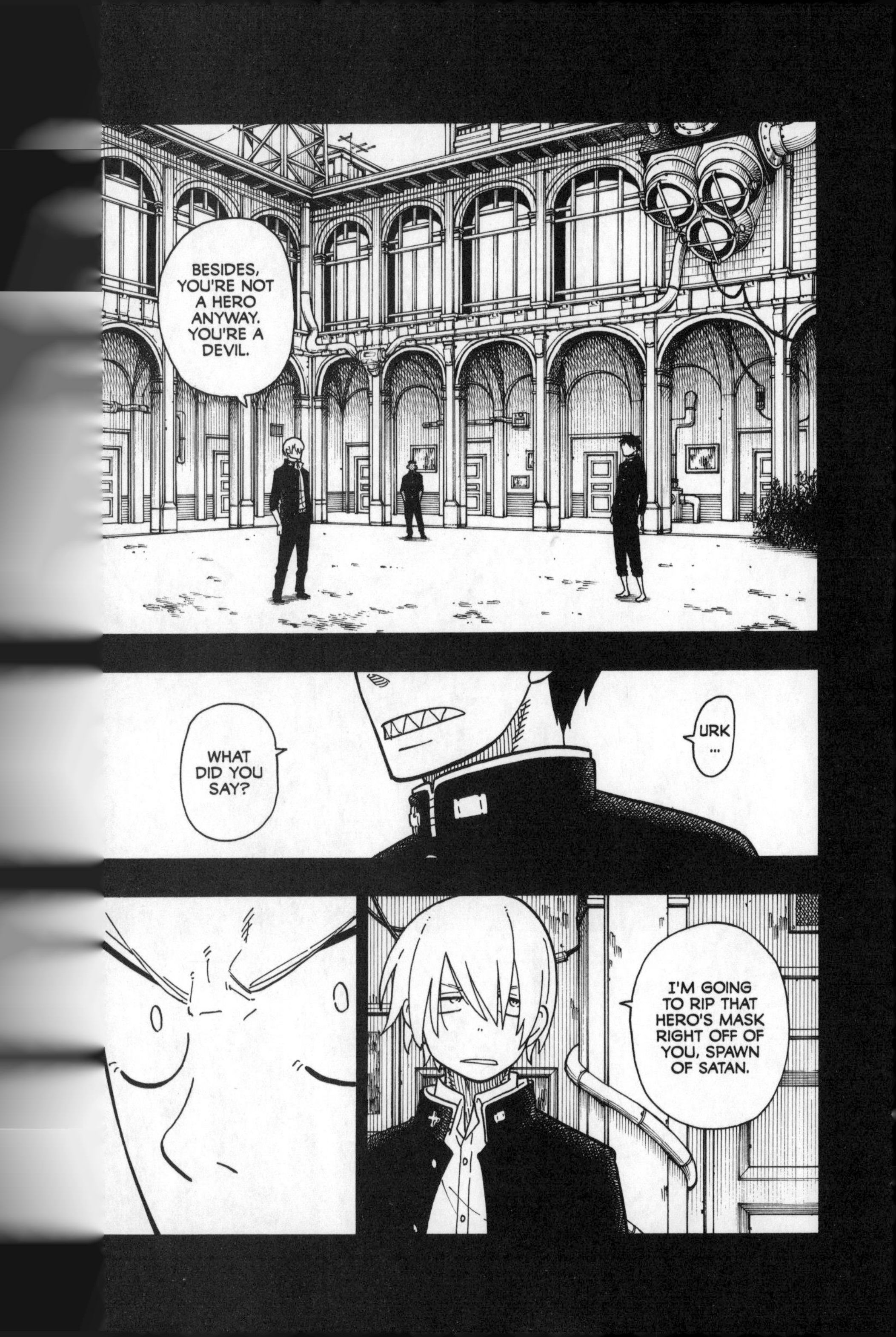
BESIDES, YOU'RE NOT A HERO ANYWAY. YOU'RE A DEVIL.
URK ...
WHAT DID YOU SAY?
I'M GOING TO RIP THAT HERO'S MASK RIGHT OFF OF YOU, SPAWN OF SATAN.

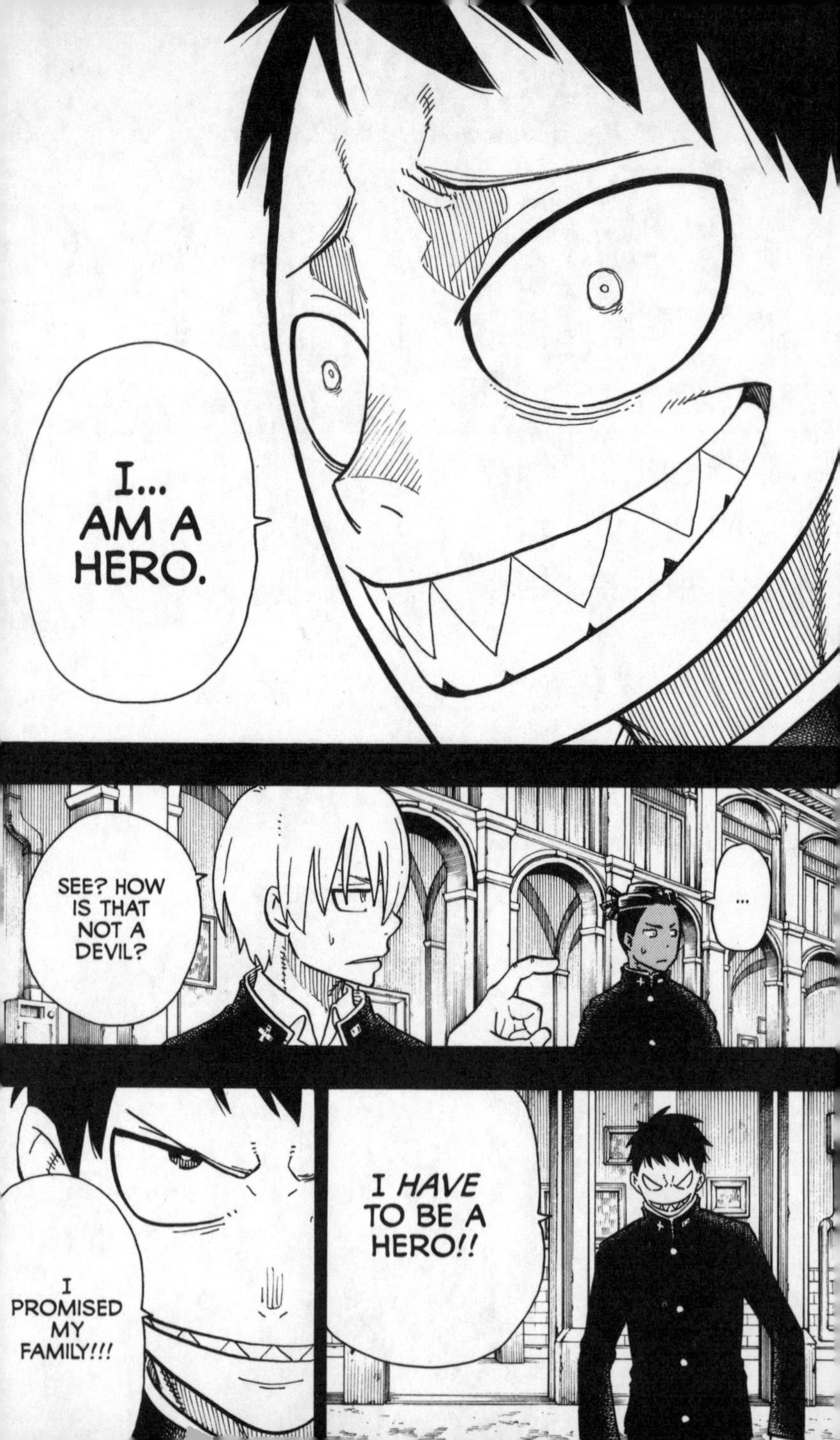

I... AM A HERO.
...
SEE? HOW IS THAT NOT A DEVIL?
I *HAVE* TO BE A HERO!!
I PROMISED MY FAMILY!!!

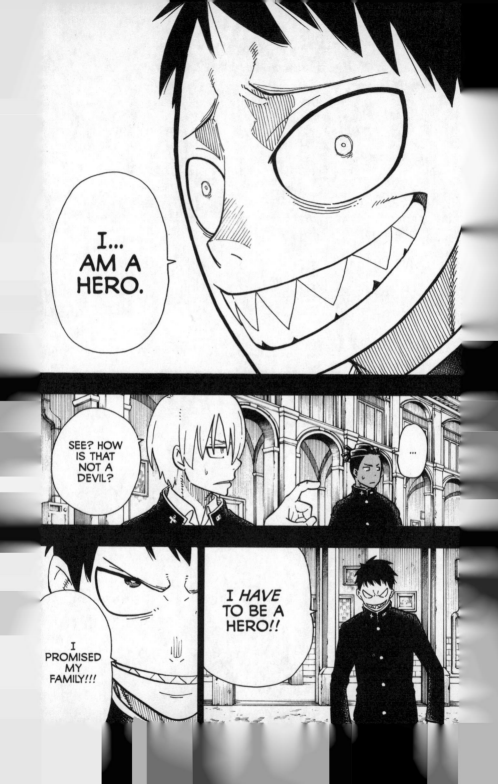

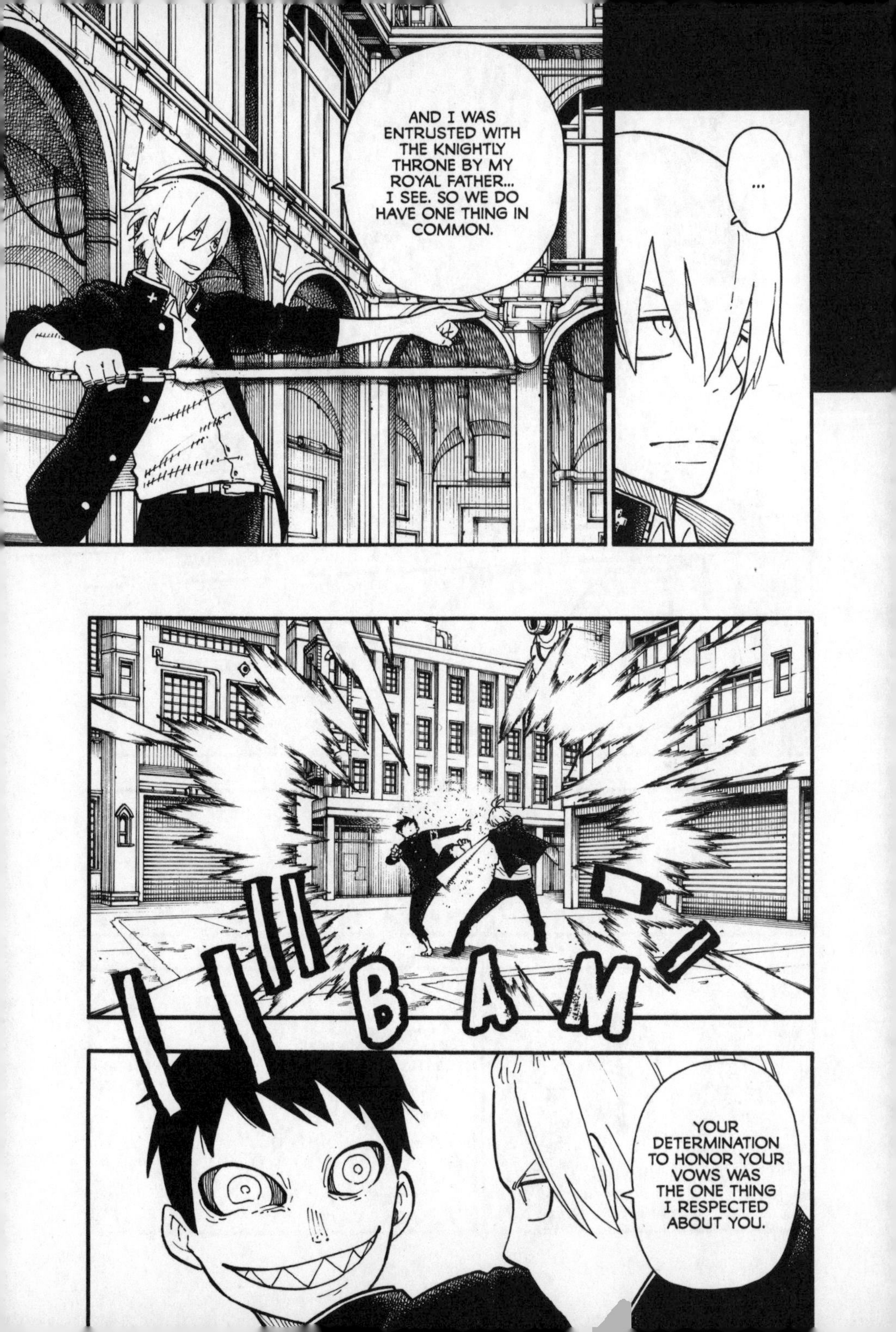
...
AND I WAS ENTRUSTED WITH THE KNIGHTLY THRONE BY MY ROYAL FATHER... I SEE. SO WE DO HAVE ONE THING IN COMMON.
BAM!!!
YOUR DETERMINATION TO HONOR YOUR VOWS WAS THE ONE THING I RESPECTED ABOUT YOU.

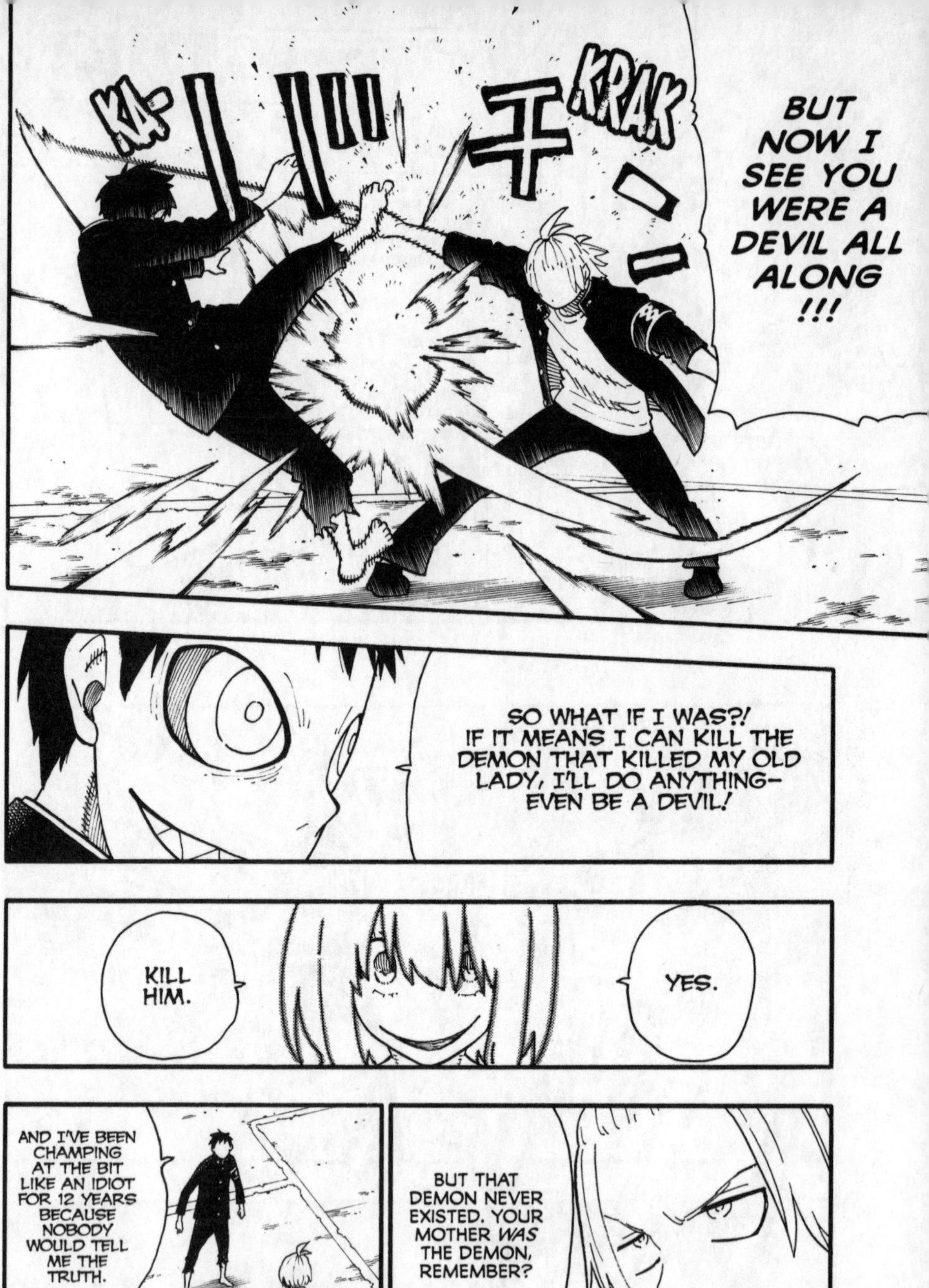
KRAK
KA-
BUT NOW I SEE YOU WERE A DEVIL ALL ALONG !!!
SO WHAT IF I WAS?! IF IT MEANS I CAN KILL THE DEMON THAT KILLED MY OLD LADY, I'LL DO ANYTHING— EVEN BE A DEVIL!
YES.
KILL HIM.
BUT THAT DEMON NEVER EXISTED. YOUR MOTHER *WAS* THE DEMON, REMEMBER?
AND I'VE BEEN CHAMPING AT THE BIT LIKE AN IDIOT FOR 12 YEARS BECAUSE NOBODY WOULD TELL ME THE TRUTH.

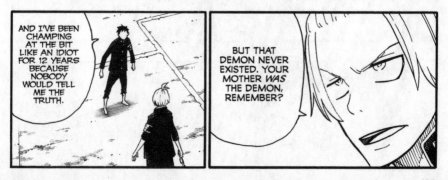

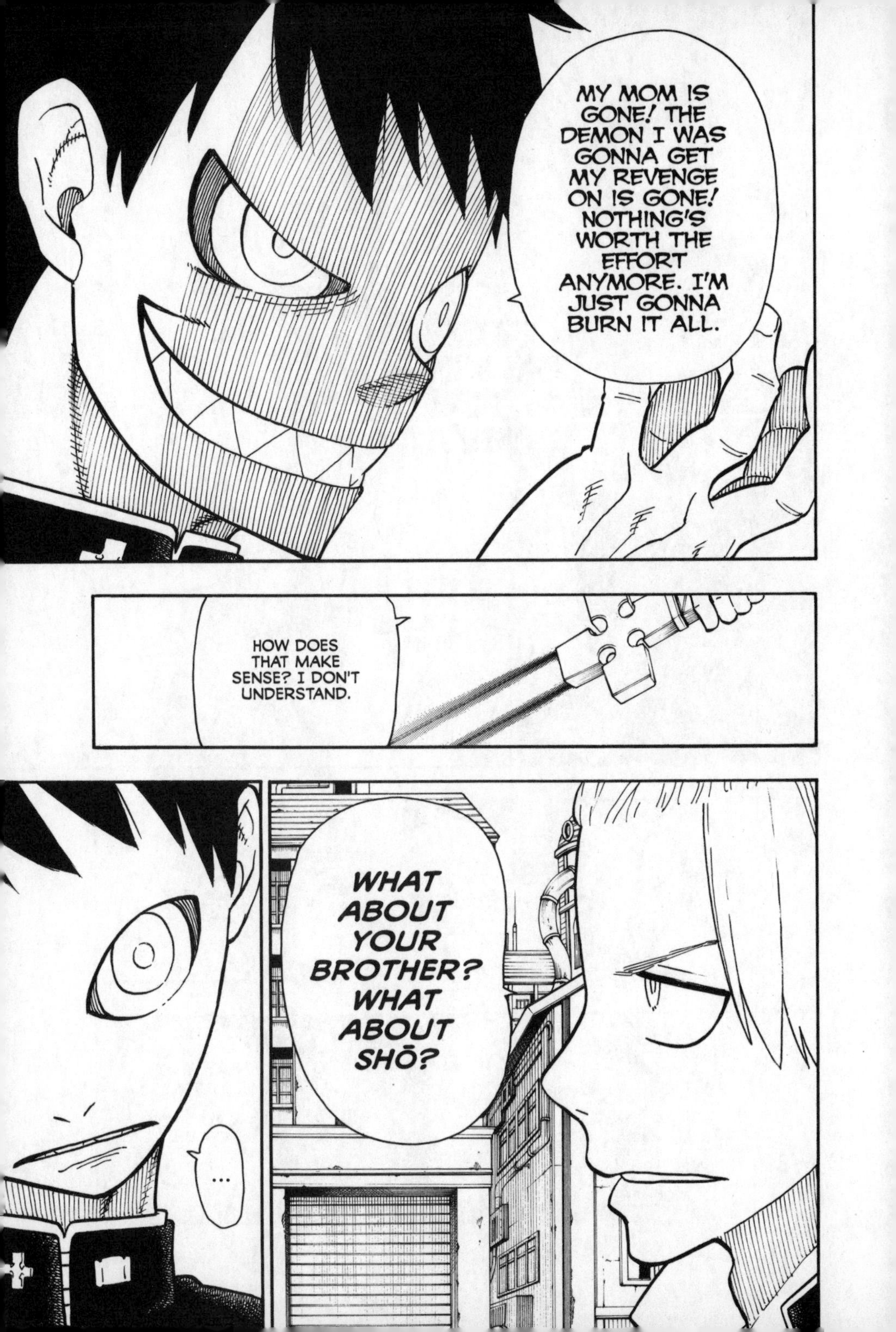
MY MOM IS GONE! THE DEMON I WAS GONNA GET MY REVENGE ON IS GONE! NOTHING'S WORTH THE EFFORT ANYMORE. I'M JUST GONNA BURN IT ALL.
HOW DOES THAT MAKE SENSE? I DON'T UNDERSTAND.
WHAT ABOUT YOUR BROTHER? WHAT ABOUT SHŌ?
...

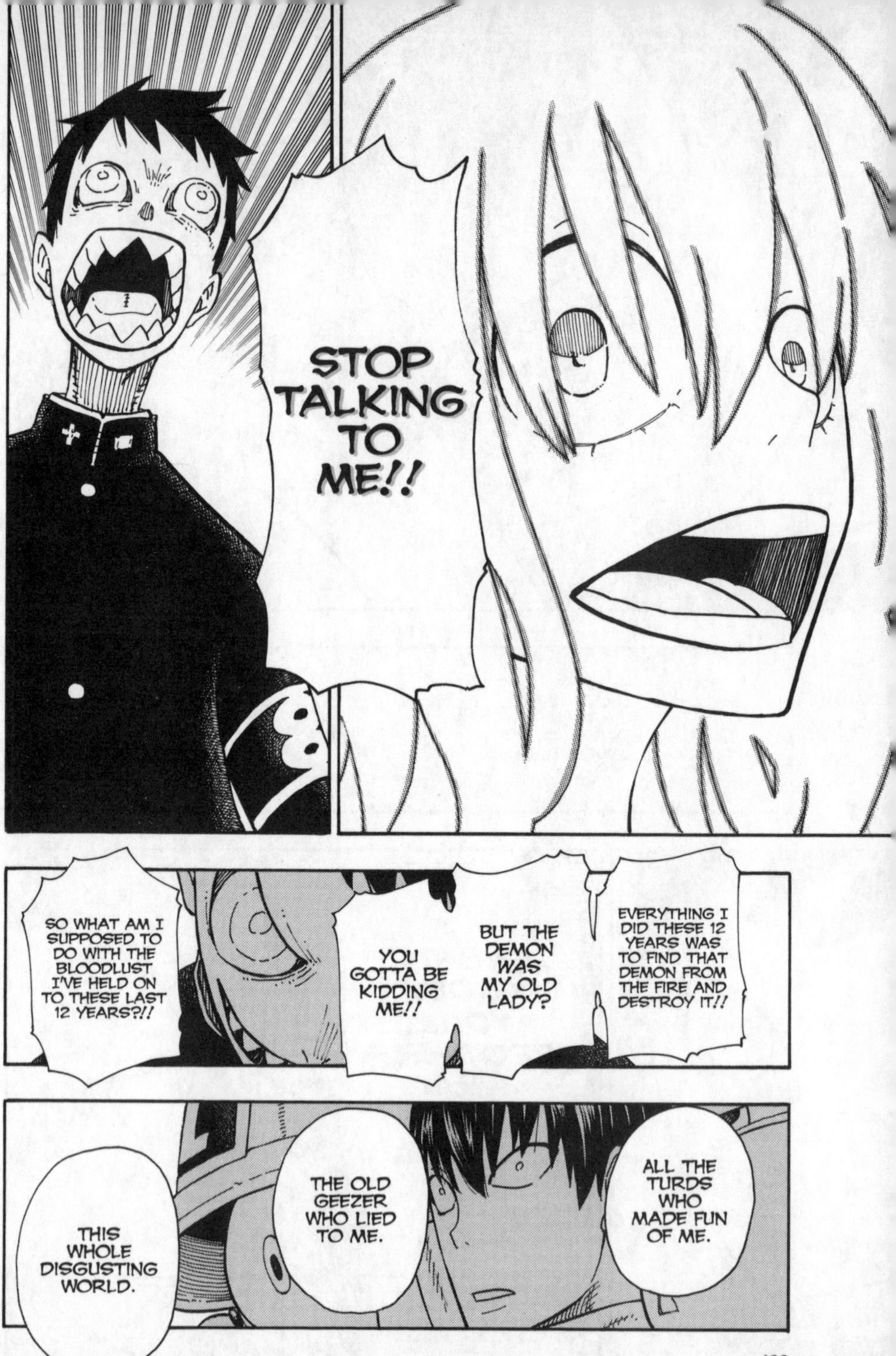
STOP TALKING TO ME!!
EVERYTHING I DID THESE 12 YEARS WAS TO FIND THAT DEMON FROM THE FIRE AND DESTROY IT!!
BUT THE DEMON WAS MY OLD LADY?
YOU GOTTA BE KIDDING ME!!
SO WHAT AM I SUPPOSED TO DO WITH THE BLOODLUST I'VE HELD ON TO THESE LAST 12 YEARS?!!
ALL THE TURDS WHO MADE FUN OF ME.
THE OLD GEEZER WHO LIED TO ME.
THIS WHOLE DISGUSTING WORLD.

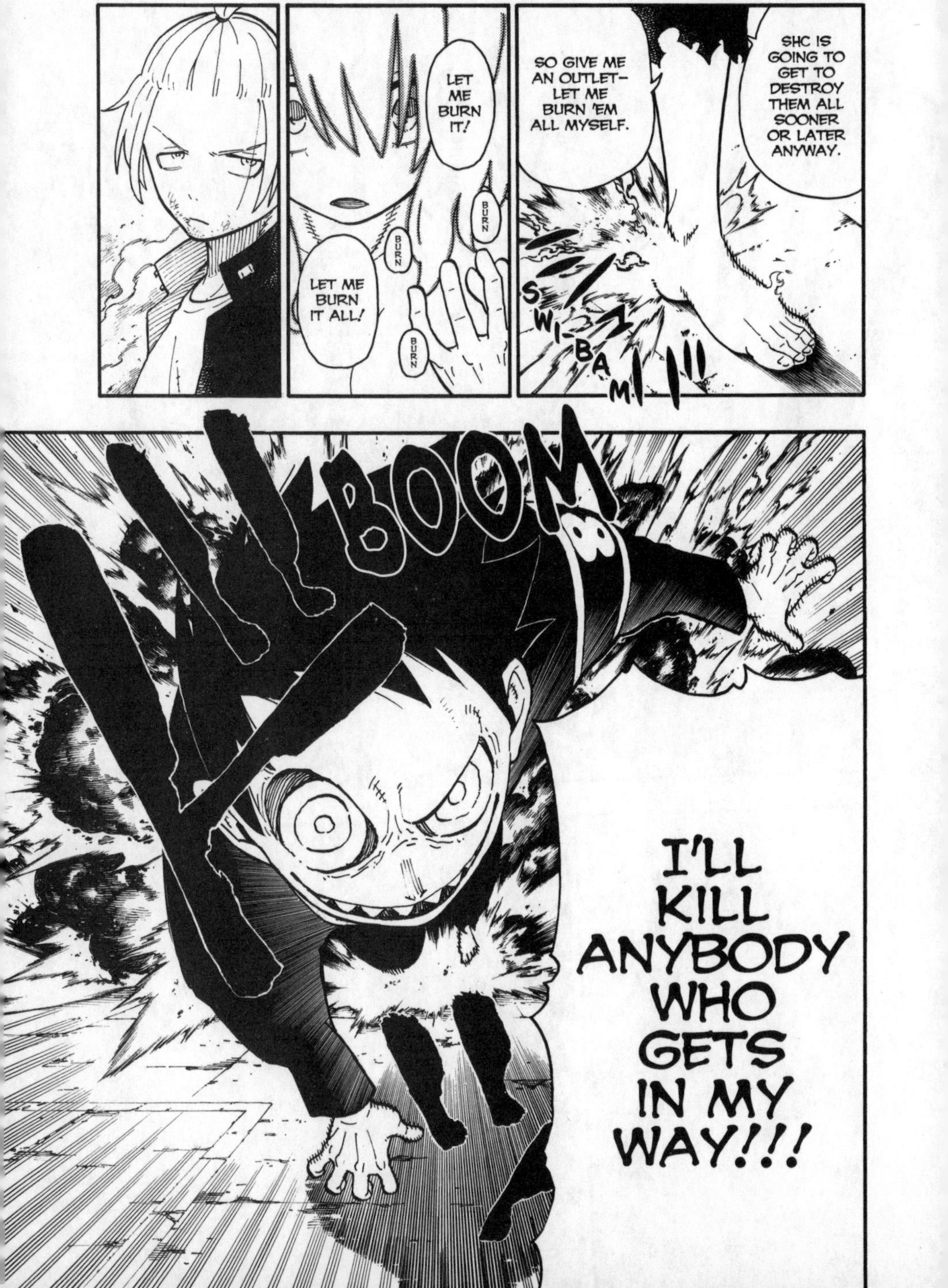
SHC IS GOING TO GET TO DESTROY THEM ALL SOONER OR LATER ANYWAY.
SO GIVE ME AN OUTLET— LET ME BURN 'EM ALL MYSELF.
SWI-BAM!!!
LET ME BURN IT!
BURN
BURN
LET ME BURN IT ALL!
BURN
BOOM
I'LL KILL ANYBODY WHO GETS IN MY WAY!!!

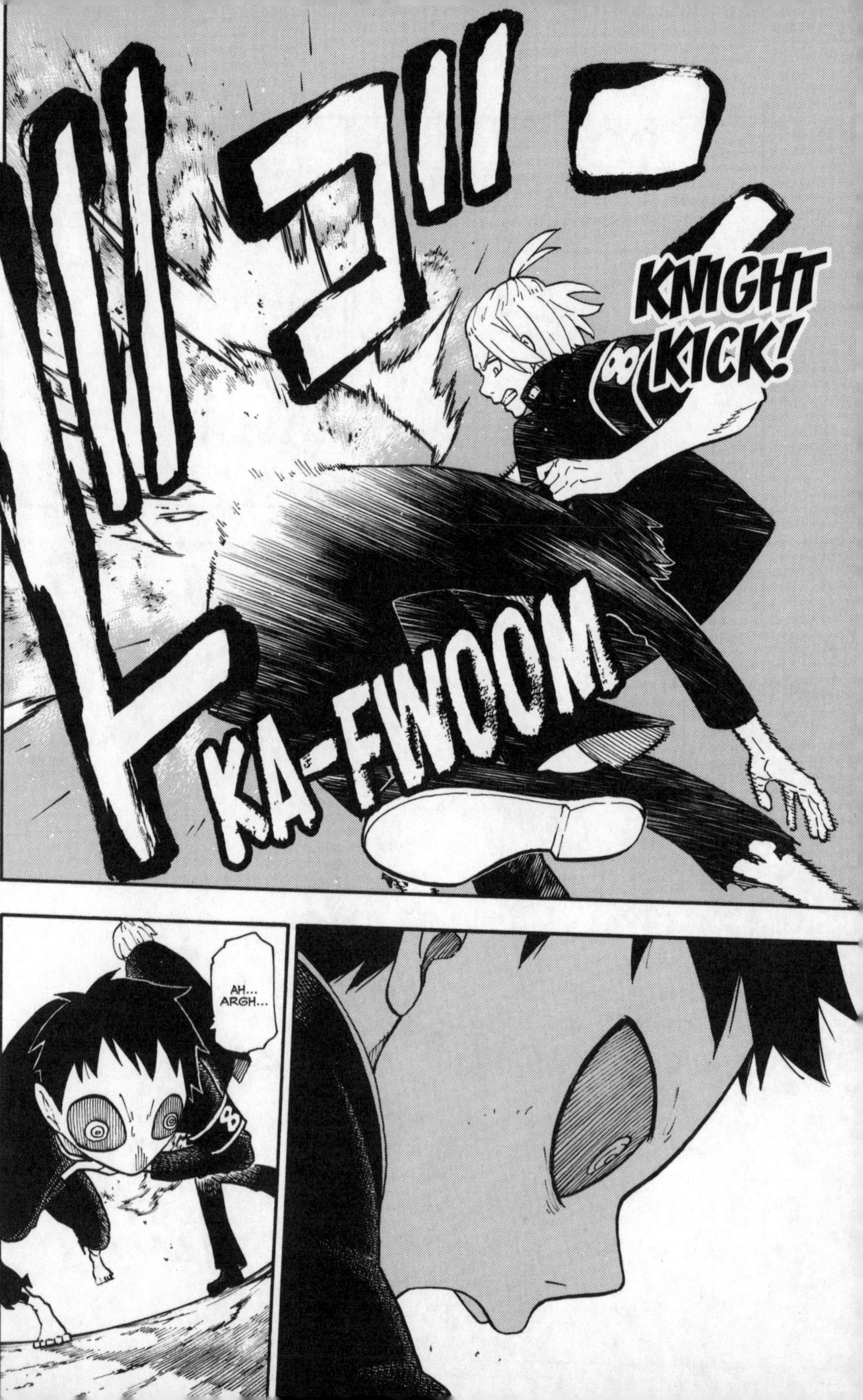
KNIGHT KICK!
KA-FWOOM
AH... ARGH...

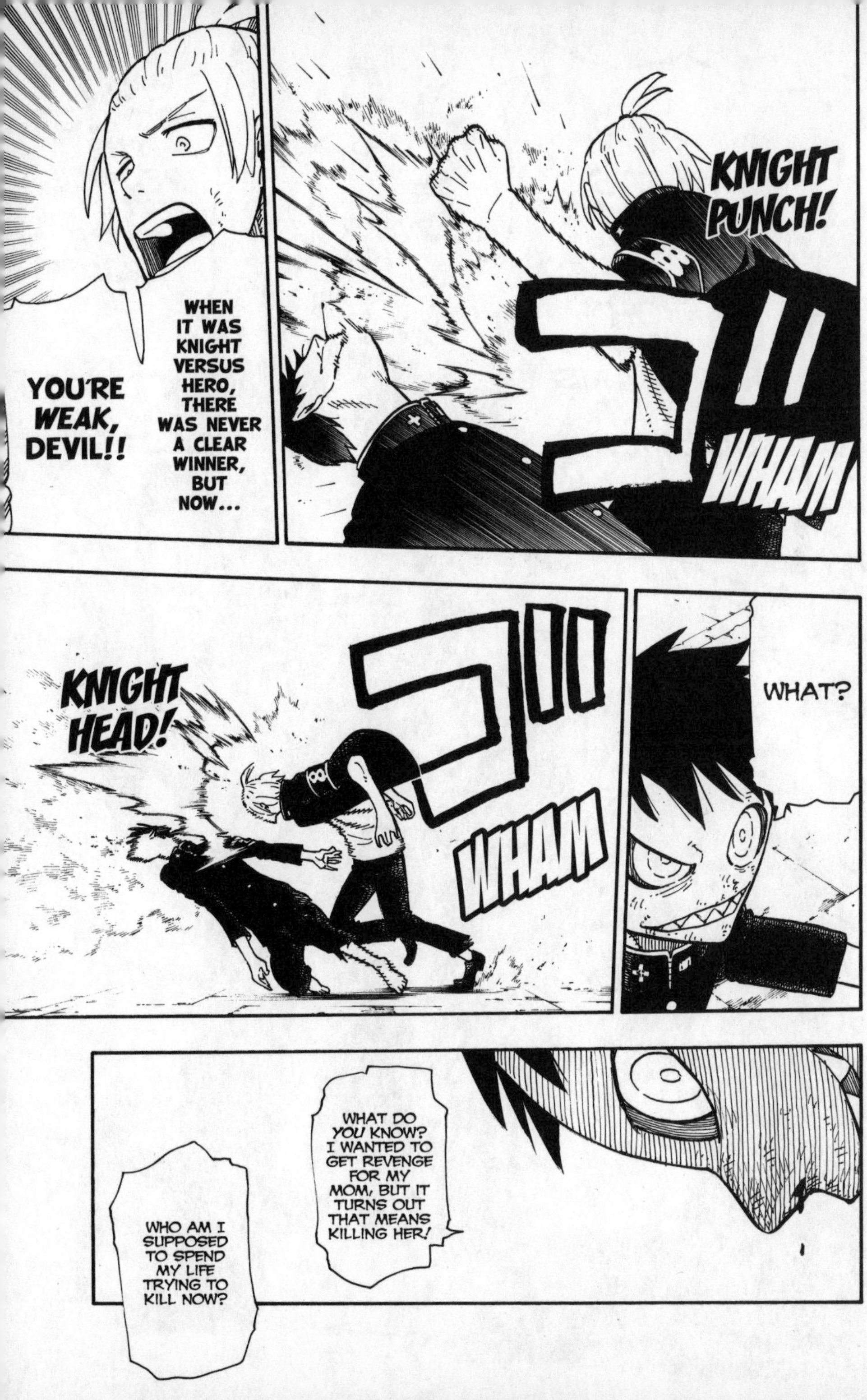
KNIGHT PUNCH!
WHAM
WHEN IT WAS KNIGHT VERSUS HERO, THERE WAS NEVER A CLEAR WINNER, BUT NOW...
YOU'RE *WEAK*, DEVIL!!
WHAT?
KNIGHT HEAD!
WHAM
WHAT DO *YOU* KNOW? I WANTED TO GET REVENGE FOR MY MOM, BUT IT TURNS OUT THAT MEANS KILLING HER!
WHO AM I SUPPOSED TO SPEND MY LIFE TRYING TO KILL NOW?

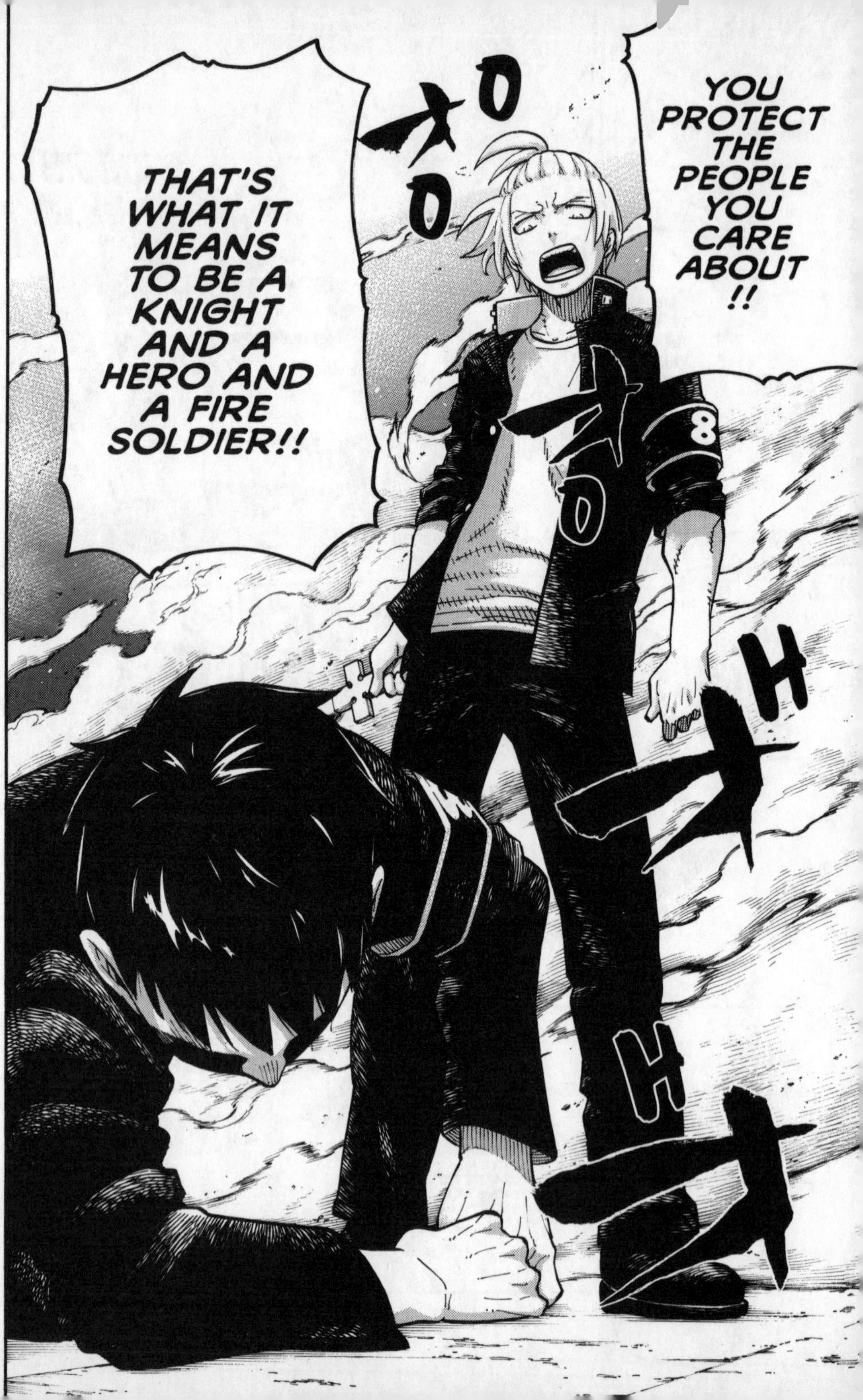
YOU PROTECT THE PEOPLE YOU CARE ABOUT !!
THAT'S WHAT IT MEANS TO BE A KNIGHT AND A HERO AND A FIRE SOLDIER!!

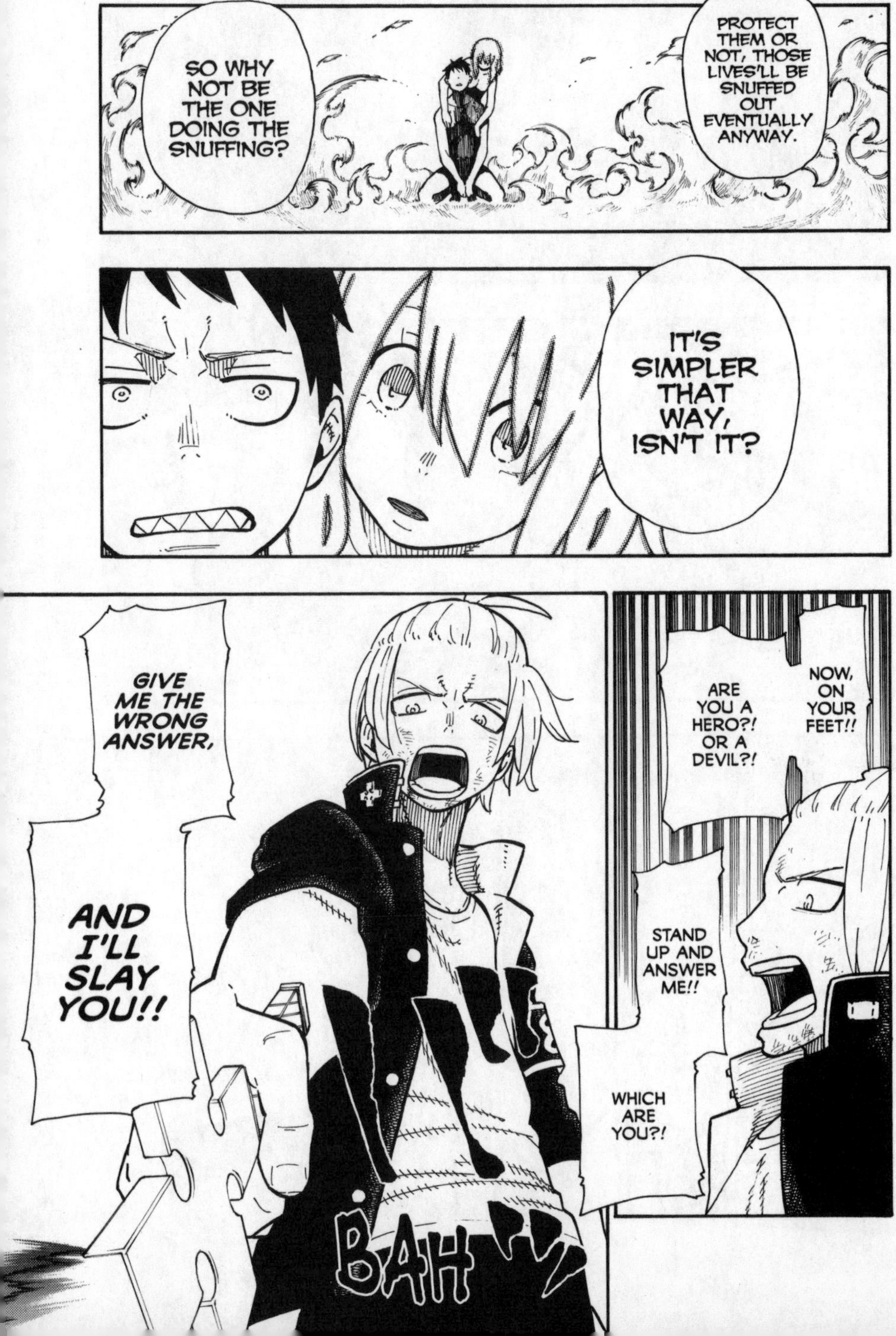
PROTECT THEM OR NOT, THOSE LIVES'LL BE SNUFFED OUT EVENTUALLY ANYWAY.
SO WHY NOT BE THE ONE DOING THE SNUFFING?
IT'S SIMPLER THAT WAY, ISN'T IT?
NOW, ON YOUR FEET!!
ARE YOU A HERO?! OR A DEVIL?!
STAND UP AND ANSWER ME!!
WHICH ARE YOU?!
GIVE ME THE WRONG ANSWER,
AND I'LL SLAY YOU!!
BAH

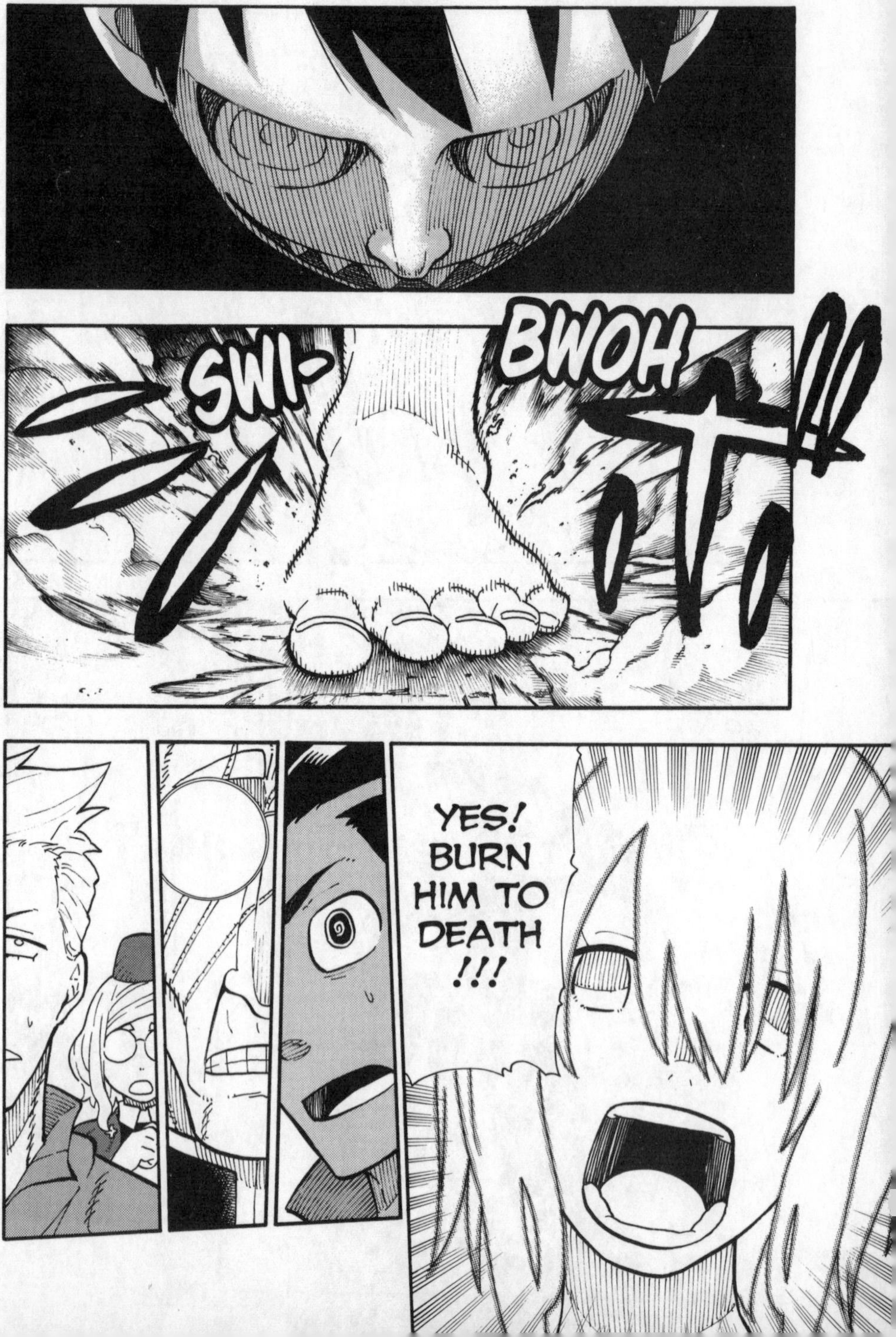
SWI-BWOH!!
YES! BURN HIM TO DEATH !!!

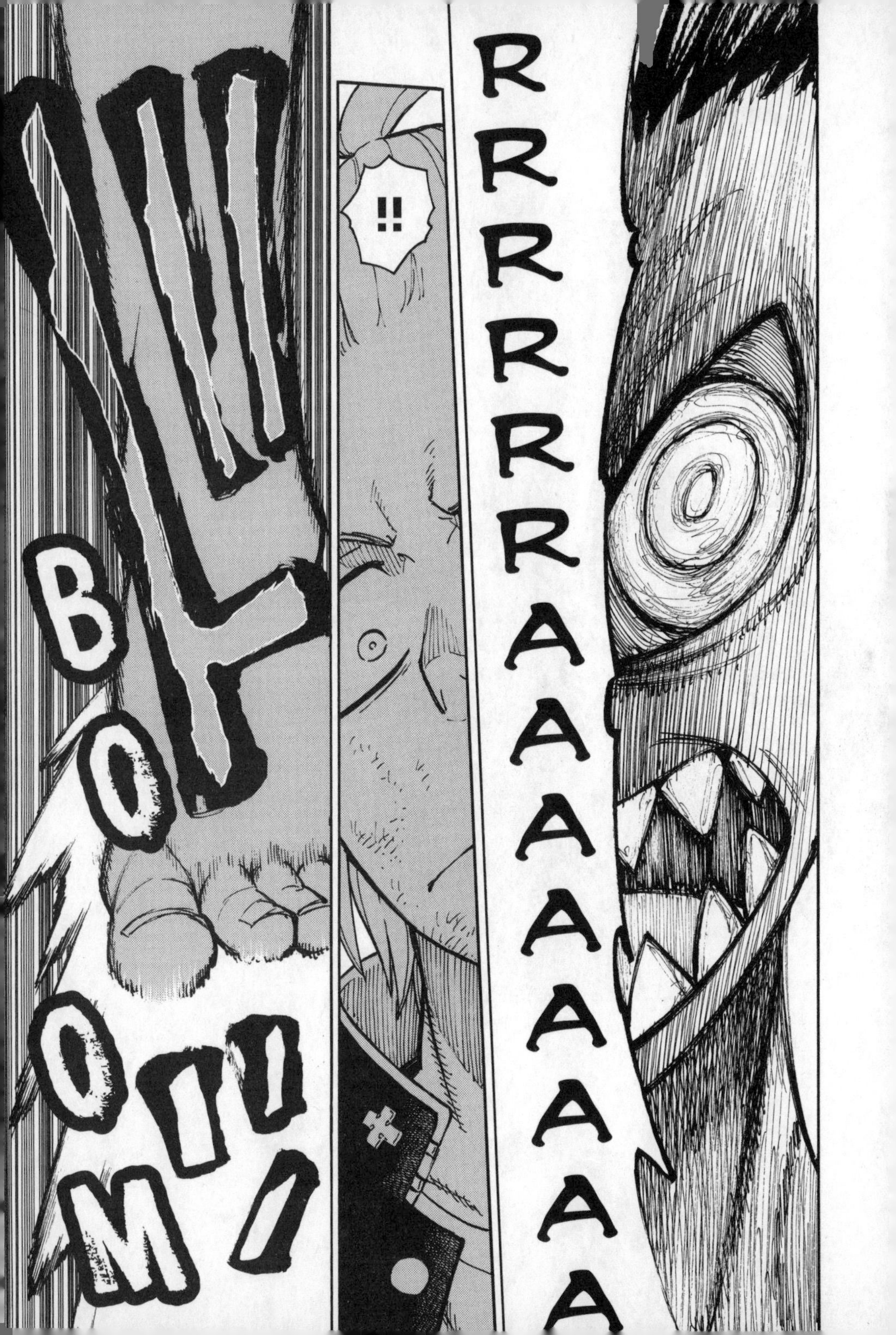

RRRRRRAAAAAAAAAA
!!
BOOM!

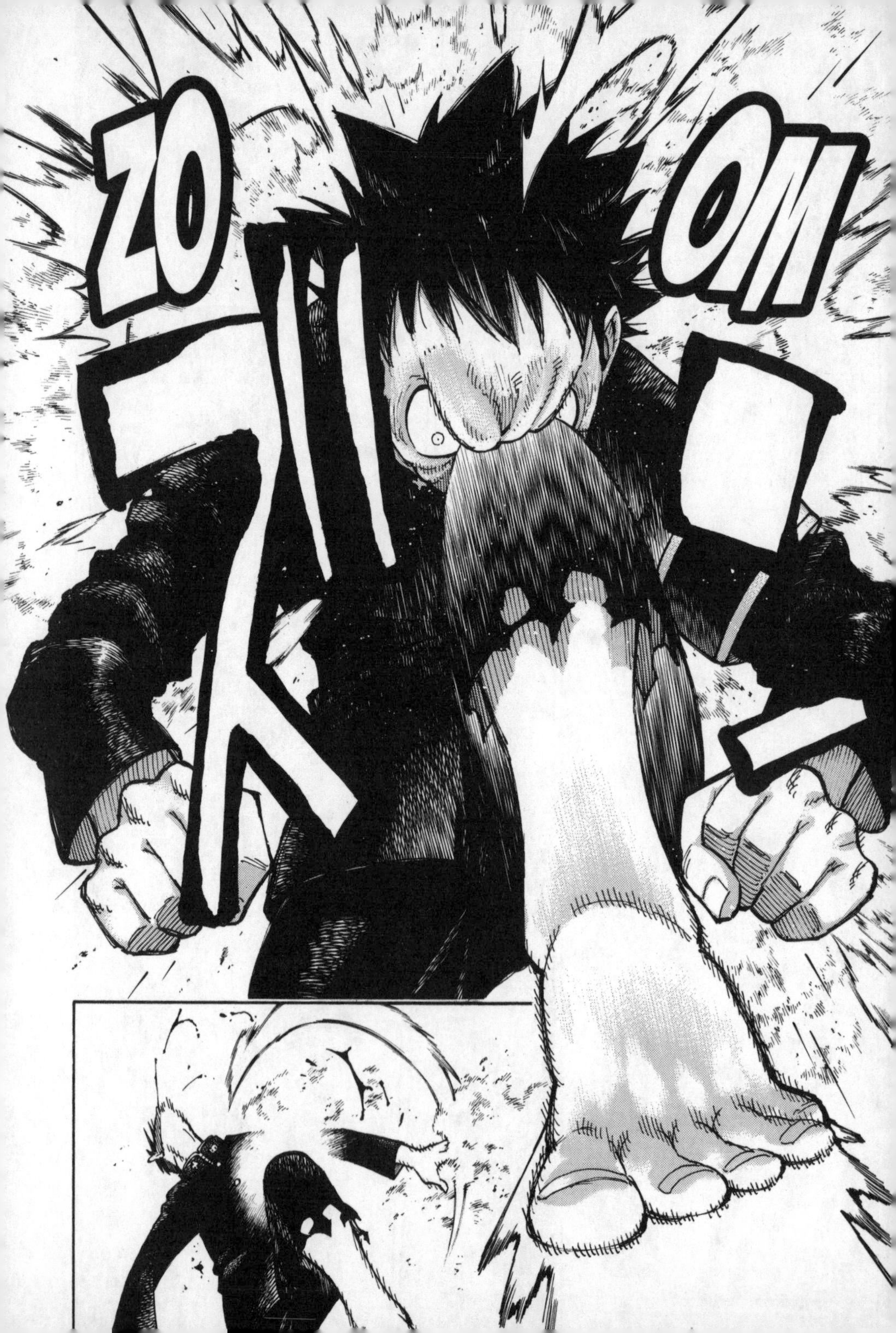
ZO OM

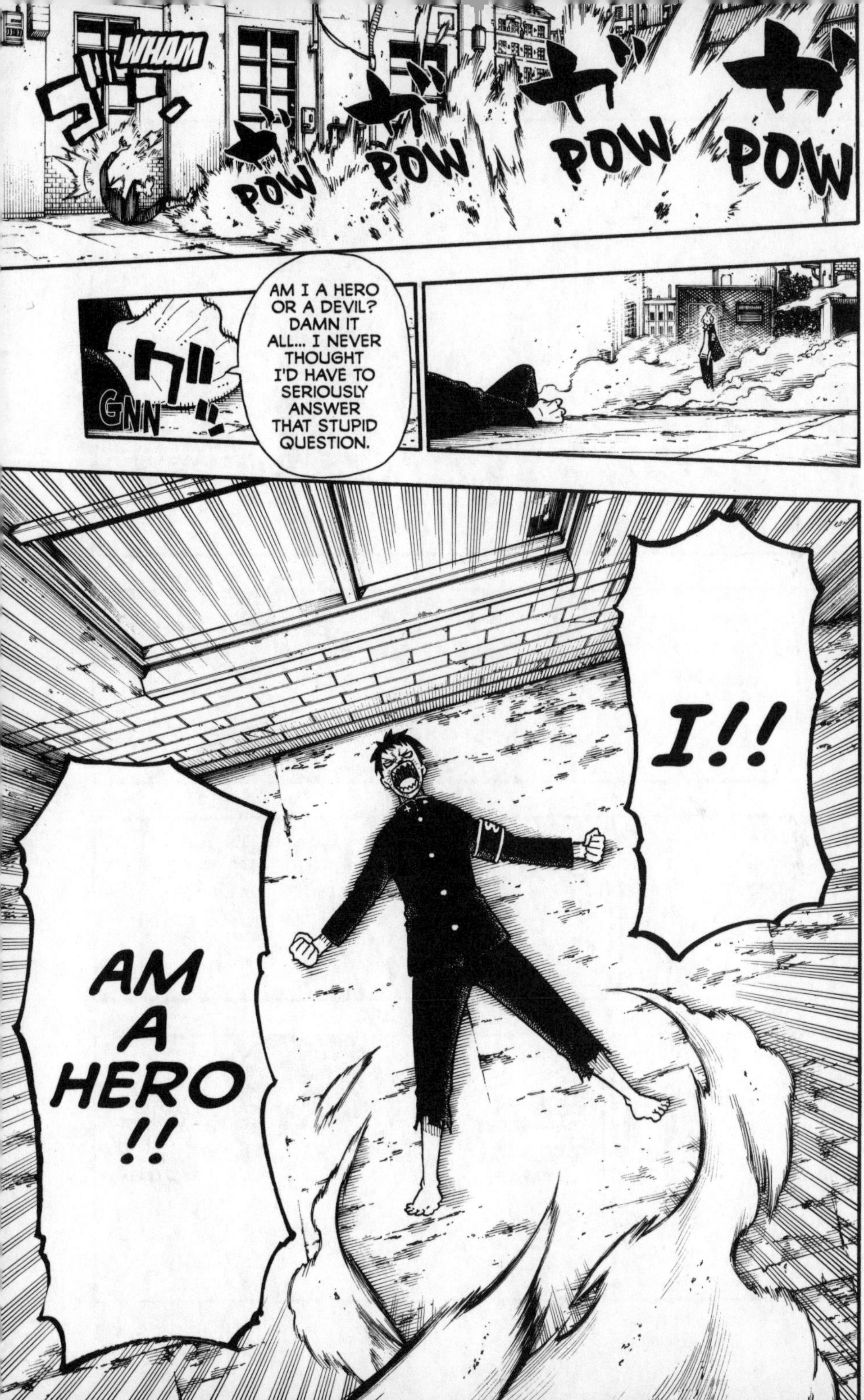
WHAM
POW
POW
POW
POW
GNN
AM I A HERO OR A DEVIL? DAMN IT ALL... I NEVER THOUGHT I'D HAVE TO SERIOUSLY ANSWER THAT STUPID QUESTION.
I!!
AM A HERO!!

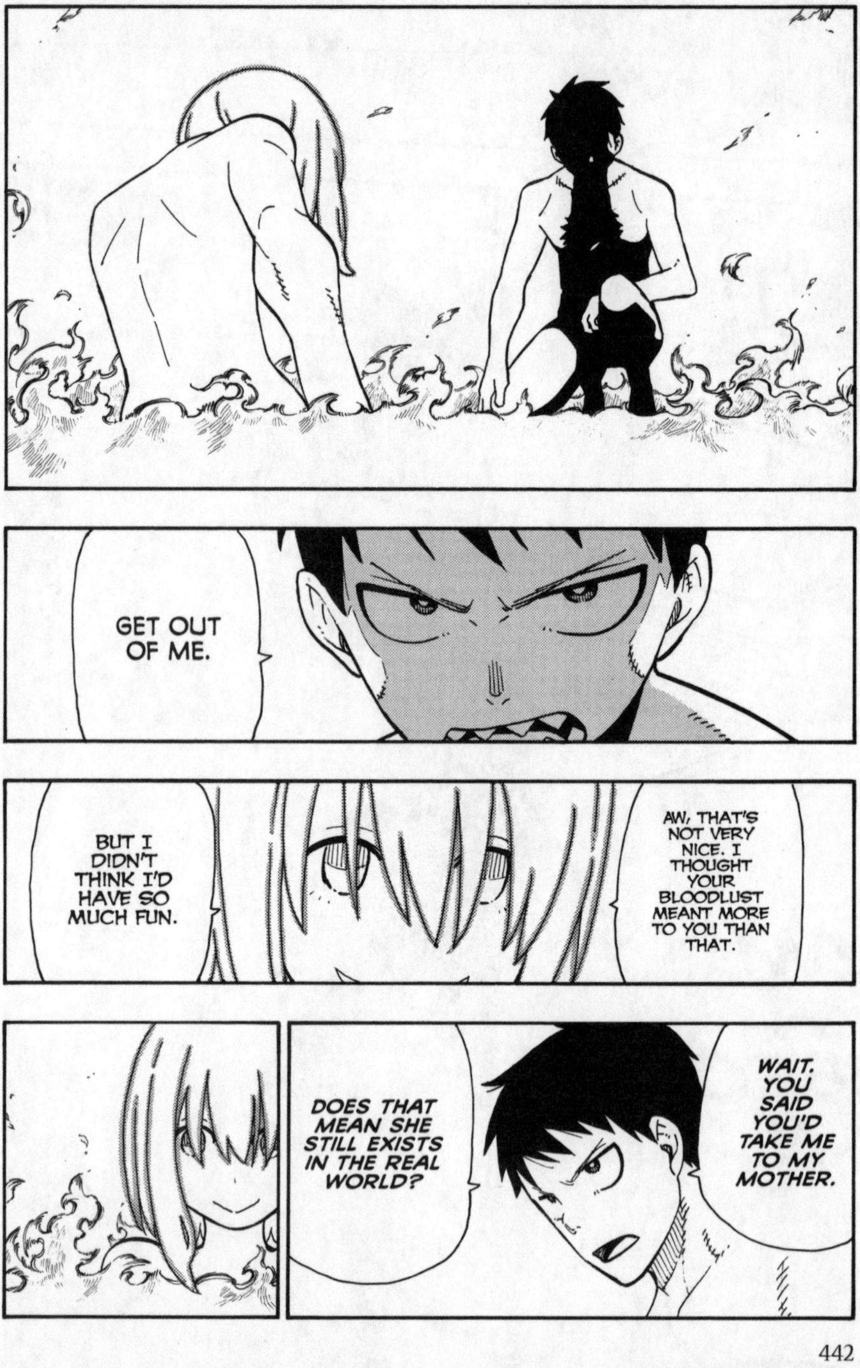
GET OUT OF ME.
AW, THAT'S NOT VERY NICE. I THOUGHT YOUR BLOODLUST MEANT MORE TO YOU THAN THAT.
BUT I DIDN'T THINK I'D HAVE SO MUCH FUN.
WAIT. YOU SAID YOU'D TAKE ME TO MY MOTHER.
DOES THAT MEAN SHE STILL EXISTS IN THE REAL WORLD?

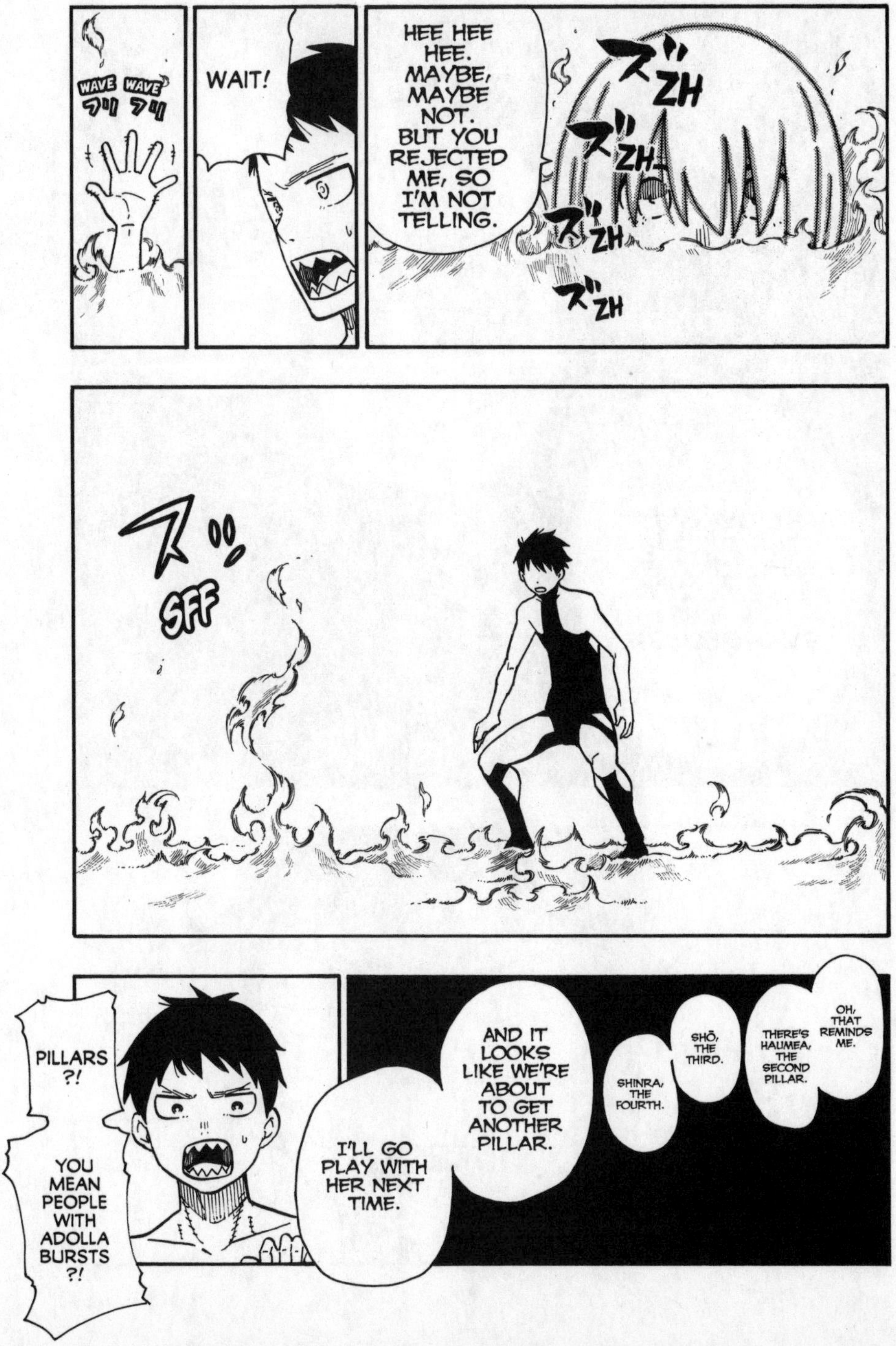
HEE HEE HEE. MAYBE, MAYBE NOT. BUT YOU REJECTED ME, SO I'M NOT TELLING.
ズZH
ズZH
ズZH
ズZH
WAIT!
WAVE WAVE
フリフリ
スSFF
OH, THAT REMINDS ME.
THERE'S HAUMEA, THE SECOND PILLAR.
SHŌ, THE THIRD.
SHINRA, THE FOURTH.
AND IT LOOKS LIKE WE'RE ABOUT TO GET ANOTHER PILLAR.
I'LL GO PLAY WITH HER NEXT TIME.
PILLARS?!
YOU MEAN PEOPLE WITH ADOLLA BURSTS?!

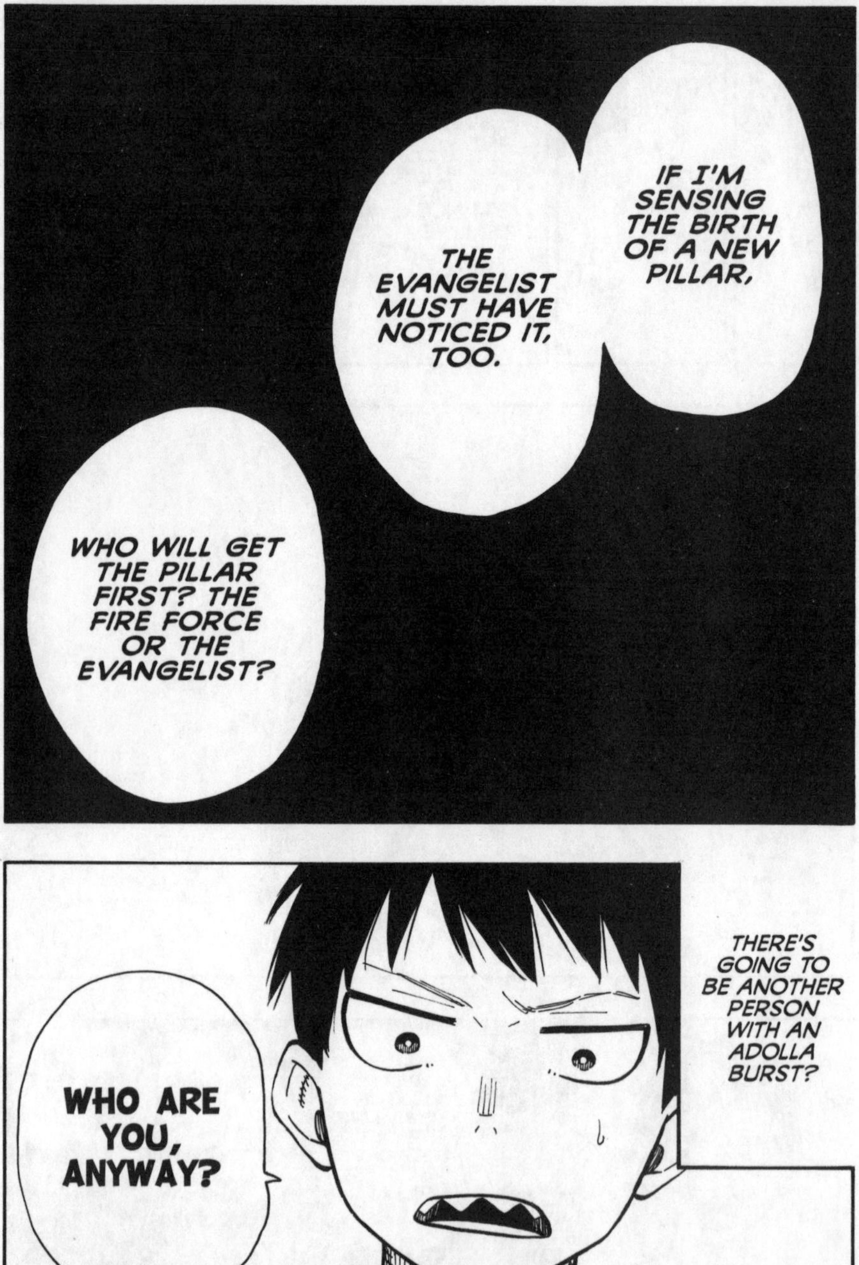
IF I'M SENSING THE BIRTH OF A NEW PILLAR,
THE EVANGELIST MUST HAVE NOTICED IT, TOO.
WHO WILL GET THE PILLAR FIRST? THE FIRE FORCE OR THE EVANGELIST?
THERE'S GOING TO BE ANOTHER PERSON WITH AN ADOLLA BURST?
WHO ARE YOU, ANYWAY?

CHAPTER XCIX: A NEW KINDLING

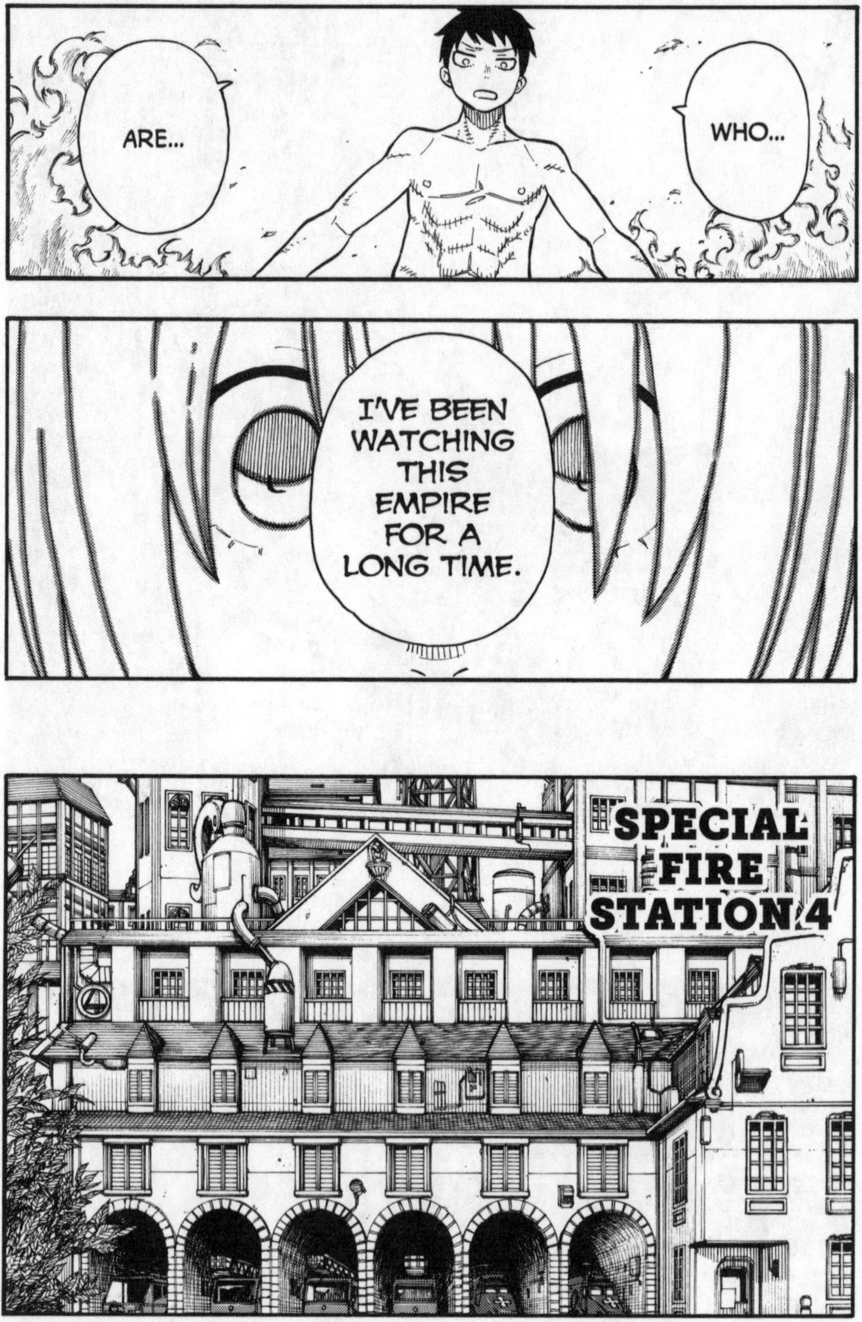
WHO...
ARE...
I'VE BEEN WATCHING THIS EMPIRE FOR A LONG TIME.
SPECIAL FIRE STATION 4

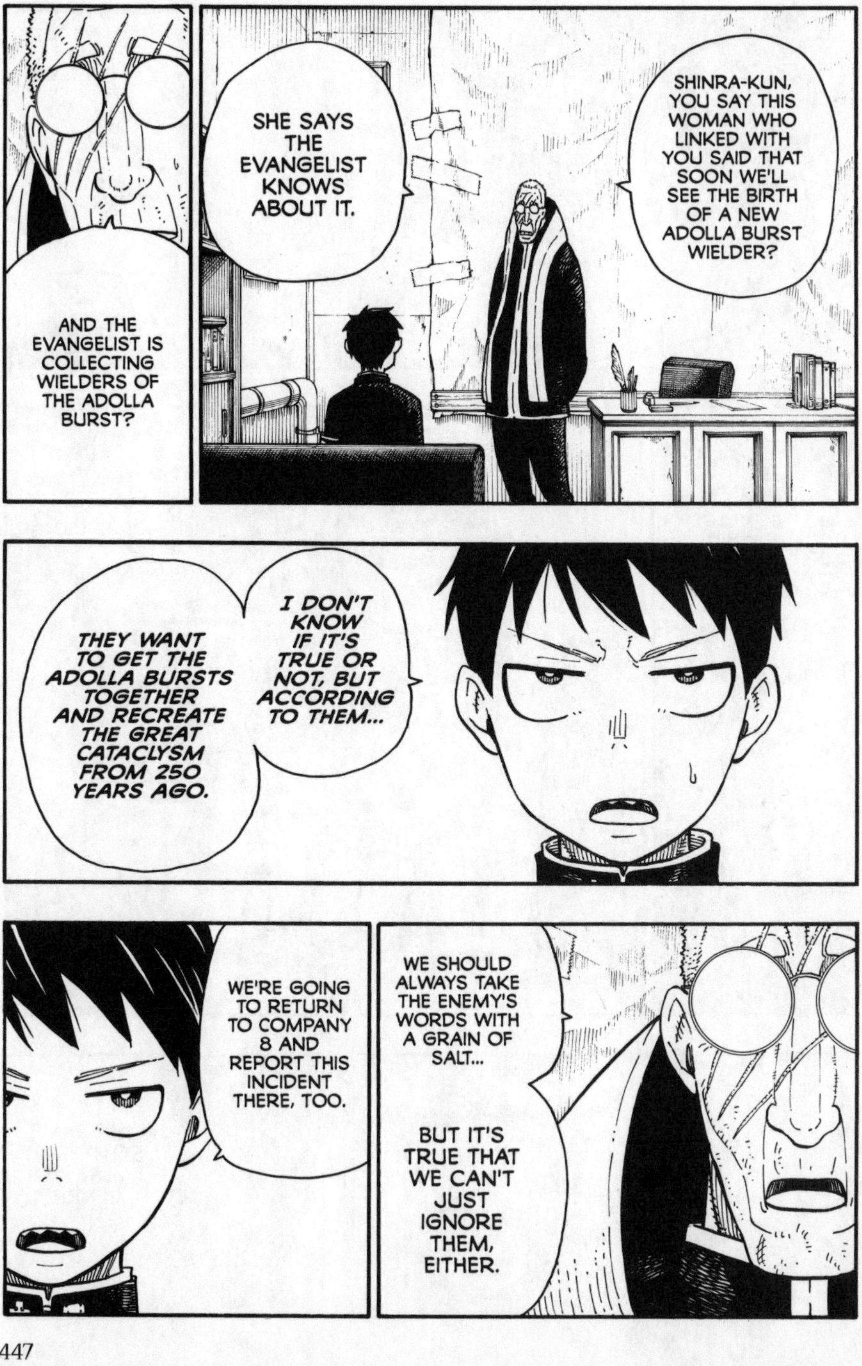
SHINRA-KUN, YOU SAY THIS WOMAN WHO LINKED WITH YOU SAID THAT SOON WE'LL SEE THE BIRTH OF A NEW ADOLLA BURST WIELDER?
SHE SAYS THE EVANGELIST KNOWS ABOUT IT.
AND THE EVANGELIST IS COLLECTING WIELDERS OF THE ADOLLA BURST?
I DON'T KNOW IF IT'S TRUE OR NOT, BUT ACCORDING TO THEM...
THEY WANT TO GET THE ADOLLA BURSTS TOGETHER AND RECREATE THE GREAT CATACLYSM FROM 250 YEARS AGO.
WE SHOULD ALWAYS TAKE THE ENEMY'S WORDS WITH A GRAIN OF SALT...
BUT IT'S TRUE THAT WE CAN'T JUST IGNORE THEM, EITHER.
WE'RE GOING TO RETURN TO COMPANY 8 AND REPORT THIS INCIDENT THERE, TOO.

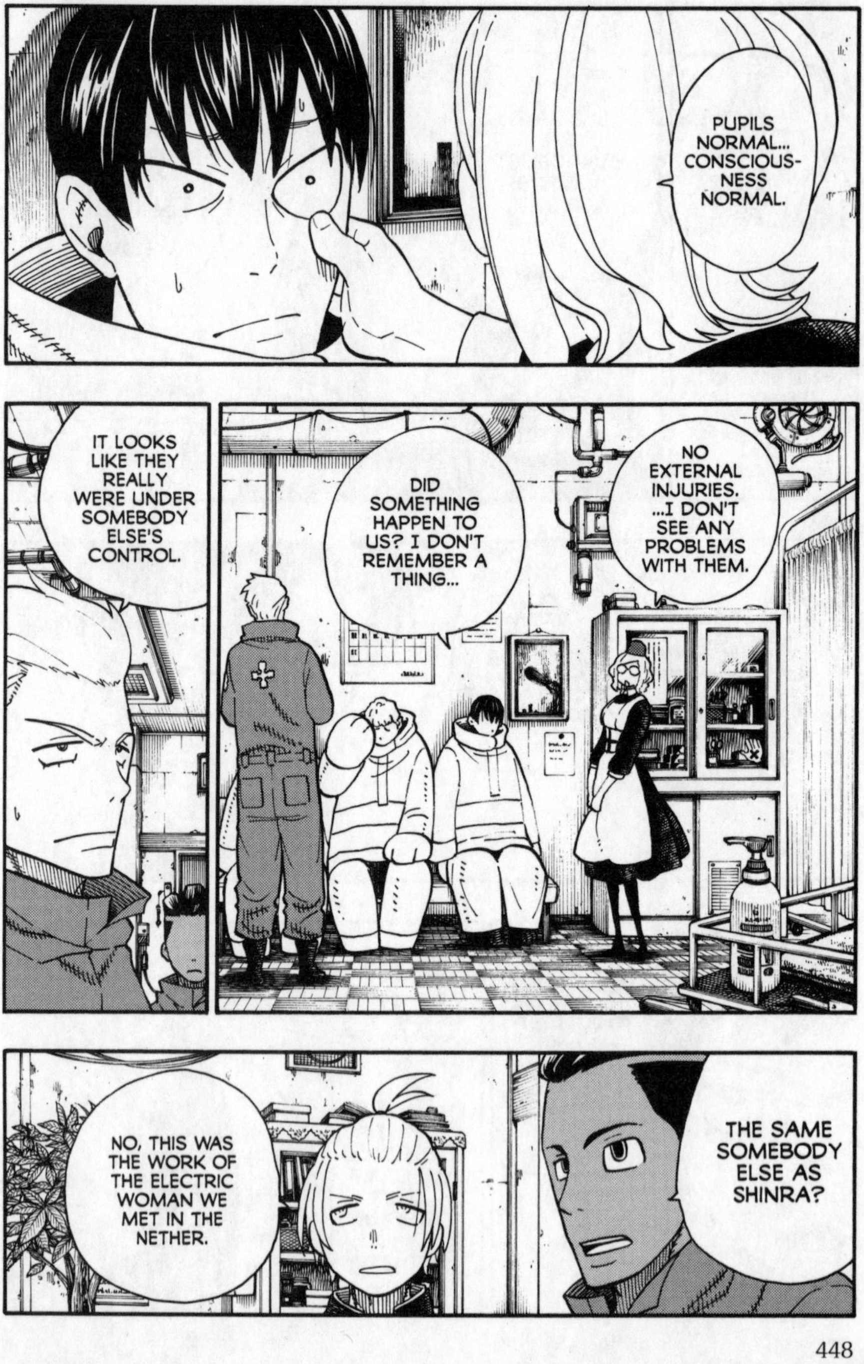
PUPILS NORMAL... CONSCIOUS-NESS NORMAL.
NO EXTERNAL INJURIES. ...I DON'T SEE ANY PROBLEMS WITH THEM.
DID SOMETHING HAPPEN TO US? I DON'T REMEMBER A THING...
IT LOOKS LIKE THEY REALLY WERE UNDER SOMEBODY ELSE'S CONTROL.
THE SAME SOMEBODY ELSE AS SHINRA?
NO, THIS WAS THE WORK OF THE ELECTRIC WOMAN WE MET IN THE NETHER.

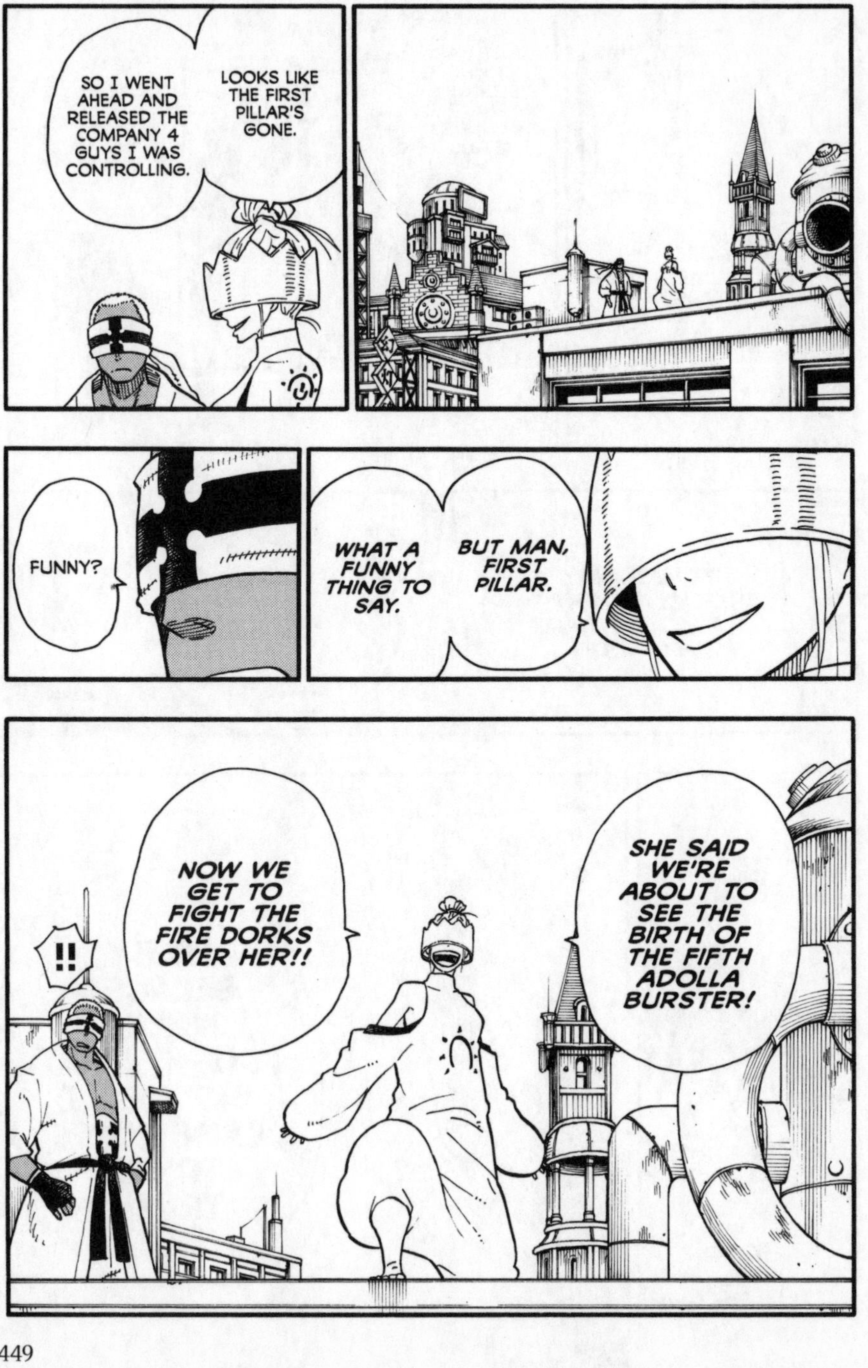
LOOKS LIKE THE FIRST PILLAR'S GONE.
SO I WENT AHEAD AND RELEASED THE COMPANY 4 GUYS I WAS CONTROLLING.
BUT MAN, FIRST PILLAR.
WHAT A FUNNY THING TO SAY.
FUNNY?
SHE SAID WE'RE ABOUT TO SEE THE BIRTH OF THE FIFTH ADOLLA BURSTER!
NOW WE GET TO FIGHT THE FIRE DORKS OVER HER!!
!!

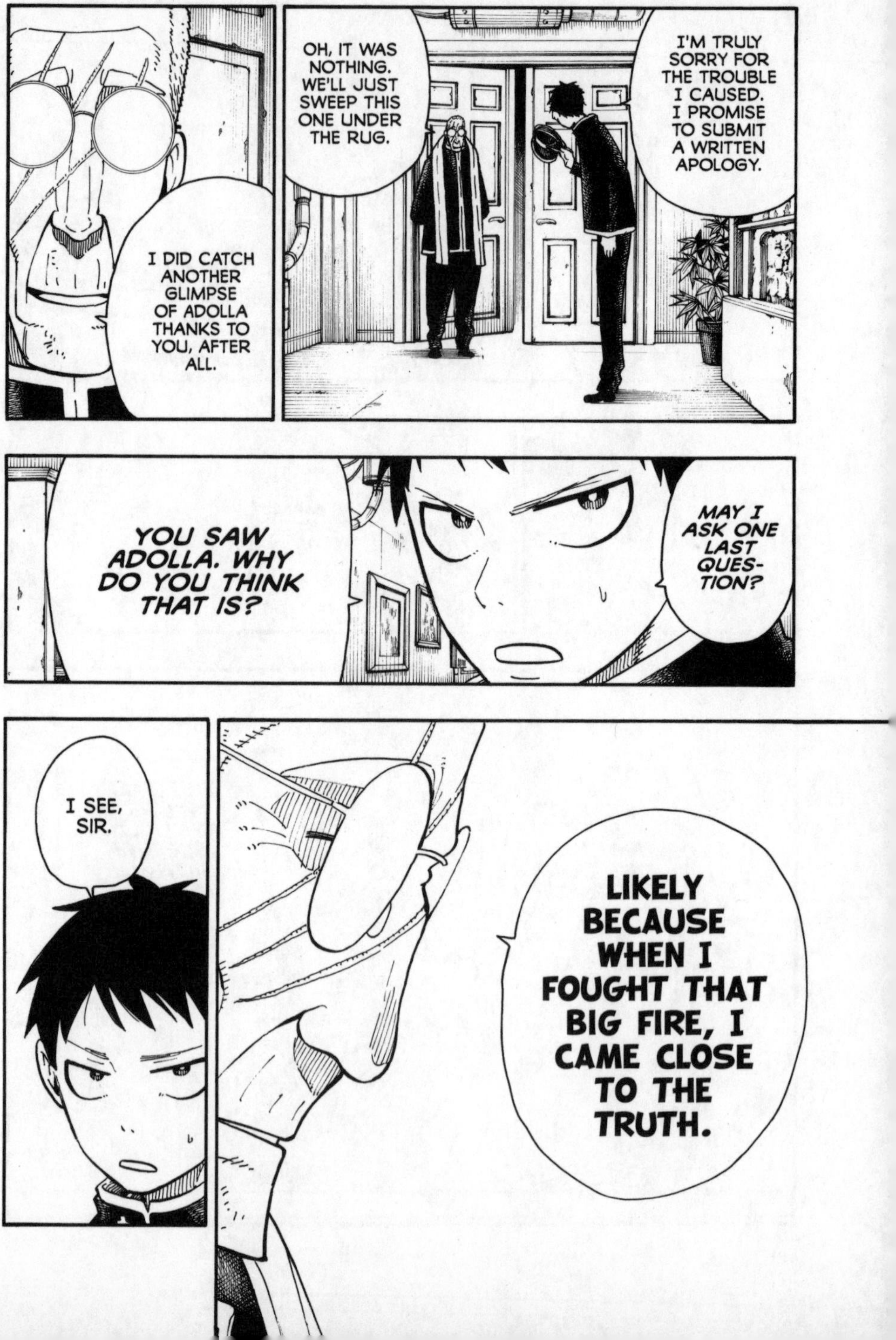
I'M TRULY SORRY FOR THE TROUBLE I CAUSED. I PROMISE TO SUBMIT A WRITTEN APOLOGY.
OH, IT WAS NOTHING. WE'LL JUST SWEEP THIS ONE UNDER THE RUG.
I DID CATCH ANOTHER GLIMPSE OF ADOLLA THANKS TO YOU, AFTER ALL.
MAY I ASK ONE LAST QUES-TION?
YOU SAW ADOLLA. WHY DO YOU THINK THAT IS?
LIKELY BECAUSE WHEN I FOUGHT THAT BIG FIRE, I CAME CLOSE TO THE TRUTH.
I SEE, SIR.

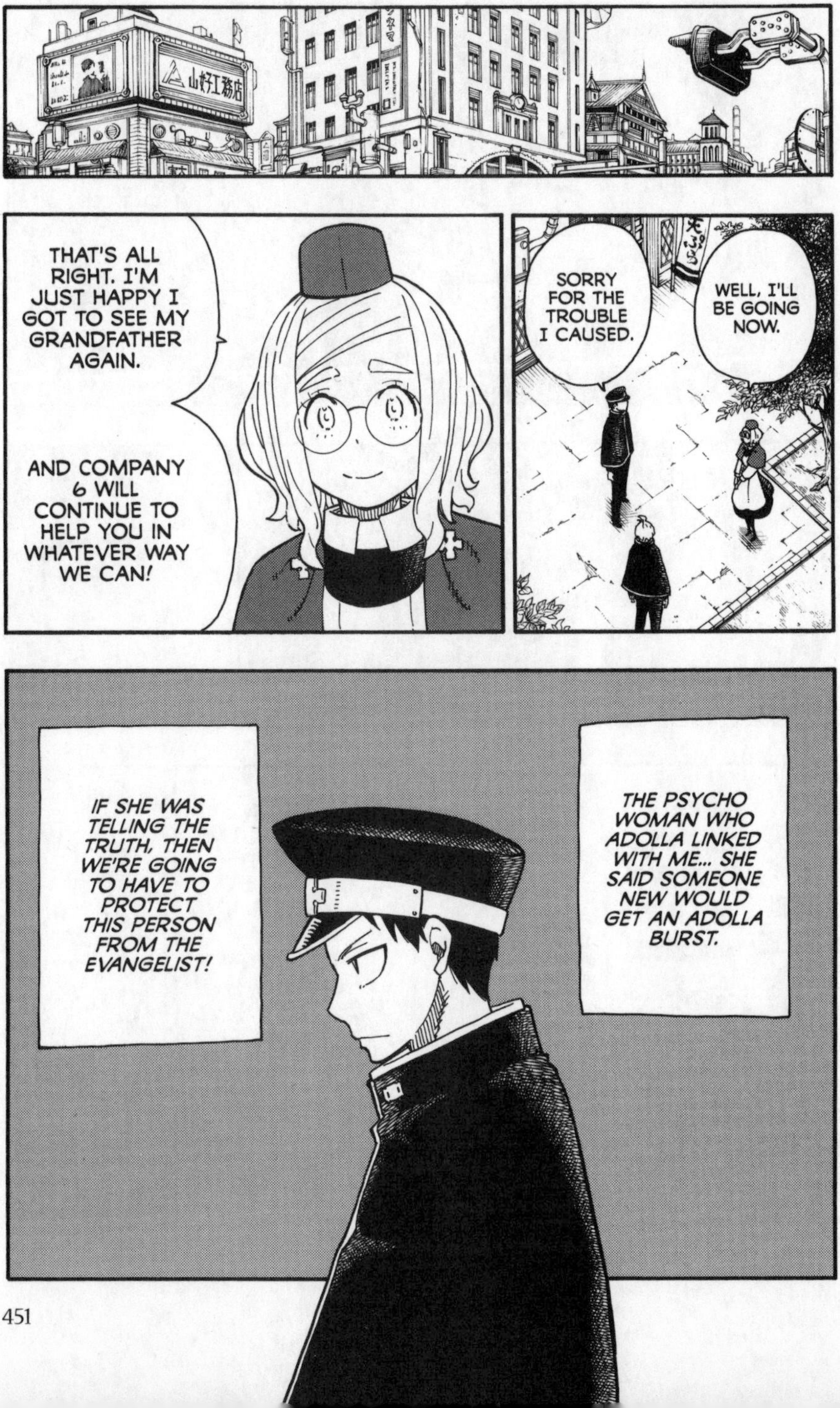
WELL, I'LL BE GOING NOW.
SORRY FOR THE TROUBLE I CAUSED.
THAT'S ALL RIGHT. I'M JUST HAPPY I GOT TO SEE MY GRANDFATHER AGAIN.
AND COMPANY 6 WILL CONTINUE TO HELP YOU IN WHATEVER WAY WE CAN!
THE PSYCHO WOMAN WHO ADOLLA LINKED WITH ME... SHE SAID SOMEONE NEW WOULD GET AN ADOLLA BURST.
IF SHE WAS TELLING THE TRUTH, THEN WE'RE GOING TO HAVE TO PROTECT THIS PERSON FROM THE EVANGELIST!

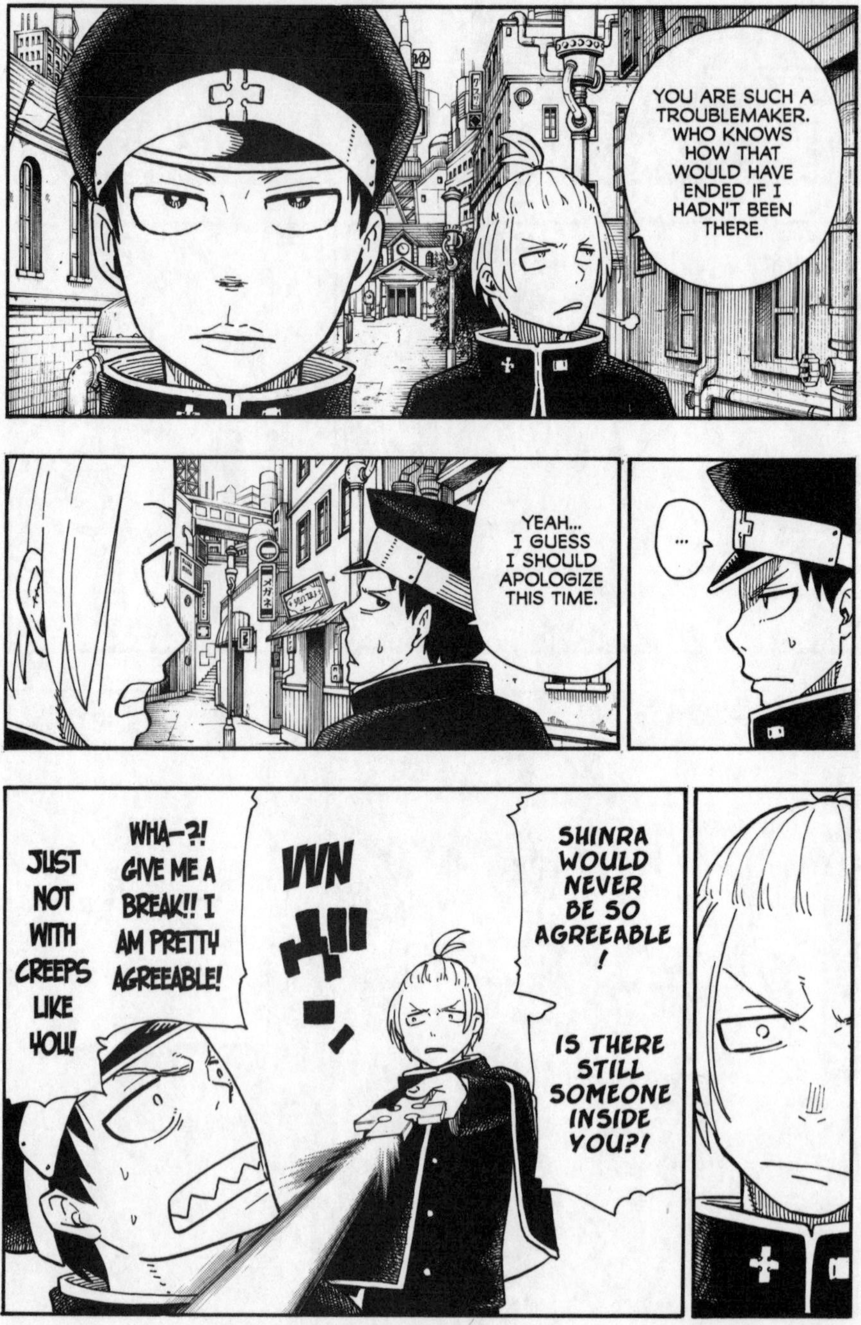
YOU ARE SUCH A TROUBLEMAKER. WHO KNOWS HOW THAT WOULD HAVE ENDED IF I HADN'T BEEN THERE.
...
YEAH... I GUESS I SHOULD APOLOGIZE THIS TIME.
SHINRA WOULD NEVER BE SO AGREEABLE!
IS THERE STILL SOMEONE INSIDE YOU?!
VVN
WHA-?! GIVE ME A BREAK!! I AM PRETTY AGREEABLE!
JUST NOT WITH CREEPS LIKE YOU!

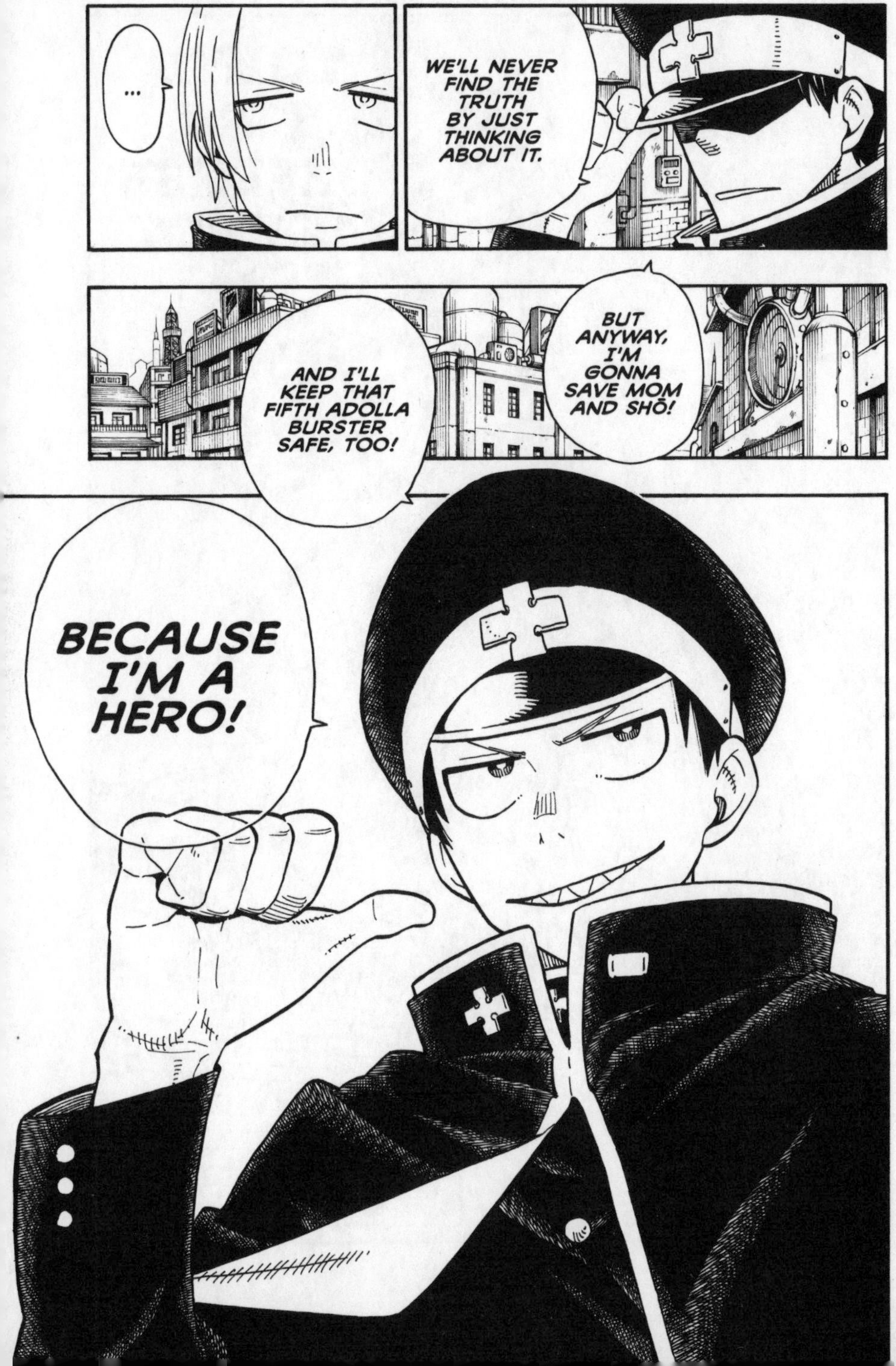
WE'LL NEVER FIND THE TRUTH BY JUST THINKING ABOUT IT.
...
BUT ANYWAY, I'M GONNA SAVE MOM AND SHŌ!
AND I'LL KEEP THAT FIFTH ADOLLA BURSTER SAFE, TOO!
BECAUSE I'M A HERO!

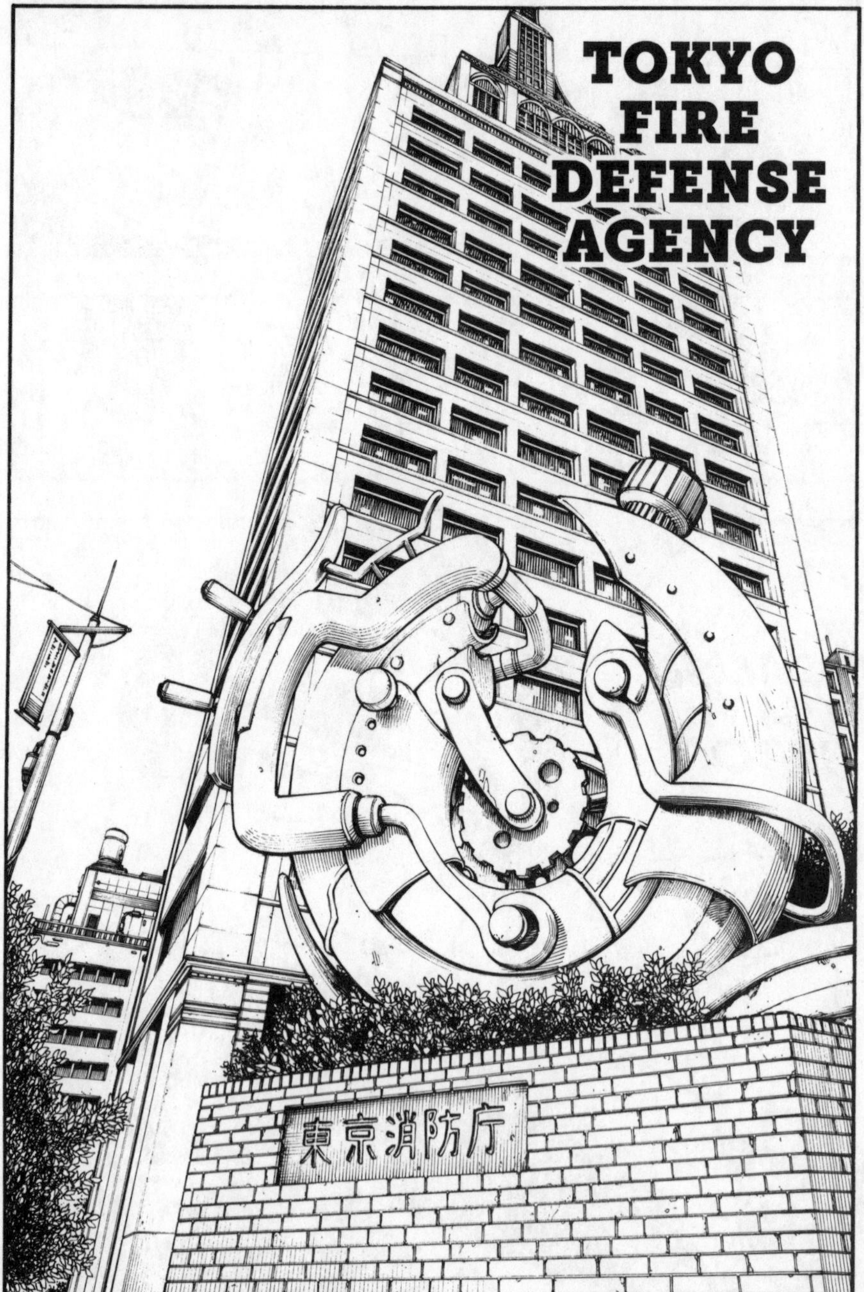
TOKYO FIRE DEFENSE AGENCY
東京消防庁

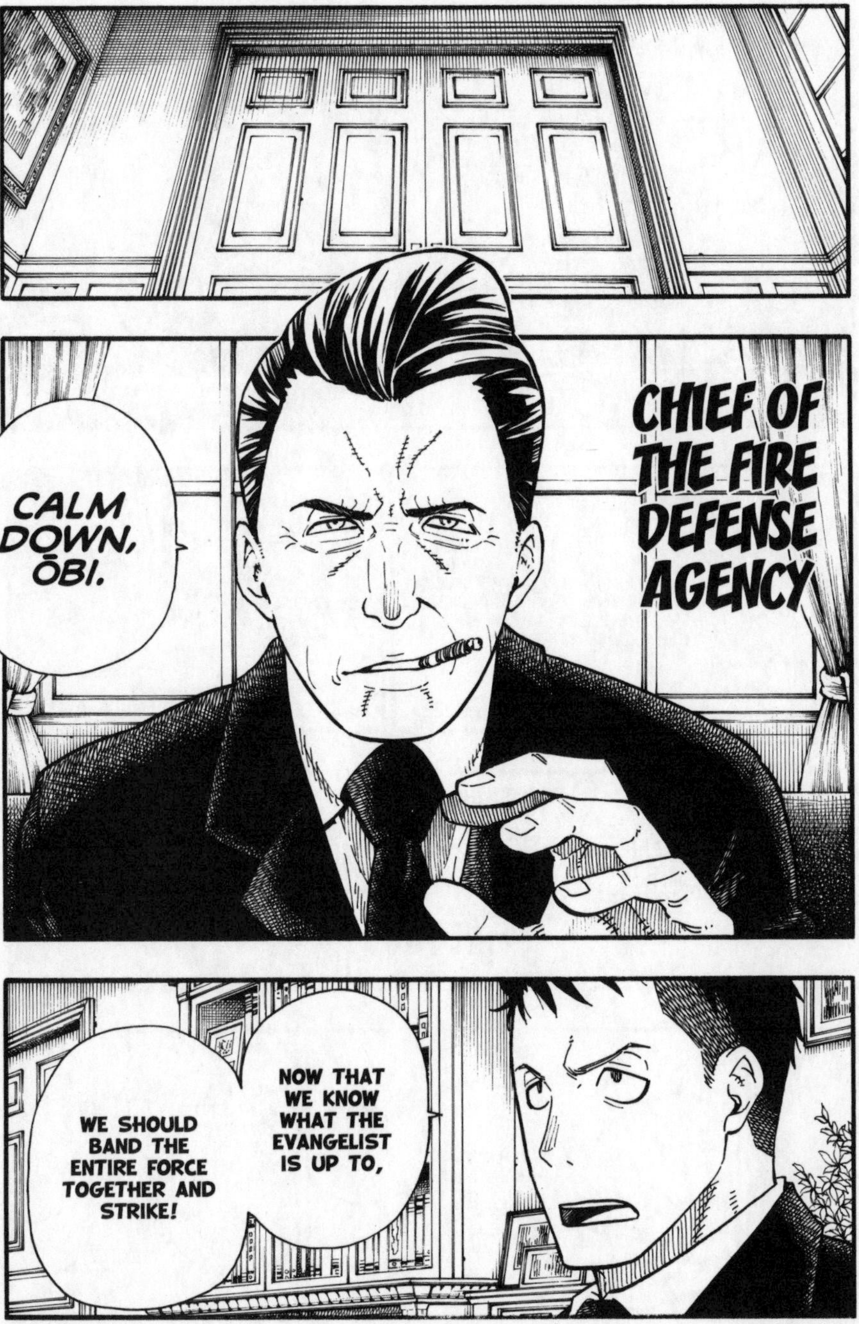
CHIEF OF THE FIRE DEFENSE AGENCY
CALM DOWN, ŌBI.
NOW THAT WE KNOW WHAT THE EVANGELIST IS UP TO,
WE SHOULD BAND THE ENTIRE FORCE TOGETHER AND STRIKE!

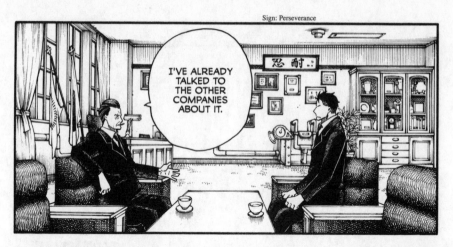

Sign: Perseverance

忍耐
I'VE ALREADY TALKED TO THE OTHER COMPANIES ABOUT IT.
WE ALSO HAD A REPORT THAT A NEW PERSON WILL BE OBTAINING AN ADOLLA BURST.
IT'S NOT EASY TO GET PEOPLE TO BELIEVE THIS.
HAIJIMA IS BEING ESPECIALLY UNCOOPERATIVE.
THE EVANGELIST IS ALREADY ARTIFICIALLY IGNITING INFERNALS.
AND THERE'S SO MUCH WE DON'T KNOW ABOUT THE ADOLLA BURST ITSELF. NO ONE KNOWS IF BRINGING THEM TOGETHER WOULD REALLY CAUSE A GREAT CATACLYSM.
I CAN'T MOBILIZE THE ENTIRE FORCE WITHOUT DEFINITE PROOF.
BUT IF WE WAIT UNTIL SOMETHING HAPPENS, IT WILL BE TOO LATE.
EXACTLY.
THAT'S WHY I PUT YOU IN CHARGE OF COMPANY 8.
...

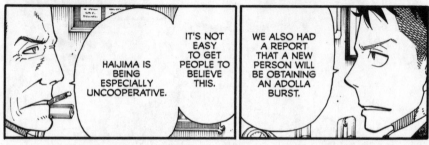

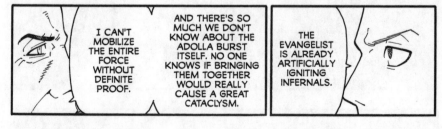

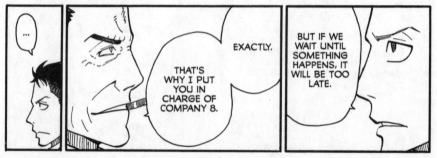

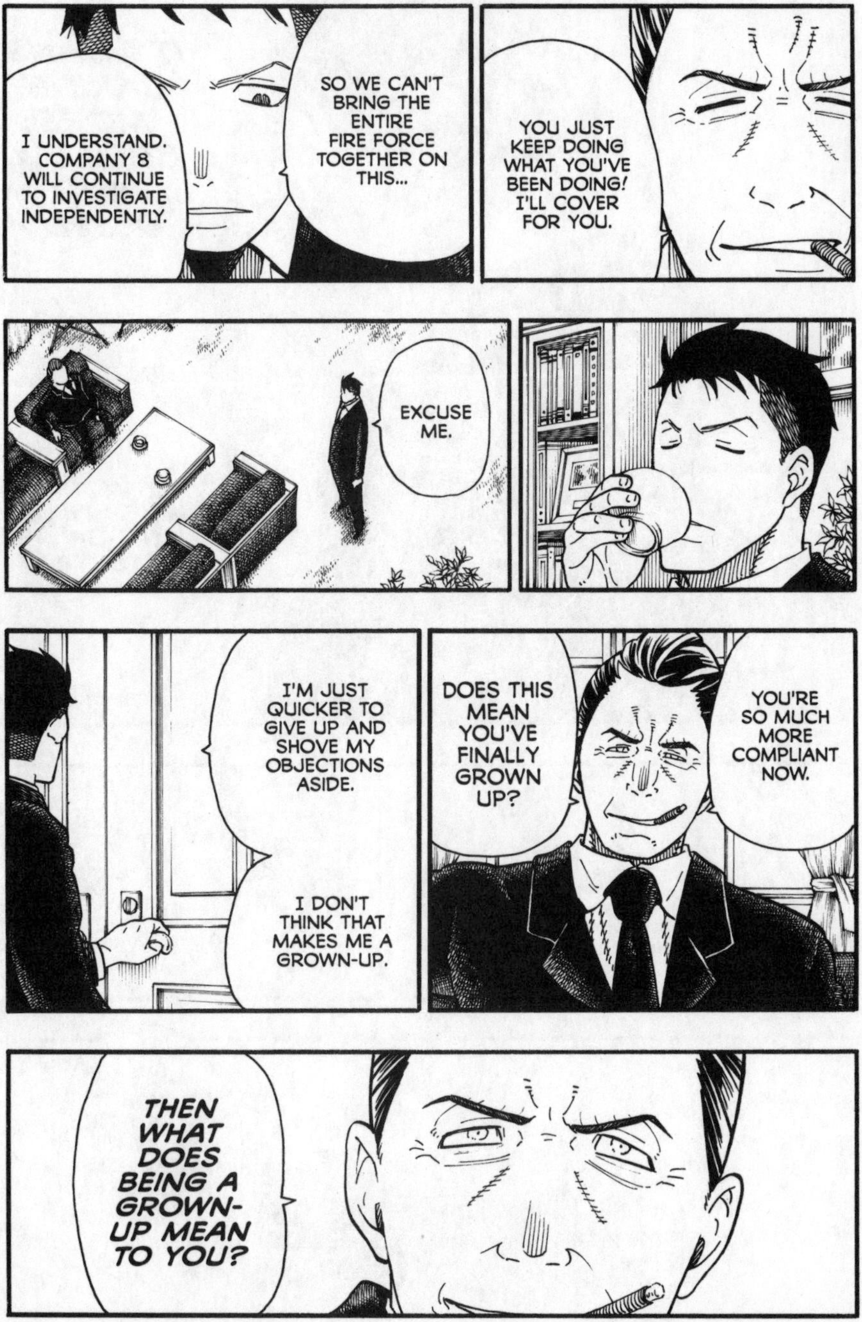
YOU JUST KEEP DOING WHAT YOU'VE BEEN DOING! I'LL COVER FOR YOU.
SO WE CAN'T BRING THE ENTIRE FIRE FORCE TOGETHER ON THIS...
I UNDERSTAND. COMPANY 8 WILL CONTINUE TO INVESTIGATE INDEPENDENTLY.
EXCUSE ME.
YOU'RE SO MUCH MORE COMPLIANT NOW.
DOES THIS MEAN YOU'VE FINALLY GROWN UP?
I'M JUST QUICKER TO GIVE UP AND SHOVE MY OBJECTIONS ASIDE.
I DON'T THINK THAT MAKES ME A GROWN-UP.
THEN WHAT DOES BEING A GROWN-UP MEAN TO YOU?

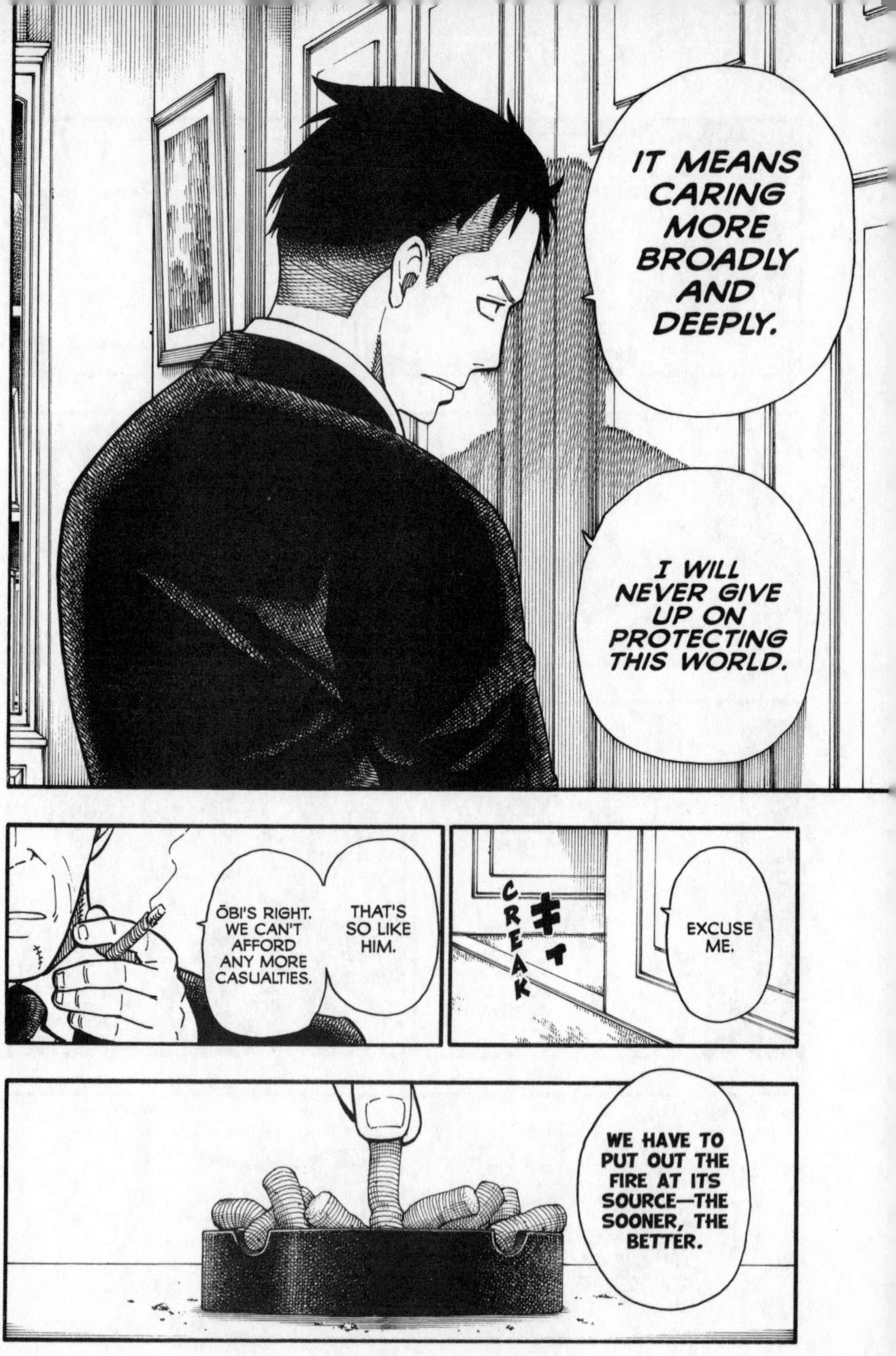
IT MEANS CARING MORE BROADLY AND DEEPLY.
I WILL NEVER GIVE UP ON PROTECTING THIS WORLD.
CREAK
キィ
EXCUSE ME.
THAT'S SO LIKE HIM.
ŌBI'S RIGHT. WE CAN'T AFFORD ANY MORE CASUALTIES.
WE HAVE TO PUT OUT THE FIRE AT ITS SOURCE—THE SOONER, THE BETTER.

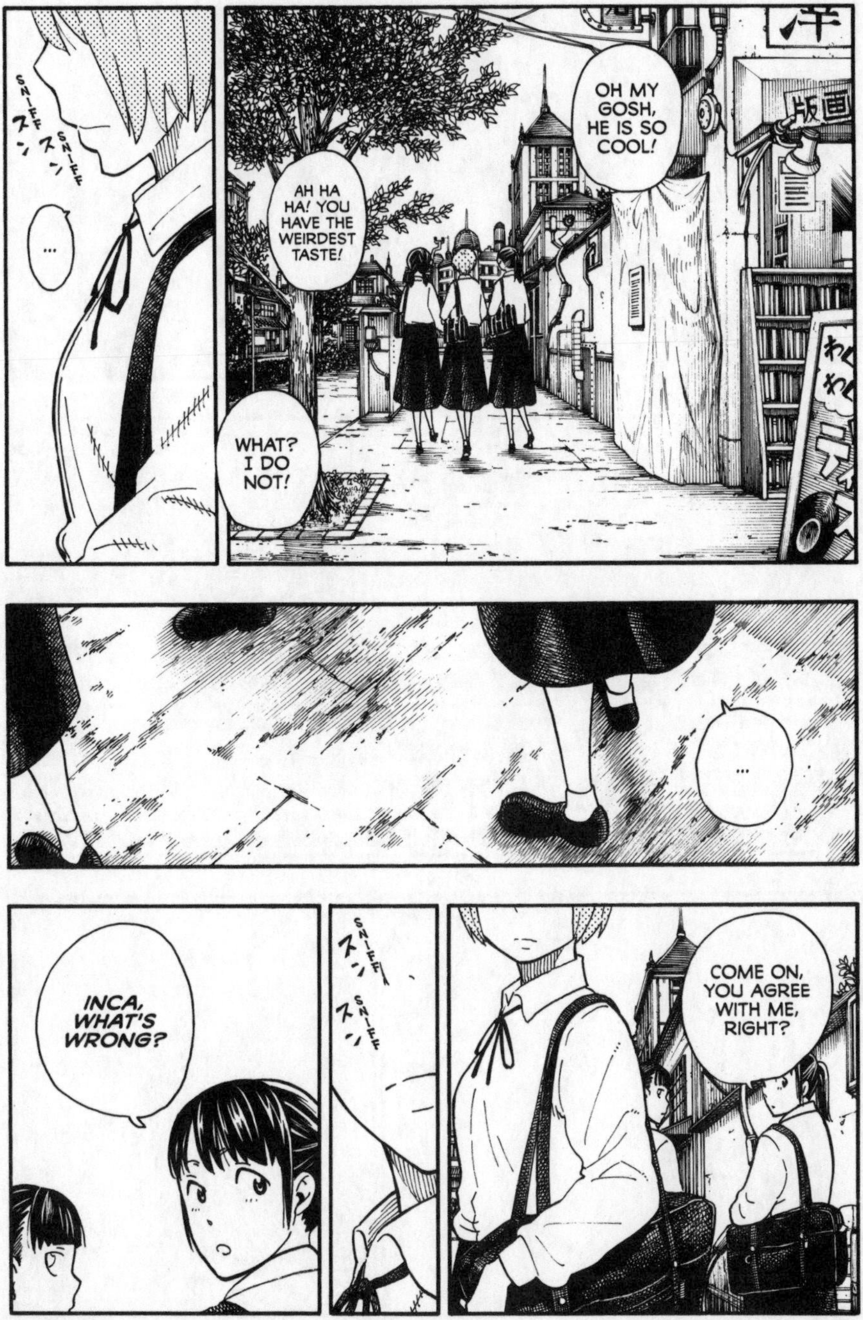
OH MY GOSH, HE IS SO COOL!
AH HA HA! YOU HAVE THE WEIRDEST TASTE!
WHAT? I DO NOT!
SNIFF スン
SNIFF スン
...
...
COME ON, YOU AGREE WITH ME, RIGHT?
SNIFF スン
SNIFF スン
INCA, WHAT'S WRONG?

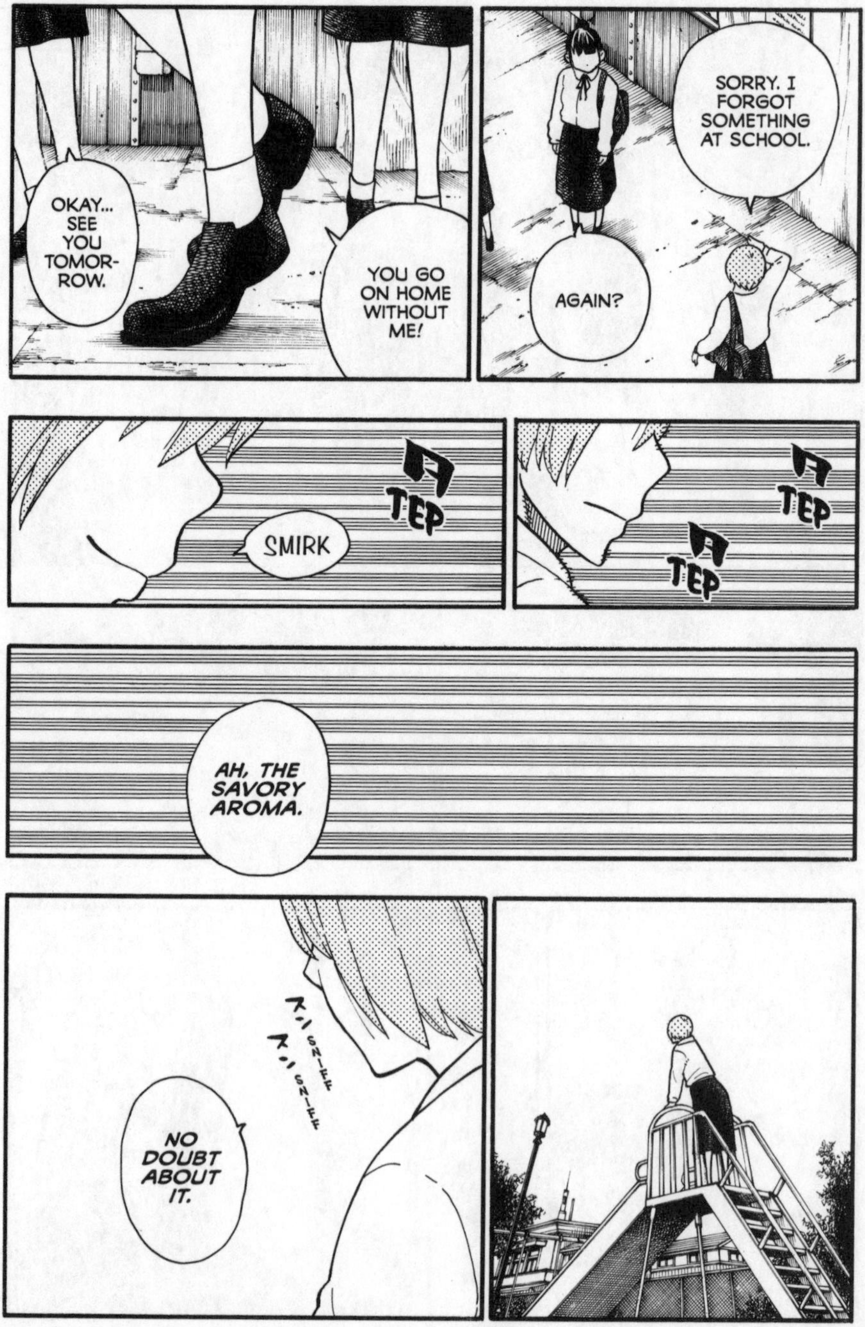
SORRY. I FORGOT SOMETHING AT SCHOOL.
AGAIN?
YOU GO ON HOME WITHOUT ME!
OKAY... SEE YOU TOMOR-ROW.
TEP
TEP
TEP
SMIRK
AH, THE SAVORY AROMA.
SNIFF
SNIFF
NO DOUBT ABOUT IT.

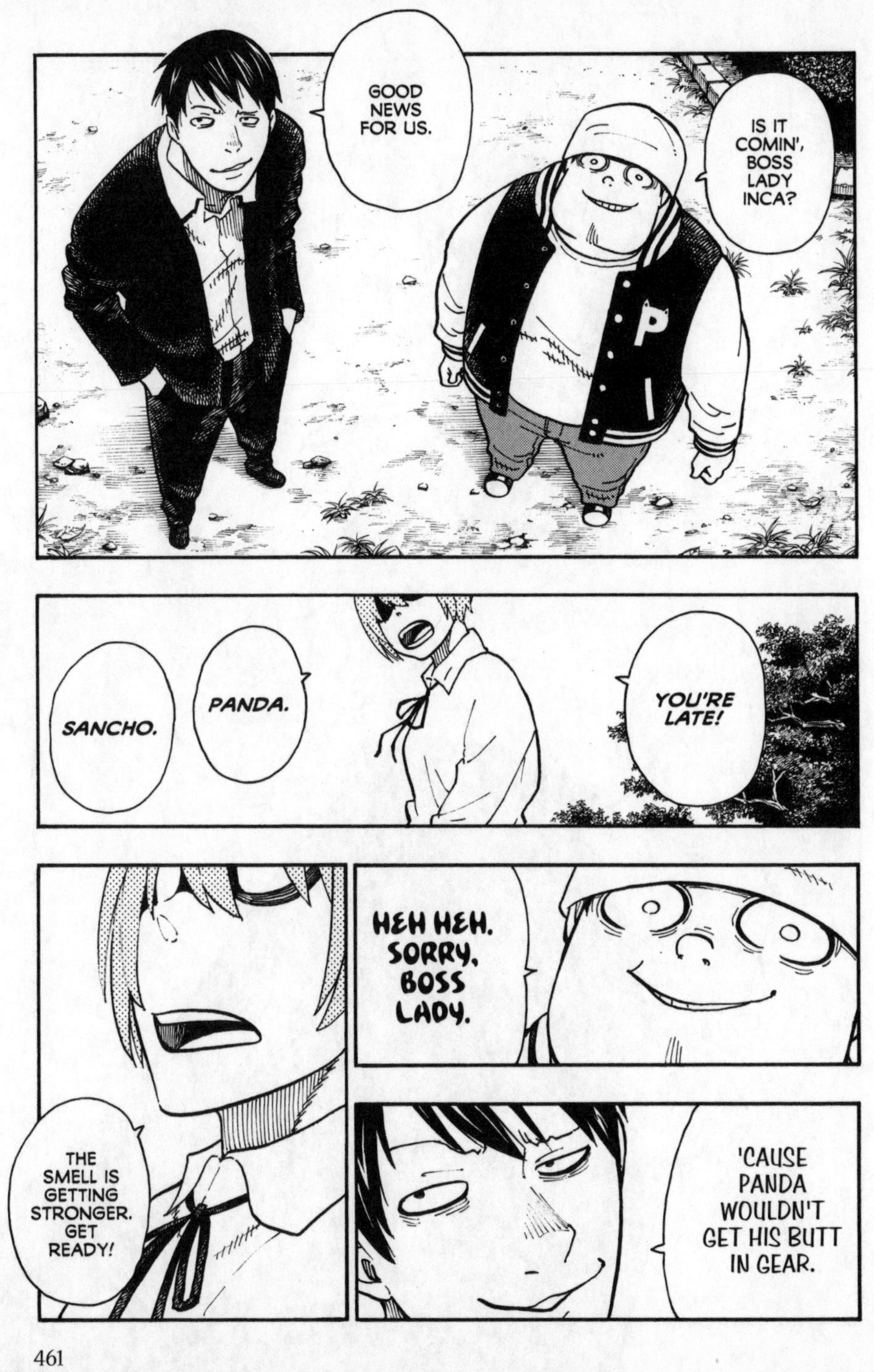
IS IT COMIN', BOSS LADY INCA?
GOOD NEWS FOR US.
YOU'RE LATE!
PANDA.
SANCHO.
HEH HEH. SORRY, BOSS LADY.
'CAUSE PANDA WOULDN'T GET HIS BUTT IN GEAR.
THE SMELL IS GETTING STRONGER. GET READY!

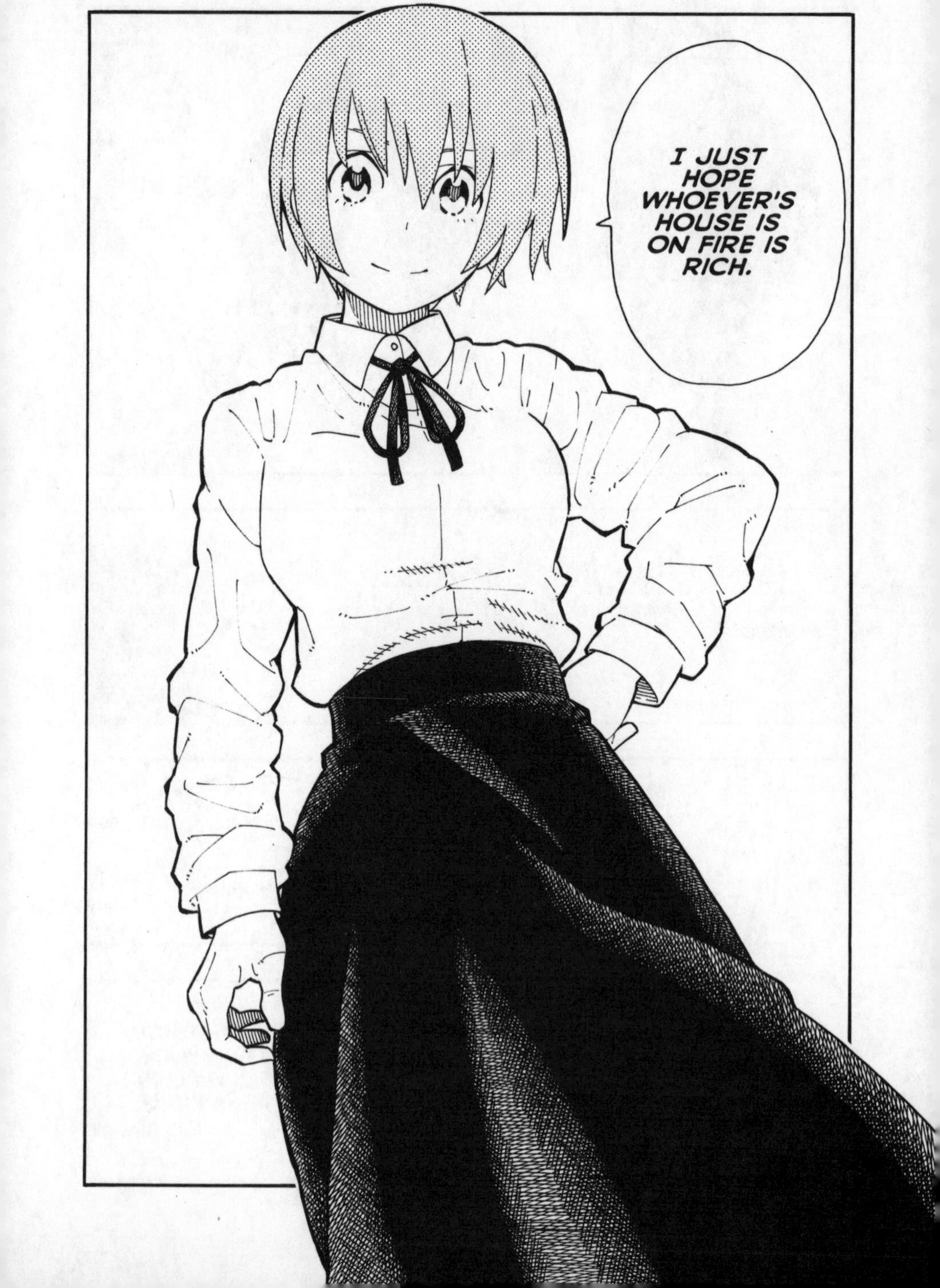
I JUST HOPE WHOEVER'S HOUSE IS ON FIRE IS RICH.

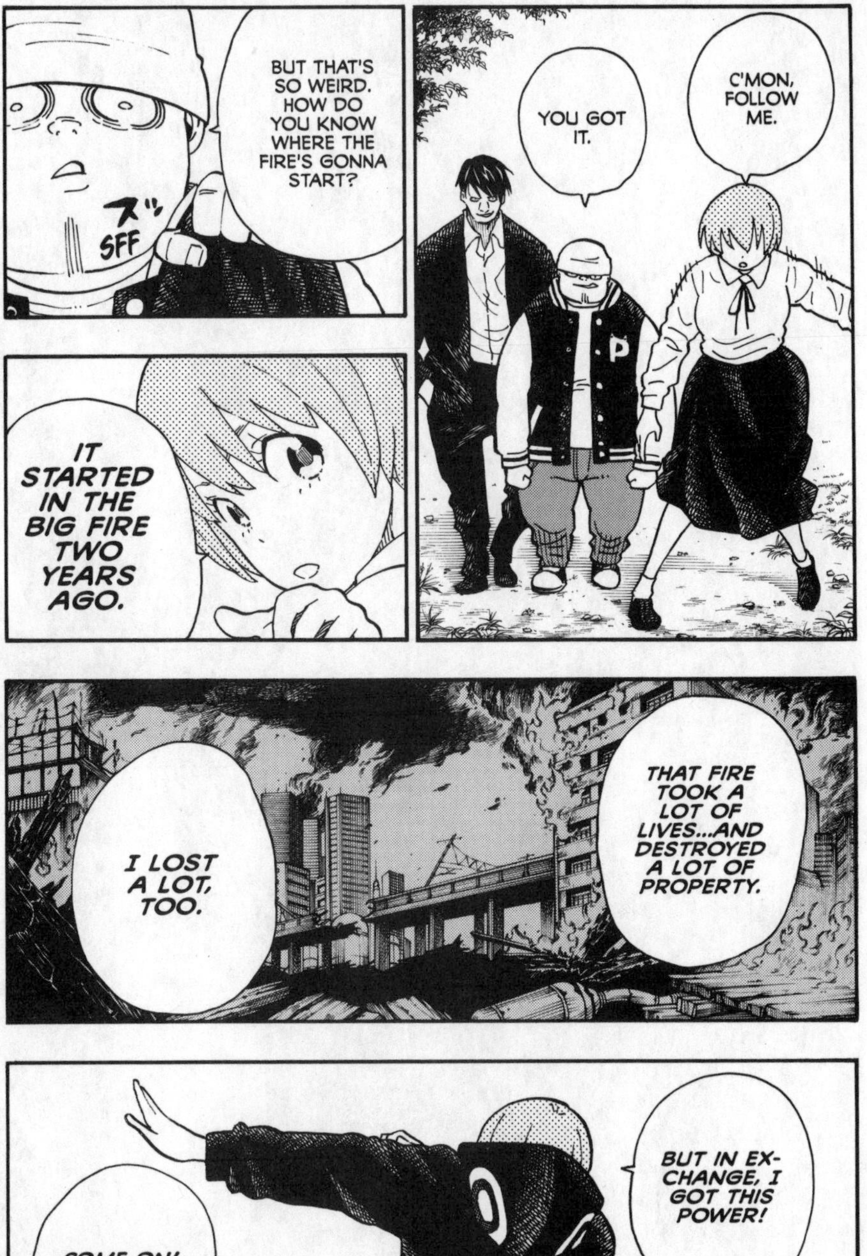
C'MON, FOLLOW ME.
YOU GOT IT.
BUT THAT'S SO WEIRD. HOW DO YOU KNOW WHERE THE FIRE'S GONNA START?
ズッ
SFF
IT STARTED IN THE BIG FIRE TWO YEARS AGO.
THAT FIRE TOOK A LOT OF LIVES...AND DESTROYED A LOT OF PROPERTY.
I LOST A LOT, TOO.
BUT IN EX-CHANGE, I GOT THIS POWER!
COME ON! THE FIRE'S STARTING!!

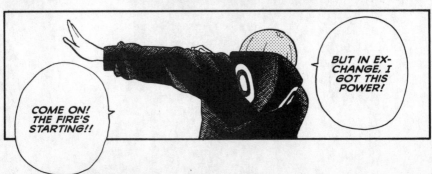

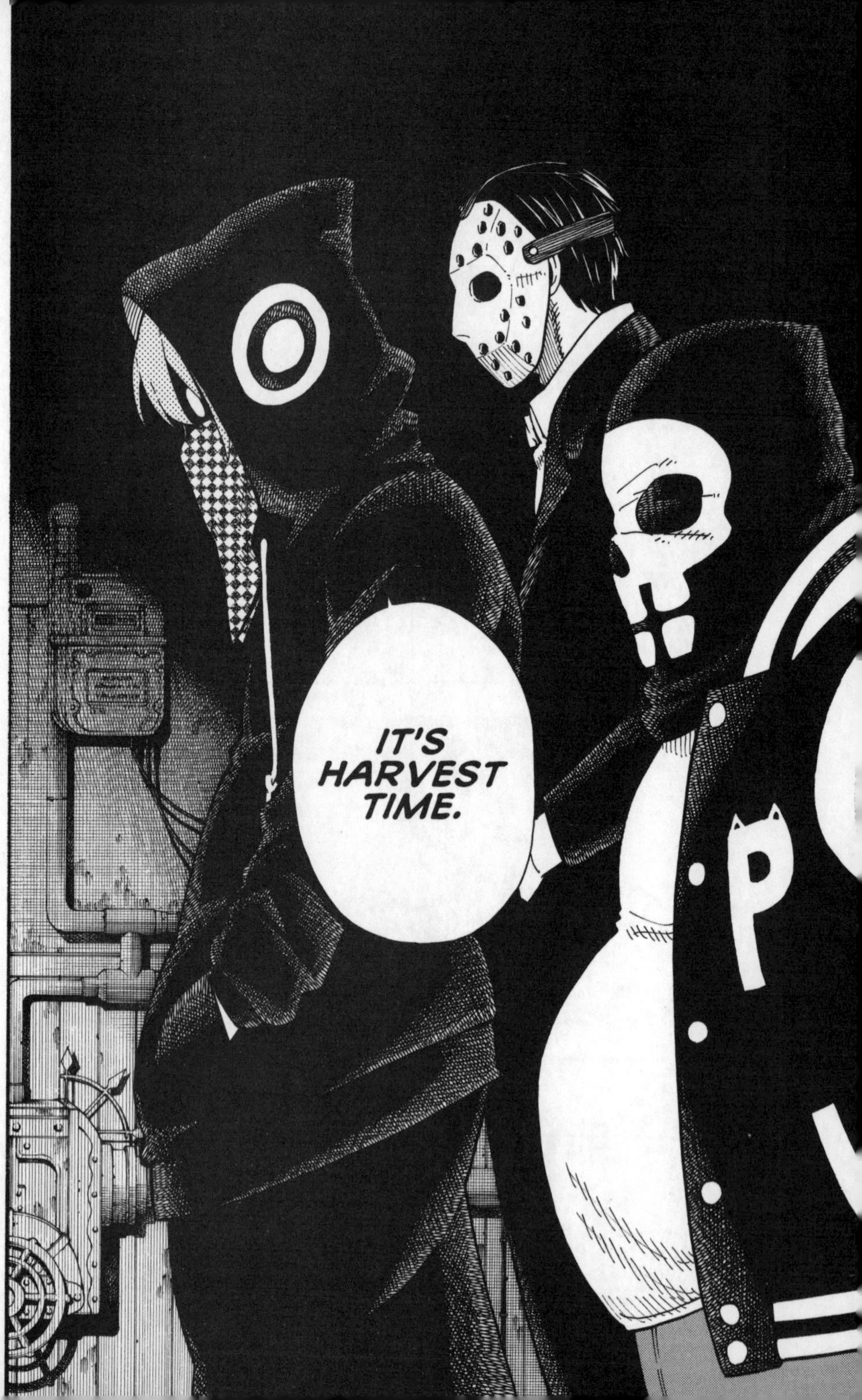
IT'S HARVEST TIME.

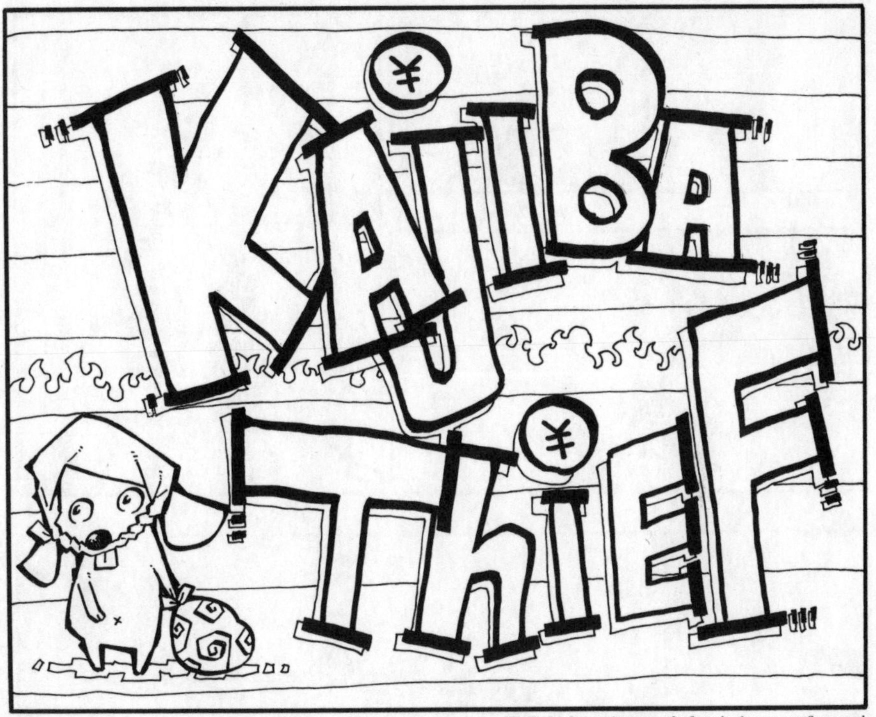
KAJIBA
THIEF

"*Kajiba*" refers to the scene of a fire, also known as a fireground.

CHAPTER C: THE SCENT OF THE FLAME

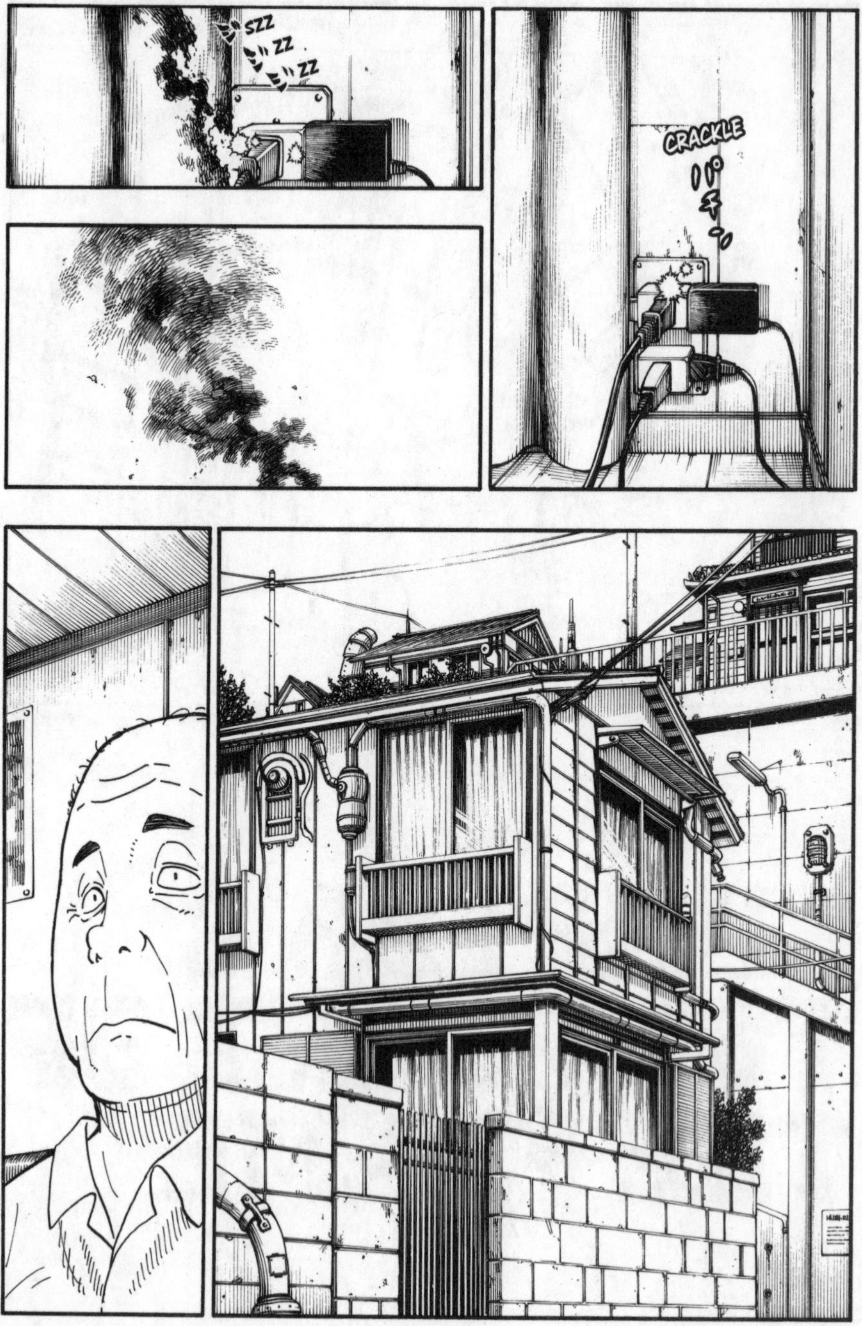
CRACKLE
SZZ
ZZ
ZZ

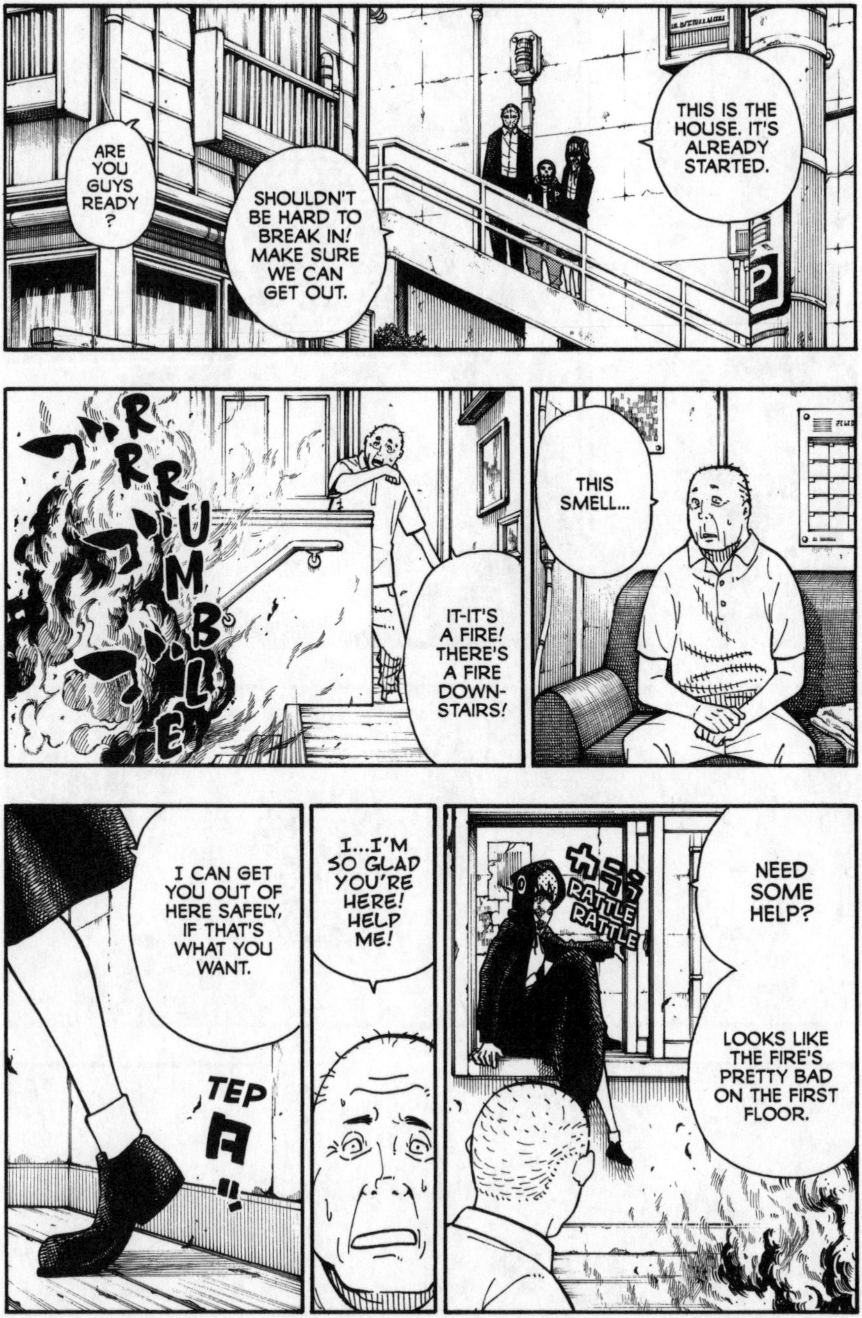
THIS IS THE HOUSE. IT'S ALREADY STARTED.
SHOULDN'T BE HARD TO BREAK IN! MAKE SURE WE CAN GET OUT.
ARE YOU GUYS READY?
THIS SMELL...
IT-IT'S A FIRE! THERE'S A FIRE DOWN-STAIRS!
RRRUMBLE
NEED SOME HELP?
RATTLE RATTLE
LOOKS LIKE THE FIRE'S PRETTY BAD ON THE FIRST FLOOR.
I...I'M SO GLAD YOU'RE HERE! HELP ME!
I CAN GET YOU OUT OF HERE SAFELY, IF THAT'S WHAT YOU WANT.
TEP

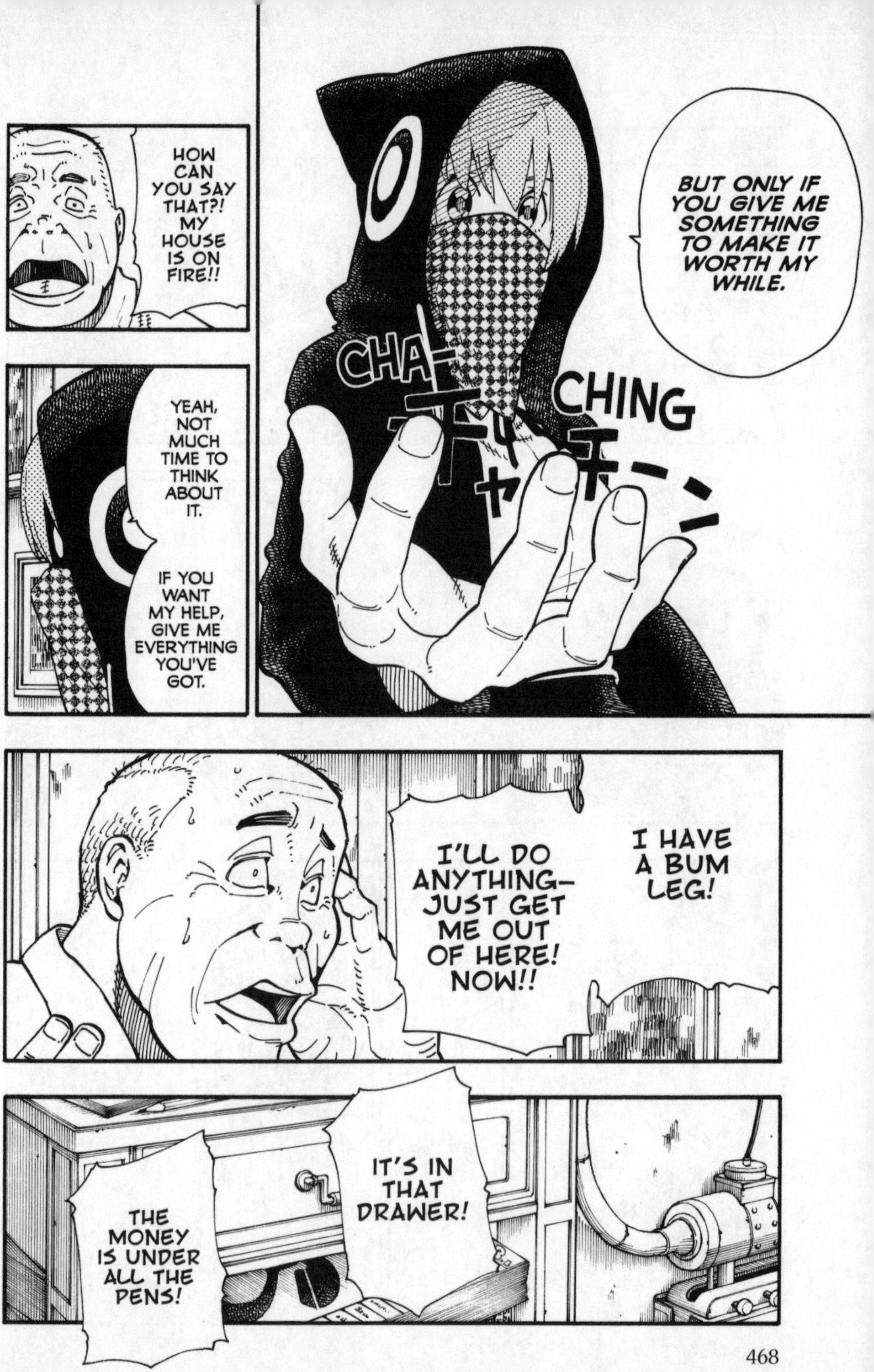
BUT ONLY IF YOU GIVE ME SOMETHING TO MAKE IT WORTH MY WHILE.
CHA-CHING
HOW CAN YOU SAY THAT?! MY HOUSE IS ON FIRE!!
YEAH, NOT MUCH TIME TO THINK ABOUT IT.
IF YOU WANT MY HELP, GIVE ME EVERYTHING YOU'VE GOT.
I HAVE A BUM LEG!
I'LL DO ANYTHING— JUST GET ME OUT OF HERE! NOW!!
IT'S IN THAT DRAWER!
THE MONEY IS UNDER ALL THE PENS!

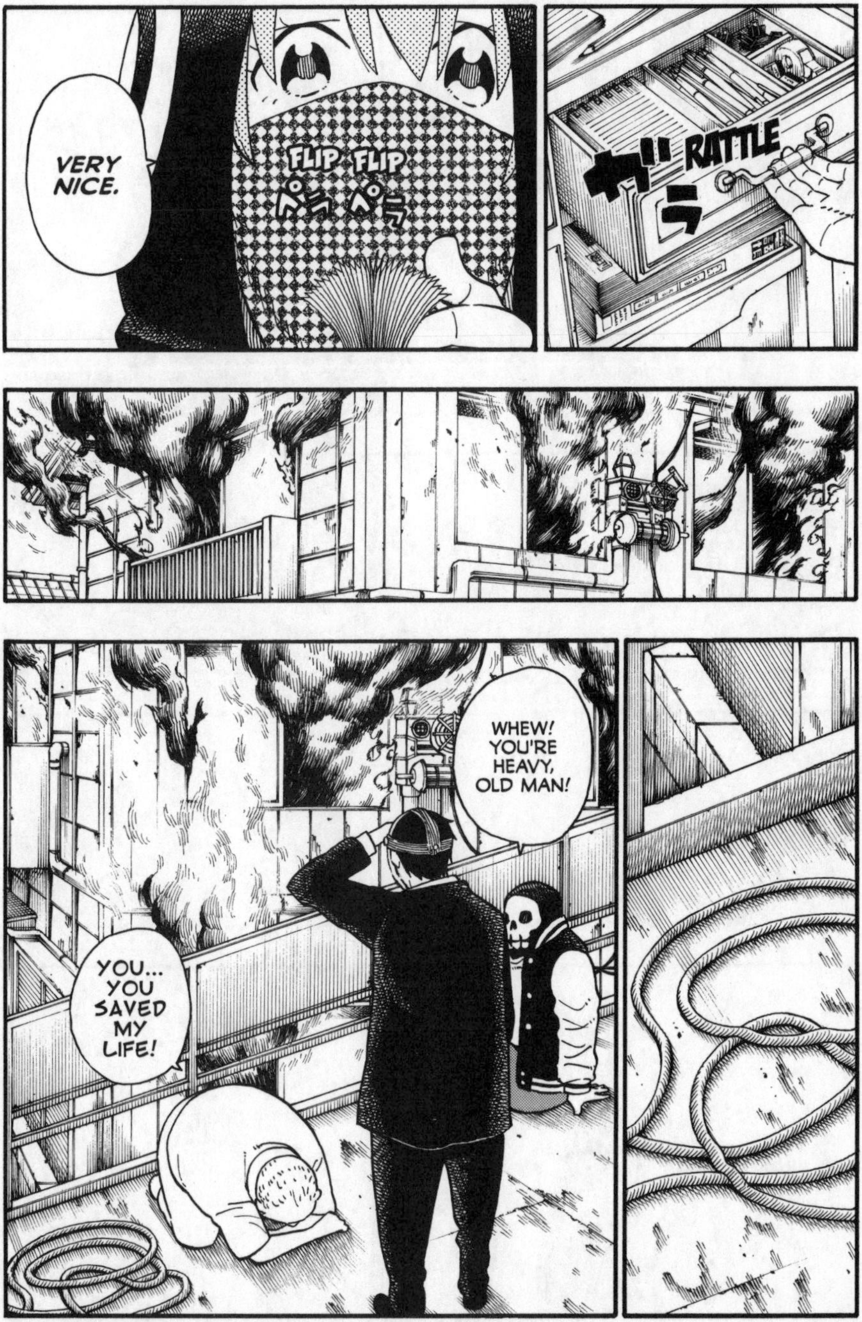
RATTLE
ガラ
VERY NICE.
FLIP FLIP
ぺらぺら
WHEW! YOU'RE HEAVY, OLD MAN!
YOU... YOU SAVED MY LIFE!

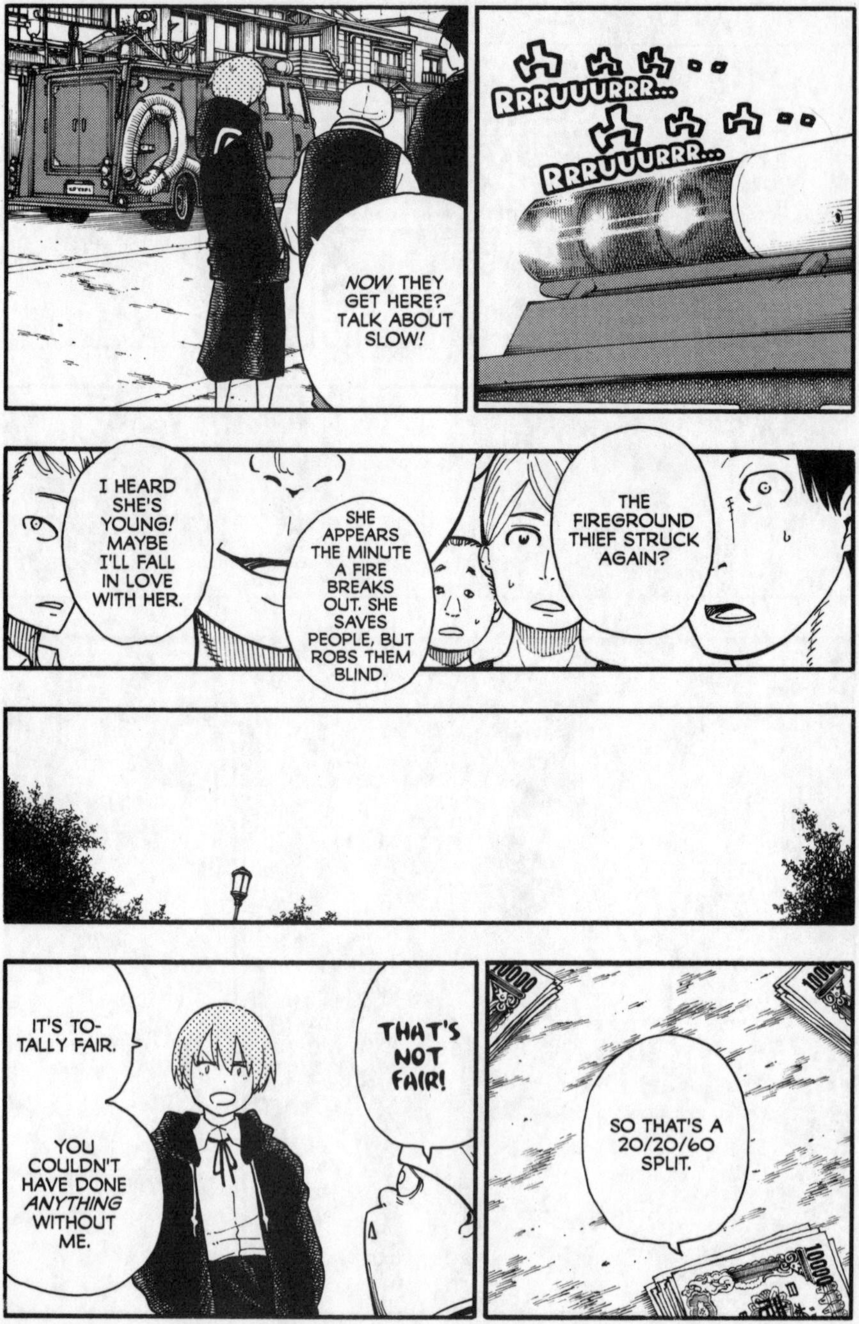
ウウウ..
RRRUUURRR...
ウウウ..
RRRUUURRR...
NOW THEY GET HERE? TALK ABOUT SLOW!
THE FIREGROUND THIEF STRUCK AGAIN?
SHE APPEARS THE MINUTE A FIRE BREAKS OUT. SHE SAVES PEOPLE, BUT ROBS THEM BLIND.
I HEARD SHE'S YOUNG! MAYBE I'LL FALL IN LOVE WITH HER.
SO THAT'S A 20/20/60 SPLIT.
THAT'S NOT FAIR!
IT'S TO-TALLY FAIR.
YOU COULDN'T HAVE DONE *ANYTHING* WITHOUT ME.

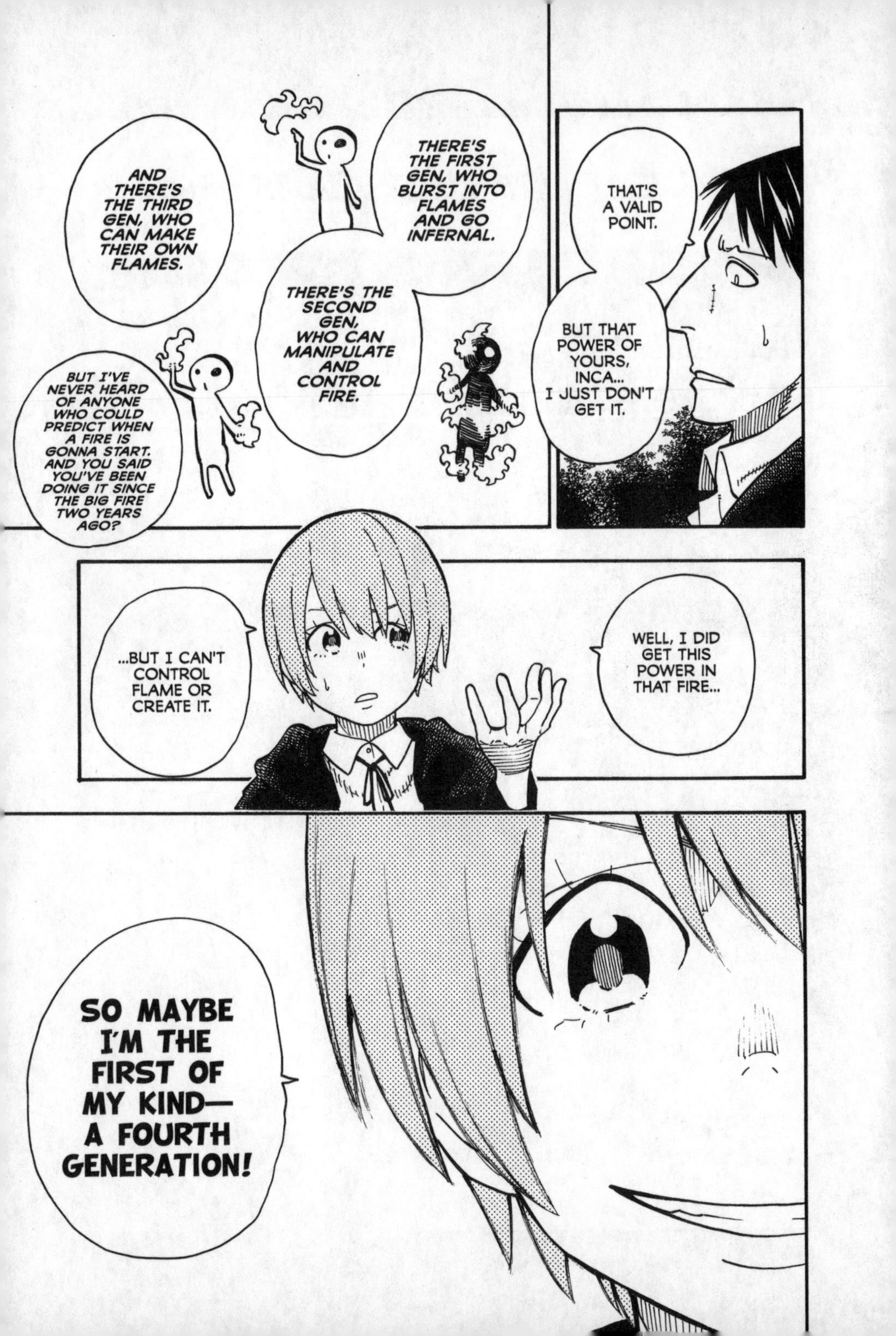
THAT'S A VALID POINT.
BUT THAT POWER OF YOURS, INCA... I JUST DON'T GET IT.
THERE'S THE FIRST GEN, WHO BURST INTO FLAMES AND GO INFERNAL.
THERE'S THE SECOND GEN, WHO CAN MANIPULATE AND CONTROL FIRE.
AND THERE'S THE THIRD GEN, WHO CAN MAKE THEIR OWN FLAMES.
BUT I'VE NEVER HEARD OF ANYONE WHO COULD PREDICT WHEN A FIRE IS GONNA START. AND YOU SAID YOU'VE BEEN DOING IT SINCE THE BIG FIRE TWO YEARS AGO?
WELL, I DID GET THIS POWER IN THAT FIRE...
...BUT I CAN'T CONTROL FLAME OR CREATE IT.
SO MAYBE I'M THE FIRST OF MY KIND— A FOURTH GENERATION!

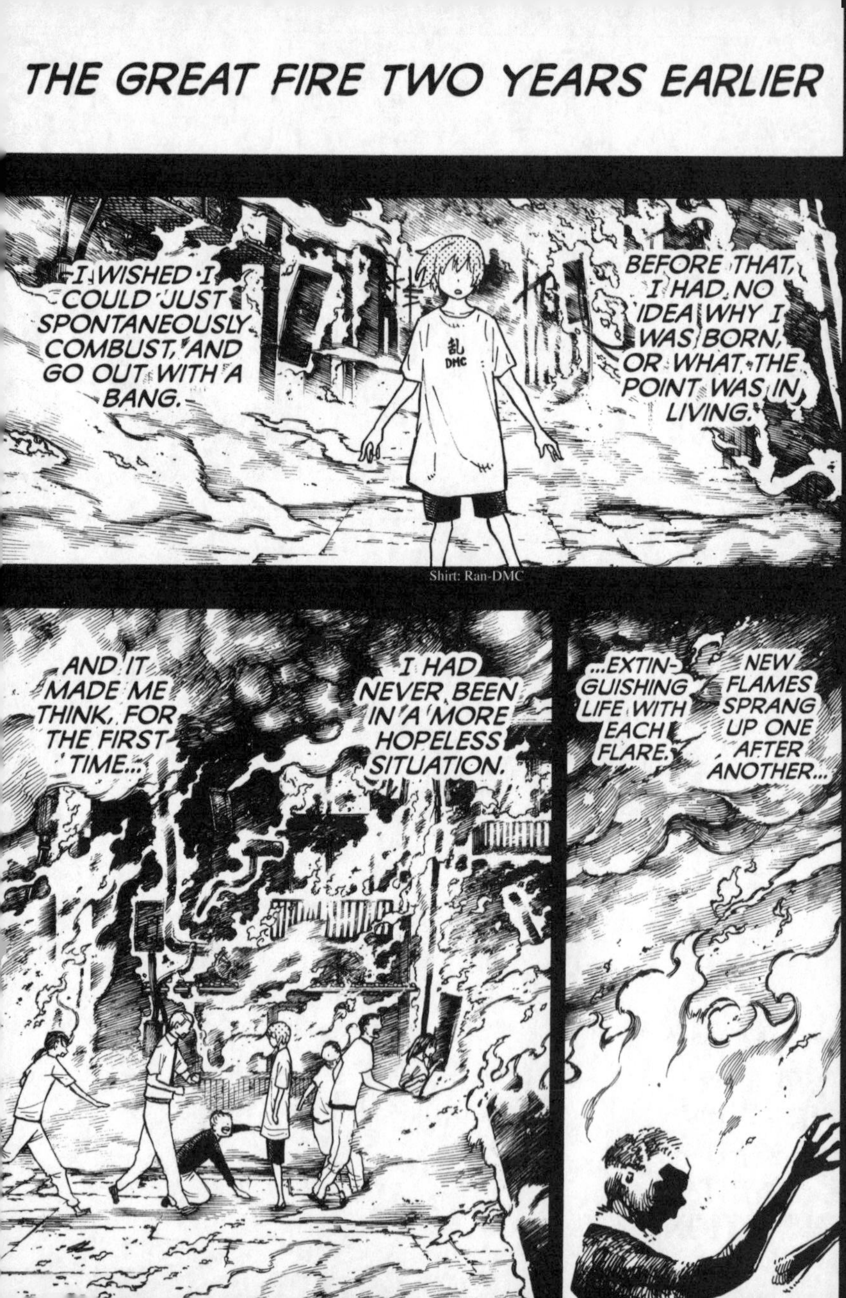
THE GREAT FIRE TWO YEARS EARLIER
BEFORE THAT, I HAD NO IDEA WHY I WAS BORN, OR WHAT THE POINT WAS IN LIVING.
I WISHED I COULD JUST SPONTANEOUSLY COMBUST, AND GO OUT WITH A BANG.
乱 DMC
Shirt: Ran-DMC
NEW FLAMES SPRANG UP ONE AFTER ANOTHER...
...EXTIN-GUISHING LIFE WITH EACH FLARE.
I HAD NEVER BEEN IN A MORE HOPELESS SITUATION.
AND IT MADE ME THINK, FOR THE FIRST TIME...

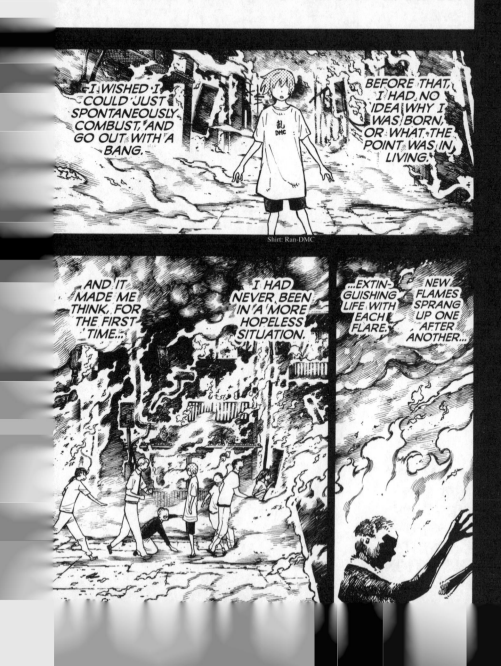

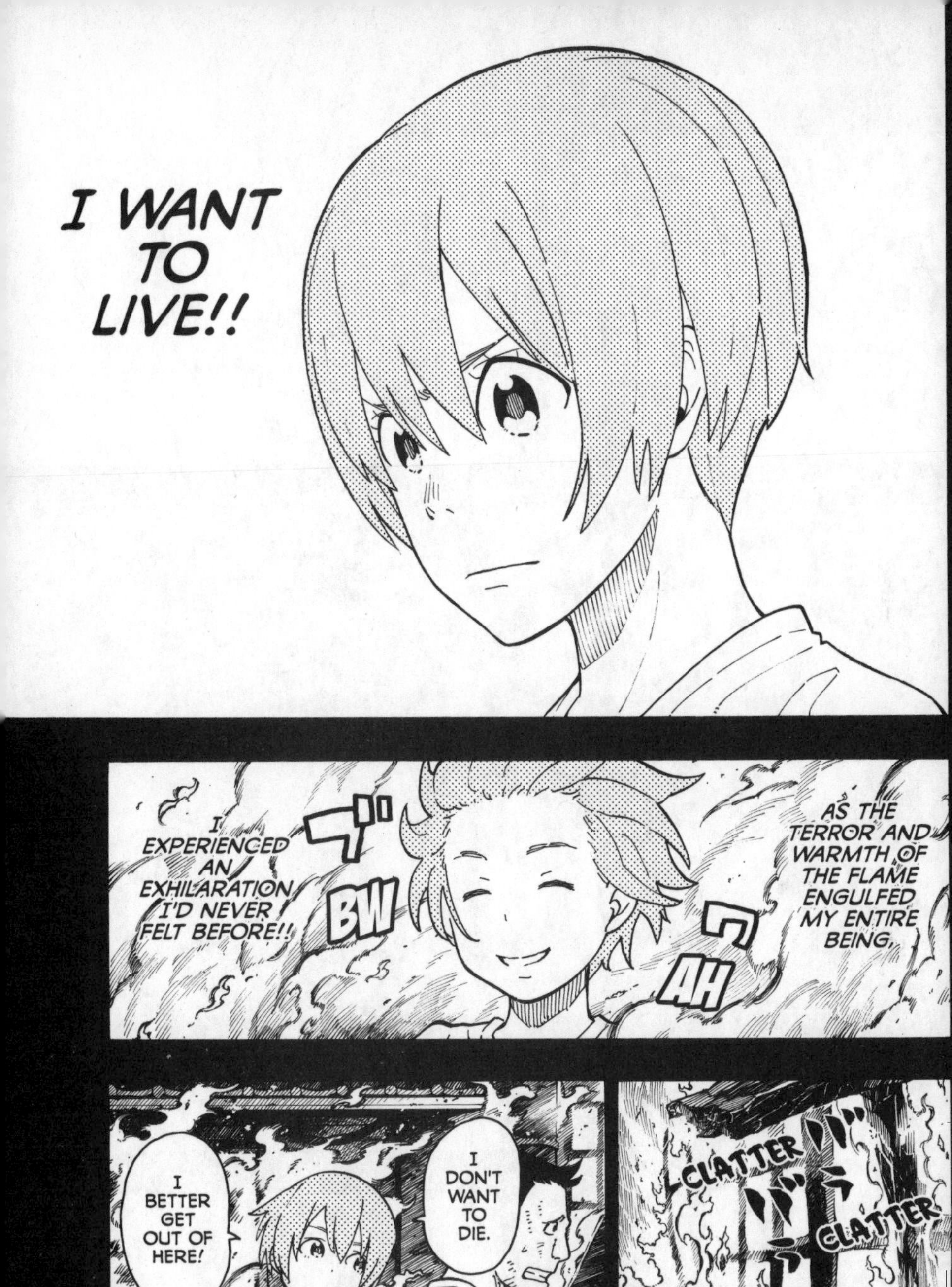
I WANT TO LIVE!!
AS THE TERROR AND WARMTH OF THE FLAME ENGULFED MY ENTIRE BEING,
AH
BW
I EXPERIENCED AN EXHILARATION I'D NEVER FELT BEFORE!!
CLATTER
CLATTER
I DON'T WANT TO DIE.
I BETTER GET OUT OF HERE!

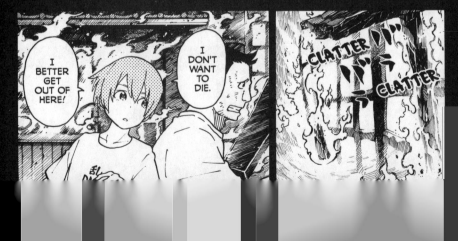

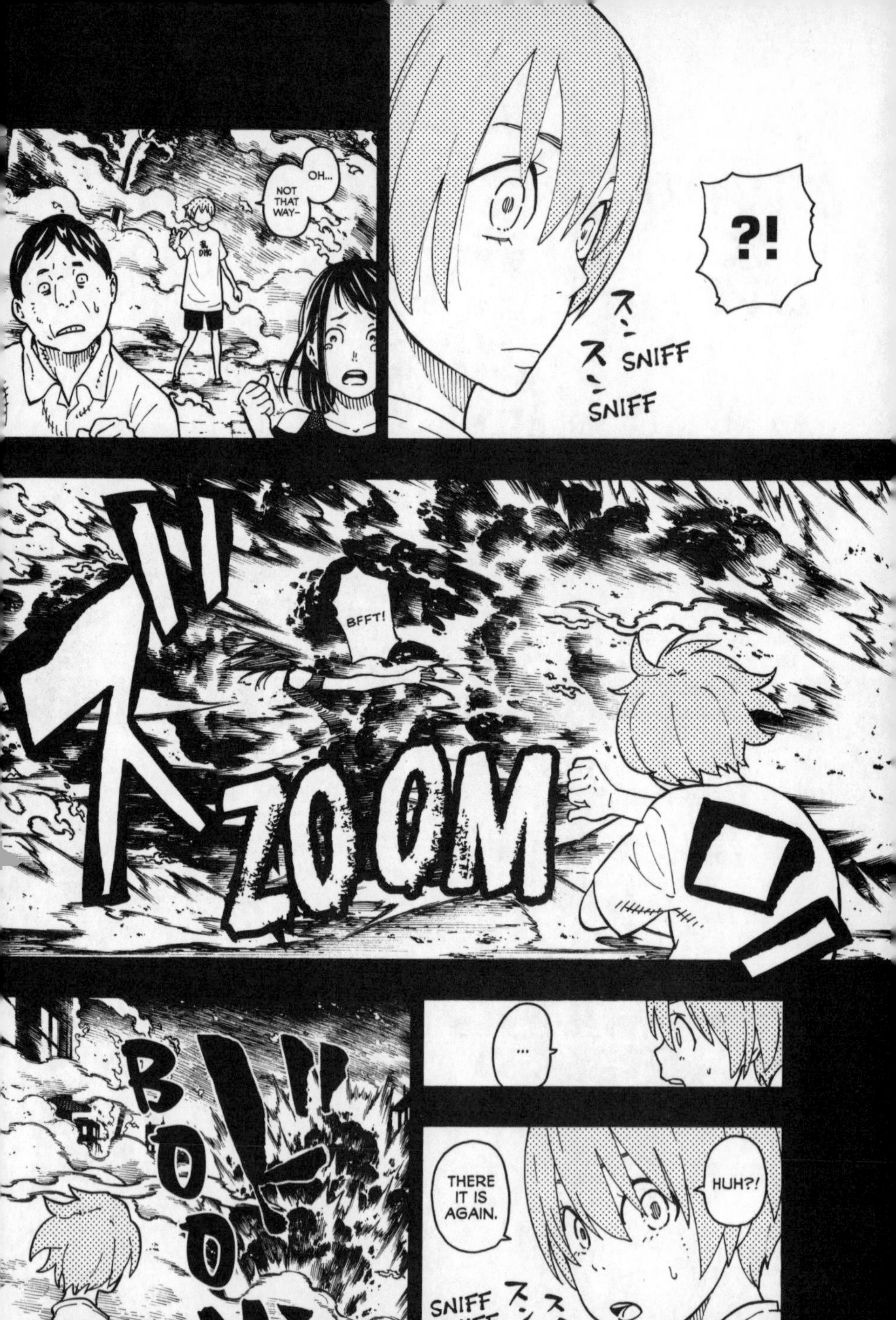
?!
スン スン
SNIFF SNIFF
OH... NOT THAT WAY-
BFFT!
ZOOM
...
HUH?!
THERE IT IS AGAIN.
スン スン
SNIFF SNIFF

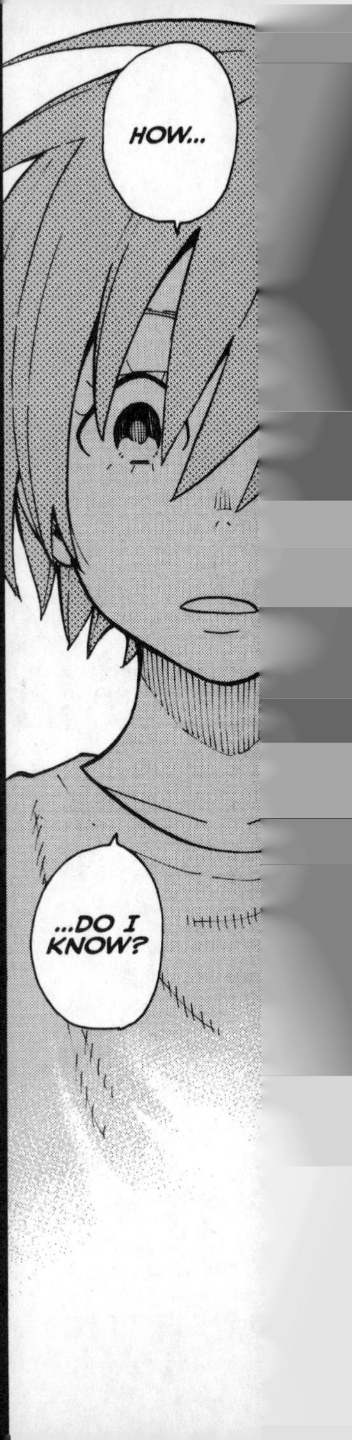
HOW...
...DO I KNOW?
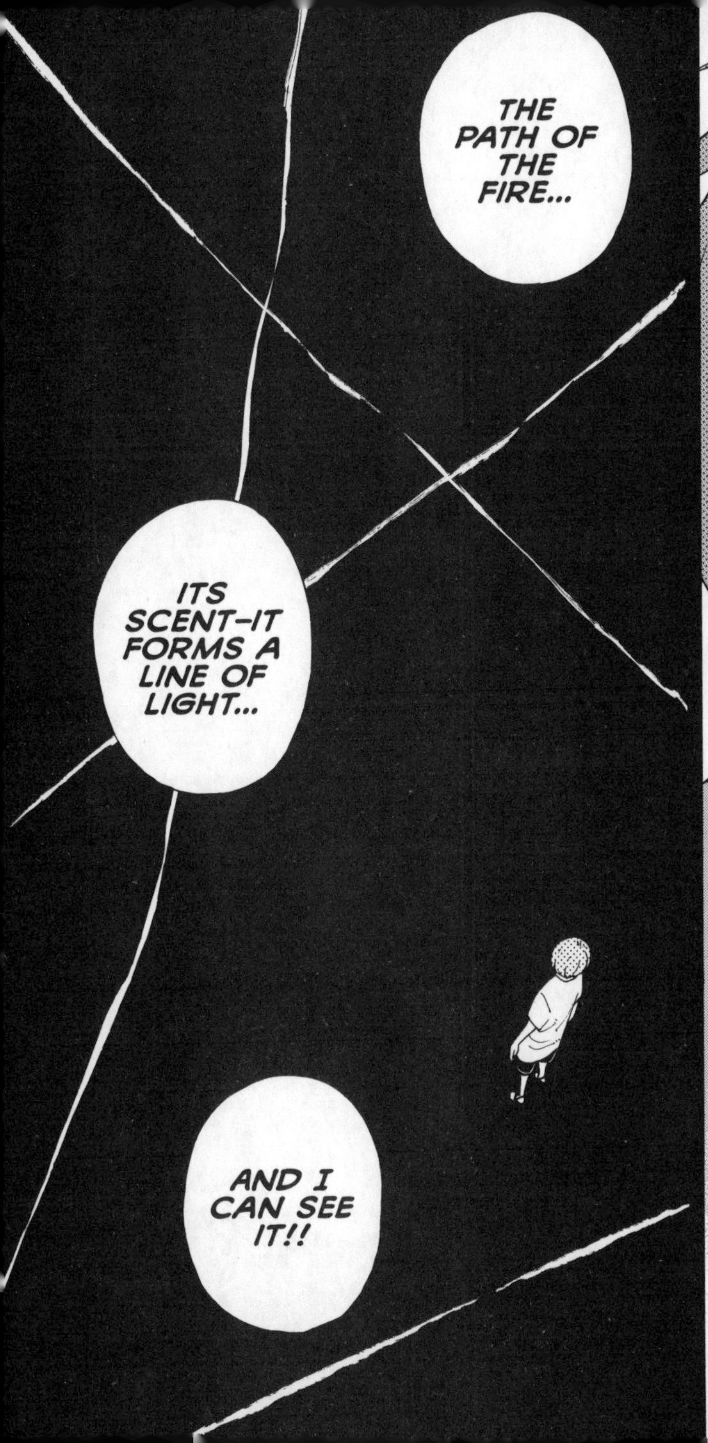
THE PATH OF THE FIRE...
ITS SCENT—IT FORMS A LINE OF LIGHT...
AND I CAN SEE IT!!

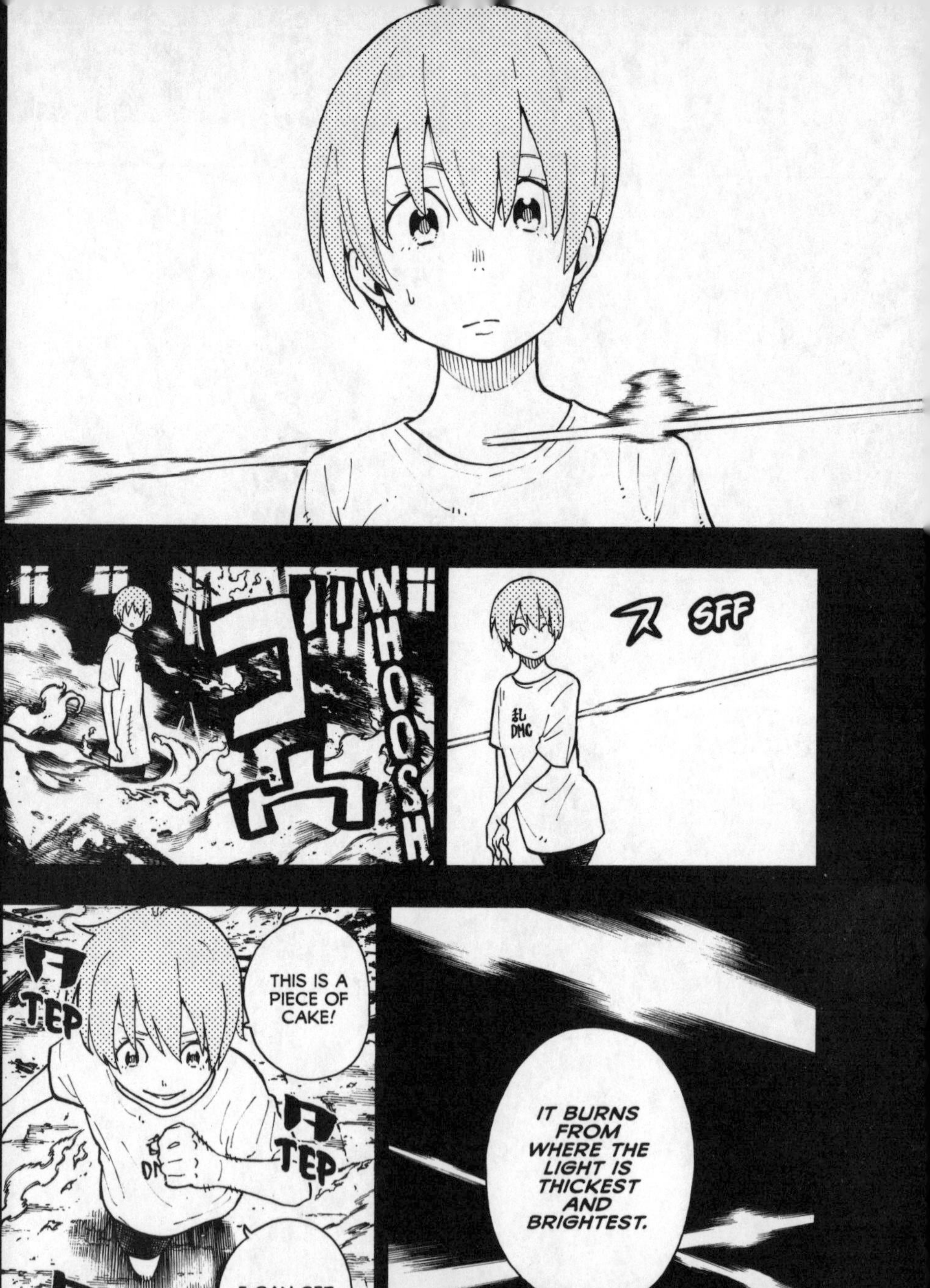
ス
SFF
WHOOSH
IT BURNS FROM WHERE THE LIGHT IS THICKEST AND BRIGHTEST.
TEP
THIS IS A PIECE OF CAKE!
TEP
I CAN GET OUT OF HERE, NO SWEAT!!
TEP

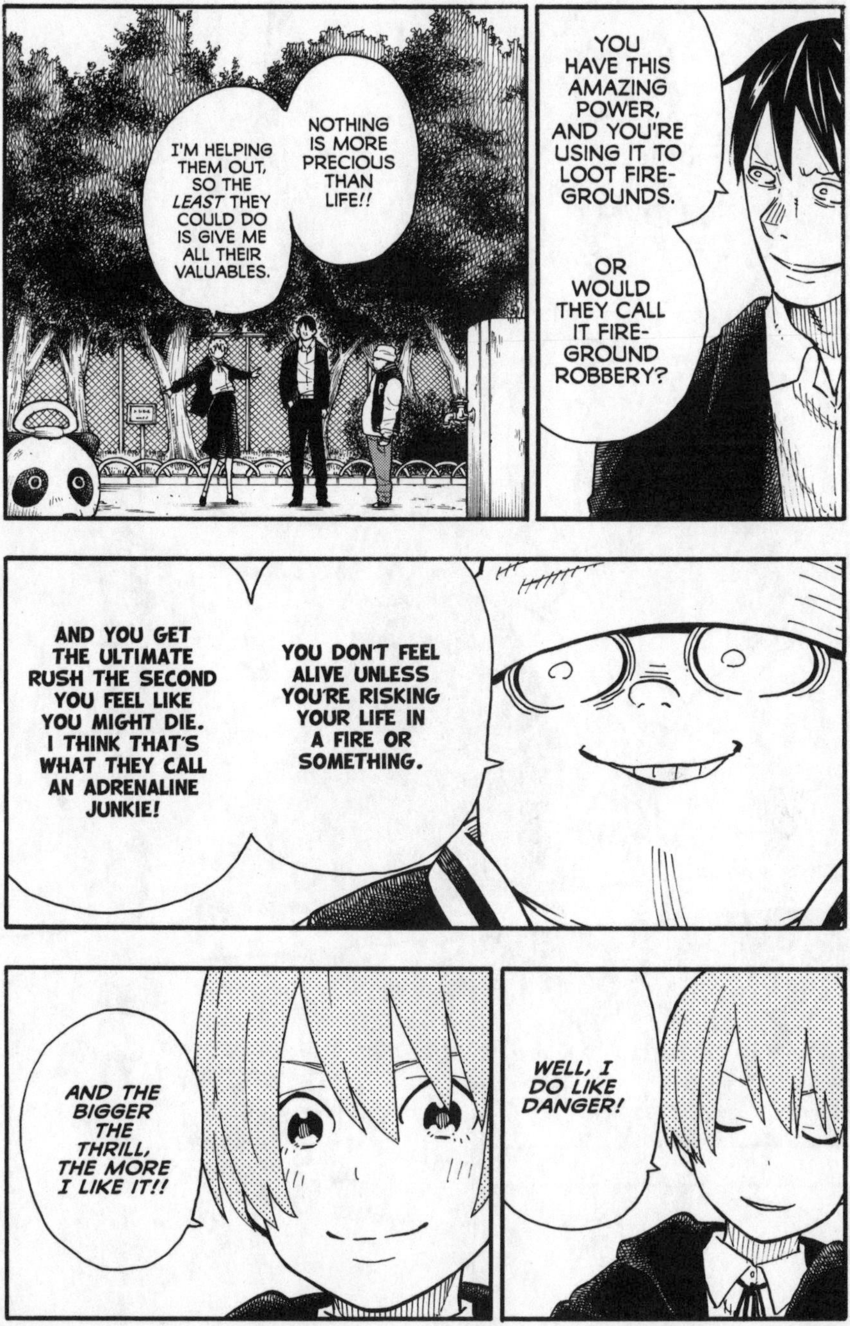

YOU HAVE THIS AMAZING POWER, AND YOU'RE USING IT TO LOOT FIRE-GROUNDS.
OR WOULD THEY CALL IT FIRE-GROUND ROBBERY?
NOTHING IS MORE PRECIOUS THAN LIFE!!
I'M HELPING THEM OUT, SO THE *LEAST* THEY COULD DO IS GIVE ME ALL THEIR VALUABLES.
YOU DON'T FEEL ALIVE UNLESS YOU'RE RISKING YOUR LIFE IN A FIRE OR SOMETHING.
AND YOU GET THE ULTIMATE RUSH THE SECOND YOU FEEL LIKE YOU MIGHT DIE. I THINK THAT'S WHAT THEY CALL AN ADRENALINE JUNKIE!
WELL, I DO LIKE DANGER!
AND THE BIGGER THE THRILL, THE MORE I LIKE IT!!

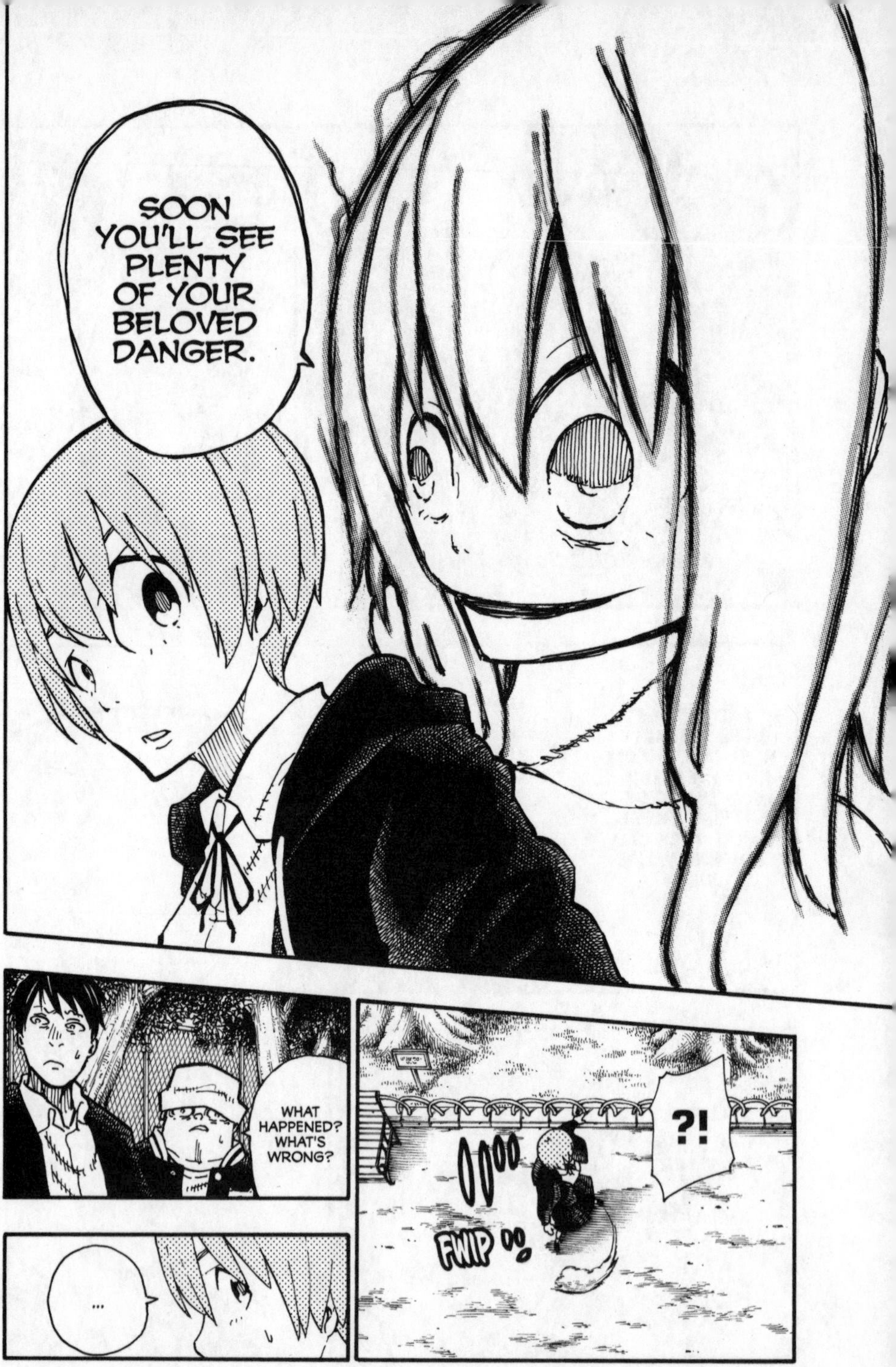
SOON YOU'LL SEE PLENTY OF YOUR BELOVED DANGER.
?!
FWIP
WHAT HAPPENED? WHAT'S WRONG?
...

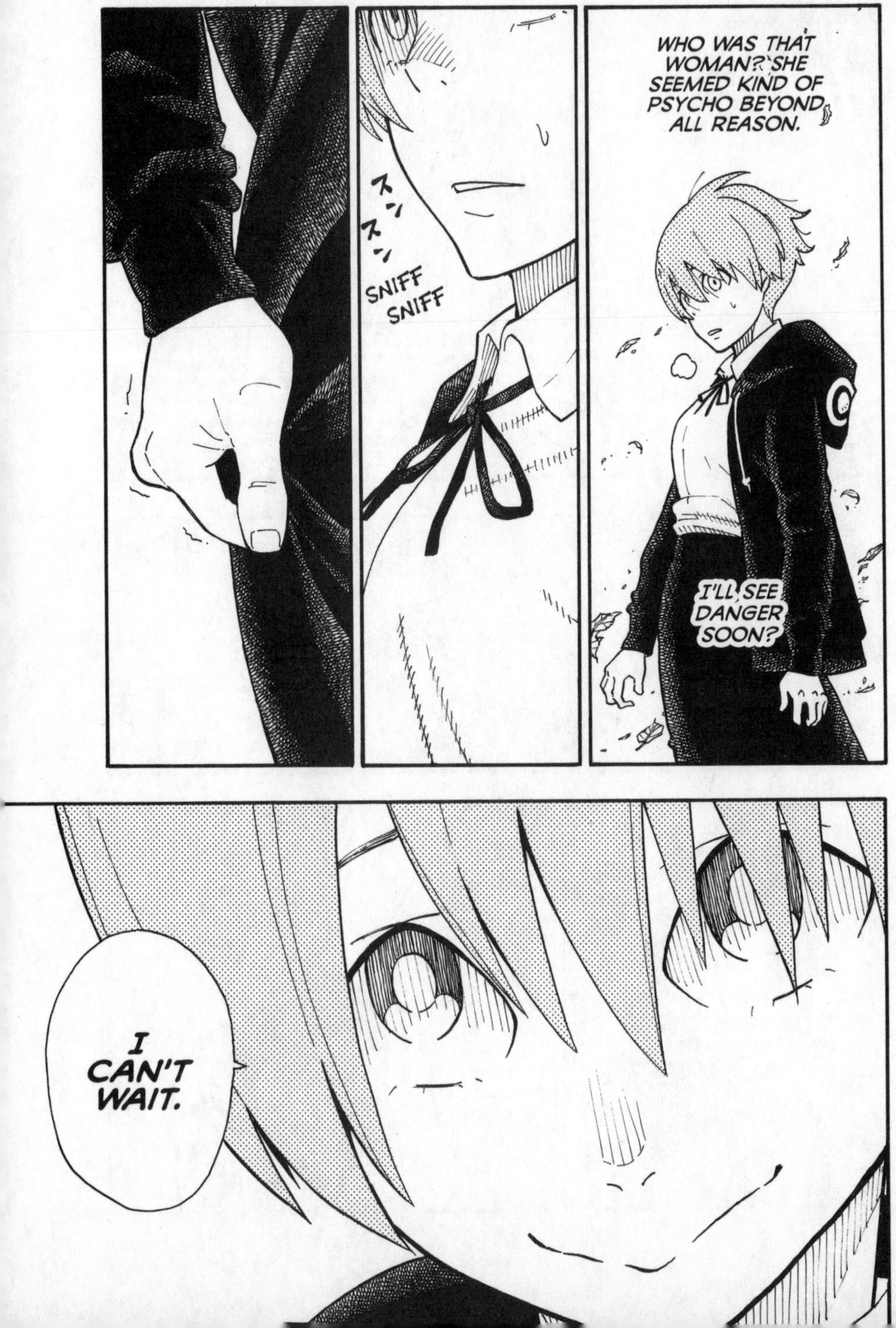
WHO WAS THAT WOMAN? SHE SEEMED KIND OF PSYCHO BEYOND ALL REASON.
I'LL SEE DANGER SOON?
スン スン
SNIFF SNIFF
I CAN'T WAIT.

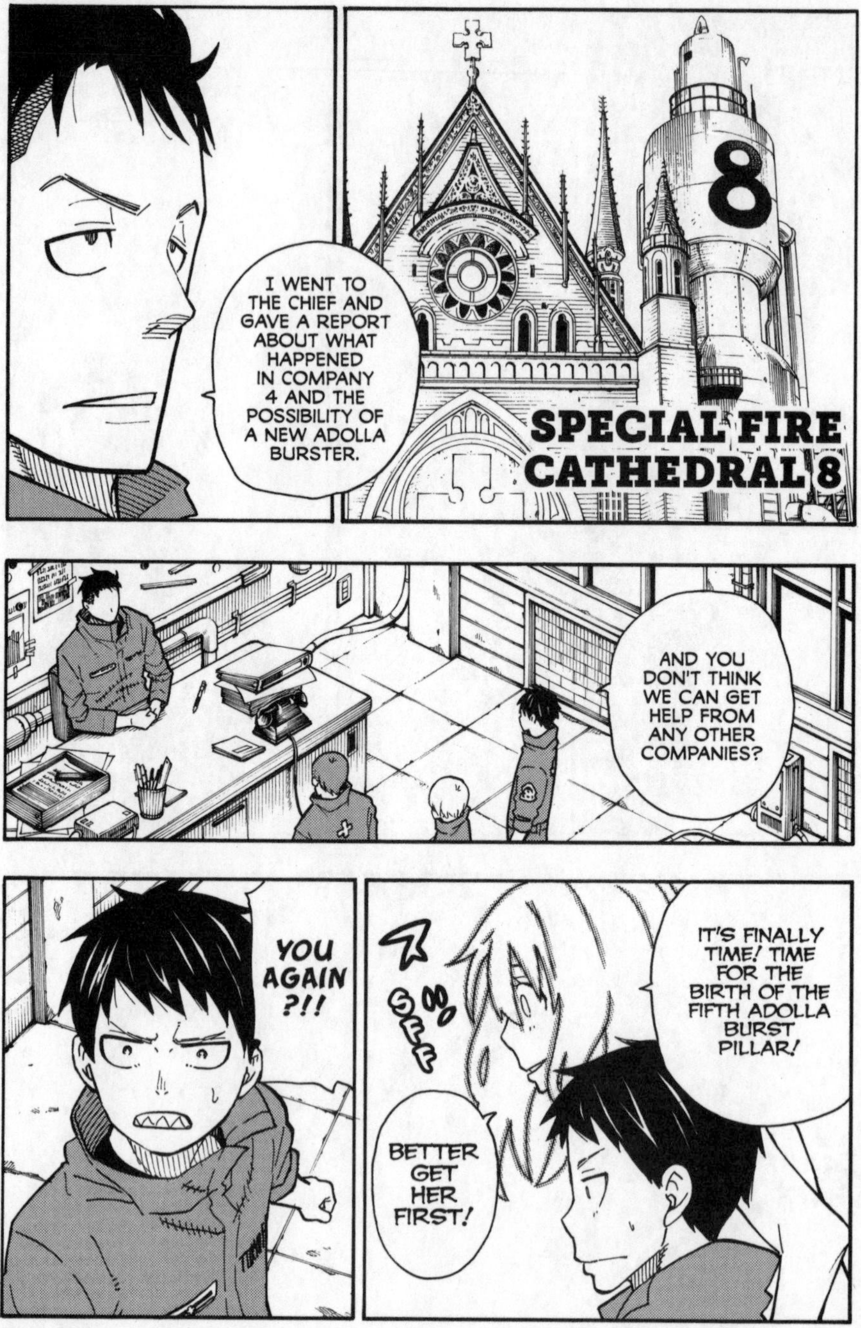
8
SPECIAL FIRE CATHEDRAL 8
I WENT TO THE CHIEF AND GAVE A REPORT ABOUT WHAT HAPPENED IN COMPANY 4 AND THE POSSIBILITY OF A NEW ADOLLA BURSTER.
AND YOU DON'T THINK WE CAN GET HELP FROM ANY OTHER COMPANIES?
IT'S FINALLY TIME! TIME FOR THE BIRTH OF THE FIFTH ADOLLA BURST PILLAR!
BETTER GET HER FIRST!
YOU AGAIN?!!

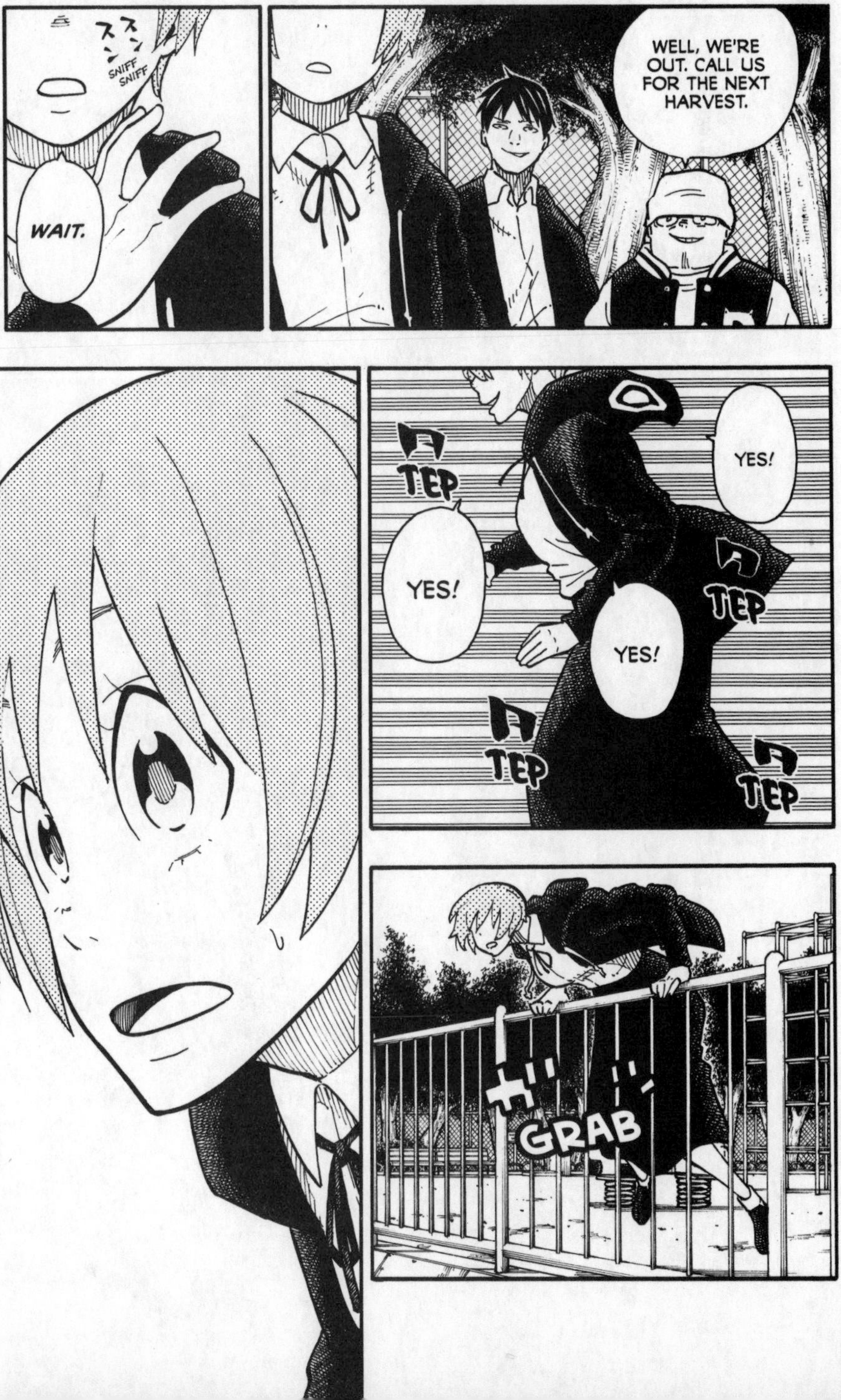
WELL, WE'RE OUT. CALL US FOR THE NEXT HARVEST.
SNIFF SNIFF
WAIT.
YES!
TEP
YES!
TEP
YES!
TEP
TEP
GRAB

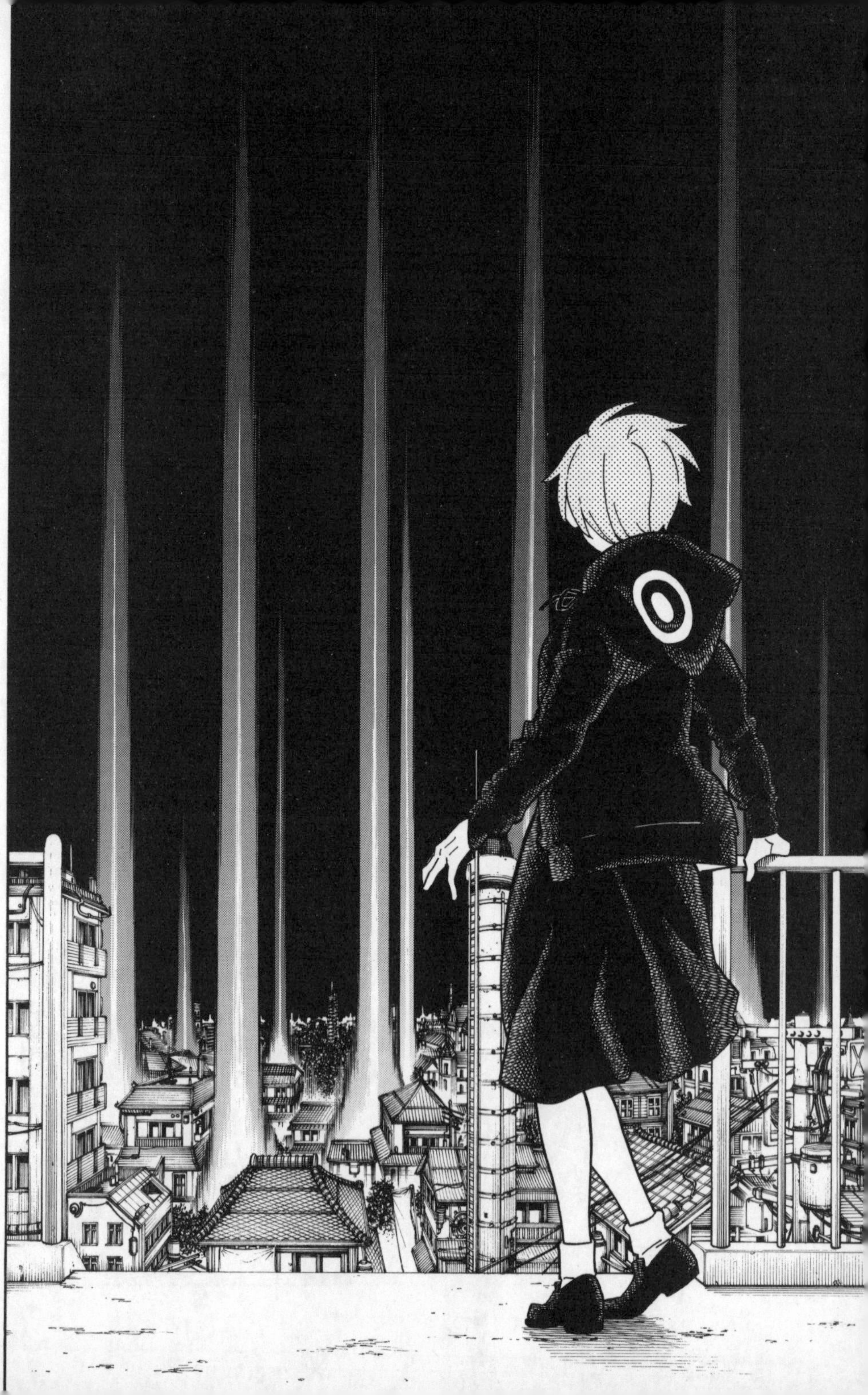

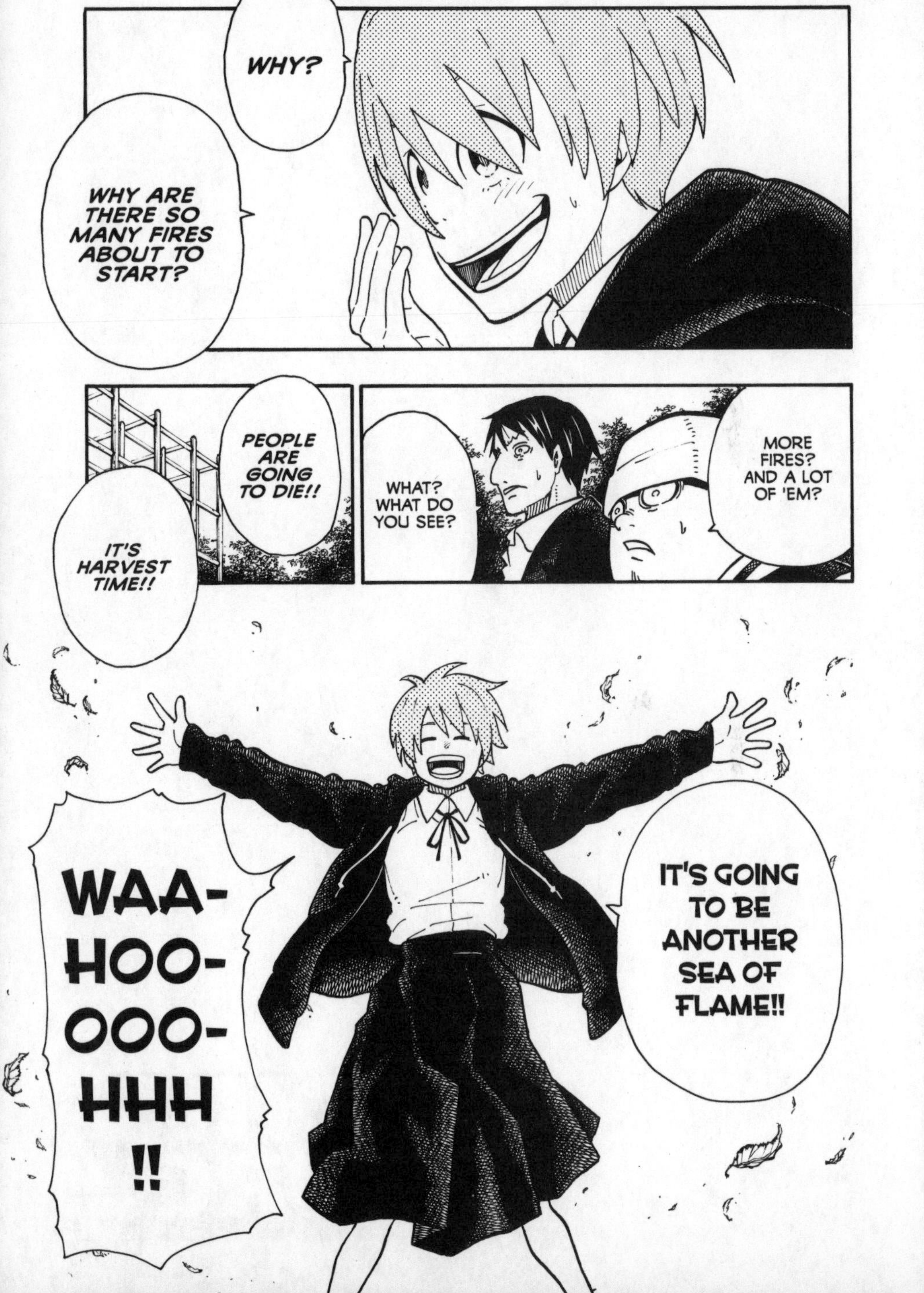
WHY?
WHY ARE THERE SO MANY FIRES ABOUT TO START?
MORE FIRES? AND A LOT OF 'EM?
WHAT? WHAT DO YOU SEE?
PEOPLE ARE GOING TO DIE!!
IT'S HARVEST TIME!!
IT'S GOING TO BE ANOTHER SEA OF FLAME!!
WAA-HOO-OOO-HHH!!

FIRE FORCE

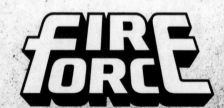

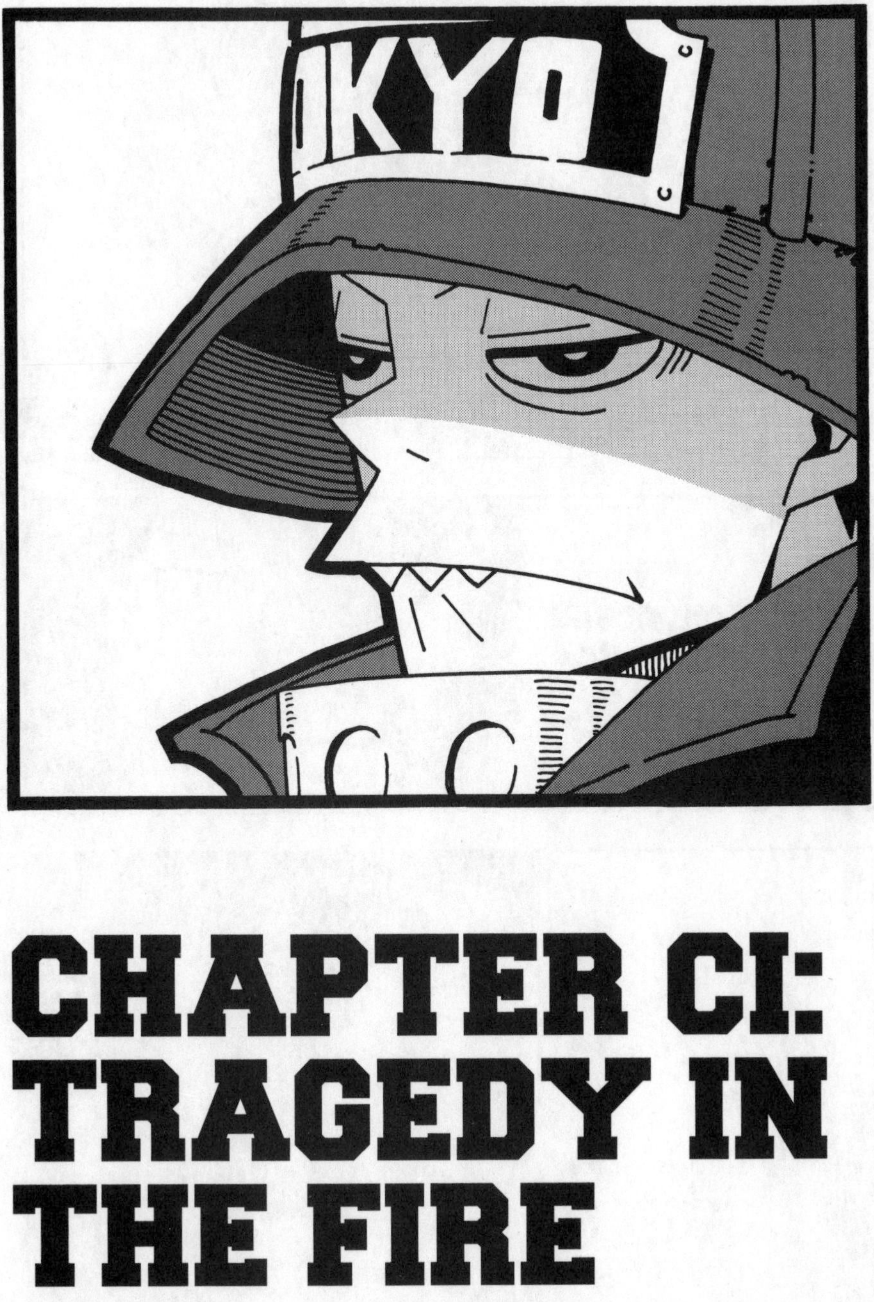
KYO 1

CHAPTER CI: TRAGEDY IN THE FIRE

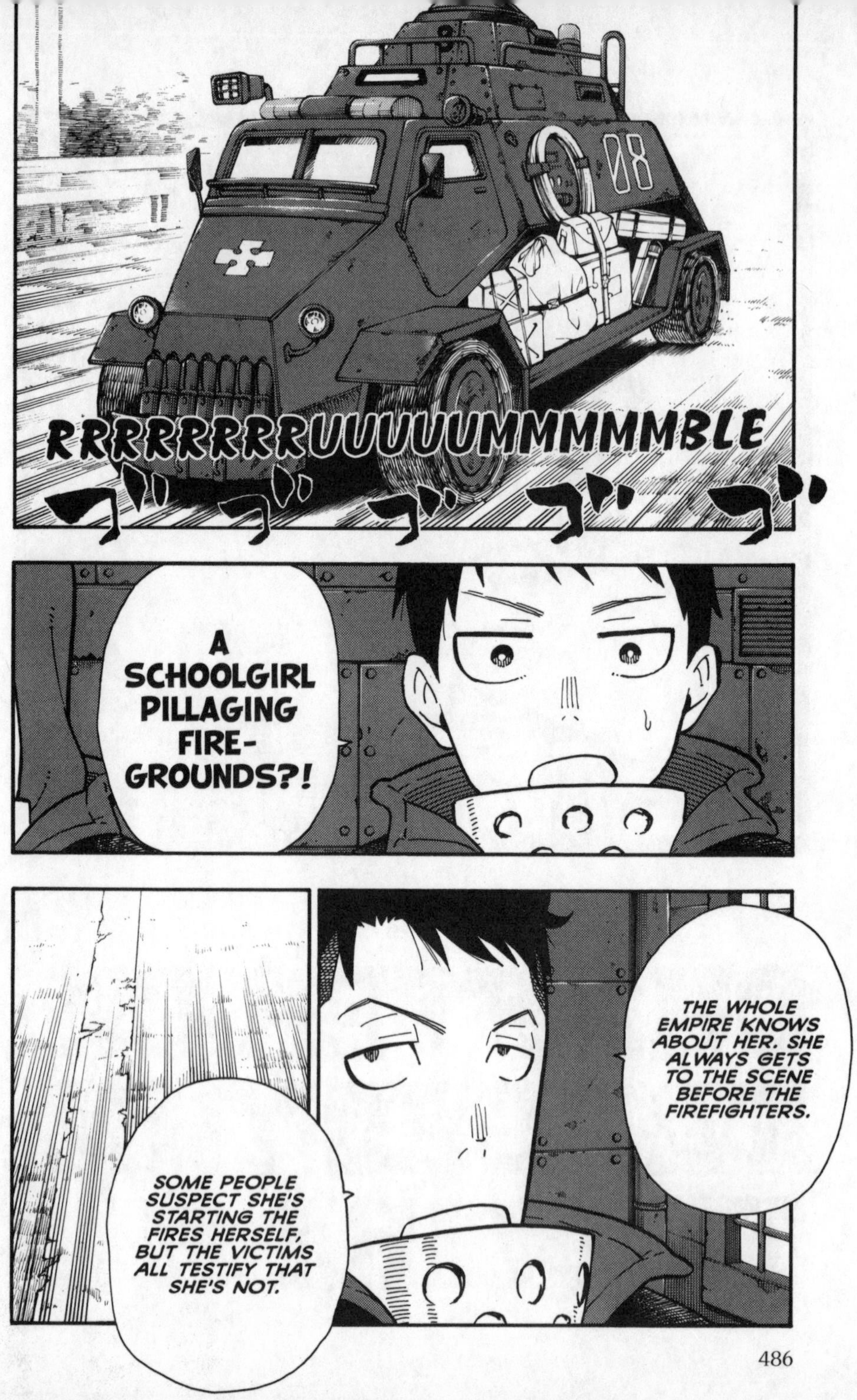
RRRRRRRRUUUUUUMMMMMBLE
ゴゴゴゴゴ
A SCHOOLGIRL PILLAGING FIRE-GROUNDS?!
THE WHOLE EMPIRE KNOWS ABOUT HER. SHE ALWAYS GETS TO THE SCENE BEFORE THE FIREFIGHTERS.
SOME PEOPLE SUSPECT SHE'S STARTING THE FIRES HERSELF, BUT THE VICTIMS ALL TESTIFY THAT SHE'S NOT.

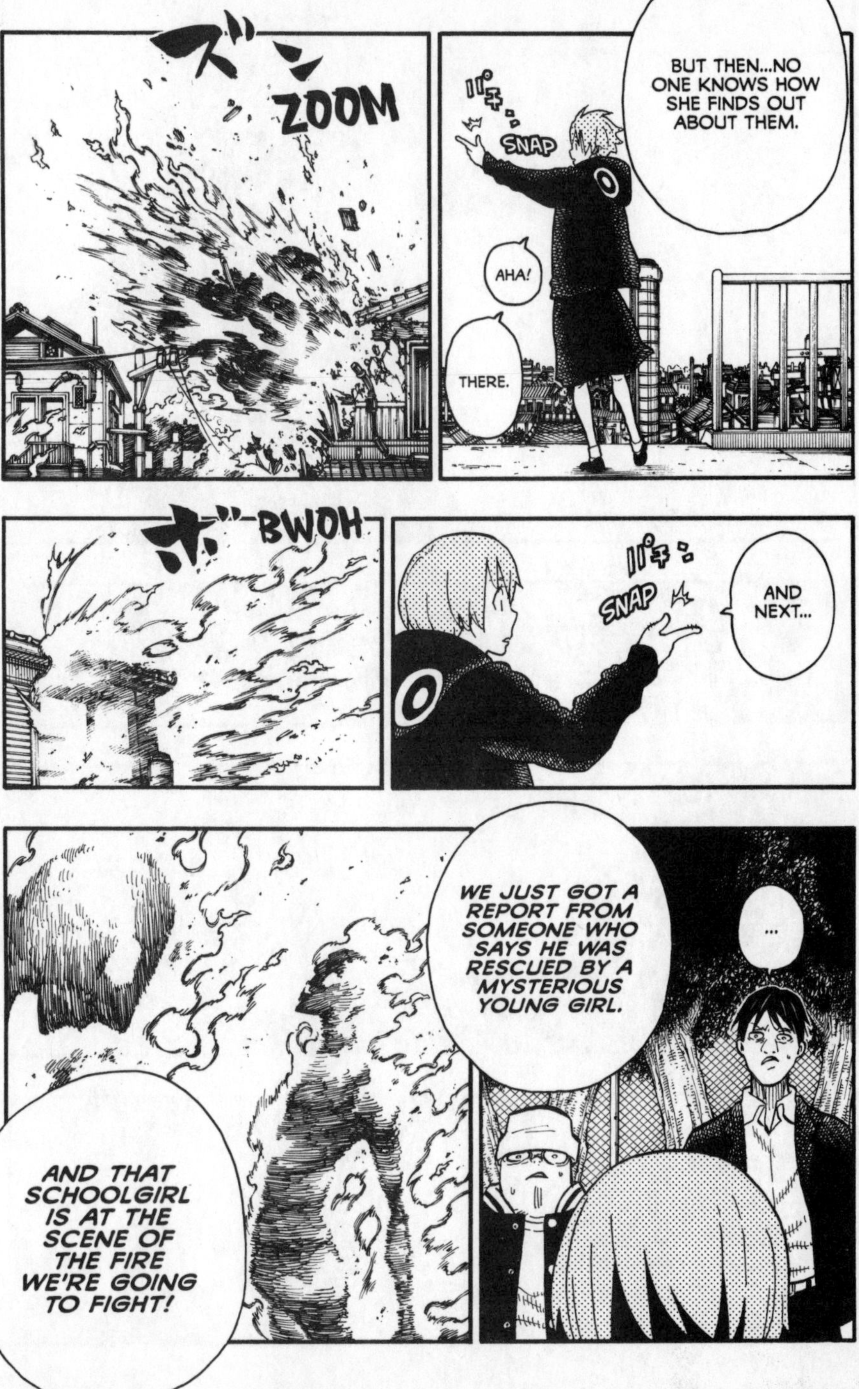
BUT THEN...NO ONE KNOWS HOW SHE FINDS OUT ABOUT THEM.
SNAP
AHA!
THERE.
ズン
ZOOM
SNAP
AND NEXT...
BWOH
...
WE JUST GOT A REPORT FROM SOMEONE WHO SAYS HE WAS RESCUED BY A MYSTERIOUS YOUNG GIRL.
AND THAT SCHOOLGIRL IS AT THE SCENE OF THE FIRE WE'RE GOING TO FIGHT!

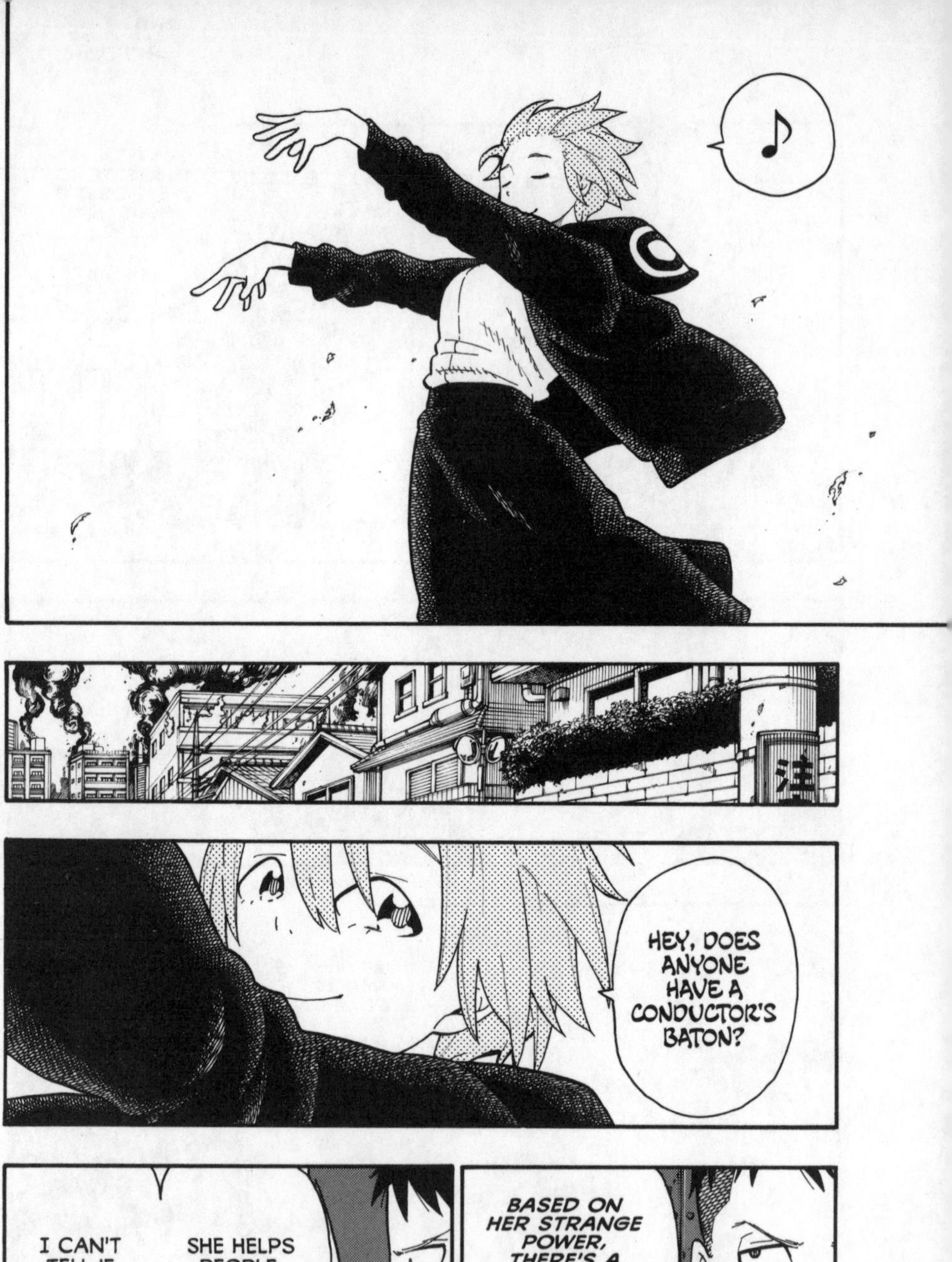
♪
HEY, DOES ANYONE HAVE A CONDUCTOR'S BATON?
BASED ON HER STRANGE POWER, THERE'S A STRONG POSSIBILITY THAT SHE WILL HAVE THE FIFTH ADOLLA BURST.
SHE HELPS PEOPLE, AND SHE TAKES THEIR VALUABLES.
I CAN'T TELL IF SHE'S GOOD OR BAD...

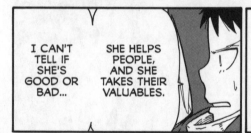

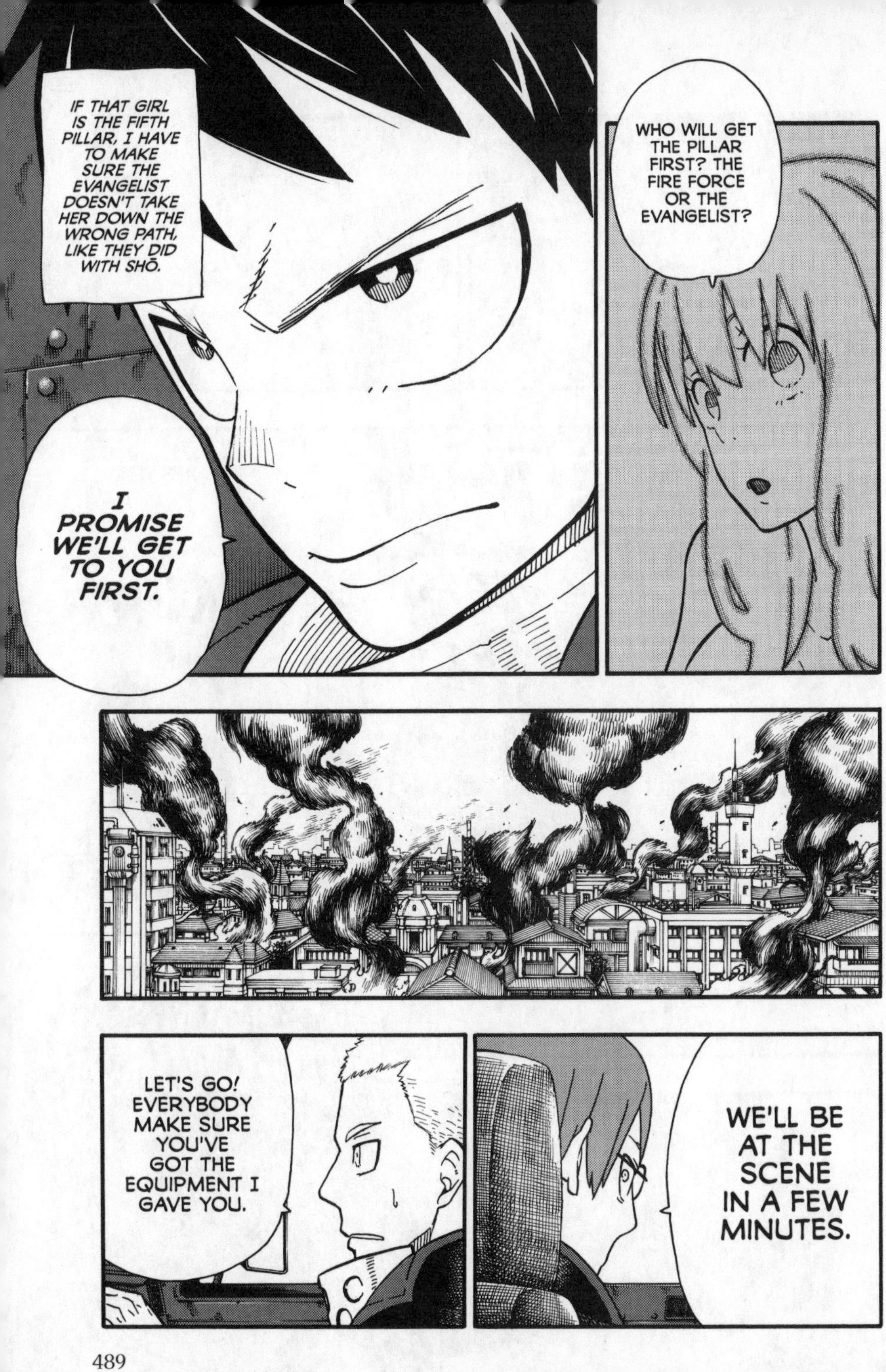
WHO WILL GET THE PILLAR FIRST? THE FIRE FORCE OR THE EVANGELIST?
IF THAT GIRL IS THE FIFTH PILLAR, I HAVE TO MAKE SURE THE EVANGELIST DOESN'T TAKE HER DOWN THE WRONG PATH, LIKE THEY DID WITH SHŌ.
I PROMISE WE'LL GET TO YOU FIRST.
WE'LL BE AT THE SCENE IN A FEW MINUTES.
LET'S GO! EVERYBODY MAKE SURE YOU'VE GOT THE EQUIPMENT I GAVE YOU.

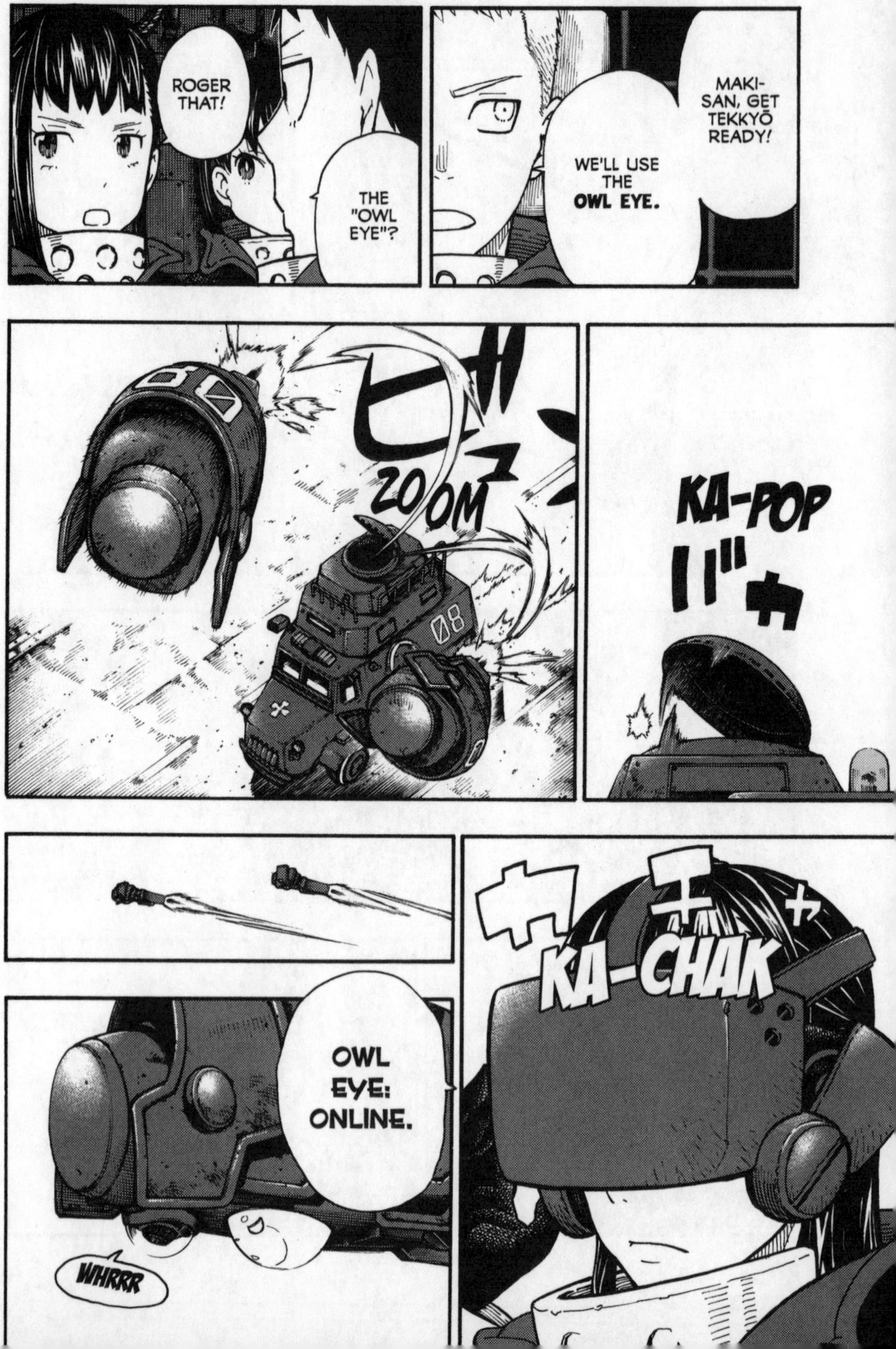
MAKI-SAN, GET TEKKYŌ READY!
WE'LL USE THE OWL EYE.
ROGER THAT!
THE "OWL EYE"?
KA-POP
ZOOM
KA-CHAK
OWL EYE: ONLINE.
WHRRR

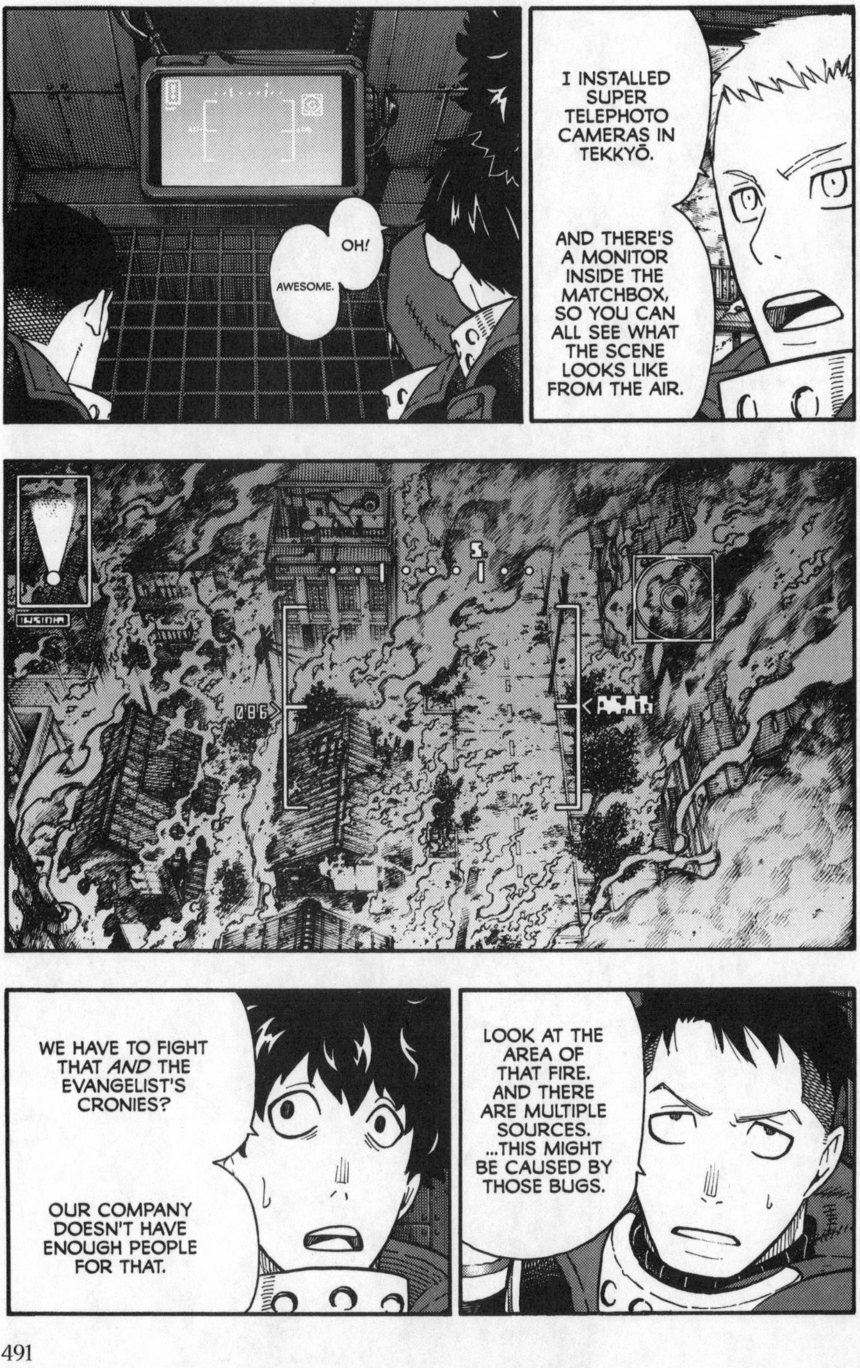
I INSTALLED SUPER TELEPHOTO CAMERAS IN TEKKYŌ.
AND THERE'S A MONITOR INSIDE THE MATCHBOX, SO YOU CAN ALL SEE WHAT THE SCENE LOOKS LIKE FROM THE AIR.
OH!
AWESOME.
LOOK AT THE AREA OF THAT FIRE. AND THERE ARE MULTIPLE SOURCES. ...THIS MIGHT BE CAUSED BY THOSE BUGS.
WE HAVE TO FIGHT THAT *AND* THE EVANGELIST'S CRONIES?
OUR COMPANY DOESN'T HAVE ENOUGH PEOPLE FOR THAT.

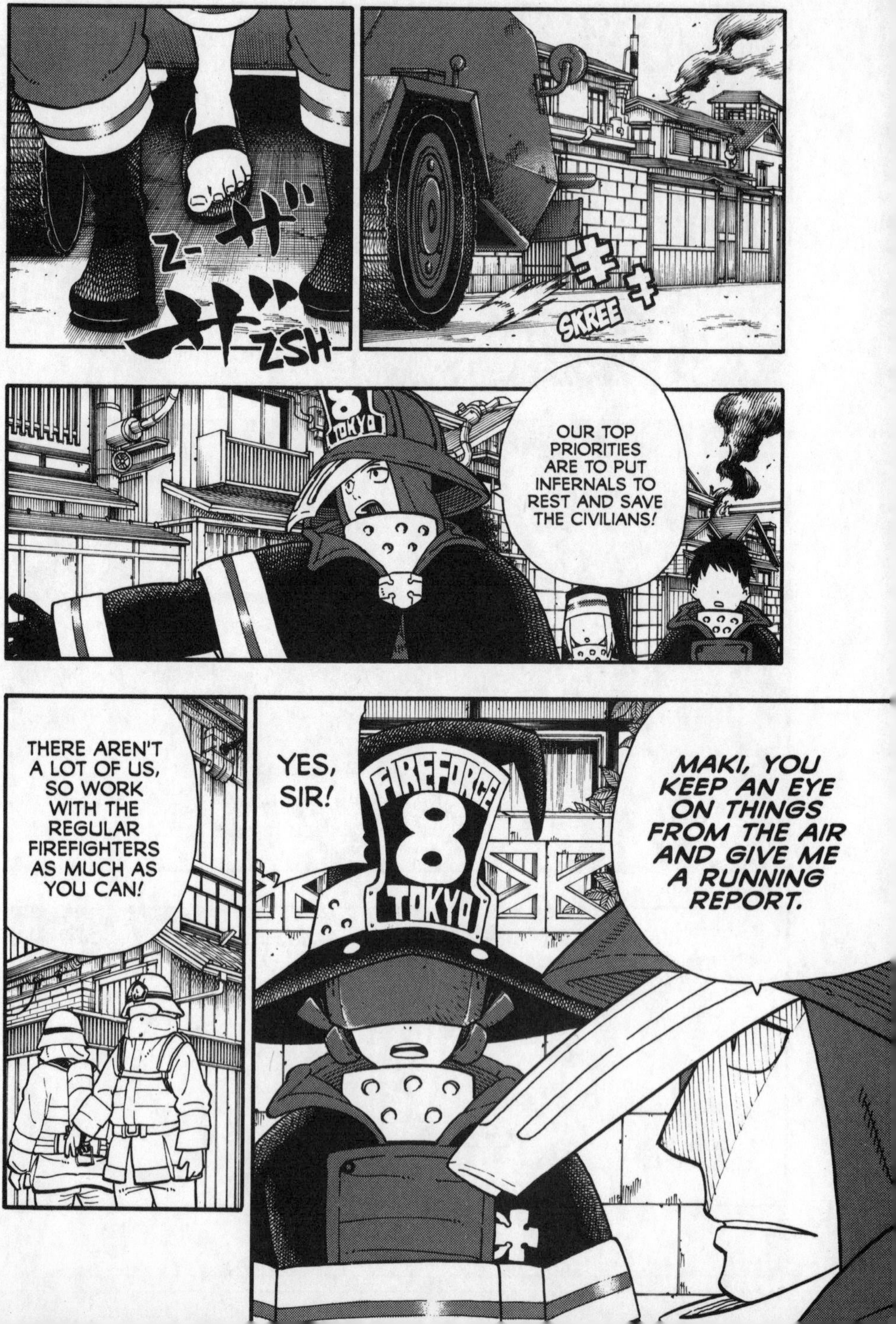
キキ
SKREE
ZSH
OUR TOP PRIORITIES ARE TO PUT INFERNALS TO REST AND SAVE THE CIVILIANS!
8 TOKYO
MAKI, YOU KEEP AN EYE ON THINGS FROM THE AIR AND GIVE ME A RUNNING REPORT.
YES, SIR!
FIREFORCE 8 TOKYO
THERE AREN'T A LOT OF US, SO WORK WITH THE REGULAR FIREFIGHTERS AS MUCH AS YOU CAN!

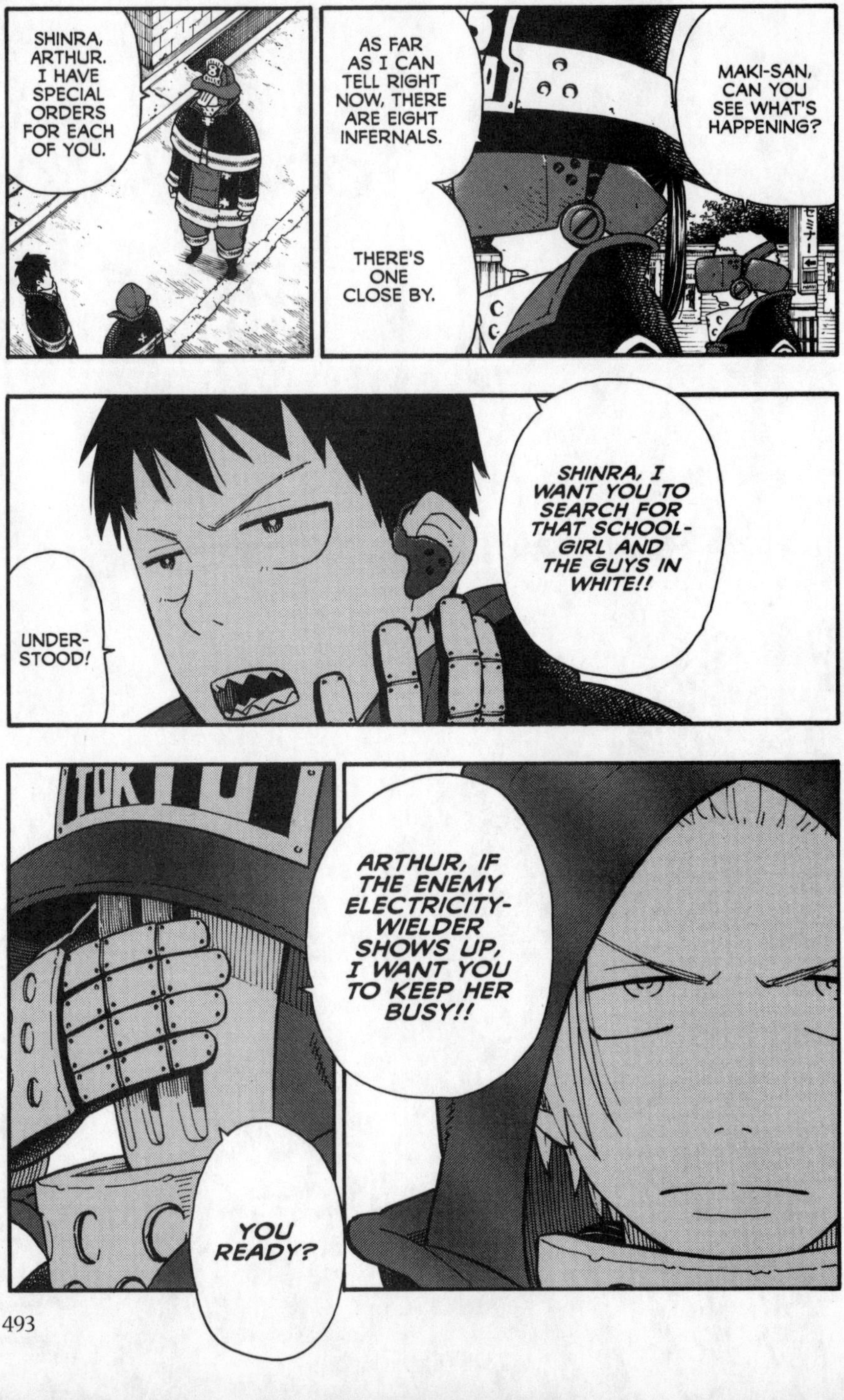
MAKI-SAN, CAN YOU SEE WHAT'S HAPPENING?
AS FAR AS I CAN TELL RIGHT NOW, THERE ARE EIGHT INFERNALS.
THERE'S ONE CLOSE BY.
SHINRA, ARTHUR. I HAVE SPECIAL ORDERS FOR EACH OF YOU.
SHINRA, I WANT YOU TO SEARCH FOR THAT SCHOOL-GIRL AND THE GUYS IN WHITE!!
UNDER-STOOD!
ARTHUR, IF THE ENEMY ELECTRICITY-WIELDER SHOWS UP, I WANT YOU TO KEEP HER BUSY!!
YOU READY?

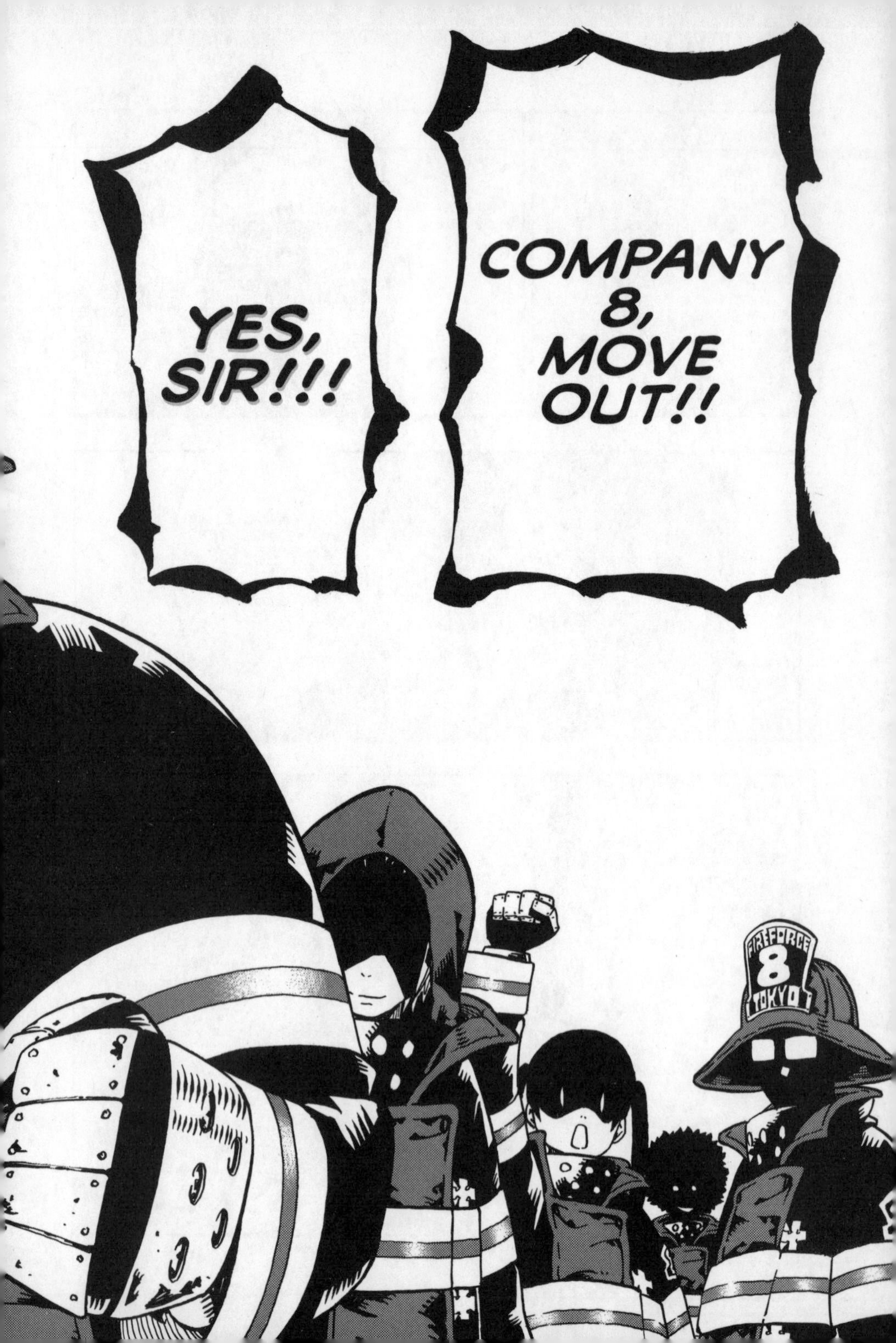
COMPANY 8, MOVE OUT!!
YES, SIR!!!
FIRE FORCE 8 TOKYO

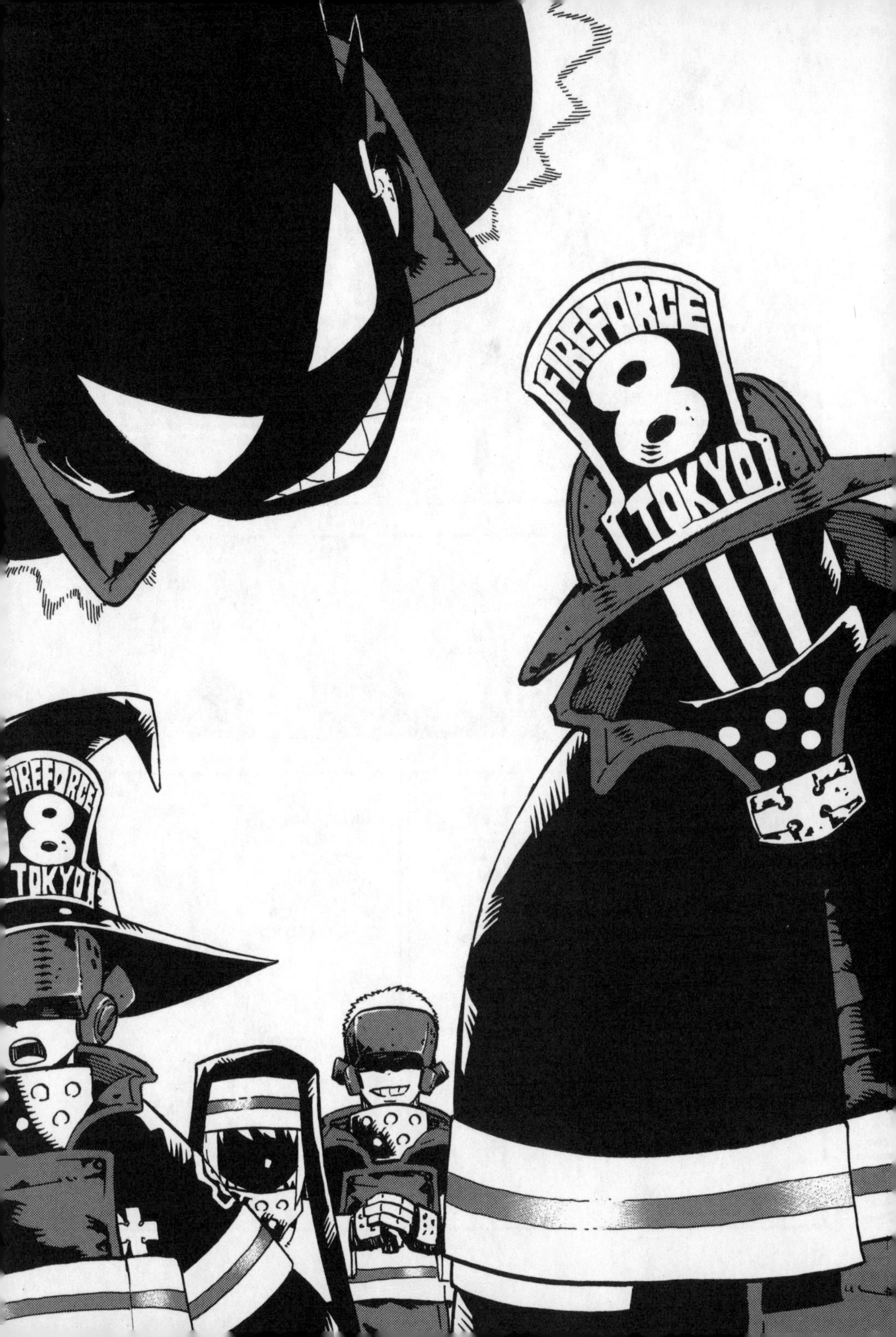
FIREFORCE
8
TOKYO
FIREFORCE
8
TOKYO

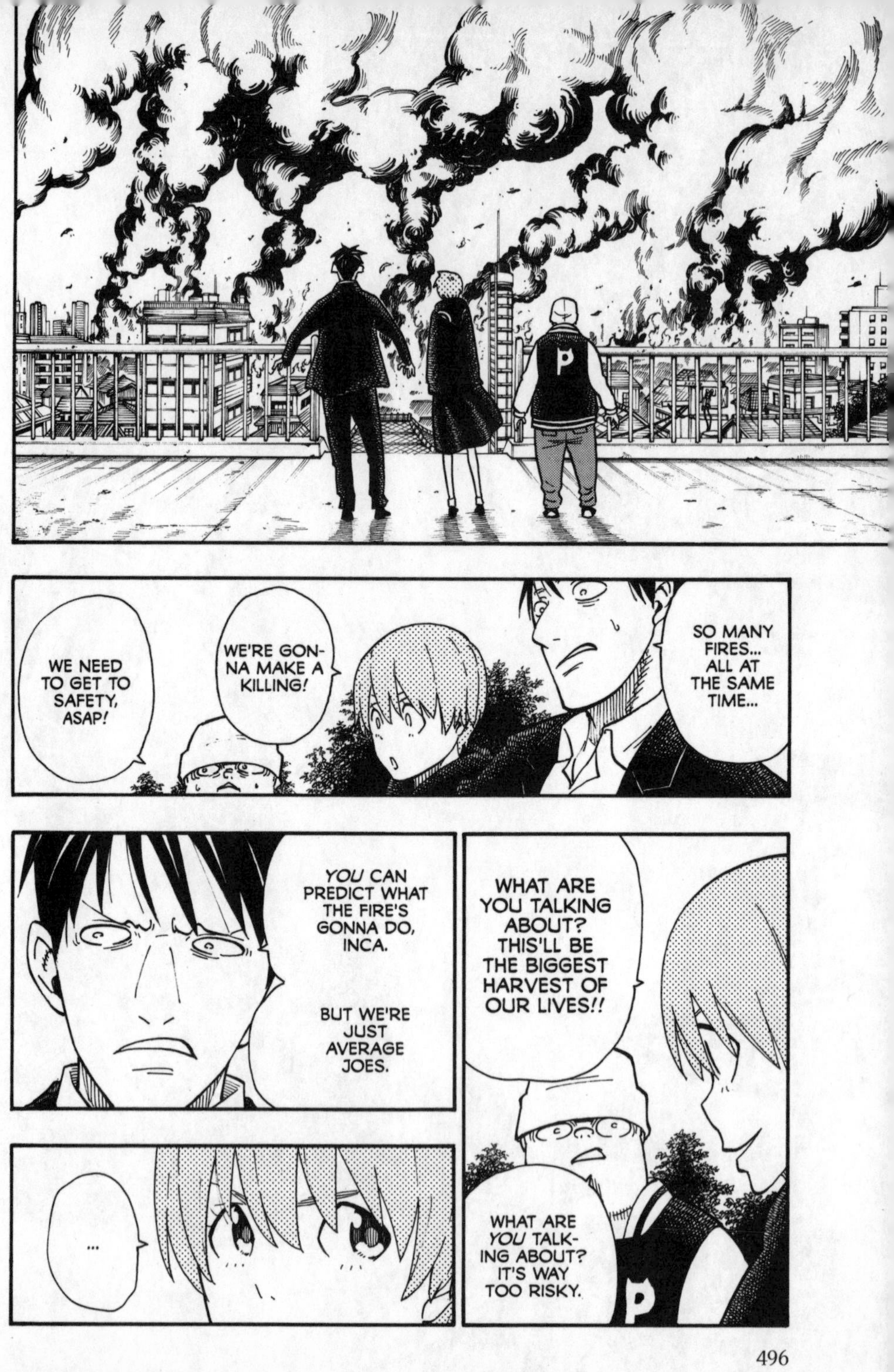
SO MANY FIRES... ALL AT THE SAME TIME...
WE'RE GON-NA MAKE A KILLING!
WE NEED TO GET TO SAFETY, ASAP!
WHAT ARE YOU TALKING ABOUT? THIS'LL BE THE BIGGEST HARVEST OF OUR LIVES!!
WHAT ARE *YOU* TALK-ING ABOUT? IT'S WAY TOO RISKY.
YOU CAN PREDICT WHAT THE FIRE'S GONNA DO, INCA.
BUT WE'RE JUST AVERAGE JOES.
...

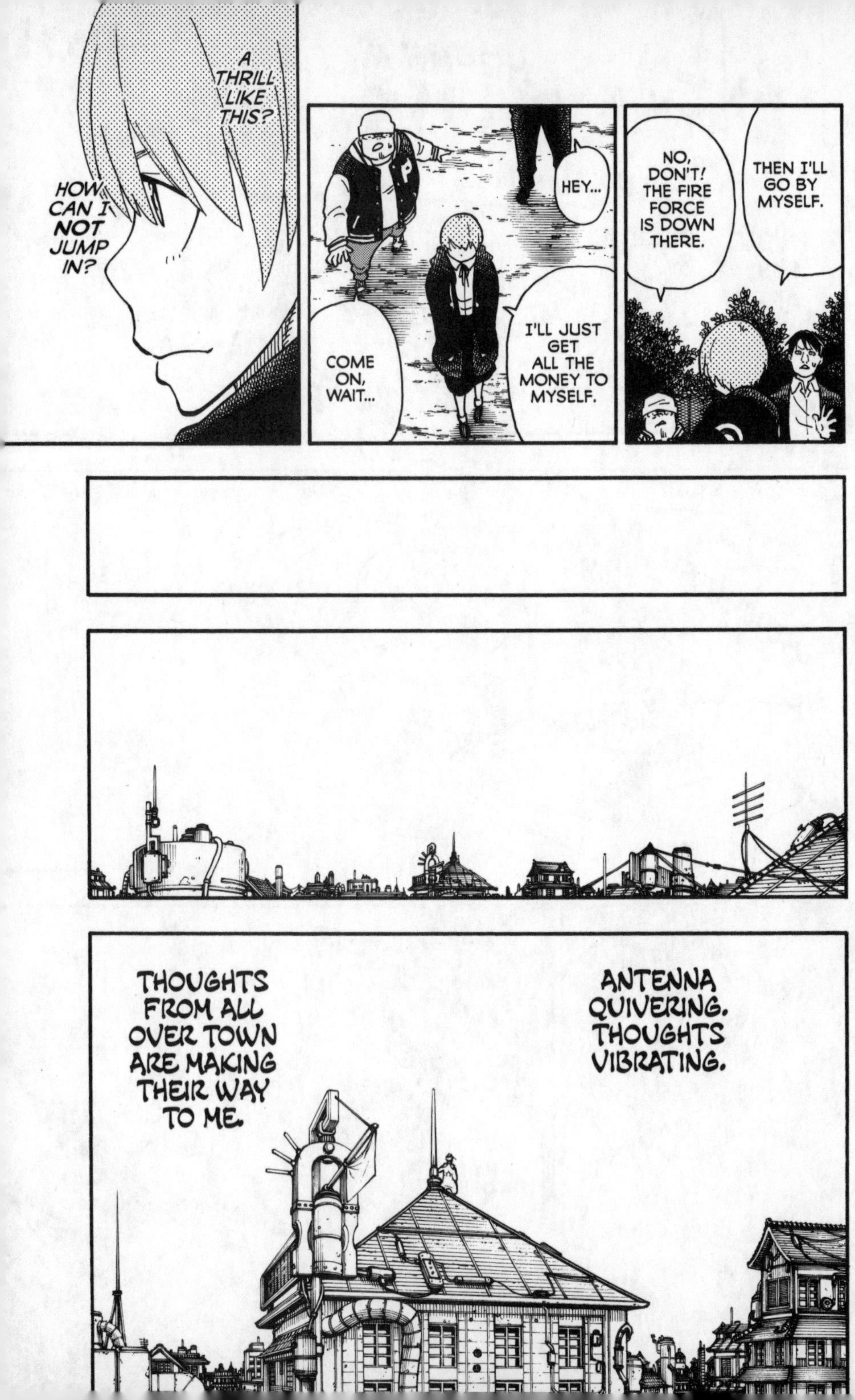
THEN I'LL GO BY MYSELF.
NO, DON'T! THE FIRE FORCE IS DOWN THERE.
HEY...
I'LL JUST GET ALL THE MONEY TO MYSELF.
COME ON, WAIT...
A THRILL LIKE THIS?
HOW CAN I NOT JUMP IN?
ANTENNA QUIVERING. THOUGHTS VIBRATING.
THOUGHTS FROM ALL OVER TOWN ARE MAKING THEIR WAY TO ME.

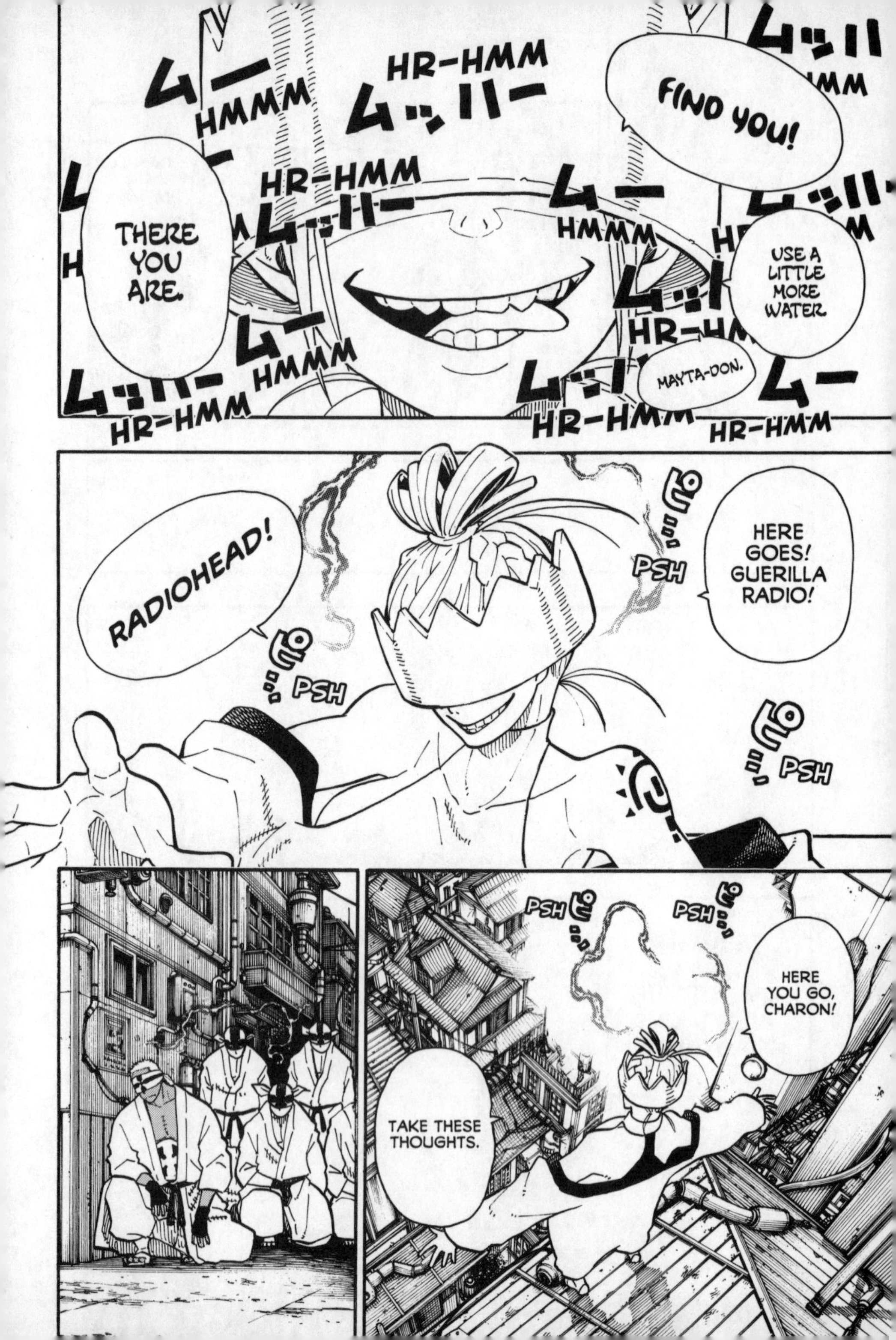
ムッハ
HMM
FIND YOU!
ムッハー
HR-HMM
USE A LITTLE MORE WATER
MAYTA-DON.
ムー
HR-HMM
HMMM
ムッハー
HR-HMM
ムー
HMMM
THERE YOU ARE.
ムッハー
HR-HMM
ムー
HMMM
ムッハー
HR-HMM
ぴ
PSH
HERE GOES! GUERILLA RADIO!
RADIOHEAD!
ぴ
PSH
ぴ
PSH
PSH
ぴ
PSH
ぴ
HERE YOU GO, CHARON!
TAKE THESE THOUGHTS.

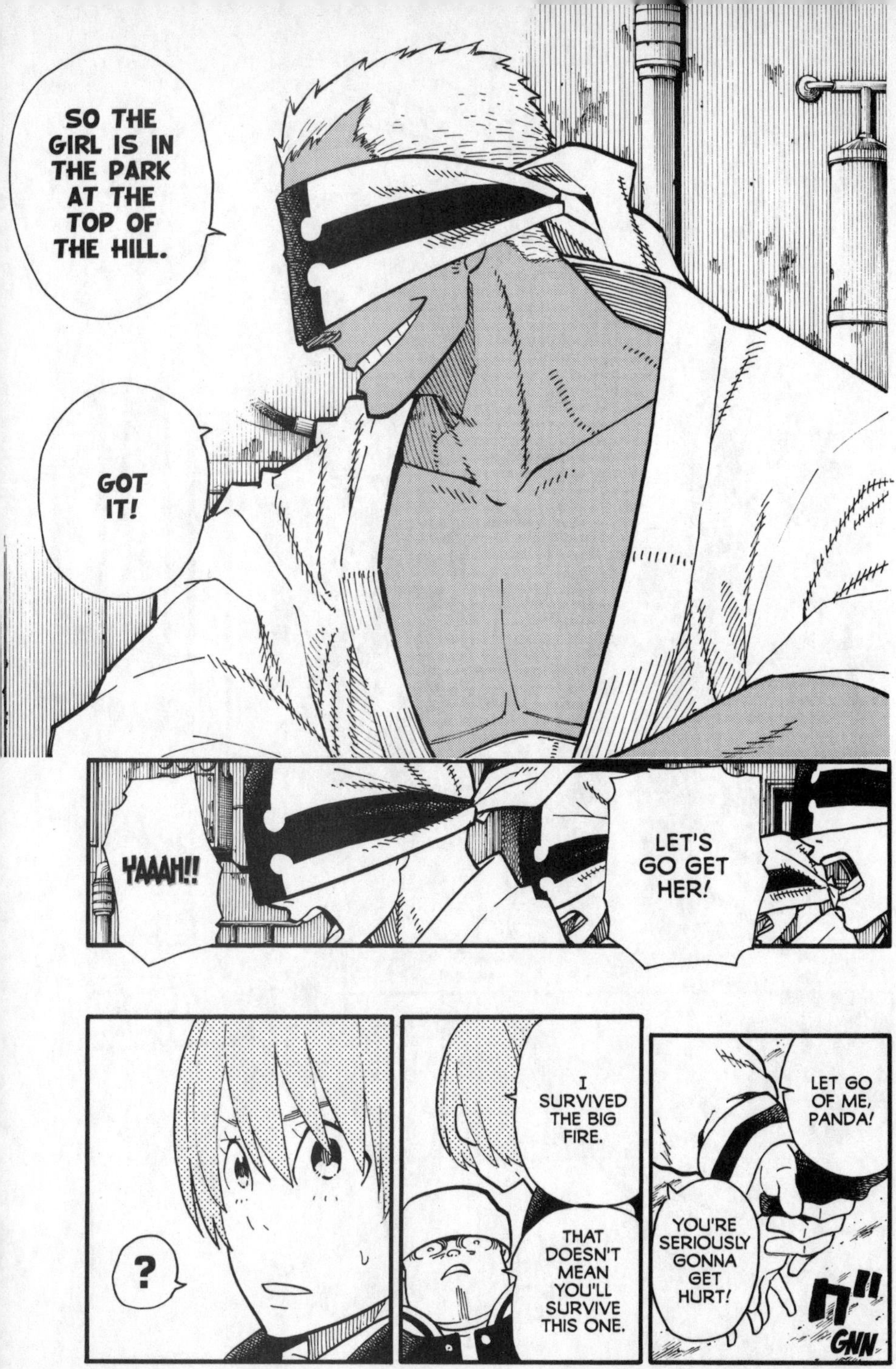
SO THE GIRL IS IN THE PARK AT THE TOP OF THE HILL.
GOT IT!
LET'S GO GET HER!
YAAAH!!
LET GO OF ME, PANDA!
YOU'RE SERIOUSLY GONNA GET HURT!
GNN
I SURVIVED THE BIG FIRE.
THAT DOESN'T MEAN YOU'LL SURVIVE THIS ONE.
?

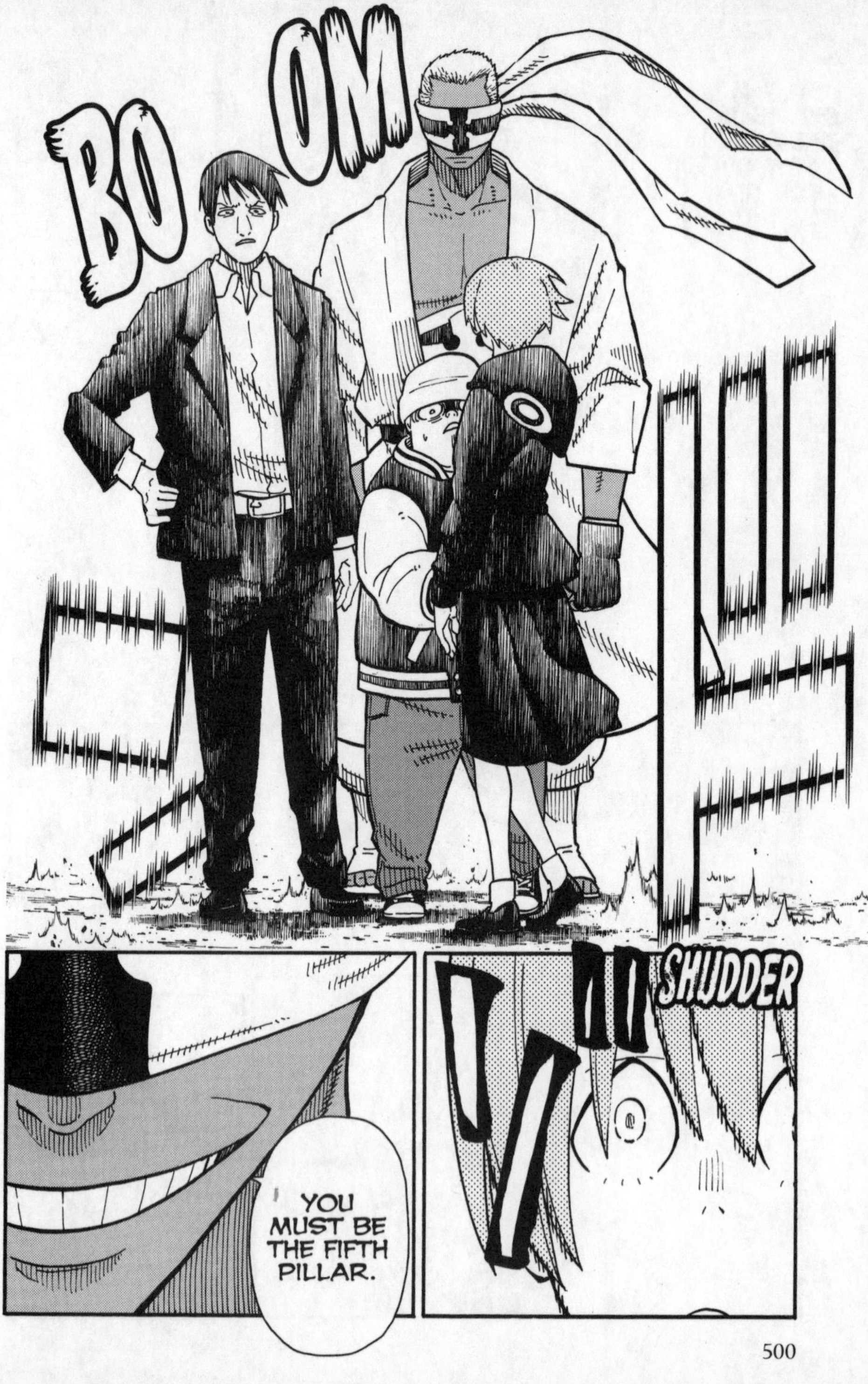
BOOM
SHUDDER
YOU MUST BE THE FIFTH PILLAR.

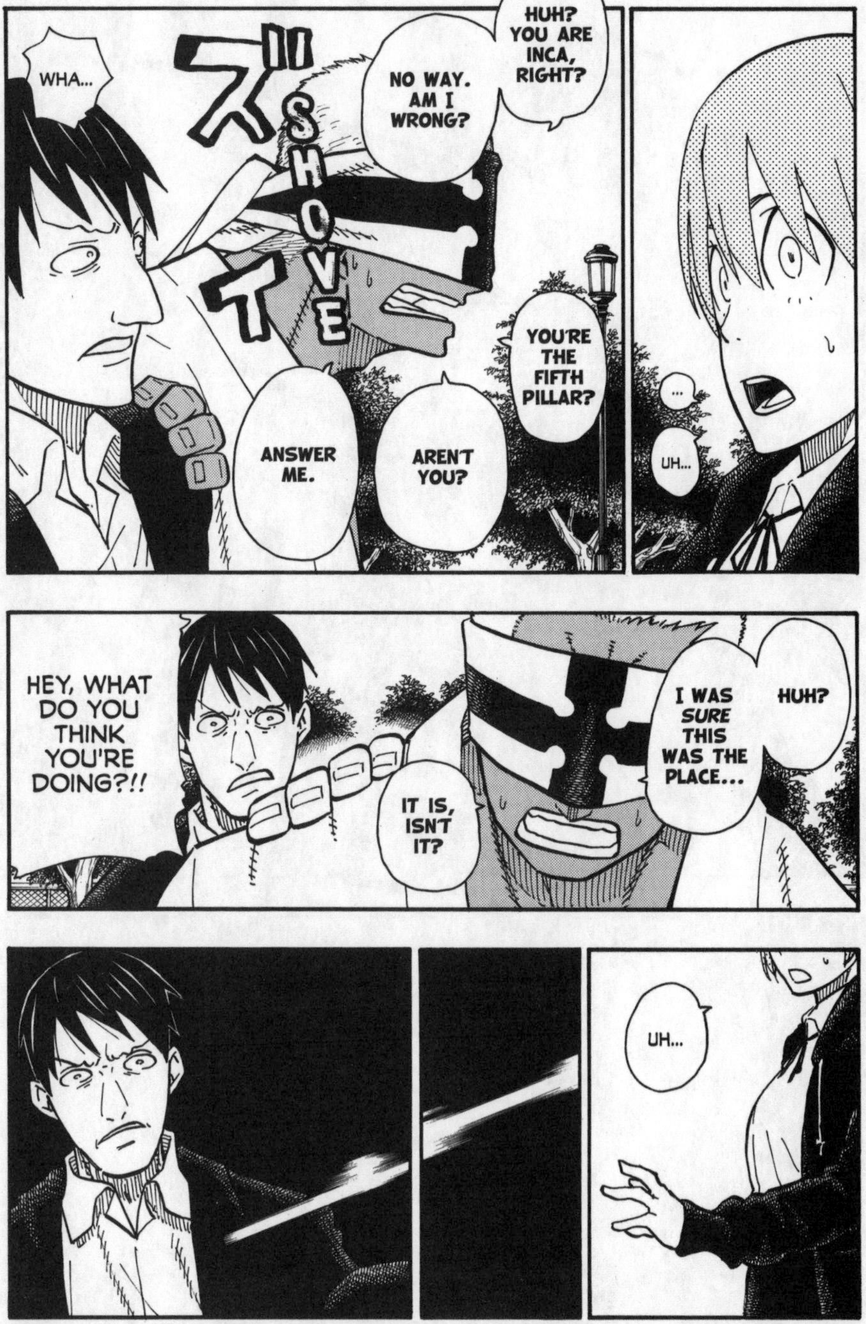
...
UH...
HUH? YOU ARE INCA, RIGHT?
NO WAY. AM I WRONG?
SHOVE
YOU'RE THE FIFTH PILLAR?
AREN'T YOU?
ANSWER ME.
WHA...
HUH?
I WAS *SURE* THIS WAS THE PLACE...
IT IS, ISN'T IT?
HEY, WHAT DO YOU THINK YOU'RE DOING?!!
UH...

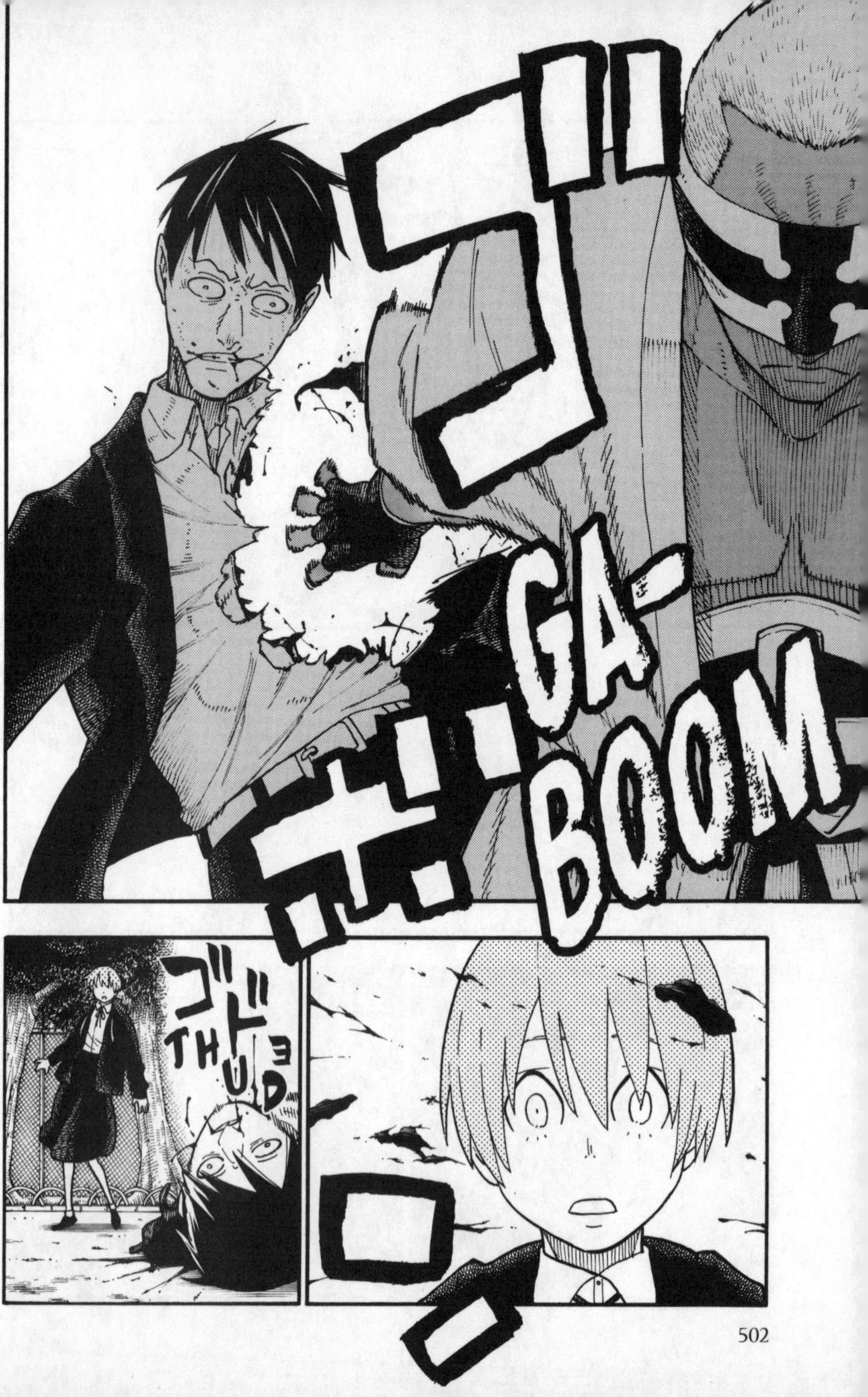
GA-BOOM
THUD

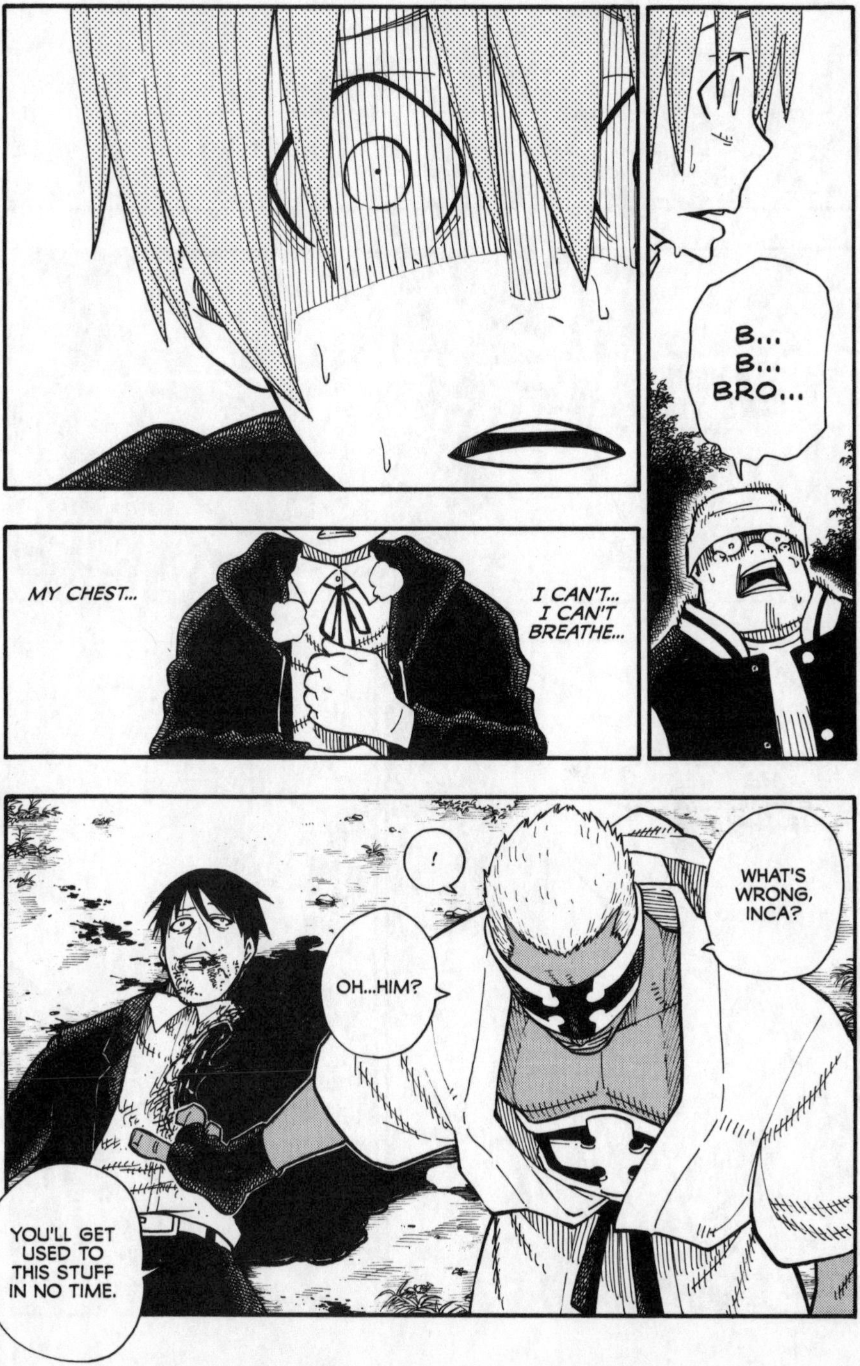
B...
B...
BRO...
I CAN'T...
I CAN'T
BREATHE...
MY CHEST...
WHAT'S
WRONG,
INCA?
!
OH...HIM?
YOU'LL GET
USED TO
THIS STUFF
IN NO TIME.

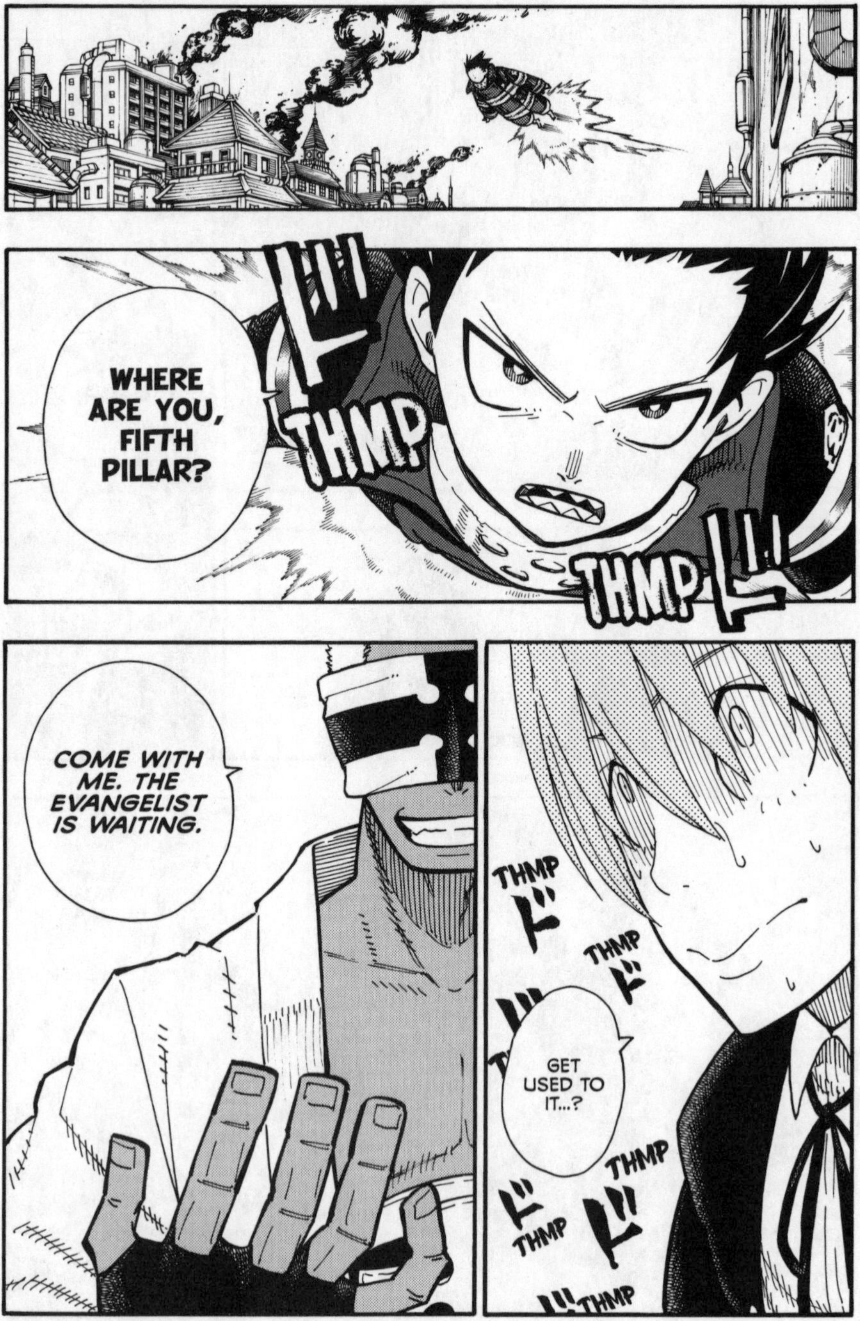
THMP
WHERE ARE YOU, FIFTH PILLAR?
THMP
THMP
THMP
GET USED TO IT...?
THMP
THMP
THMP
COME WITH ME. THE EVANGELIST IS WAITING.

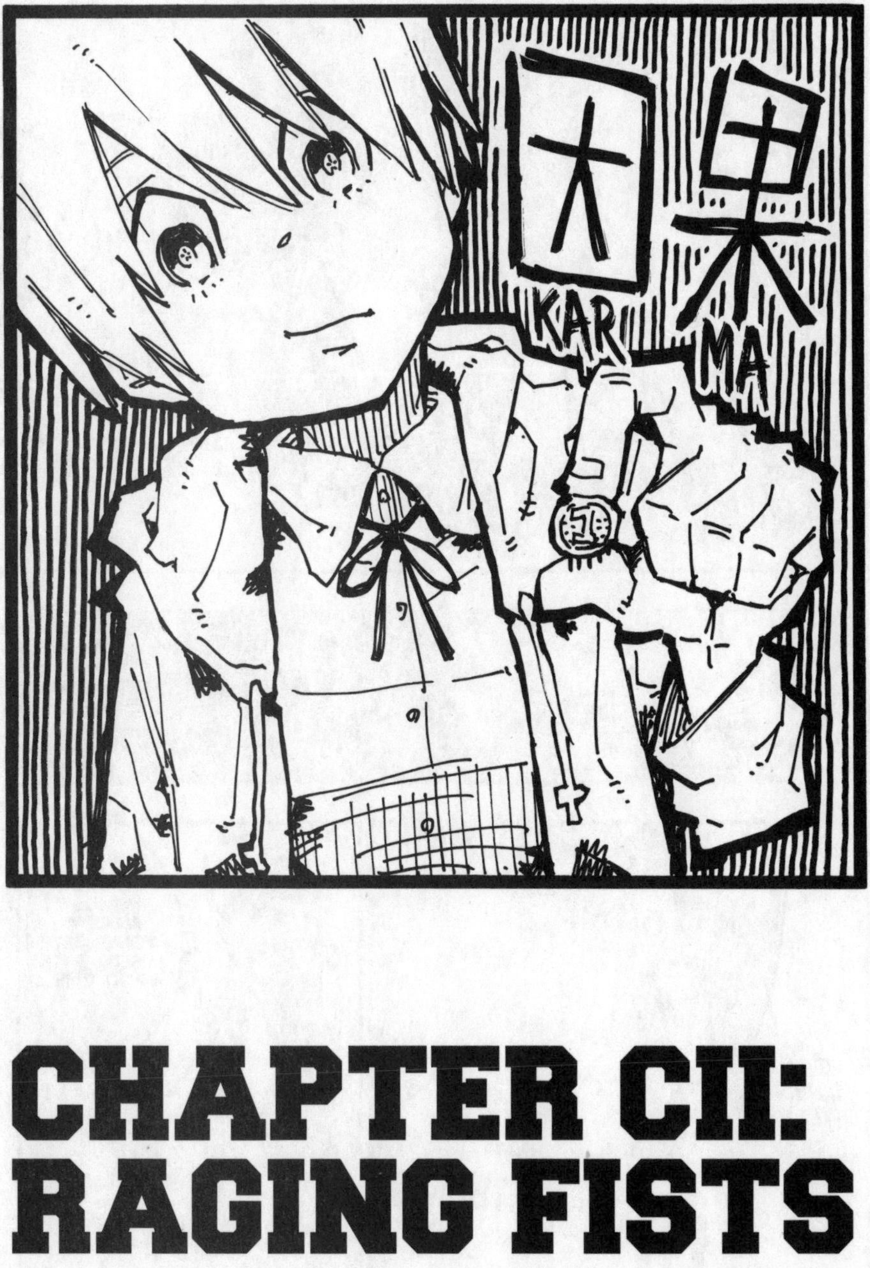

因果
KAR
MA

CHAPTER CII: RAGING FISTS

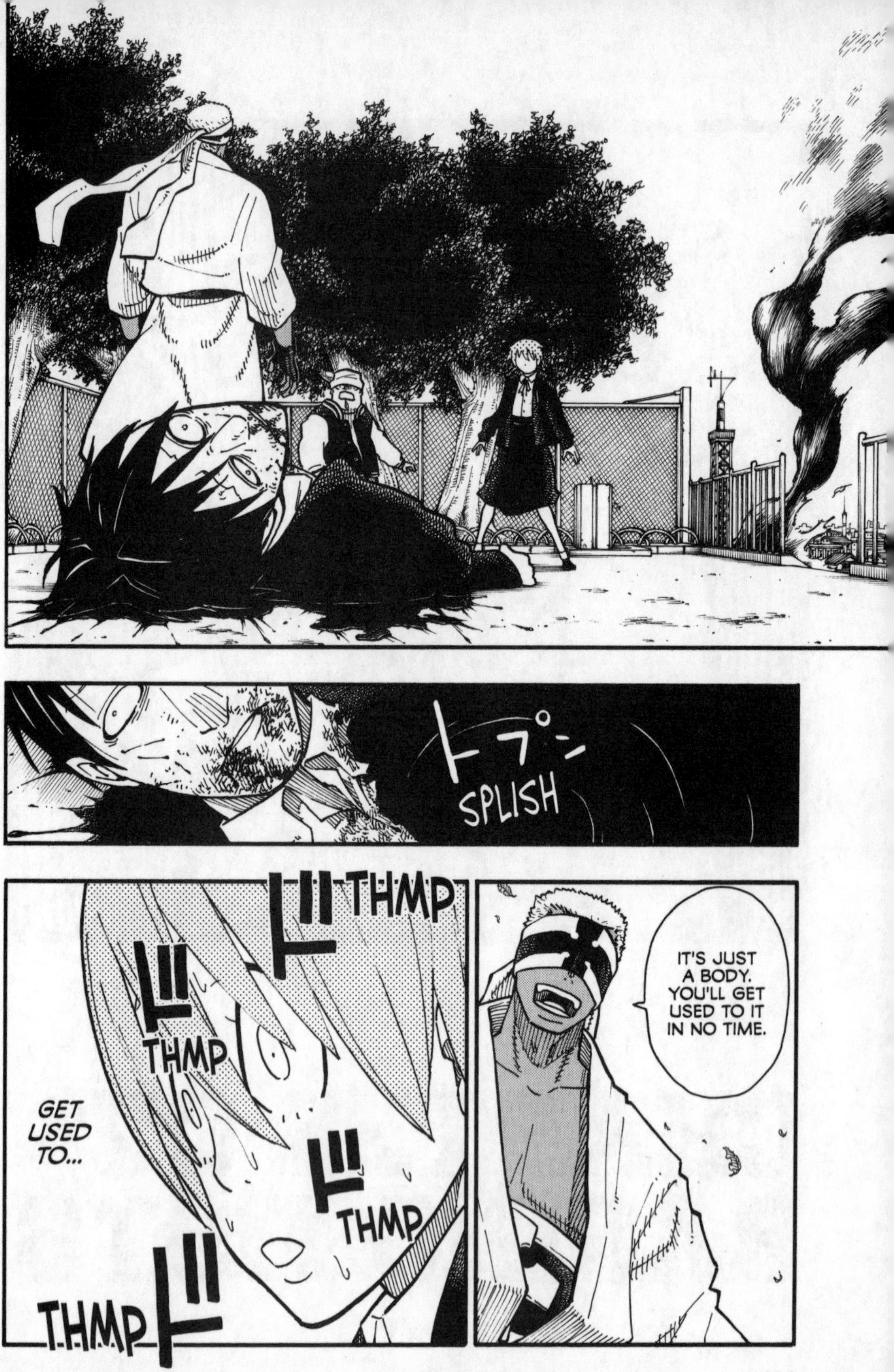
SPLISH
IT'S JUST A BODY. YOU'LL GET USED TO IT IN NO TIME.
THMP
THMP
GET USED TO...
THMP
THMP

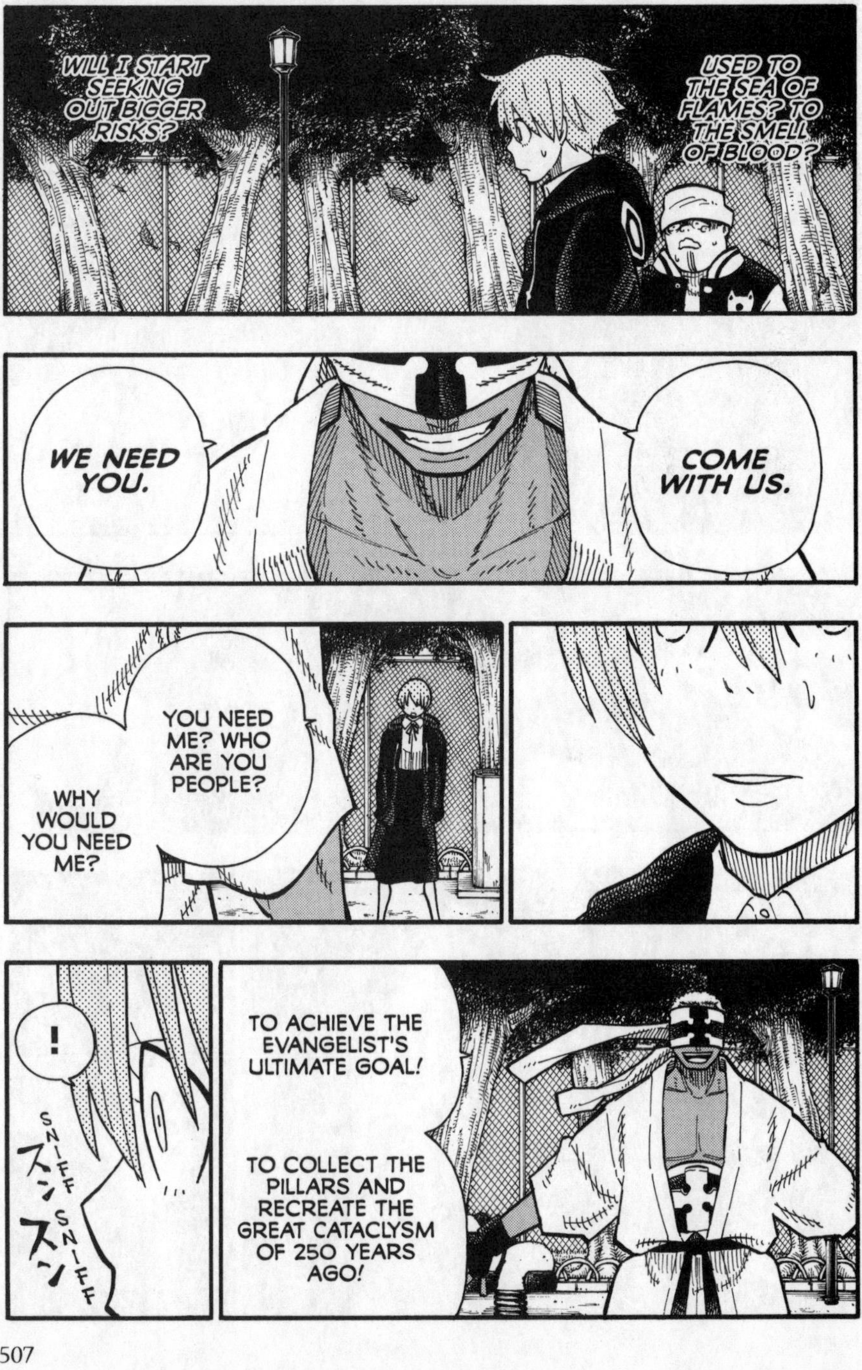
USED TO THE SEA OF FLAMES? TO THE SMELL OF BLOOD?
WILL I START SEEKING OUT BIGGER RISKS?
COME WITH US.
WE NEED YOU.
YOU NEED ME? WHO ARE YOU PEOPLE?
WHY WOULD YOU NEED ME?
TO ACHIEVE THE EVANGELIST'S ULTIMATE GOAL!
TO COLLECT THE PILLARS AND RECREATE THE GREAT CATACLYSM OF 250 YEARS AGO!
!
スン SNIFF
スン SNIFF

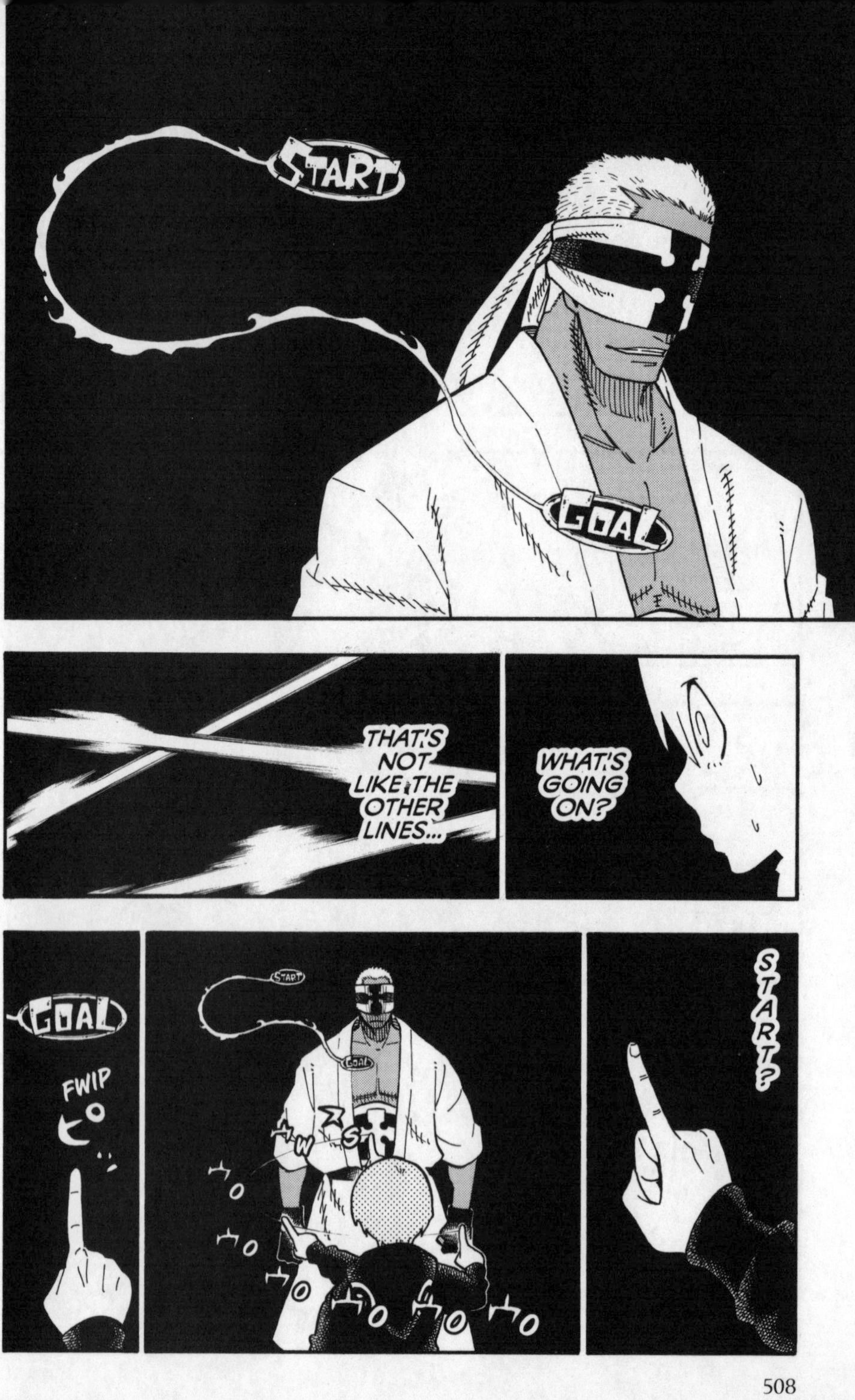
START
GOAL
WHAT'S GOING ON?
THAT'S NOT LIKE THE OTHER LINES...
START?
START
GOAL
GOAL
FWIP

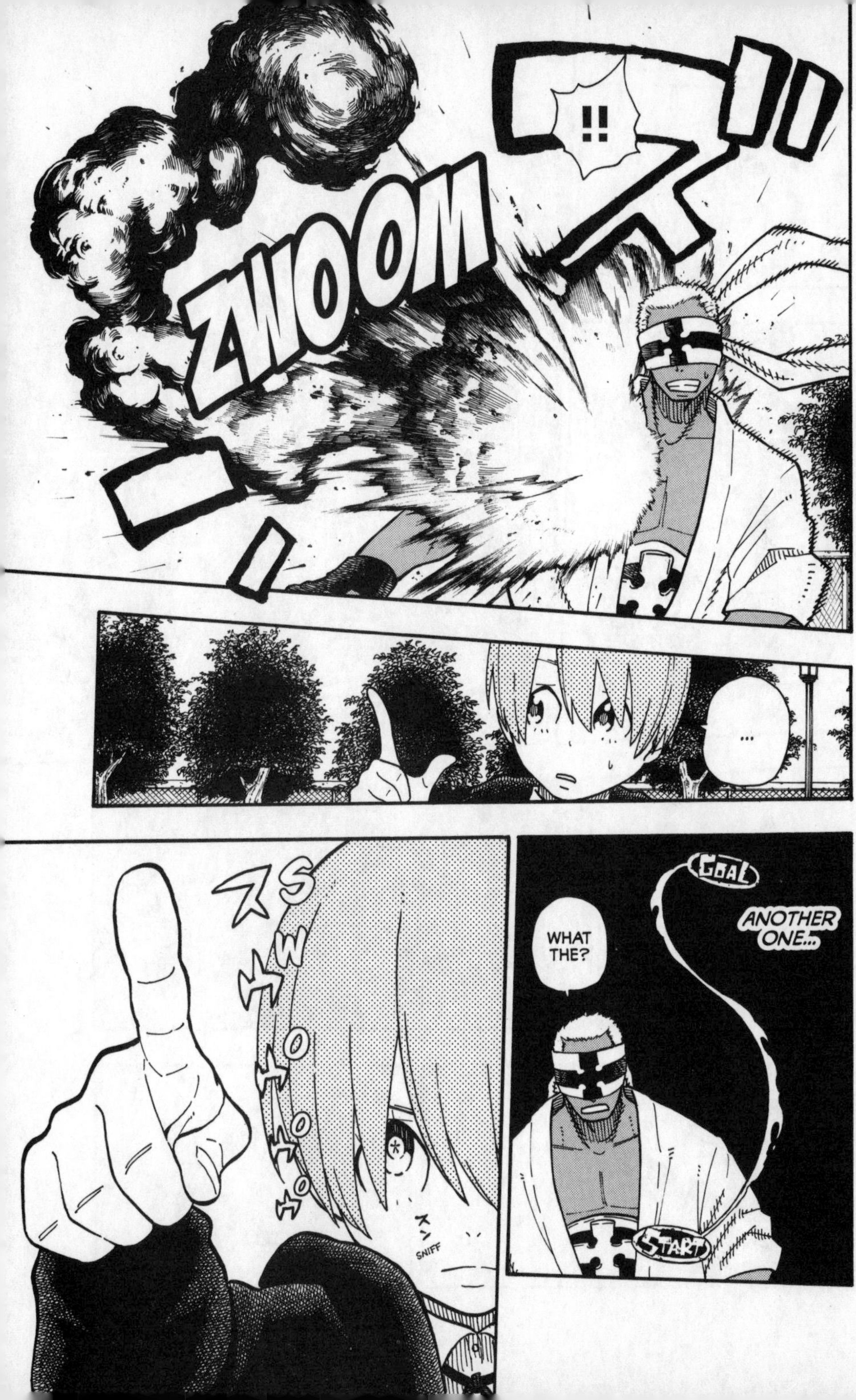
!!
ZWOOM
...
GOAL
ANOTHER ONE...
WHAT THE?
START
SWOOOO
SNIFF

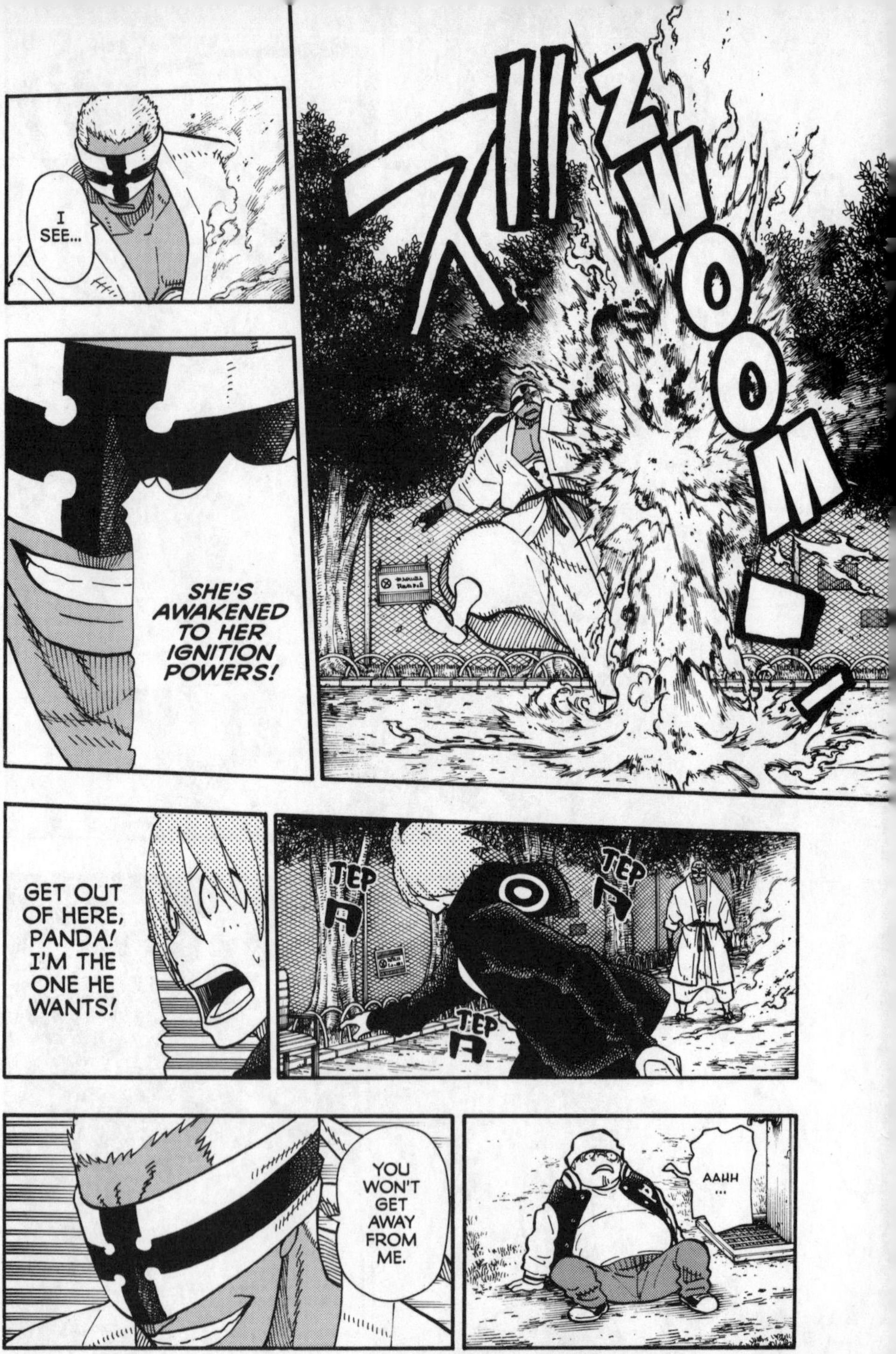
ZWOOM
I SEE...
SHE'S AWAKENED TO HER IGNITION POWERS!
TEP
TEP
TEP
GET OUT OF HERE, PANDA! I'M THE ONE HE WANTS!
AAHH ...
YOU WON'T GET AWAY FROM ME.

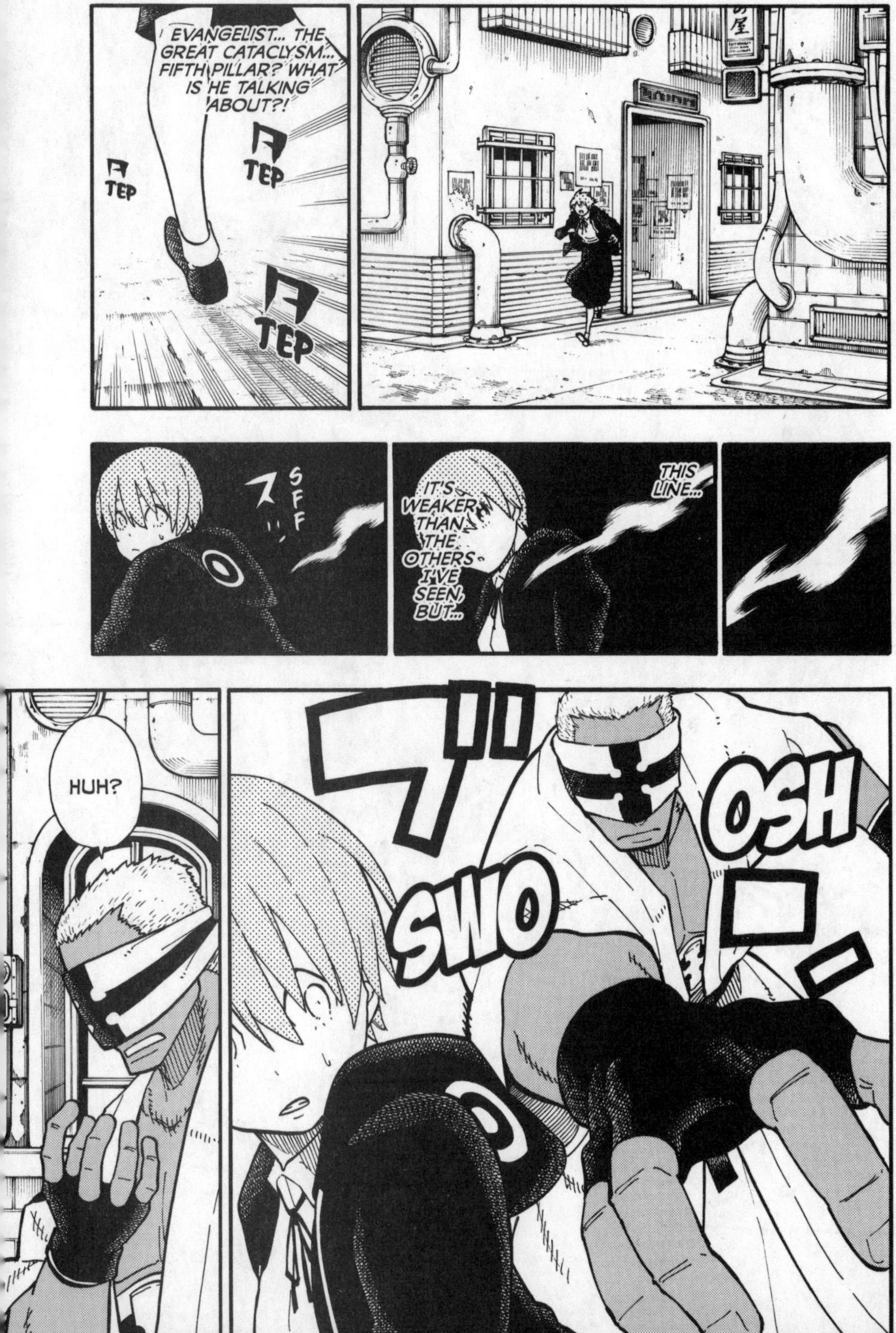
EVANGELIST... THE GREAT CATACLYSM... FIFTH PILLAR? WHAT IS HE TALKING ABOUT?!
TEP
TEP
TEP
THIS LINE...
IT'S WEAKER THAN THE OTHERS I'VE SEEN, BUT...
SFF
SWOOSH
HUH?

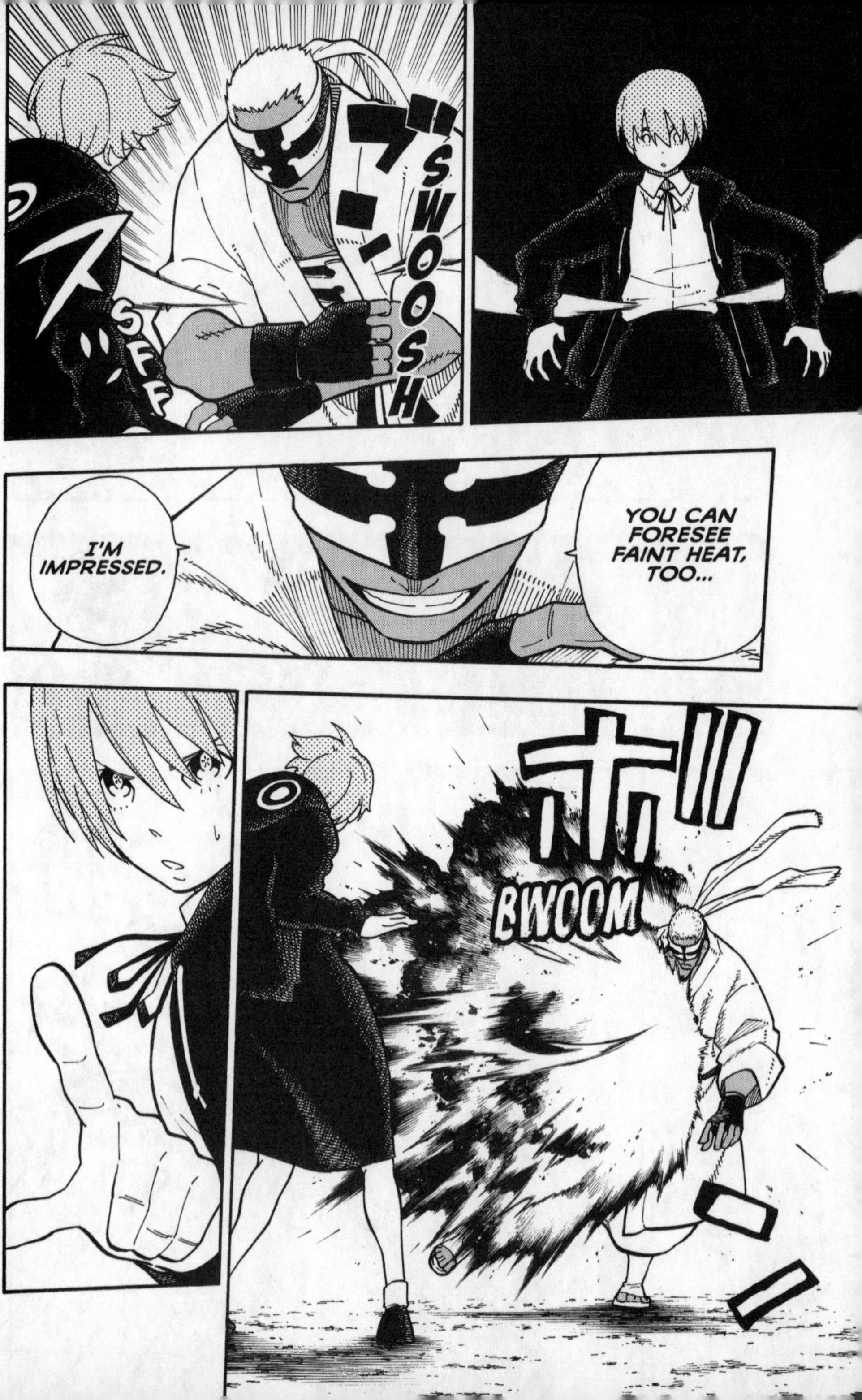
SWOOSH
SFF
YOU CAN FORESEE FAINT HEAT, TOO...
I'M IMPRESSED.
BWOOM

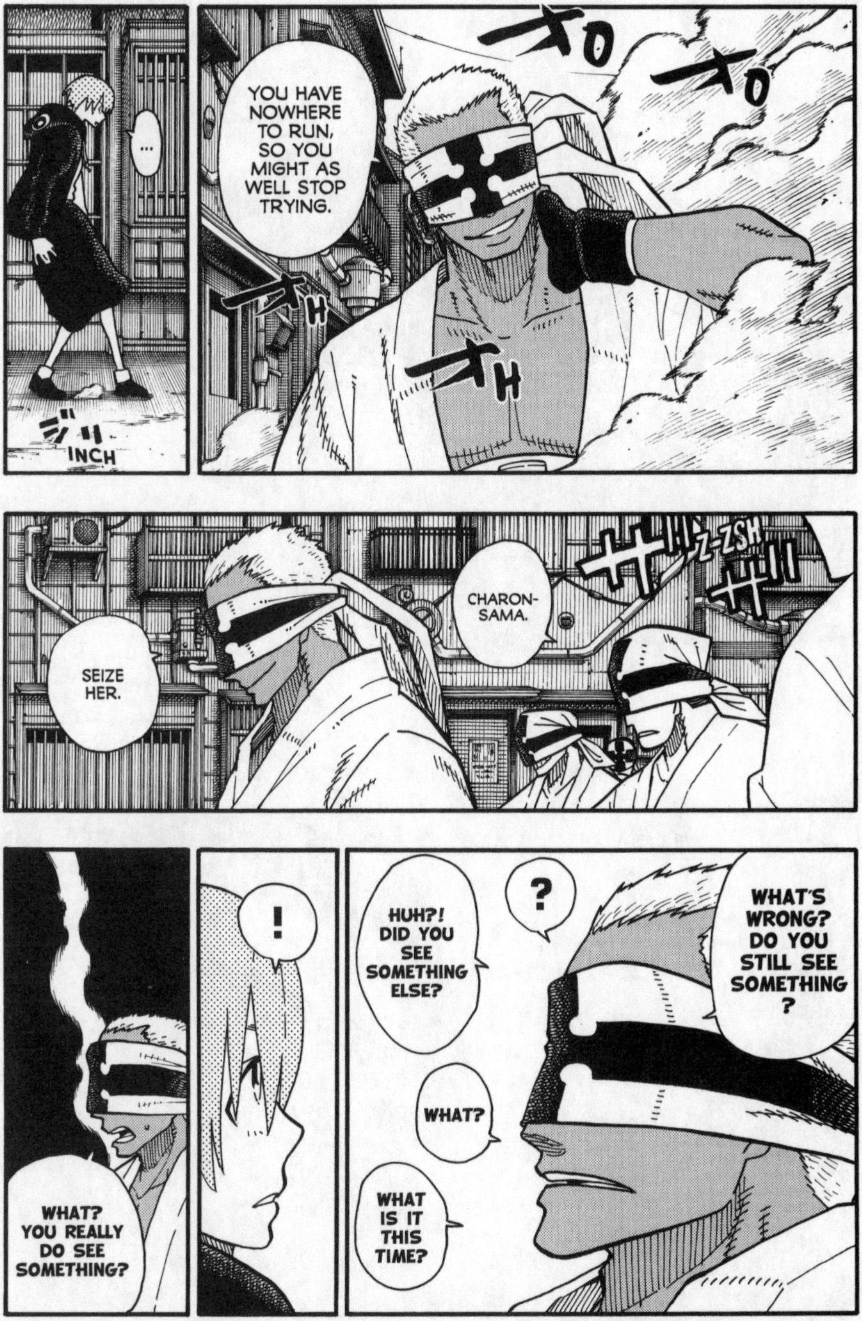
YOU HAVE NOWHERE TO RUN, SO YOU MIGHT AS WELL STOP TRYING.
...
INCH
Z-ZSH
CHARON-SAMA.
SEIZE HER.
WHAT'S WRONG? DO YOU STILL SEE SOMETHING ?
?
HUH?! DID YOU SEE SOMETHING ELSE?
WHAT?
WHAT IS IT THIS TIME?
!
WHAT? YOU REALLY DO SEE SOMETHING?

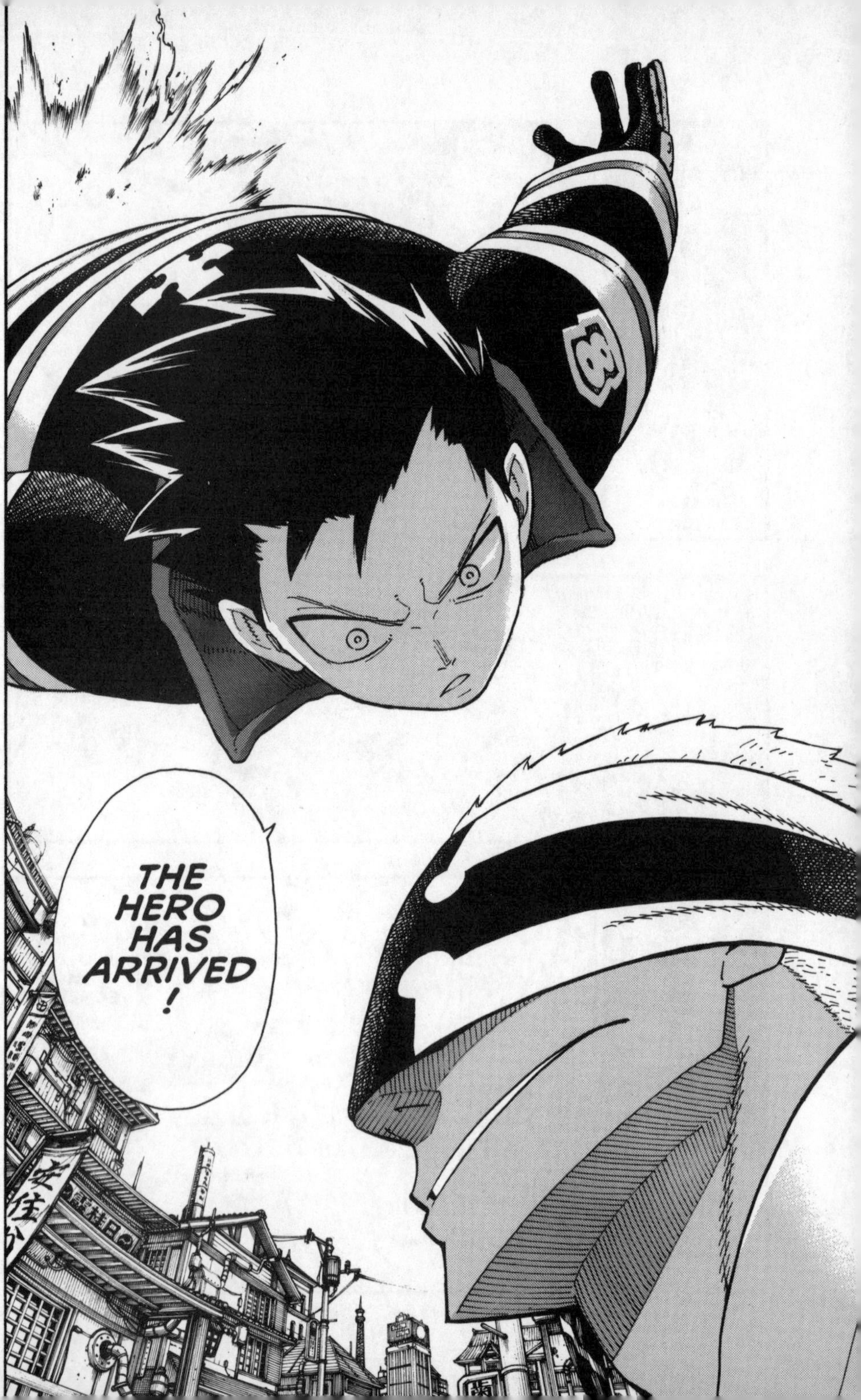
THE HERO HAS ARRIVED!

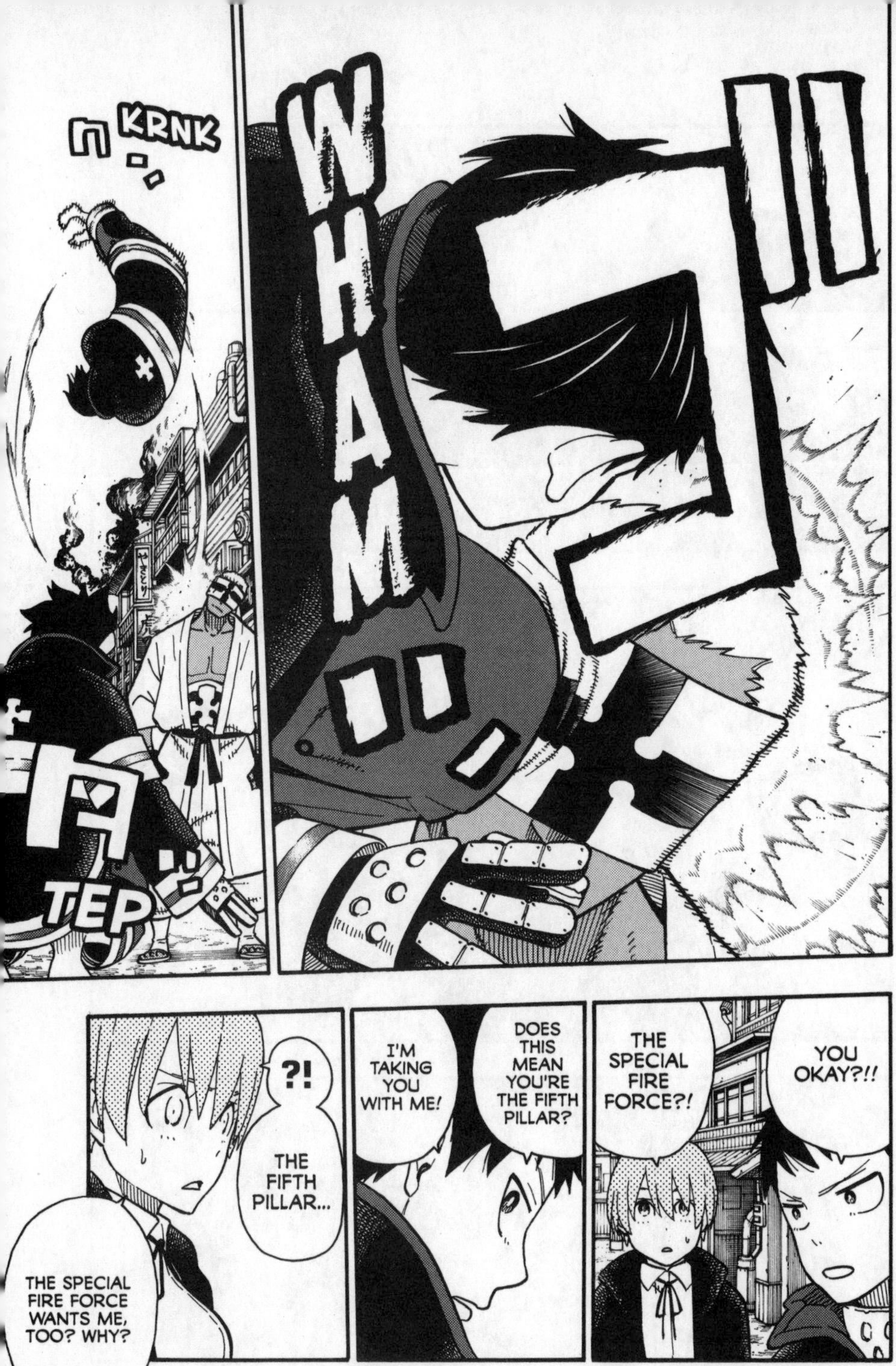

WHAM
KRNK
TEP
YOU OKAY?!!
THE SPECIAL FIRE FORCE?!
DOES THIS MEAN YOU'RE THE FIFTH PILLAR?
I'M TAKING YOU WITH ME!
?!
THE FIFTH PILLAR...
THE SPECIAL FIRE FORCE WANTS ME, TOO? WHY?

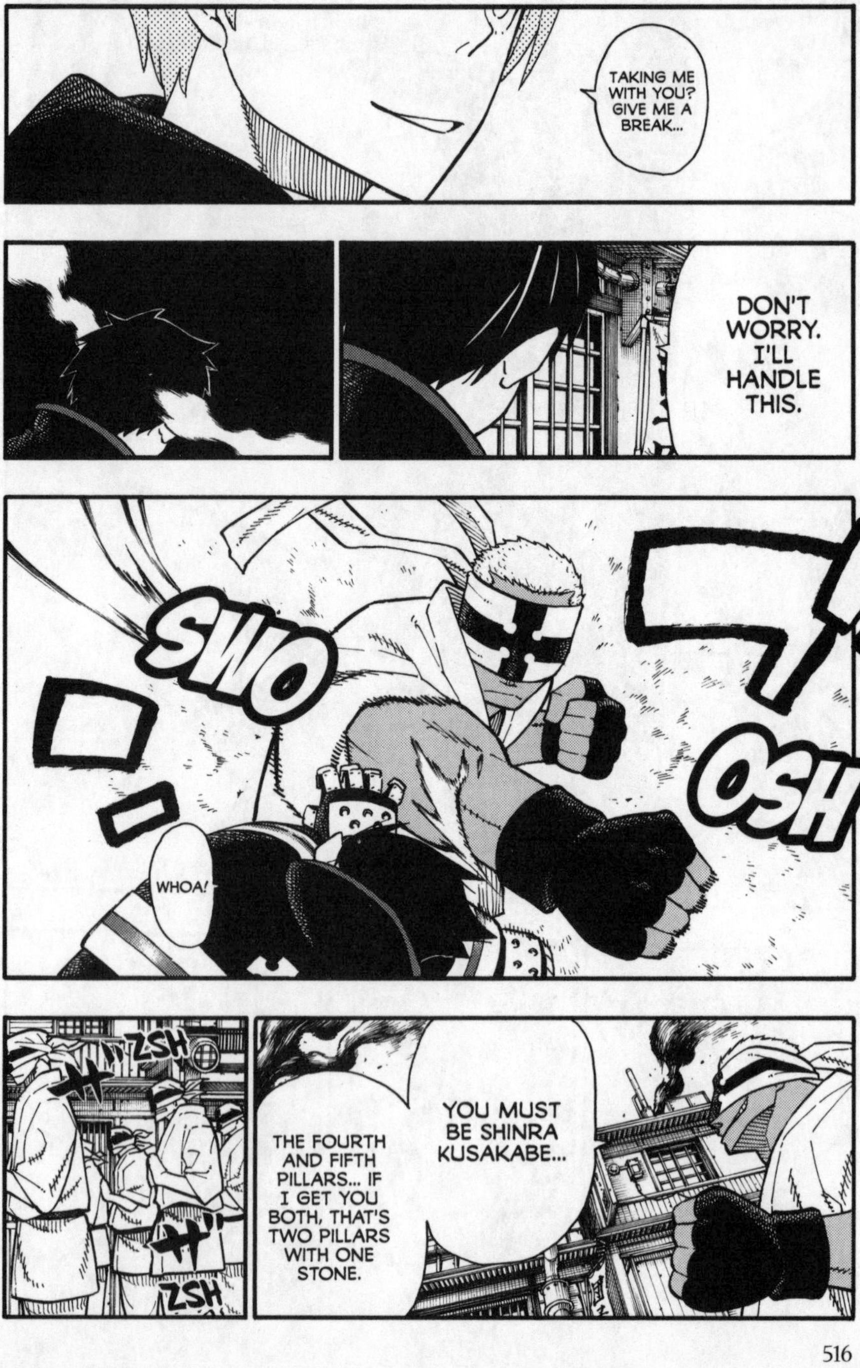
TAKING ME WITH YOU? GIVE ME A BREAK...
DON'T WORRY. I'LL HANDLE THIS.
SWO
OSH
WHOA!
YOU MUST BE SHINRA KUSAKABE...
THE FOURTH AND FIFTH PILLARS... IF I GET YOU BOTH, THAT'S TWO PILLARS WITH ONE STONE.
ZSH
ZSH

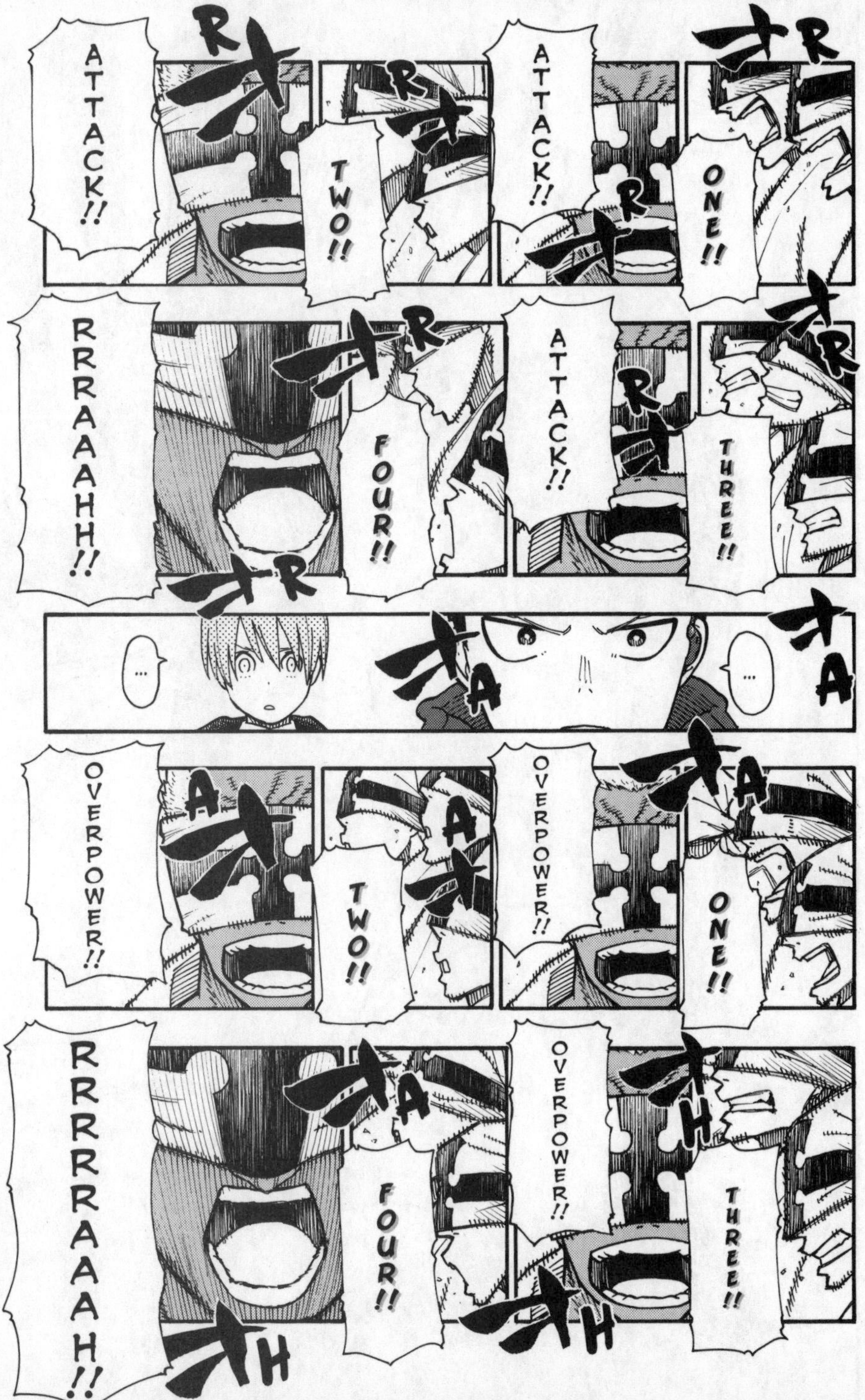
ONE!!
ATTACK!!
TWO!!
ATTACK!!
THREE!!
ATTACK!!
FOUR!!
RRRAAAHH!!
...
...
ONE!!
OVERPOWER!!
TWO!!
OVERPOWER!!
THREE!!
OVERPOWER!!
FOUR!!
RRRRRAAAH!!

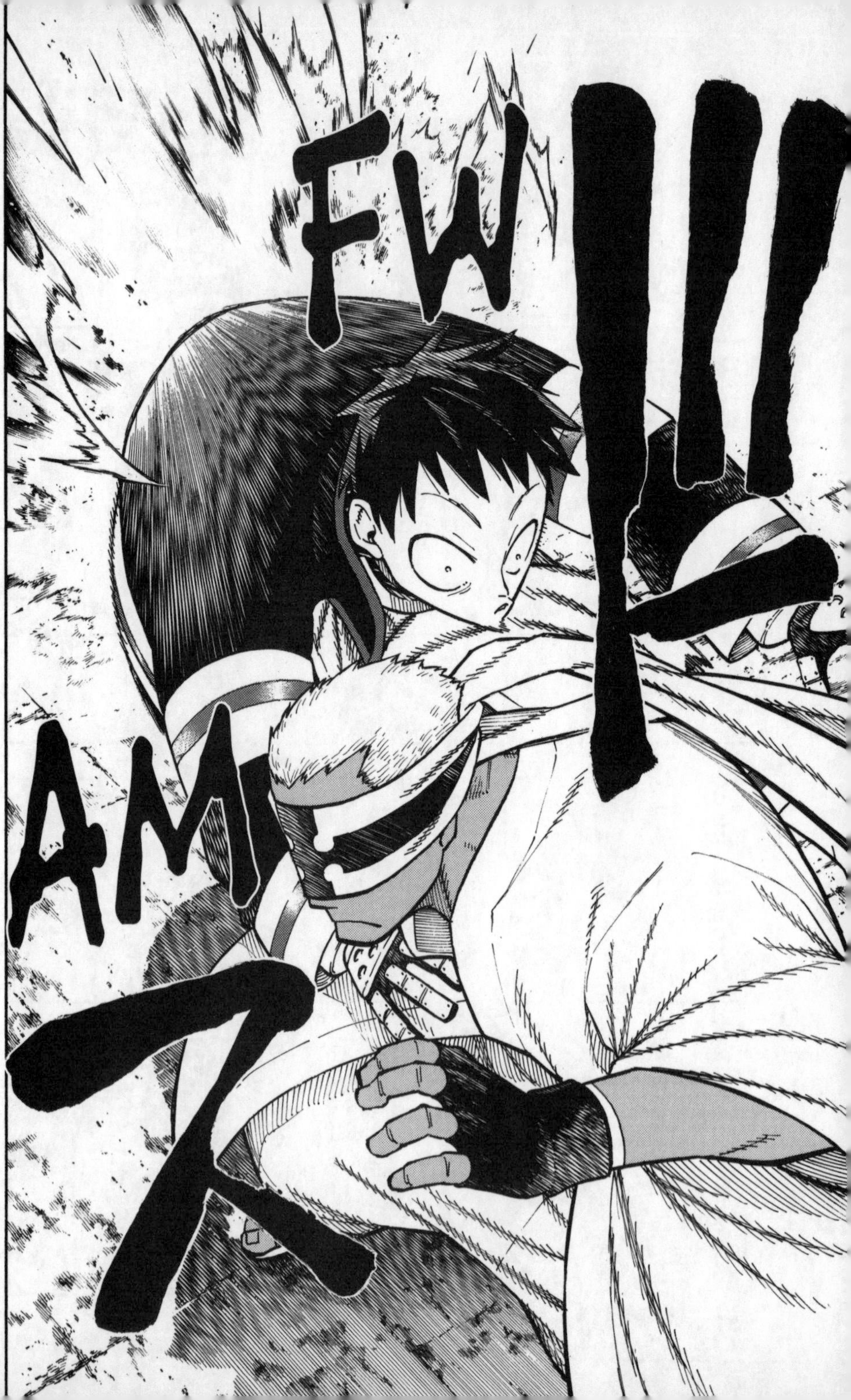
FWAM

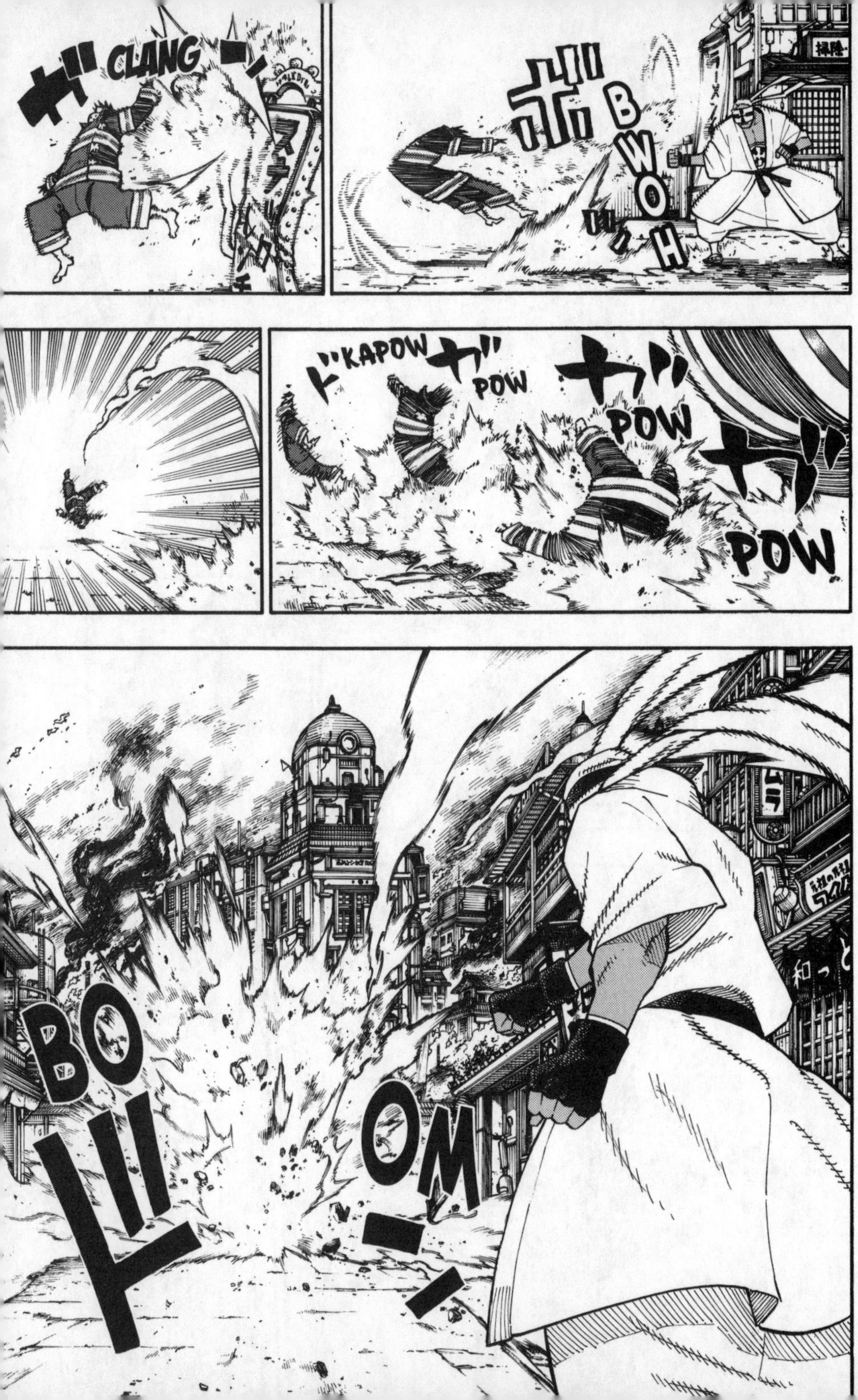
BWOOH
CLANG
KAPOW
POW
POW
POW
BOOOM

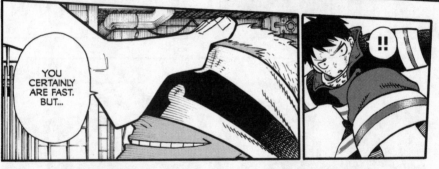

YOU CERTAINLY ARE FAST. BUT...

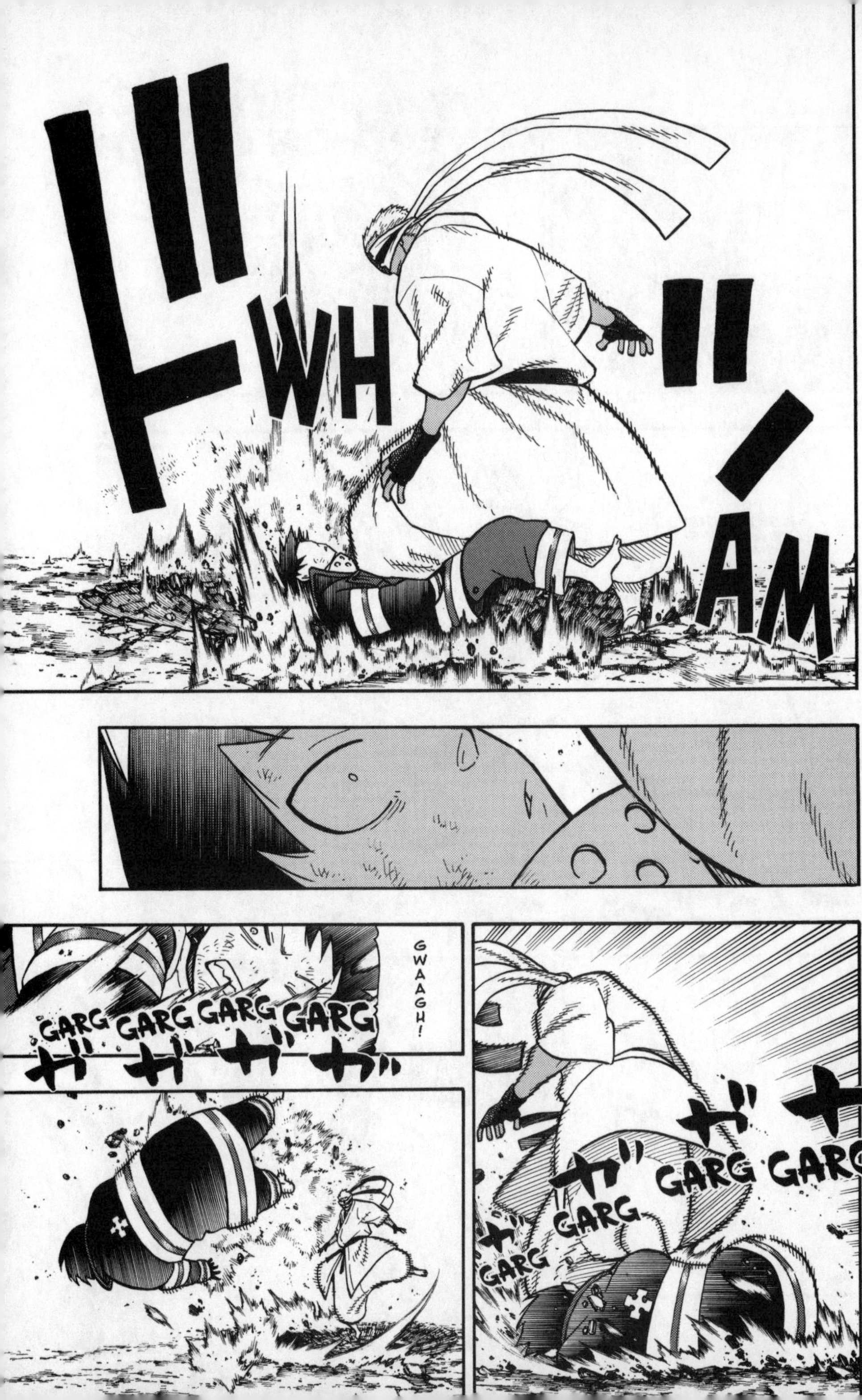
WH
AM
GARG GARG
GARG
GARG
GWAAGH!
GARG GARG GARG GARG

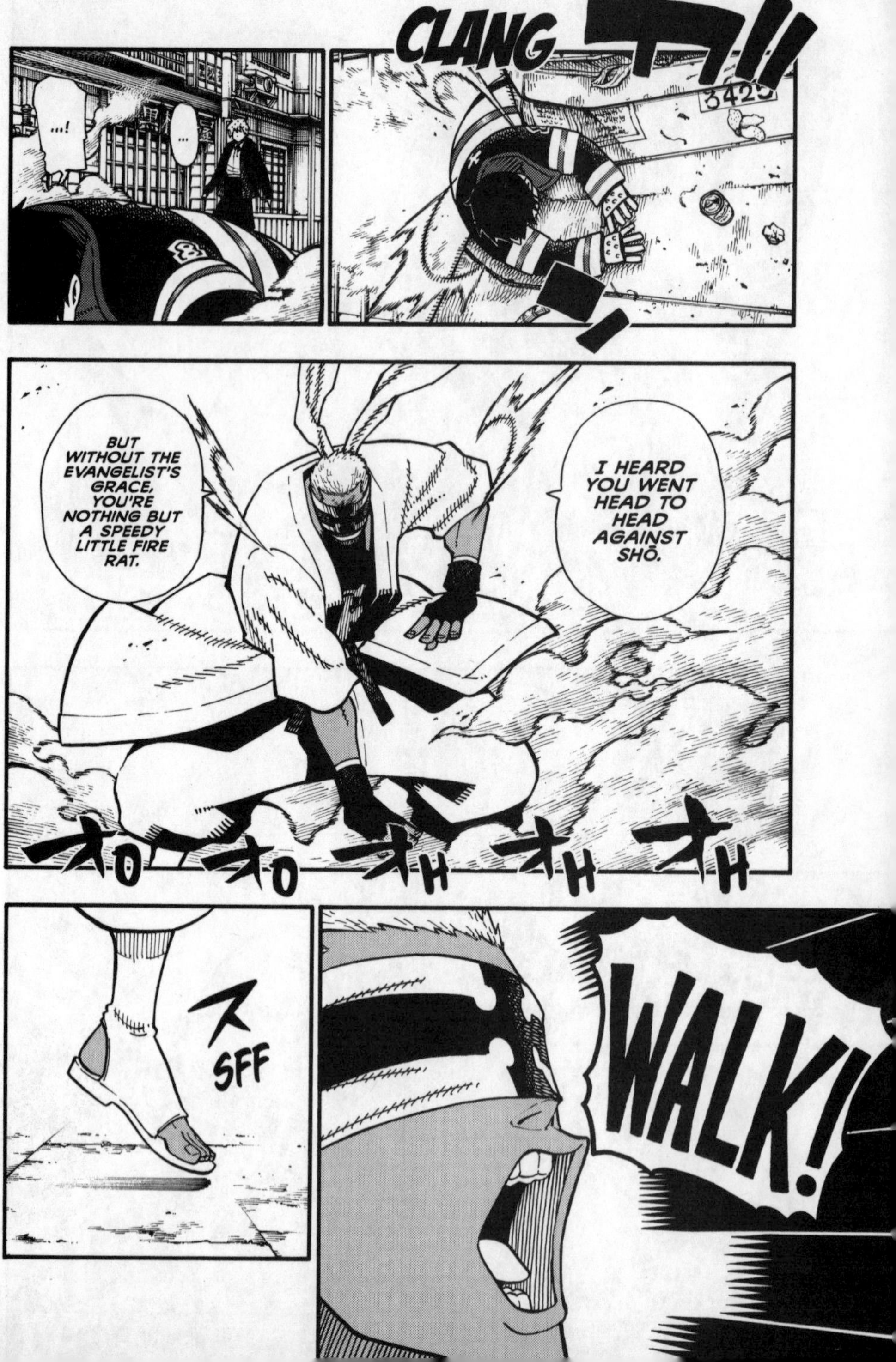
CLANG
...
...!
I HEARD YOU WENT HEAD TO HEAD AGAINST SHŌ.
BUT WITHOUT THE EVANGELIST'S GRACE, YOU'RE NOTHING BUT A SPEEDY LITTLE FIRE RAT.
H
H
H
O
O
WALK!
SFF

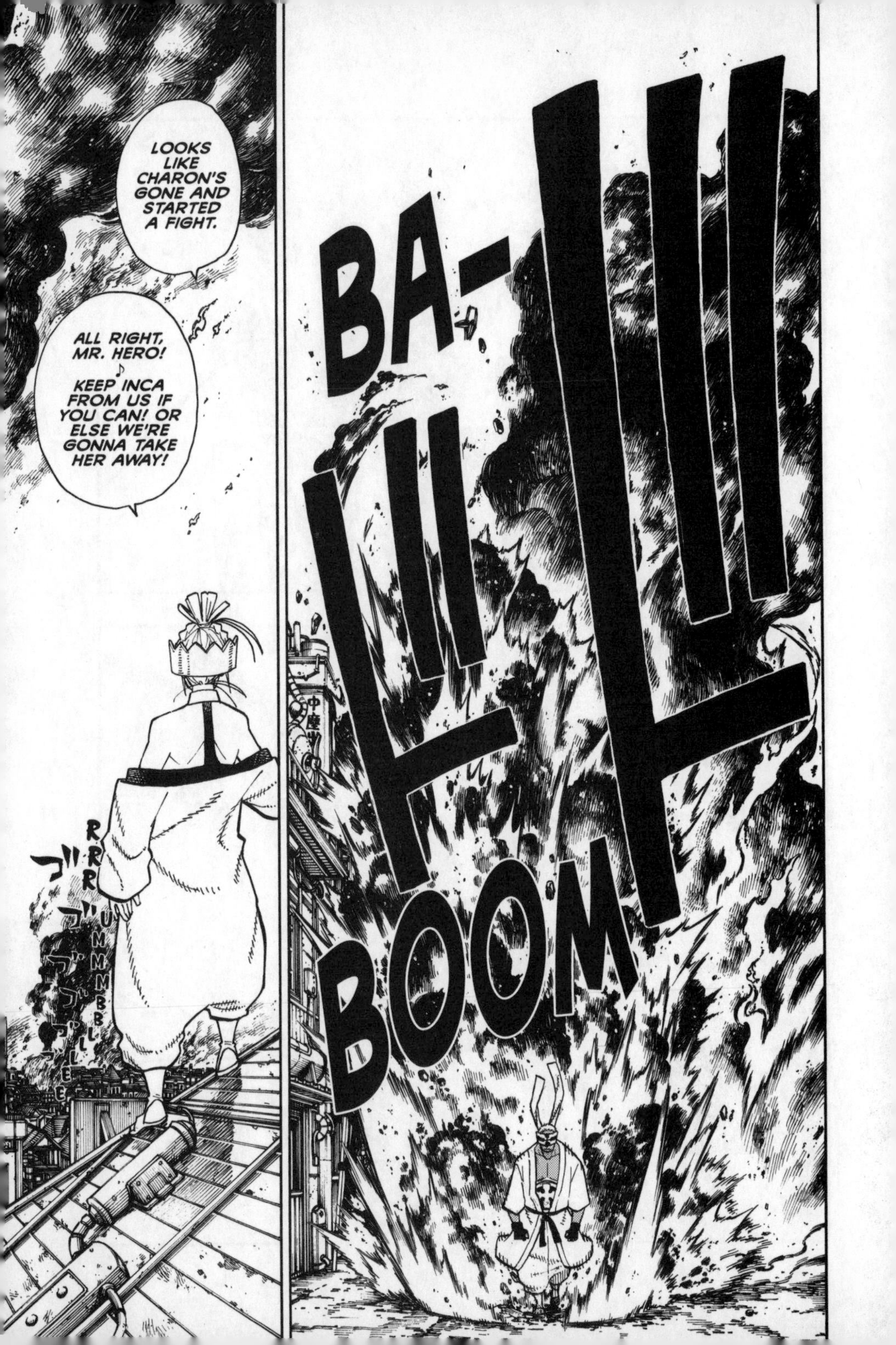
BA-
BOOM
LOOKS LIKE CHARON'S GONE AND STARTED A FIGHT.
ALL RIGHT, MR. HERO! ♪ KEEP INCA FROM US IF YOU CAN! OR ELSE WE'RE GONNA TAKE HER AWAY!
RRRUMMMBBLLLEE
ゴゴゴゴゴゴ

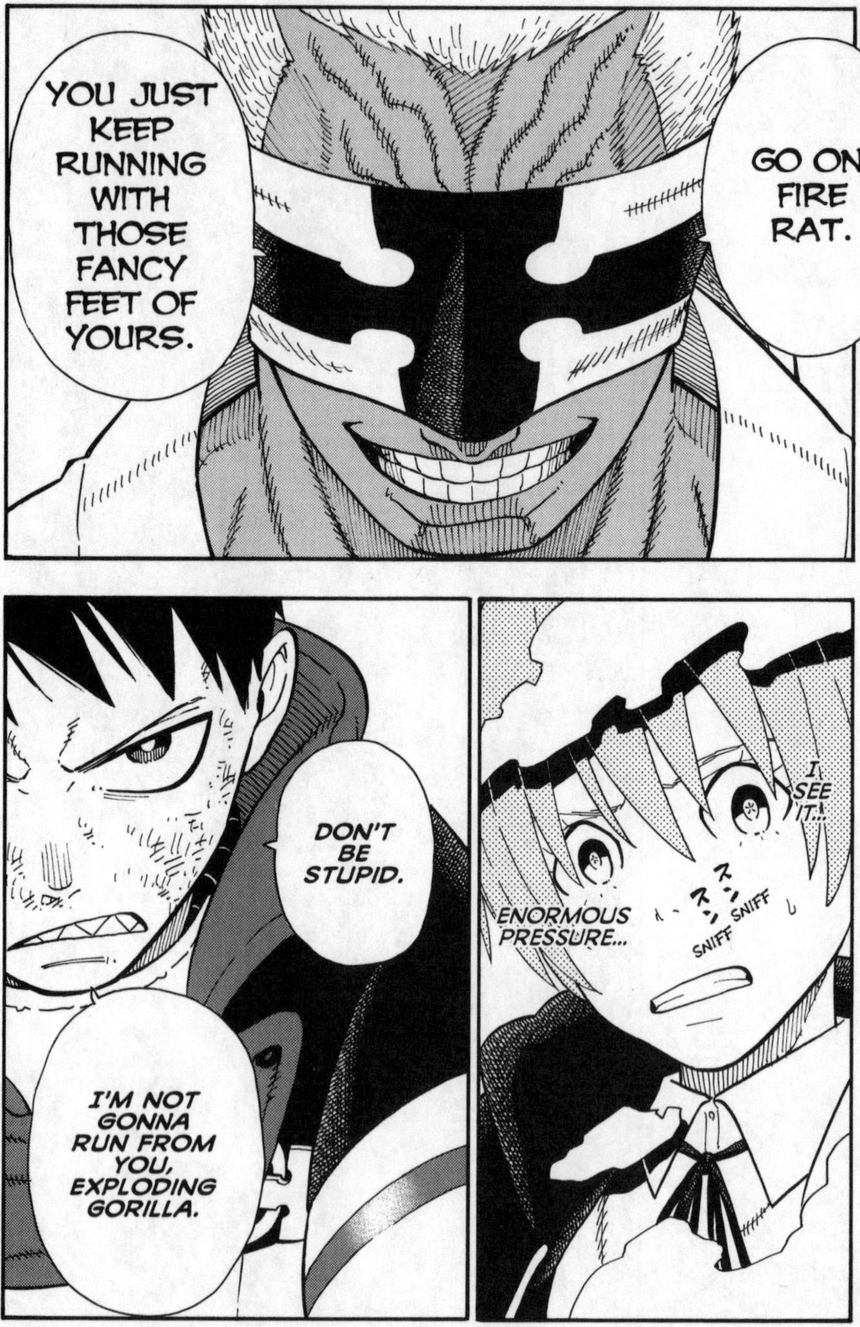
GO ON, FIRE RAT.
YOU JUST KEEP RUNNING WITH THOSE FANCY FEET OF YOURS.
I SEE IT...
SNIFF
SNIFF
ENORMOUS PRESSURE...
DON'T BE STUPID.
I'M NOT GONNA RUN FROM YOU, EXPLODING GORILLA.

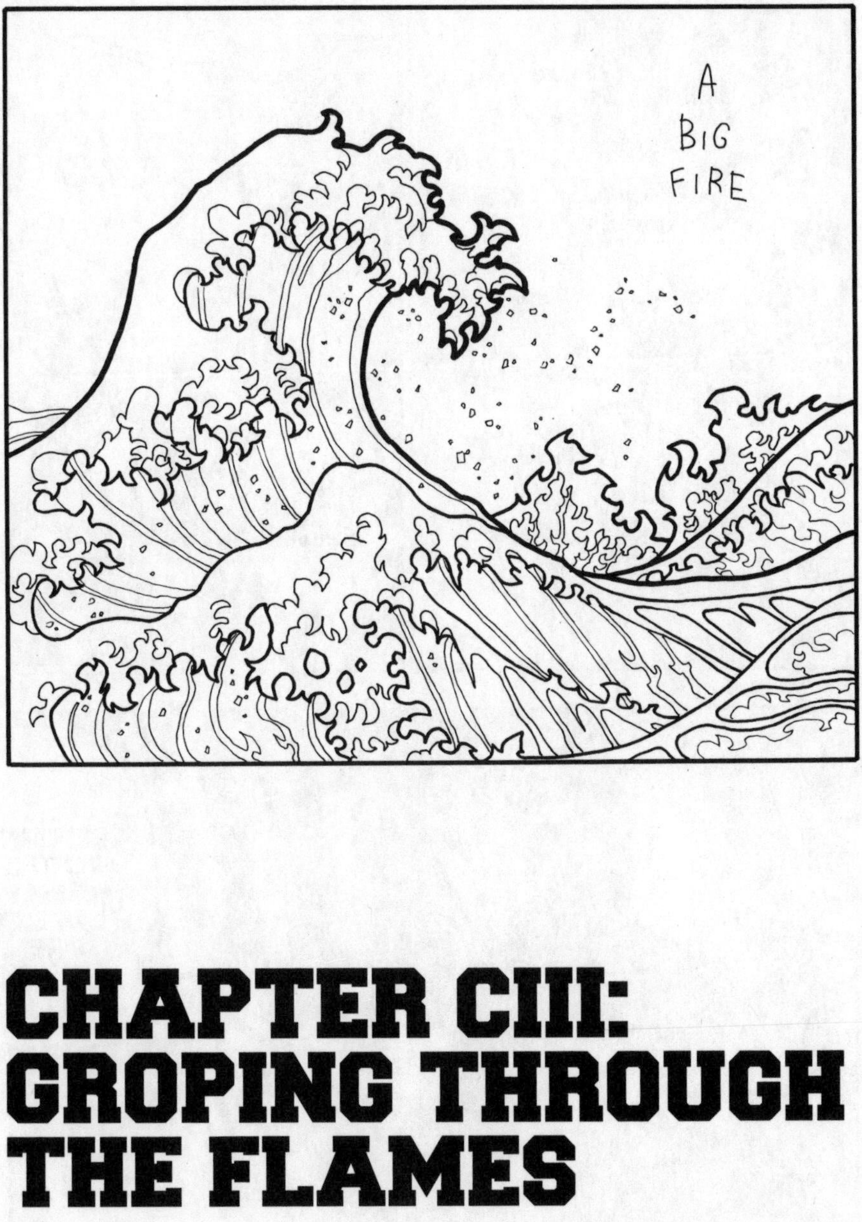
A
BIG
FIRE

CHAPTER CIII: GROPING THROUGH THE FLAMES

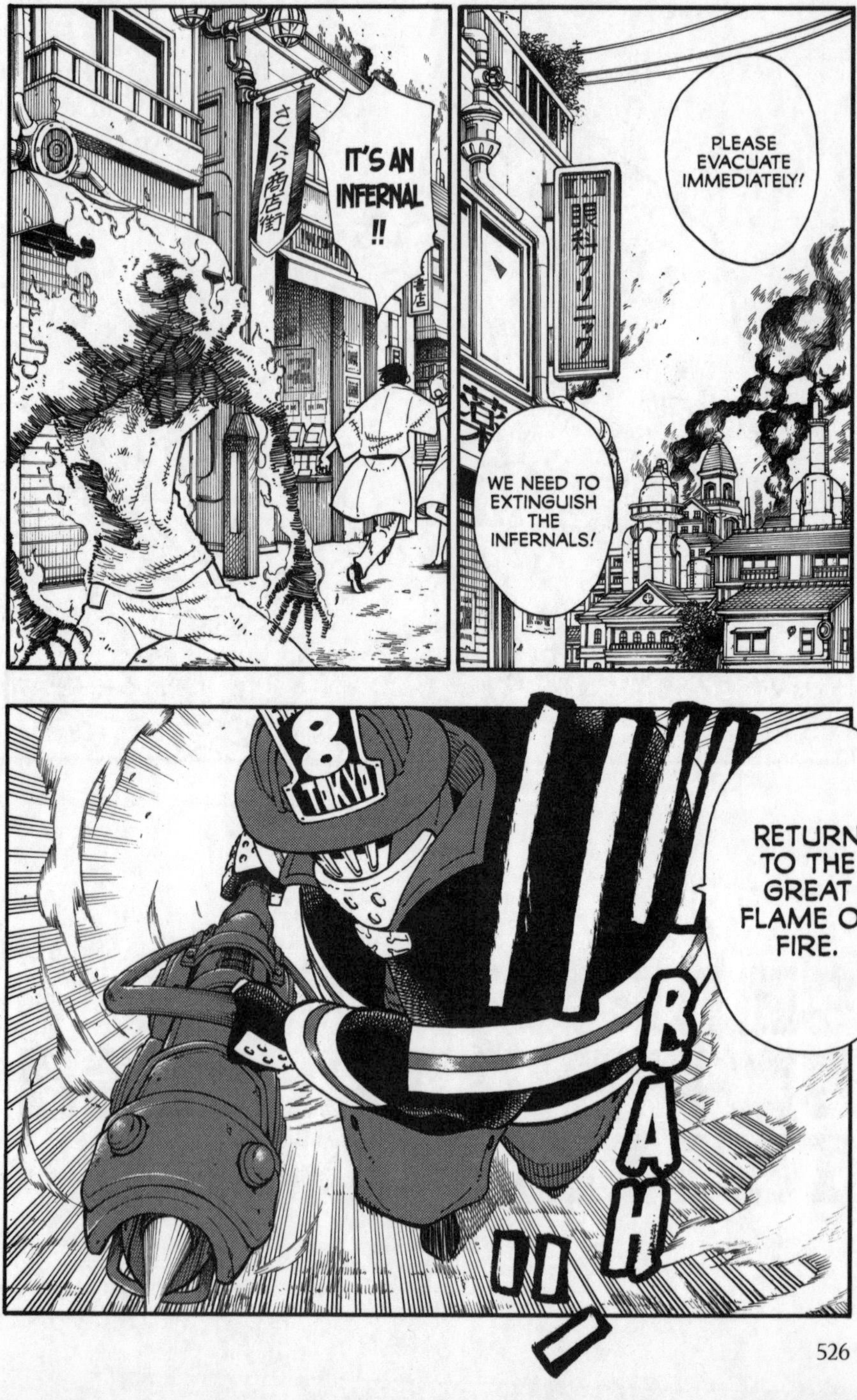
PLEASE EVACUATE IMMEDIATELY!
眼科クリニック
WE NEED TO EXTINGUISH THE INFERNALS!
さくら商店街
書店
IT'S AN INFERNAL!!
8
TOKYO
RETURN TO THE GREAT FLAME OF FIRE.
BAH!!

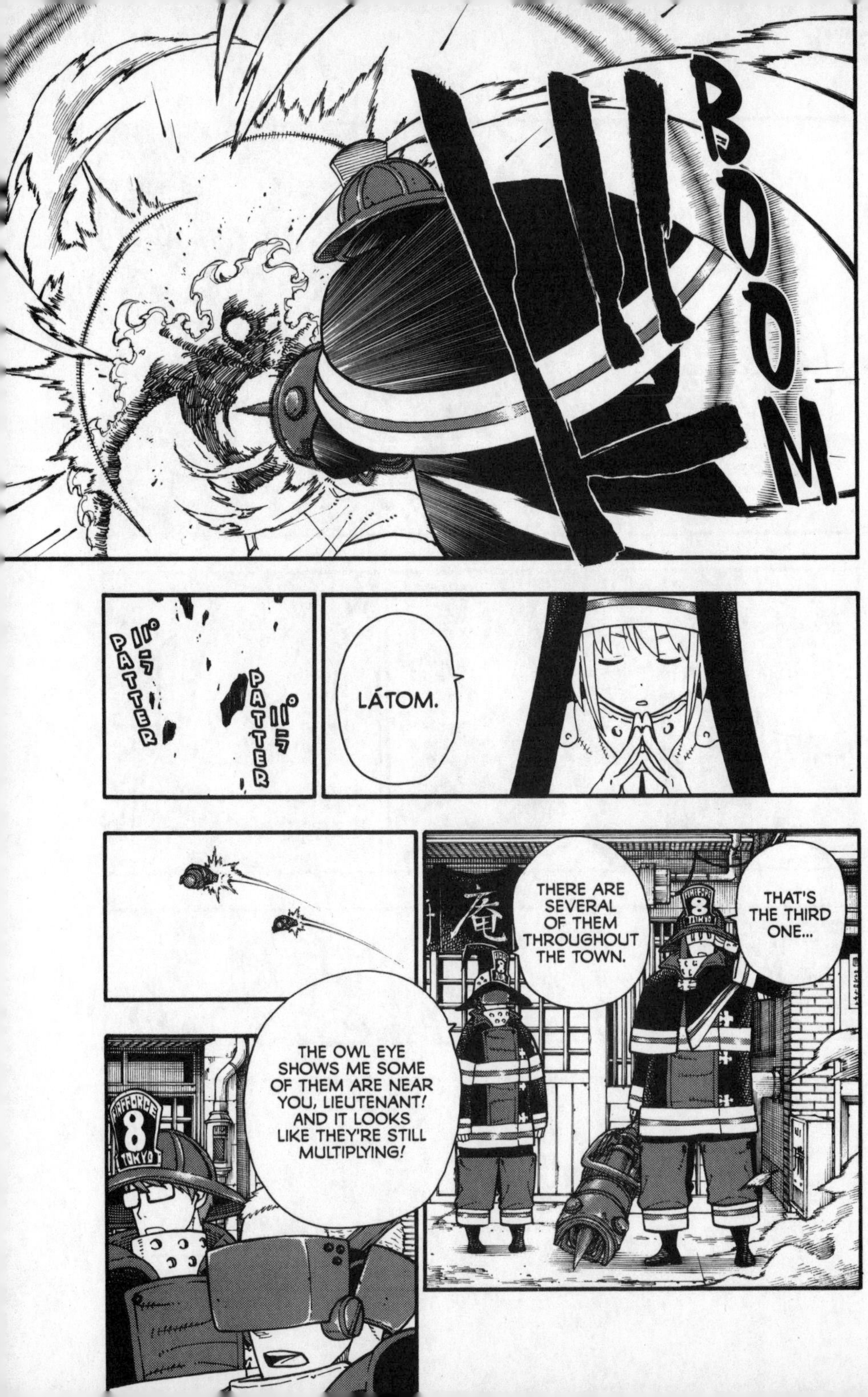
BOOM
LÁTOM.
PATTER
PATTER
THAT'S THE THIRD ONE...
THERE ARE SEVERAL OF THEM THROUGHOUT THE TOWN.
THE OWL EYE SHOWS ME SOME OF THEM ARE NEAR YOU, LIEUTENANT! AND IT LOOKS LIKE THEY'RE STILL MULTIPLYING!

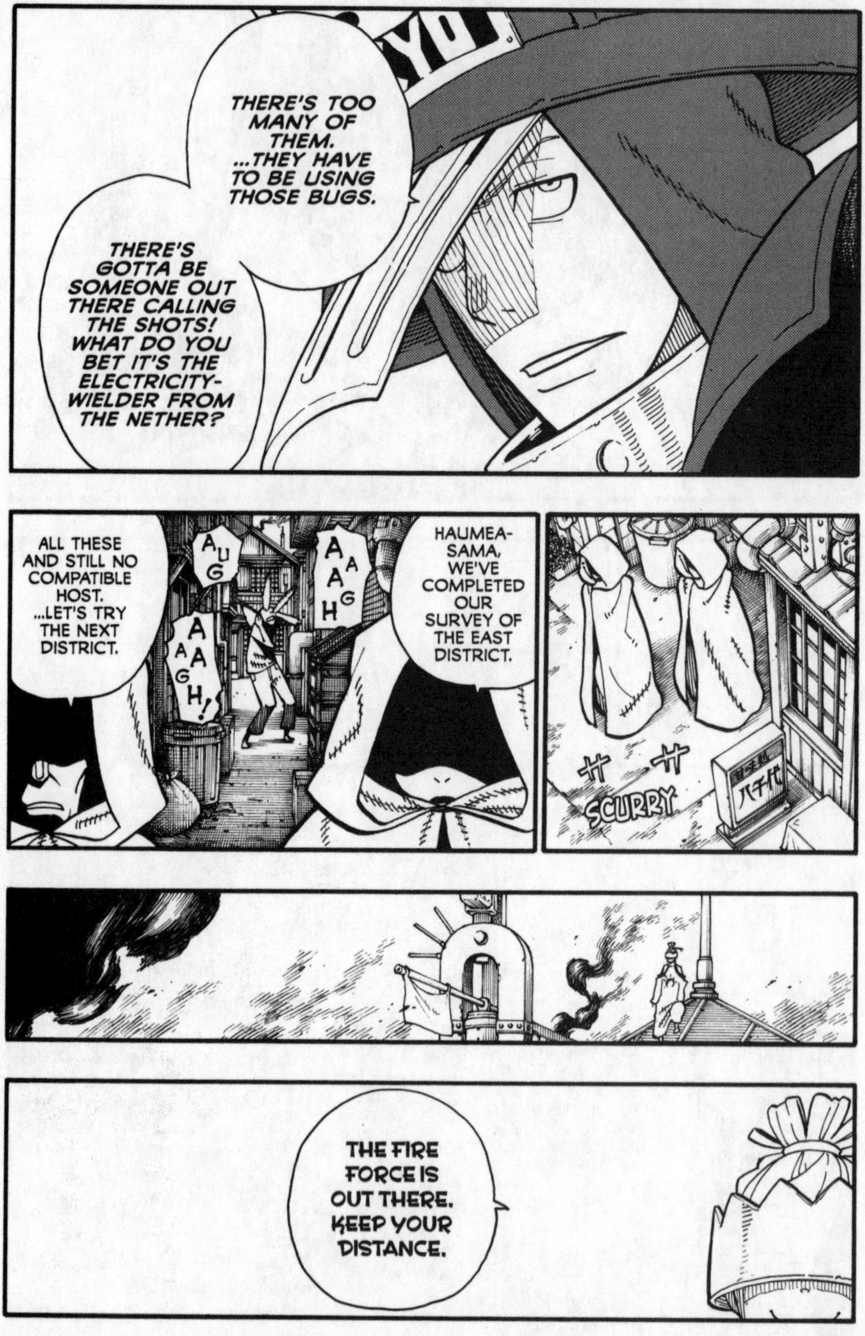
THERE'S TOO MANY OF THEM. ...THEY HAVE TO BE USING THOSE BUGS.
THERE'S GOTTA BE SOMEONE OUT THERE CALLING THE SHOTS! WHAT DO YOU BET IT'S THE ELECTRICITY-WIELDER FROM THE NETHER?
サ サ
SCURRY
八千代
HAUMEA-SAMA, WE'VE COMPLETED OUR SURVEY OF THE EAST DISTRICT.
AAAHG
AUG
AAAGH!
ALL THESE AND STILL NO COMPATIBLE HOST. ...LET'S TRY THE NEXT DISTRICT.
THE FIRE FORCE IS OUT THERE. KEEP YOUR DISTANCE.

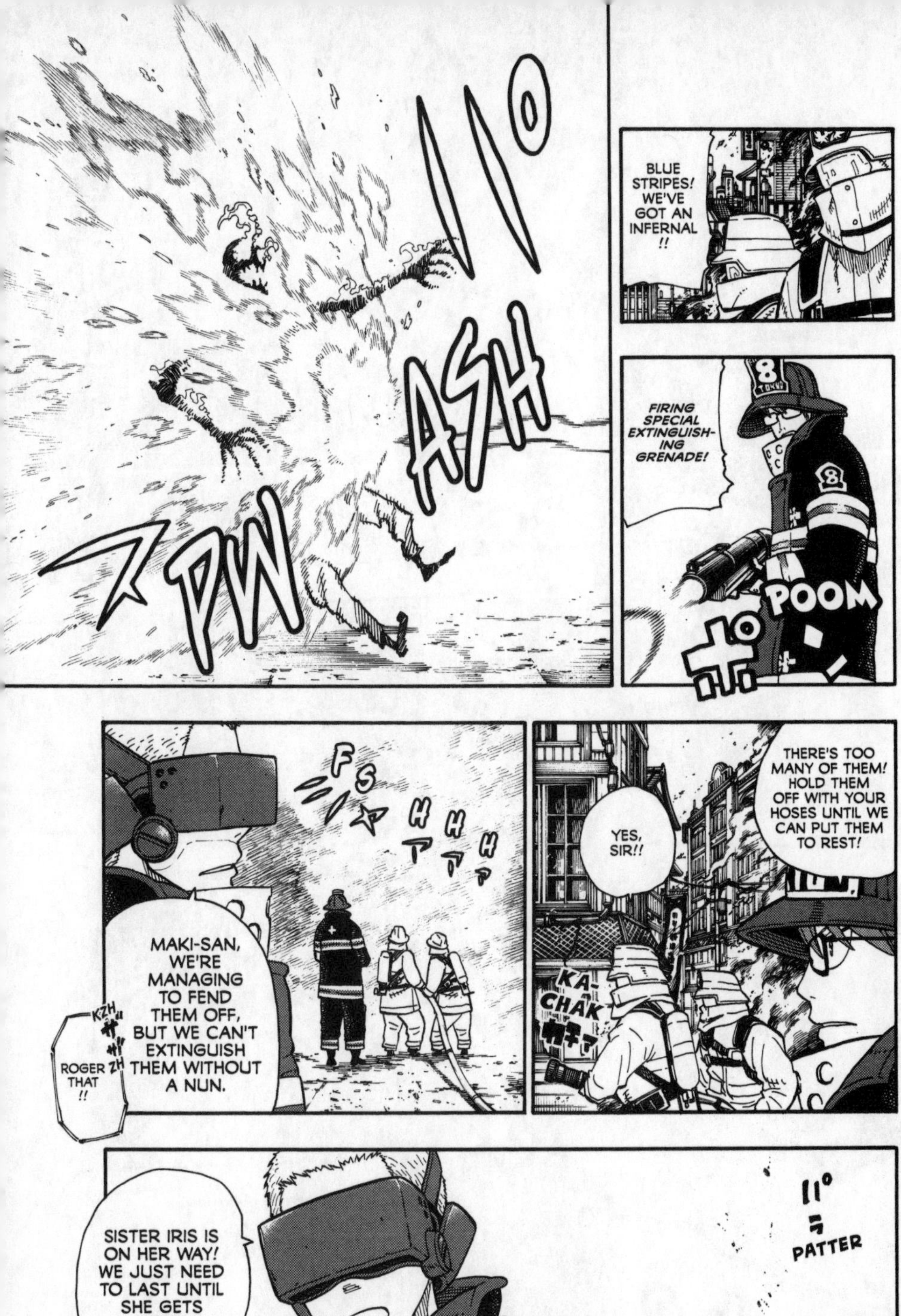
BLUE STRIPES! WE'VE GOT AN INFERNAL !!
FIRING SPECIAL EXTINGUISHING GRENADE!
POOM
PWASH
THERE'S TOO MANY OF THEM! HOLD THEM OFF WITH YOUR HOSES UNTIL WE CAN PUT THEM TO REST!
YES, SIR!!
KA-CHAK
FSHHH
MAKI-SAN, WE'RE MANAGING TO FEND THEM OFF, BUT WE CAN'T EXTINGUISH THEM WITHOUT A NUN.
KZH
ZH
ROGER THAT !!
PATTER
SISTER IRIS IS ON HER WAY! WE JUST NEED TO LAST UNTIL SHE GETS HERE!

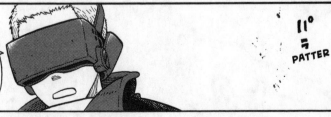

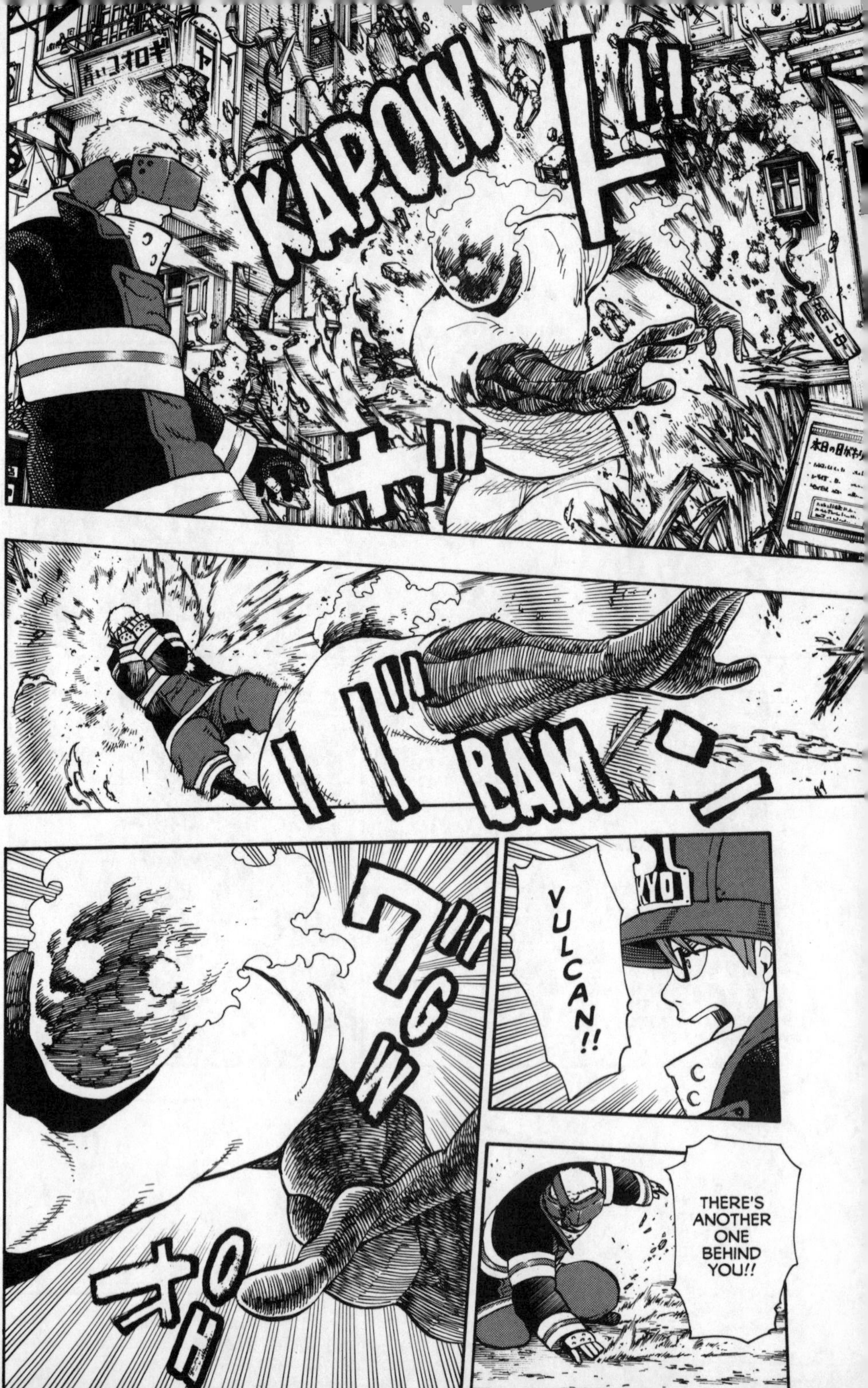
KAPOW
BAM
VULCAN!!
THERE'S ANOTHER ONE BEHIND YOU!!

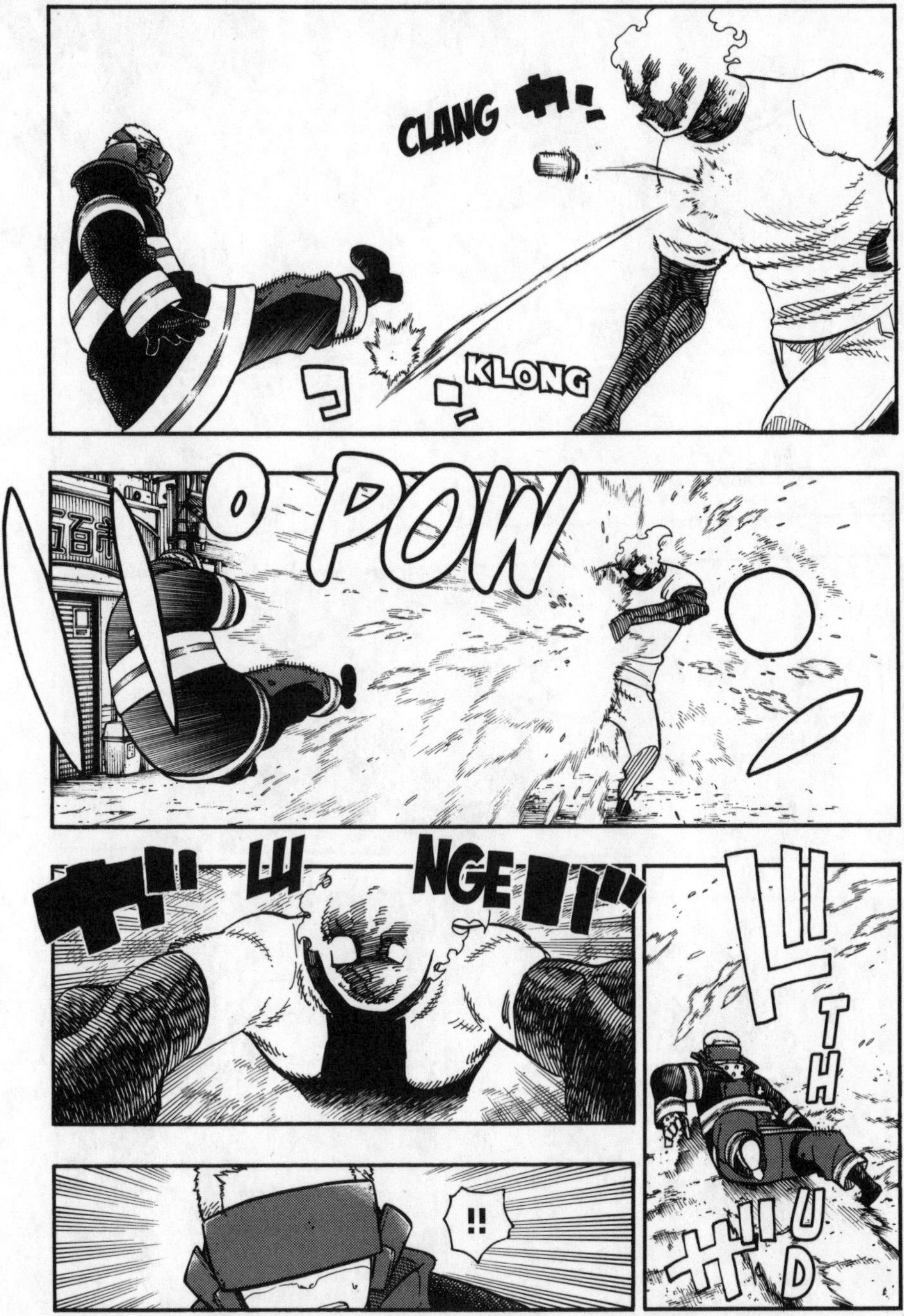
CLANG
KLONG
POW
THUD
NGE
!!

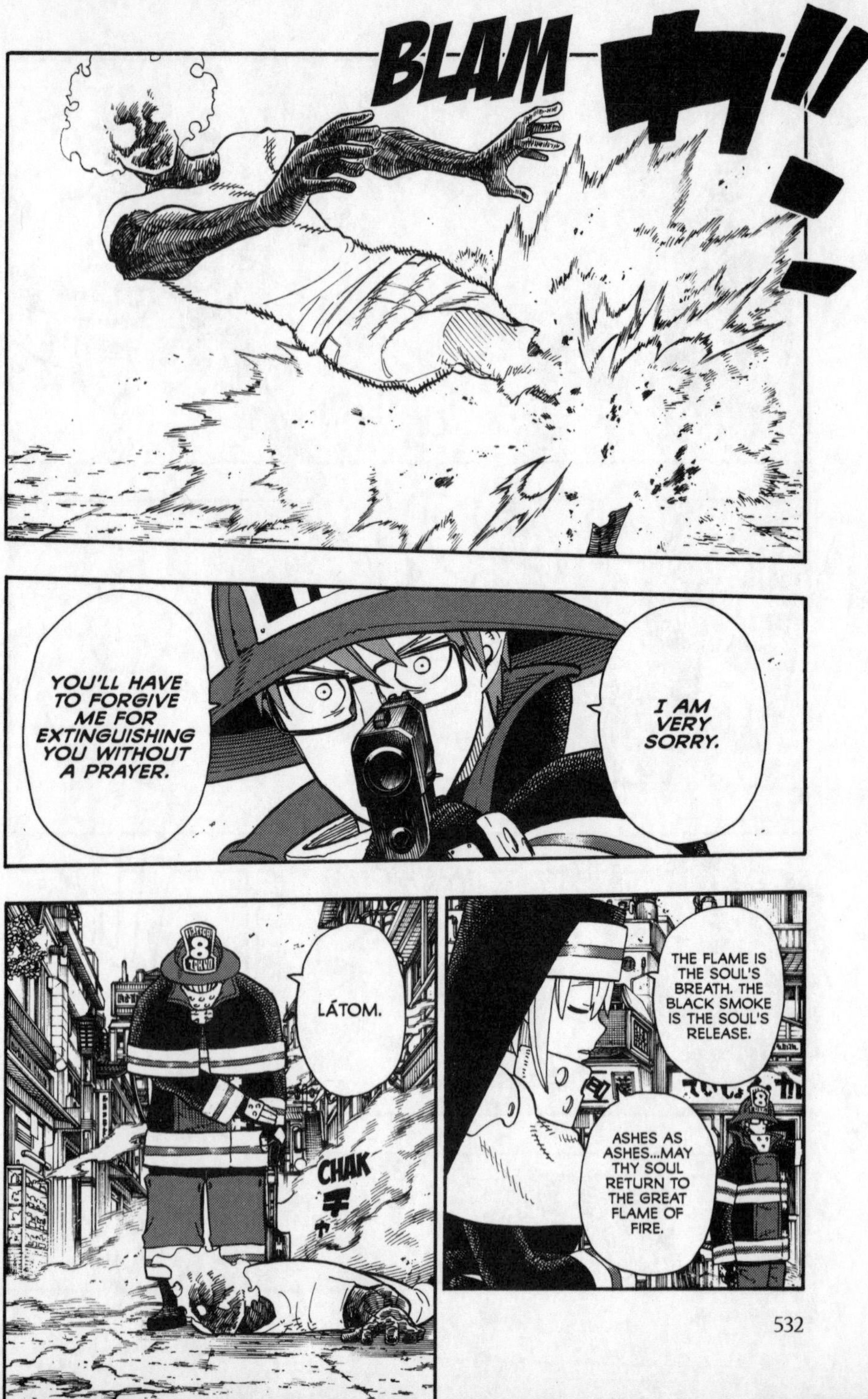
BLAM
I AM VERY SORRY.
YOU'LL HAVE TO FORGIVE ME FOR EXTINGUISHING YOU WITHOUT A PRAYER.
THE FLAME IS THE SOUL'S BREATH. THE BLACK SMOKE IS THE SOUL'S RELEASE.
ASHES AS ASHES...MAY THY SOUL RETURN TO THE GREAT FLAME OF FIRE.
LÁTOM.
CHAK

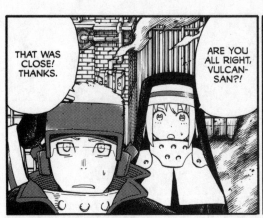

KA-KLUNK
ARE YOU ALL RIGHT, VULCAN-SAN?!
THAT WAS CLOSE! THANKS.
SORRY WE TOOK SO LONG. WE HAD TO PUT ANOTHER ONE TO REST FIRST.
KEEP FIGHTING THEM ON THE FRONT LINES! WE HAVE TO MAKE SURE THIS AREA IS CLEAR BEFORE THE REGULAR FIRE-FIGHTERS CAN PUT OUT THE FLAMES!
UNDERSTOOD.
CAN YOU HANDLE IT, VULCAN?
NO PROBLEM, SIR.
THERE WERE TWO MORE INFERNALS DOWN THIS STREET.
AAAAHHH... IF I'D KNOWN IT WAS GOING TO BE THIS BAD, I WOULDN'T HAVE COME...
THIS DISTRIBUTION OF INFERNALS IS SO UNNATURAL... I BET THEY'RE USING THE BUGS TO LURE US APART.
FIND THE ELECTRICITY-WIELDER! SHE SHOULD BE SOMEWHERE IN TOWN GIVING ORDERS!
!!

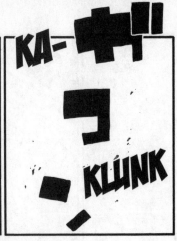

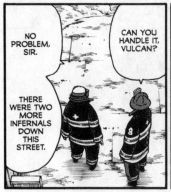

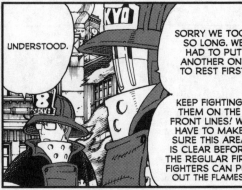

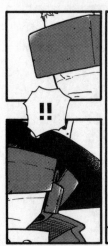

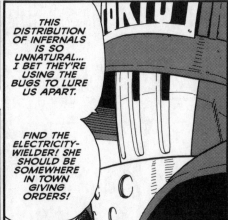

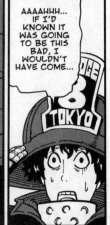

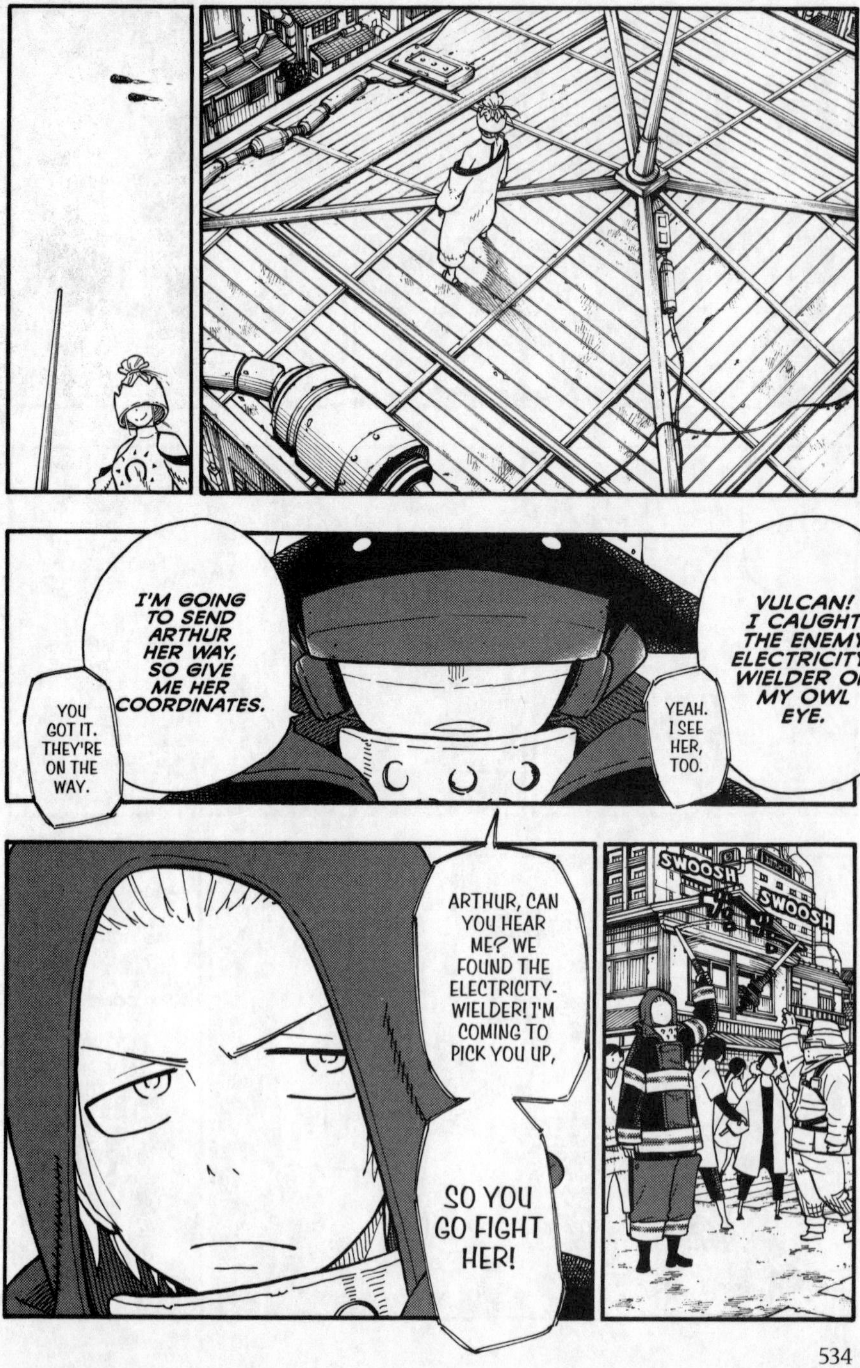
VULCAN! I CAUGHT THE ENEMY ELECTRICITY-WIELDER ON MY OWL EYE.
YEAH. I SEE HER, TOO.
I'M GOING TO SEND ARTHUR HER WAY, SO GIVE ME HER COORDINATES.
YOU GOT IT. THEY'RE ON THE WAY.
SWOOSH
SWOOSH
ARTHUR, CAN YOU HEAR ME? WE FOUND THE ELECTRICITY-WIELDER! I'M COMING TO PICK YOU UP,
SO YOU GO FIGHT HER!

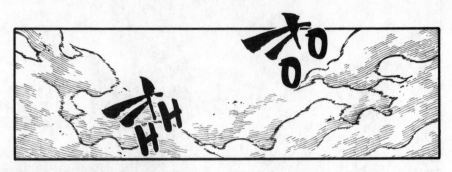

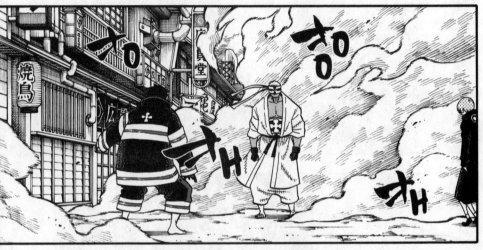

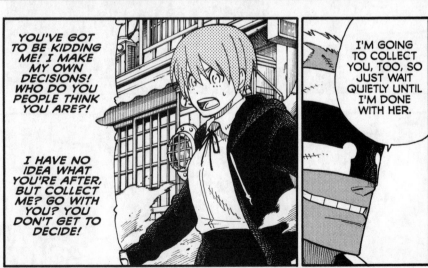

I'M GOING TO COLLECT YOU, TOO, SO JUST WAIT QUIETLY UNTIL I'M DONE WITH HER.
YOU'VE GOT TO BE KIDDING ME! I MAKE MY OWN DECISIONS! WHO DO YOU PEOPLE THINK YOU ARE?!
I HAVE NO IDEA WHAT YOU'RE AFTER, BUT COLLECT ME? GO WITH YOU? YOU DON'T GET TO DECIDE!

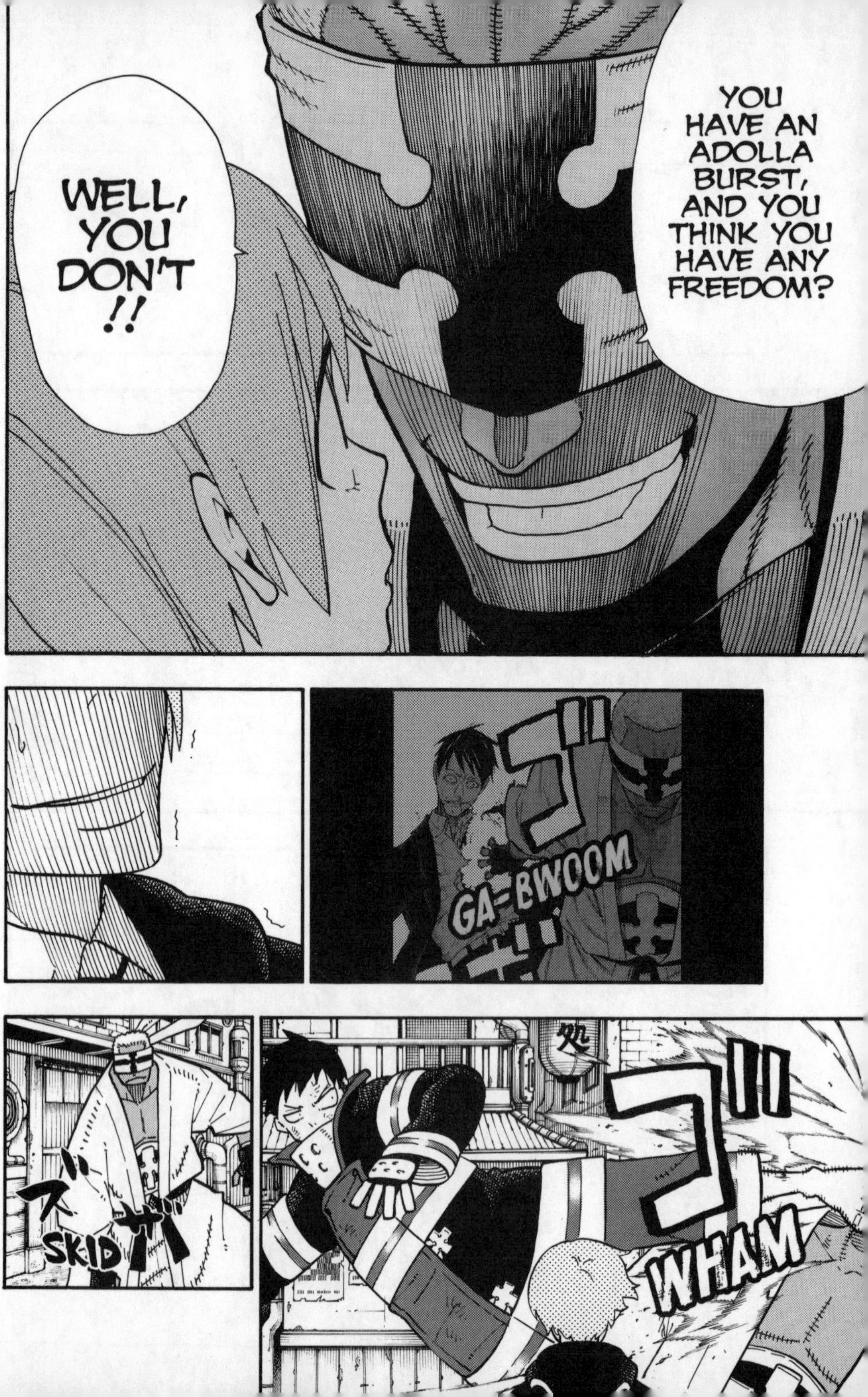
YOU HAVE AN ADOLLA BURST, AND YOU THINK YOU HAVE ANY FREEDOM?
WELL, YOU DON'T!!
GA-BWOOM
WHAM
SKID

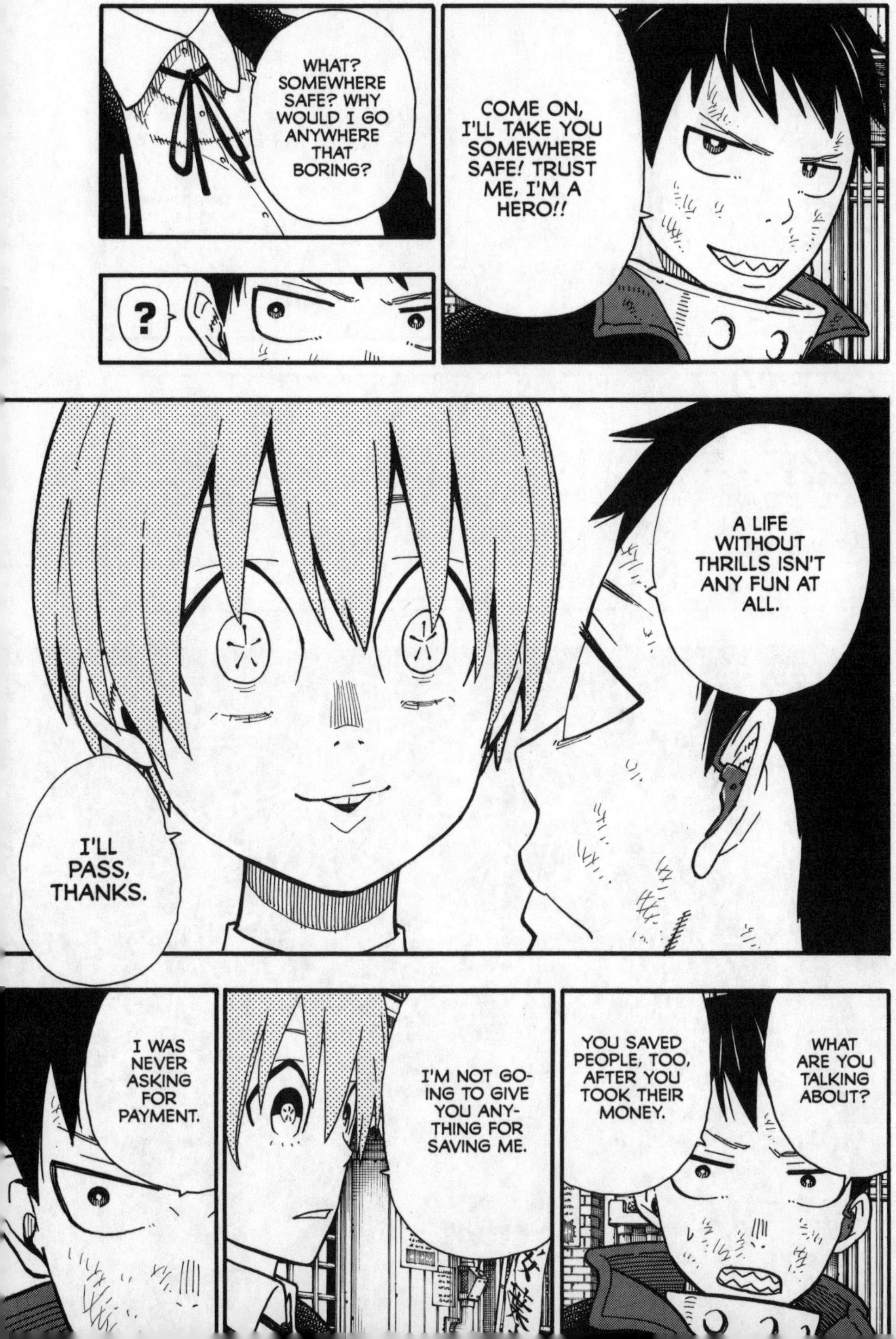
COME ON, I'LL TAKE YOU SOMEWHERE SAFE! TRUST ME, I'M A HERO!!
WHAT? SOMEWHERE SAFE? WHY WOULD I GO ANYWHERE THAT BORING?
?
A LIFE WITHOUT THRILLS ISN'T ANY FUN AT ALL.
I'LL PASS, THANKS.
WHAT ARE YOU TALKING ABOUT?
YOU SAVED PEOPLE, TOO, AFTER YOU TOOK THEIR MONEY.
I'M NOT GO-ING TO GIVE YOU ANY-THING FOR SAVING ME.
I WAS NEVER ASKING FOR PAYMENT.

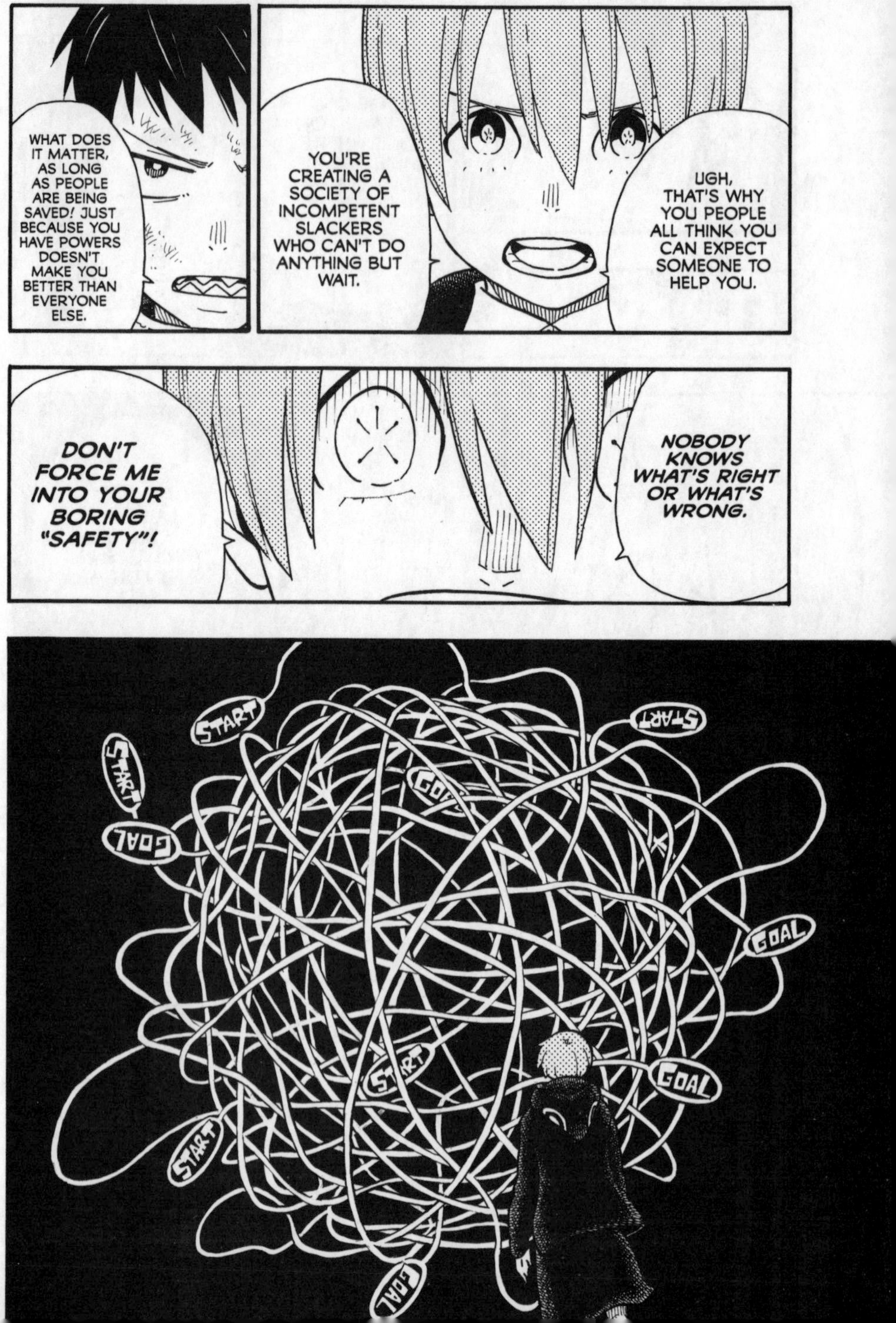
UGH, THAT'S WHY YOU PEOPLE ALL THINK YOU CAN EXPECT SOMEONE TO HELP YOU.
YOU'RE CREATING A SOCIETY OF INCOMPETENT SLACKERS WHO CAN'T DO ANYTHING BUT WAIT.
WHAT DOES IT MATTER, AS LONG AS PEOPLE ARE BEING SAVED! JUST BECAUSE YOU HAVE POWERS DOESN'T MAKE YOU BETTER THAN EVERYONE ELSE.
NOBODY KNOWS WHAT'S RIGHT OR WHAT'S WRONG.
DON'T FORCE ME INTO YOUR BORING "SAFETY"!
START
START
START
GOAL
GOAL
GOAL
START
START
GOAL

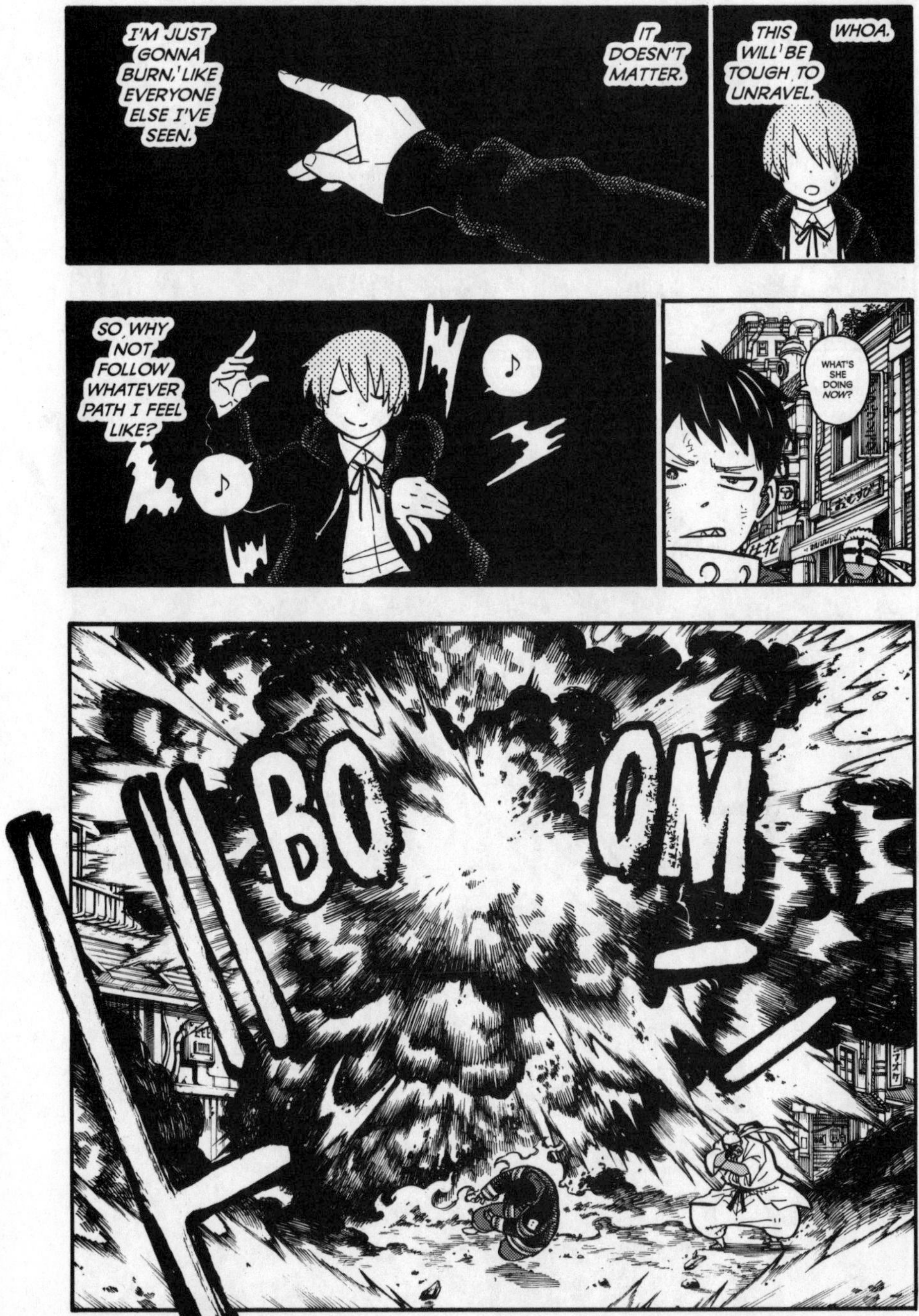
WHOA.
THIS WILL BE TOUGH TO UNRAVEL.
IT DOESN'T MATTER.
I'M JUST GONNA BURN, LIKE EVERYONE ELSE I'VE SEEN.
WHAT'S SHE DOING NOW?
SO WHY NOT FOLLOW WHATEVER PATH I FEEL LIKE?
♪
♪
BOOM

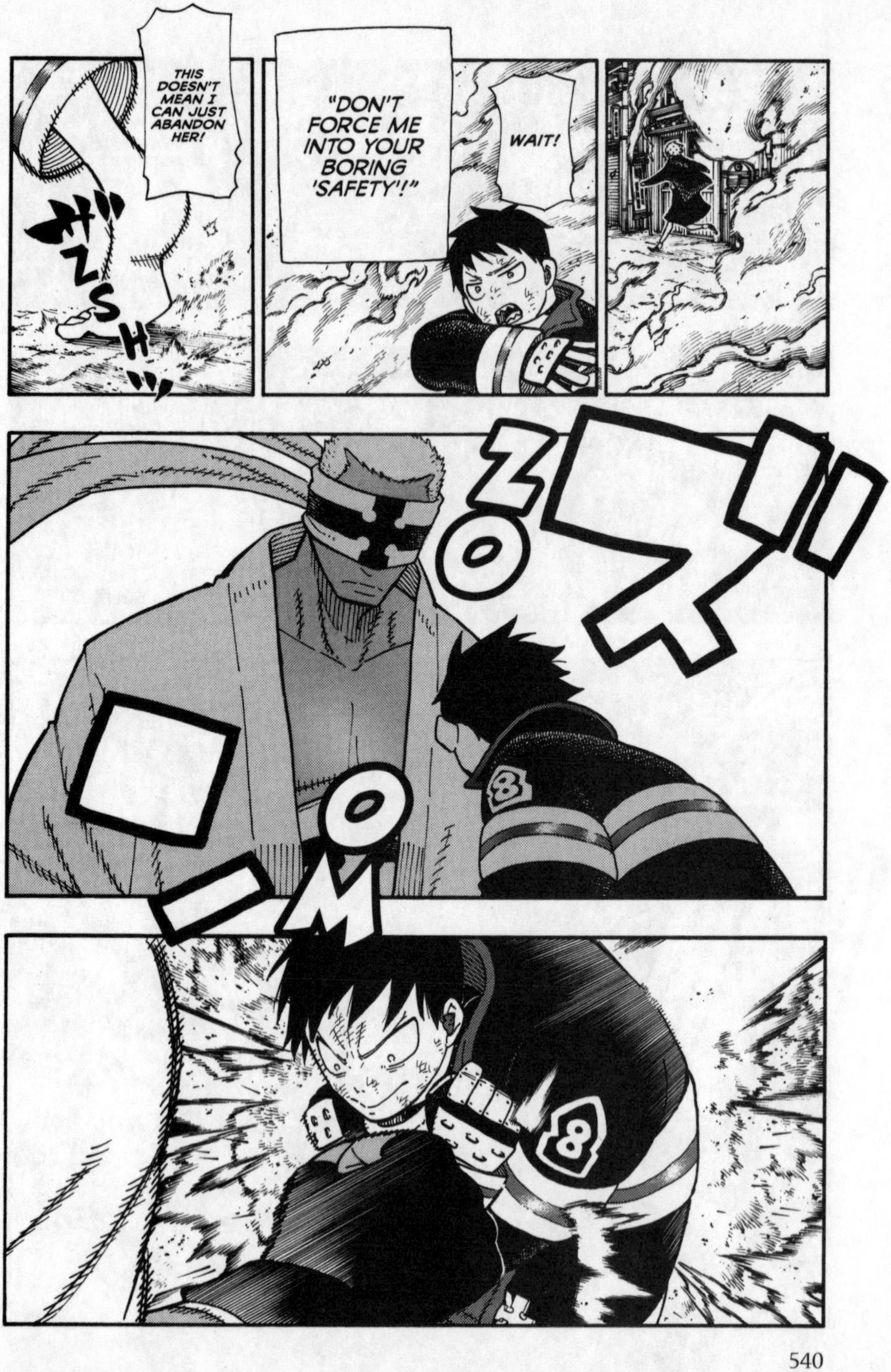

WAIT!
"DON'T FORCE ME INTO YOUR BORING 'SAFETY'!"
THIS DOESN'T MEAN I CAN JUST ABANDON HER!
ZSH
ZOOM

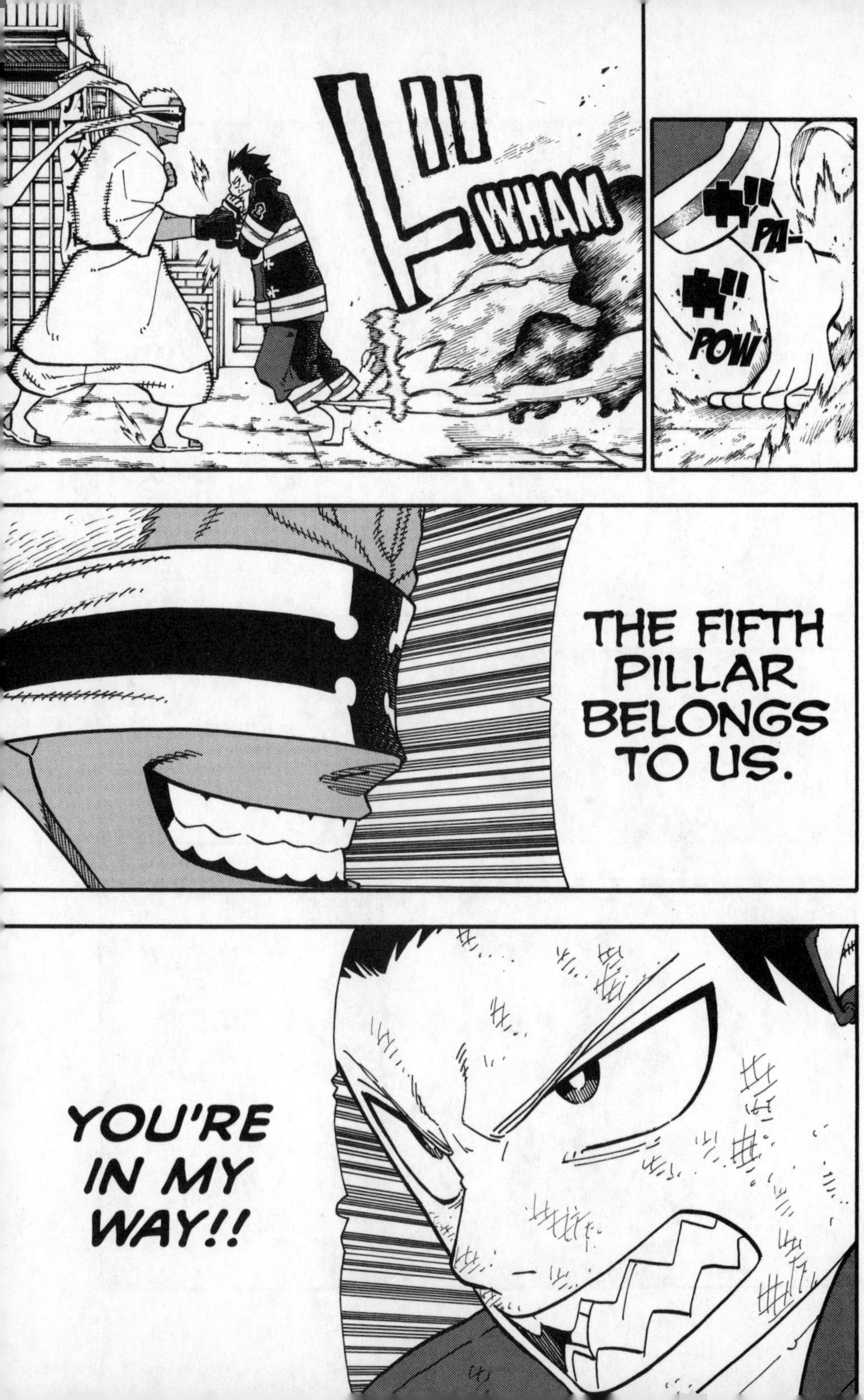
PA-
POW
WHAM
THE FIFTH PILLAR BELONGS TO US.
YOU'RE IN MY WAY!!

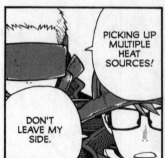

THEY'RE CLOSE... SOMEWHERE IN THIS AREA.
WATCH YOURSELF.
TEP TEP
TEP TEP
PICKING UP MULTIPLE HEAT SOURCES!
DON'T LEAVE MY SIDE.
TWO INFERNALS AT ONE O'CLOCK...
ONE AT NINE.
!
NO...THOSE AREN'T THE ONLY ONES.
I CAN SEE THAT...
HOW ARE WE SUPPOSED TO DEAL WITH ALL OF THESE INFERNALS IF WE CAN'T EXTINGUISH THEM?

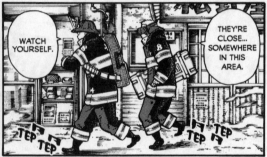

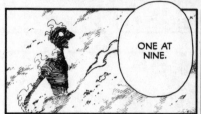

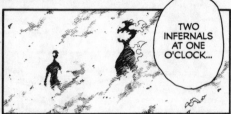

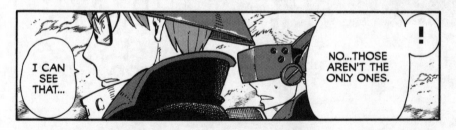

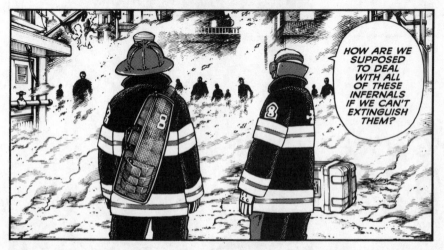

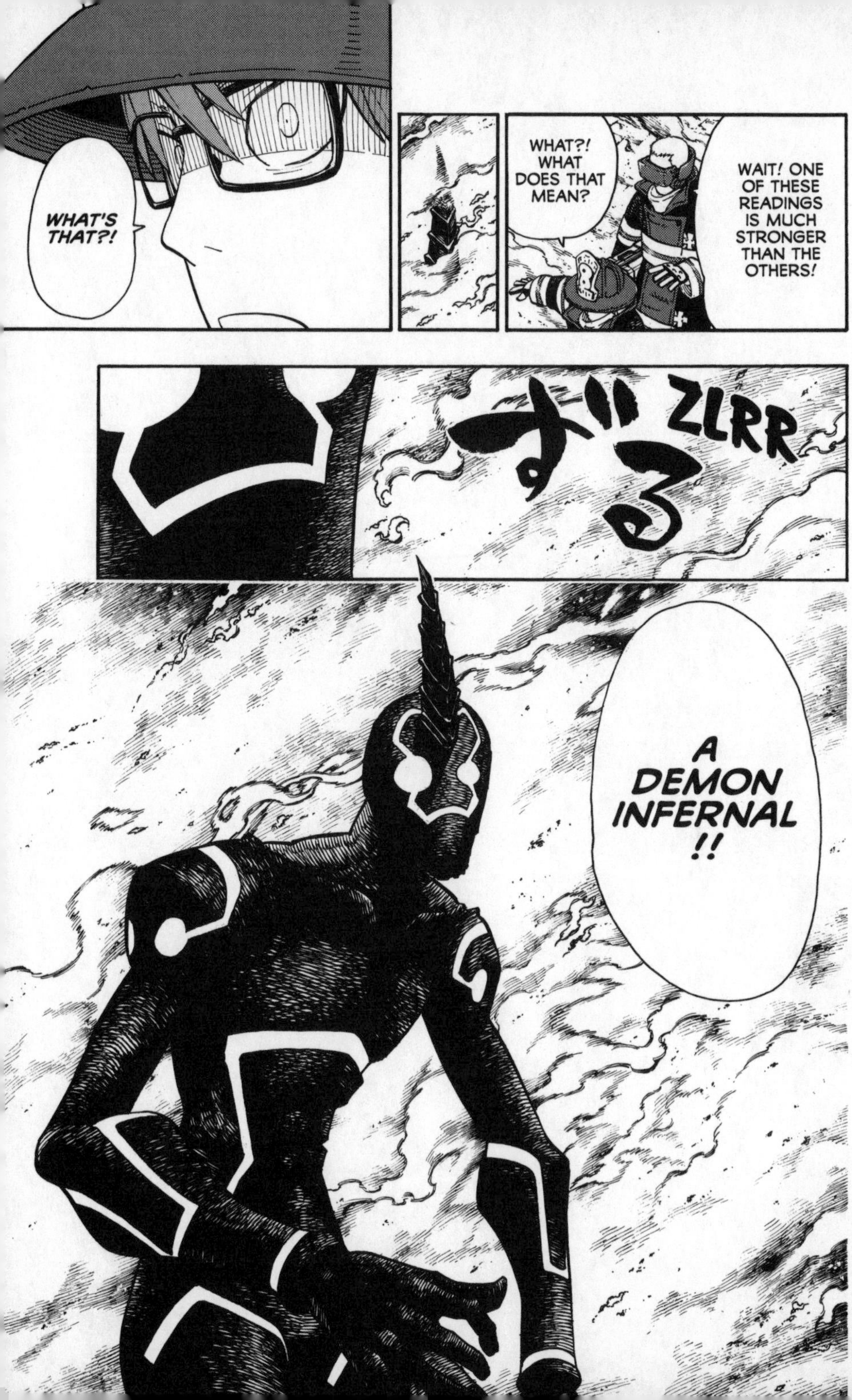
WAIT! ONE OF THESE READINGS IS MUCH STRONGER THAN THE OTHERS!
WHAT?! WHAT DOES THAT MEAN?
WHAT'S THAT?!
ZLRR
A DEMON INFERNAL!!

FIRE FORCE

人体発火

Label: Spontaneous Human Combustion

CHAPTER CIV: BONDS OF THE FIREGROUND

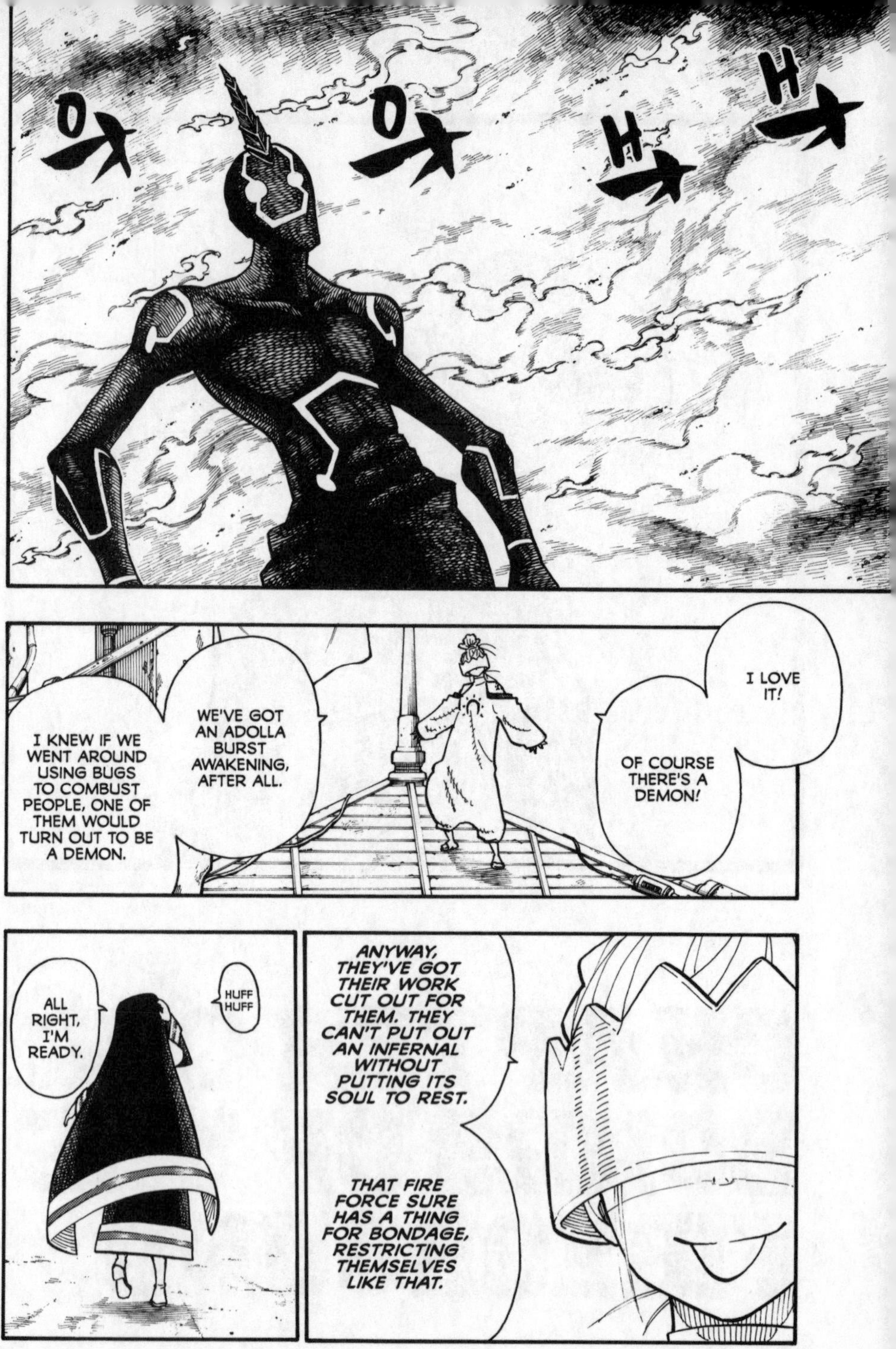
I LOVE IT!
OF COURSE THERE'S A DEMON!
WE'VE GOT AN ADOLLA BURST AWAKENING, AFTER ALL.
I KNEW IF WE WENT AROUND USING BUGS TO COMBUST PEOPLE, ONE OF THEM WOULD TURN OUT TO BE A DEMON.
ANYWAY, THEY'VE GOT THEIR WORK CUT OUT FOR THEM. THEY CAN'T PUT OUT AN INFERNAL WITHOUT PUTTING ITS SOUL TO REST.
THAT FIRE FORCE SURE HAS A THING FOR BONDAGE, RESTRICTING THEMSELVES LIKE THAT.
HUFF HUFF
ALL RIGHT, I'M READY.

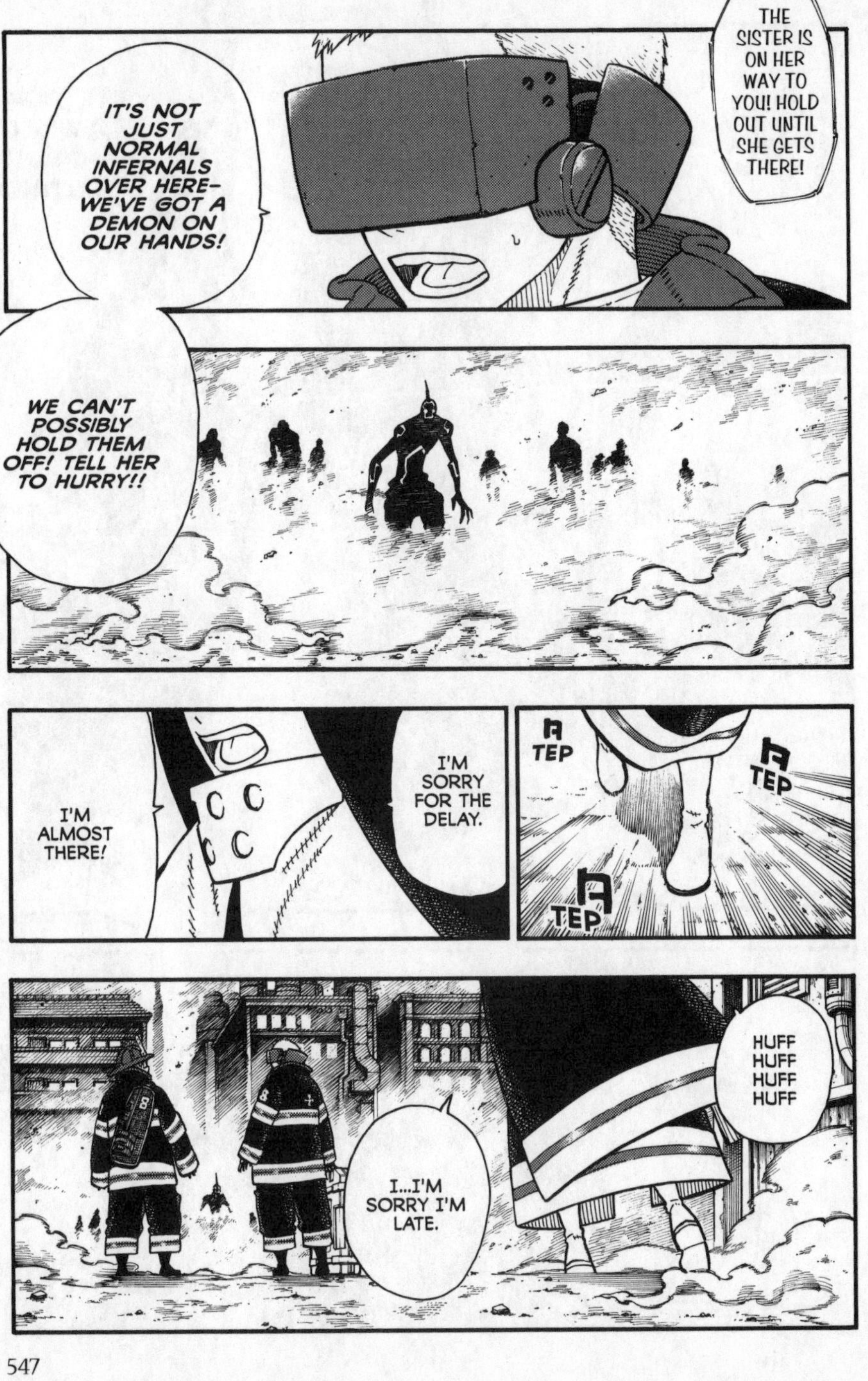
THE SISTER IS ON HER WAY TO YOU! HOLD OUT UNTIL SHE GETS THERE!
IT'S NOT JUST NORMAL INFERNALS OVER HERE—WE'VE GOT A DEMON ON OUR HANDS!
WE CAN'T POSSIBLY HOLD THEM OFF! TELL HER TO HURRY!!
TEP
TEP
TEP
I'M SORRY FOR THE DELAY.
I'M ALMOST THERE!
HUFF HUFF HUFF HUFF
I...I'M SORRY I'M LATE.

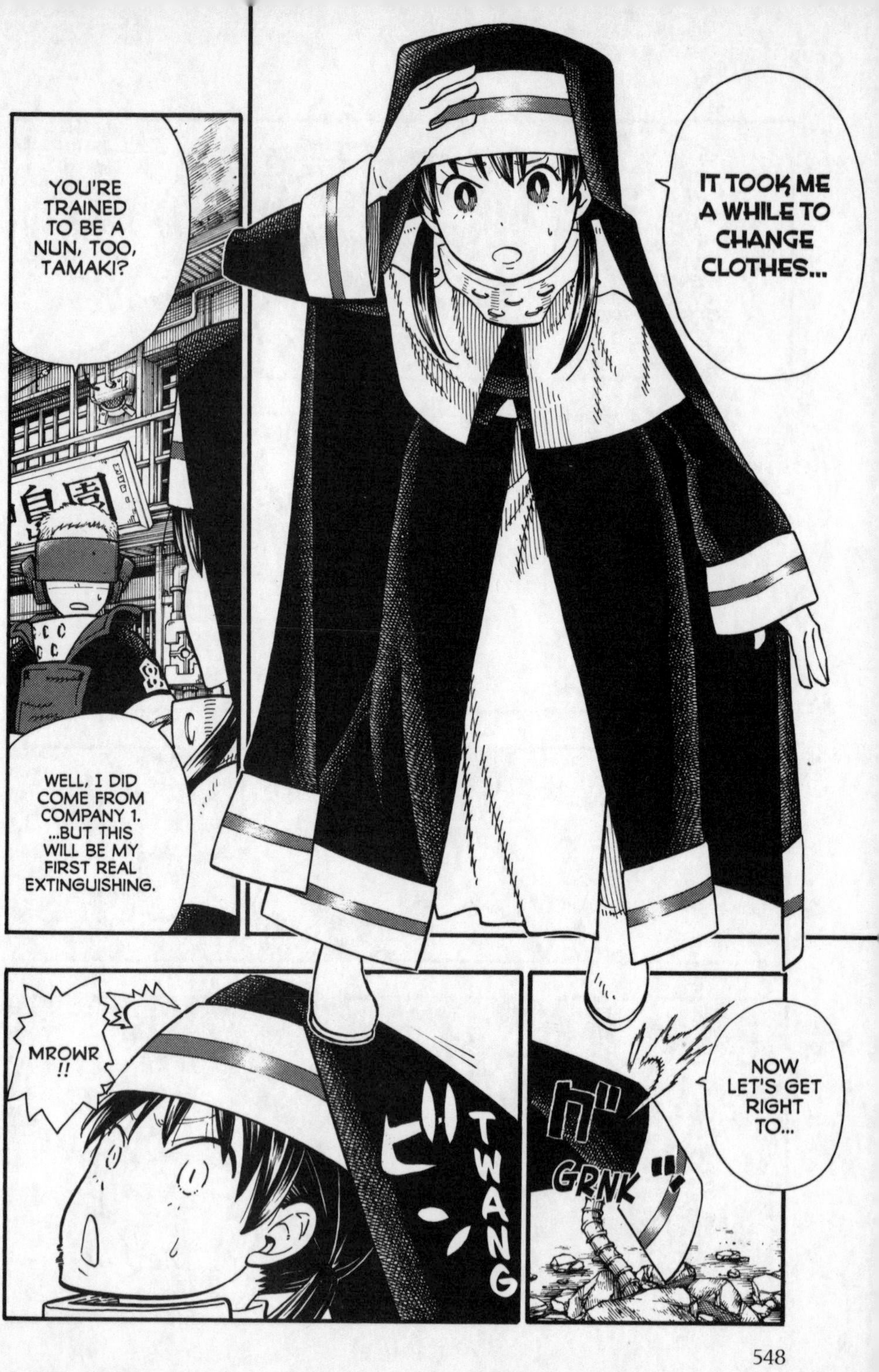
IT TOOK ME A WHILE TO CHANGE CLOTHES...
YOU'RE TRAINED TO BE A NUN, TOO, TAMAKI?
WELL, I DID COME FROM COMPANY 1. ...BUT THIS WILL BE MY FIRST REAL EXTINGUISHING.
NOW LET'S GET RIGHT TO...
ガ
GRNK
ビ
TWANG
MROWR !!

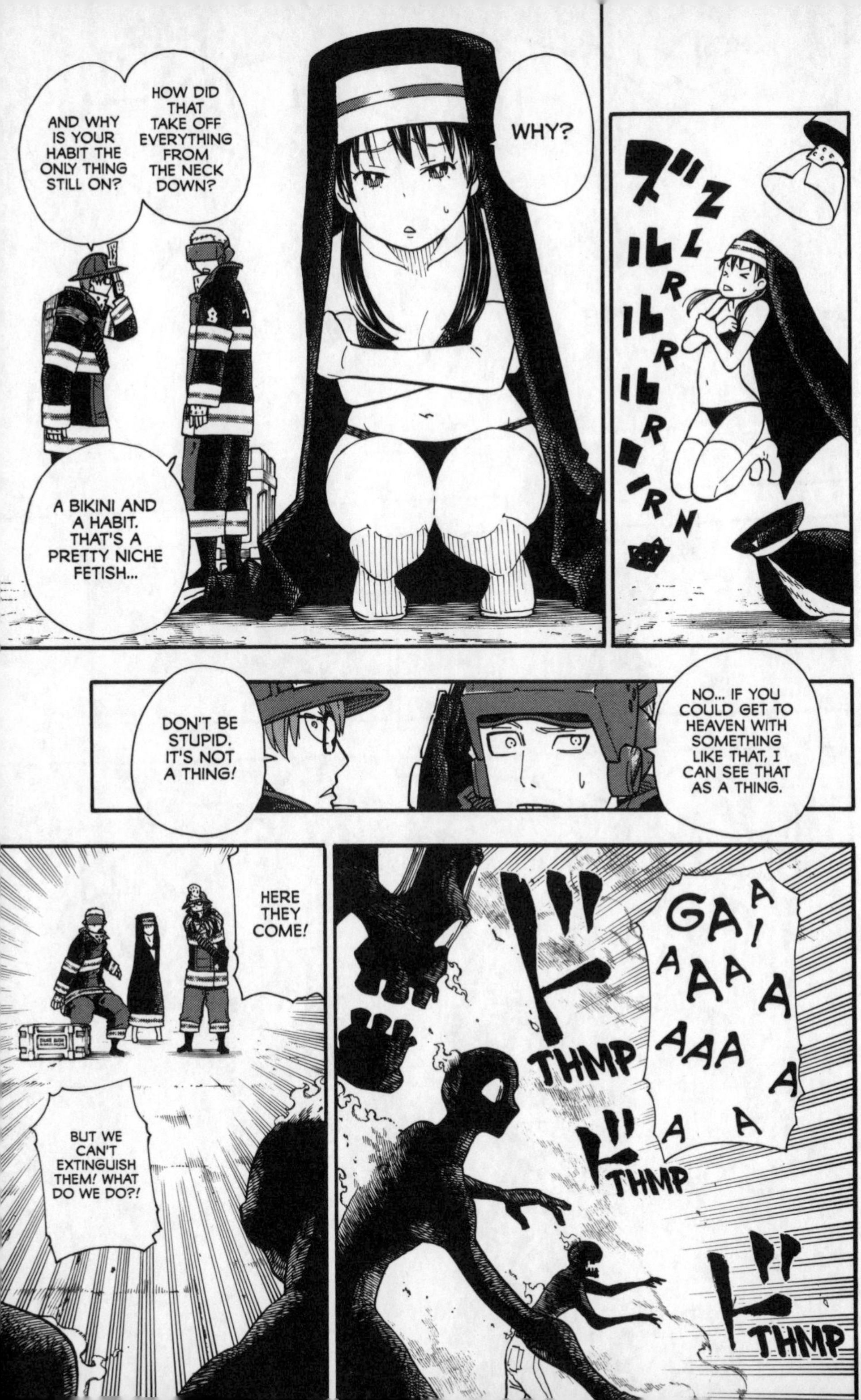
ズルルルー
ZLRRRRN
WHY?
HOW DID THAT TAKE OFF EVERYTHING FROM THE NECK DOWN?
AND WHY IS YOUR HABIT THE ONLY THING STILL ON?
A BIKINI AND A HABIT. THAT'S A PRETTY NICHE FETISH...
NO... IF YOU COULD GET TO HEAVEN WITH SOMETHING LIKE THAT, I CAN SEE THAT AS A THING.
DON'T BE STUPID. IT'S NOT A THING!
GAAAAAAAAAAAA
THMP
THMP
THMP
HERE THEY COME!
BUT WE CAN'T EXTINGUISH THEM! WHAT DO WE DO?!

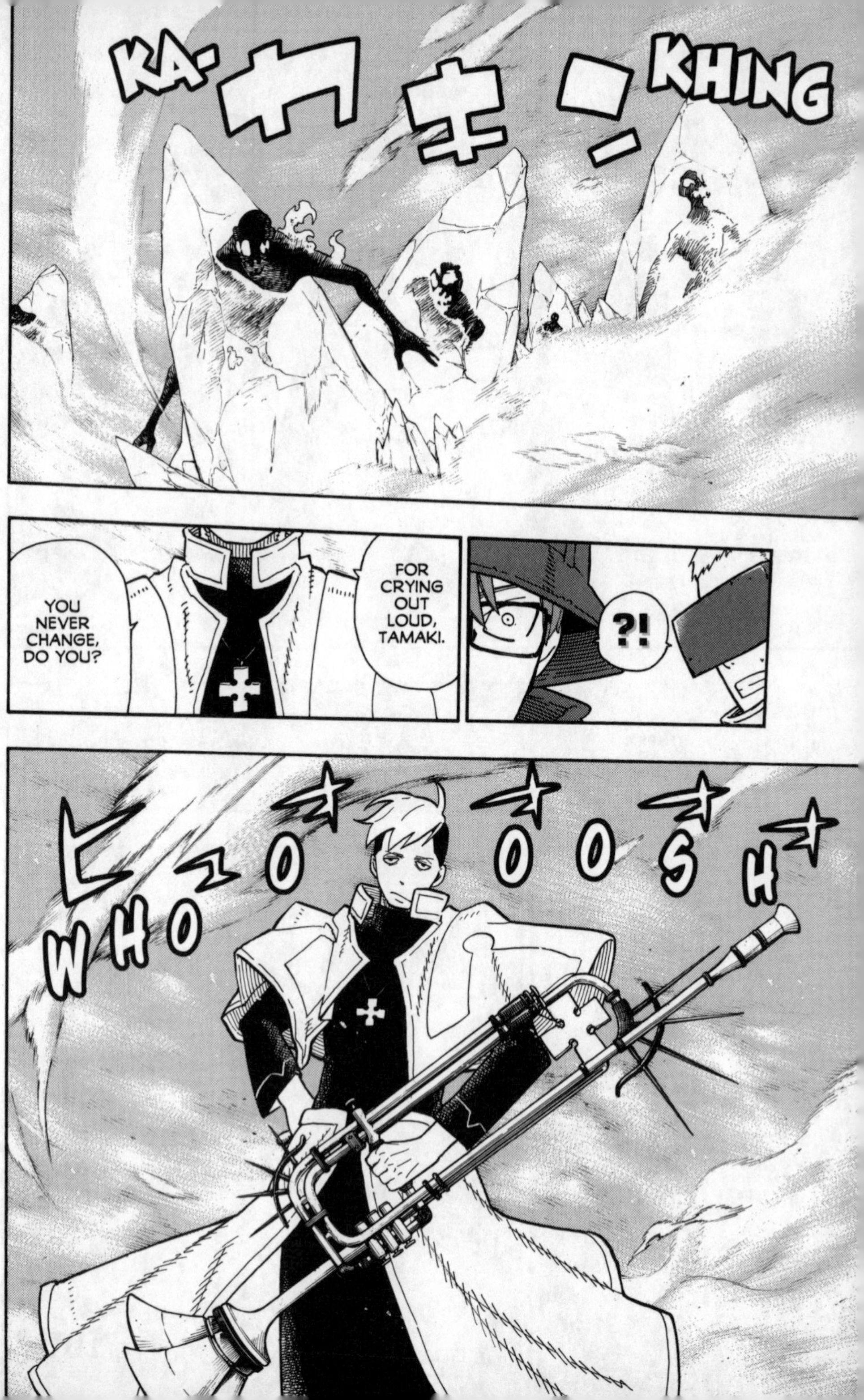

KA-KHING
?!
FOR CRYING OUT LOUD, TAMAKI.
YOU NEVER CHANGE, DO YOU?
WHOOOOOSH

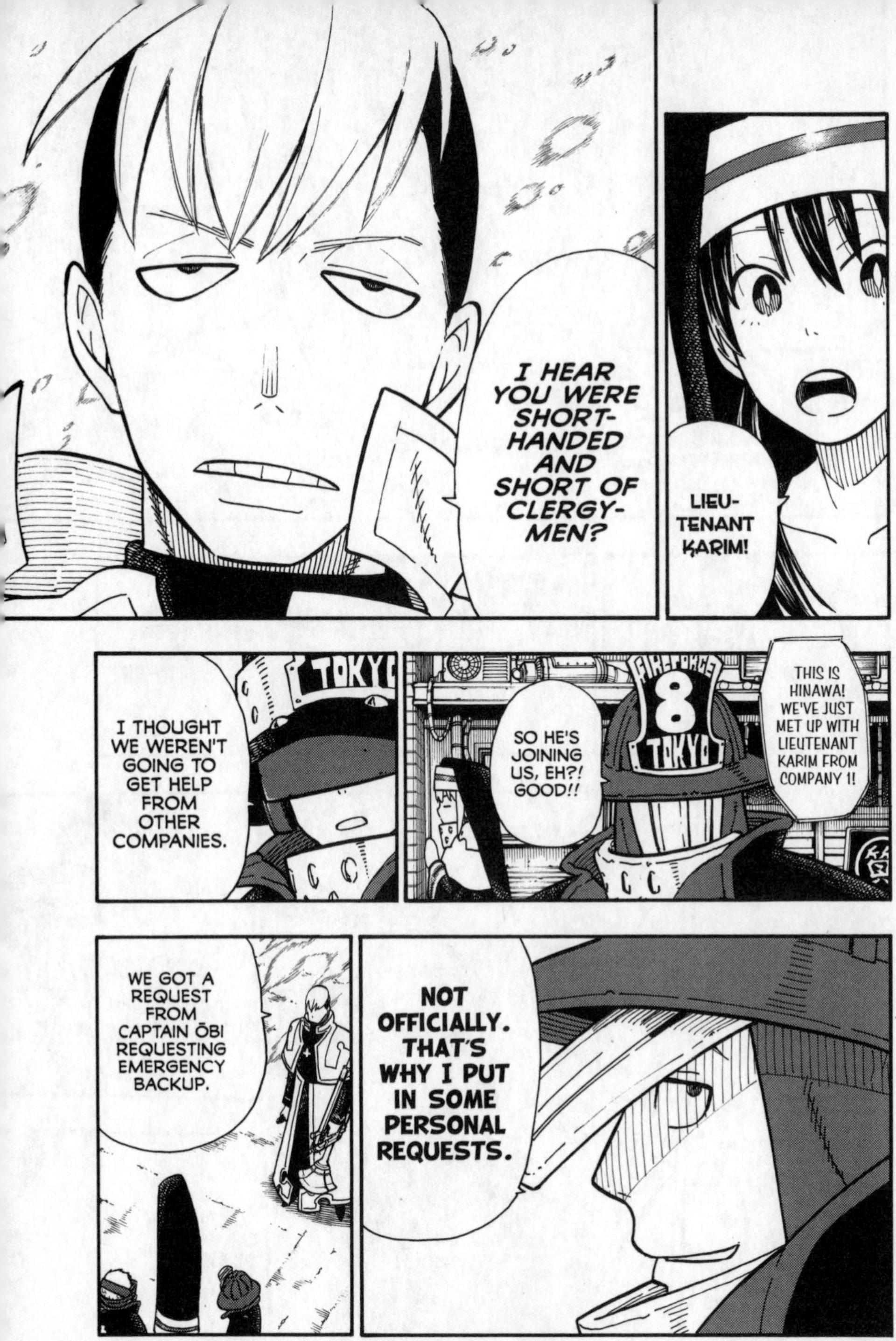
LIEU-TENANT KARIM!
I HEAR YOU WERE SHORT-HANDED AND SHORT OF CLERGY-MEN?
THIS IS HINAWA! WE'VE JUST MET UP WITH LIEUTENANT KARIM FROM COMPANY 1!
SO HE'S JOINING US, EH?! GOOD!!
I THOUGHT WE WEREN'T GOING TO GET HELP FROM OTHER COMPANIES.
NOT OFFICIALLY. THAT'S WHY I PUT IN SOME PERSONAL REQUESTS.
WE GOT A REQUEST FROM CAPTAIN ŌBI REQUESTING EMERGENCY BACKUP.

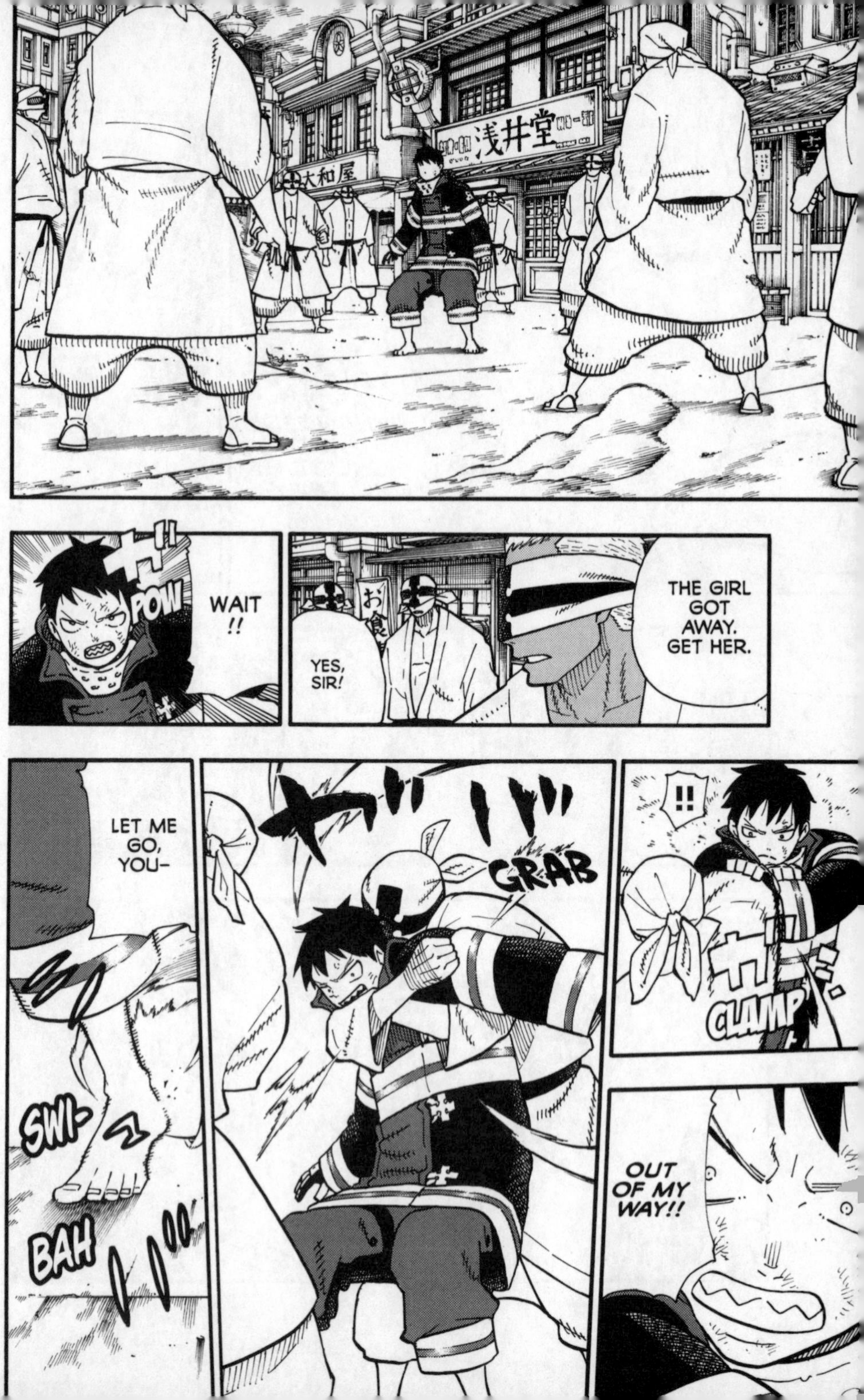

浅井堂
大和屋
THE GIRL GOT AWAY. GET HER.
YES, SIR!
お食
WAIT !!
POW
!!
CLAMP
OUT OF MY WAY!!
GRAB
LET ME GO, YOU–
SWI-
BAH

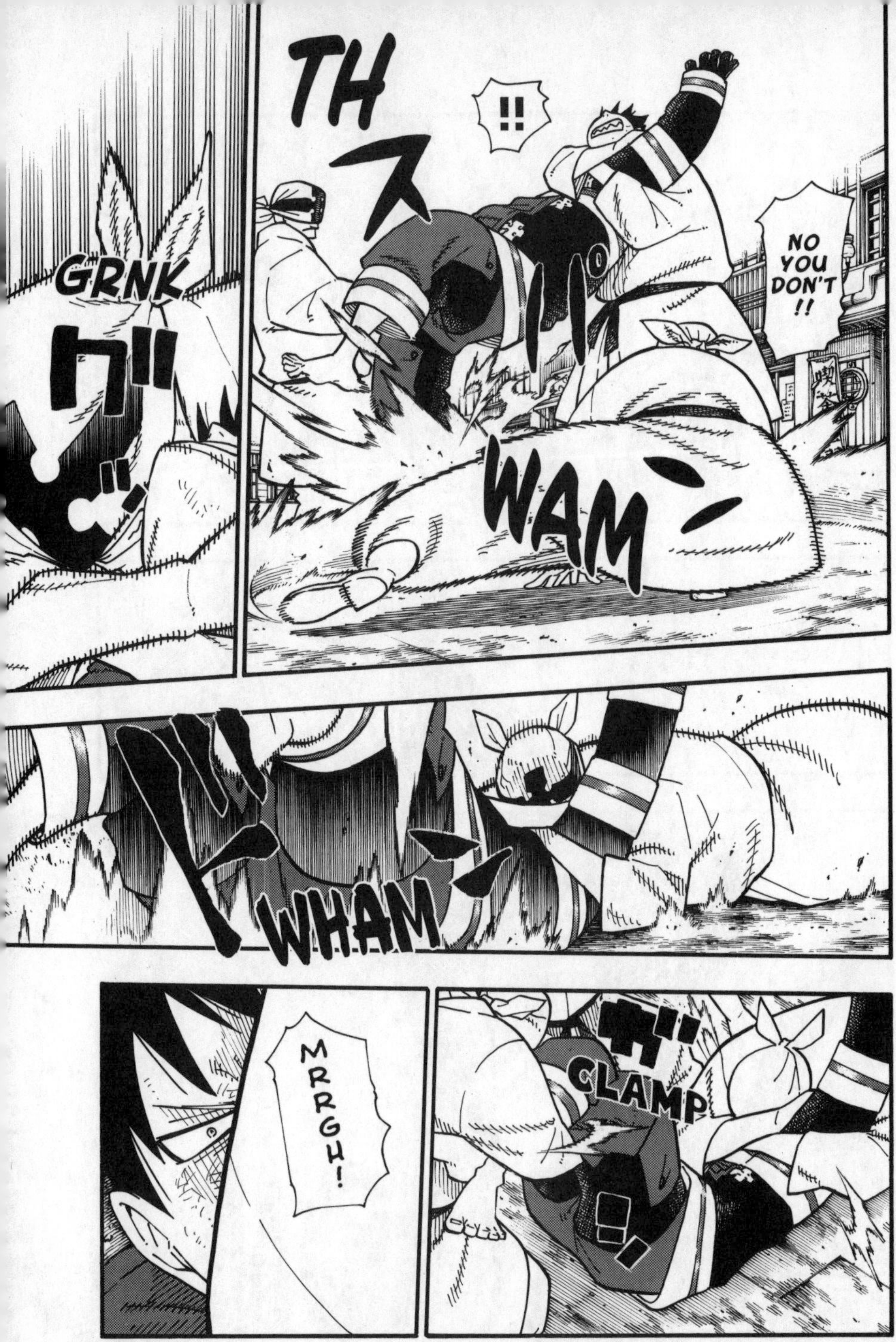
TH
ス
!!
NO YOU DON'T !!
WAM
GRNK
WHAM
CLAMP
MRRGH!

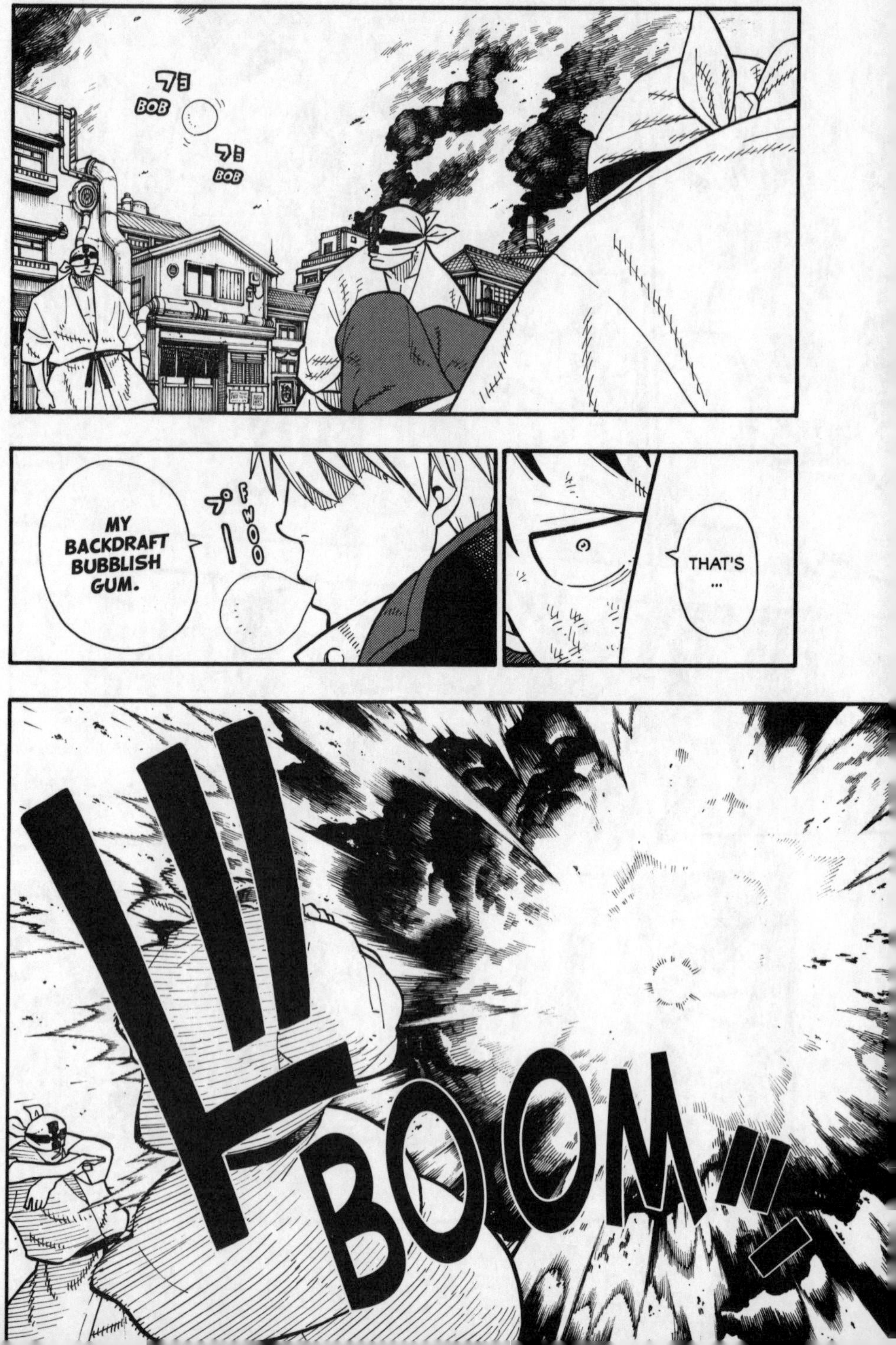
フヨ
BOB
フヨ
BOB
THAT'S ...
MY BACKDRAFT BUBBLISH GUM.
プー
FWOO
BOOM!!

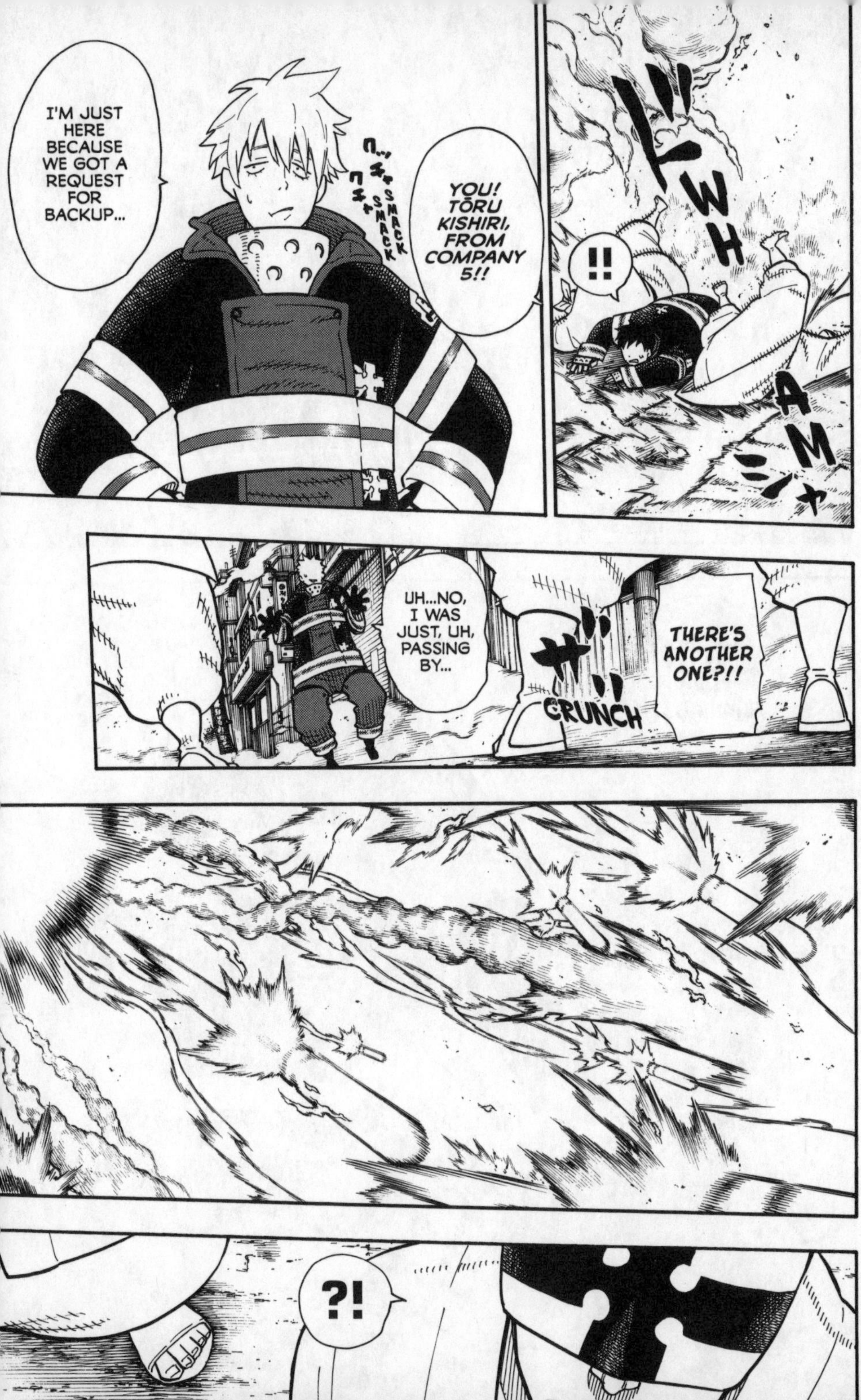
WHAM
!!
YOU! TŌRU KISHIRI, FROM COMPANY 5!!
SMACK SMACK
I'M JUST HERE BECAUSE WE GOT A REQUEST FOR BACKUP...
THERE'S ANOTHER ONE?!!
CRUNCH
UH...NO, I WAS JUST, UH, PASSING BY...
?!

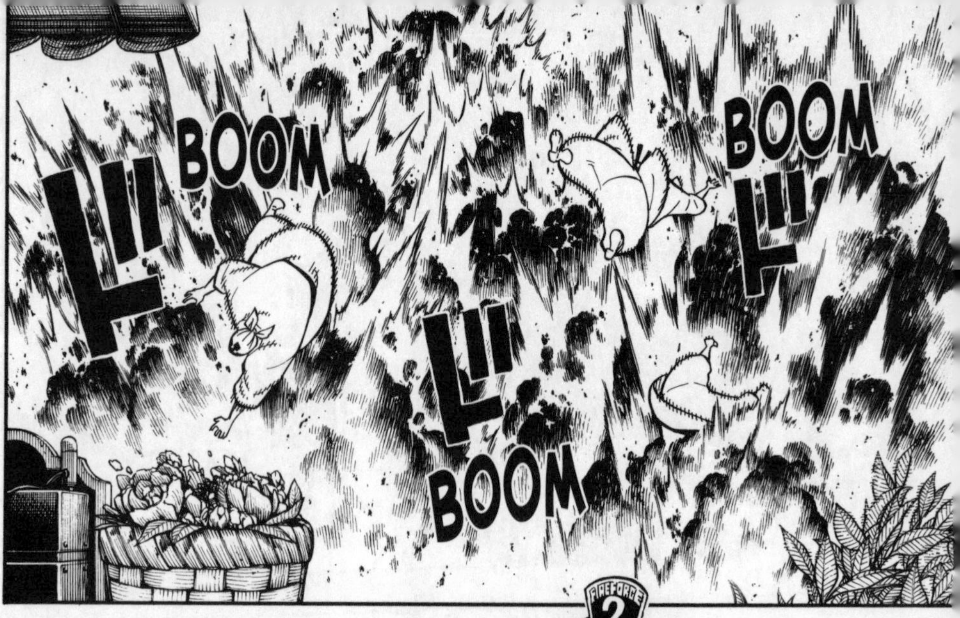
BOOM
BOOM
BOOM
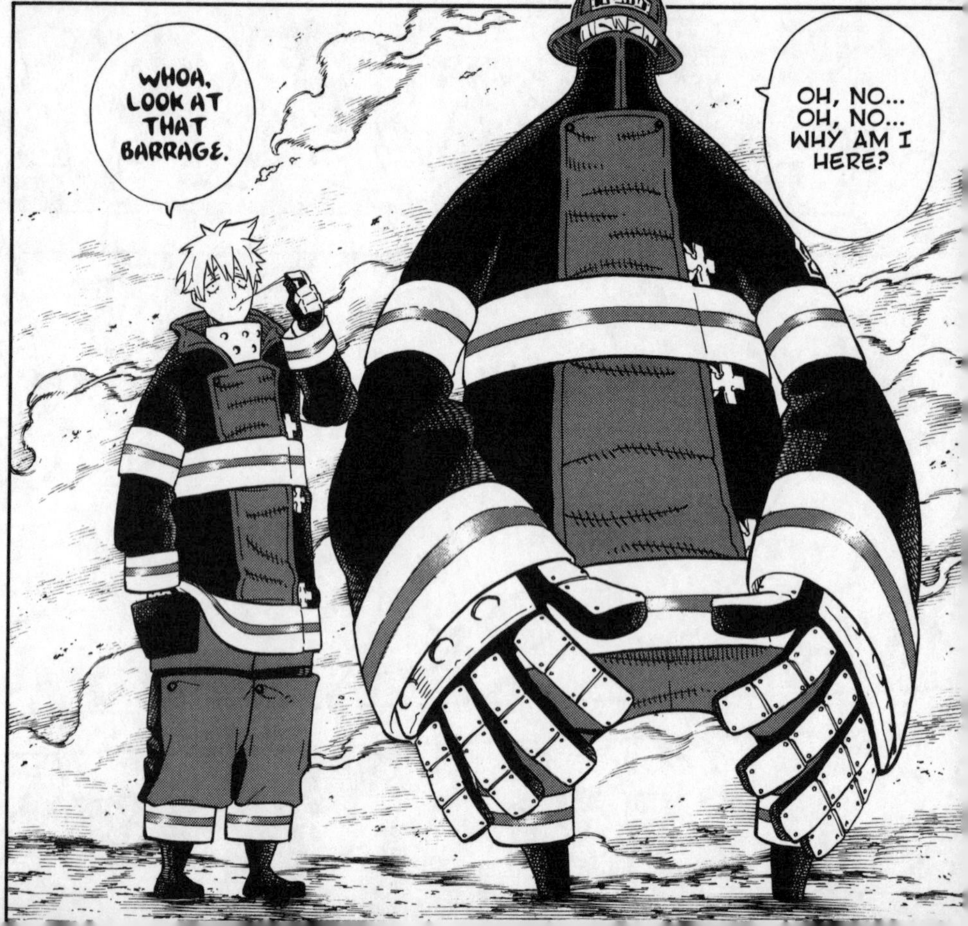
OH, NO... OH, NO... WHY AM I HERE?
WHOA, LOOK AT THAT BARRAGE.
FIREFORCE 2 TOKYO

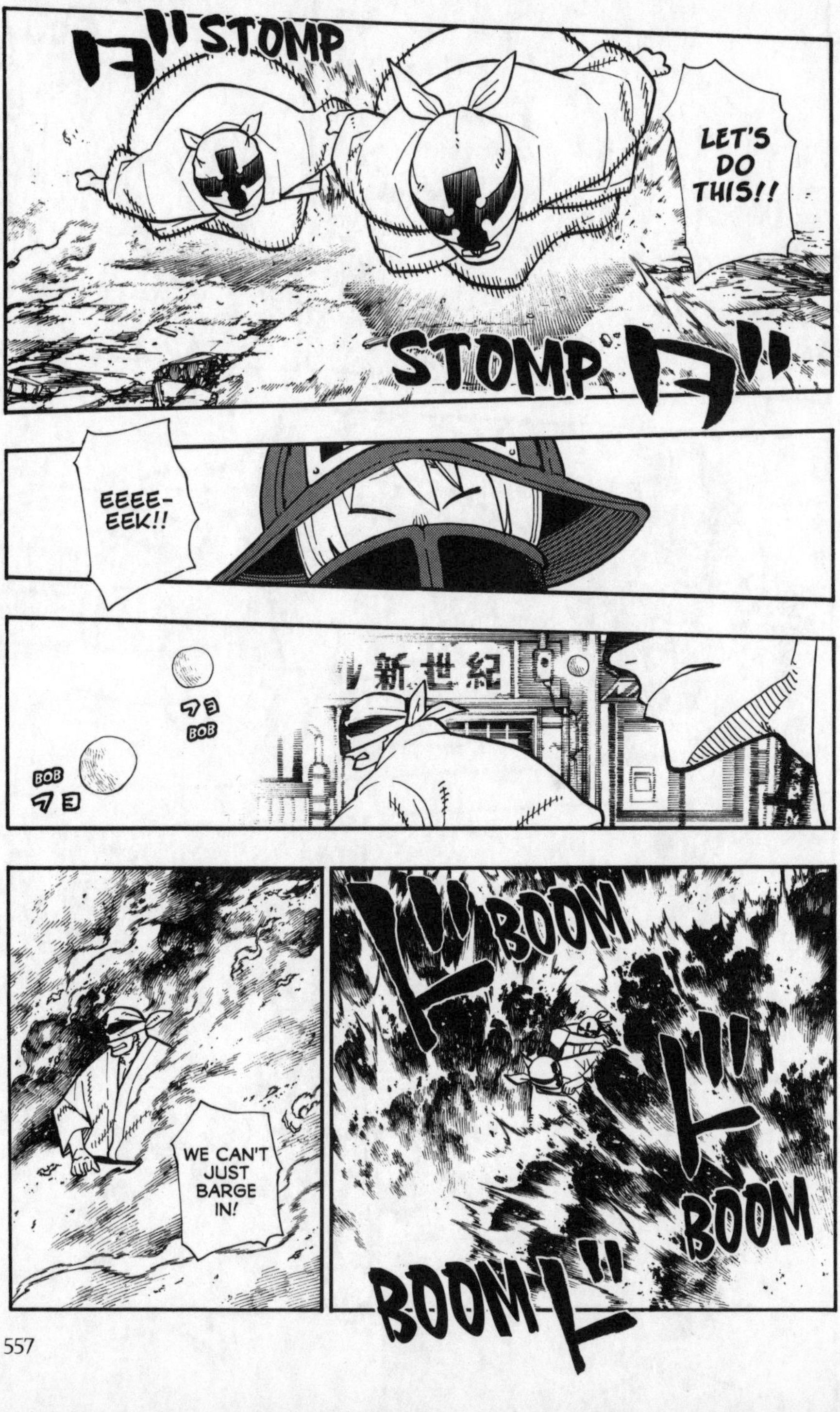
LET'S DO THIS!!
STOMP
STOMP
EEEE-EEK!!
新世紀
フヨ BOB
BOB フヨ
BOOM
BOOM
BOOM
WE CAN'T JUST BARGE IN!

AAAA GW

AAAAAAHH!!

ド THMP

ド THMP

ド THMP

ド THMP

?!

FWAM

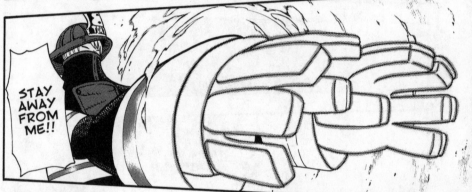

STAY AWAY FROM ME!!

TOKYO

NICE WORK, JUGGERNAUT!! I'LL MAKE SURE THEY NEVER GET ANYWHERE NEAR YOU, SO YOU JUST KEEP BACKING AWAY AND FIRE, FIRE, FIRE!

YOU BETTER!!

FW OOM

YES, SIR!

WE NEED SOME LONG-RANGE BACKUP, TOO!

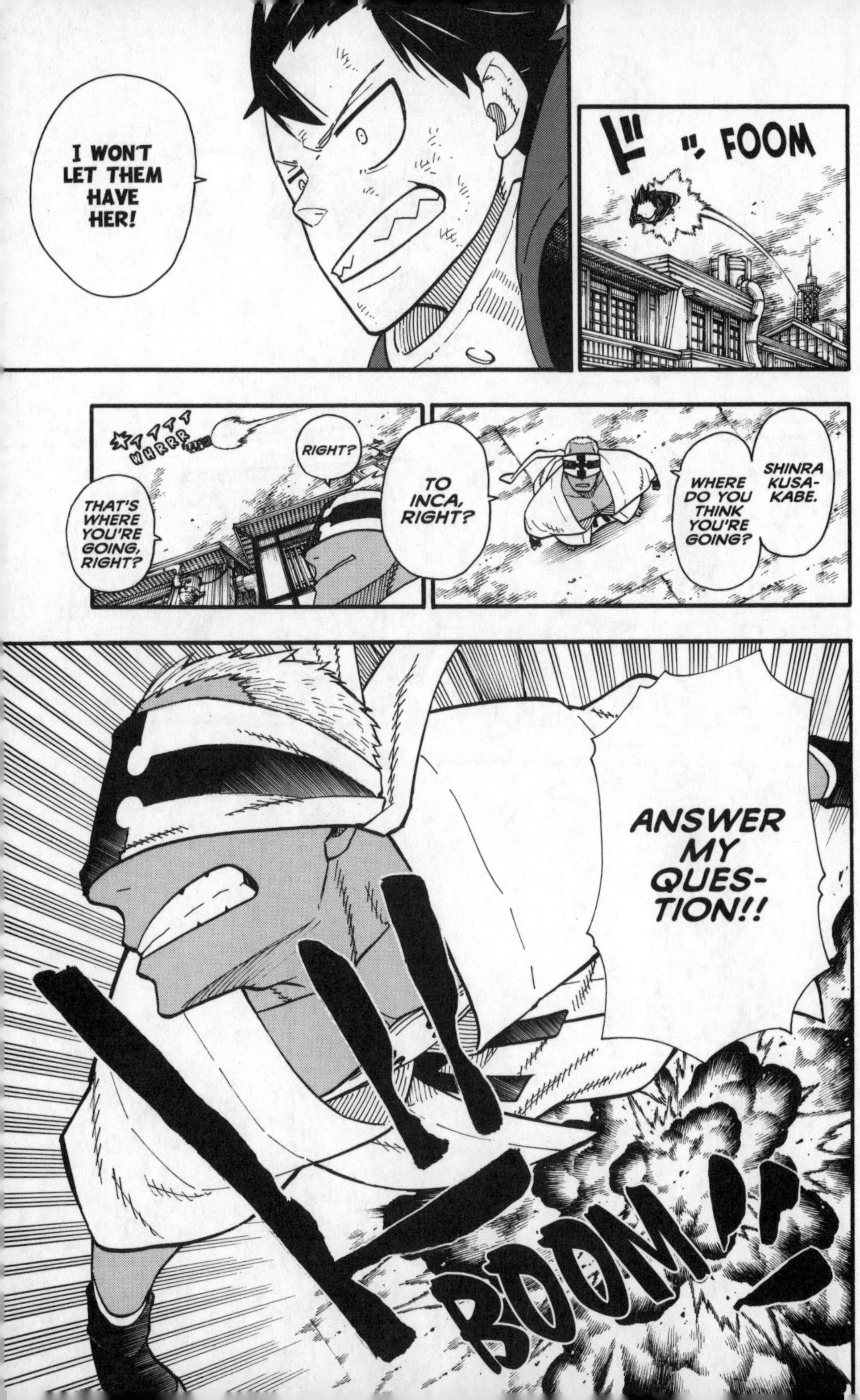
FOOM
I WON'T LET THEM HAVE HER!
SHINRA KUSA-KABE.
WHERE DO YOU THINK YOU'RE GOING?
TO INCA, RIGHT?
RIGHT?
WHRRR
THAT'S WHERE YOU'RE GOING, RIGHT?
ANSWER MY QUES-TION!!
BOOM!!

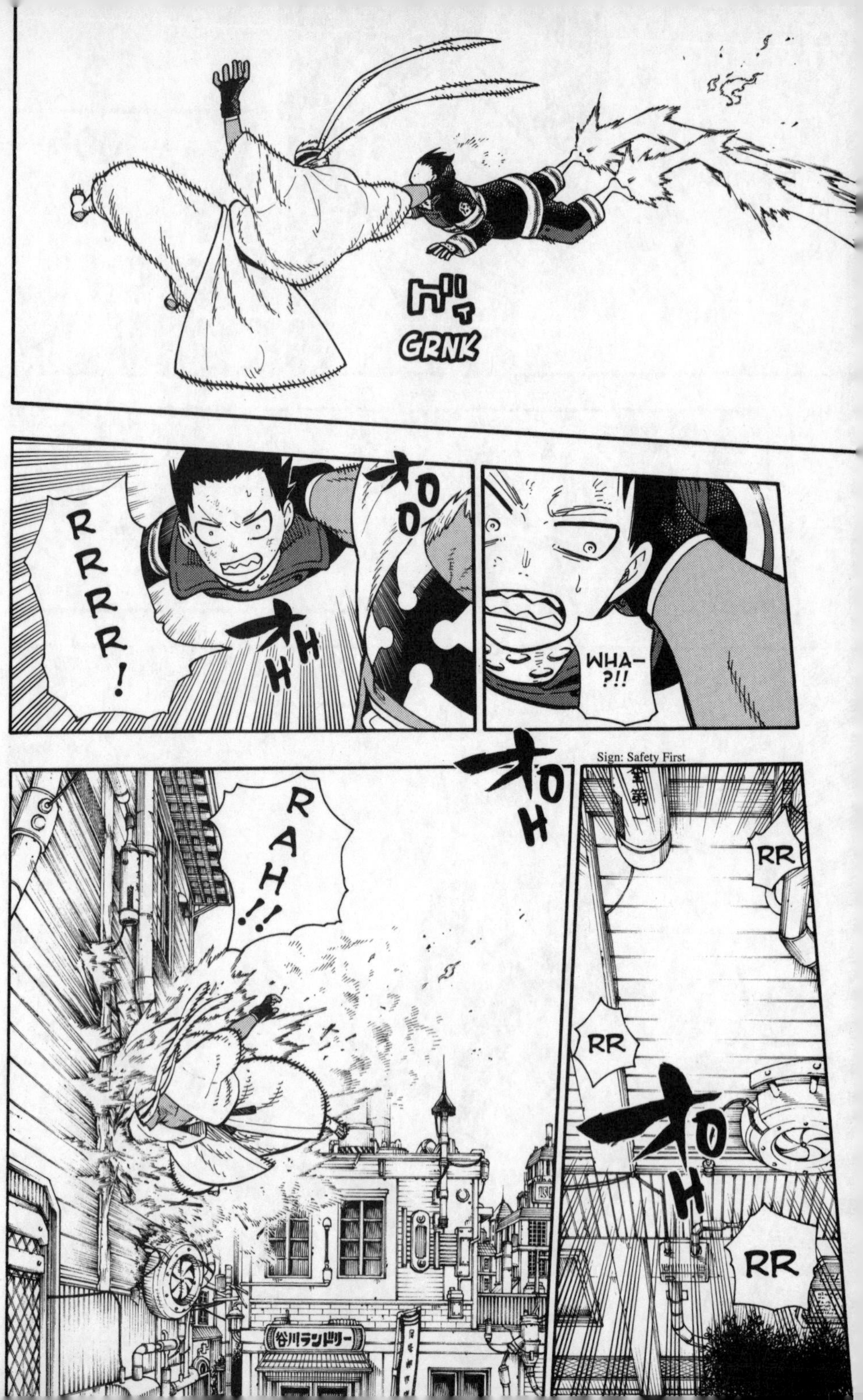
GRNK
WHA-?!!
RRRRR!
OOHH
Sign: Safety First
RR
RR
RR
OOH
OOH
RAH!!

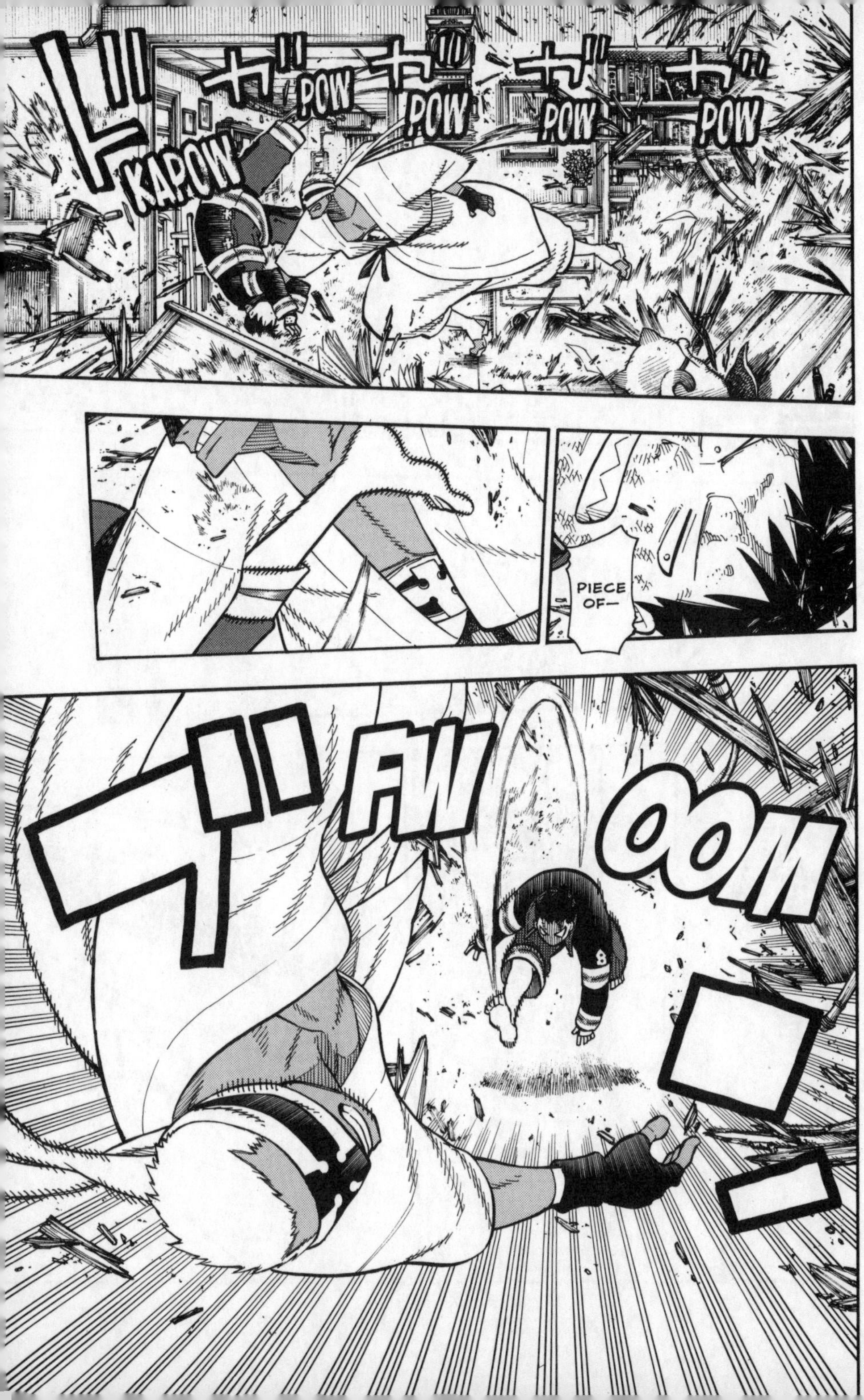
POW
POW
POW
POW
KAPOW
PIECE OF—
FWOOM

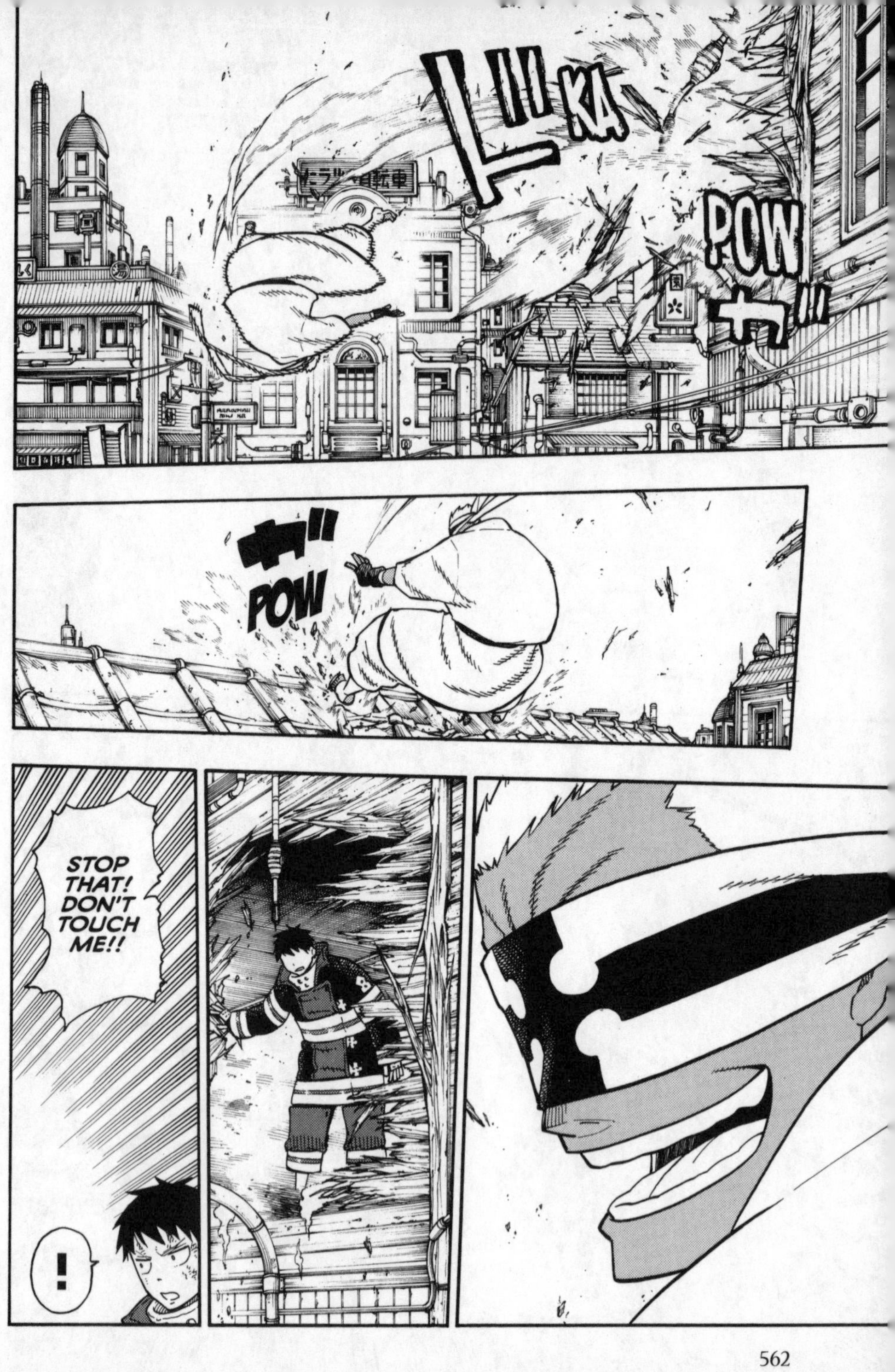

KA
POW
POW
STOP THAT! DON'T TOUCH ME!!
!

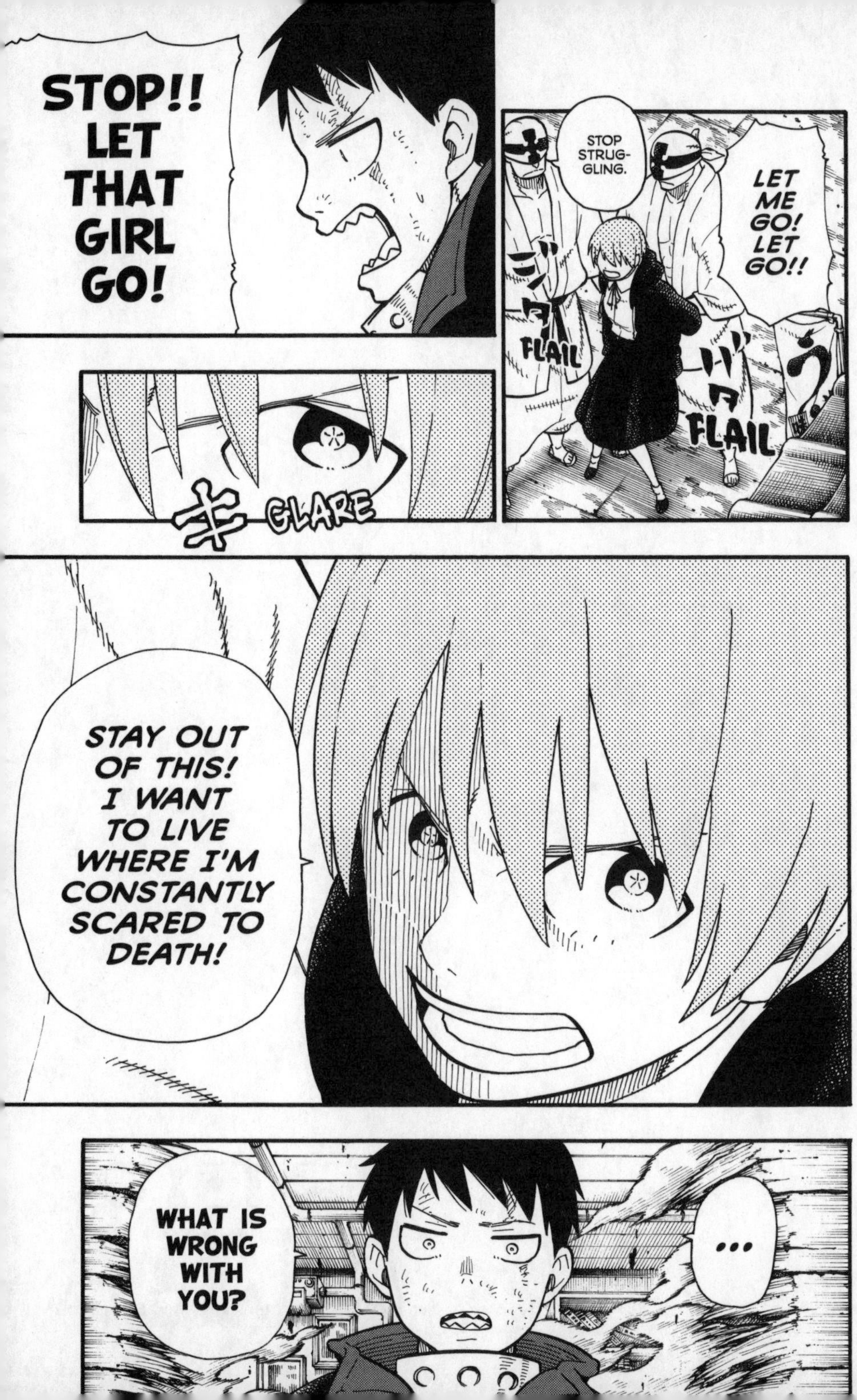
LET ME GO! LET GO!!
STOP STRUG-GLING.
FLAIL
FLAIL
STOP!! LET THAT GIRL GO!
GLARE
STAY OUT OF THIS! I WANT TO LIVE WHERE I'M CONSTANTLY SCARED TO DEATH!
...
WHAT IS WRONG WITH YOU?

FIRE FORCE

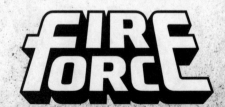

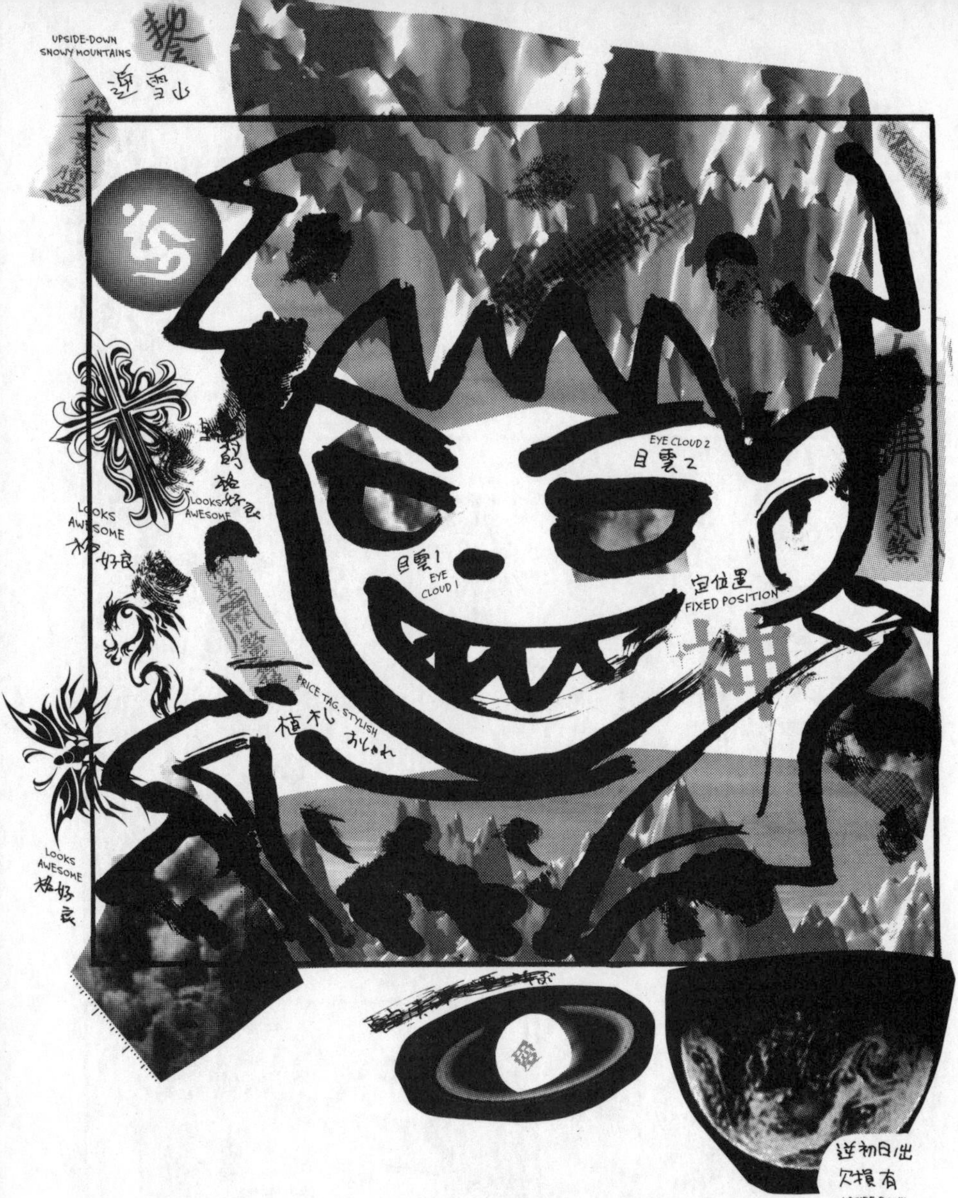
UPSIDE-DOWN SNOWY MOUNTAINS
逆雪山
EYE CLOUD 2
目雲2
LOOKS AWESOME
LOOKS AWESOME
格好良
目雲1
EYE CLOUD 1
定位置
FIXED POSITION
神
PRICE TAG, STYLISH
植札
おしゃれ
LOOKS AWESOME
格好良
逆初日出
欠損有
UPSIDE-DOWN FIRST SUNRISE (W/ IMPERFECTIONS)

CHAPTER CV: ASSEMBLE!

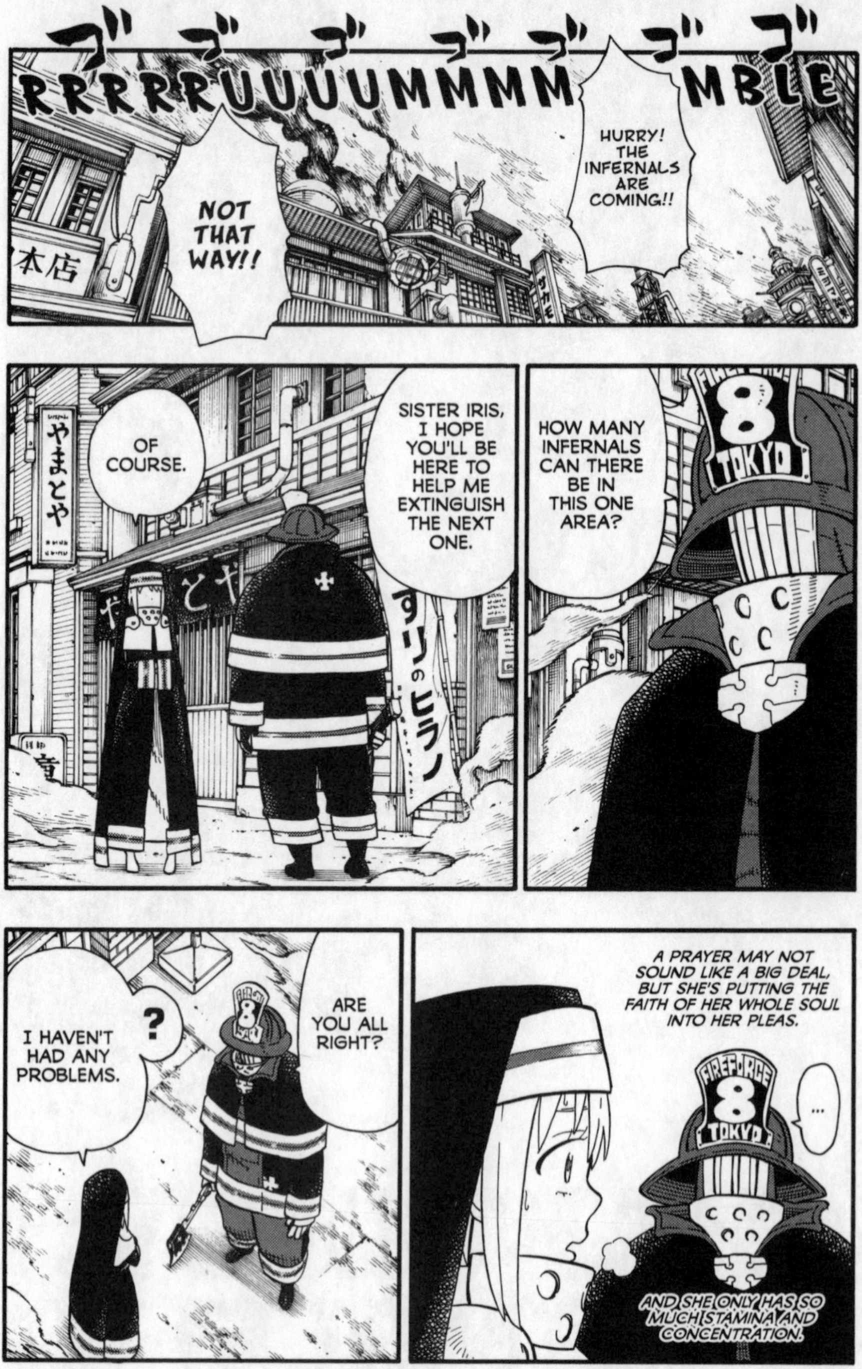
ゴ ゴ ゴ ゴ ゴ ゴ ゴ
RRRRRUUUUMMMM MBLE
HURRY! THE INFERNALS ARE COMING!!
NOT THAT WAY!!
HOW MANY INFERNALS CAN THERE BE IN THIS ONE AREA?
SISTER IRIS, I HOPE YOU'LL BE HERE TO HELP ME EXTINGUISH THE NEXT ONE.
OF COURSE.
A PRAYER MAY NOT SOUND LIKE A BIG DEAL, BUT SHE'S PUTTING THE FAITH OF HER WHOLE SOUL INTO HER PLEAS.
...
AND SHE ONLY HAS SO MUCH STAMINA AND CONCENTRATION.
ARE YOU ALL RIGHT?
?
I HAVEN'T HAD ANY PROBLEMS.

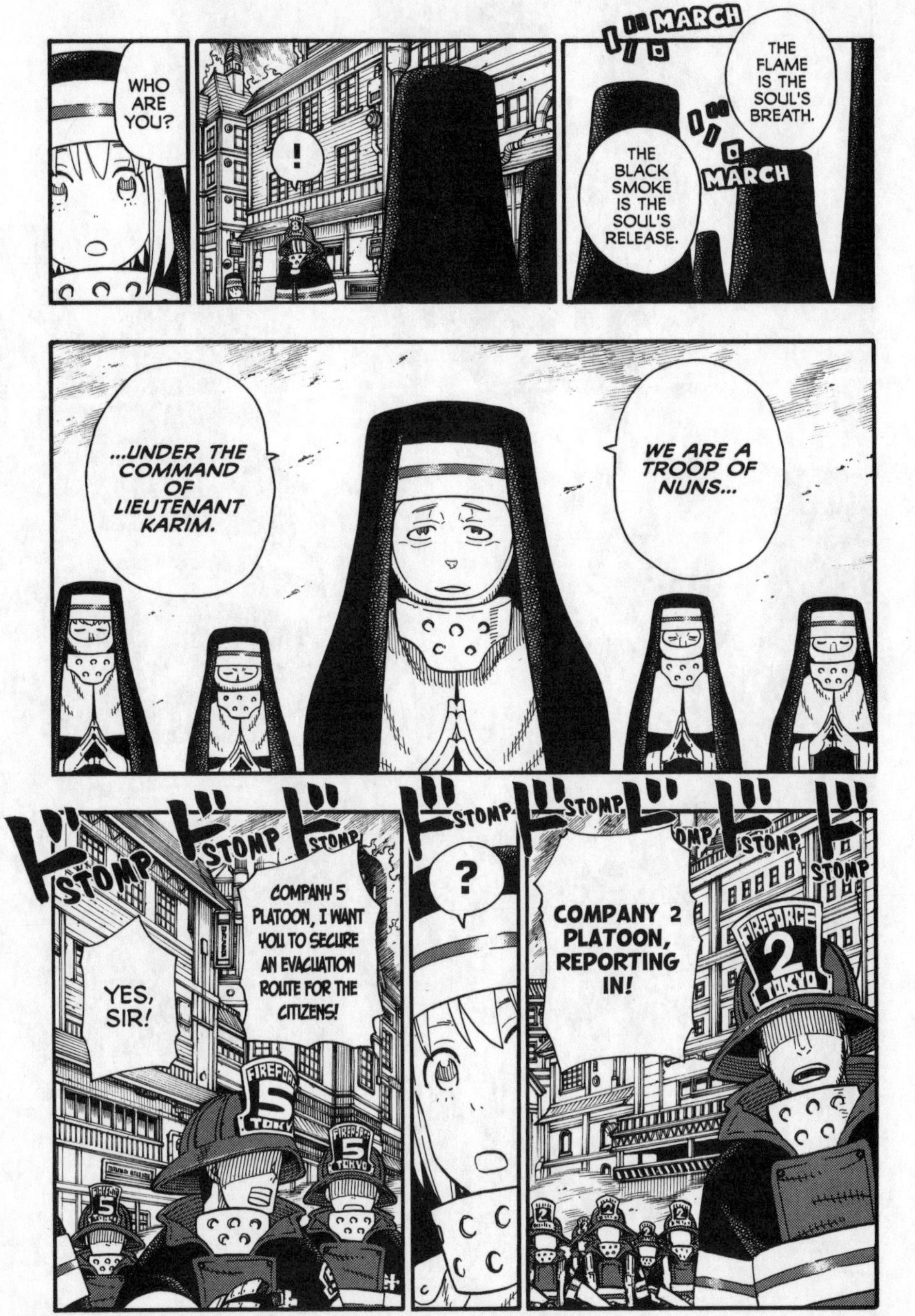
MARCH
THE FLAME IS THE SOUL'S BREATH.
THE BLACK SMOKE IS THE SOUL'S RELEASE.
MARCH
!
WHO ARE YOU?
WE ARE A TROOP OF NUNS...
...UNDER THE COMMAND OF LIEUTENANT KARIM.
STOMP STOMP STOMP STOMP STOMP STOMP STOMP STOMP
COMPANY 2 PLATOON, REPORTING IN!
?
COMPANY 5 PLATOON, I WANT YOU TO SECURE AN EVACUATION ROUTE FOR THE CITIZENS!
YES, SIR!

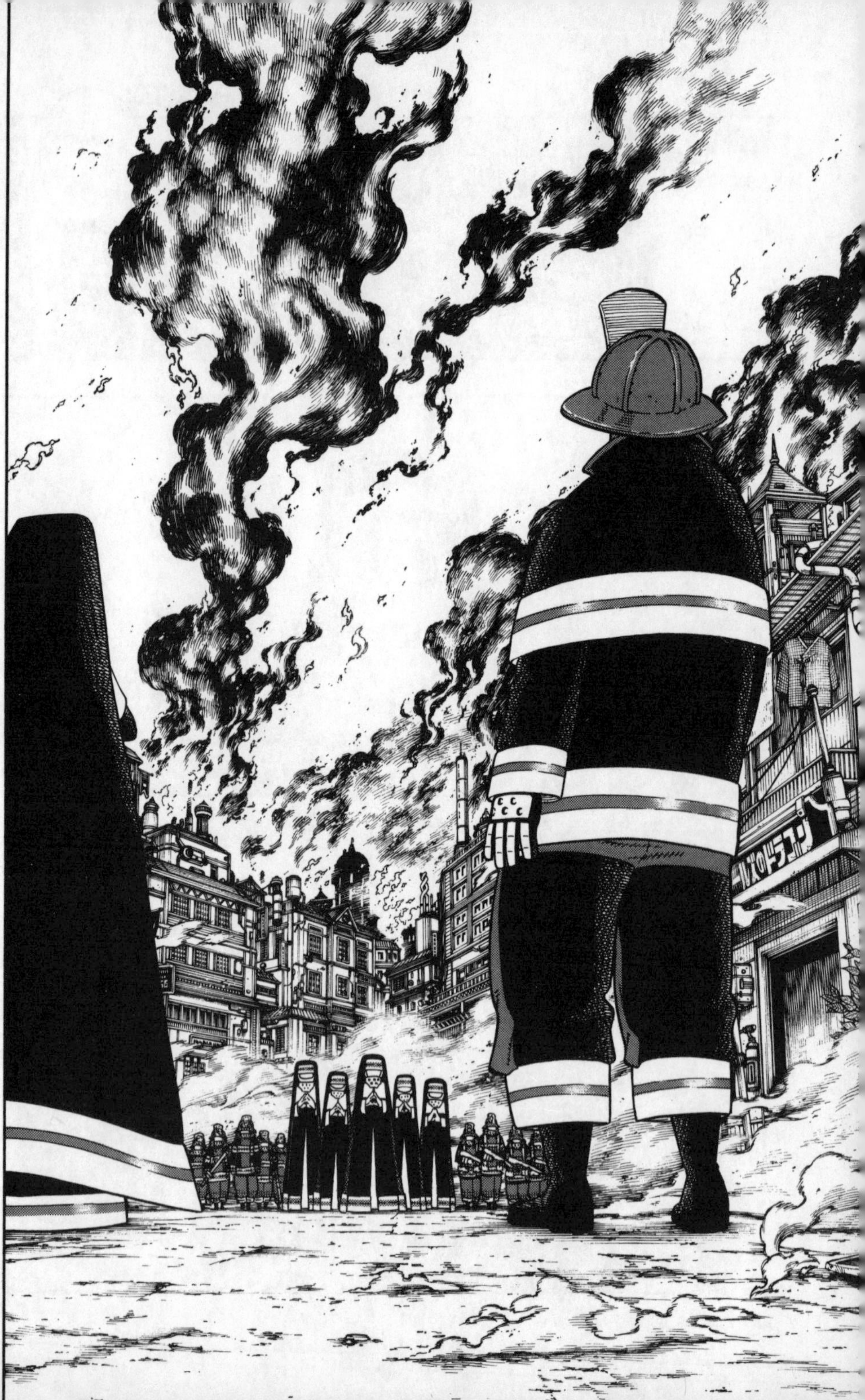

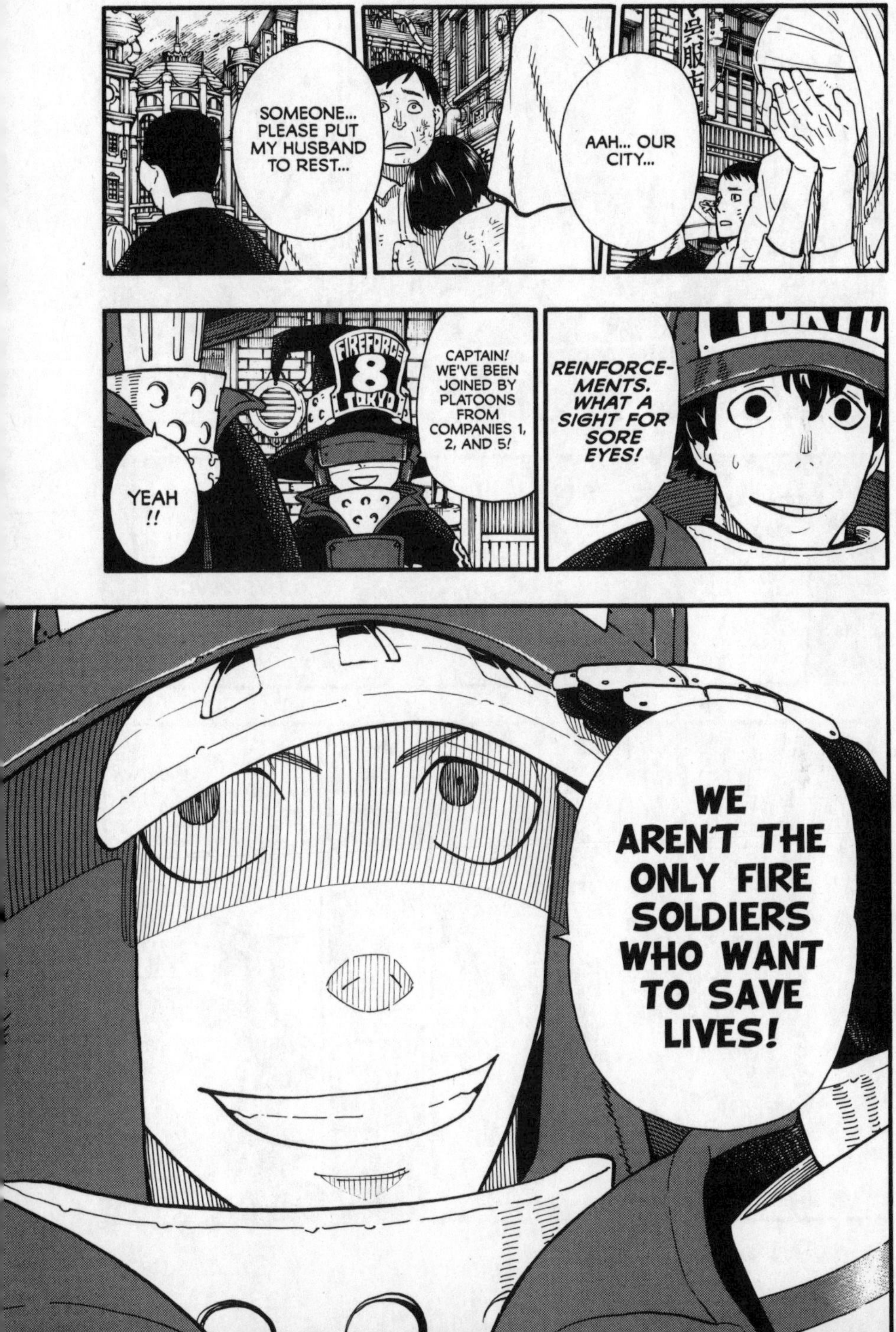
AAH... OUR CITY...
SOMEONE... PLEASE PUT MY HUSBAND TO REST...
REINFORCEMENTS. WHAT A SIGHT FOR SORE EYES!
CAPTAIN! WE'VE BEEN JOINED BY PLATOONS FROM COMPANIES 1, 2, AND 5!
YEAH!!
WE AREN'T THE ONLY FIRE SOLDIERS WHO WANT TO SAVE LIVES!

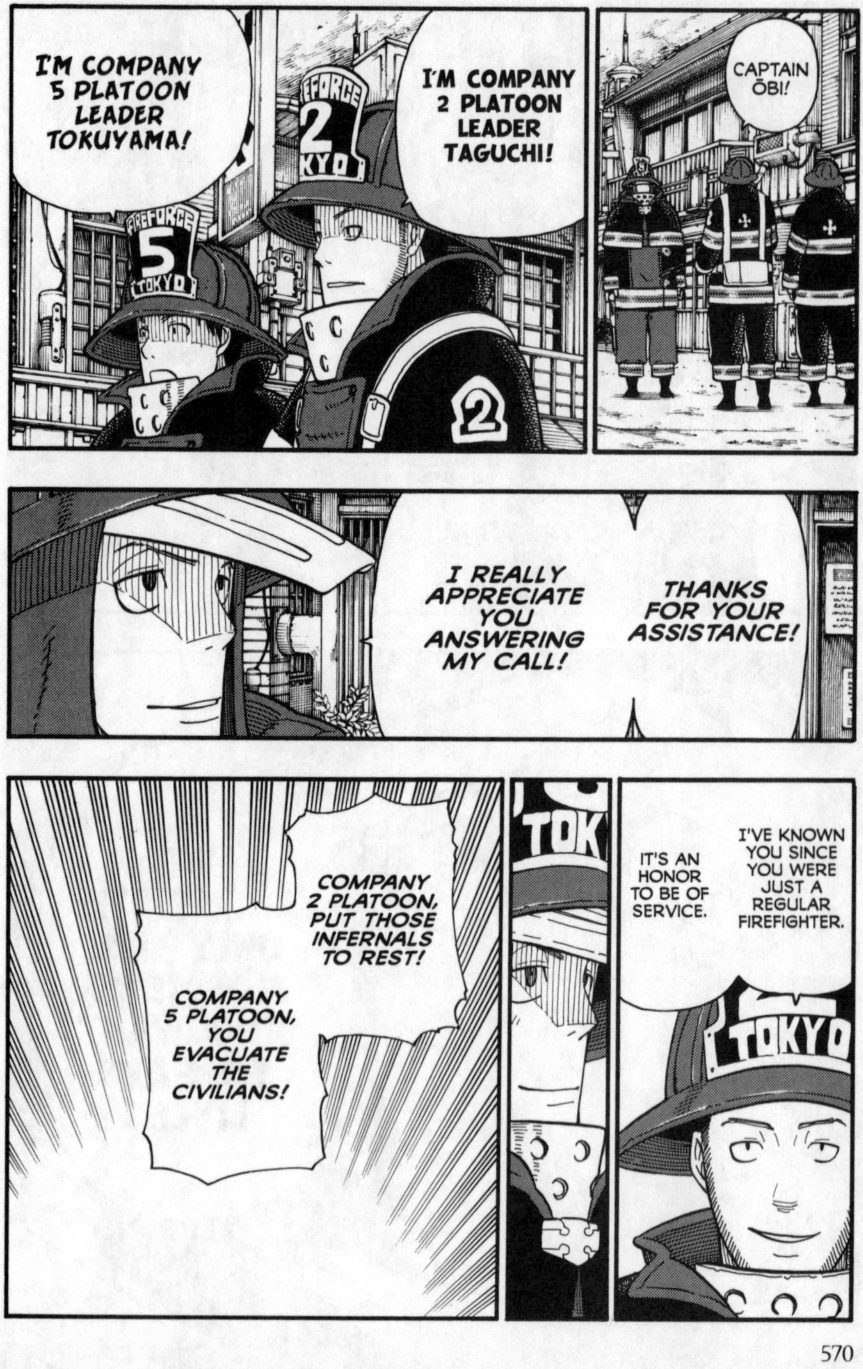
CAPTAIN ŌBI!
I'M COMPANY 2 PLATOON LEADER TAGUCHI!
I'M COMPANY 5 PLATOON LEADER TOKUYAMA!
THANKS FOR YOUR ASSISTANCE!
I REALLY APPRECIATE YOU ANSWERING MY CALL!
I'VE KNOWN YOU SINCE YOU WERE JUST A REGULAR FIREFIGHTER.
IT'S AN HONOR TO BE OF SERVICE.
COMPANY 2 PLATOON, PUT THOSE INFERNALS TO REST!
COMPANY 5 PLATOON, YOU EVACUATE THE CIVILIANS!

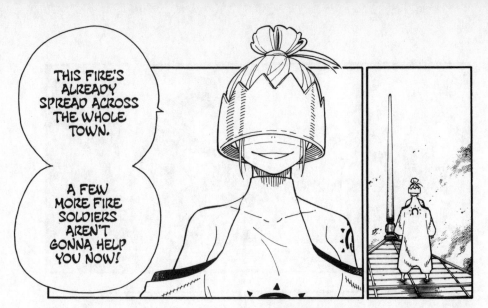

THIS FIRE'S ALREADY SPREAD ACROSS THE WHOLE TOWN.

A FEW MORE FIRE SOLDIERS AREN'T GONNA HELP YOU NOW!

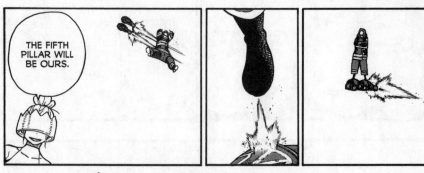

THE FIFTH PILLAR WILL BE OURS.

ACK!

KA-CRACK

CELESTIAL KNIGHT SLASH!!

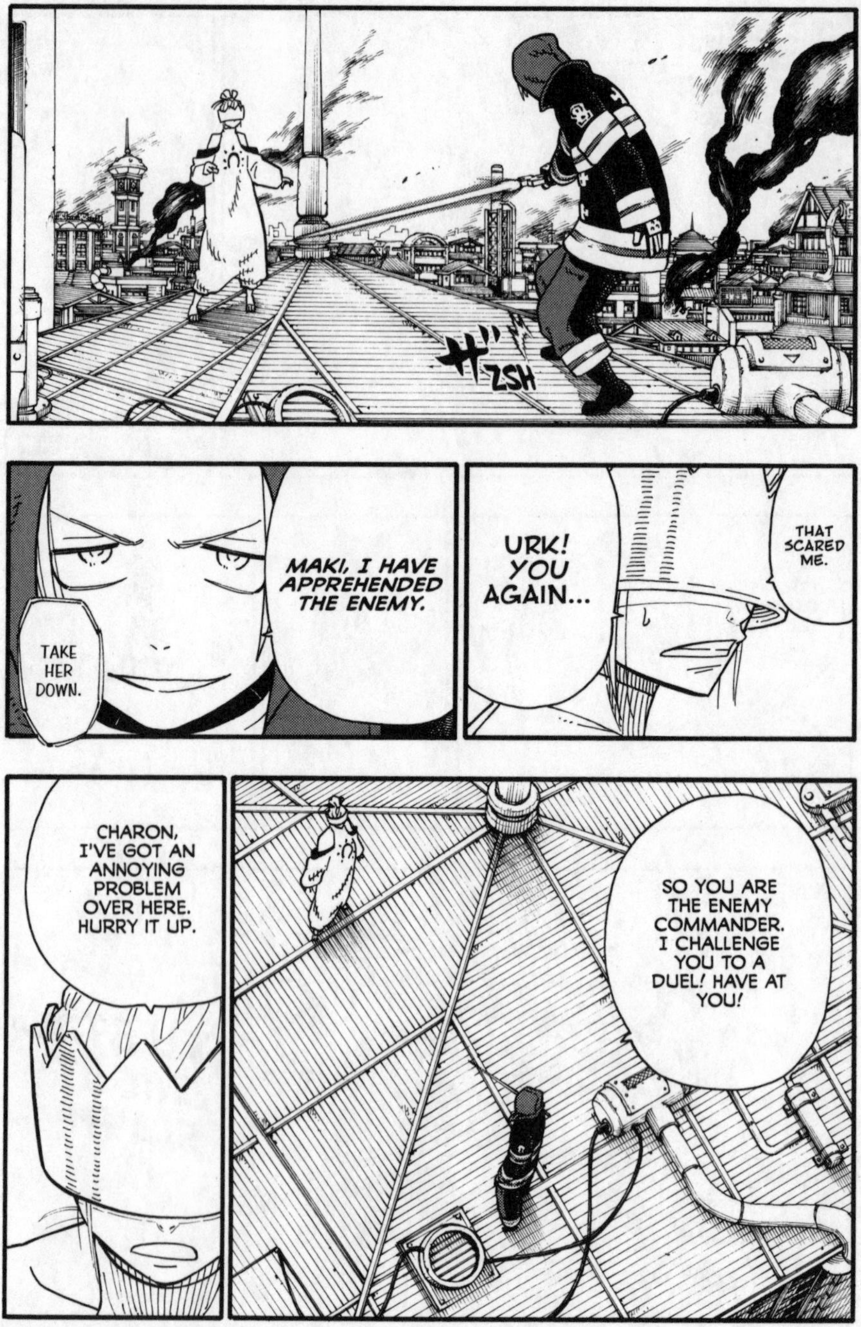
ZSH
THAT SCARED ME.
URK! YOU AGAIN...
MAKI, I HAVE APPREHENDED THE ENEMY.
TAKE HER DOWN.
SO YOU ARE THE ENEMY COMMANDER. I CHALLENGE YOU TO A DUEL! HAVE AT YOU!
CHARON, I'VE GOT AN ANNOYING PROBLEM OVER HERE. HURRY IT UP.

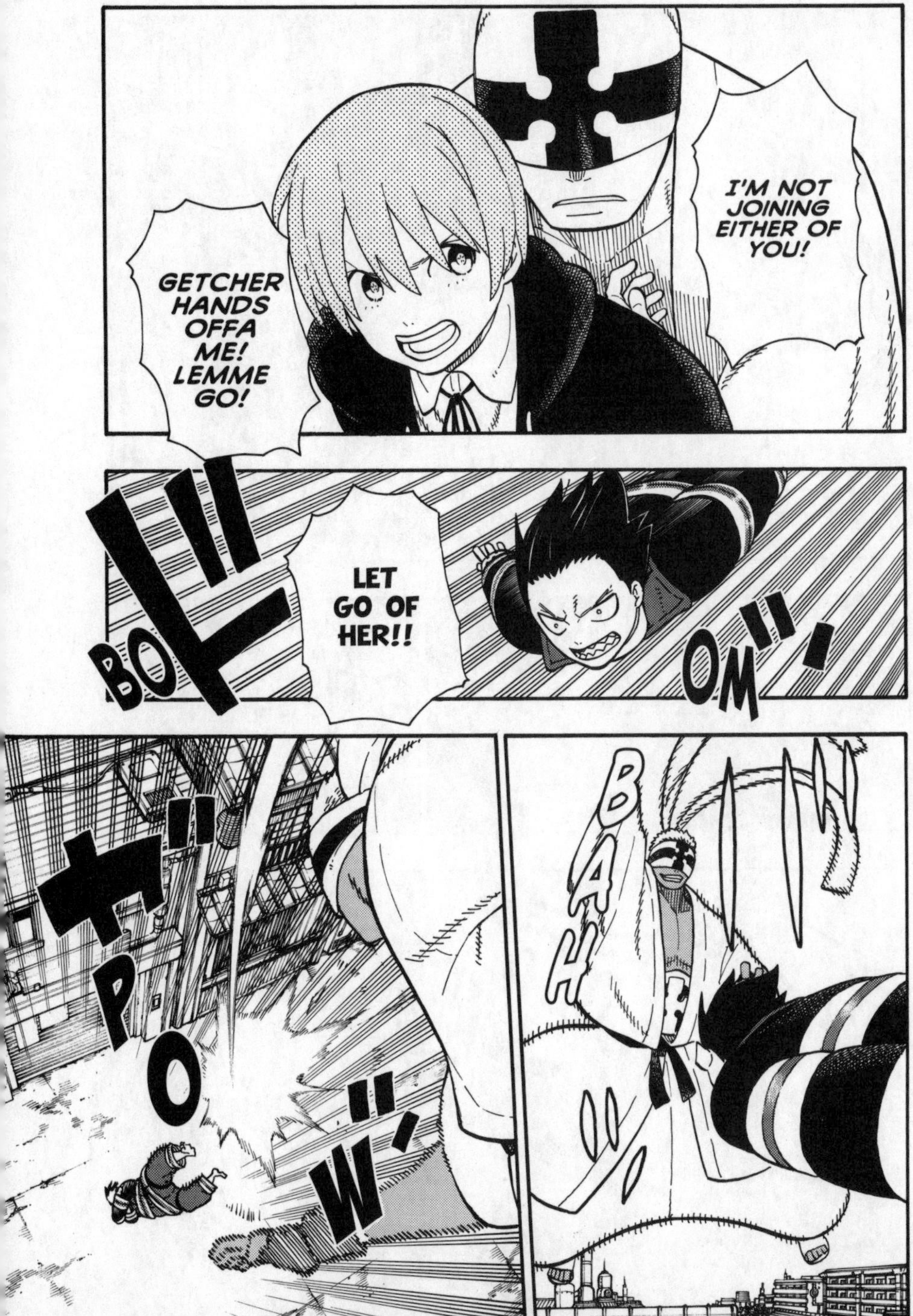
I'M NOT JOINING EITHER OF YOU!
GETCHER HANDS OFFA ME! LEMME GO!
BOOM
LET GO OF HER!!
BAAH
POW

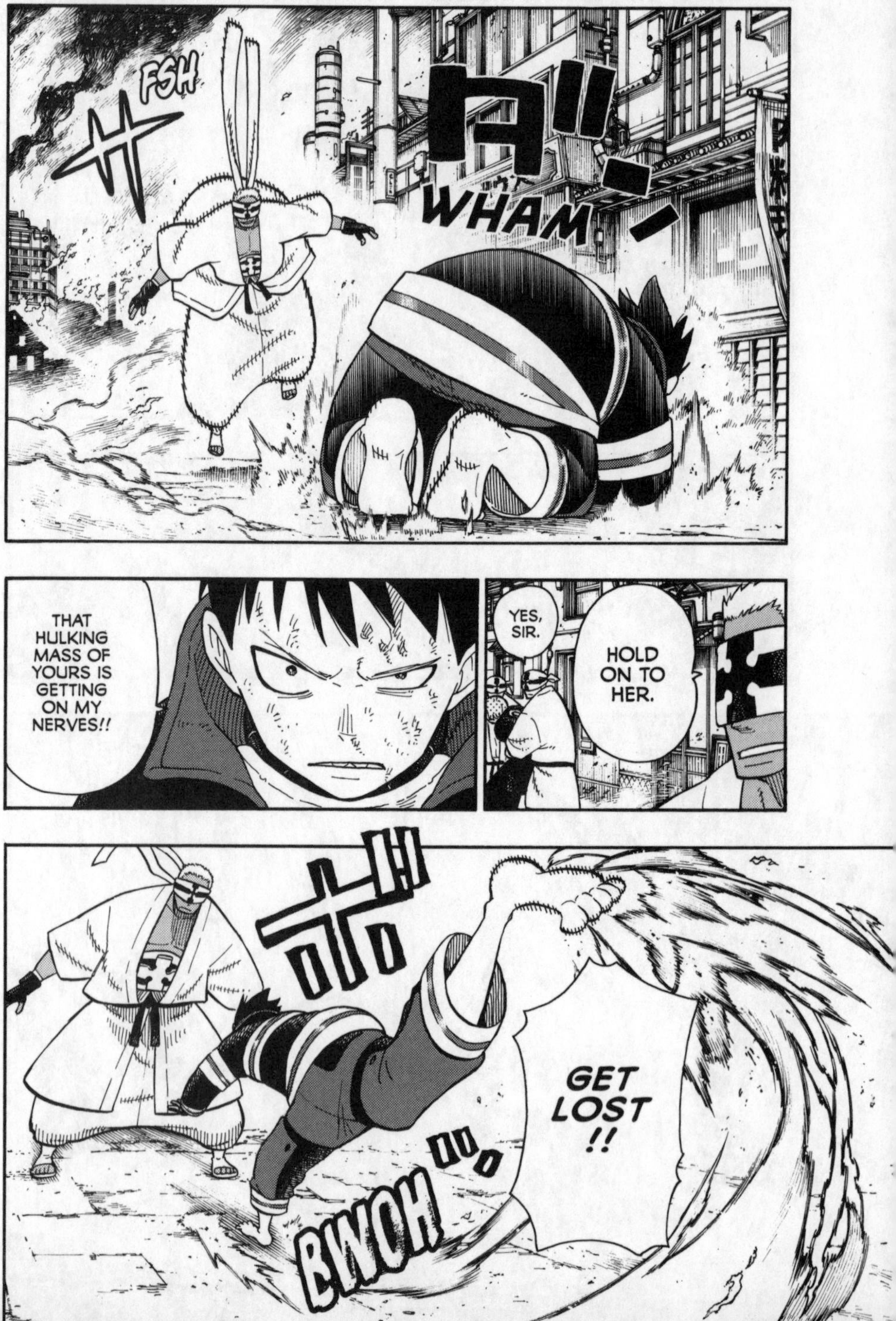
FSH
WHAM
HOLD ON TO HER.
YES, SIR.
THAT HULKING MASS OF YOURS IS GETTING ON MY NERVES!!
GET LOST !!
BWOH

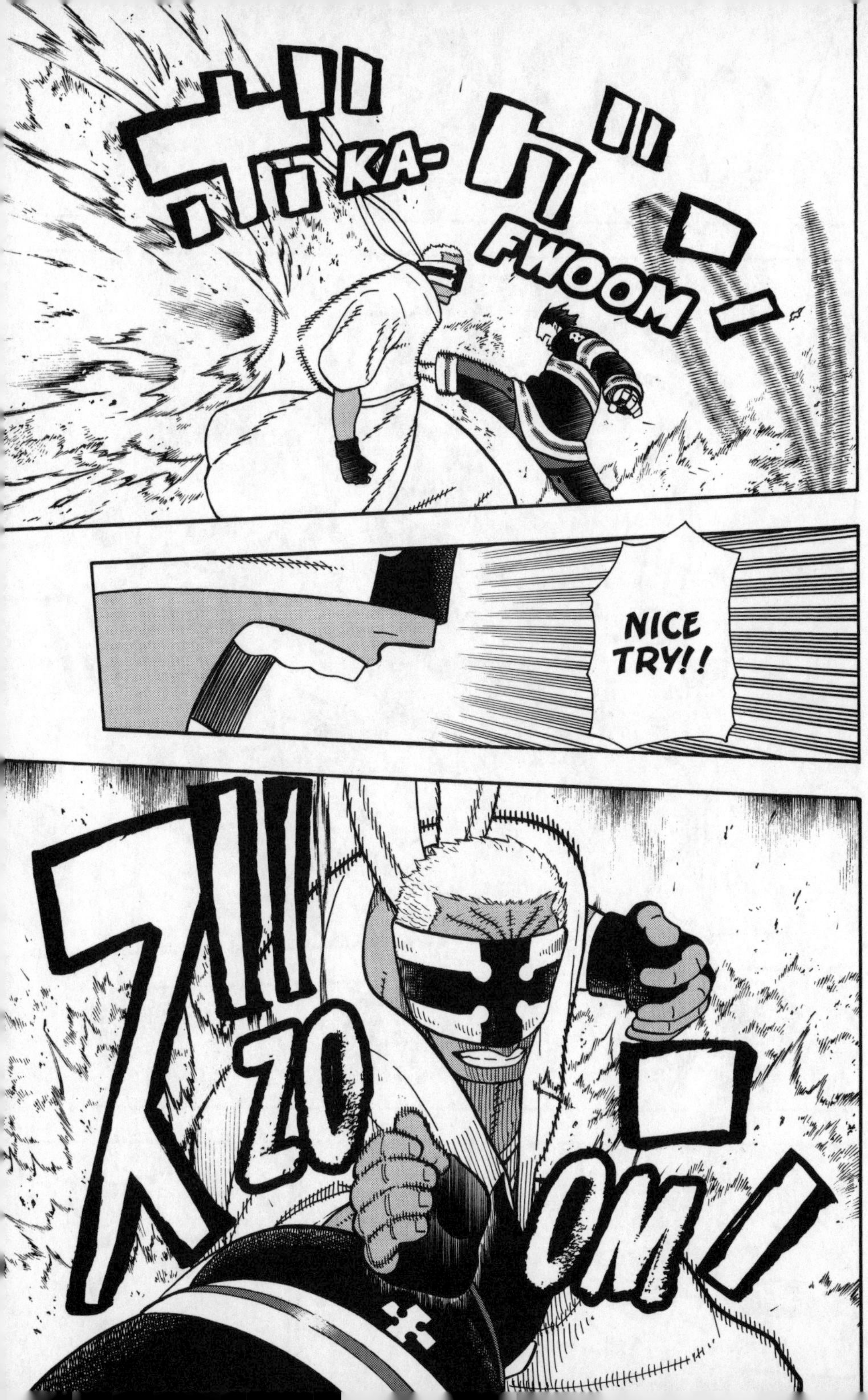
KA-
FWOOM!
NICE TRY!!
ZOOM!

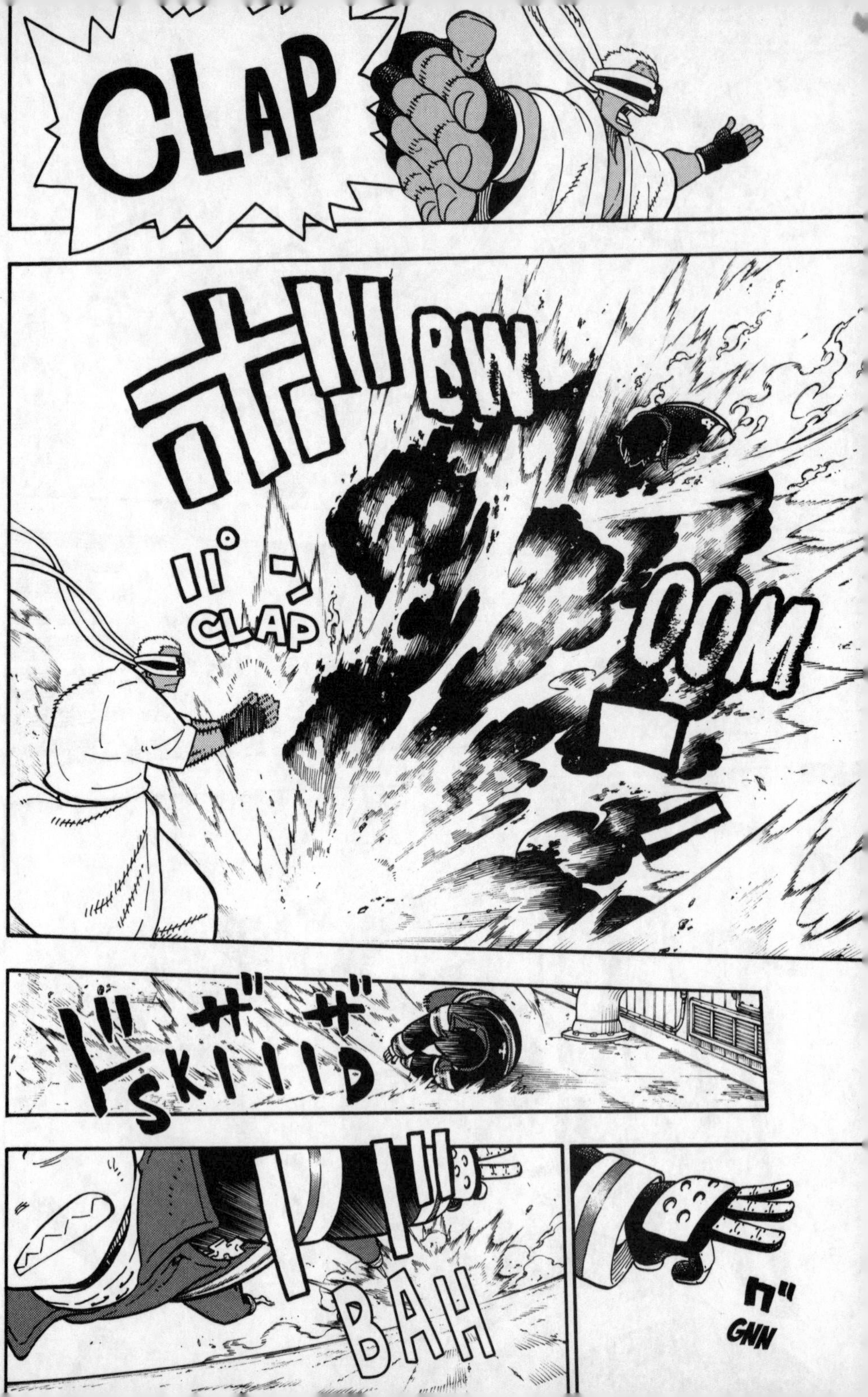
CLAP
BWOOM
CLAP
ドザザ
SKIIID
GNN
BAH

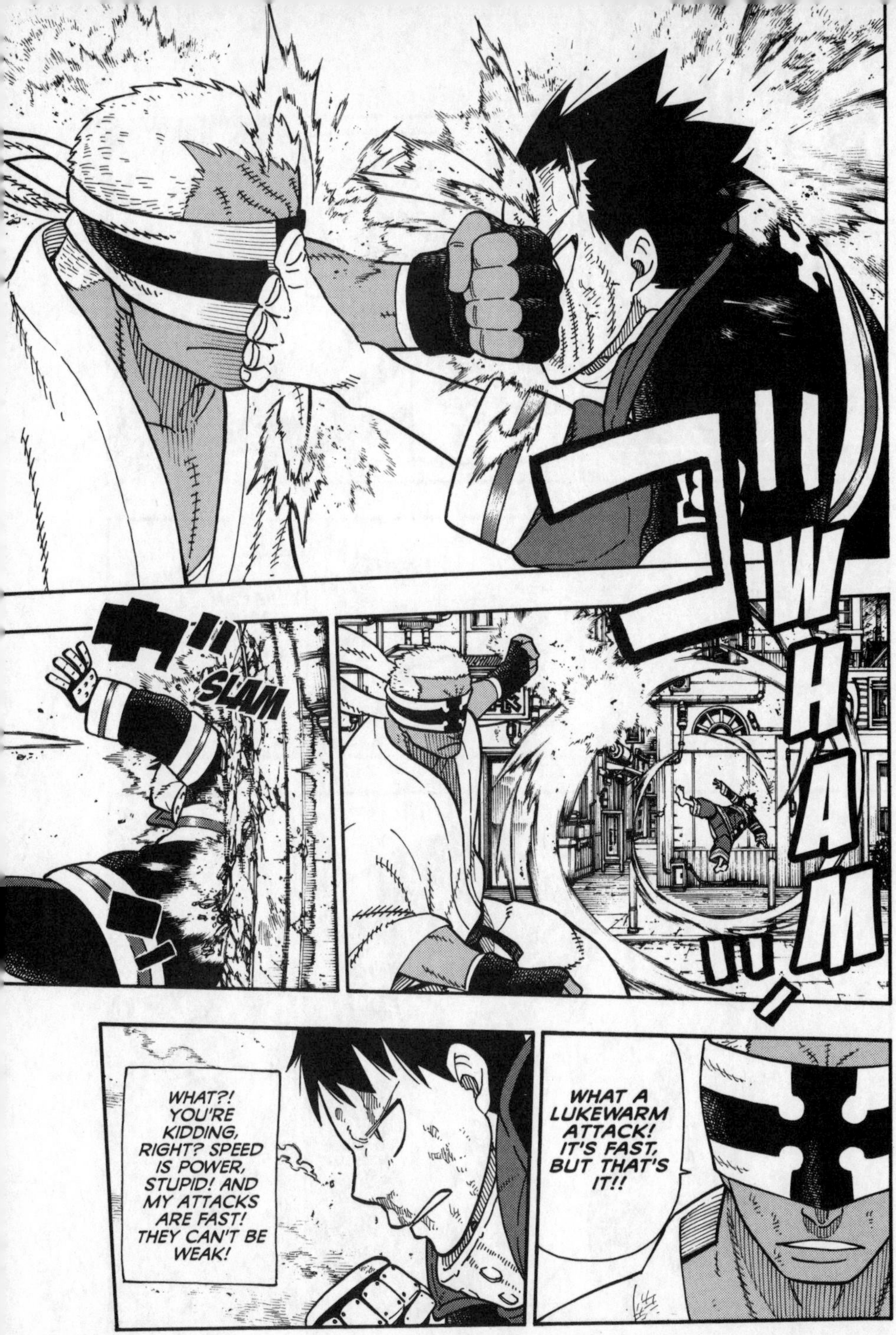
WHAM!!
SLAM
WHAT A LUKEWARM ATTACK! IT'S FAST, BUT THAT'S IT!!
WHAT?! YOU'RE KIDDING, RIGHT? SPEED IS POWER, STUPID! AND MY ATTACKS ARE FAST! THEY CAN'T BE WEAK!

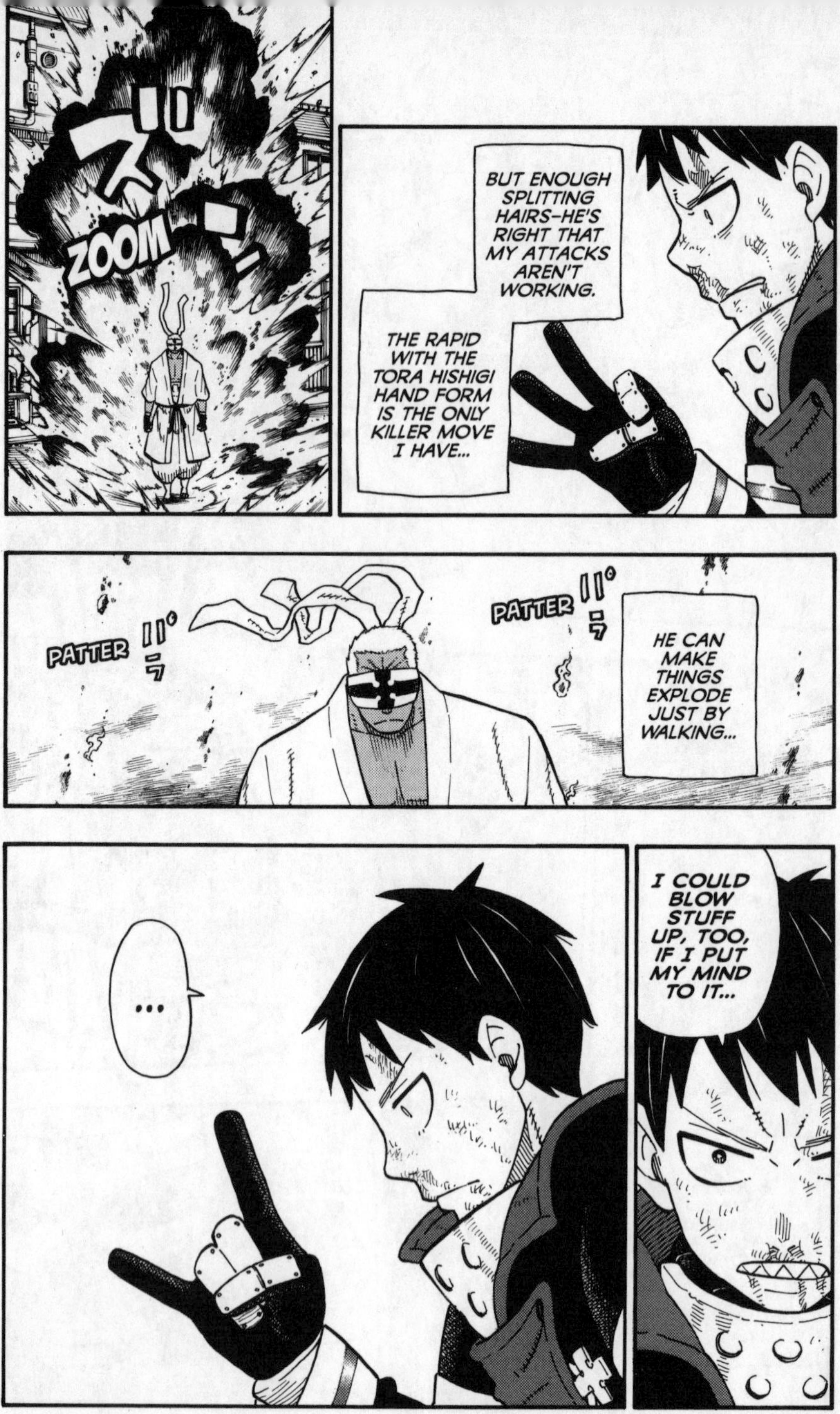
BUT ENOUGH SPLITTING HAIRS–HE'S RIGHT THAT MY ATTACKS AREN'T WORKING.
THE RAPID WITH THE TORA HISHIGI HAND FORM IS THE ONLY KILLER MOVE I HAVE...
ZOOM
HE CAN MAKE THINGS EXPLODE JUST BY WALKING...
PATTER
PATTER
I COULD BLOW STUFF UP, TOO, IF I PUT MY MIND TO IT...
...

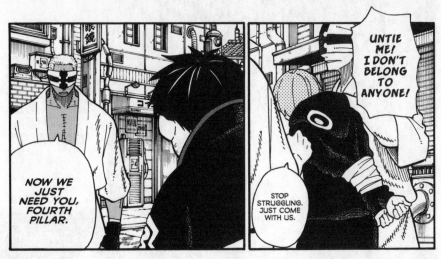

UNTIE ME! I DON'T BELONG TO ANYONE!
STOP STRUGGLING. JUST COME WITH US.
NOW WE JUST NEED YOU, FOURTH PILLAR.
IT REALLY IS WEIRD THAT HE DOESN'T HAVE A SCRATCH ON HIM... ANYWAY, IF I KEEP DOING THE SAME THING, I'LL KEEP GETTING THE SAME RESULTS.
IF I DON'T THINK OF SOMETHING DIFFERENT, I'LL NEVER BE ABLE TO BEAT HIM.
ROCK
COME TO THINK OF IT, WHEN I WENT TO COMPANY 7 TO TRAIN WITH CAPTAIN SHINMON, THERE WAS A HAND FORM THAT CAUSED AN EXPLOSION...
KA BOOM

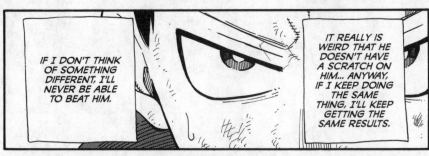

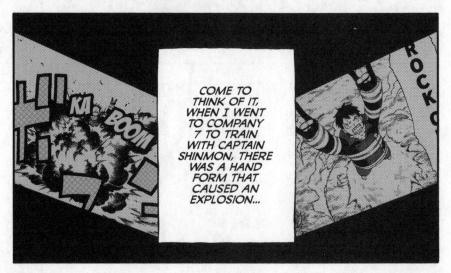

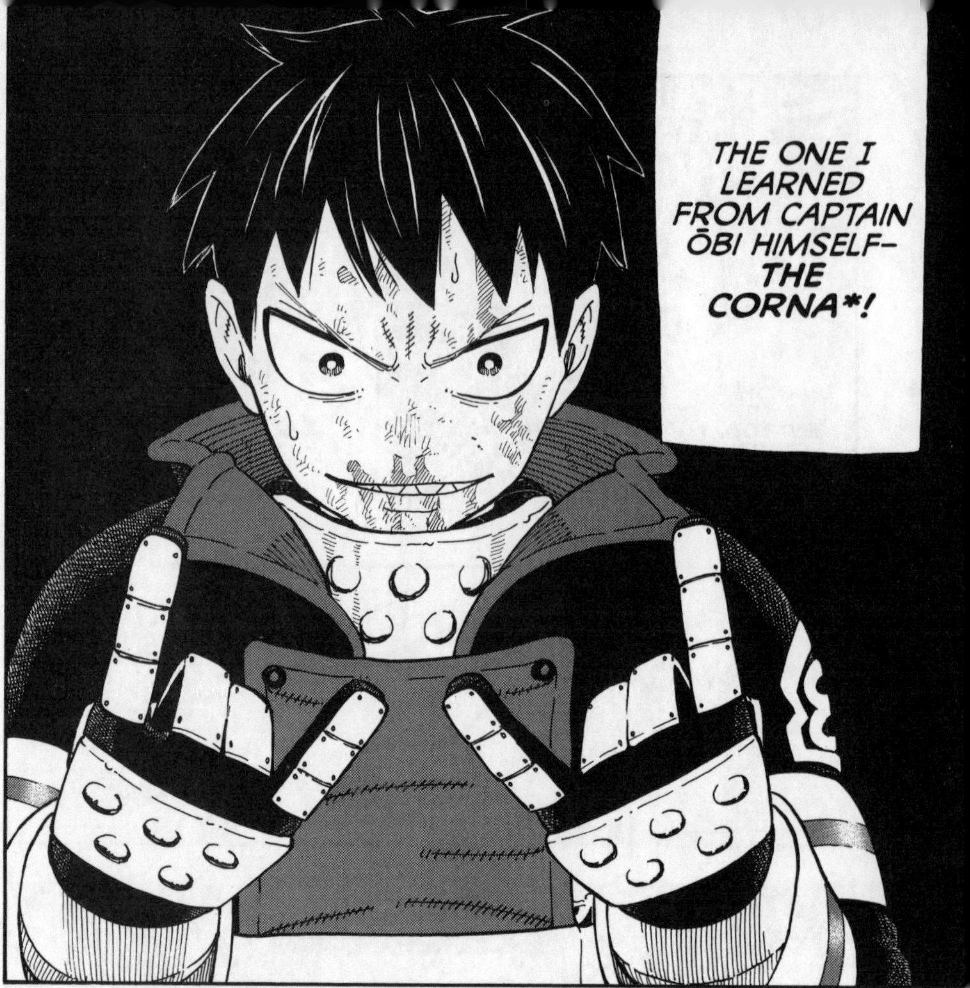
THE ONE I LEARNED FROM CAPTAIN ŌBI HIMSELF–THE CORNA*!

*The sign of the horns

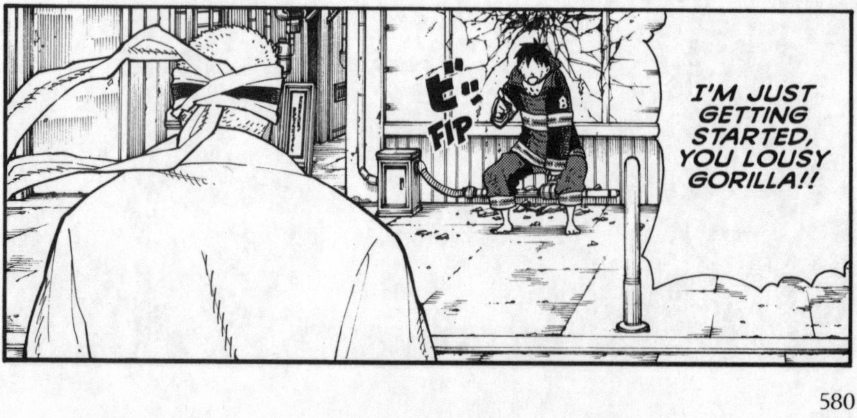
I'M JUST GETTING STARTED, YOU LOUSY GORILLA!!
ビッ
FIP

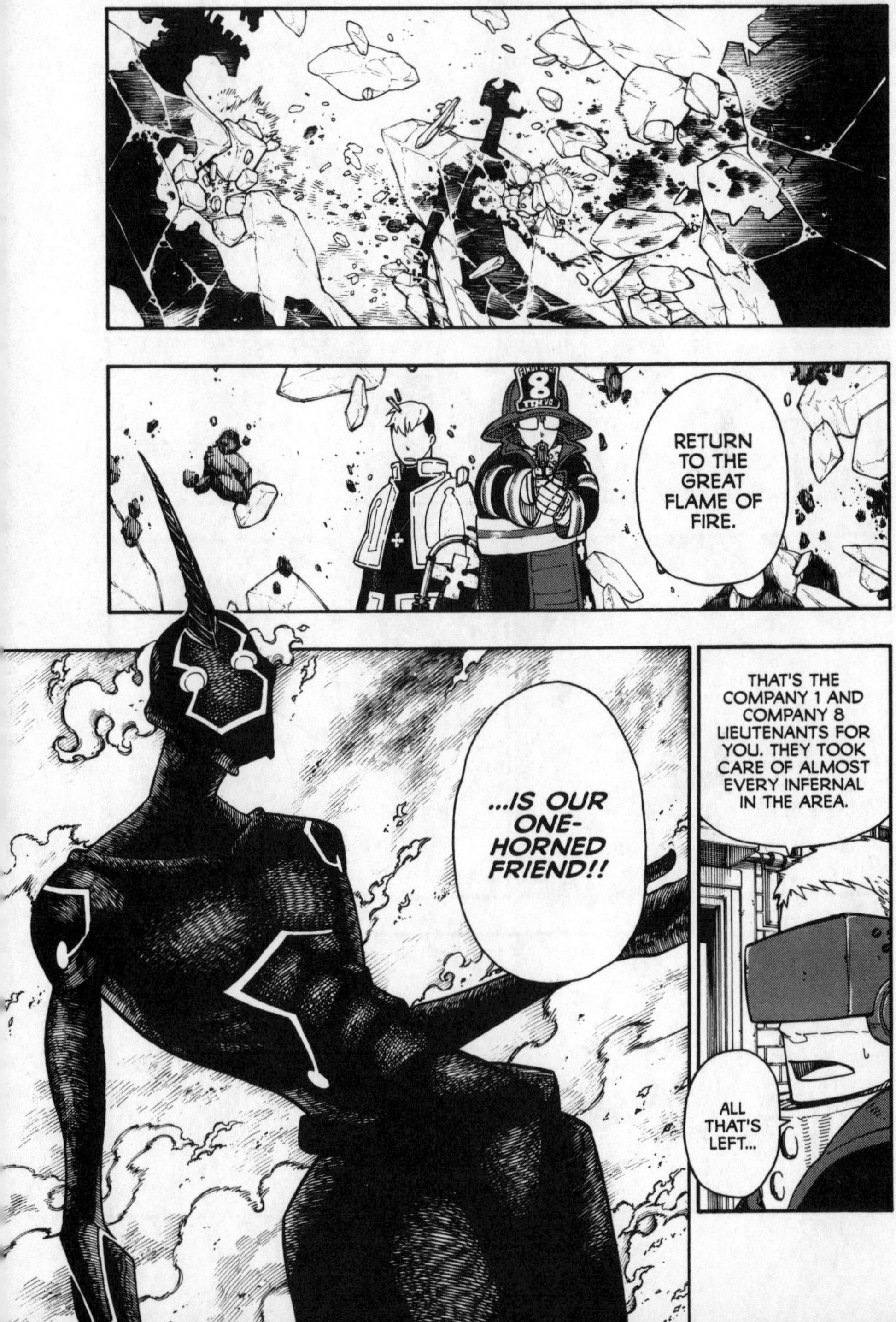
RETURN TO THE GREAT FLAME OF FIRE.
THAT'S THE COMPANY 1 AND COMPANY 8 LIEUTENANTS FOR YOU. THEY TOOK CARE OF ALMOST EVERY INFERNAL IN THE AREA.
ALL THAT'S LEFT...
...IS OUR ONE-HORNED FRIEND!!

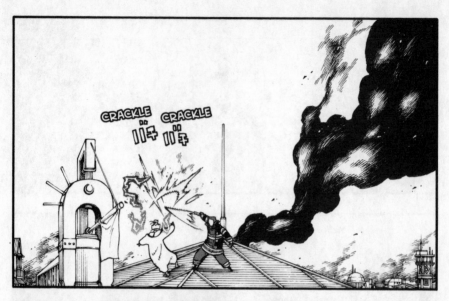

CRACKLE CRACKLE
バチバチ
DAMMIT! I CAN'T USE MY MESSENGER SYSTEM WITH YOU AROUND!
YOU REALLY ARE A PAIN IN THE ASS.
I WILL THWART YOUR EVIL AMBITIONS!
OH YOU WILL, WILL YOU?
BUT THE FIFTH PILLAR IS ALREADY OURS!!

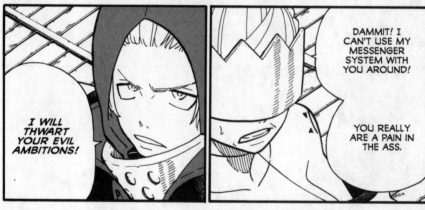

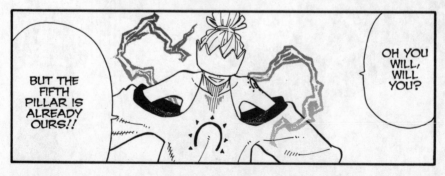

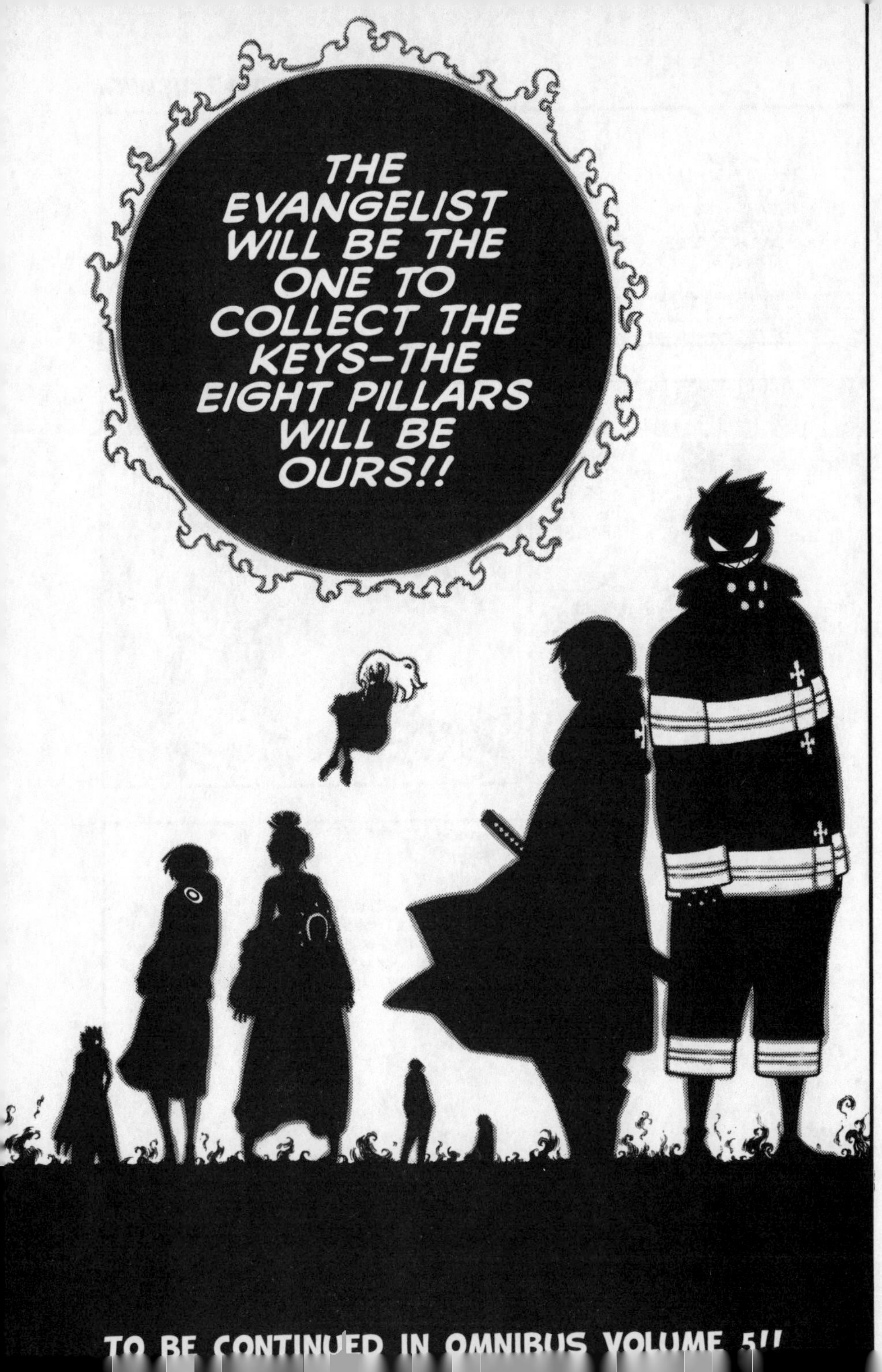
THE EVANGELIST WILL BE THE ONE TO COLLECT THE KEYS–THE EIGHT PILLARS WILL BE OURS!!
TO BE CONTINUED IN OMNIBUS VOLUME 5!!

AFTERWORD MANGA: ATSUSHIYA

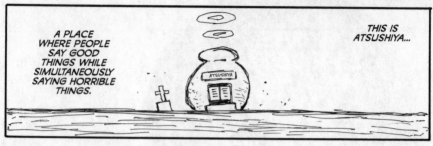

THIS IS ATSUSHIYA...
A PLACE WHERE PEOPLE SAY GOOD THINGS WHILE SIMULTANEOUSLY SAYING HORRIBLE THINGS.
ATSUSHIYA
HEY, GUYS! LISTEN TO THIS!!
RAAARR!
ROOARRR!
RAARR!
THIS PLACE IS FINALLY GETTING A FRESH FEMALE FACE!
OOOHH !!
INDEED!! INDEED!!
SPLASH
A FRESH FEMALE FACE IN THIS FILTHY DEN OF TESTOSTERONE ?!!
SURELY SHE WILL BRIGHTEN AND BEAUTIFY OUR HUMBLE ESTABLISHMENT!
DEN OF TESTOSTERONE? I DON'T KNOW ABOUT THAT. IT'S HARD TO HAVE HORMONES WHEN MOST OF US AREN'T EVEN LIVING THINGS...
HURRY, BOSS! WHERE IS THIS FRESH FEMININE FACE?
INDEED, WHERE IS THE GIRL?! INDEED!!
SPLASH
QUIT PANICKING. SHE'S RIGHT THERE IN FRONT OF YOU.

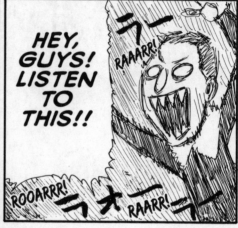

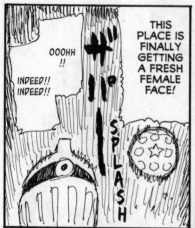

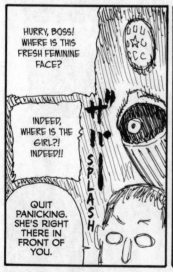

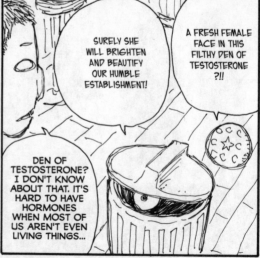

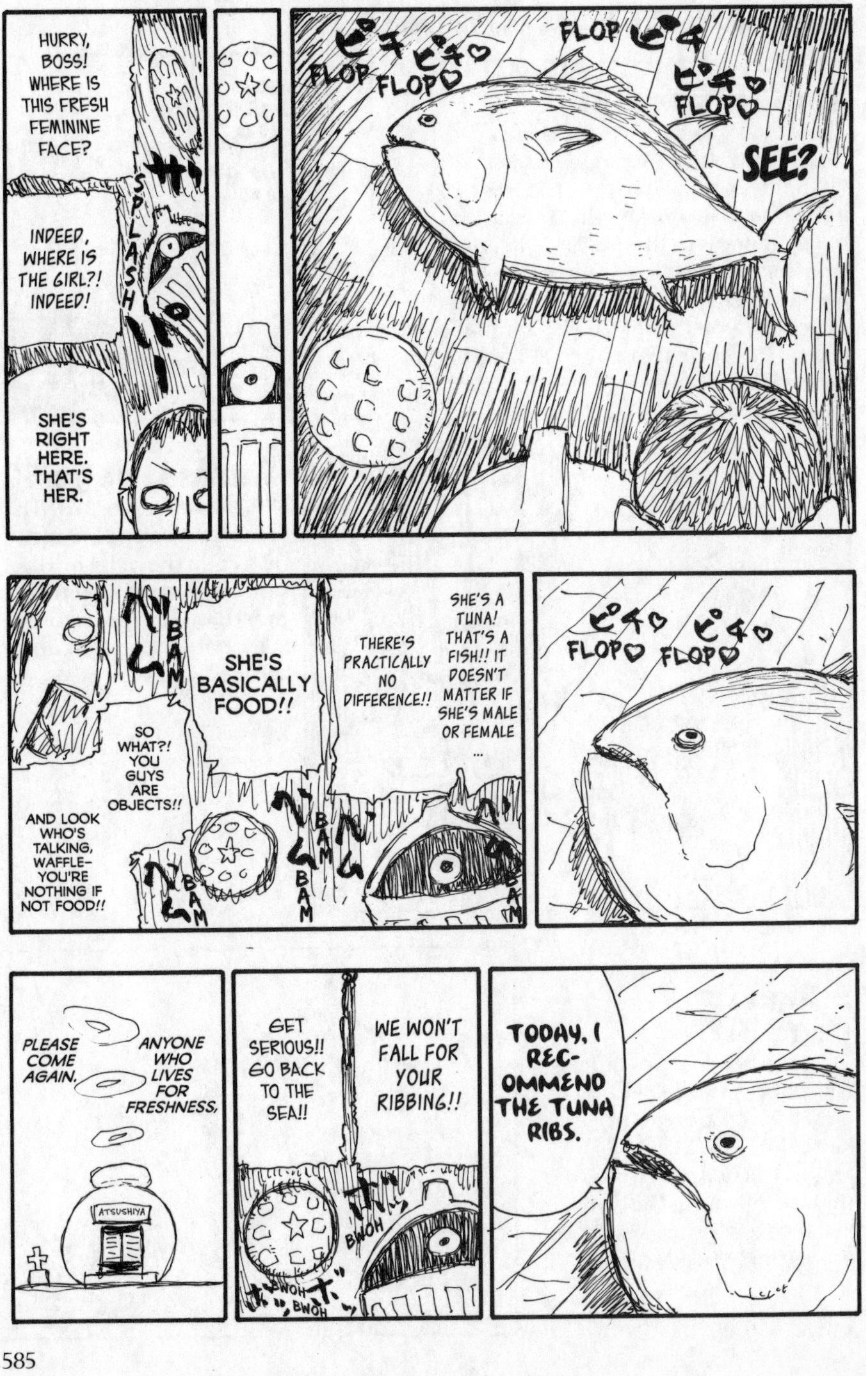
FLOP ピチ
ピチ♡ FLOP♡
SEE?
ピチ FLOP
ピチ♡ FLOP♡
HURRY, BOSS! WHERE IS THIS FRESH FEMININE FACE?
サッ SPLASH
INDEED, WHERE IS THE GIRL?! INDEED!
SHE'S RIGHT HERE. THAT'S HER.
ピチ♡ FLOP♡
ピチ♡ FLOP♡
SHE'S A TUNA! THAT'S A FISH!! IT DOESN'T MATTER IF SHE'S MALE OR FEMALE ...
THERE'S PRACTICALLY NO DIFFERENCE!!
SHE'S BASICALLY FOOD!!
バム BAM
SO WHAT?! YOU GUYS ARE OBJECTS!!
AND LOOK WHO'S TALKING, WAFFLE— YOU'RE NOTHING IF NOT FOOD!!
バム BAM
バム BAM
バム BAM
バム BAM
TODAY, I REC- OMMEND THE TUNA RIBS.
WE WON'T FALL FOR YOUR RIBBING!!
GET SERIOUS!! GO BACK TO THE SEA!!
ボッ BWOH
ボッ BWOH ボッ BWOH
ANYONE WHO LIVES FOR FRESHNESS,
PLEASE COME AGAIN.
ATSUSHIYA

Translation Notes:

Pinched pennies up in smoke, page 409

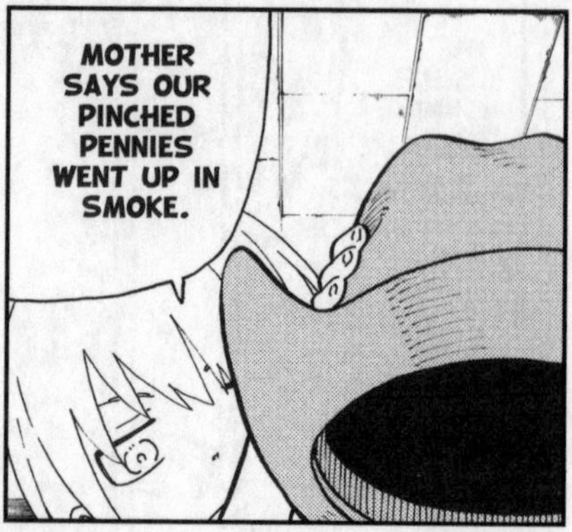
MOTHER SAYS OUR PINCHED PENNIES WENT UP IN SMOKE.

There is a Japanese term for being in financial straits, *hi no kuruma*, which literally means "fire chariot." It refers to a supernatural creature that is believed to take sinners to the afterlife—in other words, someone is in so much trouble financially that that person is on their way to hell. Here, Arthur says that their fire chariot has burned to ash, meaning what little money his family had left has also disappeared.

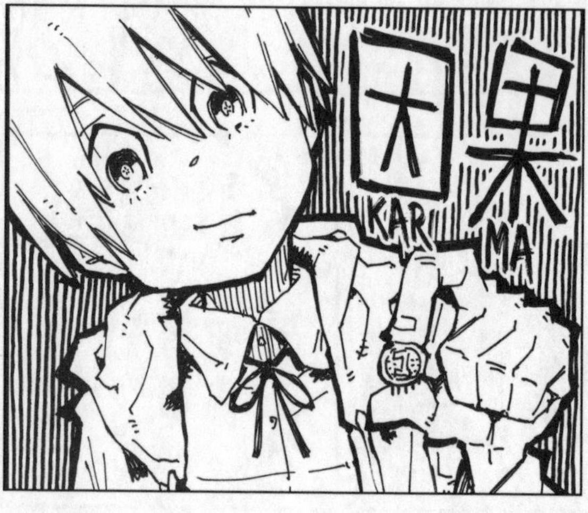
因果
KAR MA

Karma, page 505

The Japanese word used here can also mean "cause and effect," in the sense of "the effects that befall someone are caused by their actions." The word is *inga*, but can be pronounced *inka*.

A Big Fire, page 525

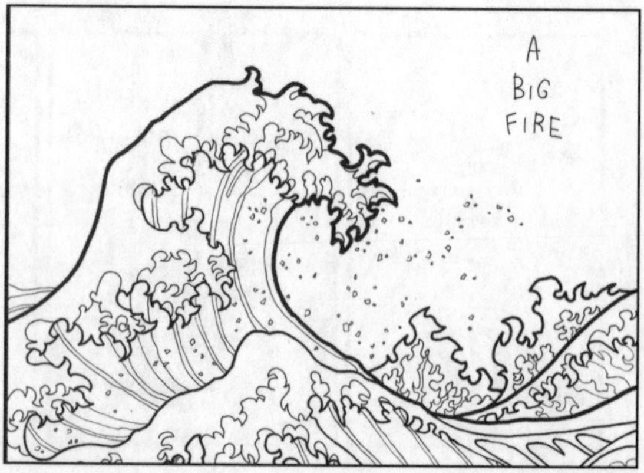
A BIG FIRE

This is an homage to a famous woodblock print called *The Great Wave Off Kanagawa* by Katsushika Hokusai. In the original version, a large wave threatens boats in the water, and frames Mt. Fuji, which can be seen far in the distance.

FIRE FORCE

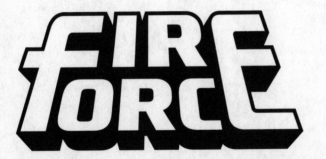

Knight of the Ice ©Yayoi Ogawa/Kodansha Ltd.

SKATING THRILLS AND ICY CHILLS WITH THIS NEW TINGLY ROMANCE SERIES!

A rom-com on ice, perfect for fans of *Princess Jellyfish* and *Wotakoi*. Kokoro is the talk of the figure-skating world, winning trophies and hearts. But little do they know... he's actually a huge nerd! From the beloved creator of *You're My Pet* (*Tramps Like Us*).

Chitose is a serious young woman, working for the health magazine *SASSO*. Or at least, she would be, if she wasn't constantly getting distracted by her childhood friend, international figure skating star Kokoro Kijinami! In the public eye and on the ice, Kokoro is a gallant, flawless knight, but behind his glittery costumes and breathtaking spins lies a secret: He's actually a hopelessly romantic otaku, who can only land his quad jumps when Chitose is on hand to recite a spell from his favorite magical girl anime!

Young characters and steampunk setting, like *Howl's Moving Castle* and *Battle Angel Alita*

Beyond the Clouds © 2018 Nicke / Ki-oon

A boy with a talent for machines and a mysterious girl whose wings he's fixed will take you beyond the clouds! In the tradition of the high-flying, resonant adventure stories of Studio Ghibli comes a gorgeous tale about the longing of young hearts for adventure and friendship!

The adorable new odd-couple cat comedy manga from the creator of the beloved *Chi's Sweet Home*, in full color!

Sue & Tai-chan

Konami Kanata

Sue is an aging housecat who's looking forward to living out her life in peace... but her plans change when the mischievous black tomcat Tai-chan enters the picture! Hey! Sue never signed up to be a catsitter! *Sue & Tai-chan* is the latest from the reigning meow-narch of cute kitty comics, Konami Kanata.

Something's Wrong With Us

NATSUMI ANDO

The dark, psychological, sexy shojo series readers have been waiting for!

A spine-chilling and steamy romance between a Japanese sweets maker and the man who framed her mother for murder!

Following in her mother's footsteps, Nao became a traditional Japanese sweets maker, and with unparalleled artistry and a bright attitude, she gets an offer to work at a world-class confectionary company. But when she meets the young, handsome owner, she recognizes his cold stare...

KC KODANSHA COMICS

A Kodansha Trade Paperback Original

Fire Force Omnibus 4 (Vol. 10–12) copyright © 2017–2018 Atsushi Ohkubo
English translation copyright © 2018 Atsushi Ohkubo

Published in the United States by
Kodansha USA Publishing, LLC, New York.

Publication rights for this English edition arranged through
Kodansha Ltd., Tokyo.

First published in Japan in 2017–2018 by Kodansha Ltd., Tokyo
as *Enen no shouboutai*, volumes 10–12.

ISBN 978-1-64651-550-9

Printed in the United States of America.

9 8 7 6 5 4 3 2 1

Translation: Alethea Nibley & Athena Nibley
Lettering: AndWorld Design
Additional Lettering: Jamil Stewart
Editing: Lauren Scanlan, Kathryn Henzler
Kodansha USA Publishing edition cover design by Abigail Blackman
Kodansha USA Publishing edition logo design by Phil Balsman

Publisher: Kiichiro Sugawara

Director of Publishing Services: Ben Applegate
Director of Publishing Operations: Dave Barrett
Publishing Services Managing Editors: Madison Salters, Alanna Ruse,
with Grace Chen
Production Manager: Emi Lotto

KODANSHA.US

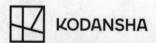

KODANSHA